INDEPENDENCE AND IMPARTIALITY
OF INTERNATIONAL ADJUDICATORS

Ius Comparatum – Global Studies in Comparative Law

Founding Editors
Jürgen Basedow, Max Planck Institute for Comparative and International Private Law, Hamburg, Germany

George A. Bermann, Columbia University, New York, USA

Former Series Editors
Katharina Boele-Woelki, Bucerius Law School, Hamburg, Germany

Diego P. Fernández Arroyo, Institut d'Études Politiques de Paris (Sciences Po), Paris, France

Series Editors
Giuditta Cordero-Moss, University of Oslo, Oslo, Norway

Gary Bell, National University of Singapore, Singapore

Series Assistant Editor
Philippine Blajan, IACL, Paris, France

Editorial Board Members
Ewa Baginska, Gdansk University, Gdansk, Poland

Vivian Curran, University of Pittsburgh, Pittsburgh, PA, USA

Nicolás Etcheverry, Universidad de Montevideo, Montevideo, Uruguay

Makane Moïse Mbengue, Université de Genève, Geneva, Switzerland

Marilda Rosado de S. Ribeiro, Universidade do Estado do Rio de Janeiro, Rio de Janeiro, Brazil

Marilyne Sadowsky, Université Paris 1 Panthéon-Sorbonne, Paris, France

Dan Wei, University of Macau, Macau, China

INDEPENDENCE AND IMPARTIALITY OF INTERNATIONAL ADJUDICATORS

Edited by
Giuditta Cordero-Moss

Cambridge – Antwerp – Chicago

Intersentia Ltd
8 Wellington Mews
Wellington Street | Cambridge
CB1 1HW | United Kingdom
Tel: +44 1223 736 170
Email: contact@larcier-intersentia.com
www.larcier-intersentia.com

Distribution for the UK and
Rest of the World (incl. Eastern Europe)
NBN International
1 Deltic Avenue, Rooksley
Milton Keynes MK13 8LD
United Kingdom
Tel: +44 1752 202 301 | Fax: +44 1752 202 331
Email: orders@nbninternational.com

Distribution for Europe
Lefebvre Sarrut Belgium NV
Hoogstraat 139/6
1000 Brussels
Belgium
Tel: +32 (0)2 548 07 13
Email: contact@larcier-intersentia.com

Distribution for the USA and Canada
Independent Publishers Group
Order Department
814 North Franklin Street
Chicago, IL 60610
USA
Tel: +1 800 888 4741 (toll free) | Fax: +1 312 337 5985
Email: orders@ipgbook.com

Independence and Impartiality of International Adjudicators
© The editor and contributors severally 2023

The editor and contributors have asserted the right under the Copyright, Designs and Patents Act 1988, to be identified as authors of this work.

No part of this book may be reproduced, stored in a retrieval system, or transmitted, in any form, or by any means, without prior written permission from Intersentia, or as expressly permitted by law or under the terms agreed with the appropriate reprographic rights organisation. Enquiries concerning reproduction which may not be covered by the above should be addressed to Intersentia at the address above.

Artwork on cover: Steve Johnson / Pexels

ISBN 978-1-83970-361-4
ISSN 2214-6881
D/2023/7849/90
NUR 820

British Library Cataloguing in Publication Data. A catalogue record for this book is available from the British Library.

FOREWORD

It is difficult to overstate the importance of impartiality and independence of arbitrators in the practice of international investment, commercial and investment alike. Users of arbitration expect tribunals to operate with impartiality and independence; arbitrators need to ensure the enforceability of their awards; arbitral institutions have an interest in ensuring the integrity of the awards they issue; national courts may set aside or decline to recognize or enforce awards rendered by tribunals that fall short in that respect; and international arbitration as a whole stakes its very legitimacy on the impartiality and independence of individuals who render awards.

International arbitration community's commitment to the impartiality and independence of arbitrators is nothing new. It is not just waking up now to those concerns. The integrity of the international arbitration process – and arbitrator impartiality and independence is central to that – is the stuff of countless articles and conferences. Arbitral institutions are promulgating their own standards and soft law instruments abound.

From this work there emerges a general consensus that impartiality and independence are of the essence. Giuditta Cordero-Moss rightly describes concern over these values as 'overarching'. The problem is itself international.

But Giuditta is not content to examine the problem internationally. She knows that, while international arbitration is of course international, it is subject in a great many respects to the particularities of national law. Notwithstanding still widely held notions to the effect that international arbitration is a fully autonomous regime, detached from national legal orders, that is simply not the case. That is as true of impartiality and independence as of any other feature of international arbitration.

With the exception of arbitration under the International Convention on the Settlement of Investment Disputes (ICSID), international arbitrations have a territorial home known as the seat, and that seat will have a law of arbitration (*lex arbitri*) determining the conditions to which arbitrations conducted locally are subject. Impartiality and independence are manifestly among the many conditions on which arbitration laws at the state level insist. Even in the presence of provisions on impartiality and independence in the arbitration law of the seat, the application of any such norms rests in the hands of national courts. Naturally, if an arbitration law happens to be silent on the matter, courts will play an even larger role. There also exist across jurisdictions distinctive legal cultures which may be reflected both in the practice of participants who are

Intersentia

v

Foreword

steeped in a given culture and, again, in the local courts. Thus there are ample opportunities to articulate and apply the particular requirements of impartiality and independence as articulated and understood in any given jurisdiction.

A distinct merit of Giuditta's inquiry is that it documents and displays the enormous number of variations on the general theme of impartiality and independence exhibited at the national level. In doing so, it necessarily employs the comparative method so as to identify both commonalities and differences (i.e. both convergences and divergences). The book focuses on arbitrator selection, but that is not a simple exercise. Parties and counsel representing them must be sensitive at the very outset to the risks that accompany appointment of an arbitrator who may eventually be found to lack impartiality and independence. Persons nominated as arbitrator may be expected, upon nomination, to determine for themselves whether they can serve with impartiality and independence, and to decline appointment if they are not sure they can. Even if they are confident in their neutrality, they must disclose any circumstances that may give rise to justifiable doubts on that score. These disclosures may lead to challenges and requests for disqualification, and means of challenging a nominee or appointee on grounds of lack of neutrality, as well as remedies, must be in place.

Although the standards and procedures studied in this book are applied at an early stage in the proceedings, their impact of may be felt later on, notably on the occasion of actions to set aside or enforce the resulting award. One can only hope that impartiality and independence are ensured at these early stages, since annulment of an award, or denial of enforcement, based upon a lack of arbitrator neutrality is very costly. An entire arbitral proceeding, consuming massive amounts of time and cost, may come to naught if policing occurs only or even primarily at the post-award stage.

Even if we focus exclusively on arbitrator selection, the ways in which legal systems differ are legion. Some differences across jurisdictions concern the most basic of issues: how impartiality and independence are to be defined, who selects the arbitrator and by what method, and by what means are obligations of impartiality and independence to be policed.

Other considerations raised by Giuditta are more narrow-gauged, but nonetheless important: waivability of the requirement of impartiality and independence, nationality and like factors as bases for disqualification, 'double-hatting', repeat appointments, and 'issue conflicts'. But what also come across in the book are a series of important dichotomies: (i) judges v. arbitrators; (ii) domestic v. international arbitration; (iii) commercial v. investment arbitration; (iv) party v. institutional appointments; (v) chair/sole arbitrator v. party-appointed arbitrator; (vi) actual v. apparent bias; (vii) pre-arbitration v. post-award enforcement; (viii) individual conflicts v. firm and related entity conflicts; (ix) arbitrator conflicts v. conflicts of others (counsel, expert witnesses, third-party funders, even tribunal secretaries); and (x) 'familiarity' v. 'extraneity', as defined by the editor.

Given this multitude of facets of impartiality and independence, it is not surprising that, as Giuditta acknowledges, harmonization of standards and practices across jurisdictions is essentially off the table, as is the development of meaningful 'international standards'. That hardly means, however, that the comparative method lacks utility. Far from it. First, those who operate within the international arbitration system need to know what, in any given case, are the obligations of impartiality and independence and how they are enforced. We need to be reminded that things may not correspond to that to which we are accustomed. This is a matter, if nothing else, of sheer professional competence. Second, legal systems stand to benefit from placing their policies and practices in a broader context, since knowing how other legal systems effectively address a common problem may facilitate domestic reform. Finally, even if harmonization is beyond reach, convergence is not.

It is rare for scholars of international arbitration to undertake as comprehensive and wide-ranging a study of an international arbitration problem as Giuditta has done. She makes genuine use of the comparative method, laying a wealth of knowledge at our feet, and inviting us to explore the myriad ways in which the imperatives of arbitrator impartiality and independence may be managed. This book is, as excellent scholarship must be, thought-provoking.

George A. Bermann

CONTENTS

Foreword. v
List of Cases xvii
List of Rapporteurs. xxxi

General Report: Independence and Impartiality of International Adjudicators
Giuditta CORDERO-MOSS. 1

1. Introduction 2
2. Independence and Impartiality as a Prerequisite of Adjudication. 7
3. The Selection Criteria. 14
4. Who Makes the Selection?. 26
5. The Selection Mechanism 32
6. Counterbalancing the Selecting Body's Influence 37
7. Breach: Consequences for the Adjudicator. 54
8. Breach: Consequences for the Decision. 56
9. Conclusion. 59

PART I. SPECIAL NON-NATIONAL REPORTS

Claims Tribunals
Maria Beatrice DELI 67

1. Introduction 68
2. The Criteria for the Selection of the Adjudicators 69
3. Which Authority Appoints the Adjudicators? 72
4. The Method for Appointing the Adjudicators 73
5. Methods to Balance the Appointing Authority's Influence on the
   Appointment of the Adjudicators. 75
6. Parameters to Ensure that the Adjudicators Act Independently
   and Impartially 75
7. Consequences for the Adjudicator of a Breach by the Adjudicator
   of the Requirement to Act Independently and Impartially. 79
8. Enforceability of a Final Decision Rendered by an Adjudicator who
   Breached the Requirement to Act Independently and Impartially 82

Intersentia

ix

Commercial Ad Hoc Arbitration
Christophe SERAGLINI and Anne-Lise MÉNAGÉ 83

1. Introduction 84
2. Analysis of the Optional Framework of Non-Administered
   Arbitration Rules... 86
3. Analysis of the Subsidiary National Legal and Judicial Frameworks 113

Commercial Institutional Arbitration
Franco FERRARI and Friedrich ROSENFELD 133

1. Introduction 133
2. A Comparative Analysis of the Institutional Framework on Independence
   and Impartiality... 134
3. A Post-Award Perspective on the Institutional Framework on
   Independence and Impartiality................................. 149
4. Conclusion.. 155

Commodities Arbitration
Yuliya CHERNYKH.. 157

1. Criteria for the Selection of Adjudicators 159
2. Which Authority Appoints Adjudicators?........................ 163
3. The Method for Appointing Adjudicators........................ 163
4. Methods to Balance the Appointing Authority's Influence on the
   Appointment of Adjudicators.................................. 165
5. Parameters to Ensure that Adjudicators Act Independently
   and Impartially 166
6. Consequences for Adjudicators of a Breach by Adjudicators
   of the Requirement to Act Independently and Impartially.......... 168
7. Enforceability of a Final Decision Rendered by an Adjudicator who
   Breached the Requirement to Act Independently and Impartially........ 169

International Administrative Tribunals
Chiara GIORGETTI 171

1. Introduction 172
2. Criteria for the Selection of Adjudicators 172
3. Which Authority Appoints the Adjudicators? 174
4. Parameters for Independence and Impartiality 175
5. Consequences and Enforceability of Final Decisions Rendered
   in Breach of Impartiality Obligations.......................... 178
6. Conclusion.. 179

The International Court of Justice and the International Tribunal
for the Law of the Sea
>   Makane Moïse MBENGUE and Damien CHARLOTIN 181

1. Introduction 181
2. Independence and Impartiality in Practice. 182
3. Adaptations in a Changing Context. 187
4. Conclusion. 191

International Sports Law
>   Antonio RIGOZZI and Erika HASLER 193

1. Introduction 194
2. The Structure of the Court of Arbitration for Sport. 195
3. The CAS List(s) of Arbitrators 203
4. The Appointment of CAS Panels 209
5. The Requirement of Independence and Impartiality. 214
6. Challenge Proceedings. 227
7. Remedies 229
8. Conclusion. 231

Investment Arbitration under Non-Treaty-Based Rules
>   Diego P. FERNÁNDEZ ARROYO and Alexandre SENEGACNIK. 233

1. The Narrow Scope of Enquiry: Investment Arbitration under NTBRs. . . . 234
2. A Comparative Study of NTBRs Used in Investment Arbitration. 235
3. Criteria for the Selection of Investment Arbitrators under NTBRs. 236
4. Appointing Authorities in Investment Arbitration under NTBRs. 240
5. The Method of Appointment in Investment Arbitration under NTBRs. . . . 242
6. Parameters to Ensure Independence and Impartiality: Preventive
    Measures 251
7. Consequences of a Breach of the Duty to Act Independently
    and Impartially: Curative Measures. 255
8. General Conclusions 261

Investment Arbitration under Treaty-Based Rules
>   Andrea K. BJORKLUND. 263

1. Criteria for the Selection of the Adjudicators. 264
2. Which Authority Appoints the Adjudicators? 265
3. The Method for Appointing the Adjudicators 267
4. Methods to Balance the Appointing Authority's Influence on the
    Appointment of the Adjudicators. 268

Contents

5. Parameters to Ensure that the Adjudicators Act Independently
   and Impartially 277
6. Consequences for the Adjudicator of a Breach of the Requirement
   to Act Independently and Impartially 280
7. Enforceability of a Final Decision that was Rendered by an Adjudicator
   who Breached the Requirement to Act Independently and Impartially . . . 281

Regional Courts
   Freya BAETENS. 283

1. Introduction 283
2. Criteria for the Selection of Adjudicators 285
3. Appointing Authority and Appointment Method 288
4. Methods and Parameters to Ensure the Independence and Impartiality
   in the Exercise of the Adjudicators' Functions 294
5. Consequences of a Breach of the Requirement to Act Independently
   and Impartially 299

Regional Human Rights Courts
   Hilary CHARLESWORTH, Emma MACFARLANE and Nikiforos PANAGIS . . . 303

1. Introduction 304
2. Criteria for the Selection of Adjudicators 306
3. Appointing Authority and Appointment Method 313
4. Tenure and Grounds for Dismissal. 320
5. Methods and Parameters to Ensure Adjudicators' Independence
   and Impartiality in the Exercise of their Functions 324

**The World Intellectual Property Organization Arbitration and Mediation
Center**
   Yuliya CHERNYKH 337

1. Criteria for the Selection of the Adjudicators. 338
2. Which Authority Appoints the Adjudicators? 340
3. The Method for Appointing the Adjudicators 342
4. Methods to Balance the Appointing Authority's Influence on the
   Appointment of the Adjudicators. 343
5. Parameters to Ensure that the Adjudicators Act Independently and
   Impartially 344
6. Consequences for the Adjudicator of a Breach by the Adjudicator
   of the Requirement to Act Independently and Impartially. 346
7. Enforceability of a Final Decision that was Rendered by an Adjudicator
   who Breached the Requirement to Act Independently and Impartially 349

xii

Intersentia

The World Trade Organization
Maria Chiara Malaguti and Giulia Poli 351

1. Settlement of Disputes within the WTO: A Paradigm Yet with Lights and Shadows 352
2. Selection of Adjudicators. 354
3. Rules of Conduct. 366
4. Conclusions. 372

PART II. SPECIAL NATIONAL REPORTS

Canada
Fabien Gélinas and Paul E. Trinel 377

1. Criteria for the Selection of Adjudicators 378
2. Which Authority Appoints Adjudicators?. 380
3. The Method for Appointing Adjudicators. 383
4. Methods to Balance the Appointing Authority's Influence on the Appointment of Adjudicators 383
5. Parameters to Ensure that Adjudicators Act Independently and Impartially 386
6. Consequences for Adjudicators of a Breach of the Requirement to Act Independently and Impartially 388
7. Enforcement of a Final Decision Rendered by an Adjudicator who Breached the Requirement to Act Independently and Impartially 390

Cyprus
Soterios Loizou 395

1. Introduction 395
2. The Legal Framework of Independence and Impartiality of Adjudicators in Cyprus 398
3. Independence and Impartiality in Litigation 399
4. Independence and Impartiality in Arbitration. 407
5. Conclusion. 411

Denmark
Kasper Steensgaard. 413

1. Introduction 413
2. Appointment of Adjudicators 414
3. Constitutional Protection, Measures and Sanctions Concerning the Domestic Judiciary. 420
4. International Aspects 423

Intersentia   xiii

France
Karim El Chazli 427

1. The Selection of Candidates for Positions as International Judges 429
2. Arbitrators' Impartiality in French Law............................ 439
3. General Conclusion 455

Greece
Eva Litina 457

1. The Fundamental Principle of Independence and Impartiality
   of Adjudicators in the Greek Legal System 458
2. The Selection of National Candidates for Positions as International
   Adjudicators... 460
3. Arbitrators 470
4. Conclusions 477

Hungary
István Varga 479

1. Introduction 480
2. The Designation of Domestic Adjudicators 480
3. The Appointment of National Candidates to Positions as International
   Adjudicators... 516
4. Conclusion... 518

Italy
Marco Torsello... 519

1. Introduction 520
2. Criteria for the Selection of Adjudicators 524
3. The Authority Appointing Adjudicators 533
4. The Method for Appointing Adjudicators........................... 536
5. Methods to Balance the Appointing Authority's Influence on the
   Appointment of Adjudicators 538
6. Parameters to Ensure that Adjudicators Act Independently and
   Impartially... 540
7. Consequences for an Adjudicator of a Breach of the Requirement
   to Act Independently and Impartially 545
8. Enforcement by a Domestic Court of Decisions Rendered by an
   Adjudicator who Breached the Requirement to Act Independently
   and Impartially 549
9. Final Remarks 552

Mexico
Rafael QUINTERO GODÍNEZ 555

1. Introduction 555
2. Historical Context of the 2021 Judicial Reform 557
3. Criteria for the Selection of Adjudicators 560
4. The Methods to Balance the Appointing Authority's Influence 569
5. Parameters to Ensure that Adjudicators Act Independently and
   Impartially 570
6. Consequences for Domestic Adjudicators of a Breach of the
   Requirement to Act Independently and Impartially 572
7. Enforcement of Final Judgments Rendered by Adjudicators in Breach
   of the Requirement to Act Independently and Impartially. 575
8. Conclusion. 576

Paraguay
Raúl PEREIRA FLEURY 579

1. Selection Criteria and Appointment Method 579
2. Appointing Authorities 583
3. Counterbalancing the Selecting Authority's Influence 584
4. Code of Conduct for Adjudicators 585
5. Consequences of Breaching the Duties of Independence and
   Impartiality 586
6. Conclusion. 589

Romania
Lucian BOJIN and Sorina DOROGA. 591

1. Preliminary Remarks 592
2. Criteria for Selection of Adjudicators 592
3. Authority Appointing the Adjudicators and Methods for Appointing
   the Adjudicators 596
4. Methods to Balance the Appointing Authority's Influence on the
   Appointment of Adjudicators 601
5. Parameters to Ensure that Adjudicators Act Independently and
   Impartially 604
6. Consequences for Adjudicators in Case of a Breach of the Requirement
   to Act Independently and Impartially 607
7. Enforcement of a Final Decision Rendered by an Adjudicator
   in Breach of the Requirement to Act Independently and Impartially 608
8. Conclusion. 610

Slovenia

Vasilka SANCIN and Domen TURŠIČ 611

1. Introduction 611
2. Appointment of Adjudicators 612
3. Independence and Impartiality of Adjudicators. 617
4. Conclusion. 619

Turkey

Didem KAYALI. 621

1. Introduction 622
2. Judges 622
3. Arbitrators 633
4. Selection of National Candidates to Positions as International
   Adjudicators. 637
5. Conclusion. 639

United States of America

Jarrod WONG 641

1. Introduction 641
2. US Judges 642
3. Arbitrators in the US 647
4. International Adjudicators in the US. 653

Vietnam

NGUYEN Thi Hoa and TRAN Hoang Tu Linh 659

1. Introduction 660
2. The Principle of Independence and Impartiality of Adjudicators
   in the Vietnamese Legal System 660
3. Mechanism to Ensure the Principle of Independence and Impartiality
   of Adjudicators 662
4. Enforcement of an Arbitral Award or a Judgment Breaching the
   Principle of Independence and Impartiality of Adjudicators 673
5. Conclusion. 677

Appendix: Questionnaire 679
Comments to the Questionnaires. 685
Index. 697

LIST OF CASES

SUPRANATIONAL

COURT OF ARBITRATION FOR SPORT

CAS 2005/A/876, *Adrian Mutu v. Chelsea Football Club*, Award of 15.12.2005 226
CAS 2006/A/1192, *Chelsea Football Club Limited v. Adrian Mutu*, Award
of 21.05.2007. 226–227
CAS 2008/A/1644, *Adrian Mutu v. Chelsea Football Club*, Award of 31.07.2009 227
CAS 2009/A/1893, *Panionios v. Al-Ahli SC*, Award of 19.11.2009. 228
CAS 2011/A/2348 and 2386, *UCI & WADA v. Contador & RFEC*, ICAS Board
Decision of 04.05.2011 224
CAS 2011/O/2574, *UEFA v. Olympique des Alpes SA/FC Sion*, Award of 31.01.2012. . . . 216
CAS 2012/A/2697, *Brescia Calcio SpA v. West Ham United FC*, Award of 26.06.2012. 228
CAS 2019/A/6148, *WADA v. Sun Yang & FINA*, Award of 22.06.2021 . . . . .228, 231
CAS 2020/A/7509, Award of 08.04.2022. 200

COURT OF JUSTICE OF THE EUROPEAN UNION

Case C-284/16 (*Achmea*). 3
Case C-741/19 (*Komstroy*) 3
Case C-109/20 (*PL Holdings*) 3
Case C-156/21 (*Hungary v. Parliament and Council*) 53
Case C-157/21 (*Poland v. Parliament and Council*). 53
Joined Cases C-585/18, C-624/18 and C-625/18 (*AK, CP, DO v. Sąd Najwyższy*) 28
Joined Cases C-83/19, C-127/19, C-195/19, C-291/19, C-355/19 and C-397/19
(*Asociatia Forumul Judecatorilor din Romania*). 608

EUROPEAN COURT OF HUMAN RIGHTS

Advance Pharma sp. z o.o v. Poland, ECtHR decision of 3 February 2022,
application no. 1469/20. . . . . .28, 53
Ali Riza and Others v. Turkey, ECtHR decision of 28 January 2020,
application nos 30226/10, 17880/11, 17887/11, 17891/11 and 5506/16. 25
BEG SpA v. Italy, ECtHR decision of 20 May 2021, application no. 5312/11. . . . . . . 4, 9–13,
48–49, 153, 551
Cyprus v. Turkey, ECtHR decision of 10 May 2001, application no. 25781/94 326
Daktaras v. Lithuania, ECtHR decision of 31 July 2012, application no. 36662/04. 37
Denisov v. Ukraine, ECtHR decision of 19 May 2019, application no. 76639/11. 12

Intersentia   xvii

List of Cases

Dolińska-Ficek and Ozimek v. Poland, ECtHR decision of 8 November 2021,
application nos 49868/19 and 57511/19 53
Grzęda v. Poland, ECtHR Grand Chamber decision of 19 May 2021,
application no. 43572/18. . . . . 8, 28, 53
Guðmundur Andri Ástráðsson v. Iceland, ECtHR decision of 1 December 2020,
application no. 26374/18. 25
Ibrahim Tokmak v. Turkey, ECtHR decision of 18 May 2021, application
no. 54540/16 . . . . 25, 55
Kamenos v. Cyprus, ECtHR decision of 31 October 2017, application
no. 147/07 401–405
Kleyn v. Netherlands, ECtHR decision of 6 May 2003, application nos 39651/98,
39343/98 and 4664/99 13
Koulias v. Cyprus, ECtHR decision of 26 May 2020, application no. 48781/12 . . . . . 396, 405
Kyprianou v. Cyprus ECtHR, ECtHR decision of 15 December 2005,
application no. 73797/01. 401–405
Mežnarić v. Croatia ECtHR decision of 15 July 2005, application no. 71615/01 405
Miracle v. Hungary, ECtHR decision of 12 January 2016, application no. 57774/13 37
Moiseyev v. Russia, ECtHR decision of 9 October 2008, application no. 62936/00. 37
Morice v. France, ECtHR Grand Chamber decision of 23 April 2015,
application no. 29369/10. . . . . 10–11, 326
Mutu and Pechstein v. Switzerland, ECtHR decision of 2 October 2018,
application nos 40575/10 and 67474/10 . . . . 4, 8–11, 15, 24–25,
31, 44, 217–220, 226
Naki and Amed Sportif Faaliyetler Kulübü Derneği v. Turkey, ECtHR decision
of 18 May 2021, application no. 48924/16 . . . . 25, 55
Nicholas v. Cyprus, ECtHR decision of 9 January 2018, application
no. 63246/10 . . . . 326, 396, 400–403
Parlov v. Croatia, ECtHR decision of 22 December 2009, application
no. 24810/06 . . . . 12, 37
Reczkowicz v. Poland, ECtHR decision of 22 July 2021, application no. 43447/19 . . . . . . 53, 561
Ringeisen v. Austria, ECtHR decision of 16 July 1971, application no. 2614/65 12
Sedat Doğan v. Turkey, ECtHR decision of 18 May 2021, application no. 48909/14 . . . . . 25, 55

INTERNATIONAL CENTRE FOR SETTLEMENT OF INVESTMENT DISPUTES

*Canepa Green Energy Opportunities I, S.Á R.L. and Canepa Green Energy
Opportunities II, S.Á R.L. v. Kingdom of Spain*, ICSID Case No. ARB/19/4,
decision on the proposal to disqualify Mr Peter Rees QC of 19 November 2019 15
Caratube International Oil Co. LLP et al. v. Republic of Kazakhstan (II), ICSID
Case No. ARB/13/13, Decision on the Proposal for Disqualification of Bruno
Boesch of 20 March 2014 270
Donatas Aleksandravicius v. Kingdom of Denmark, ICSID Case No. ARB/20/30 419
Eiser Infrastructure Ltd et al. v. Kingdom of Spain, ICSID Case No. ARB/13/36
(Proceeding on Annulment), decision of 11 June 2020 281
Tidewater v. Venezuela, ICSID Case No. ARB/10/5, decision of 23 December 2010 18
Universal Compression v. Venezuela, ICSID Case No. ARB/10/9, decision
of 20 May 2011 18

List of Cases

Urbaser SA & Consorcio de Aguas Bilbao Bizkaia, Bilbao Bizkaia Ur Partzuergoa v. The Argentine Republic, ICSID Case No. ARB/07/26, Decision on Claimant's Proposal to Disqualify Professor Campbell McLachlan, Arbitrator of 12 August 2010 274

INTER-AMERICAN COURT OF HUMAN RIGHTS

Case of González et al. ('Cotton Field') v. Mexico, Preliminary Objection, Merits, Reparations, and Costs, IACtHR Series C No. 205 (16 November 2009) 318
Case of Heliodoro Portugal v. Panama, IACtHR Series C No. 186 (12 August 2008) 330
Case of the Moiwana Community v. Suriname, IACtHR Series C No. 124 (15 March 2005) 330
Case of the Yean and Bosico Children v. The Dominican Republic, IACtHR Series C No. 130 (4 May 2004) 330

INTERNATIONAL COURT OF JUSTICE

Obligation to Negotiate Access to the Pacific Ocean (Bolivia v. Chile), Preliminary Objection, Oral Proceedings, CR 2015/18 186
Islamic Republic of Iran v. United States of America, Judgment, 3 February 2021 186
Legal Consequences of the Construction of a Wall in the Occupied Palestinian Territory, Order of 30 January 2004, I.C.J. Reports 2004 . . . . 188, 191

INTERNATIONAL CRIMINAL TRIBUNAL FOR THE FORMER YUGOSLAVIA

Prosecutor v. Furundzija, Case No. IT-95-17/1-A, Judgement, 21 July 2000 188

IRAN-US CLAIMS TRIBUNAL

US v. Iran, Case B/61, Decision on Challenge to Judge Sefi, 3 September 2010, 39 IRAN-U.S. C.T.R. 140. 189

LONDON COURT OF INTERNATIONAL ARBITRATION

Decision in LCIA No. 8086 of 30 September 1998 (2011) 27 *Arb. Int'l* 328 137
Decision in LCIA No. UN3490 of 21 October 2005, Challenge Digest (2011) 27 *Arb. Int'l* 377 588
National Grid PLC v. Argentina, LCIA No. UN7949, Decision on the Challenge to Mr Judd L. Kessler, 3 December 2007 108

Intersentia

xix

PERMANENT COURT OF ARBITRATION

CC/Devas (Mauritius) Ltd. et al. v. Republic of India, UNCITRAL, Decision
on the Respondent's Challenge to the Hon. Marc Lalonde as Presiding
Arbitrator and Prof. Francisco Orrego Vicuña as Co-Arbitrator
(30 September 2013) 273
Chagos Marine Protected Area Arbitration (Mauritius v. United Kingdom),
PCA Case No. 2011-03 186–188
Country X v. Company Q, Challenge Decision, 11 January 1995 (1997) XXII
Yearbook Commercial Arbitration 227, 234 108–109
*Guida Santiago Tawil, Serafín García Armas and Karina García Gruber v.
Bolivarian Republic of Venezuela*, Decision on the Challenge, 12 February 2018,
PCA Case No. 2013-3 50
Perenco Ecuador Limited v. the Republic of Ecuador, PCA Case No. IR-2009/1,
Decision on Challenge to the Arbitrator, 8 December 2009 188
Vito Gallo v. Government of Canada, PCA Case No. 55798, Decision on the Challenge
to Mr J. Christopher Thomas, QC, 14 October 2009, NAFTA/UNCITRAL. 108

SPECIAL COURT FOR SIERRA LEONE

Prosecutor v. Sesay, Case No. SCSL-2004-15-AR15, Decision on Defence Motion
Seeking the Disqualification of Justice Robertson from the Appeals Chamber,
13 March 2004 188

WORLD INTELLECTUAL PROPERTY ORGANIZATION

Britannia Building Society v. Britannia Fraud Prevention, Case No. D2001-0505. 347
Two Way NV/SA v. Moniker Privacy Services, LLC, Case No. D2012-2413 347

WORLD TRADE ORGANIZATION

African Countries and the WTO negotiations on the Dispute Settlement Understanding,
International Centre for Trade and Sustainable Development 2007 370
WT/DS160/15. 365
WT/DS34/R, 31 May 1999 372
WT/GC/W/753, 26 November 2018. 362

NATIONAL

BRITISH VIRGIN ISLANDS

PT Ventures SGPS SA v. Vidatel Ltd, BVIHC (COM) 2015/0017 and 2019/0067,
13 August 2020. 14

List of Cases

CANADA

Beals v. Saldanha, 2003 SCC 72, (2003) 3 SCR 416 392–393
Beauregard v. Canada (1986) 2 SCR 56 385
Black v. Chrétien, 2001 CanLII 8537 (ON CA), 54 OR (3d) 215 382
Boardwalk Regency Corp v. Maalouf (1992) 6 OR (3d) 737 392
Corporacion Transnacional de Inversiones, SA de CV v. STET International, SpA
    (1999) 45 OR (3d) 183 392
Oakwell Engineering Ltd v. EnerNorth Industries Inc., 2006 CarswellOnt 3477,
    19 BLR (4th) 11 392
R v. Valente (1985) 2 SCR 673 385
R v. Williams (1998) 1 SCR 1128 390
Reference re Remuneration of Judges of the Provincial Court of Prince Edward Island
    (1997) 3 SCR 3 384–385
Roberts v. R (2003) 2 SCR 259 391
Schreter v. Gasmac Inc. (1992) 7 OR (3d) 608 392

CYPRUS

A. Panayides Contracting Ltd v. Charalambous (2004) 1 AAD 416 398
Achtar v. The Police (2010) 2 AAD 397 406
Active Export Technologies Ltd et al. v. AAS Advanced Automation Systems Ltd
    District Court of Nicosia App. No. 3/2016 (18.11.2016) 407
Adidas Sportschufabriken Adi Dassier Stiftung and Co. Ltd v. Krashias Shoe
    Factory Ltd (No. 1) (1990) 1 AAD 873 404–406
Afoi CVAVasileiou Developers Ltd v. Ntekermendjan District Court of Limassol
    App. Nos 3995/2008 and 3834/2010 (13.03.2013) 409
Andreas Othonos & Sons Co. Ltd v. Bardsey Enterprises Ltd District Court
    of Limassol App. No. 301/2011 (19.09.2013) 409–410
Apostolidou v. The Republic (2002) 3 AAD 80 . . . . 401, 404–405
Athanasiou v. Reana Manufacturing & Trading Co. Ltd (2001) 1C AAD 1635 402
Attorney General v. Deputy Attorney General (2015) 3 AAD 484 . . . . 400, 406
Autocefalous Church of Cyprus v. House of the Representatives (No. 1)
    (1990) 3A AAD 54 401–405
Christopoulos v. The Police (2001) 2 AAD 100 . . . . 402, 406
Constantinides v. Ekdotiki Eteria Vima Ltd (1983) 1A CLR 348 398
Dionysiou v. Champi District Court of Larnaca App. Nos 1743/2008 and
    1202/2009 (09.09.2014) 411
Economides v. The Police (1983) 2 CLR 301 402–405
Efstathiou v. The Police (1990) 2 AAD 294 406
Eleftheriades v. Mavrellis (1985) 1 CLR 436 402
Ellinas v. The Republic (1989) 2 AAD 149 406
Evangelou v. Ambizas (1982) 1 CLR 41 . . . . 402, 411
General Construction Company Ltd v. Silver Leaf Developments Ltd
    District Court of Limassol App. No. 68/2016 (09.03.2018) 407–408
Grigoriou v. Trapeza Kyprou Ltd (1992) 1B AAD 1222 406
Hadjicosta v. Anastassiades (1982) 1 CLR 296 405
Koureas v. Nea SPE Geriou District Court of Nicosia App. No. 210/2014 (07.04.2017) 411

Intersentia   xxi

List of Cases

Kritiotis v. The Municipality of Paphos (1983) 3B CLR 1460 ....400–401, 405
Liasides v. The Police (2002) 2 AAD 434 398
Makolom v. Skouloukou District Court of Larnaca App. No. 2945/2005
   (26.03.2010) 409
Makrides v. The Republic (1984) 3A CLR 304............................402, 404–405
Mandritis v. SPE Polemidion District Court of Limassol App. No. 130/2004
   (12.02.2009) 409
Manolis v. Synergatiko Tamieutirio Lefkosias Ltd District Court of Nicosia
   App. No. 2662/2013 (27.09.2017) 410
Mastercon Construction Ltd v. Koukouma District Court of Nicosia
   App. No. 248/2014 (31.03.2016) 398, 410
Mediams Construction and Development Co. Ltd v. Konstantinidi District Court
   of Nicosia App. No. 44/2020 (29.06.2020) 400, 406
Michael v. SPE Morfou Ltd District Court of Limassol App. No. 444/2014
   (08.12.2016) 408, 410
Michael v. SPE Stroumpiou Supreme Court (CA) App. No. 190/2012 (28.06.2018)..... 409
Michaelides v. The Republic Supreme Court (CA) App. No. 125/2017
   (26.04.2018) 400–401, 403, 405
Miltiadous v. Synergatiko Tameio Lemesou Ltd District Court of Limassol
   App. No. 363/2013 (14.09.2018) 409
Mitidou v. K&Y Theodorou & Construction Ltd District Court of Larnaca
   App. No. 101/2011 (16.11.2012) 410–411
Neophytou v. The Police (1981) 2 CLR 195 406
Nikolaides v. The Police (2003) 2 AAD 271......................................401, 404
NK Shacolas (Merchants) Ltd v. Universal Life Insurance Co. Ltd (1984) 1 CLR 47 405
Paniccos Harakis Ltd v. The Official Receiver (1978) 1 CLR 15......................411
Papakyriakou v. The Police (2007) 2 AAD 133................................402, 406
Pastellopoulos v. The Republic (1985) 2 CLR 165 ....399, 401–402
Petridis v. Periferiaki SPE Lemesou Ltd District Court of Limassol
   App. No. 2389/2014 (29.05.2015) 407
Pitsillos v. Eugeniou (1989) 1E AAD 691........................... 401–403, 406, 411
Pitsillos v. The Republic (1994) 2 AAD 268.................................401–405
Prometheas United Ltd v. Miltiades Neophytou Civil Engineering Contractors &
   Developers Ltd District Court of Nicosia App. No. 53/2015 (04.10.2016) 410
Psaras v. The Republic (1987) 2 CLR 132..406
Psyllas v. The Police (No. 2) (2008) 2 AAD 601..................................404
Razis v. The Republic (1983) 3A CLR 309 404
Re Andronikou (2013) 1B AAD 1118...402–405
Re Cyprus Oil Refinery (No. 3) (2004) 1C AAD 1676 403
Re Kantouna Supreme Court (CA) App. No. 363/2020 (13.09.2021).................403
Re Liakou Mela (No. 1) (1998) 1B AAD 706......................................402
Re Liasides (1999) 1A AAD 185...405
Re Pericleous (1985) 1 CLR 178 407
Re Psaras (1985) 1 CLR 604 .... 401–402, 404–405
Re Symeou (2012) 1B AAD 974 .... 401–403, 405–406
Rodosthenous v. The Republic (1961) 1 RSCC 127 405
SCPA Architects Engineers Ltd v. The Cyprus Institute District Court of Nicosia
   App. No. 19/2018 (27.11.2018)..408
Sigma Radio TV Ltd v. CRA (2004) 3 AAD 134..........................400, 402–403
Silvestrou v. The Police (1996) 2 AAD 151...............................402, 406
Sofokleous v. Taveloudi (2003) 1B AAD 837................................403, 405

Solomou v. Laiki Cyprialife Ltd (2010) 1A AAD 687 407
SPE Pisteos v. Paraika District Court of Nicosia App. No. 2104/2012
    (16.04.2014) 408–409, 411
Spyrou v. Xeni Supreme Court (CA) App. No. 223/2014 (19.07.2019) 403–404, 406
STDY Ltd v. Kalaitzi District Court of Limassol App. No. 779/2013
    (29.12.2015) 408–409
Synergatiko Tamieutirio Lefkosias Ltd v. Krasari District Court of Nicosia
    App. No. 1932/2012 (01.09.2014) 408
Synergatiko Tamieutirio Lemesou Ltd v. Aleksandrou District Court of Limassol
    App. No. 259/2014 (30.01.2018) 408
Synergatiko Tamieutirio Lemesou Ltd v. Andreou District Court of Limassol
    App. No. 282/2016 (21.07.2017) 408, 410
Synergatiko Tamieutirio Lemesou Ltd v. Apostolou District Court of Limassol
    App. No. 297/2015 (15.01.2016) 410
Synergatiko Tamieutirio Lemesou Ltd v. Leonidou District Court of Limassol
    App. No. 380/2014 (01.08.2016) 409
Synergatiko Tamieutirio Lemesou Ltd v. Merki District Court of Limassol
    App. No. 499/2015 (04.02.2020) 408, 411
The Co-operative Grocery of Vasilia Ltd v. Ppirou (1962) 4 RSCC 12 408
The Police v. Athienitis (1983) 2 CLR 194 402
The Republic v. Avgoustis Supreme Court (CA) App. Nos 117/2018, 75/2019,
    76/2019, 77/2019, 79/2019, 80/2019, 84/2019, 85/2019 (16.06.2019). 400,
                                            402–403, 405
The Republic v. Florides District Court of Nicosia App. No. 477/2016
    (07.01.2021) 409
The Republic v. Mozoras (1966) 3 CLR 356. 400
The Republic v. Vassiliades (1967) 3 CLR 82 404
Themistokleous v. NSPE Lakatameias District Court of Nicosia
    App. No. 512/2011 (05.12.2011) 410
Theodorou v. The Police (1971) 2 CLR 245 404
Trapeza Kyprou Ltd v. Dynacon Ltd (1999) 1 AAD 717 . . . . 407, 409
Tympiotis v. The Republic (2004) 2 AAD 612 403–405
Typye v. The Police (2008) 2 AAD 279 402–403
Vassiliades v. Vassiliades (1941) 18 CLR 10. 401–406
Victoros v. Christodoulou (1992) 1A AAD 512. 406
Vrakas v. The Republic (1973) 2 CLR 139 402
Zampas v. Synergatikis Kypriakis Trapezas Ltd Supreme Court (CA)
    App. No. 96/2012 (06.06.2018). 408

DENMARK

Special Court of Indictment and Revision of 10.06.2021 in case no. 21/00229 420

FRANCE

CA Basse-Terre, 04.07.2022, *Sté AGI*, no. 17/00750 453
CA Paris, 14.10.1993, *Ben Nasser c. BNP et Crédit Lyonnais, Rev. arb.* 1994 450

List of Cases

CA Paris, 12.10.1995, *Raoul-Duval*, Rev. arb. 1999 453
CA Paris, 16.01.2003, *Intelcam c. France Télécom*, no. 2001/03698 450
CA Paris, 17.02.2005, *Mytilineos Holdings c. The Authority for Privatization and State Equity Administration*, no. 2003/22386 445
CA Paris, 01.07.2011, *SA Emivir c. SAS ITM Entreprises*, no. 10/10406 446
CA Paris, 30.10.2012, *Chambre Arbitrale Maritime de Paris (CAMP) et Generali Iard c. Nykcool AB*, no. 11/08277 [2013] 8 Gaz Pal 15 151
CA Paris, 17.12.2013, *Oursel c. Sermaplus*, no. 12/13053 449
CA Paris, 27.05.2014, *Huertas c. Taburno*, no. 12/05975 448
CA Paris, 14.10.2014, *S.A. Fidelidade Companhia de Seguros c. FC Nantes*, no. 13/14076 446
CA Paris, 25.11.2014, *Electroputere VFU Pascani c. Blue Engineering*, no. 13/11333 445
CA Paris, 17.02.2015, no. 13/13278 439
CA Paris, 23.06.2015, *CNAN c. CTI*, no. 13/09748 .... 448, 452
CA Paris, 27.03.2018, *Sté Saad Buzwair Automotive (SBA) c. Sté Audi Volkswagen Middle East (AVME)*, no. 16/09386 446
CA Paris, 28.06.2018, *Me C. c. Le Bâtonnier de l'Ordre des avocats de Paris*, no. 16/16859 450
CA Paris, 02.04.2019, *Patrick Desbordes*, no. 16/00136. 449
CA Paris, 25.02.2020, *Sté Dommo Energia c. Sté Barra Energia Do Brazil*, no. 19/15818 446
CA Paris, 26.01.2021, *Vidatel*, no. 19/10666 .... 49, 446
CA Paris, 16.02.2021, *Grenwich*, no. 18/07442, Rev. arb. 2022. .... 440, 445, 449
CA Paris, 23.02.2021, *Lerco*, no. 18/03068 443
CA Paris, 02.03.2021, *Rotana*, no. 18/16891 440
CA Paris, 23.03.2021, No. RG 18/05756 – No. Portalis 35L7-V-B7C-B5JUM. 241
CA Paris, 25.05.2021, *Delta Dragon c. Byd Auto*, no. 18/20625 .... 49–50, 446
CA Paris, 15.06.2021, *Pharaon*, no. 20/07999. .... 8, 447, 452
CA Paris, 12.07.2021, *Fiorilla*, no. 19/11413. .... 8, 452
CA Paris, 12.10.2021, *République du Sénégal c. Aboukhalil*, no. 19/21625 445
CA Paris, 24.11.2021, no. 20/00688 453–454
CA Paris, 14.12.2021, *Maessa c. Ecuador* 8, 14
CA Paris, 11.01.2022, *Rio Tinto France*, no. 19/19201 .... 443, 446–447
CA Paris, 14.01.2022, *République du Bénin c. Société Générale de Surveillance*. 58
CA Paris, 17.05.2022, *Sté Billionaire International AG c. SARL Sivendome*, no. 20/18020 446
CA Paris, 17.05.2022, *Sté Saudi Tumpane Company Ltd c. Sté Pizzarotti Rizzani De Eccher Saudi Ltd*, no. 20/15162 446
CA Paris, 28.06.2022, no. 21/06317 449
CA Reims, 02.11.2011, *Tecnimont c. Avax*, no. 10/02888 .... 447, 450
CA Reims, 31.01.2012, *Somoclest*, Rev. arb. 2012. 453
Cass., 09.10.1984, *Pabalk Ticaret Limited Sirketi c. Norsolor* 58
Cass., 23.03.1994, *Hilmarton Ltd. c. Omicron de traitement et de valorisation* 58
Cass., 08.07.2015, *PT Putrabali Adyamulia c. Rena Holding* 58
Cass., 09.11.2022, *Vidatel c. PT Ventures SGPS et al.*, no. 21-17.203. 151
Cass. 1re civ., 07.01.1992, *BKMI Industrieanlagen GmbH & Siemens AG c. Dutco Construction*, no. 89-18.708, 89-18.726 .... 8, 13–14, 151
Cass. 1re civ., 23.01.2007, *Médard c. Société Systeme U*, no. 06-12.946 130
Cass. 1re civ., 18.12.2014, *Sté VR services c. Sté Dukan de Nitya*, no. 14-11085 447

Cass. 1ʳᵉ civ., 04.11.2015, *Cool Carriers c. Helvetia*, no. 14-22.643 452
Cass. 1ʳᵉ civ., 16.12.2015, D14-26.279 50
Cass. 1ʳᵉ civ., 31.03.2016, no. 14-20.396.. 152
Cass. 1ʳᵉ civ., 13.01.2021, *EGPC c. NATGAS*, no. 19-22.932...................... 440
Cass. 1ʳᵉ civ., 25.05.2022, *Sté Soletanche Bachy France c. Sté Aqaba Container
    Terminal*, no. 20-23.148... 446
TGI Paris, *State of Dubai c. Halcrow* (1993) 3 *Rev. Arb.* 455 129

GERMANY

OLG Schleswig (Court of Appeal Schleswig), 24.06.1999, (2004) XXIX
    Y.B. Comm. Arb. 687 154
BayOLG (Court of Appeals Bavaria), 23.09.2004, BeckRS 2009, 21310.............. 150
OLG Köln (Court of Appeals Cologne), 26.02.2014, SchiedsVZ 2014, 203, 204–05 150
OLG München (Court of Appeals Munich), 15.01.2015, Az. U 1110/14 Kart.,
    Claudia Pechstein v. International Skating Union.............................. 221
BGH (Supreme Court of Germany), 11.12.2014, BeckRS 2015, 08903 150
BGH (Supreme Court of Germany), 07.06.2016, Az. KZR 6/15, *Pechstein v.
    International Skating Union (ISU)* 216, 221
BVerfG, *Beschluss der 2. Kammer des Ersten Senats*, 1 BvR 2103/16, 03.06.2022,
    published on 12.07.2022 221

GREECE

CA Athens 6839/1986 NOMOS.. 472
CA Thessaloniki 2525/2000 NOMOS 472
SC 1261/2021 473
SC 1509/1982 NOMOS 472
SFIC Athens 1202/2008 NOMOS 472
SFIC Athens 4778/2013, *Greek Journal Epitheorisi Politikis Dikonomias
    (EPolD)* 2013..473–474
SFIC Kerkira 360/2003 NOMOS 472

ITALY

C. Cost., 04.07.1977 529
C. Cost., 12.02.1963 529
C. Cost., 26.05.1966 529
C. Cost., 28.11.2001, No. 376 528
C. Cost., 14.07.2000, No. 283 542
Cass., 03.08.2000, No. 527.. 529
Cass., 07.09.2020, No. 18611.. 545
Cass., 08.03.2013, No. 5901... 548
Cass., 25.10.2013, No. 24153.. 529
Cass., 31.08.2017, No. 20615.. 546

List of Cases

MEXICO

SCJN Pleno, 'Acuerdo Número 14/2016' (2016) 564
SCJN Pleno, 'Acuerdo Número 6/2016' (2016) 564
SCJN Pleno, Controversia Constitucional 99/2016 (24 September 2019) 574
SCJN Pleno, Nulidad de Juicio Concluido. El Artículo 737 A, Fracciones I y VI,
   del Código de Procedimientos Civiles para el Distrito Federal Viola la Garantía
   de Seguridad Jurídica, No. P./J. 87/2008 (2008)............................... 576
SCJN Segunda Sala, Recurso de Revisión. Debe Prevalecer la Autoridad de la
   Cosa Juzgada Respecto de las Determinaciones Sobre Cuestiones
   Competenciales, No. 2a./J. 126/2012 (10a.) (2012)............................ 576

THE NETHERLANDS

Maximov v. OJCS Novolipetsky Metallurgichesky Kombinat, Dutch Supreme Court,
   24 November 2017.. 59
Telkom Malaysia v. Ghana, Hague District Court, 18 October 2004 18
Yukos Capital SARL v. Oao Rosneft, Amsterdam Court of Appeal, 28 April 2009,
   Case No. 200.005.269/01... 59

PARAGUAY

Acción de Inconstitucionalidad E. T., O. v. Art. 1 de la Ley Nº 5534/15, Supreme
   Court of Justice, Decision No. 889 dated 02.10.2018 584
*Arévalo M., María del Carmen v. Sra. Sung Choi Prop. Supermercado 'Mbocayá' s/
   cobro de guaraníes*, Labor Court of Appeals of Asunción, Chamber 1,
   Decision No. 257 dated 16.06.2005 587
Oscar A. Gonzalez Daher et al s/ Trafico de influencias, asociación criminal y otros,
   Criminal Court 35, Decision No. 2 dated 28.12.2020.......................... 584
*RHP G. M., N. B. v. Itaipú Binacional y otro s/ Indemnización de daños y perjuicios
   por responsabilidad extracontractual y otros*, Supreme Court of Justice,
   Decision No. 889 dated 04.12.2020 585
Sanatorio Cristina S.R.L. v. Rojas González, Beatriz y otro, Civil and Commercial
   Court of Appeals of Asunción, Chamber 5, Decision No. 1009 dated 26.12.2002 587

SPAIN

Tribunal Superior de Justícia de Catalunya (Superior Court of Justice of Catalonia),
   25.03.2013, (2013) XXXVIII *Y.B. Comm. Arb.* 465............................. 150

SWITZERLAND

Swiss Federal Tribunal, 08.02.1978, (1986) XI *Y.B. Comm. Arb.* 538 150
Swiss Federal Tribunal 118 II 199, Decision of 11.03.1992 230

xxvi   Intersentia

List of Cases

Swiss Federal Tribunal 118 II 361, Decision of 18.08.1992 222
Swiss Federal Tribunal 119 II 271 (*Elmar Gundel v. FEI*), Decision of 15.03.1993 214
Swiss Federal Tribunal 4P.217/1992, Decision of 15.03.1993 (unpublished version
   of the *Gundel v. FEI* decision (ATF 119 II 271)) 225
Swiss Federal Tribunal 4P.168/1999, Decision of 17.02.2000....................... 230
Swiss Federal Tribunal 4P.188/2001, Decision of 15.10.2001....................223, 225
Swiss Federal Tribunal 129 III 445 (*Larisa Lazutina & Olga Danilova v. IOC,
   FIS & CAS*), Decision of 27.05.2003 .... 195, 215–216,
                                                                         224–225
Swiss Federal Tribunal 4P.105/2006, Decision of 04.08.2006....................225–226
Swiss Federal Tribunal 4A_506/2007, Decision of 20.03.2008 223
Swiss Federal Tribunal 4A_528/2007, Decision of 04.04.2008 230
Swiss Federal Tribunal 4A_234/2008, Decision of 14.08.2008 230
Swiss Federal Tribunal 4A_612/2009, Decision of 10.02.2010 216
Swiss Federal Tribunal 4A_644/2009, Decision of 13.04.2010 229
Swiss Federal Tribunal, 06.01.2010 (2010) *ASA Bulletin* 772...................... 154
Swiss Federal Tribunal 136 III 605 (*Alejandro Valverde v. CONI, WADA & UCI*),
   Decision of 29.10.2010 ....223–225, 230
Swiss Federal Tribunal 4A_14/2012, Decision of 02.05.2012 (*X GmbH v. Y Sàrl*) 154
Swiss Federal Tribunal, DFT 4A_54/2012, Decision of 27.06.2012 154
Swiss Federal Tribunal 4A_110/2012, Decision of 09.10.2012 224–226
Swiss Federal Tribunal 142 III 521 (*X. SpA v. Y. B.V*), Decision
   of 07.09.2016...223, 230–231
Swiss Federal Tribunal 144 III 120 (*FC Seraing v. FIFA*), Decision
   of 20.02.2018.. 216
Swiss Federal Tribunal 4A_663/2018, Decision of 27.05.2019 50
Swiss Federal Tribunal 4A_318/2020, Decision of 22.12.2020 ....11, 49–50
Swiss Federal Tribunal 147 III 65 (*Sun Yang v. AMA and FINA*),
   Decision of 22.12.2020 .... 223, 226,
                                                                        231, 443
Swiss Federal Tribunal 4A_612/2020 (*Evgeny Ustyugov v. International Biathlon
   Union (IBU)*), Decision of 18.06.2021, under the reference ATF 147 III 500 199–200
Swiss Federal Tribunal 344/2021, Decision of 13.01.2022 200
Swiss Federal Tribunal 4A_404/2021, Decision of 24.01.2022 18
Swiss Federal Tribunal 4A_520/2021, Decision of 04.03.2022 .... 24, 49,
                                                                       223–225, 227
Swiss Federal Tribunal 4A_10/2022, Decision of 17.05.2022....................... 216
Swiss Federal Tribunal 4A_232/2022 (*Evgeny Ustyugov v. International Biathlon
   Union (IBU)*), Decision of 22.12.2022...................................199, 217
Swiss Federal Tribunal 4A_332/2022, Decision of 22.12.2022 200–201

TURKEY

İstanbul BAM 14. HD E.2019/2100, K.2020/74, T.30.01.2020...................... 636
Y. 4. HD E.1964/8868, K.1964/5220, T.09.11.1964 636
Y. 13. HD E.1974/2385, K.1974/2161, T.26.09.1974 636
Y. 15. HD E.1975/1617, K.1976/1052, T.10.03.1976 636
Y. 15. HD E.1991/2383, K.1991/3667, T.10.07.1991 637
Y. 15. HD E.1996/2781, K.1996/3533, T.20.06.1996 637

Intersentia   xxvii

List of Cases

Y. 15. HD E.2005/5778, K.2006/93, T.18.01.2006 636
Y. 19. HD E.2003/2061, K.2003/7606, T.10.07.2003 637
Y. 20. HD E.2002/1955, K.2002/2791, T.28.03.2002 636
Y. 20. HD E.2003/4042, K.2003/5618, T.09.07.2003 632
Y. 20. HD E.2005/1299, K.2005/1864, T.01.03.2005 632
Y. 20. HD E.2010/15448, K.2010/16428, T.21.12.2010 632
Y. 20. HD E.2012/13574, K.2012/14189, T.10.12.2012 633
Y. 20. HD E.2014/8621, K.2014/10584, T.16.12.2014 633
Y. 20. HD E.2015/13366, K.2015/12087, T.03.12.2015 633
Y. 20. HD E.2016/3456, K.2016/4496, T.14.04.2016 633

UNITED KINGDOM

A v. B [2011] EWHC 2345 129
Aldcroft v. The International Cotton Association Limited [2017]
 EWHC 642 (Comm) 161
AT&T Corp. v. Saudi Cable Co. [2000] EWCA Civ 154 129
Halliburton Company v. Chubb Bermuda Insurance Ltd [2018] EWCA Civ 817 124
*Halliburton Company v. Chubb Bermuda Insurance Ltd (formerly known
 as Ace Bermuda Insurance Ltd)* [2020] UKSC 48 .... 11, 13, 46–47, 49,
 109, 124, 152, 162
Kanda v. Government of the Federation of Malaya [1962] AC 322 400
*Manchester City Football Club Ltd v. Football Association Premier League
 Limited and others* [2021] EWHC 628 (Comm) 24
*Newcastle United Football Company Limited v. The Football Association
 Premier League Limited* [2021] EWHC 349 (Comm)........................... 50
P v. Q [2017] EWHC 148 (Comm) 129
R v. Stratford on Avon Justice ex parte Edmonds, Edmonds v. Badham
 [1973] 1 RTR 356.. 402
R v. Sussex Justices ex parte McCarthy [1924] 1 KB 256 401
W Limited v. M SDN BHD [2016] EWHC 422 (Comm) 18
Yiacoub v. R [2014] UKPC 22... 396
Yukos Capital SARL v. OJSC Rosneft Oil Company [2012] EWCA Civ 855 59

UNITED STATES OF AMERICA

ANR Coal Co., Inc. v. Cogentrix of North Carolina, Inc., 173 F.3d 493
 (4th Cir. 1999) 651
Azteca Construction, Inc. v. ADR Consulting, Inc, Court of Appeal,
 Third District, California, C045316... 155
Beebe Med. Center v. Insight Health Servs, 751 A.2d 426 (1999)................... 155
Certain Underwriting Members of Lloyds of London v. State of Fla.,
 892 F.3d 501 (2d Cir. 2018)... 116
Chromalloy Aeroservices v. Arab Republic of Egypt, United States District Court,
 District of Columbia, 31 July 1996, 94-2339 58
Commonwealth Coatings Corp. v. Cont'l Cas. Co., 393 U.S. 145 (U.S. S.Ct. 1968) 124

xxviii

Intersentia

List of Cases

Corporación Mexicana de Mantenimiento Integral v. Pemex Exploración y
Producción, Southern District for New York 2013 (2013) XXXVIII Yearbook
Commercial Arbitration 537–41 58
Delta Mine Holding Co. v. AFC Coal Properties, Inc., 280 F.3d 815 (8th Cir. 2002) 648
Esso Exploration and Production Nigeria Limited v. Nigerian National Petroleum
Corporation, United States District Court, Southern District of New York
Opinion and Order, 4 September 2019, 14cv8445 58
Fid. Fed. Bank, FSB v. Durga Ma Corp., 386 F.3d 1306, 2004 U.S. App. LEXIS 22535 154
First Options of Chicago, Inc. v. Kaplan, 514 U.S. 938 (1995) 155
Graham v. Scissor Tail, Inc., 171 Cal. Rptr. 604 (Cal.1981) 648
Hooters of America, Inc. v. Phillips, 173 F.3d 933 (4th Cir. 1999) 648
Karaha Bodas, Co., L.L.C. v. Perusahaan Pertambangan Minyak Dan Gas Bumi,
364 F.3d 274 654
Lucent Techs., Inc. v. Tatung Co., 379 F.3d 24, 2004 U.S. App. LEXIS 15907........... 154
Merit Ins. Co. v. Leatherby Ins. Co., 714 F.2d 673, 1983 U.S. App. LEXIS 25862 154
Middlesex Mut. Ins. Co. v. Levine, 675 F.2d 1197 (11th Cir. 1982)................... 650
Patrolmen's Benevolent Ass'n of N.Y. v. City of N.Y. State Public Employment
Relations Bd, 110 N.Y.S.3d 81 (N.Y. App. Div. 2019) 116
Positive Software Solutions, Inc. v. New Century Fin. Corp., 476 F.3d 278
(5th Cir. 2007) (en banc)... 651
Positive Software Solutions, Inc. v. New Century Mortgage Corp., 436 F.3d 495
(5th Cir. 2006) 652
Schmitz v. Zilveti, 20 F.3d 1043 (9th Cir. 1994) 652
Shanghai Yongrun Inv. Mgt. Co., Ltd, Plaintiff-Appellant v. Maodong Xu,
Defendant-Respondent, Kashi Galaxy Venture Capital Co., Ltd., Defendant,
New York Appellate Division, 10 March 2022, Case No. 2021-01637 57
Sphere Drake Ins., Ltd. v. All Am. Life Ins. Co., 307 F.3d 617 (7th Cir. 2002)......... 649
U.S. Life Ins. Co. v. Superior Nat. Ins. Co., 581 F.3d 1167 (9th Cir. 2010) 648
Wages v. Smith Barney Harris Upham Co., 937 P.2d 715 (Ariz.Ct.App. 1997) 652
Winfrey v. Simmons Foods, Inc., 495 F.3d 549 (8th Cir. 2007) 116

VIETNAM

Decision No. 05/2010/KDTM-PQTT of 15 January 2010 of the Appellate Court
of the Supreme People's Court in Ho Chi Minh City 673
Decision No. 120/QD-TANDTC of 19 June 2017 of the Supreme People's Court
of Vietnam promulgating regulations on handling responsibilities of judicial
cadres in people's courts 667
Decision No. 13/2019/HNGD-ST of 28 March 2019 of People's Court of District
of Thai Thuy of Thai Binh Province... 673
Decision No. 147/2017/QD-PQTT of 17 February 2017 of the People's Court
of Ho Chi Minh City.. 670
Decision No. 509/2015/QD-PQTT of 27 May 2015 of the People's Court
of Ho Chi Minh City.. 672

LIST OF RAPPORTEURS

Giuditta Cordero-Moss

Giuditta Cordero-Moss, Dr. juris (Oslo), PhD (Moscow), is Professor at the Law Faculty of the University of Oslo, where she teaches international commercial law, private international law, comparative law and Norwegian law of obligations. An originally Italian lawyer, she was a corporate lawyer for years before joining academia, where she researches the issues that she had met in her practice and meets as an arbitrator. She publishes in Norway and internationally and is often invited to lecture internationally. She held the special lectures at the Hague Academy of International Law in 2014, and was the co-director of the Academy's Centre for Studies and Research on arbitration and the applicable law (2021). She is the President of the International Academy of Comparative Law (2022–2026), and a member of the Curatorium of the Hague Academy of International Law (2019). Among the institutions in which she participates are: the Norwegian Academy of Science and Letters (since 2016); the International Court of Arbitration of the International Chamber of Commerce (since 2018); the UNCITRAL Working Group on Arbitration (since 2007); the Norwegian Governmental Tariff Board (since 2015); the Board of the Financial Supervisory Authority of Norway (Vice Chairman, since 2014); and the European Bank for Reconstruction and Development Administrative Tribunal (President (2017–2020) and Judge (2007–2020)).

Diego Fernández Arroyo

Diego P. Fernández Arroyo is a Professor at Sciences Po Law School in Paris and Honorary Professor of the Universities of Buenos Aires and Cordoba. He teaches subjects related to international dispute resolution, arbitration, private and public international law, comparative law, and global governance, and he is the director of the Sciences Po LLM in Transnational Arbitration & Dispute Settlement. Professor Fernández Arroyo is a member of the Curatorium of the Hague Academy of International Law, a member of the Institut de droit international, former President of the American Association of Private International Law (ASADIP), and former Secretary-General of the International Academy of Comparative Law. He has been invited to many universities in Europe, the Americas, Asia and Australia, and has been a Global Professor of New York University. Professor Fernández Arroyo has been a member of the Argentine Delegation before UNCITRAL (Working Groups on Arbitration and on ISDS Reform) since 2003. He is actively involved in the practice of international arbitration as an independent arbitrator. He is a member of the ICSID panels of arbitrators and conciliators appointed by Argentina. Professor Fernández Arroyo has published several books and a number of articles in publications of more than 20 countries.

Freya Baetens
Freya Baetens (Cand.Jur./Lic.Jur. (Ghent); LLM (Columbia); PhD (Cambridge)) is Professor of Public International Law (Faculty of Law, Oxford University), Head of Programmes at the Bonavero Institute of Human Rights and Fellow at Mansfield College. She is also affiliated with the PluriCourts Centre (Faculty of Law, Oslo University) and the Europa Institute (Faculty of Law, Leiden University). As a Member of the Brussels Bar, she regularly acts as counsel or expert in international and European disputes. She is listed on the EU Roster of Arbitrators and Sustainable Development (TSD) experts, the Panel of Arbitrators and Conciliators of the International Centre for the Settlement of Investment Disputes (ICSID), the South China International Economic and Trade Arbitration Commission (Shenzhen Court of International Arbitration) and the Hong Kong International Arbitration Centre (HKIAC). She is a general public international lawyer, with a particular interest in the law of treaties, responsibility of states and international organisations, privileges and immunities, law of the sea, human rights, WTO and investment law, energy law and sustainable development.

Andrea K. Bjorklund
Andrea K. Bjorklund is a Full Professor and the L. Yves Fortier Chair in International Arbitration and International Commercial Law at McGill University Faculty of Law. She acts as arbitrator and expert in both investment and commercial arbitrations and as an expert in court proceedings related to arbitration. She has been appointed to the ICSID roster of arbitrators by the Government of Canada, and is on the panel of arbitrators of the Beijing Arbitration Commission/Beijing International Arbitration Center, the Shenzen Court of International Arbitration, the International Commercial Arbitration Court of the Ukrainian Chamber of Commerce, and Industry, and AAA's International Centre for Dispute Resolution. She is also a US appointee to the NAFTA Chapter 19 (now USMCA Chapter 10) roster of arbitrators. She serves on the advisory board of the Investment Treaty Forum of the British Institute of International and Comparative Law. Professor Bjorklund has a JD from Yale Law School, an MA in French Studies from New York University, and a BA (with High Honors) in History and French from the University of Nebraska.

Lucian Bojin
Lucian Bojin is an Associate Professor at the Law Faculty of the West University of Timişoara, Romania, where he teaches international law and international relations and organisations. He has also been a practising lawyer for more than 20 years. He has authored three books and over 50 articles on international law,

human rights, European law and private law. He was an expert for the Romanian government in the Working Group II (Dispute Settlement) of the United Nations Commission on International Trade Law (UNCITRAL) between 2017 and 2020.

Hilary Charlesworth

Hilary Charlesworth is a Judge of the International Court of Justice. She has taught most recently at the University of Melbourne Law School and the Australian National University.

Damien Charlotin

Damien Charlotin is a Research Fellow at HEC Paris, as well as practitioner and academic in public international law, with a PhD from the University of Cambridge. He assists Professor Makane Moïse Mbengue in various endeavours, academic and professional. He is also a recognised expert in investment arbitration law, having worked for years as a Senior Analyst and Chief Data Officer with a renowned publication in the field. He is also a practising data scientist, teaching Legal Data Analytics to students at Sciences Po Law School, HEC and Queen Mary University, and collaborating with the Smart Law Hub at HEC.

Yuliya Chernykh

Yuliya Chernykh is Associate Professor at the Inland Norway University of Applied Sciences and Adjunct Associate Professor at the University of Oslo. Yuliya researches questions related to the interpretation of legal texts and the intersections between national law and international law in international adjudication. She also works in the fields of contract law, comparative law, legal theory and legal history. Yuliya's recent monograph *Contract Interpretation in Investment Treaty Arbitration: A Theory of the Incidental Issue* (Brill 2022) is available as an Open Access book. Yuliya has practical experience in international adjudication. She has acted as an arbitrator in numerous international arbitration proceedings and appeared as expert in Ukrainian and international law in investment treaty arbitration and before foreign courts. In 2013, the Chartered Institute of Arbitrators (UK) awarded her the qualification of Chartered Arbitrator.

Maria Beatrice Deli

Maria Beatrice Deli is Professor of International Law at the University of Molise and of International Arbitration at Roma Tre University. Since 2011 Maria Beatrice is Secretary General of the Italian Association for Arbitration. She is co-founder of ArbIt and co-director of the Certificate in International Commercial and Investment Arbitration, at Roma Tre University. She is responsible for the editorial board of the *Rivista dell'Arbitrato* and director of *Diritto del Commercio Internazionale*. She is co-founder of DeliSasson and in her professional practice she mainly focuses on international law matters and on international commercial arbitration and litigation. She regularly acts as an arbitrator in ad hoc and institutional cases. She is a speaker and lecturer at international and national symposia and seminars and author of many publications, particularly on public and private international law, national and international arbitration.

Sorina Doroga

Sorina Doroga is the vice-dean for international relations and a senior lecturer at the Faculty of Law of the West University of Timişoara, where she teaches European and public international law. She holds an LLM degree from Harvard Law School, as well as a PhD degree from the West University of Timişoara. Her research interests lie in the fields of EU international relations and international adjudication, EU competition law and EU constitutional law. She also has extensive experience in private practice and is a qualified attorney in Romania.

Karim El Chazli

Karim El Chazli has been a legal advisor at the Swiss Institute of Comparative Law (SICL) since 2013. He studied law in Egypt (Cairo University), France (Sorbonne University) and England (Oxford University). El Chazli wrote his PhD on the 'Impartiality of Arbitrators' under the supervision of Prof. Pierre Mayer (Sorbonne Law School), which was awarded the highest distinction and favourably cited by the Swiss Federal Supreme Court in the *Sun Yang* case. Karim is also a frequent guest lecturer at French and Swiss universities. He is teaching a full course on international arbitration at the Savoie Mont Blanc University (France). He is the author of several publications on arbitration, private international law, civil procedure and comparative law.

Franco Ferrari

Franco Ferrari is a professor of law at New York University School of Law, where he also directs the Center for Transnational Litigation, Arbitration, and Commercial Law. Before joining NYU full-time, he served as a professor of law at Verona University (2002–2016, on leave from 2011–2016), Bologna University (1998–2002), and Tilburg University (1995–1998). Professor Ferrari, a former legal officer at the UN Office of Legal Affairs, works and does research in the areas of international commercial law, conflict of laws, comparative law, and international commercial arbitration. He is a prolific author, who has published more than 350 law review articles, encyclopaedia entries and book chapters, and 45 books in different languages. He is a recipient of the 2018 Certificate of Merit for High Technical Craftsmanship and Utility to Practicing Lawyers and Scholars awarded by the ASIL. He also acts as an international arbitrator both in international commercial arbitrations and investment arbitrations.

Fabien Gélinas

Fabien Gélinas, Ad. E., is Sir William C. Macdonald Professor of Law at McGill University, where he teaches international arbitration, and civil and common law contracts. A former Supreme Court law clerk, he holds a doctorate in law from the University of Oxford. Fabien Gélinas was formerly general counsel of the ICC International Court of Arbitration and chair of the Canadian Arbitration Committee. He is a fellow of the Chartered Institute of Arbitrators, and serves as arbitrator in large international commercial and investment matters. He publishes widely on arbitration law and practice, including adjudicatory independence.

Chiara Giorgetti

Chiara Giorgetti (Laurea, Bologna, MSc LSE, LLM and JSD Yale) is Professor of Law at Richmond Law School and Senior Fellow at Columbia Law School's International Claims and Reparations Project on issues related to reparations for Ukraine. She teaches international law and international dispute resolution, and her numerous publications include *International Claims Commissions: Righting Wrongs After Conflict*, *The Rule, Practice and Jurisprudence of International Courts and Tribunals*, and *Litigating International Investment Disputes*. Her practice focuses on international disputes resolution, including international investment arbitration and international claims and boundaries commissions. She was appointed as a conciliator for CERD and is member of the ICSID panels of arbitrators and conciliators. She is a delegate at UNCITRAL Working Group III. She clerked at the International Court of Justice and worked for several years at the UN.

Rafael Quintero Godínez

Rafael Quintero Godínez is Lecturer at Birmingham City School of Law. He completed his PhD in 2022 at Warwick Law School, exploring the theory of social systems and its offshoots to analyse judicialisation of international investment law. He has taught a range of legal and business subjects at University of Warwick and is experienced in public policy. He has submitted recommendations on foreign investment policies to the OECD Investment Committee and investigated legal and economic consequences of voluntary versus mandatory non-financial disclosure of corporate social responsibility in the EU at the Cato Institute. His latest article published in the ELTE Law Journal proposes argumentative strategies to address the legitimacy crisis of investment arbitration. He wishes to acknowledge the financial sponsorship of the Mathias Corvinus Collegium, as it was during his visiting fellowship in 2021 that he completed most of the report.

Erika Hasler

Erika Hasler (LLM, MCIArb) is a senior associate at Lévy Kaufmann-Kohler (Geneva, Switzerland), specialising in international commercial and sports arbitration. She has authored and co-authored several contributions in these fields, and is frequently involved in arbitration-related research and publication projects.

List of Rapporteurs

Didem Kayalı

Didem Kayalı is an Assistant Professor of Private International Law at TOBB University of Economics and Technology, Faculty of Law, Ankara, Turkey. Before joining TOBB ETU in 2016, she worked for 14 years as an associate, senior associate and chief of division at the Undersecretariat of Treasury, which is one of the leading governmental bodies in Turkey. She teaches private international law, nationality and foreigners law, international investment arbitration and international commercial arbitration, and her research interests relate primarily to conflict of laws and arbitration. She is the author of several articles, including 'Smart Contracts from the Perspective of Private International Law' (*UTBA Review* 2022), 'Third-Party Funding in Investment Arbitration: How to Define and Disclose It' (*ICSID Review* 2022), 'Enforceability of Multi-Tiered Dispute Resolution Clauses' (*Journal of International Arbitration* 2010), 'The Lex Mercatoria as the Applicable Law in International Commercial Arbitration' (*Gazi University Law Journal* 2003), and a book entitled *Independence and Impartiality of Arbitrators in International Commercial Arbitration* (2015). She earned her LLB from the University of Ankara (1999), her LLM in Comparative and International Dispute Resolution from the University of London, Queen Mary College (2008), and her PhD in Private International Law from the University of Ankara (2015).

Eva Litina

Dr Eva Litina is a Legal Expert at the Hellenic Consumers' Ombudsman, and an attorney-at-law admitted to the Athens and New York Bars. She teaches commercial law at the Department of Shipping, Trade and Transport of the University of the Aegean. For her research, Eva has been awarded the Comité Maritime International (yCMI) Essay Prize 2020, the International Bar Association Dispute Resolution Section Scholarship 2017, and scholarships from the Max Planck Institute Luxembourg for International, European and Regulatory Procedural Law and the Max Planck Institute for Comparative and International Private Law in Hamburg. Her monograph, entitled *Theory, Law and Practice of Maritime Arbitration: The Case of International Contracts for the Carriage of Goods by Sea*, was published with Kluwer Law International.

Soterios Loizou

Soterios Loizou is a Senior Lecturer (Associate Professor) in Commercial Law at King's College London, where he teaches and conducts research in the areas of commercial law, conflict-of-laws and international arbitration. He has also served as TTLF Fellow at Stanford Law School, Hauser Global Fellow at the NYU School of Law, and held visiting faculty positions at the Peking University School of Transnational Law in China, the University of Ferrara in Italy and the University of Nicosia in Cyprus. For his research, Soterios has been awarded numerous awards and prizes, including the prestigious Colin B. Picker Prize by the American Society of Comparative Law (ASCL) and the Smit-Lowenfeld

Prize by the International Arbitration Club of New York (IACNY). Soterios is qualified to practice law in the State of New York (USA).

Emma Macfarlane
Emma Macfarlane is a graduate of the University of Michigan Law School, currently working at Debevoise & Plimpton LLP in New York. She was a Judicial Fellow at the International Court of Justice in 2021–2022.

Maria Chiara Malaguti
Maria Chiara Malaguti is Full Professor of International law at the Università Cattolica del Sacro Cuore (Milan/Rome, Italy). She was appointed President of UNIDROIT in 1 September 2020. She is also legal advisor to the Italian Ministry for Foreign Affairs on trade matters and to the World Bank on modernisation of payment systems, financial markets and governance. An international arbitrator for commercial disputes and foreign direct investments included in various rosters, she has supported the General Attorney's Office of Italy in all procedures opened against Italy until now for international investment law. She has various publications, mainly focusing on financial markets and sovereign debt, harmonisation of law and international investment law.

Makane Moïse Mbengue
Makane Moïse Mbengue is Professor of International Law at the Faculty of Law of the University of Geneva and Director of the Department of International Law and International Organization. He is also an Affiliated Professor at Sciences Po Paris (School of Law). Since 2017, he is the President of the African Society of International Law (AfSIL). He is also a Member of the Curatorium of the Hague Academy of International Law and an Associate Member of the Institut de droit international. Prof. Mbengue acts as counsel in disputes before international courts and tribunals (in particular, before the International Court of Justice, the International Tribunal for the Law of the Sea and in investment cases) and as advisor for governments. He also acts as an arbitrator and was the president of the first international arbitration involving two international organisations. He is the author of several publications in the field of international law.

Anne-Lise Ménagé
Anne-Lise Ménagé is an associate at Freshfields Bruckhaus Deringer in the International Arbitration Group, based in Paris, France. She has experience in both commercial and investment arbitration under a variety of rules (ICC, UNCITRAL, ICSID, LCIA), with a particular focus on the construction and energy sectors. She also has experience in proceedings for the enforcement of arbitral awards and foreign judgments, set-aside proceedings and, more generally, cases involving conflict of laws issues before the French courts. Anne-Lise holds a Master 2 in Business and Tax Law from Université Paris II Panthéon-Assas and an LLM in International Business Regulation Litigation

and Arbitration from New York University School of Law. She is a member of the Paris and New York Bars and is fluent in French and English.

Nguyen Thi Hoa
Dr Nguyen Thi Hoa has been a lecturer at Ho Chi Minh City University of Law in Vietnam since September 2019, where she teaches and researches international business law, international commercial arbitration law, international commercial contract negotiation and drafting skill. In addition, since April 2022, she is also a reviewer for the *Journal of Legal Affairs and Dispute Resolution in Engineering and Construction* (indexed on Scopus – 1st quartile in 2020–2021) of the American Society of Civil Engineering. She is also currently a member of the Executive Committee of the Society of Construction Law in Vietnam. Before becoming a lecturer, she worked as a legal adviser in the Department of Justice of Ho Chi Minh City in Vietnam (2010–August 2019) and her job involved advising on public–private partnership contracts, construction law, investment law, international dispute resolution, promotion of commercial arbitration, recognition and enforcement of decisions of foreign authorities, etc. In December 2018, she finished her PhD thesis with honours at Panthéon-Assas Paris II University in France on the topic of 'Dispute resolution procedures in the international construction sector under FIDIC forms of contracts'. From September to December 2018, she worked as an intern in a construction law firm in Paris.

Nikiforos Panagis
Nikiforos Panagis is an Associate Legal Officer at the International Court of Justice. He is also a DPhil candidate in International Law at the University of Oxford. His research spans a range of topics in international law and in constitutional law, including international dispute settlement and the separation of powers. Nikiforos has taught international law at the University of Oxford, where he has also served as Co-convenor of the Oxford Public International Law Discussion Group. He holds a master's degree in public law from the University of Athens, as well as an MJur and an MPhil in international law from the University of Oxford. He has previously worked at the European Union and in private practice.

Raúl Pereira Fleury
Raúl Pereira Fleury is a senior associate with FERRERE's international arbitration regional practice, based in Asunción. Raúl specialises in international and domestic arbitration, under different industries and arbitration rules. Before FERRERE, Raúl worked at Shearman & Sterling LLP's international arbitration group in Paris, focusing mainly on foreign investment, renewable energy, oil and gas, and construction and corporate contracts, under different rules and institutions. Raúl is a member of the arbitrators' list of the Paraguayan Arbitration

and Mediation Center, Assistant Editor at *ITA in Review*, and a representative for Paraguay before the ICC Commission on Arbitration and ADR. Raúl obtained his law degree from the Catholic University of Asunción and holds an LLM degree from the American University Washington College of Law.

Giulia Poli

Giulia Poli is a licensed attorney. Following a traineeship at UNIDROIT and by being Associate Attorney at several international law firms in the USA and Italy, she is currently practising commercial and contractual law in Rome and she is CEO's right-hand man for an international company. She developed her legal skills in Italy and USA dealing mainly with international commercial contracts cases. She was a Teaching Assistant in Florida and Italy, and she is an expert of private law at the Università degli Studi della Tuscia. She is a member of the Miami International Arbitration Society in Florida. She has published legal articles in the *ILSA Journal of International and Comparative Law*, *Arkansas Law Review* and *Albany Government Law Review*.

Antonio Rigozzi

Antonio Rigozzi is a partner at Lévy Kaufmann-Kohler, a law firm specialising in international arbitration in Geneva, Switzerland. He serves as an arbitrator, acts as counsel, co-counsel and legal expert in international and domestic commercial arbitrations, and represents parties in arbitration-related annulment or recognition and enforcement proceedings before the Swiss courts. As the head of LKK's sports arbitration practice, Antonio is known for his work advising and representing top athletes, teams, sports governing bodies and other organisations before the CAS and other tribunals, in a wide range of matters including disciplinary, governance, regulatory, contractual and commercial disputes more generally. In addition to his practice as advocate and arbitrator, Antonio is a Professor of International Arbitration and Sports Law at the University of Neuchâtel.

Friedrich Rosenfeld

Friedrich Rosenfeld is Partner at Hanefeld, a dispute resolution boutique with offices in Hamburg and Paris. He acts as counsel in international arbitrations with a focus on construction, post-M&A, commercial and investment disputes. In addition, he has been an arbitrator in cases involving a range of applicable substantive laws and seats (e.g. Austria, Denmark, England, France, Germany, Greece, Israel, Northern Macedonia, Switzerland and the United States). His expertise is recognised in international rankings. Alongside his full-time practice, Friedrich is also Global Adjunct Professor of Law at NYU Law in Paris, a Lecturer at Bucerius Law School in Hamburg and Honorary Professor at the International Hellenic University in Thessaloniki. He has published six books and various articles on arbitration.

Vasilka Sancin

Vasilka Sancin, PhD, is a Full Professor of International Law, Head of Department of International Law and Director of the Institute for International Law and International Relations at University of Ljubljana, Faculty of Law (Slovenia). She is currently a member of the United Nations Human Rights Council Advisory Committee (2022–2025) and previously served as a member (2019–2022) and Vice-Chair of the United Nations Human Rights Committee and its Special Rapporteur for the Follow-up process to Concluding Observations. Among others, she serves as ad hoc judge at the European Court of Human Rights; an arbitrator and a Bureau member of the Court of Conciliation and Arbitration within OSCE; and an expert of the OSCE Moscow mechanism on Human Rights. She has (co-)authored and (co-)edited numerous articles/books in the field of international law, and, among other professional affiliations, acts as a President of the Slovene Branch of the International Law Association (ILA).

Alexandre Senegacnik

Alexandre Senegacnik, PhD, is a lecturer at Sciences Po Law School. He is actively involved in the practice of international arbitration. His research interests include (private and public) international law, comparative law and inter/transnational dispute resolution. He has been a visiting scholar at Columbia Law School, the Max Planck Institute for Comparative Public Law and International Law in Heidelberg, Kyoto University, the National University of Singapore and the Max Planck Institute for International European and Regulatory Procedural Law in Luxembourg. He participates as an observer for ASADIP in the sessions of the Working Group III of the UNCITRAL on reform of Investor-State Dispute Settlement. He is a former Deputy Secretary-General of the International Academy of Comparative Law.

Christophe Seraglini

Christophe Seraglini is an *Avocat à la Cour* and Partner at Freshfields Bruckhaus Deringer in the Paris International Arbitration Group, Christophe Seraglini has particular experience in energy, engineering and construction, environment, high-technology sectors of industry, sale of goods, joint venture, industrial cooperation and post-M&A. He also has considerable experience in handling international investment disputes in both the role of counsel and arbitrator, brought under the auspices of the ICC, ICSID and in international ad hoc arbitration proceedings. In parallel, Christophe Seraglini is a Professor of Law at the Université Paris Sud – Paris Saclay where he teaches international arbitration, private international law, international contracts law and international business transactions. He is also member of many institutions, such as the Arbitration Academy (Secretary General), the French Committee on Arbitration, the French Committee on Private International Law, the Arbitration Law Committee of the International Law Association (French representative), the Academic Council of the ITA, IAI, ICCA, IBA, the Editorial Board (committee) of the *Cahiers de l'Arbitrage* (Paris Journal of International Arbitration) and the Scientific Council of *La Semaine Juridique – Édition Entreprises* (LexisNexis). Christophe is the author of several books and articles regarding arbitration, including *Droit de l'arbitrage*, Domat Montchrestien, with J. Ortscheidt, 2nd ed. 2019, which received the Cercle Montesquieu Award for its first edition (2013).

Kasper Steensgaard

Kasper Steensgaard, PhD, is Professor of Law at the Department of Law, Aarhus BSS, Aarhus University, and focuses on domestic and international commercial law, private international law and international commercial arbitration.

Marco Torsello

Marco is a Full Professor of Comparative Private Law and Transnational Commercial Law at Verona Law School and a Global Professor of Law at NYU School of Law (Law-Abroad Program in Paris), where he teaches European Business Law. As a visiting professor, Marco has taught at several top-tier universities, including NYU, Columbia, Sciences Po, Bucerius, Fordham, the University of Pittsburgh and many others. He is also the author of several books and papers dealing with contracts, international business transactions and transnational dispute resolution. Marco has over 25 years of experience in private practice, and he is a name partner at ARBLIT – Radicati di Brozolo Sabatini Benedettelli Torsello, a boutique firm specialising in international dispute resolution.

Tran Hoang Tu Linh

Tran Hoang Tu Linh is a lecturer at the Faculty of Commercial Law, Ho Chi Minh City University of Law, Vietnam. She is also listed as a commercial arbitrator with the Southern Trade Arbitration Centre (STAC) in Vietnam and the Thailand Arbitration Center (THAC) in Thailand. Linh completed her Master of Laws and Bachelor of Laws at the University of Melbourne, Australia, and Ho Chi Minh City University of Law, Vietnam, respectively. She has actively been working on different projects related to international law, global governance, and dispute resolution. Linh has been published in the *Journal of Legal Affairs and Dispute Resolution in Engineering and Construction*, the *Contemporary Asia Arbitration Journal* and the *Vietnamese Journal of Legal Sciences*, among others.

Paul E. Trinel

Paul E. Trinel is Research Associate at McGill University where he steers projects in the areas of international law and international arbitration in collaboration with Professors Andrea Bjorklund and Fabien Gélinas. He holds master's degrees in law from Université Paris 2 Panthéon-Assas and McGill University. His latest paper is 'Counterclaims and legitimacy in investment treaty arbitration', recently published in *Arbitration International*.

List of Rapporteurs

Domen Turšič

Domen Turšič is a PhD student at the Faculty of Law, University of Ljubljana, focusing on international investment arbitration. He was previously a Teaching Assistant (Department of International Law) at the Faculty of Law, University of Ljubljana, and a Pegasus Scholar at the Honourable Society of the Inner Temple in London. He graduated from the Faculty of Law, University of Ljubljana and obtained a Master of Law degree at the University of Cambridge, specialising in international law.

István Varga

István Varga is Professor of Civil Procedural Law at ELTE Budapest University and Head of the Litigation and Arbitration Practice Group of PROVARIS Varga & Partners. His book on taking of evidence in international commercial arbitration (C.H. Beck – Nomos 2006) was awarded the First Prize of the German Permanent Court of Arbitration (DIS). Since his admission to the Budapest Bar in 2007 he has been primarily involved in litigation and arbitration before both domestic and foreign courts as lead counsel and has also acted as counsel before the Court of Justice of the European Union. He was a member and the academic secretary of the High Committee for the Codification of the new Code of Civil Procedure and author of the Expert Proposal for the new Code. He also authored the New Permanent Arbitration Rules of the Hungarian Chamber of Commerce and Industry, he acted as a member of several case law analysis groups of the Supreme Court, and since 2020 he has been the head of the Private Law Centre at Mathias Corvinus Collegium. István Varga is visiting professor at several foreign universities (Göttingen, Leipzig, Beijing, Kyoto), Director of Studies at the Hague Academy of International Law and honorary professor at the University of Leipzig. He is a member of the ELI-UNIDROIT working group on Civil Procedure. He regularly acts as arbitrator, counsel or expert witness at several foreign and international arbitral institutions (ICC, DIS, VIAC). Between 2014 and 2021 he was a listed arbitrator of Hungary at ICSID.

Jarrod Wong

Jarrod Wong is Professor of Law and Co-Director of the Global Center for Business and Development at the University of the Pacific, McGeorge School of Law. He is a scholar in international dispute resolution and has been published in the *Yale Journal of International Law*, *Columbia Journal of Transnational Law* and the *NYU Journal of International Law and Politics*, among others. Professor Wong serves on the Academic Forum on Investor-State Dispute Settlement, as well as the Academic Council of the Institute for Transnational Arbitration. Professor Wong is also the American Society of International Law observer delegate to the United Nations Commission on International Trade Law Working Group III on Investor-State Dispute Settlement reform.

GENERAL REPORT

Independence and Impartiality of International Adjudicators

Giuditta CORDERO-MOSS

1. Introduction 2
   1.1. The Purpose of Comparative Research 4
   1.2. This General Report 5
2. Independence and Impartiality as a Prerequisite of Adjudication 7
   2.1. Standards 9
   2.2. Independence from What? 12
   2.3. Non-Waivable Principle 13
3. The Selection Criteria 14
   3.1. Incompatibility/Conflict of Interests 15
   3.2. Bias: Familiarity v. Extraneity 19
   3.3. Nationality 20
   3.4. Competence 22
   3.5. Broadness of the Field 23
   3.6. High Moral Standards 24
   3.7. Diversity 25
4. Who Makes the Selection? 26
   4.1. Appointing Authority 27
   4.2. Party Appointment 30
5. The Selection Mechanism 32
6. Counterbalancing the Selecting Body's Influence 37
   6.1. Collegial Nomination or Appointment 38
   6.2. Limiting Reappointments 39
   6.3. Limiting Double-Hatting 40
   6.4. Issue Conflict 42
   6.5. Accountability 45
   6.6. Disclosure 46
   6.7. Post-Term Duties and Rights 50

	6.8.	Codes of Conduct	52

6.8. Codes of Conduct 52
6.9. Immunity. 52
7. Breach: Consequences for the Adjudicator 54
8. Breach: Consequences for the Decision 56
9. Conclusion. 59

Résumé

Les principes d'indépendance et d'impartialité sont fondamentaux pour une bonne administration de la justice. Ce rapport général examine la manière dont ces principes sont mis en œuvre dans divers contextes : dans les tribunaux nationaux de certaines juridictions, les tribunaux internationaux et l'arbitrage international.

Le rapport général rassemble et commente les rapports spéciaux qui traitent des questions d'actualité actuellement débattues, telles que la nécessité de préserver l'indépendance du juge par rapport aux autres pouvoirs de l'État, et la nécessité de préserver la légitimité de l'arbitrage dans les litiges entre investisseurs et États. Il examine également des sujets tels que les paramètres pour l'indépendance et l'impartialité, les critères et la méthode de sélection, l'autorité chargée de la sélection (nomination par une partie ou par une autorité de désignation), les mécanismes permettant de contrebalancer l'influence pouvant être exercée par l'autorité de désignation, le devoir de divulgation de l'arbitre, l'immunité de l'arbitre, les droits et devoirs de l'arbitre après son mandat, les codes de conduite et les conséquences d'une violation de ces différents devoirs.

Le rapport général fournit une analyse comparative des mécanismes mis en œuvre dans les différents systèmes et met en évidence leurs similitudes et leurs différences. L'analyse réfute certaines des hypothèses couramment formulées dans le débat actuel sur la réforme du mécanisme de règlement des différends entre États, en particulier dans le domaine de l'arbitrage d'investissement. En particulier, l'analyse comparative des mécanismes utilisés au sein des juridictions internationales ne confirme pas l'hypothèse selon laquelle une cour permanente résoudrait les questions de légitimité qui sont actuellement débattues dans le cadre de l'arbitrage d'investissement (telles que le conflit d'intérêts, la double casquette et le conflit de questions).

1. INTRODUCTION

International adjudication is a notion used to designate disparate methods for the settlement of international disputes. It refers to a variety of disputes – ranging from private or commercial disputes, to disputes between a private party and a state or an international organisation, or disputes between states.

The notion also refers to a variety of adjudicating bodies – ranging from ad hoc or institutional commercial arbitral tribunals, arbitral tribunals established by treaty, claim tribunals, international administrative tribunals, WTO panels, permanent regional courts or permanent international courts.

The need to solve international disputes has grown in parallel with the increasing internationalisation that we witnessed in the second half of the 20th century, and it does not seem that it is decreasing at the current moment, which is instead characterised by decreasing globalisation and signs of emerging re-localisation. Possibly as a side effect of the emerging reversal of globalisation, international adjudication is the object of increasing criticism.

This applies, to varying degrees, to all forms of international adjudication.

The International Court of Justice, for example, is criticised for, inter alia, its restricted jurisdiction, its ineffectiveness and also possible bias.[1]

The WTO Dispute Resolution System is criticised for possible bias and for exceeding its power.[2] Its ability to be operative has been threatened since the US in 2018 declined to contribute to the appointment of new members, as a reaction to what the US defines as the Appellate Body's judicial overreach.[3]

The type of adjudication that has probably attracted the loudest criticism in recent years is investment arbitration. Criticism of investment arbitration led to, among other things, a mandate by the UNCITRAL to its Working Group III to work on the possible reform of investor-state dispute settlement. Among the strongest opponents of investment arbitration, at least as far as concerns its interaction with the internal division of powers within the EU, is the European Union.[4] The European Union's active position against investment arbitration resulted, inter alia, in the agreement for the termination of bilateral investment treaties between the Member States of the European Union, signed in May 2020. Among other points, the criticism regards the impact of party appointment on the impartiality and independence of arbitrators.[5]

---

[1] Gleider Ignacio Hernandez, 'Impartiality and Bias at the International Court of Justice' (2012) 1(3) *Cambridge Journal of International and Comparative Law* 183; Eric A. Posner and Miguel de Figueiredo, 'Is the International Court of Justice Biased?' (2005) 34(2) *The Journal of Legal Studies* 599.

[2] https://www.wto.org/english/thewto_e/10anniv_e/future_wto_chap6_e.pdf.

[3] https://www.wto.org/english/news_e/news18_e/ab_22jun18_e.htm. For more details, see Maria Chiara Malaguti and Giulia Poli, Special Non-National Report on the WTO, section 2.2.2.

[4] See, for example, the decisions by the EU Court of Justice (CJEU) excluding arbitrability of investment disputes involving EU law: CJEU decisions C-284/16 (*Achmea*), C-741/19 (*Komstroy*) and C-109/20 (*PL Holdings*).

[5] Note by the UNCITRAL Secretariat, Possible reform of investor-State dispute settlement (ISDS), A/CN.9/WG.III/WP.142, para. 20.

Commercial arbitration is also increasingly criticised for having become unnecessarily costly and time-consuming, as well as overregulated.[6] In part, this development is due to arbitral tribunals' increasing concern for avoiding suspicion of being partial. In an excessive effort to confirm their impartiality, arbitral tribunals refrain more and more from exercising active case management and indulge the parties in sometimes unreasonable requests that new claims or new evidence be admitted, that terms be extended, etc. – falling for what is often called 'due process paranoia' and unnecessarily inflating the duration and cost of the proceedings.

While the requirement of independence and impartiality is not the only basis for the growing criticism against international adjudication, it constitutes an important element.

1.1. THE PURPOSE OF COMPARATIVE RESEARCH

Certain fundamental principles apply to all adjudication systems, and the principle of independence and impartiality is one of them. The principle does not only stem from the legal framework applicable to the specific adjudication system, but is an overarching principle. For example, the European Court of Human Rights (ECtHR) found that the country in which arbitral proceedings are seated is liable for the legal framework of those proceedings and has to ensure that the principles enshrined in Article 6 of the European Convention of Human Rights (including independence and impartiality) are complied with even when the dispute is subject to private mechanisms for dispute resolution (such as, in the instant case, sports arbitration).[7]

The principle of independence and impartiality is, therefore, generally recognised; however, this does not necessarily mean that its specific implementation is uniform across the different forms of adjudication.

A first observation is that the content of this principle is usually not defined. Furthermore, each type of dispute and each type of adjudicating

---

[6]   See the discussions on future work for the UNCITRAL Working Group II on dispute resolution, which in 2018 led to a mandate to work on instruments ensuring a balance between efficiency and quality: Report of the United Nations Commission on International Trade Law, Fifty-first session (25 June–13 July 2018), A/73/17, para. 252. See also William W. Park, 'Arbitration's Discontents: Between the Pernicious and the Precarious', in *Mélanges en l'honneur du Professeur Bernard Audit*, LGDJ 2014, pp. 581–609, affirming that arbitration has become a victim of its own success; Giuditta Cordero-Moss, 'The Alleged Failure of Arbitration to Address Due Process Concerns: Is Arbitration under Attack?', in *Stockholm Arbitration Yearbook 2021*, pp. 251–77.

[7]   *Mutu and Pechstein v. Switzerland*, ECtHR decision of 2 October 2018, application nos 40575/10 and 67474/10. See also *BEG SpA v. Italy*, ECtHR decision of 20 May 2021, application no. 5312/11.

body has its own legal framework. Some of these rely on national law or on uniform law (i.e. national law that has been harmonised by international conventions); some rely on public international law; some on a combination. Some are constituted ad hoc for a certain dispute; others are permanent. It is not necessarily evident that features from one adjudication system can automatically have relevance for all other adjudicative systems.

What is, then, the purpose of comparative research in this field? The aim of comparative research is not necessarily to harmonise the various criteria and mechanisms.[8] Comparative research aims at shedding light on the criteria and mechanisms that each system puts in place to ensure that the principle of independence and impartiality is respected.

To the extent it exists, a convergence among the systems will be highlighted. More importantly, however, the interests that justify a divergence will be exposed and analysed. The intention is to provide an assessment of the different meanings that the principle of independence and impartiality may have and of how the different mechanisms may serve this diversity.

To this end, it is useful to assess the relevant criteria, mechanisms and remedies applicable in each system for the purpose of ensuring independence and impartiality of adjudicators.

1.2. THIS GENERAL REPORT

This general report is written in the frame of the International Academy of Comparative Law's 21st General Congress. It is based on a series of reports prepared by special national and non-national rapporteurs. Special national rapporteurs were appointed, following the Academy's tradition, by the Academy through its national committees. Special non-national rapporteurs were chosen by the general rapporteur.

The special national reports explain how the respective domestic legal system deals with independence and impartiality – both as far as concerns the domestic system of justice (i.e. the mechanisms ensuring independence and impartiality of domestic judges) and as far as concerns the national nomination of members of international adjudicating bodies (i.e. the mechanisms ensuring the independence and impartiality of national individuals who are meant to sit on international adjudicating bodies).

---

[8]   On the purpose of comparative law see the seminal articles by Rodolfo Sacco, 'Legal Formants: A Dynamic Approach to Comparative Law' (1991) 39 *American Journal of Comparative Law* 1–34 and 343–402.

The former may permit us to verify to what extent there is, among the domestic legal systems, a convergence of criteria, mechanisms and remedies regarding independence and impartiality of domestic adjudicators. In turn, this can be the basis for developing international principles.

The latter may permit us to assess, in the various legal systems, the approaches to independence and impartiality of international adjudicators. Two aspects are of particular relevance. Firstly, as far as concerns the selection of international adjudicators, there may be domestic rules, guidelines or practices for the implementation of the relevant international tribunal's rules on the selection of the adjudicators. Secondly, as far as concerns the effects of breaching the principle of independence and impartiality, of particular interest are: (i) the consequences for the adjudicator, as well as (ii) the domestic criteria, mechanisms and remedies regarding the validity and enforceability in the given state of a decision rendered by an international adjudicator in case of a breach of the independence and impartiality requirements.

The special national reports concentrate on rules and practices within domestic legal systems. However, international adjudicating bodies have their own rules and practices on independence and impartiality. This means that, once they receive a nomination from a state, adjudicating bodies will deal with it in accordance with their own rules, before proceeding to the appointment of the nominated person. The special national reports deal only with the first phase, that of nomination. As the phase of appointment depends not on national legal systems, but on international bodies, the list of special national rapporteurs needed to be complemented by a list of special non-national rapporteurs.

The special non-national reports deal each with a specific international adjudication system. They explain how the respective type of international adjudication deals with the issue of independence and impartiality.

All reports are written on the basis of a questionnaire. To fully understand the implications of the principle of independence and impartiality in international adjudication, the questionnaire addressed the issue from different angles.

Firstly, the questionnaire asked the rapporteurs to address the criteria for selecting the adjudicators and to analyse what interests they intend to protect. Secondly, it asked the rapporteurs to assess who carries out the selection and, thirdly, on the basis of what mechanism. This may permit us to assess whether the selection process actually makes it possible to achieve the protection of the interests that the selection criteria intend to protect.

Fourthly, it asked the rapporteurs to explain the parameters for the conduct of the adjudicators. Finally, it asked them to assess the remedies available in case the principle of independence and impartiality is breached. This was, in turn, divided into two parts: fifthly, the effects that the breach has on the adjudicator and, sixthly, the effects that the breach has on the decision that was rendered by an adjudicator who was not independent or impartial (e.g. invalidity or unenforceability).

This general report follows the same structure as the questionnaire. On the basis of the special national and non-national reports, it aims to give a reasoned overview of the various approaches to the issue of independence and impartiality of adjudicators. Not all the planned special national and non-national reports could be submitted, unfortunately. This general report also takes into consideration the main lines of some of the systems that are not represented among the special national and non-national reports.

This report concentrates on the requirement that adjudicators *be* independent and impartial, and not on the requirements that they *act* in such a way. Certainly, the conduct of the proceedings also has significance for the principle of independence and impartiality: acts that may qualify as partial, such as communicating only with one party or not treating the parties equally, will have an impact on other important aspects of due process, such as equality of the arms and the right to be heard. These aspects, however, do not fall within the scope of this report.

2. INDEPENDENCE AND IMPARTIALITY AS A PREREQUISITE OF ADJUDICATION

The requirement that adjudicators be impartial and independent is a fundamental principle that can be found in national law,[9] often at the level of the constitution;[10] in international law;[11] and in transnational sources of soft law,[12]

---

[9] See Article 12 of the UNCITRAL Model Law, adopted in 85 countries. According to Christophe Seraglini and Anne-Lise Ménagé, Special Non-National Report on Commercial Ad Hoc Arbitration, section 3.2.1, virtually all jurisdictions have a requirement of independence and impartiality for adjudicators.

[10] Fabien Gélinas and Paul Trinel, Special National Report on Canada, section 4.1; Soterios Loizou, Special National Report on Cyprus, section 2; Kasper Steensgaard, Special National Report on Denmark, sections 1 and 3.1; Eva Litina, Special National Report on Greece, section 1; István Varga, Special National Report on Hungary, section 2.1; Marco Torsello, Special National Report on Italy, section 2.1.1; Lucian Bojin and Sorina Doroga, Special National Report on Romania, sections 4.1 and 5.1; Vasilka Sancin and Domen Turšič, Special National Report on Slovenia, sections 1 and 2.1; Didem Kayalı, Special National Report on Turkey, section 2.2.1; Jarrod Wong, Special National Report on the USA, section 2.1; Nguyen Thi Hoa and Tran Hoang Tu Linh, Special National Report on Vietnam, section 2.

[11] See the European Convention on Human Rights, Article 6; the Universal Declaration of Human Rights, Article 10; the International Covenant on Civil and Political Rights, Article 14.

[12] See, for example, Article 1 of the ALI/UNIDROIT Principles of Transnational Civil Procedure. The text of the Principles and the accompanying commentary, adopted by the American Law Institute (ALI) in May 2004 and by the International Institute for the Unification of Private Law (UNIDROIT) in April 2004, is available at https://www.unidroit.org/english/principles/civilprocedure/ali-unidroitprinciples-e.pdf. The same requirement may be found in a corresponding text adopted by the European Law Institute (ELI) and UNIDROIT in 2020: https://www.unidroit.org/instruments/civil-procedure/eli-unidroit-rules/overview/. In this text, the requirement of independence and impartiality is not spelled out expressly, but it results from various duties of the courts, see Rules 2 (and its comment 5) and 13(1) (and its comment 1).

among which the most widespread are the International Bar Association (IBA) Guidelines on Conflicts of Interest in International Arbitration.[13] In addition, it is affirmed in arbitration rules (both for institutional[14] and ad hoc[15] arbitration) and in codes of conduct of international courts of free trade or investment agreements.[16] Independence and impartiality are deemed to be inherent to the role of adjudicator,[17] since ancient times.[18] They are part of the principle of due process,[19] also referred to as the rule of law.[20] As such, they are deemed to be part of public policy.[21]

The two terms are often used jointly[22] or interchangeably. While each of the terms denotes a different aspect of the adjudicator's autonomy, their goal is the same:[23] that the dispute be decided solely on its merits, without giving consideration to external elements. Independence relates to the adjudicator's objective ability to determine a dispute solely on the basis of its merits, without being influenced by issues that may flow from professional, economic or other links with the parties or the interests at stake. Impartiality relates to the adjudicator's subjective ability to evaluate the disputed issues solely on the

---

[13] https://www.ibanet.org/MediaHandler?id=e2fe5e72-eb14-4bba-b10d-d33dafee8918.

[14] Franco Ferrari and Friedrich Rosenfeld, Special Non-National Report on Commercial Institutional Arbitration, section 2.4; Yuliya Chernykh, Special Non-National Report on the WIPO Arbitration and Mediation Center, section 5; Special National Report on Greece, section 2.2.2.

[15] Special Non-National Report on Commercial Ad Hoc Arbitration, section 2.1.

[16] See, for example, the Code of Conduct adopted under the Comprehensive Economic and Trade Agreement (CETA) between Canada on the one part, and the European Union and its Member States on the other. See also the Draft Code of Conduct for Adjudicators in Investor-State Dispute Settlement, the third version of which was released in September 2021 by ICSID and the UNCITRAL Working Group III, available, with annotations and commentary, at https://uncitral.un.org/en/codeofconduct.

[17] Special Non-National Report on Commercial Ad Hoc Arbitration, section 1.

[18] Special Non-National Report on Commercial Institutional Arbitration, section 1.

[19] Charles T. Kotuby Jr. and Luke A. Sobota, *General Principles of Law and International Due Process*, Oxford University Press 2017, pp. 157–202, identify independence and impartiality of the adjudicator as one of the elements of the principle of due process; Special National Report on Cyprus, section 5.

[20] *Grzęda v. Poland*, ECtHR Grand Chamber decision of 19 May 2021, application no. 43572/18, paras 300 f. See also Special National Report on Cyprus, section 5; Special National Report on Italy, section 1; Rafael Quintero Godínez, Special National Report on Mexico, section 1.

[21] See, for example, French case law: Cour de Cassation, Chambre civile 1, 7 January 1992, 89-18.708, 89-18.726 (*Dutco*); Cour d'appel de Paris, Pôle 5, Chambre 16, 15 June 2021 (*CNAN & IBC v. CTI & Pharaon*); Cour d'appel de Paris, Pôle 5, Chambre 16, 12 July 2021 (*Fiorilla*); Cour d'appel de Paris, Pôle 5, Chambre 16, chambre commerciale internationale, 14 December 2021 (*Maessa v. Ecuador*); see also the Special National Report on Italy, section 8.1.2; Special Non-National Report on Commercial Institutional Arbitration, section 3.1.

[22] See for example, ECtHR decision *Mutu v. Switzerland*, para. 144.

[23] See the Special National Report on Italy, section 1; even when only one of the terms is used, it follows that both are relevant: see the Special National Report on Vietnam, section 2. See also the Note by the UNCITRAL Secretariat, Possible reform of investor-State dispute settlement (ISDS) – Background information on a code of conduct, A/CN.9/WG.III/WP.167, para. 17 on the interpretation of Article 14(1) of the ICSID Convention.

General Report

basis of the dispute's merits, without being influenced by pre-judgements or other bias. In sum, each of independence and impartiality aim at ensuring that the dispute is decided solely on its merits. It is worth noting that the Law Commission of England and Wales, in its 2022 Report on the Review of the Arbitration Act 1996, observes that there is no duty of independence of arbitrators, and is of the opinion that there is no need to impose such a duty. The Law Commission finds that the duty of impartiality, enshrined in section 33 of the Arbitration Act, is more important.[24]

2.1. STANDARDS

While there is a general consensus on the main principle that adjudicators should be independent and impartial, there is no clear definition of the content of these principles.[25]

The standard is often the same for courts and arbitration,[26] although it is sometimes affirmed that it is more stringent for courts and domestic arbitration than for international arbitration.[27] The European Court of Human Rights seems to assume that independence and impartiality may be construed flexibly when the adjudicator is party-appointed.[28] This could be interpreted as if the ECtHR considered the standard to be more flexible for arbitration than for courts. However, the observation of the ECtHR does not concern the standard, but is restricted to the circumstance that parties may waive the requirement of independence and impartiality. Having concluded that there had been no voluntary and unequivocal waiver,[29] the Court proceeds to consider the standard to be equally applicable to all systems of adjudication.[30] This observation, therefore, may not be interpreted as an assumption that the standard of independence and impartiality is lower for adjudicators who have been appointed by the parties. Similarly, often the constituting documents of international courts provide that judges who are

---

[24] Law Commission Consultation Paper 257, *Review of the Arbitration Act 1996: A consultation paper*, 2022, chapter 3.

[25] This is emphasised in the Special Non-National Report on the WTO, section 3.1; Maria Beatrice Deli, Special Non-National Report on Claims Tribunals, section 1; Makane Moïse Mbengue and Damien Charlotin, Special Non-National Report on ICJ and ITLOS, section 3; Diego P. Fernández Arroyo and Alexandre Senegacnik, Special Non-National Report on Investment Arbitration under Non-Treaty-Based Rules, section 6; Andrea Bjorklund, Special Non-National Report on Investment Arbitration under Treaty-Based Rules, section 5.

[26] See the ECtHR decision *BEG v. Italy*, para. 141; Special National Report on Cyprus, sections 1 and 4.

[27] See the Special National Report on Greece, section 2.2.1.2.

[28] See the ECtHR decision *Mutu v. Switzerland*, para. 146.

[29] On waiver, see section 2.3.

[30] ECtHR decision *Mutu v. Switzerland*, para. 139; ECtHR decision *BEG v. Italy*, para. 126.

Intersentia

appointed by a state shall act in their own capacity, and not as representatives of the state which appointed them.[31]

That judges and arbitrators are subject to the same standard of independence and impartiality is assumed in the fifth version of the ICSID/UNCITRAL draft Code of Conduct, the latest available at the time of writing this general report.[32] Adopting a Code of Conduct is one of the measures that the UNCITRAL Working Group III is developing to improve the legitimacy of investment arbitration, see section 6.8. While the first four versions of the draft did not distinguish between judges and arbitrators, the fifth version was divided into two parts: one regulating the conduct of judges, and one regulating the conduct of arbitrators. Article 3, which contains the requirement to be independent and impartial, has been drafted in full for arbitrators; for judges, the draft advises that certain adjustments may be necessary, such as explaining that 'referring to or relying on a binding judgment or interpretation of an appellate tier of the same standing mechanisms would not be considered as taking instruction'.[33] Apart from adjustments rendered necessary by the structure of a permanent court with an appellate mechanism, however, the draft does not suggest that the regulation of independence and impartiality be affected by whether the adjudicator acts as an arbitrator or as a judge.

Within arbitration, there may be two kinds of appointment, see section 5 below. It is generally assumed that party-appointed co-arbitrators are subject to the same requirements of independence and impartiality as the chair of the tribunal and sole arbitrators, who are appointed by agreement of the parties or by an independent appointing authority.[34] Nevertheless, it is sometimes affirmed that the degree of independence and impartiality that is expected of a party-appointed arbitrator is not as high as that expected of a sole arbitrator or a chair of the tribunal.[35]

Independence is usually evaluated according to an objective standard (appearance of lack of independence),[36] whereas impartiality can be evaluated both under a subjective (actual lack of impartiality) and an objective standard.[37]

---

[31] See n. 78.

[32] ICSID/UNCITRAL draft Code of Conduct, fifth draft, November 2022, available at https://uncitral.un.org/sites/uncitral.un.org/files/media-documents/uncitral/en/wp.223_advance_copy.pdf.

[33] Ibid., Commentary to Article J3.

[34] Expressly denying that party-appointed arbitrators are subject to a different standard, see the Special Non-National Report on Investment Arbitration under Non-Treaty-Based Rules, section 6. See also the General Standard No. 5 of the IBA Guidelines, specifying that the Guidelines' standards apply to all arbitrators, irrespective of the method of their appointment.

[35] Special National Report on Denmark, section 3.2; Karim El Chazli, Special National Report on France, section 2.4; Special National Report on the USA, section 3.

[36] ECtHR decision *Mutu v. Switzerland*, para. 140.

[37] ECtHR decision *Mutu v. Switzerland*, para. 141; ECtHR decision *BEG v. Italy*, para. 129; *Morice v. France*, ECtHR Grand Chamber decision of 23 April 2015, application no. 29369/10, para. 73; Special National Report on Cyprus, section 3.

The objective standard is the one generally applicable in arbitration and in domestic courts.[38] It is not settled whether the criterion of appearance applies at the ICJ and ITLOS, but it is gaining acceptance.[39]

Under the objective standard, it is not necessary to prove that the adjudicator is actually conflicted or biased.[40] It is sufficient that there is an appearance of conflict or bias. The appearance of lack of independence and impartiality is generally described as the presence of circumstances that can raise reasonable doubts as to the adjudicator's independence and impartiality. Therefore, an objective standard simplifies the burden of proof, as it does not require providing evidence that the adjudicator is actually biased.[41]

Furthermore, a mechanism preserving appearance is linked to the need to safeguard legitimacy in the adjudication system.[42] There is no uniform approach to the criterion of appearance: while some adjudication systems require justifiable doubts in the eyes of a third party,[43] others refer to doubts in the eyes of the parties to the dispute.[44]

It should also be pointed out that there may be different standards within the same adjudication system, depending on the phase of the proceedings in which independence and impartiality are evaluated. As section 6.6 will show, one of the requirements applicable to adjudicators is that they disclose any circumstances that may create the appearance of conflict or bias, even those that likely will not lead to disqualification. The purpose of the disclosure is to permit the parties to assess the circumstances and decide whether they accept the adjudicator or not. Often, the standard required for disclosure is lower than the standard required for disqualifying the adjudicator.

---

[38] See, for example, the Swiss Tribunal Fédéral decision No. 4A_318/2020; the UK Supreme Court decision *Halliburton Company (Appellant) v. Chubb Bermuda Insurance Ltd (formerly known as Ace Bermuda Insurance Ltd) (First Respondent)* [2020] UKSC 48; Special Non-National Report on the WTO, section 3.1; Special Non-National Report on Commercial Ad Hoc Arbitration, section 2.4.1; Special National Report on Greece, section 2.2.1.2; Special National Report on Slovenia, section 3.1; Special National Report on Turkey, section 3.2.3; Special National Report on the USA, section 3.

[39] Special Non-National Report on ICJ and ITLOS, section 3.1; ECtHR decision *Mutu v. Switzerland*, para. 143.

[40] ECtHR decision *BEG v. Italy*, paras 131–32, 145, 148–49; ECtHR decision *Morice v. France*, para. 75; Special National Report on Cyprus, section 3.

[41] ECtHR decision *Mutu v. Switzerland*, para. 142. See also the Report of UNCITRAL Working Group III (Investor-State Dispute Settlement Reform) on the work of its thirty-fifth session, A/CN.9/935, 2017, para. 53, and the Note by the UNCITRAL Secretariat, Possible reform of investor-State dispute settlement (ISDS) – Ensuring independence and impartiality on the part of arbitrators and decision makers in ISDS, A/CN.9/WG.III/WP.151, para. 57.

[42] ECtHR decision *Mutu v. Switzerland*, para. 143.

[43] ECtHR decision *BEG v. Italy*, paras 148–49, 153–54; ECtHR decision *Morice v. France*, para. 76; Special National Report on Canada, section 7.2; Special National Report on Cyprus, section 3; Special National Report on Slovenia, section 3.1; Special Non-National Report on Commercial Institutional Arbitration, section 2.4; Special Non-National Report on Commercial Ad Hoc Arbitration, section 2.4.1.

[44] Special Non-National Report on Commercial Institutional Arbitration, section 2.4.

2.2. INDEPENDENCE FROM WHAT?

Adjudicators are to be independent and impartial. As will be seen in sections 4 and 5, this usually implies that adjudicators shall be appointed for their competence and ability to solve disputes in a fair way, not for other reasons, such as political reasons. In some systems, however, judges are appointed for their political preferences.[45] Even these judges, however, are expected to act independently and impartially.

The classical concept of independence follows from the principle of separation of powers: the judiciary shall not be influenced by the executive or legislative powers.[46] This implies that appointment or removal of the adjudicator shall not be done, or influenced, by the government or by the parliament.

Sections 4.1 and 5 below discuss, respectively, the appointing authority and the method of appointment. These sections will show that independence from the other branches of power is achieved to a varying degree in the various adjudicating systems.

Independence from the other branches of power requires not only that the appointment of adjudicators not be influenced, but also that the other branches of power not be capable of imposing sanctions on adjudicators as a consequence of the latter's adjudicating activity, see section 6.9 on immunity.

Independence from the other branches of power often results in self-governance of the judiciary. However, independence and impartiality shall be ensured not only for the judiciary as a system, but also for the individual adjudicator. This means that safeguards are also necessary against undue influence that may be exercised from within the judiciary system.[47] To shield the adjudicators against internal influence, a series of mechanisms are useful, such as predetermined criteria for the allocation of cases (see section 5 below) and immunity from disciplinary measures and from liability (see section 6.9 below).

In addition to the independence that follows from the separation of powers and internal mechanisms, adjudicators shall be independent from the parties to the dispute.[48] This is achieved by avoiding appointing, or permitting removing,

---

[45] Special National Report on the USA, sections 2.1 and 2.2.

[46] ECtHR decision *BEG v. Italy*, para. 128; *Ringeisen v. Austria*, ECtHR decision of 16 July 1971, application no. 2614/65; Special National Report on Cyprus, section 3. For further references see Joost Sillen, 'The concept of "internal judicial independence" in the case law of the European Court of Human Rights' (2019) 15(1) *European Constitutional Law Review* 104, n. 11.

[47] For further references see Joost Sillen, 'The concept of "internal judicial independence" in the case law of the European Court of Human Rights' (2019) 15(1) *European Constitutional Law Review* 104, 109; *Parlov v. Croatia*, ECtHR decision of 22 December 2009, application no. 24810/06; *Denisov v. Ukraine*, ECtHR decision of 19 May 2019, application no. 76639/11.

[48] ECtHR decision *BEG v. Italy*, para. 128; Special National Report on Cyprus, section 3.

adjudicators who are in such a relationship with one of the parties or the issues in dispute that an appearance of conflict of interests or bias is created. As section 3.1 will show, there is a core of circumstances that are uncontroversially deemed to create a conflict. The impact on independence is less clear for other circumstances, and these are dealt with differently in different contexts, see sections 6.2 on multiple appointments, 6.3 on double-hatting and 6.4 on issue conflict.

2.3. NON-WAIVABLE PRINCIPLE

A party may accept adjudicators notwithstanding the presence of circumstances that may cast doubts on their independence and impartiality. Generally, the party's waiver of its right to challenge the adjudicator has preclusive effects, and the party may not later invoke these grounds to recuse the adjudicator or contest the validity of the decision.[49] Such a waiver may also be implied: failure to challenge an adjudicator on the basis of a circumstance that a party knew or should have known may be interpreted as a waiver of the right to challenge the adjudicator.[50]

As long as the waiver has been voluntary and unequivocal, therefore, a party may accept an adjudicator who is not independent and impartial, at least in the field of arbitration.[51]

However, the parties' possibility to waive their right to an independent and impartial adjudicator has to be balanced against society's interest in a legitimate and credible system for dispute resolution. There are some principles, often referred to as due process principles, that are meant to protect not only the parties to a specific dispute, but also the legitimacy of the adjudication system. When a principle is aimed at protecting the interests of society, it will be applied even at the cost of overriding the parties' agreement.[52]

---

[49]   See the Special National Report on Cyprus, section 4; Special National Report on France, section 2.2.3.

[50]   Special National Report on Cyprus, section 3; Special National Report on France, section 2.2.3. See also ECtHR decision *BEG v. Italy*, para. 139, assuming that a waiver may be implied.

[51]   See ECtHR decision *BEG v. Italy*, emphasising in para. 141 that case law on waiver has been developed in the context of arbitration, and explaining that the Court has not expressed an opinion on whether such a waiver is acceptable in the context of purely judicial proceedings.

[52]   *Morice v. France*; *Kleyn v. Netherlands*, ECtHR decision of 6 May 2003, application nos 39651/98, 39343/98 and 4664/99. This is also recognised in national case law, see the already mentioned French Supreme Court decision in *Dutco* and the English Supreme Court decision in *Halliburton v. Chubb*. In the USA, the parties may agree on a partial arbitrator. However, there are limits to party autonomy, see the Special National Report on the USA, section 3: an arbitration agreement reserving the drafting party complete discretion over the selection of the arbitrator is not enforceable. See also the Special National Report on Italy, section 4.1.1; Special National Report on Slovenia, section 3.1; Special Non-National Report on Commercial Ad Hoc Arbitration, section 3.2.1; Special Non-National Report on Commercial Institutional Arbitration, section 3.1.

One such principle is equality of the parties. This means that an agreement between the parties may be overridden if it infringes the principle of equality. Selection mechanisms that permit one party to determine the composition of adjudicating bodies are often deemed to be incompatible with the principle of equality of the parties. In an arbitration with a plurality of claimants (or of respondents), for example, the parties may have agreed (directly or by making reference to arbitration rules containing such regulation) that all the claimants (or, as the case may be, all the respondents) shall jointly appoint an arbitrator. If the interests of all the claimants (or of all the respondents) are not aligned, this means that each of the claimants (or of the respondents) has been deprived of the possibility to appoint an arbitrator and would lead to an arbitral tribunal that is not balanced. As a result, the arbitral tribunal in a situation like this is generally to be appointed in its entirety by the appointing authority.[53]

The principle of equality in the determination of the arbitral tribunal's composition, however, is not always implemented, see section 6.1 on the English Arbitration Act.

That certain principles of due process affect not only the parties' interests, but the credibility of the adjudicating systems, and that therefore these principles cannot be waived, is also recognised by the IBA Guidelines, which list, among the circumstances that may create the appearance of conflict or bias, some that are deemed to be so serious that they cannot be waived by the parties, see section 3.1 below.

By contrast, the ICSID/UNCITRAL draft Code of Conduct does not have restrictions on the parties' possibility to waive, as long as they do not waive the qualification requirements laid down in the treaties upon which jurisdiction is based, such as Article 14(1) of the ICSID Convention.[54]

3. THE SELECTION CRITERIA

Generally, selection criteria are aimed at ensuring that the adjudicator has the required competence and that the decision is not influenced by interests or considerations beyond the merits of the case.

A prerequisite for *independence* is that the adjudicators have no ties with involved parties that may influence the determination of the dispute, nor that they have an interest in the outcome of the dispute. This will be examined in section 3.1.

---

[53] Special National Report on Italy, sections 2.1.2 and 4.1.1. See the French Supreme Court decision in *Dutco*, and the French Court of Appeal decision in *Maessa v. Ecuador*; see also the British Virgin Islands decision *PT Ventures SGPS SA v. Vidatel Ltd*, BVIHC (COM) 2015/0017 and 2019/0067, 13 August 2020.

[54] ICSID/UNCITRAL draft Code of Conduct, Article 11(8).

A prerequisite for *impartiality* is that the adjudicators have not pre-judged the issues in dispute – whether as a consequence of bias, loyalty to one party or otherwise. There are two main competing criteria in the selection of adjudicators that may have an impact on impartiality: familiarity and extraneity. This will be examined in section 3.2.

3.1. INCOMPATIBILITY/CONFLICT OF INTERESTS

A prerequisite for independence and impartiality is that the adjudicator does not have a personal, professional or financial relationship with a party to the dispute, and that the adjudicator has no interest in the outcome of the dispute. Connections not only to the parties are relevant, but also to the other adjudicators in the panel,[55] as well as to counsel or the funders of the parties.[56] That the adjudicating system is financed by one party, however, has not been deemed to affect the independence and impartiality of the individual adjudicators.[57]

The existence of a personal, professional or financial relationship with a party to the dispute or of an interest in the outcome of the dispute may induce the adjudicator to consider the impact that the decision may have on these interests. The decision would therefore run the risk of being based not only on the merits of the dispute, but also on the desire to avoid a negative impact on the adjudicator's own interests, or to obtain a benefit, with the consequence that the adjudicator cannot be seen to be independent and impartial. Both international[58] and domestic[59] adjudication systems rely on this principle.

---

[55]   See the Special National Report on Vietnam, section 3.1.1.2.

[56]   *Canepa Green Energy Opportunities I, S.Á R.L. and Canepa Green Energy Opportunities II, S.Á R.L. v. Kingdom of Spain*, ICSID Case No. ARB/19/4, decision on the proposal to disqualify Mr Peter Rees QC of 19 November 2019, para. 73; Special National Report on Cyprus, section 3; Special National Report on France, section 2.3.2.1.

[57]   ECtHR decision *Mutu v. Switzerland*, para. 151. A similar situation is to be found in the administrative tribunals acting as an internal justice system for international organisations. The internal justice system is financed by the organisation, which regularly is the respondent in the disputes heard by the tribunals.

[58]   Hilary Charlesworth, Emma Macfarlane and Nikiforos Panagis, Special Non-National Report on Regional Human Rights Courts, section 5.1.1 on the European Court of Human Rights, section 5.2.1 on the Inter-American Court of Human Rights, and section 5.3.1 on the African Court on Human and Peoples' Rights; Special Non-National Report on the WTO, sections 2.1.1 and 3.1.1; Special Non-National Report on Investment Arbitration under Treaty-Based Rules, section 5.

[59]   Special National Report on Cyprus, section 3; Special National Report on Denmark, section 3.3; Special National Report on France, section 2.3.2; Special National Report on Greece, sections 2.1.1 and 2.2.1.2; Special National Report on Hungary, section 2.6.1; Special National Report on Italy, sections 2.1.1, 6.1.1 and 6.1.2; Special National Report on Paraguay, sections 3 and 5.1; Special National Report on Romania, section 5.1; Special National Report on Slovenia, section 3.1; Special National Report on Vietnam, section 3.1.1.

Differences may arise in the definition of the principle's content. For example, as will be seen below, approaches are not necessarily uniform to the questions of whether the existence of conflicts must be verified only in respect of the individual adjudicator, or also in respect of the adjudicator's firm; or whether it must be verified only in respect of the parties to the dispute, or also in respect of their affiliates.

To avoid conflicts of interests, in many systems adjudicators are prevented from exercising professional or other activities that may be incompatible with the role of adjudicator. Incompatibility does not require that there is a relationship with the parties to the specific dispute or an interest in the outcome of the specific dispute. It aims rather at avoiding a setting in which conflicts or bias may arise. That adjudicators shall refrain from carrying out activities or holding positions that are not compatible with the exercise of their adjudicative functions is a recurrent requirement in international[60] and domestic adjudication systems. However, this does not necessarily mean that side activities are forbidden.[61]

Some circumstances evidently create a conflict between the adjudicator's interest and the duty to act independently and impartially. The ICSID/ UNCITRAL draft Code of Conduct exemplifies typical conflicts of interests in Article 3. These are defined at a rather high level of abstraction and include: being influenced by self-interest and outside pressure; being influenced by loyalty to parties, states or funders; taking instructions on the dispute; being influenced by a past or existing financial, business, professional or personal relationship; advancing the arbitrator's own interests; and assuming obligations that may interfere with the dispute. In Article 11, the draft contains a more detailed list of circumstances that may need to be disclosed. It includes: any relationships with the parties, counsel, third-party funders, expert witnesses and the other arbitrators; any past appointments made by counsel; and any personal interests in the dispute or in issues similar to those in dispute. On the different thresholds for disclosure and disqualification, see section 6.6.

To render the principle of independence and impartiality more specific, sources of soft law have been developed by arbitral institutions, such as the 2021 ICC Note to Parties and Arbitral Tribunals on the Conduct of Arbitration.[62]

---

[60] See, for example, Freya Baetens, Special Non-National Report on Regional Courts, section 4; Special Non-National Report on ICJ and ITLOS, sections 2.1 and 3.2; Chiara Giorgetti, Special Non-National Report on Administrative Tribunals, section 4; Special Non-National Report on Regional Human Rights Courts, section 5.1.2 on the European Court of Human Rights, section 5.2.2 on the Inter-American Court of Human Rights, and section 5.3.2 on the African Court on Human and Peoples' Rights; Yuliya Chernykh, Special Non-National Report on Commodities Arbitration, section 5; Special Non-National Report on the WTO, sections 2.2.1 and 3; Special Non-National Report on Commercial Institutional Arbitration, section 2.1.

[61] Special National Report on Denmark, section 3.2.

[62] https://iccwbo.org/content/uploads/sites/3/2020/12/icc-note-to-parties-and-arbitral-tribunals-on-the-conduct-of-arbitration-english-2021.pdf.

Of particular interest are the already mentioned IBA Guidelines. They contain three lists of types of relationships between the adjudicator and the dispute or the parties. The lists are divided according to the impact that the relationship is likely to have on the outcome of the decision.

The red list contains examples of connections that are so close that an adjudicator cannot be deemed to be impartial or independent. When there is a relationship as described in the red list, the adjudicator is conflicted and cannot serve as an arbitrator. The red list is divided into two: a waivable list of situations where the arbitrator may serve on the condition that the parties expressly accept the appearance of lack of independence and impartiality, and a non-waivable list of situations where the arbitrator may not serve – not even if it is accepted by the party to whose disadvantage the conflict may be. This shows that certain safeguards provided by the principle of independence and impartiality are so fundamental to the credibility of arbitration as a method to settle disputes that they may not be waived by the parties, see section 2.3 above. The non-waivable red list includes close connections between the arbitrator and one of the parties, while the waivable red list includes the arbitrator's prior involvement in the dispute, as well as close relationships with the parties or their counsel. Examples of non-waivable circumstances are that the arbitrator is a representative of one of the parties, has a significant interest in one of the parties or in the outcome of the dispute, or regularly advises one of the parties and derives significant income therefrom. Examples of waivable circumstances are that the arbitrator has been involved in an earlier stage of the dispute, or that the arbitrator or a member of the arbitrator's family has an interest in the outcome of the dispute or has a close relationship with one of the parties.

The orange list contains situations where doubts about the arbitrator's independence and impartiality may be justifiable. These situations must be disclosed by the arbitrators, and the arbitrator may serve if the parties do not raise objections. Examples are having repeatedly been appointed by one of the parties, having acted for or against one of the parties, or having advocated an opinion on the case in dispute.

The green list contains situations that are not deemed to raise doubts about the arbitrator's independence and impartiality – such as having expressed an opinion on a legal issue that also arises in the dispute, having academic contacts with other arbitrators or with counsel, or participating in the same professional organisations.

The IBA Guidelines are widely used in international arbitration.[63] Furthermore, they are generally considered to also be useful for other types of adjudication, although this is not uncontroversial.[64]

---

[63] Special Non-National Report on Commercial Ad Hoc Arbitration, section 2.3.1; Special Non-National Report on Investment Arbitration under Non-Treaty-Based Rules, section 6; Special National Report on France, section 2.1.3.1.

[64] Special Non-National Report on ICJ and ITLOS, section 3.1, particularly n. 45.

While there is a consensus on the more obvious situations that may create a conflict of interests, such as when the arbitrator is an officer of one of the parties to the dispute, opinions vary when the relationship between the adjudicator and the party is not direct. How close the indirect connection must be to have an impact on the appearance of independence and impartiality is not clear. In this context, courts and tribunals have applied criteria diverging from those of the IBA Guidelines.[65]

For example, the circumstance that a sole arbitrator is a partner in a law firm which provides services to an affiliate of a party, and derives substantial income therefrom, was deemed not to raise any appearance of bias by the English High Court,[66] but this factor is listed in the non-waivable red list of the IBA Guidelines.[67]

By contrast, repeat appointments are on the orange list of the IBA Guidelines of circumstances that need to be disclosed, and are often deemed to create a potential conflict of interests.[68] However, they are sometimes considered to be neutral.[69]

In addition, circumstances that are not expressly listed in the IBA Guidelines have been deemed to create a conflict of interest, such as when an arbitrator in another matter also acts as counsel for a client seeking annulment of an award which was rendered in an unrelated case, but on which one of the parties relies in its pleadings before the arbitral tribunal.[70]

That a partner in the law firm of one of the arbitrators had acted as an honorary consul to a state while one of the parties was a member of that state's parliament was not considered to create a conflict by the Swiss Federal Tribunal, as the professional relationship that may give rise to a conflict only refers to activity typical of a lawyer.[71]

As pointed out in section 6.6 below, the relatively strict requirement that conflict of interests be avoided has led to a reorganisation of the law firm sector.

The requirement that adjudicators not be conflicted inspires some possible measures for counterbalancing the influence of the selecting body on the

---

[65] See the Note by the UNCITRAL Secretariat, Possible reform of investor-State dispute settlement (ISDS) – Ensuring independence and impartiality on the part of arbitrators and decision makers in ISDS, A/CN.9/WG.III/WP.151, para. 65.

[66] *W Limited v. M SDN BHD* [2016] EWHC 422 (Comm), para. 42.

[67] Article 1.4: 'The arbitrator or his or her firm regularly advises the party, or an affiliate of the party, and the arbitrator or his or her firm derives significant financial income therefrom'.

[68] Special National Report on Canada, section 6.2; Special National Report on Italy, section 2.2 on re-election; Special National Report on Vietnam, section 3.1.1.2.

[69] See the decisions on challenges in the ICSID cases *Tidewater v. Venezuela*, ICSID Case No. ARB/10/5, decision of 23 December 2010, and *Universal Compression v. Venezuela*, ICSID Case No. ARB/10/9, decision of 20 May 2011.

[70] *Telkom Malaysia v. Ghana*, Hague District Court, decision of 18 October 2004.

[71] Swiss Tribunal Fédéral decision No. 4A_404/2021.

composition of the adjudicating body, and thus on the outcome of the dispute – particularly, in respect of multiple appointments and double-hatting, see sections 6.2 and 6.3.

3.2. BIAS: FAMILIARITY v. EXTRANEITY

A prerequisite of impartiality is that the adjudicators are not biased against the parties, and that they have not pre-judged the issues in dispute. This requirement assumes a degree of extraneity from the dispute, and needs to be balanced with the requirement that the adjudicators possess competence in the field of the dispute. In turn, competence assumes a certain familiarity with the disputed issues.

Familiarity assumes that the adjudicator is selected from the environment that is involved in the dispute: for example, a judge with the same nationality as the respondent state, or an arbitrator active in the specific business area in which the dispute arose. This is deemed to ensure that decisions are taken by an adjudicator who is able to understand the legal system involved, the underlying issues, the branch uses, or other parameters that may be relevant.

On the one hand, this ensures that the adjudicator has the necessary background to permit an efficient evaluation of the disputed issues. It also favours accountability of the adjudicator.

On the other hand, familiarity with the underlying values may expose the adjudicator to bias, and accountability may create the risk of adjudicators rendering a decision that is in favour of the party to which they are accountable. These concerns inspire some possible measures for counterbalancing the influence of the selecting body on the composition of the adjudicating body, and thus on the outcome of the dispute – particularly, in respect of double-hatting and issue conflict, see sections 6.3 and 6.4.

Extraneity assumes that the adjudicator does not have any connection with the interests in dispute. While this may decrease the risk of bias, it may create the risk of misunderstandings due to the lack of insight into the legal system involved, the underlying issues, etc. Extraneity may, in other words, be incompatible with the requirement that adjudicators possess the necessary expertise.

The reports show that there is an inconsistent approach to the balance between familiarity and extraneity, and that this inconsistency is to be found irrespective of whether the adjudicating body is ad hoc or permanent. The main principle remains that the adjudicating body shall be impartial and independent, but the understanding of independence and impartiality varies depending on whether efficiency is privileged, or whether full autonomy is deemed to be a necessary requisite.

Both understandings obviously require that the adjudicator does not have any direct link with the specific dispute or any interest in its outcome. There may be differences in the appreciation of whether there is a conflict of interests or bias (see section 3.1 above), but the principle that independence and impartiality do not allow an adjudicator who has a conflict with the specific dispute or is prejudiced is common to both approaches.

Where approaches diverge is in respect of a more abstract risk of an adjudicator being tempted to identify with, or privilege, the interests of one party. The following sections highlight the main issues in this context.

3.3. NATIONALITY

Perhaps somewhat anachronistically, the risk that an adjudicator may sympathise with the position of one party is deemed to be particularly high when the adjudicator and a party have the same nationality. In these days of high mobility, the formal nationality of adjudicators does not necessarily define their affiliation to a socio-legal system: an adjudicator may be a national of country A, may have received legal education in country B, and may have resided in country C for decades. It is not necessarily evident that the legal sensibility of this adjudicator is dictated by the nationality. For this reason, some adjudication systems operate with other criteria that are more likely to reveal an actual connection, such as residence[72] or de facto nationality.[73] Other systems maintain formal nationality as a criterion;[74] yet others do not have any regulation in this respect.[75]

Whether or not the circumstance that an adjudicator has a certain nationality implies more than an ability to understand the dispute and leads to loyalty to, or sympathy with, the interests of one party depends also on the

---

[72] See the Special Non-National Report on Regional Courts, section 2, on the Court of Justice of the Common Market for Eastern and Southern Africa; the Special Non-National Report on Claims Tribunals, section 2.3 on the Eritrea–Ethiopia Claims Commission. See also the Arbitration Rules of the International Chamber of Commerce, commented on in the Special Non-National Report on Commercial Institutional Arbitration, section 2.1.

[73] See the Arbitration Rules of the London Court of International Arbitration, commented on in the Special Non-National Report on Commercial Institutional Arbitration, section 2.1.

[74] See, for example, Rule 13 of the ICSID Arbitration Rules, amended in 2022; the UNCITRAL Arbitration Rules and the UNCITRAL Model Law recommend considering the criterion of nationality, see the Special Non-National Report on Commercial Ad Hoc Arbitration, sections 2.1 and 3.2.2. See also Special Non-National Report on Regional Human Rights Courts, section 5.2.1 on the Inter-American Court of Human Rights (in cases arising from individual petitions, judges who hold the same nationality as the respondent state party must recuse themselves from the case), and section 5.3.1 on the African Court on Human and Peoples' Rights (the African Court on Human and Peoples' Rights as well as its successor court, the African Court of Justice and Human and Peoples' Rights, both prohibit judges from hearing any case in which the state of which they are a national is a state party).

[75] Special Non-National Report on Investment Arbitration under Treaty-Based Rules, section 1.

General Report

selection process, which will be discussed in section 5. If the candidates for positions as international adjudicators are selected from among members of the executive and are expected to act as representatives of the interests of the state nominating them, it is understandable that nationality be deemed to have an impact on independence and impartiality in disputes involving states. To the contrary, if the candidates are chosen for their competence and expertise, there are fewer reasons to assume that nationality has an impact on independence and impartiality.[76] This is exemplified by a proposal for reform of the WTO that was presented by the EU. To enhance independence and impartiality, the EU proposed that only non-governmental members be appointed. Similarly, a study carried out by the New York Bar showed that if the members are not affiliated with the executive, their nationality has less of an impact on the decisions.[77]

Often the constituting documents of international courts expressly provide that adjudicators are appointed in their individual capacity,[78] even though they hold the nationality of the appointing state. They should not, therefore, act as representatives of the appointing state. This is no different from party appointment in arbitration: adjudicators are expected to be independent and impartial even though they have been appointed by a party, see section 4.2.

Be that as it may, nationality is traditionally deemed to evidence a connection between the country and the adjudicator, leading to the adjudicator's understanding of the framework, assumptions and implications of positions linked to that country. This familiarity is evaluated differently in the various approaches. Some courts always include in the panel a judge from the respondent state.[79] Should there not be a judge on the bench with the same nationality as a party, an ad hoc judge will be appointed.[80] In other

---

[76] See the comments in the Special National Report on Greece, section 2.1.1.4. The same report, in section 2.2.1.3, considers members of the Council of State as being representatives of the state and therefore not independent and impartial in arbitration disputes involving the state. See also the comments in the Special National Report on France, section 1.2.1, according to which university professors may be less loyal to the state, but more influential within the panel, see also section 1.2.2.

[77] Commented on in the Special Non-National Report on the WTO, section 1.1.2.

[78] Special Non-National Report on Regional Human Rights Courts, section 2.1 on the European Court of Human Rights, section 2.2 on the Inter-American Court of Human Rights, and section 2.3 on the African Court on Human and Peoples' Rights; Special Non-National Report on the WTO, sections 2.1.1 and 3.

[79] Special Non-National Report on Regional Human Rights Courts, section 5.1.1 on the European Court of Human Rights and section 5.2.1 on the Inter-American Court of Human Rights; Special Non-National Report on Regional Courts, section 3 on the Economic Community of West African States Court; Special Non-National Report on Claims Tribunals, section 2.1 on the Iran–US Claims Tribunal and section 4.2 on the Commission for Real Property Claims of Displaced Persons. Interestingly, the Claims Resolution Tribunal for Dormant Accounts requires that only the banks' (Swiss) nationality be reflected in the composition of the tribunal, see the Special Non-National Report on Claims Tribunals, section 2.

[80] See the Special Non-National Report on ICJ and ITLOS, section 2.1, although recently ad hoc judges were appointed who were not nationals of the state who appointed them, see section 3.2.

Intersentia

21

courts[81] and in arbitration,[82] by contrast, adjudicators usually do not have the same nationality as one of the parties. Common nationality is a criterion for qualification in the former and for disqualification in the latter.

3.4. COMPETENCE

The adjudicators' expertise in the field of the dispute is generally deemed to be an essential feature of their qualification. The importance of competence is reflected, inter alia, in the requirement in many domestic systems that applicants to the position as a judge in domestic courts pass an examination.[83] Competence is also required by the constituting documents of international courts.[84]

This is also reflected in the circumstance that, in some systems, expertise is considered to be more relevant than nationality.[85] Thus, it has been affirmed that nationality as a criterion is giving way to expertise.[86]

---

[81] Special Non-National Report on Regional Human Rights Courts, section 5.3.1 on the African Court of Human and Peoples' Rights.

[82] Special Non-National Report on Commercial Institutional Arbitration, section 2.1 on the International Chamber of Commerce (ICC) and the London Court of International Arbitration Rules; Special Non-National Report on Investment Arbitration under Non-Treaty-Based Rules, section 3; Special Non-National Report on Commercial Ad Hoc Arbitration, section 2.1; Special Non-National Report on Claims Tribunals, section 2.1 on the Iran–US Claims Tribunal and section 2.3 on the Eritrea–Ethiopia Claims Tribunal; Special Non-National Report on the WTO, section 2.1.1; Special Non-National Report on the WIPO, section 1; on the position of French case law see the Special National Report on France, section 2.2.1.

[83] Special National Report on Italy, section 2.1.1; Special National Report on Mexico, section 4; Special National Report on Paraguay, section 1; Special National Report on Vietnam, section 3.1.1.2.

[84] Special Non-National Report on Regional Human Rights Courts, section 2.1 on the European Court of Human Rights, section 2.2 on the Inter-American Court of Human Rights, and section 2.3 on the African Court on Human and Peoples' Rights; Special Non-National Report on Regional Courts, section 2; Special Non-National Report on ICJ and ITLOS, section 2.1; ICSID Convention, Article 14(1); Hague Rules, Article 11(1)(b).

[85] Special Non-National Report on the WTO, section 2.2.1 on the Appellate Body; Special Non-National Report on Regional Courts, section 2 on the Caribbean Court of Justice; Special Non-National Report on ICJ and ITLOS, section 2.1, considering that the appointment of ad hoc judges is increasingly less linked to nationality, see section 3.2. For administrative tribunals, the nationality of a Member State is a criterion to be eligible to sit as a judge, but has no relevance for the specific disputes, see the Special Non-National Report on Administrative Tribunals. In addition, some arbitration rules do not have regard for nationality, see the Special Non-National Report on Commercial Institutional Arbitration, section 2.1 on the Singapore International Arbitration Centre; Special Non-National Report on Commodities Arbitration, section 1 on GAFTA and FOSFA; Special Non-National Report on the WIPO, section 1, if special circumstances require it and unless the parties agreed otherwise.

[86] Special Non-National Report on ICJ and ITLOS, section 3.2; Special National Report on Canada, section 1.2, pointing out that competence is a more important criterion than independence and impartiality.

On the one hand, the adjudicator's expertise is perceived not only as an assumption for properly assessing the disputed issues and thus for rendering efficient decisions, but also as a sufficient qualification capable of counterbalancing the connection due to nationality.[87] True independence is said to be the ability to render autonomous judgments, which is the case when the decision is based on expertise.[88]

On the other hand, expertise is often accompanied by a high level of activity in the field in which the dispute arose. This may in turn imply an involvement by the adjudicator that, even though not directly leading to conflicts of interests connected with the specific dispute, may create doubts about the complete autonomy of the adjudicator. Measures are being discussed to reduce this risk, see section 6.2 on multiple appointments.

Doubts about the complete autonomy of the adjudicator may be raised even though the adjudicator is not directly involved with the specific dispute or one of the parties. For example, the adjudicator may be active as counsel, as an expert or as an adjudicator in separate disputes between different parties but involving similar issues – and this may raise doubts about possible interests in rendering a decision as an adjudicator in one dispute that may create precedents useful to the same person in a different role in the other disputes. Measures are being discussed to reduce this risk, see section 6.3 on double-hatting.

Another possible consequence of the adjudicator's familiarity with the issues in dispute is so-called 'issue conflict': the adjudicator may on previous occasions have already dealt with issues similar to the one in dispute, or may have expressed opinions on such issues in doctrinal or professional contexts. This may create doubts about the existence of a pre-judgement – not of the specific dispute, but of the abstract issue. It is questionable whether this creates a risk that needs to be reduced, see section 6.4 on issue conflict.

3.5. BROADNESS OF THE FIELD

While adjudicators who are completely external to the field of the dispute will not give reason to doubt their independence and impartiality, an adjudicator who has never been exposed to the disputed issues is not necessarily equipped for rendering a decision efficiently. The extraneous adjudicator will need to become acquainted with the legal framework and the branch usages, and will need to be

---

[87] Special Non-National Report on Regional Human Rights Courts, section 2.1 on the European Court of Human Rights and section 2.2 on the Inter-American Court of Human Rights. Under some international investment agreements, however, the requirement of expertise does not replace, but comes in addition to, the requirement of nationality, see Special Non-National Report on Investment Arbitration under Treaty-Based Rules, section 1.2.

[88] See the comments in the Special Non-National Report on the WTO, section 1.1.2.

educated on the interests at stake. This may be quite demanding, particularly in specialised fields that require a deep understanding of complex issues. A certain familiarity with the disputed issues is therefore highly advisable to ensure the competence of the adjudicator. The balance between familiarity and extraneity varies, depending on the broadness of the field. In areas in which expertise is relatively widespread, such as, arguably,[89] investment protection, practices such as double-hatting are increasingly the object of criticism, see section 6.3. By contrast, in more specialised areas, such as maritime,[90] commodity[91] and sports arbitration,[92] the adjudicator's involvement in the field is deemed to be an inevitable prerequisite for the necessary expertise. Familiarity, therefore, trumps extraneity. The narrowness of the field even justifies deviating from the principle of equality of the parties in the appointment of adjudicators, something that has been approved by the European Court of Human Rights.[93] The Law Commission of England and Wales even finds it nearly impossible to avoid an arbitrator having connections to the parties or the subject matter of the dispute, given that arbitrators are qualified precisely for their immersive experience in the field of the dispute. What matters is not that arbitrators have connections, but that they are impartial.[94]

3.6. HIGH MORAL STANDARDS

The ability to maintain independence and impartiality notwithstanding familiarity with the disputed issues is also linked to the high moral standards required to act as an adjudicator. The European Court of Human Rights has consistently affirmed that a tribunal must be composed of judges who fulfil

---

[89] See the Note by the UNCITRAL Secretariat, Possible reform of investor-State dispute settlement (ISDS) – Ensuring independence and impartiality on the part of arbitrators and decision makers in ISDS, A/CN.9/WG.III/WP.151, para. 34, but see para. 77.

[90] Special National Report on Denmark, section 3.3; IBA Guidelines on conflict of interests, n. 5.

[91] Special Non-National Report on Commodities Arbitration, section 1; Special National Report on France, section 2.3.2.2; see also the UK Supreme Court in the mentioned *Halliburton* decision; IBA Guidelines on conflict of interests, n. 5.

[92] ECtHR decision *Mutu v. Switzerland*, para. 157; *Manchester City Football Club Ltd v. Football Association Premier League Limited and others* [2021] EWHC 628 (Comm); Swiss Tribunal Fédéral decision No. 4A_520/2021; IBA Guidelines on conflict of interests, n. 5.

[93] ECtHR decision *Mutu v. Switzerland*, para. 157, accepting the Court of Arbitration for Sports (CAS) requirement that the tribunal be composed by arbitrators chosen from a list drawn by sports organisations (closer to the interests of the federations than to the interests of the athletes).

[94] Law Commission Consultation Paper 257, *Review of the Arbitration Act 1996: A consultation paper*, 2022, chapter 3.

the requirements of technical competence and moral integrity,[95] and similar requirements are to be found in most sources.[96] However, the requirement is not found in many arbitration instruments.[97]

3.7. DIVERSITY

Where the adjudicating body is collegial, the degree of diversity in its composition may have significance for the outcome of the dispute, as well as for its legitimacy, see sections 6.1 and 6.4 below. Where the composition of the adjudicating body reflects the different interests involved in the dispute, the collegial deliberation will ensure that the different points of view are collated and thus all issues and interests are recognised and duly considered. If only the interests of one side of the dispute are represented in the adjudicating body, the principle of independence and impartiality is not respected.[98] As was seen in section 2.3, equality of the parties in the determination of the adjudicating body's composition is a non-waivable principle.

In arbitration, often each party appoints one arbitrator, and the two party-appointed arbitrators, or the appointing authority, appoint the chair.[99] For adjudicating bodies appointed in their entirety by an authority, the composition of the authority will have great significance, see below section 4.1.

The importance of a composition reflecting the diverse interests is confirmed in Article 25(2) of the ECtHR Rules, according to which the composition of the sections shall reflect the different legal systems among the Member States.

---

[95] *Guðmundur Andri Ástráðsson v. Iceland*, ECtHR decision of 1 December 2020, application no. 26374/18, paras 220–22.

[96] Special Non-National Report on Regional Human Rights Courts, section 2.1 on the European Court of Human Rights, section 2.2 on the Inter-American Court of Human Rights, and section 2.3 on the African Court on Human and Peoples' Rights; Special Non-National Report on Regional Courts, section 2; Special Non-National Report on ICJ and ITLOS, section 2.1; ICSID Convention, Article 14(1); Hague Rules, Article 11(1)(b).

[97] Special Non-National Report on Investment Arbitration under Non-Treaty-Based Rules, section 3.

[98] *Ali Riza and Others v. Turkey*, ECtHR decision of 28 January 2020, application nos 30226/10, 17880/11, 17887/11, 17891/11 and 5506/16, confirmed in *Sedat Doğan v. Turkey*, ECtHR decision of 18 May 2021, application no. 48909/14; *Naki and Amed Sportif Faaliyetler Kulübü Derneği v. Turkey*, ECtHR decision of 18 May 2021, application no. 48924/16; and *Ibrahim Tokmak v. Turkey*, ECtHR decision of 18 May 2021, application no. 54540/16. However, in its decision *Mutu v. Switzerland*, para. 157, the ECtHR assumed that it is necessary to prove the subjective lack of independence and impartiality of the individual components of the tribunal, irrespective of the circumstance that they were all chosen from a list drawn by one party, see section 3.5 above.

[99] Special Non-National Report on Commercial Ad Hoc Arbitration, sections 2.2.2 and 3.2.2.

This provision also refers to diversity in terms of geography and gender balance, reflecting a concern that is increasingly addressed in international adjudication.[100] A step in the direction of diversity is when the appointment is made on the basis of a public call for applications (see section 5 below), rather than following a closed selection carried out by the appointing authority. A public call enhances transparency and permits admission to the selection process of candidates who otherwise might have been overlooked.[101]

4. WHO MAKES THE SELECTION?

The identity of the selecting body is crucial to the selection of the adjudicator and may thus have a significant impact on the adjudicator's independence and impartiality. As the selecting body has a wide discretion in appointing the adjudicator, any lack of independence and impartiality on the part of the selecting body may be reflected in the appointment of an adjudicator who in turn is not independent or impartial. In this case, it will be necessary to counterbalance the selecting body's influence with various mechanisms, see sections 6, 7 and 8. There are two main approaches: selection can be carried out by an appointing authority, or the adjudicators may be appointed by the parties involved.

Combinations of these two approaches may also be found. A panel may be composed of both party-appointed and externally appointed adjudicators, as is often the case in arbitration: a panel of three often consists of one arbitrator appointed by each of the parties, and a presiding arbitrator appointed by the party-appointed arbitrators or by an appointing authority. Another possible combination is that a party presents a list of candidates, from which the appointing authority chooses the adjudicator, as is the case for many international courts, see section 4.2.

---

[100] Special Non-National Report on Regional Human Rights Courts, section 2.1 on the European Court of Human Rights, section 2.2 on the Inter-American Court of Human Rights, and section 2.3 on the African Court on Human and Peoples' Rights; Special Non-National Report on Commercial Institutional Arbitration, section 2.1. See the comments on the recent EU policy in the Special Non-National Report on the WTO, n. 32. Special National Report on Canada, section 1.1; Special National Report on Greece, section 2.1.1.1. See the Note by the UNCITRAL Secretariat, Possible reform of investor-State dispute settlement (ISDS) – Arbitrators and decision makers: appointment mechanisms and related issues, A/CN.9/WG.III/WP.152, paras 19–29, and the Note by the UNCITRAL Secretariat, Possible reform of investor-State dispute settlement (ISDS) – Selection and appointment of ISDS tribunal members, A/CN.9/WG.III/WP.203, paras 10–13.

[101] See the comments in the Special National Report on Greece, section 2.1.1.4.

4.1. APPOINTING AUTHORITY

The appointing authority may be a selection committee, a court or other body.[102] As pointed out in sections 3.7 and 6.1, the appointing authority must be composed in such a way as to reflect all the interests in the dispute. In addition, the composition of the appointing authority must meet the requirements of independence and impartiality, if the adjudicators that it appoints are to be independent and impartial.

Impartiality of the appointing authority is also ensured in domestic legislation for domestic courts[103] and arbitration.[104] However, there are also systems in which judges are appointed for their political preferences,[105] or in which the division of powers is not respected.[106] Where separation of powers is not ensured on a formal plan, self-imposed procedures may safeguard independence of the judiciary.[107]

The essential role of the appointing authority for the independence and impartiality of the adjudication system is the reason for a reform introduced in 2015 in the appointment regime of the ECtHR. Under the new regime, the Permanent Committee on the Election of Judges is to be composed of experts, rather than of politicians.[108] This is meant to ensure that appointments are made on the basis of competence, rather than of political considerations.

However, the national procedures for nomination are not always optimal, and influence of the executive branch on the composition of appointing authorities is still quite significant.[109]

The correlation between the independence of the appointing authority and the independence of the appointed adjudicators was emphasised, among

---

[102]   Individuals may also act as appointing authority, but an institution is preferable, see the comments in the Special Non-National Report on Commercial Ad Hoc Arbitration, section 2.2.1.1, and in the Special Non-National Report on Commercial Institutional Arbitration, section 2.2. See also the Special National Report on Hungary, section 2.2.1.

[103]   Special National Report on Denmark, section 2.1; Special National Report on Italy, section 3.1; Special National Report on Romania, sections 3.1 and 4.1.

[104]   See, for example, the Special National Report on Italy, section 2.1.2 on company law arbitration.

[105]   Special National Report on the USA, section 2.1.

[106]   Special National Report on Canada, section 2.1; Special National Report on Mexico, sections 3.1.1 and 3.2; Special National Report on Slovenia, section 2.1; Special National Report on Vietnam, sections 3.1.1 and 3.1.1.1.

[107]   Special National Report on Canada, section 4.1; Special National Report on Cyprus, section 3.

[108]   Special Non-National Report on Regional Human Rights Courts, section 3.1. Similarly, see the Special National Report on Canada, section 1.1.

[109]   Special National Report on France, section 1.1.1; Special National Report on Greece, sections 2.1.1.2 and 2.1.1.4; Special National Report on Romania, section 3.2; Special National Report on Turkey, section 4.

others, by the EU Court of Justice[110] and by the ECtHR[111] in a series of cases regarding reforms of the Polish judiciary system. The independence of the appointing authority is traditionally seen in the context of separation of powers, see section 2 above. The European Court of Human Rights found that judicial reforms introduced in Poland in 2017 did not safeguard independence and impartiality of Polish judges, because the method for composing the appointing authority no longer met the requirements of being independent from the executive and the legislature in a manner which ensured the independence of the Polish judiciary.

Additionally, just as the selection of the adjudicators needs to strike a balance between familiarity and extraneity, so does the composition of the authority appointing the adjudicators.[112]

The result of the selection will depend on the appointing authority's familiarity with the requirements for effectively adjudicating the relevant type of disputes, its understanding of the relevant legal framework and its knowledge of how to identify qualified adjudicators.

The identity of the appointing authority, therefore, may have a considerable impact not only on the independence and impartiality of the adjudicator, but also on the efficiency of the process.

This is reflected in the UNCITRAL Arbitration Rules. These rules' system for identifying the appointing authority may at first sight seem cumbersome, but is meant to ensure that the appointing authority has a certain proximity to the dispute.

The main rule under the UNCITRAL Arbitration Rules is that the appointing authority shall be chosen by agreement of the parties to the dispute (Article 6(1)). However, in the eventuality that the parties have not agreed which entity shall act as appointing authority, the Rules give a two-stage procedure: the Secretary-General of the Permanent Court of Arbitration (PCA) shall designate the body that will act as appointing authority (Article 6(2)). This division between designating and appointing authority may, at first sight, seem unnecessary. The PCA is a highly respected institution with broad expertise in international arbitration. Why not stop at this stage of the procedure and let the Secretary-General of the PCA act as appointing authority? As a matter of fact, the parties often agree that the Secretary-General of the PCA shall act as appointing authority – an option that is, of course, available to the parties, as confirmed in Article 6(1). However, the second stage of the procedure, in which the Secretary-General of the PCA designates the entity that will act as appointing authority, is meant to ensure that the appointing authority is close to the dispute

---

[110] CJEU decisions in cases C-585/18, C-624/18 and C-625/18.

[111] *Advance Pharma sp. z o.o v. Poland*, ECtHR decision of 3 February 2022, application no. 1469/20, para. 223, confirmed by the Grand Chamber decision in *Grzęda v. Poland*, paras 300, 345.

[112] ECtHR decision *Grzęda v. Poland*, para. 346.

and thus capable of better assessing the characteristics that a tribunal should have and of identifying individuals who may be appropriate as arbitrators in that dispute. The need for this designation appears clear in light of the scope of application of the UNCITRAL Arbitration Rules: these rules are applicable to disputes that may be decided by tribunals seated in any country of the world, between parties who may come from any country of the world, on all possible issues, and with values that may range from extremely low to extremely high. While the PCA has undisputed expertise within international arbitration, it does not necessarily possess the local and specialised knowledge that may be required for selecting arbitrators in this disparate range of disputes. For this reason, the UNCITRAL Arbitration Rules entrust the PCA with the task of designating the entity that may possess the local and specialised knowledge required to act as an appointing authority under the circumstances of any given dispute.

Although cumbersome, this double procedure was retained when the UNCITRAL Working Group II drafted the Rules for expedited arbitration: also under Article 6(1) of the UNCITRAL Expedited Arbitration Rules, the Secretary-General of the PCA shall act as designating authority. The purpose of the expedited rules is to permit more expedient proceedings than the ordinary. Therefore, to enhance efficiency, the expedited rules reduce the term within which the designation has to be made, and permit a party to ask that the Secretary-General of the PCA act as designating authority or as appointing authority. However, to safeguard the underlying interest, according to which the appointing authority should have closeness to the dispute, the expedited rules permit the Secretary-General of the PCA to act as designating authority even when requested by the parties to act as appointing authority (Article 6(3) of the expedited rules).

A corresponding rationale can be found in the Arbitration Rules of the International Chamber of Commerce (ICC). In addition, ICC tribunals may be seated in any country of the world. Under Article 13(3) of the ICC Arbitration Rules, the Court of International Arbitration of the ICC acts as appointing authority, but the appointments are made on the basis of proposals made by national committees.

Proximity to the dispute is thus ensured both under the UNCITRAL Arbitration Rules and under the ICC Arbitration Rules: under the former, by providing for a central authority that designates the local appointing authority; and under the latter, by providing national committees that make proposals for the central appointing authority.

Other arbitral institutions act as appointing authorities without the need for this double procedure.[113] This can be explained in light of the circumstance that

---

[113]   A variety of bodies within the institution may act as appointing authority: the board, committees, courts. See the Special Non-National Report on Commercial Institutional Arbitration, section 2.2.

Intersentia

arbitral institutions usually administer disputes decided by tribunals seated in the territory of the institution. While these disputes may also take place between parties who may come from any country of the world, on all possible issues, and with values that may range from extremely low to extremely high, they will generally be carried out in the territory of the institution and under the arbitration law prevailing in that country. Therefore, a certain closeness between the appointing authority and the dispute is ensured.

In some international courts, independence and impartiality of the appointing authority is ensured in that challenges to the appointed adjudicators are decided by a body different from that which made the appointment, see section 7 below.

4.2. PARTY APPOINTMENT

In some dispute resolution mechanisms, particularly arbitration, the appointing authority intervenes only if the parties have not succeeded in appointing the tribunal – the main rule is that the tribunal is appointed by the parties according to the arbitration agreement, to the applicable arbitration rules or to the applicable arbitration law. This mechanism is meant to ensure the principle of equality between the parties, see sections 2.3 and 6.1. Should one party not make the appointment, the appointing authority will intervene and make the appointment on the party's behalf.

The system of party appointment is not uncontroversial. On the one hand, arbitrators appointed by the parties are suspected of being biased and of being inclined to decide in favour of the party who appointed them, for the purpose of being appointed again by the same party in new disputes. Party appointment is often deemed to prejudice the legitimacy of the adjudicators. This has recently been argued in respect of investment arbitration, see section 6.2. The system of party appointment is also criticised for preventing diversity by confirming pre-existing connections, and for creating conflicts of interests when professionals belonging to the same environment appoint each other or alternatively appear as counsel and arbitrator (double-hatting), see section 6.3.

On the other hand, party appointment is the fundamental basis of a dispute settlement mechanism such as arbitration.[114] It makes it possible to select arbitrators for their expertise and their understanding of the specific area of

---

[114] Special Non-National Report on Commercial Institutional Arbitration, section 2.3. See also the Note by the UNCITRAL Secretariat, Possible reform of investor-State dispute settlement (ISDS) – Arbitrators and decision makers: appointment mechanisms and related issues, A/CN.9/WG.III/WP.152, para. 30, and the Report of UNCITRAL Working Group III (Investor-State Dispute Settlement Reform) on the work of its thirty-fifth session, A/CN.9/935, 2017, para. 83. See also William W. Park, 'Arbitration's Discontents: Between the Pernicious and the Precarious', in *Mélanges en l'honneur du Professeur Bernard Audit*, LGDJ 2014, pp. 592 f.

the dispute. There may be few qualified experts in sophisticated areas, and it may be more important to ensure that the tribunal understands the law and the underlying issues than to avoid appointing anyone who has an involvement in similar disputes. When called upon to scrutinise the appointment mechanism of the Court of Arbitration for Sport (CAS), the European Court of Human Rights found that it did not violate the principle of independence and impartiality laid down in Article 6 of the European Convention of Human Rights.[115]

Party appointment, furthermore, does not imply that parties may disregard any criteria and exercise their appointing power in a capricious way. The principle that adjudicators be independent and impartial also applies to party-appointed adjudicators (see section 2.1 above), and to a large extent it is not waivable, see section 2.3 above. This means that remedies will be available in case the principle is violated, see sections 7 and 8 below – first and foremost, party appointment is coupled with the other party's right to challenge the adjudicator if there are doubts about the adjudicator's independence and impartiality.

That party appointment is an appropriate mechanism also beyond mere commercial disputes is confirmed by the Hague Rules on Business and Human Rights Arbitration.[116] The Hague Rules emphasise that arbitration can assist in implementing the UN Guiding Principles on Business and Human Rights.[117] The Hague Rules are based on the UNCITRAL Arbitration Rules, and, therefore, prefer party appointment,[118] additionally spelling out the requirements that arbitrators shall be of high moral character and exercise independent and impartial judgment,[119] and that the presiding arbitrator shall have demonstrated expertise in international dispute resolution and in areas relevant to the dispute.[120]

The UNCITRAL Arbitration Rules, with the party appointment mechanism, are also the basis for the rules used in the Iran–US Claims Tribunal.[121]

The model of party appointment also inspires the nomination by the states of candidates to the position of adjudicator in international bodies[122] – with the difference that the Member States, who will ultimately be party to a dispute,

---

[115] ECtHR decision *Mutu and Pechstein v. Switzerland*, paras 150 ff. See also the English decision in *Halliburton*.

[116] Hague Rules on Business and Human Rights Arbitration, launched 12 December 2019, by the Centre for International Legal Cooperation and the Business and Human Rights Arbitration Working Group, chaired by former ICJ Judge Bruno Simma, available at https://www.cilc.nl/cms/wp-content/uploads/2019/12/The-Hague-Rules-on-Business-and-Human-Rights-Arbitration_CILC-digital-version.pdf.

[117] Hague Rules, Preamble, Comment No. 2. The UN Guiding Principles are available at https://www.ohchr.org/Documents/Publications/GuidingPrinciplesBusinessHR_EN.pdf.

[118] Hague Rules, Article 11(1)(c).

[119] Hague Rules, Article 11(1)(b).

[120] Hague Rules, Article 11(1)(c).

[121] Special Non-National Report on Claims Tribunals, section 2.

[122] Special National Report on France, section 1.5; Special National Report on Italy, section 3.2.

Intersentia

appoint adjudicators who will sit in the court, and not the adjudicators who will decide a specific dispute.[123] The state-appointed judge will eventually hear the specific dispute anyway, see section 3.3 above. Therefore, although state appointment to permanent courts does not permit the tailoring of the appointment to the specific issue of each dispute, it permits consideration of the candidate's profile, competence and approach. To a very large extent, therefore, it corresponds to party appointment as is practised, for example, in the context of arbitration.

Similarly, the Comprehensive Economic and Trade Agreement (CETA) provides for the establishment of a permanent court, the first instance of which is a tribunal composed of three groups: one with members from each of the parties (Canada and the EU), and one of nationals of third parties.

Here there are three major variants, which aim at enhancing the legitimacy of party appointment to international bodies: the state may nominate the candidate, and an appointing authority confirms the nomination by appointing the candidate without any substantive screening;[124] the state nominates the candidate or a list of candidates, and the appointing authority screens the nominations and proceeds to appoint the candidate whom it considers most appropriate;[125] or the state does not participate in the procedure, but applicants from the relevant state apply directly to the appointing authority.[126] The third method is not widespread, but ensures that governmental influence is kept to a minimum. The first two methods rely, to a varying extent, on the quality of the state's nominating procedure – see, on this point, section 5.

5. THE SELECTION MECHANISM

The selecting body's role in nominating or appointing the adjudicators may have a significant impact on the adjudicators' independence and impartiality. The more the selecting body may exercise influence on the outcome of the appointment or on the adjudicator's position, the more the adjudicator is exposed to the risk of not being independent or of being biased. The adjudicator

---

[123]   Special Non-National Report on ICJ and ITLOS, section 2.1.

[124]   Special Non-National Report on Regional Courts, section 3 on the EFTA Court, the Benelux Court, the Court of Justice of the Common Market for Eastern and Southern Africa and the Mercosur system.

[125]   Special Non-National Report on Regional Human Rights Courts, section 3.1 on the European Court of Human Rights, section 3.2 on the Inter-American Court of Human Rights, and section 3.3 on the African Court on Human and Peoples' Rights; Special Non-National Report on Regional Courts, section 3 on the CJEU; Special Non-National Report on the WTO, section 2.2.1; Special Non-National Report on the WIPO, section 4.

[126]   Special Non-National Report on Regional Courts, section 3 on the Economic Community of West African States Court.

may be tempted, for the purpose of achieving benefits or avoiding negative consequences, to render decisions that are likely to please the selecting body.

As was seen above, the selecting body may be a party or an appointing authority. Furthermore, there are various methods: the adjudicator may be appointed by each of the parties or by the authority, may be appointed by consent of the parties to the dispute or by consent of the represented parties. A frequent combination, particularly in arbitration, is that each party appoints an adjudicator, and the two party-appointed adjudicators, or an appointing authority, appoint the chair.[127] The absence of any formalised method may also be encountered.[128]

Often a combination of these methods may be found: the appointment may be made from a shortlist of candidates nominated by the different parties,[129] or a roster of candidates agreed between the parties.[130] Another alternative is that the appointing authority appoints the adjudicator subject to the parties' objections.[131]

Variations may also be found: the selection may be based not on the appointment of one adjudicator, but on the exclusion of all but one candidate on a list agreed between the parties.[132]

When there is a combination of nomination and appointment, the two-tier process is meant as a safeguard of independence and impartiality. The idea is that the nomination is made by a party or a potential party (i.e. a state which could potentially be involved in a dispute before the international court on which the adjudicator will sit), and the appointment is made by an appointing authority which represents the court or the totality of the Member States.[133] The appointment stage is meant to permit an objective evaluation of the nominated adjudicator's qualifications and thus to safeguard independence and impartiality. However, the goal is not necessarily achieved. The nomination

---

[127] For an overview of the variety of solution in different arbitral institutions, see Special Non-National Report on Commercial Institutional Arbitration, section 2.3.2. See also the Note by the UNCITRAL Secretariat, Possible reform of investor-State dispute settlement (ISDS) – Arbitrators and decision makers: appointment mechanisms and related issues, A/CN.9/WG.III/WP.152, paras 6–14.

[128] Special National Report on Mexico, section 3.

[129] See n. 125.

[130] Special Non-National Report on Investment Arbitration under Treaty-Based Rules, section 2.

[131] Special Non-National Report on the WTO, section 2.1.1.

[132] Special Non-National Report on Commercial Ad Hoc Arbitration, section 2.2.3.2; Special Non-National Report on Commercial Institutional Arbitration, section 2.3.1; Special Non-National Report on the WIPO, section 3; Special Non-National Report on Investment Arbitration under Treaty-Based Rules, section 2.

[133] Special Non-National Reports on Regional Courts, section 3 on the CJEU; Special Non-National Report on Regional Human Rights Courts, section 3.1 on the European Court of Human Rights, section 3.2 on the Inter-American Court of Human Rights, and section 3.3 on the African Court on Human and Peoples' Rights.

Intersentia

stage is usually left to the country's own procedures.[134] Even where the court's constituting documents regulate the nominating authority, as is the case for the ICJ and the International Criminal Court, which refer to the National Groups in the PCA, the nomination procedure is far from transparent.[135]

The nomination phase is often highly politicised and influenced by governments according to opaque mechanisms.[136] Competence and independence are not necessarily at the core of the selection process.[137] Even when the nomination is not influenced by the executive, it may aim at professional protectionism[138] or nepotism.[139]

As mentioned above, efforts are being made to improve the quality of the nomination process. The selection procedures have been reformed for the CJEU[140] and the ECtHR.[141] Transparency was introduced, and this led to an improvement of the nomination process.[142] In particular, the introduction of public calls for applications leads to more diverse lists.[143] Moreover, the appointing authority actively makes use of its right to refuse a list of candidates which was not prepared according to the procedure.[144] The parallel court to the CJEU, the EFTA Court, has not yet introduced a similar reform.[145] However, one of the three Member States of the EFTA Court, Norway, for the nomination of the Norwegian judge to the EFTA Court in 2022 spontaneously initiated a public

---

[134] Special Non-National Report on the WTO, section 2.2.1; Special Non-National Report on Regional Human Rights Courts, section 3.3 on the African Court on Human and Peoples' Rights.

[135] Special National Report on France, section 1.1.2, notwithstanding that consultations with the relevant environment are carried out, as recommended, see section 1.1.4.

[136] Special Non-National Report on Regional Human Rights Courts, section 3.1 on the European Court of Human Rights, section 3.2 on the Inter-American Court of Human Rights, and section 3.3 on the African Court on Human and Peoples' Rights; Special National Report on Greece, section 2.1.1.4; Special National Report on Italy, section 2.2; Special National Report on Mexico, section 3.2; Special National Report on Romania, section 4.2; Special National Report on the USA, section 3.2.

[137] Special Non-National Report on ICJ and ITLOS, section 1; Special National Report on Italy, section 2.2; Special National Report on Slovenia, sections 2.2 and 3.2.

[138] Special National Report on France, section 1.1.4.

[139] Special National Report on Mexico, section 2.

[140] Special Non-National Report on Regional Courts, section 3.

[141] Special Non-National Report on Regional Human Rights Courts, sections 2.1 and 3.1.

[142] Special National Report on France, section 1.3.3; Special National Report on Greece, section 2.1.1.5; Special National Report on Italy, sections 4.1.1 and 6.2.

[143] Special National Report on Denmark, sections 2.1 and 2.2.3; Special National Report on France, section 1.3.5; Special National Report on Greece, sections 2.1.1.1, 2.1.1.4 and 2.1.2.1; Special National Report on Romania, sections 2.2, 3.2 and 4.2; Special National Report on Slovenia, section 2.2.

[144] Special National Report on France, section 1.3.3; Special National Report on Greece, section 2.1.2.5. See also the Special Non-National Report on the WTO, section 2.1.1.

[145] For this reason, a complaint was filed by the former president of the EFTA Court: Special Non-National Report on Regional Courts, section 3.

consultation with the purpose of regulating the nomination mechanism in a way similar to the procedure of the CJEU.[146]

Another way to improve the quality of the appointment is to skip the nomination phase and let applicants from the relevant states apply directly to the appointing authority.[147]

Selection has also undergone professionalisation in arbitration.[148] Where selection earlier was mainly based on personal connections, it is now based on a systematic screening of the potential arbitrator's competence. An increasingly widespread practice is that of pre-appointment interviews. Potential arbitrators are asked about their availability and, only in general terms, their stance on different issues of law, both substantive and procedural. This practice is increasingly accepted,[149] at least for party-appointed arbitrators,[150] and subject to regulation.[151]

Another development that is enhancing independence and impartiality in arbitration is increased transparency, particularly in investment arbitration. In investment arbitration, there is a clear public interest in the dispute and its outcome. The arbitral tribunal is called upon to evaluate the conduct of the state, and this may involve scrutinising, inter alia, the state's policies, its balancing of conflicting policies, its management of public interests, etc. The award, furthermore, may have an impact on the state's regulations and future policies, with effects that go far beyond the legal relationship between the disputing parties. The public, therefore, has a clear interest in being informed about investment disputes, and stakeholders have an expectation of being able to present comments. Facing growing criticism for a lack of legitimacy and accountability,[152] already in 2006 the ICSID Rules were amended to introduce transparency,[153] and transparency was enhanced in the version of 2022.[154] In 2013, the UNCITRAL adopted the Rules on Transparency in Treaty-based Investor-State Arbitration. A new provision was added in Article 1(4) of the

---

[146] Letter of the Ministry of Foreign Affairs dated 11 February 2022, 21/13204.

[147] Special Non-National Report on Regional Courts, section 3 on the Economic Community of West African States Court.

[148] For an anecdotal observation of this development based on my experience see Giuditta Cordero-Moss, 'Interpretation of contracts in international commercial arbitration: diversity on more than one level' (2014/1) *European Review of Private Law* 13, 33 f.

[149] Special National Report on Cyprus, section 3. But not always is it accepted, see Special Non-National Report on the WTO, section 2.1.1 on WTO panels.

[150] Special Non-National Report on Ad Hoc Arbitration, section 2.3.1, referring to the IBA Guidelines.

[151] Special Non-National Report on Commercial Institutional Arbitration, section 2.4; Special Non-National Report on Investment Arbitration under Treaty-Based Rules, section 4.6.

[152] For references, see UNCTAD, *Transparency in IIAS: A Sequel*, UNCTAD Series on Issues in International Investment Agreements, 2012, p. 36, and UNCTAD, *World Investment Report 2015*, p. 148.

[153] https://icsid.worldbank.org/news-and-events/speeches-articles/brief-history-amendment-icsid-rules-and-regulations.

[154] https://icsid.worldbank.org/news-and-events/communiques/icsid-administrative-council-approves-amendment-icsid-rules.

UNCITRAL Arbitration Rules (which had just been revised in 2010) to incorporate the Rules on Transparency for arbitration initiated pursuant to an investment treaty concluded on or after 1 April 2014. Furthermore, with the 2014 Mauritius Convention on Transparency, parties to investment treaties concluded before 1 April 2014 express their consent to also apply the Rules on Transparency to disputes based on investment treaties concluded prior to 1 April 2014. The UNCITRAL Working Group III is also considering transparency.[155] For human rights disputes, the Hague Rules suggest a regulation that is largely based on the UNCITRAL Transparency Rules.

The calls for transparency that have recently turned around the world of investment arbitration seem to also be affecting commercial arbitration.[156] Commercial awards are being published to a greater extent than earlier,[157] institutions are being more transparent regarding the appointment and removal of arbitral tribunals,[158] and initiatives to increase transparency in commercial arbitration are flourishing.[159]

---

[155] See the Note by the UNCITRAL Secretariat, Possible reform of investor-State dispute settlement (ISDS) – Ensuring independence and impartiality on the part of arbitrators and decision makers in ISDS, A/CN.9/WG.III/WP.151, paras 80–86.

[156] Calling for transparency in commercial arbitration, see Diego Fernández Arroyo, 'Nothing is for free: the prices to pay for *arbitrabilizing* legal disputes', in Loïc Cadiet, Burkard Hess and Marta Requejo Isidro (eds), *Privatizing Dispute Resolution*, Nomos 2019, pp. 635 ff. In 2016 the then Lord Chief Justice of England and Wales, Lord Thomas, held a lecture in which he pointed out that, since many commercial parties choose arbitration to solve their disputes and appeal from arbitral awards is very restricted, courts are not participating to the desirable extent to the development of the law: Lord Thomas of Cwmgiedd, Lord Chief Justice of England and Wales, Bailii Lecture: Developing Commercial Law through the Courts: Rebalancing the Relationship between the Courts and Arbitration, 9 March 2016. The same criticism had been put forward, decades earlier, by the then Chief Justice of the Norwegian Supreme Court, Carsten Smith, 'Voldgift – domstolenes konkurrent og hjelper' (1993) *Tidsskrift for Rettsvitenskap* 474. The Norwegian Arbitration Act of 2004 acted upon this criticism and assumes that confidentiality of the awards must be agreed to by the parties. In contrast, most arbitration laws still assume confidentiality as the main rule in arbitration.

[157] Many arbitration institutions publish, in an anonymised version, a selection of the awards rendered under their rules. For example, following an amendment to the ICC Notes to the parties and arbitral tribunals on the conduct of the arbitration under the ICC Arbitration Rules dated 1 January 2019, https://iccwbo.org/publication/note-parties-arbitral-tribunals-conduct-arbitration/, section III.D, all awards rendered after 1 January 2019 may be published, unless one party objects. In addition, awards are collected in databases such as Case Law on UNCITRAL Texts (CLOUT, https://www.uncitral.org/clout/), the database on the UNIDROIT Principles and CISG Unilex (http://www.unilex.info/).

[158] See, for example, the publication by the Stockholm Arbitration Institute in 2017 of its policy for appointing arbitrators: https://sccinstitute.com/media/220131/scc-policy-appointment-of-arbitrators-2017.pdf. As from 2016, the ICC publishes information about arbitrators sitting in tribunals administered under the ICC Rules: see the ICC Notes to the parties and arbitral tribunals on the conduct of the arbitration under the ICC Arbitration Rules dated 1 January 2019, section III.B. In 2018, the London Court of International Arbitration released a database on decisions on challenges to the arbitrators: https://www.lcia.org/challenge-decision-database.aspx.

[159] See, for example, Arbitrator Intelligence, https://arbitratorintelligence.com.

The importance of the selection mechanism applies not only to the appointment of the members of an adjudicating body, but also to the allocation of cases to the different panels that may be formed within an adjudicating body.[160] The composition of the panels and the allocation of the cases to the panels may be based on a random system enhancing objectivity,[161] on predetermined criteria for rotation,[162] or on discretionary assignment. An objective or random allocation reduces the possibility of steering the allocation of specific cases to certain adjudicators, thus reducing the possible impact on the adjudicators' independence and impartiality. However, this also reduces the possibility to allocate disputes according to the specialisation of the adjudicators, and thus may give inefficient results.[163] This concern may be met by organising the adjudicating body into different sections, each specialising in certain types of disputes. This organisation may permit canalising the disputes according to an objective criterion (competence), and to preserve objectivity in the allocation within the competent section.

6. COUNTERBALANCING THE SELECTING BODY'S INFLUENCE

The more the selecting body (whether an external appointing authority or the parties) may influence the outcome of the selection, the more the adjudication system is exposed to the suspicion of not being independent. Adjudicators may be suspected of rendering decisions that they assume may be pleasing for the selecting body. There are some mechanisms to reduce any incentives that the selection system may give. However, these mechanisms may lead to disqualifying many professionals with the relevant qualifications and experience, thus giving inefficient results, see section 3.2. Some of these mechanisms are discussed below.

There are other ways of detaching the adjudication system from the states or the parties involved. Some of these ways are more organisational than merely legal, and regard, for example, the financing of the adjudication activity. These mechanisms are not discussed in this report.

---

[160] See the 2017 International Association of Judges Universal Charter of the Judge, https://www.unodc.org/res/ji/import/international_standards/the_universal_charter_of_the_judge/universal_charter_2017_english.pdf, Articles 3–4; *Daktaras v. Lithuania*, ECtHR decision of 31 July 2012, application no. 36662/04; *Moiseyev v. Russia*, ECtHR decision of 9 October 2008, application no. 62936/00; *Miracle v. Hungary*, ECtHR decision of 12 January 2016, application no. 57774/13; *Parlov v. Croatia*, ECtHR decision of 22 December 2009, application no. 24810/06.

[161] Special Non-National Report on the WTO, section 2.2.1; Special Non-National Report on Investment Arbitration under Treaty-Based Rules, section 3.

[162] Special Non-National Report on Italy, sections 2.1.1 and 4.1.1.

[163] This objection is raised in the Special National Report on Vietnam, section 3.1.1.2.

6.1. COLLEGIAL NOMINATION OR APPOINTMENT

As was explained in section 3.7, to achieve legitimacy an adjudicating body should in its composition reflect all the interests involved in the dispute, or be completely independent.[164] If the appointing authority reflects the constellation of the interests involved (see section 4.1), or if the parties participate in the appointment of the adjudicating body (see section 4.2), the different interests involved are likely to be considered when the composition of the adjudicating body is determined. That a collegial body may in its composition reflect diversity highlights an important feature of collegial decision-making: diversity leads to a dynamic in the deliberations that may result in balanced decisions. Furthermore, the interaction between the adjudicators may work as an additional guarantee of independence and impartiality, as the deliberations would reveal possible conflicts or bias. Additionally, in a collegial body the voice of a biased or conflicted adjudicator would be counterweighed by the other adjudicators. A large number of adjudicators is likely to be an efficient safeguard of independence and impartiality.[165]

What should be avoided is an appointment procedure involving only some of the disputed interests. Section 3.5 above showed that the narrowness of the field may justify departing from the principle of equality of the parties in the appointment procedure. Another mechanism that does not follow equality is laid down in section 17 of the English Arbitration Act. According to this provision, the arbitrator appointed by one of the parties shall act as a sole arbitrator as a consequence of the failure by the other party to appoint an arbitrator in a panel of three – on the condition that the party failing to appoint its own arbitrator is given notice and an opportunity to make good its default.[166] This means that, if the other party does not proceed to appoint an arbitrator, the tribunal is transformed from a three-member tribunal into a sole arbitrator, and that the sole arbitrator is appointed unilaterally by one party. In contrast, the usual approach in such a situation is that the appointing authority makes the appointment on behalf of the defaulting party. This mechanism is more in line with the principle of independence and impartiality.

As was mentioned in section 4.2, in the field of investment arbitration the method of party appointment is increasingly criticised for permitting the parties to unduly influence the composition of the tribunal. In addition to the criticism

---

[164] Special Non-National Report on Commercial Ad Hoc Arbitration, sections 2.2.2 and 3.3.1.

[165] See the considerations made in the Special Non-National Report on ICJ and ITLOS, section 2.1. See also the Note by the UNCITRAL Secretariat, Possible reform of investor-State dispute settlement (ISDS) – Standing multilateral mechanism: Selection and appointment of ISDS tribunal members and related matters, A/CN.9/WG.III/WP.213, paras 18 and 20.

[166] See the Special Non-National Report on Commercial Ad Hoc Arbitration, section 3.2.2. Similarly, see the Special Non-National Report on Investment Arbitration under Non-Treaty-Based Rules, section 5 on the London Court of International Arbitration Rules.

discussed under sections 6.2, 6.3 and 6.4, party appointment is said to prevent diversity. The criticism may be avoided if the entire tribunal is appointed by agreement of all the parties, or by the appointing authority. This applies particularly, but not only, when the tribunal is composed of a sole arbitrator, who is usually appointed either by agreement of the parties or by the appointing authority.[167] In practice, it may be difficult to obtain the consent of all the parties once a dispute has arisen – which makes it even more important that the appointing authority is independent and impartial, as well as knowledgeable of the requirements that adjudicators should meet in the specific dispute.

6.2. LIMITING REAPPOINTMENTS

An adjudicator may be interested in the prospect of being reappointed (so-called multiple or repeat appointments). This may expose the adjudicator to the suspicion of rendering decisions that are likely to encourage new appointments.[168]

Repeat appointments are generally deemed to create a potential conflict of interests. However, as was seen in section 3.1, there is no consistent standard on this matter.

A possible way to reduce the influence of this incentive is to ban reappointments.[169] Another possible way is to provide for full-time terms that

---

[167]   Special Non-National Report on Investment Arbitration under Non-Treaty-Based Rules, section 4. The importance of involving the parties is emphasised by the circumstance that institutions have procedures involving the parties even when a sole arbitrator is to be appointed by the appointing authority, see the Special Non-National Report on Commercial Institutional Arbitration, section 2.3.1.

[168]   Jan Paulsson, 'Moral hazard in international dispute resolution' (2010) 25 *ICSID Review* 339; Jan Albert Van den Berg, 'Dissenting Opinions by Party-Appointed Arbitrators in Investment Arbitration', in Mahnoush Arsanjani, Jacob Katz Cogan, Robert Sloane and Siegfried Wiessner (eds), *Looking to the Future: Essays on International Law in Honor of W. Michael Reisman*, Martinus Nijhoff 2011; for further references, see Diego Fernández Arroyo, 'Nothing is for free: the prices to pay for *arbitrabilizing* legal disputes', in Loïc Cadiet, Burkard Hess and Marta Requejo Isidro (eds), *Privatizing Dispute Resolution*, Nomos 2019, p. 627. See also Note by the UNCITRAL Secretariat, Possible reform of investor-State dispute settlement (ISDS) – Ensuring independence and impartiality on the part of arbitrators and decision makers in ISDS, A/CN.9/WG.III/WP.151, paras 22–24; Note by the UNCITRAL Secretariat, Possible reform of investor-State dispute settlement (ISDS) – Background information on a code of conduct, A/CN.9/WG.III/WP.167; Report of UNCITRAL Working Group III (Investor-State Dispute Settlement Reform) on the work of its thirty-fifth session, A/CN.9/935, 2017, paras 54, 56, 70, 73, 78.

[169]   Special Non-National Report on Regional Human Rights Courts, section 4.1 on the European Court of Human Rights; Special Non-National Report on Regional Courts, section 4 on the Economic Community of West African States Court and the Court of the Eurasian Economic Union.

are so long that seeking other appointments under the term is not possible.[170] Similarly, when judges are elected, the goal of reducing dependence on the public is in part achieved by long terms between election cycles.[171]

Where the volume of disputes is not such as to justify full-time, long-term positions for the adjudicators, the measures that can safeguard independence and impartiality consist mainly in imposing a duty to disclose repeat appointments as a circumstance that may give rise to doubts about possible conflicts or bias and give the parties the possibility to object to the appointment of that adjudicator, see sections 6.6 and 7.

6.3. LIMITING DOUBLE-HATTING

An adjudicator may be interested in being appointed to, or may hold, other functions within the dispute resolution system, such as an expert witness or counsel in other disputes. When an adjudicator holds or has acted in multiple roles, a situation usually referred to as double-hatting, independence and impartiality may be affected in several ways.[172]

Adjudicators may, through their participation in other, related disputes, have more information relevant to the dispute than the other members of the tribunal. Such asymmetric information may have an impact on the balance in the deliberations, and thus affect the outcome of the dispute.

In addition, double-hatting may expose the adjudication to bias and may raise suspicion of adjudicators rendering decisions that may serve the interests they represent in other disputes.

This is not perceived as an obstacle in areas where the degree of specialisation is high and the pool from which to choose adjudicators is not broad, see section 3.5.

---

[170] Special Non-National Report on Regional Human Rights Courts, section 4.1 on the European Court of Human Rights: the reform extended the term to nine years from the original six, without the possibility to be reappointed; Special Non-National Report on the WTO, section 2.2.2: the EU proposal for reform of the WTO contemplates a term of six to eight years without reappointment; Special Non-National Report on Regional Courts, section 4, refers to a suggestion that the system currently applicable in the CJEU (six-year renewable term) could be retained, but that non-renewals should be justified; the judges of other regional courts remain in their role until they reach the age of retirement, see Special Non-National Report on Regional Courts, section 4 on the Benelux Court and the Caribbean Court of Justice. This latter alternative is usual for domestic courts, see the Special National Report on Canada, section 4.1; Special National Report on Italy, section 5.1.1; Special National Report on Slovenia, section 2.1; Special National Report on the USA, section 2.1.

[171] Special National Report on the USA, section 2.2.

[172] For references, see the Background paper on double-hatting prepared by ICSID on 25 February 2022 for the work on a Code of Conduct: https://icsid.worldbank.org/sites/default/files/Background_Papers_Double-Hatting_(final)_2021.02.25.pdf.

General Report

Generally, however, this is perceived as a threat to the legitimacy of the adjudication system, particularly in the field of investment arbitration.[173]

On some occasions, the nomination process reflects this concern, and states advise applicants for positions as adjudicators that they are to refrain from acting in positions that would lead to double-hatting.[174] Similarly, where adjudicators are to be appointed from a closed list, on some occasions being admitted to the list is conditional on not acting as counsel before the adjudicating body for which the list is meant.[175]

Some international investment agreements contain a complete ban on double-hatting,[176] while others have a more limited prohibition affecting double-hatting before tribunals acting under the same treaty under which the arbitrator is acting and only for the duration of the proceedings in which the arbitrator is acting.[177]

The ICSID/UNCITRAL draft Code of Conduct, in its third version, offered three alternative approaches in Article 4: a full prohibition affecting any activities other than the adjudication of the dispute in question, a modified prohibition applying to activities relating to the same measures, same issue or same parties as those at issue in the dispute in question, or a duty to disclose any such other activity, with a related right to challenge the adjudicator. In the fourth version, Article 4 was based on a combination of these approaches: a modified prohibition applying to activities relating to the same measures, same issue or same parties as those at issue in the dispute in question is coupled with the possibility for the parties to waive the application of Article 4. The provision, however, was not yet in its final version, as the comments point out.[178] In the fifth, and, at the time of writing this general report, latest version, the provision was not

---

[173] Note by the UNCITRAL Secretariat, A/CN.9/WG.III/WP.142, paras 40, 41, 64; Note by the UNCITRAL Secretariat, Possible reform of investor-State dispute settlement (ISDS) – Ensuring independence and impartiality on the part of arbitrators and decision makers in ISDS, A/CN.9/WG.III/WP.151, paras 25–34; Note by the UNCITRAL Secretariat, Possible reform of investor-State dispute settlement (ISDS) – Background information on a code of conduct, A/CN.9/WG.III/WP.167, para. 25; Report of Working Group III (Investor-State Dispute Settlement Reform) on the work of its thirty-sixth session (Vienna, 29 October– 2 November 2018), A/CN.9/964, para. 72; Report of Working Group III on the work of its thirty-fifth session, A/CN.9/935, para. 78. See Malcolm Langford, Daniel Behn and Runar Lie, 'The Ethics and Empirics of Double Hatting', *SSRN Electronic Journal*, 0.2139/ssrn.3008643.

[174] See the Special National Report for France, section 1.3.5 on the ICSID roster; Special National Report for Romania, section 2.2 on the ECtHR.

[175] See, for example, in sports arbitration the CAS Code since its 2010 edition, and the CAS-CNOSF since 2020.

[176] For example, the CETA, Article 8.30.1.

[177] Special Non-National Report on Investment Arbitration under Treaty-Based Rules, section 4.2 refers to the United States–Mexico–Canada Agreement (USMCA) and the Comprehensive and Progressive Agreement for Trans-Pacific Partnership (CPTPP).

[178] ICSID/UNCITRAL draft Code of Conduct, fourth version (September 2022), paras 24 f.

Intersentia

changed. Another manner of excluding concurring activities is to provide that the adjudicator's position be full-time.[179]

The same considerations that were made in section 6.2 apply here: if the volume of cases is not such as to justify full-time positions, it may be difficult to prevent professionals active in a certain field from being involved in other cases.[180] Some situations of double-hatting may give rise to conflicts of interests, and may fall within the rule forbidding conflicts of interests, see section 3.1 above. It is also possible to restrict the possibility for adjudicators to represent parties before the adjudicating body to which they belong. In other situations, where the conflict is less clear, an appropriate mechanism is a duty of disclosure, coupled with the parties' right to object to the appointment, see sections 6.6 and 7.

6.4. ISSUE CONFLICT

An adjudicator may in the past have held functions within the dispute resolution system or within the field of the dispute, which may have led to developing certain professional opinions on issues of law or of fact which also arise in the dispute in question (so-called issue conflict). For example, an adjudicator may, in past disputes, have decided a legal issue similar to the one in dispute (such as the question of whether arbitrability is to be decided according to the lex fori or according to the law chosen by the parties to govern the contract), may have published doctrinal works on such an issue, or may have acted as an expert witness or pleaded as counsel on such an issue.

Adjudicators may be exposed to the suspicion of bias if they are called upon to decide on an issue in respect of which they already have developed an opinion. Admittedly, adjudicators who are experts on the field of the dispute are likely to have had the occasion to consider the abstract issues on which the specific dispute relies. If they have never thought about those issues, it may

---

[179] See the Special Non-National Report on Regional Human Rights Courts, section 5.1.1 on the European Court of Human Rights and section 5.2.1 on the Inter-American Court of Human Rights; the Special Non-National Report on Regional Courts, section 4 on the CJEU, the Andean Community Tribunal of Justice, the Court of the Eurasian Economic Union and the Caribbean Court of Justice; the Special Non-National Report on the WTO, section 2.2.2 on the EU proposal for reform of the WTO Appellate Body. See also the Note by the UNCITRAL Secretariat, Possible reform of investor-State dispute settlement (ISDS) – Background information on a code of conduct, A/CN.9/WG.III/WP.167. Permanent bodies with part-time positions are the African Court on Human and Peoples' Rights, see the Special Non-National Report on Regional Human Rights Courts, section 4.3; the WTO Panels and Appellate Body, see the Special Non-National Report on the WTO, section 2.1.1 and 2.2.1; the Benelux Court, see the Special Non-National Report on Regional Courts, section 4, as well as in the Special Non-National Report on Administrative Tribunals.

[180] For a criticism of the CETA's complete ban, see Special Non-National Report on Investment Arbitration under Treaty-Based Rules, section 4.2.

be questionable whether they have the necessary competence to decide the dispute.[181]

In the field of investment arbitration, the criticism goes that parties may exercise an undue influence on the composition of the tribunal by picking an arbitrator based on the position that the arbitrator has taken on certain issues.[182] However, successful challenges based on issue conflicts are rare.[183] As was mentioned in section 4.2, an important advantage of arbitration is often said to consist in the ability of the parties to select the arbitrators according to their expertise. Each party will be careful to select an arbitrator whose expertise is likely to be compatible with that party's position. It will then be the collegial character of the arbitral tribunal that will ensure a balanced consideration of all the perspectives involved, see section 6.1.

The matter of issue conflict, in any case, is not only met in investment arbitration. To give an example, administrative tribunals established to hear labour disputes involving specific international organisations are often composed of judges who sit or have sat on administrative tribunals involving other organisations, or who have other roles within the internal justice system of other organisations. The composition of administrative tribunals is accessible on the site of the relevant organisation, and a quick glance at the curricula of the judges reveals that many judges are or have been involved in the internal justice system of a plurality of organisations. These judges may already have encountered, in prior disputes or in disputes before other administrative tribunals, a legal issue that they are called on to decide (such as the question of whether administrative tribunals have jurisdiction to hear claims by appellants who are not formal employees of the organisation, but who claim to be de facto employees), and may thus have developed an opinion on how the issue shall be decided.

If a professional opinion on an abstract issue were sufficient to consider the adjudicator biased, it would lead to the absurd consequence that a deep knowledge of the law would be a ground for disqualification whenever the disputed issue is to be solved by applying the law. This would disqualify virtually all judges and experts.

As a matter of fact, often domestic courts consider judges to be conflicted if they have already been involved in the dispute in question in another capacity,

---

[181] Park ('Arbitration's Discontents: Between the Pernicious and the Precarious', in *Mélanges en l'honneur du Professeur Bernard Audit*, LGDJ 2014, p. 586) points out that 'if arbitrators must be completely sanitized from all possible external influences on their decisions, only the most naive or incompetent would be available', and (ibid., p. 592): 'It would be a shame to exclude from service those who really know something, leaving arbitration only to the ignorant.'

[182] See the Note by the UNCITRAL Secretariat, Possible reform of investor-State dispute settlement (ISDS) – Background information on a code of conduct, A/CN.9/WG.III/WP.167; see also the Report of UNCITRAL Working Group III (Investor-State Dispute Settlement Reform) on the work of its thirty-fifth session, A/CN.9/935, para. 56.

[183] Special Non-National Report on Investment Arbitration under Treaty-Based Rules, section 4.3.

for example as prosecutors or as counsel.[184] However, this applies when the judge has been involved in a prior phase of the specific dispute. It does not apply when the involvement regards the abstract legal issue or a dispute between different parties.[185]

Furthermore, the consistency and coherence of a legal system is one of the goals pursued by the administration of justice. It would run counter to this goal to seek adjudicators who do not have a basis to consider the legal issues underlying the dispute.[186]

It seems, therefore, that issue conflict is not a concern in respect of independence and impartiality,[187] unless it can be characterised as double-hatting, see section 6.3.

That the professional opinion developed by arbitrators over the course of their career does not affect the arbitrator's independence and impartiality is also assumed in the IBA Guidelines.[188] Nevertheless, it is sometimes expected that sole arbitrators or chairs of the tribunal are free from issue conflicts.[189]

Another aspect of the same matter is that adjudicators who are experts in a certain area may have developed a frame of mind that can impact on the evaluation not only of specific legal issues, but also of the general framework – such

---

[184] Special National Report on Denmark, section 3.3; Special National Report on Hungary, section 2.6.1; Special National Report on Italy, section 6.1.1; Special National Report on Paraguay, section 5.1; Special National Report on Romania, section 5.1; Special National Report on Slovenia, section 3.1.

[185] Special National Report on Cyprus, section 3, n. 61. The Norwegian Supreme Court repeatedly affirmed that having written a doctrinal analysis of a legal issue does not affect the impartiality of a judge deciding that very issue: see the decisions recorded in Rt. 2003 s. 1094, Rt. 2008 s. 602 and HR-2022-1959-A. A conflict can arise only if the analysis regards the specific case, or if the conclusions are so unconditional that it can be excluded the judge would be open to evaluate the issue with an open mind. See also the ECtHR decision *Mutu v. Switzerland*, implying in para. 162 that doubts about the impartiality of an arbitrator may be legitimate only if the arbitrator successively dealt with identical facts and had to answer the same question or, at least, that the difference between the questions that he had to address was tenuous. Similarly regarding arbitration, see the Special National Report on France, section 2.3.3.

[186] The Note by the UNCITRAL Secretariat, Possible reform of investor-State dispute settlement (ISDS) – Background information on a code of conduct, A/CN.9/WG.III/WP.167, para. 27. The Note refers to investment arbitration, but the reasoning has general application.

[187] See the Note by the UNCITRAL Secretariat, Possible reform of investor-State dispute settlement (ISDS) – Ensuring independence and impartiality on the part of arbitrators and decision makers in ISDS, A/CN.9/WG.III/WP.151, paras 35–39. See also the Special National Report on Cyprus, section 3; Special National Report on France, section 2.3.3.

[188] While an opinion expressed on the case in dispute is included in the orange list of situations that create the appearance of conflict but may be waived (Article 3.5.2), an opinion on an issue that arises also in the dispute is included in the green list of circumstances that need not being disclosed (Article 4.1.1).

[189] According to the Special Non-National Report on ICJ and ITLOS, section 3.1, the law is unsettled.

General Report

as what role regional courts should play in the development of the law.[190] The selecting authority may take into consideration the opinions of the candidate with the purpose of avoiding so-called judicial activism, see the controversial conduct of the USA that led to the stalling of the WTO Appellate Body.[191] It is at the discretion of the appointing authority to choose the adjudicator who is most appropriate. Safeguards against the appointment of inadequate candidates, as well as against the abuse of the nominating or appointing authority, lie in the independence and impartiality of the authority (section 4), in the clarity and objectivity of the selection criteria (section 3) and in the transparency of the procedures (section 5) – not in disqualifying candidates whose competence has led to developing professional opinions on abstract issues relevant to the dispute.

6.5. ACCOUNTABILITY

An adjudicator may be interested in showing to the selecting body (whether it is an external appointing authority or the parties) the extent to which the selecting body's interests have been given consideration in the deliberations. This may be done for the purpose of obtaining new appointments (see section 6.2), obtaining other benefits, or avoiding negative consequences (see section 6.9).

A possible way of reducing the accountability of the adjudicator towards the selecting body is to require that decisions are drafted in a way that does not show the different positions within the adjudicating body. There are different approaches: to ban dissenting opinions,[192] to impose secrecy of deliberations,[193] or to allow separate opinions, but anonymously.[194]

---

[190]   Special National Report on Denmark, section 2.2.4, on a position according to which activist lawyers should not be nominated.

[191]   Special National Report on the USA, section 3.2; Special Non-National Report on the WTO, section 2.2.2.

[192]   Special Non-National Report on Regional Courts, section 4 on the CJEU, the Benelux Court, the Economic Community of West African States Court, the Court of Justice of the Common Market for Eastern and Southern Africa and the Caribbean Court of Justice. See also the Special National Report on Italy, section 5.1.1.

[193]   Special Non-National Report on Regional Human Rights Courts, section 5.1.3 on the European Court of Human Rights, section 5.2.3 on the Inter-American Court of Human Rights, and section 5.3.3 on the African Court on Human and Peoples' Rights; Special Non-National Report on Regional Courts, section 4 on the Mercosur Court; Special Non-National Report on Investment Arbitration under Treaty-Based Rules, section 4.4.

[194]   Special Non-National Report on the WTO, section 3.1.2; Special Non-National Report on Claims Tribunals, section 5.1 on the Commission for Real Property Claims of Displaced Persons; Special Non-National Report on Investment Arbitration under Treaty-Based Rules, section 4.5.

Intersentia

6.6. DISCLOSURE

Among the duties imposed on adjudicators to support the principle of independence and impartiality is the duty to disclose any interests that may give rise to suspicion regarding the adjudicator's independence or impartiality.

A duty of disclosure can be found in arbitration,[195] domestic courts[196] and international courts.[197]

Disclosing circumstances that may raise doubts about possible conflicts of interests or bias permits the parties (or, in the case of party appointment, the party or parties who did not make the appointment) to evaluate whether to accept the adjudicator or not.

The duty of disclosure applies to any circumstances that may justify doubts about the presence of conflicts or bias, and does not assume that the adjudicator is in fact conflicted or biased. As was seen in section 2.1, it sufficient to establish the appearance of conflict or bias, not their actual existence. Therefore, the duty to disclose is triggered by the simple appearance, and does not imply actual conflicts or bias. An interesting development[198] is that early versions of the ICSID/UNCITRAL draft Code of Conduct provided a duty to disclose all of the arbitrator's publications. This requirement, however, is no longer contemplated – thus indicating that so-called issue conflict in itself is not a circumstance capable of creating the appearance of bias, see section 6.4.

---

[195] Special Non-National Report on Commercial Ad Hoc Arbitration, sections 2.3.1 and 3.3.1; Special Non-National Report on Commercial Institutional Arbitration, section 2.4; Special Non-National Report on Investment Arbitration under Non-Treaty-Based Rules, section 6; Special Non-National Report on Investment Arbitration under Treaty-Based Rules, section 5; Special Non-National Report on the WIPO, section 5; Special Non-National Report on the WTO, section 3.1.1; Special Non-National Report on Claims Tribunals, section 6.1 on the Iran–US Claims Tribunals; see also the fourth version of the ICSID/UNCITRAL Code of Conduct, Article 11, and the Note by the UNCITRAL Secretariat, Possible reform of investor-State dispute settlement (ISDS) – Ensuring independence and impartiality on the part of arbitrators and decision makers in ISDS, A/CN.9/WG.III/WP.151, paras 43–45. As far as arbitration law is concerned, see the Special National Report on France, section 2.2.2; Special National Report on Greece, section 2.2.1.2; see also the mentioned UK Supreme Court decision *Halliburton v. Chubb*; Special National Report on Italy, section 5.1.2. A duty of disclosure was also introduced in Swiss arbitration law as reformed in 2020, see Article 179(6) of the Private International Law Act.

[196] Special National Report on Cyprus, section 3; Special National Report on Denmark, section 3.2.

[197] See the Note by the UNCITRAL Secretariat, Possible reform of investor-State dispute settlement (ISDS) – Ensuring independence and impartiality on the part of arbitrators and decision makers in ISDS, A/CN.9/WG.III/WP.151, para. 46.

[198] See Special Non-National Report on Investment Arbitration under Treaty-Based Rules, section 4.3.

General Report

Moreover, the duty to disclose covers circumstances that do not necessarily imply the appearance of a lack of independence or impartiality: often, the threshold for the duty of disclosure is lower than the threshold for considering that an adjudicator is not independent and impartial.[199]

The rationale for the different thresholds is that, by imposing disclosure for circumstances that are not necessarily disqualifying, it will be up to the party to determine whether it trusts the adjudicator's ability to be independent and impartial notwithstanding the disclosed circumstances. An extensive duty of disclosure is, therefore, meant to empower the parties by giving the party who did not participate in the appointment an opportunity to evaluate the acceptability of the other party's choice. Because disclosure does not imply a lack of independence and impartiality, and enhances party autonomy, it is often recommended to err in favour of disclosure.[200] Arbitral institutions generally expect potential arbitrators to disclose all circumstances that may raise doubts, even though it is quite clear that they do not have a real impact on independence and impartiality.

Anecdotal evidence, however, suggests that an excess of disclosure may not necessarily succeed in enhancing the parties' confidence in the adjudicator. Some parties may indeed appreciate an excess of disclosure, which permits them to exercise their discretion to accept the arbitrator notwithstanding the disclosed circumstances. Other parties, however, may react to the disclosure with suspicion and not be willing to accept the arbitrator, even though they do not find that the disclosed circumstances raise justifiable doubts.[201] Even an extensive duty of disclosure should, in any case, not be unreasonably wide; a definition of its scope refers to circumstances which might reasonably give rise to justifiable doubts as to the adjudicator's impartiality.[202]

---

[199] Special Non-National Report on Investment Arbitration under Treaty-Based Rules, section 5; Special National Report on France, section 2.2.2. See also the Note by the UNCITRAL Secretariat, Possible reform of investor-State dispute settlement (ISDS) – Background information on a code of conduct, A/CN.9/WG.III/WP.167, para. 51. The third version of the ICSID/UNCITRAL draft Code of Conduct operated with two different standards for disqualification (Article 3: 'any circumstance capable of rising justifiable doubts in the eyes of third parties') and for disclosure (Article 10: 'any circumstance capable of rising justifiable doubts in the eyes of a party'). The fourth version introduced square brackets into the formulation of Article 10: '[, including in the eyes of the disputing parties,]' reflecting the uncertainty that the double standard may create, see the comments to the fourth version of the ICSID/UNCITRAL draft Code of Conduct, paras 59 f. The fifth version has not modified the provision.

[200] See also the fifth version of the ICSID/UNCITRAL draft Code of Conduct, Article 11(4).

[201] Park ('Arbitration's Discontents: Between the Pernicious and the Precarious', in *Mélanges en l'honneur du Professeur Bernard Audit*, LGDJ 2014, p. 601) points out that '[e]xcessive disclosure can cause as many problems as inadequate disclosure. If an overscrupulous conscience announces links that would not normally raise questions, this might cause parties to wonder whether there is more going on than meets the eye.'

[202] UK Supreme Court decision *Halliburton v. Chubb*; this formulation is recommended to be codified by the Law Commission Consultation Paper 257, *Review of the Arbitration Act 1996 Summary of Consultation Paper*, 2022, section 1.30.

Intersentia

47

Be that as it may, party autonomy is deemed to be crucial in the mechanism of disclosure. As was seen in section 2.3, however, independence and impartiality are meant not only to protect the interests of the disputing parties, but also to safeguard the legitimacy of the adjudication system. There are, therefore, certain circumstances that disqualify adjudicators even if the parties were willing to accept them.

At the other end of the scale are circumstances that are generally deemed to be disqualifying, but that in certain situations do not even need to be disclosed. It was already mentioned in section 3.5 that in highly specialised areas it is acceptable for the adjudicator and one party to have a connection due to repeat appointments.

A duty of disclosure should be balanced against the duty of confidentiality to which potential adjudicators may be subject. Furthermore, it applies to issues that are reasonably expected to be known to the potential adjudicators. This means that the adjudicator shall exercise due diligence in investigating whether there are circumstances that may raise doubts as to possible conflicts or bias, but that the duty should not require unreasonable measures that render it too cumbersome.[203] In practice, it is customary for potential adjudicators who are affiliated with a law firm to run a firm-wide conflict check, comparing all the parties involved and their affiliates to the firm's register of clients. As large international firms are likely to have or have had relationships with many clients, conflicts of interest often occur. For this reason, many professionals who desire to act mainly as arbitrators end up leaving their large firms and opening boutique firms, for which the potential of conflicts is considerably reduced.

Above it was mentioned that the duty to disclose should be balanced against the adjudicator's duty of confidentiality and interests in privacy and in effectiveness. A question that may arise is whether the duty of disclosure may be reduced by the parties' duty of diligence.

There are different approaches to the correlation between the adjudicator's duty to disclose and the party's diligence in seeking information about the adjudicator. At one end of the scale, the adjudicator is under a duty to disclose all circumstances, even those that are of common knowledge.[204] This approach implies that the parties have no duty of diligence, and that there is no presumption that they were aware of the publicly accessible circumstances. A consequence is that failure to challenge the adjudicator for circumstances that

---

[203] See the Special Non-National Report on the WTO, section 3.1.1: under the WTO Working Procedures for the Appellate Review, Rule VI, disclosure is not expected for matters without significant relevance to the dispute, the privacy of the adjudicators shall be considered, and the duty shall not be too burdensome to administrate.

[204] ECtHR decision *BEG v. Italy*, paras 138–39.

were not disclosed cannot be deemed to be a waiver of the right to do so, even when those circumstances are widely known.[205]

Other approaches assume a certain degree of diligence by the party, meaning that a party may not simply rely on the declaration of independence and impartiality made by the arbitrator. A party has a duty to investigate the arbitrator's possible conflicts or bias. However, this duty is not unlimited.

When requested to revise a CAS arbitral award, the Swiss Federal Tribunal[206] admitted the request well after the term for challenge had expired. The Chinese appellant had not been aware of the grounds for challenging the arbitrator's impartiality until a journalist published an article disclosing a series of tweets that the arbitrator had sent at the time of the dispute, and in which the arbitrator repeatedly and with extremely rude language had referred to Chinese people and their culinary traditions. Contrary to the European Court of Human Rights, the Swiss Federal Tribunal expected from the parties a certain degree of diligence. In the specific case, the Federal Tribunal found that the required level of diligence had been met by means of an internet search without results that had been made by the party's lawyer, even though the arbitrator's tweets were available on social media and could have been discovered by entering other combinations of search words. In another case, in which a party's lawyer had become aware of the arbitrator's repeat appointments and double-hatting, the Swiss Federal Tribunal found that the duty of curiosity assumes that a party formally requests clarifying details within the term for challenge – even though the lawyer had become aware of this circumstance in unrelated cases.[207]

An even higher degree of diligence is assumed by French courts: starting from the assumption that circumstances that are of common knowledge need not be disclosed, the Paris Court of Appeal concluded that information published in the specialised review GAR is well known, even though GAR is not a open-access site.[208] Furthermore, the Court found that information that becomes available by entering search words in German is publicly available even though the language of the proceedings was not German.[209]

The duty to disclose is, therefore, to a certain extent limited by the expectation that the party exercise due diligence.[210] Issues that are of common knowledge, and of which a party should therefore be aware, do not need to be disclosed. However, the threshold for considering an issue to be of common knowledge varies, as was seen above.

---

[205] ECtHR decision *BEG v. Italy*, paras 139 f.; UK Supreme Court decision *Halliburton v. Chubb*.

[206] Swiss Tribunal Fédéral decision No. 4A_318/2020.

[207] Swiss Tribunal Fédéral decision No. 4A_520/2021.

[208] Special National Report on France, section 2.2.2; Cour d'appel de Paris, 26 January 2021 (*Vidatel*).

[209] Cour d'appel de Paris, Pôle 5, Chambre 16, chambre commerciale internationale, 25 May 2021 (*Delta Dragon v. BYD*).

[210] Special Non-National Report on Commercial Institutional Arbitration, section 3.1.

There is no consensus on what the consequences are if circumstances that should be disclosed are not disclosed. Failure to disclose may justify admitting a challenge after the term for challenge has expired.[211] However, failure to disclose does not necessarily imply a manifest lack of independence and impartiality. Therefore, often failure to disclose does not automatically trigger disqualification.[212] Failure to disclose, however, is a violation of a duty. It can, therefore, be deemed to impair the integrity of the system and can generate the appearance of bias.[213]

In some systems, failure to disclose automatically triggers disqualification.[214] This seems to be an excessive measure, particularly considering that the duty to disclose is open-ended and not clearly determined.

Some international investment agreements, such as the CETA and the EU–Singapore Investment Protection Agreement, provide that all stakeholders be informed of the arbitrator's breach. Targeting the arbitrator's reputation may be quite an effective measure.[215]

6.7. POST-TERM DUTIES AND RIGHTS

Impartiality and independence do not necessarily only depend on the circumstances at the time of the dispute or of the term of office. They may be affected by past relationships, such as repeat appointments in the past (see section 6.2), or by concerns about the future, such as the desire to be appointed again (see section 6.2), to obtain an advantage in other disputes (see section 6.3),

---

[211] Swiss Tribunal Fédéral decision No. 4A_318/2020.

[212] Special National Report on France, section 2.2.2; Special Non-National Report on Investment Arbitration under Treaty-Based Rules, section 5; Special Non-National Report on the WTO, section 3.1.3; Cour d'appel de Paris, Pôle 5, Chambre 16, chambre commerciale internationale, 25 May 2021 (*Delta Dragon v. BYD*); Swiss Tribunal Fédéral decision No. 4A_663/2018; *Newcastle United Football Company Limited v. The Football Association Premier League Limited* [2021] EWHC 349 (Comm); PCA decision of 12 February 2018 on the challenge to *Guida Santiago Tawil, Serafín García Armas and Karina García Gruber v. Bolivarian Republic of Venezuela*, PCA Case No. 2013-3. See also the fifth version of the ICSID/UNCITRAL draft Code of Conduct, Article 11(7); see also para. 129 on Article 11, Comment 5 of the Practical Application of the General Standards of the IBA Guidelines.

[213] Special Non-National Report on the WTO, section 3.1.3; Special Non-National Report on Commercial Ad Hoc Arbitration, section 2.4.1; Special National Report on France, section 2.2.2; Cour de Cassation, Chambre civile 1, 16 December 2015, D14-26.279. The UK Supreme Court decision *Halliburton v. Chubb* assumes that failure to disclose may imply the appearance of bias generally, but not in the field of commodities arbitration, see section 3.5 above. See also the comments in the Special Non-National Report on Claims Tribunals, section 6.1 on the Iran–US Claims Tribunal.

[214] Special National Report on the USA, section 3; Special National Report on Italy, section 5.1.2.

[215] Special Non-National Report on Investment Arbitration under Treaty-Based Rules, section 6.

to ensure career prospects or to avoid negative consequences (see sections 6.5 and 6.9).

Some instruments impose a quarantine in respect of the parties involved in the proceedings.[216] This is a measure meant to prevent conduct that may raise doubts about the existence, already during the term of office, of ties between the adjudicators and the party.

In the preparation of the ICSID/UNCITRAL draft Code of Conduct, it was discussed whether a duty should be imposed on adjudicators to refrain from acting, after the proceedings, in a way that can create suspicion that they, during the proceedings, were not independent or impartial. Such a duty was not included in the third version of the draft. The comment points out that, under Article 8(3), the duty of confidentiality survives after the decisions are rendered, and this would cover many of the situations in which such a suspicion may have arisen.[217] While this would cover situations in which the former adjudicator discloses information about deliberations or about other aspects of the proceedings, it does not necessarily cover a situation in which the former adjudicator obtains benefits, such as employment in a profitable position in the organisation of the party who won the dispute. If these benefits are given immediately after the dispute is decided, suspicions may arise that the former adjudicator is being remunerated for the positive decision. This may undermine confidence in the adjudication system.

The time after the adjudicator's term expires may have the opposite significance: not only can an adjudicator be remunerated for a positive decision, a decision may also trigger negative reactions, such as removal from office.

It is a contribution to independence and impartiality if adjudicators do not need to worry during their term about possible repercussions or financial difficulties that may intervene after the term expires. To facilitate the return to a professional environment after the term of office has expired, the ECtHR introduced in 2013 lifelong diplomatic immunity and the right to a pension.[218] Other courts provide for immunity after the term for acts performed in the adjudicator's official capacity.[219]

---

[216] Special Non-National Report on Regional Human Rights Courts, section 5.1.1 on the European Court of Human Rights; Special Non-National Report on Investment Arbitration under Treaty-Based Rules, section 4.2.

[217] Note by the UNCITRAL Secretariat, Possible reform of investor-State dispute settlement (ISDS) – Draft Code of Conduct, A/CN.9/WG.III/WP.209, para. 52.

[218] Special Non-National Report on Regional Human Rights Courts, section 4.1 on the European Court of Human Rights.

[219] Special Non-National Report on Regional Human Rights Courts, sections 4.1 and 5.1.4 on the European Court of Human Rights; Special Non-National Report on Regional Courts, section 4 on the CJEU, the EFTA Court, the Benelux Court, the Economic Community of West African States Court and the Court of Justice of the Common Market for Eastern and Southern Africa.

6.8. CODES OF CONDUCT

Codes of conduct are widespread both for international and for domestic tribunals.[220] Generally, they affirm the duty to act independently and impartially, but they do not contain guidelines that are more specific than what has been set forth above.

Among the more detailed codes of conduct that are being developed, mention can be made of the Draft Code of Conduct for Adjudicators in Investor-State Dispute Settlement, the third version of which was released in September 2021 by ICSID and the UNCITRAL Working Group III. This Code of Conduct is intended to be a binding set of rules, rather than a set of guidelines.[221]

Among the specifications of what could constitute a conflict of interests, and thus affect the adjudicator's independence and impartiality, is the conduct described in sections 6.2, 6.3 and 6.4 above: repeat appointment, double-hatting and issue conflict.

6.9. IMMUNITY

It is uncontroversial that adjudicators should be shielded from undue influence and that they should not be held liable for their adjudicative activity (save for misconduct). Otherwise, the decisions will be based not only on the merits of the dispute, but also on concerns relating to possible consequences that the decision may have for the adjudicator.[222]

---

[220] Special Non-National Report on the WTO, section 3; Special Non-National Report on Regional Courts, section 4 on the Mercosur Court and the Caribbean Court of Justice; Special Non-National Report on Commodity Arbitration, section 5; Special National Report on Canada, section 5.2; Special National Report on Cyprus, section 3; Special National Report on Hungary, sections 2.1 and 2.7.2; Special National Report on Mexico, section 5; Special National Report on Paraguay, section 4; Special National Report on Turkey, section 3.2.2; Special National Report on the USA, sections 2.1 and 2.2. For an overview and summary of the main codes of conduct, see https://uncitral.un.org/sites/uncitral.un.org/files/media-documents/uncitral/en/annex_b_summary_of-fta_coc.docx (Annex B – Summary of Code of Conducts in Free Trade Agreements (update as of 8 May 2020, including new treaties and updated references)).

[221] Note by the UNCITRAL Secretariat, Possible reform of investor-State dispute settlement (ISDS) – Draft Code of Conduct, A/CN.9/WG.III/WP.209, para. 6.

[222] See how the situation is described in the Special National Report on Vietnam, section 3.1.1.2.

Immunity is a recurrent feature for adjudicators, and can be found in sources regulating international courts,[223] domestic courts[224] and arbitration bodies.[225]

Without immunity, and without a protection against consequences linked to their activity, adjudicators would not be in a position to render their decisions exclusively on the merits of the case, but would have to consider possible consequences for their own career, liability or even safety.

As was explained in section 2.2 above, independence must be guaranteed on various levels: from the other branches of power, from the internal justice system, and from the parties. Similarly, immunity needs to be ensured on different levels: from the other branches of power, from internal influence such as disciplinary measures or removal from office, as well as from liability – be it civil or criminal.

The importance of this principle is attracting significant attention in connection with judicial reforms introduced in Poland in 2017. The reforms imply, among other things, that judges may be exposed to disciplinary measures. Considering that these reforms violate the rule of law, Poland has been repeatedly condemned by the European Court of Human Rights,[226] and an infringement procedure was launched against Poland by the EU Commission. The EU Court of Justice found that the principle of the rule of law had been violated,[227] and the EU Commission suspended payment of funds to Poland.[228]

---

[223] Special Non-National Report on Regional Human Rights Courts, section 5.1.4 on the European Court of Human Rights, section 5.2.4 on the Inter-American Court of Human Rights, and section 5.3.4 on the African Court on Human and Peoples' Rights; Special Non-National Report on Regional Courts, section 4 on the CJEU, the EFTA Court and the Andean Community Tribunal of Justice; Special Non-National Report on ICJ and ITLOS, section 2.1; Special Non-National Report on Commercial Ad Hoc Arbitration, section 2.3.3.

[224] Special National Report on Denmark, section 3.1; Special National Report on Hungary, sections 2.6.6.3 and 2.6.7; Special National Report on Italy, sections 5.1.1 and 7.1.1; Special National Report on Romania, section 4.1; Special National Report on Turkey, section 2.2.1; Special National Report on the USA, section 2.1. See also the Special National Report on Mexico, section 6.1, 6.2 and 6.3, although immunity is quite restricted.

[225] Special Non-National Report on Commercial Ad Hoc Arbitration, section 2.3.3.

[226] The European Court of Human Rights confirmed, in its Grand Chamber decision *Grzęda v. Poland*, its previous case law on this matter: *Reczkowicz v. Poland*, ECtHR decision of 22 July 2021, application no. 43447/19; *Dolińska-Ficek and Ozimek v. Poland*, ECtHR decision of 8 November 2021, application nos 49868/19 and 57511/19; and *Advance Pharma v. Poland*.

[227] Precise references can be found in the ECtHR Grand Chamber decision *Grzęda v. Poland*, paras 16–28.

[228] The CJEU confirmed the compatibility with EU law of the conditionality mechanism which makes the receipt of financing from the Union budget subject to the respect by the Member States for the principles of the rule of law: CJEU decisions in cases C-156/21 and C-157/21.

Immunity, however, should not be abused by adjudicators. For these reasons, it is often excluded when the adjudicator's conduct may be deemed to amount to gross negligence or misconduct.[229]

7. BREACH: CONSEQUENCES FOR THE ADJUDICATOR

The effectiveness of the principle of independence and impartiality may be measured by reference to the consequences that follow a breach of the principle. As far as concerns the consequences for the adjudicator, an adjudicator who is deemed not to be independent and impartial will not be allowed to adjudicate the dispute.

This can be achieved by permitting the adjudicator to withdraw,[230] by giving the parties access to recusal or to object to the appointment,[231] or by providing for removal by the adjudicating body or the appointing authority.[232]

Withdrawal is seen as an expression of self-governance, and is the most common method to control the composition of the bench in, for example,

---

[229] Special National Report on Cyprus, section 3; Special National Report on Denmark, section 3.1; Special National Report on France, sections 2.5.2.2, 1.4 and 2.5.2.3; Special National Report on Italy, sections 7.1.1 and 7.1.2 for arbitration; Special National Report on Mexico, sections 6.1, 6.2 and 6.3, however with a wide understanding of misconduct that affirms liability for errors; Special National Report on Romania, section 6.1; Special National Report on the USA, section 2.1; Special National Report on Vietnam, section 3.1.1.2, according to which, however, misconduct is presumed; Special Non-National Report on Commercial Ad Hoc Arbitration, sections 2.3.3 and 3.3.3.

[230] Special National Report on Cyprus, section 3; Special National Report on Denmark, section 3.3; Special National Report on Italy, sections 6.1.1 and 7.1.1; Special National Report on Paraguay, section 5.1; Special National Report on Romania, section 5.1; Special National Report on Slovenia, section 3.1; Special National Report on Vietnam, section 3.2. See also the Note by the UNCITRAL Secretariat, Possible reform of investor-State dispute settlement (ISDS) – Ensuring independence and impartiality on the part of arbitrators and decision makers in ISDS, A/CN.9/WG.III/WP.151, para. 50.

[231] Special National Report on Canada, section 5.1; Special National Report on Cyprus, section 3; Special National Report on Denmark, section 3.3; Special National Report on France, section 2.5.2.1; Special National Report on Greece, section 2.2.1.2; Special National Report on Hungary, section 2.6.1; Special National Report on Italy, sections 6.1.1 and 7.1.1; Special National Report on Paraguay, section 5.1; Special National Report on Romania, section 5.1; Special National Report on Slovenia, section 3.1; Special National Report on the USA, section 3; Special Non-National Report on Commercial Ad Hoc Arbitration, sections 2.4 and 3.4.1; Special Non-National Report on Commercial Institutional Arbitration, section 2.5; Special Non-National Report on Claims Tribunals, section 6.1 on the Iran–US Claim Tribunal; Special Non-National Report on the WIPO, section 6 (for arbitration and expert determination); Special Non-National Report on Commodities Arbitration, section 6.

[232] Special Non-National Report on ICJ and ITLOS, section 2.2; Special Non-National Report on the WTO, section 3.2; Special Non-National Report on Regional Human Rights Courts, section 3.7 on the European Court of Human Rights; Special National Report on Canada, section 6.1; Special National Report on France, section 2.5.2.1; Special National Report on Hungary, section 2.6.6.2; Special National Report on Mexico, section 6.1; Special National Report on Romania, section 5.1; Special National Report on Slovenia, section 3.1.

the ICJ.[233] By contrast, the possibility of withdrawing is restricted when the adjudicator is party-appointed.[234] This is because an adjudicator who is in a position to withdraw should not have accepted the appointment in the first place. However, party-appointed adjudicators may also withdraw if circumstances intervene after the appointment that affect the adjudicator's independence and impartiality,[235] or when the adjudicator is challenged.[236]

Recusal of an adjudicator occurs rarely in some adjudication systems,[237] and very frequently in others – often with a tactical purpose of delaying the procedure.[238] Access to the possibility to challenge adjudicators for their lack of independence and impartiality is, according to the ECtHR, imposed by Article 6(1) of the European Convention of Human Rights.[239]

While the initiative is usually taken by a party in the dispute, it is also possible for the court or tribunal to initiate a process for the removal of an adjudicator. The application of this mechanism, however, is rare.[240]

There are different approaches to who can remove an adjudicator from office because of a breach of the principle of independence and impartiality: the decision may be taken by the court to which the adjudicator belongs,[241]

---

[233] Special National Report on ICJ and ITLOS, section 2.2. See also the Special Non-National Report on the WTO, section 3.2.2; Special National Report on Cyprus, section 3; Special National Report on Denmark, section 3.3.

[234] Special Non-National Report on Commercial Institutional Arbitration, section 2.5.

[235] Special Non-National Report on Investment Arbitration under Non-Treaty-Based Rules, section 7.

[236] Note by the UNCITRAL Secretariat, Possible reform of investor-State dispute settlement (ISDS) – Ensuring independence and impartiality on the part of arbitrators and decision makers in ISDS, A/CN.9/WG.III/WP.151, para. 51.

[237] Special National Report on ICJ and ITLOS, section 2.2; Special Non-National Report on Regional Human Rights Courts, sections 4.1 and 5.1.1 on the European Court of Human Rights, and section 5.2.1 on the Inter-American Court of Human Rights; Special Non-National Report on the WTO, section 4 – however, the functioning of the Appellate Body is stalled because of vetoes to appointments.

[238] Special Non-National Report on Claims Tribunals, section 6.1 on the Iran–US Claims Tribunal; Special National Report on Greece, section 1.

[239] *Sedat Doğan v. Turkey*, ECtHR decision of 18 May 2021, application no. 48909/14; *Naki and Amed Sportif Faaliyetler Kulübü Derneği v. Turkey*, ECtHR decision of 18 May 2021, application no. 48924/16; *Ibrahim Tokmak v. Turkey*, ECtHR decision of 18 May 2021, application no. 54540/16.

[240] Special Non-National Report on ICJ and ITLOS, section 2.2, according to which this has never happened so far. The initiative can be taken by any third party: Special National Report on Canada, section 6.1; Special National Report on Mexico, section 6.1.

[241] Special National Report on Cyprus, section 3; Special National Report on Italy, section 7.1.1; Special Non-National Report on Regional Human Rights Courts, section 4.1 on the European Court of Human Rights, sections 3.2 and 4.2 on the Inter-American Court of Human Rights, and section 4.3 on the African Court on Human and Peoples' Rights; Special Non-National Report on the WTO, section 3.2; Special Non-National Report on Regional Courts, section 5 on the CJEU and the EFTA Court; Special Non-National Report on Commercial Ad Hoc Arbitration, section 3.4.1, albeit with the possibility to address the appointing authority for a review; ICSID Convention, Article 58.

by the appointing authority,[242] or by a third party – such as boards, committees or bodies separate from the authority who made the appointment.[243]

To ensure full independence, and given the influence that the appointing authority has on the independence and impartiality of the adjudicator, as was seen in section 4.1, it should be possible to have recourse to the courts against decisions taken by the self-governance body of the judiciary. However, in various adjudication systems neither of these criteria is met: challenges are decided by the same authority which made the appointment, and the decisions are final.[244] The risk of abuse is mitigated by mechanisms applicable to the appointing authority, such as the selection criteria of its members, their duty to disclose any circumstances that may raise doubts about their independence and impartiality, as well as working procedures.[245]

In addition to removal of the adjudicator from office, it is possible that a breach of the duty of independence and impartiality is deemed to be a circumstance that leads to lifting the immunity of the adjudicator against civil or criminal liability, see section 6.9.

8. BREACH: CONSEQUENCES FOR THE DECISION

The effectiveness of the principle of independence and impartiality may be measured by reference to the consequences that follow if the principle is breached. A decision rendered by an adjudicator who was not independent and impartial is not a decision rendered according to the principle of due process.

The consequences that this may have for the effectiveness of the decision, however, are not uniform, and depend on the legal framework to which the particular decision is subject. The enforcement of a decision is ultimately a matter of exercise of the state's judicial power, and it is regulated by national law or by international conventions.

---

[242] Special Non-National Report on the WTO, section 3.2; Special Non-National Report on Commercial Ad Hoc Arbitration, section 2.4.2; Special Non-National Report on Commercial Institutional Arbitration, section 2.5; Special Non-National Report on Claims Tribunal, section 7.1 on the Iran–US Claims Tribunal and section 7.3 on the Eritrea–Ethiopia Claims Commission; Special Non-National Report on Regional Courts, section 5 on the Andean Community Tribunal of Justice, the Court of Justice of the Common Market for Eastern and Southern Africa, the Court of the Eurasian Economic Union and the Caribbean Court of Justice.

[243] Special Non-National Report on Commercial Institutional Arbitration, section 2.5; Special Non-National Report on Commercial Ad Hoc Arbitration, section 2.4.3; Special National Report on Canada, section 6.1; Special National Report on Paraguay, section 5.1.

[244] Special Non-National Report on Investment Arbitration under Non-Treaty-Based Rules, section 5; Special Non-National Report on Commercial Ad Hoc Arbitration, section 2.4.3; Special National Report on France, section 1.1.3.

[245] Special Non-National Report on Investment Arbitration under Non-Treaty-Based Rules, section 5.

General Report

National laws often permit a decision rendered by a domestic court to be revoked or revised, if it turns out that the adjudicator was not independent or impartial.[246] Regarding foreign decisions, the possibility to refuse recognition and enforcement is regulated in conventions,[247] regional regulations,[248] or in the internal law. In these instruments there is often a basis to refuse recognition and enforcement of a decision rendered by an adjudicator who was not independent or impartial, to the extent that recognition and enforcement would lead to an infringement of public policy. That a foreign court was not independent or impartial, however, must be proven in the specific case.[249] It cannot be presumed on the basis of the general political situation in which the court functions.[250]

Regarding decisions rendered by international courts, often the recognition and enforcement rely on states' spontaneous compliance. Usually, enforcement is resisted based on arguments relating to national sovereignty;[251] however, lack of independence and impartiality has also been invoked.[252]

In arbitration, national courts (or, in the case of ICSID arbitration, ad hoc committees) may exercise a certain control over awards. The validity of an award rendered on their territory may be verified by national courts. The criteria for validity are laid down in national law. If the arbitral tribunal was not independent or impartial, the award can usually be annulled, either because the

---

[246] Special National Report on Canada, section 7.1; Special National Report on Cyprus, section 3; Special National Report on Denmark, section 3.1; Special National Report on Hungary, sections 2.6.1 and 2.6.8; Special National Report on Italy, section 8.1.2; Special National Report on Romania, section 7.1; Special National Report on Slovenia, section 3.1; Special National Report on Vietnam, section 4.2. However, in other systems this is not possible, as it would weaken the effect of *res judicata*, see the Special National Report on Mexico, section 7.

[247] Such as the 2005 Hague Convention on Choice of Courts Agreements and the 2019 Hague Convention on Recognition and Enforcement of Foreign Judgements in Civil and Commercial Matters.

[248] Such as the Brussels I Regulation (1215/2012).

[249] See the Special Non-National Report on ICJ and ITLOS, section 4. See also the Note by the UNCITRAL Secretariat, Possible reform of investor-State dispute settlement (ISDS) – Ensuring independence and impartiality on the part of arbitrators and decision makers in ISDS, A/CN.9/WG.III/WP.151, para. 59.

[250] See, for example, *Shanghai Yongrun Inv. Mgt. Co., Ltd, Plaintiff-Appellant v. Maodong Xu, Defendant-Respondent, Kashi Galaxy Venture Capital Co., Ltd., Defendant*, New York Appellate Division, 10 March 2022, Case No. 2021-01637, enforcing a Chinese decision notwithstanding the negative evaluation of China in the State Department Country Report. According to the New York Court, Country Reports regard politically sensitive issues and are not conclusive evidence of lack of independence and impartiality of all courts in the relevant country. Enforcement requires a case-by-case approach.

[251] This is observed in the Special National Report on Italy, section 8.2.

[252] See the Special Non-National Report on ICJ and ITLOS, making reference, in section 2.2, to a case against Kenya.

Intersentia

arbitral tribunal was not constituted in accordance with the applicable law, or because recognition and enforcement would infringe public policy.[253]

National courts also exercise a certain control over awards at the stage of enforcement. Enforceability of awards is regulated by the New York Convention (for ICSID awards, it is subject to the same rules applicable to final court decisions rendered in the country of enforcement).

It must be pointed out that the standard applied by courts to evaluate the arbitral tribunal's independence and impartiality is not necessarily the same standard applied by the arbitral tribunal or the arbitral institution: courts apply their own law when annulling an award, and the New York Convention when enforcing it.[254] This may lead to inconsistent application of the principle: arbitral tribunals, arbitral institutions (if any) and courts may each have a different understanding of the principle of independence and impartiality. As was seen in section 3.1, the use of transnational sources such as the IBA Guidelines does not necessarily permit achieving uniformity. Similar inconsistency may be encountered among courts of different states. An award may, thus, have been set aside in its country of origin, and nevertheless be recognised and enforced in another country. According to the prevailing view, an award that was set aside by a national court in the award's country of origin may not be enforced in other countries under the New York Convention. However, sometimes the New York Convention is interpreted so as to permit enforcement of an award notwithstanding that it was set aside in its country of origin.[255] For what is

---

[253] Special National Report on Canada, section 7.2; Special National Report on Cyprus, section 4; Special National Report on Denmark, section 4.1.1; Special National Report on France, section 2.5.1; Special National Report on Italy, section 8.1.2; Special National Report on Romania, sections 7.1 and 7.2; Special National Report on Turkey, section 3.2.3; Special National Report on Vietnam, section 4.1.

[254] Special Non-National Report on Commercial Institutional Arbitration, section 3.1.

[255] In particular, French courts consider arbitral awards to have an international nature that cannot be affected by an annulment at the country of origin, see the French Supreme Court decisions *Pabalk Ticaret Limited Sirketi v. Norsolor*, 9 October 1984; *Hilmarton Ltd. v. Omicron de traitement et de valorisation*, 23 March 1994; and *PT Putrabali Adyamulia v. Rena Holding*, 8 July 2015. See also Cour d'appel de Paris, *République du Bénin v. Société Générale de Surveillance*, 14 January 2022. US courts have also enforced awards that had been set aside in their country of origin, although on different grounds and not consistently. The first controversial enforcement of an award that had been set aside in its country of origin, Egypt, was based on the need to implement the public policy of finality of awards (*Chromalloy Aeroservices v. Arab Republic of Egypt*, United States District Court, District of Columbia, 31 July 1996, 94-2339). Thereafter, an award that had been set aside in its country of origin, Mexico, was enforced based on the circumstance that the setting aside deprived the winning party of a fair hearing. The setting aside was based on a change in legislation that rendered the dispute not arbitrable, after the proceedings had been initiated (*Corporación Mexicana de Mantenimiento Integral v. Pemex Exploración y Producción*, Southern District for New York 2013 (2013) XXXVIII *Yearbook Commercial Arbitration* 537–41). In contrast, an award that had been set aside in its country of origin (Nigeria) was not enforced, because the Nigerian legal system provided sufficient opportunity to be heard (*Esso Exploration and Production Nigeria Limited v. Nigerian National Petroleum Corporation*, United States District Court, Southern District of New York Opinion and Order, 4 September 2019, 14cv8445).

relevant here, this is particularly so when the annulment court is deemed not to have been independent or impartial.[256]

Regarding ICSID awards, the circumstance that enforcement is subject to the same enforcement regime applying to final judgments does not necessarily mean that a breach of the principle of independence and impartiality would not have an effect on the enforceability of the award. As was seen above, a court decision may be revised even though it is final, if it turns out that the court was not independent or impartial. If this is applicable to final judgments rendered by courts in the enforcement country, it must also apply to ICSID awards that are sought to be enforced in that country.

9. CONCLUSION

The foregoing shows that there is a broad consensus on the principle that adjudicators shall be independent and impartial, but that the specific content of the principle is generally not defined. Attempts to define it are useful, but do not necessarily ensure full uniformity (see particularly section 3.1). Furthermore, the assessment of independence and impartiality is highly fact-dependent, and it is therefore difficult to regulate in detail on an abstract level.

Therefore, a comparative examination should turn to the legal framework implementing the principle: regulating criteria and mechanisms for the selection and functioning of adjudicators is an effective way to ensure their independence and impartiality.

An examination of the different regimes shows that independence and impartiality are more easily safeguarded if the adjudicators are selected on the basis of their competence in the field of the dispute, rather than of their proximity to the interests of one of the sides. Adjudicators should be able to develop considered opinions on the basis of the material that is submitted to them and on the basis of their competence and expertise – they should not be expected to identify with one side of the dispute and to act as a representative of the body that appointed them. Recognised competence and high moral standards are generally deemed to be a condition for acting independently and impartially (see, in particular, sections 3.3, 3.4 and 3.6).

Competence implies a certain familiarity with the field of the dispute, the interests at stake and the issues in dispute. This familiarity may reach a level of involvement in the dispute that impairs the adjudicator's independence and impartiality (see, in particular, section 3.2).

---

[256]   *Yukos Capital SARL v. Oao Rosneft*, Decision of the Amsterdam Court of Appeal, 28 April 2009, Case No. 200.005.269/01; *Yukos Capital SARL v. OJSC Rosneft Oil Company* [2012] EWCA Civ 855; Dutch Supreme Court, 24 November 2017, *Maximov v. OJCS Novolipetsky Metallurgichesky Kombinat.*

The assessment of whether the adjudicator is conflicted or biased is generally made on the basis of objective standards: impartiality and independence are essential to the credibility of the dispute resolution system, and it would be excessively burdensome if a challenge of the adjudicator assumed that the actual existence of a conflict or of bias were proven. Therefore, the standard generally applicable is that of an appearance of conflict or bias, also defined as justifiable doubts in the eyes of a third party (see, in particular, section 2.1).

While some situations manifestly create conflicts or bias (see, in particular, section 3.1), others are more subtle and require an assessment of all the circumstances. To enhance predictability, some measures are available for the most typical situations in which suspicions may be raised. In particular, three situations have crystallised as potentially creating an appearance of conflicts or bias: repeat appointments (see, in particular, section 6.2), double-hatting (see, in particular, section 6.3) and issue conflict (see, in particular, section 6.4). Issue conflict arises when the adjudicator has already dealt with an issue relating to the issue in dispute – for example, in scholarly writings or in other, unrelated cases that are concluded. Issue conflict is close to inevitable when the adjudicator has competence in the field of dispute, and is therefore generally not deemed to create the appearance of conflict or bias, if the involvement of the adjudicator was in a context unrelated to the dispute in question. However, issue conflict has the potential to infringe the principle of independence and impartiality when it results in double-hatting, i.e. when adjudicators are professionally involved with an issue relating to the issue in dispute, possibly in unrelated cases and in different capacities (for example as counsel or as an expert witness), and their decision as adjudicators could benefit their position in these other disputes. Repeat appointments also have the potential to infringe the principle of independence and impartiality: if adjudicators have often been appointed by the same party or counsel, and have derived considerable income from these appointments, their independence can be questioned. Furthermore, the prospect of receiving new appointments in the future may affect independence and impartiality.

The possibility of double-hatting and repeat appointments may be restricted when the adjudicators serve in a full-time position and for terms that are so long that reappointments are unlikely or even impossible. While full-time, long-term positions are an effective measure to safeguard independence and impartiality, they assume a certain consistent volume of disputes over time.

When the volume of disputes is not such as to justify a permanent position as described, a common mechanism to ensure independence and impartiality is to require that adjudicators disclose any circumstances that may give rise to doubts about the existence of conflicts or bias (see, in particular, section 6.6). On the basis of the disclosure, the parties may assess whether they accept the adjudicator or challenge the adjudicator's independence and impartiality (see, in particular, section 7). Generally, the threshold for requiring disclosure is

General Report

lower than that for disqualifying the adjudicator. While this is considered an appropriate mechanism to enhance the parties' role in the constitution of the adjudicating body, it needs to be balanced with the adjudicator's own obligations of confidentiality and interest in efficiency.

In order to ensure an objective and transparent mechanism, determination of the parties' challenges against the adjudicators is made by independent bodies. Where this precaution is not implemented, the quality of the decisions depends on the applicable procedures and on the integrity of the determining body.

Regarding the appointment mechanism, there are two major approaches: appointment may be made by the parties (see, in particular, section 4.2) or by an independent authority (see, in particular, section 4.1).

Party appointment occurs particularly in arbitration, but it is also at the basis of the appointment mechanism for several international courts. Judges are appointed on the nomination of Member States, and Member States are potential parties to the disputes that the judges will hear. The difference between party appointment for international courts and party appointment for arbitration disputes is that the former results in a long-term office, and that the specific characteristics of each dispute that will be heard by the judge is not known at the time of nomination. In arbitration, by contrast, appointment is made for the specific dispute. It is questionable whether this difference has such significance that it prevents affirming that the mechanism for international courts is also based on party appointment. While it is true that the specific disputes before the international court are not known at the moment of nomination, and that therefore it is not possible to tailor the nomination to the characteristics of the specific dispute, it is still possible to select a judge on the basis of experience, professional profile, loyalty, general approach to the field of law relevant to the court in question, etc. This permits a considerable influence to be exercised over the composition of the court, and does not depart substantially from the influence that party appointment has on an arbitral tribunal. Where differences may be more significant is in respect of the number of adjudicators: while arbitral tribunals often consist of three members, courts may have a larger number of judges sitting on the bench. This reduces the influence that each state-appointed judge may have in the deliberations, compared to arbitration.

The influence that a party may exercise on the adjudicating body by appointing an adjudicator is, in any case, compensated to the extent that the other party also exercises a corresponding influence and appoints an adjudicator (see, in particular, section 6.1). Therefore, quite irrespective of the circumstance that even party-appointed adjudicators have a duty to be and act independently and impartially, the possible impact that a tailored choice may have on the deliberations will be offset by the corresponding impact of the other party's tailored choice. In sum, the deliberations will be balanced – at least they have the theoretical potential of being balanced. Whether the specific tribunal is

Intersentia

61

balanced depends on the selection that the parties actually make. A party whose case is based on the strict application of national law is well advised to select an adjudicator who has a traditional approach to the law. Should this party instead appoint an adjudicator who considers that transnational soft law is preferable, it will not have made an appointment in its interest.

The alternative to party appointment is that the adjudicating body is appointed by an independent authority. The composition of the appointing authority is deemed to be crucial to the quality of the appointment. So is the quality of the selection process. The composition of the appointing authority should ensure that all the interests involved are represented, and the selection process should be transparent, objective and based on relevant criteria (mainly on competence, see above).

Another important aspect of independence and impartiality is that adjudicators be shielded from negative consequences due to, and liability deriving from, the adjudicating activity (see, in particular, sections 6.7 and 6.9). Immunity is generally deemed to be a prerequisite for independent and impartial adjudication, and whenever immunity is restricted, the integrity of the adjudication system is impaired.

The foregoing shows that there is a significant consensus, among domestic and international systems, on the main contours of the principle of independence and impartiality. The principle may be safeguarded by a variety of methods, the main lines of which were summarised above.

What can be drawn from this summary? Particularly considering the current debate on a reform of the dispute resolution system for investment disputes, it is clear that an important matter of controversy is whether the current system of party-appointed tribunals constituted for the specific dispute is appropriate. However, it is questionable whether party appointment and appointment for the specific dispute are the most important issues to be discussed. The considerations made above suggest that the discrimen should rather be whether the adjudicators serve in a full-time or part-time position.

As long as adjudicators serve on a part-time basis, it will be difficult to avoid appointments of professionals who are active in the field of the dispute – thus giving rise to situations that may be qualified as repeat appointments or double-hatting. However, restrictions may be imposed on the eligibility as adjudicators of professionals who represent or act for parties before the adjudication body on which they are meant to sit. While the more obvious conflicts may be avoided if the appointing party exercises self-restraint and seeks diversity, an underlying suspicion may still affect the system.

Suggestions to introduce mechanisms similar to those existing in international courts do not really address the issue, as permanent courts may include both part-time and full-time positions. In addition, as explained above, a mechanism like that existing in international courts in effect reiterates the mechanism of party appointment. Party appointment was precisely the mechanism that these suggestions were meant to correct.

Furthermore, such a mechanism would create an asymmetrical situation if one of the parties regularly is not a state, as is the case in investment disputes. To safeguard the equality of the parties in the appointment of the adjudicating body, the mechanism of party autonomy gives all parties the possibility to appoint an adjudicator. Therefore, a mechanism reproducing the appointment system for international courts would need to provide that one adjudicator is appointed from a list nominated by the states, and one from a list nominated by representatives of the opposing interests. Alternatively, the composition of the appointing authority should reflect all the interests involved.

As long as the volume of cases is not such as to justify full-time positions, however, a mechanism corresponding to that of international courts does not meet all the concerns that are voiced in relation to investment arbitration. Furthermore, the selection process for international courts is not necessarily a model to be followed, as their transparency and objectivity could be improved.

This comparative research has shown that party appointment and appointment of a tribunal for a specific dispute are not incompatible with the principle of independence and impartiality; that a permanent court does not necessarily imply appointment by an appointing authority; that a permanent court with full-time positions ensures independence and impartiality only if the appointment procedure is objective and based on competence, and if the adjudicators are protected against repercussions due to their decisions; and that a permanent court with part-time positions does not necessarily ensure independence and impartiality of the adjudicators.

There is a wide range of mechanisms that could meet many of the criteria to ensure independence and impartiality. On one end of the spectrum is a permanent court with full-time, long-term positions filled by experts who are selected, according to transparent procedures, by representatives of each of the interests that may be involved in prospective disputes. On the other end of the spectrum is a tribunal appointed by the parties for the specific dispute, with a duty on the adjudicator to disclose any circumstances that may give rise to doubts and a right of the parties to challenge the adjudicator's independence and impartiality before an independent body. Between these two ends of the spectrum there may be many variants and combinations.

PART I
SPECIAL NON-NATIONAL REPORTS

THE INDEPENDENCE AND IMPARTIALITY OF ADJUDICATORS IN CLAIMS TRIBUNALS

Maria Beatrice DELI

1. Introduction 68
2. The Criteria for the Selection of the Adjudicators 69
   2.1. The Iran–United States Claims Tribunal......................... 69
   2.2. The Claims Resolution Tribunal for Dormant Accounts 70
   2.3. The Eritrea–Ethiopia Claims Commission...................... 71
3. Which Authority Appoints the Adjudicators? 72
   3.1. The Iran–United States Claims Tribunal......................... 72
   3.2. The Claims Resolution Tribunal for Dormant Accounts 73
   3.3. The Eritrea–Ethiopia Claims Commission...................... 73
4. The Method for Appointing the Adjudicators 73
   4.1. The Iran–United States Claims Tribunal......................... 73
   4.2. The Commission for Real Property Claims of Displaced Persons..... 74
5. Methods to Balance the Appointing Authority's Influence on the
   Appointment of the Adjudicators................................... 75
6. Parameters to Ensure that the Adjudicators Act Independently and
   Impartially 75
   6.1. The Iran–United States Claims Tribunal......................... 75
   6.2. The Commission for Real Property Claims of Displaced Persons..... 79
   6.3. The Eritrea–Ethiopia Claims Commission...................... 79
7. Consequences for the Adjudicator of a Breach by the Adjudicator
   of the Requirement to Act Independently and Impartially.............. 79
   7.1. The Iran–United States Claims Tribunal......................... 79
   7.2. The Claims Resolution Tribunal for Dormant Accounts 81
   7.3. The Eritrea–Ethiopia Claims Commission...................... 81
8. Enforceability of a Final Decision Rendered by an Adjudicator
   who Breached the Requirement to Act Independently and Impartially....... 82

1. INTRODUCTION

Mixed claims commissions have been frequently established during the first half of the 20th century within Europe or among European states, the United States and Latin American states. In the majority of cases, they were created to decide post-conflict disputes and to adjudicate on compensation and damages suffered by states, state entities and/or individual citizens. The claims commission mechanism was reintroduced in the second part of the century with the establishment, in 1981, of the Iran–United States Claims Tribunal, followed by other bodies like the United Nations Compensations Commission in 1991, the Commission for Real Property Claims of Displaced Persons and Refugees in 1996, the Independent Claims Tribunal for Dormant Accounts in 1997 and the Eritrea–Ethiopia Claims Commission in 2000.[1]

The claims tribunals or commissions were all conceived to act as dispute resolution bodies where the adjudicators were appointed according to procedural rules adopted by the institutions or designated by an ad hoc appointing authority. The present report will show that in most cases the adjudicators were requested to be experts in the matter concerned, but also independent and impartial in relation to the parties and the case at stake.[2] The notion of independence and impartiality, however, in relation to each claims tribunal is rarely specified in the applicable procedural rules (or in the institutional rules) and only a few bodies have enacted a clear procedure for challenging the adjudicators and consequently replacing them in the event of a breach of these requirements.

It should be noted that the claims tribunals reported below are only those which in their respective rules of procedure (or institutional provisions) make specific reference to the appointment of 'impartial and independent' adjudicators and possibly provide for challenge or replacement.[3]

---

[1]   A. Carrillo, J. Palmer, *Transnational Mass Claim Processes (TMCPs) in International Law and Practice*, 28 *Berkeley J. Int'l L.*, 2010, p. 343; L. Brilmayer, C. Giorgetti, L. Charlton, *International claims commissions: righting wrongs after conflict*, Cheltenham, UK/Northampton, MA, 2017, p. 5 ff.; L. Brilmayer, *Understanding IMCCs: Compensation and Closure in the Formation and Function of Intentional Mass Claims Commissions*, 43 *Yale J. Int'l L.*, 2018, p. 273 ff., available at: https://digitalcommons.law.yale.edu/yjil/vol43/iss2/2; S. Giroud, S. Moss, *Mass Claims Processes under Public International Law*, in E. Lein, D. Fairgrieve, M. Otero Crespo, V. Smith (eds), *Collective Redress in Europe: Why and How?*, British Institute of International and Comparative Law, 2015, p. 481.

[2]   See A. Carrillo, J. Palmer, *Transnational Mass Claim Processes (TMCPs) in International Law and Practice*, 28 *Berkeley J. Int'l L.*, 2010, p. 403: the authors noted that '[s]uch experts, whether they are called "Judge" or "Commissioner" or any other of the terms applied to IMCP decision makers, are always appointed through a carefully balanced selection process that, while allowing for each party's input, emphasizes impartiality and expertise'.

[3]   The present report does not include the UN Compensation Commission created in 1991 as a subsidiary organ of the United Nations Security Council to process claims and pay compensation for losses and damage caused by Iraq's unlawful invasion and occupation of Kuwait in the years 1990–1991. The claims had to be submitted to 19 Panels of Commissioners

2. THE CRITERIA FOR THE SELECTION OF THE ADJUDICATORS

2.1. THE IRAN–UNITED STATES CLAIMS TRIBUNAL

The Iran–United States Claims Tribunal was established with the Algiers Declarations of 1981 in order to deal with claims between Iran nationals and the US government, between US nationals and the Iranian government, and between the two states themselves, in matters arising out of commercial, non-public issues and also intergovernmental issues involving public international law.

The Claims Settlement Declaration of 19 January 1981, under Article III, para. 2, specified that the Tribunal is expected to conduct its work in accordance with the UNCITRAL Arbitration Rules, 'except to the extent modified by the Parties or by the Tribunal to ensure that the Agreement can be carried out. The UNCITRAL rules for appointing members of the three-member tribunals shall apply *mutatis mutandis* to the appointment of the Tribunal'. This provision enacted the Rules of Procedure of the Iran–US Claims Tribunal of 3 May 1983, which 'incorporate the UNCITRAL Rules and Administrative Directives … with certain modifications to each'. The UNCITRAL Rules served to provide the necessary flexibility that allowed the Tribunal to develop its practice in its specific context, adopting modifications in order to carry out its functions in a more effective way.

According to the Claims Settlement Declaration, the Iran–United States Claims Tribunal consists of nine arbitrators to sit on three tripartite panels (Article III).[4] The Rules of Procedure deal with the appointment of members of the arbitral tribunal under Articles 6–8. The procedure adopted is quite articulated due to the complex relations between the two governments involved.[5]

One Iranian national and one United States national are appointed to each of three arbitral panels. The remaining arbitrator is appointed by mutual agreement to be reached by the members already designated by the parties.

According to Article 6, para. 4 of the Tribunal's Rules of Procedure, concerning the appointment of a sole arbitrator, the appointing authority should

---

chosen for their integrity, experience and expertise. Still the Commissioners were not 'adjudicators' but 'reporters', having the task of recommending the amount of compensation to be paid, subject to the approval by the Governing Council. Due to the non-binding character of the recommendation of the Commissioners, their role was not considered equivalent to that of the other adjudicators analysed in the present report.

4 The two states may agree on a larger number of members, in case they deem it necessary to conduct procedures in a more expeditious way.

5 The Rules of Procedure contain a Note to Articles 6–8 where it is clarified that 'the terms "party" and "parties" refer to the one or both of the two Governments'.

apply criteria and considerations that 'are likely to secure the appointment of an independent and impartial arbitrator'. In this perspective, the rule itself raises a specific issue, suggesting that the appointing authority should take into account the advisability of appointing an arbitrator who has a different nationality from the parties. In the case of a sole arbitrator, a coincidence of nationality between the arbitrator and one of the parties would therefore be considered an impediment to the expected impartiality and independence requirement. Given the hybrid nature of the claims submitted to the Iran–US Tribunal and the involvement of issues of public international law, nationality becomes therefore one of the most relevant criteria to be considered for the appointment of the adjudicators.

In any case, nationality is an element to be declared when the names of one or more persons are proposed as candidates for appointment as arbitrators (Article 8, para. 2).

2.2. THE CLAIMS RESOLUTION TRIBUNAL FOR DORMANT ACCOUNTS

With a Memorandum of Understanding in 1996, the World Jewish Restitution Organization, the World Jewish Congress and the Swiss Bankers Association established the Independent Committee of Eminent Persons (ICEP). The ICEP and the Swiss Federal Banking Commission then established in 1997 a Claims Resolution Tribunal (CRT-I) with the purpose of identifying accounts in Swiss banks that had belonged to victims of Nazi persecution and had remained dormant since 1945. The founders aimed at allowing the owners of the accounts, or their heirs, to claim their property.[6]

The Rules of Procedure adopted in 1997 for the Claims Resolution Process provided that the members of the Claims Resolution Tribunal were appointed by the Board of Trustees 'to serve as independent, impartial and objective arbitrators of claims to dormant accounts'. The Tribunal had to be also independent and impartial from the Swiss banks.[7] The Tribunal was composed of a Chairman, a Vice-Chairman

---

[6]   The CRT-I and II operated in Zurich and New York under the supervision of the United States District Court for the Eastern District of New York. The accounts adjudicated by CRT-I dated from 1933 to 1945 and had remained open and dormant. The Claims Resolution Tribunal had received over 32,000 claims from Nazi victims or their heirs to assets deposited in Swiss banks in the period before and during World War II. The claims process is part of the settlement of the Holocaust Victim Assets class action litigation. The Claims Resolution Tribunal was later charged with the processing of Deposited Assets claims and that activity was known as CRT-II. See S. Beauchamp, *The New Claims Resolution Tribunal for Dormant Accounts in Switzerland Distribution Organ Mass Claims Adjudicative Body or Sui Generis Entity?*, *Journal of World Investment*, 2002, p. 999; R. Alford, *The Claims Resolution Tribunal and Holocaust Claims Against Swiss Banks*, 20 *Berkeley J. Int'l L.*, 2002, p. 250.

[7]   See the features of the Claims Tribunal, available at https://www.crt-ii.org/_crt-i/features.html.

and up to 15 arbitrators, 'chosen for their extensive experience in international arbitration or banking matters and … appointed to resolve claims in a fair and just manner'.[8] The arbitrators would then be appointed to a Claims Panel composed of the members of the Tribunal, making sure to include a Swiss member with two international members. The inclusion of a member with Swiss nationality is motivated by the fact that the Swiss banks had a fundamental role in the claims concerned.[9]

2.3. THE ERITREA–ETHIOPIA CLAIMS COMMISSION

After a long and full-scale war, a few months after the ceasefire, on 12 December 2000, Eritrea and Ethiopia signed a peace treaty, known as the Algiers Agreement. The Agreement provided for the creation, among other bodies, of an arbitral tribunal, known as the Commission, to decide claims concerning the loss, damage or injuries by one government against the other, or resulting from violations of international and international humanitarian law (Article 5 of the Agreement). The parties could submit claims on their own behalf and on behalf of their nationals (natural and legal persons) and in limited cases also on behalf of persons of only Ethiopian or Eritrean origin.[10]

The Commission's premises were in The Hague. The Rules of Procedure were adopted in 2001 and were essentially based on the 1992 Permanent Court of Arbitration Optional Rules for Arbitration Disputes Between Two States.[11]

The Commission was composed of five arbitrators, supported in their work by the staff of the Permanent Court of Arbitration. Each party was requested

---

[8]   See https://www.crt-ii.org/_crt-i/overview.html and the Rules of Procedure for the Claims Resolution Process, Foreword and Article 25.

[9]   Article 1 of the Rules of Procedure stated that the Rules governed all claims relating 'i) to accounts opened by non-Swiss nationals or residents that are dormant since May 9, 1945 and were made public by the Swiss Bankers Association on July 23, 1997 or at a later date; ii) and to accounts opened by Swiss nationals that are dormant ever since May 9, 1945 and will be made public by the Swiss Bankers Association in October 1997 or at a later date, if and to the extent a Sole Arbitrator determines, after consultation with ICEP, that such accounts may have been held by a Swiss intermediary for a victim of Nazi persecution'.

[10] Article 5 of the Agreement states that the Commission will 'decide through binding arbitration all claims for loss, damage or injury by one Government against the other, and by nationals (including both natural and juridical persons) of one party against the Government of the other party or entities owned or controlled by the other party that are (a) related to the conflict that was the subject of the Framework Agreement, the Modalities for its Implementation and the Cessation of Hostilities Agreement, and (b) result from violations of international humanitarian law, including the 1949 Geneva Conventions, or other violations of international law'. See C. Gray, *The Eritrea-Ethiopia Claims Commission Oversteps its Boundaries: A Partial Award?*, 17 Eur. J. Int'l L., 2006, p. 699 ff.; A. Dybnis, *Was the Eritrea-Ethiopia Claims Commission Merely a Zero-Sum Game? Exposing the Limits of Arbitration in Resolving Violent Transnational Conflict*, 33 Loy.L.A. Int'l & Comp. L.Rev., 2011, p. 255 ff.

[11] The Commission delivered 15 partial and final awards on liability and delivered its final awards on damages on 17 August 2009, when it concluded its work.

to appoint two members, 'neither of whom shall be nationals or permanent residents of the party making the appointment'. The president of the Commission was to be chosen by the party-appointed arbitrators and was requested to be a third-country national, and in any case the Agreement required that he or she not be a permanent resident of either state party.[12]

3. WHICH AUTHORITY APPOINTS THE ADJUDICATORS?

3.1. THE IRAN–UNITED STATES CLAIMS TRIBUNAL

The parties are encouraged to agree on the appointment (and if necessary, replacement) of their own arbitrators if possible. If the parties cannot agree, they have to resort to an appointing authority on whom the parties have agreed, and the decision will be made by that independent authority.

In case a sole arbitrator is to be appointed, Article 6, para. 1 provides that either party may propose to the other one or more names of persons to serve as sole arbitrator. In the event of disagreement on the names proposed, each party can propose to the other the names of one or more institutions or persons that could serve as appointing authority.

If no agreement is reached by the parties as to the arbitrator and the parties cannot agree on the selection of the appointing authority, either party can request the Secretary-General of the Permanent Court of Arbitration – acting as an independent authority – to designate the appointing authority charged with the appointment of the sole arbitrator or the third arbitrator. The role of the PCA Secretary-General is, therefore, limited to designating an 'appointing authority' to choose the arbitrators if the parties cannot agree on one.[13]

This two-step process was considered an effective and practical way to guarantee that an able and authoritative person or institution would be available in the event of disagreement between the parties.[14] For this reason, the appointing authority has played a fundamental role in mitigating tensions between the governments involved, helping the system to act in an efficient way.[15]

---

[12] Article 5, paras 2–3.

[13] S.A. Baker, M.D. Davis, *Establishment of an Arbitral Tribunal Under the UNCITRAL Rules: The Experience of the Iran-United States Claims Tribunal*, The International Lawyer, 1989, p. 107 ff.

[14] High-level individuals and professionals have been designated as appointing authority: Judge Charles Moons, former Chief Justice of the Supreme Court of the Netherlands; Sir Robert Jennings, former President of the International Court of Justice; and W.E. Haak and Judge Geert J.M. Corstens, both having served as Chief Justice of the Supreme Court of the Netherlands.

[15] S.A. Baker, M.D. Davis, *Establishment of an Arbitral Tribunal under the UNCITRAL Rules: The Experience of the Iran-United States Claims Tribunal*, The International Lawyer, 1989,

3.2. THE CLAIMS RESOLUTION TRIBUNAL FOR DORMANT ACCOUNTS

According to the Rules of Procedure, upon the submission of a claim, it was for the Chairman of the Claims Resolution Tribunal to appoint the Sole Arbitrator or a Claims Panel, depending on the circumstances.[16] The Claims Panel should be composed of three members, a Swiss arbitrator and two international members, selected from among those serving in the Claims Resolution Tribunal (Article 6).

3.3. THE ERITREA–ETHIOPIA CLAIMS COMMISSION

In the event that a party failed to appoint one or both of its party-appointed arbitrators, or when the parties did not reach an agreement to nominate the president, the neutrality in the appointment was guaranteed by the designation as appointing authority of the Secretary-General of the United Nations. For the appointment of the president of the Commission the UN Secretary-General was requested to have prior consultation with the parties.

4. THE METHOD FOR APPOINTING THE ADJUDICATORS

4.1. THE IRAN–UNITED STATES CLAIMS TRIBUNAL

Given the peculiarity of the institutional character of this claims tribunal,[17] the two governments involved seemed to agree that the state-appointed arbitrators could communicate with their respective governments with regard to the selection of the third-country arbitrators, without making any reference to substantive issues or the merits of the cases.

---

p. 81; D.D. Caron, L.M. Caplan, *The UNCITRAL Arbitration Rules. A Commentary*, 2nd ed., 2013; L.M. Caplan, *Arbitrator Challenges at the Iran-United States Claims Tribunal*, in C. Giorgetti (ed.), *Challenges and Recusals of Judges and Arbitrators in International Courts and Tribunals*, 2015, p. 115 ff.

16   The Rules provide for fast-track arbitrations at the request of the Swiss bank or upon agreement of all parties involved or for the ordinary procedure, see Article 28.

17   It is to be noted that in the Iran–United States Tribunal only the two governments are allowed to appoint arbitrators or request the appointing authority to appoint them and not the private parties involved in the disputes.

The Procedural Rules do not contain any distinction between party-appointed and non-party-appointed arbitrators in connection with the issue of impartiality and independence.[18]

The practice of the Iran–United States Claims Tribunal also includes party-appointed arbitrators. The members of the Tribunal appointed by the US and Iranian governments respectively are requested to be as independent and impartial as the third-country arbitrators acting as chairs of the Tribunal. Their strict application of those standards is demonstrated by several cases in which the party-appointed arbitrators have chosen to withdraw or recuse themselves whenever they could not maintain a neutral position.[19]

4.2. THE COMMISSION FOR REAL PROPERTY CLAIMS OF DISPLACED PERSONS

The parties to the Dayton Peace Agreement of 1995, which concluded the Bosnian War, created a specific institution, the Commission for Real Property Claims of Displaced Persons and Refugees, to resolve the various issues associated with the deprivation of the real property of refugees and displaced persons that occurred in the course of the hostilities since 1991.[20] Claims might be raised for the return of the property or only for compensation.

The Commission, which started its activities in March 1996 and terminated in 2003, consisted of three international members and six national members. The three international commissioners were appointed by the President of the European Court of Human Rights. The Federation of Bosnia and Herzegovina and the Republika Srpska, being the two constituent entities of the Republic of Bosnia and Herzegovina, appointed two Bosniak and two Croat commissioners, while two Serb members were appointed by the Republika Srpska.[21] The peculiarity of the Commission, from the perspective of the standards of independence and impartiality, is that although the Dayton Agreement provided that the Commission 'might' sit in panels,[22] a structure composed of three panels, each

---

[18]　R.M. Mosk, *The Role of Party-Appointed Arbitrators in International Arbitration: The Experience of the Iran-United States Claims Tribunal*, 1 *Transnational Lawyer*, 1988, p. 253, esp. 266.

[19]　See S.A. Baker, M.D. Davis, *Establishment of an Arbitral Tribunal Under the UNCITRAL Rules: The Experience of the Iran-United States Claims Tribunal, The International Lawyer*, 1989, p. 122.

[20]　Dayton Peace Agreement, Annex 7, Agreement on Refugees and Displaced Persons, Articles VII–XVI. See H. van Houtte, *Mass Property Claim Resolution in a Post-War Society: The Commission for Real Property Claims in Bosnia and Herzegovina*, 48 *The International and Comparative Law Quarterly*, 1999, p. 625 ff.

[21]　Article IX, para. 1.

[22]　Article IX under para. 3 states that '[t]he Commission may sit in panels, as provided in its rules and regulations'.

consisting of one international and two national members, was not considered suitable since each panel would lack a representative of the third ethnic group (Bosniak, Serb or Croat), generating a possible threat to independence and impartiality. For this reason, the Commission adopted a different practice and took its decisions in plenary meetings.[23]

5. METHODS TO BALANCE THE APPOINTING AUTHORITY'S INFLUENCE ON THE APPOINTMENT OF THE ADJUDICATORS

The Commission for Real Property Claims of Displaced Persons

The deliberations of the Commission were to be kept secret and not disclosed to the public so that the minutes of the meetings could not reflect the members' individual positions, in order to avoid any kind of pressure by the respective national authorities.[24]

6. PARAMETERS TO ENSURE THAT THE ADJUDICATORS ACT INDEPENDENTLY AND IMPARTIALLY

6.1. THE IRAN–UNITED STATES CLAIMS TRIBUNAL

The requirement of impartiality and independence of the members of the Iran–United States Claims Tribunal has no autonomous definition, but it is to be generally derived from the provisions indicated in the Tribunal Rules of Procedure of 1983. It should observed that the Tribunal has adopted accompanying 'Notes' in the Rules which clarify and emphasise the duties of the arbitrators.

The basic element seems to be the absence of 'circumstances likely to give rise to justifiable doubts as to his impartiality or independence' with respect to the given case (Article 6, para. 4). No other references are recalled as to the meaning to be attributed to impartiality and independence or to the establishment of this requirement. It was noted that impartiality and independence are defined only 'by indirection'.[25]

---

[23] Commission for Real Property Claims of Displaced Persons and Refugees, Executive Summary: End of Mandate Report, 1996–2003, available at http://www.nuhanovicfoundation. org/user/file/emr-part1-coverexec1-summary-emr.pdf.

[24] See on this point H. van Houtte, *Mass Property Claim Resolution in a Post-War Society: The Commission for Real Property Claims in Bosnia and Herzegovina*, 48 *The International and Comparative Law Quarterly*, 1999, p. 629.

[25] S.A. Baker, M.D. Davis, *Establishment of an Arbitral Tribunal Under the UNCITRAL Rules: The Experience of the Iran-United States Claims Tribunal*, *The International Lawyer*, 1989, p. 117.

As mentioned above, due to the nature of the Claims Tribunal, the Rules of Procedure modified the corresponding UNCITRAL Rules on disclosure, providing for the notification of the occurrence of 'circumstances likely to give rise to justifiable doubts as to his impartiality or independence' to the President of the Tribunal rather than to the parties and leaving the President discretion in deciding whether the information could or should be disclosed to the parties. This is to limit frivolous and unnecessary challenges, reserving the decision to a neutral and authoritative personality (at least at a preliminary stage).

The climate of distrust between the two governments characterised the long and highly productive activity of the Iran–US Claims Tribunal.[26] The Tribunal hence experienced a certain number of cases where the concepts of independence and impartiality were raised and put under discussion with challenges.[27] This experience therefore could be considered a useful reference in the context of the activity of this intergovernmental/hybrid dispute settlement mechanism.

A famous challenge was lodged in 1988 against Judge Briner in one of the largest cases to be decided by the Iran–United States Tribunal. The government of Iran challenged Judge Briner acting as Chairman in the case of *Amoco Iran Oil Company v. Iran*, objecting that there were preceding professional relations between the arbitrator and the subsidiary of the corporate employer (Morgan Stanley & Company) which was involved as an expert witness in the case. This connection was not previously disclosed to the parties, and 'his failure to fulfil his disclosure was an additional basis for challenge'. Judge Briner denied any duty of disclosure, declaring in a letter that the subsidiary at issue was not active and that in his position he had no contact with the entity or any of the individuals involved. The challenge was submitted to the appointing authority, but Judge Briner withdrew before the decision was taken, 'in the overall best interest of the Tribunal'.[28]

Judge Briner was addressed of another challenge in 1988, when he was elected President of the Tribunal. On that occasion Iran contested Judge Briner's continuous service at the Tribunal, claiming that he had made use of a confidential memorandum he was given by a US arbitrator.[29]

---

[26] The Iran–US Claims Tribunal has successfully resolved over 3,900 claims, awarding large sums to nationals and companies.

[27] More than 20 challenges were lodged against various members of the Tribunal, and others were brought against the appointing authority. The majority of the challenges came from governmental parties and only few from private litigants. For an overview see L.M. Caplan, *Arbitrator Challenges at the Iran-United States Claims Tribunal*, in C. Giorgetti (ed.), *Challenges and Recusals of Judges and Arbitrators in International Courts and Tribunals*, 2015, p. 138 f.

[28] See C.N. Brower, J.D. Brüschke, *The Iran-United States Claims Tribunal*, 1998, p. 173; L.M. Caplan, *Arbitrator Challenges at the Iran-United States Claims Tribunal*, in C. Giorgetti (ed.), *Challenges and Recusals of Judges and Arbitrators in International Courts and Tribunals*, 2015, p. 123 f.

[29] L.M. Caplan, *Arbitrator Challenges at the Iran-United States Claims Tribunal*, in C. Giorgetti (ed.), *Challenges and Recusals of Judges and Arbitrators in International Courts and Tribunals*, 2015, p. 124.

Other challenges were made under quite peculiar circumstances. This is the case of the first challenge ever to occur, when in 1984 Iran accused the Swedish Judge Mangard of unduly favouring the United States. The dismissal of the challenge caused a wild reaction by the Iranian co-arbitrators, who physically attacked Judge Mangard, thus leading to a further challenge for lack of independence and impartiality against the Iranian arbitrators themselves. This case is well known, but does represent a unicum, and this was not an occurrence ever contemplated in any list of factors relevant for challenges in any arbitral institution.[30] The United States government also lodged a challenge against the Iranian arbitrators, asserting that they were engaged in a scheme to kick back portions of their salaries to the Iranian government.

In the various challenges made over the years in the Iran–United States Claims Tribunal, recurrent grounds for disqualification of arbitrators involved connections of members of the Tribunal with entities, organisations or professional activities, or breaches of confidentiality of deliberations, as well as alleged financial dependence on one of the parties involved. Often these challenges have been considered unsubstantiated.[31]

Compared with the relatively general provisions of Article 6, the Tribunal Rules contain a more extensive set of provisions for challenging an arbitrator when lack of impartiality or independence is called into question. According to Article 9, para. 1, it is expected that the prospective arbitrator, when proposed as a member of the Tribunal, has a duty to disclose 'to those who approach him in connection with his possible appointment' any occurrence that could affect his impartiality or independence in order to avoid future challenges.[32] The same is true for the arbitrator already appointed by the appointing authority or designated by the parties, who has a duty to disclose 'any circumstances likely to give rise to justifiable doubts as to his impartiality or independence'. The duty to disclose continues until the award is rendered.

As to disclosure, arbitrators appointed by both governments provided detailed disclosure whenever necessary, according to rules generally applicable in

---

[30] The United States argued that '[t]he attack on Mr Mangard, the continued threats of future attacks, and the arbitrators' stated reasons for their attack are in themselves proof of unacceptable partiality and lack of necessary independence'. See C.N. Brower, J.D. Brüschke, *The Iran-United States Claims Tribunal*, 1998, p. 170.

[31] See also the challenges against Judge Arangio Ruiz, L.M. Caplan, *Arbitrator Challenges at the Iran-United States Claims Tribunal*, in C. Giorgetti (ed.), *Challenges and Recusals of Judges and Arbitrators in International Courts and Tribunals*, 2015, p. 128 f., or against President Skubiszewski, see on the case M. Zenkiewicz, *Judge Skubiszewski at the Iran-United States Claims Tribunal*, 18 *International Community Law Review*, 2016, p. 151 ff., and more recently against Judge Brower, for alleged interference with the functions of the appointing authority.

[32] The duty to disclose is limited to issues regarding the arbitrator him- or herself and is not directed to disclosing circumstances affecting other members' impartiality or independence, see R. Teitelbaum, *Challenges of Arbitrators at the Iran-United States Claims Tribunal*, 23 *Journal of International Arbitration*, 2006, p. 550.

international commercial arbitration.[33] Cases of connection were more frequent with US arbitrators, possibly involved with other roles (e.g. as counsel) in previous cases where the non-governmental claimants were parties. This was not often the case with Iranian arbitrators, because almost all cases before the Claims Tribunal involved governmental parties. Iranian arbitrators still provided disclosures whenever they were involved in cases which they could have an interest in or when they have served in the legal office of the Tribunal assisting the Iranian government.[34]

In addition to the duty to disclose under para. 1, Article 9 also provides under para. 2 for the case in which a member of the Tribunal becomes aware of circumstances 'likely to give rise to justifiable doubts as to his impartiality or independence' with respect to the dispute at stake. In such a case, the arbitrator has the duty to disclose the circumstances to the President and if he or she 'so determines, to the arbitrating parties in the case' and 'if appropriate' the arbitrator has to disqualify him- or herself.[35]

One last point concerns a possible adverse effect of non-disclosure in establishing independence and impartiality. As already mentioned, the Rules do not state the criteria to determine when disqualification is to be considered appropriate and similarly do not clarify whether non-disclosure can be interpreted in itself as a ground for disqualification. Non-disclosure could be motivated by the exercise of the individual discretion of the arbitrator, who did not consider certain facts relevant under Article 9, but could also be non-intentional and determined by an omission or even an act of negligence by the arbitrator. In support of the various challenges based on the failure by an arbitrator to disclose, Iran or the United States recalled the IBA Guidelines on Conflicts of Interest, underlining that failure to disclose generates an appearance of bias and could be a ground for disqualification. However, the appointing authority has never mentioned the IBA Guidelines in its decisions, nor has it sustained a challenge on that basis. Therefore, it seems reasonable to conclude that a violation of the duty to disclose under Article 9, even if it gives rise to justifiable doubts, does not establish such doubts and does not entail disqualification.[36]

---

[33]   R.M. Mosk, *The Role of Party-Appointed Arbitrators in International Arbitration: The Experience of the Iran-United States Claims Tribunal*, 1 *Transnational Lawyer*, 1988, p. 253, esp. 267.

[34]   It was noted that given the particularly sensitive situation between the two countries, and the differences between the legal systems involved, the parties before the Tribunal 'were aware at all times of the possibility of any actual partiality or lack of independence ... The Tribunal and the parties demonstrated the necessary flexibility to cope with any deviations from the standards normally applicable to party-appointed arbitrators in international arbitration', see R.M. Mosk, *The Role of Party-Appointed Arbitrators in International Arbitration: The Experience of the Iran-United States Claims Tribunal*, 1 *Transnational Lawyer*, 1988, p. 270.

[35]   See S.A. Baker, M.D. Davis, *Establishment of an Arbitral Tribunal Under the UNCITRAL Rules: The Experience of the Iran-United States Claims Tribunal*, *The International Lawyer*, 1989, p. 116 f.

[36]   See S.A. Baker, M.D. Davis, *Establishment of an Arbitral Tribunal Under the UNCITRAL Rules: The Experience of the Iran-United States Claims Tribunal*, *The International Lawyer*, 1989,

6.2. THE COMMISSION FOR REAL PROPERTY CLAIMS OF DISPLACED PERSONS

The Agreement on Refugees and Displaced Persons, annexed to the Dayton Agreement, does not make any reference to independence and impartiality of the members of the Commission instituted to take decisions on the return and reintegration of real property for the individuals concerned. The members of the Commission – besides the issue of combination of nationalities with the countries involved (as mentioned above) – are only requested to be 'of recognized high moral standing'.[37]

6.3. THE ERITREA–ETHIOPIA CLAIMS COMMISSION

The Rules of Procedure of the Eritrea–Ethiopia Claims Commission do not contain any notion of independence and impartiality as standards of neutrality requested of the arbitrators appointed as members of the Commission. Besides the issue of nationality, recalled above, under the provisions concerning the challenge of arbitrators, Article 5 of the Rules states that a prospective arbitrator has the duty to disclose 'to those who approach him/her in connection with his/her possible appointment any circumstances likely to give rise to justifiable doubts as to his/her impartiality or independence'. The arbitrator who has already been appointed has the same duty of disclosure towards the parties of the occurrence of circumstances of which he or she was not aware before.

7. CONSEQUENCES FOR THE ADJUDICATOR OF A BREACH BY THE ADJUDICATOR OF THE REQUIREMENT TO ACT INDEPENDENTLY AND IMPARTIALLY

7.1. THE IRAN–UNITED STATES CLAIMS TRIBUNAL

In the event of a breach or presumed breach of the requirement to be independent and impartial, the Rules of Procedure provide the possibility for the parties to raise a challenge against the member of the Tribunal. Given the specific political climate between the governments, the number of challenges made against the Tribunal's arbitrators is remarkable.

---

p. 120; R. Teitelbaum, *Challenges of Arbitrators at the Iran-United States Claims Tribunal*, 23 *Journal of International Arbitration*, 2006, p. 555 ff.

[37] Article IX, para. 2.

Maria Beatrice Deli

There are two types of challenge procedure: a specific challenge to the capacity of the arbitrator to serve in a particular case, or a general challenge to his or her capacity to serve as a member of the Tribunal. When the challenge is sustained, the effects in relation to the first case could be that the member of the Tribunal withdraws and the case is assigned to another Chamber, while in the second case the member of the Tribunal is removed and a new arbitrator is appointed.[38]

Besides the case provided for under Article 9, paras 1 and 2, Articles 10–12 deal with the possibility that one of the parties raises a challenge against one arbitrator if the party becomes aware after the appointment that circumstances exist that give rise to justifiable doubts as to the arbitrator's impartiality or independence. In particular, the arbitrator can be challenged by the party that has appointed him or her only 'for reasons of which he becomes aware after the appointment' (Article 10, para. 2). The challenge should be notified to the counterparty, the arbitrator and the other members of the arbitral tribunal within 15 days from the appointment and the notification should include the reasons for the challenge. If the other party does not agree with the challenge or the challenged arbitrator does not withdraw, the decision on the challenge will be for the appointing authority to make (Article 12).

The Notes to Articles 9–12, however, clarify that the arbitrating parties can challenge a member only with regard to circumstances relating to the particular case at stake and not 'upon any general grounds which also relate to other cases'. This latter kind of challenge can only be made by one of the two governments (Notes, para. 1) and can be initiated at any time.[39]

Time limits, notice requirements and methods for challenging, removing or replacing an arbitrator are provided for under Articles 11 and 12. The party who intends to submit a challenge should proceed within 15 days after the appointment or after the circumstances for the challenge have become known. The challenge is to be notified to the other party and to the members of the Tribunal through a written notice containing the grounds for the challenge. The decision on the challenge is made, according to Article 12 of the Rules of Procedure, by the appointing authority that made the appointment or that would have made the appointment or would have been designated.

It has been noted that the role of the appointing authority in relation to challenges made against members of the Iran–United States Claims Tribunal 'has gone far beyond the procedures of other institutions, and has gone far

---

[38]   C.N. Brower, J.D. Brüschke, *The Iran-United States Claims Tribunal*, 1998, p. 163 ff.

[39]   R. Teitelbaum, *Challenges of Arbitrators at the Iran-United States Claims Tribunal*, 23 *Journal of International Arbitration*, 2006, p. 547 ff.; H. Holtzmann, E. Kristjánsdóttir (eds), *International Mass Claims Processes: Legal and Practical Perspectives*, 2007, p. 192.

beyond the role apparently envisioned by the Tribunal Rules of Procedures'.[40] The character of the in camera analysis conducted by the appointing authority in dealing with the challenges against one arbitrator under the Claims Tribunal was unanimously considered to be a real investigation aimed at establishing facts and circumstances. With particular reference to the activity carried out by Judge Moons as appointing authority,[41] he was considered an 'investigating judge', not limiting himself to hearing arguments and witnesses to sustain the challenge. In the end, having decided on the admissibility/sustainability of a significant number of challenges made by the parties, he set out quite consistent jurisprudence relating to every single case, complete in all details. This also allowed for greater transparency of the decision-making process.

7.2. THE CLAIMS RESOLUTION TRIBUNAL FOR DORMANT ACCOUNTS

According to Article 8 of the Rules of Procedure, a sole arbitrator or a panel member could challenged whenever 'circumstances exist that give rise to legitimate doubts concerning his or her independence or integrity'. The challenge had to be submitted to the Chairman of the Claims Resolution Tribunal, indicating the facts and circumstances upon which the challenge was grounded. If the challenge was not accepted by the arbitrator involved, the Board of Trustees of the Independent Claims Resolution Foundation had the right to finally decide on the challenge.

7.3. THE ERITREA–ETHIOPIA CLAIMS COMMISSION

Article 6 of the Rules of Procedure of the Eritrea–Ethiopia Claims Commission regulates the procedure for challenging one of the members of the arbitral tribunal. The challenge might be made by one of the parties, once the circumstances that give rise to justifiable doubts as to an arbitrator's impartiality or independence became known to that party. The arbitrator, after the challenge,

---

[40] R. Briner, *The Appointing Authority*, in D.D. Caron, J.R. Crook (eds), *The Iran-United States Claims Tribunal and the Process of International Claims Resolutions*, 2000, p. 157, also recalled in R. Teitelbaum, *Challenges of Arbitrators at the Iran-United States Claims Tribunal*, 23 *Journal of International Arbitration*, 2006, p. 550. See also S.A. Baker, M.D. Davis, *Establishment of an Arbitral Tribunal Under the UNCITRAL Rules: The Experience of the Iran-United States Claims Tribunal*, *The International Lawyer*, 1989, p. 108 f.

[41] Judge Moons was Chief Justice of the Hoge Raad and later became appointing authority. On his role and on the criteria of independence and impartiality required for the appointing authority, see D.D. Caron, L.M. Caplan, *The UNCITRAL Arbitration Rules. A Commentary*, 2nd ed., 2013, p. 341 ff.

might withdraw from his or her office and this decision was not to be intended as a confirmation of the grounds of the challenge.

If the other party did not agree with the challenge, an appointing authority was to be designated by the UN Secretary-General to decide on the challenge, and if this was sustained, a new arbitrator was appointed according to the ordinary procedure provided for under Article 5 of the Rules.

The Rules do not contain any further specification on the meaning of independence and impartiality, nor does the practice of the Commission – which decided a number of claims – present any cases relating to these requirements.

8. ENFORCEABILITY OF A FINAL DECISION RENDERED BY AN ADJUDICATOR WHO BREACHED THE REQUIREMENT TO ACT INDEPENDENTLY AND IMPARTIALLY

This issue is not evidenced in the rules and practice of any of the claims tribunals examined by the present report.

THE INDEPENDENCE AND IMPARTIALITY OF ADJUDICATORS IN COMMERCIAL AD HOC ARBITRATION

Christophe Seraglini and Anne-Lise Ménagé

1. Introduction 84
2. Analysis of the Optional Framework of Non-Administered
   Arbitration Rules... 86
   2.1. Requirements Regarding the Arbitrators 87
   2.2. Constitution of the Arbitral Tribunal 90
      2.2.1. Third-Party Appointing Authority...................... 91
         2.2.1.1. The UNCITRAL Arbitration Rules 91
         2.2.1.2. Other Procedural Rules....................... 94
      2.2.2. Number of Arbitrators 94
      2.2.3. Appointment of Arbitrators........................... 95
         2.2.3.1. Party Appointment and Intervention of
                  a Third-Party Appointing Authority 96
         2.2.3.2. Selection Process Led by the Third-Party
                  Appointing Authority 97
   2.3. Duties of Arbitrators and Safeguards 100
      2.3.1. Continuous Disclosure Obligation...................... 100
      2.3.2. Duty to Treat the Parties Equally and Prohibition
             of Ex Parte Communications 104
      2.3.3. Immunity from Civil Liability......................... 105
   2.4. Consequences of a Breach of the Requirement of Independence
        and Impartiality 106
      2.4.1. Grounds for Challenging an Arbitrator................. 106
      2.4.2. Challenge Procedures................................. 109
      2.4.3. Challenge Decisions 112
3. Analysis of the Subsidiary National Legal and Judicial Frameworks 113
   3.1. Requirements Regarding the Arbitrator's Person 113
      3.1.1. Requirements of Independence and Impartiality......... 114
      3.1.2. Nationality Requirements 116

3.2.	Constitution of the Arbitral Tribunal	117
	3.2.1. Number of Arbitrators	117
	3.2.2. Appointment of Arbitrators	119
3.3.	Duties of Arbitrators and Safeguards	122
	3.3.1. Continuous Disclosure Obligation	122
	3.3.2. Duty to Treat the Parties Equally and Prohibition of Ex Parte Contact	124
	3.3.3. Immunity from Civil Liability	125
3.4.	Consequences of a Breach of the Requirement of Independence and Impartiality	126
	3.4.1. Challenges of Arbitrators	127
	3.4.2. Annulment and Denial of Recognition and Enforcement of Arbitral Awards	130

1. INTRODUCTION

According to a recent survey, ad hoc commercial arbitration represents around 20% of the caseload of practitioners surveyed.[1] Although ad hoc arbitration is not used as often as institutional arbitration to resolve commercial disputes, it is nevertheless quite popular. In comparison to institutional arbitration, where proceedings are conducted with the support of an administering authority and pursuant to specific institutional procedural rules, ad hoc arbitration grants parties significant freedom and flexibility to determine how to resolve their disputes.

In ad hoc commercial arbitration, to avoid the burdensome and time-consuming drafting of a detailed arbitration agreement and the difficulties of reaching an agreement after a dispute arises, practitioners widely recommend the selection of a pre-existing set of procedural rules designed to govern ad hoc arbitrations. These rules will have been drafted and revised by experts based upon decades of practical experience.[2] When the parties have not referred to such rules, applicable national arbitration legislation and national courts will generally be available to assist the parties and the arbitrator(s) in shaping the procedure.

---

[1] G. Feld and M.-L. Bizeau, '"Pour vivre heureux vivons cachés" – Mythes, réalité et pratique de l'arbitrage commercial ad hoc' (2021) 1 *Revue de l'Arbitrage* 57, 64. This number may vary depending on the practitioners' jurisdictions as some of them might not recognise ad hoc arbitration.

[2] G. Born, *International Arbitration and Forum Selection Agreements: Drafting and Enforcing*, 6th ed., Kluwer Law International, Alphen aan den Rijn 2021, p. 67.

The 2021 Queen Mary Survey sets out various procedural regimes used in ad hoc arbitration.[3] The most popular regime identified by the survey is the 2013 United Nations Commission on International Trade Law Arbitration Rules (UNCITRAL Arbitration Rules) (selected by 76% of the surveyed practitioners),[4] a comprehensive set of procedural rules for arbitration of commercial disputes, dating back to 1976 and subsequently revised in 2010 and 2013. National arbitration laws were identified as the second most popular regime in the survey (selected by 28% of the surveyed practitioners), and bespoke regimes based on agreement of the parties were identified in the survey as the third most popular (selected by 26% of the surveyed practitioners).[5] However, even when the parties have agreed on the procedure, national arbitration laws will apply to remedy procedural missteps in the arbitration and safeguard important public policies. The survey also refers to other non-administered arbitration rules, namely:

- the 2021 London Maritime Arbitrators Association Terms (LMAA Terms) (selected by 13% of the surveyed practitioners);
- the 2016 Construction Industry Model Arbitration Rules (CIMAR) (selected by 5% of the surveyed practitioners);
- the 2018 Conflict Prevention & Resolution International Non-Administered Arbitration Rules (CPR Arbitration Rules) which, although not widely used (they were selected by 4% of the surveyed practitioners), include a useful set of rules for ad hoc arbitrations;[6] and lastly
- the 2016 Grain and Feed Trade Association Arbitration Rules No. 125 (GAFTA Arbitration Rules), selected by 5% of the surveyed practitioners.

Virtually all non-administered arbitration rules and national arbitration laws require arbitrators to be independent and impartial, although in some jurisdictions there may be differences in the standard and scope of the requirement. This is an inherent and vital aspect of the arbitrators' adjudicatory role, defined by the International Bar Association (IBA) Rules of Ethics for International Arbitrators (1987) (IBA Rules of Ethics) in the following way:

> Partiality arises when an arbitrator favours one of the parties, or where he is prejudiced in relation to the subject-matter of the dispute. Dependence arises from relationships between an arbitrator and one of the parties, or with someone closely connected with one of the parties.[7]

---

3   '2021 International Arbitration Survey: Adapting Arbitration to a Changing World', Queen Mary 2021, p. 9, https://arbitration.qmul.ac.uk/media/arbitration/docs/LON0320037-QMUL-International-Arbitration-Survey-2021_19_WEB.pdf.
4   Ibid.
5   Ibid.
6   Ibid.
7   IBA Rules of Ethics, Article 3(1).

This means that arbitrators must be free from subjective biases, predispositions or affinities that would prevent them from fairly and impartially deciding the dispute. They must also be free from personal, contractual or other relationships that would impact their independence.

Section 2 of this report analyses the requirement of independence and impartiality when the parties have chosen to refer to a pre-existing set of procedural rules, and in particular how these rules ensure compliance with this requirement. This includes the support of a third-party appointing authority in the constitution of the tribunal, as well as procedures for arbitrator challenges and replacements. The analysis focuses on the UNCITRAL Arbitration Rules, which, as explained above, are the set of non-administered arbitration rules most frequently used in commercial ad hoc arbitration and, as will be explained, the most sophisticated. The UNCITRAL Arbitration Rules are generally representative of other non-administered arbitration rules, although there may be differences, which we will describe.[8]

Section 3 performs the same analysis with respect to situations where the parties have not referred to a pre-existing set of procedural rules, and describes the different approaches taken by national arbitration laws, including the support of national courts in the constitution of the tribunal as well as in arbitrator challenges and replacements.

2. ANALYSIS OF THE OPTIONAL FRAMEWORK OF NON-ADMINISTERED ARBITRATION RULES

Like most non-administered arbitration rules, the UNCITRAL Arbitration Rules grant the parties the right to agree on the criteria and requirements applicable to arbitrators, with at least one limit: they require arbitrators to be impartial and independent (section 2.1).

To ensure that arbitrators are impartial and independent, in the absence of specific agreement of the parties, the UNCITRAL Arbitration Rules and other non-administered arbitration rules contain default rules and mechanisms relating to the number of arbitrators and the appointment process. These include the support of a third-party appointing authority to assist the parties in the constitution of the arbitral tribunal (section 2.2).

They also provide for duties and safeguards applicable to arbitrators before their appointment, throughout the proceedings and after (section 2.3), and

---

[8] Our analysis of non-administered arbitration rules is limited to those mentioned in the '2021 International Arbitration Survey: Adapting Arbitration to a Changing World', Queen Mary 2021, https://arbitration.qmul.ac.uk/media/arbitration/docs/LON0320037-QMUL-International-Arbitration-Survey-2021_19_WEB.pdf.

they provide for the possibility to challenge arbitrators before the third-party appointing authority when justifiable doubts exist as to their independence and impartiality (section 2.4).

2.1. REQUIREMENTS REGARDING THE ARBITRATORS

The UNCITRAL Arbitration Rules impose a general requirement that arbitrators, whether party-appointed or not,[9] be independent and impartial.[10]

The UNCITRAL Arbitration Rules do not provide criteria and requirements to be considered by the parties when appointing arbitrators. Thus, the parties are free to determine these criteria and requirements, to the extent that they include the requirement of independence and impartiality and that they comply with the requirements of national arbitration laws (as explained in section 3 below). In practice, the parties will tend to favour the appointment of arbitrators who are familiar with the elements of the underlying dispute, which may impact the arbitrators' independence and impartiality.

The UNCITRAL Arbitration Rules, however, provide for criteria to be considered by a third party acting as the appointing authority under the rules, thereby indirectly regulating the selection of arbitrators. These criteria, which are general and non-binding, specifically aim at ensuring that the appointed arbitrators are independent and impartial: pursuant to Article 6(7), '[t]he appointing authority shall have regard to such *considerations as are likely to secure the appointment of an independent and impartial arbitrator* and shall take into account the *advisability of appointing an arbitrator of a nationality other than the nationalities of the parties*' (emphasis added).

In practice, the appointing authority will seek to strike the right balance between, on the one hand, the requirement that arbitrators be independent and impartial and, on the other hand, their familiarity with elements of the underlying dispute (which may expose them to bias). Factors relating to an arbitrator's familiarity with the dispute include, for example: the place and language(s) of the arbitration; the amount in dispute; the subject matter and complexity of the dispute; the qualifications, experience and language abilities of the arbitrator; and the nationalities of the parties and the prospective arbitrator.[11]

The arbitrator's nationality may indeed expose the arbitrator to bias if one of the parties is of the same nationality. Under the UNCITRAL Arbitration

---

9   D. Caron and L. Caplan, *The UNCITRAL Arbitration Rules: A Commentary*, 2nd ed., Oxford University Press, Oxford 2013, pp. 209–11.
10   UNCITRAL Arbitration Rules (2013), Articles 6(7), 11 and 12(1).
11   PCA, 'Spotlight on the PCA's Appointing Authority Activities', https://docs.pca-cpa. org/2019/04/EN-Spotlight-on-the-PCAs-Appointing-Authority-Activities-1.pdf.

Rules, '[t]he appointing authority ... *shall take into account the advisability* of appointing an arbitrator of a nationality other than the nationalities of the parties' (emphasis added). However, there is no obligation to do so and there is no rule according to which the sole arbitrator or the presiding arbitrator must be of a nationality other than those of the parties. This differs from most leading institutional arbitration rules, which generally impose a more direct prohibition on the nationality of sole and presiding arbitrators.[12]

Therefore, it will be up to the appointing authority acting under the UNCITRAL Arbitration Rules to take into consideration the arbitrator's nationality on a case-by-case basis if it believes that it may have an impact on the arbitrator's independence and impartiality. In practice, as one author indicates, '[i]n applying Article 6(7) [of the UNCITRAL Arbitration Rules], ... appointing authorities should as a rule not appoint a sole or presiding arbitrator with the same nationality as one, but not the other, party'; '[d]oing so violates the basic principle of international neutrality that underlies the arbitral process, particularly in the eyes of the "foreign" party'.[13] In particular, when leading arbitral institutions act as appointing authorities, which is very often the case (see section 2.2.1 below), they are 'very unlikely to appoint a sole or presiding arbitrator with the same nationality as one (but not the other) party' (see sections 2.2.1.1 and 2.2.3.2 below).[14]

Other non-administered arbitration rules take varying approaches. Although the CPR Arbitration Rules are similar to the UNCITRAL Arbitration Rules in some respects,[15] they provide that, unless otherwise agreed, an arbitrator not appointed by a party shall be a member of a closed group of individuals – 'a member of the CPR Panels of Distinguished Neutrals ("CPR Panels")'.[16] This mechanism may help achieve the right balance between the appointment of independent arbitrators and the appointment of qualified arbitrators. As explained by the CPR on its website, on the one hand, '[t]he Neutrals, when selected for a matter, are independent contractors'; '[t]hey have no ownership

---

[12]   See e.g. those of the ICC, the LCIA, the International Centre for Dispute Resolution (ICDR) and HKIAC; a contrario, other rules such as those of SIAC and the China International Economic and Trade Arbitration Commission (CIETAC) do not include such a requirement.

[13]   G. Born, *International Commercial Arbitration*, 3rd ed., Kluwer Law International, Alphen aan den Rijn 2021, pp. 1869–70.

[14]   Ibid., p. 1870.

[15]   The CPR Arbitration Rules impose a general requirement that arbitrators, whether party-appointed or non-party-appointed, be independent and impartial (see Rules 7.1, 7.3 and 7.5). They do not specify criteria to be taken into account by the parties when appointing arbitrators, but they indirectly regulate the selection of arbitrators through a few criteria to be considered by a third party acting as appointing authority under the Rules, which aim at ensuring, inter alia, that the appointed arbitrators are independent and impartial (see Rules 6.4 and 6.5).

[16]   CPR Arbitration Rules, Rule 5.1.

interest in CPR, a not-for-profit organization, and receive no funding from CPR.'[17] On the other hand, the CPR Panels 'includ[e] prominent attorneys, retired state and federal judges, academics, as well as highly-skilled business executives, legal experts and dispute resolution professionals' and there are CPR Panels specialised in various sectors (including, for example, construction, energy, oil and gas, environment, cross-border disputes, cyber, biotech, banking, accounting and financial services).[18]

The GAFTA Arbitration Rules similarly require arbitrators to be independent and impartial[19] and provide that an arbitrator appointed under these rules shall be a member of a closed group of individuals.[20] While the rules do not include any specific criteria to be considered in appointing arbitrators, GAFTA has enacted guidelines for appointments to be made by it. These guidelines include a non-exhaustive list of criteria pertaining to independence and impartiality, good standing, and relevant knowledge and expertise of the arbitrator.[21]

Other procedural rules we have analysed provide indirectly for independence and impartiality of arbitrators, but do not specify additional considerations to be taken into account. The LMAA Terms, for example,[22] merely indicate that the default seat of the arbitration is England and thus 'the arbitral proceedings ... shall

---

[17]   'Who Are Our Neutrals', Who Are Our Neutrals | CPR International Institute for Conflict Prevention & Resolution (cpradr.org).

[18]   Ibid.

[19]   First, they provide that the arbitrator 'shall not be interested in the transaction nor directly interested as a member of a company or firm named as a party to the arbitration, nor financially retained by any such company or firm, nor a member of nor financially retained by any company or firm financially associated with any party to the arbitration' (GAFTA Arbitration Rules, Rule 3.7). Second, the Rules provide that the seat of arbitration shall be England and refer to the English Arbitration Act 1996, which applies to 'every arbitration and/or appeal under these Rules save insofar as such provisions are expressly modified by, or are inconsistent with, these Rules' (see GAFTA Arbitration Rules, Rules 1.1 and 1.2) and which provides that arbitrators shall be 'impartial' (see English Arbitration Act, sections 1(a), 24(1), 33(1) and 68(1) and (2)).

[20]   GAFTA Arbitration Rules, Rule 3.7.

[21]   See the Guidelines for GAFTA Appointment of Arbitrators, according to which appointments are made by GAFTA on a case-by-case basis taking into account a number of selection criteria pertaining to diversity, independence, impartiality and good standing of arbitrators, as well as their knowledge and expertise relevant to the dispute at stake. According to Guideline 4, GAFTA should: (i) '[a]void nominating arbitrators where there is an *actual or perceived conflict of interest*. It is, however, the responsibility of both the parties to the dispute and the individual arbitrator(s) to inform Gafta immediately if they believe there is, or is likely to be, a conflict' (emphasis added); and (ii) '[m]aintain impartiality'. Under Guideline 2, arbitrators should comply with all relevant rules and regulations of GAFTA, including the General Code of Conduct Applicable to All Members and the Rules and Code of Conduct for Qualified Arbitrators and Qualified Mediators (which, in particular, enumerates specific circumstances where a Qualified Arbitrator *will not* be eligible to act in an arbitration – see Rules and Code of Conduct for Qualified Arbitrators and Qualified Mediators, Article 6.1).

[22]   See also CIMAR, Articles 1.1, 1.4 and 1.6.

be in all respects governed by the [English Arbitration Act 1996]'.[23] The English Arbitration Act, in turn, includes the requirement that arbitrators be 'impartial'.[24] This requirement should also apply when the seat is not in England, since virtually almost all national arbitration laws provide that arbitrators should be independent and impartial (see section 3 below).[25] In practice, it seems to us that parties and appointing authorities will nevertheless balance considerations of independence and impartiality with considerations of familiarity with the underlying dispute.

Lastly, if the appointing authority is an arbitral institution, the institution may have issued rules, guidelines or practice notes setting out, with more or less detail, requirements or criteria to be considered when appointing arbitrators. These rules, guidelines or practice notes should be taken into consideration in addition to the applicable procedural rules chosen by the parties. The Hong Kong International Arbitration Centre (HKIAC), for example, has published a detailed Practice Note on Appointment of Arbitrators (HKIAC Practice Note), which applies when it acts as appointing authority in ad hoc arbitrations brought under the UNCITRAL Arbitration Rules and other arbitrations. The HKIAC Practice Note contains more details than the UNCITRAL Arbitration Rules and other non-administered arbitration rules, providing that arbitrators are normally appointed from a panel or list of arbitrators published on the HKIAC's website,[26] taking into account factors that aim at striking the right balance between, on the one hand, the arbitrators' independence and impartiality and, on the other hand, their qualifications and familiarity with the dispute.[27] The Practice Note adds that the HKIAC 'generally will not appoint a sole or presiding arbitrator of the same nationality as any of the parties unless the parties expressly agree otherwise'[28] or '[i]n appropriate circumstances and where no party objects within a time limit set by HKIAC'.[29]

2.2. CONSTITUTION OF THE ARBITRAL TRIBUNAL

With respect to the constitution of the tribunal, the UNCITRAL Arbitration Rules, like most other rules, are based on party autonomy but provide for default

---

23   LMAA Terms, sections 6(b) and 7(a).
24   English Arbitration Act, sections 1(a), 24(1), 33(1), and 68(1) and (2). As explained in section 3.3 below, it is well established under English law that this requirement is one of impartiality and *independence*.
25   Please also note that the LMAA Terms, in section 3, provide that 'the arbitrators at all times are under a duty to act fairly and impartially between the parties.'
26   HKIAC Practice Note on Appointment of Arbitrators, section 2.2.
27   Ibid., section 2.3.
28   Ibid., section 3.1.
29   Ibid., section 3.2.

rules and mechanisms regarding the number of arbitrators (section 2.2.2) and their appointment (section 2.2.3). These default rules and mechanisms include the support of a third-party appointing authority (section 2.2.1).

2.2.1. Third-Party Appointing Authority

The identity of the appointing authority, and therefore the way it is selected (i.e. by the parties or by other means), may have an impact on the independence and impartiality of the arbitrator(s) it appoints. This is because close connection between one of the parties and the appointing authority may affect the independence of the appointed arbitrator(s). We examine below the identity of the appointing authority and the way it is selected under, on the one hand, the UNCITRAL Arbitration Rules (section 2.1.1.1) and, on the other hand, other procedural rules (section 2.1.1.2).

2.2.1.1. The UNCITRAL Arbitration Rules

Under Article 6(1) of the UNCITRAL Arbitration Rules, the parties may choose the appointing authority at any time, although it is recommended that they do so as early as possible.[30]

The parties may choose an established institution[31] such as the International Chamber of Commerce (ICC), the Singapore International Arbitration Centre (SIAC), the HKIAC or the London Court of International Arbitration (LCIA). These institutions have extensive experience in selecting arbitrators in complex commercial disputes since they also provide this service in arbitrations administered by them. As explained in section 2.1 above, when acting as appointing authorities in ad hoc arbitrations, these institutions usually follow their own rules, guidelines or practice notes. According to these rules, guidelines or practice notes, decisions are generally taken by a committee or, at least, in consultation with other members of the institution. For example, for the ICC, the function of appointing authority is carried out exclusively by the ICC International Court of Arbitration (ICC Court).[32] Under the HKIAC Practice

---

[30] Hence, the model arbitration clause in the Annex to the UNCITRAL Arbitration Rules includes a provision to that effect (see the model arbitration clause in the Annex to the UNCITRAL Arbitration Rules).

[31] UNCITRAL Arbitration Rules, Article 6(1).

[32] 'Rules of ICC As Appointing Authority in UNCITRAL or Other Arbitration Proceedings', 2018 (Rules of ICC As Appointing Authority), Article 1(2), https://iccwbo.org/content/uploads/sites/3/2017/12/2018-rules-of-icc-as-appointing-authority-english.pdf.

Note, the appointment is made by the HKIAC's Appointment Committee and members of the Committee are not eligible for appointment.[33]

The parties may also choose an individual as appointing authority, including the Secretary-General of the Permanent Court of Arbitration (PCA).[34] Since this individual will make the appointment decision alone, utmost care is required in selecting him or her. It is recommended that the individual be the PCA Secretary-General or another experienced arbitration practitioner. The PCA Secretary-General has experience in appointing arbitrators under the UNCITRAL Arbitration Rules. To date, it has received 787 requests to act as appointing authority or to designate an appointing authority under the UNCITRAL Arbitration Rules (under Article 6(2), the PCA Secretary-General may indeed designate the appointing authority, as explained below).[35]

Overall it seems preferable to designate an institution rather than an individual since, as explained above, an institution 'usually has a comprehensive panel of experienced arbitrators or other established procedures by which to choose a qualified person for the case concerned'[36] and it 'can offer procedural safeguards such as overriding frivolous objections, appointing arbitrators when acceptable nominations are not forthcoming, and disposing efficiently of groundless challenges, all of which help to keep the case on track.'[37] Designating an institution rather than an individual (other than the PCA Secretary-General) should also limit the risk of a close connection between the appointing authority and a party, which may impact the appointed arbitrator's independence and impartiality.

Pursuant to Article 6(2) of the UNCITRAL Arbitration Rules, if the parties have not been able to jointly designate the third-party appointing authority within 30 days after a party has made a proposal and that proposal has been received by all other parties, 'any party may request the Secretary-General of the PCA to designate the appointing authority' (but it cannot designate itself).[38] Thus, not only can the PCA Secretary-General be chosen to serve as appointing authority, it also serves as

---

[33] HKIAC Practice Note, section 2.1, which provides for one exception: 'a member's designation as arbitrator by a party or the co-arbitrators in an arbitration may be confirmed by HKIAC'.

[34] UNCITRAL Arbitration Rules, Article 6(1).

[35] These requests related to a wide variety of cases: arbitrations between states under public international law, proceedings involving international organisations, treaty-based investment arbitrations between an investor and a state, contract-based arbitrations involving a state or state-entity, contract-based arbitrations between private parties, and other forms of dispute resolution. See PCA, 'Spotlight on the PCA's Appointing Authority Activities', https://docs.pca-cpa.org/2019/04/EN-Spotlight-on-the-PCAs-Appointing-Authority-Activities-1.pdf.

[36] H. Jonkman, 'The Role of the Secretary-General of the Permanent Court of Arbitration Under the UNCITRAL Arbitration Rules' (1995) 8 *Leiden Journal of International Law* 185, 191.

[37] A.M. Whitesell, 'Independence in ICC Arbitration: ICC Court practice concerning the Appointment, Confirmation, Challenge and Replacement of Arbitrators' (2007) *ICC International Court of Arbitration Bulletin, Special Supplement* 7, 39.

[38] T. Webster, *Handbook of UNCITRAL Arbitration: Commentary, Precedents and Materials for UNCITRAL Based Arbitration Rules*, Sweet & Maxwell, London 2010, p. 100, para. 6-3.

the default authority under the UNCITRAL Arbitration Rules for designating the appointing authority in case the parties cannot reach an agreement.

The UNCITRAL Arbitration Rules do not provide any instructions to the PCA Secretary-General regarding the criteria to be considered in selecting the appointing authority. Nevertheless, a former PCA Secretary-General explains that, in practice, the PCA Secretary-General takes into consideration circumstances analogous to those established for arbitrators under Article 6 of the UNCITRAL Arbitration Rules – i.e. all such circumstances that are likely to secure the designation of an independent and impartial appointing authority, and the advisability of designating an authority of a nationality other than that of the parties[39] – as well as their qualifications, availability and familiarity with the underlying dispute.[40]

Although the choice of the appointing authority belongs to the PCA Secretary-General, the Secretary-General 'may require from any party and the arbitrators the information [it] deem[s] necessary and [it] shall give the parties and, where appropriate, the arbitrators, an opportunity to present their views in any manner they consider appropriate. All such communications to and from the appointing authority ... shall also be provided by the sender to all other parties'.[41] The parties may therefore influence the Secretary-General's choice, but to a limited extent.

Consistent with the general view that it is preferable to designate an institution rather than an individual, the former PCA Secretary-General mentioned above indicates that '[a]s a rule, the Secretary-General prefers to designate *an institution*' (emphasis added).[42]

Once the PCA Secretary-General has designated an appointing authority, the parties are not entitled to refuse, accept or challenge that appointing authority. For this reason, 'utmost care in selecting the authority is ... required' from the PCA Secretary-General.[43] Nevertheless, as some authors point out, this indirect appointment by the PCA 'provides a global system that is likely to yield a particularly knowledgeable appointing authority' and '[i]n practice ... has functioned well under the Rules'.[44]

---

[39]   H. Jonkman, 'The Role of the Secretary-General of the Permanent Court of Arbitration Under the UNCITRAL Arbitration Rules' (1995) 8 *Leiden Journal of International Law* 185, 190–91.
[40]   Ibid.
[41]   UNCITRAL Arbitration Rules, Article 6(5).
[42]   H. Jonkman, 'The Role of the Secretary-General of the Permanent Court of Arbitration Under the UNCITRAL Arbitration Rules' (1995) 8 *Leiden Journal of International Law* 185, 191.
[43]   Ibid.
[44]   D. Caron and L. Caplan, *The UNCITRAL Arbitration Rules: A Commentary*, 2nd ed., Oxford University Press, Oxford 2013, pp. 152–53.

2.2.1.2. Other Procedural Rules

All other procedural rules we have analysed directly designate an appointing authority to proceed with the appointment of arbitrators in given circumstances, with no possibility for the parties to make that designation themselves:

- the CPR Arbitration Rules designate an authority in charge of remedying difficulties in the appointment of arbitrators, which is the *International Institute for Conflict Prevention & Resolution* (CPR);[45]
- the LMAA Terms provide that the third-party appointing authority is the *President of the LMAA*[46] (except for small claims procedures);[47]
- under the CIMAR, *the English courts* will act as appointing authority under section 18 of the English Arbitration Act;[48] and
- lastly, *GAFTA* will act as the appointing authority under the GAFTA Arbitration Rules.[49]

This direct designation of the appointing authorities by the rules decreases the risk of close connection between the appointing authorities and one of the parties.

2.2.2. *Number of Arbitrators*

The UNCITRAL Arbitration Rules include a default rule in case the parties have not agreed on the number of arbitrators: in that case, 'three arbitrators shall be appointed',[50] with two arbitrators appointed by the parties and the chair appointed by the two party-appointed arbitrators.[51]

While some of the delegates of the Working Group charged with revising the UNCITRAL Arbitration Rules favoured a default rule that would have resulted in a sole arbitrator, the Working Group ultimately opted for three arbitrators.

---

[45] CPR Arbitration Rules, Rule 6.
[46] LMAA Terms, sections 11–12.
[47] LMAA Small Claims Procedure, section 2(b).
[48] CIMAR, Rules 2.2 and 2.4.
[49] GAFTA Arbitration Rules, Rules 3.1, 3.2 and 3.3. See also Rule 3.9 regarding revocations and replacements of arbitrators. This will involve the participation of several individuals and bodies among the organisation: 'the Arbitration Team', 'the Director General of Gafta', 'the Gafta's Appointment Panel ... consist[ing] of certain Current Officers and Past Presidents of Gafta' (see Guidelines for GAFTA Appointment of Arbitrators, Guideline 3).
[50] UNCITRAL Arbitration Rules, Article 7(1): 'If the parties have not previously agreed on the number of arbitrators, and if within 30 days after the receipt by the respondent of the notice of arbitration the parties have not agreed that there shall be only one arbitrator, three arbitrators shall be appointed.'
[51] Ibid., Article 9(1).

One reason for this was that it was found that 'a three-member tribunal could "enhance the legitimacy of the arbitral tribunal and better guarantee impartiality and fairness of the proceedings"'[52] as the presiding arbitrator may counterbalance the co-arbitrators' potential bias when these two co-arbitrators are appointed by the parties.

The UNCITRAL Arbitration Rules nevertheless encourage the parties to agree on a sole arbitrator if appropriate. The default rule of Article 7(1) applies in circumstances where the parties have not previously agreed on the number of arbitrators *and* 'if within 30 days after the receipt by the respondent of the notice of arbitration the parties have not agreed that there shall be only one arbitrator'.[53] Moreover, there is one exception set forth in Article 7(2), according to which the appointing authority, at the request of the claimant, may appoint a sole arbitrator where a party has failed to respond to a proposal on the number of arbitrators within 30 days after the claimant has submitted its notice of arbitration. In this case, the appointing authority may reverse the default rule in favour of three arbitrators, if warranted by the circumstances of the case.

Most other procedural rules also provide that when the parties have not agreed on the number of arbitrators, three arbitrators shall be appointed, with two arbitrators appointed by the parties and the chair appointed by the two party-appointed arbitrators.[54]

2.2.3. Appointment of Arbitrators

The method for the appointment of arbitrators may also have a significant impact on the arbitrators' independence and impartiality: the more the parties are involved in the appointment process, the more they can influence it, in which case the arbitrators' independence and impartiality may suffer. The UNCITRAL Arbitration Rules, like most other procedural rules, prefer party appointments. However, in case of difficulties, the third-party appointing authority will appoint an arbitrator (section 2.2.3.1). In that case, the UNCITRAL Arbitration Rules and other procedural rules provide some guidance as to how the third-party appointing authority should select the arbitrators, whether in consultation with the parties or not (section 2.2.3.2).

---

[52]   D. Caron and L. Caplan, *The UNCITRAL Arbitration Rules: A Commentary*, 2nd ed., Oxford University Press, Oxford 2013, p. 158.

[53]   UNCITRAL Arbitration Rules, Article 7(1).

[54]   See LMAA Terms, section 8(a) and (b); CPR Arbitration Rules, Rules 5.1 and 5.2; GAFTA Arbitration Rules, Rule 3.

2.2.3.1. Party Appointment and Intervention of a Third-Party Appointing Authority

Under the UNCITRAL Arbitration Rules, the parties are free to jointly appoint the sole arbitrator[55] or, if three arbitrators are to be appointed, they are free to each appoint an arbitrator; these two party-appointed arbitrators will then jointly appoint the third and presiding arbitrator.[56] In that case, the parties may significantly influence the appointment process, particularly the appointment of the two party-appointed arbitrators in a three-arbitrator tribunal.

The third-party appointing authority mentioned in section 2.2.1 above will only come into play and appoint an arbitrator, upon the request of a party, when:

- the parties have failed to jointly agree on the appointment of the sole arbitrator within *30 days* after the receipt by all other parties of a proposal for the appointment of the sole arbitrator;
- a party has failed to appoint the arbitrator to be appointed by it within *30 days* after the receipt of the other party's notification of the appointment of the arbitrator to be appointed by it; and
- the party-appointed arbitrators have failed to appoint the presiding arbitrator within *30 days* after the appointment of the second party-appointed arbitrator.

The appointing authority will proceed to replacements of arbitrators in similar circumstances[57] and also when the appointing authority determines that, given exceptional circumstances (for instance, in the event of abusive resignations intended to delay the proceedings), a party should be denied the right to appoint a replacement arbitrator.[58]

The appointing authority therefore plays a major role, since without its intervention in making the necessary appointments, the process of arbitration would come to a halt.

Other analysed procedural rules similarly provide that the third-party appointing authority will intervene, upon an application of either party or an arbitrator, when the parties or the party-appointed arbitrators have failed to appoint the arbitrators or the presiding arbitrator.[59] One notable difference can nevertheless be found in the LMAA Terms, which provide that, when the party bringing the arbitration has appointed its arbitrator and requested the

---

[55] UNCITRAL Arbitration Rules, Article 8(1).
[56] Ibid., Article 9(1).
[57] Ibid., Article 14(2).
[58] PCA, 'Spotlight on the PCA's Appointing Authority Activities', https://docs.pca-cpa.org/2019/04/EN-Spotlight-on-the-PCAs-Appointing-Authority-Activities-1.pdf.
[59] CPR Arbitration Rules, Rules 5.2 and 5.3; LMAA Terms, sections 8(b), 9(a) and (b), and 11; CIMAR, Articles 2.3 and 2.4 referring to section 18 of the English Arbitration Act; GAFTA Arbitration Rules, Rule 3.3.

other party to appoint its own arbitrator, if the other party does not do so within 14 days, the party bringing the arbitration will appoint its own arbitrator as sole arbitrator.[60] The LMAA Terms nevertheless provide that the LMAA President will intervene when the parties have agreed to a sole arbitrator but have failed to jointly appoint him or her, or when the tribunal is to consist of three arbitrators (or two arbitrators and an umpire) and the party-appointed arbitrators have failed to appoint a presiding arbitrator (or an umpire).[61]

2.2.3.2. Selection Process Led by the Third-Party Appointing Authority

Under the UNCITRAL Arbitration Rules, there are two different appointment processes: (i) for the appointment of arbitrators who were supposed to be appointed by a party; and (ii) for the appointment of sole or presiding arbitrators. In the first scenario, the parties in principle are not to participate in the appointment process. Pursuant to Article 9(2) of the Rules, the appointment is left to the discretion of the appointing authority.[62] In the second scenario, the appointing authority will follow a so-called 'list-procedure' pursuant to Articles 8(2) and 9(3) of the Rules, unless the parties agree that the list-procedure should not be used or the appointing authority determines that the use of the list-procedure is not appropriate for the case. The list-procedure, described as follows, is to be carried out in consultation with the parties, who may therefore influence the appointing authority's choice to some extent:

- the appointing authority communicates a list of at least three names to the parties;
- the parties return the list after having deleted the name(s) to which they object and numbered the remaining names in order of preference;
- the appointing authority appoints the arbitrator from the list returned to it, in accordance with the order of preference as indicated by the parties.[63]

---

[60] LMAA Terms, section 10: 'A party wishing to refer a dispute to arbitration in accordance with paragraph 8(b)(i) or paragraph 9(a) above shall appoint its arbitrator and send notice of such appointment in writing to the other party, requiring the other party to appoint its own arbitrator within 14 calendar days of the notice, and stating that the requesting party will appoint its own arbitrator as sole arbitrator unless the other party appoints its own arbitrator and gives notice that it has done so within the 14 days specified. If the other party does not appoint its own arbitrator and give notice that it has done so within the 14 days specified in the notice, the party referring a dispute to arbitration may, without the requirement of any further prior notice to the other party, appoint its arbitrator as sole arbitrator and shall advise the other party accordingly.'

[61] LMAA Terms, sections 8(b), 9(a) and (b), and 11.

[62] UNCITRAL Arbitration Rules, Article 9(2); see also PCA, 'Spotlight on the PCA's Appointing Authority Activities', https://docs.pca-cpa.org/2019/04/EN-Spotlight-on-the-PCAs-Appointing-Authority-Activities-1.pdf.

[63] UNCITRAL Arbitration Rules, Articles 8(2) and 9(3).

Intersentia

The parties may jointly request the appointing authority to adopt alternative approaches, which include: (i) a list-procedure excluding strikes;[64] (ii) a list-procedure on the basis of a closed list/roster;[65] (iii) selection between several options submitted by the parties;[66] or (iv) selection at the complete discretion of the appointing authority.[67]

In both scenarios, the appointing authority will 'have regard to such considerations as are likely to secure the appointment of an independent and impartial arbitrator and ... take into account the advisability of appointing an arbitrator of a nationality other than the nationalities of the parties' (see section 2.1 above).[68] It is not required to appoint an actually independent and impartial arbitrator, which would be 'an unreasonably high standard in practice', 'but rather one that is *likely* to have these characteristics'.[69]

Moreover, even when it is not required to consult the parties (e.g. in the first scenario), the appointing authority 'may require from any party and the arbitrators the information [it] deem[s] necessary and [it] shall give the parties and, where appropriate, the arbitrators, an opportunity to present their views in any manner they consider appropriate. All such communications to and from the appointing authority ... shall also be provided by the sender to all other parties'.[70] The parties may therefore influence the appointing authority's choice, although only to a limited extent.

The appointment process under the CPR Arbitration Rules is similar to the appointment process under the UNCITRAL Arbitration Rules.[71] The other procedural rules we have analysed simply provide that appointments shall be

---

64   The parties are limited to ranking candidates on the list and/or commenting on the relative qualifications and suitability of candidates. See PCA, 'Spotlight on the PCA's Appointing Authority Activities', https://docs.pca-cpa.org/2019/04/EN-Spotlight-on-the-PCAs-Appointing-Authority-Activities-1.pdf.

65   The appointing authority's choice is limited to persons nominated to a closed list of arbitrators (see ibid.).

66   Following bilateral discussion, the parties jointly submit a shortlist of candidates to the appointing authority, who will then select one candidate for appointment (ibid.).

67   Finally, the selection of the sole or presiding arbitrator (or, indeed, all arbitrators) may be placed in the hands of the appointing authority. While the parties may be invited to provide general comments on the required profile of the arbitrator, they have no role in proposing or commenting on any specific candidates for appointment (see ibid.).

68   UNCITRAL Arbitration Rules, Article 6(7).

69   D. Caron and L. Caplan, *The UNCITRAL Arbitration Rules: A Commentary*, 2nd ed., Oxford University Press, Oxford 2013, p. 155.

70   UNCITRAL Arbitration Rules, Article 6(5).

71   CPR Arbitration Rules, Rules 6.1–6.4. Note, however, that the CPR shall suggest more candidates to the parties than the appointing authority acting under the UNCITRAL Arbitration Rules (the CPR 'shall submit to the parties a list of not less than five candidates if one arbitrator remains to be selected, and of not less than seven candidates if two or three arbitrators are to be selected' – Rule 6.4(b)).

made at the discretion of the appointing authority, taking into consideration the requirement of independence and impartiality, as well as the circumstances surrounding the underlying dispute (as explained in section 2.1 above).[72]

When an arbitral institution acts as appointing authority, the procedure may also depend upon the specific rules, guidelines or practice notes of that institution if they provide a method for the appointment of arbitrators. Generally, these rules, guidelines or practice notes broadly follow the approaches taken by the UNCITRAL Arbitration Rules and other sets of non-administered arbitration rules (i.e. a list-procedure involving the parties' participation or an discretionary decision of the appointing authority).[73] The Guidelines for GAFTA Appointment of Arbitrators, however, are quite different as they provide for a detailed selection process involving several GAFTA individuals and bodies, to the exclusion of the parties.[74] Nevertheless, the parties should not be completely excluded from the process, notably because the guidelines indicate that, while GAFTA should consider actual or perceived conflicts of interest, '[i]t is the responsibility of both the parties to the dispute … to inform Gafta immediately if they believe there is, or is likely to be, a conflict'.[75]

---

[72] See e.g. LMAA Terms, section 11 (regarding the appointment of sole arbitrators by the LMAA President: '(c) the party applying to the President shall give a concise explanation of the issues likely to arise, and as to whether any particular expertise on the part of the arbitrator is required but shall not suggest any particular names of potential arbitrators; (d) the President, having considered the nature of the dispute, shall appoint a sole arbitrator and give notice of such appointment to the parties'); CIMAR, Rule 2.4 referring to section 18 of the English Arbitration Act (according to which the powers of the court are 'to make any necessary appointments itself'); GAFTA Arbitration Rules, Rule 3.5 ('Upon applications being made to Gafta under Rule 3 for the appointment(s) of an arbitrator(s), Gafta will make the appointment(s) and will give notice of the name(s)of the arbitrator(s) appointed to the parties').

[73] See e.g. the Rules of ICC As Appointing Authority, Articles 6(2)–(5) and 7(2): first, the ICC Court, when appointing arbitrators in ad hoc proceedings conducted pursuant to the UNCITRAL Arbitration Rules, should follow the methods set out in the UNCITRAL Arbitration Rules, depending on whether the ICC Court appoints, on the one hand, arbitrators who were supposed to be appointed by a party (i.e. at the appointing authority's discretion) or, on the other hand, sole or presiding arbitrators (i.e. following the list-procedure); second, when appointing arbitrators in other arbitration proceedings, the rules provide that 'the Court shall exercise its discretion, taking into account the parties' agreement and any applicable rules'. See also the HKIAC Practice Note, Article 2.5, providing that '[i]n all cases where HKIAC is to appoint an arbitrator, it will first propose *at least one candidate* to the parties and set a time limit for comments. If no party objects to or raises any justifiable concerns about the proposed candidate, HKIAC will generally proceed to appoint that candidate' (emphasis added).

[74] See Guidelines for GAFTA Appointment of Arbitrators, Guideline 3, involving the 'Arbitration Team', the 'Director General of GAFTA' and the 'GAFTA Appointment Panel'.

[75] Guidelines for GAFTA Appointment of Arbitrators, Guideline 4.

2.3. DUTIES OF ARBITRATORS AND SAFEGUARDS

Under the UNCITRAL Arbitration Rules and most other procedural rules, arbitrators are subject to a continuous duty to disclose circumstances likely to give rise to justifiable doubts as to their independence and impartiality (section 2.3.1). In addition to requiring arbitrators to *be* independent and impartial, the rules also require them to *conduct* the proceedings in a fair and impartial way (section 2.3.2). Moreover, some of these procedural rules provide that arbitrators are immune from liability, at least partially (section 2.3.3). This immunity and the duties imposed on arbitrators support the principle of independence and impartiality.

2.3.1. *Continuous Disclosure Obligation*

The UNCITRAL Arbitration Rules impose a continuous disclosure obligation on arbitrators.[76] This helps avoid selecting an arbitrator (or having an arbitrator in the tribunal) who may later be successfully challenged[77] and is also important for reasons of estoppel: '[a]cceptance of arbitrators in the face of circumstances likely to give rise to justifiable doubts as to impartiality or independence lays the basis for possible estoppel of the accepting party later seeking to challenge the award in the appropriate municipal court'.[78]

The duty first applies to the prospective arbitrator from the moment he or she is approached up until the point he or she is appointed (or not appointed). During this time period, disclosure should be made to the parties and, if the parties have called on an appointing authority to help with the constitution of the tribunal, to the appointing authority. The arbitrator candidate should disclose circumstances likely to give rise to justifiable doubts as to his or her independence and impartiality, even if these circumstances arose after he or she was initially approached but before he or she was appointed or chosen.

The duty then also applies after the arbitrator's appointment, throughout the whole proceedings. During this time period, disclosure should be made to the parties and the other arbitrators.

---

[76] UNCITRAL Arbitration Rules, Article 11 ('When a person is approached in connection with his or her possible appointment as an arbitrator, *he or she shall disclose any circumstances likely to give rise to justifiable doubts as to his or her impartiality or independence.* An arbitrator, from the time of his or her appointment and throughout the arbitral proceedings, shall without delay disclose any such circumstances to the parties and the other arbitrators unless they have already been informed by him or her of these circumstances' (emphasis added)).

[77] D. Caron and L. Caplan, *The UNCITRAL Arbitration Rules: A Commentary*, 2nd ed., Oxford University Press, Oxford 2013, p. 195.

[78] Ibid.

Overall, the standard for disclosure is an objective one ('justifiable doubts'), i.e. the candidate/arbitrator must put him- or herself in the shoes of a reasonable third party and determine whether that reasonable party would conclude that a given circumstance is likely to give rise to justifiable doubts as to the candidate/arbitrator's impartiality or independence.[79] Moreover, 'likely to give rise to justifiable doubts' implies that the candidate/arbitrator determines whether the reasonable third party would believe the circumstances would *more likely than not* support a challenge,[80] not that they would *in fact* cause a party to bring a challenge or, if a challenge is brought, that they would be found to *actually* give rise to reasonable doubts.[81]

It follows from the above that the circumstances that must be disclosed are broad. They may arise from past and present professional, business and other relationships with the parties[82] and they are left to the candidate/arbitrator's discretion, although he or she should take into account the requirements of independence and impartiality as provided by the applicable national arbitration law (see section 3.3.1 below).

The parties may have incorporated ethical rules or guidelines by reference in their arbitration agreement, such as the IBA Rules of Ethics or the IBA Guidelines on Conflicts of Interest in International Arbitration (2014) (IBA Guidelines on Conflicts of Interest).[83] In that case, the candidate/arbitrator should take them into account, at least as guidance.[84] Although the IBA Guidelines on Conflicts of Interest are not binding (they are 'guidelines') and have been criticised, they reflect best practices in international arbitration with respect to disclosure.[85] For this reason, they can also serve as guidance even when the parties have not expressly referred to them.

---

[79] T. Webster, *Handbook of UNCITRAL Arbitration: Commentary, Precedents and Materials for UNCITRAL Based Arbitration Rules*, Sweet & Maxwell, London 2010, p. 159, para. 11-20.

[80] D. Caron and L. Caplan, *The UNCITRAL Arbitration Rules: A Commentary*, 2nd ed., Oxford University Press, Oxford 2013, pp. 196–97.

[81] Ibid.

[82] See the UNCITRAL Model statements of independence in the Annex of the UNCITRAL Arbitration Rules: the second statement ('Circumstances to disclose') indicates that the prospective arbitrator wishes to disclose certain '*past and present professional, business and other relationships with the parties and ... any other relevant circumstances*', while maintaining the view that 'those circumstances do not affect [his or her] impartiality' (D. Caron and L. Caplan, *The UNCITRAL Arbitration Rules: A Commentary*, 2nd ed., Oxford University Press, Oxford 2013, p. 198 (emphasis added)).

[83] Referring to a previous version of those Guidelines: T. Webster, *Handbook of UNCITRAL Arbitration*, Sweet & Maxwell, London 2010, p. 169. See also the AAA/ABA Code of Ethics for Arbitrators in Commercial Disputes.

[84] T. Webster, *Handbook of UNCITRAL Arbitration: Commentary, Precedents and Materials for UNCITRAL Based Arbitration Rules*, Sweet & Maxwell, London 2010, p. 159, para. 11-19, p. 169, para. 12-4.

[85] G. Born, *International Arbitration and Forum Selection Agreements: Drafting and Enforcing*, 6th ed., Kluwer Law International, Alphen aan den Rijn 2021, p. 88 (the author explains that

The guidelines are useful in that they include three non-exhaustive lists of circumstances which need not, may or must be disclosed:

- the *Red List* includes situations which, depending on the facts of a given case, a reasonable third-party would think give rise to doubts as to the arbitrator's impartiality and independence and therefore must be disclosed;[86]
- the *Orange List* includes situations which, depending on the facts of a given case, may, in the eyes of the parties, give rise to doubts as to the arbitrator's impartiality or independence, in which case they must be disclosed;[87] and
- the *Green List* includes situations where no appearance and no actual conflict of interest exists from an objective point of view: thus, the arbitrator has no duty to disclose situations falling within the Green List.[88]

Among the situations listed in the Green List is the arbitrator's 'initial contact with a party, or an affiliate of a party (or their counsel) prior to appointment, if this contact is limited to the arbitrator's availability and qualifications to serve, or the names of possible candidates for a chairperson, and did not address the merits or procedural aspects of the dispute, other than to provide the arbitrator with a basic understanding of the case'.[89] This is indeed common and ordinarily unobjectionable practice with respect to party-appointed arbitrators,[90] as is

---

although the IBA Guidelines on Conflicts of Interest 'have been the subject of some criticism on the grounds that they are needlessly detailed and susceptible of encouraging challenges to both arbitrators and awards', '[t]hey nonetheless provide an important perspective on customary attitudes towards an arbitrator's obligations of independence and impartiality – notably, the circumstances that should be disclosed'). See also T. Webster, *Handbook of UNCITRAL Arbitration: Commentary, Precedents and Materials for UNCITRAL Based Arbitration Rules*, Sweet & Maxwell, London 2010, p. 158, paras 11-14 to 11-16 ('Experience shows that challenges raise a great variety of circumstances in which parties allege that there has been a failure to disclose information that is arguably relevant. The practical issue for the arbitrator is how and where to draw the line as to disclosure. It is impractical for an arbitrator to review cases where challenges have been upheld based on a failure to disclose. Those challenges provide a very limited view of circumstances that an arbitrator should have disclosed as many challenges are dealt with by arbitral institutions and Appointing Authorities. These decisions are rarely published and in some instances when challenged, an arbitrator resigns. The most practical course therefore is for the arbitrator to seek to apply a reasonably objective standard in deciding what to disclose. The IBA Guidelines deal with the issue of conflicts of interest and disclosure by arbitrators in some detail and are intended to provide that standard' (footnotes omitted)).

[86] IBA Guidelines on Conflicts of Interest, Part II, paras 1–2.
[87] Ibid., para. 3.
[88] Ibid., para. 4.
[89] Ibid., para. 4.4.1.
[90] G. Born, *International Commercial Arbitration*, 3rd ed., Kluwer Law International, Alphen aan den Rijn 2021, p. 1813.

also reflected in the IBA Rules of Ethics[91] and the ICDR International Dispute Resolution Procedures (including Mediation and Arbitration Rules) (2021) (ICDR Rules).[92] The situation is different with respect to sole and presiding arbitrators because of the difference in nature of their roles, as compared to the role of co-arbitrators. It is generally considered inappropriate for a party or its counsel to 'interview' the prospective sole or presiding arbitrator alone, prior to his or her selection, in the manner that is common with co-arbitrators.[93]

As to the CPR Arbitration Rules, they also provide for a continuous disclosure obligation.[94] The other analysed procedural rules, however, do not include such an express requirement, although we believe that arbitrators should in principle make such disclosures, as it is standard practice in international arbitration[95]

---

[91]   IBA Rules of Ethics, Rule 5.1 ('When approached with a view to appointment, a prospective arbitrator should make sufficient enquiries in order to inform himself whether there may be any justifiable doubts regarding his impartiality or independence; whether he is competent to determine the issues in dispute; and whether he is able to give the arbitration the time and attention required. He may also respond to enquiries from those approaching him, provided that such enquiries are designed to determine his suitability and availability for the appointment and provided that the merits of the case are not discussed').

[92]   ICDR Rules, Rule 14.6 ('No party or anyone acting on its behalf shall have any ex parte communication relating to the case with any arbitrator, or with any candidate for party-appointed arbitrator, except to advise the candidate of the general nature of the controversy and of the anticipated proceedings and to discuss the candidate's qualifications, availability, or impartiality and independence in relation to the parties, or to discuss the suitability of candidates for selection as a presiding arbitrator where the parties or party-appointed arbitrators are to participate in that selection').

[93]   The IBA Rules of Ethics provide that '[i]n the event that a prospective sole arbitrator or presiding arbitrator is approached by one party alone, or by one arbitrator chosen unilaterally by a party (a "party-nominated" arbitrator), he should ascertain that the other party or parties, or the other arbitrator, has consented to the manner in which he has been approached. In such circumstances he should, in writing or orally, inform the other party or parties, or the other arbitrator, of the substance of the initial conversation' (IBA Rules of Ethics, Rule 5.1). However, '[i]f a party-nominated arbitrator is required to participate in the selection of a third or presiding arbitrator, it is acceptable for him (although he is not so required) to obtain the views of the party who nominated him as to the acceptability of candidates being considered' (IBA Rules of Ethics, Rule 5.2). Similarly, the ICDR Rules provide that '[n]o party or anyone acting on its behalf shall have any ex parte communication relating to the case with any candidate for presiding arbitrator' (ICDR Rules, Rule 14.6).

[94]   CPR Arbitration Rules, Rule 7.3.

[95]   IBA Guidelines on Conflicts of Interest, General Standard 3(a) ('If facts or circumstances exist that may, in the eyes of the parties, give rise to doubts as to the arbitrator's impartiality or independence, the arbitrator shall disclose such facts or circumstances to the parties, the arbitration institution or other appointing authority (if any, and if so required by the applicable institutional rules) and the co-arbitrators, if any, prior to accepting his or her appointment or, if thereafter, as soon as he or she learns of them'); IBA Rules of Ethics, Rules 4.1 and 4.3 (Rule 4.1: 'A prospective arbitrator should disclose all facts or circumstances that may give rise to justifiable doubts as to his impartiality or independence. Failure to make such disclosure creates an appearance of bias, and may of itself be a ground for disqualification even though the non-disclosed facts or circumstances would not of themselves justify disqualification'; Rule 4.3: 'The duty of disclosure continues throughout the arbitral proceedings as regards new facts or circumstances').

and is provided for by most national arbitration laws (as explained in section 3.3 below).[96]

2.3.2. Duty to Treat the Parties Equally and Prohibition of Ex Parte Communications

In addition to requiring arbitrators to be independent and impartial, all rules also require them to conduct the proceedings in a fair and impartial way.[97] This includes ensuring that communications are always sent to both parties (i.e. that there are no ex parte communications), as provided by the UNCITRAL Arbitration Rules, according to which:

> the arbitral tribunal may conduct the arbitration in such manner as it considers appropriate, *provided that the parties are treated with equality and that at an appropriate stage of the proceedings each party is given a reasonable opportunity of presenting its case.* The arbitral tribunal, in exercising its discretion, shall conduct the proceedings as to avoid unnecessary delay and expense and to *provide a fair* and efficient *process for resolving the parties' dispute* (emphasis added);[98] and

---

[96] For example, the LMAA Terms provide that the default seat of the arbitration is in England and, in that case, the arbitral proceedings shall be governed by the English Arbitration Act (LMAA Terms, sections 6(b) and 7(a)). As explained in section 3.3.1 below, although the English Arbitration Act is silent as to the existence of a disclosure obligation applying to arbitrators, the English courts have confirmed that such obligation exists under English law in a recent decision in the case of *Halliburton v. Chubb*. The CIMAR and the GAFTA Arbitration Rules are similar to the LMAA Terms with respect to disclosure (see CIMAR, Rules 1.6(b), 1.1 and 1.4; see also GAFTA Arbitration Rules, Rule 1.1). The Guidelines for GAFTA Appointment of Arbitrators, however, add that '[i]t is ... the responsibility of ... the individual arbitrator(s) to inform Gafta immediately if they believe there is, or is likely to be, a conflict' (emphasis added) (see Guidelines for GAFTA Appointment of Arbitrators, Guideline 4).

[97] In addition to Article 17(1) and (4) of the UNCITRAL Rules cited below, see LMAA Terms, section 3 ('[t]he arbitrators *at all times* are *under a duty to act fairly and impartially between the parties*' (emphasis added)) and section 33(1) of the English Arbitration Act for arbitrations conducted under the LMAA Terms when the seat is in England ('[t]he tribunal shall – (a) *act fairly and impartially as between the parties*, giving each party a reasonable opportunity of putting his case and dealing with that of his opponent' (emphasis added)); CIMAR, Rule 1.4; GAFTA Arbitration Rules, Rule 1.1; and GAFTA Rules and Code of Conduct for Qualified Arbitrators and Qualified Mediators, Rules 8.2 and 8.3. As to the CPR Arbitration Rules, although they do not expressly require arbitrators *to act* fairly and impartially between the parties, arbitrators acting under the CPR Arbitration Rules are undoubtedly bound by a duty to act as such, since: (i) as explained in section 2.1 above, arbitrators are required to be independent and impartial; and (ii) Rule 7.4 prohibits ex parte communications.

[98] UNCITRAL Arbitration Rules, Article 17(1). It has been considered that Article 17(1) of the UNCITRAL Arbitration Rules, applying to arbitrators, should also, in practice, apply to appointing authorities acting under the rules: see D. Caron and L. Caplan, *The UNCITRAL Arbitration Rules: A Commentary*, 2nd ed., Oxford University Press, Oxford 2013, p. 272.

All communications to the arbitral tribunal by one party shall be communicated by that party to all other parties. Such communications shall be made at the same time, except as otherwise permitted by the arbitral tribunal if it may do so under applicable law.[99]

2.3.3. Immunity from Civil Liability

Some procedural rules may also provide that arbitrators shall be immune from civil liability.[100] This immunity is similar to the immunity applicable to state judges, which is limited to their mission to judge,[101] and is intended 'to limit [their] exposure to frivolous lawsuits and thus reinforc[e] the[ir] independence'.[102] One author explains that, like the judge, 'the arbitrator should remain immune from the pressures of the parties during and after the trial in order that they can make their decision with calmness of mind and see that justice be done.'[103]

Therefore, the UNCITRAL Arbitration Rules, in Article 16, provide that:

[s]ave for intentional wrongdoing, the parties waive, to the fullest extent permitted under the applicable law, any claim against the arbitrators, the appointing authority and any person appointed by the arbitral tribunal based on any act or omission in connection with the arbitration.[104]

This limitation of liability is partial (arbitrators are immune from liability save for 'intentional wrongdoing').[105]

The CPR Arbitration Rules also provide that arbitrators should be immune from civil liability.[106] However, unlike the UNCITRAL Arbitration Rules, they do not include an exception for intentional wrongdoing.[107] The CPR Arbitration

---

[99]   UNCITRAL Arbitration Rules, Article 17(4).

[100] See e.g. UNCITRAL Arbitration Rules, Article 16; CPR Arbitration Rules, Rule 20.

[101] M. Danis and M. Valentini, 'The Civil Liability Regime of Arbitrators and Arbitration Institutions', August Debouzy, 2021, https://www.august-debouzy.com/en/blog/1698-clarification-of-the-civil-liability-regime-of-arbitrators-and-arbitration-institutions.

[102] D. Caron and L. Caplan, *The UNCITRAL Arbitration Rules: A Commentary*, 2nd ed., Oxford University Press, Oxford 2013, p. 326, regarding Article 16 of the UNCITRAL Arbitration Rules.

[103] R. Mullerat, 'The Liability of Arbitrators: a Survey of Current Practice', International Bar Association, 2006, https://www.josemigueljudice-arbitration.com/xms/files/02_TEXTOS_ARBITRAGEM/01_Doutrina_ScolarsTexts/arbitrators__impartiality_and_independence/mullerat_ilability_arbs.pdf.

[104] UNCITRAL Arbitration Rules, Article 16.

[105] Ibid.

[106] CPR Arbitration Rules, Rule 20 ('Neither CPR nor any arbitrator shall be liable to any party for any act or omission in connection with any arbitration conducted under these Rules').

[107] Ibid.

2.4. CONSEQUENCES OF A BREACH OF THE REQUIREMENT OF INDEPENDENCE AND IMPARTIALITY

The effectiveness of the principle of independence and impartiality may also be measured by reference to the consequences that follow if the principle is breached. When parties have chosen to refer to non-administered arbitration rules, these consequences are usually threefold:

1. First, most (although not all)[108] non-administered arbitration rules, including the UNCITRAL Arbitration Rules,[109] provide for the possibility to challenge the arbitrator and have him or her removed from the tribunal during the proceedings.
2. Second, the parties may also obtain a court order for the payment of civil damages by the arbitrator in question, but this will depend on the applicable national arbitration laws.
3. Third, once the arbitral award has been rendered, the award may be challenged at the seat of arbitration and enforcement and recognition may be refused. Again, this will depend on the applicable national arbitration laws.

These last two points are analysed in sections 3.3.3 and 3.4.2 below.

Turning back to arbitrator challenges under non-administered arbitration rules, we will examine in turn the grounds for challenging an arbitrator (section 2.4.1), the challenge procedure, including who can initiate the challenge and who can remove the arbitrator (section 2.4.2), and the decision on the challenge (section 2.4.3).

2.4.1. Grounds for Challenging an Arbitrator

When it is reasonable to believe that an arbitrator has breached his or her duty of independence and impartiality, the UNCITRAL Arbitration Rules,[110]

---

[108] The LMAA Terms and the CIMAR are silent on this point, although removal may be provided by the applicable national arbitration law(s).

[109] UNCITRAL Arbitration Rules, Article 12(1) and (2). See also the CPR Arbitration Rules (Rule 7.5) and the GAFTA Arbitration Rules (Rule 3.9(a)).

[110] UNCITRAL Arbitration Rules, Article 12 ('1. Any arbitrator may be challenged if circumstances exist that give rise to justifiable doubts as to the arbitrator's impartiality or

the CPR Arbitration Rules[111] and the GAFTA Arbitration Rules,[112] like most leading institutional arbitration rules, provide that the parties may challenge the arbitrator and have him or her removed from the tribunal during the proceedings.

Whether the arbitrator is de facto independent and impartial is not necessarily relevant.[113] 'Doubts' will suffice. This leaves 'sufficient flexibility to address situations which, even in the absence of actual bias or dependence, nevertheless create a sufficiently negative perception about an arbitrator's impartiality and independence to justify his or her removal.'[114]

As a commentary of the UNCITRAL Arbitration Rules indicates, the drafters of the rules thought of creating a list of examples of possible circumstances of partiality or dependence which could give rise to justifiable doubts.[115] However, that list would have had to be exhaustive, an impossible task; so the drafters preferred a broader and generic wording,[116] i.e. 'circumstances ... that give rise to justifiable doubts as to the arbitrator's impartiality or independence'.[117]

---

    independence. 2. A party may challenge the arbitrator appointed by it only for reasons of which it becomes aware after the appointment').

[111] CPR Arbitration Rules, Rule 7.5 ('Any arbitrator may be challenged if circumstances exist or arise that give rise to justifiable doubt regarding that arbitrator's independence or impartiality, provided that a party may challenge an arbitrator whom it has appointed only for reasons of which it becomes aware after the appointment has been made').

[112] GAFTA Arbitration Rules, Rule 3.9(a) (the arbitrator's 'authority is revoked by the Gafta pursuant to the Gafta Rules and Regulations and Code of Conduct for Qualified Arbitrators', which themselves provide that '[a]rbitrators must always act with impartiality between the parties and avoid saying or doing anything which even gives the impression that they are not or may not be impartial' and 'any person may make a complaint ... regarding an Arbitrator's eligibility to act in a particular case, on any of the following grounds: (a) that he is not impartial or there are doubts as to his impartiality' – see GAFTA Rules and Regulations and Code of Conduct for Qualified Arbitrators, Rules 8.3 and 7.1.1).

[113] N. Lindström, 'Challenges to Arbitrators – Decisions by the SCC Board During 2008–2010 10–12', p. 2, https://sccinstitute.com/media/93825/challenges-to-arbitrators-decisions-by-the-scc-board-during-2008.pdf; M.N. Cleis, *The Independence and Impartiality of ICSID Arbitrators: Current Case Law, Alternative Approaches, and Improvement Suggestions,* Brill, Leiden 2017, pp. 126, 143; see also D. Caron and L. Caplan, *The UNCITRAL Arbitration Rules: A Commentary,* 2nd ed., Oxford University Press, Oxford 2013, p. 214 ('*sustaining a challenge of an arbitrator under Article 12 does not necessarily require proof of an arbitrator's actual lack of impartiality or independence. The* appearance *of these deficiencies may alone suffice in certain circumstances to disqualify an arbitrator.* Article 12 notably requires only that "doubts" as to an arbitrator's impartiality or independence be proven to be justifiable, not that an arbitrator is, in fact, biased or dependent on a party. Article 12 thus establishes a standard with sufficient flexibility to address situations which, even in the absence of actual bias or dependence, nevertheless create a sufficiently negative perception about an arbitrator's impartiality and independence to justify his or her removal' (emphasis added)).

[114] D. Caron and L. Caplan, *The UNCITRAL Arbitration Rules: A Commentary,* 2nd ed., Oxford University Press, Oxford 2013, p. 214.

[115] Ibid., p. 211.

[116] Ibid.

[117] UNCITRAL Arbitration Rules, Article 12(1).

In practice, the following circumstances have been found to *potentially* justify doubts as to an arbitrator's impartiality and independence:

> an arbitrator's (1) relationship with a witness; (2) financial relationship with a party through shareholdings; (3) financial relationship with a party through potential control over arbitrator salaries; (4) previous employment by the parent corporation of a party; (5) representation in another forum that is adverse to a party; (6) previous advocacy on behalf of a country formerly adverse to a party; (7) representation of a third party with a right to intervene in the proceedings; (8) handling of the proceedings; (9) statement regarding a party or the dispute; (10) decision-making; (11) breach of confidentiality of deliberations; (12) physical assault of a fellow arbitrator.[118]

Here again, the IBA Guidelines on Conflicts of Interest and their Red, Orange and Green Lists of situations may serve as guidance.[119]

It should be noted that, while an arbitrator's failure to disclose given circumstances[120] may give rise to justifiable doubts as to his or her impartiality or independence, it does not per se establish the existence of justifiable doubts as to his or her impartiality or independence. The issue is then: what is the standard applicable to determine whether circumstances *actually* give rise to justifiable doubts as to the arbitrator's impartiality or independence?

Under the UNCITRAL Arbitration Rules and the CPR Arbitration Rules, the inclusion of the word 'justifiable' to define one's doubts as to the arbitrator's independence and impartiality clearly indicates that the standard is also an objective one,[121] i.e. whether an objective third party would find it reasonable that such doubts exist.[122] In one precedent, the relevant appointing authority deciding the challenge under the UNCITRAL Arbitration Rules referred to an 'objective observer', being a 'well informed but disinterested commercial

---

[118] D. Caron and L. Caplan, *The UNCITRAL Arbitration Rules: A Commentary*, 2nd ed., Oxford University Press, Oxford 2013, pp. 214–15, further elaborated on pp. 215–25.

[119] See section 2.3.1 above.

[120] I.e. a failure to disclose under e.g. Article 11 of the UNCITRAL Arbitration Rules or Rule 7.3 of the CPR Arbitration Rules.

[121] D. Caron and L. Caplan, *The UNCITRAL Arbitration Rules: A Commentary*, 2nd ed., Oxford University Press, Oxford 2013, p. 208: 'The inclusion of the word "justifiable" in Article 12(1), to define the kind of doubt required to sustain a challenge, reflects UNCITRAL's clear intention of establishing an objective standard for impartiality and independence. While a party's subjective concerns about an arbitrator's bias may prompt a challenge, it is the objective reasonableness of these concerns that is ultimately determinative.'

[122] *Country X v. Company Q*, Challenge Decision, 11 January 1995 (1997) XXII *Yearbook Commercial Arbitration* 227, 234, paras 23–24; *National Grid PLC v. Argentina*, Decision on the Challenge to Mr Judd L. Kessler, 3 December 2007, LCIA Case No. UN7949, para. 80; *Vito Gallo v. Government of Canada*, Decision on the Challenge to Mr J. Christopher Thomas, QC, 14 October 2009, NAFTA/UNCITRAL, PCA Case No. 55798, para. 19.

person assessing the matter without specific expertise but aware of the political background against which the matter arises and of the nature of a lawyer's professional services.'[123] Yet it may be difficult to assess what an objective observer would find reasonable in multicultural settings.[124]

As to the standard applicable under the GAFTA Arbitration Rules, there is no indication in the rules as to whether it is an objective or a subjective one. However, as explained above, the rules expressly provide that GAFTA arbitrations are seated in England and are conducted under the English Arbitration Act,[125] and the standard under English law is an objective one.[126]

2.4.2. Challenge Procedures

Under both the UNCITRAL Arbitration Rules[127] and the CPR Arbitration Rules,[128] it is the parties who initiate challenges. A party that intends to challenge an arbitrator shall do so in writing, indicating the reasons for doing so,[129] and within a certain time period from the notification of the appointment of the challenged arbitrator or the moment it became aware of the circumstance giving rise to justifiable doubts – 15 days under the UNCITRAL Arbitration Rules[130] and 10 days under the CPR Arbitration Rules.[131] If a party does not raise a challenge within this timeframe, it will be deemed to have waived its right to challenge the arbitrator. These requirements aim at preventing abusive challenges intended to unduly influence the arbitrator.

When a party brings a challenge, the challenged arbitrator may withdraw on his or her own initiative, without prejudice, or the parties can both agree on the challenge, without prejudice as well.[132] Therefore, as an author explains, because 'the challenged arbitrator has a direct and significant interest in his or her reputation', 'given the provisions for agreement and withdrawal, it seems unlikely that a meritorious challenge would ever reach the point of decision.'[133]

---

123   *Country X v. Company Q*, Challenge Decision, 11 January 1995 (1997) XXII *Yearbook Commercial Arbitration* 227, 234, para. 31.
124   D. Caron and L. Caplan, *The UNCITRAL Arbitration Rules: A Commentary*, 2nd ed., Oxford University Press, Oxford 2013, p. 213.
125   GAFTA Arbitration Rules, section 1.1.
126   English Arbitration Act, section 24 ('circumstances exist that give rise to *justifiable* doubts as to his impartiality' (emphasis added)); *Halliburton Company v. Chubb Bermuda Insurance Ltd (formerly known as Ace Bermuda Insurance Ltd)* [2020] UKSC 48.
127   UNCITRAL Arbitration Rules, Article 13.
128   CPR Arbitration Rules, Rules 7.6–7.8.
129   '[W]ith specificity' according to Rule 7.6 of the CPR Arbitration Rules.
130   UNCITRAL Arbitration Rules, Articles 13.1–13.2.
131   CPR Arbitration Rules, Rule 7.6.
132   UNCITRAL Arbitration Rules, Article 13.3; CPR Arbitration Rules, Rule 7.7.
133   D. Caron and L. Caplan, *The UNCITRAL Arbitration Rules: A Commentary*, 2nd ed., Oxford University Press, Oxford 2013, p. 272.

Nevertheless, if the challenged arbitrator does not voluntarily withdraw and the parties cannot agree on the challenge, the appointing authority designated under the rules will decide the challenge upon the request of the challenging party.[134] This is the same authority empowered by the rules to appoint arbitrators in the circumstances described in section 2.2.3.1 above, although deciding upon a challenge requires legal and judicial skills which are not required in making an appointment.[135] The drafters of the UNCITRAL Rules were concerned that this same authority could potentially lack independence and impartiality,[136] but '[u]ltimately, [they] were satisfied that even if the appointing authority who made the original appointment would decide the challenge under Article 12(1) of the Rules, the assumption of neutrality and impartiality could be maintained: "[e]xperience has shown that arbitral institutions and appointing authorities were deeply concerned with preserving their reputation for integrity"'.[137]

As to the procedure to be followed by the appointing authority, the rules do not include many details.[138] The UNCITRAL Arbitration Rules merely provide that, when deciding a challenge, as for an appointment, the appointing authority will be able to 'require from any party and the arbitrators the information [it] [will] deem necessary and … give the parties and, where appropriate, the arbitrators, an opportunity to present their views in any manner they consider appropriate.'[139] The CPR Arbitration Rules, for their part, provide that CPR shall 'provid[e] the non-challenging party and each member of the Tribunal with an opportunity to comment on the challenge'.[140] According to an author commenting on the UNCITRAL Arbitration Rules, '[t]he drafters of the UNCITRAL Rules apparently chose to leave these issues up to the discretion of the appointing authority, presumably to ensure sufficient flexibility so the process could be tailored to the circumstances of each arbitration and could avoid taking on a life of its own'.[141] Accordingly, in practice, the appointing authority will

---

[134]   UNCITRAL Arbitration Rules, Article 13.4; CPR Arbitration Rules, Rule 7.8.

[135]   D. Caron and L. Caplan, *The UNCITRAL Arbitration Rules: A Commentary*, 2nd ed., Oxford University Press, Oxford 2013, p. 270 ('Appointment is not particularly a legal task, but rather involves knowledge of potential arbitrators and appreciation for the importance of the place of arbitration. *Deciding upon a challenge, in contrast, is distinctively legal and judicial* requiring both application of the law, assessment of the evidence and fair, yet firm, administration of procedure. It may be the case that the institution or person that served as the appointing authority making the original appointment also possesses the skills necessary to decide upon a challenge, but that is not necessarily always the case' (emphasis added)).

[136]   D. Caron and L. Caplan, *The UNCITRAL Arbitration Rules: A Commentary*, 2nd ed., Oxford University Press, Oxford 2013, p. 269.

[137]   Ibid.

[138]   Ibid., p. 271.

[139]   UNCITRAL Arbitration Rules, Article 6(5).

[140]   CPR Arbitration Rules, Rule 7.8.

[141]   D. Caron and L. Caplan, *The UNCITRAL Arbitration Rules: A Commentary*, 2nd ed., Oxford University Press, Oxford 2013, p. 271.

allow written submissions by both parties and/or oral submissions, and will also give the challenged arbitrator an opportunity to comment on the challenge.[142]

The challenge procedure under the GAFTA Arbitration Rules is similar: (i) the parties also initiate challenges; (ii) prior to bringing a challenge, the parties must 'use all reasonable endeavours to resolve the matter informally with the Arbitrator'[143] (this resembles the possibility for the arbitrator, under the UNCITRAL Arbitration Rules and the CPR Arbitration Rules, to withdraw, or for the parties to agree on the challenge). However, unlike the UNCITRAL Arbitration Rules and the CPR Arbitration Rules, the authority deciding the challenge if the parties cannot resolve the matter with the arbitrator will not be the same authority in charge of appointments. Additionally, there are two levels of authorities: (i) the party who wishes to challenge the arbitrator may first bring the matter to the GAFTA Director General; (ii) if the matter cannot be resolved by the Director General, the party will be required to submit a written complaint to an 'Arbitration Complaints Committee' – a committee composed, in principle, of three council members of GAFTA.[144] There is no specific procedure to be followed by the Director General and the Arbitration Complaints Committee, so that the process can be tailored to the circumstances of each arbitration.[145]

---

[142] See the practice of the PCA Secretary-General acting as appointing authority under the UNCITRAL Arbitration Rules, explained in PCA, 'Spotlight on the PCA's Appointing Authority Activities', https://docs.pca-cpa.org/2019/04/EN-Spotlight-on-the-PCAs-Appointing-Authority-Activities-1.pdf. It may also be useful to check the rules, guidelines or practice notes of institutions acting as appointing authorities under the UNCITRAL Arbitration Rules. See e.g. Rules of ICC As Appointing Authority, Article 6(7) ('The Court will take decisions on challenges submitted by any party under Article 13(4) of the UNCITRAL Rules after the Secretariat has afforded an opportunity for the arbitrator concerned, the other party or parties, and any other members of the arbitral tribunal to comment in writing within a suitable period of time. Such comments shall be communicated to the parties and the arbitrators before being submitted to the Court').

[143] GAFTA Rules and Code of Conduct for Qualified Arbitrators and Qualified Mediators, Rule 7.1.2.

[144] Ibid., Rule 7.1.1.

[145] Ibid., Rule 7.1.5 ('The Committee shall investigate the matter as it sees fit' – the decision is therefore left at the Committee's discretion), Rule 7.1.6 ('The Committee shall use its reasonable endeavours to reach a determination of the complaint within 14 working days of the date on which the complaint has been referred to it' – this ensures a speedy resolution of the challenge so that the arbitration can proceed), Rule 7.1.7 ('At any time, The Committee may, at its discretion, seek legal advice from the Association's General Counsel. Such advice shall be confidential and privileged to The Committee and/or the Council' – as explained above, '[d]eciding upon a challenge … is distinctively legal and judicial requiring both application of the law, assessment of the evidence and fair, yet firm, administration of procedure'; thus, this possibility to request legal advice ensures the Committee reaches the right decision in law).

2.4.3. Challenge Decisions

Under the UNCITRAL Arbitration Rules and the CPR Arbitration Rules, the appointing authority will decide to uphold or dismiss the challenge, while under the GAFTA Rules and Code of Conduct for Qualified Arbitrators and Qualified Mediators, the Arbitration Complaints Committee will have three options: dismiss the complaint, revoke the arbitrator's authority, or (again) seek to resolve the matter by agreement between the parties.[146] In all cases, if a challenge is upheld, a substitute arbitrator will be appointed pursuant to the same procedure that was applicable to the appointment of the arbitrator being replaced.[147]

Neither the UNCITRAL Arbitration Rules nor the CPR Arbitration Rules provide for the possibility to challenge the appointing authority's decisions on challenges, whether the appointing authority has upheld or dismissed the challenge. If a challenge is upheld, 'the matter is generally terminated';[148] '[u]nder the Rules and applicable law, an arbitrator who is successfully challenged at that level does not have any further recourse';[149] '[t]his is based on the primary concern of having the dispute resolved'.[150] If the challenge is dismissed, 'then the ultimate decision as to the challenge or the effect of the challenged arbitrator's participation in the proceedings is generally subject to the decisions of the state courts at the place of arbitration or at the place of enforcement'.[151] In other words, the party that challenged the arbitrator may seek annulment of the award (or resist enforcement and recognition) based on the arbitrator's lack of independence and impartiality, subject to the conditions set forth in the applicable arbitration laws, as explained in section 3.4.2 below. This is all subject to the applicable national arbitration law(s), which may provide specific remedies against decisions of third-party appointing authorities, as explained in section 3.4.1 below.

As to GAFTA arbitrations, the GAFTA Rules and Code of Conduct for Qualified Arbitrators and Qualified Mediators expressly provide that the decisions of the Arbitration Complaints Committee 'shall be final and binding on the parties to the complaint'.[152] Here as well, the party that challenged the arbitrator may seek the annulment of the award (or resist enforcement and

---

[146] Ibid., Rule 7.1.9.

[147] UNCITRAL Arbitration Rules, Article 14.1; CPR Arbitration Rules, Rule 7.9; GAFTA Arbitration Rules, Rule 3.9(a).

[148] T. Webster, *Handbook of UNCITRAL Arbitration: Commentary, Precedents and Materials for UNCITRAL Based Arbitration Rules*, Sweet & Maxwell, London 2010, p. 204, para. 13-9.

[149] Ibid.

[150] Ibid.

[151] Ibid., p. 204, para. 13-10.

[152] GAFTA Rules and Code of Conduct for Qualified Arbitrators and Qualified Mediators, Rule 7.1.12.

recognition) based on the arbitrator's lack of independence and impartiality, subject to the conditions set forth in the applicable arbitration laws.

3. ANALYSIS OF THE SUBSIDIARY NATIONAL LEGAL AND JUDICIAL FRAMEWORKS

If the parties have not referred to institutional rules or non-administered arbitration rules such as the UNCITRAL Arbitration Rules, the arbitration will be governed by any substantive provisions of the parties' agreement and, subsidiarily, by default rules and mechanisms provided for in the applicable national arbitration laws. In this section, we will focus on the provisions of national arbitration laws relating to the independence and impartiality of arbitrators.

As we understand that the special national reports will cover the specificities of many jurisdictions in relation to the requirement of independence and impartiality, we will set out below the main approach taken by a majority of jurisdictions and, when relevant, some of the different approaches adopted by other states. There has indeed been a movement toward harmonisation with respect to the duty of independence and impartiality in most jurisdictions, in particular pro-arbitration ones, and many of these jurisdictions follow the approach taken by the UNCITRAL Model Law on International Arbitration (1985) with amendments as adopted in 2006 (Model Law), as well as other soft law instruments such the IBA Guidelines on Conflicts of Interest.

We first discuss the requirements regarding the arbitrator's person, which relate to independence and impartiality (section 3.1). We then examine the constitution of the arbitral tribunal (section 3.2). National arbitration laws also provide duties and safeguards applicable to arbitrators to ensure they are and remain independent and impartial throughout the proceedings (section 3.3), as well as remedies in case of a breach of the requirement of independence and impartiality (section 3.4).

3.1. REQUIREMENTS REGARDING THE ARBITRATOR'S PERSON

According to most national arbitration laws, and similarly to most non-administered arbitration rules, the parties are free to require arbitrators to possess certain qualifications and characteristics. These national arbitration laws nevertheless impose professional incompatibilities and requirements, including requirements of legal capacity and requirements that aim at ensuring that arbitrators are independent and impartial. A duty of independence and impartiality exists in virtually almost all jurisdictions (section 3.1.1). Other requirements may be present that have a potential impact on the arbitrator's

3.1.1. Requirements of Independence and Impartiality

National arbitration legislation in virtually all jurisdictions imposes requirements of independence and impartiality on international arbitrators. Most of them follow the approach of the UNCITRAL Model Law, whether they have adopted it or not.[153]

The Model Law's approach is identical to that of the UNCITRAL Arbitration Rules. In the Model Law, the requirement of independence and impartiality, which applies to both party-appointed arbitrators and sole/presiding arbitrators, is set out in relation to: (i) the arbitrator/arbitrator candidate's duty to disclose 'circumstances likely to give rise to justifiable doubts';[154] (ii) the appointment by an appointing authority or the local court 'hav[ing] due regard ... to such considerations as are likely to secure the appointment of an independent and impartial arbitrator';[155] (iii) the possibility to challenge the arbitrator when there exist 'circumstances that give rise to justifiable doubts';[156] and (iv) the possibility to challenge/refuse recognition or enforcement of an award.[157] There is no indication as to what circumstances would require disclosure or would be considered as a breach of that duty. Therefore, whether an arbitrator must disclose a given circumstance or whether he or she should be considered has having breached that duty must be decided on a case-by-case basis. The standard under the Model Law is an objective one and does not require proof of a certainty of partiality or dependence (instead requiring 'justifiable doubts'). For this reason, the precise contours of that requirement will depend on the circumstances of each case and the practice of the courts of each relevant state. Parties, arbitrators and national courts may also refer for guidance to guidelines and codes of conduct which reflect best practices, as explained in section 2.

---

[153] See e.g. Belgium (Article 1685(2) and (5) of the Belgian Judicial Code (enacted in 1967 and revised in 2020)); Germany (sections 1035–1036 of the Code of Civil Procedure (enacted in 1877 and revised in 2021) (the German ZPO)); Hong Kong (sections 24, 25, and 46(3) of the Arbitration Ordinance (Cap. 609 of the Laws of Hong Kong) (2011) (enacted in 2010 and revised in 2021) (the Hong Kong Arbitration Ordinance) in conjunction with Rule 7(1) of the Arbitration (Appointment of Arbitrators and Mediators and Decision on Number of Arbitrators) Amendment Rules 2019); Switzerland (Articles 179(6), 180(1) and (2), and 190(2) of the Swiss Private International Law Act (enacted in 1987 and revised in 2020) (the Swiss PILA)); the Netherlands (Articles 1023, 1033(1) and 1065 of the Dutch Code of Civil Procedure (enacted in 1837 and revised in 2020) (the Dutch CCP)).

[154] UNCITRAL Model Law, Article 12(1).

[155] Ibid., Article 11(5).

[156] Ibid., Article 12(2).

[157] Ibid., Article 34(2).

There may be some differences or specificities in the arbitration laws of some states. For example, in England, although the requirement of independence and impartiality applies to both party-appointed and sole/presiding arbitrators, there is an exception when two co-arbitrators cannot reach an agreement and the dispute is referred to an *umpire*. While prior to referral to the umpire the two arbitrators are obligated to act impartially, their roles cease to be impartial and become those of advocates after their failure to decide the matter unanimously.[158] However, the umpire system, which also exists in other common law jurisdictions, is increasingly rare. In addition, in the United States Federal Arbitration Act (FAA), the requirement is stated only with respect to the annulment of arbitral awards. Pursuant to section 10(a)(2) of the FAA, an award may be vacated '[w]here there was evident partiality or corruption in the arbitrators, or either of them'.[159] Courts impose a duty to disclose on arbitrators[160] but there is no possibility to challenge an arbitrator during the arbitration, unless this is provided by the applicable arbitration rules.[161]

One important issue is whether, in ad hoc arbitrations, the parties may agree on heightened or reduced standards of independence and impartiality and therefore derogate from the standards set out in the relevant national arbitration laws.[162] The Model Law does not answer that question and there does not seem to be any reported authority under the Model Law considering whether its standards are mandatorily applicable, regardless of the parties' agreement.[163] The national arbitration laws and judicial decisions do not always provide an answer. Regarding whether the parties may agree on heightened standards of independence and impartiality, as an author explains, there is no reported authority denying effect to such agreement.[164] This author adds, and we agree with him, '[i]t is difficult to see why parties should not be permitted to agree upon a standard of heightened impartiality for all arbitrators, with the arbitrators being free from any conceivable prior connection with, or predisposition towards, either party'.[165] As to whether the parties may agree on reduced standards of independence and impartiality, most national arbitration laws lack language addressing the parties' ability to reach such agreement.[166]

---

[158]   G. Born, *International Commercial Arbitration*, 3rd ed., Kluwer Law International, Alphen aan den Rijn 2021, pp. 1796–97.

[159]   The United States Federal Arbitration Act (enacted in 1925 and revised in 1990), section 10(a)(2).

[160]   See section 3.3.1 below.

[161]   See sections 3.3.1 and 3.4.1 below.

[162]   G. Born, *International Commercial Arbitration*, 3rd ed., Kluwer Law International, Alphen aan den Rijn 2021, pp. 1947–54.

[163]   Ibid., p. 1949.

[164]   Ibid., p. 1948.

[165]   Ibid.

[166]   Ibid., p. 1949.

In a few jurisdictions, however, national arbitration legislation fairly explicitly imposes mandatory prohibitions against agreements on partial co-arbitrators.[167] For example, sections 4(1) and 33(1)(a) of the English Arbitration Act require all arbitrators to act fairly and impartially 'notwithstanding any agreement to the contrary' – with the exception of co-arbitrators in the umpire system, as explained above. This is different from the United States, where it is well settled under the FAA and state law that parties may agree on reduced standards of independence and impartiality for co-arbitrators.[168]

3.1.2. Nationality Requirements

The Model Law, which many jurisdictions follow,[169] provides that '[n]o person shall be precluded by reason of his nationality from acting as an arbitrator, unless otherwise agreed by the parties'[170] – thus, the parties may require that arbitrators be nationals of a given country, which may negatively impact the arbitrators' independence and impartiality.

---

[167] See e.g. ibid., n. 1063, referring inter alia to the Arbitration Law of the People's Republic of China (enacted in 1994 and revised in 2017), Article 34(3) (requiring, without exception, that arbitrator 'must withdraw' in case of potential impartiality), and the Brazilian Arbitration Act (enacted in 1996 and revised in 2015), Article 14 ('Individuals somehow linked to the parties or to the submitted dispute, by any of the relationships resulting in the impediment or suspicion of Court members, are prevented from acting as arbitrators').

[168] While historically there was a presumption in US domestic arbitrations that party-appointed arbitrators are not neutral, recent domestic US practice has started to abandon that presumption (see G. Born, *International Commercial Arbitration*, 3rd ed., Kluwer Law International, Alphen aan den Rijn 2021, pp. 1935–36; T.G. Nelson and C.P. McInerney, 'Constituting the Arbitral Tribunal: FAA, Chapter 1, section 5, and Challenges to Arbitrators' in L. Shore et al. (eds), *International Arbitration in the United States*, Kluwer Law International, Alphen aan den Rijn 2017, pp. 233–34; see a contrario e.g. *Certain Underwriting Members of Lloyds of London v. State of Fla.*, 892 F.3d 501, 510 (2d Cir. 2018); *Winfrey v. Simmons Foods, Inc.*, 495 F.3d 549, 551 (8th Cir. 2007); *Patrolmen's Benevolent Ass'n of N.Y. v. City of N.Y. State Public Employment Relations Bd*, 110 N.Y.S.3d 81 (N.Y. App. Div. 2019)). Notably, the presumption has been removed from the 2004 Revision of the American Arbitration Association (AAA)/American Bar Association (ABA) Code of Ethics for Arbitrators in Commercial Cases. The 2013 AAA Commercial Arbitration Rules and Mediation Procedures nevertheless allow parties to appoint non-neutral arbitrators, as long as they behave with integrity, loyalty and good faith (see sections R-13(b) and R-18(b) of the Rules).

[169] See e.g. Hong Kong (section 24 of the Hong Kong Arbitration Ordinance referring to Article 11 of the UNCITRAL Model Law). Other countries, which have not adopted the Model Law, nevertheless follow a similar approach – such as France (see Article 1450 of the French Code of Civil Procedure (enacted in 1806/1975 and revised in 2019) (the French CCP)); see also C. Seraglini and J. Ortscheidt, *Droit de l'Arbitrage Interne et International*, 2nd ed., LGDJ, Paris 2019, paras 218–33 regarding domestic arbitration and paras 733–42 regarding international arbitration); Italy (see Article 812 of the Italian Code of Civil Procedure (enacted in 1865/1940 revised in 2019) (the Italian CCP)); Belgium (see Article 1685(1) of the Belgian Judicial Code); the Netherlands (see Article 1023 of the Dutch CCP).

[170] UNCITRAL Model Law, Article 11(1).

Commercial Ad Hoc Arbitration

It also adds that '[t]he court or other authority, in appointing an arbitrator, ...,
in the case of a sole or third arbitrator, shall take into account as well the
advisability of appointing an arbitrator of a nationality other than those of the
parties',[171] which is almost identical to the UNCITRAL Arbitration Rules (as
explained in section 2.1 above). This provision aims at ensuring that arbitrators
are independent and impartial. However, as in the UNCITRAL Arbitration
Rules, there is no obligation to take into account their nationalities and there
is no rule according to which the sole arbitrator or the presiding arbitrator
shall necessarily be of a different nationality than those of the parties. While, as
explained above, arbitral institutions acting as appointing authorities tend, as a
rule, not to appoint a sole or presiding arbitrator with the same nationality as
one of the parties, it is not certain that other appointing authorities, including
local courts, would do the same.

A few states may depart from the Model Law and require arbitrators to have
the nationality of a given state or prohibit appointments of foreign arbitrators,
although this is rare.[172]

3.2. CONSTITUTION OF THE ARBITRAL TRIBUNAL

National arbitration laws contain default rules and mechanisms relating to the
number of arbitrators (section 3.2.1) and the appointment process (section 3.2.2),
in the absence of a specific agreement of the parties, including the support of
local courts or a third-party appointing authority.

3.2.1. Number of Arbitrators

Some jurisdictions[173] have adopted an approach similar to the Model Law's,
according to which '[t]he parties are free to determine the number of arbitrators',
whether even or uneven,[174] and '[f]ailing such determination, the number of
arbitrators shall be *three*' (emphasis added).[175] As explained in section 2 above, a

---

[171] Ibid., Article 11(5).
[172] G. Born, *International Commercial Arbitration*, 3rd ed., Kluwer Law International, Alphen
aan den Rijn 2021, p. 1871, referring to Saudi Arabia and Ecuador, which used to have such
requirements in place that have now been repealed. In addition, according to G. Born, India
recently adopted legislation that appears to indirectly impose a nationality requirement
(arbitrators in Indian-seated arbitrations should be qualified to practise law in India).
[173] See e.g. Germany (section 1034(1) of the German ZPO); Sweden (sections 12–16 of the
Swedish Arbitration Act (enacted in 1999 and revised in 2018) (the Swedish Arbitration
Act)).
[174] G. Born, *International Commercial Arbitration*, 3rd ed., Kluwer Law International, Alphen
aan den Rijn 2021, p. 1789.
[175] UNCITRAL Model Law, Article 10(2).

Intersentia

117

three-member tribunal may 'enhance the legitimacy of the arbitral tribunal and better guarantee impartiality and fairness of the proceedings'.[176]

Other jurisdictions, however, prohibit arbitrations by an even number of arbitrators. This includes, for example, France and Switzerland (with respect to domestic arbitrations), the Netherlands, Belgium, Spain and Egypt.[177] In some of these states, including France, local legislation or judicial authorities convert(s) agreements on even numbers of arbitrators into agreements on uneven numbers of arbitrators by providing for the appointment of an additional arbitrator.[178] Under French law, in domestic arbitrations, where an arbitrator has not been added on the tribunal to reach an uneven number of arbitrators and the tribunal renders an award, the award may be set aside.[179] In other states, local legislation simply invalidates any arbitration agreement that specifies an even number of arbitrators, rather than substituting an uneven number of arbitrators. This is the case, for example, in Egypt.[180] As an author indicates, '[t]he rationale of such prohibitions is that an even number of arbitrators may not be capable of finally resolving a dispute (if the two arbitrators disagree)' and these prohibitions are 'inappropriate as a matter of legislative policy'.[181]

It is also interesting to note that, in England, there is no prohibition against arbitration by an even number of arbitrators. However, there is an interpretative presumption in favour of an uneven number of arbitrators if the parties have not agreed otherwise.[182] If the parties have opted for an even number of arbitrators and in case of deadlocks, the parties would be able to refer the dispute to an umpire (as explained above).

---

[176] D. Caron and L. Caplan, *The UNCITRAL Arbitration Rules: A Commentary*, 2nd ed., Oxford University Press, Oxford 2013, p. 158, referring to *Report of Working Group II (Arbitration and Conciliation) on the Work of its Forty-Ninth Session* (Vienna, 15–19 September 2008), UNCITRAL, 42nd Session, UN Doc A/CN.9/665, 12, para. 58.

[177] See France (Article 1451 of the French CCP); Switzerland (Article 360(2) of the Swiss Code of Civil Procedure (enacted in 2008 and revised in 2020) (the Swiss CCP)); the Netherlands (Article 1026(1) of the Dutch CCP); Belgium (Article 1684(1) of the Belgian Judicial Code); Spain (Article 12 of the Spanish Arbitration Act (enacted in 2003 and revised in 2015) (the Spanish Arbitration Act)); Egypt (Article 15(2) of the Egyptian Arbitration Law (enacted in 1994 and revised in 2000) (the Egyptian Arbitration Law)).

[178] See e.g. France (Article 1451(3) of the French CCP regarding domestic arbitrations); Switzerland (Article 360(2) of the Swiss CCP regarding domestic arbitrations); the Netherlands (Article 1026(3) of the Dutch Code of Civil Procedure); Belgium (Article 1684(2) of the Belgian Judicial Code).

[179] C. Seraglini and J. Ortscheidt, *Droit de l'Arbitrage Interne et International*, 2nd ed., LGDJ, Paris 2019, para. 250.

[180] Egyptian Arbitration Law, Article 15(2).

[181] G. Born, *International Commercial Arbitration*, 3rd ed., Kluwer Law International, Alphen aan den Rijn 2021, p. 1790.

[182] English Arbitration Act, section 15 (while paragraph 1 provides that '[t]he parties are free to agree on the number of arbitrators to form the tribunal and whether there is to be a chairman or umpire', paragraph 2 provides that '[u]nless otherwise agreed by the parties, an agreement that the number of arbitrators shall be two or any other even number shall be understood as requiring the appointment of an additional arbitrator as chairman of the tribunal').

Some jurisdictions also provide for a sole arbitrator instead of a three-arbitrator tribunal as a default solution. This is mostly the case in common law jurisdictions, including England,[183] although some civil jurisdictions, such as Spain, have adopted this default rule as well.[184] Other different approaches include:

- Hong Kong where, if the parties fail to agree on the number of arbitrators, '[t]he number of arbitrators ... is to be *either 1 or 3 as decided by HKIAC*' (emphasis added);[185]
- the Netherlands where, if the parties have not otherwise agreed, the number of arbitrators shall be fixed by the national courts;[186] and
- a few modern arbitration acts, which do not include a default rule for the number of arbitrators; in that case, as an author indicates, 'national courts should have the authority ... to specify the appropriate number of arbitrators'[187] – this is the case in France for example.[188]

3.2.2. Appointment of Arbitrators

As stated in section 2 above, the method for the appointment of arbitrators and the identity of the appointing authority (i.e. whether the parties or a third party) may affect the arbitrators' independence and impartiality. The mainstream approach is that of the Model Law,[189] which in Article 11(2)–(4) provides for:

---

[183] England (section 15(3) of the English Arbitration Act); United States (section 5 of the FAA); Singapore (section 9 of the Singapore International Arbitration Act (Chapter 143A) (enacted in 1994 and revised in 2002) (the Singapore International Arbitration Act)).

[184] Spanish Arbitration Act, Article 12.

[185] Hong Kong Arbitration Ordinance, section 23(3). Note that, in 2019, pursuant to section 13(3) of the Ordinance, the HKIAC adopted rules to facilitate the performance of its functions under inter alia section 23, with the approval of the Chief Justice: the Rules as Appointing Authority. These rules provide that, in deciding the number of arbitrators, the HKIAC must take into account a number of factors: the amount in dispute; the complexity of the claim; the nationality of the parties; the relevant customs of the trade, business or profession involved in the dispute; whether there are any appropriate arbitrators; and the urgency of the case (see HKIAC Rules as Appointing Authority, Rule 9(1)). Moreover, the HKIAC must allow the other party or parties to give brief written reasons in support of their positions (see HKIAC Rules as Appointing Authority, Rule 9(2)).

[186] Dutch CCP, Article 1026(2).

[187] G. Born, *International Commercial Arbitration*, 3rd ed., Kluwer Law International, Alphen aan den Rijn 2021, p. 1805.

[188] See Article 1454 of the French CCP, applicable to both domestic arbitrations and international arbitrations by reference of Article 1506 of the same Code, according to which when there is a difficulty in relation to the appointment of the tribunal, the matter should be referred to the person in charge of administering the arbitration or the support judge.

[189] Whether the states have adopted the Model Law or not, they generally follow its approach. See e.g. Belgium (Article 1685 of the Belgium Judicial Code); Hong Kong (section 24 of

(i) party autonomy to directly agree upon a particular individual as arbitrator, or on a procedure for the selection of the arbitrator(s),[190] and (ii) failing such agreement, default rules and mechanisms regarding the appointment of arbitrators:

- 'in an arbitration with three arbitrators, each party shall appoint one arbitrator, and the two arbitrators thus appointed shall appoint the third arbitrator';[191]
- 'if a party fails to appoint the arbitrator within thirty days of receipt of a request to do so from the other party, or if the two arbitrators fail to agree on the third arbitrator within thirty days of their appointment, the appointment shall be made, upon request of a party, by the court or other authority specified in article 6' (according to which, '[t]he functions referred to in articles 11(3), 11(4), 13(3), 14, 16(3) and 34(2) shall be performed by ... [Each State enacting this model law specifies the court, courts or, where referred to therein, other authority competent to perform these functions]')[192] – the court(s) referred to herein is also commonly designated as a 'support judge';[193]
- 'in an arbitration with a sole arbitrator, if the parties are unable to agree on the arbitrator, he shall be appointed, upon request of a party, by the court or other authority specified in article 6'.[194]

Moreover, if the parties have agreed on a procedure for the appointment of arbitrators but the parties are unable to constitute the tribunal, 'any party may request the court or other authority specified in article 6 to take the necessary measure'.[195]

Judicial/third-party involvement in the selection of arbitrators under Article 11(3) and (4) of the Model Law is therefore subsidiary, either because the parties' agreed mechanism for choosing the arbitrator has failed to function (e.g. when a party or a designated appointing authority has refused to act) or, in the absence of any mechanism agreed by the parties, because they (or the arbitrators) have not been able to select an arbitrator. It is not authorised as an independent basis for choosing the arbitrators irrespective of the parties' agreement.

---

the Hong Kong Arbitration Ordinance); Singapore (sections 8, 9A and 9B of the Singapore International Arbitration Act); France (Articles 1444, 1451–1454, 1508 and 1506 of the French CCP); Switzerland (Article 179(1)–(5) of the Swiss PILA); the Netherlands (Article 1027 of the Dutch CCP); United States (section 5 of the FAA).

190 UNCITRAL Model Law, Article 11(2).
191 Ibid., Article 11(3)(a).
192 Ibid., Article 11(3)(a).
193 France and Switzerland have designated the national courts acting as appointing authorities and deciding arbitrator challenges as the 'support judge' (*juge d'appui*).
194 UNCITRAL Model Law, Article 11(3)(b).
195 Ibid., Article 11(4).

While most jurisdictions have opted for judicial involvement under Article 6 of the Model Law, Hong Kong and Singapore have preferred to refer these matters to local arbitral institutions (in Hong Kong, the HKIAC (in particular, an 'Appointment Advisory Board' constituted under Part 2 of the HKIAC Rules as Appointing Authority (2019)),[196] and in Singapore, the President of SIAC).[197]

When appointing arbitrators under Article 11(3) and (4), the support judge or other authority 'shall have due regard to any qualifications required of the arbitrator by the agreement of the parties and to such considerations as are likely to secure the appointment of an independent and impartial arbitrator and, in the case of a sole or third arbitrator, shall take into account as well the advisability of appointing an arbitrator of a nationality other than those of the parties' – as explained in section 3.1 above.[198] For arbitrations seated in Hong Kong, the HKIAC Rules as Appointing Authority indicate that the Appointment Advisory Board of the HKIAC

> must appoint a suitable person to be an arbitrator, having regard to – (a) the nature of the dispute; (b) whether the arbitrators who possess the required qualifications would be available to accept the appointment; (c) the identity and nationality of the parties to the arbitration agreement; (d) any considerations in respect of the independence and impartiality of the person to be appointed as an arbitrator; (e) any stipulations in the relevant agreement; and (f) any suggestions made by the parties themselves.[199]

Thus, for these arbitrations seated in Hong Kong, even when a party fails to appoint the arbitrator it has to appoint, it will be able to participate to some extent in the selection process led by the HKIAC.

According to the Model Law, these decisions of the support judge or other authority 'shall be subject to no appeal'.[200]

---

[196] See Hong Kong Arbitration Ordinance, sections 13 and 24(1)–(4).

[197] Singapore International Arbitration Act, section 8(2).

[198] UNCITRAL Model Law, Article 11(5).

[199] HKIAC Rules as Appointing Authority, Rule 7(1).

[200] UNCITRAL Model Law, Article 11(5). See also e.g. France (Articles 1460 and 1506 of the French CCP – although there is an exception when the support judge found that the arbitration agreement was manifestly void or manifestly inapplicable and refused to appoint the arbitrator(s) pursuant to Article 1455 of the same Code); Switzerland (for international arbitration, see Article 179(2) of the Swiss PILA; for domestic arbitration, see Article 356(2)(a) of the Swiss CCP; see also M. Orielli, 'Commentary on Chapter 12 PILS, Article 179 [Arbitral tribunal: constitution of the arbitral tribunal]' in M. Arroyo (ed.), *Arbitration in Switzerland: The Practitioner's Guide*, 2nd ed., Kluwer Law International, Alphen aan den Rijn 2018, pp. 112–13, paras 46–47(a); Hong Kong (section 24(5) of the Hong Kong Arbitration Ordinance); Singapore (the UNCITRAL Model Law is attached as the First Schedule to the Singapore International Arbitration Act (as per section 3)).

While, in England, the English Arbitration Act also provides for the appointment of arbitrators by the support judge in most situations of default, it departs from the Model Law on at least two points. First, pursuant to section 17(1), if both parties to an arbitration agreement are to appoint an arbitrator and one party refuses to do so, or fails to do so within the time specified, unless the parties have otherwise agreed, 'the other party, having duly appointed his arbitrator, may give notice in writing to the party in default that he proposes to appoint his arbitrator to act as sole arbitrator'.[201] Then, if the party in default does not make the required appointment and notify the other party that it has done so, the other party may appoint his or her arbitrator as sole arbitrator.[202] The party in default may apply to the court to have the appointment set aside.[203] Second, the decisions of the English support judge may be appealed with the leave of the court.[204]

3.3. DUTIES OF ARBITRATORS AND SAFEGUARDS

Most jurisdictions require prospective arbitrators and arbitrators to disclose circumstances that may create doubts as to their independence and impartiality (section 3.3.1). They also require arbitrators to conduct the proceedings in an independent and impartial way – including to treat the parties equally and refrain from ex parte contact (section 3.3.2). An arbitrator's breach of these duties, if it is found that the arbitrator actually lacked independence and impartiality, may lead to the sanctions set out in section 3.4 below.

Moreover, most jurisdictions afford arbitrators a broad immunity from civil liability, in order to protect their independence (section 3.3.3).

3.3.1. *Continuous Disclosure Obligation*

The Model Law, in Article 12(1), expressly provides for a continuous disclosure requirement applicable to prospective arbitrators and arbitrators (whether co-arbitrators or presiding/sole arbitrators). The wording is almost identical to Article 11 of the UNCITRAL Arbitration Rules, and the standard for disclosure is similarly objective ('any circumstances likely to give rise to justifiable doubts'), as explained in sections 2.3.1 and 3.1 above. What has to be disclosed is left to the discretion of the prospective arbitrator(s), who may refer for guidance to guidelines and codes of conduct which reflect best practices and, in that case,

---

[201] English Arbitration Act, section 17(1).
[202] Ibid., section 17(2).
[203] Ibid., section 17(3).
[204] Ibid., section 17(4).

should read them in conjunction with national laws and court decisions. The precise contours of that requirement therefore depend on the circumstances of each case, the applicable law and the practice of the relevant courts.

Article 12(1) of the Model Law is representative of statutory disclosure requirements in many jurisdictions, whether they have adopted the Model Law or not.[205] One notable difference is the standard for disclosure in France, which is both a subjective and an objective one: arbitrators shall disclose any facts or circumstances which might be of such nature as to call into question the arbitrator's independence and impartiality in the eyes of the parties, as well as any circumstances that could give rise to reasonable doubts as to the arbitrator's independence and impartiality.[206] Not only should these facts or circumstances be likely to give rise to doubts as to the arbitrator's independence and impartiality, they should also be relevant for the arbitrator's views on the case and his or her decision.[207]

While Article 12(1) of the Model Law relieves arbitrators of their duty to disclose circumstances from their appointment and throughout the arbitral proceedings when 'the parties … have already been informed of [these circumstances] by [the arbitrators]', in France and in Switzerland arbitrators are not required to disclose matters which the parties *reasonably should have known* – either because these matters are public or because they are easily accessible.[208] According to recent French court decisions, for the arbitrator to be relieved of his or her duty to disclose a particular matter, the parties should have reasonably known of the matter before the start of the arbitration.[209]

Some jurisdictions do not impose a statutory disclosure requirement, but their courts have imposed a similar requirement. This is the case, for example, in England and the United States. In England, the Arbitration Act does not include

---

[205] See e.g. France (see Articles 1456 and 1506 of the French CCP); Switzerland (see Article 179(6) of the Swiss PILA for international arbitration, and Article 363 of the Swiss CCP for domestic arbitration); Spain (see Article 17(2) of the Spanish Arbitration Act); Hong Kong (see section 25 of the Hong Kong Arbitration Ordinance); Singapore (see, for international arbitration, Singapore International Arbitration Act, attaching the UNCITRAL Model Law as First Schedule); United Arab Emirates (see Article 10(4) of the UAE Federal Arbitration Law (enacted in 2018)).

[206] C. Seraglini and J. Ortscheidt, *Droit de l'Arbitrage Interne et International*, 2nd ed., LGDJ, Paris 2019, para. 746.

[207] Ibid., para. 746; J. Jourdan-Marques, 'Chronique d'arbitrage : déflagration dans le recours en annulation' (2020) *Dalloz Actualité*, https://www.dalloz-actualite.fr/flash/chronique-d-arbitrage-deflagration-dans-recours-en-annulation#.YdcbQtDMKUk.

[208] C. Seraglini and J. Ortscheidt, *Droit de l'Arbitrage Interne et International*, 2nd ed., LGDJ, Paris 2019, para. 746; G. Born, *International Commercial Arbitration*, 3rd ed., Kluwer Law International, Alphen aan den Rijn 2021, pp. 2041–42.

[209] J. Jourdan-Marques, 'Chronique d'arbitrage : déflagration dans le recours en annulation' (2020) *Dalloz Actualité*, https://www.dalloz-actualite.fr/flash/chronique-d-arbitrage-deflagration-dans-recours-en-annulation#.YdcbQtDMKUk.

a disclosure requirement. This omission was deliberate; as an author explains, the 'drafters concluded that a formal disclosure and challenge procedure was unduly cumbersome and likely to result in delays to constitution of the tribunal'.[210] No such duty was imposed by the English courts until a recent decision of the English Court of Appeal in the case of *Halliburton v. Chubb*.[211] In this case, the Court of Appeal held that arbitrators are required to disclose circumstances which 'would or might give rise to justifiable doubts as to [their] impartiality'.[212] In the United States, the FAA does not impose any express statutory disclosure requirement on prospective arbitrators/arbitrators, but the US courts have regularly imposed such requirement, absent an agreement of the parties to the contrary.[213]

3.3.2. Duty to Treat the Parties Equally and Prohibition of Ex Parte Contact

Not only must arbitrators be independent and impartial, they must also conduct themselves and the arbitration independently and impartially. For this reason, almost all states require that arbitrators treat the parties equally and fairly, and prohibit ex parte contact between an arbitrator and a party during the arbitral proceedings.[214]

The Model Law is representative of these requirements, providing that '[t]he parties shall be treated with equality and each party shall be given a full opportunity of presenting his case';[215] '[a]ll statements, documents or other information supplied to the arbitral tribunal by one party shall be communicated to the other party';[216] '[a]lso any expert report or evidentiary document on which

---

[210] G. Born, *International Commercial Arbitration*, 3rd ed., Kluwer Law International, Alphen aan den Rijn 2021, p. 2042.

[211] *Halliburton Company v. Chubb Bermuda Insurance Ltd (formerly known as Ace Bermuda Insurance Ltd)* [2020] UKSC 48 (holding that there is a legal duty to disclose facts that might give rise to the appearance of bias).

[212] *Halliburton Company v. Chubb Bermuda Insurance Ltd* [2018] EWCA Civ 817, para. 71; affirmed in *Halliburton Company v. Chubb Bermuda Insurance Ltd (formerly known as Ace Bermuda Insurance Ltd)* [2020] UKSC 48, paras 74–81.

[213] G. Born, *International Commercial Arbitration*, 3rd ed., Kluwer Law International, Alphen aan den Rijn 2021, pp. 2037–40, referring to inter alia *Commonwealth Coatings Corp. v. Cont'l Cas. Co.*, 393 U.S. 145, 149 (U.S. S.Ct. 1968).

[214] G. Born, *International Commercial Arbitration*, 3rd ed., Kluwer Law International, Alphen aan den Rijn 2021, p. 2012.

[215] UNCITRAL Model Law, Article 18. See also e.g. in France, Article 1510 of the French CCP (regarding international arbitration proceedings); in Switzerland, Article 182(3) of the Swiss PILA (regarding international arbitration proceedings); in England, section 33 of the English Arbitration Act; in the Netherlands, Article 1036(2) of the Dutch CCP; in Hong Kong, section 46 of the Hong Kong Arbitration Ordinance; in Spain, section 24(1) of the Spanish Arbitration Act; in Singapore, Articles 18 and 24(3) of the UNCITRAL Model Law are attached as the First Schedule to the Singapore International Arbitration Act (as per section 3).

[216] UNCITRAL Model Law, Article 24(3).

the arbitral tribunal may rely in making its decision shall be communicated to the parties.'[217]

With respect to ex parte contact during the arbitral proceedings, many jurisdictions, both civil and common law, regard this contact as improper when it relates to the substance of the arbitration.[218] However, they usually find that ex parte contact regarding 'purely logistical, scheduling and similar matters', or which does not relate to the arbitration, is acceptable.[219] In practice, many arbitrators will nevertheless prefer to avoid ex parte contact, even regarding procedural aspects.[220]

3.3.3. Immunity from Civil Liability

In almost all jurisdictions, arbitrators enjoy a broad immunity from civil liability for actions and omissions performed in their adjudicative functions, whether imposed by law or by the courts,[221] and these immunities are usually mandatory.[222] As explained in section 2.3.3 above, this is intended to reinforce the independence of arbitrators, who should remain free from pressures exercised by the parties, and is provided by most leading institutional arbitration rules and non-administered arbitration rules (including the UNCITRAL Arbitration Rules). Surprisingly, however, the Model Law is silent on this point.

From an analysis of the existing statutory immunities in various jurisdictions, we note that there are two main approaches. Either statutes provide that arbitrators will not be liable, except in circumstances as provided by law (i.e. the so-called 'negative approach'),[223] or they provide that arbitrators will be liable in given circumstances provided by law (i.e. the so-called 'affirmative approach').[224] An example of the negative approach is section 29 of the English Arbitration Act, according to which '[a]n arbitrator is not liable for anything done or omitted in the discharge or purported discharge of his functions as arbitrator unless the act or omission is shown to have been in bad faith.' An example of the affirmative approach is Article 21(1) of the Spanish Arbitration Act, which provides that '[a]cceptance obliges the arbitrators and, where applicable, the arbitral institution

---

[217] Ibid.

[218] G. Born, *International Commercial Arbitration*, 3rd ed., Kluwer Law International, Alphen aan den Rijn 2021, p. 2012.

[219] Ibid., p. 2013.

[220] Ibid.

[221] Ibid., p. 2177.

[222] Ibid., p. 2178.

[223] See e.g. English Arbitration Act, section 29. See also e.g. Irish Arbitration Act (enacted in 2010), section 22(1); Portuguese Law on Voluntary Arbitration (enacted in 2012), Article 9(4).

[224] See e.g. Spanish Arbitration Act, Article 21(1); Austrian Code of Civil Procedure (enacted in 1895 and revised in 2020) (the Austrian ZPO), Article 594(4); Italian CCP, Article 813(2).

to comply faithfully with their responsibilities, being, if they do not do so, liable for the damage and losses they cause by reason of bad faith, recklessness or fraud.' In substance these two types of statutory civil immunities are similar, as they both afford arbitrators immunity.

In most jurisdictions, whether common or civil law jurisdictions, the arbitrators' civil immunity is broad, as liability will be incurred only in very limited circumstances: in cases of 'intentional wrongdoing', 'bad faith', 'gross negligence', 'reckless conduct' or 'fraud'.[225] In some jurisdictions, however, other circumstances can also trigger an arbitrator's civil liability.[226] In France, for example, it is well settled that arbitrators should be liable for any breach of their duty of independence and impartiality (including a breach of their duty to disclose when this breach led to the annulment of the arbitral award), as an exception to their immunity from civil liability for actions or omissions performed in their adjudicative functions.[227]

3.4. CONSEQUENCES OF A BREACH OF THE REQUIREMENT OF INDEPENDENCE AND IMPARTIALITY

Pursuant to almost all national arbitration laws, when the duty of independence and impartiality has been breached, the following remedies are available to the parties, depending on when the parties learn of the litigious circumstances: during the proceedings, they can challenge the arbitrator and, once the award has been issued, the award can be set aside or can be denied recognition and enforcement. In addition, as already explained in section 3.3.3 above, in some jurisdictions, arbitrators may be held liable for damages, as a breach of independence and impartiality may qualify as an exception to the arbitrator's traditional immunity from civil liability.

---

[225] See e.g. English Arbitration Act, section 29; Spanish Arbitration Act, Article 21(1); G. Born, *International Commercial Arbitration*, 3rd ed., Kluwer Law International, Alphen aan den Rijn 2021, pp. 2180–82 referring to case law and doctrine in inter alia the United States, Singapore, Hong Kong, Belgium, the Netherlands and Germany.

[226] In addition to the example of France, the arbitration laws of some Arab countries provide that arbitrators should be liable for unjustified resignations during the arbitral proceedings. See e.g. Bahrain (Article 234 of the Bahraini Code of Civil and Commercial Procedure (enacted 1971 and revised in 1999)); Lebanon (Article 769 of the Lebanese New Code of Civil Procedure (enacted in 1993 and revised in 2002)); Libya (Article 748 of the Libyan Code of Civil and Commercial Procedure (enacted in 1954)); Qatar (Article 194 of the Qatari Code of Civil and Commercial Procedure (enacted in 1990)); Syria (Article 17(2) of the Syrian Arbitration Act (enacted in 2008)); Tunisia (Article 11 of the Tunisian Arbitration Code (enacted in 1993) (the Tunisian Arbitration Code)); G. Born, *International Commercial Arbitration*, 3rd ed., Kluwer Law International, Alphen aan den Rijn 2021, pp. 2183–84.

[227] C. Seraglini and J. Ortscheidt, *Droit de l'Arbitrage Interne et International*, 2nd ed., LGDJ, Paris 2019, paras 246, 294, 759; Paris Court of Appeal, 12 October 1995 (1999) *Revue de l'Arbitrage* 324.

Commercial Ad Hoc Arbitration

This section will focus, on the one hand, on arbitrator challenges (section 3.4.1) and, on the other hand, on annulment, recognition and enforcement of arbitral awards (section 3.4.2) in national arbitration legislation.

3.4.1. Challenges of Arbitrators

Like Article 12(2) of the Model Law and Article 12 of the UNCITRAL Arbitration Rules, almost all jurisdictions allow challenges of arbitrators during proceedings when, after their appointments, it appears there exist circumstances giving rise to doubts as to their independence and impartiality.[228] One exception is the legal regime under the United States FAA, under which it is not possible to challenge an arbitrator for lack of independence and impartiality.[229] Parties in arbitrations seated in the United States, however, may have agreed on a challenge procedure in the arbitration agreement or may have referred to procedural rules that provide for one.

As explained in section 3.1 above, there may be differences in the standards applicable to the national requirements of independence and impartiality, depending on the laws and practices of the domestic courts of each state. Jurisdictions may also have different approaches regarding challenge procedures, which this section therefore focuses on, although one common pattern can be noted: most of them grant expansive powers to the support judge.

On the one hand, a number of jurisdictions incorporate or broadly follow the challenge procedure set out in Article 13 of the Model Law,[230] pursuant to which:

- the parties may agree on a procedure for challenging the arbitrators (see Article 13(1));

---

[228] G. Born, *International Commercial Arbitration*, 3rd ed., Kluwer Law International, Alphen aan den Rijn 2021, pp. 2065–77. See e.g. jurisdictions where circumstances giving rise to justifiable doubts as to the arbitrators' independence and impartiality open the door for a challenge: England (section 24(1) of the English Arbitration Act); Switzerland (for international arbitration: Article 180 of the Swiss PILA); Spain (Article 17(3) of the Spanish Arbitration Act); Germany (section 1036(2) of the German ZPO); Belgium (Article 1686(2) of the Belgian Judicial Code); the Netherlands (Article 1033 of the Dutch CCP); Hong Kong (section 25 of the Hong Kong Arbitration Ordinance); Singapore (the UNCITRAL Model Law is attached as the First Schedule to the Singapore International Arbitration Act, as per section 3). See also France, where arbitrators may be challenged by the parties when they have not revealed a circumstance likely to create doubts in the parties' minds as to the arbitrators' independence and impartiality (Articles 1456–1458 and 1506 of the French CCP).

[229] In the United States, there is no possibility to challenge arbitrators but the award may be set aside if 'there was evident partiality or corruption in the arbitrators' (see FAA, section 10(a)(2)).

[230] See e.g. Germany (section 1037 of the German ZPO); Austria (Article 589 of the Austrian ZPO); Singapore (the UNCITRAL Model Law is attached as the First Schedule to the Singapore International Arbitration Act as per section 3); Hong Kong (section 26 of the Hong Kong Arbitration Ordinance); Japan (Article 19 of the Japanese Arbitration Law (enacted in 2003)); Sweden (section 10 of the Swedish Arbitration Act).

Intersentia

- absent an agreement of the parties, and unless the challenged arbitrator withdraws from his office or the other party agrees to the challenge, the challenge will be decided *by the arbitral tribunal* (see Article 13(2)); and
- if the challenge is rejected, any of the parties may request the *support judge or another authority* designated by law to decide the challenge (see Article 13(3)) (jurisdictions that follow the Model Law have opted for judicial involvement, except Singapore where the decision on challenge belongs to the President of SIAC).[231]

A party who intends to challenge an arbitrator under the default procedure provided by Article 13(2) has 15 days after becoming aware of the constitution of the arbitral tribunal, or after becoming aware of a circumstance giving rise to justifiable doubts as to the arbitrator's impartiality or independence, to bring the challenge.[232] If a party does not raise a challenge within this time period, it will be deemed to have waived its right of challenge. In addition, it must do so in writing and state the reasons for the challenge.[233] Then, if the challenge is rejected pursuant to the procedure agreed by the parties or, in the absence of an agreement of the parties, by the arbitral tribunal, the party who has challenged the arbitrator has 30 days after having received notice of the decision rejecting the challenge to request the local courts or another authority designated by law to decide the challenge.[234] These requirements are similar to those of Article 13(1) and (2) of the UNCITRAL Arbitration Rules[235] and, as explained in section 2.4.2 above, are meant to prevent abusive challenges which are brought in order to exercise undue influence on the arbitrator.

The Model Law, in Article 13(3), adds that 'while such a request [before the local courts or another authority designated by law] is pending, the arbitral tribunal, including the challenged arbitrator, may continue the arbitral proceedings and make an award.' This is also meant to limit the impact of potentially abusive challenges.

On the other hand, some jurisdictions have departed from the Model Law. Some of them, for example, have excluded the involvement of arbitrators in the challenge procedure, unless the parties have expressly provided for it. In these cases, challenges are decided by the support judge, when the parties have not

---

[231] Singapore International Arbitration Act, section 8(2), in combination with UNCITRAL Model Law, Article 6, referred to by section 3 of the Act.

[232] UNCITRAL Model Law, Article 13(2).

[233] Ibid.

[234] Ibid., Article 13(3).

[235] Ibid., Article 13: '1. A party that intends to challenge an arbitrator shall send notice of its challenge within 15 days after it has been notified of the appointment of the challenged arbitrator, or within 15 days after the circumstances mentioned in articles 11 and 12 became known to that party. 2. The notice of challenge shall be communicated to all other parties, to the arbitrator who is challenged and to the other arbitrators. The notice of challenge shall state the reasons for the challenge.'

Commercial Ad Hoc Arbitration

decided otherwise or as a last resort. This is the case inter alia of England,[236] the Netherlands,[237] France,[238] Switzerland,[239] Belgium[240] and Tunisia.[241] In the Netherlands, it can also be noted that, once a challenge is raised, the arbitral tribunal 'may suspend the proceedings'.[242] This departs from Article 13(3) of the Model Law, pursuant to which 'the arbitral tribunal … may continue the arbitral proceedings and make an award', as explained above. Another interesting difference can be found in France and Switzerland where, if the parties have agreed on a procedure to deal with arbitrator challenges, the French and Swiss support judges will *not* entertain the challenges – even in last resort;[243] the party's sole recourse is to seek to annul the award on the ground that the arbitral tribunal was not regularly constituted.[244]

In jurisdictions other than France and Switzerland, where the parties have granted an institution or another authority the power to decide challenges against the arbitrator(s), and that institution or authority rejects the challenge, an issue may arise as to the weight that the national courts thereafter seized of the challenge should give to the institution or authority's decision on the challenge. This will depend on the practice of the courts of each state. In England, for instance, the answer is not clear cut. Although institutional arbitration rules may provide that the authority's decision on the challenge is subject to no appeal, English courts deciding challenges on the basis of section 24(1)(a) of the English Arbitration Act have ruled that they have the power to review that institution's decision.[245] They will take into consideration the institution's decision and reasons (if those are set out in the decision) but they are not bound by them.[246]

Lastly, in France, not only is it possible for a party to challenge an arbitrator before the support judge when the parties have not agreed on another procedure,

---

[236] English Arbitration Act, sections 23 and 24 (see in particular section 24(2), providing that '[i]f there is an arbitral or other institution or person vested by the parties with power to remove an arbitrator, the court shall not exercise its power of removal unless satisfied that the applicant has first exhausted any available recourse to that institution or person').

[237] Dutch CCP, Article 1035.

[238] French CCP, Articles 1456–1458 and 1506.

[239] Swiss PILA, Article 180(a) (regarding international arbitration).

[240] Belgian Judicial Code, Article 1687.

[241] Tunisian Arbitration Code, Article 58.

[242] Dutch CCP, Article 1035(5).

[243] In France, see TGI Paris, *State of Dubai v. Halcrow* (1993) 3 *Revue de l'Arbitrage* 455; T. Webster, *Handbook of UNCITRAL Arbitration: Commentary, Precedents and Materials for UNCITRAL Based Arbitration Rules*, Sweet & Maxwell, London 2010, p. 209, paras 13-25 to 13-26. In Switzerland, see Swiss PILA, Article 180(a).

[244] Ibid.

[245] *AT&T Corp. v. Saudi Cable Co.* [2000] EWCA Civ 154 (English Court of Appeal); *P v. Q* [2017] EWHC 148 (Comm) (English High Court); *A v. B* [2011] EWHC 2345 (English High Court).

[246] Ibid.

Intersentia

but it is also possible for a party who has appointed an arbitrator to ask the support judge to confirm that appointment.[247]

3.4.2. Annulment and Denial of Recognition and Enforcement of Arbitral Awards

Many legal systems provide for annulment of awards (and similarly denial of recognition and enforcement of awards) if, after the award was issued, it turns out that an arbitrator was not independent and impartial and it can be proven that this impacted the tribunal's decision in the award.[248] This ground for annulment is not expressly provided by Article 34(2) of the Model Law or Article V of the New York Convention on the Recognition and Enforcement of Foreign Arbitral Awards (1958), although it is undoubtedly covered by either one of the following grounds:

- the party making the applicable was unable to present its case;[249] or
- the tribunal was not constituted in accordance with the parties' agreement or the applicable law.[250]

The differences that there may be in the standards applicable to the national requirements of independence and impartiality, as explained in section 3.1 above, also apply in the context of annulment proceedings, as well as enforcement and recognition proceedings.

As indicated in section 3.4.1 above, in almost all jurisdictions, an arbitrator lacking independence and impartiality may be challenged during the proceedings and a party who wishes to challenge an arbitrator should do so as soon as it learns of the circumstances creating doubts as to the arbitrator's independence and impartiality. For this reason, this ground may only be invoked after the award was issued if these circumstances were not known by the party during the proceedings. If the party knew of these circumstances but did not challenge the arbitrator, in most jurisdictions, it will be held to have waived its right to seek annulment of the award or resist recognition and enforcement on this ground.[251]

If a party challenged an arbitrator during the proceedings, that challenge was rejected and the party later challenges the award before the courts of the seat on

---

[247] E. Loquin, *Fasc. 1015: ARBITRAGE. – L'arbitre. – Conditions d'exercice. – Statut* (2021), para. 60, referring to French Court of Cassation, 1ʳᵉ civ., 23.01.2007, *Médard c. Société Systeme U*, no. 06-12.946 (2007) *Revue de l'Arbitrage* 284, observations of E. Teynier.

[248] G. Born, *International Commercial Arbitration*, 3rd ed., Kluwer Law International, Alphen aan den Rijn 2021, pp. 3562–68.

[249] UNCITRAL Model Law, Article 34(2)(a)(ii); New York Convention, Article V(1)(b).

[250] UNCITRAL Model Law, Article 34(2)(a)(iv); New York Convention, Article V(1)(d).

[251] G. Born, *International Commercial Arbitration*, 3rd ed., Kluwer Law International, Alphen aan den Rijn 2021, pp. 2060, 2080–82, 3568.

the same ground, the national courts seized of the matter are either bound by the earlier decision on the arbitrator's challenge, or should take it into consideration, depending on the applicable law. In France and in Switzerland, for example, if the arbitrator challenge was previously decided by an arbitral institution or another person or authority designated by the parties, the annulment judge should not be bound by their decision on the challenge when ruling on the action to set aside the award (unless there are new circumstances creating doubt as to the arbitrator's independence and impartiality).[252] If, however, the challenge was decided by the support judge, that decision of the support judge is binding on the annulment judge (in Switzerland, the decision is both final and binding;[253] in France, the decision cannot be appealed, except on the ground of excessive use of powers, and is binding).[254] This is because an arbitral institution's decision on an arbitrator challenge is not a judicial decision; therefore, it is not *res judicata*, as opposed to the support judge's decision on the arbitrator challenge.[255] Moreover, in France, if an arbitrator was designated by the support judge, that arbitrator's designation cannot be later raised as a ground to seek the annulment of the award.[256]

---

[252] E. Loquin, *Fasc. 1015: ARBITRAGE. – L'arbitre. – Conditions d'exercice. – Statut* (2021), paras 57 and 64; E. Loquin, *Fasc. 1800-72: ARBITRAGE. – La décision arbitrale. – Voies de recours* (2021), para. 60; C. Seraglini and J. Ortscheidt, *Droit de l'Arbitrage Interne et International*, 2nd ed., LGDJ, Paris 2019, paras 242, 277, 750 and 752; M. Orielli, 'Commentary on Chapter 12 PILS, Article 180 [Arbitral tribunal: challenge to an arbitrator]' in M. Arroyo (ed.), *Arbitration in Switzerland: The Practitioner's Guide*, 2nd ed., Kluwer Law International, Alphen aan den Rijn 2018, pp. 126–27. This similarly applies in recognition and enforcement proceedings before the French and Swiss courts.

[253] Swiss PILA, Article 180(a)(2); M. Orielli, 'Commentary on Chapter 12 PILS, Article 180 [Arbitral tribunal: challenge to an arbitrator]' in M. Arroyo (ed.), *Arbitration in Switzerland: The Practitioner's Guide*, 2nd ed., Kluwer Law International, Alphen aan den Rijn 2018, pp. 127–28, paras 36–37.

[254] French CCP, Article 1460 (applicable to domestic arbitration, and also to international arbitration through Article 1506).

[255] C. Seraglini and J. Ortscheidt, *Droit de l'Arbitrage Interne et International*, 2nd ed., LGDJ, Paris 2019, paras 242, 277, 750 and 752.

[256] Ibid., para. 277.

THE INDEPENDENCE AND IMPARTIALITY OF ADJUDICATORS IN COMMERCIAL INSTITUTIONAL ARBITRATION

Franco FERRARI and Friedrich ROSENFELD

1. Introduction 133
2. A Comparative Analysis of the Institutional Framework
   on Independence and Impartiality.............................. 134
   2.1. Criteria for the Selection of Arbitrators 135
   2.2. The Authority Appointing or Confirming Arbitrators and
        the Methods for Balancing its Influence................. 137
   2.3. The Method for the Appointment of Arbitrators.......... 141
        2.3.1. Sole Arbitrators................................ 142
        2.3.2. Modalities of Appointing Three-Member Tribunals.... 142
        2.3.3. Modalities of Constituting the Tribunal in Multi-Party
               Arbitrations 143
   2.4. The Standards for Independence and Impartiality 144
   2.5. Consequences of a Breach................................ 146
   2.6. Interim Conclusion 148
3. A Post-Award Perspective on the Institutional Framework
   on Independence and Impartiality.............................. 149
   3.1. Scope of Review 149
   3.2. Standard of Review 154
4. Conclusion... 155

1. INTRODUCTION

The proposition that decision-makers must be neutral is a fundamental aspect of every judicial procedure. The idea goes back to ancient times, when early representations of justice were of a blindfolded lady holding a balance and a sword.[1]

---

[1] For further references, see F. Ferrari and F. Rosenfeld, *International Commercial Arbitration – A Comparative Introduction*, Elgar, Cheltenham, UK/Northampton, MA, USA 2021, p. 74.

Intersentia

Today, the requirement of adjudicative neutrality[2] is as relevant as ever, and it applies with equal force in international arbitration proceedings.[3]

An important source of the legal framework governing international arbitration proceedings are the rules of arbitral institutions, which administer the majority of today's arbitrations.[4] Such institutional arbitration rules offer a robust framework on independence and impartiality, which shall be the focus of this report.

The analysis will be done in three steps. Section 2 offers a comparative analysis of the institutional framework governing the independence and impartiality of arbitrators. The analysed rules include those of the ICC, DIS, SIAC, HKIAC, LCIA and ICDR (the Analysed Rules). Section 3 shows how this institutional regime is enforced at the post-award stage. Section 4 concludes.

2. A COMPARATIVE ANALYSIS OF THE INSTITUTIONAL FRAMEWORK ON INDEPENDENCE AND IMPARTIALITY

If one takes a closer look at the Analysed Rules, it does not take long to realise that the requirement of independence and impartiality of arbitrators features prominently in them. While the Analysed Rules are marked by a considerable degree of convergence in this respect, one can identify distinct nuances in their regulatory approaches towards independence and impartiality. These differences will be addressed below. Our focus will be on how the requirement of independence and impartiality affects the criteria for the selection of arbitrators (section 2.1), the authority appointing arbitrators (section 2.2) and the method for the constitution of the tribunal (section 2.3). We will then review the specific standards of independence and impartiality (section 2.4) as well the consequences of a breach of the arbitrator's obligation to be and remain independent and impartial (section 2.5).

---

[2] S.D. Franck, 'The Role of International Arbitrators' (2006) 12 *ILSA J. Int'l & Comp. L.* 499, 501 (where the author also refers to a different type of neutrality, namely 'neutrality of forum, where the place of dispute resolution does not unfairly benefit either party or create a "homecourt" advantage').

[3] See D.A. Lawson, 'Impartiality and Independence of International Arbitrators – Commentary on the 2004 IBA Guidelines on Conflict of Interests in International Arbitration' (2005) 23 *ASA Bulletin* 22, 23 ('The fundamental right enshrined in the second part of [Article 10 of the 1948 Universal Declaration of Human Rights], part of customary public international law and an important element of the Rule of Law, is equally applicable in national and international arbitration and is restated in many other international and regional treaties and conventions'); T. Cole, 'Authority and Contemporary International Arbitration' (2010) 70 *La. L. Rev.* 801, 839 ('it is an unquestionable tenet of contemporary international arbitration that all arbitrators on a panel, including the two party-nominated arbitrators, must be neutral between the parties').

[4] F. Ferrari and F. Rosenfeld, *International Commercial Arbitration – A Comparative Introduction*, Elgar, Cheltenham, UK/Northampton, MA, USA 2021, pp. 6–9.

2.1. CRITERIA FOR THE SELECTION OF ARBITRATORS

As far as the criteria for the selection of arbitrators are concerned, the Analysed Rules exhibit no more than subtle differences.

To begin with, the majority of the Analysed Rules only indirectly regulate the selection of arbitrators by the parties.[5] Put differently, they do not expressly set limits on whom parties may select as arbitrators; they indirectly subject the parties' choice to a requirement of confirmation by the arbitral institution. In this process of confirming arbitrators nominated by the parties (or when appointing arbitrators selected by the arbitral institution absent a nomination by the parties), the arbitral institution will consider various factors, including 'considerations that are relevant to the impartiality or independence of the arbitrator'.[6] The DIS Rules differ from this approach by expressly stating that the parties' nomination – and not only the confirmation by the DIS – must also respect the requirement of independence and impartiality.[7]

The Analysed Rules also differ in terms of how much of their normative content is specified ex ante. Some rules are phrased as broad standards and, thus, leave discretion on how to interpret them. The ICDR Rules, for example, state that the Administrator shall endeavour 'to appoint suitable arbitrators, taking into account their availability to serve'.[8] The ICDR Rules do not further define when an arbitrator is suitable and, thus, leave a considerable degree of flexibility to the Administrator.[9] The only further clarification they make is that the Administrator 'may appoint nationals of a country other than that of any of the parties'.[10] Other rules are more prescriptive and contain detailed guidance in supplementary texts such as practice notes or guidelines. The 2018 Practice Notice on the Appointment of Arbitrators under the HKIAC Rules (2018 Practice Note) is evidence of such an approach. It lists a large number of criteria to be considered for the appointment of arbitrators, including:

(a) any qualifications agreed by the parties;
(b) any qualifications or candidates suggested by any of the parties;
(c) the identity of the parties, counsel and co-arbitrators (if any);
(d) the nationality of the parties;
(e) the nationality of the arbitrator;
(f) the place of residence of the arbitrator;

---

[5] Cf. the LCIA Rules (2020), the SIAC Rules (2016), the ICC Rules (2021), the HKIAC Rules (2018), and the ICDR Rules (2021).

[6] See e.g. Article 13.2 SIAC Rules (2016).

[7] Article 9.2 DIS Rules (2018).

[8] Article 12.4 ICDR Rules (2021).

[9] M. Gusy and J. Hosking, *A Guide to the ICDR International Arbitration Rules*, 2nd ed., OUP, Oxford 2019, p. 124 (discussing the previous version of the ICDR Rules).

[10] Article 12.4 ICDR Rules (2021).

(g)   the availability of the arbitrator;
(h)   the proposed fee of the arbitrator;
(i)   the nature and complexity of the dispute;
(j)   the amount in dispute;
(k)   the governing law of the contract(s);
(l)   the seat of arbitration;
(m)   the language of the arbitration and underlying contract(s);
(n)   the number of previous appointments of the arbitrator in HKIAC cases; and
(o)   HKIAC's previous experience with the arbitrator and any party feedback.[11]

The 2018 Practice Note also contains a commitment to diversity. It provides that HKIAC 'will include, wherever possible, qualified female candidates and qualified candidates of any age, ethnic group, legal or cultural background among those it considers for arbitrator appointments'.[12]

Finally, some of the Analysed Rules mention secondary criteria for the assessment of independence and impartiality. We use the term 'secondary criteria' to designate criteria other than independence and impartiality, which may, however, be relevant for the assessment of an arbitrator's independence and impartiality. Under the ICC Rules, for example, the ICC Court or Secretary-General 'shall consider the prospective arbitrator's nationality, residence and other relationships with the countries of which the parties or the other arbitrators are nationals'.[13] The fact that the Court shall only 'consider' these secondary criteria shows that the Rules leave considerable discretion to the Court in its decision to appoint or confirm an arbitrator. The Court's discretion is more limited in situations in which the Court is to appoint the sole arbitrator or president of the arbitral tribunal. In such a scenario, the Court shall appoint a candidate whose nationality differs from those of the parties.[14] Only in suitable circumstances and provided that none of the parties objects in a timely manner may the sole arbitrator or president be chosen from a country of which any of the parties is a national.[15] For example, where all parties share the same nationality, the Court may appoint an arbitrator having the same nationality of the parties. The Court will usually not do so in situations where the dispute is nevertheless international in nature.[16]

---

[11]   HKIAC Practice Note on the Appointment of Arbitrators, effective 1 November 2018, para. 2.3, https://www.hkiac.org/arbitration/rules-practice-notes/practice-notes.
[12]   Para. 4.1 2018 Practice Note.
[13]   Article 13.1 ICC Rules (2021).
[14]   Article 13.5 ICC Rules (2021).
[15]   Article 13.5 ICC Rules (2021).
[16]   ICC Note to the Parties and Arbitral Tribunals on the Conduct of the Arbitration under the ICC Rules of Arbitration (2021), para. 44. In treaty-based arbitrations, no arbitrator shall have the same nationality of any party to the arbitration unless otherwise agreed. See Article 13.6 ICC Rules (2021).

The nationality of arbitrators also features prominently under the LCIA Rules as a secondary criterion to be considered for the appointment of arbitrators.[17] The LCIA Court has applied a substantive test to assess an arbitrator's nationality. It has ruled that 'a person would be deemed a de facto national of [a] country in circumstances where [his or her] connection to it were so concentrated that [his or her] technical nationality did not ensure neutrality'.[18] One may critically observe that such a definition of de facto nationality defeats its purpose as a secondary criterion to assess an arbitrator's neutrality. After all, there is a logical fallacy in any attempt to define nationality by reference to an arbitrator's neutrality in order to then assess an arbitrator's neutrality by his or her nationality. Against this background, it is understandable that some arbitral rules forego an express reference to the criterion of nationality to assess an arbitrator's independence and impartiality.[19]

The overall conclusion to be drawn is that the Analysed Rules exhibit some differences in how they rely on independence and impartiality as criteria for the selection of arbitrators. Having said this, one should not attach too much weight to these textual differences. In practice, there is a considerable degree of convergence regarding the criteria that arbitral institutions consider when appointing or confirming arbitrators.

2.2. THE AUTHORITY APPOINTING OR CONFIRMING ARBITRATORS AND THE METHODS FOR BALANCING ITS INFLUENCE

The Analysed Rules also show some variations in respect of the authority appointing or confirming the arbitrator. They notably differ as to the specific organ in charge of the appointment or confirmation as well as the methods for balancing this organ's influence.

Some rules provide for the appointment by an organ composed of one natural person. For example, under the ICDR Rules, the authority to appoint arbitrators is vested with the Administrator.[20] Under the SIAC Rules, it is the President of SIAC who is responsible for the appointment of arbitrators.[21]

---

17 M. Scherer, L. Richman and R. Gerbay, *Arbitrating under the 2020 LCIA Rules: A User's Guide*, Kluwer, Alphen aan den Rijn 2021, Chapter 9, paras 36, 61. See also Article 6 LCIA Rules: in assessing the nationality of a party, one must also consider the nationality of its controlling shareholders. The LCIA Rules further specify that a person who is a citizen of two or more states shall be treated as a national of each state.

18 Decision in LCIA No. 8086 of 30 September 1998 (2011) 27 *Arb. Int'l* 328, para. 3.2; for a comment on this decision, see T.W. Walsh and R. Teitelbaum, 'The LCIA Court Decisions on Challenges to Arbitrators: An Introduction' (2011) 27 *Arb. Int'l* 283, 291.

19 See e.g. SIAC Rules (2016).

20 Article 13.6 ICDR Rules (2021).

21 Article 9.3 SIAC Rules (2016). See also J. Choong, M. Mangan and N. Lingard, *A Guide to the SIAC Arbitration Rules*, 2nd ed., OUP, Oxford 2018, pp. 133–34.

Other rules provide for the appointment by an organ composed of a representative number of practitioners and academics:

- For example, the LCIA Court consists of eminent practitioners and academics with different nationalities.[22] The functions of the LCIA Court may be performed by the President of the LCIA Court or any of its Vice-Presidents, Honorary Vice-Presidents or former Vice-Presidents. Alternatively, they may be performed by a division of three or more members of the LCIA Court appointed by its President or any Vice-President.[23]
- In a similar vein, the ICC Court is composed of eminent arbitration practitioners and academics. Where the ICC Court is responsible for appointing an arbitrator, it shall make the appointment upon the proposal of an ICC National Committee or Group that it considers to be appropriate.[24] The ICC Court may under limited circumstances directly appoint any person whom it regards as suitable.[25] As an exception to this regime, the Secretary-General of the ICC may also confirm prospective arbitrators. This presupposes that their statement contains no qualification regarding impartiality or independence or that a qualified statement regarding their impartiality and independence has not given rise to any objections.[26]
- Under the DIS Rules, the body equivalent to the ICC or LCIA Court is the DIS Appointment Committee.[27] The Appointment Committee shall consist of three main members and three alternate members with practical experience in domestic and international arbitration.[28] In the event that no party has objected in a timely manner to the appointment of a prospective arbitrator, the appointment may also be decided upon by the Secretary-General of the DIS.[29]
- The HKIAC Rules provide for a different organ depending on whether what is at stake is the confirmation of an arbitrator nominated by the parties or the appointment of an arbitrator by the institution. The decision on confirmation

---

[22] M. Scherer, L. Richman and R. Gerbay, *Arbitrating under the 2020 LCIA Rules: A User's Guide*, Kluwer, Alphen aan den Rijn 2021, Chapter 1, para. 13.

[23] Article 3.1 LCIA Rules (2020).

[24] Article 13.3 ICC Rules (2021).

[25] Article 13.4 ICC Rules, with reference to the following three situations: (i) arbitrations in which one or more of the parties is a state or may be considered to be a state entity; (ii) the ICC Court considers that it would be appropriate to appoint an arbitrator from a country or territory where there is no National Committee or Group; or (iii) the President certifies to the ICC Court that circumstances exist which make a direct appointment necessary and appropriate.

[26] Article 13.2 ICC Rules (2021).

[27] Article 13.2 DIS Rules (2018). See also A. Meier and L. Gerhardt, '§2.03: The Arbitral Tribunal, Article 13, Appointment of the Arbitrators' in G. Flecke-Giammarco et al. (eds), *The DIS Arbitration Rules – An Article-by-Article Commentary*, Kluwer, Alphen aan den Rijn 2020, pp. 228–29.

[28] Article 6.1 DIS Internal Rules (Annex I).

[29] Article 13.3 DIS Rules (2018).

is taken by the HKIAC,[30] which includes the Council of the HKIAC or any other body or person designated by it to perform the functions referred to in the HKIAC Rules.[31] Where applicable, it may also include the Secretary-General of the HKIAC and other staff members.[32] The appointment of arbitrators, in turn, is done by the Appointments Committee.[33] Where the HKIAC appoints an arbitrator under the Arbitration Ordinance, it will consult with at least three members of the Appointment Advisory Board. The HKIAC must consider their advice but is not bound by it. The Appointment Advisory Board includes members nominated by 11 Hong Kong professional and interest groups.[34]

Clearly, the involvement of a representative organ in the appointment process offers the benefit of the 'wisdom of the crowd'. As economists have shown, 'averaging several independent judgments (or measurements) yields a new judgment, which is less noisy ... than the individual judgments'.[35] Put simply, the decision taken by a representative organ of experts may be more reliable than the one taken by one individual person. At the same time, however, the involvement of an alternating group of external experts whose mandate is limited in time makes it more difficult to establish consistency in the appointment process. Arbitral institutions may reduce the risk of such inconsistencies through working procedures that facilitate the transfer of knowledge and information on practices in the appointment process. Under the DIS Rules, for example, the Secretariat advises the members of the Appointing Committee on existing practices in comparable situations and makes non-binding recommendations.[36] Other arbitral institutions publish information regarding their practices on appointments and challenges.[37]

And still, the considerable degree of authority that the organs in charge of appointments have gives cause to ask the question that the Roman poet Juvenal famously articulated in his *Satires*: 'Quis custodiet ipsos custodes?'[38] Who controls the guardians? How can it be ensured that the organs in charge of appointments do not misuse their powers?

The answer is that arbitral institutions have devised a number of mechanisms in order to prevent abuses of powers. These mechanisms already come into

---

30 Article 9 HKIAC Rules (2018). See also C. Bao and M. Moser, *A Guide to the HKIAC Rules*, OUP, Oxford 2017, pp. 97–98 (discussing the previous version of the HKIAC Rules).

31 Article 2.4 HKIAC Rules (2018).

32 Article 2.4 HKIAC Rules (2018).

33 Para. 2.1 2018 Practice Note.

34 Para. 24 2018 Practice Note.

35 D. Kahnemann, O. Sibony and C.R. Sunstein, *Noise – A Flaw in Human Judgment*, Little, Brown Spark, New York/Boston/London 2021, p. 84.

36 Article 6.7 DIS Internal Rules (Annex I).

37 This, for example, is the case for the LCIA and the ICC.

38 Juvenal, Satire VI, lines 347–48 ('Who will guard the guards themselves?').

play at the time of selecting the individuals to serve as members of the organ in charge of the appointment process. Generally, arbitral institutions provide that the members of the organ in charge of the appointment of arbitrators are appointed by another, external organ. The LCIA Court Members, for example, are not appointed by the LCIA Court Members whose terms are ending. Rather, they are appointed by the LCIA Board of Directors, which is not involved in the administration of dispute resolution procedures.[39] Similar observations hold true for the members of the DIS Appointment Committee, who are appointed by the DIS Board of Directors.[40] The ICC Court Members are appointed by the ICC World Council based on the proposal of an ICC National Committee or Group.[41] Alternate members as well as Vice-Presidents are appointed based on the suggestion by the President of the Court.[42] Upon selection, the members of the organ in charge of appointment have a limited term, which is typically renewable only once.[43]

The selection of the members of the appointment authority is not the only parameter that is subject to such safeguards. Arbitral institutions have also set up working procedures in order to balance the influence of the organ in charge of appointment during the appointment process. The LCIA Rules provide, for example, that the President of the LCIA Court shall only be eligible if the parties agree to nominate him or her as sole or presiding arbitrator.[44] Restrictions also apply with respect to the nomination of Vice-Presidents and the Chairman of the LCIA Board of Directors. They are only eligible to serve as arbitrators if nominated in writing by at least one party or by the other arbitrators, provided that they will not have taken or will not take any part thereafter in any function of the LCIA Court or LCIA relating to such arbitration.[45] The HKIAC Rules provide for a similar regime.[46]

Far-reaching safeguards to ensure the integrity of the appointment process are also foreseen in the DIS Rules. Pursuant to the DIS Rules, every member of the Appointing Committee has an obligation to 'promptly disclose' any conflict of interest. Upon disclosure, that member may no longer participate in decisions pertaining to the given arbitration.[47] An alternative member is designated to act in lieu of the conflicted member.[48] The DIS Appointing Committee Members shall

---

[39] M. Scherer, L. Richman and R. Gerbay, *Arbitrating under the 2020 LCIA Rules: A User's Guide*, Kluwer, Alphen aan den Rijn 2021, Chapter 1, para. 10.
[40] Article 6.2 DIS Internal Rules (Annex I).
[41] Article 3(3) Statutes of the International Court of Arbitration (Appendix I).
[42] Article 3(2) and (3) Statutes of the International Court of Arbitration (Appendix I).
[43] Article 3(5) Statutes of the International Court of Arbitration (Appendix I).
[44] Article 5.10 LCIA Rules (2020).
[45] Article 5.10 LCIA Rules (2020).
[46] Para. 2.1 2018 Practice Note on Appointment of Arbitrators.
[47] Article 6.4 DIS Internal Rules (Annex I).
[48] Article 6.5 DIS Internal Rules (Annex I).

abide by section 3 of the DIS Integrity Principles. These principles provide, inter alia, that the DIS Appointing Committee Members shall not appoint members of the Board of Directors, the Advisory Board, the DIS Secretariat or the DIS's external auditors as arbitrators, nor shall they accept mandates as arbitrators in arbitration proceedings under the DIS Arbitration Rules during their term of office.[49]

In conclusion, the Analysed Rules all provide for a specific organ in charge of the appointment process. Various mechanisms ensure the independence and impartiality of the organ itself. Apart from rules regarding the composition of the organ, the term of the organ's members and the ability of the organ's members to serve as arbitrators, the Analysed Rules include working procedures on how the organ reaches its decisions.

2.3. THE METHOD FOR THE APPOINTMENT OF ARBITRATORS

It is not only the authority appointing arbitrators itself that may have an impact upon their independence and impartiality. The specific method of appointment also matters. In this respect, there has been a lively debate as to whether it is time to depart from the existing paradigm of party involvement in the selection of arbitrators. The question has been raised whether it would be preferable to have an arbitral institution or the competent appointing authority select all arbitrators.[50] Without doubt, this way of proceeding could lead to a more balanced tribunal in situations of information asymmetries between the parties and it might be conducive to securing the independence and impartiality of the arbitrators. After all, there would no longer be any basis for concerns about bias created by the prospect of repeat appointments by one of the parties.

However, there are also strong reasons militating against this approach. Specifically, a party's ability to influence the composition of the arbitral tribunal is said to be one of the main advantages of arbitration, which has contributed to its success.[51] This ability to participate in the composition of the arbitral tribunal is a basis for trust in the entire arbitral process, which enhances the legitimacy of the proceedings. It may also contribute to the quality of the proceedings, as the parties will likely have superior knowledge of the case that may allow them to select arbitrators who are well versed in the matters relevant to a given case.[52] Against this background, institutional rules endorse a disputing parties paradigm for the constitution of the arbitral tribunal.

---

[49]   Article 6.1 DIS Internal Rules (Annex I) and section 3 DIS Integrity Principles.

[50]   J. Paulsson, 'Moral Hazard in International Dispute Resolution' [2010] *ICSID Review* 339.

[51]   Queen Mary University and White & Case, *2018 International Arbitration Survey: The Evolution of International Arbitration*, Queen Mary University, London 2018, http://www.arbitration.qmul.ac.uk/research/2018/.

[52]   G. Born, *International Commercial Arbitration*, 3rd ed., Kluwer, Alphen aan den Rijn 2021, pp. 1766–67.

2.3.1. Sole Arbitrators

As far as the modalities for the selection of sole arbitrators are concerned, various institutions provide – by way of a default rule – that the arbitrator be jointly nominated by the parties.[53] The Analysed Rules accord a large degree of discretion to the parties to agree on a specific procedure for this purpose.[54]

Absent such a joint nomination, the appointment shall be made by the institution.[55] In this respect, some arbitral institutions provide for a formalised process involving the parties. For example, the HKIAC will propose at least one candidate to the parties and set a time limit for comments. If no party objects or raises justifiable concerns, the HKIAC will generally proceed to appoint that candidate.[56]

Under the ICDR Rules, a list procedure applies absent any other agreement by the parties.[57] The Administrator shall simultaneously send an identical list of candidates to the parties. If the parties cannot agree on a candidate, they have 15 days to strike names they object to and rank the remaining candidates. The Administrator shall invite an arbitrator to serve from the persons approved on the lists and in accordance with the order of mutual preference.[58]

Under the ICC Rules, the parties may agree that the appointment should occur in consultation between the parties and the Secretariat. For this purpose, they may agree on a list procedure.[59]

2.3.2. Modalities of Appointing Three-Member Tribunals

Where a tribunal has to be composed of three members, many arbitral institutions allow each party to designate one co-arbitrator.[60] The two co-arbitrators are then as a default rule invited to nominate the presiding arbitrator.[61] Where a party or the two co-arbitrators do not nominate an arbitrator, the arbitral institutions become responsible for the selection and appointment.[62]

Things look different under the ICC and SIAC Rules; there, the appointment of the presiding arbitrator through the institution is the default rule and it applies

---

[53] Article 10.1 SIAC Rules (2016).
[54] Article 7.3 HKIAC Rules (2018) and Article 12.2 ICDR Rules (2021).
[55] Article 7.1 HKIAC Rules (2018).
[56] Para. 25 2018 Practice Note.
[57] Article 13.1 ICDR Rules (2021). See also M. Gusy and J. Hosking, *A Guide to the ICDR International Arbitration Rules*, 2nd ed., OUP, Oxford 2019, pp. 128–29 (discussing the previous version of the ICDR Rules).
[58] Article 13.6 ICDR Rules (2021).
[59] ICC Note to the Parties and Arbitral Tribunals on the Conduct of the Arbitration under the ICC Rules of Arbitration (2021), para. 38.
[60] Article 12.1 DIS Rules (2018).
[61] Article 8.1 HKIAC Rules (2018); Article 12.2 DIS Rules (2018).
[62] Article 12.2 and 12.3 DIS Rules (2018).

unless otherwise agreed by the parties.[63] Under the ICC Rules, in exceptional cases, the Court may even override an agreement by the parties on the method of constitution of the arbitral tribunal and appoint each member of the arbitral tribunal. The Court may do so 'to avoid a significant risk of unequal treatment and unfairness that may affect the validity of the award'.[64]

2.3.3. Modalities of Constituting the Tribunal in Multi-Party Arbitrations

Special rules apply in situations of multi-party arbitrations. In this respect, the Analysed Rules generally provide that the claimant or claimants jointly and the respondent or respondents jointly shall nominate one co-arbitrator. The co-arbitrators or the arbitral institution shall then respectively nominate and appoint the presiding arbitrator. As we will explain in greater detail below, the Analysed Rules thereby reflect restrictions imposed by the regulatory framework mandating equal treatment of the parties.[65]

The rules differ as to what happens in the event that the claimant or claimants jointly or the respondent or respondents jointly do not agree on a joint nomination of a co-arbitrator:

- The LCIA Rules provide that where (i) there are more than two parties and (ii) these parties have agreed that each party may nominate an arbitrator and (iii) the parties have not agreed that the disputing parties represent collectively two sides, the LCIA Court shall appoint the arbitral tribunal.[66] The SIAC Rules take a similar approach and state that the President shall appoint all three arbitrators absent a joint nomination by the claimants or respondents.[67]
- The HKIAC Rules provide for some more flexibility. Where the parties fail to designate co-arbitrators or if they do not all agree that they represent two separate sides (as claimant and respondent) for the purposes of designating arbitrators, the HKIAC *may* appoint all members with or without regard to the designation made by the parties.[68] The ICC Rules[69] and the ICDR Rules[70] endorse a similar approach.

---

[63] Article 11.5 ICC Rules (2021); Article 11.3 SIAC Rules (2016).
[64] Article 12.9 ICC Rules (2021).
[65] See below section 3.1 with reference to the *Dutco* decision.
[66] Article 8.1 LCIA Rules (2020).
[67] Article 12.2 SIAC Rules (2016). J. Choong, M. Mangan and N. Lingard, *A Guide to the SIAC Arbitration Rules*, 2nd ed., OUP, Oxford 2018, pp. 142–43.
[68] Article 8.2(c) HKIAC Rules (2018). See also C. Bao and M. Moser, *A Guide to the HKIAC Rules*, OUP, Oxford 2017, pp. 93–96 (discussing the previous version of the HKIAC Rules).
[69] Article 12.6 ICC Rules (2021); Article 12.8 ICC Rules (2021).
[70] Article 13.5 ICDR Rules (2021). See also M. Gusy and J. Hosking, *A Guide to the ICDR International Arbitration Rules*, 2nd ed., OUP, Oxford 2019, p. 125 (discussing the previous version of the ICDR Rules).

- Under the DIS Rules, the Appointing Committee may either, after consultation with the parties, select and appoint a co-arbitrator for the parties who have not jointly nominated a co-arbitrator and appoint the co-arbitrator nominated by the opposing side or select and appoint the co-arbitrators for both sides, in which case a prior party nomination shall be deemed void.[71]

From the foregoing, it can be derived that the Analysed Rules are evidence of a considerable degree of convergence regarding the requirements relating to the constitution of the arbitral tribunal.

2.4. THE STANDARDS FOR INDEPENDENCE AND IMPARTIALITY

As far as the specific standards of independence and impartiality are concerned, similar observations can be made.

First, the Analysed Rules all oblige arbitrators to be and remain impartial and independent of the parties throughout the entire proceedings.[72] The Analysed Rules typically require arbitrators to sign a declaration confirming their independence and impartiality.[73] Some rules offer more detailed guidance in this respect. The LCIA Rules, for example, specify that no arbitrator shall act in the arbitration as an advocate for any party and that no arbitrator shall advise any party on the parties' dispute or the outcome of the arbitration.[74]

Second, the Analysed Rules all provide for a duty of disclosure.[75] This duty of disclosure helps to overcome information asymmetries between the prospective arbitrator and the parties, thus allowing the parties to get a better picture of potential conflicts which may be triggered by information in the possession of the arbitrators. By sharing the disclosed information with the parties, the arbitrator establishes transparency. The parties are in turn able to determine whether they agree with the potential arbitrator's assessment that the facts disclosed do not impact his or her independence or impartiality.[76] If they do not agree, they may decide to object to the appointment of the arbitrator or

---

[71] Article 20.3 DIS Rules (2018). See also A. Sessler and P. Heckel, '§2.04: Multi-Contract Arbitration, Multi-Party Arbitration, Joinder, Article 20: Three-Member Arbitral Tribunal in Multi-Party Arbitrations' in G. Flecke-Giammarco et al. (eds), *The DIS Arbitration Rules – An Article-by-Article Commentary*, Kluwer, Alphen aan den Rijn 2020, pp. 312–13.

[72] Article 9.1 DIS Rules (2018); Article 11.1 ICC Rules (2021); Article 13.1 ICDR Rules (2021); Article 13.1 SIAC Rules (2016).

[73] Article 9.4 DIS Rules (2018); Article 11.2 ICC Rules (2021); Article 13.2 ICDR (2021); Article 11.4 HKIAC Rules (2018).

[74] Article 5.3 LCIA Rules (2020).

[75] Article 11.4 HKIAC Rules (2018); Article 13.5 SIAC Rules (2016).

[76] F. Ferrari and F. Rosenfeld, *International Commercial Arbitration – A Comparative Introduction*, Elgar, Cheltenham, UK/Northampton, MA, USA 2021, pp. 75–76.

to raise a challenge if he or she has already been appointed. If they fail to do so, they risk being precluded from relying upon the disclosed fact as a basis to object to the arbitrator at a later point in time or to seek post-award relief. This duty of disclosure is ongoing and subject to a requirement of timeliness during the proceedings.

However, the Analysed Rules differ as to whether one should examine an arbitrator's independence and impartiality from the perspective of the parties, an objective bystander or both.

- The ICDR Rules reference a merely objective criterion by focusing on circumstances and facts that could give rise to 'justifiable doubts' about an arbitrator's independence and impartiality.[77]
- The ICC Rules, in contrast, refer to the perspective of the parties for assessing an arbitrator's independence. They require disclosing 'any facts or circumstances which might be of such a nature as to call into question the arbitrator's independence in the eyes of the parties, as well as any circumstances that could give rise to reasonable doubts as to the arbitrator's impartiality.'[78]
- Other arbitration rules require the assessment to be made from the perspective of 'a reasonable person in the position of a party'.[79]

Some arbitration rules also impose a duty of disclosure on the parties. For example, under the ICC Rules, each party must inform the Secretariat, the arbitral tribunal and other parties of the existence of any third-party funder having an economic interest in the outcome of the arbitration.[80] Inter-company funding within a group of companies, fee arrangements between a party and its counsel as well as indirect interests such as those of a bank having granted a loan in the ordinary course of its ongoing activities are generally not captured by this provision.[81] Yet another approach has been adopted under the ICDR Rules, which also stipulate a duty of disclosure for the parties.[82] If a party fails to comply with this duty within a reasonable period of time after it becomes aware of the circumstances to be disclosed, it is considered to have waived its right to challenge the arbitrator on that ground.[83]

Third, the Analysed Rules also offer, in one way or another, guidance on ex parte communications. The general approach taken is in the Analysed Rules is

---

[77] Article 13.2 ICDR Rules (2021).
[78] Article 11.2 ICC Rules (2021).
[79] Article 9.4 DIS Rules (2018); Article 5.4 LCIA Rules (2020).
[80] Article 11.7 ICC Rules (2021).
[81] ICC Note to the Parties and Arbitral Tribunals on the Conduct of the Arbitration under the ICC Rules of Arbitration (2021), para. 21.
[82] Article 13.3 ICDR Rules (2021).
[83] Article 13.5 ICDR Rules (2021).

that ex parte communications are not permitted.[84] Exceptions apply during the formation of the arbitral tribunal. Many rules provide that a party may have limited ex parte communications with a prospective party-appointed arbitrator to advise the candidate of the general nature of the controversy and to discuss the candidate's qualifications, availability, or impartiality and independence.[85] Some arbitral rules also allow for ex parte communications between a co-arbitrator and a party to discuss the suitability of candidates for selection as presiding arbitrator in the scenario where the parties have a say in this selection.[86] The parties may be required to reach a separate agreement for this purpose. For example, the ICC Note provides that arbitrators may communicate with parties or party representatives on an ex parte basis for the purpose of selecting the president to the extent that all parties agree.[87] Ex parte communications with the presiding arbitrator him- or herself are generally not allowed.[88]

2.5. CONSEQUENCES OF A BREACH

Where an arbitrator fails to comply with his or her duty of independence and impartiality, the parties may challenge the arbitrator. Unsurprisingly, all the Analysed Rules provide for a challenge mechanism. However, the procedure to be followed for a challenge, the body deciding the challenge and the precise standards governing the decision regarding the challenge differ.

As far as the timeliness of the challenge is concerned, the Analysed Rules provide deadlines within a range of 14[89] to 30[90] days after the party filing the challenge first became aware of the facts and circumstances giving rise to the challenge.

The institution usually transmits the challenge to the challenged arbitrator, the other arbitrators and the other party, who are granted the opportunity to comment within a fixed period of time.[91] Things look different under the ICDR Rules, which provide that the challenge shall not be sent to any member of the tribunal.[92] Rather, the Administrator shall notify the other party of the challenge

---

[84] Article 3 ICC Rules (2021); Article 11.4 LCIA Rules (2020); Article 4.5 DIS Rules (2018); Article 14.6 ICDR Rules (2021).

[85] Article 11.5 HKIAC Rules (2018); Article 11.5 LCIA Rules (2020); Article 13.6 SIAC Rules (2016).

[86] Article 13.6 ICDR Rules (2021).

[87] ICC Note to the Parties and Arbitral Tribunals on the Conduct of the Arbitration under the ICC Rules of Arbitration (2021), para. 68.

[88] Article 11.5 HKIAC Rules (2018); Article 13.6 ICDR Rules (2021); Article 13.6 SIAC Rules (2016).

[89] Article 15.2 DIS Rules (2018); Article 10.3 LCIA Rules (2020).

[90] Article 14.2 ICC Rules (2021).

[91] Article 15.3 DIS Rules (2018); Article 14.3 ICC Rules (2021).

[92] Article 15.1 ICDR Rules (2021).

and give that party an opportunity to respond. The Administrator shall then notify the tribunal that a challenge has been received without identifying the party challenging. The Administrator may request additional information from the challenged arbitrator relating to the challenge.[93]

As far as the further challenge procedure is concerned, the LCIA Rules clarify that the decision on the challenge may require further materials and information from the challenging party, the challenged arbitrator, other parties and other members of the arbitral tribunal.[94] In exceptional cases, the LCIA Court has granted a request to hold a hearing on the challenge.[95] While the challenge is pending, the arbitral tribunal may proceed with the arbitration.[96]

Differences exist as to the body deciding upon the challenge: under the DIS Rules, the body deciding upon the challenge is the Arbitration Council.[97] This organ consists of at least 15 members who shall be 'nationals of at least five different countries' and 'have practical experience in domestic and international arbitration'.[98] The Council Members are appointed by the DIS Board of Directors for a four-year term, which is renewable once.[99] Decisions are taken by a Case Committee to which an arbitration has been assigned.[100] Such a Case Committee shall consist of three Council Members.[101] The Secretariat prepares a written statement advising the Case Committee of any existing practice of other Case Committees in comparable cases. It may also contain non-binding recommendations.[102] Decisions are taken by majority and require a quorum of two of its members.[103] The reasons are not communicated.[104]

Under the ICC Rules, the Court will decide on the admissibility and merits of the challenge.[105] Upon request of any party, the Court will communicate the reasons for its decision regarding the challenge.[106] In exceptional cases, however,

---

[93]   Article 15.2 ICDR Rules (2021).

[94]   Article 10.4 LCIA Rules (2020).

[95]   See T.W. Walsh and R. Teitelbaum, 'The LCIA Court Decisions on Challenges to Arbitrators: An Introduction' (2011) 27 *Arb. Int.* 283, 286; see also M. Scherer, L. Richman and R. Gerbay, *Arbitrating under the 2020 LCIA Rules: A User's Guide*, Kluwer, Alphen aan den Rijn 2021, Chapter 11, para. 22.

[96]   Article 15.5 DIS Rules (2018); Article 11.9 HKIAC Rules (2018).

[97]   Article 15.4 DIS Rules (2018); see A. Meier and L. Gerhardt, '§2.03: The Arbitral Tribunal, Article 15, Appointment of the Arbitrators' in G. Flecke-Giammarco et al. (eds), *The DIS Arbitration Rules – An Article-by-Article Commentary*, Kluwer, Alphen aan den Rijn 2020, p. 245.

[98]   Article 3.1 DIS Internal Rules (Annex I).

[99]   Article 3.2 and 3.3 DIS Internal Rules (Annex I).

[100]   Article 3.6 DIS Internal Rules (Annex I).

[101]   Article 4.1 DIS Internal Rules (Annex I).

[102]   Article 4.1 DIS Internal Rules (Annex I).

[103]   Article 4.4 DIS Internal Rules (Annex I).

[104]   Article 9.3 DIS Internal Rules (Annex I).

[105]   Article 14.3 ICC Rules (2021).

[106]   ICC Note to the Parties and Arbitral Tribunals on the Conduct of the Arbitration under the ICC Rules of Arbitration (2021), para. 46 and Article 5 of Appendix II.

the Court may decide not to communicate the reasons for its decision.[107] Similarly, the LCIA Court decides on challenges under the LCIA Rules. The LCIA's decision is made in writing with reasons.[108] Under the ICDR Rules, the Administrator shall decide on the challenge in its discretion.[109]

The Analysed Rules also differ in terms of the specific standards for a challenge. While the Analysed Rules typically refer to 'justifiable doubts'[110] about an arbitrator's independence and impartiality, the DIS Rules merely refer to non-compliance with the requirement of independence and impartiality under Article 9.1 without further specifying the applicable standard.[111] Some rules also allow for a challenge if an arbitrator becomes unable or unfit to act. Under the LCIA Rules, unfitness to act is given if an arbitrator (i) acts in deliberate violation of the Arbitration Agreement, (ii) does not act fairly or impartially as between the parties, or (iii) does not conduct or participate in the arbitration with reasonable efficiency, diligence and industry.[112]

Finally, the Analysed Rules diverge as to whether a challenged arbitrator may withdraw on his or her own initiative. Under the ICC Rules and the DIS Rules, such a unilateral withdrawal is not possible. Unless the parties agree otherwise, the competent organ must accept the challenge or resignation of the arbitrator.[113] Other rules provide for a different regime. The ICDR Rules, for example, provide that an arbitrator may withdraw absent agreement on the challenge after consultation with the Administrator. Such withdrawal shall not be deemed to imply the acceptance of the grounds for a challenge.[114] The LCIA Rules, SIAC Rules and the HKIAC Rules reflect a similar approach.[115]

2.6. INTERIM CONCLUSION

The interim conclusion to be drawn is that the Analysed Rules display a considerable degree of convergence in the approaches towards independence and impartiality. However, there remain subtle differences in the regulatory approaches. The regime on independence and impartiality is not uniform.

---

[107] Ibid., para. 47.
[108] Article 10.6 LCIA Rules (2020). See also M. Scherer, L. Richman and R. Gerbay, *Arbitrating under the 2020 LCIA Rules: A User's Guide*, Kluwer, Alphen aan den Rijn 2021, Chapter 11, para. 23.
[109] Article 15.3 ICDR Rules (2021).
[110] Article 10.1 LCIA Rules (2020); Article 11.6 HKIAC Rules (2018); Article 15.1 ICDR Rules (2021); Article 14 SIAC Rules (2016); Article 10.1 LCIA Rules (2016).
[111] Article 15.1 in conjunction with Article 9.1 of the DIS Rules (2018).
[112] Article 10.2 LCIA Rules (2020).
[113] Article 16.1 DIS Rules (2018); Article 15.1 ICC Rules (2021).
[114] Article 15.2 ICDR Rules (2021).
[115] Article 10.5 and 10.6 LCIA Rules (2020); Article 10.9 and 10.10 HKIAC Rules (2018); Article 10.5 SIAC Rules (2016).

3. A POST-AWARD PERSPECTIVE ON THE INSTITUTIONAL FRAMEWORK ON INDEPENDENCE AND IMPARTIALITY

At this juncture, it may well be useful to take a step back and look at the regime outlined above from a post-award perspective. In what follows below, we will do so, making a distinction between the scope and the standard of review.

3.1. SCOPE OF REVIEW

The scope of review concerns the question of which issues courts can examine at the post-award stage.[116] Generally speaking, it is clear that courts can review issues of independence and impartiality in the context both of domestic setting-aside proceedings and of recognition and enforcement proceedings under the New York Convention.

Under the New York Convention, there are two main gateways to consider issues of independence and impartiality: on the one hand, courts may refuse recognition and enforcement of an arbitral award under Article V(2)(b), if the enforcement would be contrary to the public policy of the state in which enforcement is sought.[117] On the other hand, courts may refuse recognition and enforcement of an arbitral award under Article V(1)(d), if the arbitral authority or the procedure was not in line with the parties' agreement or, absent such agreement, the law of the seat.[118] By selecting a set of arbitration rules, parties reach agreement on the provisions contained therein. A deviation from these rules may therefore constitute a ground for refusal of recognition and enforcement.

When interpreting Article V(1)(d) of the New York Convention, many courts apply a threshold. This means that they require the deviation to be significant, be outcome-determinative, cause prejudice or otherwise have a weight equivalent to that of the other grounds for refusal of recognition and enforcement under

---

[116] On the scope of post-award review, see F. Ferrari and F. Rosenfeld, *International Commercial Arbitration – A Comparative Introduction*, Elgar, Cheltenham, UK/Northampton, MA, USA 2021, pp. 173–90.

[117] For recent comments regarding this provision, see A. Bonomi, 'The Concept of Public Policy under the 1958 Convention: An Autonomous Interpretation?' in F. Ferrari and F. Rosenfeld (eds), *Autonomous versus Domestic Concepts under the New York Convention*, Kluwer, Alphen aan den Rijn 2021, pp. 315–47.

[118] In respect of this provisions, see most recently F. Ferrari and F. Rosenfeld, 'The Interplay of Autonomous Concepts and Municipal Law under Article V (1) (d) of the New York Convention' in F. Ferrari and F. Rosenfeld (eds), *Autonomous versus Domestic Concepts under the New York Convention*, Kluwer, Alphen aan den Rijn 2021, pp. 273–97.

the New York Convention.[119] However, courts have applied rather low standards when examining whether the lack of independence and impartiality of the tribunal affected the outcome of the arbitration.[120] For example, in a case where one of three arbitrators had been successfully challenged, the court held that this constituted a ground for refusal of recognition and enforcement, even though the tribunal had reached a unanimous decision and the two remaining arbitrators could have rendered the same award by themselves. The court reasoned that judicial decision-making is a deliberative process, which may well be affected by the participation of a biased arbitrator.[121]

Exceptionally, parties have sought to invoke issues of independence and impartiality through the prism of other Convention grounds. A case decided by the Superior Court of Justice of Catalonia stands as an example.[122] The case concerned an arbitral award that had been rendered under the rules of the Independent Film and Television Association (IFTA) in Los Angeles. The Spanish respondent, Wide Pictures, argued that this institution lacked the required independence and impartiality to administer arbitration proceedings, because it allegedly represented the interests of North American film producers, including the US claimant, Sierra Affinity. For this reason, Wide Pictures argued, the arbitration agreement was invalid.

The Supreme Court of Catalonia rejected this argument. It found that the IFTA was constituted by both American and foreign producers and distributors, including Spanish companies. According to the Court, the parties were at liberty to agree to arbitrate under the rules of such an institution. It held:

> It is not illegal for professionals of the same sector to group in associations and to decide, in the exercise of their autonomy in respect of matters of which they may freely dispose [*de libre disposición*], to solve the disputes among themselves by arbitration. Things would be different if, because of one party being a member and the other not, the former influenced the administration of the specific arbitration or occupied directive positions in the association at the time of [the arbitration's] administration, or if the arbitrator

---

[119] Restatement of the U.S. Law of International Commercial and Investor-State Arbitration (Proposed Final Draft 1), Am. L. Inst. 2019, Section 4.13; OLG Köln (Court of Appeals Cologne), 26.02.2014, SchiedsVZ 2014, 203, 204–05; BayOLG (Court of Appeals Bavaria), 23.09.2004, BeckRS 2009, 21310; Bundesgericht (Supreme Court of Switzerland), 08.02.1978, (1986) XI *Y.B. Comm. Arb.* 538.

[120] C. Borris and R. Hennecke, 'Improper Tribunal Composition or Flawed Proceedings, Article V (1)(d)' in R. Wolff (ed.), *New York Convention: Article by Article Commentary*, 2nd ed., Beck/Hart/Nomos, Munich/Worcester/Baden-Baden 2019, 355.

[121] See BGH (Supreme Court of Germany), 11.12.2014, BeckRS 2015, 08903. The decision concerned an application for the setting aside of an arbitral award. The applicable standard mirrored that of Article V(1)(d) of the New York Convention.

[122] Tribunal Superior de Justícia de Catalunya (Superior Court of Justice of Catalonia), 25.03.2013, (2013) XXXVIII *Y.B. Comm. Arb.* 465, para. 28.

Commercial Institutional Arbitration

appointed by IFTA had a relation with Claimant or the parties were given an unequal treatment. This is neither argued nor proved in any manner in this case.[123]

Whatever the ground upon which a lack of independence and impartiality is based, courts may be required to examine institutional arbitration rules at the post-award stage. This interface between the post-award regime and institutional arbitration rules risks producing norm collisions. Such norm collisions may result from the fact that institutional rules are privately set norms applicable by virtue of the parties' autonomous choice to arbitrate under these rules. The parties' choice may in a given case be contrary to mandatory norms and breach public policy.

One decision illustrating these tensions between party autonomy and mandatory norms is the *Dutco* decision of the French Supreme Court,[124] which arose from the following facts. In 1981, the companies Siemens, BKMI and Dutco had entered into an agreement for the construction of a plant in Oman. The agreement provided for ICC arbitration with three arbitrators. In 1986, Dutco commenced ICC arbitration proceedings against Siemens and BKMI. Dutco appointed one co-arbitrator and Siemens and BKMI jointly nominated a co-arbitrator, but did so under protest. The two co-arbitrators nominated the presiding arbitrator. The ICC Court confirmed all three arbitrators in accordance with the then applicable ICC Rules. At the post-award stage, the French Supreme Court held that the ICC framework regarding the constitution of the tribunal resulted in the unequal treatment of the parties. This was because it had permitted a single claimant to nominate one arbitrator, while multiple respondents with diverging interests had to rely on a joint nomination. The French Supreme Court found that this was contrary to public policy.[125]

Another example is the *Nykcool* decision, which concerned the setting aside of an arbitral award rendered under the rules of the Chambre Arbitrale Maritime de Paris.[126] The award debtor sought the setting aside of the arbitral award on the ground that the arbitrators lacked the required independence and impartiality. The award creditor objected on the ground that the award debtor had not raised a challenge in a timely manner as foreseen under the rules of the Chambre Arbitrale Maritime de Paris. These rules provided that challenges of an arbitrator had to be brought 15 days after the initiation of the arbitral proceedings irrespective of whether the respective party had obtained knowledge of the

---

[123] Ibid.

[124] Cass. 1re civ., 07.01.1992, *BKMI Industrieanlagen GmbH & Siemens AG v. Dutco Construction*, no. 89-18.708, 89-18.726.

[125] As set forth above, the current ICC Rules contemplate that the ICC Court may appoint all members of the arbitral tribunal to prevent such a form of unequal treatment. See also Cour de Cassation, 09.11.2022, *Vidatel v. PT Ventures SGPS et al.*, no. 21-17.203.

[126] Cour d'appel Paris, 30.10.2012, *Chambre Arbitrale Maritime de Paris (CAMP) et Generali Iard v. Nykcool AB*, no. 11/08277 [2013] 8 Gaz Pal 15.

Intersentia

circumstances giving rise to the challenge by that date. However, the Court of Appeals found that such a 15-day deadline was invalid and dismissed the defence of procedural estoppel.[127] The Court of Cassation confirmed the Court of Appeal's decision.[128]

The UK Supreme Court has also shown a marked willingness to examine issues of independence and impartiality irrespective of what the parties agreed to when selecting institutional arbitration rules. It ruled in the recent *Halliburton* decision:

> It is not necessary to determine whether the tests as to the nature of the doubts in the UNCITRAL Model Law, the IBA Guidelines and the LCIA Rules are precisely the same as those of English law. The important point is that the test in English law, involving the fair-minded and informed observer, requires objectivity and detachment in relation to the appearance of bias.[129]

Based on a similar reasoning, the Court adopted a test of disclosure that differs from the ones provided for by the LCIA and ICC Rules. It held:

> Article 11 of the ICC Arbitration Rules and article 5.4 of the LCIA Rules relating to disclosure have a similar focus on the perceptions of the parties to an arbitration. This subjective approach to the duty of disclosure in the ... rules of the arbitral institutions addresses the perception of the parties to an arbitration who are people or entities involved in a stressful and often expensive dispute. English law, by contrast, adopts an objective test by looking to the judgment of the fair-minded and informed observer.[130]

One could continue to list such decisions, which show that the standards of independence and impartiality as applicable at the post-award stage may differ from those agreed under institutional rules.

Some authorities question this approach and argue that state courts should respect the parties' agreement on the applicable standards of independence and impartiality, even when the parties agree on lower standards of independence and impartiality. Gary Born, for example, argues that 'there is substantial presumptive force to the position that parties should generally be free to agree upon predisposed arbitrators, provided that this is done transparently and that the parties are treated equally'.[131] Born posits that jurisdictions such as the United States have clearly acknowledged the parties' freedom to agree upon

---

[127] Ibid.

[128] Cass 1re civ., 31.03.2016, no. 14-20.396.

[129] *Halliburton Company v. Chubb Bermuda Insurance Ltd (formerly known as Ace Bermuda Insurance Ltd)* [2020] UKSC 48, para. 54.

[130] Ibid., para. 72.

[131] G. Born, *International Commercial Arbitration*, 3rd ed., Kluwer, Alphen aan den Rijn 2021, p. 1948.

non-neutral co-arbitrators.[132] This would be consistent with the principle of party autonomy[133] being 'one of the defining characteristics of arbitration'.[134] In support of his position, Born points to the fact that arbitration statutes allow objections to an arbitrator's independence and impartiality to be waived.[135]

However, this position may well be criticised. Arbitration has a dual foundation in party autonomy and the applicable arbitration framework.[136] It is the applicable arbitration framework, including arbitration statutes and the New York Convention, that defines to what extent state courts are required to uphold the parties' exercise in party autonomy. While some jurisdictions are more liberal and allow parties to define autonomously the standards of independence and impartiality,[137] most jurisdictions do not.

Restrictions may also apply with respect to the possibility of waiving objections to an arbitrator's independence and impartiality. The European Court of Human Rights (ECtHR) confirmed this in the case of *Beg SpA v. Italy*.[138] This case arose from an arbitration under the Arbitration Chamber of the Rome Chamber of Commerce (ACR) between the applicant Beg SpA (Beg) and the Italian company ENELPOWER. ENELPOWER appointed arbitrator N.I., who was at that time representing ENELPOWER's mother company ENEL in a civil dispute and had previously been vice-chairman and on the board of ENEL. N.I. did not disclose this and did not make any statement as to his independence and impartiality when accepting his appointment. Beg did not raise a challenge at the time but only raised the lack of independence and impartiality after the award had been rendered. The Italian courts rejected Beg's actions as untimely and noted that N.I.'s links with ENEL were well known at the time of the arbitration; Beg's failure to raise a challenge amounted to a waiver.[139] The ECtHR took a different view. According to the ECtHR, Beg could assume that no relationships and/or economic interests of N.I. existed.[140] It held that the Italian courts had incorrectly presumed Beg's knowledge of the circumstances giving rise to the challenge. Therefore, the ECtHR found that Beg had not waived the requirement of impartiality by failing to raise an objection or a challenge to N.I.'s appointment.[141] Applying autonomous standards of impartiality, the

---

[132] Ibid.
[133] Ibid., p. 1950.
[134] Ibid.
[135] Ibid.
[136] G.A. Bermann, 'International Arbitration and Private International Law' (2015) 381 *Recueil des cours* 41, 57; F. Ferrari and F. Rosenfeld, *International Commercial Arbitration – A Comparative Introduction*, Elgar, Cheltenham, UK/Northampton, MA, USA 2021, p. 49.
[137] See Restatement, §4.11.
[138] *Beg SpA v. Italy*, ECtHR decision of 20 May 2021, application no. 5312/11.
[139] Ibid., paras 25, 27.
[140] Ibid., para. 139.
[141] Ibid., para. 140.

ECtHR found that Italy had breached Article 6 of the European Convention on Human Rights.

One may certainly have a discussion as to whether this decision is correct and whether an arbitrator's duty of disclosure finds its limits in a duty to investigate on the part of the parties.[142] The rapporteurs do not want to revisit this question here, which they have discussed elsewhere.[143] The point to be made is simply that party autonomy is subject to limitations.[144] When exercising their post-award review, state courts are therefore not necessarily bound to apply the standards of independence and impartiality as applicable under institutional arbitration rules.

3.2. STANDARD OF REVIEW

A matter distinct from the scope of review is that of the standard of review, i.e. the question of whether a court at the post-award stage should pay deference to a prior determination by an arbitral institution or whether it should review decisions de novo.

Courts across jurisdictions have shown some reluctance to pay deference to decisions by arbitral institutions on challenges of arbitrators.[145] Swiss courts, for example, have emphasised that the authority to decide on a challenge cannot be finally delegated to an arbitral institution. They held that it would be incompatible with the Swiss legal order to entrust private bodies with the task of ensuring the independence and impartiality of the members of an arbitral tribunal.[146] For this reason, state courts would remain competent to 'review freely' whether or not there was an irregularity in the composition of the arbitral tribunal.[147]

---

[142] In case law, see e.g. *Fid. Fed. Bank, FSB v. Durga Ma Corp.*, 386 F.3d 1306, 2004 U.S. App. LEXIS 22535; *Lucent Techs., Inc. v. Tatung Co.*, 379 F.3d 24, 2004 U.S. App. LEXIS 15907. For the opposite view, see *Merit Ins. Co. v. Leatherby Ins. Co.*, 714 F.2d 673, 1983 U.S. App. LEXIS 25862 ('We do not want to encourage the losing party to every arbitration to conduct a background investigation of each of the arbitrators in an effort to uncover evidence of a former relationship with the adversary. This would only increase the cost and undermine the finality of arbitration, contrary to the purpose of the United States Arbitration Act of making arbitration a swift, inexpensive, and effective substitute for judicial dispute resolution').

[143] F. Ferrari and F. Rosenfeld, *International Commercial Arbitration – A Comparative Introduction*, Elgar, Cheltenham, UK/Northampton, MA, USA 2021, p. 78.

[144] Cf. G. Born, *International Commercial Arbitration*, 3rd ed., Kluwer, Alphen aan den Rijn 2021, p. 1952.

[145] For an exception, see OLG Schleswig (Court of Appeal Schleswig), 24.06.1999, (2004) XXIX *Y.B. Comm. Arb.* 687. The German court noted that the ICC Court's dismissal of the challenge constituted 'the end of the matter' as it did not appear to be 'clearly defective, e.g., for evident bias'.

[146] Swiss Federal Tribunal, *X GmbH v. Y Sàrl*, 02.05.2012, docket no. 2012, 4A_14/2012; Swiss Federal Tribunal, 06.01.2010, (2010) *ASA Bulletin* 772.

[147] Bundesgericht (Federal Supreme Court of Switzerland), 27.06.2012, DFT 4A_54/2012, 2.1.

US courts have propounded similar views. A US federal court was, for example, not willing to pay deference to a challenge decision of the American Arbitration Association. Considering the crucial importance of an arbitrator's neutrality, the Court found that the legislature had not intended to delegate decisions about this issue 'to the unfettered discretion of private business'.[148] Likewise, the Chancery Court of Delaware ruled in *Beebe Med. Center v. Insight Health Servs.* that agreeing to arbitrate under the Rules of the American Arbitration Association did not amount to a waiver of independent judicial review at the post-award stage.[149]

That said, the Court did not rule out that parties could agree to accept a challenge decision of an arbitral institution as final and binding by explicitly stating so in the arbitration agreement. This accords with the principle underlying the *First Options* decision:[150] insofar as parties can delegate competence-competence to an arbitral tribunal, it suggests that they are able to delegate powers to decide on the independence and impartiality of arbitrators to arbitral institutions.

4. CONCLUSION

In conclusion, the arbitrators' neutrality features prominently in institutional arbitration rules. While the Analysed Rules show a considerable degree of convergence, one can identify subtle nuances in their regulatory stances towards independence and impartiality. At the post-award regime, state courts may review whether an arbitral tribunal lacked the required independence and impartiality. At the interface between the post-award regime and institutional arbitration rules, norm collisions may occur. These may entail that states disregard the standards set forth in institutional arbitration rules and apply autonomous standards, as set forth in the applicable arbitration law. State courts show a marked hesitance to exercise deference when performing this review. This is a testament to the great value that legal orders attach to neutrality as one of the key pillars of justice in general, and arbitral justice in particular.

---

[148]   *Azteca Construction, Inc. v. ADR Consulting, Inc*, Court of Appeal, Third District, California, C045316.
[149]   *Beebe Med. Center v. Insight Health Servs*, 751 A.2d 426 (1999).
[150]   *First Options of Chicago, Inc. v. Kaplan*, 514 U.S. 938, 943 (1995).

Intersentia

THE INDEPENDENCE AND IMPARTIALITY OF ADJUDICATORS IN COMMODITIES ARBITRATION

Yuliya Chernykh[*]

1.	Criteria for the Selection of Adjudicators	159
2.	Which Authority Appoints Adjudicators?	163
3.	The Method for Appointing Adjudicators	163
4.	Methods to Balance the Appointing Authority's Influence on the Appointment of Adjudicators	165
5.	Parameters to Ensure that Adjudicators Act Independently and Impartially	166
6.	Consequences for Adjudicators of a Breach by Adjudicators of the Requirement to Act Independently and Impartially	168
7.	Enforceability of a Final Decision Rendered by an Adjudicator who Breached the Requirement to Act Independently and Impartially	169

Numerous trade associations offer arbitration to resolve disputes arising out of the global trade of commodities, such as metal, grain, cocoa, cotton, sugar vegetable oils, seeds, fats, etc. Among them are the London Metal Exchange (LME), the Grain and Feed Trade Association (GAFTA), the Federation of Oils, Seeds and Fats Associations (FOSFA), the Federation of Cocoa Commerce (FCC), the International Cotton Association (ICA), the British Coffee Association (BCA), the Refined Sugar Association (RSA), the Royal Dutch Grain and Feed Trade Association (Het Comité), etc. Each association develops a range of regularly updated standard contracts which incorporate arbitration clauses referring to the arbitration rules specifically designed by the respective trade associations.

While the precise approach towards the appointment and challenge of arbitrators may somewhat vary under the arbitration rules of these associations,

---

[*]   This report was finalised in August 2021.

they nevertheless share many similar features. Party appointments usually take place in the first-tier proceedings in cases where the proceedings are two-tiered, whereas in second-tier proceedings the parties have no role to play in the formation of the appeal boards.[1] For first-tier proceedings, associations as a rule maintain lists or directories of arbitrators. Arbitrators who are listed are professional traders or otherwise professionally involved in trade. With some exceptions,[2] none outside of the list of arbitrators can be appointed by the parties. Because of the maintained lists of arbitrators coupled with the limited community of traders and other special features of commodities trade, such as string arbitration,[3] *repeat* and *multiple* appointments raise less concern if compared with similar appointments in ordinary/conventional international commercial arbitration under the arbitration rules of non-specialist arbitration institutes. There is accordingly less expectation from arbitrators about the duty to disclose involved in commodities arbitration.

To give a meaningful overview of the regime governing impartiality and independence of arbitrators in commodities arbitration, this report relies on the regulation by two powerful trade associations: the Grain and Feed Trade Association (GAFTA) and the Federation of Oils, Seeds and Fats Associations (FOSFA). With more than 1,900 members in 100 countries, GAFTA assures that 80% of global trade in grain is conducted under its standard contract forms that incorporate the GAFTA Arbitration Rules No. 125.[4] With 1,190 members in

---

[1] Proceedings under the arbitration rules of GAFTA, FOSFA, the FCC, the ICA, the BCA and Het Comité are all two-tiered, whereas proceedings under the arbitration rules of the LME and the RSA are single-tiered. Rather exceptionally to the common approach, the FCC appoints the entire tribunal in the first-tier proceedings. The RSA also appoints the entire tribunal in its single-tiered arbitration proceedings.

[2] As a rare exception to the general rule, Het Comité accepts appointments of those who are not in the list upon its consent (Article 5 of the Conditions for Arbitration of Disputes subject to German-Dutch Contracts and Other C.I.F. and C.&F. Contracts).

[3] String arbitration arises out of string contracts, i.e. contracts that relate to the same goods successively resold between diverse parties on essentially the same terms, except for the price. Because a broad range of parties may be affected by the same problem, the entire idea behind such arbitration is to ensure that uniform solutions equally affect the initial seller and the ultimate buyer. Uniformity may be ensured only if all parties agree to the proceedings. The GAFTA Arbitration Rules No. 125 define string arbitration in the following words: '7.1 If a contract forms part of a string of contracts which contain materially identical terms (albeit that the price may vary under each contract), the tribunal may hold a single arbitration to determine the dispute between the first seller and the last buyer in the string as though they were parties who had contracted with each other, provided all the parties in the string of contracts agree to it in writing.'

[4] Information on the extent of the use of GAFTA's standard contract forms is available at https://www.gafta.com/All-Contracts. For completeness, it should be observed that in addition to the commonly used GAFTA Arbitration Rules No. 125, GAFTA also offers a specific set of rules for simplified proceedings – the GAFTA Expedited Arbitration Rules No. 126 and GAFTA Mediation Rules No. 128.

86 countries, FOSFA in turn affirms that 85% of global trade in oilseeds, oils and fats is conducted under its standard contracts forms that incorporate the FOSFA Rules of Arbitration and Appeal.[5]

1. CRITERIA FOR THE SELECTION OF ADJUDICATORS

Experience in trade is among the key criteria for the selection of arbitrators. Both GAFTA and FOSFA set the requirement of trade experience of no less than 10 years. Throughout the period of their listing, arbitrators are expected to maintain their engagement in trade, follow continuing professional development and annually notify the respective associations of their progress. Familiarity with the trade serves not only as a qualifying criterion for inclusion in the list or directory of arbitrators in the first place, but also as an important relevant consideration for individual appointment from the otherwise qualified arbitrators included in the respective lists. FOSFA enables all its trading, full broker and full non-trading member company representatives to act as arbitrators, provided that they are listed on the FOSFA website, are under the age of 75, and are active in the trade. At the same time, the association also holds a directory of those who regularly accept appointments and it is this directory which is commonly used as a list of arbitrators. GAFTA follows a more common path of a list separate from other members and limits the parties' right to appoint arbitrators to this list only. Arbitrators included in the lists or directories further 'compete' in terms of individual experience in various sub-fields (types of commodities), precise years in trade, their exact capacity of involvement in trade, etc.

Double-hatting, in the sense that arbitrators may also appear in the industry in other capacities rather than exclusively serving as arbitrators, of itself does not raise serious concerns. Qualified arbitrators are meant to be *active* in their trade.[6] They may secure involvement in the trade through various means, including acting as trade representatives or brokers. This somewhat more tolerant perception of the playing of various roles in comparison with investor-state dispute settlement (ISDS) should not mislead the reader. A general duty of independence and impartiality in commodities arbitration is still governed by the relevant laws of the seat, on most occasions the Arbitration Act of England and Wales 1996, and specific requirements of the applicable arbitration rules

---

[5] Information on the extent of the use of FOSFA standard contract forms is available at https://www.fosfa.org/about-us/.

[6] See para. 2(b) of the FOSFA Rules of Arbitration and Appeal, para. 1 of the Rules and Code of Conduct for Qualified Arbitrators and Qualified Mediators and a general overview of the current requirements for GAFTA qualified arbitrators available at https://www.gafta.com/Gafta-Qualified-Arbitrator-Status.

and codes of conduct. Arbitrators' previous direct involvement in either of the capacities in a particular transaction that gives rise to a dispute would inevitably undermine their duty of independence and impartiality and would not be tolerated, whereas mere active participation in a trade in various capacities would not be considered as an impermissible sign of apparent or actual bias. Both GAFTA and FOSFA expressly exclude the opportunity for first-tier arbitrators to accept trade representation roles in the respective second-tier proceedings or for a first-tier arbitrator to appear as a member of an appeal board in second-tier proceedings.[7]

Interestingly, legal training or experience in legal practice does not necessarily appear to be a competitive advantage. If combined with active private legal practice, it may even serve as an obstacle to inclusion in the list of arbitrators. Trade associations attempt to oppose unnecessary judicialisation of trade disputes and restrict the inclusion of lawyers fully engaged in legal practice in the list of arbitrators. By way of example, GAFTA specifies that '[i]n-house lawyers working for Gafta members are eligible, but not those working primarily in private practice'.[8] Similarly, FOSFA explains that '[n]o person wholly or principally engaged in private legal practice shall be eligible to act as an arbitrator'.

In contrast, nationality does not as a rule appear to be a sensitive consideration in the appointment of arbitrators in commodities disputes. Neither the GAFTA Arbitration Rules No. 125 nor the FOSFA Rules of Arbitration and Appeal provide for any limitation on the nationality of the presiding arbitrator or a sole arbitrator vis-à-vis the nationality of the parties or otherwise address the nationality of appointed arbitrators. The structural peculiarities of the industry again explain this tolerance: traders of the same trading house frequently use trading vehicles registered in various (rather common) jurisdictions and therefore the nationality of a formal party to a dispute does not necessarily reflect the centre of gravity of the party/its holding company. Furthermore, with limited pools of arbitrators, any requirement of neutral nationality might be impractical.

Generally, the system of commodities arbitration accepts more readily repeat and multiple appointments by the same party. The IBA Guidelines on Conflict of Interests recognises this peculiarity of exempting commodities arbitration from the general requirement that makes it mandatory for arbitrators to disclose appointments by the same party within the last three years if made on two or more occasions.[9] The Guidelines explain the exemption by 'a smaller or specialised

---

[7]   Rule 6.1.4 of the GAFTA Code of Conduct for Qualified Arbitrators and Qualified Mediators; FOSFA Code of Conduct for Arbitrators, pp. 3, 5.

[8]   An overview of the current requirements for GAFTA qualified arbitrators is available at https://www.gafta.com/Gafta-Qualified-Arbitrator-Status.

[9]   IBA Guidelines on Conflicts of Interest in International Arbitration, n. 5, available at https://www.ibanet.org/MediaHandler?id=e2fe5e72-eb14-4bba-b10d-d33dafee8918.

pool of individuals' and knowledge of all participants of this peculiarity.[10] At the same time, it remains not entirely clear how many appointments by the same party and within which period raise concerns or if there is any discrepancy in the perception of bias across trade associations.

Neither GAFTA nor FOSFA have chosen to issue guidance on this in terms of concrete numbers of limitations. GAFTA generally encourages parties to '[a]void nominating arbitrators where there is an actual or perceived conflict of interest',[11] and '[m]aintain impartiality by seeking to make, insofar as it is reasonably practicable to do so, as wide a range of arbitration appointments from the list of Qualified Arbitrators as is possible, and, in doing so, reflect the diversity of its membership by promoting representation from different age groups, ethnicities, nationalities and genders'.[12] FOSFA similarly specifies the duty of arbitrators 'to adjudicate jointly and impartially on the dispute between the parties and not to act as agents or advocates of either party'[13] and further clarifies that '[i]f at any stage it becomes evident that an arbitrator, his/her company or firm has any interest, direct or indirect, in the transaction in dispute then he/she should withdraw as no longer eligible'.[14]

Rather indirectly through analysis of the court's jurisprudence one can find some indication about the approaches and methods utilised to balance the influence of the appointing authority on the appointment of adjudicators. The widely discussed decision in *Aldcroft v. The International Cotton Association Limited*[15] has revealed, for instance, that GAFTA considers problematic five appointments in a year from the same party.[16] Yet GAFTA has not intervened in proceedings and its official position remains unknown. The entire case turned on the legitimacy of the restrictions of repeat and concurrent appointments in proceedings under the ICA arbitration rules. In particular, the ICA limits the permissible number of repeat appointments to three from the same or related party in a calendar year and imposes a restriction of no more than eight active first-tier cases at any one time. In an attempt to show that the rule does not unduly limit party autonomy, the ICA's representative referred to GAFTA practice. Having considered the relevance of the doctrine of trade restraints, the court found no violations of the ICA's rules in regard to the number of repeat and concurrent appointments.

---

[10] Ibid.
[11] Guidelines for GAFTA Appointment of Arbitrators, available at https://www.gafta.com/ Guidelines-for-Gafta-Appointment-of-Arbitrators.
[12] Ibid.
[13] The FOSFA Code of Practice for Arbitrators, p. 3, available at https://www.fosfa.org/wp-content/uploads/2022/04/The-Code-of-Practice-for-Arbitrators-April-2018.pdf.
[14] Ibid.
[15] *Aldcroft v. The International Cotton Association Limited* [2017] EWHC 642 (Comm).
[16] Ibid., para. 69.

In a more recent case related to multiple appointments by the same party in related proceedings, *Halliburton v. Chubb*,[17] GAFTA did intervene, arguing that such appointments in themselves do not give rise to the appearance of bias in the case of arbitrators adjudicating in commodities arbitration. The Supreme Court of the UK recognised this peculiarity. The Court, in particular, observed that:

> It is clear from the parties' and interveners' initial cases and from their further submissions that there is a variety of arbitral practices in relation to the disclosure of multiple appointments in different contexts. In this context I use the expression 'multiple appointments' to cover the acceptance of appointments in multiple references concerning the same or overlapping subject matter with only one common party as described in issue 1 in para 2 above. What is appropriate for arbitration in which the parties have submitted to institutional rules, such as those of ICC and LCIA, differs from the practice in GAFTA and LMAA arbitrations. There are practices in maritime, sports and commodities arbitrations, as the IBA Guidelines recognise (para 133 below), in which engagement in multiple overlapping arbitrations does not need to be disclosed because it is not generally perceived as calling into question an arbitrator's impartiality or giving rise to unfairness.[18]

The Court further concluded:

> because of the custom and practice of specialist arbitrators in specific fields, such as ... commodities and maybe others, such multiple appointments are a part of the process which is known to and accepted by the participants. In such circumstances no duty of disclosure would arise.[19]

Appointments by the same law firm appear to be far less clear than repeat and multiple appointments. From one side, the limits of the pool of arbitrators equally affects the parties and the law firms representing the parties. From another side, trade associations do not appear to specifically address appointments made by law firms on behalf of their clients and the possible appearance of bias in the case of repeat appointments made by the same law firm. One may connect this lack of clarification with the somewhat discouraging attitude towards lawyers' participation in proceedings where trade associations permit compensation of legal fees only in the case of the parties' joint agreement. Not much clarity may be found in the IBA Guidelines on Conflict of Interest, which, while regarding the situations of repeat appointments by the same party in commodities arbitration as an exception, make no similar exception in relation to a duty of an arbitrator to disclose repeated appointments if the arbitrator has, within the past three

---

[17] *Halliburton v. Chubb* [2020] UKSC 48.
[18] Ibid., para. 87.
[19] Ibid., para. 135.

years, been appointed on more than three occasions by the same counsel or the same law firm (para. 3.3.8 of the IBA Guidelines on Conflict of Interest).

2. WHICH AUTHORITY APPOINTS ADJUDICATORS?

Both parties' appointments and appointments by appointing authorities are normally made in commodities arbitration in various combinations. As mentioned earlier, parties normally possess a right to appoint an arbitrator in first-tier proceedings, whereas the composition of the second-tier, or appeal boards/panels, fully remains within the authority of the respective trade association. In addition to the appointments made in second-tier tribunals, trade associations may also intervene in first-tier proceedings for default appointments instead of/on behalf of either of the parties as well as the appointments of a presiding arbitrator or sole arbitrator.

When appointing authorities are involved, their role is exercised by the relevant trade association and is not delegated to a third (independent) party. Who precisely within respective trade associations decides on appointments depends on their institutional structures. Some associations, like GAFTA, have more transparent internal appointment procedures, whereas others, like FOSFA, choose not to disclose the same. In GAFTA proceedings, several internal bodies of the association are normally engaged in appointing arbitrators. Relying on the selection criteria set out in the Guidelines for GAFTA Appointment of Arbitrators, the Arbitration Team first recommends the appointment to the Director General of GAFTA. Upon the approval of the Director General, the GAFTA Appointing Panel, consisting of some current GAFTA executives and previous presidents of GAFTA, decides on the final approval of the Arbitration Team's recommended appointment. If the GAFTA Appointing Panel does not approve the appointment, the procedure has to start again.

3. THE METHOD FOR APPOINTING ADJUDICATORS

The precise method for appointing arbitrators depends upon the arbitration rules involved, the stage of the proceedings, the number of arbitrators to be appointed and the actual exercise of the appointment by the parties, when applicable. Despite the existent diversity, some common features can still be summarised in the examples of the GAFTA and FOSFA arbitration rules.

In GAFTA and FOSFA proceedings, the parties can appoint arbitrators only in the first-tier proceedings.[20] In the case of three-member tribunals, each party

---

[20] Rule 3 of the GAFTA Arbitration Rules No. 125; Rule 2 of the FOSFA Rules of Arbitration and Appeal.

appoints one arbitrator and the appointing authority appoints the presiding arbitrator. Appointing authorities also appoint an arbitrator if the parties fail to do so or upon the parties' application. In the case of a sole arbitrator, the parties may jointly agree on the candidacy of the sole arbitrator. If they do not agree, the appointing authority appoints the sole arbitrator.

Previously, FOSFA arbitration proceedings were known for their specific arrangement whereby the parties appointed one arbitrator each. Two arbitrators were supposed to reach an agreement on how to resolve the dispute in question. If they failed to do so, they had to appoint an *umpire* to effectively decide the dispute. The arrangement was abandoned in favour of a classical model of three-member tribunals in 2018, with the presiding arbitrator being appointed by the association.[21] According to the FOSFA Code of Practice for Arbitrators, the introduction of the model was 'a measure to provide a degree of control of the case as well as accountability'.[22]

In relation to the formation of second-tier tribunals, as identified earlier, trade associations possess exclusive authority in their selection. For GAFTA proceedings, the number of appeal members depends on the composition of the tribunal in the first tier: if there were three arbitrators in the first-tier proceedings, a five-member panel would be appointed for the second-tier tribunal; if there was a sole arbitrator in the first-tier proceedings, a three-member tribunal would be selected for the second-tier tribunal. For FOSFA proceedings, an appeal board consists of five members. Arbitrators sitting in the second-tier proceedings normally undergo more stringent control over their qualification. The overall number of these arbitrators or panellists is substantially less than the number of those competent to resolve disputes in the first-tier proceedings. This even more limited pool of adjudicators may raise further concerns about possible apparent or actual bias of adjudicators regularly appointed by the trade associations.

Overall, the appointing authorities' actual exercise of appointments either in the first-tier proceedings or in the second-tier proceedings remains entirely private. Trade associations do not release information about how many arbitrators they appoint on behalf of the parties, as a presiding arbitrator or as a member of appeal boards, nor do they disclose who were appointed.[23] Policy guidelines on the exercise of appointments are not common either. Rather exceptionally in this regard stands GAFTA, with its recent Guidelines for GAFTA Appointment of

---

[21] John Rollason, 'FOSFA Arbitration Rules Simplified', available at https://www.hfw.com/FOSFA-arbitration-rules-simplified-May-2018.

[22] The FOSFA Code of Practice for Arbitrators, p. 3.

[23] The lack of disclosure is in contrast to the practice of commercial arbitration institutes such as the ICC International Court of Arbitration or the Vienna International Arbitration Centre, which publishes the names of appointed arbitrators and the method of their appointments.

Arbitrators, referred to later.[24] The document provides a general account of the appointing methods and selection criteria. In particular, GAFTA acknowledges that the appointing authority does not exercise any rotation in the appointment. Appointments are considered 'on a case-by-case method basis with the intention of selecting the most appropriate arbitrator for that case irrespective of that arbitrator's geographical location'.[25]

4. METHODS TO BALANCE THE APPOINTING AUTHORITY'S INFLUENCE ON THE APPOINTMENT OF ADJUDICATORS

Trade associations as appointing authorities may be viewed as having considerable control over arbitrators. In GAFTA and FOSFA proceedings, their extensive appointing role can be observed in all default appointments and appointments of the presiding arbitrators in first-tier proceedings as well as in the entire formation of the appeal members. When coupled with the limited pools of arbitrators, this power to form the tribunals makes repeat and multiple appointments rather unavoidable for the appointing authorities.

And while repeat and multiple appointments appear to be a recognised feature of commodities arbitration, the problem is not entirely resolved. One may still raise questions about unknown practices of trade associations in the exercise of their appointing authority in light of the limited pools of arbitrators. By way of example, the 2020 list of GAFTA arbitrators, one of the most extensive lists in the industry of commodities trade, contains 78 arbitrators competent to resolve disputes in first-tier proceedings and 43 arbitrators as appeal board members. All 43 appeal board members may also resolve disputes in first-tier proceedings. With 291 new arbitration cases registered, 109 awards issued and 28 appeal proceedings launched in 2020, it is highly probable that the same or partially the same compositions of arbitrators will consider disputes in first- and second-tier proceedings. Similarly, the same arbitrators may decide disputes in relation to the same party. While each situation of repeat and multiple appointments, no doubt, has to be resolved on a case-by-case basis, more specific guidance from the trade associations in relation to appointments by the same parties and the same law firms would be welcome. This guidance could shed more light on the methods to balance the influence of parties and appointing authorities. A larger,

---

[24] See Guidelines for GAFTA Appointment of Arbitrators, available at https://www.gafta.com/Guidelines-for-Gafta-Appointment-of-Arbitrators.

[25] Ibid., para. 4.

more inclusive list of arbitrators would also assist in satisfying the growing expectations of independence and impartiality even for industries where repeat and multiple appointments are traditionally justified by party autonomy and the specificity of custom and trade usages.

In relation to other possible parameters that attempt to maintain tribunals' independence and impartiality in cases where their appointments are exercised by a trade association, one can observe that there are various aspects of the proceedings which serve to secure a tribunal's independence and impartiality. For example, there is no formal procedure for the approval of awards; there are no deviations from the general rule on confidentiality of deliberations; there is no formal ban on dissenting opinions (yet such opinions are not normally given); appointed arbitrators are normally financially secure as parties pay deposits to the respective trade associations in advance. Furthermore, one cannot ignore the role of codes of conduct developed by trade associations, which put pressure on arbitrators in their assessment of proper conduct and integrity. Ultimately, GAFTA's efforts in making the appointing process more transparent and in introducing the Guidelines for GAFTA Appointment of Arbitrators show a good pattern to follow for other trade associations.

5. PARAMETERS TO ENSURE THAT ADJUDICATORS ACT INDEPENDENTLY AND IMPARTIALLY

To give guidance for arbitrators and to ensure that arbitrators act independently and impartially, trade associations have formulated codes of conduct. GAFTA expects its arbitrators to comply with the GAFTA Rules and Code of Conduct for Qualified Arbitrators and Qualified Mediators[26] and FOSFA makes it mandatory for arbitrators to comply with the FOSFA Code of Practice for Arbitrators. The codes do not circumvent other relevant legal frameworks consisting of the law of the seat, arbitration rules, and other regulations and by-laws mandatory for members of the respective trade associations to follow.

The GAFTA Rules and Code of Conduct for Qualified Arbitrators and Qualified Mediators specify that arbitrators act in 'a judicial capacity'[27] and that 'basic requirements of justice'[28] shall be observed. The GAFTA Code further explains that all these requirements are satisfied if arbitrators 'have acted with

---

[26] https://www.gafta.com/write/MediaUploads/Arbitration/Rules_and_Code_of_Conduct_for_Qualified_Arbitrators_and_Qualified_Mediators_July_2021.pdf.

[27] The GAFTA Rules and Code of Conduct for Qualified Arbitrators and Qualified Mediators, para. 8.2.

[28] Ibid.

fairness towards both the parties'[29] and avoid even giving 'the impression that they are not or may not be impartial'.[30] Apart from these general principles safeguarding impartiality and independence, the Rules provide more specific guidelines by listing specific occasions when arbitrators are ineligible. Qualified arbitrators would become ineligible in the situations as follows:

> Where they have an interest in the transaction being the subject of the reference, including but not limited to, an interest arising from being a party thereto, or as a broker, agent, consultant, or superintendent acting in the transaction.

> Where they have involvement in any other capacity which links them to either of the disputing parties, including but not limited to, an involvement arising from being a member of an organisation named as party to the arbitration or mediation, or from being financially retained by any such party, or from being a member of or being financially retained by any organization financially associated with any such party.

> Where they are so closely associated with a party as to cast doubt on their ability to conduct the reference impartially.

> At appeal hearings, as either party's representative or as a board member where they participated as an arbitrator in the arbitration against which the appeal has been lodged.

> Where another employee of the same organisation or associated organisation or firm, as that of the Qualified Arbitrator or Qualified Mediator is appointed to act as Arbitrator, Appeal Board Member or Mediator in the same case.

> In cases involving a former employer who is a party to the arbitration, for a period of 5 years from leaving their employment. Retired employees shall always be ineligible to serve on any case where their last employer is a party to the arbitration. For avoidance of doubt a law firm shall not be considered to be a party to the arbitration.[31]

The FOSFA Code of Practice for Arbitrators also instructs arbitrators to 'act fairly'[32] to both parties and observe 'the generally accepted but not specifically defined "rules of natural justice"'.[33] The Code specifies, among other things, that arbitrators have to verify before their appointment that they or their company or firm have no direct or indirect interest in the transaction in dispute and that they have not already advised or been consulted by one of the parties to the dispute in respect of the specific dispute. If at any stage it becomes evident that an arbitrator has any such direct or indirect interest, he or she should withdraw.

---

[29]   Ibid.
[30]   Ibid., para. 8.3.
[31]   Ibid., para. 6.
[32]   FOSFA Code of Practice for Arbitrators, pp. 1–2.
[33]   Ibid.

To exclude any ambiguity, the Code chooses to expressly state that arbitrators are not supposed to act as agents or advocates of either of the parties.

6. CONSEQUENCES FOR ADJUDICATORS OF A BREACH BY ADJUDICATORS OF THE REQUIREMENT TO ACT INDEPENDENTLY AND IMPARTIALLY

The law of the seat together with applicable arbitration rules and codes of conduct define the consequences for adjudicators for a breach of the requirement to act independently and impartially. As identified earlier, the Arbitration Act of England and Wales 1996 serves as the law of the seat for many commodity arbitrations. In addition to being highlighted in this report, proceedings under the GAFTA and FOSFA arbitration rules, and proceedings under the arbitration rules of other trade associations, including the LME, FCC, ICA, BCA and RSA, all have London as the seat of arbitration. In contrast to the jurisdictions based on the UNCITRAL Model Arbitration Law, the Act provides in section 24 for an opportunity for a state court to remove an arbitrator if circumstances exist that give rise to justifiable doubts as to his or her impartiality, failure or resistance to duly conduct the proceedings. While exhaustion of internal arbitral procedures does not serve as a jurisdictional impediment to filing an application and initiating proceedings, the court shall not carry out removal of arbitrators unless all internal procedures have been duly exhausted.[34]

As a rule, each association stipulates its own internal rules for the removal of arbitrators. Both grounds for their removal and the procedures may vary. By way of example, GAFTA lists seven grounds for the removal of arbitrators in its Code of Conduct for Qualified Arbitrators and Qualified Mediators. These grounds directly mention lack of independence and impartiality and further some other related grounds, including a failure or refusal to conduct the proceedings properly, incapacity to act or where the arbitrator acts or proposes to act in excess of their jurisdiction, a failure to use all reasonable dispatch in conducting the arbitration or making an award, etc. The procedure may be triggered by any person. That person shall first attempt to resolve the matter informally with an arbitrator in question and only when such attempts do not lead to an acceptable solution should they file a complaint with the Director General of GAFTA. The Director General of GAFTA shall in turn attempt to ensure that the matter is resolved by agreement. If the matter cannot be so resolved, the Arbitration Complaints Committee steps in. The Arbitration

---

[34] Robert Merkin QC and Louis Flannery QC, *Merkin and Flannery on the Arbitration Act 1996*, 6th ed., Routledge, 2019, p. 272.

Complaints Committee decides the matter itself if there are no signs of unprofessional conduct as defined by GAFTA. The Arbitration Complaints Committee may either dismiss the complaint or seek to resolve it by agreement between the parties or revoke the arbitrator's authority to act in the case at hand or in any specified future category of cases. All unprofessional conduct is to be resolved in accordance with another procedure determined by the Association's Complaints and Disciplinary Regulations. As a result of consideration, not only may an arbitrator be removed from a tribunal, but he or she may also be excluded from the list of qualified arbitrators. The only occasion which is expressly addressed by FOSFA as a ground for removal of an arbitrator relates to delays in the proceedings. The procedure for removal of an arbitrator also encourages amicable settlement where an arbitrator/tribunal is provided with an opportunity to give an explanation and to carry out the necessary actions within the set deadline, if requested by FOSFA and thus to react proactively to the delay. In the case of failure by an arbitrator or arbitrators to explain or to take the required next steps, FOSFA has a right to request their resignation. The arbitrator or arbitrators are deemed to have resigned 14 consecutive days after the despatch of FOSFA's written requirement if not otherwise decided by the federation. The removed arbitrator's right to act as an arbitrator or to serve on the FOSFA Appeal Panel in the future may also be suspended or revoked.

There is no public information on the internal challenges exercised by GAFTA, FOSFA and other trade associations. Whether and how often trade associations have intervened to secure the impartiality and independence of arbitrators remain entirely unclear.

7. ENFORCEABILITY OF A FINAL DECISION RENDERED BY AN ADJUDICATOR WHO BREACHED THE REQUIREMENT TO ACT INDEPENDENTLY AND IMPARTIALLY

If a final award is rendered by an arbitrator who has breached the requirement to act independently and impartially, the award can be set aside or enforcement thereof may be refused. Despite some harmonisation achieved among the states, the result of the procedures on setting aside and enforcement still largely depends on the law of the seat and the law where the enforcement is being sought. The approaches adopted by judges in a given jurisdiction for the assessment of independence and impartiality of arbitrators would be determinative. There is no guarantee that domestic courts in other jurisdictions than the seat of arbitration (often England and Wales) would demonstrate tolerance to repeat multiple appointments in commodities arbitration.

In addition to applications under section 24(1) of the Arbitration Act of England and Wales 1996, the Act enables one to challenge an award under section 68 because of apparent or actual bias. The same circumstances as those falling under section 24(1) of the Act may be qualified as serious irregularity and serve as a reason for challenging an issued award under section 68(1) of the Act. As both procedures apply the same standard towards the impartiality and independence of a tribunal, they can be effectively combined.[35] The reason for the combination primarily lies in the necessity to exclude a situation where the same arbitrator participates in decision-making anew if the court returns an award back to the tribunal to cure the defects.

In relation to enforcement, while the New York Convention on the Recognition and Enforcement of Foreign Arbitral Awards has reached an impressive geographic spread,[36] the content of some provisions, including those on due process and public policy, still continues to be informed by domestic practices. Accordingly, repeat and multiple appointments may find less tolerance in regard to commodities trade in some jurisdictions in comparison with the practice established in England and Wales even despite the exception made in the IBA Guidelines on Conflict of Interests.

When the apparent or actual bias of arbitrators is premised on other circumstances which are not specific to commodities arbitration, there is a possibility to challenge an arbitrator and award or to resist enforcement thereof, the same as in the context of conventional international commercial arbitration. As a rule, neither impartiality nor independence has a statutory definition and therefore local practices in a given jurisdiction play a significant role in setting the precise content for the standard thus exercised and assessed.

---

[35]   Ibid., p. 702.

[36]   According to the data available on the official site of UNCITRAL as of 25 February 2023, the New York Convention has 172 contracting members: https://uncitral.un.org/en/texts/arbitration/conventions/foreign_arbitral_awards/status2.

THE INDEPENDENCE AND IMPARTIALITY OF ADJUDICATORS IN INTERNATIONAL ADMINISTRATIVE TRIBUNALS

Chiara GIORGETTI

1. Introduction 172
2. Criteria for the Selection of Adjudicators 172
   2.1. World Bank Administrative Tribunal 172
   2.2. International Monetary Fund Administrative Tribunal 173
   2.3. United Nations Dispute Tribunal............................. 173
   2.4. Inter-American Development Bank Administrative Tribunal...... 173
   2.5. European Bank for Reconstruction and Development
        Administrative Tribunal 173
   2.6. International Labour Organization Administrative Tribunal 174
3. Which Authority Appoints the Adjudicators? 174
   3.1. World Bank Administrative Tribunal 174
   3.2. International Monetary Fund Administrative Tribunal 174
   3.3. United Nations Dispute Tribunal............................. 174
   3.4. Inter-American Development Bank Administrative Tribunal...... 175
   3.5. European Bank for Reconstruction and Development
        Administrative Tribunal 175
   3.6. International Labour Organization Administrative Tribunal 175
4. Parameters for Independence and Impartiality 175
   4.1. World Bank Administrative Tribunal 176
   4.2. International Monetary Fund Administrative Tribunal 176
   4.3. United Nations Dispute Tribunal............................. 176
   4.4. Inter-American Development Bank Administrative Tribunal...... 177
   4.5. European Bank for Reconstruction and Development
        Administrative Tribunal 177
   4.6. International Labour Organization Administrative Tribunal 177
5. Consequences and Enforceability of Final Decisions Rendered
   in Breach of Impartiality Obligations............................. 178
   5.1. World Bank Administrative Tribunal 178
   5.2. International Monetary Fund Administrative Tribunal 178

Intersentia

5.3.	United Nations Dispute Tribunal.	178
5.4.	Inter-American Development Bank Administrative Tribunal.	179
5.5.	European Bank for Reconstruction and Development Administrative Tribunal	179
5.6.	International Labour Organization Administrative Tribunal	179
6.	Conclusion.	179

1. INTRODUCTION

International organisations possess the juridical personality necessary to enter into legal relations in pursuit of their core functions. An integral part of this is the ability to hire employees, but complications arise from the fact that international organisations enjoy immunity from suit and legal process before national courts. This immunity extends to allegations of violations of employment contracts. To reconcile this conflict, international organisations are required to make available the settlement of employment disputes, and it is this function that international administrative tribunals accomplish.[1]

2. CRITERIA FOR THE SELECTION OF ADJUDICATORS

Organisations predominantly select experts in the field of employment law, the law of international organisations, and the international civil service, arbitration and dispute resolution.

2.1. WORLD BANK ADMINISTRATIVE TRIBUNAL

Selection for the seven judges of the World Bank Administrative Tribunal (WBAT) specify that they must be nationals of the Member States of the Bank (but no two may be the same nationality) and possess high moral character and recognised qualifications in relevant fields.[2] Relevant fields include employment relations, international civil service and international organisation administration.

---

[1] Olufumi Elias and Melissa Thomas, 'Administrative Tribunals of International Organizations' in Chiara Giorgetti (ed.), *The Rules, Practice, and Jurisprudence of International Courts and Tribunals*, 2012, pp. 159–88.

[2] Article III, WBAT Statute.

2.2. INTERNATIONAL MONETARY FUND ADMINISTRATIVE TRIBUNAL

Selection for the five judges of the International Monetary Fund Administrative Tribunal (IMFAT) requires that they be nationals of a member country of the IMF at the time of appointment, and possess the qualifications required for appointment to high judicial office or be jurisconsults of recognised competence.[3]

2.3. UNITED NATIONS DISPUTE TRIBUNAL

The United Nations Dispute Tribunal (UNDT) has nine judges in total, three of whom are full-time and six of whom are part-time. For valid selection, members must be of high moral character and impartial, possess at least 10 years of judicial experience in administrative law or equivalent practice, and be fluent, both orally and in writing, in English or French.[4]

2.4. INTER-AMERICAN DEVELOPMENT BANK ADMINISTRATIVE TRIBUNAL

Selection for the seven judges of the Inter-American Development Bank Administrative Tribunal (IADBAT) requires that they be nationals of member countries (but no two may be the same nationality), have recognised professional competence and integrity, have qualifications necessary to occupy a similar position in the highest judicial courts of their countries or be jurisconsults of similar recognised competence.[5]

2.5. EUROPEAN BANK FOR RECONSTRUCTION AND DEVELOPMENT ADMINISTRATIVE TRIBUNAL

Selection for the five judges of the European Bank for Reconstruction and Development Administrative Tribunal (EBRDAT) requires that they be nationals of different Member States of the Bank, possess high moral character, have qualifications required for appointment to high judicial office, or be lawyers or arbitrators expert in the areas of employment relations, international civil service, or the administration of international organisations.[6]

---

[3] Article VII, Statute of the Administrative Tribunal of the International Monetary Fund.
[4] Article 4, Statute of the UNDT.
[5] Article III, Statute of the Administrative Tribunal of the IADB Group.
[6] Rule 2.02, Rules of Procedure of the Administrative Tribunal of the EBRD.

2.6. INTERNATIONAL LABOUR ORGANIZATION ADMINISTRATIVE TRIBUNAL

Selection for the seven judges of the International Labour Organization Administrative Tribunal (ILOAT) requires that they all have different nationalities, possess high moral character, impartiality and integrity, and must have been appointed to, or possess the required qualifications for appointment to, the highest judicial office of their countries.[7] Judges must also have excellent knowledge of one of the working languages of the ILO, and ideally will possess basic comprehension of the other working language. The selection process will also give due consideration to the geographical distribution and gender balance of the tribunal.

3. WHICH AUTHORITY APPOINTS THE ADJUDICATORS?

3.1. WORLD BANK ADMINISTRATIVE TRIBUNAL

The Executive Directors of the Bank appoint judges from a list of candidates nominated by the President of the Bank.[8] The President makes these nominations after appropriate consultations with a four-member advisory committee.

3.2. INTERNATIONAL MONETARY FUND ADMINISTRATIVE TRIBUNAL

The Managing Director of the IMF appoints the President of the Tribunal, subject to consultations with the Staff Association and the approval of the Executive Board.[9] Other members are appointed by the Managing Director after appropriate consultation.

3.3. UNITED NATIONS DISPUTE TRIBUNAL

Judges are appointed by the General Assembly on the recommendation of the Internal Justice Council.[10] This Council is composed of three external

---

[7]   Article III, Statute of the Administrative Tribunal of the ILO.
[8]   Article III, WBAT Statute.
[9]   Article VII, Statute of the Administrative Tribunal of the IMF.
[10]   Article 4, Statute of the UNDT.

expert jurists and two UN staff members and will give due consideration to geographical distribution in providing its views and recommendations to the General Assembly.[11]

3.4. INTER-AMERICAN DEVELOPMENT BANK ADMINISTRATIVE TRIBUNAL

Judges are appointed by the Board of Directors from a list of candidates presented by the Nominating Committee for the Tribunal, which consists of five members within the Bank, including the Chairperson of Human Resources, who heads the committee.[12] Meetings of the Committee are called as necessary to fill open positions on the Tribunal, and a quorum requires all five members of the Committee.

3.5. EUROPEAN BANK FOR RECONSTRUCTION AND DEVELOPMENT ADMINISTRATIVE TRIBUNAL

Judges of the Tribunal are appointed by the Board of Directors on recommendation of the President, who must first consult with the Vice-President of HR & Administration, the General Counsel and the Staff Council.[13] In addition, the President may appoint a selection committee to assist him in recommending appointees.

3.6. INTERNATIONAL LABOUR ORGANIZATION ADMINISTRATIVE TRIBUNAL

Judges are appointed by the International Labour Conference on a recommendation of the Governing Body of the International Labour Office.[14]

4. PARAMETERS FOR INDEPENDENCE AND IMPARTIALITY

As a baseline rule, members of tribunals are typically appointed for set terms, which may or may not be renewable. In addition, many organisations, such as

---

[11] Resolution 62/228, General Assembly.
[12] Article III, Statute of the Administrative Tribunal of the IADB Group.
[13] Rule 2.02, Rules of Procedure of the Administrative Tribunal of the EBRD.
[14] Article III, Statute of the Administrative Tribunal of the ILO.

Intersentia

the World Bank and the IMF, prevent or restrict the eligibility of current or former staff members to be appointed to the administrative tribunal.

4.1. WORLD BANK ADMINISTRATIVE TRIBUNAL

Members are appointed for a five-year term and may be reappointed for one additional five-year term. The founding statute specifies that the Tribunal is a body fully independent from the management of the World Bank that may not be interfered with, and it possesses independent power to design and implement its own rules and procedure.[15] Current and former staff members are not eligible to serve on the Tribunal, and members of the Tribunal may not be employed by the Bank Group following their service.[16] A member of the Tribunal must recuse him- or herself from any case that presents a conflict of interest or other circumstances that so require it.[17]

4.2. INTERNATIONAL MONETARY FUND ADMINISTRATIVE TRIBUNAL

Judges are appointed for a four-year term and may be reappointed for a maximum of two additional terms. No person with a prior or present employment relationship with the IMF may be appointed to the Tribunal, nor will they be permitted to seek subsequent employment at the IMF. The Tribunal is completely independent in the exercise of its duties, with no instructions or constraints permissible from the governing body. However, the Managing Director does retain the power to terminate the appointment of a member who, in the unanimous opinion of the other members, is unsuited for service.[18] A member of the Tribunal must recuse himself where there is a conflict of interest in a case.[19]

4.3. UNITED NATIONS DISPUTE TRIBUNAL

Members are appointed for a non-renewable seven-year term. All judges of the Tribunal enjoy full independence, and any judge who has or appears to have a conflict of interest must recuse himself from a case.[20] A party may also request a recusal, and that decision is made by the President of the Tribunal. The Tribunal's

---

[15]   Article I, WBAT Statute.
[16]   Article IV, WBAT Statute.
[17]   Rule V, Rules of Procedure of the Administrative Tribunal of the IMF.
[18]   Article VII, Statute of the Administrative Tribunal of the IMF.
[19]   Ibid.
[20]   Article 4, Statute of the UNDT.

rules of procedure specify that a conflict arises where a case involves: (i) a person with whom the judge has a personal, familial or professional relationship; (ii) a matter in which the judge has previously served in another capacity; or (iii) any other circumstances that would make it appear to a reasonable and impartial observer that the judge's participation would be inappropriate.[21]

4.4. INTER-AMERICAN DEVELOPMENT BANK ADMINISTRATIVE TRIBUNAL

Members are appointed for one non-renewable six-year term and should recuse themselves from any case that presents a conflict of interest or other inappropriate circumstances.[22] A party may challenge a member of the Tribunal for any of the following: (i) being a close friend of or manifestly unfriendly to any of the parties; (ii) being a relative of any of the counsellors, advisors, attorneys or representatives of a party; and (iii) having expressed an opinion on a case currently before the Tribunal.[23] A member may contest a challenge, and the President of the Tribunal will ultimately decide the issue. If upheld, the member will be barred from hearing the case.

4.5. EUROPEAN BANK FOR RECONSTRUCTION AND DEVELOPMENT ADMINISTRATIVE TRIBUNAL

Members are appointed for a single three-year term, except for the President, who may be reappointed for an additional term. The Tribunal must act independently and impartially in the exercise of its duties, including the obligation of members to recuse themselves where a conflict exists, and it may not receive instruction on any issues from the Bank or an outside source.[24]

4.6. INTERNATIONAL LABOUR ORGANIZATION ADMINISTRATIVE TRIBUNAL

Members are appointed for a five-year term and may be reappointed for a single additional term. The Tribunal is completely independent from the ILO and performs its functions without instruction or constraints.[25] Members are

---

[21] Article 27, UNDT Rules of Procedure.
[22] Article III, Statute of the Administrative Tribunal of the IADB Group.
[23] Article 10, Rules of Procedure of the IADB Tribunal.
[24] Rule 2.02–2.04, Rules of Procedure of the Administrative Tribunal of the EBRD.
[25] Article III, Statute of the Administrative Tribunal of the ILO.

Chiara Giorgetti

expected to recuse themselves from any case where there is a conflict of interest or other inappropriate circumstances.

5. CONSEQUENCES AND ENFORCEABILITY OF FINAL DECISIONS RENDERED IN BREACH OF IMPARTIALITY OBLIGATIONS

5.1. WORLD BANK ADMINISTRATIVE TRIBUNAL

All judgments are final and without appeal.[26] However, a party to a case in which a judgment has been delivered may request that the Tribunal revise its judgment in light of new facts, such as an undisclosed conflict, that would have had a decisive influence on the outcome of the case.[27] If neither the Tribunal nor that party had knowledge of the facts at the time of the judgment, a request for revision may be made within a six-month period after the party acquired knowledge of the new facts.

5.2. INTERNATIONAL MONETARY FUND ADMINISTRATIVE TRIBUNAL

All judgments are final and without appeal.[28] However, the IMF Statute has a provision identical to the World Bank for revision of a judgment if new material evidence or facts come to light.[29] The party may request revision within six months after that party acquired knowledge of the fact or evidence.

5.3. UNITED NATIONS DISPUTE TRIBUNAL

Judgments of the Dispute Tribunal are binding on the parties but are subject to appeal to the UN Appeals Tribunal.[30] Either party may apply to the Tribunal for a revision of a judgment on the basis of the discovery of a new fact that was previously unknown at the time the judgment was rendered. However, ignorance of such facts must not be due to the party's own negligence. An application for revision must be made within 30 days of the discovery of the fact, and within one year of the date of the judgment.

---

[26]   Article XI, WBAT Statute.
[27]   Article XIII, WBAT Statute.
[28]   Article XIII, Statute of the Administrative Tribunal of the IMF.
[29]   Article XVI, Statute of the Administrative Tribunal of the IMF.
[30]   Article 32, Statute of the UNDT. See also Article 2, Statute of the UN Appeals Tribunal.

5.4. INTER-AMERICAN DEVELOPMENT BANK ADMINISTRATIVE TRIBUNAL

Judgments are final and without appeal. The Tribunal's procedure for revising judgments is identical to that of the UNDT, including timing.[31] However, there is no appellate body.

5.5. EUROPEAN BANK FOR RECONSTRUCTION AND DEVELOPMENT ADMINISTRATIVE TRIBUNAL

All decisions are final and binding on the parties to the proceedings. A decision is not subject to any type of appeal by either of the parties, including a request for a revision.[32]

5.6. INTERNATIONAL LABOUR ORGANIZATION ADMINISTRATIVE TRIBUNAL

Judgments are final and without appeal. However, the Tribunal may consider applications for interpretation, execution or review of a judgment. The ILO Statute and procedure do not specify further on what grounds a party may apply for review of a judgment.

6. CONCLUSION

International administrative tribunals provide essential access to justice to employees of international organisations. They also provide the only available venue to international civil servants for their labour disputes, and it is therefore essential that they work well and are staffed by independent and impartial judges. The statutes of the international administrative tribunals examined in this report show a certain degree of uniformity consistency among the different tribunals. Existing provisions guarantee independence and impartiality of judges, including by requiring certain characteristics of judges, for example in relation to nationality. This report also highlights the consequences and enforceability of final decisions rendered in breach of impartiality obligations.

---

[31]   Article 28, Rules of Procedure of the IADB Tribunal.
[32]   Rule 8.08, Rules of Procedure of the Administrative Tribunal of the EBRD.

THE INDEPENDENCE AND IMPARTIALITY OF ADJUDICATORS IN THE INTERNATIONAL COURT OF JUSTICE AND THE INTERNATIONAL TRIBUNAL FOR THE LAW OF THE SEA

Makane Moïse MBENGUE and Damien CHARLOTIN

1. Introduction 181
2. Independence and Impartiality in Practice. 182
   2.1. The Role of Structural Features 183
   2.2. A Tradition of Self-Governance. 185
3. Adaptations in a Changing Context. 187
   3.1. Independence and Impartiality: New Expectations 187
   3.2. Recent Practice by the ICJ and ITLOS 189
4. Conclusion. 191

1. INTRODUCTION

The growth of international law in the 20th century has coincided with the creation of international courts. Instead of relying on diplomats hashing out compromises on the basis of political and extra-legal considerations, states have agreed to respect judgments rendered by standing international adjudicators applying international rules and norms.[1] The International Court of Justice (ICJ) and the International Tribunal for the Law of the Sea (ITLOS) are prime examples of this model of international adjudication.

---

[1] This is 'the substitution of judicial sense of responsibility for diplomatic sense of responsibility' called for by Elihu Root, in his Address Opening the National Arbitration and Peace Congress, New York City, 15 April 1907, as quoted by E. Gordon, 'Observations on the Independence and Impartiality of the Members of the International Court of Justice' (1987) 2 *Connecticut Journal of International Law* 397, 413.

This model relies however on a kind of paradox: while these two courts are meant to be ruled (and rule) by law, they are surrounded by politics. States agreed to submit to international adjudication in large part because they control the design and composition of international courts. Only states can select judges, and it is no secret that elections for the ICJ or the ITLOS are a highly politically laden exercise. Extra-legal criteria are bound to enter the matrix, and there is little to prevent some judges being appointed for reasons beyond their legal abilities.[2] It is notably striking that few of the states participating in international judicial elections allow for such a practice at home.

The solution to this paradox can, to some extent, be found in the requirement for all judges to adhere to some standards of conduct, and notably to remain independent and impartial. In this respect, the Statutes of both the ICJ and the ITLOS provide that they should be composed of 'independent' judges,[3] and that those judges shall 'exercise [their] powers impartially and conscientiously.'[4] A number of further provisions in both Statutes relate to the same concern for attaching judges to the legal domain, and for ensuring their independence and impartiality.[5]

Decades after this solution presided over the creation of both the ICJ and the ITLOS, these provisions seem to have mostly been successful, though likely because the courts have been proactive in averting potential conflicts (section 2). Yet, as other international disputes bear witness that the standards of independence and impartiality are shifting, the practice of both bodies may have to evolve (section 3).

2. INDEPENDENCE AND IMPARTIALITY IN PRACTICE

In reviewing the judicial standards of independence and impartiality for ICJ and ITLOS judges, it is useful first to consider how these courts were designed to deal with judicial bias in theory and practice. As we shall see, a number of structural features entail that the salience, meaning and enforcement of these standards display specific characteristics that may place these courts apart from other systems of international adjudication (section 2.1). These features also explain the significant emphasis these courts put on self-governance, as well as their concern for dealing with potential conflicts pre-emptively, through the use, primarily, of self-recusals (section 2.2).

---

[2] On this matter see e.g. R. Mackenzie, K. Malleson, P. Martin and P. Sands, *Selecting International Judges: Principle, Process, and Politics*, OUP, Oxford 2010.

[3] ICJ Statute, Article 2; ITLOS Statute, Article 2.

[4] ICJ Statute, Article 20; ITLOS Statute, Article 11.

[5] D. Robinson, 'The Role of Politics in the Election and the Work of Judges of the International Court of Justice' (2003) 97 *Proceedings of the ASIL Annual Meeting* 277, 279: 'The ICJ Statute on paper goes to considerable length to reduce the effect of raw politics on the election process'.

2.1. THE ROLE OF STRUCTURAL FEATURES

As noted, states likely agree to submit disputes to elected international judges because those judges are bound by standards of independence and impartiality.[6] While these standards are not further developed in the ICJ and the ITLOS Statutes, they should be read and understood against the background of a number of other structural features characterising such international standing bodies.

In dealing with the structure of these permanent bodies, it is helpful to contrast appointment to the ICJ and the ITLOS with arbitration, since the ICJ's predecessor (the Permanent Court of International Justice) was partly designed in opposition to the arbitral model (while the ITLOS was later set up on the model of the ICJ). Notably, parties to an ICJ or ITLOS dispute cannot appoint the judges who will decide that dispute in particular.[7] This entails fewer opportunities for post-appointment challenges, as states should be less concerned that an adjudicator had been appointed for his or her sympathy for the appointing party, or has pre-judged the case at hand, or that appointees will rule in a certain way to receive further appointments down the line. Instead, ICJ and ITLOS judges are elected for long, renewable terms of nine years,[8] and can only be removed from the Court by the agreement of all their colleagues.[9]

Meanwhile, the number of adjudicators on their benches (15 judges for the ICJ, and 21 members at the ITLOS) departs considerably from the historical norms of three or five arbitrators, and lessens the role of the individual in these proceedings.[10] While international disputes, which are often highly political, offer a number of opportunities for judges to exercise and/or conceal bias,[11] the possible predispositions of a single judge are expected to be offset by a large number of unbiased, unconcerned judges.

---

[6]   Note however that an alternative story can also be told, according to which international courts maintain a margin of uncertainty as to the independence and impartiality of their members *precisely* so as for states to agree on international adjudication. See e.g. the remarks by R. Falk on the panel, 'The Independence and Impartiality of International Judges' (1989) 83 *Proceedings of the ASIL Annual Meeting* 508, 516–17.

[7]   With the exception of the Chamber procedure and the appointment of judges ad hoc.

[8]   ICJ Statute, Article 13; ITLOS Statute, Article 5(1).

[9]   ICJ Statute, Article 18; ITLOS Statute, Article 9.

[10]   See the remarks by E. Gordon on the panel, 'The Independence and Impartiality of International Judges' (1989) 83 *Proceedings of the ASIL Annual Meeting* 508, 510. However, recent psychological research has cast doubt over this intuition, as the most polarised jury members often have an outsized influence over a jury – think of the movie *12 Angry Men*. On this, see more generally D. Kahneman, O. Sibony and C.R. Sunstein, *Noise: a Flaw in Human Judgment*, Little, Brown Spark, New York 2021.

[11]   I.e. international law's lack of development on certain issues might offer more flexibility in concealing a (biased) legal solution, while the fact that both the ICJ and the ITLOS sit at the apex of their respective fields means that there is no correcting mechanism against biased decisions.

Both institutions are nonetheless concerned with making sure only proper individuals sit on their benches. ICJ judges and ITLOS members are therefore meant to be elected, respectively, from 'among persons of high moral character, who possess the qualifications required in their respective countries for appointment to the highest judicial offices', and from 'among persons enjoying the highest reputation for fairness and integrity and of recognized competence in the field of the law of the sea.'[12]

Historically, allegations of bias and partiality have focused on the nationality of the adjudicators. Both courts however entertain a complex relationship with the national origins of their members. On the one hand, both Statutes seek to make nationality irrelevant: judges are elected 'regardless of their nationality',[13] though no two of them can be of the same nationality,[14] and national groups are meant to diversify the nationalities of their nominees for the ICJ.[15] Elected judges and members also become members of the international community: they enjoy 'diplomatic privileges and immunities',[16] which are also meant to protect their independence. On the other hand, both Statutes allow states to appoint a judge ad hoc to the Bench if they have no nationals sitting.[17] While this appears contradictory,[18] it has been advanced that the institution of judges ad hoc actually bolsters the ICJ and the ITLOS's independence and impartiality.[19] In any case, judges ad hoc are subject to the same requirement regarding character or impartiality as permanent judges.[20]

The Statutes make efforts to centre the nomination and election process on the legal character and background of judges.[21] Yet the individual personality of candidates may remain a source of complications. This is not surprising: to the extent that nations are meant to appoint judges from among prestigious individuals accomplished in international legal matters, such individuals are

---

[12]   ICJ Statute, Article 2; ITLOS Statute, Article 2.

[13]   ICJ Statute, Article 2.

[14]   ICJ Statute, Article 3(1); ITLOS Statute, Article 3(1).

[15]   ICJ Statute, Article 5(2).

[16]   ICJ Statute, Article 19; ITLOS Statute, Article 10.

[17]   ICJ Statute, Article 31; ITLOS Statute, Article 17.

[18]   C. Giorgetti, 'The Challenge and Recusal of Judges of the International Court of Justice' in C. Giorgetti (ed.), *Challenges and Recusals of Judges and Arbitrators in International Courts and Tribunals*, Brill Nijhoff, Leiden 2015, p. 12: 'Once the Bench is constituted, it is peculiar that nationality should play a role again when specific cases enter the docket.'

[19]   C. Brower and M. Lando, 'Judges *Ad Hoc* of the International Court of Justice' (2020) 33 *Leiden Journal of International Law* 467.

[20]   ICJ Statute, Article 31(6); ITLOS Statute, Article 17(6). See also ICJ Practice Direction VII, advising against appointing as judge ad hoc 'individuals who have appeared as agent, counsel or advocate in another case before the Court'.

[21]   For instance, in the fact that each national groups is advised to consult 'its highest court of justice, its legal faculties and schools of law, and its national academies and national sections of international academies devoted to the study of law' before nominating candidates to the election: ICJ Statute, Article 6.

The International Court of Justice and the International Tribunal for the Law of the Sea

likely to have résumés that entail possible conflicts of interests when they are elected.[22] This is why both Statutes provide for a number of incompatibilities with the role of a judge.[23] Notably, ICJ judges and ITLOS members cannot act as 'agent, counsel, or advocate' during their term,[24] and are barred from hearing a dispute in which they officiated as such in the past.[25]

2.2. A TRADITION OF SELF-GOVERNANCE

Given these structural features, how have the ICJ and ITLOS fared with respect to the independence and impartiality of their judges and members? While the practice took time to develop,[26] the Court and the Tribunal now display a preference for self-governance and a pre-emptive resolution of conflicts, instead of a reliance on post hoc challenges by parties.

Certainly, states have not been particularly active (at least at the post-election stage) about insisting on the independence and impartiality of ICJ judges and ITLOS members. In contrast with arbitral proceedings, requests for disqualification have been exceedingly rare before the Court and the Tribunal: three at the ICJ (all unsuccessful), none for the ITLOS.[27] And while the possibility for disputes to be heard before a Chamber (and not the full Court or Tribunal) has been cited as a device that could soothe concerns over independence and impartiality,[28] parties have rarely availed themselves of this opportunity.

Instead, it has been noted that '[v]oluntary (or self) recusals are by far the most common method to control the composition of the ICJ bench and ensure its independence and impartiality.'[29] A survey by Chiara Giorgetti in 2015 found

---

[22] E. Ivanova, 'Election of Judges: International Tribunal for the Law of the Sea', *MPEPIL* (2021), at 62: 'nearly all of the current members of the Tribunal served as legal advisors to their governments'.

[23] ICJ Statute, Article 16(1); ITLOS Statute, Article 7.

[24] ICJ Statute, Article 17(1); ITLOS Statute, Article 7.

[25] ICJ Statute, Article 17(2); ITLOS Statute, Article 8(1).

[26] As noted by Chiara Giorgetti, the ICJ in the first decades of its functioning 'accepted situations that would be seen as problematic in the present context of international litigation': C. Giorgetti, 'The Challenge and Recusal of Judges of the International Court of Justice' in C. Giorgetti (ed.), *Challenges and Recusals of Judges and Arbitrators in International Courts and Tribunals*, Brill Nijhoff, Leiden 2015, p. 8.

[27] Ibid., pp. 28–31, for a review of these three requests.

[28] E.g., in the *Gulf of Maine* case, the Canada and the US reportedly preferred a Chamber so as to make sure only judges they agree on could hear their dispute: see D. Robinson, 'The Role of Politics in the Election and the Work of Judges of the International Court of Justice' (2003) 97 *Proceedings of the ASIL Annual Meeting* 277, 280.

[29] C. Giorgetti, 'The Challenge and Recusal of Judges of the International Court of Justice' in C. Giorgetti (ed.), *Challenges and Recusals of Judges and Arbitrators in International Courts and Tribunals*, Brill Nijhoff, Leiden 2015, p. 17. She also noted one instance of a 'non-voluntary' recusal, under Article 24(2) of the Statute, when President Spender asked Judge Zafrullah Khan not to sit in the *South West Africa* (*Ethiopia & Liberia v. South Africa*) cases.

Intersentia

185

36 known cases of self-recusals.[30] While judges have offered a variety of grounds to recuse themselves, a substantial number of instances remain unexplained, and the whole practice defies easy categorisation.[31]

Recusals have continued since Giorgetti's survey, although keeping track of the practice is made difficult, since the Court rarely indicates why, let alone when, a judge decided to step down from hearing a case, leaving one to seek gaps in the Court's roll, or hope for an indication at the oral hearing.[32] Recent practice indicates that Judges Crawford and Greenwood recused themselves from considering the *Chagos* advisory opinion,[33] undoubtedly for their roles as (respectively) counsel and arbitrator in a related arbitration.[34] Judge Crawford also sat out the *Bolivia/Chile* case,[35] while Judge Donoghue recused herself from the two recent *Iran/US* cases.[36]

That self-governing system of recusal might however be under strain. As recusals have become ever more common,[37] parties have come to expect, and then to demand, such recusals when they think it warranted – with the inevitable disappointment when judges decline to step down. The recent proceedings in *Somalia v. Kenya*[38] are a case in point, as (then) President Yusuf refused to recuse

---

[30] Ibid., with a summary table pp. 18–25. By contrast, there was seemingly no recusal or disqualification in the ITLOS's 25-year history – a fact maybe due to the relatively low number of disputes received by the Tribunal so far.

[31] Article 24(1) of the ICJ Statute, which offers the basis for recusals, only provides that judges can recuse themselves 'for some special reason'.

[32] For instance, Peter Tomka was seemingly not on the Bench to decide *Immunities and Criminal Proceedings (Equatorial Guinea v. France)*, Preliminary Objections, Judgment, I.C.J. Reports 2018, p. 292, though he is listed as taking part in the vote in the final judgment dated 11 December 2020; Mohamed Bennouna is not listed as participating in the two *ICAO Council* appeal decisions, without any reason being given why.

[33] *Legal Consequences of the Separation of the Chagos Archipelago from Mauritius in 1965*, Advisory Opinion, I.C.J. Reports 2019, p. 95. See in this respect D. Akande and A. Tzanakopoulos, 'Composition of the Bench in ICJ Advisory Proceedings: Implications for the Chagos Islands case' (*EJIL:Talk!*, 10 July 2017), https://www.ejiltalk.org/composition-of-the-bench-in-icj-advisory-proceedings-implications-for-the-chagos-islands-case/.

[34] *Chagos Marine Protected Area Arbitration (Mauritius v. United Kingdom)*, PCA Case No. 2011-03.

[35] *Obligation to Negotiate Access to the Pacific Ocean (Bolivia v. Chile)*, Preliminary Objection, Oral Proceedings, CR 2015/18, p. 10.

[36] *Alleged Violations of the 1955 Treaty of Amity, Economic Relations, and Consular Rights (Islamic Republic of Iran v. United States of America)*, Judgment, 3 February 2021, para. 7. Her recusal is however not recorded in judgments and orders in the second pending case, *Certain Iranian Assets (Islamic Republic of Iran v. United States of America)*.

[37] C. Giorgetti, 'The Challenge and Recusal of Judges of the International Court of Justice' in C. Giorgetti (ed.), *Challenges and Recusals of Judges and Arbitrators in International Courts and Tribunals*, Brill Nijhoff, Leiden 2015, p. 8: 'of the thirty-six known cases of self-recusals, twenty-one occurred after the year 2000.'

[38] While there were media reports that Pakistan should ask for Judge Bhandari's recusal in the *Jadhav* case, it seems that the state never took that step: see LatestLaws.com, 'India decides to Re-Nominate Justice Dalveer Bhandari to the International Court of Justice' (19 June 2017).

himself when invited to do so by Kenya. It is telling that Kenya did not opt for a more formal disqualification procedure; instead, President Yusuf's steadfastness weighed strongly in the state's decision not to appear at the hearing, and to decry the ICJ judgment as 'biased' after it was rendered.[39]

Finally, it bears mentioning that both Statutes provide that judges can be removed through a unanimous agreement to this effect by their members.[40] This has never happened so far.

3. ADAPTATIONS IN A CHANGING CONTEXT

As a result of the few reasoned decisions on challenges against ICJ and ITLOS judges and members, and because the practice of self-recusal defies easy categorisation, the standards of 'independence and impartiality' have not been greatly developed in the context of these two international bodies. Yet the ICJ and the ITLOS are not insulated from other parts of international law, and developments in these contexts (section 3.1) indicate that the practice of both courts might have to evolve – though to an extent, it already has (section 3.2).

3.1. INDEPENDENCE AND IMPARTIALITY: NEW EXPECTATIONS

It is widely accepted that all international adjudicators (not only ICJ and ITLOS members) are subject to obligations of 'independence and impartiality'. Having received application in other international fora, these terms have been developed in ways that, perhaps, are now out of step with the ICJ and the ITLOS's respective practices. While the application of these developments to ICJ and ITLOS proceedings is debatable,[41] they remain relevant in indicating the ways in which the Court and the Tribunal's practice could (some say, should)[42] evolve.

Most of these developments can be retraced to international arbitrations, of the interstate or investor-state kinds. Self-evidently, the Court and the Tribunal's

---

[39]   BBC, 'ICJ rejects Kenya case in Somalia maritime border row' (12 October 2021), https://www.bbc.com/news/world-africa-58885535.

[40]   ICJ Statute, Article 18; ITLOS Statute, Article 9.

[41]   See in particular *Chagos Marine Protected Area Arbitration (Mauritius v. United Kingdom)*, Reasoned Decision on Challenge, PCA Case No. 2011-03, paras. 165–68, holding that developments in non-state-only arbitrations were irrelevant for disputes involving only states, and in particular 'cannot be considered as a source of law as regards judges of ITLOS or the ICJ'.

[42]   Y. Shany and S. Horovitz, 'Judicial Independence in The Hague and Freetown: A Tale of Two Cities' (2008) 21 *Leiden Journal of International Law* 113, 129, decrying the ICJ's 'conservative approach' with respect to the evolving understanding of independence and impartiality in international law.

preference for proactive self-recusal is irrelevant in a context where adjudicators are appointed by the parties (and therefore agreed to such appointment). Instead, arbitration proceedings have seen frequent uses of disqualification mechanisms as provided under the relevant arbitral rules. This resulted in a substantial jurisprudence over the meaning of the standard of conduct expected of arbitrators. That jurisprudence has been accompanied by international efforts to better define the standard: under the auspices of the United Nations Commission on International Trade Law (UNCITRAL), states are currently negotiating a draft Code of Conduct for international arbitrators that seeks to embody their view of what this standard should mean in investor-state proceedings.[43]

In this respect, a growing number of states and stakeholders agree that international adjudicators should not only be free of biases, but they should also avoid the 'appearance' of bias.[44] It is an open question whether the application of such 'appearance of bias' standard would have changed anything in the Court's past practice.[45] Of particular interest, however, is that when the Court dismissed a request for disqualification in the 2004 *Wall* advisory opinion, the sole ICJ judge to vote in favour of the challenge did so on the basis of the 'appearance of bias' standard.[46] It is likewise striking that one of the arguments for the disqualification of Judge Elaraby in those advisory proceedings, namely the fact that some of his public statements allegedly created an appearance of bias, led to the successful challenge of a number of arbitrators and international judges in other contexts.[47]

While the 'appearance of bias' standard is receiving broader acceptance, other developments are more debated. Notably, the jurisprudence is somewhat conflicted on the relevance of the so-called 'issue conflict' concept, i.e. when an adjudicator has already ruled, or taken a doctrinal position, on a given legal

---

[43] For an update on the negotiations, see UNCITRAL, Code of Conduct, available at https://uncitral.un.org/en/codeofconduct.

[44] This standard was notably applied by the ICTY in *Prosecutor v. Furundzija*, Case No. IT-95-17/1-A, Judgement, 21 July 2000, para. 189.

[45] But see *Chagos Marine Protected Area Arbitration (Mauritius v. United Kingdom)*, Reasoned Decision on Challenge, PCA Case No. 2011-03, para. 169: 'the Tribunal is not convinced that the Appearance of Bias Standard as presented by Mauritius and derived from private law sources is of direct application in the present case'.

[46] *Legal Consequences of the Construction of a Wall in the Occupied Palestinian Territory*, Order of 30 January 2004, I.C.J. Reports 2004, p. 3, Dissenting Opinion of Judge Buergenthal, paras. 10–14.

[47] See, notably, Special Court for Sierra Leone, *Prosecutor v. Sesay*, Case No. SCSL-2004-15-AR15, Decision on Defence Motion Seeking the Disqualification of Justice Robertson from the Appeals Chamber, 13 March 2004, in which a judge was disqualified for statements he wrote in a book preceding his appointment. See also *Perenco Ecuador Limited v. the Republic of Ecuador*, PCA Case No. IR-2009/1, Decision on Challenge to the Arbitrator, 8 December 2009, when Charles Brower (himself a frequent ad hoc judge at the ICJ) was disqualified from an investor-state arbitration on account of comments he made to a legal publication.

The International Court of Justice and the International Tribunal for the Law of the Sea

question.[48] When the United States sought to disqualify Judge Seifi from the Iran–US Claims Tribunal on account of such an alleged 'issue conflict', the appointing authority (Judge Haak) side-stepped the question after finding that Judge Seifi was under no obligation to disclose the past arbitration that allegedly created this conflict.[49] Though international law remains unsettled on the matter, allegations of conflicts will only increase in number at the ICJ and ITLOS, as the judges keep writing ever more individual opinions in a growing body of cases.

Finally, and more recently, a number of arbitrators in investor-state proceedings have been removed from tribunals on account of their straddling appointments in cases sharing some factual and/or merits relationship – with the justification that the inherent 'asymmetry of information' enjoyed by that arbitrator (compared to the co-arbitrators) was an issue warranting disqualification.[50] Here as well, the frequent overlap of international disputes between different fora, and the activity of ICJ and ITLOS judges as arbitrators, might give salience to such arguments in future cases – if it is not pre-emptively resolved by self-recusals.

3.2. RECENT PRACTICE BY THE ICJ AND ITLOS

These developments in broader international legal proceedings evidence a shift in what parties to international disputes might deem important in relation to independence and impartiality. It echoes developments in the practice of both the ICJ and the ITLOS.

Notably, the traditional concerns centred on the nationality of international judges have remarkably lost in salience before both bodies. In recent years, states before the ICJ have taken to appointing judges ad hoc that are not their nationals,[51]

---

[48] It is debatable whether Principle 9.2 of the International Law Association's *Burgh House Principles on the Independence of the International Judiciary* refers to 'issue conflict' situations; as stated ('Judges shall not serve in a case with the subject-matter of which they have had any other form of association that may affect or may reasonably appear to affect their independence or impartiality'), Principle 9.2 remains a tautology, since it refers back to the standard of independence and impartiality.

[49] *US v. Iran*, Case B/61, Decision on Challenge to Judge Sefi, 3 September 2010, 39 IRAN-U.S. C.T.R. 140, para. 33. Judge Haak however opined that '[w]hile not the case in this instance, one might be able to conceive of situations where the past activities of an incoming or current Member of the Tribunal might subject him or her to potential issue conflicts'. It is also notable that, in contrast with the *Chagos* tribunal, Judge Haak considered that the norms and resources applicable in arbitral proceedings (such as the IBA Guidelines on Conflict of Interest) remained relevant in the context of state-to-state arbitral proceedings.

[50] L.E. Peterson, 'Arbitrator is Disqualified from Poland Bilateral Investment Treaty Arbitration' (*Investment Arbitration Reporter*, 8 November 2021).

[51] See the numbers collected by C. Brower and M. Lando, 'Judges Ad Hoc of the International Court of Justice' (2020) 33 *Leiden Journal of International Law* 467, 478. They note that, in the original PCIJ Statute until a 1929 revision, judges ad hoc were *required* to be nationals of their appointing state.

Intersentia

frequently preferring to appoint judges who have already sat on the Court.[52] This has often been the case as well at the ITLOS.[53] And while the ICJ Statute's requirement that judges be elected 'regardless of their nationality' has long been belied by the fact that members of the Security Council consistently maintained a judge of their own on the Bench, that tradition came to an end with the 2017 election.[54]

Instead, the focus has shifted to an important extent to the position of the adjudicator in a network of relationships, often mediated by his or her extra-judicial functions. In this respect, a number of guidelines adopted by the ICJ in 2018 (but published only in late 2020) has now clarified the scope of activities that are available for judges while they sit on the Court,[55] and stressed that judges 'are required to give absolute priority to the exercise of their judicial functions over their external activities'.[56] ICJ judges are in particular forbidden from participating in investor-state or commercial arbitrations,[57] and limited to sitting on 'one inter-State arbitration procedure at a time'.[58] While these guidelines were reportedly adopted in view of the Court's busy docket,[59] it is telling that their adoption and publication coincided with criticisms levelled against the activity of some of ICJ judges (so-called 'moonlighting') in investor-state disputes.[60]

While the ITLOS, seemingly, has not adopted similar guidelines, it has been a forerunner in regulating the activities of its members: besides the 'Incompatible Activities' already prohibited in the ICJ Statute, Article 7 of the ITLOS Statute provides that its members cannot be involved in activities related to the 'the exploration for or exploitation of the resources of the sea or the seabed or other commercial use of the sea or the seabed'. As states and private enterprises are gearing up to start industrial exploitation of the Area,[61] it is to be expected that this provision will acquire greater salience in the years to come.

---

[52] C. Brower and M. Lando, 'Judges Ad Hoc of the International Court of Justice' (2020) 33 *Leiden Journal of International Law* 467, 472–75.

[53] E. Ivanova, 'Election of Judges: International Tribunal for the Law of the Sea', *MPEPIL* (2021), at 47.

[54] The United Kingdom's nominee was not elected. See IJRC, 'After Contested Election, UK Withdraws ICJ Candidate' (21 November 2017), https://ijrcenter.org/2017/11/21/after-contested-election-uk-withdraws-icj-candidate/.

[55] ICJ, *Compilation of Decisions Adopted by the Court concerning the External Activities of its Members*, adopted on 2 October 2018 and 8 September 2020, https://www.icj-cij.org/en/other-texts/compilation-decisions.

[56] Ibid., B.(a).1.

[57] Ibid., A.1.

[58] Ibid., A.5.

[59] Speech by H.E. Mr Abdulqawi A. Yusuf, President of the International Court of Justice, on the occasion of the Seventy-Third Session of the United Nations General Assembly, 25 October 2018.

[60] See D. Charlotin, 'On heels of an ICJ Judge accepting China's invitation to sit in investor-state arbitration, the Court makes public its guidelines designed to curb such appointments' (*Investment Arbitration Reporter*, 23 December 2020).

[61] K. Lyons, 'Deep-sea mining could start in two years after Pacific nation of Nauru gives UN ultimatum' (*The Guardian*, 30 June 2021).

4. CONCLUSION

In his dissenting opinion in the *Wall* advisory opinion, Judge Buergenthal rightly noted that '[j]udicial ethics are not matters strictly of hard and fast rules ... – I doubt they can ever be exhaustively defined – they are matters of perception and of sensibility to appearances that courts must continuously keep in mind to preserve their legitimacy'.[62] If anything, history has proven and is proving him right, as the standards of independence and impartiality at the ICJ and ITLOS have evolved, and will likely continue to evolve, together with the rest of international law.

---

[62] *Legal Consequences of the Construction of a Wall in the Occupied Palestinian Territory*, Order of 30 January 2004, I.C.J. Reports 2004, p. 3, Dissenting Opinion of Judge Buergenthal, para. 10.

THE INDEPENDENCE AND IMPARTIALITY OF ADJUDICATORS IN INTERNATIONAL SPORTS LAW – CAS ARBITRATION

Antonio Rigozzi and Erika Hasler

1. Introduction 194
2. The Structure of the Court of Arbitration for Sport................... 195
   2.1. The International Council of Arbitration for Sport.............. 195
   2.2. The Court of Arbitration for Sport 198
        2.2.1. The CAS Ordinary Division 198
        2.2.2. The CAS Appeals Division........................... 199
        2.2.3. The CAS Anti-Doping Division 199
        2.2.4. The CAS Ad Hoc Division........................... 202
        2.2.5. The CAS Director General........................... 202
        2.2.6. The CAS Court Office............................... 203
3. The CAS List(s) of Arbitrators 203
   3.1. The General List and Other Lists of CAS Arbitrators............ 204
   3.2. The Criteria for the Inclusion of Arbitrators on the CAS Lists 206
   3.3. The Authority Appointing the Arbitrators on the List(s) and
        the Appointment Procedure................................. 208
   3.4. Removal from the CAS Arbitrator Lists 209
4. The Appointment of CAS Panels 209
   4.1. CAS Ordinary Division.................................... 210
   4.2. CAS Appeals Division 210
   4.3. CAS Anti-Doping Division.................................. 211
   4.4. CAS Ad Hoc Division 212
   4.5. Confirmation of Party-Appointed Arbitrators and Appointment
        of an Ad Hoc Clerk 212
5. The Requirement of Independence and Impartiality.................. 214
   5.1. Structural Independence.................................... 214
   5.2. Personal Independence and Impartiality 221
6. Challenge Proceedings... 227
7. Remedies 229
8. Conclusion... 231

1. INTRODUCTION

The idea that the state would recognise the outcome of an arbitration as the equivalent of a state court judgment only to the extent that the arbitration process provides sufficient guarantees of independence and impartiality is self-evident. While in commercial arbitration the focal point of inquiry is the personal independence of the arbitrators, in international sports arbitration the issue also goes to the structural independence of the arbitral institution.

The only truly international system capable of resolving the full range of disputes arising in the world of sports is that of the Court of Arbitration for Sport (CAS), under the Code of Sports-related Arbitration (CAS Code). The CAS was established in the early 1980s, at the behest of the International Olympic Committee (IOC), primarily to insulate sports litigation from the intervention of state courts, by offering a specialised tribunal to resolve sports-specific disputes according to uniform rules, regardless of the parties' domicile or of the competition's location, in a final, binding and judicially recognised manner.

Since its 1994 edition, the CAS Code foresees two principal kinds of arbitral proceedings, the 'Ordinary Arbitration Procedure' and the 'Appeal Arbitration Procedure', which provide for different methods for the appointment of the arbitrators. A third kind of CAS arbitration proceedings is available under the Arbitration Rules applicable to the CAS Ad Hoc Division, which (since 1996) is set up to operate on site at the Olympic Games and other major international sports events. Finally, a permanent Anti-Doping Division was established within the CAS in 2019. These different kinds of arbitration proceedings at the CAS have one common feature that is of particular interest for the present report: only individuals who appear on a CAS list of arbitrators can be appointed to sit in the arbitral tribunals (called panels in the CAS system) that are constituted under the CAS rules.

Another provision that is found in all sets of CAS procedural rules mandatorily fixes the seat of the arbitration in Lausanne, Switzerland, which entails that CAS proceedings are always governed by the Swiss lex arbitri, and subject to the supervisory jurisdiction of the Swiss Supreme Court (Tribunal fédéral, SFT).

Accordingly, this report will examine the CAS's rules relating to the independence and impartiality of arbitrators under Swiss law and by reference to the European Convention on Human Rights (ECHR), to which Switzerland is a party.

2. THE STRUCTURE OF THE COURT OF ARBITRATION FOR SPORT

The CAS Code states in its opening provision, Article S1,[1] that: '[i]n order to resolve sports-related disputes through arbitration ..., two bodies are hereby created: [(i)] the International Council of Arbitration for Sport (ICAS) [and (ii)] the Court of Arbitration for Sport (CAS).'

2.1. THE INTERNATIONAL COUNCIL OF ARBITRATION FOR SPORT

Article S2 of the CAS Code provides that '[t]he purpose of ICAS is to facilitate the resolution of sports-related disputes through arbitration ... and to safeguard the independence of CAS and the rights of the parties. It is also responsible for the administration and financing of CAS'. The CAS Code is silent with respect to the legal nature of the ICAS, but it is common knowledge that it is incorporated as a foundation within the meaning of Articles 80 et seq. of the Swiss Civil Code.[2]

According to Articles S4 and S5 of the CAS Code, the 'ICAS is composed of twenty-two members,[3] experienced jurists', 'appointed for one or several renewable period(s) of four years' as follows:

a. six members are appointed by the International Sports Federations (IFs), viz. five by the Association of Summer Olympic IFs (ASOIF) and one by the Association of Winter Olympic IFs (AIOWF), chosen from within or outside their membership;

b. four members are appointed by the Association of the National Olympic Committees (ANOC), chosen from within or outside its membership;

---

[1]   The current (2022) edition of the CAS Code and many of the previous ones can be found on the CAS website, at https://www.tas-cas.org/en/arbitration/code-procedural-rules. html. The CAS Code is divided into two parts, namely the Statutes of the Bodies Working for the Settlement of Sports-Related Disputes (Articles S1–S26) and the Procedural Rules (Articles R27–R70).

[2]   See e.g. ATF 129 III 445 (*Larisa Lazutina & Olga Danilova v. IOC, FIS & CAS*), Decision of 27.05.2003, para. 3.3.1. The ICAS's Annual Reports, which it started publishing at the end of 2021, indicate that the ICAS is 'a Swiss foundation of private law and of public interest' and that it is 'governed by the rules of the Swiss Civil Code' (see e.g. ICAS Annual Report 2020, published in December 2021, pp. 5 and 15, available at https://www.tas-cas.org/fileadmin/user_ upload/ICAS_2020_Annual_Report_and_Financial_Statements_.pdf).

[3]   Until 1 November 2022 (and since its first edition, issued in 1994), the CAS Code provided that the ICAS was composed of 20 members. An ICAS Media Release published on 11 October 2022 indicated that '[i]n view of the significant increase of the number of arbitrations related to football conducted by CAS, ICAS has decided to increase the number of ICAS members from 20 to 22 in order to guarantee a better representation of football stakeholders'.

c. four members are appointed by the International Olympic Committee (IOC), chosen from within or outside its membership;

d. four members are appointed by the fourteen members of ICAS listed above, after appropriate consultation with a view to safeguarding the interests of the athletes;

e. four members are appointed by the eighteen members of ICAS listed above, chosen from among personalities independent of the bodies designating the other members of the ICAS.

The way in which both the appointment of the 14 members who are directly chosen by the sports governing bodies (SGBs) listed in Article S4(a)–(c) and the co-optation of the remaining eight members pursuant to Article S4(d)–(e) are decided is unknown. The list of current ICAS members (in place for the 2023–2026 term) is published on the CAS website, with a short CV for each member.[4] Until not long ago, no information was provided by the CAS as to which entity had appointed which ICAS member, or, as the case may be, which members were co-opted, and for the latter, on which basis (Article S4(d) or (e)). Since 2021, this information can be found, in very concise form, in the ICAS's Annual Report and Financial Statement.[5]

Among the prerogatives of the ICAS, as listed in Article S6 of the CAS Code, the following are particularly relevant for the present report:

- It elects from among its members for one or several renewable period(s) of four years ... the President of the Ordinary Arbitration Division, the President of

---

[4] https://www.tas-cas.org/en/icas/members-2023-2026/.

[5] In the latest Annual Report (covering the year 2021), which was published in November 2022 and can be found at https://www.tas-cas.org/fileadmin/user_upload/ICAS_Annual_Report___Financial_Statements_2021.pdf, the ICAS included, in the captions under its members' portraits (at p. 8), a shorthand indication, in brackets, of each member's appointing entity, or, for co-opted members, of whether they had been appointed 'with a view to safeguarding the interests of the athletes' (portraits captioned with '(Athlete)'), or 'chosen from among personalities independent of the bodies appointing the other members' (portraits captioned with '(Independent)'). Prior to the 2020 Annual Report, published in 2021, a CAS Media Release dated 28 December 2018 (the 2018 Media Release) also provided this information with regard to the ICAS's composition for the 2019–2022 term. In fact, the 2018 Media Release provided more information than the ICAS's Annual Reports, as it also indicated, for each member, whether he or she had been 'chosen from within [or from outside] the [ASOIF's or AIOWF's/ANOC's/IOC's] membership' (in accordance with Article S4(a)–(c)), as well as who was a new member (and, indirectly, who had been re-elected); see https://www.tas-cas.org/fileadmin/user_upload/ICAS_media_release_-_ICAS_2019-2022.pdf. The latest CAS Media Release breaking down the ICAS's composition for the current term (2023–2026), was published on 16 December 2022 (the 2022 Media Release) and can be found at https://www.tas-cas.org/fileadmin/user_upload/ICAS_Media_Release_-_Composition_of_ICAS_2023-2026.pdf. Unlike the 2018 Media Release, the 2022 Media Release does not highlight newly elected members, nor expressly indicate, for those among them who are ANOC/ASOIF/AIOWF and IOC appointees, whether they have been selected from within or outside the memberships of those organisations.

the Anti-doping Division and the President of the Appeals Arbitration Division of the CAS ... [as well as] the deputies of the three Division Presidents who can replace them in the event they are prevented from carrying out their functions;
- It appoints the arbitrators who constitute the list of CAS arbitrators ... on the proposal of the CAS Membership Commission. It can also remove them from those lists;
- It resolves challenges to and the removal of arbitrators through its Challenge Commission, and performs any other functions identified in the Procedural Rules.

With respect to the election of the ICAS President, Article S8(3) provides that '[a]ny ICAS member is eligible to be a candidate for the ICAS Presidency' and that the term of appointment is four years. The CAS Code does not specify the ICAS President's prerogatives, other than stating in Article S9 that '[t]he President of ICAS is also President of CAS [and that] [s]he/he is responsible for the ordinary administrative tasks pertaining to the ICAS'.[6]

According to Article S7 of the CAS Code, the ICAS 'exercises its functions itself or through its Board ... or [its] permanent commissions'.[7] The ICAS Board is composed of 'the President, the two Vice-Presidents of the ICAS, the President of the Ordinary Arbitration Division and the President of the Appeals Arbitration Division'.[8]

As mentioned, Article S7 of the CAS Code further provides that the ICAS may exercise its functions through its permanent commissions, including the Challenge Commission, which was introduced in the 2019 edition of the CAS Code to exercise the functions foreseen in Articles R34 and R35 of the Code, namely determining challenges against arbitrators and deciding on their removal

---

6   The current President of ICAS is Mr John Coates, who is also Vice-President of the IOC.
7   The ICAS Board may carry out all functions listed under Article S6 of the CAS Code, except those listed at paras 1, 2, 6.2 and 6.3, namely: adopting and amending the CAS Code (Article S6(1) of the CAS Code); electing the President, the two Vice-Presidents, the President of the Ordinary Arbitration Division, the President of the Anti-doping Division, the President of the Appeals Arbitration Division and the deputies of the three Division Presidents (Article S6(2) of the CAS Code); approving the ICAS budget (Article S6(6.2) of the CAS Code); and approving the annual report and financial statements of the ICAS (Article S6(6.3) of the CAS Code).
8   The current Vice-Presidents of the ICAS are Ms Elisabeth Steiner (elected to replace Ms Tjasa Andree-Prosenc, who retired before the end of her term) and Mr Michael Lenard, and the Presidents of the Ordinary and Appeals Arbitration Division are Ms Carole Malinvaud and Ms Corinne Schmidhauser. According to a Media Release published on 16 December 2022, at a meeting held on 2 December 2022, the ICAS 'voted to amend Article S6.2 [of the CAS Code] so that for the 2023–2026 cycle onwards, ICAS will be composed of three, rather than two, Vice-Presidents, meaning that the ICAS Board will count 6 members' (see https://www.tas-cas.org/fileadmin/user_upload/ICAS_Media_Release_-_Composition_of_ICAS_2023-2026.pdf). As indicated in that same Media Release, elections for the positions of ICAS President and Vice-Presidents, as well as President and Deputy President of the Ordinary, Appeals and Anti-Doping Divisions, will be held on 31 May 2023.

from CAS panels. The Challenge Commission is 'composed of an ICAS Member to be appointed from outside the IOC, IFs and ANOC selection and membership and who shall act as commission chair, any by the 3 Division Presidents and their Deputies'.[9] Article S7(2)(c) clarifies that the Division President and the Deputy President of the Division concerned by a challenge procedure before the Commission shall be 'automatically disqualified' from the proceedings.

Another of the ICAS's permanent commissions (also introduced with the 2019 Code) is the CAS Membership Commission, which is 'responsible to propose the nomination of new CAS arbitrators and mediators to the ICAS [or to] suggest the removal of arbitrators and mediators from the CAS lists'.[10] The CAS Membership Commission is composed of two ICAS members (from among those who have been appointed in accordance with Article S4(d) or (e) CAS Code, i.e. with a view to safeguarding the interests of athletes or in view of their independent status vis-à-vis SGBs) and the Presidents of the Ordinary, Appeals and Anti-Doping Divisions.[11]

2.2. THE COURT OF ARBITRATION FOR SPORT

According to Article S3 of the CAS Code, the 'CAS maintains one or more list(s) of arbitrators and provides for the arbitral resolution of sports-related disputes through arbitration conducted by Panels composed of one or three arbitrators'.

CAS panels operate within specialised CAS Divisions, dedicated to the management of the different types of CAS procedures, according to specific sets of rules. Article S3 provides that there are three permanent CAS Divisions, namely the CAS Ordinary Division, the CAS Appeals Division, and the CAS Anti-Doping Division. In addition, as mentioned at the outset, the CAS operates an Ad Hoc Division, which is only set up for finite periods of time, to resolve disputes on the occasion of major sports events. CAS arbitration proceedings are administered by the CAS Court Office, which is managed by the CAS Director General.

2.2.1. The CAS Ordinary Division

The CAS Ordinary Division constitutes panels of one or three arbitrators to resolve sports-related commercial disputes, such as media or image rights

---

[9] The current members of the Challenge Commission are listed in the ICAS's 2021 Annual Report, pp. 9–10, available at https://www.tas-cas.org/fileadmin/user_upload/ICAS_Annual_Report___Financial_Statements_2021.pdf.

[10] Article S7(2)(a) CAS Code.

[11] The current members of the Membership Commission are listed in the ICAS's 2021 Annual Report, p. 10, available at https://www.tas-cas.org/fileadmin/user_upload/ICAS_Annual_Report___Financial_Statements_2021.pdf.

disputes, or matters relating to licensing, sponsorship, agency and other commercial agreements. The jurisdiction of the CAS Ordinary Division to hear the disputes brought before it is based on specific submission or arbitration agreements, concluded ad hoc or included in the parties' contracts. The Ordinary Division's role is to 'ensure the efficient running' of the arbitral proceedings within its remit, which are conducted in accordance with the procedural rules contained in Articles R27–R46 and R64–R70 of the CAS Code.[12]

2.2.2. The CAS Appeals Division

The CAS Appeals Division constitutes panels of one or three arbitrators to resolve challenges against the decisions rendered by SGBs in a variety of contexts, be they disciplinary (including anti-doping) or related to governance, eligibility, contractual or other matters. Its jurisdiction is generally based on an arbitration clause contained in the relevant SGB's regulations or other instruments, providing that the SGB's decisions may be impugned before the CAS upon exhaustion of the applicable internal remedies.[13] The Appeals Division's role is to manage and 'ensure the efficient running' of the arbitral proceedings within its remit, which are governed by Articles R27–R37 and R47–R70 of the CAS Code.[14]

2.2.3. The CAS Anti-Doping Division

As mentioned, the permanent CAS Anti-Doping Division (CAS ADD) is a recent creation. It was established in 2019 in order 'to hear and decide anti-doping cases as a first-instance authority pursuant to a delegation of powers from the [IOC], International Federations of sports on the Olympic programme (Olympic IFs), and any other signatories to the World Anti-Doping Code (WADC)'.[15] In accordance with Articles A1, A2, A14, A16 and A21 of the ADD Rules, the cases submitted to the CAS ADD operating in this capacity are decided by panels composed of a sole arbitrator and can be appealed before the CAS Appeals Division.

A recent case[16] has raised the question whether CAS ADD panels qualify as genuine arbitration tribunals, and their decisions as arbitral awards, within the meaning of the Swiss lex arbitri. Indeed, as just noted, the CAS ADD decides anti-doping cases as a first-instance authority, by delegation (i.e. on behalf)

---

[12] Article S20(a) of the CAS Code.

[13] See Article R47 of the CAS Code.

[14] Article S20(b) of the CAS Code.

[15] Article A1 of the CAS ADD Rules.

[16] SFT 4A_612/2020 (*Evgeny Ustyugov v. International Biathlon Union (IBU)*), Decision of 18.06.2021, reproduced in part in the SFT's reports on leading cases, under the reference ATF 147 III 500; and SFT 4A_232/2022 (*Evgeny Ustyugov v. International Biathlon Union (IBU)*), Decision of 22.12.2022, also slated for publication in the SFT's collection of leading cases.

of the SGBs that opt to entrust it with this role.[17] This means that when the CAS ADD rules on a case in this capacity, it is acting as a substitute for the SGB's internal adjudicatory organs that would otherwise be called to determine (in the first instance and subject to appeal before the CAS) whether there has been an anti-doping violation and impose the appropriate sanction for any such violation.[18]

Under Swiss law, decisions rendered by the internal organs of a sports federation do not qualify as arbitration awards; they are considered as manifestations of the federation's will rather than judicial acts.[19]

This position was confirmed – and its ramifications with regard to the CAS ADD's status clarified – in a very recent decision rendered by the SFT in the *Evgeny Ustyugov v. International Biathlon Union (IBU)* case, where the athlete challenged the jurisdiction and regularity of the constitution of both the CAS ADD and the CAS Appeals Division panel hearing the case on appeal.[20]

After a first application for annulment brought by Ustyugov against the CAS ADD's first-instance 'award' was declared inadmissible by the SFT on the ground that the applicant had failed to exhaust the available remedies,[21] a CAS Appeals Division panel constituted in accordance with Article A21 ADD Rules issued a preliminary award upholding both the CAS ADD's and its own jurisdiction to hear the case, and dismissing the athlete's challenge to the regularity of the constitution and structural independence of both panels.[22]

---

[17]   At present, more than a dozen SGBs have delegated the adjudication of alleged anti-doping violations in accordance with their regulations to the CAS ADD.

[18]   See Articles 8 (Results Management: Right To a Fair Hearing and Notice of Hearing Decision) and 13 (Results Management: Appeals) of the World Anti-Doping Code (WADC).

[19]   See e.g. SFT 344/2021, Decision of 13.01.2022, para. 5.2, with further references; SFT 4A_612/2020, Decision of 18.06.2021, para. 4 (see also the discussion of the SFT's *Gundel* and *Lazutina* decisions in section 5.1 below). As such, the federations' decisions are not open to annulment or revision before the SFT in the same way as arbitral awards. In accordance with Swiss association law, an athlete who intends to challenge his or her federation's disciplinary decisions, can, once any available internal remedies have been exhausted, bring the case for a final and binding judicial determination before the competent court or, if a valid arbitration agreement so provides (as is often the case), before an arbitral tribunal (almost invariably, in such cases, the CAS).

[20]   SFT 4A_332/2022, Decision of 22.12.2022.

[21]   SFT 4A_612/2020 (ATF 147 III 500), Decision of 18.06.2021, paras 4–5.

[22]   CAS 2020/A/7509, Award of 08.04.2022. In disputing the CAS ADD's and (relatedly) the CAS Appeals Division's jurisdiction under the applicable (2019) IBU regulations, Ustyugov argued that, having retired as a professional biathlete in 2014, at a time when the IBU regulations provided for first-instance proceedings before the IBU Anti-Doping Hearing Panel (ADHP) and appeal proceedings before the CAS Appeals Division, he was not bound by the IBU's later decision to replace the ADHP with the CAS ADD (see the summary of the parties' arguments and of the CAS Appeals Division panel's reasoning in SFT 4A_332/2022, Decision of 22.12.2022, paras 5.3–5.5). In essence, Ustyugov argued that either the CAS ADD lacked jurisdiction for this reason (the ADHP should have heard his case in the first instance), and thus the CAS Appeals Division also had no jurisdiction to hear an appeal against the CAS ADD decision, or, if the CAS ADD was to be considered as a genuine arbitral tribunal, its jurisdiction (and that of the CAS Appeals Division on appeal) could not be validly imposed on him, given that he had never consented to it (since the relevant regulations were adopted after his retirement).

Ustyugov again sought the annulment of this award before the SFT.[23] Here, the SFT recalled that, to qualify as an arbitral award, a decision must be rendered by a tribunal meeting the fundamental requirements of impartiality and independence and drawing its power to adjudicate the case (in lieu of the otherwise competent courts) from a valid arbitration agreement.[24] In this regard, the SFT noted that, even though the CAS ADD is not itself an organ of the sports federation, its power to rule as a first-instance tribunal, applying the federation's anti-doping rules and deciding cases on its behalf, arises from a unilateral decision of the relevant SGB (in this case, the IBU) to delegate that power to the ADD instead of exercising it directly through its internal organs. Under this configuration, there is no basis for a finding that either of the parties to the dispute, i.e. the SGB and the athlete accused of an anti-doping rule violation, have intended to confer jurisdiction to the CAS ADD panel to determine their dispute in a final and binding manner, in lieu of the competent courts of law. Regardless of the terminology used in the CAS ADD Rules, which refer to the proceedings before the ADD as 'arbitration' and to the resulting decisions as 'awards', the CAS ADD's authority vis-à-vis Ustyugov did not rest on actual arbitration agreement, and as a consequence, its decision could not qualify as a genuine arbitral award.[25] On the other hand, in line with its longstanding case law, the SFT held that the CAS Appeals Division panel hearing the case on appeal was a validly constituted arbitral tribunal, with the jurisdictional mission to finally adjudicate the dispute instead of the otherwise competent state courts, based on the parties' mutual submission to the relevant provisions in the IBU regulations.[26]

In *Ustyugov*, the CAS ADD operated in accordance with the 'default' two-tier procedure under the ADD Rules, which, as noted, mandatorily provides for the CAS ADD award to be rendered by a sole arbitrator, subject to a subsequent appeal before a CAS Appeals Division panel (consisting of one or three arbitrators). However, the CAS ADD Rules also allow the parties to agree to have their case decided by a three-member panel as the *sole* adjudicating instance. The procedure for the conclusion of such an agreement is set out in subsections of Articles A13–A15 ADD Rules. As Article A15 makes clear, '[w]hen the parties agree to have a three-member Panel instead of a Sole Arbitrator, they also agree to forgo their right of appeal before the CAS Appeals Division.' Although the CAS ADD Rules still permit certain (non-participating) third parties to bring an appeal against the CAS ADD award,[27] as far as the original parties are concerned, the award is final.

---

23   SFT 4A_332/2022, Decision of 22.12.2022.
24   Ibid., para. 5.2.
25   Ibid., paras 5.9.1–5.9.3.
26   Ibid., para. 5.9.5. As noted in n. 22 above, the IBU regulations to which Ustyugov had adhered (prior to his retirement) already provided for the CAS Appeal Division's jurisdiction to hear appeals against the IBU's first-instance decisions in anti-doping matters.
27   Article A15(4)(a) and (b) CAS ADD Rules, with reference to Article 13.2.3 WADC.

While the SFT did not rule on this point in the *Ustyugov* decision, it is submitted (in line also with the SFT's reasoning in that case) that in this particular configuration and by virtue of the separate and specific arbitration agreement concluded by the parties in accordance with Articles A13–A15 ADD Rules, the CAS ADD's ruling is to be deemed a genuine arbitral award, subject to review by the Swiss courts in accordance with the Swiss lex arbitri, including its provisions governing the independence and impartiality of arbitrators. Accordingly, the provisions governing CAS ADD 'sole instance' proceedings will be examined, where relevant, in the following sections.

2.2.4. The CAS Ad Hoc Division

As mentioned, the CAS also comprises a non-permanent Ad Hoc Division, which is set up specifically on the occasion of major international sporting events (including, beyond the Summer and Winter Olympic Games, the Commonwealth Games, the Asian Games, the UEFA European Championship, and the FIFA World Cup).

Each CAS Ad Hoc Division only exists and operates for a predetermined period of time, to deal with any disputes as may arise in the run-up to the event's official opening and throughout its duration.[28] Given the dynamic competition context in which the Ad Hoc Division operates, the proceedings are highly expedited and the resulting awards must normally be rendered within 24 hours from the lodging of the application.[29]

Since the Summer Olympic Games of 2016, a CAS Ad Hoc Anti-Doping Division has also been operating, alongside the 'classic' Ad Hoc Division, on a temporary basis and on site, at major international sports events.

2.2.5. The CAS Director General

The CAS Director General, who formerly carried the title of Secretary General,[30] is appointed by the ICAS. The Code does not set out a limit to the duration of the Director General's mandate.[31]

---

[28] For instance, Article 1 of the Arbitration Rules applicable to the CAS Ad Hoc Division for the Olympic Games (CAS Arbitration Rules for the Olympic Games) provides, in conjunction with Article 61 of the Olympic Charter, that the CAS Ad Hoc Division is competent to adjudicate any disputes 'arising on the occasion of, or in connection with, the Olympic Games', 'insofar as they arise during the Olympic Games or during a period of ten days preceding the Opening Ceremony of the Olympic Games.'

[29] See, in particular, Articles 14–18 of the CAS Arbitration Rules for the Olympic Games.

[30] The change in title, which was implemented in the CAS Code's 2020 edition, has been reportedly decided by the ICAS to 'better reflect the managerial role of the chief executive of CAS through the years and acknowledg[e] the person's supervision of the activities of the CAS Court Office' (CAS Bulletin 2020/1, p. 3).

[31] The current Director General, Mr Matthieu Reeb, has been in office for 23 years (see 'Important Dates', at https://www.tas-cas.org/en/general-information/statistics.html, indicating that

According to Articles S8(4) and S10 of the CAS Code, the CAS Director General takes part in the decision-making of the ICAS and ICAS Board with a consultative voice, acts as Secretary to the ICAS and ICAS Board, and supervises the activities of the CAS Court Office.

One prerogative of the CAS Director General, which, as will be seen below, has made the object of challenges before the CAS itself and in various courts, is the so-called scrutiny of awards. In this regard, Articles R46 and R59 of the CAS Code provide, for awards rendered by panels sitting in the Ordinary and Appeals Divisions, that 'before the award is signed, it shall be transmitted to the CAS Director General who may make rectifications of pure form and may also draw the attention of the Panel to fundamental issues of principle.' A similar provision is found in Article A21 of the CAS ADD Rules, which entrusts the Managing Counsel of the CAS ADD with the scrutiny of ADD awards. The CAS Ad Hoc Division Rules provide that the scrutiny of the award is performed by the President of the Ad Hoc Division.[32]

2.2.6. The CAS Court Office

According to Article S22 of the CAS Code, the CAS 'includes a Court Office composed of the Director General and one or more Counsel, who may represent the Director General when required',[33] and '[t]he Court Office performs the functions assigned to it by this Code'.

The functions carried out by the CAS Court Office are mentioned in several provisions throughout the Code. Among others, the CAS Court Office receives and issues communications to and from the parties and the CAS, including with regard to the process of constitution of CAS panels and any procedural incidents arising from or related to such process (e.g. disclosures and challenges). Similar functions are performed by the CAS ADD Office under the CAS ADD Rules.

3. THE CAS LIST(S) OF ARBITRATORS

Both the CAS Code[34] and the court decisions that have reviewed the CAS system generally refer to the 'CAS list' of arbitrators in the singular form. In reality there is nowadays, within the CAS, a complex system of lists, special lists and sub-lists.

Mr Reeb was appointed in 1999. The previous CAS Secretary Generals were Messrs Jean-Philippe Rochat (1994–1999), and Gilbert Schwaar (1984–1994)).

[32] Article 19 CAS Arbitration Rules for the Olympic Games.

[33] According to the CAS website, the CAS Court Office currently employs 13 CAS Counsel and two Clerks (https://www.tas-cas.org/en/general-information/addresses-and-contacts.html).

[34] See in particular, in the CAS Statutes, Articles S5, S6, S13, S14 and S19, and, in the CAS Procedural Rules, Articles R33, R38, R39, R40.2 and R48. Article S3 was amended in 2019 to reflect the possibility for CAS of maintaining 'one or more list(s) of arbitrators', and, since

3.1. THE GENERAL LIST AND OTHER LISTS OF CAS ARBITRATORS

Ever since the start of its operations in 1984,[35] the CAS works with a mandatory list of arbitrators, meaning that the parties can only appoint individuals from the list to serve as arbitrators on CAS panels.[36]

Initially, the CAS list of arbitrators consisted of 60 names. Starting in 1994 (as a result of the structural and institutional reforms prompted by the SFT's *Gundel* decision, which will be discussed below)[37] and until 2021, the CAS Code provided that the list should include at least 150 names. The current (2022) wording of Article S13 provides that '[t]here shall be not less than three hundred arbitrators' on the CAS list of arbitrators. The latest version of the list is publicly available on the CAS website, under the tab 'general list'.[38] At the time of drafting the present report there were 376 arbitrators on this 'general list'. Arbitrators appearing on the general list can be appointed to sit in proceedings administered by the Ordinary, Appeals and Ad Hoc Divisions.

The CAS website also refers to a 'football list', which currently contains 111 names.[39] The existence of the 'football list' is not expressly contemplated by the CAS Code but is understood to be the result of an agreement between the CAS and the Fédération Internationale de Football Association (FIFA) when the latter decided to join the CAS system in 2002. It is further understood that the composition of this list is based on recommendations of arbitrators with specific expertise in football matters, made to ICAS by football stakeholders. Several arbitrators on the football list also appear on the general list. That said, arbitrators who only appear on the CAS football list can also be appointed in cases that do not concern football. In connection with the recent renewal of this agreement between FIFA and the CAS it has reportedly been decided to expand the 'football list' and to allow arbitrators who are not on the 'football list' to act as sole or presiding arbitrators in football disputes only if the parties so agree or the President of the Appeals Division so decides in exceptional circumstances.[40]

Since 2018, there is an additional sub-list, selected from the general list, to form a 'special list' of arbitrators who are designated to handle cases concerning

---

1 November 2022, Article R54 of the Code expressly refers to the existence of special list(s) of arbitrators 'in relation to a particular sport or event' in connection with the appointment of sole or presiding arbitrators in appeals proceedings (see section 4.2 below).

[35] For a brief history of the CAS, see https://www.tas-cas.org/en/general-information/history-of-the-cas.html, and G. Kaufmann-Kohler and A. Rigozzi, *International Arbitration – Law and Practice in Switzerland*, OUP, Oxford 2015, paras 1.122–28.

[36] Article R33(2) CAS Code.

[37] Section 5.1.

[38] https://www.tas-cas.org/en/arbitration/liste-des-arbitres-liste-generale.html.

[39] https://www.tas-cas.org/en/arbitration/list-of-arbitrators-football-list.html.

[40] See Article R54(4) of the 1 November 2022 edition of the CAS Code and section 4.2 below.

non-compliance with the WADC by signatory sports organisations.[41] This list has now become a sub-list of the list of arbitrators composing the recently established CAS ADD.

Indeed, since 2019, there is a 'new list of arbitrators specialized in anti-doping regulations (the CAS ADD list)',[42] who constitute the CAS ADD. According to the CAS, the CAS ADD list 'is separated from the CAS general list of arbitrators in order to avoid that the same arbitrators be eligible in first instance and in appeal. However, the CAS ADD arbitrators ... remain eligible to decide cases submitted to the CAS Ordinary Division'.[43] In addition, Article A9 of the CAS ADD Rules provides for a special 'sub-list' of ADD 'arbitrators who shall exclusively act as Presidents of three-member CAS ADD Panels or as Sole Arbitrators', and who will not be 'eligible to be nominated by parties involved in CAS ADD procedures, except where the parties agree on such nomination'.

There are currently 22 arbitrators who are eligible for party nomination on the CAS ADD list, 24 on the list of Panel Presidents/Sole Arbitrators and nine arbitrators who are eligible for appointment in WADC non-compliance issues.[44]

Yet another list of CAS arbitrators is set up on a temporary basis, on the occasion of the establishment of a CAS Ad Hoc Division and CAS Ad Hoc ADD Division to operate at the Olympic Games and other major sports events. According to Article 2 of the CAS Arbitration Rules for the Olympic Games, 'the ad hoc Division consists of arbitrators appearing on a special list, a President, a Co-president and a Court Office'. According to Article 3 of the same Rules, the arbitrators selected to appear in the ad hoc list of arbitrators for the Olympics are drawn from ('appear on') the CAS general list. Article 3 further specifies that '[n]one of these arbitrators may act for the CAS [ADD] during the same edition of the [Olympics], nor thereafter in matters connected to the said edition of the [Olympics]'.

In recent years, the CAS Ad Hoc Division and Ad Hoc ADD Division lists of arbitrators have generally included between six and 12 names, depending on the event.[45]

---

41 While the jurisdiction of CAS to decide on these issues is provided for by Article 24.1.6 WADC, the existence of the 'list of arbitrators specifically designated by CAS for cases arising under [WADC] Article 24.1' is contemplated in Articles 9.3.2 and 9.4.2 of WADA's International Standard for Code Compliance by Signatories.

42 M. Reeb, 'Editorial', CAS Bulletin 2019/2, p. 4.

43 Ibid. See also Article A8 CAS ADD Rules, and Article S18(1) of the CAS Code, as amended in the Code's 2020 edition.

44 https://www.tas-cas.org/en/add/list-of-arbitrators-cas-add.html.

45 At the London 2012 and Rio 2016 Summer Olympics, the ad hoc list of arbitrators consisted of 12 names. At the Tokyo 2021 Olympics, the list consisted of 10 names (see https://www.tas-cas.org/fileadmin/user_upload/CAS_Media_Release_Tokyo_Announcement.pdf). At the last three editions of the Winter Olympics (Sochi 2014, Pyeongchang 2018 and Beijing 2022), the ad hoc list of arbitrators consisted of nine names (see, most recently, https://www.tas-cas.org/fileadmin/user_upload/CAS_Media_Release_Beijing2022_18.01.22.pdf). The lists of

3.2. THE CRITERIA FOR THE INCLUSION OF ARBITRATORS ON THE CAS LISTS

With respect to the CAS general list of arbitrators, Article S14(1) ab initio of the CAS Code provides that 'ICAS shall appoint personalities to the list of CAS arbitrators with appropriate legal training, recognized competence with regard to sports law and/or international arbitration, a good knowledge of sport in general and a good command of at least one CAS working language', namely French, English or Spanish. Until 31 December 2011, candidate arbitrators could only be proposed for inclusion in the list by 'the IOC', 'the IFs' or 'the NOCs [National Olympic Committees]'.[46] This limitation was lifted in the 2012 edition of the Code. Under the current version of Article S14(1), the ICAS may select arbitrators 'whose names and qualifications are brought to [its] attention, *including* by the IOC, the IFs, the NOCs and by the athletes' commissions of the IOC, IFs and NOCs' (emphasis added). Hence, theoretically, a proposal can now come from virtually anyone and prospective arbitrators are not precluded from submitting personal applications.

Article S14(1) in fine of the CAS Code adds that the 'ICAS may identify the arbitrators having a specific expertise to deal with certain types of disputes'. It is understood that this provision is the basis for the existence of the above-mentioned 'football list' and the 'special list' for WADC non-compliance matters. There are no express requirements that are specifically set out for arbitrators to be included in these two lists, though one would assume that the individuals selected for inclusion will have particular expertise in football and anti-doping matters, respectively.

Similarly, there are no special (express) requirements for inclusion in the list of arbitrators for the CAS Ad Hoc Divisions. The CAS Media Releases issued on 9 July 2021 and 18 January 2022, announcing the composition of the CAS Ad Hoc Divisions for the Tokyo and Beijing Olympics, stated that all the selected arbitrators 'are … experienced lawyers, judges or professors specialized in sports law, anti-doping regulations and arbitration'.[47]

---

arbitrators for the Ad Hoc CAS ADD Divisions that operated at the Olympic Games in Rio, Pyeongchang and Tokyo each consisted of six names (see, most recently, https://www.tas-cas.org/fileadmin/user_upload/CAS_Media_Release_Tokyo_Announcement.pdf).

[46] Specifically, one-fifth of the arbitrators were ('in principle') to be 'selected from among the persons proposed by the IOC, chosen from within its membership or from outside'; one-fifth were to be 'selected from among the persons proposed by the IFs, chosen from within their membership or outside'; one-fifth were to be 'selected from among the persons proposed by the NOCs, chosen from within their membership or outside'; one-fifth were to be 'chosen, after appropriate consultations, with a view to safeguarding the interests of the athletes'; and one-fifth were to be 'chosen from among persons independent of the bodies responsible for proposing arbitrators in conformity with the present article.'

[47] https://www.tas-cas.org/fileadmin/user_upload/CAS_Media_Release_Tokyo_Announcement.pdf; https://www.tas-cas.org/fileadmin/user_upload/CAS_Media_Release_Beijing2022_18.01.22.pdf.

The CAS Code also provides, in Article S16, that '[w]hen appointing arbitrators ... the ICAS shall consider continental representation and the different juridical cultures'. It is likely for this reason that one version of the CAS general list published on the CAS website displays the arbitrators' names by continents and countries of nationality.[48] Until very recently, Article S16's recommendation was the only express reference to diversity requirements with regard to arbitrators in the CAS Code.[49] As will be seen in section 4.2 below, the 2022 edition of the CAS Code has introduced a new provision, addressing arbitrator diversity more comprehensively, in connection with the selection, by the President of the Appeals Division, of sole and presiding arbitrators at the panel appointment stage.

Finally, Article S18(3) of the CAS Code prohibits so-called double-hatting, providing that 'CAS arbitrators ... may not act as counsel or expert for a party before the CAS'. Hence, candidates for appointment to the list of arbitrators will have to renounce acting in other capacities, even in unrelated cases, in CAS proceedings. Article S18(3) was first introduced in 2010.[50] At the time, the CAS was one of the first major arbitral institutions to introduce an express

---

[48] https://www.tas-cas.org/fileadmin/user_upload/Liste_des_arbitres_par_nationalite_2022__sans_ADD__.pdf (status: January 2023). In this regard, it may be worth noting that, contrary to other institutional arbitration rules, the CAS Code does not contain express nationality-based restrictions to panel appointments (i.e. one or more of the arbitrators on a panel may have the same nationality as one of the parties).

[49] In this connection it may be worth noting that recent studies have found that there remain significant disparities in terms of, inter alia, gender and nationality, not only in the make-up of the CAS list(s) of arbitrators (with male arbitrators from a limited number of countries counting for a large proportion of the names on the lists), but, more importantly, when it comes to the arbitrators who are actually appointed to sit in panels, as opposed to simply appearing on the CAS lists (see in particular J. Lindholm, *The Court of Arbitration for Sport and Its Jurisprudence: An Empirical Inquiry into Lex Sportiva*, Asser Press, The Hague 2019, and R. Sethna, 'A Data Analysis Of The Arbitrators, Cases And Sports At The Court Of Arbitration For Sport', LawInSport, 4 July 2019, https://www.lawinsport.com/topics/item/a-data-analysis-of-the-arbitrators-sports-and-cases-at-the-court-of-arbitration-for-sport#_Qualifications). Nevertheless, it is worth noting that, in recent years, the ICAS has seemed to pay more attention to these aspects, as it indicated in Media Releases it published on the occasion of its revisions of the list of arbitrators in 2017 and 2018, where it stated that, in selecting new names to add to the list, its focus was 'on geographic spread as well as on gender and knowledge of the sports world in order to achieve a balanced list of independent legal specialists (attorneys-at-law, judges, professors) equipped to meet the unique challenges of global sports arbitration' (see https://www.tas-cas.org/fileadmin/user_upload/2018.01.26_New_CAS_members.pdf; https://www.tas-cas.org/fileadmin/user_upload/ICAS_release_Jan_17_new_arbitrators_and_mediators_corrected_Bennett_Canada_instead_of_Australia_.pdf (sic) (status: January 2023)).

[50] As worded in the 2010 edition of the CAS Code and several subsequent iterations, the provision (originally found in Article S18(2)) only precluded arbitrators from acting as counsel. Since the 2021 edition, and in what is now Article S18(3), appointments as expert are also incompatible with inclusion in the CAS list of arbitrators.

rule prohibiting double-hatting. That said, as noted elsewhere,[51] the CAS's rule's effectiveness in actually preventing conflicts of interest is limited by the fact that it does not prohibit other members of CAS arbitrators' law firms from acting as counsel or experts in CAS cases.

Upon their appointment, CAS arbitrators are required to sign an 'official declaration' whereby they undertake to 'exercise their functions personally with total objectivity, independence and impartiality and in conformity with the provisions of [the CAS Code]'.[52]

3.3. THE AUTHORITY APPOINTING THE ARBITRATORS ON THE LIST(S) AND THE APPOINTMENT PROCEDURE

As mentioned, the various lists of CAS arbitrators are compiled by the ICAS,[53] and, since the entry into force of the CAS Code's 2019 edition, the new members are appointed to the lists upon the proposal of the ICAS's Membership Commission.[54]

As was also seen above, proposals to the CAS Membership Commission can be put forward not only by 'the IOC, the IFs, the NOCs and by the athletes' commissions of the IOC, IFs and NOCs', but also by any other stakeholder, and nothing in the rules prevents the CAS Membership Commission from considering spontaneous applications.

Neither the CAS Code nor the CAS website provide any information on the application process. It is understood that individuals who wish to be considered for inclusion in the list can request an application form from the CAS Court Office.[55] The form requires applicants to state their personal details, including their nationality, domicile 'education (legal)', 'current function', language skills, and whether they have any experience in arbitration and/or sports law and/or experience in sports 'as an athlete, as an official or as a manager'. In addition, applicants are asked to provide '2 or 3 letters of reference of persons who could be consulted and who are specialized in international arbitration ..., sports law or sports management.'[56]

---

[51] A. Rigozzi, 'The Recent Revision of the Code of Sports-Related Arbitration (CAS Code)', *Jusletter*, 13 September 2010, p. 3.

[52] Article S18(1) CAS Code.

[53] Article S3 CAS Code.

[54] Article S7(2)(a) CAS Code.

[55] An older specimen of the form was reproduced in D. Mavromati and M. Reeb, *The Code of the Court of Arbitration for Sport – Commentary, Cases and Materials*, Kluwer Law, Alphen aan den Rijn 2015, pp. 155–56.

[56] The form (in its 2020 edition on file with the rapporteurs) indicates that it should be sent to the CAS's general postal address (and/or by e-mail to info@tas-cas.org), and that, although applications can be submitted at any time, '[t]he review process of applications by the ICAS takes place twice a year'.

Candidates are not interviewed and it is understood that the decision not to appoint them does not state the reasons for non-appointment.

3.4. REMOVAL FROM THE CAS ARBITRATOR LISTS

Article S7(2)(a) of the CAS Code provides that the CAS Membership Commission, 'may … suggest the removal of arbitrators … from the CAS lists'. Article S19(2) also provides that 'ICAS may remove an arbitrator … from the list of CAS members, temporarily or permanently, if she/he violates any rule of this Code or if her/his action affects the reputation of ICAS/CAS'. As ICAS is not a permanent body, it is understood that the initial call for removal is a matter for the CAS Director General.

According to Article S13, arbitrators can appear on the list 'for one or several renewable period(s) of four years'. Beyond acting to remove an arbitrator in the course of an ongoing four-year 'tenure' period, in accordance with Articles S7 and S19 of the CAS Code, the CAS Membership Commission can obviously also choose not to renew an arbitrator's appointment to the list after one or more four-year period(s). The reasons for removal or non-reappointment are not set out in the CAS Code, and it is understood that they were not, in the past, communicated to the non-renewed arbitrators. It remains to be seen whether the language most recently added in Article S13, providing that 'CAS arbitrators … who have not been reappointed shall be informed accordingly'[57] means that, in addition to being notified of their non-reappointment, arbitrators will also be informed of the reasons for the decision not to reappoint them and be allowed to comment on such reasons.

As far as the Ad Hoc Divisions are concerned, removal from the list would not normally occur, given the Divisions' short-term tenure (a new Ad Hoc Division (and the corresponding list of arbitrators) is appointed for each of the concerned sports events). That said, the Arbitration Rules for the Olympic Games do reserve the faculty for the ICAS Board to 'modify' the Ad Hoc List after it has been published.[58]

4. THE APPOINTMENT OF CAS PANELS

The modalities according to which panels are constituted differ depending on the applicable CAS arbitration proceedings.

---

[57] Article S13(1) in fine, as amended with effect on 1 November 2022.
[58] Article 3.

4.1. CAS ORDINARY DIVISION

Article R40.1 of the CAS Code provides that Panels in the CAS Ordinary Division are composed of one or three arbitrators, depending on the parties' agreement. If there is no such agreement,[59] the President of the Ordinary Division 'shall determine the number [of arbitrators], taking into account the circumstances of the case'.[60]

Article R40.2 gives priority to the parties' autonomy and thus to their agreement also with respect to the modalities of appointment of the arbitrators (subject always to the requirement that appointees must be selected from the (relevant) CAS list). In the absence of an agreement, it provides that, if a sole arbitrator is to be appointed, the appointment will be made directly by the Division President. Where the Division President determines that the panel is to be constituted of three arbitrators, the claimant will be expected to nominate an arbitrator within the time limit set by the CAS to that effect, failing which the arbitration will be deemed withdrawn. If, on the other hand, the respondent fails to appoint its arbitrator within the set time limit, the Division President will make the appointment. The two co-arbitrators will then select the President of the Panel by mutual agreement, failing which the Division President will make the appointment.

4.2. CAS APPEALS DIVISION

Article R50 of CAS Code, entitled 'Number of arbitrators', sets out a default rule, providing for the appointment of a three-member panel, unless the parties have agreed to have their dispute heard by a sole arbitrator, or, absent an agreement between the parties, if the President of the Appeals Division 'decides to submit the appeal to a sole arbitrator, taking into account the circumstances of the case, including whether or not the Respondent pays its share of the advance of costs within the time limit fixed by the CAS Court Office'.

The room left to party autonomy is significantly reduced with regard to the appointment of the panels in CAS Appeals Division cases, given that, under Article R54, if a sole arbitrator is to be appointed, the appointment will be made by the President of the Appeals Division, with no direct input from the parties. If the case is to be heard by a three-member panel, while each party may appoint a

---

[59] Article R40.1 was amended in the 1 November 2022 edition of the Code to expressly provide that '[i]f the arbitration agreement does not specify the number of arbitrators', the parties may agree to a panel composed of a sole arbitrator 'at the outset of the procedure.'

[60] In particular, the Division President may choose to appoint a sole arbitrator when the claimant so requests and the respondent fails to pay its share of the advance on costs.

co-arbitrator,[61] the President of the Panel (who, importantly, will have a casting vote in case the panel cannot reach a majority decision)[62] will be appointed by the President of the Appeals Division, again with no direct input from the parties.[63]

As already mentioned, for cases where a special list of arbitrators is established in relation to a particular sport (e.g. the football list), the 2022 edition of the Code has introduced a further limitation to the effect that the sole arbitrator or the president of the panel must be a person appearing on the special list, unless the parties agree otherwise, or the President of the Appeals Division so decides in exceptional circumstances (when appointing either the sole arbitrator or the president of the panel).[64]

The 2022 edition of the Code has also added a requirement (which, for unclear reasons, is spelled out only with regard to appeals proceedings) that, when selecting sole and presiding arbitrators, the President of the Appeals Division shall consider the criteria of 'expertise, availability, diversity, equality and turnover of arbitrators'.[65]

4.3. CAS ANTI-DOPING DIVISION

Article A15 of the CAS ADD Rules sets out the appointment procedure that applies when a three-member CAS ADD Panel is to be appointed to operate as a single-instance arbitral tribunal, by virtue of an agreement between the parties, as provided in Article A14. In these cases, the claimant, then the respondent, are each to nominate an arbitrator from the CAS ADD list (and, as noted in section 3.1 above, the parties may agree to the appointment of co-arbitrators drawn from the special list of CAS ADD Presidents, in accordance with

---

[61]   The 1 November 2022 edition of the CAS Code has been amended to clarify that, as also provided with regard to ordinary proceedings (Article R40.2), where a three-member panel is to be appointed by virtue of a decision made by the President of the Appeals Division, 'the Appellant shall appoint an arbitrator within the time limit set by the President of the Division, failing which the appeal shall be deemed withdrawn.'

[62]   Articles R46 and R59 CAS Code.

[63]   According to Article R54(2), the President of the Appeals Division will proceed with the appointment of the presiding arbitrator 'after having consulted the [co-]arbitrators'.

[64]   Article R54(4) CAS Code (2022 edition): '[i]n case a special list of arbitrators exists in relation to a particular sport or event, the Sole Arbitrator or the President of the Panel shall be appointed from such list, unless the parties agree otherwise or the President of the Division decides otherwise due to exceptional circumstances'. This provision is rather obscure, particularly to the extent it refers to a special list for 'a particular sport event', as in that case the appointment is done directly by the President of the Ad Hoc Division and arbitrators who are not on the list will not be at the venue of the event.

[65]   Article R54(3) CAS Code (2022 edition). It is submitted that the same criteria should be taken into consideration when CAS (Ordinary or Appeals) Division Presidents appoint arbitrators in lieu of defaulting respondents (in accordance with Articles R40.2(3) and R53 in fine of the CAS Code).

Article A9). If either party fails to nominate its arbitrator, the appointment is made on that party's behalf by the President of the CAS ADD.

With regard to the presiding arbitrator, Article A15 provides that he or she 'shall be appointed from the special list of Presidents for CAS ADD, either by mutual agreement of the parties ... or, failing such agreement, by the President of CAS ADD'.

4.4. CAS AD HOC DIVISION

Given the expedited nature of the proceedings in the Ad Hoc Division, it is the President of the Ad Hoc Division that directly appoints a three-member panel (and, within that panel, the presiding arbitrator) or – where he or she deems it appropriate – a sole arbitrator to hear each incoming case, with no input from the parties. This rule applies to both the 'general' CAS Ad Hoc Division and the CAS Ad Hoc Anti-Doping Division.[66]

4.5. CONFIRMATION OF PARTY-APPOINTED ARBITRATORS AND APPOINTMENT OF AN AD HOC CLERK

In the CAS Ordinary, Appeals and ADD Divisions, party-appointed arbitrators must be confirmed by the President of the relevant Division, who is required by the CAS Code to proceed with the confirmation only after having 'ensure[d] that the arbitrators comply with the requirements of Article R33 [of the CAS Code]'.[67] In CAS Ad Hoc Divisions, this step is not required given that panels are exclusively and directly appointed by the Ad Hoc Division President.

Article R33 of the CAS Code sets out the fundamental requirements of independence and impartiality for all CAS arbitrators,[68] and provides that each arbitrator shall 'immediately disclose any circumstances which may affect her/his independence with respect to any of the parties.'[69]

In practice, upon their proposed appointment, CAS arbitrators in the Ordinary, Appeals and ADD Divisions must fill in and sign a form entitled

---

[66]   Article 11 Arbitration Rules for the Olympic Games; Article 11 of the CAS Ad Hoc ADD Rules.

[67]   Articles R40.3 and R54 CAS Code; Article A17 CAS ADD Rules.

[68]   Article R33(1); see section 5.2 below. In addition, Article R33(2) requires, as seen in section 3.1 above, that '[e]very arbitrator shall appear on the list [of arbitrators] drawn up by the ICAS' and that he or she 'shall have a good command of the language of the arbitration and shall be available as required to complete the arbitration expeditiously.'

[69]   Similarly, Article 12 of the Arbitration Rules for the Olympic Games requires arbitrators to 'disclose immediately any circumstance likely to compromise their independence.'

'Arbitrator's Acceptance and Statement of Independence'.[70] In this form, appointee arbitrators confirm their ability and availability to serve in the case at hand, and are asked to declare that there are no facts or circumstances that 'might be of such a nature as to compromise [the appointee arbitrator's] independence in the eyes of any of the parties', or to disclose any such facts or circumstances.[71] In the rapporteurs' experience, the CAS Court Office's practice with regard to the timing of communication to the parties of prospective arbitrators' Acceptance and Statement of Independence forms is not entirely consistent, in that the forms may or may not be circulated for comments prior to the Division President's confirmation of the arbitrators' appointment.[72]

Be that as it may, once (all) the arbitrator(s) is/are confirmed, the panel's appointment is recorded in a document entitled Notice of Formation of Panel, which includes copies of the Arbitrator(s)' Statement(s) of Independence (with any disclosures) and is circulated by the CAS Court Office to the parties. As from service of the Notice of Formation (and throughout the arbitration proceedings), any challenges to the panel's composition must be raised by the parties within seven days of their becoming aware of the relevant facts or circumstances, in accordance with the procedure described in section 6 below.[73]

The CAS Code further mentions that '[a]n ad hoc clerk, independent of the parties, may be appointed to assist the Panel'.[74] Upon their appointment (which generally occurs after the panel's formation), CAS ad hoc clerks are also required to fill in a Statement of Independence form, similar to the one filled in by the arbitrators. In practice, the ad hoc clerk's statement is only circulated to the parties if it contains any disclosures (and if the panel has confirmed to the CAS Court Office that it wishes to retain the ad hoc clerk, notwithstanding

---

[70] A sample of this form was reproduced in D. Mavromati and M. Reeb, *The Code of the Court of Arbitration for Sport – Commentary, Cases and Materials*, Kluwer Law, Alphen aan den Rijn 2015, pp. 151–52.

[71] Obviously, an arbitrator who makes a disclosure in the Acceptance and Statement of Independence form considers that the circumstances so disclosed do not affect his or her independence, or else he or she should decline the appointment.

[72] When an arbitrator's Acceptance and Statement of Independence form containing a disclosure is circulated by the CAS Court Office to the parties prior to the arbitrator's confirmation, the CAS's cover letter mentions that 'pursuant to Article R34 of the CAS Code, the time limit to bring a challenge against an arbitrator is seven days after the ground for the challenge has become known'. As noted and discussed more thoroughly elsewhere, Article R34's time limit for bringing a challenge runs from the *confirmation* of the appointment (see G. Kaufmann-Kohler and A. Rigozzi, *International Arbitration – Law and Practice in Switzerland*, OUP, Oxford 2015, para. 4.137). That said, if a party considers that the disclosure reveals facts or circumstances that may justify a challenge, it must immediately raise any objections it may have or seek any clarifications it may need in that regard, reserving its right to bring a challenge should the arbitrator be confirmed.

[73] Article R34 CAS Code; Article A10 CAS ADD Rules.

[74] Articles R40.3 and R54 CAS Code; Article A17 CAS ADD Rules. There is no provision for the appointment of an ad hoc clerk in CAS Ad Hoc Division proceedings.

such disclosure(s)).[75] Although, unlike CAS arbitrators, ad hoc clerks are not required to appear on a CAS list, the CAS keeps an internal list of specialised lawyers from different countries who can be called upon to act as ad hoc clerks in CAS proceedings.[76]

5. THE REQUIREMENT OF INDEPENDENCE AND IMPARTIALITY

5.1. STRUCTURAL INDEPENDENCE

The issue of the CAS's structural independence has long been a subject of debate within the sports law and arbitration community.[77] Time and again over the years, it has also come before the highest national and international judicial authorities.

As noted above, the CAS was established in 1983, at the initiative of the IOC, and it started operating in 1984, with a list of 60 arbitrators. In accordance with the CAS Statutes of the time, half of the arbitrators on the list were appointed by the IOC, which also financed all of the CAS's operations.[78] In its landmark *Gundel* decision of 15 March 1993,[79] the SFT ruled that, in light of the close financial and organisational ties between the CAS and the IOC, this system would not qualify as genuine arbitration in disputes involving the IOC,[80] meaning that a resulting CAS award would then be considered an IOC decision, subject to the Swiss courts' full scrutiny (and not the limited review to which arbitral awards are subject).

In the wake of the *Gundel* decision, the IOC undertook a reform of the CAS system. The resulting 1994 Paris Agreement[81] and newly adopted CAS Code provided for the establishment of the ICAS, as a separate and independent body

---

[75] D. Mavromati and M. Reeb, *The Code of the Court of Arbitration for Sport – Commentary, Cases and Materials*, Kluwer Law, Alphen aan den Rijn 2015, ad Article R40.3, paras 40–41.

[76] Ibid., para. 36.

[77] See e.g. A. Rigozzi, *L'arbitrage international en matière de sport*, Helbing & Lichtenhahn, Basel 2005, pp. 273–307; D.Y. Yi, *Turning Medals into Metal: Evaluating the Court of Arbitration for Sport as an International Tribunal*, Student Scholarship Papers, Yale Law School May 2006, available at https://openyls.law.yale.edu/handle/20.500.13051/5650; A. Vaitiekunas, *The Court of Arbitration for Sport: Law-Making and the Question of Independence*, Stämpfli, Berne 2014, pp. 121–200 (all with numerous further references to the relevant scholarship and case law).

[78] https://www.tas-cas.org/en/general-information/history-of-the-cas.html.

[79] ATF 119 II 271 (*Elmar Gundel v. FEI*), Decision of 15.03.1993.

[80] Ibid., para. 3(b).

[81] Agreement Related to the Constitution of the International Council of Arbitration for Sport (ICAS) (Paris Agreement), signed in Paris on 22 June 1994 (reproduced in M. Reeb, *Digest of CAS Awards II 1998–2000*, Kluwer Law, Alphen aan den Rijn 2002, pp. 883–85).

International Sports Law

overseeing and managing the CAS, and responsible for compiling the list of CAS arbitrators according to the modalities described in the preceding sections. The Paris Agreement also overhauled the CAS's funding system, providing that IFs and NOCs would participate in the financing of the CAS, alongside the IOC.[82] Almost 10 years later, in the well-known *Lazutina* decision of 27 May 2003,[83] the SFT reviewed the reformed CAS system and found it to be consistent with the minimal requirements of structural independence, and thus capable of qualifying as genuine arbitration under Swiss law.[84]

In *Lazutina*, the SFT acknowledged that the CAS's mandatory list limits the parties' autonomy in the selection of arbitrators, but held that, since the 1994 reform, with the establishment of ICAS as an autonomous body responsible for compiling and overseeing the list, the IOC was no longer in a position to influence its composition. Further, the SFT found that the list was long enough to provide the parties with 'a wide range of names to choose from', including from a pool of arbitrators which had been selected, in accordance with Article S14 of the CAS Code, with a view to protecting the interests of the athletes.[85] It also noted that the obligation to appoint the arbitrators from a closed list was based on legitimate interests, in particular the benefit of specialisation in cases where awards need to be rendered without delay (as is generally the case in the world of competitive sports), and the necessity of ensuring a 'degree of consistency' in the decisions rendered.[86] The unbalanced composition of ICAS, and in particular the fact that all of its appointed members are nominated by the SGBs, and that only a minority of its co-opted members are appointed 'with a view to safeguarding the interests of the athletes', was not discussed as such in the decision.[87] The fact that, back then,[88] the arbitrators on the list could only be proposed by the IOC, IFs or NOCs also did not appear to be of concern to the SFT. However, the SFT did suggest that it would be desirable for the list to carry an indication, for each arbitrator, of the category (among those listed in Article S14 of Code) to which he or she belonged (i.e. whether the arbitrator's appointment had been proposed by the IOC, by an IF (and if so, which one), or

---

[82]   Article 3 of the Paris Agreement. See also G. Kaufmann-Kohler and A. Rigozzi, *International Arbitration – Law and Practice in Switzerland*, OUP, Oxford 2015, para. 1.127.

[83]   ATF 129 III 445 (*Larisa Lazutina & Olga Danilova v. IOC, FIS & CAS*), Decision of 27.05.2003.

[84]   Ibid., para. 3.3.4.

[85]   Ibid., para. 3.3.3.2, at pp. 457–58.

[86]   Ibid., at p. 456.

[87]   The athletes' challenge was focused on the IOC's alleged control over the ICAS: in this regard, the SFT did dismiss (finding it to be irrelevant *in casu*) their argument based on the 'rather theoretical possibility' that the 12 appointed members of ICAS could potentially, in accordance with Article S4 of the CAS Code, all be selected from within the IOC membership (ATF 129 III 445 (*Larisa Lazutina & Olga Danilova v. IOC, FIS & CAS*), Decision of 27.05.2003, para. 3.3.3.2, at p. 456).

[88]   As provided in Article S14 of the CAS Code until the end of 2011.

Intersentia

215

by a NOC (and if so, which one)), or if the arbitrator was part of the quota that was to be appointed 'with a view to safeguarding the interests of the athletes' or 'from among persons independent of [the IOC, IFs and NOCs]'.[89] Despite initial indications by the CAS, in the aftermath of the *Lazutina* decision, that this recommendation would be implemented, the CAS list of arbitrators still does not provide this information.

In a more recent case, where the independence of the CAS specifically vis-à-vis FIFA was challenged by the Belgian club FC Seraing,[90] the SFT noted that the changes made in 2012 with regard to the way arbitrators are proposed for inclusion in the CAS list (eliminating the preponderant influence of the SGBs) represented a positive development.[91] In this decision, the SFT also re-examined the role played by the SGBs, and by FIFA more particularly, in the financing of the CAS, concluding that the existing system did not establish a dependence relationship of the latter vis-à-vis the former.[92] Addressing another recurrent criticism of the CAS system raised by the applicant,[93] the SFT reaffirmed its position that the rule requiring the scrutiny of the award by the CAS Director General is not per se problematic, as it does not call into question the arbitrators' ultimate and exclusive power to decide the case before them.[94] In its *Seraing* decision, the SFT referenced the judgment rendered in 2016 by the German Supreme Court in the *Pechstein v. ISU* case, which had also examined and upheld the CAS system, having considered many of the same criticisms.[95]

Even more recently, Russian high jumper Aleksandr Shustov sought the annulment of the CAS award confirming his four-year ban for violations of World Athletics' anti-doping rules, arguing, inter alia, that the CAS lacked structural independence and impartiality vis-à-vis SGBs. Mr Shustov criticised in particular Article R54's rule, providing that the panel's president in appeals cases is to be appointed by the President or Deputy President of the Appeals Division, and more generally the 'totally opaque [manner] in which the CAS list of arbitrators is constituted'.[96] In the *Shustov* case, the athlete's arguments

---

[89]   ATF 129 III 445 (*Larisa Lazutina & Olga Danilova v. IOC, FIS & CAS*), Decision of 27.05.2003, para. 3.3.3.2, at pp. 458–59.

[90]   ATF 144 III 120 (*FC Seraing v. FIFA*), Decision of 20.02.2018.

[91]   Ibid., para. 3.4.3, at pp. 126–27.

[92]   Ibid., pp. 127–28.

[93]   See in particular SFT 4A_612/2009, Decision of 10.02.2010, para. 3.3, as well as CAS 2011/O/2574, *UEFA v. Olympique des Alpes SA/FC Sion*, Award of 31.01.2012, paras 257–61. The provision for the scrutiny of the award by the (then) CAS Secretary General was also challenged by Ms Claudia Pechstein, a German speed-skater, both before the ECtHR (in the *Pechstein v. Switzerland* case), and the German Supreme Court (in the case of *Pechstein v. International Skating Union (ISU)*), which are discussed below.

[94]   ATF 144 III 120 (*FC Seraing v. FIFA*), Decision of 20.02.2018, para. 3.4.3, at p. 128.

[95]   Ibid., paras 3.4.1 and 3.4.3 (referring to the decision rendered by the Bundesgerichtshof in case Az. KZR 6/15, *Pechstein v. International Skating Union (ISU)*, 07.06.2016).

[96]   SFT 4A_10/2022, Decision of 17.05.2022, para. 5.3.1.

International Sports Law

against the CAS were not sufficiently substantiated, and his complaints were clearly inadmissible as he only raised them at the annulment stage. Nevertheless, Mr Shustov's challenge, which relied primarily on a reference to the Dissenting Opinion accompanying the European Court of Human Rights' decision in the *Pechstein* case, to which this report will turn in the following paragraphs, shows that the mechanism for the panels' appointment in CAS appeals cases, as well as the way in which individuals are designated to the CAS's mandatory and closed list of arbitrators, are persistent 'pain points' when it comes to users' (and the public's) perception of the CAS's ability to operate as an independent and impartial tribunal in disputes between sportspersons and SGBs.

Finally and most recently, in the *Ustyugov* case, the applicant challenged, in various respects, the structural independence of the CAS ADD system operating in accordance with its two-tier procedure, i.e. with a CAS ADD sole arbitrator ruling in the first instance, subject to appeal before the CAS Appeals Division.[97] The athlete contended, in particular, that the 'organic links' existing between the CAS ADD and the Appeals Division, which are both part of the CAS and placed under the oversight of the ICAS, would impair the Divisions' ability to rule in an independent and impartial manner on the same case. The SFT dismissed this argument, noting that the coexistence of first-instance and appeal divisions within the same court is not unusual, including in international courts and tribunals like the ECtHR, and thus not, per se, sufficient to call into question the independence of the CAS ADD and Appeals Division vis-à-vis each other in relation to the same case. The SFT also underscored that the CAS ADD and Appeals Divisions have separate lists of arbitrators,[98] and that Article A8 of the CAS ADD Rules, which provides that CAS ADD arbitrators cannot sit in Appeals Division cases, further guarantees the mutual independence of the CAS ADD and Appeals Division.[99]

As just noted, the issue of the CAS's structural independence has also landed on the docket of the European Court of Human Rights (ECtHR), in the well-known *Pechstein v. Switzerland* matter.[100] Ms Pechstein claimed in substance that the SFT's case law acknowledging the CAS as an independent arbitral tribunal constituted a breach of Article 6(1) ECHR.[101]

---

[97] SFT 4A_232/2022, Decision of 22.12.2022, para. 6.7.

[98] Ibid.; see section 3.1 above.

[99] Ibid., para. 6.7.

[100] *Mutu & Pechstein v. Switzerland*, ECtHR decision of 2 October 2018, application nos 40575/10 and 67474/10. Only the 'Pechstein limb' of the judgment is discussed in this section of the report, as Mr Mutu did not challenge the CAS's structural independence, but rather the lack of independence and impartiality, on an individual basis, of two of the arbitrators who had sat on the CAS panels that had handled his case. The ECtHR's assessment of Mr Mutu's challenge will be discussed in the following section, which deals with the issue of personal independence and impartiality.

[101] For a critical examination of this decision, see in particular A. Rigozzi, 'Sports Arbitration and the ECHR – Pechstein and Beyond' in C. Muller et al. (eds), *New Developments in International Commercial Arbitration 2020*, Schulthess, Zurich 2020, available at https://lk-k.com/wp-content/

The ECtHR considered that given the non-consensual nature of CAS arbitration in disputes between athletes and SGBs, Article 6(1) ECHR was fully applicable, and assessed the CAS system in light of its case law regarding the guarantees enshrined in that provision.[102] The ECtHR considered the following principles to be of particular relevance in the case at hand:

- A 'tribunal' within the meaning of Article 6(1) ECHR must be understood in a 'substantive sense', i.e. focusing on its judicial function, 'that is to say' the fact that it 'determin[es] matters within its competence on the basis of legal rules, with full jurisdiction and after proceedings conducted in a prescribed manner', and that it must 'satisf[y] a number of requirements, such as independence from the executive and also from the parties'.[103]
- The independence of a tribunal must be determined taking into account, inter alia, 'the manner of appointment of its members and their term of office, the existence of guarantees against outside pressure and the question whether the body presents an appearance of independence'.[104]
- Impartiality under Article 6(1) ECHR, being 'the absence of prejudice or bias', must be determined both subjectively, i.e. 'on the basis of the personal conviction and conduct of a particular judge', and objectively, i.e. based on 'whether the court offered, in particular through its composition, guarantees sufficient to exclude any legitimate doubt about [its] impartiality'.[105]
- The objective test is particularly important as it might 'be difficult to procure evidence with which to rebut the presumption of a judge's subjective impartiality'. In this context, the ECtHR emphasised that 'justice must not only be done, it must also be seen to be done', as ultimately what is at stake 'is the confidence which the courts in a democratic society must inspire in the public'.[106]

Applying these principles to the facts of the case, the ECtHR found (in a majority decision of five votes to two)[107] that there were insufficient grounds for

---

uploads/2020/12/RIGOZZI-in-M%C3%9CLLER-et-al.-Eds-New-Developments-in-Intl-Comm.-Arb.-2020-2020-Sports-Arb.-ECHR-Pechstein-beyond-pp.-77-130-1.pdf; and A. Duval, 'The "Victory" of the Court of Arbitration for Sport at the European Court of Human Rights: The End of the Beginning for the CAS', *Asser International Sports Law Blog*, 10 October 2018, https://www.asser.nl/SportsLaw/Blog/post/the-victory-of-the-court-of-arbitration-for-sport-at-the-european-court-of-human-rights-the-end-of-the-beginning-for-the-cas.

[102] *Mutu & Pechstein v. Switzerland*, ECtHR decision of 2 October 2018, application nos 40575/10 and 67474/10, paras 109–15.

[103] Ibid., para. 139.

[104] Ibid., para. 140.

[105] Ibid., para. 141.

[106] Ibid., para. 143.

[107] Judges Georgios Serghides of Cyprus and Helen Keller of Switzerland dissented, co-authoring a 'Joint Partly Dissenting, Partly Concurring Opinion' (the Dissenting Opinion), annexed to the ECtHR's judgment.

it to reject the SFT's settled case law to the effect that the CAS system meets the constitutional requirements of independence and impartiality, and, therefore, that the proceedings in the CAS Appeals Division can be assimilated to those before a judicial authority, independent of the parties.[108]

In a nutshell, the ECtHR held, making an analogy with state courts in disputes between litigants and the state, that the fact that the CAS is largely financed by SGBs does not mean that the requirements of structural independence are not met in CAS proceedings between athletes and sports federations.[109]

The ECtHR further examined the list of arbitrators as it was composed at the relevant time, i.e. in application of the 2004 edition of the CAS Code, and in particular the fact that the ICAS was required to choose only one-fifth of the listed arbitrators from individuals who had no relationships with the SGBs involved in disciplinary cases such as Ms Pechstein's.[110] Noting that ICAS itself was composed of individuals directly or indirectly appointed by SGBs,[111] the ECtHR acknowledged that 'the organizations which were likely to be involved in disputes with athletes before the CAS had real influence over the mechanism for appointing arbitrators', but, crucially, went on to state that it could not 'conclude that, solely on account of this influence, the list of arbitrators, or even a majority thereof, was composed of arbitrators who could not be regarded as independent and impartial, on an individual basis, whether objectively or subjectively, vis-à-vis those organizations'.[112]

---

[108] *Mutu & Pechstein v. Switzerland*, ECtHR decision of 2 October 2018, application nos 40575/10 and 67474/10, para. 157. In their Dissenting Opinion, Judges Serghides and Keller disagreed with this finding, holding (at para. 28) that 'the structural problems of [the CAS] should have led the Court to find a violation of Article 6 §1'. For an in-depth analysis of the relevant points in the Dissenting Opinion, see in particular A. Rigozzi, 'Sports Arbitration and the ECHR – Pechstein and Beyond' in C. Muller et al. (eds), *New Developments in International Commercial Arbitration 2020*, Schulthess, Zurich 2020, pp. 92–94, and A. Rigozzi, 'Chronique de jurisprudence arbitrale en matière sportive' (2019) *Revue de l'arbitrage* 914, available at https://lk-k.com/wp-content/uploads/2019/11/BESSON-RIGOZZI-Rev.-Arb.-2019-903-974-Chronique-jurisprudence-arb.-sportive.pdf.

[109] *Mutu & Pechstein v. Switzerland*, ECtHR decision of 2 October 2018, application nos 40575/10 and 67474/10, para. 151.

[110] Ibid., para. 153.

[111] Ibid., para. 154.

[112] Ibid., para. 157. This point in particular was criticised by the dissenting judges (at paras 5–16 of the Dissenting Opinion), who held that the Court's majority had gone 'beyond what the [ECtHR's case law] requires' by demanding proof, on an individual basis, of the CAS members' lack of independence and/or impartiality. Given in particular the existing links between the SGBs and ICAS, which the dissenting judges deemed 'worrying', as well as the SGBs' 'disproportionate and unjustified' influence, under the applicable rules, over the procedure for selecting arbitrators to be included in the CAS (closed) list, and the role played by the Division Presidents (who are also ICAS members) in the appointment of CAS panels, Judges Serghides and Keller considered that the concerns raised by Ms Pechstein with regard to the CAS as an institution were 'objectively justified' within the meaning of the ECtHR's case law, which should have led the majority to find a breach of Article 6(1) ECHR, without

Finally, the ECtHR also dismissed Ms Pechstein's challenge of the CAS Secretary General (now Director General)'s power to scrutinise the award prior to its signature, in accordance with Article R59 CAS Code, which the athlete considered to be a further illustration of the lack of independence and impartiality of the CAS vis-à-vis the SGBs, by noting that 'the applicant has not provided evidence to show that the award ... was amended by the intervention of the Secretary General, still less in a manner which was unfavourable to her.'[113]

The CAS welcomed the ECtHR's decision as 'another confirmation, this time at a continental level, that CAS is a genuine arbitration tribunal', all the while stating that, while the ECtHR proceedings were pending, the ICAS had undertaken to review 'its own structures and rules in order to strengthen the independence and the efficiency of the CAS year after year'.[114]

On the occasion of its 2018 Dispatch on the proposed revision of the Swiss law governing international arbitration, which was issued shortly after the ECtHR decision, the Swiss government indicated that while it had refrained from including special provisions regarding sports arbitration in the revision bill, it intended to continue monitoring the evolution in that area closely. Interestingly, the government observed that it had taken due notice of the CAS's statements in reaction to the ECtHR's *Pechstein* ruling, which it understood to be an indication of the CAS's 'will to take the [ECtHR's] remarks seriously' and to 'proceed with improvements'. The government's Dispatch also made it a point to underscore that, going forward, the SFT would continue to ensure, in its supervisory capacity, that the CAS would maintain the level of independence required for it to be deemed the equivalent of the state courts.[115]

Meanwhile, in parallel to her ECtHR application, Ms Pechstein has pursued her challenge of the CAS system as part of a damages claim she brought against the International Skating Union before the German courts. In 2015, she succeeded in obtaining a decision from the Oberlandesgericht in Munich that invalidated her consent to CAS arbitration, on the ground that she had been obliged to

---

requiring that the applicant demonstrate bias or a lack of independence on the part of the individual arbitrators appointed to hear her case.

[113] *Mutu & Pechstein v. Switzerland*, ECtHR decision of 2 October 2018, applications nos 40575/10 and 67474/10, para. 158.

[114] Statement of the Court of Arbitration for Sport (CAS) on the Decision Made by the European Court of Human Rights (ECHR) in the Case Between Claudia Pechstein/Adrian Mutu and Switzerland – The ECHR Recognizes that CAS Fulfils the Requirements of Independence and Impartiality, 2 October 2018, https://www.tas-cas.org/fileadmin/user_upload/Media_Release_Mutu_Pechstein_ECHR.pdf. In particular, the CAS's Statement noted that: 'ICAS is now composed of a large majority of legal experts coming from outside the membership of sports organizations and has achieved an equal representation of men and women. The list of arbitrators has been increased and the privilege reserved to sports organizations to propose the nomination of arbitrators on the CAS list has been abolished'.

[115] Swiss Federal Council (Conseil fédéral), *Message concernant la modification de la loi fédérale sur le droit international privé (Chapitre 12: Arbitrage international)*, 24 October 2018, FF 2018 7153, pp. 7171–73, available at https://www.fedlex.admin.ch/eli/fga/2018/2548/fr.

International Sports Law

accept CAS jurisdiction even though it did not provide for an impartial and independent system of adjudication, due to its structural imbalance favouring SGBs.[116] However, this decision was overturned by the highest civil court in Germany, the Bundesgerichtshof, in 2016,[117] which re-examined and upheld the validity of the athlete's consent to CAS arbitration and rejected her arguments on the (impact of the) structural imbalance of the CAS. Ms Pechstein continued her legal fight and challenged the Bundesgerichtshof's ruling before the German Constitutional Court (Bundesverfassungsgericht), arguing that the mandatory submission of her dispute to the CAS violated her constitutional right of access to justice. In a landmark decision rendered on 3 June 2022,[118] the Constitutional Court, relying on the ECtHR's judgment in Ms Pechstein's case, ruled that the Bundesgerichtshof had failed to uphold the athlete's right of access to justice by dismissing her case notwithstanding the fact that she had been denied a public hearing before the CAS, in breach of her fundamental right to effective legal protection in accordance with the rule of law. On this basis, the Constitutional Court did not have to address the issue of the CAS's structural independence, and explicitly left that question open.[119]

5.2. PERSONAL INDEPENDENCE AND IMPARTIALITY

Given that CAS arbitrations are seated in Switzerland[120] and thus subject to the Swiss lex arbitri,[121] CAS arbitrators must meet the Swiss statutory requirements of independence and impartiality. These are set out in Chapter 12 of the Private International Law Act (PILA),[122] which governs international arbitrations,

---

[116] OLG München, Az. U 1110/14 Kart., *Claudia Pechstein v. International Skating Union*, 15.01.2015.

[117] Bundesgerichtshof, Az. KZR 6/15, *Pechstein v. International Skating Union (ISU)*, 07.06.2016.

[118] BVerfG, *Beschluss der 2. Kammer des Ersten Senats*, 1 BvR 2103/16, 03.06.2022, published on 12.07.2022 (https://www.bundesverfassungsgericht.de/SharedDocs/Entscheidungen/DE/2022/06/rk20220603_1bvr210316.html); an English translation of the decision is now available at https://www.bundesverfassungsgericht.de/SharedDocs/Entscheidungen/EN/2022/06/rk20220603_1bvr210316en.html.

[119] Ms Pechstein's case has now been remanded to the Oberlandesgericht in Munich for further consideration. For a full review of the *Pechstein* legal saga to date, covering also the Bundesverfassungsgericht's decision, and discussing the case's direct and indirect implications for the CAS system, see A. Rigozzi, 'Claudia Pechstein v. Court of Arbitration for Sport: Advantage CAS?', *Football Legal*, June 2022, pp. 108–19, https://lk-k.com/wp-content/uploads/2022/07/RIGOZZI-Claudia-Pechstein-v.-Court-of-Arbitration-for-Sport-Football-Legal-17-2022-pp.-108-119.pdf.

[120] See Article R28 of the CAS Code; Article A3 ADD Rules; Article 7 of the Arbitration Rules for the Olympic Games.

[121] See n. 123 below.

[122] Loi fédérale sur le droit international privé du 18 décembre 1987, RS 291, Articles 176–94 (https://www.fedlex.admin.ch/eli/cc/1988/1776_1776_1776/fr). An English translation of

---

Intersentia

221

and, for the rare sports cases that fall under the regime governing domestic arbitrations,[123] Part 3 of the Swiss Code of Civil Procedure (CCP).[124] The rules on independence and impartiality are in any event identical under these two regimes, and in turn reflect the guarantees applicable to court judges in Switzerland, as set out in Article 30(1) of the Swiss Constitution and Article 6(1) ECHR.[125]

Chapter 12 PILA, which was enacted in 1987, recently made the object of a revision,[126] which resulted in the inclusion of new black-letter provisions codifying certain developments in the SFT's case law on the requirements of independence and impartiality for arbitrators and the related obligations (discussed in this section), as well as on the challenge proceedings and available remedies in cases giving rise to complaints of lack of independence and impartiality (as discussed in the following two sections).

Article 180(1)(c) PILA provides[127] that '[a]n arbitrator may be challenged ... if circumstances exist that give rise to justifiable doubts as to [his or her] independence or impartiality.' This provision is mandatory, in the sense that the parties cannot waive it in advance, by agreeing to submit their arbitration to a set of rules providing for a lower standard of independence and impartiality.[128]

Articles R33 and R34 of the CAS Code mirror the statutory requirements by providing that '[e]very arbitrator shall be and remain impartial and independent of the parties',[129] and that '[a]n arbitrator may be challenged if the circumstances give rise to legitimate doubts over her/his independence or over her/his impartiality',[130] and Articles A8 and A10 of the CAS ADD Rules are drafted in almost identical language.[131] Article 12 of the CAS Arbitration Rules for the

---

Chapter 12 PILA can be found at https://www.swissarbitration.org/wp-content/uploads/2021/05/20210129-Chapter-12-PILA_Translation_English.pdf.

[123] The scope of application of Chapter 12 PILA is governed by its Article 176(1), which provides that: 'the provisions of this Chapter shall apply to arbitrations with their seat in Switzerland if at least one of the parties to the arbitration agreement, at the time of its conclusion, did not have its domicile, habitual residence or seat in Switzerland'. While many of the major SGBs have their seat in Switzerland, the clubs, athletes or other sports entities or persons appearing opposite them in CAS disputes are, in the vast majority of cases, domiciled outside Switzerland.

[124] Code de procédure civile du 19 décembre 2008, RS 272, Articles 353–99. An English translation of Part 3 CCP can be found at https://www.swissarbitration.org/wp-content/uploads/2021/05/CCP_Translation.pdf.

[125] ATF 118 II 361, para. 3c; G. Kaufmann-Kohler and A. Rigozzi, *International Arbitration – Law and Practice in Switzerland*, OUP, Oxford 2015, para. 4.108.

[126] RO 2020 4179, https://www.fedlex.admin.ch/eli/oc/2020/767/fr. The revised law entered into force on 1 January 2021.

[127] As does Article 367(1)(c) CCP, in substantively similar language.

[128] G. Kaufmann-Kohler and A. Rigozzi, *International Arbitration – Law and Practice in Switzerland*, OUP, Oxford 2015, para. 4.107.

[129] Article R33 ab initio.

[130] Article R34 ab initio.

[131] Article 8 of the CAS ADD Rules is identical, in its relevant part, to Article R33, and Article 10 provides that '[a]n arbitrator may be challenged if the circumstances give rise to legitimate doubts regarding independence or impartiality.'

Olympic Games sets out that arbitrators 'must be independent of the parties', and Article 13 provides that an arbitrator 'may be challenged by a party if circumstances give rise to legitimate doubts as to his or her independence.'

The SFT emphasises in its case law that it is not possible to 'formulate immutable principles' for the purpose of assessing an arbitrator's independence and impartiality, which always requires an examination of the circumstances of the case.[132] However, the SFT's case law does establish that the relevant circumstances must be examined objectively, i.e. from the point of view of a reasonable third person, and that what is required is not actual proof of bias, but a demonstration that, 'viewed objectively, the circumstances create an appearance of bias'.[133]

In its assessment of the relevant circumstances, the SFT also regularly refers to the IBA Guidelines on Conflicts of Interest in International Arbitration (IBA Guidelines), which it has described as 'a useful working instrument, susceptible of contributing to the harmonization and unification of the standards applied to the resolution of conflicts of interests in the field of international arbitration'.[134]

A notable ruling with regard to allegations of bias vis-à-vis one of the parties was issued in the well-known *Sun Yang* case, where the SFT found that a series of tweets published by the President of a CAS Panel before and during the arbitration raised legitimate doubts as to his impartiality vis-à-vis the athlete, a Chinese swimmer, in view of the language used in the tweets to condemn the acts of certain Chinese nationals, and even if the tweets concerned facts that were completely unrelated to the issues at stake in the arbitration.[135]

Beyond the parties to the dispute, an arbitral tribunal must also be independent and impartial vis-à-vis the parties' counsel and other participants in the proceedings, such as experts and other witnesses, as well as vis-à-vis third parties that are related to the litigants and/or may have an interest in the outcome of the dispute.[136]

When examining the relevant relationships, the SFT highlights that although arbitral tribunals are subject to the same constitutional standards of impartiality and independence as court judges, the specificities of arbitration, and in particular the fact that the profession involves frequent encounters between

---

[132] ATF 136 III 605 (*Alejandro Valverde v. CONI, WADA & UCI*), Decision of 29.10.2010, para. 3.3.3, at p. 615. For in-depth analysis and examples of the SFT's determinations in specific situations, see for instance G. Kaufmann-Kohler and A. Rigozzi, *International Arbitration – Law and Practice in Switzerland*, OUP, Oxford 2015, paras 4.111–24.

[133] SFT 4P.188/2001, Decision of 15.10.2001.

[134] See e.g. ATF 142 III 521, Decision of 07.09.2016, para. 3.1.2, at p. 537; SFT 4A_520/2021, Decision of 04.03.2022, para. 5.1.3; SFT 4A_506/2007, Decision of 20.03.2008, para. 3.3.2.2.

[135] ATF 147 III 65 (*Sun Yang v. WADA & FINA*), Decision of 22.12.2020, para. 6.5.

[136] G. Kaufmann-Kohler and A. Rigozzi, *International Arbitration – Law and Practice in Switzerland*, OUP, Oxford 2015, paras 4.112–21.

practitioners in a variety of settings, must be taken into account.[137] With regard to CAS arbitrators more specifically, the SFT has underscored time and again that the circumstances that only arbitrators on the CAS list can be appointed, and that in order to be included in the list arbitrators must have both legal training and a demonstrated competence in sports law, make it inevitable that they may end up building relationships with other individuals working in the same field, which relationships cannot automatically be assumed to compromise their impartiality and independence.[138]

As opined elsewhere, while the SFT's approach correctly takes into account the specificities of CAS arbitration in assessing the independence and impartiality of arbitrators on a case-by-case basis, more attention should be given, in the Court's decisions, to the fundamental differences between the situation of commercial parties, freely choosing to resolve their disputes by arbitration, and that of athletes who have no choice but to agree to CAS arbitration (including its closed-list system), as mandated by the regulations governing participation in their sport.[139] The existence of this constraint has significant consequences, which become apparent in particular in disputes brought by athletes against SGBs, which, contrary to their opponents, are 'repeat players' before the CAS, familiar with the system and its workings.[140]

In this context, one specific concern that has already given rise to challenges before the SFT is that of repeat appointments of the same arbitrator(s) by the same SGB.[141] When dealing with challenges to repeat appointments, both the ICAS[142] and the SFT[143] have placed significant emphasis on footnote 5 to paragraph 3.1.3 of the IBA Guidelines, which carves out an exception to the 'orange list' obligation for arbitrators to disclose the fact that they have been

---

[137]   ATF 129 III 445 (*Larisa Lazutina & Olga Danilova v. IOC, FIS & CAS*), Decision of 27.05.2003, para. 4.2.2.2, at p. 466.

[138]   Ibid.; ATF 136 III 605 (*Alejandro Valverde v. CONI, WADA & UCI*), Decision of 29.10.2010, para. 3.3.3, at p. 614, noting that it would be counterproductive to disregard these specificities as doing so would prompt an increase in challenges, 'which would be contrary to the objective of securing the speedy resolution of sports disputes by specialized tribunals presenting sufficient guarantees of independence and impartiality'.

[139]   For more extensive developments on this point, see, in particular, G. Kaufmann-Kohler and A. Rigozzi, *International Arbitration – Law and Practice in Switzerland*, OUP, Oxford 2015, paras 4.126–28.

[140]   Ibid. This gap can only partially be filled, on the athlete's side, by instructing specialised counsel (an option that, in any event, may not always be available, for financial or other reasons).

[141]   See SFT 4A_110/2012, Decision of 09.10.2012, and, most recently, SFT 4A_520/2021, Decision of 04.03.2022.

[142]   CAS 2011/A/2348 and 2386, *UCI & WADA v. Contador & RFEC*, ICAS Board Decision of 04.05.2011 (unpublished), relating to a challenge against an arbitrator who had been appointed by WADA four times in less than three years, and a dozen times since WADA had recognised CAS jurisdiction to deal with doping disputes in 2003.

[143]   SFT 4A_110/2012, Decision of 09.10.2012; SFT 4A_520/2021, Decision of 04.03.2022.

appointed by one of the parties on two or more occasions in the preceding three years. Footnote 5 acknowledges that:

[i]t may be the practice in certain types of arbitration, such as maritime, sports or commodities arbitration, to draw arbitrators from a smaller or specialised pool of individuals. If in such fields it is the custom and practice for parties to frequently appoint the same arbitrator in different cases, no disclosure of this fact is required, where all parties in the arbitration should be familiar with such custom and practice.

As noted elsewhere,[144] the addition (in the 2014 edition of the IBA Guidelines) of sports arbitration to the types of specialised arbitrations that can be exempted from the general rule proscribing repeat appointments is unwarranted, not only because the non-consensual nature of sports arbitration rules out any analogy with commodities or maritime arbitration, but also because repeat appointments exclusively benefit repeat players, i.e. in CAS arbitration the SGBs, and the list of CAS arbitrators is anything but a 'small pool' that would make repeat appointments inevitable.[145]

The duty of arbitrators to disclose 'without delay the existence of circumstances that could give rise to legitimate doubts as to [their] independence or impartiality' is now expressly set out in Article 179(6) PILA,[146] where it is also made clear that the duty applies 'throughout the entire proceedings.' That said, contrary to what may be the case in other jurisdictions, the SFT considers that a breach of the duty to disclose is not per se a ground for annulment of the award.[147]

The recent revision of Chapter 12 PILA has also brought about the express codification (in Article 180(2) PILA and Article 367(1)(c) CCP) of a principle that was originally enunciated in the SFT's case law on sports arbitration,[148]

---

[144]   G. Kaufmann-Kohler and A. Rigozzi, *International Arbitration – Law and Practice in Switzerland*, OUP, Oxford 2015, para. 4.128.

[145]   On this point, in the decision referenced in n. 142 above, the ICAS Board agreed with WADA's argument that '[g]iven the limited number of arbitrators who have specific qualifications in doping and the fact that WADA regularly proceeds before CAS, the frequency [of the challenged arbitrator's] appointments is not a sufficient ground to challenge him.' WADA's and the ICAS's reliance on footnote 5 is difficult to reconcile with the SFT's case law justifying the parties' obligation to draw arbitrators from the CAS list. Indeed, if the *raison d'être* of the list is that it allows parties to choose from a pool of specialised arbitrators, then arguments to the effect that only some of the arbitrators on that list have the requisite competence to resolve certain types of CAS disputes raises the question whether the list actually serves its purpose.

[146]   This rule is also expressly stated in Article 363 CCP.

[147]   SFT 4P.188/2001, Decision of 15.10.2001, para. 2f. For a more in-depth analysis of this point, with further references, see G. Kaufmann-Kohler and A. Rigozzi, *International Arbitration – Law and Practice in Switzerland*, Oxford, OUP 2015, paras 4.157–65. See also, most recently, SFT 4A_520/2021, Decision of 04.03.2022, para. 5.5.

[148]   ATF 136 III 605 (*Alejandro Valverde v. CONI, WADA & UCI*), Decision of 29.10.2010, para. 3.2.2; ATF 129 III 445 (*Larisa Lazutina & Olga Danilova v. IOC, FIS & CAS*), Decision of 27.05.2003, para. 4.2.2.1; SFT 4A_110/2012, Decision of 09.10.2012, para. 2; SFT 4P.105/2006, Decision

namely that, while arbitrators must disclose conflicts, the parties themselves are subject to a so-called 'duty of curiosity' (or duty of inquiry), meaning that they cannot simply rely on the arbitrator's duty of disclosure, but are, in turn, under an obligation to diligently undertake any reasonable and necessary investigations about an arbitrator's independence and impartiality.[149] A failure to conduct appropriate and timely investigations may result in the loss of the right to challenge the arbitrator.[150] In the *Sun Yang* decision, the SFT clarified that while the exact scope of the parties' duty of curiosity will always depend on the circumstances of the case, it is not without limits, particularly when it comes to the investigations that can and should be conducted on the internet, and more specifically on social media.[151]

Notwithstanding the outcome in an exceptional case like *Sun Yang*, all in all, commentators tend to agree that the SFT's case law has set a relatively high bar for challenges against arbitrators to succeed.[152]

In the aforementioned *Mutu and Pechstein* decision, the ECtHR was also asked to re-examine the challenges, which had been rejected by the SFT, against the personal independence and impartiality of three CAS arbitrators. In the case of *Pechstein v. Switzerland*, the ECtHR dismissed the athlete's challenge against the Panel's President, which it found to be based on an argument that had not been raised before the SFT, and, in any event, resting on allegations that were too vague and hypothetical.[153] In the case of *Adrian Mutu v. Switzerland*, the applicant complained of a lack of impartiality and independence on the part of two of the arbitrators who had sat on the last of the three separate panels which had dealt with different aspects of his contractual dispute with Chelsea FC.[154]

---

of 04.08.2006, para. 4; SFT 4P.217/1992, Decision of 15.03.1993 (unpublished version of the *Gundel v. FEI* decision (ATF 119 II 271)).

[149] The requirement that the parties apply, throughout the proceedings, the requisite level of 'due diligence' in investigating the existence of possible conflicts of interest or other grounds for challenge is now stated as follows in the revised wording of Article 180(2) PILA (and Article 367(1)(c) CCP): '[a] party may challenge an arbitrator whom it has appointed or in whose appointment it has participated solely for reasons of which, *despite having exercised due diligence*, it became aware only after the appointment.'

[150] B. Berger and F. Kellerhals, *International and Domestic Arbitration in Switzerland*, 4th ed., Stämpfli, Berne 2021, para. 882; G. Kaufmann-Kohler and A. Rigozzi, *International Arbitration – Law and Practice in Switzerland*, Oxford, OUP 2015, para. 8.137; SFT 4A_110/2012, Decision of 09.10.2012, para. 2; SFT 4P.105/2006, Decision of 04.08.2006, para. 4.

[151] ATF 147 III 65 (*Sun Yang v. AMA and FINA*), Decision of 22.12.2020, para. 6.5.

[152] See e.g. L. Beffa, 'Challenge of international arbitration awards in Switzerland for lack of independence and/or impartiality of an arbitrator – Is it time to change the approach?' (2011) *ASA Bulletin* 598; J. Marguerat, 'Indépendance et impartialité de l'arbitre – Le devoir de l'arbitre de révéler éclipsé', *Jusletter*, 15 April 2013.

[153] *Mutu & Pechstein v. Switzerland*, ECtHR decision of 2 October 2018, application nos 40575/10 and 67474/10, para. 150.

[154] Ibid., paras 160–68. The relevant awards were rendered in the following matters: CAS 2005/A/876, *Adrian Mutu v. Chelsea Football Club*, Award of 15.12.2005; CAS 2006/A/1192,

Mr Mutu challenged the award in case CAS 2008/A/1644, arguing that the Panel's President (arbitrator 'L.F.') had failed to disclose that Chelsea FC's owner was among his law firm's clients, a circumstance the player claimed to have discovered after the award had been rendered. In addition, Mr Mutu challenged the fact that arbitrator 'D.-R.M.', who had been appointed as the President of the Panel that rendered the first award (on the question whether the player had unilaterally breached his employment contract), was confirmed as Chelsea's co-arbitrator in the third Panel, which was seized with the player's appeal against the damages FIFA had ordered him to pay as a consequence of that breach. Here too, the ECtHR dismissed the challenges on the merits, upholding the SFT's findings that the player had failed to: (i) adduce any evidence in support of his challenge against L.F., and (ii) establish (as required for a finding of lack of impartiality in such a case) that not only the facts, but also the legal questions submitted to the two panels in which D.-R.M. had sat as an arbitrator were the same.[155]

In closing, it should be noted that challenges for lack of independence and impartiality can also be brought against tribunal secretaries or assistants assuming similar functions,[156] such as ad hoc clerks in CAS arbitration, as has happened recently in a CAS case.[157]

6. CHALLENGE PROCEEDINGS

Article 180(a) PILA and Article 369 CCP set out the (default) procedural rules that apply to challenges against arbitrators in Swiss-seated arbitrations, 'unless the parties have agreed otherwise'. By submitting to CAS arbitration, the parties agree to follow the challenge procedure provided in the CAS Code, as well as, where applicable, the CAS ADD Rules and CAS Ad Hoc Division Rules.

Article R34(1) of the CAS Code, which applies to both ordinary and appeals proceedings, provides that a challenge must be brought within seven days from the time the challenging party has become aware of the ground(s) for challenge.

Chelsea Football Club Limited v. Adrian Mutu, Award of 21.05.2007; CAS 2008/A/1644, *Adrian Mutu v. Chelsea Football Club*, Award of 31.07.2009.

[155] Ibid., paras 166–68.

[156] See e.g. B. Berger and F. Kellerhals, *International and Domestic Arbitration in Switzerland*, 4th ed., Stämpfli, Berne 2021, para. 1009.

[157] SFT 4A_520/2021, Decision of 04.03.2022. D. Mavromati and M. Reeb, *The Code of the Court of Arbitration for Sport – Commentary, Cases and Materials*, Kluwer Law, Alphen aan den Rijn 2015 (ad Article R40.3, para. 41), considered that the challenge procedure of Article R34 (examined in the following section) should not apply to CAS ad hoc clerks. However, that position seems now to have been disavowed by the ICAS, since the CAS Challenge Commission recently heard and dealt with an application for challenge filed against an ad hoc clerk (at the same time as a challenge against the Panel's President), as can be read in SFT 4A_520/2021, Decision of 04.03.2022, para. B, p. 5.

The challenge must be lodged 'in the form of a petition setting forth the facts giving rise to the challenge', with the CAS Court Office, and 'shall be determined by the Challenge Commission, which has the discretion to refer a case to ICAS'.

Article R34(2) further provides that '[t]he Challenge Commission or ICAS shall rule on the challenge after the other party (or parties), the challenged arbitrator and the other arbitrators, if any, have been invited to submit written comments. Such comments shall be communicated by the CAS Court Office ... to the parties and [if the case is heard by a three-member panel] to the other arbitrators'.

It may occur that the challenged arbitrator opts to step down upon being notified of a challenge, in which case the procedure for his or her replacement (in accordance with Article R36) will be initiated, without the need for a ruling on the challenge.[158] Where the arbitrator contests the challenge, Swiss law provides that unless the parties agree otherwise, the arbitration may proceed while the challenge is being heard.[159] The CAS Code does not contain a specific provision in this regard. In practice, CAS panels will determine whether to stay the proceedings based on the specific circumstances of the case, including the apparent merit of the challenge and the procedural stage in which it is raised.[160]

Article R34(2) requires that the Challenge Commission's or ICAS's decision 'give brief reasons' for the outcome of the challenge, and provides that the CAS 'may decide to publish [the decision]'.[161] If the challenge is successful, the arbitrator is removed and replaced in accordance with Article R36 of the CAS Code.

The procedure set out in Article A10 of the CAS ADD Rules is identical to that provided in Article R34 CAS Code, with the sole difference that the challenge must be lodged with the CAS ADD Office. Article A10 also adds an

---

[158] See e.g. CAS 2019/A/6148, *WADA v. Sun Yang & FINA*, Award of 28.02.2020, para. 55.

[159] Article 180(a)(3) PILA and Article 369(4) CCP.

[160] M. Noth and U. Haas, 'Commentary to Article R34 of the CAS Code' in M. Arroyo (ed.), *Arbitration in Switzerland: The Practitioner's Guide*, 2nd ed., Kluwer Law International, Alphen aan den Rijn 2018, para. 9; see e.g. CAS 2019/A/6148, *WADA v. Sun Yang & FINA*, Award of 28.02.2020, paras 46–50.

[161] To the rapporteurs' knowledge, no decision on challenge has been published by CAS to date. However, two decisions were reproduced in D. Mavromati and M. Reeb, *The Code of the Court of Arbitration for Sport - Commentary, Cases and Materials*, Kluwer Law, Alphen aan den Rijn 2015, pp. 166–80 (in the matters CAS 2009/A/1893, *Panionios v. Al-Ahli SC*, Decision of 19.11.2009, where the challenge was rejected, and CAS 2012/A/2697, *Brescia Calcio SpA v. West Ham United FC*, Decision of 26.06.2012, where the challenge was upheld). The latest ICAS Annual Report, published in November 2022, provides some recent statistics on challenges against CAS arbitrators, indicating that, in 2021, parties to CAS proceedings filed 11 petitions for challenge, of which 10 were dismissed and one upheld by the CAS Challenge Commission (*ICAS 2021 Annual Report and Financial Statements*, https://www.tas-cas.org/fileadmin/user_upload/ICAS_Annual_Report___Financial_Statements_2021.pdf, p. 19).

express provision that, in the event of a challenge, '[t]he challenged arbitrator remains on duty until her/his replacement, if any.' If the challenge is successful, the disqualified arbitrator is replaced in accordance with Article A12.

Given the highly expedited nature of proceedings in the CAS Ad Hoc Division, the applicable rules necessarily put the strongest possible emphasis on speed with regard to the resolution of arbitrator challenges. Accordingly, Article 13 of the CAS Arbitration Rules for the Olympic Games provides that a challenge 'must be brought as soon as the reason for the challenge becomes known' and that '[t]he President of the ad hoc Division is competent to take cognizance of any challenge requested by a party. She/he shall decide upon the challenge immediately after giving the parties and the arbitrator concerned the opportunity to be heard, insofar as circumstances permit'. This provision does not require that reasons be given for the decision on the challenge. If the challenge is successful, 'the President of the ad hoc Division shall immediately appoint an arbitrator to fill the vacancy.'

The decisions rendered by the ICAS, its Challenge Commission and the President of the Ad Hoc Division are final, in the sense that they are not subject to further recourse within the CAS system.[162] Because they do not qualify as arbitral awards, they are also not amenable to immediate review by the SFT under Article 190 PILA (or Article 393 CCP).[163] A party seeking to overturn a CAS challenge decision must bring its complaint against the (first) award rendered by the panel including the impugned arbitrator(s), as set out in the following section.

7. REMEDIES

A party who wishes to contest a CAS decision rejecting a challenge must raise its complaint in annulment proceedings brought against the award rendered by the panel comprising the impugned arbitrator(s).[164] If the panel issues more than one award, the first award rendered by the panel in the impugned composition must be challenged, failing which the right to call into question the arbitrator's

---

[162] D. Mavromati and M. Reeb, *The Code of the Court of Arbitration for Sport – Commentary, Cases and Materials*, Kluwer Law, Alphen aan den Rijn 2015, ad Article R34, para. 80.

[163] SFT 4A_644/2009, Decision of 13.04.2010, para. 1. For a discussion of the problematic nature of this restriction with regard to the time-sensitivity of many sports disputes, in particular in disciplinary cases, see G. Kaufmann-Kohler and A. Rigozzi, *International Arbitration – Law and Practice in Switzerland*, Oxford, OUP 2015, para. 4.146.

[164] This is expressly provided in Article 369(5) CCP for domestic cases, and results from the SFT's case law for cases governed by Chapter 12 PILA (ATF 118 II 359, para. 3b; see also B. Berger and F. Kellerhals, *International and Domestic Arbitration in Switzerland*, 4th ed., Stämpfli, Berne 2021, para. 909).

independence or impartiality (on the grounds invoked in the original challenge) is deemed to have been forfeited.[165]

The applicable ground for annulment is set out, in identical terms, in Article 190(2)(a) PILA and Article 393(a) CCP, which provide that the award may be challenged if 'the sole arbitrator was not properly appointed or the arbitral tribunal was not properly constituted'.

The SFT's case law makes it clear that, in deciding the challenge, the SFT relies on the facts as established in the lower-instance challenge decision.[166] If the SFT upholds the challenge, the award is annulled, and the SFT, if so requested, will order the removal of the arbitrator.[167]

An application to annul an award can only be brought within a strict time limit of 30 days from the date of notification of the award.[168] As a consequence, grounds for challenge discovered after that time limit cannot be invoked to seek the annulment of the award.

In a landmark decision of 1992,[169] the SFT decided that the exceptional remedy of revision, which permits the revocation (on very narrow grounds) of a decision after the expiry of the time limit to request its annulment, was also available against international arbitral awards, even though this was not expressly provided in Chapter 12 PILA.[170] In this regard, the question had also long remained open, in the SFT's case law, whether the discovery, after the 30-day time limit for annulment, of a ground for challenging an arbitrator could be relied upon to request the revision of the award.[171]

That question has been given an affirmative answer in the revised version of Chapter 12 PILA: Article 190a now provides that the remedy of revision is available against international arbitral awards, including in cases where 'despite

---

[165]   SFT 4P.168/1999, Decision of 17.02.2000, para. 1b–c. G. Kaufmann-Kohler and A. Rigozzi, *International Arbitration – Law and Practice in Switzerland*, Oxford, OUP 2015, para. 8.21.

[166]   ATF 136 III 605 (*Alejandro Valverde v. CONI, WADA & UCI*), Decision of 29.10.2010, para. 3.4.1, at p. 616.

[167]   Ibid., para. 3.3.4. If the challenge was brought against a preliminary or partial award, the parties or the panel will have to decide whether the proceedings can be continued with a newly appointed arbitrator from the point where the disqualified arbitrator ceased to perform his or her duties, or whether any prior procedural steps need to be repeated, the default rule under the Code being in favour of direct continuation (see Article R36 in fine: 'unless otherwise agreed by the parties or otherwise decided by the Panel, the proceedings shall continue without repetition of any aspect thereof prior to the replacement'). For a discussion of the CAS's practice in this regard, see D. Mavromati and M. Reeb, *The Code of the Court of Arbitration for Sport – Commentary, Cases and Materials*, Kluwer Law, Alphen aan den Rijn 2015, ad Article R36 CAS Code, paras 19–23.

[168]   Article 100(1) Swiss Supreme Court Act (SCA).

[169]   ATF 118 II 199, Decision of 11.03.1992.

[170]   The CCP (which was enacted in 2008) makes express provision for the revision of domestic arbitral awards (in Articles 396–99), as did the statute governing domestic arbitrations prior to the entry into force of the CCP.

[171]   SFT 4A_528/2007, Decision of 04.04.2008, para. 2.5; SFT 4A_234/2008, Decision of 14.08.2008, para. 2.1; ATF 142 III 521 (*X. SpA v. Y. B.V*), Decision of 07.09.2016, para. 2.

[the applicant's] diligence, a ground for challenge under Article 180(1)(c) was not discovered until after the conclusion of the arbitration and no other remedy is available.'[172] In the landmark *Sun Yang* decision, rendered just a few days before the entry into force of this statutory provision, the SFT took note of the imminent legislative change, and, as seen above,[173] upheld an application for revision of a CAS award on the ground that there existed legitimate doubts as to the impartiality of the Panel's President.[174]

Under the new legislative regime (which is in line with what the CCP already provided for domestic awards), an application for revision must be brought within 90 days from the discovery of the ground for challenge, and not more than 10 years from the notification of the award.[175] The court of competent jurisdiction to determine applications for revision in international arbitrations is the SFT,[176] whereas applications in domestic arbitrations should be filed with the competent cantonal court at the seat of the arbitration.[177]

If the application is granted, the challenge is upheld and (if the corresponding request is made by the applicant) the arbitrator is disqualified; the award is annulled and the matter is remanded to a new tribunal, to be constituted (without the disqualified arbitrator, or, depending on the circumstances, in an entirely new composition) in accordance with the originally agreed procedure.[178] This procedure was followed in the *Sun Yang* case, resulting in a second award rendered by an entirely new Panel.[179]

8. CONCLUSION

From the very beginning of the CAS's operations, the requirement that arbitrators be selected from the institution's closed list of arbitrators, as well as

---

[172] Article 190a(c) PILA. Article 396 CCP has also been amended, with effect as of 1 January 2021, to include this ground for revision. The other grounds for revision available against both international and domestic awards are: (i) the subsequent discovery of (pre-existing) relevant facts or conclusive evidence; and (ii) the fact that criminal proceedings have established that the award was influenced, to the detriment of the applicant, by a crime or misdemeanour (Article 190a(a)–(b) PILA and Article 396(a)–(b) CCP).

[173] Section 5.2.

[174] ATF 147 III 65 (*Sun Yang v. AMA and FINA*), Decision of 22.12.2020, para. 6.

[175] Article 190a(2) PILA; Article 397 CCP.

[176] Article 191 PILA.

[177] Article 396(1) CCP.

[178] ATF 142 III 521, Decision of 07.09.2016, para. 2.1.

[179] CAS 2019/A/6148, *WADA v. Sun Yang & FINA*, Award of 22.06.2021. Upon receipt of the SFT's Decision of 22.12.2020, the CAS noted that the proceedings in case CAS 2019/A/6148 were 'reopened' (CAS 2019/A/6148, *WADA v. Sun Yang & FINA*, Award of 22.06.2021, para. 76). The Panel was entirely reappointed after the athlete challenged both of the co-arbitrators who had sat in the first Panel, and the latter both decided to step down shortly thereafter, 'in the interest of expedition of the procedure' (ibid., paras 74–90).

the rules prescribing the modalities of constitution of the list, have been a focal point of scrutiny before the different judicial instances that have been called to review the independence and impartiality of CAS panels and arbitrators. Still today, almost four decades later and after several revisions of the CAS Code, the closed list(s) of arbitrators remain(s) a defining feature of CAS arbitration, and, as this report has shown, its most problematic aspect.

THE INDEPENDENCE AND IMPARTIALITY OF ADJUDICATORS IN INVESTMENT ARBITRATION UNDER NON-TREATY-BASED RULES

Diego P. Fernández Arroyo and Alexandre Senegacnik

1. The Narrow Scope of Enquiry: Investment Arbitration under NTBRs ... 234
2. A Comparative Study of NTBRs Used in Investment Arbitration........ 235
3. Criteria for the Selection of Investment Arbitrators under NTBRs 236
4. Appointing Authorities in Investment Arbitration under NTBRs 240
5. The Method of Appointment in Investment Arbitration under NTBRs 242
6. Parameters to Ensure Independence and Impartiality: Preventive Measures 251
7. Consequences of a Breach of the Duty to Act Independently and Impartially: Curative Measures................................. 255
8. General Conclusions 261

The present special report aims to respond to general rapporteur Giuditta Cordero Moss' questionnaire with a view to providing an overview of the unescapable topic of independence and impartiality of international adjudicators. This report will focus on investment arbitrators operating under 'non-treaty based-rules' (NTBRs). The specific scope of enquiry entrusted to the special rapporteurs will be discussed before turning to each of the general issues raised in the questionnaire.[1]

---

[1] The issue of the enforceability of a final investment decision/award that was rendered by an arbitrator who breached the requirement to act independently and impartially is left to the national courts or the ICSID ad hoc committee and will thus not be explored in this special report.

Intersentia

1. THE NARROW SCOPE OF ENQUIRY: INVESTMENT ARBITRATION UNDER NTBRs

For the purpose of this project under the aegis of the International Academy of Comparative Law, investment arbitration under treaty-based rules (TBRs) includes investment disputes subject to arbitration rules contained in treaties (e.g. the 1965 Convention on the Settlement of Investment Disputes Between States and Nationals of Other States). By opposition, investment arbitration under NTBRs includes investment disputes subject to arbitration rules which are not based on treaties, e.g. the UNCITRAL Arbitration Rules or the Rules of the International Chamber of Commerce (ICC) headquartered in Paris. Whether the claim is based on a treaty is accordingly irrelevant for the present distinction. This delimitation calls for two preliminary observations.

Firstly, one must necessarily anticipate a possible overlap between this narrow scope of enquiry and other special reports commissioned by the general rapporteur, namely on commercial arbitration (institutional and ad hoc). Investment arbitrations under NTBRs are conducted either pursuant to the UNCITRAL Arbitration Rules or the typical rules used in the framework of commercial arbitration, such as the ICC Rules, etc. The only exception to this finding is the existence of NTBRs specifically designed for investment arbitration, as will be discussed hereafter. Keeping this narrow scope in mind, and the need to avoid any overlaps, the primary aim of this report was accordingly to identify possible specificities developed for investment disputes conducted under NTBRs traditionally used in the context of commercial arbitration.

Figure 1. Investment arbitration under NTBRs

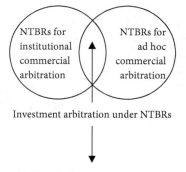

Source: Produced by the rapporteurs.

Secondly, the report cannot only focus on the NTBRs but needs, where possible, to consider the application of the rules in practice. In this regard, it can be regretted that the available data is certainly not exhaustive. Surely one can hardly deny that the push for transparency has found its greatest expression and practical anchor in the field of international investment arbitration – the particular role of the ICSID in this regard must be acknowledged. Yet the available data on awards is uneven when one compares institutional investment arbitration conducted under TBRs and investment arbitration conducted under NTBRs. The role of private news providers is certainly effective in reducing the existing discrepancy, but much remains to be done. Accordingly, no comprehensive and exhaustive screening of case law can be conducted in this regard. This does not mean that the available data is not scarce: out of the 1,104 reported cases on the UNCTAD database, at least 424 correspond to the category of investment arbitration under NTBRs.[2] It appears that around 38% of publicly known cases are conducted under NTBRs.

2. A COMPARATIVE STUDY OF NTBRs USED IN INVESTMENT ARBITRATION

The UNCTAD Database identified the following NTBRs as having been applied at least once in publicly known arbitrations:

- CRCICA (Cairo Regional Center for International Commercial Arbitration) (1);
- ICC (International Chamber of Commerce) (19);
- LCIA (London Court of International Arbitration) (1);
- MCCI (Moscow Chamber of Commerce and Industry) (3);
- SCC (Stockholm Chamber of Commerce) (49); and
- UNCITRAL (351).

A comparative analysis of NTBRs will be made for each of the topics identified in the questionnaire. The following rules have been retained for the purpose of the analysis:

- ICC (International Chamber of Commerce);
- LCIA (London Court of International Arbitration);
- SIAC Investment Rules (Singapore International Arbitration Center);
- SCC (Stockholm Chamber of Commerce); and
- UNCITRAL.

---

[2]   See https://investmentpolicy.unctad.org/investment-dispute-settlement.

The CRCICA and MCCI Arbitration Rules have been taken out as they were used only in four cases in total and the rules in question are not specifically designed for international investment arbitration, but rather for commercial arbitration. The SIAC Investment Rules (2017), which are not identified in the UNCTAD Database, were included despite the absence of publicly known cases as they contain some adjustments in comparison to the classical SIAC Rules largely used in international commercial arbitration. Lastly, the LCIA Rules were kept despite the fact that only one case appears on the UNCTAD Database; they, however, offer a unique set of rules with specific language on the issues relevant to this special report.

3. CRITERIA FOR THE SELECTION OF INVESTMENT ARBITRATORS UNDER NTBRs

The studied NTBRs do not provide an exhaustive set of criteria to take into account. They do offer some guidance but largely defer the question to the parties, who will be able to express their wishes prior to the appointment.

The criteria for selecting the adjudicators can evidently be expected to have a significant impact on any adjudicator's independence and impartiality. The general rapporteur invited the special rapporteurs to consider two main competing interests in the selection of adjudicators: representation and independence. It appears that NTBRs certainly focus on the necessity of independence (and impartiality). In doing so, NTBRs do not present independence and impartiality as an optional criterion but – understandably so – as a mandatory requirement. This aspect will be further discussed in the following sections.

In addition, some NTBRs make occasional references to possible criteria which may be taken into account by the parties or the competent appoint authority, for example: the arbitrator's nationality, residence and other relationships with the countries of which the parties or the other arbitrators are nationals; the arbitrator's availability and ability to conduct the arbitration in accordance with the applicable Rules; the transaction(s) at issue; the type of dispute, particularly when it is based on a treaty; the nature and circumstances of the dispute; the monetary amount or value of the dispute; the relevant location(s) and language(s) of the parties; and the number of parties. General catch-all formulas allow the taking into account of all other factors which may be considered relevant in the circumstances. SIAC Rule 10.3 for instance invites one to pay due regard to 'considerations that are relevant to the impartiality or independence of the arbitrator' without however providing any concrete example.

Investment Arbitration under Non-Treaty-Based Rules

Table 1. Comparison of Select Non-Treaty Based Rules: Selected Extracts

ICC (2021)	LCIA (2020)	SCC (2017)	UNCITRAL (2013)	SIAC (2017)
Article 13	Article 5	Article 17	Article 11	Rule 8
1. In confirming or appointing arbitrators, the Court shall consider the prospective *arbitrator's nationality, residence and other relationships with the countries of which the parties or the other arbitrators are nationals and the prospective arbitrator's availability and ability to conduct the arbitration in accordance with the Rules.* The same shall apply where the Secretary General confirms arbitrators pursuant to Article 13(2).	... 5.3 All arbitrators shall be and *remain at all times impartial and independent of the parties;* and *none shall act in the arbitration as advocate for or authorised representative of any party. No arbitrator shall give advice to any party on the parties' dispute or the conduct or outcome of the arbitration.*	... 6. If the parties are of different nationalities, the sole arbitrator or the Chairperson of the Arbitral Tribunal shall be of a *different nationality than the parties,* unless the parties have agreed otherwise or the Board otherwise deems it appropriate. 7. When appointing arbitrators, the Board shall consider the *nature and circumstances of the dispute, the applicable law, the seat and language of the arbitration and the nationality of the parties.*	When a person is approached in connection with his or her possible appointment as an arbitrator, he or she shall disclose any circumstances likely to give rise to justifiable doubts as to his or her *impartiality or independence.* An arbitrator, from the time of his or her appointment and throughout the arbitral proceedings, shall disclose without delay any such circumstances to the parties and the other arbitrators unless they have already been informed by him or her of these circumstances.	In making the appointment of the arbitrator(s) ... the Court shall use the following list-procedure, unless the Parties agree that the list-procedure shall not be used or unless the Court determines, in its discretion, that the use of the list-procedure is not appropriate for the case: a) The Court shall invited *the Parties' views on any qualifications of the arbitrator(s) prior to compiling the list of* candidates. The Court shall not be bound by the Parties'
2. The Secretary General may confirm as co-arbitrators, sole arbitrators and presidents of arbitral tribunals persons nominated by the parties or pursuant to their particular agreements, provided that *the statement they have submitted contains no qualification regarding impartiality or independence or that a qualified statement regarding impartiality or independence has not given rise to objections.* ...	5.4 Before appointment by the LCIA Court, each arbitrator candidate shall furnish to the Registrar (upon the latter's request) a brief written summary of his or her *qualifications and professional positions (past and present); the candidate shall also agree in writing fee rates conforming to the Schedule of Costs; the candidate shall sign a written declaration stating: (i) whether*	Article 18 1. Every arbitrator must be *impartial and independent.* 2. Before being appointed, a prospective arbitrator shall disclose any circumstances that may give rise to justifiable doubts		

(continued)

Table 1 *continued*

ICC (2021)	LCIA (2020)	SCC (2017)	UNCITRAL (2013)	SIAC (2017)
5. Where the Court is to appoint the sole arbitrator or the president of the arbitral tribunal, such sole arbitrator or president of the arbitral tribunal shall be of a *nationality other than those of the parties.* … 6. *Whenever the arbitration agreement upon which the arbitration is based arises from a treaty, and unless the parties agree otherwise, no arbitrator shall have the same nationality of any party to the arbitration.* **General Observation:** **The ICC Rules do list several criteria to take into account (nationality/ availability) in addition to the traditional reference to impartiality and independence.**	there are any circumstances currently known to the candidate which are likely to give rise in the mind of any party to any justifiable doubts as to his or her *impartiality or independence* and, if so, specifying in full such circumstances in the declaration; and (ii) whether the candidate is ready, willing and able to *devote sufficient time, diligence and industry to ensure the expeditious and efficient conduct of the arbitration.* … 5.9 The LCIA Court shall appoint arbitrators with due regard for any particular method or criteria of selection agreed in writing by the parties. The LCIA Court shall also take into account the *transaction(s) at issue, the nature and circumstances of the dispute,*	as to the prospective arbitrator's *impartiality or independence.* 3. Once appointed, an arbitrator shall submit to the Secretariat a signed statement of *acceptance, availability, impartiality and independence,* disclosing any circumstances that may give rise to justifiable doubts as to the arbitrator's impartiality or independence. The Secretariat shall send a copy of the statement of acceptance, availability, impartiality and independence to the parties and the other arbitrators. **General Observation:** **The SCC Rules list several criteria to take into account (nationality/availability) in addition to the traditional reference to impartiality and independence. Article 17.7 provides a specific list of criteria to take into account.**	**General Observation:** **The UNCITRAL Rules do not list criteria to take into account but contain a traditional reference to impartiality and independence.**	recommendations, but it shall take the Parties' views and the circumstances of the case into account when compiling the list of candidates. … Rule 10 *10.1 Any arbitrator appointed in an arbitration under these Rules, whether or not nominated by the Parties, shall be and remain at all times independent and impartial.* *10.2 In appointing an arbitrator under these Rules, the Court shall have due regard to any qualifications required of the arbitrator by the agreement of the*

its monetary amount or value, the location and languages of the parties, the number of parties and all other factors which it may consider relevant in the circumstances.

Article 6

6.1 Upon request of the Registrar, the parties shall each inform the Registrar and all other parties of their nationality. Where the parties are of different nationalities, a sole arbitrator or the presiding arbitrator shall not have the *same nationality* as any party unless the parties who are not of the same nationality as the arbitrator candidate all agree in writing otherwise.

General Observation:
The LCIA Rules list several criteria to take into account (nationality/availability) in addition to the traditional reference to impartiality and independence.
Article 5.9 specifically opens the door for any dispute-relevant circumstance to be taken into account.

Parties and to such considerations that are relevant to the impartiality or independence of the arbitrator.

…

10.3 The Court shall also consider whether the arbitrator has *sufficient availability to determine the case in a prompt and efficient manner that is appropriate given the nature of the arbitration.*

General Observation:
The SIAC Rules list specific qualifications and contain a traditional reference to impartiality and independence.

In stark contrast with other rules applicable to the resolution of investment disputes, there is no general reference to higher standards of morality or specific expertise in law.[3] In practice, however, the parties will evidently take into account these factors when considering the possible candidates who could be appointed as arbitrators for a given dispute. The rules recognise the parties' discretion in this regard by mainly pointing to possible limits to the choice which could encroach on due process considerations and endanger the dispute resolution process as a whole.

It can be highlighted that the ideal number of arbitrators is further to be determined by taking into account the specific circumstances of the dispute.

The only criteria which appears to be particularly sensitive concerns the nationality of the arbitrator(s). The studied NTBRs address this by requiring the appointment of a presiding or sole arbitrator who does not have the nationality of the parties. In addition, the ICC Rules require the appointment of arbitrators with a nationality other than that of the parties, where the claim is based on a treaty.

It can be noted that the studied NTBRs do not explicitly address the issue of repeat appointments or double-hatting. The rules, however, invite the arbitrators to disclose any relevant facts which may call into question their independence or impartiality, as will be discussed later.

4. APPOINTING AUTHORITIES IN INVESTMENT ARBITRATION UNDER NTBRs

The studied NTBRs all envisage an appointing authority whose function is certainly not limited to a default role in cases where the parties are unable to proceed with the appointment of the arbitral tribunal. The appointing authority in institutional settings plays a supervisory role to ensure the integrity of the procedure.

An important distinction must be made in this case between institutional NTBRs on the one hand, and the UNCITRAL Rules on the other hand. Arbitral institutions directly provide for an independent appointing authority whose composition, functioning and work is comprehensively regulated. In contrast, within the non-institutional framework of UNCITRAL arbitration, the parties are invited to select an appointing authority. By default, the UNCITRAL Rules empower the Secretary-General of the PCA to designate the appointing authority.[4] The PCA is further regularly designated by parties as the appointing authority.[5]

---

[3]   See e.g. Article 14 ICSID Convention, requiring that persons designated to serve on the Panels be persons of high moral character and recognised competence in the fields of law, commerce, industry or finance, who may be relied upon to exercise independent judgment.

Table 2. Comparison of Select Non-Treaty Based Rules: Selected Extracts

ICC (2021)	LCIA (2020)	SCC (2017)	UNCITRAL (2013)	SIAC (2017)
Article 12	Article 5	Article 17	Articles 6, 8 and 9	Rules 6.2, 7.3, 8, 9.1 and 9.2
Parties and/or ICC Court	*Parties and/or LCIA Court*	*Parties and/or SCC Board*	*Parties and/or Appointing authority.*	*Parties and/or Court*
	NB: Article 7 explicitly contemplates the possibility for an arbitrator to be nominated by a third person (other than the LCIA Court)		Article 6 1. Unless the parties have already agreed on the choice of an appointing authority, a party may at any time propose the name or names of one or more institutions or persons, including the Secretary-General of the Permanent Court of Arbitration at The Hague (hereinafter called the 'PCA'), one of whom would serve as appointing authority. 2. If all parties have not agreed on the choice of an appointing authority within 30 days after a proposal made in accordance with paragraph 1 has been received by all other parties, any party may request the Secretary-General of the PCA to designate the appointing authority.	

The appointing authority aims to protect the legitimacy of the dispute resolution system by ensuring equal treatment of the parties in the appointment process, and to intervene in case of any difficulties or more generally a reluctance to proceed with the appointment.

Party appointment is systematically envisaged and encouraged: the NTBRs considered for this study all confirm that the parties are offered an opportunity to appoint one or several arbitrators. The involvement of the appointing authority is still necessary for the appointment of a presiding arbitrator for three-member tribunals. It can further become necessary for the appointment of a sole arbitrator, depending on the specific circumstances of the case and the parties' ability to reach an agreement on the sole arbitrator.

---

[4] While the UNCITRAL Rules specifically provide for the designation of an appointing authority by the PCA Secretary-General, one may note an interesting ad hoc case based on the Investment Agreement of the Organisation for Islamic Cooperation where the PCA Secretary-General was asked to intervene to appoint an authority as the OIC's Secretary-General had failed to make a default appointment. The Paris Court of Appeal found in March 2021 that the PCA lacked the power to step in. See Cour d'appel de Paris, Pôle 5, Chambre 16, chambre commerciale internationale, 23.03.2021, No. RG 18/05756 – No. Portalis 35L7-V-B7C-B5JUM.

[5] See for instance the arbitration agreement in the *Centerra Gold Inc., Kumtor Gold Company CJSC and Kumtor Operating Company CJSC v. The Kyrgyz Republic and Kyrgyzaltyn OJSC (III)* case providing that 'if the Parties fail to agree to an Arbitrator, the PCA shall act as the Appointing Authority pursuant to the UNCITRAL Arbitration Rules.'

5. THE METHOD OF APPOINTMENT IN INVESTMENT ARBITRATION UNDER NTBRs

Table 3. Comparison of Select Non-Treaty Based Rules: Selected Extracts

ICC (2021)	LCIA (2020)	SCC (2017)	UNCITRAL (2013)	SIAC (2017)
Article 11	Article 5	Article 16	Article 8	Rule 5
4. *The decisions of the Court as to the appointment, confirmation, challenge or replacement of an arbitrator shall be final.*	5.6. The *LCIA Court shall appoint the Arbitral Tribunal* promptly following delivery to the Registrar of the Response or, if no Response is received, promptly after 28 days from the Commencement Date (or such other lesser or greater period to be determined by the LCIA Court pursuant to Article 22.5).	1. The *parties may agree on the number of arbitrators.*	1. If the parties have agreed that a sole arbitrator is to be appointed and if within 30 days after receipt by all other parties of a proposal for the appointment of a sole arbitrator *the parties have not reached agreement thereon, a sole arbitrator shall, at the request of a party, be appointed by the appointing authority.*	5.1 The Parties may agree that the Tribunal shall be composed of *one, three or any other odd number of arbitrators.*
Article 12		2. Where the parties have not agreed on the number of arbitrators, the Board shall decide whether the Arbitral Tribunal shall consist of a sole arbitrator or three arbitrators, having regard to the complexity of the case, the amount in dispute and any other relevant circumstances.		5.2 *Three arbitrators shall be appointed in any arbitration under these Rules unless the Parties have otherwise agreed;* or it appears to the Court, giving due regard to any proposals by the Parties, that the complexity, the quantum involved or other relevant circumstances of the dispute, warrants the appointment of a sole arbitrator.
1. The disputes shall be decided by a sole arbitrator or by three arbitrators.	5.7 No party or third person may appoint any arbitrator under the Arbitration Agreement: *the LCIA Court alone is empowered to appoint arbitrators (albeit taking into account any written agreement or joint nomination by the parties or nomination by the other candidates or arbitrators).*		2. The appointing authority shall appoint the sole arbitrator as promptly as possible. In making the appointment, the appointing authority shall *use the following list-procedure, unless the parties agree that the list-procedure should not be used or unless the appointing authority determines in its discretion that the use of the list-procedure is not appropriate for the case:*	
2. Where the *parties have not agreed* upon the number of arbitrators, the Court shall appoint a sole arbitrator, save where it appears to the Court that the dispute is such as to warrant the appointment of three arbitrators. In such case, the *claimant shall nominate an arbitrator within 15 days from receipt of the notification of the decision of the Court, and the respondent shall nominate*		Article 17		5.3 If the Parties have agreed that any arbitrator is to be appointed by one or more of the Parties, or by any third person including by the arbitrators already appointed, that agreement shall be deemed
		1. The *parties may agree on a procedure for appointment of the Arbitral Tribunal.*		
		2. Where the parties have not agreed on a procedure, or if the Arbitral Tribunal has not been appointed within the time period agreed by the parties or, where the parties have not		

agreed on a time period, within the time period set by the Board, the appointment shall be made pursuant to paragraphs (3)–(7). 3. *Where the Arbitral Tribunal is to consist of a sole arbitrator, the parties shall be given 10 days to jointly appoint the arbitrator. If the parties fail to appoint the arbitrator within this time, the Board shall make the appointment.* 4. *Where the Arbitral Tribunal is to consist of more than one arbitrator, each party shall appoint an equal number of arbitrators and the Board shall appoint the Chairperson. Where a party fails to appoint arbitrator(s) within the stipulated time period, the Board shall make the appointment.* 5. *Where there are multiple Claimants or Respondents and the Arbitral Tribunal is to consist of more than one arbitrator, the multiple*	(a) The appointing authority shall communicate to each of the parties an identical list containing at least three names; (b) Within 15 days after the receipt of this list, each party may return the list to the appointing authority after having deleted the name or names to which it objects and numbered the remaining names on the list in the order of its preference; (c) After the expiration of the above period of time the appointing authority shall appoint the sole arbitrator from among the names approved on the lists returned to it and in accordance with the order of preference indicated by the parties; (d) If for any reason the appointment cannot be made according to this procedure, the appointing authority may exercise its discretion in appointing the sole arbitrator.	an agreement to nominate an arbitrator under these Rules. 5.4 In all cases, the arbitrators nominated by the Parties, or by any third person including by the arbitrators already appointed, *shall be subject to appointment by the Court in its discretion.* 5.5 The Court shall appoint an arbitrator as soon as practicable. Any decision by the Court to appoint an arbitrator under these Rules shall be final and not subject to appeal. 5.6 The Court may appoint an arbitrator whose appointment has already been suggested or proposed in the arbitral proceedings. 5.7 *Where the Parties are of different nationalities, the Court shall appoint a sole arbitrator or a presiding arbitrator of a different nationality than the Parties, unless the Parties have otherwise agreed or unless the Court otherwise determines it*
5.8 A sole arbitrator shall be appointed unless the parties have agreed in writing otherwise or the LCIA Court determines that in the circumstances a three-member tribunal is appropriate (or, exceptionally, more than three). 5.9 The LCIA Court shall appoint arbitrators with due regard for any particular *method or criteria of selection agreed in writing by the* parties. The LCIA Court shall also take into account the transaction(s) at issue, the nature and circumstances of the dispute, its monetary amount or value, the location and languages of the parties, the number of parties and all other factors which it may consider relevant in the circumstances. 5.10 *The President of the LCIA Court shall only be eligible to be appointed as an arbitrator if the parties agree in writing to nominate him or her as the*	*an arbitrator within 15 days from receipt of the notification of the nomination made by the claimant. If a party fails to nominate an arbitrator, the appointment shall be made by the Court.* 3. *Where the parties have agreed that the dispute shall be resolved by a sole arbitrator, they may, by agreement, nominate the sole arbitrator for confirmation. If the parties fail to nominate a sole arbitrator within 30 days from the date when the claimant's Request for Arbitration has been received by the other party or parties, or within such additional time as may be allowed by the Secretariat,* the sole arbitrator shall be appointed by the Court. 4. *Where the parties have agreed that the dispute shall be resolved by three arbitrators, each party shall nominate in the Request and the Answer, respectively, one arbitrator for confirmation. If a party fails*	

(continued)

Table 3 *continued*

ICC (2021)	LCIA (2020)	SCC (2017)	UNCITRAL (2013)	SIAC (2017)
to nominate an arbitrator, the appointment shall be made by the Court. 5. Where the dispute is to be referred to three arbitrators, *the third arbitrator, who will act as president of the arbitral tribunal, shall be appointed by the Court, unless the parties have agreed upon another procedure for such appointment, in which case the nomination will be subject to confirmation pursuant to Article 13.* Should such procedure not result in a nomination within 30 days from the confirmation or appointment of the co-arbitrators or any other time limit agreed by the parties or fixed by the Court, the third arbitrator shall be appointed by the Court. 6. Where there are multiple claimants or multiple respondents, and where the dispute is to be referred to	sole or presiding arbitrator; and the Vice Presidents of the LCIA Court and the Chair of the LCIA Board of Directors (the latter being ex officio a member of the LCIA Court) shall only be eligible to be appointed as arbitrators if nominated in writing by a party or parties or by the other candidates or arbitrators – provided that no such nominee shall have taken or shall take thereafter any part in any function of the LCIA Court or LCIA relating to such arbitration. Article 7 7.1 If the parties have agreed howsoever that any arbitrator is to be appointed by one or more of them or by any third person (other than the LCIA Court), that agreement shall be treated under the Arbitration Agreement as an agreement to nominate an arbitrator for all	Claimants, jointly, and the multiple Respondents, jointly, shall appoint an equal number of arbitrators. If either side fails to make such joint appointment, the Board may appoint the entire Arbitral Tribunal. 6. If the parties are of different nationalities, the sole arbitrator or the Chairperson of the Arbitral Tribunal shall be of a different nationality than the parties, unless the parties have agreed otherwise or the Board otherwise deems it appropriate. 7. When appointing arbitrators, the Board shall consider the nature and circumstances of the dispute, the applicable law, the seat and language of the arbitration and the nationality of the parties.	Article 9 1. *If three arbitrators are to be appointed, each party shall appoint one arbitrator. The two arbitrators thus appointed shall choose the third arbitrator who will act as the presiding arbitrator of the arbitral tribunal.* 2. If within 30 days after the receipt of a party's notification of the appointment of an arbitrator the other party has not notified the first party of the arbitrator it has appointed, the first party may request the appointing authority to appoint the second arbitrator. 3. *If within 30 days after the appointment of the second arbitrator the two arbitrators have not agreed on the choice of the presiding arbitrator, the presiding arbitrator shall be appointed by the appointing authority in the same way as a sole arbitrator would be appointed under article 8.*	*to be appropriate having regard to the circumstances of the case.* … Rule 6 6.1 If a sole arbitrator is to be appointed, either Party may propose to the other Party the names of one or more persons to serve as the sole arbitrator. *Where the Parties have reached an agreement on the nomination of a sole arbitrator, Rule 5.4 shall apply.* 6.2 If within 42 days after the date of commencement of the arbitration, or within the period otherwise agreed by the Parties or set by the Registrar, the Parties have not reached an agreement on the nomination of a sole arbitrator, or if at any time either Party so requests, *the Court shall appoint the sole arbitrator in accordance with the procedure under Rule 8.*

three arbitrators, the multiple claimants, jointly, and the multiple respondents, jointly, shall nominate an arbitrator for confirmation pursuant to Article 13. 7. Where an *additional party* has been joined (Article 7(1)), and where the dispute is to be referred to three arbitrators, the additional party may, jointly with the claimant(s) or with the respondent(s), nominate an arbitrator for confirmation pursuant to Article 13 and subject to Article 7(5). 8. In the absence of a joint nomination pursuant to Articles 12(6) or 12(7) and where all parties are unable to agree to a method for the constitution of the arbitral tribunal, *the Court may appoint each member of the arbitral tribunal and shall designate one of them to act as president.*	*purposes.* Such nominee may only be appointed by the LCIA Court as arbitrator subject to that nominee's compliance with Articles 5.3 to 5.5; and *the LCIA Court shall refuse to appoint any nominee if it determines that the nominee is not so compliant or is otherwise unsuitable.* 7.2 Where the parties have howsoever agreed that the Claimant or the Respondent or any third person (other than the LCIA Court) is to nominate an arbitrator and such nomination is not made within time (in the Request, Response or otherwise), the LCIA Court may appoint an arbitrator notwithstanding the absence of a nomination. The LCIA Court may, but shall not be obliged to, take into consideration any late nomination. 7.3 *In the absence of written agreement between the Parties, no party may unilaterally nominate a sole arbitrator or presiding arbitrator.*		Article 10 1. For the purposes of article 9, paragraph 1, where three arbitrators are to be appointed and there are multiple parties as claimant or as respondent, unless the parties have agreed to another method of appointment of arbitrators, the multiple parties jointly, whether as claimant or as respondent, shall appoint an arbitrator. 2. If the parties have agreed that the arbitral tribunal is to be composed of a number of arbitrators other than one or three, the arbitrators shall be appointed according to the method agreed upon by the parties. 3. *In the event of any failure to constitute the arbitral tribunal under these Rules, the appointing authority shall, at the request of any party, constitute the arbitral tribunal and, in doing so, may revoke any appointment already made and appoint or reappoint each of the arbitrators and designate one of them as the presiding arbitrator.*	7. Multiple Arbitrators 7.1 *If three or more arbitrators are to be appointed, the Claimant and the Respondent shall each nominate an equal number of arbitrators.* 7.2 If a Party fails to nominate its arbitrator(s) within 35 days after receipt of the other Party's nomination of its arbitrator(s), or within the period otherwise agreed by the Parties or set by the Registrar, *the Court shall proceed to appoint the arbitrator(s) on its behalf.* 7.3 Unless the Parties have agreed upon another procedure for appointing the presiding arbitrator, or if such agreed procedure does not result in a nomination within the period agreed by the Parties or set by the Registrar, *the Court shall appoint the presiding arbitrator in accordance with the procedure under Rule 8.* Rule 8 In making the appointment of the arbitrator(s) under Rule 6.2,

(continued)

Table 3 *continued*

ICC (2021)	LCIA (2020)	SCC (2017)	UNCITRAL (2013)	SIAC (2017)
In such cases, the Court shall be at liberty to choose any person it regards as suitable to act as arbitrator, applying Article 13 when it considers this appropriate. 9. Notwithstanding any agreement by the parties on the method of constitution of the arbitral tribunal, *in exceptional circumstances the Court may appoint each member of the arbitral tribunal to avoid a significant risk of unequal treatment and unfairness that may affect the validity of the award.* Article 13 *1. In confirming or appointing arbitrators, the Court shall consider the prospective arbitrator's nationality, residence and other relationships with the countries of which the parties or the other arbitrators are nationals and the prospective arbitrator's availability*	Article 8 8.1 Where the Arbitration Agreement entitles each party howsoever to nominate an arbitrator, the parties to the dispute number more than two and such parties have not all agreed in writing that the disputant parties represent collectively two separate 'sides' for the formation of the Arbitral Tribunal (as Claimants on one side and Respondents on the other side, each side nominating a single arbitrator), *the LCIA Court shall appoint the Arbitral Tribunal without regard to any party's entitlement or nomination.*			Rule 7.3, Rule 9.1 and Rule 9.2, *the Court shall use the following list-procedure, unless the Parties agree that the list-procedure shall not be used or unless the Court determines, in its discretion, that the use of the list-procedure is not appropriate for the case:* a) The Court shall invite the Parties' views on any qualifications of the arbitrator(s) prior to compiling the list of candidates. The Court shall not be bound by the Parties' recommendations, but it shall take the Parties' views and the circumstances of the case into account when compiling the list of candidates. b) The Court shall communicate to each of the Parties an identical list containing at least five names. c) Within 15 days after the receipt of such list, or within the period otherwise agreed by the Parties or set by the

and ability to conduct the arbitration in accordance with the Rules. The same shall apply where the Secretary General confirms arbitrators pursuant to Article 13(2). 2. The Secretary General may confirm as co-arbitrators, sole arbitrators and presidents of arbitral tribunals persons nominated by the parties or pursuant to their particular agreements, provided that the statement they have submitted contains no qualification regarding impartiality or independence or that a qualified statement regarding impartiality or independence has not given rise to objections. Such confirmation shall be reported to the Court at one of its next sessions. *If the Secretary General considers that a co-arbitrator, sole arbitrator or president of an arbitral tribunal should not be confirmed, the matter shall be submitted to the Court.*				Registrar, each Party shall return the list directly to the Registrar, without need to copy in the other Party, after having deleted the name or names to which it objects and numbered the remaining names on the list in the order of its preference. d) After the expiry of the above period of time, the Court shall appoint the arbitrator(s) from among the names approved on the lists returned to the Registrar and in accordance with the order of preference indicated by the Parties. e) *If for any reason the appointment cannot be made according to this procedure, the Court may exercise its discretion in appointing the arbitrator(s), including appointing the arbitrator(s) from outside the list communicated to the Parties.*

(continued)

Table 3 *continued*

ICC (2021)	LCIA (2020)	SCC (2017)	UNCITRAL (2013)	SIAC (2017)
3. *Where the Court is to appoint an arbitrator, it shall make the appointment upon proposal of an ICC National Committee or Group that it considers to be appropriate.* If the Court does not accept the proposal made, or if the National Committee or Group fails to make the proposal requested within the time limit fixed by the Court, the Court may repeat its request, request a proposal from another National Committee or Group that it considers to be appropriate, or appoint directly any person whom it regards as suitable. 4. *The Court may also appoint directly to act as arbitrator any person whom it regards as suitable where*: a) one or more of the parties is a state or may be considered to be a state entity;				Rule 9 9.1 Where there are more than two Parties to the arbitration, and a sole arbitrator is to be appointed, *the Parties may agree to jointly nominate the sole arbitrator.* In the absence of such joint nomination having been made within 42 days of the date of commencement of the arbitration or within the period otherwise agreed by the Parties or set by the Registrar, *the Court shall appoint the sole arbitrator in accordance with the procedure under Rule 8.* 9.2 Where there are more than two Parties to the arbitration, and three or more arbitrators are to be appointed, *the Claimant(s) and Respondent(s) shall each jointly nominate an equal number of arbitrators. The presiding arbitrator shall be*

b) the Court considers that it would be appropriate to appoint an arbitrator from a country or territory where there is no National Committee or Group; or c) the President certifies to the Court that circumstances exist which, in the President's opinion, make a direct appointment necessary and appropriate. 5. Where the Court is to appoint the sole arbitrator or the president of the arbitral tribunal, such sole arbitrator or president of the arbitral tribunal shall be of a nationality other than those of the parties. However, in suitable circumstances and provided that none of the parties objects within the time limit fixed by the Secretariat, the sole arbitrator or the president of the arbitral tribunal may be chosen from a country of which any of the parties is a national.				*appointed in accordance with Rule 7.3.* In the absence of both such joint nominations having been made within 42 days of the date of commencement of the arbitration or within the period otherwise agreed by the Parties or set by the Registrar, *the Court shall appoint all the arbitrators in accordance with the procedure under Rule 8 and shall designate one of them to be the presiding arbitrator.*

The studied NTBRs all *afford the parties a possibility to play a direct role in the appointment of arbitrator(s)*. The NTBRs however provide a series of default mechanisms to determine the number of arbitrators and ultimately appoint one or sometimes even all arbitrators. Several provisions aim to ensure equal treatment of the parties by contemplating adjustments for the nomination of arbitrators in case of multiple parties or added parties.

The appointing authority plays an open and direct role to not only provide solutions in case of difficulties with the appointment. The appointing authority directly supervises and controls the appointment process.

The following observations can be made when contrasting these appointment procedures under the different NTBRs:

1. *Number of arbitrators*: the NTBRs provide different methods and default rules to determine the number of arbitrators. Strikingly, the SIAC Rules reverse the default rule to be found for instance in the ICC and LCIA Rules by opting for three-member tribunals except if the parties ask otherwise.

2. *List-procedure*: the SIAC and UNCITRAL explicitly envisage a list-procedure which allows the parties to express their preferences and be involved in the appointment process. This list-procedure can however be excluded by the parties.

3. *Final say of the appointing authority*: the appointing authority has the final say over the appointment, even if it will take into account any nomination agreement which may directly come from the parties or, occasionally, emanate from a third party designated by the parties. The wording of LCIA Article 5.7 leaves no room for ambiguity: the LCIA Court alone is empowered to appoint arbitrators (albeit taking into account any written agreement or joint nomination by the parties or nomination by the other candidates or arbitrators).

4. *Unilateral party appointment is exceptionally possible*: the LCIA Rules explicitly authorise the parties to agree in writing to a unilateral appointment by one party only of a sole arbitrator or presiding arbitrator.

5. *No challenge of decisions to appoint*: the NTBRs (or related instruments applicable to the functioning of the appointing authority) do not allow the parties to challenge a decision made by the appointing authority

6. *Limitations on appointment of appointing authority members*: The appointing authority itself is typically subject to limitations for its members to be appointed as arbitrators. This is explicitly provided in the ICC and LCIA Rules, limiting (albeit not excluding) the possibility to appoint members of the ICC or LCIA Court.

The particularity for UNCITRAL is twofold: firstly, it provides for a default list-procedure for the appointment of sole arbitrators; secondly, it entrusts by default not the appointing authority but the two party-appointed arbitrators to select the presiding arbitrator in case of three-member tribunals. The appointing authority would thus only intervene if the party-appointed arbitrators failed to appoint a presiding arbitrator.

6. PARAMETERS TO ENSURE INDEPENDENCE AND IMPARTIALITY: PREVENTIVE MEASURES

All the studied NTBRs provide for a preventive mechanism to ensure the fundamental requirements of impartiality and independence of arbitrators. This preventive mechanism consists in the duty for any prospective arbitrator, in order to be appointed, to *disclose any relevant facts which may casts doubts, in the eyes of the parties, on his or her independence and impartiality*. Where it is involved, the arbitral institution will provide a specific form and guide the arbitrators in this regard. This traditional mechanism exists in investment arbitration conducted under TBRs as well as for commercial arbitration. There is accordingly no specific alternative regulation provided for investment arbitrations conducted under NTBRs.

The following observations can be made:

1. *NTBRs used for investment arbitration contain only generic reference to independence and impartiality*: the NTBRs do not provide any benchmarks or guidelines which could be used to assess the existing of possible conflicts.
2. *Use of IBA Guidelines on Conflict of Interest in Investment Arbitration under NTBRs*: In practice, the IBA Guidelines on Conflict of Interest (2014) will typically be considered by prospective arbitrators, parties and even the appointing authorities to determine whether a specific situation should prevent an arbitrator from being appointed. For the purpose of this special report, it can be observed that the IBA Guidelines on Conflict of Interest do not distinguish between investment arbitration and commercial arbitration. In practice, the Guidelines have been equally applied in the framework of Commercial and Investment Arbitration.
3. There is no distinct standard of independence and impartiality for party-appointed arbitrators and non-party appointed arbitrators.
4. After appointment, all arbitrators remain under a continuing duty to disclose any new facts which may give rise to doubts as to the impartiality or independence.
5. The 2021 ICC Rules explicitly require the disclosure of information related to third-party funders.

Table 4. Comparison of Select Non-Treaty Based Rules: Selected Extracts

ICC (2021)	LCIA (2020)	SCC (2017)	UNCITRAL (2013)	SIAC (2017)
Article 11 1. Every arbitrator must be and remain impartial and independent of the parties involved in the arbitration. 2. Before appointment or confirmation, a prospective arbitrator shall sign a statement of acceptance, availability, impartiality and independence. The prospective arbitrator shall disclose in writing to the Secretariat any facts or circumstances which might be of such a nature as to call into question the arbitrator's independence in the eyes of the parties, as well as any circumstances that could give rise to reasonable doubts as to the arbitrator's impartiality. The Secretariat shall provide such information to the parties in writing and fix a time limit for any comments from them.	Article 5 … 5.4 Before appointment by the LCIA Court, each arbitrator candidate shall furnish to the Registrar (upon the latter's request) a brief written summary of his or her qualifications and professional positions (past and present); the candidate shall also agree in writing fee rates conforming to the Schedule of Costs; the candidate shall sign a written declaration stating: (i) whether there are any circumstances currently known to the candidate which are likely to give rise in the mind of any party to any justifiable doubts as to his or her impartiality or independence and, if so, specifying in full such circumstances in the declaration; and (ii) whether the candidate is ready, willing and able to devote sufficient	Article 18 1. Every arbitrator must be impartial and independent. 2. Before being appointed, a prospective arbitrator shall disclose any circumstances that may give rise to justifiable doubts as to the prospective arbitrator's impartiality or independence. 3. Once appointed, an arbitrator shall submit to the Secretariat a signed statement of acceptance, availability, impartiality and independence, disclosing any circumstances that may give rise to justifiable doubts as to the arbitrator's impartiality or independence. The Secretariat shall send a copy of the statement of acceptance, availability, impartiality and independence to the parties and the other arbitrators.	Article 11 When a person is approached in connection with his or her possible appointment as an arbitrator, he or she shall disclose any circumstances likely to give rise to justifiable doubts as to his or her impartiality or independence. An arbitrator, from the time of his or her appointment and throughout the arbitral proceedings, shall without delay disclose any such circumstances to the parties and the other arbitrators unless they have already been informed by him or her of these circumstances.	Rule 10 10.1 Any arbitrator appointed in an arbitration under these Rules, whether or not nominated by the Parties, shall be and remain at all times independent and impartial. 10.2 In appointing an arbitrator under these Rules, the Court shall have due regard to any qualifications required of the arbitrator by the agreement of the Parties and to such considerations that are relevant to the impartiality or independence of the arbitrator. … 10.4 A nominated arbitrator shall disclose to the Parties and to the Registrar any circumstances that may give rise to justifiable doubts as to his impartiality or independence as soon as reasonably practicable and in any event before his appointment.

3. An arbitrator shall immediately disclose in writing to the Secretariat and to the parties any facts or circumstances of a similar nature to those referred to in Article 11(2) concerning the arbitrator's impartiality or independence which may arise during the arbitration.

4. The decisions of the Court as to the appointment, confirmation, challenge or replacement of an arbitrator shall be final.

5. By accepting to serve, arbitrators undertake to carry out their responsibilities in accordance with the Rules.

6. Insofar as the parties have not provided otherwise, the arbitral tribunal shall be constituted in accordance with the provisions of Articles 12 and 13. | time, diligence and industry to ensure the expeditious and efficient conduct of the arbitration. The candidate shall promptly furnish such agreement and declaration to the Registrar.

5.5 Each arbitrator shall assume a continuing duty, until the arbitration is finally concluded, forthwith to disclose in writing any circumstances becoming known to that arbitrator after the date of his or her written declaration (under Article 5.4) which are likely to give rise in the mind of any party to any justifiable doubts as to his or her impartiality or independence, to be delivered to the LCIA Court, any other members of the Arbitral Tribunal and all parties in the arbitration. | 4. An arbitrator shall immediately inform the parties and the other arbitrators in writing if any circumstances that may give rise to justifiable doubts as to the arbitrator's impartiality or independence arise during the course of the arbitration. |
| | | 10.5 An arbitrator shall immediately disclose to the Parties, to the other arbitrators and to the Registrar any circumstances that may give rise to justifiable doubts as to his impartiality or independence that may be discovered or arise during the arbitration.

10.6 No Party or person acting on behalf of a Party shall have any ex parte communication relating to the case with any arbitrator or with any candidate for appointment as party-nominated arbitrator, except to advise the candidate of the general nature of the controversy and of the anticipated proceedings; to discuss the candidate's qualifications, availability or independence in relation to the Parties; or to discuss the suitability of candidates for selection as the presiding arbitrator where the Parties or |

(continued)

Table 4 *continued*

ICC (2021)	LCIA (2020)	SCC (2017)	UNCITRAL (2013)	SIAC (2017)
7. In order to assist prospective arbitrators and arbitrators in complying with their duties under Articles 11(2) and 11(3), each party must promptly inform the Secretariat, the arbitral tribunal and the other parties, of the existence and identity of any non-party which has entered into an arrangement for the funding of claims or defences and under which it has an economic interest in the outcome of the arbitration.				Party-nominated arbitrators are to participate in that selection. No Party or person acting on behalf of a Party shall have any *ex parte* communication relating to the case with any candidate for presiding arbitrator.

7. CONSEQUENCES OF A BREACH OF THE DUTY TO ACT INDEPENDENTLY AND IMPARTIALLY: CURATIVE MEASURES

Table 5. Comparison of Select Non-Treaty Based Rules: Selected Extracts

ICC (2021)	LCIA (2020)	SCC (2017)	UNCITRAL (2013)	SIAC (2017)
Article 14	Article 10	Article 19	Article 12	Rule 11
1. *A challenge of an arbitrator, whether for an alleged lack of impartiality or independence, or otherwise, shall be made by the submission to the Secretariat of a written statement specifying the facts and circumstances on which the challenge is based.* 2. *For a challenge to be admissible, it must be submitted by a party either within 30 days from receipt by that party of the notification of the appointment or confirmation of the arbitrator, or within 30 days from the date when the party making the challenge was informed of the facts and circumstances on which the challenge is based if such date is subsequent to the receipt of such notification.*	10.1 *The LCIA Court may revoke any arbitrator's appointment upon its own initiative, at the written request of all other members of the Arbitral Tribunal or upon a written challenge by any party if: … (iii) circumstances exist that give rise to justifiable doubts as to that arbitrator's impartiality or independence.* 10.2 *The LCIA Court may determine that an arbitrator is unfit to act under Article 10.1 if that arbitrator: (i) acts in deliberate violation of the Arbitration Agreement; (ii) does not act fairly or impartially as between the parties; or (iii) does not conduct or participate in the arbitration with reasonable efficiency, diligence and industry.*	1. *A party may challenge any arbitrator if circumstances exist that give rise to justifiable doubts as to the arbitrator's impartiality or independence or if the arbitrator does not possess the qualifications agreed by the parties.* 2. *A party may challenge an arbitrator it has appointed, or in whose appointment it has participated, only for reasons it becomes aware of after the appointment was made.* 3. A party wishing to challenge an arbitrator shall submit a written statement to the Secretariat stating the reasons for the challenge, within 15 days from the date the circumstances giving rise to	1. *Any arbitrator may be challenged if circumstances exist that give rise to justifiable doubts as to the arbitrator's impartiality or independence.* 2. *A party may challenge the arbitrator appointed by it only for reasons of which it becomes aware after the appointment has been made.* 3. *In the event that an arbitrator fails to act or in the event of the de jure or de facto impossibility of his or her performing his or her functions, the procedure in respect of the challenge of an arbitrator as provided in article 13 shall apply.*	11.1 *Any arbitrator may be challenged if circumstances exist that give rise to justifiable doubts as to the arbitrator's impartiality or independence or if the arbitrator does not possess any requisite qualification on which the Parties have agreed.* 11.2 *A Party may challenge the arbitrator nominated by it only for reasons of which it becomes aware after the appointment has been made.* Rule 12 12.1 A Party that intends to challenge an arbitrator shall file a notice of challenge with the Registrar in accordance with the requirements of Rule 12.2 *within 28 days after receipt of the notice of*

(continued)

Table 5 *continued*

ICC (2021)	LCIA (2020)	SCC (2017)	UNCITRAL (2013)	SIAC (2017)
3. *The Court shall decide on the admissibility and, at the same time, if necessary, on the merits of a challenge after the Secretariat has afforded an opportunity for the arbitrator concerned, the other party or parties and any other members of the arbitral tribunal to comment in writing within a suitable period of time. Such comments shall be communicated to the parties and to the arbitrators.*	10.3 A party challenging an arbitrator under Article 10.1 shall, *within 14 days of the formation of the Arbitral Tribunal or (if later) within 14 days of becoming aware of any grounds described in Article 10.1 or 10.2, deliver a written statement of the reasons for its challenge to the LCIA Court, the Arbitral Tribunal and all other parties. A party may challenge an arbitrator whom it has nominated, or in whose appointment it has participated, only for reasons of which it becomes aware after the appointment has been made by the LCIA Court.* 10.4 *If all other parties agree in writing to the challenge within 14 days of receipt of the written statement, the LCIA Court shall revoke that arbitrator's appointment (without reasons).* 10.5 Unless the parties so agree or the challenged arbitrator resigns in writing within 14 days	the challenge became known to the party. *Failure to challenge an arbitrator within the stipulated time constitutes a waiver of the party's right to make the challenge.* 4. The Secretariat shall notify the parties and the arbitrators of the challenge and *give them an opportunity to submit comments.* 5. If the other party agrees to the challenge, the arbitrator shall resign. *In all other cases, the Board shall take the final decision on the challenge.* Article 20 1. The Board shall release an arbitrator from appointment where: (i) the Board accepts the resignation of the arbitrator; (ii) a challenge to the arbitrator under Article 19 is sustained; or (iii) the arbitrator is otherwise unable or fails to perform the arbitrator's functions.	Article 13 1. A party that intends to challenge an arbitrator shall send *notice of its challenge within 15 days after it has been notified of the appointment of the challenged arbitrator, or within 15 days after the circumstances mentioned in articles 11 and 12 became known to that party.* 2. The notice of challenge shall be communicated to all other parties, to the arbitrator who is challenged and to the other arbitrators. *The notice of challenge shall state the reasons for the challenge.* 3. When an arbitrator has been challenged by a party, all parties may agree to the challenge. The arbitrator may also, after the challenge, withdraw from his or her office. In neither case does this imply acceptance of the validity of the grounds for the challenge.	*appointment of the arbitrator who is being challenged or within 28 days after the circumstances specified in Rule 11.1 or Rule 11.2 became known or should have reasonably been known to that Party.* 12.2 *The notice of challenge shall state the reasons for the challenge.* The date of receipt of the notice of challenge by the Registrar shall be deemed to be the date the notice of challenge is filed. The Party challenging an arbitrator shall, at the same time as it files a notice of challenge with the Registrar, send the notice of challenge to the other Party, the arbitrator who is being challenged and the other members of the Tribunal (or if the Tribunal has not yet been constituted, any appointed arbitrator), and shall notify the Registrar that it has done so, specifying the mode of service employed and the date of service.

	of receipt of the written statement, the LCIA Court shall decide the challenge. *The LCIA Court may conduct the challenge proceedings in any manner it considers to be appropriate in the circumstances but shall in any event provide the other parties and the challenged arbitrator a reasonable opportunity to comment on the challenging party's written statement.* The LCIA Court may require at any time further information and materials from the challenging party, the challenged arbitrator, other parties, any authorised representative of a party, other members of the Arbitral Tribunal and the tribunal secretary (if any). 10.6 *The LCIA Court's decision shall be made in writing, with reasons*; and a copy shall be transmitted by the Registrar	2. Before the Board releases an arbitrator, the Secretariat may give *the parties and the arbitrators an opportunity to submit comments.*	4. If, within 15 days from the date of the notice of challenge, all parties do not agree to the challenge or the challenged arbitrator does not withdraw, the party making the challenge may elect to pursue it. *In that case, within 30 days from the date of the notice of challenge, it shall seek a decision on the challenge by the appointing authority.*	12.3 *The Party making the challenge shall pay the requisite challenge fee under these Rules in accordance with the applicable Schedule of Fees. If the Party making the challenge fails to pay the challenge fee within the time limit set by the Registrar, the challenge shall be considered as withdrawn.* 12.4 After receipt of a notice of challenge under Rule 12.2, the Registrar may order a suspension of the arbitral proceedings until the challenge is resolved. Unless the Registrar orders the suspension of the arbitral proceedings pursuant to this Rule 12.4, *the challenged arbitrator shall be entitled to continue to participate in the arbitration pending the determination of the challenge by the Court in accordance with Rule 13.*

(continued)

Table 5 *continued*

ICC (2021)	LCIA (2020)	SCC (2017)	UNCITRAL (2013)	SIAC (2017)
	to the parties, the challenged arbitrator and other members of the Arbitral Tribunal (if any). If the challenge is upheld, the LCIA Court shall revoke that arbitrator's appointment. A challenged arbitrator who resigns in writing prior to the LCIA Court's decision shall not be considered as having admitted any part of the written statement.			12.5 Where an arbitrator is challenged by a Party, the other Party may agree to the challenge, and the Court shall remove the arbitrator if all Parties agree to the challenge. The challenged arbitrator may also voluntarily withdraw from office. In neither case does this imply acceptance of the validity of the grounds for the challenge. 12.6 If an arbitrator is removed or withdraws from office in accordance with Rule 12.5, a substitute arbitrator shall be appointed in accordance with the procedure applicable to the nomination and appointment of the arbitrator being replaced. This procedure shall apply even if, during the process of appointing the challenged arbitrator, a Party failed to exercise its right to

				nominate an arbitrator. The time limits applicable to the nomination and appointment of the substitute arbitrator shall commence from the date of receipt of the agreement of the other Party to the challenge or the challenged arbitrator's withdrawal from office.
				Rule 13
				13.1 If, within 21 days of receipt of the notice of challenge under Rule 12, the other Party does not agree to the challenge and the arbitrator who is being challenged does not withdraw voluntarily from office, the Court shall decide the challenge. *The Court may request comments on the challenge from the Parties, the challenged arbitrator and the other members of the Tribunal (or if the Tribunal has not yet been constituted, any appointed arbitrator), and set a schedule for such comments to be made.*
				13.2 If the Court accepts the challenge to an arbitrator, the Court shall remove the

(continued)

Table 5 *continued*

ICC (2021)	LCIA (2020)	SCC (2017)	UNCITRAL (2013)	SIAC (2017)
				arbitrator, and a substitute arbitrator shall be appointed in accordance with the procedure applicable to the nomination and appointment of the arbitrator being replaced. The time limits applicable to the nomination and appointment of the substitute arbitrator shall commence from the date of the Registrar's notification to the Parties of the decision by the Court.

13.3 If the Court rejects the challenge to an arbitrator, the challenged arbitrator shall continue with the arbitration.

13.4 *The Court's decision on any challenge to an arbitrator under this Rule 13 shall be reasoned, unless otherwise agreed by the Parties, and shall be issued to the Parties by the Registrar. Any such decision on any challenge by the Court shall be final and not subject to appeal.* |

All the studied NTBRs provide for a curative mechanism to ensure the fundamental requirements of impartiality and independence of arbitrators. This curative mechanism consists in a possibility for any party *to challenge an arbitrator and to obtain the replacement of the arbitrator*. Here again, this traditional mechanism exists in investment arbitration conducted under TBRs as well as for commercial arbitration. There is accordingly no specific alternative regulation provided for investment arbitrations conducted under NTBRs.

The following observations can be made:

1. *NTBRs all provide for a limited possibility to challenge an arbitrator*: the NTBRs studied for this report all provide different time periods for the filing of a challenge. Parties cannot challenge an arbitrator outside of the stipulated time period.
2. Challenge procedures allow the arbitrator(s) and parties to file comments.
3. The appointing authorities are generally required to motivate their decisions on arbitrator challenges but their decisions are final.
4. Parties may occasionally jointly agree to revoke the arbitrator(s).
5. *Arbitrators may voluntarily resign after a challenge and NTBRs confirm that such resignation does not imply an acceptance of the validity of the grounds for the challenge*: this should be highlighted as it certainly finds an echo in the general practice where arbitrators are also regularly approached (or 'tapped') without ultimately being confirmed as arbitrators. This banalisation of the disclosure procedure aims to facilitate the handling of challenges by allowing an easy way out for arbitrators without any substantial impact on their reputation.
6. The SIAC Rules explicitly request the payment of a challenge fee while other rules remain silent or general about the costs associated to the challenge.

8. GENERAL CONCLUSIONS

The main conclusions of the present special report can be summarised as follows.

Investment arbitrations conducted under NTBRs are governed by the same rules and procedures as classical commercial arbitration cases submitted to the NTBRs.

The studied NTBRs confirm that the appointment of investment arbitrators primarily rests on the parties, which are free to agree on one or several arbitrators, depending on the specific context of the procedure and the case. Institutional settings supervise and directly control the appointment process. Nominations by the parties are taken into account but in exceptional circumstances the competent appointing authority may disregard such nomination.

The role of the appointing authority is to supervise and ultimately legitimise the dispute resolution process by ensuring the proper appointment of arbitrators.

There is no authoritative list of criteria for the appointment of investment arbitrators to be found in the NTBRs but occasional mention is made of the need for arbitrators to be available. NTBRs otherwise provide a general reference to circumstances of the case (type of dispute, nature, claims, etc.) which must be taken into account by the appointing authority.

Independence and impartiality of arbitrators are cardinal and mandatory requirements which are explicitly enshrined in all NTBRs. The same standards of independence and impartiality apply to party-appointed arbitrators and other arbitrators appointed by default or through a different mechanism.

Investment arbitrators under NTBRs must, prior to appointment, disclose any relevant facts which may cast doubt in the eyes of the parties as to their independence or impartiality. They remain in any event under a continuing duty to promptly disclose such facts as they may appear during the course of the proceedings.

Strikingly, however, the concrete requirements to ensure such independence and impartiality are nowhere to be found in the NTBRs. No guidelines or comprehensive rules are to be found in the NTBRs in this regard.

Soft rules such as the IBA Guidelines on Conflict of Interest fill this gap and are regularly taken into account in the course of investment arbitrations under NTBRs. There is no specific difference in this regard between commercial and investment arbitration.

Parties have the possibility to challenge investment arbitrators under NTBRs just as is the case in the commercial context. There is no derogatory regime which would provide for a different level of scrutiny when deciding on the proposed challenge of an investment arbitrator as opposed to a commercial arbitrator.

THE INDEPENDENCE AND IMPARTIALITY OF ADJUDICATORS IN INVESTMENT ARBITRATION UNDER TREATY-BASED RULES

Andrea K. BJORKLUND[*]

1. Criteria for the Selection of the Adjudicators...........................264
    1.1. Nationality..264
    1.2. Qualifications 265
2. Which Authority Appoints the Adjudicators? 265
3. The Method for Appointing the Adjudicators 267
4. Methods to Balance the Appointing Authority's Influence on the Appointment of the Adjudicators...................................268
    4.1. Repeat Appointments 269
    4.2. 'Double-Hatting'..271
    4.3. Issue Conflicts...273
    4.4. Secrecy of Deliberations 274
    4.5. Dissenting Opinions 275
    4.6. Ex Parte Communications between Parties and Arbitrators 276
5. Parameters to Ensure that the Adjudicators Act Independently and Impartially 277
6. Consequences for the Adjudicator of a Breach of the Requirement to Act Independently and Impartially 280
7. Enforceability of a Final Decision that was Rendered by an Adjudicator who Breached the Requirement to Act Independently and Impartially 281

---

[*] Special thanks to Paul Trinel, McGill LLM, for his assistance in the preparation of this report.

Andrea K. Bjorklund

1. CRITERIA FOR THE SELECTION OF THE ADJUDICATORS

When it comes to establishing criteria for the selection of adjudicators, investment treaties have usually had recourse to two different sets of criteria: those based on the nationality of prospective adjudicators and those based on their expertise.[1] Additional considerations are that adjudicators be independent and impartial, a topic that will be considered further in section 5 infra.

1.1. NATIONALITY

Many sets of arbitral rules do not contain any provisions on nationality. If, however, one looks at the most common institution through which investment treaty disputes are solved, the International Centre for Settlement of Investment Disputes (ICSID), Article 39 of the ICSID Convention states that the majority of the arbitrators in a dispute must be nationals of states other than the respondent state and the home state of the claimant investor, unless the parties agree otherwise. Given the fact that the majority of arbitral tribunals constituted under the ICSID Convention have three members, this means that, in practice, most often none of the arbitrators have the nationality of one the parties to the dispute.[2]

The Comprehensive Economic and Trade Agreement (CETA) signed between the European Union and Canada is another interesting case study, most notably because it lays out a new procedure for the resolution of disputes which is not international arbitration per se. Indeed, CETA calls for the establishment of a two-tiered permanent court. Its first-instance tribunal will be composed of 15 members appointed by the CETA Joint Committee; out of those 15 members, five will be nationals of European Union states, five will be nationals of Canada, and five will be nationals of third countries.[3] Nationals of other states can be appointed by Canada or the EU, but they are to be regarded as nationals of the entity that selected them for purposes of the investment court system.[4]

Another way in which some investment treaties try to influence the selection of arbitrators is by implementing a roster. For example, the North American Free

---

[1]   Andrea K. Bjorklund, Marc Bungenberg, Manjiao Chi and Catherine Titi, 'Selection and Appointment of International Adjudicators: Structural Options for ISDS Reform', UNCITRAL Academic Forum on ISDS Concept Paper 2019/11 (24 September 2019), available at https://www.jus.uio.no/pluricourts/english/projects/leginvest/academic-forum/papers/papers/11-bjorklund-et-al-selection-and-appointment-isds-af-11-2019.pdf.

[2]   Ibid., p. 3.

[3]   Comprehensive Economic and Trade Agreement (Canada–European Union), 30 October 2016, provisional application 21 September 2017, Art. 8.27(2).

[4]   CETA is not yet in force, so this system has yet to be put to work in practice. As of 6 June 2023, 17 of the 27 EU Member States had ratified CETA. The remaining 10 need to ratify before it enters into force.

Trade Agreement (NAFTA) called for the establishment of a roster of arbitrators from which the Secretary-General of ICSID could appoint presiding arbitrators in the absence of an agreement between the parties on the tribunal president. The assumption was that each state would nominate 15 people to the roster, but that 'roster members shall be appointed by consensus and without regard to nationality'.[5] However, this roster was never constituted.[6]

1.2. QUALIFICATIONS

The second criterion often used by investment treaties concerns the expertise of prospective adjudicators. Thus, Article 14(1) of the ICSID Convention requires that the members of ICSID's Panel of Arbitrators be 'persons of high moral character and recognized competence in the fields of law, commerce, industry or finance, who may be relied upon to exercise independent judgment'. While competence in the field of law is deemed to be of particular importance when it comes to arbitrators, it is not the only area in which competence may be required. Depending on the dispute, other types of expertise, for example in financial services or oil and gas law, might be desirable.

Some instruments have their own requirements. For example, Articles 8.27(4) and 8.28(4) of CETA, dealing with the constitution of the first-instance and appellate tribunals, state that their members 'shall possess the qualifications required in their respective countries for appointment to judicial office, or be jurists of recognised competence'. This language is found in the appointment criteria for many international tribunals. CETA also provides that adjudicators must have demonstrated expertise in public international law, and it would be 'preferable' that they also command similar expertise in international trade and investment law, and in the resolution of disputes arising out of international investment or trade agreements.

2. WHICH AUTHORITY APPOINTS THE ADJUDICATORS?

Most investment treaty arbitrations are decided by three-person arbitral tribunals, although sole arbitrators are a possibility, or indeed a larger odd number of decision-makers. In practice this means that each party appoints its arbitrator,

---

5   North American Free Trade Agreement (Canada–Mexico–United States), 17 December 1992, 32 ILM 289 (1993), Art. 1124(4).

6   Andrea K. Bjorklund, Marc Bungenberg, Manjiao Chi, and Catherine Titi, 'Selection and Appointment of International Adjudicators: Structural Options for ISDS Reform', UNCITRAL Academic Forum on ISDS Concept Paper 2019/11 (24 September 2019), p. 15, available at https://www.jus.uio.no/pluricourts/english/projects/leginvest/academic-forum/papers/papers/11-bjorklund-et-al-selection-and-appointment-isds-af-11-2019.pdf.

and that either the parties themselves, or the arbitrators, appoint the presiding arbitrator. This latter question depends on the applicable investment treaty and, in the absence of specification in that instrument, on the applicable arbitration rules. This process is essentially the same as that used in commercial arbitration.

In the absence of party agreement on the presiding arbitrator, or in the event a disputing party fails to appoint its arbitrator, either the treaty itself or the applicable rules will provide for an appointing authority to fulfil that role. For example, the ICSID Convention and its associated arbitration rules, which are used in the majority of investment treaty cases, provide in Article 38 that, if no tribunal has been constituted 'within 90 days after notice of registration of the request has been dispatched by the Secretary-General ... or such other period as the parties may agree', the Chairman of the ICSID Administrative Council (who is the President of the World Bank Group)[7] will appoint the arbitrator(s) from the ICSID Panel of Arbitrators.[8] This rule thus covers both situations in which a party fails to appoint its arbitrator and when the parties cannot agree on a presiding arbitrator within the requisite time. In either case the Chairman is constrained to appoint from the ICSID roster of arbitrators. In a treaty-based arbitration under the UNCITRAL Rules the Secretary-General of the PCA designates an appointing authority. That person makes the necessary selection and is not restricted to a roster (unless the treaty in question imposes such a limit).

If a party successfully requests the annulment of an ICSID award, the Chairman of the Administrative Council appoints the members of the annulment committee, again from the ICSID Panel of Arbitrators.[9]

When it comes to the CETA, members of its tribunals are to be appointed by the CETA Joint Committee.[10] This Committee is to be composed of representatives of Canada and the EU and is co-chaired by the Minister for International Trade of Canada and the member of the European Commission responsible for Trade.[11] Cases will be heard by panels consisting of three judges appointed by the President of the relevant Tribunal (first instance or appellate), who must be a national of a third country.[12]

Finally, one can refer to the identity of the appointing authority regarding the rosters that are provided for in some investment agreements. Theoretically,

---

[7] Convention on the Settlement of Investment Disputes between States and Nationals of Other States, 575 UNTS 159, 3 March 1965, Art. 5.

[8] Ibid., Art. 38.

[9] Ibid., Art. 52(3).

[10] Comprehensive Economic and Trade Agreement (Canada–European Union), 30 October 2016, provisional application 21 September 2017, Art. 8.27(2).

[11] Ibid., Art. 26.1.

[12] Ibid., Art. 8.27(7) and (8). Cf. also Art. 2(4) and (5) of Decision No. 001/2021 of the CETA Joint Committee of 29 January 2021 regarding the functioning of the Appellate Tribunal, available at https://www.international.gc.ca/trade-commerce/trade-agreements-accords-commerciaux/agr-acc/ceta-aecg/appellate-tribunal-dappel.aspx?lang=eng.

presiding arbitrators in NAFTA cases should have been appointed by the Secretary-General of ICSID from the NAFTA roster of arbitrators; in the absence of that roster, he or she appoints from the ICSID Panel of Arbitrators.[13] The ICSID Secretary-General is also designated as the appointing authority in investment disputes in the United States–Mexico–Canada Agreement (USMCA), but with no requirement that the arbitrator be selected from the ICSID Panel.[14] Under the NAFTA the stipulation was that he or she not appoint a presiding arbitrator with the nationality of any of the parties; under the USMCA he or she cannot do so 'unless the disputing parties agree otherwise'.[15]

3. THE METHOD FOR APPOINTING THE ADJUDICATORS

Some of the methods for appointing adjudicators under treaty-based rules have been covered in the preceding sections of this report, but for ease of reference they will be summarised here. In investment treaty arbitration, whether under the ICSID Convention or another set of rules, the primary concern is party autonomy. The parties first of all attempt to agree on the number of arbitrators composing the tribunal: according to the text of the ICSID Convention, it can be either one or any odd number of arbitrators.[16] If the parties cannot agree on that number, the Convention holds that the arbitral tribunal shall comprise three arbitrators, including one presiding arbitrator.[17] Each party must then appoint one arbitrator, and the two must agree on the choice of a presiding arbitrator.[18]

As has been described supra, if the parties cannot agree on such a choice and therefore cannot constitute the tribunal, it becomes the Chairman's role, upon request by one of the parties, to do so by appointing arbitrators from the ICSID Panel of Arbitrators. He or she is required to 'consult both parties as far as possible'.[19] Before resorting to the default appointment of the arbitrators by the Chairman, ICSID follows a 'ballot procedure': a ballot containing the names of several candidates, who might or might not be members of the Panel, is provided to each party. They must indicate on the ballot which candidates they deem acceptable; and if they agree on a candidate, he or she shall be considered

---

[13]   North American Free Trade Agreement (Canada–Mexico–United States), 17 December 1992, 32 ILM 289 (1993), Art. 1124.
[14]   United States–Mexico–Canada Agreement, entry into force 1 July 2020, Art. 14.D.6(2).
[15]   Ibid., Art. 14.D.6(3).
[16]   Convention on the Settlement of Investment Disputes between States and Nationals of Other States, 575 UNTS 159, 3 March 1965, Art. 37(2)(a).
[17]   Ibid., Art. 37(2)(b).
[18]   ICSID Convention Arbitration Rules (2006), Rule 3.
[19]   Ibid., Rule 4(4).

Intersentia

appointed by agreement of the parties.[20] If there is still no possibility of an agreement, then the Chairman steps in as the appointing authority.

Because they establish permanent tribunals, the systems of dispute resolution envisaged by the CETA and the other recent European trade and investment agreements do not allow for party nomination of adjudicators. They will be selected by the CETA Joint Committee. In a given case, the President of the Tribunal is responsible for the nomination of the members of the Tribunal composing the division that will hear the case, within 90 days of its submission. These appointments are supposed to be made on a rotation basis, in order to ensure that 'the composition of the divisions is random and unpredictable, while giving equal opportunity to all Members of the Tribunal to serve'.[21] Similar wording is used regarding the functioning of the Appellate Tribunal,[22] as well as in other European investment treaties, such as the EU–Vietnam[23] and the EU–Singapore Investment Protection Agreements.[24]

4. METHODS TO BALANCE THE APPOINTING AUTHORITY'S INFLUENCE ON THE APPOINTMENT OF THE ADJUDICATORS

Disputing parties themselves usually appoint their party-appointed arbitrators and agree on the presiding arbitrator (or entrust the party-appointed arbitrators with the authority to select the presiding arbitrator, often in consultation with the parties). At present, the biggest constraint on this exercise of party autonomy is the requirement that arbitrators be independent and impartial. Arbitrators are supposed to police themselves, but they can also be subject to challenge in the event one of the disputing parties believes the arbitrator fails to fulfil the requirements of independence and impartiality. The ICSID Convention also imposes a nationality constraint (unless the parties agree otherwise) in that a majority of the arbitrators must be from states that are neither the host state nor the investor's home state. When an appointing authority is called upon to choose, the authority might face constraints on nationality or might be constrained to appoint from a particular roster or Panel, as described above.

---

[20]   https://icsid.worldbank.org/services/arbitration/convention/process/selection-appointment.

[21]   Comprehensive Economic and Trade Agreement (Canada–European Union), 30 October 2016, provisional application 21 September 2017, Art. 8.27(7).

[22]   Art. 2(6) of Decision No. 001/2021 of the CETA Joint Committee of 29 January 2021 regarding the functioning of the Appellate Tribunal, available at https://www.international.gc.ca/trade-commerce/trade-agreements-accords-commerciaux/agr-acc/ceta-aecg/appellate-tribunal-dappel.aspx?lang=eng.

[23]   European Union–Vietnam Investment Protection Agreement, 30 June 2019, Arts 3.38(7) and 3.39(9).

[24]   European Union–Singapore Investment Protection Agreement, 15 October 2018, Arts 3.9(8) and 3.10(8).

These relatively limited constraints have led to concerns about certain practices – 'repeat' appointments and 'double-hatting' – described more fully below. Other areas of interest are the confidentiality of deliberations and the role of dissenting opinions, as well as the regulation of ex parte communications.

4.1. REPEAT APPOINTMENTS

Investment treaty arbitrations are initiated by investors submitting claims against a host state under an investment treaty. Some arbitrators have become known for repeat appointments by the same party (or counsel). There are concerns that this continued relationship establishes a financial link between an arbitrator and the party that repeatedly appoints him or her that jeopardises the arbitrator's independence. A related issue is that of the 'investor-appointed' arbitrator or the 'state-appointed' arbitrator – while they might not be repeatedly appointed by the same party, certain arbitrators are repeatedly appointed by the same side (i.e. investor or state), giving rise to concerns about impartiality.[25] There is also some concern that an arbitrator might develop loyalty (whether consciously or subconsciously) to the party that repeatedly appoints him or her. Repeat appointments also make it difficult for new entrants to break in to the field.

At the time of writing (May 2023), UNCITRAL and ICSID had created a Code of Conduct for Arbitrators in International Investment Dispute Resolution. The draft Code of Conduct was adopted by UNCITRAL's Working Group III at its forty-fourth and forty-fifth working sessions in January and March 2023.[26] It is expected to be adopted by the Commission at its meeting in July 2023. A separate code has been created to cover judges; thus this report focuses on the provisions applicable to arbitrators. Throughout the various iterations of the Code of Conduct repeat appointments have not been explicitly prohibited, though they have been matter of concern. The draft Code provides in Article 3(2)(c) that the obligation to be independent and impartial means that an arbitrator cannot '[b]e influenced by any past, present or prospective financial, business, professional or personal relationship'. This falls short of an outright prohibition. Article 11(2) requires that an arbitrator disclose any financial, business, professional or personal relationship in the past five years with any disputing party, legal representative of a disputing party, other arbitrators and expert witness, and any other interested entity, such as a third-party funder. A disputing party that was concerned about repeat appointments could thus challenge the

---

[25] See Malcolm Langford, Daniel Behn and Runer Lie, 'The Revolving Door in International Investment Arbitration' (2017) 20 *Journal of International Economic Law* 301, 310.

[26] UNCITRAL, Draft code of conduct for arbitrators in international investment dispute resolution and commentary, Note by the Secretariat, A/CN.9/1148 (28 April 2023). Unless otherwise noted, references to the Code of Conduct in this report are to this version.

arbitrator's appointment and the disclosure obligation would mean it would likely have the requisite knowledge to do so.

Because it establishes a permanent two-tiered court system, with a Tribunal and an Appellate Tribunal, the Code of Conduct annexed to the Canada–EU CETA does not deal directly with repeat appointments. Indeed, parties to a CETA dispute do not appoint the judges that will decide their case; judges are chosen on a rotation basis from the roster in a manner designed in order to be random and unpredictable.[27] The same comments apply to other EU treaties that establish a permanent court system as well, such as the EU–Singapore and the EU–Vietnam Investment Protection Agreements.

When looking at the case law of international investment arbitral panels, it does not appear that the number of times an arbitrator has been appointed by the same party has been, in and of itself, determinative in a disqualification request. Tribunals have been more interested in the similarities, both in terms of facts and substantive issues discussed, of the relevant cases. For instance, one can look at the decision in *Caratube v. Kazakhstan*, which states that multiple appointments by the same firm, without anything more, do not constitute an objective circumstance that would demonstrate the arbitrator's inability to exercise independent and impartial judgment.[28] Repeat appointments in cases involving similar facts and legal issues, however, might give rise to a successful challenge.[29]

In instruments specific to the investment sphere, there is no express limit on the number of times an arbitrator can be appointed by the same party or by the same counsel. The IBA Guidelines on Conflicts of Interest require disclosure and place on its 'orange' list a situation where an arbitrator has, in the past three years, been appointed as an arbitrator on two or more occasions by one of the parties, or by an affiliate of one of the parties.[30] Orange list items require disclosure and an assessment on a case-by-case basis of whether there are justifiable doubts about an arbitrator's independence and impartiality.

---

[27] Comprehensive Economic and Trade Agreement (Canada–European Union), 30 October 2016, provisional application 21 September 2017, Art. 8.27(7).

[28] For more information on repeat appointments, see ICSID, Code of Conduct – Background Papers, available at https://icsid.worldbank.org/sites/default/files/Background_Papers_Repeat_Appointments_final_25.2.2021.pdf.

[29] *Caratube International Oil Co. LLP et al. v. Republic of Kazakhstan (II)*, ICSID Case No. ARB/13/13, Decision on the Proposal for Disqualification of Bruno Boesch (20 March 2014).

[30] IBA Guidelines on Conflicts of Interest in International Arbitration, 3.1.3, available at https://www.ibanet.org/MediaHandler?id=e2fe5e72-eb14-4bba-b10d-d33dafee8918. In paragraph 132 of Version V of the ICSID–UNCITRAL draft Code of Conduct, the UNCITRAL Secretariat included a note to the working group that it might consider whether a provision similar to the IBA Guidelines should be included. UNCITRAL, Possible reform of investor-State dispute settlement (ISDS), Draft Codes of Conduct and Commentary, Note by the Secretariat, A/CN.9/WG.III/WP.223 (23 November 2022).

4.2. 'DOUBLE-HATTING'

Another recurrent problem in investment treaty arbitration is so-called 'double-hatting', that is to say the concerns raised in a situation where an arbitrator also acts as counsel or as an expert witness in other cases. The situation is fairly frequent in international arbitral practice, notably because of the fact there are no tenured appointments, so it can be difficult for someone to act solely as an arbitrator whilst ensuring a regular income. Serving multiple roles arguably gives rise to a number of concerns regarding independence and impartiality. One is that an adjudicator might consciously or subconsciously decide in a way that is advantageous to his or her interests, or the interests of his or her client. For instance, an arbitrator might behave in a certain way and produce certain legal arguments in the hope of being subsequently appointed as counsel by potential future clients, and vice versa. Another is simply the appearance of impropriety in the ability of one person to occupy multiple and sometimes apparently conflicting roles. A related problem, discussed more fully infra, is that of the 'issue conflict', which can arise in the 'multiple role' context.

There is some variety as to how different international investment agreements have chosen to tackle the issue; most do not address it at all. One option is to provide for a complete ban on double-hatting. Article 8.30.1 of CETA provides that as soon as they are nominated, members of the Tribunal must refrain from acting as counsel, witness or expert in any kind of international investment dispute. It is quite common in the context of a permanent court that such a ban be imposed; judges are generally forbidden from acting as counsel during their time on the bench. Given that CETA calls for a semi-permanent court in which tribunal or appellate body members are appointed on a part-time basis, the prohibition on double-hatting could limit those who can be appointed to the relevant panels.

Related to the idea of a concurrent ban is the question of a 'cooling-off' period after an individual has completed his or her service. Article 5(2) of the CETA Code of Conduct indicates that there is a period of three years after their term as a member of the Tribunal or Appellate Tribunal ended during which former adjudicators are precluded from acting as representative of 'any of the disputing parties in investment disputes' in front of a CETA Tribunal.[31] The Code does not specify whether the word 'representative' means 'lawyer' or 'counsel' only, or if it is also to be applied to situations in which the former adjudicator is called upon to serve as an expert. This restriction is also temporal, limited to three years after the term of the member of the Tribunal has ended.

---

[31] Art. 5(2) of Decision No. 001/2021 of the Committee on Services and Investment of 29 January 2021 adopting a code of conduct for Members of the Tribunal, Members of the Appellate Tribunal and mediators, available at https://www.international.gc.ca/trade-commerce/trade-agreements-accords-commerciaux/agr-acc/ceta-aecg/code-conduct-conduite.aspx?lang=eng.

This temporal and treaty-specific prohibition of double-hatting is the method that seems to have been chosen by most of those international investment agreements that address the issue For instance, Article 14.D.65(c) of Annex 14-D of the USMCA provides that when an arbitrator is appointed to a tribunal set up in accordance with the Agreement, he or she cannot act as counsel or a party-appointed expert or witness in any other USMCA arbitration for the duration of the proceedings. This prohibition is therefore temporal (limited to the duration of the proceedings) and treaty-based (only concerned with other USMCA arbitrations, and not all investment-related disputes). The same approach is to be found in Article 3(d) of the Code of Conduct of the Comprehensive and Progressive Agreement for Trans-Pacific Partnership (CPTPP).

Other international investment agreements also provide for a temporal restriction on double-hatting, but without limiting it to disputes under a specific treaty. For instance, Article 20(5) of the Dutch Model Bilateral Investment Agreement provides that in order to be appointed as an arbitrator, a person shall not have acted as legal counsel for the last five years preceding their appointment, in 'investment disputes under this or any other international agreement'. While the restriction seems to only concern work as counsel and not as an expert, it is noticeably stricter that the one contained in the CPTPP or the USMCA, as it concerns the five years prior to the appointment as an arbitrator and is not limited to claims presented under the same investment agreement.

The question of double-hatting has been a vexing problem in the ICSID–UNCITRAL draft Code of Conduct. In some earlier versions the proposed language permitted the disputing parties to agree that double-hatting would not pose a problem to them, on the grounds that prohibitions on double-hatting can be described as limiting the parties' choice to nominate the arbitrators whom they deem to be the most qualified to solve their present dispute. In order for that consent to be valid, however, it must be informed, which is why an arbitrator's past work as counsel or as an expert is subject to an expansive disclosure obligation.[32] The 2023 draft Code of Conduct permits the disputing parties to agree to permit multiple roles, but otherwise provides that:

> Unless the disputing parties agree otherwise, an Arbitrator shall not act concurrently as a legal representative or an expert witness in any other IID proceeding involving:
>
> (a) The same measure(s);
> (b) The same or related party (parties); or
> (c) The same provision(s) of the same instrument of consent.[33]

---

[32] The breadth of the disclosure obligation has changed somewhat, though it remains extensive.
[33] UNCITRAL, Draft code of conduct for arbitrators in international investment dispute resolution and commentary, Note by the Secretariat, A/CN.9/1148 (28 April 2023), Art. 4(1).

A further provision provides:

> For a period of three years, a former Arbitrator shall not act as a legal representative or an expert witness in any other related IID or any other proceeding involving the same measure(s) unless the dispute parties agree otherwise.[34]

Similar prohibitions extend to proceedings involving the same or related parties (found in Art. 4(3)). A shorter period – one year – applies to proceedings involving the same instrument of consent (Art. 4(4)). Dispute parties can also agree to waive those restrictions.

4.3. ISSUE CONFLICTS

Another matter that has come up in the discussions surrounding the independence and impartiality of arbitrators in investment treaty arbitration is what has been termed the 'issue conflict'. An issue conflict can arise when an arbitrator has publicly – in a published article, for instance – taken a position regarding a legal controversy that is at stake in the dispute in which he or she is acting as an arbitrator. That position could be on legal issues, factual issues or both. There can also be an overlap between issue conflict and double-hatting – a person might make an argument as counsel on a subject that must be decided in the case in which he or she is sitting as an arbitrator; he or she might be on an arbitral tribunal in which the decision (which is likely to be made public) will potentially be relevant to his or her argument as counsel in another case. Another aspect of the issue conflict is whether an arbitrator has an unalterable opinion about an issue that will arise in the case.

Successful challenges of arbitrators based on an alleged issue conflict are quite rare in investment jurisprudence, notwithstanding the attention paid to issue conflicts in discussions about investment arbitration. Some examples do exist, such as in *Devas Ltd. v. India*,[35] but such challenges are much more likely to fail than to succeed. For instance, in *Urbaser v. Argentina*, the claimants' proposal to disqualify one of the members of the arbitral tribunal was rejected because the rest of the tribunal held that the arbitrator's scholarly opinions '[did] not meet the threshold of presenting an appearance that he is not

---

[34] Ibid., Art. 4(2).
[35] *CC/Devas (Mauritius) Ltd. et al. v. Republic of India*, UNCITRAL, Decision on the Respondent's Challenge to the Hon. Marc Lalonde as Presiding Arbitrator and Prof. Francisco Orrego Vicuña as Co-Arbitrator (30 September 2013). See generally ICSID, Code of Conduct – Background Papers, available at https://icsid.worldbank.org/sites/default/files/ Background_Papers_Issue_Conflict_Final_2.26.2021.pdf.

prepared to hear and consider each Parties' position with full independence and impartiality'.[36]

An earlier version of the ICSID–UNCITRAL draft Code of Conduct inserted 'a list of all publications by the adjudicator or candidate [and their relevant public speeches]' as part of the adjudicators' disclosure obligations.[37] However, this reference has been removed in the latest version of the Code. This change likely reflects general agreement with the opinion of the *Urbaser* tribunal that an arbitrator's familiarity with a legal issue, and even expertise about that issue, does not preclude him or her from keeping an open mind in response to arguments in an individual case.

4.4. SECRECY OF DELIBERATIONS

Given the practice of party appointment, disputing parties are presumed to want to know as much as possible about an arbitrator's preferences. Thus the fact of confidentiality of deliberations is one means of keeping in check the parties' influence over the appointment of arbitrators. Keeping proceedings confidential helps ensure that the parties are as much as possible unaware of the potential biases existing among arbitrators. It also frees arbitrators to express opinions or hazard ideas without the repercussions that might ensue from the public airing of what might be preliminary ideas. The possibility to exploit arbitrators' biases exposed through deliberations could be seen as imperilling their independence and impartiality.

In the latest version of the ICSID–UNCITRAL draft Code of Conduct, Article 8 sets out general and straightforward obligations regarding confidentiality. These obligations are perpetual and do not end once the award is delivered to the parties. As a general principle, the candidates and adjudicators can neither disclose nor use any information they may have acquired concerning an international investment dispute, except for the purposes of the proceedings.

Most particularly, the deliberations of the tribunal are confidential.[38] Any view expressed by an adjudicator will be kept hidden by the secrecy of

---

[36]   *Urbaser SA & Consorcio de Aguas Bilbao Bizkaia, Bilbao Bizkaia Ur Partzuergoa v. The Argentine Republic*, ICSID Case No. ARB/07/26, Decision on Claimant's Proposal to Disqualify Professor Campbell McLachlan, Arbitrator (12 August 2010), para. 58.

[37]   Draft Code of Conduct for Adjudicators in Investor-State Dispute Settlement, Art. 5(2)(d) ('A list of all publications by the adjudicator or candidate [and their relevant public speeches]').

[38]   UNCITRAL, Draft code of conduct for arbitrators in international investment dispute resolution and commentary, Note by the Secretariat, A/CN.9/1148 (28 April 2023), Art. 8(2).

deliberations. This rule is not subject to any exception. Similar rules are to be found in the CETA[39] and CPTPP.[40]

In the draft Code, arbitrators cannot disclose drafts of decisions.[41] Nevertheless, the Code defers to applicable rules or treaties, which might have some individual exceptions, or to party consent on the circulation of drafts. Indeed, a few treaties suggest that arbitrators submit draft rulings to the parties in order to obtain their comments. The CETA Code of Conduct does not contain such an exception.[42]

4.5. DISSENTING OPINIONS

Another debate related to the confidentiality issues in investment treaty arbitration regards whether arbitrators can issue dissenting opinions or not, and if they can sign them by name. Dissenting opinions potentially offer a way for arbitrators to signal to parties (i) arguments for the potential annulment or setting aside of the award and (ii) indicia as to where the arbitrator's point of view lay on certain disputed substantive issues. In the words of Alan Redfern: 'Why do some arbitrators dissent? Some, no doubt, do so out of a sense of duty or loyalty to their appointing party, which weighs more heavily than their duty to be and to remain independent and impartial. Others … [b]y expressing a detailed dissenting opinion … are in effect saying to anyone who is interested: "this is how I would have decided the dispute, if I had been the sole arbitrator".[43] Dissenting opinions also need to be careful not to betray the secrecy of tribunal

---

[39] Art. 6(3) of Decision No. 001/2021 of the Committee on Services and Investment of 29 January 2021 adopting a code of conduct for Members of the Tribunal, Members of the Appellate Tribunal and mediators, available at https://www.international.gc.ca/trade-commerce/trade-agreements-accords-commerciaux/agr-acc/ceta-aecg/code-conduct-conduite.aspx?lang=eng.

[40] Comprehensive and Progressive Agreement for Trans-Pacific Partnership, Chapter 9, Section B, Art. 8(c).

[41] UNCITRAL, Draft code of conduct for arbitrators in international investment dispute resolution and commentary, Note by the Secretariat, A/CN.9/1148 (28 April 2023), Art. 8(1).

[42] Art. 6(2) of Decision No. 001/2021 of the Committee on Services and Investment of 29 January 2021 adopting a code of conduct for Members of the Tribunal, Members of the Appellate Tribunal and mediators, available at https://www.international.gc.ca/trade-commerce/trade-agreements-accords-commerciaux/agr-acc/ceta-aecg/code-conduct-conduite.aspx?lang=eng ('Members shall not disclose an order, decision, award or parts thereof prior to its publication').

[43] Alan Redfern, 'The 2003 Freshfields Lecture – Dissenting Opinions in International Commercial Arbitration: the Good, the Bad and the Ugly' (2004) 20 *Arbitration International* 223, 241.

deliberations, though inevitably they will include arguments on which the dissenter did not prevail.[44]

Most dissenting opinions are written by the arbitrator appointed by the losing party, who might have done so in order to signal his or her views on the case, and perhaps to maximise the possibility of being appointed again in future. *Klöckner v. Cameroon* was an extreme example of this, as the arbitrator who wrote the dissenting opinion then became counsel for the losing party, and used the arguments developed in his opinion before the ad hoc Annulment Committee. Despite these observations, however, in general dissenting opinions are permitted in investment treaty arbitration. Indeed, Article 48(4) of the ICSID Convention provides that 'any individual member of the Tribunal may attach his individual opinion to the award, whether he dissents from the majority or not, or a statement of his dissent'. We did not find any investment treaty that explicitly prohibits dissenting opinions.

One interesting way of tackling the problem can be found in the Japan–Australia Economic Partnership Agreement. In Article VII.3 of its Code of Conduct (for state–state arbitration), it is specified that 'a covered person shall not at any time disclose which arbitrators are associated with any majority or minority opinions in the award of the arbitral tribunal'. Dissenting opinions are therefore authorised, but it is not possible to know exactly which arbitrator is behind which opinion. This would likely alleviate the concerns about arbitrators 'virtue signalling' to parties via dissenting opinions, although idiosyncrasies in writing style might still make it possible to identify the author.

4.6. EX PARTE COMMUNICATIONS BETWEEN PARTIES AND ARBITRATORS

When it comes to limiting the appointing party's influence on the adjudicator, Article 7 of the ICSID–UNCITRAL draft Code of Conduct is worthy of note. The article is concerned with the authorised scope of communication in ex parte communications. They are defined in the commentary to the draft Code as 'any communication concerning the IID with a disputing party, its legal representative, affiliate, subsidiary or other related person (for example, a parent company of the dispute party or a third-party funder) and taking place without the other disputing party or its legal representative being present or having knowledge of the communication taking place'. While it is perfectly in line with

---

[44]   Indeed, this is why a German court set aside a commercial award for violating public policy; the judge concluded that dissenting opinions violate the confidentiality of deliberations, pose a threat to the integrity of the proceedings, and undermine the independence of the arbitral tribunal. See e.g. Peter Bert, 'Frankfurt Court of Appeal Finds That Dissenting Opinion Violates Public Policy', *Kluwer Arbitration Blog* (21 June 2020), Oberlandesgericht, docket no. 26 Sch 14/18.

the expected advantages of party-appointed adjudicators that these parties might want to communicate with candidates prior to appointment to know whether they are suitable arbitrators or not, these communications must remain within appropriate boundaries.

Article 7(2) and (3) of the draft Code of Conduct are designed to accommodate the practice of pre-appointment interviews within said boundaries. They allow ex parte communications between a candidate and a disputing party, but only to the extent that it concerns the candidate's 'expertise, experience, competence, skills, availability, and the existence of any potential conflict of interest'.[45] Candidates are therefore prohibited from discussing 'procedural or substantive issues relating to the IID proceeding or those that a Candidate or an Arbitrator can reasonably anticipate will arise in the IID proceeding'.[46]

5. PARAMETERS TO ENSURE THAT THE ADJUDICATORS ACT INDEPENDENTLY AND IMPARTIALLY

When it comes to the obligations of adjudicators to remain independent and impartial, the majority of international investment agreements rely on broad obligations and open-ended language. For example, Article 3A of the ICSID–UNCITRAL draft Code of Conduct states that 'adjudicators shall be independent and impartial'. Article 3A(2) then spells out a non-comprehensive list of situations that are encompassed by this core obligation, such as the obligations for adjudicators not to take any instructions from governments and not to let any financial relationship influence their judgment. The commentary underscores that any determination of a breach of the duty of independence and impartiality by adjudicators is highly fact-dependent, and no exhaustive list can be made, although it indicates that examples can be found in the commentaries. Such broad obligations are also thought of as allowing for a safety net to be cast in situations that would fall outside the black letter of the Code but that could still be considered as breaches of the fundamental obligation for adjudicators to remain independent and impartial.

Most codes of conduct and international investment protection agreements have adopted the same strategy when it comes to the fundamental obligations of adjudicators. Article 4(2) of the CETA thus spells out similar independence and impartiality obligations.[47]

---

[45] UNCITRAL, Draft code of conduct for arbitrators in international investment dispute resolution and commentary, Note by the Secretariat, A/CN.9/1148 (28 April 2023), Art. 7(2).

[46] Ibid., Art. 7(3).

[47] Art. 4(1) of Decision No. 001/2021 of the Committee on Services and Investment of 29 January 2021 adopting a code of conduct for Members of the Tribunal, Members of the Appellate

Andrea K. Bjorklund

These general obligations of independence and impartiality are supplemented and made operational by disclosure obligations, the common requirement that candidates for appointment and adjudicators alike are required to fulfil by various international instruments. The philosophy behind disclosure is to provide parties with the largest amount of information possible, so they can make informed choices and potentially challenge adjudicators if necessary. Failure to comply with disclosure obligations is not, in and of itself, a breach of the adjudicators' obligations and thus does not lead to sanctions and enforcement procedures.[48] Rather, the content of the non-disclosed information is relevant for determining whether there is a breach. Nonetheless, repeated failures to disclose could give rise to a violation of the obligation of independence and impartiality found in Article 3.

In the ICSID–UNCITRAL draft Code of Conduct, the requirement to disclose is presented first as a general obligation to 'disclose any circumstances likely to give rise to justifiable doubts[, including in the eyes of the disputing parties,] as to his or her independence or impartiality'.[49] Article 11 then indicates in a more precise manner what kind of information must be part of the adjudicators' disclosure. We have already reviewed above that information related to repeat appointments and double-hatting has to be disclosed according to the Code. The other pieces of information that fall under the disclosure obligations mostly relate to conflicts of interest. Indeed, adjudicators must disclose 'any financial, business, professional or close personal relationship' they have had within the past five years with the parties, their legal representatives, the other adjudicators, the expert witnesses and any third-party funder or other interested party.[50] In the same vein, any personal or financial interest the adjudicator might have in the outcome of the proceedings or the outcome of any other proceeding involving the same measures will have to be disclosed,[51] as well as any involvement as a legal representative, an expert or an adjudicator in an investment case and any such involvement with either disputing party that occurred in the past five years, or that is in prospect and thus potentially concurrent.[52] The duty to disclose is continuous and does not arise only at the time of appointment. Adjudicators have an obligation to disclose any newly discovered information as soon as they become aware of it.[53] Furthermore, it is indicated that as a general rule, they should 'err in favour of disclosure if they have any doubt'.[54]

Tribunal and mediators, available at https://www.international.gc.ca/trade-commerce/trade-agreements-accords-commerciaux/agr-acc/ceta-aecg/code-conduct-conduite.aspx?lang=eng ('Members shall be and shall appear to be independent and impartial').

[48] Cf. UNCITRAL, Draft code of conduct for arbitrators in international investment dispute resolution and commentary, Note by the Secretariat, A/CN.9/1148 (28 April 2023), Art. 11(7)).

[49] Ibid., Art. 11(1).

[50] Ibid., Art. 11(2)(a).

[51] Ibid., Art. 11(2)(b).

[52] Ibid., Art. 11(2)(c), (d) and (e).

[53] Ibid., Art. 11(3).

[54] Ibid., Art. 11(5).

The CETA Code of Conduct provides in Article 3 that disclosure 'should cover at least the last five years prior to a candidate submitting an application or otherwise becoming aware that he or she is under consideration for selection as a Member'.[55] The language of the different existing codes and treaties related to disclosure obligations appears to be quite similar. Most often, words such as 'independence or impartiality', 'impropriety' or 'appearance of bias' are the standard used in order to evaluate whether particular information must be disclosed by the candidate/adjudicator or not. Most recent EU agreements thus have chosen open-ended language in order to be as broad as possible. While older agreements left it to the arbitrators decide exactly what to disclose, the majority of 'new-generation' investment agreements contain disclosure obligations that combine such general obligations with a non-comprehensive list of information that the adjudicator is clearly expected to disclose.

Finally, the ICSID–UNCITRAL draft Code also contains an Article 6 entitled 'Integrity and competence' listing adjudicators' obligations that cannot strictly be considered to fall within the scope of 'independence and impartiality' but that nonetheless have been highlighted as qualities that adjudicators should display. Under Article 6 an arbitrator should '[c]onduct the IID proceeding competently and in accordance with high standards of integrity, fairness and civility'.[56] Candidates shall also 'possess the necessary competence and skills and make all reasonable efforts to maintain and enhance the knowledge, skills and qualities necessary to perform his or her duties'.[57] Finally the arbitrator must not delegate his or her decision-making function.[58] These indeed appear to be essential qualities for an adjudicator to be able to help solve highly complex international investment disputes. It is another example of how the draft Code tries to maintain some flexibility in its approach to these questions. However, it remains to be seen how the enforcement of such standards will work in practice. Apart from rather extreme cases, it could be the case that allowing parties to challenge arbitrators based on their alleged skills or their civility would lead to more challenges being used as potential delaying tactics.

---

[55] Art. 3(1) of Decision No. 001/2021 of the Committee on Services and Investment of 29 January 2021 adopting a code of conduct for Members of the Tribunal, Members of the Appellate Tribunal and mediators, available at https://www.international.gc.ca/trade-commerce/trade-agreements-accords-commerciaux/agr-acc/ceta-aecg/code-conduct-conduite.aspx?lang=eng.

[56] UNCITRAL, Draft code of conduct for arbitrators in international investment dispute resolution and commentary, Note by the Secretariat, A/CN.9/1148 (28 April 2023), Art. 6(a).

[57] Ibid., Art. 6(b).

[58] Ibid., Art. 6(c).

6. CONSEQUENCES FOR THE ADJUDICATOR OF A BREACH OF THE REQUIREMENT TO ACT INDEPENDENTLY AND IMPARTIALLY

If an adjudicator fails in his or her duties, the ultimate sanction is removal from the office of arbitrator in accordance with the rules applicable to the case at hand. When it comes to investment arbitrations initiated under the auspices of the ICSID Convention, the procedure for disqualification of an arbitrator is spelled out in Articles 57 and 58 of the Convention. The two grounds that are currently accepted for the disqualification of an arbitrator are (i) a manifest lack of the qualities required by paragraph 1 of Article 14 of the Convention[59] and (ii) ineligibility of the arbitrator for the appointment to the tribunal according to Section 2 of Chapter IV of the Convention (Articles 37–40, which are rules on the nationality of arbitrators). For our purposes, it is interesting to note that among the qualities required by Article 14(1), one can find the 'capacity to exercise independent judgment'.

Article 8.30.2 of CETA spells out a procedure in which the President of the International Court of Justice will be called upon to decide on challenges to the appointment of members of the Tribunal, most notably on one of the grounds set out in Article 8.30.1 of the Agreement. Furthermore, the CETA Code of Conduct deals with breaches of any part of the Code that might have been committed by former members of the Tribunal or Appellate Tribunal. According to Article 5(4) of the Code, after having heard the arguments of the member alleged to have committed the breach, it will be the duty of the President of the Tribunal or Appellate Tribunal to inform other interested parties of that alleged breach. These are: the professional body or association of said member; Canada and the EU; the disputing parties that might be concerned by the particular breach; and the 'President of any other relevant international court or tribunal'. Thus, we can see that the CETA Code of Conduct has elected to deal with adjudicators alleged to have breached their ethical obligations by targeting their reputation and informing any relevant institution that might then have the power to take action.

Other international investment agreements have taken the same route. For instance, the EU–Singapore Investment Protection Agreement spells out a procedure in paragraph 18 that is similar to that found in the CETA Code of Conduct. If a former member of the Tribunal or Appellate Tribunal is alleged to have breached his or her obligations concerning a lack of bias, repeat appointments or double-hatting, the President of the relevant Tribunal will inform the relevant stakeholders and make public its finding. This action

---

[59]   Cf. infra section 1.

can also be seen as a reputational sanction. Other than that, the Code of the EU–Singapore Investment Protection Agreement has elected not to address directly breaches of its obligations by adjudicators.

7. ENFORCEABILITY OF A FINAL DECISION THAT WAS RENDERED BY AN ADJUDICATOR WHO BREACHED THE REQUIREMENT TO ACT INDEPENDENTLY AND IMPARTIALLY

Investment treaty arbitrations that fall under the ICSID Convention are subject to annulment under the Convention. Two of the grounds for annulment are that the tribunal was improperly constituted or that it departed from a fundamental rule of procedure. In 2020 an ICSID award was annulled on both of these grounds on the basis that an arbitrator had failed to disclose a longstanding relationship with one of the experts in the case dating from his practice as counsel.[60] Under the ICSID Convention, the annulment of an award means it is no longer enforceable. Thus, an arbitrator's lack of independence and impartiality can indeed influence the enforceability of a final award, though the circumstance has not arisen on very many occasions.

Similar outcomes are possible in national courts making decisions under their own control mechanisms or in enforcement proceedings under the New York Convention. Those decisions occur under laws applicable to both commercial and treaty-based arbitration and thus will not be discussed here.

---

[60]   *Eiser Infrastructure Ltd et al. v. Kingdom of Spain*, ICSID Case No. ARB/13/36 (Proceeding on Annulment), Decision (11 June 2020).

THE INDEPENDENCE AND IMPARTIALITY OF ADJUDICATORS IN REGIONAL COURTS

Freya BAETENS*

1. Introduction 283
2. Criteria for the Selection of Adjudicators 285
3. Appointing Authority and Appointment Method 288
4. Methods and Parameters to Ensure the Independence and
   Impartiality in the Exercise of the Adjudicators' Functions 294
5. Consequences of a Breach of the Requirement to Act Independently
   and Impartially 299

1. INTRODUCTION

This report reviews the framework of regional courts (excluding human rights courts) with respect to the issues raised in the questionnaire. Account is taken of the following courts:

1. The Court of Justice of the European Union (CJEU) is the court established under the Treaty of the European Union (and its predecessors) with the mandate to 'ensure that in the interpretation of the [constitutive treaties of the European Union] the law is observed'.[1] The CJEU comprises two courts: the Court of Justice and the General Court.

2. The EFTA Court is established under Article 108(2) of the Agreement on the European Economic Area[2] as the judicial organ having jurisdiction over the states that are parties both to the EFTA Convention and to the EEA Agreement – currently, Iceland, Liechtenstein and Norway – with respect to matters concerning the latter Agreement.

---

* This work was partly supported by the Research Council of Norway through its Centres of Excellence funding scheme (project number 223274) and the FRIPRO Young Research Talents (project number 274946).

[1] Article 19(1) of the Treaty on European Union, OJ C 202, vol. 59, 7 June 2016, p. 13 (TEU).

[2] Agreement on the European Economic Area (signed 2 May 1992, entered into force 1 January 1994), 1793 UNTS 3 (EEA Agreement).

Intersentia

3. The Benelux Court is the principal judicial body of the Benelux Union between Belgium, the Netherlands and Luxembourg, with the 'task of promoting uniformity in the application of rules of law common to the Benelux countries.'[3]

4. The Andean Community Tribunal of Justice (ATJ) was founded in 1979 as the judicial body of the Andean Community,[4] which had been established in 1969 under the Cartagena Agreement.[5] The structure and function of the ATJ are modelled on those of the CJEU; the vast majority of its docket concerns intellectual property rights within the Andean Community.[6]

5. The Community Court of Justice is one of the principal institutions of the Economic Community of West African States (ECOWAS Court).[7]

6. The Court of Justice of the Common Market for Eastern and Southern Africa (COMESA Court) is a judicial organ founded under the Treaty establishing that organisation for the purpose of 'ensur[ing] the adherence to law in the interpretation and application of th[at] Treaty.'[8]

7. The Court of the Eurasian Economic Union (EEU Court) is the judicial body of the Eurasian Economic Union, which was founded under the Treaty on the Eurasian Economic Union.[9]

8. Mercosur is a regional organisation aimed at liberalising commerce between its Member States, as well as between them and third states.[10] The Olivos Protocol for the Settlement of Disputes in Mercosur,[11] which entered

---

[3] Article 1(2) of the Treaty concerning the establishment and the statute of a Benelux Court of Justice (signed 31 March 1965; entered into force 1 January 1974), 924 UNTS 2 (Statute of the Benelux Court).

[4] Treaty creating the Court of Justice of the Cartagena Agreement (signed 28 May 1979, entered into force 19 May 1983), 18 ILM 1203, as codified by Decision 472 of the Commission of the Andean Community of 28 May 1996, 483 Official Gazette of the Cartagena Agreement (17 September 1999) (ATJ Treaty).

[5] Agreement on Andean Subregional Integration (1969) 8 ILM 910; this agreement was subsequently amended significantly by the Modifying Protocol of the Andean Subregional Integration Agreement (Cartagena Agreement) of 10 March 1996 and was codified by Decision 406 of the Commission of the Andean Community of 25 June 1997, 273 Official Gazette of the Cartagena Agreement (4 July 1997).

[6] Karen J. Alter and Laurence R. Helfer, *Transplanting International Courts: The Law and Politics of the Andean Tribunal of Justice* (Oxford: OUP 2017) 3–4.

[7] Article 15 Revised Treaty of the Economic Community of West African States (ECOWAS) (signed 24 July 1993, entered into force 23 August 1995), 2373 UNTS 233; see also ibid., Article 6(1)(e).

[8] Article 19(1) of the Treaty establishing the Common Market for Eastern and Southern Africa (signed 5 November 1993, entered into force 8 December 1994), 2314 UNTS 265.

[9] Article 1 of the Statute of the Court of the Eurasian Economic Union, Annex 2 to the Treaty on the Eurasian Economic Union (signed 29 May 2014, entered into force 1 January 2015), 3042 UNTS (partial publication) (Statute of the EEU Court).

[10] Jan Peter Schmidt, 'MERCOSUR', *Max Planck Encyclopedia of Public International Law online* (entry last updated September 2017), para. 5.

[11] Olivos Protocol for the Settlement of Disputes in MERCOSUR (signed 18 February 2002, entered into force 1 January 2004), 2251 UNTS 243.

Regional Courts

into force in 2004, significantly reshaped the dispute settlement system in that regional organisation by creating a two-pronged mechanism of legal dispute settlement before ad hoc arbitral tribunals and/or a Permanent Review Court (PRC).[12]

9. The Caribbean Court of Justice (CCJ) is a hybrid judicial body: it is an international court of the Caribbean Community (CARICOM) and a national court of last instance of the Caribbean states that are parties to its constitutive instrument.[13]

2. CRITERIA FOR THE SELECTION OF ADJUDICATORS

In the European Union, the Court of Justice consists of one judge from each Member State of the EU (currently 27).[14] Under the TEU, the General Court must include at least one judge from each Member State;[15] currently, it has two. The precursor to the current constitutive treaties of the EU, the 1951 Treaty instituting the European Coal and Steel Community, simply provided that the judges of the Court were to be 'appointed for six years by agreement among the governments of the member States from among persons of recognized independence and competence.'[16] The Treaty of Rome of 1957 simply required that the judges be chosen 'from among persons of indisputable independence who fulfil the conditions required for the holding of the highest judicial office in their respective countries or who are jurists of a recognized competence.'[17] This formulation echoes the one concerning the selection of judges at the ICJ, who are to be selected 'from among persons of high moral character, who possess the qualifications required in their respective countries for appointment

---

[12] Ad hoc arbitration had already been introduced through the Brasília Protocol for the Solution of Controversies (signed 17 December 1991, entered into force 22 April 1993), 2145 UNTS 252, which was superseded by the Olivos Protocol: see Article 55 Brasília Protocol.

[13] Agreement establishing the Caribbean Court of Justice (signed 14 February 2001, entered into force 23 July 2002), 2255 UNTS 319 (CCJ Agreement). 11 states have ratified the Agreement: Barbados, Belize, Dominica, Grenada, Guyana, Jamaica, St Kitts and Nevis, St Lucia, St Vincent and the Grenadines, Suriname, and Trinidad and Tobago.

[14] Article 19(2), subparagraph 2, of the TEU.

[15] Article 19(2), subparagraph 2, of the TEU.

[16] Article 32 of the Treaty instituting the European Coal and Steel Community (signed 18 April 1951, entered into force 23 July 1952), 261 UNTS 140; upon the establishment of the EEC in 1957, this provision was amended and brought in line with the one concerning the judges of the Court of the EEC: see Article 4 of the Convention relating to certain institutions common to the European Communities (signed 25 March 1957, entered into force 1 January 1958) 298 UNTS 267.

[17] Article 167 of the Treaty establishing the European Economic Community (signed 25 March 1957, entered into force 1 January 1958) 298 UNTS 3.

Intersentia

285

to the highest judicial offices, or are jurisconsults of recognized competence in international law.'[18] Primary EU law stresses no fewer than three times that the judges of both courts 'shall be chosen from persons whose independence is beyond doubt and who possess the qualifications required for appointment to the highest judicial offices in their respective countries or who are jurisconsults of recognised competence'.[19] No other specific criteria are laid down in the treaties.

The Agreement establishing the EFTA Court was concluded in 1992 and replicates, to a large extent, the provisions applicable at the time with respect to the appointment and status of judges of the EU courts.[20] Thus, it provides that the Court's judges shall be appointed by common accord of the EFTA states 'from persons whose independence is beyond doubt and who possess the qualifications required for appointment to the highest judicial offices in their respective countries or who are jurisconsults of recognized competence'.[21]

Since the latest revision of its Statute entered into force in 2016, the Benelux Court comprises nine conseillers and six judges, and an equal number of alternate conseillers and alternate judges.[22] It is perhaps exceptional among international courts, insofar as no substantive criteria are established for the selection of its members. The only formal criterion is that the conseillers and judges (as well as their alternate counterparts) be members of the highest domestic courts or the appellate domestic courts, respectively, of the three countries: as Article 3(1) of the Benelux Court Treaty stipulates, the conseillers and alternate conseillers are appointed from among the members of the Hoge Raad der Nederlanden and from among the members of the Court of Cassation of Belgium and, in the case of Luxembourg, from among the members of the Superior Court of Justice and the Administrative Court, whereas the judges and alternate judges are appointed from among the members of the Gerechtshoven of the Netherlands, the Court of Cassation of Belgium and the Court of Appeal of Luxembourg.

The ATJ comprises one judge from each of Member State of the Andean Community (currently four: Bolivia, Colombia, Ecuador and Peru).[23] Echoing

---

[18]   Article 2 of the Statute of the International Court of Justice.

[19]   Article 19(2), subparagraph 3, of the TEU; Article 253(1) Treaty on the Functioning of the European Union, OJ C 202, vol. 59, 7 June 2016, p. 47 (TFEU); Article 254(1) of the TFEU; see already Articles 167, subparagraph 1, and 168a(3) of the Treaty establishing the European Community, OJ C 224, vol. 35, 31 August 1992.

[20]   Agreement between the EFTA States on the establishment of a surveillance authority and a Court of Justice (signed 2 May 1992, entered into force 1 January 1994), OJ L 344, 31 December 1994, p. 1.

[21]   Article 30, subparagraph 1, of the EFTA Agreement.

[22]   Article 3(1) of the Statute of the Benelux Court, as amended by the Protocol amending the Treaty of 31 March 1965 concerning the establishment and the statute of a Benelux Court of Justice (signed 15 October 2012, entered into force 1 December 2016), Reg. No. 13176.

[23]   Article 7 of the ATJ Treaty, as amended by Article 1 of Decision 633 of the Council of Ministers for Foreign Affairs of 12 June 2006, 1356 Official Gazette of the Cartagena

the Statute of the ICJ and of other international courts (like the CJEU) drafted in its image, the judges of the ATJ must be nationals of the Member States, and they must 'be of high moral reputation and fulfill the standards required in their countries of origin for undertaking the highest judicial functions, or be jurisconsults of recognized competence.'[24]

Similarly to what applies for the above-mentioned courts, the ECOWAS Protocol on the Community Court of Justice stipulates that the judges 'are persons of high moral character, and possess the qualification required in their respective countries for appointment to the highest judicial officers, or are jurisconsults of recognized competence in international law, particularly in areas of Community Law or Regional Integration Law.'[25] Furthermore, eligible candidates must have at least 20 years of professional experience.[26]

The COMESA Court consists of 12 judges chosen 'from among persons of impartiality and independence who fulfill the conditions required for the holding of high judicial office in their respective countries of domicile or who are jurists of recognised competence.'[27] Perhaps unusually, judges at the COMESA Court are appointed on the basis of their domicile, rather than nationality, although nationality serves as a negative criterion, in the sense that no two nationals of the same Member State can serve as judges.[28] Accordingly, non-nationals of COMESA Member States may be appointed as judges to the Court, as indeed they have been in the past.[29]

The EEU Court comprises two judges from each of the five Member States of the EEU, who must be 'of high moral character' and highly qualified in the field of international and domestic law; the Court's Statute also provides that the judges 'shall *usually* meet the requirements applicable to judges of the highest judicial authorities of the Member States', suggesting that this sole formal requirement is not mandatory, unlike the first two substantive requirements.[30]

Under the Olivos Protocol on the Mercosur, the arbitrators of ad hoc arbitral tribunals and the PRC 'shall be lawyers having recognized expertise in the fields

---

Agreement (15 June 2006). The authority to amend the number of judges by the Council of Ministers is provided under Article 6, subparagraph 3, of the ATJ Treaty.

[24]   Article 6, subparagraph 1, of the ATJ Treaty.

[25]   Article 3(1) of the Statute of the ECOWAS Court, as amended by Article 2 of Supplementary Protocol A/SP.2/06/06 amending Article 3 paragraphs 1, 2 and 4, Article 4 paragraphs 1, 3 and 7 and Article 7 paragraph 3 of the Protocol on the Community Court of Justice.

[26]   Article 3(1) of the Statute of the ECOWAS Court, as amended by Article 2 of Supplementary Protocol A/SP.2/06/06 amending Article 3 paragraphs 1, 2 and 4, Article 4 paragraphs 1, 3 and 7 and Article 7 paragraph 3 of the Protocol on the Community Court of Justice. The requirement that candidates be between 40 and 60 years old, under Article 3(7) of the 1991 Protocol, was abrogated by Article 7 of the 2006 Supplementary Protocol.

[27]   Article 20(2) of the COMESA Treaty.

[28]   Article 20(2) of the COMESA Treaty.

[29]   Bilika H. Simamba, 'Appointment and Term of Office of Judges of International Courts: Innovations from Africa?' (2008) 34 *Commonwealth Law Bulletin* 515, 519–20.

[30]   Article 9 of the Statute of the EEU Court (emphasis added).

that may be the subject matter of disputes, and shall be acquainted with the body of Mercosur regulations.'[31] In addition, they are to be appointed 'on the basis of their objectiveness, reliability and good judgment.'[32]

The CCJ comprises the President and at most nine judges, 'of whom at least three shall possess expertise in international law including international trade law.'[33] The CCJ Agreement stands out among other constitutive instruments of 'purely' international courts insofar as it sets rather detailed criteria for the appointment of judges. In particular, candidates must have either served for at least five years as judges of a domestic court in a state exercising 'jurisprudence common to Contracting Parties' (e.g. a state of the Commonwealth, but not necessarily a Member State), or they must have engaged in the teaching of law for at least 15 years in such a state; in either case, candidates must have distinguished themselves in that function.[34] In addition, the Agreement lists a set of criteria that an eligible candidate should have to be appointed: 'high moral character, intellectual and analytical ability, sound judgment, integrity, and understanding of people and society.'[35] These criteria are perhaps explained by the fact that the CCJ potentially acts as a domestic court of last instance replacing the Judicial Committee of the Privy Council for the states that have accepted this appellate jurisdiction; although only three out of 11 states – Barbados, Guyana and Belize – have accepted the Court's appellate jurisdiction, it is this jurisdiction that takes up the majority of the Court's work.

3. APPOINTING AUTHORITY AND APPOINTMENT METHOD

The evolution and development of the method for the selection of adjudicators in regional courts is best illustrated by the example of the EU. Since the revision of the EU treaties in 2009, the method of appointing judges at the two courts proceeds in three stages: first, the Member State selects a candidate, in accordance with its own domestic procedures; then the panel established under Article 255 TFEU delivers an advisory opinion as to the candidate's suitability; finally, the candidate is appointed as judge by common accord of the Member

---

[31]   Article 35(1) of the Olivos Protocol.
[32]   Article 35(2) of the Olivos Protocol.
[33]   Article IV(1) of the CCJ Agreement; currently, the CCJ has six judges and its President.
[34]   Article IV(10) of the CCJ Agreement.
[35]   Article IV(11) of the CCJ Agreement. It is not entirely clear whether fulfilment of these criteria is a mandatory precondition for appointment (see the difference of wording between Article IV(10) and IV(11)); in any event, their fulfilment is ultimately a matter of judgement.

States.[36] Article 255 TFEU replicates verbatim a provision first appearing in the (ultimately defeated) project of Constitution.[37] The provision envisages the establishment of a panel to opine on the candidates' suitability to perform judicial duties. Under Article 255, the panel 'shall comprise seven persons chosen from among former members of the Court of Justice and the General Court, members of national supreme courts and lawyers of recognised competence, one of whom shall be proposed by the European Parliament', appointed by the Council of the European Union on the initiative of the President of the CJEU.[38]

The operating rules of the panel were laid down by the Council in its Decision 2010/124/EU,[39] and they offer only a broad framework of the applicable system. The operating rules provide that the panel's seven members are appointed for a period of four years, renewable once, but do not contain any additional factors (e.g. gender, nationality) to be taken into account by the Council when appointing panel members, potentially leaving much to the discretion of the CJEU President (as the proposing authority) and the Council itself.[40] Perhaps more importantly, the operating rules do not set out the criteria to be used by the panel itself for the assessment of a candidate's suitability for the office of judge at the CJEU.[41] They only stipulate that the panel conducts a private interview with the candidate, unless he or she is proposed for reappointment as judge, that the panel deliberates in private with a quorum of five members, and that its opinion to the Member States ought to be reasoned.[42] The panel itself has indicated that it concentrates on the candidate's legal expertise, professional experience, language skills, ability to perform judicial duties as part of a team in an international legal environment, and – perhaps most relevantly for present purposes – on whether the candidate's 'independence, impartiality, probity and integrity are beyond doubt.'[43]

---

[36] Tomás Bumbrovsky, Bilyana Petkova and Marijn van der Sluis, 'Judicial appointments: the Article 255 TFEU advisory panel and selection procedures in the Member States' (2014) 51 *CMLRev* 455, 457.

[37] Article III-357 of the Treaty establishing a Constitution for Europe, OJ C 310, vol. 47, 16 December 2004.

[38] Article 255, subparagraph 2, of the TFEU. The panel's current composition was set up in Council Decision (EU, Euratom) 2017/2262 of 4 December 2017, OJ L 324, 8 December 2017, p. 50, as amended by Council Decision (EU) 2020/359 of 15 April 2020, OJ L 122, 20 April 2020, p. 1 and by Council Decision (EU) 2021/47 of 21 January 2021, OJ L 21, 22 January 2021, p. 1.

[39] Council Decision 2010/124/EU of 25 February 2010, OJ L 50, 27 December 2010, p. 18.

[40] Henri de Waele, 'Appointment of Judges: Court of Justice of the European Union', *Max Planck Encyclopedia of International Procedural Law online* (entry last updated January 2019), para. 9.

[41] Ibid., para. 20.

[42] Council Decision 2010/124/EU of 25 February 2010, OJ L 50, 27 December 2010, p. 18, paras 5, 7, 8.

[43] Council of the European Union, 'Sixth Activity Report of the panel provided for by Article 255 of the Treaty on the Functioning of the European Union', October 2019, p. 17; see also

The panel under Article 255 has no binding authority in the selection process of judges at the European courts. Since the conception of the EU, the power to appoint judges has rested with the Member States, which act 'by common accord'.[44] However, the introduction of the screening procedure of the panel under Article 255 TFEU seems to have somewhat constrained the Member States' otherwise unfettered discretion. In this connection, it has been argued that an unfavourable opinion by the panel would practically require unanimity by Member States to be overruled.[45] Besides, it is likely that the establishment of the screening process has triggered the introduction of new procedures in several Member States seeking to present more robust candidates and to avoid future disqualifications.[46]

Replicating the provisions applicable at the time of its conclusion with respect to the appointment and status of judges of the EU courts, the EFTA Agreement provides that the Court's judges shall be appointed by common accord of the EFTA states.[47] Currently, the EFTA Court comprises three judges, plus six judges ad hoc that sit in cases of recusal of a regular judge, and each of the three states party to EFTA and EEA nominate one judge and two judges ad hoc.[48] The introduction of an advisory panel for the appointment of EU judges in 2009 has not yet been mirrored in the procedure for selecting EFTA Court judges, and a proposal to that effect by the EFTA Court itself in 2011 seems to have fallen on deaf ears.[49] It appears that the longest-serving former President of the EFTA Court, joined by three academics, filed a complaint to the EFTA Surveillance Authority contending that the absence of a panel comparable to the one existing under Article 255 TFEU violates core principles of EEA law, including the principle of homogeneity with EU law and protection of

---

the implicit approval of these criteria by the Council itself in Regulation 2015/2422 of 16 December 2015, OJ L 341, 24 December 2015, p. 14, preambular paragraph 7.

[44] Article 253, subparagraph 1, of the TFEU; Article 254, subparagraph 2, of the TFEU.

[45] Henri de Waele, 'Appointment of Judges: Court of Justice of the European Union', *Max Planck Encyclopedia of International Procedural Law online* (entry last updated January 2019), para. 25. As the panel's opinion remain confidential, this assertion cannot be tested.

[46] Tomás Bumbrovsky, Bilyana Petkova and Marijn van der Sluis, 'Judicial appointments: the Article 255 TFEU advisory panel and selection procedures in the Member States' (2014) 51 *CMLRev* 455, 481.

[47] Article 30, subparagraph 1, of the EFTA Agreement.

[48] Halvard Haukeland Fredriksen, 'Court of Justice of the European Free Trade Association (EFTA Court)', *Max Planck Encyclopedia of International Procedural Law online* (entry last updated June 2018), para. 10.

[49] Carl Baudenbacher, *Judicial Independence: Memoirs of a European Judge* (St Gallen: Springer 2019) 29–30. The proposed provision is quoted in Carl Baudenbacher and Michael-James Clifton, 'Courts of Regional Economic and Political Integration Agreements' in Cesare P.R. Romano, Karen J. Alter and Yuval Shany (eds), *The Oxford Handbook of International Adjudication* (Oxford: OUP 2014) 257, n. 53, without indication as to its provenance.

individual and fundamental rights;[50] under Article 36, subparagraph 2, of the EFTA Agreement, the complaint may be eventually heard by the EFTA Court itself.

The conseillers, alternate conseillers, judges and alternate judges of the Benelux Court are appointed by the Committee of Ministers of the Benelux Union – the main political decision-making organ of the Union, which consists of representatives at ministerial level from each Member State.[51] The Committee of Ministers issues its decision based on proposals made by the governments of the three members of the Benelux Union, demonstrating the states' tight control over the selection process.[52]

In the ATJ, each of the four Member States proposes a list of candidates to fill one of the four seats on the tribunal; one of these candidates is appointed by unanimous decision of the Member States.[53]

Under the original 1991 Statute of the ECOWAS Court, each Member State nominated up to two candidates to fill the seven seats of the Court; the Council of Ministers proposed a shortlist of 14 persons, from among whom the Authority of Heads of State and Government appointed the seven judges.[54] The 2006 Supplementary Protocol altered the procedure significantly. The Authority of Heads of State and Government allocates the vacant seats – now five in total[55] – to specific Member States, inviting interested applicants that are nationals of those states to apply directly at the ECOWAS. A Judicial Council of the Community is established, composed of the Chief Justices of the Supreme Courts of Member States that have not been allocated a vacant seat, with the task of reviewing the candidatures and interviewing the applicants, with a view to selecting three candidates for each vacant seat.[56] The Authority of the Heads of

---

50   Complaint to the EFTA Surveillance Authority regarding the lack of an Article 255 TFEU panel in the EFTA pillar of the European Economic Area (22 March 2021) (on file with the rapporteur).

51   Article 3(2) of the Statute of the Benelux Court and Article 7 of the Treaty revising the Treaty establishing the Benelux Economic Union signed on 3 February 1958 (signed 17 June 2008, entered into force 1 January 2012), 2868 UNTS 26.

52   Mehdi Belkahla, 'Benelux Court of Justice', *Max Planck Encyclopedia of International Procedural Law online* (entry last updated February 2016), para. 4.

53   Article 7 of the ATJ Treaty; it is reported that each Member State presents a list of three candidates: Carl Baudenbacher and Michael-James Clifton, 'Courts of Regional Economic and Political Integration Agreements' in Cesare P.R. Romano, Karen J. Alter and Yuval Shany (eds), *The Oxford Handbook of International Adjudication* (Oxford: OUP 2014) 261.

54   Article 3 of the Statute of the ECOWAS Court.

55   Decision A/Dec.2/5/17 of the Authority of Heads of State and Government (2017); the ECOWAS Court considered that this decision, which took effect at the end of the tenure of seven judges in 2018, was lawful (https://elombah.com/ecowas-court-dismisses-falanas-suit-challenging-its-decision-on-judges/).

56   Article 3(4)(i) of the Statute of the ECOWAS Court, as introduced by Article 2 of the 2006 Protocol.

State and Government appoints one judge from among the three candidates to fill each vacant seat.[57] The elements of the new procedure – allocation of vacant seats to Member States on effectively a rotating basis, call for applications from interested individuals directly, and a vetting stage by the Judicial Council – serves to reduce the influence of state governments in the selection of judges. In addition, the introduction of the Judicial Council in particular enhances the influence of the domestic judiciary in the selection process.[58]

The 12 judges at the COMESA Court are appointed by the Authority of the Heads of State and Government of the Member States.[59]

Judges at the EEU Court are appointed by the Supreme Eurasian Economic Council, the 'supreme body' of the EEU comprising the Heads of State of the Member States,[60] on the proposal of Member States.[61] The fact that Member States directly propose their national judges may be seen as a setback compared to the procedure for the appointment of judges in the judicial organ of the EEU's predecessor, the Eurasian Economic Community.[62] Under that system, judges were appointed by the Inter-Parliamentary Assembly of the Eurasian Economic Community on the proposal of the Interstate Council of the Community.[63]

In the Mercosur dispute settlement system, Member States retain strong control over the selection of arbitrators. Each Member State compiles a list of 12 arbitrators; when a dispute arises, the Member State appoints one of them to sit in the three-person ad hoc tribunal.[64] Each Member State also proposes four candidates for a list of 'third arbitrators' – namely, the list from which the presiding arbitrators of ad hoc tribunals are to be selected.[65] The nomination of 'third arbitrators' is approved unless other Member States object thereto.[66] When a specific dispute arises, the disputing parties are to select jointly the third (presiding) arbitrator of the ad hoc tribunal from among that list.[67]

---

[57]   Article 3(1) of the Statute of the ECOWAS Court.
[58]   Karen J. Alter, Laurence R. Helfer and Jacqueline R, McAllister, 'A New International Human Rights Court for West Africa: The ECOWAS Community Court of Justice' (2013) 107 *AJIL* 737, 760.
[59]   Article 20(1) of the COMESA Treaty.
[60]   Article 10 of the EEU Treaty.
[61]   Article 10 Statute of the EEU Court.
[62]   Alain Zamaria, 'Court of the Eurasian Economic Union', *Max Planck Encyclopedia of International Procedural Law online* (entry last updated June 2019), para. 17.
[63]   Article 8 of the Treaty establishing the Eurasian Economic Community (signed 10 October 2000, entered into force 30 May 2001), 2212 UNTS 257.
[64]   Articles 11(1) and 10(2)(i) of the Olivos Protocol.
[65]   Articles 11(2), subparagraph 1, and 10(3) of the Olivos Protocol.
[66]   Article 11(2)(ii) of the Olivos Protocol.
[67]   Article 10(3)(i) of the Olivos Protocol. The Administrative Secretariat of Mercosur is empowered to fill any vacancies resulting from the failure of the parties to appoint arbitrators: Article 10(2)(ii) and (3)(ii) of the Olivos Protocol.

The PRC comprises five arbitrators: each Member State appoints one (as well as an alternate), while the fifth arbitrator is chosen unanimously by the Member States from a list of eight candidates (two candidates proposed by each Member State).[68] The four state-appointed arbitrators serve for a period of two years, renewable twice, while the fifth arbitrator serves for a non-renewable period of three years.[69] The PRC normally sits in a three-person formation, consisting of a national of each disputing party and a third arbitrator (the presiding arbitrator) chosen by lot from among the remaining arbitrators who are not nationals of the disputing parties.[70]

Unlike other courts, judges of the CCJ are not appointed directly by unanimous decision of the Member States. Rather, appointment of judges, much like most other acts pertaining to the oversight of the Court, is entrusted to the Regional Judicial and Legal Services Commission (RJLSC), which votes by majority.[71] The RJLSC is a body comprising the Court's President (serving ex officio as Chair of the Commission); two persons nominated jointly by the Organisation of the Commonwealth Caribbean Bar Association and the Organisation of Eastern Caribbean States Bar Association; one chairperson of the Judicial Services Commission of a Member State selected in rotation in English alphabetical order for a period of three years; the chair of a Public Service Commission of a Member State selected in rotation in reverse English alphabetical order for a period of three years; two persons from civil society nominated jointly by the Secretary-General of the Community and the Director General of the Organisation of Eastern Caribbean States for a period of three years following consultations with regional NGOs; two distinguished jurists nominated jointly by the Dean of the Faculty of Law of the University of the West Indies, the Deans of the Faculties of Law of any of the Member States and the chair of the Council of Legal Education; and two persons nominated jointly by the Bar or Law Associations of the Member States.[72] The President of the Court is the only member of the Court appointed directly by the Member States; in that case, the Member States act on the recommendation of the RJLSC and vote by qualified majority of three-quarters.[73]

---

68 Article 18(2)–(3) of the Olivos Protocol. If Member States fail to reach a unanimous decision, the fifth arbitrator is selected by lot: Article 18(3), subparagraph 3, of the Olivos Protocol.
69 Article 18(2)–(3) of the Olivos Protocol.
70 Article 20(1) of the Olivos Protocol.
71 Article IV(7) of the CCJ Agreement; see also Article V(3)(1)(a) of the CCJ Agreement.
72 Article V(1) of the CCJ Agreement.
73 Article IV(6) of the CCJ Agreement.

Freya Baetens

4. METHODS AND PARAMETERS TO ENSURE THE INDEPENDENCE AND IMPARTIALITY IN THE EXERCISE OF THE ADJUDICATORS' FUNCTIONS

Judges at the CJEU serve a six-year term but may be reappointed repeatedly.[74] The relatively short period of office (six years), coupled with the (unlimited) possibility of reappointment allows Member States to retain control, because sitting judges might adapt their behaviour to retain the favour of their government.[75] On the other hand, it has been argued that a non-renewable but longer term (e.g. nine years, as in the European Court of Human Rights) would be unworkable in the CJEU due to the rather long adaptation period required for judges and the frequent turnover in registry staff; with this in mind, it has been argued that the current system should be retained but that Member States should justify their proposal not to renew the mandate of sitting judges.[76]

Judges at the CJEU take an oath to perform their duties impartially and conscientiously and to preserve the secrecy of deliberations, and they are required not to hold any political or administrative office or to engage in any occupation, whether remunerated or not, unless the Council of the EU grants a specific exemption.[77] Judges enjoy immunity from legal proceedings while in office, and retired judges enjoy immunity in respect of acts performed in their official capacity, including opinions expressed.[78] This immunity may only be waived by the Court of Justice, sitting as a full court.[79]

Judges at the CJEU may not participate in cases in which they have previously acted for one of the parties or have been called upon to pronounce in any capacity (e.g. as members of a court).[80] Decisions on this matter are resolved by the Court of Justice.[81] Moreover, in the CJEU, not only are the deliberations secret,[82] but so are the opinions of individual judges: only one judgment by the

---

[74] Article 19(2), subparagraph 3, of the TEU; Article 253, subparagraph 4, and Article 254, subparagraph 2, of the TFEU.

[75] J.H.H. Weiler, 'Epilogue: Judging the Judges – Apology and Critique' in Maurice Adams, Henri de Waele, Johan Meeusen and Gert Straetmans (eds), *Judging Europe's Judges: The Legitimacy of the Case Law of the European Court of Justice* (London: Hart Publishing 2013), 251–52.

[76] Francis G. Jacobs, 'The Court of Justice in the Twenty-First Century: Challenges Ahead for the Judicial System?' in Alan Rosas, Egils Levits and Yves Bot (eds), *The Court of Justice and the Construction of Europe: Analyses and Perspectives on Sixty Years of Case-law* (The Hague: Asser Press and Springer 2013) 58–59.

[77] Articles 2 and 4 of the Statute of the Court of Justice of the European Union (Protocol No. 3 to the Treaty of the European Union and the Treaty on the Functioning of the European Union).

[78] Article 3, subparagraph 1, of the Statute of the CJEU.

[79] Article 3, subparagraph 2, of the Statute of the CJEU.

[80] Article 18, subparagraph 3, of the Statute of the CJEU.

[81] Article 18, subparagraph 3, of the Statute of the CJEU.

[82] Article 35 of the Statute of the CJEU.

Court is issued.[83] This ensures that governments do not know the opinions of each judge, which in turn alleviates any external pressures that might jeopardise judicial independence.[84]

In broad terms, the rules applicable to the EFTA Court are similar to those of the CJEU, from which they are drawn. More specifically, judges serve a six-year term, which may be renewed repeatedly.[85] The provisions concerning the judicial oath and incompatibilities, as well as immunities, are identical to those governing the judges of the CJEU.[86] Like in the CJEU, a judge of the EFTA Court is required not participate in cases in which he or she has previously acted for one of the parties or has been called upon to pronounce in any capacity; decisions on that matter are taken by the other two judges of the EFTA Court.[87] The individual judges are not allowed to append individual opinions to the decisions of the EFTA Court.[88]

Unlike the judges of other international courts, members of the Benelux Court – who are judges in higher domestic courts – continue to serve in their respective domestic courts.[89] They also serve at the Benelux Court for as long as they are on active service in those domestic courts, while judges having reached retirement age in their respective countries may serve at the Benelux Court until the age of 70.[90] However, resignations are frequent in practice, so that members seldom hold office for more than a decade.[91] With the exception of travel and subsistence costs, members of the Benelux Court receive no remuneration for their service at that court.[92] Members of the Benelux Court are in principle not subject to legal proceedings or any form of inquiry, even after the end of service; their immunity may only be waived by the First Chamber of the Court, which comprises the conseillers and alternate conseillers.[93] When their immunity

---

[83] See Article 36 of the Statute of the CJEU and Article 87 of the Rules of Procedure of the Court of Justice (as of 25 September 2012).

[84] European Parliament, *Dissenting opinions in the Supreme Courts of the Member States* (2012), p. 37; see also Sophie Turenne, 'Institutional constraints and collegiality at the Court of Justice of the European Union: A sense of belonging?' (2017) 24(4) *MJECL* 565, 573.

[85] Article 30, subparagraph 2, of the EFTA Agreement.

[86] Articles 4 and 6 of the Statute of the EFTA Court, and Article 7 of Protocol 7 on the legal capacity, privileges and immunities of the EFTA Court. The exemption for undertaking extra-judicial occupation is granted by the governments of the EFTA states acting by common accord: Article 6, subparagraph 3, of the Statute of the EFTA Court.

[87] Article 15 of the Statute of the EFTA Court; see also Article 30, subparagraph 4, of the EFTA Agreement.

[88] Article 32 of the Statute of the EFTA Court; see also Article 60 of the Rules of Procedure.

[89] Mehdi Belkahla, 'Benelux Court of Justice', *Max Planck Encyclopedia of International Procedural Law online* (entry last updated February 2016), para. 9.

[90] Article 3(2) of the Statute of the Benelux Court.

[91] Mehdi Belkahla, 'Benelux Court of Justice', *Max Planck Encyclopedia of International Procedural Law online* (entry last updated February 2016), para. 10.

[92] Article 4(5) of the Statute of the Benelux Court.

[93] Article 4*quater*(1)–(1*bis*) of the Statute of the Benelux Court.

is waived, the members of the Benelux Court are tried by the domestic court competent to try persons performing comparable functions to theirs (i.e. judges of higher or supreme courts).[94]

The members of the Benelux Court take an oath to discharge their duties 'with integrity, exactitude and impartiality' and to maintain the secrecy of the deliberations.[95] To that effect, they are required to recuse themselves when they have participated as members of a national jurisdiction in a case brought before the Benelux Court.[96] Judgments and orders are issued by the Court, individual judges not being allowed to append their individual opinions.[97]

Like in the CJEU and EFTA, judges at the ATJ serve a six-year term; unlike those two courts, however, they may only be reappointed once.[98] Under the ATJ Treaty, the members of the Tribunal 'shall be fully independent in the exercise of their functions, they may not undertake any other professional activities, whether or not remunerated, except those, of a professorial nature, and they shall abstain from any activity incompatible with the nature of their office.'[99] They must also recuse themselves in cases where they have acted for one of their parties, have an interest in the outcome of the case, have been called upon to pronounce on the case in a different capacity, or have manifest friendship or enmity with one of the parties; in cases of doubt as to whether there exist grounds of recusal, the decision rests with the Tribunal.[100] The privileges and immunities provided for in the Vienna Convention on Diplomatic Relations are applicable to judges of the ATJ by analogy, and they may be waived by unanimous decision of the Member States.[101]

The Statute of the ECOWAS Court originally stipulated that judges would hold office for a term of five years, renewable once.[102] This was amended in 2006, so that judges now serve for a non-renewable four-year term.[103] The judges of the ECOWAS Court take an oath or make a solemn declaration to exercise their powers honourably, faithfully, impartially and conscientiously.[104] During their tenure, judges enjoy privileges and immunities 'identical to those enjoyed by

---

[94]   Article 4quater(2) of the Statute of the Benelux Court.
[95]   Article 4(2) of the Statute of the Benelux Court.
[96]   Article 5(3) of the Statute of the Benelux Court.
[97]   See Article 1.59 of the Rules of Procedure of the Benelux Court.
[98]   Article 8 of the ATJ Treaty.
[99]   Article 6, subparagraph 2, of the ATJ Treaty.
[100]   Articles 67–69 of the Statute of the ATJ, as codified by Decision 500 of the Council of Ministers for Foreign Affairs, 680 Official Gazette of the Cartagena Agreement (28 June 2001) (Statute of the ATJ).
[101]   Articles 6, 10, and 12 of the Statute of the ATJ.
[102]   Article 4(1) of the Statute of the ECOWAS Court (1991).
[103]   Article 4(1) of the Statute of the ECOWAS Court, as amended by Article 4 of Supplementary Protocol A/SP.2/06/06 amending Article 3 paragraphs 1, 2 and 4, Article 4 paragraphs 1, 3 and 7 and Article 7 paragraph 3 of the Protocol on the Community Court of Justice.
[104]   Article 5 of the Statute of the ECOWAS Court.

diplomatic missions and diplomatic agents in the territory of Member States, as well as those normally accorded to international courts and the members of such courts', and they may not be prosecuted or arrested for acts or statements made in the exercise of their functions.[105] The deliberations of the Court are secret, and individual judges are not allowed to append their opinion to the judicial decisions, which are issued by the Court collectively.[106]

Judges at the COMESA Court hold office for a five-year term, renewable once.[107] They are immune from legal action for acts and omissions in the exercise of their functions.[108] Judges of the COMESA Court are required to report any instances where they may be directly or indirectly interested in a case before the Court, in order for the Authority of Heads of State and Government to decide, upon the advice of the Court's President, whether to appoint a temporary judge for the specific case.[109] Disputing parties may also request the recusal of a judge for the same reason.[110] Like in the ECOWAS Court, the deliberations of the Court are secret, and individual judges are not allowed to append their opinion to the judicial decisions, which are issued by the Court collectively.[111]

Under the EEU Treaty, the judges of the EEU Court serve for nine years.[112] Given that neither the Statute nor the Rules of Procedure of the Court explicitly permit reappointment, it has been argued that reappointment is not permissible.[113] Under the Statute of the EEU Court, judges may not represent the interests of any public or private entities or engage in any income-generating activities, with the exception of research and teaching activities.[114] Besides, judges are required to recuse themselves if they have participated in any capacity in a dispute before the Court.[115] Furthermore, the EEU Statute provides that the proceedings are to be conducted on the basis of the principles of judicial independence, transparency of proceedings, publicity, equality of the parties to the dispute, competitiveness and collegiality.[116]

In the Mercosur system, there appears to be no limit on the number of ad hoc tribunals in which arbitrators are allowed to sit: their appointment on specific

---

[105] Article 6 of the Statute of the ECOWAS Court.
[106] See Article 19(3) of the Statute of the ECOWAS Court and Article 60 of the Rules of the Community Court of Justice of the ECOWAS.
[107] Article 21(1) of the COMESA Treaty.
[108] Article 39 of the COMESA Treaty.
[109] Article 22(4) of the COMESA Treaty.
[110] Kenneth K. Mwenda, 'Court of Justice of the Common Market for Eastern and Southern Africa (COMESA)', *Max Planck Encyclopedia of International Procedural Law online* (entry last updated February 2019), para. 33.
[111] See Article 31(2) of the COMESA Treaty.
[112] Article 8 of the Statute of the EEU Court.
[113] Alain Zamaria, 'Court of the Eurasian Economic Union', *Max Planck Encyclopedia of International Procedural Law online* (entry last updated June 2019), para. 18.
[114] Article 18 of the Statute of the EEU Court.
[115] Article 19 of the Statute of the EEU Court.
[116] Article 53 of the Statute of the EEU Court.

cases depends solely on the will of the disputing parties. By contrast, the terms of office of arbitrators serving at the PRC is limited: the four state-appointed arbitrators serve for a period of two years, renewable twice, while the fifth arbitrator serves for a non-renewable period of three years.[117] All arbitrators are also bound by a code of conduct that requires them, among other things, to avoid direct and indirect conflicts of interest,[118] to maintain the secrecy of deliberations,[119] to avoid contacts with either disputing party in the absence of the other disputing party,[120] and to refrain from taking instructions from the disputing parties or any third party.[121] Individual opinions in judgments of the ad hoc tribunals and the PRC are permissible but infrequent.[122]

Once appointed, judges of the CCJ have life tenure until mandatory retirement at 72, which may be extended to 75 by decision of the RJLSC when 'special circumstances so require'.[123] The President holds office for a non-renewable term of seven years, unless he or she reaches the age of mandatory retirement of 72 before then.[124] Judges, as well as the President, continue in office for a maximum of three months so as to complete pending cases.[125] In addition, the CCJ Agreement guarantees that the salaries and allowances of the members of the Court, as well as their other terms and conditions of service, shall not be altered to their disadvantage during their term of office; more importantly, no seat can be abolished during a judge's term of office.[126]

The CCJ has adopted a Code of Judicial Conduct with a view to upholding the principles of independence, propriety, integrity, impartiality, equality, competence and diligence, and accountability.[127] To that effect, judges are required to avoid conduct, even in their personal relations, that might reasonably

---

[117] Article 18(2)–(3) of the Olivos Protocol.

[118] Article 2(c) of the Code of Conduct (MERCOSUR/CMC/DEC No. 31/11, 19 December 2011).

[119] Article 2(d) of the Code of Conduct (MERCOSUR/CMC/DEC No. 31/11, 19 December 2011).

[120] Article 2(g) of the Code of Conduct (MERCOSUR/CMC/DEC No. 31/11, 19 December 2011).

[121] Article 2(j) of the Code of Conduct (MERCOSUR/CMC/DEC No. 31/11, 19 December 2011); see also Articles 21 and 32 of the Rules of Procedure (MERCOSUR/CM/DEC No. 37/03, 15 December 2003).

[122] See e.g. Advisory Opinion (Opinión Consultiva) No. 01/2007, *Norte S.A. Imp. Exp. c/ Laboratorios Northia Sociedad Anónima, Comercial, Industrial, Financiera, Inmobiliaria y Agropecuaria s/Indemnización de Daños y Perjuicios y Lucro Cesante.*

[123] Article IX(3) of the CCJ Agreement; Article II(1) of the Protocol to the Agreement establishing the Caribbean Court of Justice relating to the tenure of office of judges of the Court.

[124] Article IX(2) of the CCJ Agreement.

[125] Article IX(2)–(3) of the CCJ Agreement.

[126] Articles XXVIII(3) and IX(1) of the CCJ Agreement.

[127] Preamble to the Code of Judicial Conduct (adopted 26 May 2020), available at https://ccj.org/wp-content/uploads/2021/03/CCJ-Code-of-Judicial-Conduct-REV-June-30.pdf.

give rise to the suspicion or appearance of favouritism, partiality, bias[128] or political partisanship,[129] to only exceptionally receive compensation for the (limited) extra-judicial activities that are permissible to them (e.g. research and teaching activities),[130] and to recuse themselves from proceedings where there might be a reasonable perception of lack of impartiality.[131]

The deliberations of the CCJ when it exercises its original jurisdiction are private and confidential; the view of the majority is reflected in the Court's judgment or advisory opinion, while no separate or dissenting opinions are allowed.[132] By contrast, judgments under the appellate jurisdiction may contain dissenting opinions.[133]

5. CONSEQUENCES OF A BREACH OF THE REQUIREMENT TO ACT INDEPENDENTLY AND IMPARTIALLY

A judge of the CJEU may only be deprived of his or her office or right to a pension or other benefits if, in the unanimous opinion of the Judges and Advocates General of the Court of Justice, he or she 'no longer fulfils the requisite conditions or meets the obligations arising from his [or her] office.'[134] By contrast, there seems to be no recourse against a judicial decision that is rendered with the participation of a judge acting allegedly or definitively in breach of his or her duty to act independently and impartially. The situation is identical for the EFTA Court.[135]

As mentioned above, members of the Benelux Court serve for as long as they fulfil the requisite conditions – namely, for as long as they are sitting judges in their domestic courts – and may not be removed from office.[136]

Member States of the Andean Community may request the removal of a judge of the ATJ only if he or she commits a serious violation of the Court's Statute in the exercise of his or her functions.[137] The Statute itself lists what are considered

---

[128] Principle 2.4 of the Code of Judicial Conduct.
[129] Principles 2.8 and 2.9 of the Code of Judicial Conduct.
[130] Principle 2.24 of the Code of Judicial Conduct.
[131] Principles 4.6 and 4.7 of the Code of Judicial Conduct.
[132] Article 3.3 of the Original Jurisdiction Rules 2019.
[133] Carl Baudenbacher and Michael-James Clifton, 'Courts of Regional Economic and Political Integration Agreements' in Cesare P.R. Romano, Karen J. Alter and Yuval Shany (eds), *The Oxford Handbook of International Adjudication* (Oxford: OUP 2014) 270.
[134] Article 6, subparagraph 1, of the Statute of the CJEU; the judge concerned does not participate in this decision.
[135] Article 6, subparagraph 1, of the Statute of the EFTA Court.
[136] Mehdi Belkahla, 'Benelux Court of Justice', *Max Planck Encyclopedia of International Procedural Law online* (entry last updated February 2016), para. 10.
[137] Article 10 of the ATJ Treaty.

serious violations: manifest misconduct; any action incompatible with the position; repeated failure to fulfil duties inherent in the function; carrying out professional activities other than teaching or academic duties; and breach of the oath taken at the assumption of office.[138] Having heard the judge in question at a special sitting, the representatives of the Member States may remove the judge from office only by unanimous and reasoned decision.[139]

Leaving aside instances of death, resignation, and physical or mental inability, judges at the COMESA Court can only be removed by the Authority of Heads of State and Government 'for stated misbehaviour or for inability to perform the functions of [their] office ... due to any other specified cause'.[140] These grounds are not further specified, potentially leaving a wide margin of discretion to the inter-governmental body holding the power to remove sitting judges.

Judges of the EEU Court are removed by the Supreme Eurasian Economic Council on the proposal of the Member State whose nationality the judge holds, of the Court, or of the judge himself or herself.[141] Among the permissible grounds for removal, two are related to the question of independence or impartiality: 'participation in activities incompatible with the office of a judge' and 'serious misconduct incompatible with the high status of a judge'.[142]

The Code of Arbitral Conduct of the Mercosur provides that an investigation is instituted whenever a disputing party alleges, by a letter addressed to the Common Market Group, that an arbitrator has breached any of its duties under the applicable framework.[143] Pending the investigation, the Common Market Group may decide on the suspension of any ongoing dispute settlement proceedings, their continuation with the arbitrator under investigation, or their continuation after the definitive replacement of the arbitrator by his or her alternate arbitrator.[144] The investigation is conducted by the group of ad hoc arbitrators, which advises the Common Market Group as to the appropriate action: if the Common Market Group finds that there has been a breach of duty, the arbitrator is replaced by the corresponding alternate arbitrator in all ongoing proceedings, and he or she is removed from the list of ad hoc arbitrators.[145]

Judges of the CCJ are removed only for inability to perform their functions or for misbehaviour.[146] Removal of members of the CCJ occurs in the same way

---

[138]   Article 11 of the Statute of the ATJ.
[139]   Article 10 of the ATJ Treaty and Article 12, subparagraph 3, Statute of the ATJ.
[140]   Article 22(1) of the COMESA Treaty.
[141]   Articles 11 and 13 of the Statute of the EEU Court.
[142]   Article 12, clauses 5 and 8, of the Statute of the EEU Court.
[143]   Article 4(1) of the Code of Conduct of arbitrators, experts, and officials of the Mercosur acting under the Olivos Protocol.
[144]   Article 4(2) of the Code of Conduct of arbitrators, experts, and officials of the Mercosur acting under the Olivos Protocol.
[145]   Article 6 of the Code of Conduct of arbitrators, experts, and officials of the Mercosur acting under the Olivos Protocol.
[146]   Article IX(4)–(5) of the CCJ Agreement.

as appointment: in the case of regular judges, by a majority vote in the RJLSC; and in the case of the President, by a three-quarters majority vote of the Member States on the recommendation of the RJLSC.[147] In either case, the question of the removal must have been considered by an advisory tribunal established for that purpose.[148]

As a final point, the instruments constituting the above-mentioned regional courts and governing their procedure do not contain provisions governing situations where a judicial decision is issued with the participation of a judge acting contrary to the duties of independence and impartiality.

---

[147] Article IV(6)–(7) of the CCJ Agreement.
[148] Article IX(5)–(6) of the CCJ Agreement.

THE INDEPENDENCE AND IMPARTIALITY OF ADJUDICATORS IN REGIONAL HUMAN RIGHTS COURTS

Hilary CHARLESWORTH, Emma MACFARLANE
and Nikiforos PANAGIS*

1. Introduction 304
2. Criteria for the Selection of Adjudicators 306
   2.1. The European Court of Human Rights 306
   2.2. The Inter-American Court of Human Rights 310
   2.3. The African Court on Human and Peoples' Rights 311
   2.4. A Brief Comparison 312
3. Appointing Authority and Appointment Method 313
   3.1. The European Court of Human Rights 313
   3.2. The Inter-American Court of Human Rights 316
   3.3. The African Court on Human and Peoples' Rights 318
   3.4. A Brief Comparison 319
4. Tenure and Grounds for Dismissal 320
   4.1. The European Court of Human Rights 320
   4.2. The Inter-American Court of Human Rights 321
   4.3. The African Court on Human and Peoples' Rights 322
   4.4. A Brief Comparison 323
5. Methods and Parameters to Ensure Adjudicators' Independence and
   Impartiality in the Exercise of their Functions 324
   5.1. The European Court of Human Rights 324
      5.1.1. Limitations on Judges' Abilities to Hear Cases 324
      5.1.2. Limitations on Judges' Roles Outside the Court 327
      5.1.3. Judicial Deliberations and Delivery of the Court's
             Judgments 327
      5.1.4. Benefits, Privileges and Immunities 328

---

* Many thanks to Georgie Clough for her valuable research assistance.

Intersentia

5.2. The Inter-American Court of Human Rights. 328
    5.2.1. Limitations on Judges' Abilities to Hear Cases 328
    5.2.2. Limitations on Judges' Roles Outside the Court. 330
    5.2.3. Judicial Deliberations and Delivery of the Court's
           Judgments. 331
    5.2.4. Benefits, Privileges and Immunities 331
5.3. The African Court on Human and Peoples' Rights. 332
    5.3.1. Limitations on Judges' Abilities to Hear Cases 332
    5.3.2. Limitations on Judges' Roles Outside the Court. 332
    5.3.3. Judicial Deliberations and Delivery of the Court's
           Judgments. 333
    5.3.4. Benefits, Privileges and Immunities 334
5.4. A Brief Comparison. 334

1. INTRODUCTION

This report provides an overview of the methods and practices of three international human rights courts in relation to the independence and impartiality of judges.

The European Court of Human Rights (ECtHR) was established in 1959 by the Convention for the Protection of Human Rights and Fundamental Freedoms (European Convention), an international treaty which guarantees fundamental civil and political rights to all individuals within the jurisdiction of states of the Council of Europe.[1] The mandate of the Court is to ensure the observance of such engagements undertaken by the Member States of the Council of Europe.[2] The ECtHR is financed by the Council of Europe.[3] It is located in Strasbourg, France and functions on a permanent basis.[4]

The Inter-American Court of Human Rights (IACtHR) was established by the Organization of American States (OAS) in 1978 under the American Convention on Human Rights (American Convention).[5] The IACtHR is competent 'with respect to matters relating to the fulfilment of the commitments made by the State Parties' to the American Convention.[6] The Court is financed

---

[1] See Convention for the Protection of Human Rights and Fundamental Freedoms (concluded 4 November 1950, entered into force 3 September 1953) 213 UNTS 221, as amended.
[2] European Convention, Art. 19.
[3] Ibid., Art. 50.
[4] Ibid., Art. 19.
[5] American Convention on Human Rights (concluded 22 November 1969, entered into force 18 July 1978) 1144 UNTS 123, chapter VIII.
[6] Ibid., Art. 33.

304   Intersentia

by the Organization of American States.[7] The seat of the IACtHR is in San José, Costa Rica.

The African Court on Human and Peoples' Rights (ACtHPR) was established in 1998 by Article 1 of the Protocol to the African Charter on Human and Peoples' Rights on the Establishment of an African Court on Human and People's Rights (1998 Protocol).[8] The 1998 Protocol entered into force in 2004 following the ratification of 15 countries.[9] The ACtHPR's mission is to ensure the attainment of the objectives of the African Charter on Human and Peoples' Rights, namely the promotion and protection of human and peoples' rights, freedoms and duties through 'complement[ing] and reinforc[ing] the functions of the African Commission on Human and Peoples' Rights'.[10] The ACtHPR is financed by the African Union (AU)[11] and located in Arusha, Tanzania.[12] A change to the structure and functions of the ACtHPR has been in development for more than a decade, although the proposed initiative has not yet come to fruition. In 2008, the AU adopted a Protocol on the Statute of the African Court of Justice and Human Rights (2008 Protocol), to which it subsequently made amendments in 2014 (2014 Protocol).[13] The 2008 Protocol merges the ACtHPR with the Court of Justice of the African Union, the latter being a judicial body dedicated to questions arising under the law of the African Union.[14] The merger foreshadowed in the 2008 Protocol would create the African Court of Justice and Human Rights, since renamed the African Court of Justice and Human and

---

7   Ibid., Art. 72.
8   Protocol to the African Charter on Human and People's Rights on the Establishment of an African Court on Human and Peoples' Rights (concluded 10 June 1998, entered into force 25 January 2004), https://www.african-court.org/wpafc/wp-content/uploads/2020/10/2-PROTOCOL-TO-THE-AFRICAN-CHARTER-ON-HUMAN-AND-PEOPLES-RIGHTS-ON-THE-ESTABLISHMENT-OF-AN-AFRICAN-COURT-ON-HUMAN-AND-PEOPLES-RIGHTS.pdf, Art. 1.
9   African Union, 'List of countries which have signed, ratified/acceded to the Protocol to the African Charter on Human and Peoples' Rights on the Establishment of an African Court on Human and Peoples' Rights' (15 June 2017), https://au.int/sites/default/files/treaties/36393-sl-protocol_to_the_african_charter_on_human_and_peoplesrights_on_the_estab.pdf.
10   1998 Protocol, preambular paras 3 and 7.
11   Ibid., Art. 32.
12   'Basic Information', https://www.african-court.org/wpafc/basic-information/; see also 1998 Protocol, Art. 25 (the African Union was formerly known as the Organization of African Unity, or OAU).
13   Protocol on the Statute of the African Court of Justice and Human Rights (concluded 1 July 2008), https://au.int/sites/default/files/treaties/36396-treaty-0035_-_protocol_on_the_statute_of_the_african_court_of_justice_and_human_rights_e.pdf; Protocol on Amendments to the Protocol on the Statute of the African Court of Justice and Human Rights (concluded 27 June 2014), https://au.int/sites/default/files/treaties/36398-treaty-0045_-_protocol_on_amendments_to_the_protocol_on_the_statute_of_the_african_court_of_justice_and_human_rights_e-compressed.pdf.
14   Protocol of the Court of Justice of the African Union (concluded 11 July 2003, entered into force 11 February 2009), https://au.int/en/treaties/protocol-court-justice-african-union, Art. 19.

Intersentia

Peoples' Rights (ACtJHPR) by the 2014 Protocol. The 2008 Protocol requires 15 ratifications to enter into force; as of June 2022, it had only attracted eight, with the most recent state accession occurring in February 2020.[15] At times, there are variations between the provisions concerned with independence and impartiality in the 2008 Protocol and the 2014 Protocol, as compared to those of the 1998 Protocol and Rules of Court. These divergences are identified below.

2. CRITERIA FOR THE SELECTION OF ADJUDICATORS

2.1. THE EUROPEAN COURT OF HUMAN RIGHTS

The ECtHR has the same number of judges as there are state parties to the European Convention (currently 47).[16] The judges sit on the Court in their individual capacity.[17]

Originally, the drafters of the European Convention proposed a Court composition of nine judges in an effort to distinguish the Court from a 'political council of Member States'.[18] Smaller states resisted this proposal, driven by the concern that their interests would not be reflected in such an institution.[19] The resultant compromise was that the number of judges is equal to that of the parties to the European Convention.[20]

Further adjustments have been made to the Court's structure and operations to improve representation of smaller states. For example, in its original procedures, the ECtHR followed the 'standard nationality limit' wherein no two judges could be elected at the same time who were nationals of the same state.[21] The entry into

---

[15]   African Union, 'List of countries which have signed, ratified/acceded to the Protocol on the Statute of the African Court of Justice and Human Rights' (18 June 2020), https://au.int/en/treaties/protocol-statute-african-court-justice-and-human-rights. The 2014 Protocol also requires 15 ratifications to enter into force; as of May 2019, no states have ratified it. African Union, 'List of countries which have signed, ratified/acceded to the Protocol on Amendments to the Protocol on the Statute of the African Court of Justice and Human Rights' (20 May 2019), https://au.int/en/treaties/protocol-amendments-protocol-statute-african-court-justice-and-human-rights.

[16]   European Convention, Art. 20; '47 Members States', https://www.coe.int/en/web/portal/47-members-states; 'Composition of the Court', https://www.echr.coe.int/Pages/home.aspx?p=court/judges&c.

[17]   European Convention, Art. 21(3).

[18]   J. Limbach, *Judicial Independence: Law and Practice of Appointments to the European Court of Human Rights* (Report, Interrights, May 2003) 7.

[19]   Ibid., 7–8.

[20]   Ibid., 8.

[21]   See T. Dannenbaum, 'Nationality and the International Judge: The Nationalist Presumption Governing the International Judiciary and Why It Must Be Reversed' (2012) 45(1) *Cornell International Law Journal* 77, 97; European Convention, Art. 38 (prior to the amendment by Protocol No. 11, restructuring the control machinery established thereby (concluded 11 May 1994, entered into force 1 November 1998) ETS 155, Art. 1).

force of Protocol No. 11 to the European Convention (1998) removed this rule.[22] In theory, this better enables smaller states' nominations of qualified candidates by widening the pool of candidates to those who are nationals of other states. States have taken advantage of this provision. For example, Lichtenstein has nominated judges of Swiss and Canadian nationalities to take its allotted seat on the Court.[23] In practice states usually nominate candidates of their own nationality, and thus the same nationality is rarely represented by more than one judge on the Court.[24]

The European Convention sets out three main criteria for the appointment of judges.[25] First, they must be of high moral character.[26] Second, they must either possess the qualifications required for appointments to high judicial office or be jurisconsults of recognised competence.[27] Finally, at the time when the list of any state's three candidates is requested by the Council of Europe Parliamentary Assembly, the prospective candidate must be less than 65 years old.[28] Any appointed judge ad hoc must meet the same criteria.[29] Two documents in particular have clarified the criteria implicit in the general requirements for judicial appointment.

The first document was created in 2010. In 2009, the President of the ECtHR, Jean-Paul Costa, called a conference of high-level representatives of state parties to the European Convention.[30] Costa envisioned the object of the conference as re-emphasising contracting states' commitment to the Court, to clarify the necessary roles of national authorities and the Court between one another and within the European Convention's system, and to establish a roadmap outlining

---

[22] Protocol No. 11 to the Convention for the Protection of Human Rights and Fundamental Freedoms, restructuring the control machinery established thereby (concluded 11 May 1994, entered into force 1 November 1998) ETS 155.

[23] T. Dannenbaum, 'Nationality and the International Judge: The Nationalist Presumption Governing the International Judiciary and Why It Must Be Reversed' (2012) 45(1) *Cornell International Law Journal* 77, 97 n. 132. See also European Parliamentary Association, Candidates for the European Court of Human Rights, P 11, 2d Sess., Doc. No. 11243 (2007); G. Sturgess and P. Chubb, *Judging the World: Law and Politics in the World's Leading Courts* (Butterworths 1988) 537.

[24] T. Dannenbaum, 'Nationality and the International Judge: The Nationalist Presumption Governing the International Judiciary and Why It Must Be Reversed' (2012) 45(1) *Cornell International Law Journal* 77, 97.

[25] See European Convention, Art. 21.

[26] Ibid., Art. 21(1).

[27] Ibid.

[28] Ibid., Art. 21(2).

[29] ECtHR Rules of Court (2022), Rule 29(1)(c).

[30] A. Mowbray, 'The Interlaken Declaration – The Beginning of a New Era for the European Court of Human Rights?' (2010) 10(3) *Human Rights Law Review* 519, 519–20. See also Memorandum of the President of the European Court of Human Rights to the States with a View to preparing the Interlaken Conference (3 July 2009), https://www.echr.coe.int/Documents/Speech_20090703_Costa_Interlaken_ENG.pdf.

the short- to long-term goals of the Court.[31] The conference took place over two days in February 2010 and culminated in the adoption of the Interlaken Declaration.[32] Among other things, the Interlaken Declaration emphasised the importance of preserving judicial independence and impartiality, and thus the quality of the Court.[33] It called upon parties to improve the transparency and quality of the judicial selection process by ensuring the European Convention's criteria for judicial office were fully satisfied.[34] The Interlaken Declaration also stressed knowledge of public international law and national legal systems, and proficiency in at least one of the official languages of the Court.[35]

The second clarifying document was issued in 2020. The Advisory Panel of Experts, a seven-member body created in 2010 to advise the Parliamentary Assembly on nominees, issued a Short Guide on the minimum qualifications required a judicial candidate.[36] On the first requirement concerning high moral character, which includes the ability to be independent and impartial, the Short Guide notes that, generally, the Advisory Panel must assume that judicial nominees have the following qualities: 'integrity, a high sense of responsibility, courage, dignity, diligence, honesty, discretion, respect for others and the absence of conviction of crimes ... as well as (obviously) independence and impartiality'.[37]

Only when the absence of one of these qualities is 'manifestly apparent' from a candidate's curriculum vitae may the Advisory Panel make a negative judgement of character.[38] Regarding the second, general criteria of high qualifications or appointment to high judicial office, the Short Guide elaborates on the Parliamentary Assembly's responsibility in screening proposed candidates: they must be of 'mature professional experience and possess unquestionable qualifications for the exercise of a high judicial function on the international plane'.[39] This is further defined as candidates requiring 'professional experience of long duration at a high level'.[40]

---

[31]   Memorandum of the President of the European Court of Human Rights to the States with a View to preparing the Interlaken Conference (3 July 2009) 1, 3, https://www.echr.coe.int/Documents/Speech_20090703_Costa_Interlaken_ENG.pdf.

[32]   Interlaken Declaration (19 February 2010), https://www.echr.coe.int/Documents/2010_Interlaken_FinalDeclaration_ENG.pdf.

[33]   Ibid.

[34]   Ibid.

[35]   Ibid.

[36]   Council of Europe, *The Advisory Panel of Experts on Candidates for Election as Judge to the European Court of Human Rights: A short guide to the Panel's role and the minimum qualifications required of a candidate* (October 2020) 7, https://rm.coe.int/short-guide-panel-pdf-a5-2757-1197-8497-v-1/1680a0ae31.

[37]   Ibid.

[38]   Ibid.

[39]   Ibid.

[40]   Ibid.

Beyond the official requirements for the consideration of individual candidates, the Rules of Court outline policies with respect to the overall composition of judges. Three rules in particular focus on initiatives to bolster gender and geographical inclusion. First, the Court must pursue a policy aimed at securing the balanced representation of sexes in appointing both the President and Vice-Presidents of the Court and its Sections.[41] Second, each list of proposed judges ad hoc must include both sexes.[42] Finally, the composition of the Chambers and the Court must be balanced geographically and in gender, and reflect the different legal systems among the parties.[43]

Resolutions by the Parliamentary Assembly and Advisory Opinions from the Court have further outlined the contours of the Court's preferred composition, with evolving modifications. In Resolution 1366 (2004), the Parliamentary Assembly resolved that it would not consider lists of state nominations that only nominated candidates of one sex.[44] However, after considering the underrepresentation of women on the Court, the Parliamentary Assembly later added an exception to this rule permitting a list of candidates of the same sex if they are a sex which has less than 40% representation on the Court.[45] Additionally, in deciding between two candidates of equal merit, the Parliamentary Assembly resolved that, when possible, preference should be given to the candidate of the sex which is underrepresented at the Court.[46] In a 2008 Advisory Opinion, the Court itself held that the Parliamentary Assembly's practice of rejecting single-sex lists of nominees without permitting any exceptions was incompatible with the European Convention.[47] Instead, an exception to the preferred practice should apply

> where a Contracting Party has taken all the necessary and appropriate steps with a view to ensuring that the list contains a candidate of the under-represented sex, but without success, and especially where it has followed the Assembly's recommendations advocating an open and transparent procedure involving a call for candidatures.[48]

---

[41]   ECtHR Rules of Court (2022), Rule 14. The Court has never had a female President. At present, only one woman is Vice-President (and President of a Section) of the Court; all other Presidents and Vice-Presidents of the five Sections, including the Vice-President of the Court, are men.

[42]   Ibid., Rule 29(1)(a).

[43]   Ibid., Rule 25(2).

[44]   Council of Europe Parliamentary Assembly, 'Candidates for the European Court of Human Rights', Resolution 1366 (2004).

[45]   Council of Europe Parliamentary Assembly, 'Candidates for the European Court of Human Rights', Resolution 1426 (2005).

[46]   Council of Europe Parliamentary Assembly, 'Candidates for the European Court of Human Rights', Resolution 1366 (2004).

[47]   *Advisory Opinion on Certain Legal Questions Concerning the Lists of Candidates Submitted with a View to the Election of Judges to the European Court of Human Rights*, A47-2008-001 (12 February 2008), para. 54 (if such a list fulfilled all the requirements of Article 21 of the European Convention it would be deemed admissible).

[48]   Ibid.

In Resolution 1627 (2008), the Parliamentary Assembly accordingly amended its earlier Resolutions to provide that it would consider single-sex lists in exceptional circumstances where a party had taken all the necessary and appropriate steps, but was still unable to find a candidate of the underrepresented sex who satisfied all the requirements of Article 21 of the European Convention (as outlined above).[49] This was further amended by Resolution 1841 (2011) to provide that the exceptional circumstances must be so considered by a two-thirds majority of the votes cast by the members of the Subcommittee on the Election of Judges.[50]

2.2. THE INTER-AMERICAN COURT OF HUMAN RIGHTS

The IACtHR has seven judges, each of whom must be a national of a Member State of the OAS.[51] The judges are elected

> in an individual capacity from among jurists of the highest moral authority and of recognized competence in the field of human rights, who possess the qualifications required for the exercise of the highest judicial functions in conformity with the law of the state of which they are nationals or of the state that proposes them as candidates.[52]

Any judge ad hoc must possess the same qualifications.[53] The American Convention further stipulates that no two judges may be nationals of the same state.[54]

Requirements with respect to gender parity do not appear in the American Convention. However, in June 2017, the General Assembly of the OAS adopted a resolution encouraging states to

> nominate and elect persons that would ensure a membership that provides balance in terms of gender, representation of the different regions, population groups, and legal systems of the Hemisphere, while guaranteeing the requirements of independence, impartiality, and recognized competence in the field of human rights.[55]

---

[49] Council of Europe Parliamentary Assembly, 'Candidates for the European Court of Human Rights', Resolution 1627 (2008), para. 4. For discussion of the background to this amendment, see S. Hennette Vauchez, 'More Women – But Which Women? The Rule and Politics of Gender Balance at the European Court of Human Rights' (2015) 26 *European Journal of International Law* 195.

[50] Council of Europe Parliamentary Assembly, 'The amendment of various provisions of the Rules of Procedure of the Parliamentary Assembly – implementation of Resolution 1822 (2011) on the reform of the Parliamentary Assembly', Resolution 1841 (2011), para. 6.3.

[51] American Convention, Art. 52(1).

[52] Ibid., Art. 52(1).

[53] Ibid., Art. 55(4).

[54] Ibid., Art. 52(2).

[55] General Assembly of the Organization of American States, 'Promotion and Protection of Human Rights' (21 June 2017) AG/RES 2908 (XLVII-O/17), Section xv, para. 1.

The same resolution also committed to instruct the OAS Permanent Council to invite the judicial candidates proposed by Member States to deliver a public presentation to the Council prior to their election in order to describe their 'vision, proposals, and initiatives' that they might undertake if elected.[56] The resolution envisioned such presentations by the candidates would be 'disseminated as widely as possible' prior to the elections.[57]

2.3. THE AFRICAN COURT ON HUMAN AND PEOPLES' RIGHTS

The ACtHPR has 11 judges, each of whom is a national of the Member States of the AU.[58] No two judges may be nationals of the same state.[59] Each judge is elected in their individual capacity, with the requirement that they are a 'jurist[] of high moral character and of recognized practical, judicial or academic competence and experience in the field of human and peoples' rights'.[60] All judges are eligible for re-election.[61]

The Assembly of Heads of State and Government of the AU (Assembly) – namely, those who elect the Court's judges from a prepared list of candidates – must ensure that there is suitable representation of the main regions of Africa and of their principal legal traditions, as well as adequate gender representation among the judges.[62] The principles of gender parity, representation of primary legal traditions and geographical representation of the main continental regions further extend to the offices of the President and Vice-President (collectively the 'Bureau').[63] The Bureau follows a rotation system, as far as possible.[64]

Building on such rules concerning representation, in January 2016 the Executive Council of the AU adopted a resolution applicable to all AU organs and institutions, including the ACtHPR.[65] Noting that the ACtHPR was one of the AU organs where women were least represented in both elections and in the Court itself, the resolution proposed (but fell short of mandating) that at least half of the members of AU organs and institutions should be women.[66]

---

56 Ibid., Section xv, para. 2.
57 Ibid.
58 1998 Protocol, Art. 11(1).
59 Ibid., Art. 11(2).
60 Ibid., Art. 11(1).
61 Ibid., Art. 15(1).
62 Ibid., Art. 14(1)–(2).
63 ACtHPR Rules of Court (2020), Rule 10(2).
64 Ibid.
65 See Executive Council of the African Union, 'Modalities on the Implementation of the Criteria of Equitable Geographical and Gender Representation in AU Organs and Institutions', EX.CL/953(XXVIII) (23–28 January 2016).
66 Ibid., paras 13, 14, 26.

The most significant difference between the ACtJHPR and the ACtHPR is that the former will have 16 judges who are nationals of state parties to the AU rather than 11.[67] The provisions surrounding the ACtJHPR judges' qualifications and nationalities along with requirements of gender parity and geographical representation are nearly identical to those of the ACtHPR.[68]

2.4. A BRIEF COMPARISON

Within this section, perhaps the largest difference between the three Courts is the number of judges on each bench. With 47 judges, the ECtHR appointments dwarf those of the ACtHPR and IACtHPR, with 11 and seven judges respectively.[69] The ECtHR also stands alone in imposing no nationality limit on its judges, whereas both the ACtHPR and IACtHPR prohibit more than one judge of the same nationality.[70] In varying language, all three Courts require their judges to have a high moral character and recognised competence in the field of human rights.[71] Finally, the composition of each Court is subject to guidelines or rules concerning diversity in gender and geographic representation.[72] While geographic diversity has been observed in all three Courts, they have a mixed record relating to gender. In 2022 of the current 47 judges of the European Court of Human Rights, 16 are women;[73] three out of seven judges are women at the Inter-American Court of Human Rights;[74] and in the African Court on Human and Peoples' Rights, six of the 11 judges are women.[75]

---

[67] 2008 Protocol, Art. 3(1).

[68] See ibid., Arts 3(2)–(4) and 4, as amended by 2014 Protocol, Arts 2 and 3 of the Annex.

[69] European Convention, Art. 20; '47 Members States', https://www.coe.int/en/web/portal/47-members-states; 'Composition of the Court', https://www.echr.coe.int/Pages/home.aspx?p=court/judges&c.

[70] Protocol No. 11 to the Convention for the Protection of Human Rights and Fundamental Freedoms, restructuring the control machinery established thereby (concluded 11 May 1994, entered into force 1 November 1998) ETS 155; 1998 Protocol, Art. 11(2); American Convention, Art. 52(2).

[71] European Convention, Art. 21(1); 1998 Protocol, Art. 11(1); American Convention, Art. 52.(1).

[72] ECtHR Rules of Court (2022), Rules 14, 25(2), 29(1)(a); 1998 Protocol, Art. 14(1)–(2); General Assembly of the Organization of American States, 'Promotion and Protection of Human Rights' (21 June 2017) AG/RES 2908 (XLVII-O/17), Section xv, para. 1.

[73] 'Composition of the Court', https://www.echr.coe.int/Pages/home.aspx?p=court/judges&c.

[74] 'Meet the Judges', https://www.corteidh.or.cr/composicion.cfm?lang=en.

[75] 'Current Judges', https://www.african-court.org/wpafc/current-judges/.

3. APPOINTING AUTHORITY AND APPOINTMENT METHOD

3.1. THE EUROPEAN COURT OF HUMAN RIGHTS

The provisions of the European Convention concentrate all power of final judicial appointment for the ECtHR within the Parliamentary Assembly.[76] In electing the judge for each position allotted to the respective state parties, the Parliamentary Assembly chooses from a list of three candidates nominated by each state party.[77]

The ECtHR judicial appointment process has been criticised on a number of grounds, prompting several reforms over the years. Commentators have speculated that the 'delicate politics' which came hand-in-hand with the adoption of the European Convention contributed to the alleged shortcomings in the Court's appointment procedures.[78] Somewhat surprisingly, the European Convention's *travaux préparatoires* do not contain any record of discussions of judicial nominations procedures.[79] Subsequent reports indicate that drafters originally envisioned the judges would be elected by a simple majority: votes would be cast in separate, independent elections within the Council of Europe Committee of Ministers and the Parliamentary Assembly.[80] The discussion then evolved to consider the appointment of judges by an absolute majority of votes by the same two bodies.[81] However, the final adopted text excludes any reference to the Committee of Ministers within the judicial appointment process.[82]

The appointment requirements for the ECtHR were initially derived principally from Articles 21 and 22.[83] Neither article includes guidance or requirements with respect to the lists of nominees prepared by national governments.[84] Judicial nominations entailed a three-step procedure in which the national government would nominate three candidates for their allotted state slot, frequently ranking the candidates in order of the state's preference;[85]

---

[76] European Convention, Art. 22. See also J. Limbach, *Judicial Independence: Law and Practice of Appointments to the European Court of Human Rights* (Report, Interrights, May 2003) 7.

[77] European Convention, Art. 22.

[78] See J. Limbach, *Judicial Independence: Law and Practice of Appointments to the European Court of Human Rights* (Report, Interrights, May 2003) 7.

[79] Ibid.

[80] Ibid.

[81] Ibid.

[82] European Convention, Art. 22.

[83] B. Çali and S. Cunningham, 'Judicial Self Government and the Sui Generis Case of the European Court of Human Rights' (2018) 19(7) *German Law Journal* 1977, 1979.

[84] European Convention, Arts 21–22.

[85] J. Limbach, *Judicial Independence: Law and Practice of Appointments to the European Court of Human Rights* (Report, Interrights, May 2003) 8.

an ad hoc subcommittee of the Parliamentary Assembly would review the lists of candidates and their curricula vitae, granting each candidate a 15-minute interview;[86] then a full plenary vote by the Parliamentary Assembly would take place, at which time the candidate who received the majority of votes would be elected.[87]

Lacking any formal guidance from the Council of Europe, such procedures of state nominations within countries were criticised as opaque and politicised.[88] For instance, in the early to mid-2000s, members of the international legal community complained that the Court's appointment procedures were not conducive to installing judges of the requisite quality.[89] Further, observers argued that the review of candidates' applications was more pro forma than substantial, checking only that the applicants had the requisite language abilities and met other basic checklist requirements for a position on the Court.[90]

Reforms began in 1996 and continued over more than a decade to improve the credibility of the election process and, in turn, the quality of candidates appointed to the Court.[91] Resolutions between 1996 and 2009 standardised the formats of candidates' curricula vitae along with the Parliamentary Assembly's candidate interview process;[92] introduced recommendations for how the national selection process should be conducted, such as ensuring the candidates have experience in the field of human rights, and delivering the candidates' names to the Parliamentary Assembly in alphabetical order;[93] made clear that the Parliamentary Assembly would refuse to consider candidates that have not strictly complied with the criteria specified by the European Convention and subsequent Parliamentary Assembly resolutions;[94] required states to describe the process for the preparation of the lists of nominees when submitting

---

[86]   Ibid., 8–9.

[87]   Ibid., 9; B. Çali and S. Cunningham, 'Judicial Self Government and the Sui Generis Case of the European Court of Human Rights' (2018) 19(7) *German Law Journal* 1977, 1981.

[88]   J. Limbach, *Judicial Independence: Law and Practice of Appointments to the European Court of Human Rights* (Report, Interrights, May 2003) 8.

[89]   See United Kingdom House of Commons: International Affairs and Defence Section, *The European Court of Human Rights: the election of judges* (SN/IA/5949, 4 May 2011) 3–4.

[90]   J. Limbach, *Judicial Independence: Law and Practice of Appointments to the European Court of Human Rights* (Report, Interrights, May 2003) 8.

[91]   B. Çali and S. Cunningham, 'Judicial Self Government and the Sui Generis Case of the European Court of Human Rights' (2018) 19(7) *German Law Journal* 1977, 1979–80.

[92]   Council of Europe Parliamentary Assembly, 'Procedure for examining candidatures for the election of judges to the European Court of Human Rights', Resolution 1082 (1996).

[93]   Council of Europe Parliamentary Assembly, 'National procedures for nominating candidates for election to the European Court of Human Rights', Recommendation 1429 (1999).

[94]   Council of Europe Parliamentary Assembly, 'Candidates for the European Court of Human Rights', Resolution 1366 (2004) as modified by Resolutions 1426 (2005), 1627 (2008), 1841 (2011), 2002 (2014) and 2278 (2019).

that list;[95] and resolved to reject lists of nominees compiled 'in the absence of a fair, transparent and consistent national selection procedure'.[96]

The Committee of Ministers has also issued guidelines for the selection of candidates.[97] In 2010, the Committee of Ministers established an Advisory Panel of Experts to advise the Parliamentary Assembly on the nominees.[98] The Advisory Panel is made up of seven experts – both judges and lawyers – and must have geographical and gender balance.[99] Members of the Advisory Panel are appointed by the Committee of Ministers following consultation with the President of the Court.[100]

Before states submit their three nominees to the Parliamentary Assembly, they must first forward their lists to the Advisory Panel.[101] The role of the Advisory Panel is to review states' lists of prospective nominees and then advise the state on the suitability of its candidates.[102] The Panel's review process is written, and it does not conduct interviews.[103] When a state's list is later considered by the Parliamentary Assembly, the Advisory Panel makes its views available on a confidential basis.[104] As the Advisory Panel's final recommendations to states are non-binding, states may (and occasionally do) choose to submit their list of candidates to the Parliamentary Assembly despite a negative assessment

---

[95]   Council of Europe Parliamentary Assembly, 'Nomination of candidates and election of judges to the European Court of Human Rights', Resolution 1646 (2009).

[96]   Ibid.

[97]   Committee of Ministers of the Council of Europe, Resolution CM/Res(2012)40 (2012) 'Guidelines of the Committee of Ministers on the selection of candidates for the post of judge at the European Court of Human Rights' (29 March 2012).

[98]   Committee of Ministers of the Council of Europe, Resolution CM/Res(2010)26 (2010) 'Establishment of an Advisory Panel of Experts on Candidates for Election as Judge to the European Court of Human Rights' (10 November 2010).

[99]   Ibid.

[100] Ibid.

[101] Ibid., Art. 2. In 2014, a Resolution of the Committee of Ministers reiterated that states should supply their lists of nominees to the Advisory Panel prior to submission to the Parliamentary Assembly. See Committee of Ministers of the Council of Europe, Resolution CM/Res(2014)44 (2014) Amending Resolution CM/Res(2010)26 on the Establishment of an Advisory Panel of Experts on Candidates for Election to the European Court of Human Rights (26 November 2014).

[102] Committee of Ministers of the Council of Europe, Resolution CM/Res(2010)26 (2010) 'Establishment of an Advisory Panel of Experts on Candidates for Election as Judge to the European Court of Human Rights' (10 November 2010).

[103] Council of Europe, *The Advisory Panel of Experts on Candidates for Election as Judge to the European Court of Human Rights: A short guide to the Panel's role and the minimum qualifications required of a candidate* (October 2020) 4, https://rm.coe.int/short-guide-panel-pdf-a5-2757-1197-8497-v-1/1680a0ae31.

[104] Committee of Ministers of the Council of Europe, Resolution CM/Res(2010)26 (2010) 'Establishment of an Advisory Panel of Experts on Candidates for Election as Judge to the European Court of Human Rights' (10 November 2010).

of one or more candidates' suitability from the Advisory Panel.[105] This has contributed to concerns from both within and outside the Advisory Panel about the effectiveness of its role and the measure of positive impact that it brings to an intensely political process.[106] Proponents of the Advisory Panel's work however note that its recommendations have helped outline consistent expectations for ECtHR nominees, particularly with respect to prior work experience.[107]

Another initiative to improve the credibility of the election process of the ECtHR took place in 2015, at which time the ad hoc subcommittee of the Parliamentary Assembly was replaced by a permanent Committee on the Election of Judges to the European Court of Human Rights composed of legal experts instead of politicians.[108] Unlike the Advisory Panel, this Committee carries the responsibility of interviewing candidates.[109] Following the interview, the Committee makes a recommendation to the Parliamentary Assembly on the suitability of the candidate in question.[110] A representative of the Advisory Panel is also invited to participate in a briefing session held by the Committee before it carries out the interviews.[111]

3.2. THE INTER-AMERICAN COURT OF HUMAN RIGHTS

Each state party to the American Convention is permitted to propose up to three candidates for consideration during judicial elections.[112] The candidates may be nationals of the state that proposes them, or a national of any of other Member State within the OAS.[113] If a state chooses to nominate three candidates, at least one candidate must be a national of another OAS state.[114] From this list, the IACtHR judges are elected by an absolute majority vote conducted by secret ballot by the state parties to the American Convention during the General Assembly of the OAS.[115]

---

[105] B. Çali and S. Cunningham, 'Judicial Self Government and the Sui Generis Case of the European Court of Human Rights' (2018) 19(7) *German Law Journal* 1977, 1985–86.

[106] Ibid.

[107] Ibid.

[108] Council of Europe Parliamentary Assembly, 'Evaluation of the implementation of the reform of the Parliamentary Assembly', Resolution 2002 (2014).

[109] Council of Europe, *The Advisory Panel of Experts on Candidates for Election as Judge to the European Court of Human Rights: A short guide to the Panel's role and the minimum qualifications required of a candidate* (October 2020) 5, https://rm.coe.int/short-guide-panel-pdf-a5-2757-1197-8497-v-1/1680a0ae31.

[110] Ibid.

[111] Ibid.

[112] American Convention, Art. 53(2).

[113] Ibid.

[114] Ibid.

[115] Ibid., Art. 53(1).

Regional Human Rights Courts

No OAS resolutions or guidelines have attempted to regulate the national selection process.[116] Moreover, no OAS body is empowered to review the selection process or the qualifications of the proposed nominees.[117] The IACtHR nomination process has been criticised in light of the OAS's hands-off approach; a 2017 report co-authored by the International Commission of Jurists and Open Society Justice found that OAS states rarely exercise their right to nominate more than one candidate, which in turn contributes to a lack of diverse gender representation, underrepresentation of certain social groups and geographic regions, and limited competition at a regional level within the Americas.[118] The same study expressed doubt that OAS states had seriously considered the implementation of incentive structures to increase the number of qualified persons to apply for judgeships within the IACtHR.[119]

In contrast, the OAS has taken some steps to create transparency in the election process once the nominations are submitted by state parties. For example, a 2006 Resolution of the OAS General Assembly instructed the General Secretariat to publish the curriculum vitae of each nominee on its website and issue an accompanying press release so as to better inform OAS Member States and civil society of the judicial candidates' qualifications and backgrounds.[120]

The state parties may act within their complete discretion in their appointment of a judge ad hoc, provided that they meet the qualifications for all judges outlined by Article 52 of the American Convention.[121] In past cases, upon a challenge to the qualifications of an appointed judge ad hoc, the Court itself has scrutinised the qualifications of the judge in question. For example, in *González et al. v. Mexico* (2009), the Court rejected the appointment of a judge ad hoc after representatives of alleged victims within the case objected to the

---

[116] See International Commission of Jurists and Open Society Justice Initiative, *Strengthening from Within: Law and Practice in the Selection of Human Rights Judges and Commissioners* (2017) 41.

[117] Ibid.; O. Ruiz-Chiriboga, 'The Independence of the Inter-American Judge' (2012) 11(1) *The Law and Practice of International Courts and Tribunals* 111, 118 ('the entire process of appointment rests solely in the discretion of the States Parties').

[118] International Commission of Jurists and Open Society Justice Initiative, *Strengthening from Within: Law and Practice in the Selection of Human Rights Judges and Commissioners* (2017) 16.

[119] Ibid.

[120] General Assembly of the Organization of American States, 'Public Presentation of Candidates for Membership on the Inter-American Commission on Human Rights and the Inter-American Court of Human Rights' (6 June 2006) paras 2–3. See also General Assembly of the Organization of American States, 'Presentation of Candidates for Membership on the Inter-American Commission of Human Rights and the Inter-American Court of Human Rights' (7 June 2005) AG/RES 2120 (XXXV-O/05).

[121] O. Ruiz-Chiriboga, 'The Independence of the Inter-American Judge' (2012) 11(1) *The Law and Practice of International Courts and Tribunals* 111, 124; American Convention, Arts 52 and 55(4).

Intersentia

317

judge's appointment on the grounds that he did not fulfil the requirements of Article 52 of the American Convention.[122]

3.3. THE AFRICAN COURT ON HUMAN AND PEOPLES' RIGHTS

The appointment of judges to the ACtHPR begins with a request from the Secretary-General of the AU to each state party to present its nominees for the office of judge within 90 days.[123] State parties may each propose up to three candidates, at least two of whom must be nationals of that state.[124] The AU Assembly has not adopted a legal framework to regulate procedures for the nomination of candidates to the ACtHPR. However, the AU Commission (the AU's secretariat) has developed a practice of circulating a *note verbale* with accompanying guidelines in the lead-up to an election.[125] This includes information such as highlighting upcoming vacancies on the Court, reminding states of deadlines to submit lists of candidates, and providing a model curriculum vitae format for prospective candidates.[126]

Once the AU has received the nominations, the AU Office of the Legal Counsel (OLC) will process the nominations to ensure the candidates meet the criteria contained within the 1998 Protocol.[127] The OLC also checks for incompatibility with gender and regional balance quotas.[128] Following the OLC's vetting, the Secretary-General prepares a list of all candidates in alphabetical order.[129] This list is transmitted to the AU Member States at least 30 days before the next session of the Assembly.[130] A period of campaigning typically takes place at this time, with AU states arranging formal events to share and promote the profile of their respective candidates.[131] The Assembly elects the judges of

---

[122] *González et al. ('Cotton Field') v. Mexico*, Preliminary Objection, Merits, Reparations, and Costs, IACtHR Series C No. 205 (16 November 2009), n. 1. See also O. Ruiz-Chiriboga, 'The Independence of the Inter-American Judge' (2012) 11(1) *The Law and Practice of International Courts and Tribunals* 111, 124.

[123] 1998 Protocol, Art. 13(1).

[124] Ibid., Art. 12(1).

[125] International Commission of Jurists and Open Society Justice Initiative, *Strengthening from Within: Law and Practice in the Selection of Human Rights Judges and Commissioners* (2017) 44.

[126] Ibid.

[127] Ibid., 45.

[128] Ibid.

[129] 1998 Protocol, Art. 13(2). See also International Commission of Jurists and Open Society Justice Initiative, *Strengthening from Within: Law and Practice in the Selection of Human Rights Judges and Commissioners* (2017) 45.

[130] 1998 Protocol, Art. 13(2).

[131] International Commission of Jurists and Open Society Justice Initiative, *Strengthening from Within: Law and Practice in the Selection of Human Rights Judges and Commissioners* (2017) 45.

the Court.[132] Each judge is elected by secret ballot from the list prepared by the Secretary-General.[133]

The procedures of the ACtJHPR will differ in certain respects from those of the ACtHPR. The 2014 Protocol stipulates that following the receipt of state nominations, three alphabetical lists of candidates will be created by the Chairperson of the Commission of the AU.[134] List A will contain the names of candidates having recognised competence and experience in international law; List B will contain those which have competence and experience in international human rights and humanitarian law; and List C will contain the names of candidates with competence and experience in international criminal law.[135] During the first election, five judges will be elected from candidates on Lists A and B, and six from List C.[136] In contrast to the ACtHPR, the ACtJHPR will only allow the submission of two candidates from each state party.[137] Finally, whereas the ACtHPR requires states to take into account 'adequate' gender representation in the nomination process,[138] the ACtJHPR will require states to go one step further by taking account of 'equitable' gender representation in the nomination process.[139]

3.4. A BRIEF COMPARISON

The three Courts' judicial nomination and election procedures are similar in two key respects: each Court permits a nomination of up to three candidates,[140] and all three Courts elect judges by a vote of a body of representatives of state parties to the founding Convention or Protocol.[141] The Courts vary in their approach to oversight of the state nomination process. The ECtHR exercises the most control over the national selection process, going as far as to require states to describe their processes in the preparation of their lists of nominees.[142] Comparatively, states submitting their candidates to the ACtHPR and IACtHR have more autonomy over the national selection process. The main contributions of the AU and OAS to national selection procedures come after state nominees have been

---

[132]   1998 Protocol, Arts 14(1) and 13(2).
[133]   Ibid., Art. 14(1).
[134]   2008 Protocol, Art. 6(1), as amended by 2014 Protocol, Art. 4 of the Annex.
[135]   Ibid.
[136]   Ibid., Art. 6(3).
[137]   2008 Protocol, Art. 5(2).
[138]   1998 Protocol, Art. 12(2).
[139]   2008 Protocol, Art. 5(2).
[140]   European Convention, Art. 22; 1998 Protocol, Art. 12(1); American Convention, Art. 53(2).
[141]   European Convention, Art. 22; 1998 Protocol, Art. 14(1); American Convention, Art. 53(1).
[142]   Council of Europe Parliamentary Assembly, 'Nomination of candidates and election of judges to the European Court of Human Rights', Resolution 1646 (2009).

Intersentia

submitted. For instance, the AU OLC checks for incompatibilities with gender and regional balance quotas and ensures candidates meet the criteria contained within the 1998 Protocol,[143] and the OAS issues press releases of the nominees' profiles for the benefit of its Member States.[144]

4. TENURE AND GROUNDS FOR DISMISSAL

4.1. THE EUROPEAN COURT OF HUMAN RIGHTS

Judges are elected to the ECtHR for a period of nine years and they may not be re-elected.[145] Originally, judges were elected for a period of six years and could be re-elected once.[146] The nine-year term limit was introduced by Protocol No. 14 (2004),[147] designed to secure judicial independence by freeing judges from re-election concerns.[148] When re-election was on the table, judges may have felt pressure to perform their functions at the Court in a way that satisfied their national government so as to better their chances of a second nomination.[149] However, with the nine-year term came potential challenges vis-à-vis judges' reintegration into their national systems following their tenure at the ECtHR.[150] Resolution 1914 (2013) was designed to smooth the transition for the judges' return to their respective legal communities.[151] Resolution 1914 calls upon state parties to give judges and their families lifelong diplomatic immunity; to appoint judges to a position of similar calibre within their national judiciary, providing they have not reached the age of retirement; to include the judges' terms of office at the ECtHR within their national employment record; and to

---

[143]   International Commission of Jurists and Open Society Justice Initiative, *Strengthening from Within: Law and Practice in the Selection of Human Rights Judges and Commissioners* (2017) 45.

[144]   Ibid., 16.

[145]   European Convention, Art. 23(1).

[146]   European Convention, Art. 23, as amended by Protocol No. 11 to the Convention for the Protection of Human Rights and Fundamental Freedoms, restructuring the control machinery established thereby (concluded 11 May 1994, entered into force 1 November 1998) ETS 155. Prior to the reforms to the monitoring system introduced by Protocol No. 11, judges were elected for a period of nine years, which could be renewed: European Convention (original), Art. 40(1).

[147]   Protocol No. 14 to the Convention for the Protection of Human Rights and Fundamental Freedoms, amending the control system of the Convention (concluded 13 May 2004, entered into force 1 June 2010) ETS 194, Art. 2.

[148]   B. Çali and S. Cunningham, 'Judicial Self Government and the Sui Generis Case of the European Court of Human Rights' (2018) 19(7) *German Law Journal* 1977, 1991.

[149]   Ibid.

[150]   Ibid.

[151]   Ibid.

ensure that judges receive a pension equivalent to judges of the highest national court.[152]

Under Article 23(3) of the European Convention, a judge may only be dismissed from office if the other judges on the bench decide by a majority of two-thirds that the judge in question has ceased to fulfil the required conditions of holding office.[153] The Explanatory Report to Protocol No. 11 to the European Convention (1994) explains that this provision was designed to ensure the independence of the Court.[154] Before being removed from office, each judge is given the opportunity to be heard in a plenary session by the Court.[155] Any judge on the Court may set in motion the procedure for another's dismissal from their office.[156] There have been no reports of the initiation of dismissal proceedings against an ECtHR judge.[157]

4.2. THE INTER-AMERICAN COURT OF HUMAN RIGHTS

Judges on the IACtHR are elected for a period of six years and are eligible for re-election once.[158] At all times following their appointment to office, judges of the Court must conduct themselves in a manner that is 'in keeping with the office of those who perform an international judicial function'.[159]

Judges are accountable to the Court for their conduct.[160] This includes any violation, act of negligence or omission committed in the exercise of their functions as a judge of the Court.[161] The OAS General Assembly has disciplinary authority over the judges.[162] However, it may only exercise its authority over any judge at the request of the Court composed of the remaining judges.[163] When the Court requests that the OAS General Assembly discipline of one of its judges, it must detail its reasons for doing so in the request.[164] The abilities of the OAS General Assembly in this regard remain obscure as there are no

---

[152] Council of Europe Parliamentary Assembly, 'Ensuring the viability of the Strasbourg Court: structural deficiencies in States parties', Resolution 1914 (2013).
[153] European Convention, Art. 23(3).
[154] 'Council of Europe: Explanatory Report and Protocol No. 11 to the Convention for the Protection of Human Rights and Fundamental Freedoms, Restructuring the Control Machinery Established Thereby' (1994) 33 *International Legal Materials* 943, 953.
[155] ECtHR Rules of Court (2022), Rule 7.
[156] Ibid.
[157] W. Schabas, *The European Convention on Human Rights: A commentary* (OUP 2015) 672.
[158] American Convention, Art. 54(1).
[159] Statute of the Inter-American Court of Human Rights (1979), Art. 20(1).
[160] Ibid.
[161] Ibid.
[162] Ibid., Art. 20(2).
[163] Ibid.
[164] Ibid.

reported instances of judicial discipline or removal of IACtHR judges. This may suggest that disciplinary actions are more commonly conducted through informal avenues.[165]

4.3. THE AFRICAN COURT ON HUMAN AND PEOPLES' RIGHTS

The judges on the ACtHPR are elected for a period of six years and are eligible for re-election once.[166] The Court follows a system of staggered elections, which generally results in four judges' terms ending every two years.[167] All judges perform their duties of office on a part-time basis.[168]

A judge may only be suspended or removed from office if they no longer fulfil the required conditions to be a judge of the Court.[169] This decision must be made unanimously by the other judges of the Court.[170] Such a decision is final, unless the Assembly decides to set aside the finding at its next session.[171] When the removal of a judge from office is under consideration, the President (or if necessary, the Vice-President) will inform the judge in question by a written statement, including any relevant evidence and the potential grounds for dismissal.[172] A closed sitting of the Court shall be convened to discuss the grounds for dismissal; to permit the concerned judge to make a statement, along with providing any explanation or further information deemed salient; and to supply answers either orally or in writing to any questions posed by the other judges.[173] A second closed sitting shall then convene where the judge whose removal from office is under consideration shall not be present.[174] All judges shall state their opinion on the matter and, if required, a vote shall be taken on the suspension or removal of the judge in question.[175] Any decision in favour of suspension or removal will then be communicated to the Chairperson of the AU Commission.[176] No suspension or removal of an ACtHPR judge has been reported.

---

[165] See N. Tsereteli and H. Smekal, 'The Judicial Self-Government at the International Level – A New Research Agenda' (2018) 19(7) *German Law Journal* 2137, 2156–57.
[166] 1998 Protocol, Art. 15(1).
[167] Ibid. See also R. Smith, *International Human Rights Law* (9th ed., OUP 2020) 134.
[168] 1998 Protocol, Art. 15(4).
[169] Ibid., Art. 19(1).
[170] Ibid.
[171] Ibid., Art. 19(2).
[172] ACtHPR Rules of Court (2020), Rule 8(1).
[173] Ibid., Rule 8(2).
[174] Ibid., Rule 8(3).
[175] Ibid.
[176] Ibid., Rule 8(4).

Regional Human Rights Courts

In contrast to the ACtHPR, judges on the ACtJHPR will be elected for a single, non-renewable term of nine years.[177] The judges will be elected in staggered terms and perform their functions on a part-time basis.[178] With respect to the removal or suspension of a judge, the ACtJHPR strikes a different institutional balance between the judges and the Assembly, compared to the ACtHPR. While the unanimous vote of judges is required within the ACtHPR, their decision is effective unless enough support is gained in the Assembly to set it aside. By contrast, a lower majority of two-thirds of judges is required to trigger the procedure of removal or suspension of a judge from office in the ACtJHPR. Such a recommendation must receive enough support in the Assembly, which takes the final decision on the matter.[179]

4.4. A BRIEF COMPARISON

Judges are elected to both the ACtHPR and IACtHPR for six-year terms and are eligible for re-election once.[180] The ECtHR followed the same procedures until 2010, at which time the Court introduced nine-year terms without the option of re-election.[181]

In both the ECtHR and the ACtHPR, the dismissal of a judge hinges on the votes of the remaining judges on the bench. In the ECtHR, a two-thirds vote of the remaining judges is required for dismissal,[182] whereas the ACtHPR requires a unanimous decision.[183] Both the ECtHR and ACtHPR offer the judge in question an opportunity to make a statement before the Court votes on their dismissal.[184] The procedures for removal within the IACtHR are less certain, as neither its Rules of Procedure nor the American Convention provide information on this question. The only guidance comes from the IACtHR Statute, which states that the OAS General Assembly has 'disciplinary authority' over the judges.[185]

---

[177] 2008 Protocol, Art. 8(1), as amended by 2014 Protocol, Art. 5 of the Annex.
[178] Ibid., Art. 8(1)–(2), (4), as amended by 2014 Protocol, Art. 5 of the Annex.
[179] 2008 Protocol, Art. 9(2) and (4).
[180] 1998 Protocol, Art. 15(1); American Convention, Art. 54(1).
[181] Protocol No. 14 to the Convention for the Protection of Human Rights and Fundamental Freedoms, amending the control system of the Convention (concluded 13 May 2004, entered into force 1 June 2010) ETS 194.
[182] European Convention, Art. 23(3).
[183] 1998 Protocol, Art. 19(1).
[184] ECtHR Rules of Court (2022), Rule 7; ACtHPR Rules of Court (2020), Rule 8(2).
[185] Statute of the Inter-American Court of Human Rights (1979), Art. 20(2).

Intersentia

5. METHODS AND PARAMETERS TO ENSURE ADJUDICATORS' INDEPENDENCE AND IMPARTIALITY IN THE EXERCISE OF THEIR FUNCTIONS

5.1. THE EUROPEAN COURT OF HUMAN RIGHTS

The European Convention and Rules of Court each contain provisions to ensure the independence and impartiality of the Court's judges in the exercise of their functions. Over the years, these provisions have been strengthened in an effort to further increase the independence and impartiality of the Court.

5.1.1. Limitations on Judges' Abilities to Hear Cases

As with other international courts, the ECtHR has paid special attention to the consideration of whether a judge that is a national of a state party may (or should) sit on the case. For a clear understanding of the Court's procedure in this realm, a brief background on the Court's procedural methods in its consideration of cases is valuable. Taking into account the large size of the bench (47 judges, today),[186] the Court has the option to consider cases brought before it in a single-judge formation, in Committees of three judges, in Chambers of seven judges, and in a Grand Chamber of 17 judges.[187] The question of whether a judge who is a national of the state party concerned may or should sit on a case depends on the judicial formation in which the Court considers the case.

When the Court sits as a Committee of three judges, the Committee may invite the judge having the nationality of the state concerned to take the place of one of its existing members.[188] In making this decision, the Committee may take account of all relevant factors, including whether the state party has contested the Committee's decision to render a judgment on the merits.[189] When the Court sits as a Chamber of seven judges or in a Grand Chamber of 17 judges, the judge holding the nationality of the state party in question must be placed as an ex officio member of the Chamber or Grand Chamber.[190] In instances where there is no national judge of that state party, or if there is such a judge but they are unable to sit, the President of the Court shall choose an individual to serve in the capacity of a judge holding the nationality of the state party.[191] The judge

---

[186] 'Composition of the Court', https://www.echr.coe.int/Pages/home.aspx?p=court/judges&c.
[187] European Convention, Art. 26(1).
[188] Ibid., Art. 28(3).
[189] Ibid.
[190] Ibid., Art. 26(4).
[191] Ibid.

ad hoc will be chosen from a list of individuals submitted in advance by that state party.[192] When the Court considers the case as a single judge, that judge may not examine any application against their own national government or (if different) the state party by which they have been elected.[193] Further, in circumstances in which a party requests the referral of a decision of a Chamber to the Grand Chamber, the panel of judges that considers the referral request may not include a judge elected by the state party concerned, nor one who holds the nationality of that state party.[194]

Beyond nationality, additional rules govern whether a judge may consider a case. First, judges may not consider a case if they have a personal interest in its outcome or relationships with any of the parties.[195] This includes any spousal, parental, personal, professional, subordinate or close family relationship.[196] Second, a judge may not take part in the consideration of a case if they have previously acted in that case as an agent, advocate or adviser; if they had an interest in the case; if they were a member of another national or international tribunal or commission of inquiry; or if they took part in 'any other capacity'.[197] Third, if a judge continues to deal with a case in which they have participated in the consideration of the merits after the end of their term in office,[198] the judge will be removed from the case if they begin to take part in any administrative, political or professional activity which is incompatible with the judge's independence or impartiality.[199] Fourth, if the judge has expressed a public opinion that may 'objectively adversely affect their impartiality', the judge will be barred from consideration of a case.[200] Finally, a catch-all rule applies: if for any reason a judge's independence or impartiality may legitimately be called into question, the judge may not take part in the consideration of a case.[201] This is underscored by the oath or declaration that all judges and judges ad hoc must take at the beginning of the term to exercise their functions as a judge 'honourably, independently and impartially'.[202]

A 2020 study commissioned by the European Centre of Law and Justice found that judges withdrew from 313 cases between 2009 and 2019.[203] In the

---

[192]   Ibid.
[193]   ECtHR Rules of Court (2022), Rule 27(3); European Convention, Art. 26(3).
[194]   ECtHR Rules of Court (2022), Rule 24(5)(c).
[195]   Ibid., Rule 28(2)(a).
[196]   Ibid.
[197]   Ibid., Rule 28(2)(b).
[198]   See ibid., Rule 26(3).
[199]   Ibid., Rule 28(2)(c).
[200]   Ibid., Rule 28(2)(d).
[201]   Ibid., Rule 28(2)(e).
[202]   Ibid., Rule 3(1).
[203]   Delphine Loiseau, 'Annex no. 4 : les déports de juges de la CEDH entre 2009 et 2019', *European Center for Law and Justice* (January 2020), http://media.aclj.org/pdf/Annexe-4-Les-d%C3%A9ports-des-juges-%C3%A0-la-CEDH-entre-2009-et-2019.pdf.

majority of the cases, Rule 28 of the Rules of Court was cited as the reason for withdrawal – namely, the provision which addresses withdrawal for circumstances that call into question a judge's independence or impartiality.[204] In instances where a judge withdraws or is disqualified under Rule 28, the rationale behind the Court's decision to remove the judge is rarely publicly disclosed.[205] For example, in *Cyprus v. Turkey* (2001), Turkey objected to the judge elected by Cyprus before the Grand Chamber.[206] In response to Turkey's objections, the Grand Chamber decided that the judge in question should withdraw from the case, citing Rule 28.[207] The challenge was addressed in one paragraph in the final judgment without further explanation of the Grand Chamber's reasoning for the judge's disqualification.[208] In the same case, the judge elected by Turkey withdrew from consideration of the case of their own volition.[209] In describing the judge's withdrawal, the Court's final judgment again cited Rule 28 without further explanation.[210]

While the Court has not elaborated on the criteria applicable to challenges to the impartiality of the Court itself, it may be reasonable to assume that they should be similar to those that the Court has set out with respect to domestic courts. For the purposes of defining the right to a fair trial 'by an independent and impartial tribunal' under Article 6 of the European Convention, the ECtHR clarified that 'impartiality' normally denotes the absence of any prejudice or bias on the part of judges.[211] The Court uses two tests to assess the impartiality of domestic tribunals. The subjective test considers the personal beliefs and behaviour of individual judges, and examines whether a judge holds personal prejudice or bias in a particular case.[212] The Court presumes that domestic judges are impartial until there is proof of the contrary.[213] The objective test assesses whether, among other aspects, the composition of the tribunal in question adequately guarantees the exclusion of any legitimate doubt of its impartiality.[214] The Court acknowledges that there may at times be overlap between the subject matter of the two tests.[215]

---

[204]   Ibid. See also ECtHR Rules of Court (2022), Rule 28.

[205]   W. Schabas, *The European Convention on Human Rights: A commentary* (OUP 2015) 695.

[206]   *Cyprus v. Turkey*, ECtHR decision of 10 May 2001, application no. 25781/94, para. 8.

[207]   Ibid. See also ECtHR Rules of Court (2022), Rule 28(4).

[208]   *Cyprus v. Turkey*, ECtHR decision of 10 May 2001, application no. 25781/94, para. 8.

[209]   Ibid.

[210]   Ibid. See also ECtHR Rules of Court (2022), Rule 28.

[211]   *Nicholas v. Cyprus*, ECtHR decision of 9 January 2018, application no. 63246/10, para. 49.

[212]   Ibid. (citing *Morice v. France*, ECtHR decision of 23 April 2015, application no. 29369/10, para. 73).

[213]   Ibid., para. 50.

[214]   Ibid., para. 49 (citing *Morice v. France*, ECtHR decision of 23 April 2015, application no. 29369/10, para. 73).

[215]   Ibid., paras 51–52.

Specific rules govern the behaviour of former judges and judges ad hoc. A former judge may not represent a party or third party in proceedings relating to an application lodged with the Court before the date on which they ceased to hold office.[216] Moreover, former judges may not represent a party or third party in any capacity in proceedings before the Court until two years after they cease to hold office.[217] In a similar vein, judges ad hoc may not represent any party or third party in any capacity in proceedings before the Court for the duration of their appointment.[218]

5.1.2. Limitations on Judges' Roles Outside the Court

Judges' roles outside the Court are also limited by the European Convention and the Rules of Court in order to preserve the appearance and fact of independence and impartiality. During a judge's term in office, the judge may not engage in any activity that is incompatible with their independence or impartiality, or with the demands of their full-time role as a judge of the Court.[219] More specifically, the Rules of Court prohibit participation in political, administrative or professional activities that are incompatible with a judge's independence or impartiality or otherwise interfere with the demands of a full-time office.[220] Both the Rules of Court and the European Convention state that any question as to a judge's activities bearing on independence and impartiality shall be decided by the Court.[221] The Rules of Court further specify that judges shall declare to the President of the Court any additional activity in which they are partaking.[222] If the President and judge disagree on the nature of the activity – that is, whether it is incompatible with the judge's duty of independence and impartiality or interferes with the demands of a full-time office – the plenary Court decides the matter.[223]

5.1.3. Judicial Deliberations and Delivery of the Court's Judgments

Deliberations among judges must take place in private and remain secret.[224] The secrecy requirement only appears in the Rules of Court (drafted by the judges themselves) rather than in the European Convention.[225] The decision to keep deliberations secret is reinforced by the oath or declaration that all new judges

---

[216] ECtHR Rules of Court (2022), Rule 4(2).
[217] Ibid.
[218] Ibid., Rule 29(1)(c).
[219] European Convention, Art. 21(4).
[220] ECtHR Rules of Court (2022), Rule 4(1).
[221] Ibid., Rule 4(1); European Convention, Art. 21(4).
[222] ECtHR Rules of Court (2022), Rule 4(1).
[223] Ibid.
[224] Ibid., Rule 22(1).
[225] N. Arold, *The Legal Culture of the European Court of Human Rights* (Brill 2007) 76.

and judges ad hoc are required to take at the beginning of their terms.[226] Only the judges may take part in the deliberations.[227] Except for the Registrar and interpreters whose assistance is deemed necessary, any other person must obtain an exception to be present during the deliberations through a special decision of the Court.[228] Before voting on any matter in Court, the President may request each or any of the judges to state their opinions on it.[229]

In the delivery of the Court's judgment, any judge who has taken part in the consideration of the case is entitled to annex a separate opinion concurring with or dissenting from that judgment or, alternatively, to attach a simple statement of dissent.[230]

5.1.4. Benefits, Privileges and Immunities

The judges of the Court are afforded certain benefits, privileges and immunities in order to better preserve their independence and impartiality. For instance, the judges are guaranteed certain standards of remuneration, medical and social insurance, and pension entitlements.[231] Under the European Convention, judges are also entitled to those privileges and immunities that are outlined in Article 40 of the Statute of the Council of Europe – namely, those 'reasonably necessary for the fulfilment of their functions'.[232] Such privileges have been upheld in practice. For example, in a 2011 case before the ECtHR considering the investigation of the wife of a former judge for fraud, the Court underscored that diplomatic immunity for judges and their families must be maintained, barring an official waiver of immunity.[233]

5.2. THE INTER-AMERICAN COURT OF HUMAN RIGHTS

5.2.1. Limitations on Judges' Abilities to Hear Cases

The IACtHR distinguishes between judges' abilities to hear cases in interstate proceedings on the one hand, and proceedings referred by the Inter-American

---

[226] ECtHR Rules of Court (2022), Rule 3(1).

[227] Ibid., Rule 22(2).

[228] Ibid.

[229] Ibid., Rule 22(3).

[230] European Convention, Art. 45(2); ECtHR Rules of Court (2022), Rule 74(2).

[231] Committee of Ministers of the Council of Europe, Resolution CM/Res(2009)5 on the Status and Conditions of Service of Judges of the European Court of Human Rights (23 September 2009).

[232] European Convention, Art. 51; Statute of the Council of Europe (concluded 5 May 1949, entered into force 3 August 1949) 87 UNTS 103, Art. 40.

[233] B. Çali and S. Cunningham, 'Judicial Self Government and the Sui Generis Case of the European Court of Human Rights' (2018) 19(7) *German Law Journal* 1977, 1999. See also

Commission on Human Rights on behalf of an individual ('individual petitions') on the other.

Before 2009, judges of the IACtHR were permitted to hear cases against state parties of whom they themselves were nationals.[234] If such a judge were to hear a case against their own country and the respondent state did not have a corresponding judge of its own nationality on the Court – or alternatively, if this latter judge withdrew from the case – the respondent state was permitted to appoint a judge ad hoc.[235] This position is codified in both the American Convention and the Statute of the IACtHR.[236] However, in a September 2009 Advisory Opinion, the Court created an exception to this rule, choosing to distinguish between interstate proceedings and cases arising from individual petitions.[237] The Court reasoned that the judge ad hoc system had been designed to ensure procedural equity between the parties.[238] Thus, the Court decided that the right of a respondent state to appoint a judge ad hoc in a proceeding was not applicable in cases arising from individual petitions, but to interstate cases alone.[239] The Court also held that, in cases arising from individual petitions, judges who hold the same nationality as the respondent state party must recuse themselves from that case.[240] This final policy adjustment was intended to bolster the perceptions of judicial impartiality at the Court.[241] The Rules of Procedure have since been amended to reflect each of these new positions.[242]

Judges on the IACtHR are also prohibited from considering matters in which they have previously participated as agent, counsel, advocate, member of a national or international court or investigatory committee, or in any other

---

V. Pop, 'Strasbourg backs Romanian judge in jewellery-for-verdicts case', *EU Observer* (20 October 2011), https://euobserver.com/justice/114006.

[234] R. Muscat and G.C. Palomares, 'Internal Organisation of Regional Human Rights Courts: The European Court of Human Rights and the Inter-American Court of Human Rights' in P. Pinto de Albuquerque and K. Wojtyczek (eds), *Judicial Power in a Globalized World* (Springer 2019) 313, 317.

[235] Ibid.

[236] American Convention, Art. 55(1); Statute of the Inter-American Court of Human Rights (1979), Art. 10(1).

[237] See *Article 55 of the American Convention on Human Rights*, Advisory Opinion, Inter-American Court of Human Rights, Series A No. 20 (29 September 2009).

[238] Ibid., paras 36–37.

[239] Ibid., paras 44–45. See also R. Muscat and G.C. Palomares, 'Internal Organisation of Regional Human Rights Courts: The European Court of Human Rights and the Inter-American Court of Human Rights' in P. Pinto de Albuquerque and K. Wojtyczek (eds), *Judicial Power in a Globalized World* (Springer 2019) 313, 317.

[240] *Article 55 of the American Convention on Human Rights*, Advisory Opinion, Inter-American Court of Human Rights, Series A No. 20 (29 September 2009), paras 84–86.

[241] Ibid., paras 84–86. See also R. Muscat and G.C. Palomares, 'Internal Organisation of Regional Human Rights Courts: The European Court of Human Rights and the Inter-American Court of Human Rights' in P. Pinto de Albuquerque and K. Wojtyczek (eds), *Judicial Power in a Globalized World* (Springer 2019) 313, 318.

[242] Rules of Procedure of the Inter-American Court of Human Rights, Rule 19.

capacity.[243] If a judge considers that there is cause for their own disqualification under the Statute of the Court, they must alert the President and provide their reasoning.[244] If the President disagrees with the assessment of the judge, the Court shall decide the matter.[245] The Court will also decide the matter if the President believes there is reason for a judge's disqualification and the judge in question disagrees.[246]

Judges have been disqualified from the consideration of cases in a number of instances. For example, in the *Case of Yean and Bosico Children v. The Dominican Republic* (2004), a judge ad hoc was disqualified as she had previously represented the Dominican Republic in proceedings before the Inter-American Commission on Human Rights, where the same parties had attempted to settle the case.[247] In the *Case of the Moiwana Community v. Suriname* (2005), the Court ordered a judge ad hoc to withdraw from the case after filings revealed that the judge had served as counsel to the state party in interim injunction proceedings.[248] In the *Case of Heliodoro Portugal v. Panama* (2008), a national newspaper revealed that the government of Panama had made a US\$45,000 payment to the appointed judge ad hoc.[249] The judge ad hoc subsequently recused himself from the case, which the President accepted.[250]

5.2.2. Limitations on Judges' Roles Outside the Court

Throughout their terms of office, judges of the IACtHR are prohibited from becoming members of or high-ranking officials in the executive branch of government, with two exceptions: first, those positions that do not place the judge under the direct control of the executive branch; second, diplomatic agent positions that are not Chiefs of Missions to the OAS or to any of its Member States.[251] Judges may also not hold office within an international organisation nor

---

[243] Statute of the Inter-American Court of Human Rights (1979), Art. 19(1).

[244] Ibid., Art. 19(2).

[245] Ibid.

[246] Ibid., Art. 19(3).

[247] *Case of the Yean and Bosico Children v. The Dominican Republic*, IACtHR Series C No. 130 (4 May 2004), para. 10 and operative para. 1. See also O. Ruiz-Chiriboga, 'The Independence of the Inter-American Judge' (2012) 11(1) *The Law and Practice of International Courts and Tribunals* 111, 128.

[248] *Case of the Moiwana Community v. Suriname*, IACtHR Series C No. 124 (15 March 2005), paras 8–12. See also O. Ruiz-Chiriboga, 'The Independence of the Inter-American Judge' (2012) 11(1) *The Law and Practice of International Courts and Tribunals* 111, 128.

[249] O. Ruiz-Chiriboga, 'The Independence of the Inter-American Judge' (2012) 11(1) *The Law and Practice of International Courts and Tribunals* 111, 129. See also *Case of Heliodoro Portugal v. Panama*, IACtHR Series C No. 186 (12 August 2008).

[250] O. Ruiz-Chiriboga, 'The Independence of the Inter-American Judge' (2012) 11(1) *The Law and Practice of International Courts and Tribunals* 111, 129; *Case of Heliodoro Portugal v. Panama*, IACtHR Series C No. 186 (12 August 2008), n. 2.

[251] Ibid., Art. 18(1)(a).

Regional Human Rights Courts

take up any other position that might affect their independence and impartiality, prevent the discharge of their duties, or compromise the dignity and prestige of their office.[252]

5.2.3. Judicial Deliberations and Delivery of the Court's Judgments

Both the Statute of the Court and the Court's Rules of Procedure dictate that all deliberations take place in private.[253] The contents of deliberations remain secret unless the Court decides otherwise.[254] All judges must take an oath or make a declaration to this effect at the beginning of their tenure.[255] Both the hearings and deliberations of the Court are preserved on audio recordings.[256]

In the delivery of the Court's judgments, any judge who has taken part in consideration of the case is entitled to append a separate, reasoned opinion to the judgment either concurring or dissenting.[257]

5.2.4. Benefits, Privileges and Immunities

The judges receive emoluments set in accordance with the obligations imposed on them in respect of their service, bearing in mind the importance and independence of their functions.[258] The judges ad hoc also receive emoluments established by the Court's regulations and within its budget.[259] Further, judges receive per diem and travel allowances, when appropriate.[260]

From the beginning of their term in office, all judges of the Court enjoy the immunities extended to diplomatic agents in accordance with international law.[261] During the exercise of their official functions, they also enjoy diplomatic privileges necessary for the performance of their duties.[262] Judges of the IACtHR are not liable for any decision or opinion issued in the exercise of their functions.[263]

---

[252] Ibid., Art. 18(1)(b)–(c).
[253] Ibid., Art. 24(1); Rules of Procedure of the Inter-American Court of Human Rights, Rule 67(1).
[254] Statute of the Inter-American Court of Human Rights (1979), Art. 24(2).
[255] Rules of Procedure of the Inter-American Court of Human Rights, Rule 9(1); Statute of the Inter-American Court of Human Rights (1979), Art. 11(1).
[256] Rules of Procedure of the Inter-American Court of Human Rights, Rule 15(4).
[257] Ibid., Rule 65(2).
[258] American Convention, Art. 72.
[259] Statute of the Inter-American Court of Human Rights (1979), Art. 17(2).
[260] American Convention, Art. 72; Statute of the Inter-American Court of Human Rights (1979), Art. 17(3).
[261] American Convention, Art. 70(1).
[262] Ibid.
[263] Ibid., Art. 70(2).

Intersentia

5.3. THE AFRICAN COURT ON HUMAN AND PEOPLES' RIGHTS

5.3.1. Limitations on Judges' Abilities to Hear Cases

The ACtHPR prohibits judges from hearing any case in which the state of which they are a national is a state party,[264] or if the state that nominated that judge to the Court is a state party.[265] Equally, judges are prevented from hearing cases in which they have a manifest conflict of interest. This includes any personal interest in the case, such as a spousal, parental, personal, professional, subordinate or other close family relationship with any of the parties; if the judge has previously acted in the case as agent, counsel, advocate or as a member of a national or international court or commission of inquiry (or in any other capacity); if the judge has expressed a public opinion that may objectively adversely affect their impartiality; or if for any other reason the judge's independence or impartiality may legitimately be called into doubt.[266] The 1998 Protocol ties the guarantees of judicial independence and impartiality to the standards applicable under international law.[267]

The ACtJHPR also prohibits judges of the same nationality of a state party before the Court to consider that case.[268] Like the ACtHPR, there are no rules which govern whether a judge must take a case when a state party of their own nationality is concerned. The 2008 Protocol contains similar provisions to those governing the ACtHPR on a judge's recusal based on conflicting interests.[269]

5.3.2. Limitations on Judges' Roles Outside the Court

With the exception of the President of the Court, each judge performs their functions in a part-time role.[270] Thus, judges are permitted to engage in work and activities extraneous to the Court, albeit with certain limitations. The Court names 'judicial independence from any partisanship, bias, influence, whether it comes from States, NGOs, funding agencies or individuals' as one of its core values.[271] In line with these principles, both the 1998 Protocol and the Rules of Court state that the position of a judge is incompatible with any activity that might interfere with the independence or impartiality of the judge, or with the demands of the office.[272] The Rules of Court further maintain that judges are

---

[264]   1998 Protocol, Art. 22; ACtHPR Rules of Court (2020), Rule 9(2).
[265]   ACtHPR Rules of Court (2020), Rule 9(3).
[266]   Ibid., Rule 9(4).
[267]   1998 Protocol, Art. 17(1).
[268]   2008 Protocol, Art. 14(3).
[269]   Ibid., Art. 14(1).
[270]   1998 Protocol, Art. 15(4).
[271]   'Basic Information', https://www.african-court.org/wpafc/basic-information/.
[272]   Ibid., Art. 18; ACtHPR Rules of Court (2020), Rule 5(1).

prohibited from holding political, diplomatic or administrative positions, and may not function as government legal advisers.[273] Judges are bound to declare 'any activity' to the Court which may raise such issues of incompatibility.[274] In an effort to address such concerns upfront, the AU Commission issues guidelines prior to each election instructing candidates' résumés to be as detailed as possible, including 'political and other associations' and 'activism'.[275] The latter category is broadly defined.[276]

Like the ACtHPR, the ACtJHPR will prohibit its judges from engaging in all activities which might infringe on their independence or impartiality.[277]

5.3.3. Judicial Deliberations and Delivery of the Court's Judgments

The deliberations of the Court are held in camera and classified as confidential.[278] The Registrar, the Deputy Registrar, other legal officers of the Registry and any translators deemed necessary may also sit in on the deliberations; all are bound by the same rules of confidentiality.[279] All new judges must take an oath or make a declaration to preserve the confidentiality of judicial deliberations, even after their term in office has expired.[280] The Court's deliberations last for two consecutive, ordinary sessions following the close of pleadings.[281]

Any judge who has heard the case is permitted to append a separate or dissenting opinion which shall be published along with the decision of the Court.[282] Alternatively, a judge who wishes to differ from the majority without providing a reason may do so by way of a declaration.[283]

Regarding the ACtJHPR, no provisions on the secrecy of deliberations are contained within the 2008 Protocol or 2014 Protocol. Presumably, such provisions will eventually appear in the Rules of Court. Like the ACtHPR, the ACtJHPR will require its judges to make a solemn declaration at the beginning of their tenure pledging their impartiality and commitment to preserving the integrity of the Court.[284] Finally, the ACtJHPR will follow the ACtHPR in

---

273 ACtHPR Rules of Court (2020), Rule 5(2).
274 Ibid., Rule 5(3).
275 International Commission of Jurists and Open Society Justice Initiative, *Strengthening from Within: Law and Practice in the Selection of Human Rights Judges and Commissioners* (2017) 44.
276 Ibid.
277 2008 Protocol, Art. 13(1).
278 ACtHPR Rules of Court (2020), Rule 67(2).
279 Ibid.
280 Ibid., Rule 3(1).
281 Ibid., Rule 67(3).
282 Ibid., Rule 70(1)–(2).
283 Ibid., Rule 70(3).
284 2008 Protocol, Art. 11(1).

permitting any judge to append a separate or dissenting opinion to the Court's judgment.[285]

5.3.4. Benefits, Privileges and Immunities

Throughout their terms of office, judges of the ACtHPR enjoy the immunities of diplomatic agents in accordance with international law.[286] The 1998 Protocol further states that no judge of the Court shall be held liable for any decision or opinion issued in the exercise of their functions.[287]

The judges on the ACtJHPR will enjoy the same privileges and immunities as those on the ACtHPR.[288]

5.4. A BRIEF COMPARISON

Several methods to ensure judges' independence and impartiality are replicated throughout all three Courts. First, each Court requires their judges to take an oath or make a declaration at the beginning of their tenure to perform their duties of office honourably and impartially.[289] Second, each Court requires its judges to abstain from any activity that is incompatible with their independence or impartiality, or the demands of their office.[290] Third, all the Courts' deliberations take place in secret, and the judges of each office must take an oath or declaration to preserve the confidentiality of the deliberations.[291] Fourth, judges on all three Courts may append a separate opinion to the final judgment of a case.[292] Finally, all three Courts allow their judges the benefit of certain privileges and immunities.[293]

The main respect in which the Courts differ within this section is on the question of whether a judge who holds the same nationality as a state party may (or in some instances, must) take part in the consideration of that case.

---

[285] Ibid., Art. 44.

[286] 1998 Protocol, Art. 17(3).

[287] Ibid., Art. 17(4).

[288] 2008 Protocol, Art. 15.

[289] ECtHR Rules of Court (2022), Rule 3(1); ACtHPR Rules of Court (2020), Rule 4(1); Statute of the Inter-American Court of Human Rights (1979), Art. 11(1).

[290] European Convention, Art. 21(4); 1998 Protocol, Art. 18; ACtHPR Rules of Court (2020), Rule 5(1); Statute of the Inter-American Court of Human Rights (1979), Art. 18(1)(b)–(c).

[291] ECtHR Rules of Court (2022), Rules 3(1) and 4(1); ACtHPR Rules of Court (2020), Rules 3(1) and 67(2); Statute of the Inter-American Court of Human Rights (1979), Arts 11(1) and 24(2); Rules of Procedure of the Inter-American Court of Human Rights, Rule 9(1).

[292] European Convention, Art. 45(2); ECtHR Rules of Court (2022), Rule 74(2); ACtHPR Rules of Court (2020), Rule 70; Rules of Procedure of the Inter-American Court of Human Rights, Rule 65(2).

[293] European Convention, Art. 51; 1998 Protocol, Art. 17(3); American Convention, Art. 70(1).

The approach of the ECtHR hinges on how the Court hears a case. For example, if the case is considered by a single judge, that judge is barred from considering cases against their own national government (or the state party by which they have been elected).[294] In contrast, if the Court considers the case in a Chamber or Grand Chamber, a judge holding the nationality of the state party in question must be placed as an ex officio member of the Chamber or Grand Chamber.[295] The ACtHPR goes a step further than the ECtHR. Here, judges are prohibited from hearing any case in which the state of which they are a national is a state party,[296] or if the state that nominated that judge to the Court is a state party.[297] The IACtHR takes a more nuanced approach, choosing to distinguish between interstate proceedings and those on behalf of the individual. In the latter instance, judges who hold the same nationality as the respondent state party must recuse themselves from that case.[298] No such requirement is present in interstate proceedings.

---

[294]   ECtHR Rules of Court (2022), Rule 27(3); European Convention, Art. 26(3).

[295]   European Convention, Art. 26(4).

[296]   1998 Protocol, Art. 22; ACtHPR Rules of Court (2020), Rule 9(2).

[297]   ACtHPR Rules of Court (2020), Rule 9(3).

[298]   *Article 55 of the American Convention on Human Rights*, Advisory Opinion, Inter-American Court of Human Rights, Series A No. 20 (29 September 2009), paras 84–86.

THE INDEPENDENCE AND IMPARTIALITY OF ADJUDICATORS AT THE WORLD INTELLECTUAL PROPERTY ORGANIZATION ARBITRATION AND MEDIATION CENTER

Yuliya CHERNYKH[*]

1. Criteria for the Selection of the Adjudicators 338
2. Which Authority Appoints the Adjudicators? 340
3. The Method for Appointing the Adjudicators 342
4. Methods to Balance the Appointing Authority's Influence on the Appointment of the Adjudicators 343
5. Parameters to Ensure that the Adjudicators Act Independently and Impartially 344
6. Consequences for the Adjudicator of a Breach by the Adjudicator of the Requirement to Act Independently and Impartially 346
7. Enforceability of a Final Decision that was Rendered by an Adjudicator who Breached the Requirement to Act Independently and Impartially 349

In existence as of 1994, the World Intellectual Property Organization (WIPO) Arbitration and Mediation Center (WIPO Center) provides alternative dispute resolution services for IP- and technology-related disputes. Apart from international arbitration, the WIPO Center also offers mediation, expert determination and domain name dispute resolution.[1] International arbitration takes one of two forms (ordinary arbitration proceedings or expedited arbitration proceedings) and results in arbitral awards enforceable under the New York Convention on the Recognition and Enforcement of Foreign Arbitral

---

[*]   This report was finalised in August 2021.
[1]   For domain name disputes, the WIPO Center operates as one of the service providers under the Rules for Uniform Domain Name Dispute Resolution Policy.

Intersentia

Awards. Save for agreements to the contrary, expert determination is binding and results in expert decisions of a contractual nature that have binding force on the parties. Decisions of the domain name panel are administrative in nature and subject to execution without any additional procedures by a relevant domain name registrar. Overall, the procedures before the WIPO Center are governed by five sets of rules: the WIPO Mediation Rules, the WIPO Arbitration Rules, the WIPO Expedited Arbitration Rules, the WIPO Expert Determination Rules, and the Rules for Uniform Domain Name Dispute Resolution Policy used together with the WIPO Supplemental Rules for Uniform Domain Name Dispute Resolution Policy. While setting a somewhat different regime for the appointment and challenge of mediators, arbitrators, experts and domain name panellists, all WIPO rules nevertheless expressly require them to be independent and impartial.[2]

This report focuses on the standard of independence and impartiality for those adjudicators who *resolve* disputes under the WIPO rules, such as arbitrators, experts and panellists in domain name disputes. Because mediators *facilitate* the parties' settlement but do not settle disputes, they are not addressed in the analysis.

1. CRITERIA FOR THE SELECTION OF THE ADJUDICATORS

Rather unsurprisingly, specialist knowledge and expertise appear to be natural factors for the choice of prospective adjudicators. While the WIPO rules do not set any express criteria for adjudicators relating to their experience or knowledge in the field of IP and technology disputes, the requirement nevertheless may be said to be implicit in the overarching specialisation of the WIPO Center and the maintained list of mediators, arbitrators, experts and panellists for domain name disputes – the WIPO List of Neutrals.

In relation to the specialisation of the arbitral institute, the WIPO Center indeed reports on a broad range of IP- and technology-related disputes being submitted for resolution under its rules. According to the WIPO Center's statistics, the following types of agreements are typical of its caseload:

- licensing agreements (involving trademarks, patents, copyright, software);
- research and development agreements;
- technology transfer agreements;

---

[2]   Article 8 of the WIPO Mediation Rules, Article 22 of the WIPO Arbitration Rules, Article 17 of the WIPO Expedited Arbitration Rules, Article 10 of the WIPO Expert Determination Rules, and Article 7 of the UDRP Rules used together with the WIPO Supplemental Rules.

The World Intellectual Property Organization Arbitration and Mediation Center

- distribution agreements and franchising agreements;
- information technology agreements;
- data processing agreements;
- joint venture agreements;
- consultancy agreements;
- art marketing agreements;
- digital copyright;
- TV distribution and formats;
- film production;
- copyright collective management; and
- cases arising out of agreements in the settlement of prior court litigation.[3]

In addition to the identified types of agreements, disputes relating to domain names have constantly been growing since 2013 and in 2020 exceeded 4,000 cases a year.[4]

The specificity of the disputes submitted to the WIPO Center for adjudication makes specialist knowledge and experience important components of its efficient dispute resolution and requires the arbitral institution to run the WIPO List of Neutrals. The directory includes over 2,000 arbitrators, mediators, experts and panellists from more than 90 jurisdictions.[5] Inclusion in the list is not automatic and requires a decision by the specially designed WIPO Center Neutrals Committee. In its decision on approval or rejection, the WIPO Center Neutrals Committee takes into account such factors as legal or technical qualifications, professional experience (including in the areas of intellectual property law and technical or business areas), professional experience in dispute resolution, publications and professional memberships.

The operation of the List of Neutrals is somewhat unusual. It is not formally binding, nor is it publicly accessible in its entirety. It is only possible to get a complete understanding of who is included only in relation to the domain name panellists, whose names and expertise are made fully accessible on the WIPO site,[6] but not in relation to other neutrals. And while some domain name panellists may also adjudicate disputes as arbitrators or experts, the full list of all adjudicators included in the list remains unknown. The WIPO Center uses the WIPO List of Neutrals in its own appointments, whereas the parties to arbitration and expert determination still, if the circumstances so permit and subject to the ultimate approval by the WIPO Center, may nominate arbitrators and experts as they wish. In their nominations (in arbitration and expert determination), the

---

3   WIPO Caseload Summary available at https://www.wipo.int/amc/en/center/caseload.html.
4   Ibid.
5   WIPO List of Neutrals, available at https://www.wipo.int/amc/en/neutrals/index.html.
6   WIPO List of Panelists, available at https://www.wipo.int/amc/en/domains/panel/panelists.jsp.

parties are not bound to ensure nominations of those adjudicators who are on the WIPO List of Neutrals.

The absence of a formal requirement in the rules on the experience or qualifications of an adjudicator does not preclude the parties agreeing on specific criteria for their adjudicators. This party autonomy makes sense for arbitration and expert determination, where a broad range of disputes of varying character may pop up and the parties are in a position to anticipate the specialisation and other criteria needed for their adjudicators, but not for domain name disputes, where disputes are rather uniform and where the parties or appointing authorities select from the list of competent panellists. If the parties agree on the qualifications, the terms of their agreement shall be observed regardless of who makes nominations and appointments.[7]

Finally, the WIPO Arbitration Rules and the WIPO Expedited Arbitration Rules also expressly enable the parties to agree on the nationality of their arbitrators.[8] If the parties have not agreed, a neutral nationality shall be preferred unless 'special circumstances' (such as particular qualifications) require the appointment of a particular person regardless of his or her nationality.[9]

2. WHICH AUTHORITY APPOINTS THE ADJUDICATORS?

Which authority appoints the adjudicators depends on the type of proceedings. Parties enjoy a varying scope of autonomy in defining who makes an appointment. For arbitration and expert determination, the parties may jointly decide which authority appoints their adjudicators. For domain name disputes, parties do not choose the procedure for appointment; they nevertheless agree on the identity of the presiding panellist if an administrative panel consists of three arbitrators. If the parties do not determine a specific procedure for the appointment of their arbitrators or experts or do not agree on the identity of the presiding panellist for domain name disputes, the default regulation under the respective rules applies. These rules allocate a critical role to the WIPO Center as an appointing authority in the approvals/confirmations of the parties' nominations in arbitration, and the exercise of direct appointment of arbitrators and experts or election and

---

[7] A right to agree on the qualification of adjudicators follows (expressly or implicitly) from the provisions of Article 19(b)(i) of the WIPO Arbitration Rules, Article 14(b)(i) of the WIPO Expedited Arbitration Rules, and Article 9(c) and (d)(i) of the WIPO Expert Determination Rules.

[8] Article 20(a) of the WIPO Arbitration Rules and Article 15(a) of the WIPO Expedited Arbitration Rules.

[9] Article 20(b) of the WIPO Arbitration Rules and Article 15(b) of the WIPO Expedited Arbitration Rules.

selection from the list of candidates or the (general) WIPO list of domain name panellists for domain name disputes.

Below is a summary of the default regulation of authorities involved in the appointment of adjudicators in arbitration, expert determination and procedures on domain name disputes.

In WIPO arbitration, the parties *nominate* arbitrators. *Nominated* arbitrators become *appointed* arbitrators only after their approval by the WIPO Center. Whether a nomination of a prospective arbitrator is individual or joint (by both parties) depends upon the number of adjudicators on the panel. Individual nomination takes place if the panel consists of three arbitrators and each party nominates its own arbitrator, while joint nomination is used in the case of a sole arbitrator.[10] Apart from the parties, the appointed arbitrators in tribunals of three members are also entrusted with the right to nominate the presiding arbitrator. As with any nomination, this nomination of the presiding arbitrator is also subject to the WIPO Center's approval. *Direct appointments* by the WIPO Center take place in cases where the parties fail to make their individual or joint nominations or two appointed arbitrators fail to nominate a presiding arbitrator.

In the case of expert determination, if the parties have not agreed on the expert or the procedure for appointment, the WIPO Center shall appoint a sole expert. Like in arbitration proceedings, the WIPO Center possesses the right to decide that more than one expert is appropriate in the circumstances. Unlike in arbitration proceedings, there is no formal procedure for the parties' nomination, and subject to the parties' agreement to the contrary, it is the WIPO Center which carries out the appointment of an expert.

In domain name disputes, the WIPO Center plays a critical role on all occasions, though the precise modus of the exercise of this role may vary depending on the number of panellists. If either of the parties elects that a three-member tribunal should resolve the dispute instead of a sole panellist, the WIPO Center *elects* a panellist from a list of three candidates suggested by each party. For the presiding panellists, the WIPO Center prepares a list of five candidates and invites the parties to comment. Notwithstanding this, and as mentioned earlier, the parties may jointly agree on the identity of the presiding panellists and notify the WIPO Center. In the case of a sole panellist, the WIPO Center *selects* him or her directly from the (general) WIPO list of domain name panellists.

---

10   Overall, the WIPO Arbitration Rules and the WIPO Expedited Arbitration Rules provide for a sole arbitrator as a default regulation; in exceptional circumstances and in the case of ordinary arbitration as opposed to expedited arbitration, the WIPO Center may at its absolute discretion deviate from a default number for a sole arbitration and decide that a tribunal of three persons shall resolve a dispute.

3. THE METHOD FOR APPOINTING THE ADJUDICATORS

Combined methods are used for the appointment of adjudicators in proceedings under the WIPO rules. In arbitration, the WIPO Center either *approves nominations* or *carries out direct appointment*, or both. In expert determination procedures, the WIPO Center *directly appoints* experts. In domain name disputes, the WIPO Center either *elects* panellists from the lists prepared by the parties or prepared by the WIPO Center and commented on by the parties, or *selects* panellists from the (general) WIPO List of Domain Name Panellists.

In one form or another, the WIPO Center engages with the parties' feedback. It does so in relation to arbitrators, experts and domain name panellists. Illustrations for these occasions follow below. When the WIPO Center carries out direct appointment of arbitrators, a specific form of consultation with the parties usually takes place. This form of consultation is often referred to as 'a list procedure',[11] because the WIPO Center prepares a list of candidates for appointment and enables both parties to comment on it within a set timeframe. The list usually contains the names of three candidates in alphabetical order and a statement of their qualifications. Each party may delete the names of those to whose appointment the party objects and indicate the order of priority for each remaining candidate. The WIPO Center takes into account the parties' preferences and objections in appointments from the list; the parties' failure to comment upon the list is understood as an assent to all candidates indicated. While making all efforts to consider the list, the WIPO Center may deviate from the list in three circumstances: (i) if the resulting comments do not show that any arbitrator is acceptable to both parties; (ii) if a person proposed to be an arbitrator cannot or is not willing to accept the appointment and there are no other candidates remaining on the list acceptable to both parties; or (iii) if the WIPO Center exercises the discretion to determine that the list procedure is inappropriate for the case.

When the WIPO Center appoints experts, the procedure for consultation with the parties is less detailed. The WIPO Rules on Expert Determination specify in Article 9 that the WIPO Center takes into account 'any views expressed by the parties' and for that purpose 'the Center may communicate to the parties the details of one or more candidates for appointment and invite the parties to communicate their views'.

In the appointment of panellists for domain name disputes, the WIPO Center takes note of the parties' feedback in relation to the list of three candidates

---

[11]   https://www.wipo.int/amc/en/neutrals/index.html.

prepared by each party in the case of a three-member panel or to the list of five candidates prepared by the WIPO Center for the presiding panellists.

4. METHODS TO BALANCE THE APPOINTING AUTHORITY'S INFLUENCE ON THE APPOINTMENT OF THE ADJUDICATORS

The decisive role of the WIPO Center in the appointment of adjudicators is counterbalanced by the parties' involvement at various stages and in various forms, such as:

- for arbitration:
  - opportunity for joint parties' nomination of a sole arbitrator in tribunals consisting of a sole arbitrator;
  - a party nomination of an arbitrator in tribunals consisting of three arbitrators;
  - joint nomination of the presiding arbitrator by the appointed arbitrators in a tribunal consisting of three arbitrators;
  - parties' influence on default appointments exercised by the WIPO Center through the so-called 'list procedure';
- for expert determination:
  - taking into account the parties' views on the potential candidates for appointment;
- for domain name disputes
  - parties' participation in the formation of the list of potential panellists prepared in the case of a three-member panel;
  - parties' feedback on the list of potential presiding panellists prepared by the WIPO Center.

Of particular interest to counterbalancing mechanisms are limitations imposed by the WIPO Rules on the right of the WIPO Center *not to approve* parties' nominations. This authority is not unlimited. Non-approval takes place only in the case of possible violations of *the duty of impartiality and independence of an adjudicator*. By way of example, Article 14(c) of the WIPO Arbitration Rules addresses this limitation as follows: 'Any nomination of an arbitrator made by the parties pursuant to Articles 16 [appointment of a sole arbitrator], 17 [appointment of three arbitrators] and 18 [appointment of three arbitrators in the case of multiple claimants or respondents] shall be confirmed by the Center provided that the requirements of Articles 22 [impartiality and independence] and 23 [availability, acceptance and notification] have been met.' Further the Commentary to the WIPO Arbitration Rules specifies: 'The only bases upon which the Center may refuse to confirm are bias and unavailability. Therefore it would appear that if a party nominee does not fulfil qualities which the parties have stipulated as necessary for an arbitrator, the Center has no power to intervene and refuse the nomination.'[12] Similarly, Article 14(a) of the WIPO Expedited Arbitration Rules makes it clear that the WIPO Center confirms the appointment of a sole arbitrator if the latter complies with the requirements on impartiality and independence in Article 17 and availability, acceptance and notification in Article 18.

5. PARAMETERS TO ENSURE THAT THE ADJUDICATORS ACT INDEPENDENTLY AND IMPARTIALLY

The WIPO rules impose an express duty on adjudicators to be independent and impartial: Article 22(a) of the WIPO Arbitration Rules, Article 17(a) of the WIPO Expedited Arbitration Rules, Article 10(a) of the WIPO Expert Determination Rules, and Article 7 of the Rules for Uniform Domain Name Dispute Resolution Policy used together with the WIPO Supplemental Rules for Uniform Domain Name Dispute Resolution Policy.

The WIPO Center also imposes an express duty on arbitrators, experts and panellists to disclose any circumstances that may undermine their independence and impartiality: Article 22(b) and (c) of the WIPO Arbitration Rules, Article 17(b) and (c) of the WIPO Expedited Arbitration Rules, Article 10(b) and (c) of the WIPO Expert Determination Rules, and Article 7 of the Rules for Uniform Domain Name Dispute Resolution Policy used together with the WIPO Supplemental Rules for Uniform Domain Name Dispute Resolution Policy. All adjudicators involved have to make a special declaration regarding their independence and impartiality.

To further enhance full disclosure on the part of arbitrators, the WIPO Arbitration Rules and the WIPO Expedited Arbitration Rules further impose on the parties a duty to disclose the identity of third-party funders as of 1 July 2021: Articles 9(vii) and 11(b) of the WIPO Arbitration Rules, and Articles 9(v) and 11(b) of the WIPO Expedited Arbitration Rules.

Neutral nationality also appears among the traditional safeguards of adjudicators' impartiality and independence. The WIPO Arbitration Rules specify in Article 20(b) that the nationality of the sole or presiding arbitrator shall be other than the nationality of either of the parties. Two exceptions exist to this rule: (i) the parties reach agreement on addressing the nationality

---

[12] Phillip Landolt and Alejandro García, *Commentary of WIPO Arbitration Rules* (WIPO Arbitration and Mediation Center 2017) 16.

requirement in some other way, or (ii) there are special circumstances such as the need to appoint a person who has particular qualifications. Article 15(b) of the WIPO Expedited Arbitration Rules contains the same regulation. While the WIPO Rules on Expert Determination do not contain any express provision on neutral nationality, the rules nevertheless make it clear in Article 9(VI)[13] that nationality is among the relevant considerations in the appointment of an expert. Similarly to the WIPO expert determination procedure, the rules applicable in domain name disputes do not expressly provide for neutral nationality of panellists, but the rules nevertheless enable nationality to be taken into account along with other relevant considerations through the parties' lists of candidates and the parties' comments on the list of candidates prepared by the WIPO Center.

The WIPO Rules also introduce some additional safeguards in relation to the combination of the various roles of adjudicators. This makes particular sense because the WIPO Center proposes model (escalation) dispute resolution clauses[14] and encourages the parties to choose that combination of dispute resolution methods which in the parties' view might suit their particular set of relationships best. In the context of adjudicators covered by this report, the limitation relates to experts. According to Article 10(d) of the WIPO Expert Determination Rules, an expert shall not appear in any other capacity in relation to the matter referred to the expert unless required by a court of law or authorised in writing by the parties. The restriction aims to ensure neutrality of adjudicators and to limit their exposure to unnecessary information.

Finally, because the WIPO Center appears to be one of the service providers for domain name disputes, it is important to address a general concern about the possible bias of service providers in their formation of administrative panels. The core criticism goes to the specificity of domain name dispute resolution, where it is the *complainant* who initially chose the service provider who then exercises a decisive role in the formation of the administrative panel. Critics suggest that this initial choice of service provider creates an additional incentive for the service provider to appoint panellists who might be more supportive of the complainant and not the respondent. Opponents of critics invoke three grounds to refute decision-making bias: (i) domain name resolution services

---

13   Overall Article 9 contains the following non-exhaustive list of factors which the WIPO Center considers in the appointment of experts: any views expressed by the parties; the matter on which the determination is sought; the expert's relevant expertise; the ability of the expert to complete the expert determination with due expedition; the language of the expert determination; the place and nationality of the expert and the parties.

14   Among others, the WIPO Center offers model clauses for: mediation followed, in the absence of a settlement, by (expedited) arbitration; mediation followed, in the absence of a settlement, by expert determination; mediation followed, in the absence of a settlement, by court litigation; and expert determination, binding unless followed by (expedited) arbitration; available at https://www.wipo.int/amc/en/clauses/index.html.

Intersentia

are not profit-making and service providers do not have any material interest in favouring one party in a dispute; (ii) it is not the service provider but the panellists who decide the outcome of a dispute; and (iii) there is a lack of empirical evidence of biased decision-making.[15] These three grounds make sense and may be further supported by some additional safeguards which the WIPO Center has introduced to strike a balanced approach towards the influence of both parties in a dispute in the formation of an administrative panel. According to Article 8(a) of the WIPO Supplemental Rules, the parties are supposed to provide their candidates in *the order of priority* and this priority *shall be respected by the WIPO Center*. According to Article 8(b)(ii), parties may also provide the order of priority for the list of candidates of presiding panellists prepared by the WIPO Center.

6. CONSEQUENCES FOR THE ADJUDICATOR OF A BREACH BY THE ADJUDICATOR OF THE REQUIREMENT TO ACT INDEPENDENTLY AND IMPARTIALLY

Save for some exceptions, the challenging of an adjudicator appears to be a natural consequence of a breach of the requirement to act independently and impartially. A similar violation may also lie below a bigger picture of incapacity or failure of neutrals to adjudicate and lead to them ultimately being released from their mandate. Regarding procedures which enable some control by the state courts over decisions issued, such as for ordinary arbitration or expedited arbitration, a violation of the duty to act impartially and independently may, together with other relevant factors, qualify as one of the grounds for setting aside of an issued decision and may lead to its subsequent annulment. One has to bear in mind, however, that the WIPO Arbitration Rules (Article 66(a)) and the WIPO Expedited Arbitration Rules (Article 59(a)) contain an inbuilt waiver of the right to apply for the setting aside of a decision. This waiver will be observed if the seat for arbitration is in those jurisdictions which, like Switzerland,[16] permit the parties to waive setting-aside procedures.

Below is a brief overview of the internal WIPO regulation on challenge and release procedures with some critical observations.

---

[15] Andrew F. Christie, 'WIPO and IP Dispute Resolution' in Sam Ricketson (ed.), *Research Handbook on the World Intellectual Property Organization: The First 50 Years and Beyond* (Edward Elgar Publishing 2020) 276–79.

[16] Article 192 of the Swiss Private International Law Act enables parties not domiciled in Switzerland to waive the action for annulment of an arbitral award 'by an express statement in the arbitration agreement or by a subsequent written agreement'.

Interestingly enough, not all WIPO rules provide for the opportunity to challenge an adjudicator because of the violation of impartiality and independence. While the WIPO Expert Determination Rules, the WIPO Arbitration Rules and the WIPO Expedited Arbitration Rules contain specific rules on challenging adjudicators, the Rules for Uniform Domain Name Dispute Resolution Policy, used together with the WIPO Supplemental Rules, do not have any express rules for challenging adjudicators.

For arbitration and expert determination, the rules on bringing a challenge are identical and rather straightforward. If justifiable doubts exist as to the independence and impartiality of an arbitrator or an expert, either party may initiate a *challenge* under Article 24 of the WIPO Arbitration Rules, Article 19 of the WIPO Expedited Arbitration Rules or Article 11 of the WIPO Expert Determination Rules. If the other party does not agree to initiate a challenge or an adjudicator does not resign voluntarily, the WIPO Center decides on the challenge. The practice of the WIPO Center remains unknown, though some commentaries identify that challenges are rarely initiated.[17] On some occasions in relation to arbitration when the seat of arbitration so permits, the challenge may also be heard by the state court. If this happens, internal procedures shall be tried first.[18]

In relation to domain name dispute resolution, the absence of express regulation makes it important to see the approaches adopted in jurisprudence. The WIPO practice demonstrates that the right to ask the WIPO Center to disqualify or recuse a panellist because of their failure to comply with the requirements of independence and impartiality is maintained in the case of a panel consisting of a sole panellist[19] but not in the case of a three-member panel.[20] The reason for this different treatment is explained by the specific quasi-administrative nature of the domain name dispute resolution system and the greater involvement of the parties in the formation of panels in the case of three panellists as opposed to a panel consisting of a sole panellist. *Two Way NV/SA v.*

---

[17] Phillip Landolt and Alejandro García, *Commentary of WIPO Arbitration Rules* (WIPO Arbitration and Mediation Center 2017) 23.

[18] Some jurisdictions might provide for the authority of the state courts to challenge arbitrators. By way of example, section 24 of the English Arbitration Act 1996, discussed in more detail in the special report on Impartiality and Independence of Arbitrators in Commodities Arbitration, specifies that: 'If there is an arbitral or other institution or person vested by the parties with power to remove an arbitrator, the court shall not exercise its power of removal unless satisfied that the applicant has first exhausted any available recourse to that institution or person.'

[19] Administrative Panel Decision in *Britannia Building Society v. Britannia Fraud Prevention*, Case No. D2001-0505, available at https://www.wipo.int/amc/en/domains/decisions/html/2001/d2001-0505.html.

[20] Administrative Panel Decision in *Two Way NV/SA v. Moniker Privacy Services, LLC*, Case No. D2012-2413, available at https://www.wipo.int/amc/en/domains/search/text.jsp?case=D2012-2413.

Moniker Privacy Services, LLC, which denied an opportunity to challenge a panellist in a three-member panel, provides a valuable explanation:

> Furthermore, taken as a whole, the characteristics of the dispute resolution process implemented by the Policy and Rules mean that *it is not appropriate to read into the Policy a basis for such a challenge which is certainly not there in express terms.* That is so because the UDRP process is not a conventional arbitration process based on privacy and, frequently, consent between the parties on the appointment of arbitrators. Essentially, it is a 'purpose built' public, mandatory quasi-administrative/legal dispute resolution system wherein the legal bases of its decisions are limited, with such decisions to be taken in an abbreviated time-frame; the overall cost to parties is comparatively small, especially when compared with conventional arbitration and litigation; allowable evidence is restricted; the remedy is automatic in its execution and carried out by a registrar at the direction of the panel; and a court challenge is provided for where the parties can have fuller discovery and hearing if they avail themselves of that opportunity. Accordingly, it is important that all participants act within their designed roles and perform their roles so that the integrity of the panel system is preserved. The UDRP Rules (paragraph 7) assist this purpose by providing a mechanism that places obligations on panelists and providers to manage impartiality and independence *in a manner proportionate to the system.*
>
> ...
>
> It is therefore clear from this analysis that the selection process for a three-member panel is deliberately designed to ensure that each party may make a significant contribution to the selection of one panel member and to the decision by the provider on the third member of the panel. In these circumstances, it is not surprising that there is no express provision in the Policy or the Rules for one party to challenge the appointment of the other party's panelist or the appointment of the presiding panelist. For the same reason it is difficult to imply such a right when the whole structure of the system is to give an unchallenged right to parties in three-member panel cases to nominate one panelist and influence, to some extent, the choice of the third panelist.[21] (emphasis added)

In addition to initiating challenges, another internal WIPO procedure on *release* may also be initiated jointly by the parties or by the WIPO Center. Yet again the procedures are available for arbitration and expert determination only. The release procedure does not aim to address direct failures to observe the duty of impartiality and independence, but may address the concern associated with these violations indirectly. Release requires rather exceptional circumstances when 'the arbitrator has become de jure or de facto unable to fulfill, or fails to fulfill, the duties of an arbitrator'[22] or when 'the Expert is unable to make a

---

[21] Ibid.

[22] Article 32 of the WIPO Arbitration Rules and Article 27 of the WIPO Expedited Arbitration Rules.

Determination in accordance with these Rules for any reason".[23] The difference between challenge and release lies in the object that the procedure aims to address. While a challenge specifically addresses issues of *independence and impartiality*, the release procedure focuses on the *capacity to fulfil* the respective functions of an arbitrator or an expert. In this context one may say that release may address problems with independence and impartiality when an incapacity or failure to act properly has the underlying reason of lack of impartiality and independence.

Overall, while the WIPO system appears to have balancing mechanisms that aim to preclude any lack of independence and impartiality of the parties, the system of reaction to the possible lack of independence and impartiality still has some room for improvement. Two considerations are important here. First, it would bring about more transparency and trust in the system if the WIPO Center were to follow the LCIA example[24] and not only make it mandatory to state the reasons for challenges but actually publish the reasons in an anonymised form. Second, the lack of an express right to challenge an adjudicator in domain name disputes and the practice differences between sole-member panels and panels consisting of three members raises concerns. Instead of the focus on what kind of precautions are built into the system to enhance independence and impartiality, consideration should be given to what remedies are being made available in case something goes wrong even with those panellists whose appointment the party influenced.

7. ENFORCEABILITY OF A FINAL DECISION THAT WAS RENDERED BY AN ADJUDICATOR WHO BREACHED THE REQUIREMENT TO ACT INDEPENDENTLY AND IMPARTIALLY

This report deals with diverse types of procedures, not all of which may need enforcement procedures at first. While expert determination decisions are contractually binding on the parties (save for decisions to the contrary), they do not have the force of an arbitral award. Similarly, administrative decisions in domain name disputes do not have the power of arbitral awards and are actually executed by a domain name registrar without any additional procedure. The only type of decision which actually necessitates enforcement is an arbitral award

---

23 Article 12 of the WIPO Expert Determination Rules.
24 According to Article 10.6 of the LCIA Arbitration Rules 2020, 'the LCIA Court's decision shall be made in writing, with reasons'. See also the database of the decisions on challenge available at https://www.lcia.org/challenge-decision-database.aspx.

Intersentia

Yuliya Chernykh

in ordinary arbitration procedures and in expedited arbitration procedures. Awards may not be enforced if there is the existence of any of the grounds indicated in the New York Convention that have achieved global acceptance.[25] While lack of impartiality and independence is not captured verbatim in the Convention, some of the grounds for non-enforcement, such as violations of due process or public policy, may nevertheless cover violations associated with lack of impartiality and independence. Much would depend on the local practice of application of the New York Convention.

---

[25] For a few countries which have not ratified the New York Convention, the regime of enforcement may be defined either bilaterally or on the basis of the principle of mutual recognition or some other basis.

THE INDEPENDENCE AND IMPARTIALITY OF ADJUDICATORS AT THE WORLD TRADE ORGANIZATION

Maria Chiara Malaguti and Giulia Poli

1. Settlement of Disputes within the WTO: A Paradigm Yet with Lights and Shadows 352
2. Selection of Adjudicators.. 354
    2.1. Panels.. 354
          2.1.1. DSU Rules 354
          2.1.2. Proposals for Reform 356
    2.2. Appellate Body 358
          2.2.1. Pre-Selection Practices and DSU Rules.............. 358
          2.2.2. The Current Deadlock in the Appointment Process of AB Members..................................... 361
    2.3. Arbitration.. 364
          2.3.1. DSU Rules 364
          2.3.2. The Proposal to (Temporarily) Resort to Article 25 Arbitration to Address the Current AB Crisis 365
3. Rules of Conduct... 366
    3.1. Shaping Independence and Impartiality...................... 367
          3.1.1. Self-Disclosure................................... 368
          3.1.2. Confidentiality................................... 369
          3.1.3. Material Violations 370
    3.2. Implementation 371
          3.2.1. Procedures 371
          3.2.2. Concrete Cases of Recusal......................... 372
4. Conclusions.. 372

1. SETTLEMENT OF DISPUTES WITHIN THE WTO: A PARADIGM YET WITH LIGHTS AND SHADOWS

The World Trade Organization (WTO) is one of the most significant global governance organisations. Its legal system is fundamental to this reality, and its well-established system of procedures for managing and resolving disputes between WTO Member States is one of its most relevant features. One of the specificities of the system is that it is structured into a two-tier mechanism comprising ad hoc panels (Panel) as a first layer of assessment, and a permanent body (Appellate Body, or AB) to address appeals against the decision of a Panel. Finally, recourse to arbitration is further contemplated in the implementation phase.

The Dispute Settlement Understanding (DSU),[1] together with the AB Working Procedures,[2] contains the rules for dispute settlement by establishing procedures for selection of the members of Panels, of the Appellate Body and the arbitrators, as well as those to conduct each phase of such proceedings. The Dispute Settlement Body (DSB) administers such rules and procedures and, except as otherwise provided in a covered agreement, the dispute settlement provisions of the covered agreements. Accordingly, the DSB has the authority to establish Panels, adopt Panel and Appellate Body reports, maintain surveillance of the implementation of rulings and recommendations, and authorise suspension of concessions and other obligations under the covered agreements.

More precisely, when a dispute arises, the procedure starts with consultation between the relevant parties.[3] Only if a mutually agreed solution is not reached and one of the parties asks for it is a Panel is established.[4] The Panel examines the matter in meetings with the parties,[5] and can have recourse to the help of experts.[6] This first stage concludes with a report issued first to the parties,[7] and then to the DSB.[8] The report can be reviewed by the Appellate Body, which issues an appellate report.[9] The losing party can propose the implementation of the report within a reasonable period of time,[10] and in case of disagreement on the consistency of such measures with the relevant WTO agreement, that

---

[1] Annex 2 to the WTO Agreement, https://www.wto.org/english/tratop_e/dispu_e/dsu_e.htm.
[2] Working procedures for appellate review, WT/AB/WP/6, 16 August 2010, https://www.wto.org/english/tratop_e/dispu_e/ab_e.htm.
[3] Art. 4 DSU.
[4] Art. 6 DSU.
[5] Art. 12 DSU.
[6] Art. 13 DSU; Appendix 4.
[7] Art. 12.8; Appendix 3 para. 12(k).
[8] Art. 12.9; Appendix 3 para. 12(k).
[9] Art. 16.4 DSU.
[10] Art. 21.3 DSU.

dispute is decided through recourse to the dispute settlement procedures, including wherever possible resort to the original Panel.[11]

If the Member concerned fails to bring the measure found to be inconsistent with a covered agreement into compliance or to otherwise comply with the recommendations and rulings, that Member must, if so requested, enter into negotiations with any party having invoked the dispute settlement procedures, with a view to agreeing mutually acceptable compensation. If no satisfactory compensation is agreed, any party having invoked the dispute settlement procedures may request authorisation from the DSB to suspend the application to the Member concerned of concessions or other obligations under the covered agreements.[12] However, if the Member concerned objects to the level of suspension proposed, or claims that the relevant principles and procedures have not been followed where a complaining party has requested authorisation to suspend concessions or other obligations, the matter is referred to arbitration. Such arbitration is carried out by the original Panel, if members are available, or by an arbitrator appointed by the Director-General.[13] In addition, the 'reasonable period of time' to implement the recommendations requested by the DSU can be established by arbitration.[14]

Moreover, except as otherwise provided in the DSU, at any time arbitration can be chosen by parties to settle their dispute under commonly agreed rules and procedures.[15]

The Rules of Conduct, established on 11 December 1996, are designed to maintain integrity, impartiality and confidentiality of the proceedings, to strengthen the operation of the DSU, and, consequently, to enhance confidence in the dispute settlement mechanism.[16] Despite the structural differences between ad hoc Panels/arbitration and the standing AB, the Rules of Conduct apply indiscriminately to members of Panels and of the AB, as well as arbitrators. Moreover, these apply to the Secretariat, the chairperson and experts participating to the dispute settlement mechanism, as well as to administrative and legal support staff.[17]

Assessment of the independence and impartiality of adjudicators within the WTO shall thus consider the intertwining of such sets of provisions (on appointment of adjudicators, conduct and management of procedures), and bear in mind that the Rules of Conduct, although indistinctly applicable, may lead to different results depending on the specificities of each body. Moreover, independence and impartiality of adjudicators should be understood not (only)

---

[11]   Art. 21.5 DSU.
[12]   Art. 22.2 DSU.
[13]   Art. 22.6 DSU.
[14]   Art. 21.3(c) DSU.
[15]   Art. 25 DSU.
[16]   Rules of Conduct, Preamble.
[17]   Rules of Conduct, Section IV.

as a value per se, but (also) for their role as to ensure integrity and impartiality of the proceedings.

Finally, it is known that the Appellate Body is currently stalled because no agreement was reached in the appointment of new members, and that this is the result of vetoes by the USA as a measure intended to oppose, inter alia, perceived 'judicial overreach' by the AB. The intimate link between this issue and the role of independence and impartiality of adjudicators is evident and at the core of the matter. Indeed, some Member States have expressly warned that any reform to limit the risk of 'judicial overreach' should be careful not to compromise to any extent adjudicators' independence.

Any assessment of the mechanism must thus highlight its points of brightness but also its shadows, which have led to a process (albeit slow and controversial) of reform. Within such process of reform, it is also interesting to see how a mechanism of arbitration (under Article 25 DSU, see below) has been proposed by the European Union and adhered to by some states to temporarily substitute for the functions of the Appellate Body until an agreed solution is adopted to restore the (reformed) dispute settlement architecture.[18]

2. SELECTION OF ADJUDICATORS

2.1. PANELS

A Panel is an impartial body constituted by the DSB to decide on a dispute under the mandate it specifically receives from the DSB. Since there are no permanent panels or panellists in the WTO, an ad hoc Panel must be formed for each individual dispute.

2.1.1. DSU Rules

Panel members must be selected with a view to ensuring the independence of the members, a sufficiently diverse background and a wide spectrum of experience.[19]

To that end, Article 8 DSU establishes that Panels can be composed of well-qualified governmental or non-governmental individuals. These can include persons who have served on or presented a case to a Panel, or served as a representative of a Member State, as a representative to the Council or Committee of any covered agreement, or in the Secretariat. Panels can also include scholars on international trade law or policy, or individuals who have

---

[18] For an articulated analysis of the adjudicating bodies of the WTO, see R. Malacrida and G. Marceau, 'The WTO Adjudicating Bodies' in R. Howse, H. Ruiz-Fabri, G. Ulfstein and M.Q. Zang, *The Legitimacy of International Trade Courts and Tribunals*, Cambridge University Press, Cambridge 2018, pp. 20–69.

[19] Art. 8.2 DSU.

served as a senior trade policy official of a Member State. However, citizens of Members whose governments are parties to the dispute or have an interest in the dispute at stake cannot serve on a Panel, unless the parties to the dispute agree otherwise. When a dispute arises between a developing country Member and a developed country Member, the Panel must include at least one panellist from a developing country Member at the developing country Member's request.

To assist in the selection of panellists, the Secretariat maintains an indicative list of governmental and non-governmental individuals, from which panellists may be drawn as appropriate. Members may periodically suggest names of governmental and non-governmental individuals for inclusion on the indicative list. For each of the individuals on the list, the latter indicates specific areas of experience or expertise of the individuals in the sectors or subject matter of the covered agreements. However, there is no obligation to draw panellists from such rosters, and in fact many panellists are appointed outside of such list.

Many panellists are traditionally WTO trade delegates or capital-based trade officials, but former Secretariat officials, retired government officials and academics also appear on Panels on a regular basis. Panellists perform their functions on a part-time basis in addition to their regular jobs.[20]

The Secretariat also assists in the selection of the panellists by proposing nominations for the Panel to the parties to the dispute, to which the latter should not object except for compelling reasons. In reality, many Members make considerable use of this clause and often reject nominees. There is no examination of whether the reasons offered are convincing in such circumstances. Instead, the Secretariat suggests new names.[21] On the other hand, parties are not allowed to interview potential Panel members.

If there is no agreement on the panellists within 20 days after the date of the establishment of a Panel, at the request of either party, the Director-General, in consultation with the Chairperson of the DSB and the Chairperson of the relevant Council or Committee, determines the composition of the Panel by appointing the panellists whom the Director-General considers most appropriate in accordance with any relevant rules or procedures of the covered agreement(s) at issue in the dispute, after consulting with the parties. The Chairperson of the DSB then inform the Members of the composition of the Panel thus formed.

The existence of this method is considered crucial because it prevents a respondent from impeding the entire Panel's proceedings by delaying the Panel's composition, as is occasionally the case in other international dispute resolution systems. However, the parties are free to spend more than 20 days trying to reach an agreement on the Panel's composition, as long as none of them asks the Director-General to intervene.[22]

---

[20]   https://www.wto.org/english/tratop_e/dispu_e/disp_settlement_cbt_e/c6s3p2_e.htm.
[21]   Ibid.
[22]   Ibid.

Panellists serve in their individual capacities and not as government representatives, nor as representatives of any organisation. Members shall therefore not give them instructions nor seek to influence them as individuals with regard to matters before the Panel.

In the case of multiple complainants, i.e. more than one Member requesting the formation of a Panel for the same matter, Article 9.1 DSU applies, requiring the DSB to form a single Panel to investigate these complaints, taking into account the rights of all Members involved, whenever possible.[23]

If it is not possible to form a single Panel and more than one is formed, the same people should serve as panellists on each of the distinct Panels as much as practicable, and the timelines should be synchronised.[24] These two options ensure that the legal approach to the various concerns is consistent. With several Panels made up of different panellists working individually and not knowing each other's reasons and decisions (Panel processes are kept confidential until the report is distributed), there is a possibility that the various Panel reports will disagree with and even contradict one another.[25]

2.1.2. Proposals for Reform

Under the 1998–1999 DSU review, the European Union (at that time the European Community) made a proposal for a standing Panel Body of 15–24 members, then restated this proposal in 2002 in the Doha negotiations. This proposal was not exclusively meant to address independence. However, the EU suggested that a permanent panel system would inter alia enhance the legitimacy and credibility of the panel process in the eyes of the public, as the possibility of conflicts of interests would be eliminated and the independence of the panellists would be protected. More experienced panellists would also be more comfortable with judicial concepts such as the application of adverse inferences if a party fails to present evidence on a certain point. The attractiveness of the permanent Panel Body proposal would rest upon the proposition that the Panel Body would be chosen for expertise rather than for political considerations.[26]

The original proposal by the EU to form Panels from the permanent roster using a random mechanism also included the suggestion that Panels be formed exclusively

---

[23] For example, despite a separate request from India, the DSB agreed to establish a single panel in the US – Shrimp case (WT/DS58/9), following the establishment of a panel at the joint request of Malaysia and Thailand and a separate request from Pakistan. The feasibility of forming a single panel is obviously dependent on circumstances like the time of the many conflicts being similar.

[24] In EC – Hormones, for example, two distinct Panels constituted of the same personnel assessed Canada's (WT/DS48) and the United States' (WT/DS26) complaints.

[25] https://www.wto.org/english/tratop_e/dispu_e/disp_settlement_cbt_e/c6s3p2_e.htm.

[26] W.J. Davey, 'Mini-Symposium on the Desirability of a WTO Permanent Panel Body' (2003) 6(1) JIEL 175.

356

The World Trade Organization

of non-government members. This latter feature was then modified following comments by other Members that this would prevent some developing countries from proposing individuals with adequate competence. The EU then modified its proposal to permit the inclusion of governmental officials on leave, whose independence would be supported by rules on conflicts of interest. The DSB would include persons on the roster for six-year terms and no person could be reappointed.

Although the proposal by the EU was not adopted, the debate also continued outside negotiations. In 2005, the Association of the Bar of the City of New York published a study that highlighted some issues in the selection of panellists: the major point was that too much weight was given to nationality as a criterion for selection rather than true concerns regarding independence. While the independence of panellists having the same nationality as parties to a dispute may have been a legitimate concern under the old GATT dispute settlement system, in which these were generally government officials, the authors of the study consider that it should be less so under the DSU, which allows Panels to be drawn from a more diverse group.[27]

Firstly, the authors notice that, since nationals of a Member State taking part in a procedure cannot be selected unless the parties to the dispute agree, and countries such as the EU and the US often intervene in disputes as third-party interested countries, nationals of such countries would be automatically disqualified despite those members having a large pool of qualified individuals with the necessary expertise. While this obstacle would be overcome if the parties to the dispute consented, the authors state that this rarely occurs. Instead, appointment of panellists is a contentious process, and in most cases the Director-General must compose the Panel.[28]

---

[27] Association of the Bar of the City of New York, The Committee on International Trade, *Composition of WTO Dispute Settlement Panels – International Trade Committee Proposal*, August, 2005.

[28] The study relies upon WTO Doc. TN/DS/W/7 (30 May 2002), from which it emerges that of 23 Panels composed in 2001–2002, 16 were composed by the Director-General. The annex to this publication indicates that 14 out of 24 Panels in 2000–April 2002 were composed by the Director-General, four out of nine Panels were composed by the Director-General in 2000, and since then 10 out of 15, or two-thirds, have been composed by the Director-General. It also mentions the works of Professor William J. Davey, the first Director of Legal Affairs for the WTO, who has described the nationalities of the 119 individuals who had filled 186 panellist positions at the time he wrote on the subject. He found that the majority were from Switzerland (19 positions filled), New Zealand (17), Australia (12), Brazil (11), Hong Kong (11), South Africa (9), Canada (7), Czech Republic (6), Poland (6), Chile (5), Egypt (5), Germany (5), India (5), Norway (5), Sweden (5) and Thailand (5). The EC has filled 26 positions, the United States 4 and Japan 2. Overall, 73 positions have been filled by panellists from developing countries (39%) and 17 by Eastern European panellists (9%). In terms of regions, the developing country panellists have come from Africa (14), Asia (28), the Indian Ocean (1) and Latin America (30). 20% of positions have been filled by women (W.J. Davey, 'A Permanent Panel Body for WTO Dispute Settlement: Desirable or Practical?' in D.L.M. Kennedy and J.D. Southwick (eds), *The Political Economy of International Trade Law: Essays in Honour of Robert E. Hudec*, Cambridge University Press, Cambridge 2002, p. 500).

Intersentia

Secondly, they affirm that true independence should instead be based on expertise, and thus the capability of autonomous judgment and to resist any form of influence by Members. To achieve this objective, they propose a permanent roster of panellists not employed full-time by the WTO but who would serve when they come up in the roster rotation. The panel roster would be relatively large, thus allowing a greater diversity of expertise. Further, the panel roster would be set up so that individual Panels would be chosen without regard to geography, randomly from the panel roster. However, each Panel should have one member with experience in the specific sector in dispute (separate rosters or 'wheels' being maintained for this purpose), the other two having general experience in trade law. Further, the fact that a dispute might involve a panellist's home country as a party or third party should not disqualify that panellist, unless the panellist elects to recuse him- or herself on the ground that he or she cannot be impartial. Each member of the Panel should have a different nationality. However, there should be a proviso that if either the complaining party or the respondent is a developing country, then at least one of the panellists must come from a developing country.

To preserve independence, as well as the appearance of independence, persons on the roster should not be members of any current government of Member States. They do not need to be lawyers, but all should possess appropriate trade-related experience. Further, it should be specified that to sit on a particular dispute, they cannot have been involved in the dispute being heard, whether as government officials or as private lawyers or advisers.

Although the point that competence may ensure independence and impartiality better than nationality has some value, proposals in that direction did not receive wide support. As said, the proposal of having a permanent Panel Body was also abandoned. However, discussions continue within a wider spectrum of amendments to the DSU.

2.2. APPELLATE BODY

The Appellate Body is the second and last level of the dispute resolution system's adjudicatory process. The establishment of this second adjudicatory step, which did not exist in the original GATT 1947 dispute settlement system, was one of the key novelties of the Uruguay Round.

2.2.1. Pre-Selection Practices and DSU Rules

The AB is a standing adjudicating body composed of seven members who are appointed for four-year periods, with the possibility of being reappointed for one more term. Vacancies are filled on a case-by-case basis. Individual appeals are handled by three-member AB divisions, with members allocated on a rotating

The World Trade Organization

basis and utilising a mechanism designed to create random, unpredictable results as well as opportunities for all members to serve regardless of nationality.[29]

The DSU contains few rules on the selection of members of the Appellate Body and their qualities. In particular, Article 17.3 DSU states that the AB shall comprise persons of recognised authority, with demonstrated expertise in law, international trade and the subject matter of the covered agreements generally. Unlike the members of a Panel, they shall be unaffiliated with any government. Moreover, the Appellate Body membership must be broadly representative of membership in the WTO. Although they are not to work full time, all persons serving on the Appellate Body must be available at all times and on short notice and stay abreast of dispute settlement activities and other relevant activities of the WTO. They shall not participate in the consideration of any disputes that would create a direct or indirect conflict of interest.

Aside from Article 17.3, the DSU does not go into further detail about nominating and appointing AB members. Any member can propose one or more candidates. In practice, nominating governments pre-select nominees, and the DSB subsequently chooses the AB member through a consensus decision.[30]

The most important process, according to close observers,[31] is in fact the pre-selection stage, in which nominating governments look for potential candidates who have demonstrated knowledge of the WTO system, share the nominating country's concerns, and have the standing to influence other members of the Appellate Body. Candidates' views on DSU reforms are also considered when considering the possibility for a DSB appointment.

Each country or region has its own internal procedures or practices for pre-selection. In the EU, for instance, Member States propose candidates, who are then shortlisted and assessed by a committee of experts through demanding interviews. The Council then chooses from the names proposed by the Committee those who will be proposed to the DSB. No rule seems to exist to ensure rotation in terms of nationality inside the Union, and not all Member States have always proposed a candidate in past experience. No special attention was devoted to gender equality either, until the last selection, although in the meantime the EU policy has become much more gender-sensitive and any future selection might thus adopt a different approach.[32]

---

[29]   Article 17 DSU; Rule 6(2) of the AB's Working Procedures.

[30]   Despite the fact that the Appellate Body membership must be broadly representative of membership in the WTO, some criticise the prevalence of some countries/regions in imposing their candidates. See E. Voeten, 'The Politics of International Judicial Appointments' (2009) 9 *Chi. J. Int'l. L.* 387, 402, arguing that the United States and the European Union in particular have in fact assured seats, as well as an important influence on the candidates from other countries.

[31]   See R. Howse, 'Appointment with Destiny: Selecting WTO Judges in the Future', NYU Law School, Global Policy Volume 12, Supplement 3, April 2021.

[32]   Communication from the Commission to the European Parliament, the Council, the European Economic and Social Committee and the Committee of the Regions, 'A Union of Equality: Gender Equality Strategy 2020–2025', COM(2020) 152 final, https://eur-lex.europa. eu/legal-content/EN/TXT/PDF/?uri=CELEX:52020DC0152&from=EN.

Intersentia

Once candidates are presented to the organisation, a Selection Committee is constituted to help the DSB with the task of making a recommendation for appointment. The Director-General and the chairs of the WTO General Council, the DSB, and the WTO Councils for Trade in Goods, Trade in Services and TRIPS make up the Committee.[33] The Committee examines the candidates and meets with members individually or obtains written feedback before issuing a recommendation. Individual Member States often invite prospective candidates for interviews as well.

Dunoff and Pollack go into more detail on the AB member selection procedure: prospective members are subjected to a thorough vetting process. They meet for several hours, for example, with the Selection Committee.[34] Candidates are tested on their knowledge of WTO legislation, their stance on contentious legal issues and their approach to trade disputes at this time, among other things. Candidates also meet with country delegations and WTO ambassadors in Geneva for in-depth discussions of trade law and policy, and they are sometimes interviewed in major cities. Keeping in mind the WTO's consensus norm, after all interviews are completed, the Selection Committee has many 'private confessional sessions with WTO members' to evaluate levels of support for various candidates.[35] The Selection Committee is expected to present candidates who will be accepted by WTO membership consensus. The WTO's consensus decision-making mechanism allows any WTO member to veto any candidate's election or re-election. States have not been hesitant to use this authority. As a result, reaching unanimity on any person or slate of candidates has proven difficult at times. In such situations, the Selection Committee will not send any names and will instead suggest a new selection procedure. Dunoff and Pollack confirm, also based on third-party scholarly research, that the amount of scrutiny applied to candidates, as well as the related politicisation of the nomination and election processes, has risen significantly over time.[36]

Most AB members were previously either former or current government officials. Academics and/or private legal practitioners have made up the majority of the remaining AB members.[37]

---

[33] See R. Howse, H. Ruiz-Fabri, G. Ulfstein and M.Q. Zang, *The Legitimacy of International Trade Courts and Tribunals*, Cambridge University Press, Cambridge 2018.

[34] J.L. Dunoff and M.A. Pollack, 'The Judicial Trilemma' (2017) 111 *AJIL* 225.

[35] Ibid.

[36] Ibid., p. 263.

[37] https://www.wto.org/english/tratop_e/dispu_e/ab_members_descrp_e.htm. See also R. Malacrida and G. Marceau, 'The WTO Adjudicating Bodies' in R. Howse, H. Ruiz-Fabri, G. Ulfstein and M.Q. Zang, *The Legitimacy of International Trade Courts and Tribunals*, Cambridge University Press, Cambridge 2018, p. 20; M.N. Creis, *The Independence and Impartiality of ICSID Arbitrators – Current Case Law, Alternative Approaches, and Improvement Suggestions*, Brill, Leiden 2017, chapter on 'Alternative Standards of Independence and Impartiality', p. 88.

The World Trade Organization

2.2.2. *The Current Deadlock in the Appointment Process of AB Members*

From January 1995, when the WTO was established, until December 2019, the Appellate Body functioned as the highest instance of WTO dispute settlement, upholding, modifying or reversing legal findings and conclusions of the Panels. For over two decades, the Appellate Body consisted of seven members serving four-year terms.

Between 1995 and 2020, WTO members launched consultations, initiating a dispute, 598 times; of these, 365 disputes led to the creation of a Panel to adjudicate a dispute between members, and Panel reports were issued in 265 cases, the conclusions of which were appealed in 174 disputes. That two-thirds of Panel reports were appealed highlights the deference members gave to the Appellate Body and the importance of a higher instance in a dispute settlement procedure.

In addition, members largely complied with the rulings in disputes: only 19% of disputes that involved a Panel report resulted in the creation of a compliance proceeding (where parties disagree about whether compliance has occurred by the end of the implementation period).[38]

At the moment, the Appellate Body is stalled. In 2011, the USA refused for the first time to reappoint an Appellate Body member for a second term, in the case of Jennifer Hillman. At the time, the US Trade Representative did not provide clear reasons for the refusal. In 2016, the reappointment of Appellate Body member Seung Wha Chang was also blocked, reportedly due to US concerns over judicial overreach. The blockage of nominations continued, and the Appellate Body gradually stopped functioning as the terms of existing members expired. Whilst in the early 1990s the USA was among the countries that most favoured the establishment of a mechanism for binding and enforceable dispute settlement at the WTO, the country has since taken issue with several practices. In 2018, the US Trade Representative (USTR) communicated US concerns with WTO dispute settlement in the US President's Trade Policy Agenda. In February 2020, this was followed by an in-depth report on the Appellate Body of the WTO.[39]

Among the various criticisms, one concerns judicial overreach. This inevitably also touches upon and has an impact on the issue of scope and preservation of independence and impartiality of adjudicators within the WTO dispute settlement system.[40]

---

[38]   Source is the WTO website, which also contains more information of number of proceedings and distribution according to the relevant years: https://www.wto.org/english/tratop_e/dispu_e/dispustats_e.htm.

[39]   Office of the United States Trade Representative Ambassador Robert E. Lighthizer, Report on the Appellate Body of the World Trade Organization, February 2020, https://ustr.gov/sites/default/files/Report_on_the_Appellate_Body_of_the_World_Trade_Organization.pdf.

[40]   Ibid., p. 160: 'Appendix B1: Statements by U.S. Trade Representatives or their Deputies on Appellate Body Overreach: Deputy U.S. Trade Representative Michael Punke and USTR General Counsel Timothy Reif (2016): WTO members created a system of rules according

Intersentia

361

High-level consultations on how to resolve the longstanding impasse over the appointment of AB members are still under way. Some of the issues at stake and the proposals to solve them deserve some reflection.

Early on, some Members proposed inter alia to establish an annual process for meetings between the Appellate Body and the WTO Members to allow Members to express concerns about any particular Appellate Body's approaches, systemic issues or trends in the jurisprudence. This could allow Member States to concretely express their concerns, but possibly in an open discussion and without thus impairing the independence and impartiality of the body. A concrete proposal reads:

> Meetings with the Appellate Body – Once a year, the DSB shall meet in the presence of the Appellate Body. At such meetings, any Member may express its views on adopted Appellate Body reports. The meetings shall be open to all Members and their conduct shall be respectful of the independence and impartiality of the Appellate Body. The DSB shall adopt the rules applicable to such meetings on a proposal from the Chairperson of the DSB and in consultation with the Appellate Body.[41]

In this context, the European Commission proposed additional and more structural amendments to that end, which would address concerns but also mitigate the risk of impairing adjudicators' independence and impartiality. One of these is 'to provide for one single but longer (6–8 years) term for Appellate Body members. The objective is to enhance the independence of the Appellate Body and its members, which is needed in view of the experience of recent years and also in view of the other amendments proposed in document WT/GC/W/752.'[42] The EU proposal included to raise the number of AB members to nine and to impose that they do not engage in any other occupation of a professional nature. Thus, on the one hand AB members would work full-time and their number would be broadened to permit more diversity, and on the

---

to which reappointment of AB members is not automatic, but rather subject to approval by all WTO members. The right and responsibility to consider reappointments is one way that members ensure the integrity of the dispute resolution system. The US respects and supports the independence of AB members. But the AB is not independent from the rules established by WTO members themselves. Indeed, a core tenet that gives WTO members faith in the integrity of the AB is that it will not add to the obligations nor diminish the rights created through WTO agreements.

To maintain the credibility of the dispute settlement system, the US in evaluating candidates for the AB has made clear the importance of such candidates adhering to the rules of the WTO, not inventing law that goes beyond the contours of agreements negotiated by WTO members, not substituting their own judgment of facts beyond those established by the record, nor inventing their own claims and arguments not presented by the parties'.

[41] Communication from the European Union, China, Canada, India, Norway, New Zealand, Switzerland, Australia, Republic of Korea, Iceland, Singapore and Mexico to the General Council, WT/GC/W/752, 26 November 2018.

[42] WT/GC/W/753, 26 November 2018.

other hand a single term would reduce the risk of them feeling the pressure to be reconfirmed in their role.[43]

The systemic proposal by the EU was already highlighted in its 2018 Position Paper, where it warned against the risk of challenging AB members. It related in particular to the previous episodes of specific vetoes to reappoint an individual AB member because of her positions. The EU affirmed that it shared many of the US's concerns and called for reform, but stressed that such reforms should not go in the direction of weakening AB members' independence:

> Without prejudice to EU position on whether the concerns formulated by the United States are well founded, this paper explores avenues in which addressing these concerns could lead to the improvement of the system, while preserving and further strengthening its main features and principles.

> In order to achieve balance, this paper also explores other potential improvements. In particular, in 2016, following the US' veto against the re-appointment of one Appellate Body member, there was a wide recognition that a systemic solution was needed in order to preserve the independence and impartiality of Appellate Body members. Indeed, the non-reappointment of an Appellate Body member for reasons related to the content of particular rulings has created a situation in which there may be doubts as to whether decisions of particular Appellate Body members are influenced by such threat of non-reappointment. This situation is not tenable and needs to be addressed systemically.

> These various solutions should be seen as part of one package. In particular, the strengthening of the independence of the Appellate Body and its members allows for introducing an additional mechanism for their interaction with the WTO Members without fear that such interaction may unduly influence their decisions.[44]

---

[43] See P. Mavroidis and E.Y. Kim, *Dissenting Opinions in the WTO Appellate Body: Drivers of Their Issuance & Implications for the Institutional Jurisprudence*, European University Institute, Robert Schuman Centre for Advanced Studies, Global Governance Programme Working Paper No. RSCAS 2018/51 (2018), https://scholarship.law.columbia.edu/faculty_scholarship/2287. The dependence of adjudicators on states because of reappointment is one of the matters mostly discussed as affecting independence. When discussing the role of separate and dissenting opinions by AB members (see below on confidentiality of deliberations), Mavroidis and Kim provocatively state: 'Multiple factors can affect the overall attitude of judges towards issuing dissents, and their relative weights are often difficult to measure because they vary depending on personal preferences. Individuals' different moral standards, for example, have varying impact on the way judges approach disputes. Guided by nationalistic sentiments or personal interests, some AB members might be more inclined than others to lend a sympathetic ear to the voices of their respective governments and rule in favor of them. In principle, of course, this should not be the case, pursuant to Article 17.3 of DSU. But AB members still might overlook this statutory guidance, especially if their post-AB employment is largely in the hands of the governments that nominated them. In the WTO, after all, member nations have always nominated their own citizens to the AB through formal proposals: there has never been a case where a WTO member nominated a foreigner, even though the DSU does not prohibit such action' (p. 7).

[44] 2018 European Commission Position Paper, p. 15, https://ec.europa.eu/commission/presscorner/detail/en/IP_18_5786.

The above proposals were not accepted, and high-level negotiations are still in progress to find common agreement on systemic reforms.

2.3. ARBITRATION

As an alternative to adjudication by Panels and the Appellate Body, the parties to a dispute can resort to arbitration under Article 25 DSU.

2.3.1. DSU Rules

Under Article 25 DSU, the parties to a dispute must agree on the arbitration as well as the procedures to be followed. They are thus free to depart from the standard procedures of the DSU and to agree on the rules and procedures they deem appropriate for the arbitration, including the selection of the arbitrators. The parties must also clearly define the issues in dispute.

As already stated, two other forms of arbitration are foreseen in the DSU for specific situations and questions in the process of implementation of DSB rulings and recommendations. The first such situation which an arbitrator may be called to decide on is the establishment of the 'reasonable period of time' granted to the respondent for implementation under Article 21.3(c) DSU. The second is where a party subject to retaliation may also request arbitration if it objects to the level or the nature of the suspension of obligations proposed under Article 22.6 DSU. These two forms of arbitration are thus limited to clarifying very specific questions in the process of implementation and they result in decisions that are binding for the parties.

To date, in only one dispute have the parties resorted to arbitration under Article 25 DSU. The procedure was not used as an alternative to the Panel and Appellate Body procedure, but at the stage of implementation, when the Panel report had already been adopted. The parties asked the arbitrators to determine the level of nullification or impairment of benefits caused by the violation established in the Panel report.[45] As stated, under the standard procedures of the DSU, parties can indeed obtain a binding determination of the level of nullification or impairment by recourse to arbitration under Article 22.6 DSU. A prerequisite for such arbitration is that the complainant has requested the DSB's authorisation for the suspension of obligations and that the respondent disagrees with the proposed level of retaliation. In the case where the parties resorted to arbitration under Article 25 DSU, they agreed that the award of the arbitrators would be final.

The parties requested the Chairperson of the DSB to contact the original panellists in the dispute to determine their availability to serve as arbitrators.

---

[45] United States – section 110(5) of the US Copyright Act, WT/DS160/ARB25/1.

The Chairperson of the original Panel and one member were no longer available. In accordance with the agreed procedures for the selection of the arbitrators, the Director-General appointed two arbitrators to replace them.[46]

So far, all arbitrations under Article 21.3(c) have been conducted by a member of the Appellate Body acting in his or her personal capacity.[47]

2.3.2. The Proposal to (Temporarily) Resort to Article 25 Arbitration to Address the Current AB Crisis

Although the Member States continue to seek the resolution of the Appellate Body crisis, in order to find a temporary solution to the impasse the EU and a number of trade partners set up a Multiparty Interim Appeal Arbitration Arrangement (MPIA), which they agreed to use as a second instance as long as the situation continues. The MPIA is also open for more WTO members to join.[48]

More precisely, the EU and its Member States together with 15 other WTO Members decided to develop an independent appeals mechanism in January–April 2020. As a result, the MPIA was established on 30 April 2020, based on Article 25 DSU, under mutual agreement between the parties. The signatories must also agree to the eventual arbitration award, thus rendering the appeal procedure binding upon themselves.

In July 2020, the MPIA became operational when a pool of 10 standing arbitrators was confirmed, following candidate nominations by the participants.

Under the MPIA, the pool of arbitrators comprises persons of recognised authority, with demonstrated expertise in law, international trade and the WTO Agreements.[49] In a process that started in June 2020, MPIA participants put forward

---

[46] WT/DS160/15.

[47] A table is provided of ongoing arbitrations and awards that have been issued pursuant to Article 21.3(c), arranged according to the year the arbitrator was appointed, at https://www. wto.org/english/tratop_e/dispu_e/arbitrations_e.htm.

[48] Statement on a Mechanism for Developing, Documenting and Sharing Practices and Procedures in the Conduct of WTO Disputes – Addendum: Multi-Party Interim Appeal Arbitration Arrangement Pursuant to Article 25 of the DSU, JOB/DSB/1/Add.12.

[49] Ibid.: '3. The appeal arbitration procedure will be based on the substantive and procedural aspects of Appellate Review pursuant to Article 17 of the DSU, in order to keep its core features, including independence and impartiality, while enhancing the procedural efficiency of appeal proceedings. The appeal arbitration procedure is set out in Annex 1.
4. In particular, the participating Members envisage that, under the appeal arbitration procedure, appeals will be heard by three appeal arbitrators selected from the pool of 10 standing appeal arbitrators composed by the participating Members in accordance with Annex 2 (hereafter the "pool of arbitrators"). The pool of arbitrators will comprise persons of recognized authority, with demonstrated expertise in law, international trade and the subject matter of the covered agreements generally. They will be unaffiliated with any government. They will not participate in the consideration of any disputes that would create a direct or indirect conflict of interest. The composition of the pool of arbitrators will ensure an appropriate overall balance.

candidates, conducted interviews, and agreed on the 10 individuals who will serve as arbitrators under the arrangement. In any WTO dispute between participants where a party triggers an appeal against a WTO panel report, three members of the pool are selected randomly to hear an appeal under the arrangement.[50]

3. RULES OF CONDUCT

As stated, the Rules of Conduct for the Understanding on Rules and Procedures Governing Dispute Settlement were developed in 1996 to contribute to the preservation of the integrity and impartiality of each body that is part of the WTO dispute settlement mechanism. This is achieved through maintenance of independence and impartiality by all persons covered by the Rules of Conduct, the avoidance of direct or indirect conflicts of interest and respect for the confidentiality of proceedings.[51] Since the very final purpose is to ensure the integrity of the system, the Rules of Conduct apply not only to adjudicators, but

---

5. Members of the pool of arbitrators will stay abreast of WTO dispute settlement activities and will receive all documents relating to appeal arbitration proceedings under the MPIA. In order to promote consistency and coherence in decision-making, the members of the pool of arbitrators will discuss amongst themselves matters of interpretation, practice and procedure, to the extent practicable.

6. The selection from the pool of arbitrators for a specific dispute will be done on the basis of the same principles and methods that apply to form a division of the Appellate Body under Article 17.1 of the DSU and Rule 6(2) of the Working Procedures for Appellate Review, including the principle of rotation. The WTO Director General will notify the parties and third parties of the results of the selection.'

[50] Annex 2 to Multi-Party Interim Appeal Arbitration Arrangement Pursuant to Article 25 of the DSU: '1. Each participating Member may nominate one candidate, by notifying the other participating. Members [For greater certainty, current or former Appellate Body members may be nominated as candidates. If nominated as candidates, they will not undergo the pre-selection process set out in paragraph 3 of this Annex]. ... 3. The candidates will undergo a pre-selection process in order to ensure that the pool of arbitrators comprises only persons of recognised authority, with demonstrated expertise in law, international trade and the subject matter of the covered agreements generally. The participating Members envisage that this pre-selection process will be carried out by a preselection committee composed of the WTO Director General, and the Chairperson of the DSB, the Chairpersons of the Goods, Services, TRIPS and General Councils. The pre-selection committee will, after appropriate consultations, recommend to the participating Members the candidates who meet the above criteria. ... 4. The participating Members will compose the pool of arbitrators by consensus. The participating Members will endeavour to compose the pool of arbitrators within three months following the date of this communication. They will notify the pool of arbitrators to the DSB, as addendum to this communication. The composition of the pool of arbitrators will ensure an appropriate overall balance.'

[51] Article II – Governing Principle. See D. Steger, 'The founding of the Appellate Body' in G. Marceau and R. Azevêdo (ed.), *A History of Law and Lawyers in the GATT/WTO: The Development of the Rule of Law in the Multilateral Trading System*, Cambridge University Press, Cambridge 2018, pp. 482–506.

The World Trade Organization

also to any supporting staff and relevant members of the Secretariat, although of course the main target are adjudicators.[52]

The Rules of Conduct complement the DSU: the Rules themselves stress that the main way to maintain independence and impartiality (thus ensuring the integrity of the system) is indeed to adhere strictly to the provisions of the DSU (respect for which was indeed at the basis of the US's concerns, as described above).[53] However, the DSU elaborates little on standards for independence and impartiality of adjudicators: 'independence' is mentioned in the DSU a single time, in relation to the appointment of panellists,[54] and it stipulates that panellists shall serve in their individual capacities and not as government representatives, nor as representatives of any organisation, and that consequently Members shall not give them instructions nor seek to influence them as individuals with regard to matters before a Panel.[55] To the same extent, the AB Working Procedures only contain a few provisions that directly matter: AB members must reject other professional responsibilities that are inconsistent with their role in the WTO,[56] as well as avoid instructions and advice from any international, governmental or non-governmental organisations or any private source.[57] Thus, the Rules of Conduct, although in turn not directly elaborating on independence and impartiality, become a fundamental source of reference because of the connection they establish between independence and impartiality, avoidance of conflict of interests, and confidentiality.

3.1. SHAPING INDEPENDENCE AND IMPARTIALITY

As said, the Rules of Conduct do not contain a definition of independence or impartiality, nor do they delve into detail on these two concepts. They instead

---

[52] The role of the Secretariat and of supporting staff is outside the scope of this work. However, it should not be underestimated how their organisation and working bear upon if not independence and impartiality directly, at least upon their outside perception. For instance, the fact that AB members do not have individual staff assigned to them but these rotate case by case, make the surrounding organisation help reinforce collegiality, consistency of legal reasoning and thus the overall integrity and legitimacy of the body.

[53] Article 3 of the Rules of Conduct, referring to Article 2, containing the Governing Principle of the Rules: '1. Each person covered by these Rules (as defined in paragraph 1 of Section IV below and hereinafter called "covered person") shall be independent and impartial, shall avoid direct or indirect conflicts of interest and shall respect the confidentiality of proceedings of bodies pursuant to the dispute settlement mechanism, so that through the observance of such standards of conduct the integrity and impartiality of that mechanism are preserved. These Rules shall in no way modify the rights and obligations of Members under the DSU nor the rules and procedures therein.'

[54] Article 8.2 DSU: 'Panel members should be selected with a view to ensuring the independence of the members, a sufficiently diverse background and a wide spectrum of experience.'

[55] Article 8.9 DSU.

[56] Article 2.3 Working Procedures.

[57] Article 2.4 Working Procedures.

Intersentia

367

elaborate on these by imposing a duty of disclosure of any material interest, relationship or matter that may lead to impairment of independence and impartiality, or that might lead to a perception of such. In addition, covered persons must take due care in the performance of their duties to fulfil these expectations, including through avoidance of any direct or indirect conflicts of interest in respect of the subject matter of the proceedings.

3.1.1. Self-Disclosure

Under Article VII, each covered person has a duty of disclosure. To that end, each person requested to serve on a Panel, on the Standing Appellate Body, as an arbitrator or as an expert shall, at the time of the request, receive from the Secretariat the Rules of Conduct, which include an illustrative list of examples of the matters subject to disclosure.

The illustrative list includes:

1. financial interests (e.g. investments, loans, shares, interests, other debts), business interests (e.g. directorships or other contractual interests), and property interests relevant to the dispute in question;
2. professional interests (e.g. a past or present relationship with private clients, or any interests the person may have in domestic or international proceedings, and their implications, where these involve issues similar to those addressed in the dispute in question);
3. other active interests (e.g. active participation in public interest groups or other organisations which may have a declared agenda relevant to the dispute in question);
4. considered statements of personal opinion on issues relevant to the dispute in question (e.g. publications, public statements); and
5. employment or family interests (e.g. the possibility of any indirect advantage or any likelihood of pressure which could arise from their employer, business associates or immediate family members).

This list should however be read having in mind that Article 8.1 DSU explicitly stipulates that Member States shall permit their officials to serve as panellists. As such, this is thus not considered to be a potential source of conflict of interests.

It is up to the relevant person to judge whether certain information is relevant to the case, whilst information considered not to be relevant does not need to be disclosed. To that end, covered individuals are expected to disclose any information that could *reasonably* be known to them at the time which, falling within the scope of the Rules, would be *likely to affect or give rise to justifiable doubts* as to their independence or impartiality. Reasonableness is the standard of assessment, while relevant facts to be disclosed are not only those that

The World Trade Organization

actually impair independence or impartiality, but also those that might create the appearance of lack of independence and impartiality. Moreover, the personal privacy of those to whom the Rules apply acts as a limit.[58] Finally, disclosure must not be so administratively burdensome as to make it impracticable for otherwise qualified persons to serve on panels, the Standing Appellate Body or in other dispute settlement roles.

Panellists, arbitrators and experts, prior to confirmation of their appointment, complete a disclosure form. Such information is then provided to the Chair of the DSB for consideration by the parties to the dispute.

For their part, members of the Standing Appellate Body who, through rotation, are selected to hear the appeal of a particular Panel case, based on the factual portion of the Panel report, complete the same form. Such information is disclosed to the Standing Appellate Body for its consideration of whether the member concerned should hear a particular appeal.

3.1.2. Confidentiality

According to Article VII of the Rules of Conduct, each covered person must, at all times, maintain the confidentiality of both dispute settlement deliberations and proceedings, as well as of any information identified by one of the parties as confidential. Moreover, no covered person must at any time use such information to gain personal advantage or advantage for others. Finally, during the proceedings, no covered person may engage in ex parte contact concerning matters under consideration.

On the other hand, no covered person is allowed to make any statements on the proceedings or the issues in dispute in which that person is participating, until the report of the Panel or the Standing Appellate Body has been derestricted.

In the light of Article 14 DSU, Panel deliberations are also confidential. Moreover, the reports of Panels are drafted without the presence of the parties to the dispute, and opinions expressed in the Panel report by individual panellists stay anonymous. Under Article 17 DSU, the same applies to the AB proceedings: proceedings of the Appellate Body are confidential, reports of the Appellate Body are drafted without the presence of the parties, and opinions expressed in the Appellate Body report by individuals serving on the Appellate Body are anonymous.[59] Moreover, as per Article 3.2 of the Working Procedures, the members of the AB division are expected to 'make every effort to take their

---

[58] This applies despite the fact that the Chair of the DSB, the Secretariat, the parties to the dispute, and other individuals involved in the dispute settlement mechanism are requested to maintain the confidentiality of any information revealed through the disclosure process, even after the Panel process and its enforcement procedures, if any, are completed.

[59] Arts 17.10 and 17.11 DSU.

Intersentia

369

decisions by consensus' and thus avoid separate opinions, which in fact are rare in the adopted appellate reports.[60] Rules on confidentiality of deliberations as well as preference for consensus should reinforce independence and impartiality, both of each individual and of the body as a whole. However, the possibility for an adjudicator to express a dissenting opinion has been called for at times. This was rarely based on independence, but rather on the benefit for legal discourse,[61] and so far has gained very little support.

3.1.3. Material Violations

Not all violations are relevant. Only material violations of the obligations established by the Rules of Conduct that may impair the integrity, impartiality or confidentiality of the dispute settlement mechanism lead to the disqualification of the covered person.[62] Moreover, failure to disclose a relevant interest, relationship or matter as such is not a sufficient ground for disqualification unless there is also evidence of materiality.[63]

No definition of materiality exists in the Rules, nor in any other document. To the same extent, the relevance of matters to be considered in the proceedings as not pertinent is not qualified.

On the other hand, in order to challenge a covered person, concrete evidence of a material fact that is able to impair independence or impartiality, or at least their appearance, must be shown.[64] Finally, it cannot be excluded from the language of the Rules that those challenging the covered person should also prove that through the violation of the standards of conduct established by the Rules the integrity and impartiality of that mechanism are infringed. In any event, the latter element – a link between the materiality of the violation and the preservation of the integrity and impartiality of that mechanism – is also a component of the standard of conduct.

---

[60] See P. Mavroidis and E.Y. Kim, *Dissenting Opinions in the WTO Appellate Body: Drivers of Their Issuance & Implications for the Institutional Jurisprudence*, European University Institute, Robert Schuman Centre for Advanced Studies, Global Governance Programme Working Paper No. RSCAS 2018/51 (2018), https://scholarship.law.columbia.edu/faculty_scholarship/2287.

[61] See text for the African Group Proposals on Dispute Settlement Understanding Negotiations, TN/DS/W/42 (24 January 2003). See also K. Addo and E. Kessie, *African Countries and the WTO Negotiations on the Dispute Settlement Understanding*, International Centre for Trade and Sustainable Development 2007.

[62] Art. VIII.1.

[63] Art. VIII.2.

[64] See G. Marceau, 'Rules on Ethics for the New World Trade Organization Dispute Settlement Mechanism: The Rules of Conduct for the Understanding on Rules and Procedures Governing the Settlement of Disputes' (1998) 32 *J. World Trade* 57, 67.

3.2. IMPLEMENTATION

Once a party to a dispute or another member of the adjudicating body has evidence of a material violation, it must submit such evidence to the Chair of the DSB, the Director-General or the Standing Appellate Body, as appropriate according to the respective procedures (the Chair of the DSB when the challenged person is a panellist, an arbitrator or an expert; the Director-General when he or she is a member of the Secretariat; and the Standing Appellate Body when the challenged person is a member of the Standing Appellate Body or of the Standing Appellate Body support staff) in a written statement specifying the relevant facts and circumstances.

3.2.1. *Procedures*

When evidence regards panellists, arbitrators and experts, the Chair of the DSB will transmit such evidence to the person for his or her consideration.[65] Subsequently, the Chair of the DBS will inform the parties to the dispute.

The challenged person may decide to resign. In that case, the Chair of the DSB shall inform the parties to the dispute and, as the case may be, the panellists, arbitrator(s) or experts. If the person does not resign, consultation will follow and the Chair of the DSB, with the Director-General and a number of Chairs of the relevant Council(s), after having provided a reasonable opportunity for the views of the person concerned and the parties to the dispute to be heard, will decide whether a material violation actually occurred. If the parties also agree on the existence of a material violation, disqualification would be expected to follow.

In the meantime, the person who is the subject of the evidence continues to participate in the consideration of the dispute unless it is decided that a material violation of these Rules has in fact occurred.

If a material violation is ascribable to an Appellate Body member, or to a member of its support staff, this is disclosed to the Appellate Body. Upon receipt of the evidence, the Appellate Body provides it to the person who is the subject of such evidence, for his or her consideration. It is up to the Appellate Body to take any appropriate action after having provided a reasonable opportunity for the views of the person concerned and the parties to the dispute to be heard. The Appellate Body then informs the parties to the dispute and the Chair of the DSB of its decision. Another member of the AB will be selected in rotation.[66]

---

[65] Art. VIII.5–10 DSU.

[66] Art. VIII.14–20 DSU. If evidence of a material violation of the Secretariat is discovered, it shall be communicated to the Director-General of the WTO, who will take appropriate steps following Staff regulations, and inform the parties to the dispute, the Panel and the Chair of the DSB of its decision (Art. VIII.11–13).

The procedure thus differs for panellists and arbitrators, on the one hand, and the AB members, on the other. In both cases, the person is granted the opportunity to not only elaborate on and explain the evidence, but also to voluntarily step back. However, whilst in the case of panellists and arbitrators the DSB, together with the Director-General and some Chairs of relevant committees, takes the final decision, in the case of an AB member it is the Appellate Body itself that decides upon challenges to its own integrity.

3.2.2. Concrete Cases of Recusal

Panellists have voluntarily resigned as a consequence of alleged violation of standards of conduct only very exceptionally.[67] In *Turkey – Restrictions on Imports of Textile and Clothing Products*, a panellist apparently withdrew after one of the parties complained that an unpublished conference paper he had previously authored on the subject matter was relevant to the proceeding.[68]

According to Renouf, Appellate Body members have recused themselves on several occasions, but without formal challenge proceedings being initiated.[69] It appears that no material violation of the Rules of Conduct has been found to have occurred so far.[70]

4. CONCLUSIONS

Standards for independence and impartiality of adjudicators within the WTO follow similar paths as other international courts or arbitration tribunals.

---

[67]   G.J. Spak and R. Kendler, 'Selection and Recusal in the WTO Dispute Settlement System' in C. Giorgetti (ed.), *Challenges and Recusals of Judges and Arbitrators in International Courts and Tribunals*, Brill, Leiden 2015. See also M.N. Creis, *The Independence and Impartiality of ICSID Arbitrators – Current Case Law, Alternative Approaches, and Improvement Suggestions*, Brill, Leiden 2017.

[68]   WT/DS34/R (31 May 1999), 1.5/1.6, where only the resignation of the panellist is reported, with no mention of the reasons.

[69]   Y. Renouf, 'Challenges in Applying Codes of Ethics in a Small Professional Community: The Example of the WTO Rules of Conduct for the Understanding on Rules and Procedures Governing the Settlement of Disputes' in C. de Cooker (ed.), *Accountability, Investigation and Due Process in International Organizations*, Nijhoff Law Specials, Brill, Leiden 2005, p. 127.

[70]   M.N. Creis, *The Independence and Impartiality of ICSID Arbitrators – Current Case Law, Alternative Approaches, and Improvement Suggestions*, Brill, Leiden 2017, p. 104, referring in turn to G.J. Spak and R. Kendler, 'Selection and Recusal in the WTO Dispute Settlement System' in C. Giorgetti (ed.), *Challenges and Recusals of Judges and Arbitrators in International Courts and Tribunals*, Brill, Leiden 2015, p. 174, as well as P. Van den Bossche and W. Zdouc, *The Law and Policy of the World Trade Organization*, 5th ed., Cambridge University Press, Cambridge 2021, p. 217.

Despite this, it has been noticed that many fewer attempts to disqualify either panellists or AB members have been experienced, in particular if compared with ICSID arbitration cases. In fact, these have been almost inexistent.[71]

Although the matter of disqualification has not received too much attention from scholars, those who have devoted reflections to it have attributed this different trend to various reasons, mainly linked to the way adjudicators are selected, or possibly to the structural differences between WTO and ICSID parties (as the latter involve private parties).

However, whatever the reason for that difference, what appears to be of relevance is that, against almost inexistent attempts to disqualify individual panellists or AB members, the AB mechanism is now stalled because of vetoes precisely of reappointment, first, and new appointment, second, while negotiations for reform are proceeding very slowly because of obvious disagreement on a number of issues. Structural reform will most probably also affect the issue of independence and impartiality of adjudicators.

Indeed, independence and impartiality are a central feature of the WTO dispute settlement mechanism, which has meant it has strongly departed from the previous mechanism under the GATT47. These standards are linked to the quasi-judicial nature of the mechanism. However, such system is part of a more complex context, where the role of Members is still quite dominant.

Moreover, the WTO dispute settlement mechanism is the only one where a hybrid system exists, with ad hoc Panels on the one hand, where parties have to agree on adjudicators to pronounce on the individual case, and a standing Appellate Body on the other, where adjudicators are randomly selected from a limited number of permanent members, irrespective of their nationality or any other characteristic, and where an individual adjudicator is exonerated from the case only if a material conflict of interests is proved. Moreover, as has been seen, at any point in time any of these procedures may be substituted by arbitration, where the parties are at liberty to fix autonomous rules and procedures.

Independence and impartiality in this context, which are vital for the perseveration of the integrity of the system itself, make implementation of standards of conduct challenging to many extents. However, we would say that it is precisely because of its light and shadows that this system can provide a significant paradigm for the assessment of independence and impartiality of adjudicators in international courts.

---

[71] See M.N. Creis, *The Independence and Impartiality of ICSID Arbitrators – Current Case Law, Alternative Approaches, and Improvement Suggestions*, Brill, Leiden 2017, for a synthesis of this debate.

PART II
SPECIAL NATIONAL REPORTS

THE INDEPENDENCE AND IMPARTIALITY OF ADJUDICATORS IN CANADA

Fabien GÉLINAS and Paul E. TRINEL

1. Criteria for the Selection of Adjudicators 378
   1.1. Domestic Adjudicators 378
   1.2. National Candidates for Positions as International
        Adjudicators 379
2. Which Authority Appoints Adjudicators? 380
   2.1. Domestic Adjudicators 380
   2.2. National Candidates for Positions as International
        Adjudicators 382
3. The Method for Appointing Adjudicators 383
   3.1. Domestic Adjudicators 383
   3.2. National Candidates for Positions as International
        Adjudicators 383
4. Methods to Balance the Appointing Authority's Influence on the
   Appointment of Adjudicators 383
   4.1. Domestic Adjudicators 383
   4.2. National Candidates for Positions as International
        Adjudicators 386
5. Parameters to Ensure that Adjudicators Act Independently
   and Impartially 386
   5.1. Domestic Adjudicators 386
   5.2. Nationals Appointed to Positions as International
        Adjudicators 387
6. Consequences for Adjudicators of a Breach of the Requirement
   to Act Independently and Impartially 388
   6.1. Domestic Adjudicators 388
   6.2. Nationals Appointed to Positions as International Adjudicators 389
7. Enforcement of a Final Decision Rendered by an Adjudicator
   who Breached the Requirement to Act Independently
   and Impartially 390
   7.1. Decisions by Domestic Adjudicators 390
   7.2. Decisions by Foreign or International Tribunals or Adjudicators 390

Intersentia

Fabien Gélinas and Paul E. Trinel

1. CRITERIA FOR THE SELECTION OF ADJUDICATORS

1.1. DOMESTIC ADJUDICATORS

Canada is a federal country. Each one of the federated entities, the provinces, as well as the federal state itself, has different processes and rules related to their judiciary. In this report, we will focus on the federal judiciary and highlight trends that are common to Canadian courts as a whole. When relevant, provincial particularities will be discussed.

To begin with, all members of the Canadian judiciary come from the legal profession.[1] A candidate to the federal judiciary, as specified in both the Judges Act[2] and the Supreme Court Act,[3] must have spent at least 10 years as a member of a provincial bar before appointment.

Competence and merit are the relevant factors for judicial appointments, as overt political nominations are no longer considered acceptable. Merit is understood broadly: it now includes the candidate's potential contribution to diversity on the bench.[4]

Appointments are made from lists of names recommended by independent Judicial Advisory Committees. The Office of the Commissioner for Federal Judicial Affairs Canada informs Canadians that the primary assessment criteria used by independent Judicial Advisory Committees is 'professional competence and overall merit'.[5] A non-exhaustive list of factors is provided. It includes three categories: professional competence and experience (general proficiency in the law, capacity to exercise sound judgments, capacity to handle stress and pressures of the isolation of the judicial role, etc.); personal characteristics (sensitivity to and understanding of gender, racial equity and aboriginal justice issues, sense of ethics, patience, humility, etc.); and potential impediments to appointment (any debilitating physical or mental condition, any past or current disciplinary actions, any past civil or criminal actions, etc.). The Office also reiterates Canada's commitment to diversity, stating that '[c]ommittees must strive to create a pool of candidates that is gender-balanced and reflective of the diversity of each jurisdiction' and give 'due consideration to all legal experience, including that outside of mainstream legal practice'.

---

[1] F. Gélinas, 'Judicial Independence in Canada: A Critical Overview' in A. Seibert-Fohr (ed.), *Judicial Independence in Transition: Strengthening the Rule of Law in the OSCE Region*, Springer, Heidelberg 2011, p. 573.

[2] Judges Act, RSC 1985, c J-1, s 3.

[3] Supreme Court Act, RSC 1985, c S-26, s 5.

[4] Ibid.

[5] https://www.fja.gc.ca/appointments-nominations/committees-comites/guidelines-lignes-eng.html#Assessments.

378

Intersentia

Canada

1.2. NATIONAL CANDIDATES FOR POSITIONS AS INTERNATIONAL ADJUDICATORS

The Privy Council's Office lists several criteria that are to guide Governor-in-Council (GIC) appointments, which includes nominations to international adjudicative positions (cf. infra).[6] The selection process is open to all Canadian citizens and is based on merit. According to the Privy Council, the selection process 'seeks individuals who have the qualifications (education, experience, knowledge, skills and abilities) and personal suitability to fill the position, and who are able to meet any statutory and/or other conditions that may be required'.[7] The fact that the candidate reflects Canada's diversity, be that in terms of gender, languages or membership of ethnic or cultural minority groups, is also a factor to be considered when making an appointment.

More specifically, the federal government of Canada has published detailed lists of requirements for candidates wishing to be appointed to certain international panels or tribunals.[8] For instance, when it comes to the International Centre for the Settlement of International Disputes (ICSID) panels of conciliators and arbitrators, the candidate must fulfil the following criteria:

- A minimum of ten years of experience as counsel, judge, tribunal member, government official, academic or other similar role (or a combination thereof) in the area of private international law and/or public international law or
- A minimum of five years of experience as a judge, tribunal member, arbitrator, mediator or similar role (or combination thereof) in a process of formal dispute settlement, including alternative dispute settlement or
- Experience as lead counsel, lead advisor, tribunal member or other similar role (or combination thereof) in one or more specialized tribunals related to international trade law, trade remedies, international investment law or financial services
- Recognized competence in the fields of law, commerce, industry or finance
- Experience in international investment law or the practice of international commercial arbitration as a lead litigator or an arbitrator/conciliation
- Experience in managing complex disputes would be an asset and
- Proficiency in Spanish would be an asset.[9]

The Canada–Costa Rica Free Trade Agreement (CCRFTA) is an example of a bilateral investment treaty setting up a roster of arbitrators that will then be

---

6 https://www.canada.ca/en/privy-council/programs/appointments/governor-council-appointments/general-information/appointments.html.

7 Ibid.

8 https://appointments.gc.ca/slctnPrcs.asp?menu=1&lang=eng&SelectionProcessId=DC452E7C-6064-4410-92A5-38768DA57F37.

9 Ibid.

Intersentia

379

called upon to settle disputes regarding interpretation and/or application of the treaty. The criteria that the candidate is supposed to fulfil are the following:

- A minimum of ten years of experience as counsel, judge, tribunal member, government official, academic or other similar role (or a combination thereof) in the area of private international law and/or public international law or
- A minimum of five years of experience as a judge, tribunal member, arbitrator, mediator or similar role (or combination thereof) in a process of formal dispute settlement, including alternative dispute settlement or
- Experience as lead counsel, lead advisor, tribunal member or other similar role (or combination thereof) in one or more specialized tribunals related to international trade law, trade remedies, international investment law or financial services
- Expertise or experience in law, international trade, other matters covered by the CCRFTA, or the resolution of disputes arising under international trade agreements and
- Proficiency in Spanish would be an asset.[10]

As can be inferred from the two examples detailed above, the qualifications demanded of candidates for international adjudicative positions mostly put the stress on knowledge in the relevant field of law and procedural experience, be that as an adjudicator or as a party representative.

Three requirements common to these different positions can also be highlighted: that the candidate should not be 'currently affiliated with or take instruction from a government (federal or sub-federal) of Canada or any Party to the agreement governing the roster to which [he or she] is appointed', that the candidate should have sufficient time to fulfil his or her obligations, and that he or she be willing to travel across Canada and internationally.[11]

Thus, apart from the loosely worded requirement that the candidate not be currently affiliated with or take instruction from any Canadian government, the requirements highlighted for GIC appointments to positions of international adjudicators are focused on experience and knowledge rather than on independence and impartiality.

2. WHICH AUTHORITY APPOINTS ADJUDICATORS?

2.1. DOMESTIC ADJUDICATORS

The federal structure of Canada means that there are different authorities – at the federal and the provincial levels of government – with the competence to appoint

---

[10] Ibid.
[11] Ibid.

national adjudicators. One must turn to sections 96–100 of the Constitution Act, 1867, in order to know which level of government is responsible for what type of courts.[12] In any case, the system generally relies on the judicious exercise of an executive discretion which is still widely considered absolute.[13]

Superior Provincial Courts, also called Section 96 Courts, are courts of 'inherent jurisdiction', which means that they can hear any case, except when statutes limit their authority. Judges sitting on Section 96 Courts are appointed by the federal government, despite these being provincial courts. In 1988, provincial committees were established so that they can issue recommendations leading to federal appointments. They are managed by the Commissioner for Federal Judicial Affairs.[14] Their recommendation for a particular vacancy is evaluated by the Minister of Justice, who then issues an advice to the Governor General, who is formally responsible for proceeding to the appointment.[15]

Section 92 Courts, or Provincial Courts, are the courts that handle the bulk of the cases. The exact process varies from one province to another, but in most provinces, the Minister of Justice, Attorney General or Lieutenant Governor of the province is responsible for the appointment of the judges,[16] after candidates' applications have been considered by a selection committee composed typically of members of the judiciary and the legal profession, as well as from the public.[17]

Federal Courts, or Section 101 Courts, are outside the provincial justice system, and have their own particular areas of jurisdiction. Judges are appointed following the same process as the one that was discussed above in respect of Superior ('Section 96') Courts. A federal court appointment is a GIC appointment.[18]

Finally, when it comes to the Supreme Court of Canada, it is the Prime Minister of Canada who, through the federal Minister of Justice, makes the

---

[12] Constitution Act, 1867, 30 & 31 Victoria, c 3, ss 96–100.

[13] K. Eltis and F. Gélinas, 'Judicial Independence and the Politics of Depoliticization' (2009) *Social Science Research Network*, https://papers.ssrn.com/sol3/papers.cfm?abstract_id=1366242, p. 4.

[14] F. Gélinas, 'Judicial Independence in Canada: A Critical Overview' in A. Seibert-Fohr (ed.), *Judicial Independence in Transition: Strengthening the Rule of Law in the OSCE Region*, Springer, Heidelberg 2011, p. 574.

[15] K. Eltis and F. Gélinas, 'Judicial Independence and the Politics of Depoliticization' (2009) *Social Science Research Network*, https://papers.ssrn.com/sol3/papers.cfm?abstract_id=1366242, p. 7.

[16] F. Gélinas, 'Judicial Independence in Canada: A Critical Overview' in A. Seibert-Fohr (ed.), *Judicial Independence in Transition: Strengthening the Rule of Law in the OSCE Region*, Springer, Heidelberg 2011, p. 575.

[17] K. Eltis and F. Gélinas, 'Judicial Independence and the Politics of Depoliticization' (2009) *Social Science Research Network*, https://papers.ssrn.com/sol3/papers.cfm?abstract_id=1366242, p. 9.

[18] Ibid., p. 12.

appointments to the highest court of the country. Section 4(2) of the Supreme Court Act provides that 'judges shall be appointed by the Governor in Council by letters patent under the Great Seal'.[19] In 2016, the Independent Advisory for Supreme Court of Canada Judicial Appointments, whose mandate is to provide non-binding merit-based recommendations to the Prime Minister, was established.[20] Also, in the recent past, there have been examples of candidates for appointment to the Supreme Court who have been interviewed by parliamentary committees. However, this practice remains controversial and has yet to be firmly established.[21]

2.2. NATIONAL CANDIDATES FOR POSITIONS AS INTERNATIONAL ADJUDICATORS

As mentioned above, national positions as international adjudicators are usually filled through GIC appointments. The Governor General, representative of the King of Canada as the Head of State, formally makes these appointments, on the advice of the Cabinet.[22] In practice, this means that it is the Prime Minister of Canada who has the final say on these appointments.

Sometimes, the law explicitly gives the power of making appointments to certain international adjudicative bodies to the GIC. For instance, section 11 of the Settlement of International Investment Disputes Act states that the GIC may designate persons to the ICSID panels of conciliators and arbitrators.[23] This can also be done indirectly: when it comes to the USMCA, the GIC must appoint a Minister responsible for its implementation who will then have the power, according to the law, to appoint individuals to the roster of arbitrators.[24] When that power is not explicitly delegated through law, the royal prerogative relating to the conduct of foreign affairs will justify the powers of the GIC to nominate Canadians to adjudicative positions in international bodies.[25]

---

[19] Supreme Court Act, RSC 1985, c S-26, s 4(2).
[20] https://www.fja-cmf.gc.ca/scc-csc/2021/establishment-creation-eng.html.
[21] F. Gélinas, 'Judicial Independence in Canada: A Critical Overview' in A. Seibert-Fohr (ed.), *Judicial Independence in Transition: Strengthening the Rule of Law in the OSCE Region*, Springer, Heidelberg 2011, p. 574.
[22] https://www.canada.ca/en/privy-council/programs/appointments/governor-council-appointments/general-information/appointments.html.
[23] Settlement of International Investment Disputes Act, SC 2008, c 8, s 11.
[24] Canada–United States–Mexico Agreement Implementation Act, SC 2020, c 1, ss 10 and 16(c).
[25] For a discussion of the prerogative powers, see *Black v. Chrétien*, 2001 CanLII 8537 (ON CA) at paras 23 ff., 54 OR (3d) 215.

Canada

3. THE METHOD FOR APPOINTING ADJUDICATORS

3.1. DOMESTIC ADJUDICATORS

The different methods for appointing judges to the different courts are detailed in section 3 above.

3.2. NATIONAL CANDIDATES FOR POSITIONS AS INTERNATIONAL ADJUDICATORS

There are generally two stages to GIC appointments: a selection process and an appointment process.[26] Firstly, a selection committee is established so that it can determine the relevant criteria. The opportunity is then communicated to the public and prospective candidates are invited to register and apply for the position. The selection committee must then assess the candidates in order to give to the Minister in charge of the appointment a list of the most highly qualified candidates.

Based on this advice, the Minister can make his or her recommendation to the GIC. That is when the selection process ends and the appointment process starts. A due diligence process is conducted regarding the selected candidate, who is then informed of the proposed compensation and other conditions of employment. At the end of the process, the Cabinet prepares an Order in Council, which is formalised by the Governor General.

4. METHODS TO BALANCE THE APPOINTING AUTHORITY'S INFLUENCE ON THE APPOINTMENT OF ADJUDICATORS

4.1. DOMESTIC ADJUDICATORS

As detailed above, the executive branch of the government is responsible for the appointment of judges in Canada. Appointments have been largely depoliticised as a result of self-imposed processes whereby independent committees vet the candidates and provide a shortlist from which the government must make the appointment. Once these processes stabilise over time, it is likely that their existence will become constitutionally required.

---

[26] https://www.canada.ca/en/privy-council/programs/appointments/governor-council-appointments/general-information/appointments.html#toc14.

Once the appointment is made, the constitutional principle of judicial independence afford strong protections from executive interference. The separation of powers doctrine has also been recognised as a fundamental constitutional principle in Canada.[27] These two concepts of separation of powers and judicial independence are intertwined in Canadian doctrine and jurisprudence. 'The separation of powers interfaces with and strengthens the now independently recognized constitutional principle of the independence of the judiciary'.[28] According to the Supreme Court of Canada, 'the legislature and the executive cannot, and cannot appear to, exert political pressure on the judiciary'.[29]

In Canadian doctrine, judicial independence is defined as having three main components as well as two overarching dimensions. The three components are: security of tenure, financial security, and administrative autonomy. The two dimensions result from the fact that judicial independence involves both individual (the independence of each individual judge) and institutional (the independence of the tribunal taken holistically in its dealings with the government and the legislature) relationships.[30]

Security of tenure is therefore the first aspect of judicial independence in Canada. Basically, it signifies that, once appointed, a judge is protected by constitutional safeguards from the interference of the executive. Judges whose tenure is protected can focus on delivering decisions based on the law and not on what they think the government that appointed them is expecting. They may sit until the age of retirement and can only be removed for cause, following an independent investigation and parliamentary intervention.[31] The Canadian Judicial Council (CJC), an independent body made up of members of the judiciary, has been entrusted with judicial discipline[32] by the federal Judges Act.[33] A summary of the procedure is discussed in subsection 6.1 of this report.

When it comes to administrative tribunals and agencies, which could be considered as 'domestic adjudicators', the situation is different. Members of these tribunals are indeed generally appointed for a fixed term, which raises issues of

---

[27] *Reference re Remuneration of Judges of the Provincial Court of Prince Edward Island* (1997) 3 SCR 3 at para. 139.

[28] F. Gélinas, 'Judicial Independence in Canada: A Critical Overview' in A. Seibert-Fohr (ed.), *Judicial Independence in Transition: Strengthening the Rule of Law in the OSCE Region*, Springer, Heidelberg 2011, p. 592.

[29] *Reference re Remuneration of Judges of the Provincial Court of Prince Edward Island* (1997) 3 SCR 3 at para. 140.

[30] K. Eltis and F. Gélinas, 'Judicial Independence and the Politics of Depoliticization' (2009) *Social Science Research Network*, https://papers.ssrn.com/sol3/papers.cfm?abstract_id= 1366242, p. 2.

[31] Ibid., p. 13.

[32] Ibid., p. 17.

[33] Judges Act, RS 1985, c J-1 at paras 59–71.

Canada

independence linked to the prospect of reappointment.[34] These tribunals fall under the supervisory jurisdiction of superior courts, however, and as detailed above, these courts enjoy security of tenure.

The second defining component of judicial independence in Canada is financial security. Financial security ensures that judges are less susceptible to corruption and to undue influence by the executive in the determination of their pay. Members of the judiciary therefore enjoy levels of remuneration that are comparable to the salaries of deputy ministers.[35] In the seminal case *R v. Valente*, the Supreme Court of Canada defined the essence of financial security and decided that 'the right to salary and pension should be established by law and not be subject to arbitrary interference by the Executive in a manner that could affect judicial independence'.[36] In *Remuneration Reference*[37] and *Beauregard*,[38] the Court made it clear that although the Parliament of Canada has the power to fix the salaries and pensions of judges, that power was not unlimited and a 'basic minimum level' of remuneration is constitutionally guaranteed.[39] Following *Remuneration Reference*, independent remuneration commissions were established at the provincial and federal levels throughout Canada.[40]

The third and last constitutive element of judicial independence in the Canadian doctrine and jurisprudence is administrative autonomy. Because of its institutional past and its British imperial heritage, Canada follows an executive model of court administration.[41] In other words, in each province, the judicial system is administered through the Ministry of the Attorney General, and not as a separate department or branch of government. Once again, this situation evidently creates risks for the independence of judges, which is why Canadian courts have long considered that a core area of administrative autonomy is protected from interference by the executive and the legislature. Since *R v. Valente*, the courts are responsible for and have 'control over the administrative decisions that bear directly and immediately on the exercise of the judicial function'.[42] A non-exhaustive list of decisions that benefit from constitutional

---

[34]   F. Gélinas, 'Judicial Independence in Canada: A Critical Overview' in A. Seibert-Fohr (ed.), *Judicial Independence in Transition: Strengthening the Rule of Law in the OSCE Region*, Springer, Heidelberg 2011, p. 576.

[35]   Ibid., p. 578.

[36]   *R v. Valente* (1985) 2 SCR 673, p. 704.

[37]   *Reference re Remuneration of Judges of the Provincial Court of Prince Edward Island* (1997) 3 SCR 3.

[38]   *Beauregard v. Canada* (1986) 2 SCR 56.

[39]   *Reference re Remuneration of Judges of the Provincial Court of Prince Edward Island* (1997) 3 SCR 3 at para. 137.

[40]   F. Gélinas, 'Judicial Independence in Canada: A Critical Overview' in A. Seibert-Fohr (ed.), *Judicial Independence in Transition: Strengthening the Rule of Law in the OSCE Region*, Springer, Heidelberg 2011, p. 580.

[41]   Ibid., p. 569.

[42]   *R v. Valente* (1985) 2 SCR 673, p. 712.

Intersentia

protection would include the assignment of judges and the allocation of court room as well as the administrative staff. Even if by convention the courts are most often consulted on decisions that affect them, the executive still has some important administrative areas, such as the establishment of budgets, within its discretionary purview.

4.2. NATIONAL CANDIDATES FOR POSITIONS AS INTERNATIONAL ADJUDICATORS

As will be detailed in subsection 5.2 below, guidelines that apply to GIC appointees aim at ensuring that they refrain from taking part in any kind of political activity. This can be seen as a way of maintaining the necessary independence between the Canadian government (the appointing authority) and the candidates that are appointed to positions as international adjudicators.

5. PARAMETERS TO ENSURE THAT ADJUDICATORS ACT INDEPENDENTLY AND IMPARTIALLY

5.1. DOMESTIC ADJUDICATORS

In Canada, the notions of judicial independence and judicial impartiality are often seen as overlapping. Indeed, in section 11(d) of the Canadian Charter of Rights and Freedom, the right for any person to be heard 'by an independent and impartial tribunal' is enshrined. Therefore, the discussion related to the independence and impartiality of domestic adjudicators can be found in section 4 above. Section 11(d) 'remains but one manifestation among many others of that cardinal principle', that is to say judicial independence.[43]

Because of the constitutional requirement of administrative autonomy (cf. supra), it is the courts themselves who are in charge of the assignment of cases. The executive has no role to play in that regard. However, recusal exists in order to resolve situations which give rise to a reasonable apprehension of bias. Examples of such situations include the judge having a pecuniary interest in the outcome of the case, or a personal connection to one of the litigants.[44] In order to preserve the impartiality of their office, judges are expected to make

---

[43] K. Eltis and F. Gélinas, 'Judicial Independence and the Politics of Depoliticization' (2009) *Social Science Research Network*, https://papers.ssrn.com/sol3/papers.cfm?abstract_id= 1366242, p. 5.

[44] F. Gélinas, 'Judicial Independence in Canada: A Critical Overview' in A. Seibert-Fohr (ed.), *Judicial Independence in Transition: Strengthening the Rule of Law in the OSCE Region*, Springer, Heidelberg 2011, p. 582.

disclosures and to recuse themselves when appropriate. A scant body of case law governs recusal in common law provinces. The province of Quebec has codified what may be labelled a Canada-wide practice.[45] In general, when a party requests a recusal, it is the impugned judge him- or herself who will rule on the issue. That decision is in turn subject to appeal.

5.2. NATIONALS APPOINTED TO POSITIONS AS INTERNATIONAL ADJUDICATORS

As public office holders, appointees to international adjudicative positions must comply with a number of guidelines set up by the Canadian government that aim at ensuring their impartiality in the conduct of their duties.

The first set of guidelines that is explicitly referenced in respect of GIC appointments for international dispute settlement is the Ethical and Political Activity Guidelines for Public Office Holders.[46] Four general watchwords are highlighted: Ethical Standard, Public Scrutiny, Decision Making and Government Property. The general principle of these guidelines is that 'a public office holder should not participate in a political activity that is, or that may reasonably be seen, to be incompatible with the public office holder's duties, or reasonably be seen to impair his or her ability to discharge his or her public duties in a politically impartial fashion, or would cast doubt on the integrity or impartiality of the office'.[47] Furthermore, GIC appointees to international adjudicative positions are considered '[q]uasi-judicial Governor-in-Council appointees, whether full or part-time' within the meaning of the Guidelines. This means that they are subject to a much more stringent standard and that they should, as a rule, avoid all political activities other than voting.

Canada's nominees must also comply with the requirements of the Conflict of Interest Act, whose aim is to 'minimize the possibility of conflicts arising between the private interests and public duties of the public office holders'.[48] The focus of the Act is on the conflicts of interest that may arise during the public office holder's tenure, but also on post-employment issues.

These two sets of rules ensure that Canada's appointees are impartial when exercising their jurisdiction, in the sense that they are free from undue political influence and from conflicts of interest.

---

[45] Code of Civil Procedure, RSQ, c C-25 at paras 234–42.

[46] https://appointments.gc.ca/slctnPrcs.asp?menu=1&lang=eng&SelectionProcessId=DC452E 7C-6064-4410-92A5-38768DA57F37.

[47] https://pm.gc.ca/en/news/backgrounders/2015/11/27/open-and-accountable-government #Part_I.

[48] Conflict of Interest Act, SC 2006, c 9, s 3.

When appointed to a particular roster of arbitrators, GIC appointees are also expected to comply with the specific Codes of Conduct which may have been established under the agreement that forms the basis of their jurisdiction. For example, the Canada–European Union Comprehensive Economic and Trade Agreement (CETA) comprises a Code of Conduct that applies to its dispute settlement provisions. This is rendered possible by the fact that Canada follows the dualist model of receiving international law; the legislative basis is the law incorporating the treaty into national law.[49]

6. CONSEQUENCES FOR ADJUDICATORS OF A BREACH OF THE REQUIREMENT TO ACT INDEPENDENTLY AND IMPARTIALLY

6.1. DOMESTIC ADJUDICATORS

When Canadian judges act in such a way as to put themselves in breach of their obligations of impartiality and independence, it becomes a matter of discipline. As explained in section 4, discipline within the federal judiciary is largely dealt with by the Canadian Judicial Council (CJC) under the 1985 Judges Act.[50] In Canada, the only sanction that can be faced by a judge is removal from office for improper conduct. It has to be said, however, that in practice such cases of judicial removal are extremely rare and that most often, complaints about judicial conduct are resolved outside the formal process that will be detailed below.[51]

As per the Constitution Act, 1867, judges hold office during 'good behaviour' and can only be removed from office by the Governor General, acting upon a joint address of the House of Commons and the Senate.[52] It must be noted at this stage that, although we are discussing impartiality and independence in this report, breach of good behaviour includes 'non-behaviour' in the sense of being incapacitated to the point of not being able to conduct the judicial role.[53]

The Canadian Judicial Council can examine complaints it receives from any member of the public, from the federal Minister of Justice or from the

---

[49] See for example Canada–European Union Comprehensive Economic and Trade Agreement Implementation Act, SC 2017, c 6.

[50] Judges Act, RS 1985, c J-1 at paras 59–71.

[51] K. Eltis and F. Gélinas, 'Judicial Independence and the Politics of Depoliticization' (2009) *Social Science Research Network*, https://papers.ssrn.com/sol3/papers.cfm?abstract_id= 1366242, p. 16.

[52] Constitution Act, 1867, 30 & 31 Victoria, c 3, s 99(1).

[53] K. Eltis and F. Gélinas, 'Judicial Independence and the Politics of Depoliticization' (2009) *Social Science Research Network*, https://papers.ssrn.com/sol3/papers.cfm?abstract_id= 1366242, p. 17.

Attorney General of one of the provinces. The procedure will change depending on who lodged the complaint, but the important point to consider is that the CJC handles the complaint independently. It follows a two-stage process: it must first decide whether the judge is 'incapacitated or disabled from the due execution of the office of judge'; then it determines whether a recommendation for removal is warranted.[54] In lighter cases, the judge is simply reprimanded. The criterion for a recommendation of removal is the following: 'Is the conduct alleged so manifestly and profoundly destructive of the concept of the impartiality, integrity, and independence of the judicial role, that public confidence would be sufficiently undermined to render the judge incapable of executing the judicial office?'.[55]

The CJC's recommendation is made to the Minister of Justice of Canada. The removal only happens if both the House of Commons and the Senate agree with the CJC's opinion, which is not binding upon them; however, in practice, most judges facing a recommendation of removal will resign before Parliament can discuss their case.[56]

When it comes to provincially appointed judges, the CJC has its equivalents in the different provinces. Each one of them has its own procedure for handling complaints.[57] For instance, in Quebec, the Judicial Council conducts an independent inquiry and has the authority to recommend removal to the provincial Minister of Justice. Unlike the federal process, however, the Quebec process has the Quebec Court of Appeal making the final decision.[58]

6.2. NATIONALS APPOINTED TO POSITIONS AS INTERNATIONAL ADJUDICATORS

There is not one body of rules that details the consequences of breaches by international adjudicators of the requirement to act independently and impartially. As no precedent exists, the discussion contained in this subsection is purely theoretical. Some of the guidelines and obligations detailed above that are common to most public office holders impose penalties in cases of breach. For instance, the Conflict of Interest Act provides for the administrative

---

[54]   F. Gélinas, 'Judicial Independence in Canada: A Critical Overview' in A. Seibert-Fohr (ed.), *Judicial Independence in Transition: Strengthening the Rule of Law in the OSCE Region*, Springer, Heidelberg 2011, p. 585.

[55]   Ibid.

[56]   K. Eltis and F. Gélinas, 'Judicial Independence and the Politics of Depoliticization' (2009) *Social Science Research Network*, https://papers.ssrn.com/sol3/papers.cfm?abstract_id=1366242, p. 18.

[57]   F. Gélinas, 'Judicial Independence in Canada: A Critical Overview' in A. Seibert-Fohr (ed.), *Judicial Independence in Transition: Strengthening the Rule of Law in the OSCE Region*, Springer, Heidelberg 2011, p. 584.

[58]   Courts of Justice Act, RQS, c T-16, s 95.

imposition of monetary penalties on public office holders who were found to be in contravention of its provisions.[59]

It must be noted that the majority of candidates nominated to international adjudicative positions serve a fixed term. For instance, designated individuals to the ICSID panel of arbitrators remain in office for six years.[60] These terms are also often renewable. This means that, unlike national judges (cf. supra section 4), appointees to international adjudicative positions do not benefit from security of tenure. It can be seen as an impediment to their impartiality, as it also means that the government can choose not to reappoint them if it ends up not being satisfied with them.

7. ENFORCEMENT OF A FINAL DECISION RENDERED BY AN ADJUDICATOR WHO BREACHED THE REQUIREMENT TO ACT INDEPENDENTLY AND IMPARTIALLY

7.1. DECISIONS BY DOMESTIC ADJUDICATORS

The disciplinary procedure described in subsection 6.1 above must be clearly distinguished from the appeal of a decision rendered by a judge who may have departed from his or her obligation to remain independent and impartial. The CJC's determination has therefore no influence on the fate of the decision rendered by the impugned judge.

As mentioned above, Canadian courts have to respect the provisions of the Canadian Charter of Rights and Freedoms. Its section 11(d) guarantees a trial by an 'independent and impartial tribunal'. When a judge or a jury has been found to be in breach of this requirement, the appeal process allows for the case to be tried by a new tribunal. For instance, in *R v. Williams*, the widespread racial prejudice among members of the jury led the Supreme Court of Canada to direct a new trial.[61]

7.2. DECISIONS BY FOREIGN OR INTERNATIONAL TRIBUNALS OR ADJUDICATORS

When it comes to the international tribunals discussed so far in this report, most of their final decisions take the form of international arbitral awards. Some of these international adjudicative bodies have built-in mechanisms for the challenge

---

[59]   Conflict of Interest Act, SC 2006, c 9, s 52.
[60]   ICSID Convention, Article 15(1).
[61]   *R v. Williams* (1998) 1 SCR 1128.

of awards, like the ICSID. In its Article 52, the ICSID Convention provides that after the conclusion of an arbitration, a party can commence annulment proceedings for breach of the requirement of independence and impartiality by the arbitral tribunal.[62] However, these are specificities unique to ICSID arbitration. Indeed, the majority of international arbitral awards are enforced under the rules of the 1958 Convention on the Recognition and Enforcement of Foreign Arbitral Awards, also known as the 'New York Convention', according to which enforcement of a foreign award can only be refused based on very specific grounds laid out in its Article V. Canada adhered to the Convention in the 1980s and in its wake, the provinces each adopted and implemented the United Nations Commission on International Trade Law (UNCITRAL) Model Law on International Commercial Arbitration.[63] The situation in Quebec is slightly different as the province chose to implement the Model Law through provisions of the Code of Civil Procedure, and not by separate implementing legislation like in common law provinces.[64]

In these different implementing laws as well as in the original Model Law, the fact that the arbitrators did not respect their obligation to remain independent and impartial does not appear explicitly as one of the grounds for refusing recognition and enforcement of an international arbitral award in the province.[65] The reason for this is that when circumstances exist that give rise to justifiable doubts as to the arbitrator's independence or impartiality, the Model Law and its implementing legislation allow the parties to challenge the impugned arbitrator before the award is rendered by the arbitral tribunal.[66] It is then the arbitral tribunal or an appointing authority that must rule on the challenge. If that challenge is not successful, then the matter will be referred to the courts of the relevant province, which will render a final decision, not subject to appeal.[67] In *Roberts v. R*, the Supreme Court of Canada laid out the test for reasonable apprehension of bias: 'what would an informed person, viewing the matter realistically and practically – and having thought the matter through – conclude. Would he think that it is more likely than not that [the decision-maker], whether consciously or unconsciously, would not decide fairly'.[68]

The challenge procedure is, however, only available to parties while the arbitration is pending. When the award has been rendered, there is no point

---

[62] ICSID Convention, Article 52. See also M.N. Cleis, *The Independence and Impartiality of ICSID Arbitrators: Current Case Law, Alternative Approaches, and Improvement Suggestions*, Brill, Leiden 2017.

[63] F. Bachand and F. Gélinas, 'The Implementation and Application of the New York Arbitration Convention in Canada' (2014) 92 *Canadian Bar Review* 457, 458.

[64] Code of Civil Procedure, RSQ, c C-25.

[65] See e.g. International Commercial Arbitration Act, RSBC 1996, c 233, s 36.

[66] Ibid., s 12.

[67] See e.g. Code of Civil Procedure, RSQ, c C-25, s 627.

[68] *Roberts v. R* (2003) 2 SCR 259 at para. 60.

in challenging the arbitrator. If, at this stage, an element emerges that is susceptible to give rise to justifiable doubts in the mind of one of the parties as to an arbitrator's independence and impartiality, it is probable that it can fall under Article 36(1)(b)(ii) of the Model Law, that is to say that recognition and enforcement of the award would be considered contrary to public policy. Indeed, Canadian courts have said that an award could be refused enforcement if it fundamentally offends the most basic and explicit principles of justice and fairness,[69] if it offends local principles of justice and fairness in a fundamental way,[70] or if it is contrary to the essential morality of the relevant jurisdiction.[71] While no jurisprudence to that effect can be found at the time of the writing of this report, these formulations tend to signify that an international arbitral award rendered by an arbitrator who clearly breached his or her obligations to act independently and impartially would be refused recognition and enforcement in Canada.

In Canada, foreign judgments are usually recognised and enforced in two different ways. The first method is based on reciprocal enforcement legislation that details the enforcement procedure of judgments hailing from one particular country. Each one of the Canadian provinces has enacted a variety of reciprocal enforcement laws. For instance, the Ontario legislature has passed the Reciprocal Enforcement of Judgments (U.K.) Act.[72] These laws contain rules peculiar to each one of them concerning the situations in which the enforcement of a foreign judgment can be refused by the Canadian courts.

The other route by which a foreign judgment can be enforced in Canada is via the common law method, following the jurisprudence developed by the Supreme Court of Canada. In that case, defences are available to parties wishing to argue that the foreign judgment should not be recognised and enforced by the Canadian courts. To begin with, recognition and enforcement of a foreign judgment can be refused on public policy grounds. According to the Supreme Court of Canada in *Beals v. Saldanha*, 'the public policy defence guards against the enforcement of a judgment rendered by a foreign court proven to be corrupt or biased'.[73] When it comes to a foreign tribunal that breached the requirements of independence and impartiality, there is little doubt that it can be characterised as corruption or bias depending on the circumstances. In *Oakwell Engineering Ltd v. EnerNorth Industries Inc.*, the Ontario Court of Appeal underscored that 'the party asserting bias must prove actual corruption or bias'.[74] In the province

---

[69]   *Corporacion Transnacional de Inversiones, SA de CV v. STET International, SpA* (1999) 45 OR (3d) 183.

[70]   *Schreter v. Gasmac Inc.* (1992) 7 OR (3d) 608.

[71]   *Boardwalk Regency Corp v. Maalouf* (1992) 6 OR (3d) 737.

[72]   Reciprocal Enforcement of Judgments (U.K.) Act, RSO 1990, c R.6.

[73]   *Beals v. Saldanha*, 2003 SCC 72, (2003) 3 SCR 416 at para. 72.

[74]   *Oakwell Engineering Ltd v. EnerNorth Industries Inc.*, 2006 CarswellOnt 3477, 19 BLR (4th) 11 at para. 22.

of Quebec, where recognition and enforcement of all non-Quebec judgments is dealt with in the Code of Civil Procedure, enforcement will similarly be refused if the outcome of the decision is found to be manifestly contrary to any moral, social, political or economic values underlying the international legal order. This formulation undoubtedly includes situations in which the foreign court is found to be lacking independence or impartiality.

Canadian courts will also refuse to enforce a foreign judgment when it is found that there has been a 'lack of natural justice' in the foreign proceedings.[75] When the foreign system of justice does not offer guarantees of judicial independence, Canadian courts can characterise it as a 'lack of natural justice' and refuse recognition and enforcement of the foreign judgment.[76] This clearly aims at shielding the Canadian justice system from foreign courts that, because of the way the judicial system in the relevant country works, would be systematically found in breach of Canadian standards regarding the independence and impartiality of its judges.

---

[75] *Beals v. Saldanha*, 2003 SCC 72, (2003) 3 SCR 416 at paras 59–70.

[76] Ibid., para. 60.

INDEPENDENCE AND IMPARTIALITY OF ADJUDICATORS IN CYPRUS

Soterios Loizou

Εγώ __ διαβεβαιώ ότι θα υπηρετήσω καλώς και πιστώς την Δημοκρατίαν της Κύπρου εις το αξίωμα του __ και θα απονέμω το δίκαιον εις πάντας συμφώνως προς τους νόμους και τα έθιμα της Δημοκρατίας της Κύπρου, άνευ φόβου ή ευνοίας, προκαταλήψεως ή πάθους.

[I __ assure that I will serve the Republic of Cyprus well and faithfully in the position of __ and I will do justice to all in accordance with the laws and customs of the Republic of Cyprus, without fear or favour, prejudice or passion.][1]

1. Introduction 395
2. The Legal Framework of Independence and Impartiality of Adjudicators in Cyprus 398
3. Independence and Impartiality in Litigation 399
4. Independence and Impartiality in Arbitration 407
5. Conclusion 411

1. INTRODUCTION

The Republic of Cyprus was founded in 1960 after an almost century-long British colonial rule on the island. Located in the south-eastern corner of the Mediterranean Sea and with a population of approximately one million residents and nearly half a million expats, Cyprus is classified as a small state. For the purposes of this special national report, the analysis focuses on the regulatory framework, guidelines, judgments and arbitral awards linked to the southern part of the island, where the government of the Republic exercises effective control. Laws, judgments and awards linked to the so-called

---

[1]   Oath of judges, Courts of Justice Law, 1960, L 14/1960, as amended, Anx, Sch., Art. 9(I).

'Turkish Republic of Northern Cyprus', a self-proclaimed state entity, which has not been recognised by the United Nations, will not be considered.[2] Similarly, the analysis will not examine the practice of law in the two Sovereign Base Areas of Akrotiri and Dhekeleia (SBA), which as British Overseas Territories on the island enjoy unique status.[3]

Cyprus is a mixed legal order caught in a constant balance between its British colonial common law past and the civil law influences from neighbouring Greece.[4] Pursuant to section 29(1) of the Courts of Justice Law, courts must consider and apply the Constitution of the Republic, the laws enacted under the Constitution, all pre-independence laws unless repealed or rendered obsolete by subsequent legislation, the common law and the principles of equity, the principles of Ottoman properties (*Vakfs*), and EU law.[5]

Notwithstanding the small size of its territory and economy, the comparatively seamless merging of civil and common law traditions, the political stability in the country, the investor-friendly legal and tax regimes, and the accumulation of foreign assets in Cypriot banks have contributed to the rise of Cyprus as an important international dispute resolution hub. Granted, the suitability of Cyprus as a case study regarding the independence and impartiality of adjudicators is attributed not only to its classification as a mixed legal system and its role in international dispute resolution, but also to the unique scenarios of justice administration that arise in small states. Indeed, as noted by the ECtHR:

> Cyprus is a small country, with smaller firms and a smaller number of judges than larger jurisdictions; therefore, [independence and impartiality enquiries are] likely to arise more often ... [C]omplaints alleging bias should not be capable of paralysing a ... State's legal system and ... in small jurisdictions, excessively strict standards in respect of such motions could unduly hamper the administration of justice.[6]

Granted, legal scholarship on independence and impartiality of adjudicators in Cyprus is both scarce and limited in scope, thus amplifying deference to the judiciary.[7] Interestingly, this focus on case law has led to the holistic regulation

---

[2]   See UN Security Council, 'Resolution 541' (18 November 1983) S/RES/541; UN Security Council, 'Resolution 550' (11 May 1984) S/RES/550.

[3]   Treaty concerning the Establishment of the Republic of Cyprus, UN Treaty Series No. 5476 (1960). For independence and impartiality issues linked to the two Sovereign Base Areas, see e.g. *Yiacoub v. The Queen* [2014] UKPC 22.

[4]   See generally Nikitas E. Hatzimihail, 'Cyprus as a Mixed Legal System' (2013) 6 *Journal of Civil Law Studies* 37; Symeon C. Symeonides, 'The Mixed Legal System of the Republic of Cyprus' (2003) 78 *Tulane Law Review* 441.

[5]   Arts 1A, 100 Constitution.

[6]   *Nicholas v. Cyprus*, ECtHR decision of 9 January 2018, application no. 63246/10, para. 63. Accord *Koulias v. Cyprus*, ECtHR decision of 26 May 2020, application no. 48781/12, para. 62.

[7]   See e.g. Achilles C. Emilianides, *Constitutional Law in Cyprus* (2nd ed., Kluwer Law International 2019); Costas Paraskeva, *Cyprus Constitutional Law: Fundamental Rights*

of the matter, irrespective of the type or internationality of the dispute. Private and public disputes, domestic and international cases, litigation and arbitration proceedings: they all share a common underpinning, i.e. the right of access to justice before an impartial tribunal.

The importance of this report is further augmented by information and statistics published in various international reports. Specifically, Cyprus has been placed at 28 among 140 countries in the Global WJP Rule of Law Index, albeit comparatively low at 28 among 43 high-income countries and 21 among 31 countries in the region (EU, EFTA and North America).[8] In addition, recent Eurobarometer studies reveal that only 50% of the general public and 46% of the companies surveyed could describe the perceived independence of the national justice system in Cyprus as very or fairly good.[9] Among those with a negative perception, the concerns were raised mainly due to the interference or pressure from government politicians (general public: 88%; companies: 73%), interference or pressure from economic or other specific interests (general public: 88%; companies: 81%), and the status and position of judges not sufficiently guaranteeing their independence (general public: 63%; companies: 54%). Regarding investment protection, 65% of respondents noted that they were fairly or very unconfident about the adequate judicial protection of investments. Interestingly, 67% of those with a negative perception identified the difficulty to enforce their rights in court due to concerns about the quality, efficiency or independence of justice in the country as one of the main reasons for their lack of confidence in the judicial system in Cyprus.

In exploring the independence and impartiality of adjudicators in Cyprus, this report delineates the regulatory framework of the independence and impartiality of adjudicators in the country (section 2); focuses on the legal practice in state court litigation (section 3) and, at a second stage, explores independence and impartiality in the arbitration setting (section 4); finally, it draws some overall conclusions on the topic (section 5).

---

    and Liberties (Nomiki Vivliothiki 2015) 526–33; Achilles C. Emilianides, 'Principles for the Disqualification of Judges' (2010) 6 *Cyprus and European Law Review* 179; Georghios M. Pikis, *Constitutionalism – Human Rights – Separation of Powers: The Cyprus Precedent* (Martinus Nijhoff Publishers 2006) 72–77.

[8]   World Justice Project, Rule of Law Index 2022, available at https://worldjusticeproject. org/rule-of-law-index/country/2022/Cyprus. See the 2022 EU Justice Scoreboard: Communication from the Commission to the European Parliament, the Council, the European Central Bank, the European Economic and Social Committee and the Committee of the Regions COM(2022)23420; 2021 Rule of Law Report: Cyprus, SWD(2012) 704 final (Brussels, 20 July 2021).

[9]   Flash Eurobarometer 503: Perceived Independence of the National Justice Systems in the EU among the General Public (2022); Flash Eurobarometer 504: Perceived Independence of the National Justice Systems in the EU among Companies (2022).

2. THE LEGAL FRAMEWORK OF INDEPENDENCE AND IMPARTIALITY OF ADJUDICATORS IN CYPRUS

The independence and impartiality of adjudicators has been enshrined as a fundamental tenet of justice in Article 30(2) of the Constitution. This provision constitutes a nearly verbatim adoption of Article 6(1) of the European Convention on Human Rights (ECHR), which has been introduced into the Cypriot legal order by Law 39/1962.[10] Article 30(2) of the Constitution and Article 6 ECHR have been consistently cited by courts in Cyprus as pillars of natural justice in dispute resolution proceedings,[11] to such an extent that to maintain the authority and impartiality of the judiciary, the right to freedom of speech and expression may be limited or restricted.[12]

Turning to arbitration, provisions mandating an independent and impartial arbitral tribunal have been included in both domestic and international arbitration regimes. In particular, sections 9(1) and 20 of the Arbitration Law of 1944,[13] which applied to all arbitrations until 1987 and to domestic arbitrations thereafter,[14] ensure that the arbitrator's bias or prejudice will not taint the proceedings and the arbitral award. Similar rules have been enshrined in the International Commercial Arbitration Law of 1987,[15] which fully adopts Article 12 of the UNCITRAL Model Law. Law 101/1987 also enshrines Articles 34 and 36 of the Model Law on the setting aside and the grounds for refusing the recognition and enforcement of arbitral awards. These provisions are essentially identical to the grounds delineated in Article V of the 1958 New York Convention, which was ratified by Law 84/1979.[16]

Relevant rules safeguarding the independence and impartiality of mediators and arbitrators for consumer disputes have also been enshrined in

---

[10] Law on the European Convention for the Protection of Human Rights and Fundamental Freedoms together with the Amending Protocol (Ratification), 1962, L 39/1962. Cf. Art. 10 Universal Declaration of Human Rights; Art. 47 EU Charter of Fundamental Rights. Cf. also Arts 2, 19 TEU.

[11] See e.g. A. *Panayides Contracting Ltd v. Charalambous* (2004) 1 AAD 416, civil case; *Liasides v. The Police* (2002) 2 AAD 434, criminal case.

[12] Art. 19(3) Constitution; *Constantinides v. Ekdotiki Eteria Vima Ltd* (1983) 1A CLR 348, 358. See Nikolaos D. Koulouris, *Cypriot Civil Procedure* (Nomiki Vivliothiki 2017) 308. Cf. Art. 10(2) ECHR.

[13] Arbitration Law, 1944 (Cap 4), as amended. Cf. *Mastercon Construction Ltd v. Koukouma* District Court of Nicosia App. No. 248/2014 (31.03.2016), noting that English case law and treatises are very helpful in the interpretation of Cap 4.

[14] Art. 3(3) L 101/1987.

[15] Law on International Commercial Arbitration and Relevant Matters, 1987, L 101/1987.

[16] Law on the Convention and Enforcement of Foreign Arbitral Awards (Ratification), 1979, L 84/1979.

Cyprus

Articles 10(1), 10(2) and 8(f) of the Mediation Law of 2012[17] and Articles 7(1)(b) and 7(1)(e) of the Consumer ADR Law of 2017.[18]

3. INDEPENDENCE AND IMPARTIALITY IN LITIGATION

To begin with the default dispute resolution mechanism in the country, as clearly ruled by the Supreme Court:

> [t]he term 'independent' refers to the independence of the Court from the Executive and from the parties. A judge's independence includes enjoyment of a certain stability that does not necessarily imply that it should be stability for life but at least for a specific period. The judge should not be subject to any authority in the performance of his duties as a judge.[19]

A manifestation of the separation of powers principle, the external independence of the judiciary from the executive power is a cardinal feature of the Cypriot legal system.[20] It has been enshrined in Articles 35 and 157(2) of the Constitution and requires that the appointment of judges be free from political influences.[21] Hence, judges are appointed by the Supreme Council of Judicature[22] from the ranks of lawyers in private practice or from members of the Attorney General's office, who have five years of experience of practice – upon interview and without a competition.[23] Regarding appointments to the Supreme Court, the judges at the highest court in the country are appointed by the President of the Republic.[24] To safeguard the independence of the judiciary, by constitutional practice, all presidents so far have consulted with the existing members of the Supreme Court and the Cyprus Bar Association, and, with one exception, appointed from within the ranks of presidents of the first-instance courts, typically on the basis of seniority.[25] The President of the Supreme Court is appointed by the President of the Republic from within the ranks of the Supreme Court judges.[26] Hence, this informal cooptation process ensures the practical depoliticisation of

---

[17] Law on Certain Aspects of Mediation in Civil Matters, 2012, L 159(I)2012.
[18] Law on the Alternative Dispute Resolution of Consumer Disputes, 2017, L 85(I)2017.
[19] *Pastellopoulos v. The Republic* (1985) 2 CLR 165, 184.
[20] Emilianides, *Constitutional Law in Cyprus* (n. 7) para. 394; Koulouris (n. 12) 34.
[21] See Art. 153 Constitution; Art. 10 Law on the Administration of Justice (Miscellaneous Provisions), 1964, L 33/1964.
[22] The Supreme Court of Judicature is composed of all the members of the Supreme Court.
[23] Koulouris (n. 12) 35–36; Pikis (n. 7) 72–73.
[24] Emilianides, *Constitutional Law in Cyprus* (n. 7) para. 258; Pikis (n. 7) 73.
[25] Emilianides, *Constitutional Law in Cyprus* (n. 7) paras 258–59; Koulouris (n. 12) 35; Pikis (n. 7) 73, noting that the President as a rule follows the advice of the Supreme Court.
[26] Art. 3(4) L 33/1964.

Intersentia

399

appointments to the Supreme Court. Once appointed, judges become members of the Judicial Service of the Republic and remain independent from the executive.[27]

Independence also relates to the lack of connections between the judge and the parties or the dispute – so-called internal independence. In that respect, the Supreme Court has devised core guidelines entitled the Code of Judicial Practice and the Guide of Judicial Conduct for the recusal of judges.[28] Specifically, the Code of Judicial Practice is rather succinct and provides that judges are precluded from sitting on cases where the legal counsel appearing before them maintains a close relationship by blood or affinity with the judge. In parallel, the Guide of Judicial Conduct, currently in its fifth edition (June 2022), drawing inspiration from the corresponding UK Guide of Judicial Conduct and adopting the Bangalore Principles of Judicial Conduct (including its extensive Commentary of 2007),[29] sets forth detailed guidelines that the judiciary in Cyprus must follow.[30] Notably, the provisions elaborate on the duties of independence and impartiality, striking a balance between the adage *nemo iudex in casua sua*[31] and the practical limitations of the judicial system in Cyprus, such as the small population of the island and the even smaller circle of law practitioners. To conclude on the duty of independence, a court that maintains links with the parties or the dispute cannot satisfy the requirements of impartiality.[32] Still, an independent adjudicator does not necessarily entail his or her impartiality. Put differently, independence is neither a judicial privilege nor an end in itself – it is a prerequisite of and exists to serve impartiality.

---

[27]   Koulouris (n. 12) 35. See Art. 153 Constitution; Art. 6 L 33/1964.

[28]   See *Mediams Construction and Development Co. Ltd v. Konstantinidi* District Court of Nicosia App. No. 44/2020 (29.06.2020), where the judge expressly referred to both the Code of Judicial Practice and the Guide of Judicial Conduct to determine whether he should recuse himself from continuing to hear the case.

[29]   Bangalore Principles of Judicial Conduct, E/CN.3/2003/65 (2002). See Commission on Human Rights Res. No. 2003/43 (23 April 2003) and Economic & Social Council (ECOSOC) Res. Nos 2006/23 (27 July 2006) and 2007/22 (26 July 2007), inviting their respective members to encourage their judiciaries to take into consideration the Bangalore Principles.

[30]   See *The Republic v. Avgoustis* Supreme Court (CA) App. Nos 117/2018, 75/2019, 76/2019, 77/2019, 79/2019, 80/2019, 84/2019, 85/2019 (16.06.2019). For case law adopting the Bangalore Principles even before the entry into force of the Guide of Judicial Conduct in Cyprus in 2019, see e.g. *Michaelides v. The Republic* Supreme Court (CA) App. No. 125/2017 (26.04.2018); *Attorney General v. Deputy Attorney General* (2015) 3 AAD 484.

[31]   'No person shall be the judge of his or her own cause.' See *The Republic v. Mozoras* (1966) 3 CLR 356, 399: 'The two essential elements of natural justice are in modern times usually expressed as follows: (a) no man shall be judge in his own cause; and (b) both sides shall be heard, or audi alteram partem.' Cf. *Kanda v. Government of the Federation of Malaya* [1962] AC 322, 337 (Eng.).

[32]   *Sigma Radio TV Ltd v. CRA* (2004) 3 AAD 134, 185.

Impartiality, in turn, focuses on safeguarding the final decision from the adjudicator's own interests, prejudice or bias.[33] Such an interest or bias could exist because of a connection between the judge and either one of the parties or the subject matter of the dispute.[34] Impartiality is determined under a subjective and an objective test.[35] Granted, as put by the ECtHR:

> there is no watertight division between subjective and objective impartiality since the conduct of a judge may not only prompt objectively held misgivings as to impartiality from the point of view of the external observer … but may also go to the issue of his or her personal conviction … Thus, in some cases where it may be difficult to procure evidence with which to rebut the presumption of the judge's subjective impartiality, the requirement of objective impartiality provides a further important guarantee.[36]

Specifically, the subjective criterion focuses on the personal conviction and behaviour of the judge, examining whether the judge actually held any personal prejudice or bias in the case at hand.[37] 'Bias is or may be an unconscious thing and a man may honestly say that he was not actually biased and did not allow his interest to affect his mind, although, nevertheless, he may have allowed it unconsciously to do so.'[38] Be that as it may, judges are presumed impartial, unless proven otherwise.[39]

In addition to the relatively rare instances of subjective bias where the presumption has been successfully rebutted, there is also an objective criterion of impartiality, which manifests as 'apparent bias' of the judge.[40] 'It is not actual or real bias but a likelihood of bias.'[41] The focus is on whether the judge offered

---

[33] For an impressive delineation of case law from Cyprus and other common law jurisdictions on the impartiality of adjudicators, see *Kritiotis v. The Municipality of Paphos* (1983) 3B CLR 1460, 1466–79. See also *Nicholas v. Cyprus* (n. 6) para. 49; *Kamenos v. Cyprus*, ECtHR decision of 31 October 2017, application no. 147/07, para. 96; *Kyprianou v. Cyprus*, ECtHR decision of 15 December 2005, application no. 73797/01, para. 118.

[34] *Apostolidou v. The Republic* (2002) 3 AAD 80, 85.

[35] *Pitsillos v. Eugeniou* (1989) 1E AAD 691, 695.

[36] *Nicholas v. Cyprus* (n. 6) para. 51. *Accord Kamenos v. Cyprus* (n. 33) para. 98; *Kyprianou v. Cyprus* (n. 33) para. 119.

[37] *Re Symeou* (2012) 1B AAD 974, 983. See *Nicholas v. Cyprus* (n. 6) para. 49; *Kamenos v. Cyprus* (n. 33) para. 96; *Kyprianou v. Cyprus* (n. 33) para. 118.

[38] *Re Psaras* (1985) 1 CLR 604, 610.

[39] *Michaelides v. The Republic* (n. 30); *Re Symeou* (n. 37) 983; *Nikolaides v. The Police* (2003) 2 AAD 271, 293. See *Koulias v. Cyprus* (n. 6) para. 50; *Nicholas v. Cyprus* (n. 6) para. 50; *Kamenos v. Cyprus* (n. 33) para. 97; *Kyprianou v. Cyprus* (n. 33) para. 119.

[40] *Michaelides v. The Republic* (n. 30).

[41] *Re Psaras* (n. 38) 610.

sufficient guarantees to exclude any legitimate doubt in respect of his or her impartiality.[42] This test corresponds with the well-established principle that justice should not only be done but should also manifestly and undoubtedly be seen to be done;[43] the judge should not only be impartial but should also be perceived as impartial.[44]

This can be achieved by maintaining a distanced approach to the resolution of the dispute. In discharging his or her duties, the judge must operate as an impartial arbiter of the strength of the case of the adversaries, distancing him- or herself from the arena of trial.[45] Any departure from this stance could compromise the judge's impartiality in the eyes of the parties and the public,[46] and he or she could also be viewed as advancing the position of either party.[47] Nonetheless, this should not be deemed inconsistent with the powers vested in the court to control the proceedings.[48] On the contrary, this power is necessary to safeguard the independence of the judiciary and sustain the faith of the public in the judicial process.[49] What is at stake is the confidence which the courts inspire in the public in a democratic society.[50]

---

[42] *Re Symeou* (n. 37) 983. See *Nicholas v. Cyprus* (n. 6) para. 49; *Kamenos v. Cyprus* (n. 33) para. 96; *Kyprianou v. Cyprus* (n. 33) para. 118.

[43] *R v. Sussex Justices ex parte McCarthy* [1924] 1 KB 256, 259 (Eng.); *Vrakas v. The Republic* (1973) 2 CLR 139, 156–60, expounding on the principle with further references to English case law. In Cypriot case law, see *Michaelides v. The Republic* (n. 30); *Re Symeou* (n. 37) 983; *Pitsillos v. The Republic* (1994) 2 AAD 268, 273; *Autocefalous Church of Cyprus v. House of the Representatives (No. 1)* (1990) 3A AAD 54, 65; *Pitsillos v. Eugeniou* (n. 35) 695; *Pastellopoulos v. The Republic* (n. 19) 184; *Re Psaras* (n. 38) 610: 'all Judges like Caesar's wife should be above suspicion'; *Kritiotis v. The Municipality of Paphos* (n. 33) 1466; *Vassiliades v. Vassiliades* (1941) 18 CLR 10, 22. See also *Nicholas v. Cyprus* (n. 6) para. 54; *Kamenos v. Cyprus* (n. 33) para. 101.

[44] *Sigma Radio TV Ltd v. CRA* (n. 32) 185; *Pitsillos v. Eugeniou* (n. 35) 695.

[45] *Christopoulos v. The Police* (2001) 2 AAD 100, 108; *Silvestrou v. The Police* (1996) 2 AAD 151, 151; *Eleftheriades v. Mavreliis* (1985) 1 CLR 436, 444–45; *The Police v. Athienitis* (1983) 2 CLR 194, 243; *Evangelou v. Ambizas* (1982) 1 CLR 41, 61–62.

[46] *Evangelou v. Ambizas* (n. 45) 62.

[47] *Athanasiou v. Reana Manufacturing & Trading Co. Ltd* (2001) 1C AAD 1635, 1642.

[48] See *Evangelou v. Ambizas* (n. 45) 61–62. That questions asked by the court to clarify aspects of the case do not indicate bias of the judge, see e.g. *Christopoulos v. The Police* (n. 45) 108; *Re Liakou Mela (No. 1)* (1998) 1B AAD 706, 706. But see *Papakyriakou v. The Police* (2007) 2 AAD 133, 141–42, admitting, during the trial, a key prosecution witness at the judge's private chambers, finding the witness trustworthy before the completion of the oral hearings, and receiving evidence from the father of the accused without immediately disclosing this to the opposing party, was found objectionable as the judge had lost his objective impartiality; *Silvestrou v. The Police* (n. 45) 160, noting that questions indicating that the judge has already formed an opinion that the accused party was guilty or promoting the position of the accusing party might reveal bias of the court. Cf. *R v. Stratford on Avon Justice ex parte Edmonds, Edmonds v. Badham* [1973] 1 RTR 356 (Eng.).

[49] *The Police v. Athienitis* (n. 45) 243.

[50] *Sigma Radio TV Ltd v. CRA* (n. 32) 185; *Pastellopoulos v. The Republic* (n. 19) 184; *Re Psaras* (n. 38) 610. See *Nicholas v. Cyprus* (n. 6) para. 54; *Kamenos v. Cyprus* (n. 33) para. 101.

Hence, the relevant enquiry is whether an objective observer, having knowledge of the key aspects of the dispute, would consider that there were valid reasons for the exclusion of the judge.[51] As put by the Supreme Court:

> [t]his objective observer is certainly not the random uninformed person who could form a hasty impression, carried away by his subjective one-sided and fragmentary perception, but one who has complete information and understanding of the procedural framework so that he can form an objective opinion.[52]

In addition, a justified impression or real possibility of bias in the mind of a reasonable person must be established – mere suspicions would not suffice.[53] Certainly, the observer must bear in mind that judges and lawyers are trained and experienced practitioners of law, hence they are expected to rise to the occasion in any given case.[54] Although the perception of the party requesting the exclusion of the judge is important, it is not conclusive. What matters is whether the impartiality concerns are reasonable and objectively justified.[55]

Case law has identified a good number of examples that illustrate bias or prejudice of the court, such as direct or personal interest – including financial or other business interest – of the judge in the outcome of the dispute,[56] personal friendship or close acquaintance between the judge and the parties, legal counsel or witnesses,[57] and past or current employment, hierarchical or other relationships between the judge and parties with an interest in the outcome

---

[51] *Re Kantouna* Supreme Court (CA) App. No. 363/2020 (13.09.2021); *Re Andronikou* (2013) 1B AAD 1118, 1124; *Re Symeou* (n. 37) 984. See *Re Psaras* (n. 38) 609–10; *Makrides v. The Republic* (1984) 3A CLR 304, 308; *Economides v. The Police* (1983) 2 CLR 301, 309, noting that this should not be taken as a hard-and-fast rule for all cases. See also *Nicholas v. Cyprus* (n. 6) para. 49; *Kamenos v. Cyprus* (n. 33) para. 96; *Kyprianou v. Cyprus* (n. 33) para. 118.

[52] *Typye v. The Police* (2008) 2 AAD 279, 286.

[53] *Michaelides v. The Republic* (n. 30); *Re Symeou* (n. 37) 984; *Tympiotis v. The Republic* (2004) 2 AAD 612, 645; *Re Cyprus Oil Refinery (No. 3)* (2004) 1C AAD 1676, 1684; *Sofokleous v. Taveloudi* (2003) 1B AAD 837, 842; *Pitsillos v. The Republic* (n. 43) 274; *Autocefalous Church of Cyprus v. House of the Representatives (No. 1)* (n. 43) 65–66; *Pitsillos v. Eugeniou* (n. 35) 695; Pikis (n. 7) 74. See *The Republic v. Avgoustis* (n. 30).

[54] *Typye v. The Police* (n. 52) 287.

[55] *Sigma Radio TV Ltd v. CRA* (n. 32) 185. See *Nicholas v. Cyprus* (n. 6) para. 52; *Kamenos v. Cyprus* (n. 33) para. 99; *Kyprianou v. Cyprus* (n. 33) para. 118.

[56] *The Republic v. Avgoustis* (n. 30); *Michaelides v. The Republic* (n. 30); *Vassiliades v. Vassiliades* (n. 43) 21: 'The simplest type of bias is where the Judge is shown to have any pecuniary interest in the result of the proceedings: in that case it will be hold at once that he is disqualified, however small the interest and however clear it may be that his mind could not have been affected.' But see *Sigma Radio TV Ltd v. CRA* (n. 32) 185–86, noting, with further references to ECtHR case law, that there can be no violation of Art. 6(1) ECHR if the financial interest of the judge has been disclosed and the parties have been provided with the opportunity to raise a challenge.

[57] *The Republic v. Avgoustis* (n. 30); *Michaelides v. The Republic* (n. 30).

of the case.[58] Especially regarding the first scenario, it has been ruled that the existence of direct or personal interest creates a presumption of actual bias, which results in the automatic disqualification of the judge, independently of a reasonable suspicion of prejudice or the financial nature of the interest, simply because one should not be the adjudicator of one's own cause.[59]

Conversely, challenges raised on the grounds that the counsel of the plaintiffs was part of the legal team representing the majority of District Court judges, including the challenged judge, in a case of an allegedly unconstitutional law affecting all and pursued by all judges in the country, or because the son of the challenged judge was retained as counsel by a company that had a business relationship with the applicant regarding the liquidation of another company linked to the criminal charges in examination, have been dismissed as not indicating bias.[60] Rather, such scenarios illustrate the difficulties arising in close-knit legal circles.

In addition to the virtually omnipresent personal or professional ties of parties and judges in a small jurisdiction, the limited availability of judges has also resulted in judicial appointments in similar cases, as well as appointments of the same judge in disputes involving the same party. Regarding such scenarios, Cypriot courts have consistently found that a judge's pronouncement on a legal issue does not preclude him or her from entertaining the same or similar questions in subsequent cases.[61] Indeed, 'if a different view was taken, ... there would be hardly judges available to try cases as time and again the same legal issues come up for determination by the Courts'.[62] In like manner, the appointment of the same judge in different cases involving the same party does not indicate bias of the adjudicator.[63] Granted, no judge shall sit upon the

---

[58]   *Re Cyprus Oil Refinery (No. 3)* (n. 53) 1680; *Nicholas v. Cyprus* (n. 6) para. 53: 'It must ... be decided in each individual case whether the relationship in question is of such a nature and degree as to indicate a lack of impartiality on the part of the tribunal'; *Kamenos v. Cyprus* (n. 33) para. 100; *Kyprianou v. Cyprus* (n. 33) para. 121.

[59]   *Spyrou v. Xeni* Supreme Court (CA) App. No. 223/2014 (19.07.2019); *Michaelides v. The Republic* (n. 30).

[60]   *Re Andronikou* (n. 51) 1124; *Spyrou v. Xeni* (n. 59).

[61]   *Tympiotis v. The Republic* (n. 53) 646; *Apostolidou v. The Republic* (n. 34) 84–86; *Pitsillos v. The Republic* (n. 43) 274; *Razis v. The Republic* (1983) 3A CLR 309, 311–12; Pikis (n. 7) 75. See *Autocefalous Church of Cyprus v. House of the Representatives (No. 1)* (n. 43) 65–66 and 68, where the judge's participation in the legislative committee of the country's new family law did not preclude him from hearing the case; *Makrides v. The Republic* (n. 51) 309; *Economides v. The Police* (n. 51) 309; *Theodorou v. The Police* (1971) 2 CLR 245, 252.

[62]   *Razis v. The Republic* (n. 61) 311.

[63]   *Psyllas v. The Police (No. 2)* (2008) 2 AAD 601, 603–04; *Adidas Sportschufabriken Adi Dassier Stiftung and Co. Ltd v. Krashias Shoe Factory Ltd (No. 1)* (1990) 1 AAD 873, 877–79; *Economides v. The Police* (n. 51) 309; *Theodorou v. The Police* (n. 61) 259.

hearing of an appeal in a judgment or order made by him or to which she was a party, whether concurring or dissenting.[64]

A unique situation arises from the conduct of the judge during the trial as judges must avoid leaving an impression of bias or prejudice.[65] Although judges must refrain from passing prejudicial or unnecessary comments,[66] characterisations – even harsh ones – based on the behaviour of the accused and justified by the facts of the case do not imply that the judge is biased.[67] Of course, these do not

> condon[e] discourtesy on the part of judges to counsel or anyone for that matter – witnesses or members of the public. Discourtesy lowers the dignity of the Court and may weaken confidence in the patience of the judiciary to transact judicial business in a climate of calm essential for the administration of justice. Patience combined with firmness are the two essential attributes for robust judgmentship.[68]

As put in another case, however, '[j]udges … are only human, and their patience is sometimes sorely tried by counsel and litigants. It is always to be regretted if their patience even appears to give way.'[69]

In the interest of justice, a judge has a duty to identify any impediments to his or her participation in the trial, disclose any pertinent facts to the parties, affording the latter an opportunity to be heard and challenge his or her participation, and explore the possibility of recusal on his or her own motion.[70] If an objection is raised for want of impartiality, the court must consider and decide on the matter itself before proceeding further with the dispute.[71] Be that as it may, the aforementioned subjective and objective criteria of the judge's impartiality must

---

64   *Re Psaras* (n. 38) 609; *The Republic v. Vassiliades* (1967) 3 CLR 82; *Rodosthenous v. The Republic* (1961) 1 RSCC 127. Cf. *Kyprianou v. Cyprus* (n. 33) para. 121; *Mežnarić v. Croatia*, ECtHR decision of 15 July 2005, application no. 71615/01, para. 36.

65   Pikis (n. 7) 75. See *Kyprianou v. Cyprus* (n. 33) para. 121.

66   *Silvestrou v. The Police* (n. 45) 159; *Evangelou v. Ambizas* (n. 45) 62; Pikis (n. 7) 76–77.

67   *Nikolaides v. The Police* (n. 39) 293.

68   *NK Shacolas (Merchants) Ltd v. Universal Life Insurance Co. Ltd* (1984) 1 CLR 47, 52. See Pikis (n. 7) 76: 'Discourtesy on the part of the Judge cannot be countenanced in the conduct of judicial proceedings.'

69   *Vassiliades v. Vassiliades* (n. 43) 22.

70   See Emilianides, *Constitutional Law in Cyprus* (n. 7) para. 394; Pikis (n. 7) 74. See also *Nicholas v. Cyprus* (n. 6) paras 54, 64; *Koulias v. Cyprus* (n. 6) para. 63.

71   *Re Liasides* (1999) 1A AAD 185, 195 and 197–98; *Economides v. The Police* (n. 51) 310; *Kritiotis v. The Municipality of Paphos* (n. 33) 1479, noting that objection to a judge, where bias or reasonable suspicion of bias is alleged, must be taken at the earliest stage in the proceedings; Pikis (n. 7) 74.

tally with the proper functioning of the judicial system.[72] Whereas concerns about the adjudicator's lack of impartiality are not to be taken lightly, parties should not be able to determine the composition of the court at their whim by invariably and without valid reasons challenging the independence and impartiality of the appointed judge.[73] In like manner, although self-exclusion of a judge for personal or other reasons constitutes a manifestation of his or her freedom to operate as an adjudicator,[74] recusing him- or herself without good reason would amount to abdication of duty.[75] Interestingly, Cypriot courts have also grappled with cases where the accused party in criminal proceedings challenged the judge's decision to excuse himself.[76]

It is a question of substance and fact whether the objection is good.[77] The judge's failure to conform to these fundamental elements of fair trial and natural justice renders all proceedings void and the judgment is set aside.[78] To fill the gap, new proceedings will have to be instated, provided that there can be a fair trial.[79] In addition, if he or she has misconducted him- or herself or the proceedings, the adjudicator would be subject to disciplinary action.[80] For that reason, complaints for lack of impartiality must be made only after careful consideration and be substantiated by concrete and detailed explanations so that the independence and impartiality of the judge can be determined in the case at hand.[81]

---

[72]   *The Republic v. Avgoustis* (n. 30), noting also that when it is impossible to form a court composed exclusively of independent and impartial judges, the doctrine or rule of necessity may require departure from the principle and allow a judge, who would otherwise be excluded to hear and decide a case.

[73]   Ibid.; *Re Symeou* (n. 37) 984; *Tympiotis v. The Republic* (n. 53) 645; *Sofokleous v. Taveloudi* (n. 53) 842; *Pitsillos v. The Republic* (n. 43) 273; *Autocefalous Church of Cyprus v. House of the Representatives (No. 1)* (n. 43) 65. See *Adidas Sportschufabriken Adi Dassier Stiftung and Co. Ltd v. Krashias Shoe Factory Ltd (No. 1)* (n. 63) 877–78; *Re Psaras* (n. 38) 610. See also *Kritiotis v. The Municipality of Paphos* (n. 33) 1480; *Hadjicosta v. Anastassiades* (1982) 1 CLR 296, 299.

[74]   *Apostolidou v. The Republic* (n. 34) 85–86; Pikis (n. 7) 74.

[75]   *Mediams Construction and Development Co. Ltd v. Konstantinidi* (n. 28); *The Republic v. Avgoustis* (n. 30); *Michaelides v. The Republic* (n. 30); *Re Andronikou* (n. 51) 1124; *Makrides v. The Republic* (n. 51) 310–11; *Hadjicosta v. Anastassiades* (n. 73) 299; Emilianides, *Constitutional Law in Cyprus* (n. 7) para. 394.

[76]   See e.g. *Re Symeou* (n. 37).

[77]   *Vassiliades v. Vassiliades* (n. 43) 21.

[78]   *Re Symeou* (n. 37) 984; *Papakyriakou v. The Police* (n. 48) 142; *Christopoulos v. The Police* (n. 45) 111; *Silvestrou v. The Police* (n. 45) 160; *Grigoriou v. Trapeza Kyprou Ltd* (1992) 1B AAD 1222, 1224; *Victoros v. Christodoulou* (1992) 1A AAD 512, 519; *Efstathiou v. The Police* (1990) 2 AAD 294, 303; *Ellinas v. The Republic* (1989) 2 AAD 149, 168; *Pitsillos v. Eugeniou* (n. 35) 695; *Psaras v. The Republic* (1987) 2 CLR 132, 157–58; *Neophytou v. The Police* (1981) 2 CLR 195, 198; Pikis (n. 7) 84.

[79]   *Christopoulos v. The Police* (n. 45) 111; Pikis (n. 7) 84.

[80]   *Attorney General v. Deputy Attorney General* (n. 30), exploring judicial misconduct with references to a wealth of case law, guidelines and soft law instruments.

[81]   *Spyrou v. Xeni* (n. 59), amplifying that such arguments by lawyers should be made sparingly and not for the sake of creating impressions; *Achtar v. The Police* (2010) 2 AAD 397, 412.

4. INDEPENDENCE AND IMPARTIALITY IN ARBITRATION

The same rigour in safeguarding the independence and impartiality of the adjudicator applies to arbitral proceedings too. In the words of the Supreme Court:

> The task of the arbitrators is quasi-judicial. Their mission is judicial too. ... The appropriate conduct of the arbitrators is not only related to the guarantees of impartiality but also to the behaviour expected from a person acting in court. The parties and the public justifiably expect that those in charge of judicial duties behave in a manner consistent with the mission of an impersonal and indispensable adjudicator. Deviating from these established practices tends to shake the confidence in the adjudicators and to lose public's faith in the actors of justice.[82]

Indeed, case law has extended the application of the state court approach to the independence and impartiality of judges also to the members of arbitral tribunals.[83] Granted, the relevant standards that must be attained in arbitration have not been clearly set in either statutory law or soft law instruments. Whereas in litigation proceedings the Code of Judicial Practice and Guide of Judicial Conduct offer concrete guidelines to consider, there are no such instructions in the context of arbitral proceedings – domestic or international.[84] Rather, the independence and impartiality of the arbitrators are determined in light of the general principles of due process as clarified in scholarly writings and case law.[85] Interestingly, Cypriot courts have not grappled with cases involving the application of soft law instruments, such as the IBA Guidelines on Conflicts of Interest in Commercial Arbitration (2014).

Still, illuminating examples from case law set the tone regarding natural justice and the duty of the arbitral tribunal members to be and remain independent and impartial throughout the arbitral process.

To begin, it is trite that arbitrators are typically appointed by the parties.[86] In this context, communications between the prospective arbitrator and one of

---

[82] *Trapeza Kyprou Ltd v. Dynacon Ltd* (1999) 1 AAD 717, 724.

[83] See e.g. *General Construction Company Ltd v. Silver Leaf Developments Ltd* District Court of Limassol App. No. 68/2016 (09.03.2018); *Petridis v. Periferiaki SPE Lemesou Ltd* District Court of Limassol App. No. 2389/2014 (29.05.2015).

[84] The continuity of arbitration regimes and the cross referencing of cases as authorities without distinguishing between international and domestic arbitration mandate the simultaneous examination of both. See e.g. *Active Export Technologies Ltd et al. v. AAS Advanced Automation Systems Ltd* District Court of Nicosia App. No. 3/2016 (18.11.2016).

[85] See *Solomou v. Laiki Cyprialife Ltd* (2010) 1A AAD 687, 705, arbitrators must abide by the fundamental principles of law.

[86] Arts 9–12 Cap 4; Art. 11 L 101/87.

the parties to confirm the former's interest and availability to sit on the arbitral tribunal do not, without else, impact his or her impartiality.[87] As an exception to the general rule of appointment by the parties, regarding disputes between cooperative creditor companies and debtors, the law provides for arbitration before a sole arbitrator, who is selected by the Registrar of the Co-Operative Companies Service.[88] Numerous challenges – invariably unsuccessful – have been raised by debtors complaining mainly about the constitution of the arbitral tribunal and the identity of the arbitrator.

Certainly, attacks have been mounted against arbitral awards on the ground that the appointment of the arbitrator by the Registrar tainted the arbitral process. Against such allegations, it has been ruled that the unilateral appointment of the arbitrator by the Registrar does not, without else, indicate bias in favour of the cooperative creditor.[89] On the contrary, because the duties of the Registrar have been clearly delineated in the laws of the Republic and the appointment process has been set forth in both the domestic legislation and the credit agreement between the parties, the independence and impartiality of the arbitral tribunal is guaranteed.[90]

Regarding the identity of the arbitrator, a past employment relationship between the arbitrator and one of the parties is not decisive indication of the arbitrator's bias.[91] That the arbitrator used to be employed by the supervisory authority of the creditor did not impact on the independence and impartiality of the arbitrator.[92] On the contrary, the arbitrator's experience over the years at the Service was deemed beneficial for the resolution of disputes between creditors and debtors.[93] Nevertheless, it has also been ruled that when confronted with such allegations for lack of impartiality due to a past employment relationship with one of the parties, arbitrators should address the parties' concerns and note

---

[87] *SCPA Architects Engineers Ltd v. The Cyprus Institute* District Court of Nicosia App. No. 19/2018 (27.11.2018).

[88] On the constitutionality of arbitration for such disputes, see *The Co-operative Grocery of Vasilia Ltd v. Ppirou* (1962) 4 RSCC 12; *Re Pericleous* (1985) 1 CLR 178, 184–85. See also *Zampas v. Synergatikis Kypriakis Trapezas Ltd* Supreme Court (CA) App. No. 96/2012 (06.06.2018).

[89] *Synergatiko Tamieutirio Lemesou Ltd v. Merki* District Court of Limassol App. No. 499/2015 (04.02.2020).

[90] *Synergatiko Tamieutirio Lemesou Ltd v. Andreou* District Court of Limassol App. No. 282/2016 (21.07.2017); *Michael v. SPE Morfou Ltd* District Court of Limassol App. No. 444/2014 (08.12.2016).

[91] See *General Construction Company Ltd v. Silver Leaf Developments Ltd* (n. 83), where it was sufficient for the removal of the arbitrator that the arbitrator maintained a business relationship with a key witness in the dispute, who had also been employed in the past by one of the parties.

[92] *Synergatiko Tamieutirio Lemesou Ltd v. Aleksandrou* District Court of Limassol App. No. 259/2014 (30.01.2018); *Synergatiko Tamieutirio Lefkosias Ltd v. Krasari* District Court of Nicosia App. No. 1932/2012 (01.09.2014).

[93] *Synergatiko Tamieutirio Lemesou Ltd v. Aleksandrou* (n. 92).

their response in the record so that the supervising court can review the matter at a later stage.[94]

Another important consideration that has manifested in arbitrations in Cyprus pertains to the venue of the arbitral proceedings. Whereas judicial proceedings always take place in court and no sensible doubts can be raised as to the independence and impartiality of the judge regarding the place where the proceedings were conducted, the venue of the arbitration might indicate bias of the arbitrator. This has mainly arisen in domestic arbitrations between debtors and cooperative creditors, which routinely take place at the premises of the latter. In such cases, although it has been noted that the practice of holding proceedings at the premises of one of the parties should be avoided,[95] the venue of the arbitral proceedings alone cannot substantiate bias of the arbitrator.[96] Together with other elements, however, it could taint the arbitral process.[97]

The requirement to abide by the principle of independence and impartiality is not limited to the appointment of the arbitrator; it extends throughout the arbitral process until the pronouncement of the tribunal as *functus officio*. Hence, arbitrators have a continuous duty to be vigilant and to disclose any circumstances that may raise justifiable doubts regarding their independence and impartiality. In addition, arbitrators must be careful to not misconduct themselves or the proceedings.

Undeniably, the case must be handled with care and the proceedings must be conducted in a manner that would guarantee the fair and just resolution of the dispute. Since the administration of the proceedings by the tribunal can influence the legal outcome of the dispute, the exercise of the tribunal's discretion may, seemingly, 'favour' one party over the other, thus indicating bias of the tribunal toward the party that benefits from the tribunal's conduct.[98] Arbitrators must also avoid verbal or other confrontations with the parties, their lawyers or witnesses.[99] Expressing a different opinion, however, should

---

[94] *The Republic v. Florides* District Court of Nicosia App. No. 477/2016 (07.01.2021), where the court found misconduct of the arbitrator, who did not elaborate on the allegation that the spouse of one of the parties used to be his supervisor at his previous employment.

[95] *Synergatiko Tamieutirio Lemesou Ltd v. Leonidou* District Court of Limassol App. No. 380/2014 (01.08.2016); *STDY Ltd v. Kalaitzi* District Court of Limassol App. No. 779/2013 (29.12.2015); *SPE Pisteos v. Paraika* District Court of Nicosia App. No. 2104/2012 (16.04.2014).

[96] *STDY Ltd v. Kalaitzi* (n. 95); *SPE Pisteos v. Paraika* (n. 95).

[97] *Miltiadous v. Synergatiko Tameio Lemesou Ltd* District Court of Limassol App. No. 363/2013 (14.09.2018); *Michael v. SPE Stroumpiou* Supreme Court (CA) App. No. 190/2012 (28.06.2018).

[98] See *Afoi CVAVasileiou Developers Ltd v. Ntekermendjan* District Court of Limassol App. Nos 3995/2008 and 3834/2010 (13.03.2013); *Makolom v. Skouloukou* District Court of Larnaca App. No. 2945/2005 (26.03.2010); *Mandritis v. SPE Polemidion* District Court of Limassol App. No. 130/2004 (12.02.2009).

[99] *Andreas Othonos & Sons Co. Ltd v. Bardsey Enterprises Ltd* District Court of Limassol App. No. 301/2011 (19.09.2013).

not be equated to confrontation.[100] Comments or even the overall demeanour of the arbitrator might impact the arbitral proceedings.[101] Comments by the arbitrators and communications between the arbitrators and the parties should also be avoided after the completion of the hearings but before the delivery of the final decision.[102]

Three further points must be made regarding the independence and impartiality of adjudicators in arbitrations linked to Cyprus. These relate to the timeliness of the challenge for lack of independence and impartiality, the allocation of the corresponding burden of proof, and the standard of proof that must be attained.

The party raising an objection for lack of independence and impartiality by the arbitrator must challenge the adjudicator within the tight timelines set forth in the law.[103] Any challenges raised after that point will be dismissed on the grounds of waiver and/or abuse of rights and estoppel,[104] even if the delay were to be attributed to a good faith mistake.[105] Definitely, the challenging party should have made use of all procedural tools available to challenge the independence and impartiality of the arbitrator without waiting for the arbitral process to be concluded and the final arbitral award to be rendered.[106]

The ground of waiver has been explicated in *Mastercon Construction Ltd v. Koukouma*.[107] Although one of the parties complained about the appointment of the arbitrator, by attending the appointment confirmation meeting without raising any objections, the party was deemed to have consented to the appointment, thus waiving its right to challenge the arbitrator.[108] Nevertheless, simply because the parties remained in the arbitral process notwithstanding the original complaint about the arbitrator's misconduct does not necessarily mean that they cannot challenge again the independence and impartiality of the arbitrator in light of all the facts of the case.[109] Then again, if the arbitration was

---

[100]   Ibid.

[101]   Ibid.

[102]   *Trapeza Kyprou Ltd v. Dynacon Ltd* (n. 82) 724.

[103]   Art. 52(4) L 22/85; Arts 13(3), 34(3) L 101/87.

[104]   *Themistokleous v. NSPE Lakatameias* District Court of Nicosia App. No. 512/2011 (05.12.2011).

[105]   *Synergatiko Tamieutirio Lemesou Ltd v. Apostolou* District Court of Limassol App. No. 297/2015 (15.01.2016).

[106]   *Synergatiko Tamieutirio Lemesou Ltd v. Andreou* (n. 90); *Michael v. SPE Morfou Ltd* (n. 90).

[107]   *Mastercon Construction Ltd v. Koukouma* (n. 13).

[108]   Ibid. See also *Manolis v. Synergatiko Tamieutirio Lefkosias Ltd* District Court of Nicosia App. No. 2662/2013 (27.09.2017); *Andreas Othonos & Sons Co. Ltd v. Bardsey Enterprises Ltd* (n. 99), where the court explored the doctrine of waiver to decide whether a challenge for misconduct of the proceedings could be raised one year after the relevant information had been brought to the attention of the parties.

[109]   *Mitidou v. K&Y Theodorou & Construction Ltd* District Court of Larnaca App. No. 101/2011 (16.11.2012).

Cyprus

properly conducted, it would be unfair and unreasonable for the party to rely on a procedural shortcoming that it could have complained about but, eventually, did not.[110]

Regarding abuse of process, the case of *Prometheas United Ltd v. Miltiades Neophytou Civil Engineering Contractors & Developers Ltd* is illuminating.[111] One of the parties promptly and diligently raised a challenge of the arbitrator's impartiality, only to unequivocally withdraw the allegations emphasising that they were not true. After the final arbitral award was rendered, that party attempted to challenge again the impartiality of the arbitrator, but the challenge was summarily dismissed by the court for abuse of process.[112]

Similar to state court litigation, the test for establishing bias is objective and focuses on the perception of the average reasonable person and not the perception of the party making the allegation.[113] Furthermore, the lack of the arbitrator's independence and impartiality must be established by the challenging party in detail so that the allegation does not remain general, abstract and unsubstantiated.[114] If successfully raised, the violation of due process in the arbitral proceedings will lead to the removal of the arbitrator,[115] or the setting aside or the limited enforceability of the arbitral award.[116] Nevertheless, not every breach of due process warrants the setting aside or the refusal of recognition and enforcement of an arbitral award, as minor or trivial violations would only warrant a remission of the award to the arbitral tribunal. Indeed, as noted by the Supreme Court, the litmus test is whether 'there is misconduct which makes it impossible for the parties, or for the Court, to trust an arbitrator.'[117]

5. CONCLUSION

It has become clear that the independence and impartiality of adjudicators form an integral part of due process and are inseparably linked to the rule of law and the proper administration of justice in Cyprus.[118] The legislator has provided a

---

[110] Ibid.

[111] *Prometheas United Ltd v. Miltiades Neophytou Civil Engineering Contractors & Developers Ltd* District Court of Nicosia App. No. 53/2015 (04.10.2016).

[112] Ibid.

[113] *Dionysiou v. Champi* District Court of Larnaca App. Nos 1743/2008 and 1202/2009 (09.09.2014); *Mitidou v. K&Y Theodorou & Construction Ltd* (n. 109), with further references to English case law.

[114] *Synergatiko Tamieutirio Lemesou Ltd v. Merki* (n. 89); *Dionysiou v. Champi* (n. 113); *SPE Pisteos v. Paraika* (n. 95). See *Koureas v. Nea SPE Geriou* District Court of Nicosia App. No. 210/2014 (07.04.2017).

[115] Art. 20(1) Cap 4; Arts 12–13 L 101/87.

[116] Art. 20(2) Cap 4; Arts 34–35 L 101/87; Art. V L 84/79.

[117] *Paniccos Harakis Ltd v. The Official Receiver* (1978) 1 CLR 15, 22.

[118] *Pitsillos v. Eugeniou* (n. 35) 695; *Evangelou v. Ambizas* (n. 45) 62.

Intersentia

411

rigorous normative framework safeguarding the independence and impartiality of adjudicators. Simultaneously, courts and arbitral tribunals have strived to preserve public faith in litigation and arbitral proceedings. This is confirmed by a wealth of case law illustrating the development of procedural standards in the country and the sensitivity of judges and arbitrators regarding such matters. As challenging a task as the preservation of the adjudicator's independence and impartiality may be, especially in a small jurisdiction with a close-knit society and a small circle of law practitioners, jurisprudence attests to both the high level of due process protection afforded to the parties and the high quality of justice achieved in the country.

THE INDEPENDENCE AND IMPARTIALITY OF ADJUDICATORS IN DENMARK

Kasper STEENSGAARD*

1. Introduction 413
2. Appointment of Adjudicators 414
   2.1. Domestic Judges 414
   2.2. Judges at International Courts 417
        2.2.1. Appointment Authority 417
        2.2.2. Judges at the Court of Justice of the European Union 417
        2.2.3. Judges at the European Court of Human Rights 418
        2.2.4. General Attitude Towards Independence and
               Impartiality of International Adjudicators 419
   2.3. Investment Arbitration 419
3. Constitutional Protection, Measures and Sanctions Concerning
   the Domestic Judiciary....................................... 420
   3.1. Constitutional Protection of the Judiciary's Independence 420
   3.2. Regulation and Disclosure of External Activities 421
   3.3. Recusal in Individual Cases 422
4. International Aspects 423
   4.1. Enforcement of International Arbitral Awards 423
   4.2. Enforcement of Foreign Judgments......................... 424

1. INTRODUCTION

Impartiality and independence of adjudicators is a cornerstone in any legal system adhering to the rule of law, domestic or international. With that in mind, Section 3 of the Danish Constitution prescribes the separation of powers into legislative, judicial and executive branches. This provision is not an empty policy declaration but establishes a fundamental pillar in the organisation of

---

* I owe my thanks to Attorney Johan Tufte-Kristensen, PhD, for his insightful and invaluable comments during the production of this report.

Danish society. Accordingly, the judiciary is a self-governing entity that functions independently of the other governmental branches.

The Danish legal system is rooted in the philosophy of 'Scandinavian pragmatism', which, inter alia, is reflected in concise legislation that leaves a wide margin of appreciation. An example of the phenomenon is Section 36 of the Danish Contracts Act, which essentially allows the courts to *amend* or set aside unfair agreements. The courts are granted this discretion in reliance on their commitment to apply the law in a pragmatic, just and reasonable way.

The combination of an independent judiciary and legislation with a significant interpretative leeway exposes the Danish legal system to a potential abuse of adjudicative powers. Nevertheless, Denmark consequently ranks low on Transparency International's 'Corruption Perceptions Index' (2020),[1] and the general trust in Danish courts is among the highest in the EU and the world.[2] In practice, the trust in the courts is rarely misplaced.

These realisations help explain why issues of partial or non-neutral adjudicators are not an immediate priority for the legislator. It has, nonetheless, implemented some more general rules and principles to pre-empt issues from arising. I will try to present these schemes in the following. It does not appear, however, that special measures have been put into place specifically for international adjudicatory bodies. Because of this, and considering the scope of the special reports, I am only able to contribute with some very general observations on matters concerning the independence and impartiality of international adjudicators.

2. APPOINTMENT OF ADJUDICATORS

2.1. DOMESTIC JUDGES

The authority to appoint judges rests formally with the Monarch of Denmark – for the past more than 50 years, Queen Margrethe II.[3] However, the Danish Monarchy is constitutional, and thus, in practice, the Minister of Justice nominates one candidate for each vacant seat at the courts. The Queen then approves the Minister's choice by ceremonially signing the letter of appointment.[4]

Although the Minister of Justice formally nominates the candidate to the Queen, the actual assessment and selection is made by the so-called Judicial

---

[1]   See e.g. https://www.transparency.org/en/cpi/2020/table/dnk.

[2]   Compare World Justice Project's Rule of Law Index (2021) at https://worldjusticeproject.org/our-work/research-and-data/wjp-rule-law-index-2021 and the EU Justice Scoreboard (2021) at https://ec.europa.eu/info/files/eu-justice-scoreboard-2021.

[3]   Section 42(1) of the Administration of Justice Act (AJA).

[4]   Interim judges may be appointed by the Minister of Justice alone, ss. 44–45 AJA.

Appointments Council. The Judicial Appointments Council was instituted in 1998 in response to an apparent tendency that the Ministry of Justice almost exclusively appointed applicants from the judiciary and the Ministry of Justice itself.[5] Although former ministry officials were undoubtedly qualified as judges, the appearance of such a tendency was, of course, untenable.[6] Therefore, upon the recommendation of the Permanent Commission on Administration of Justice, the Judicial Appointments Council was established as an independent, self-contained entity with the commission to nominate candidates for vacant seats at the courts to the Minister of Justice. Until now, the Minister of Justice has followed the decisions of the Council in all cases.[7] This way, entrusting the selection procedure to an independent body has heightened transparency and diversity in the hiring and recruitment of judges.[8]

The Judicial Appointments Council consists of a lawyer, two representatives of the public (laypeople), and three judges (one from the Supreme Court, one from a High Court, and one from a District Court).[9] Each member serves a term of four years, and reappointments are prohibited.[10] Like any other 'ordinary' public authority, the impartiality and independence of the Council and its members is governed by Chapter 2 of the Public Administration Act.[11]

Vacant judgeships are advertised on platforms relevant to prospective applicants. The formal requirements are few. To be appointed as a judge, one must have Danish citizenship,[12] a Danish domicile and an advanced law degree from a Danish university (cand.jur.).[13] Furthermore, to sit as a judge, one must be of full capacity and proper standing (displays of conduct that, in the eyes of the public, would disqualify one from assuming or discharging the office

---

[5] See Commission Report no. 1319 of 1993, pp. 13–15. On pp. 217–18 and 242, the Report mentions that the courts had an almost decisive influence on the selection. One can speculate whether this contributed to a somewhat self-perpetuating bench. Today, society has an influence on the appointments.

[6] Compare B. Gomard and M. Kistrup, *Civilprocessen*, 8th ed., Karnov Group, Copenhagen 2020, p. 67, who notes that under the previous scheme the Ministry of Justice consulted with the higher courts before any appointments were made.

[7] See J.P. Christensen, J.A. Jensen and M.H. Jensen, *Dansk Statsret*, 3rd ed., Jurist- og Økonomforbundets Forlag, Copenhagen 2020, p. 136.

[8] Ibid., p. 137.

[9] Section 43 b(1)–(4) AJA. The members are appointed by the Danish Bar and Law Society (Advokatrådet), Local Government Denmark (Kommunernes Landsforening), Danish Adult Education Association (Dansk Folkeoplysnings Samråd), the Supreme Court, the High Courts jointly and the Association of Danish Judges (Den Danske Dommerforening).

[10] Section 43 b(6) AJA.

[11] The personal impartiality and independence of judges in their adjudicatory function is regulated under ss. 60 and 61 AJA, see below section 3.3.

[12] Section 27 of the Danish Constitution.

[13] Section 42(3) AJA. See U.R. Bang-Pedersen, L.H. Christensen and C.S. Petersen, *Den civile retspleje*, Hans Reitzels Forlag, Copenhagen 2020, pp. 39–41.

may bar the appointment).[14] Finally, the applicant must be younger than the retirement age of 70 years.[15]

According to Section 43 of the Administration of Justice Act, the Judicial Appointments Council must perform a comprehensive assessment of the applicant's qualifications and attribute decisive importance to his or her legal and personal skills. In practice, the bar is set very high.[16] In addition, the provision requires that the applicant's breadth of experience and the diversity within the courts be considered.

Section 42 of the Administration of Justice Act sets out a test of the applicant's aptitude in practice. A prospective Supreme Court justice must serve as a 'shadow judge' in four deliberations at the Supreme Court in order to prove his or her eligibility.[17] This tradition dates back to 1753 and was – until the establishment of the Judicial Appointments Council – an important safeguard that enabled the judiciary to resist unbecoming appointments by the Ministry of Justice.[18] Each applicant to a judgeship at a high or district court is normally required to have demonstrated satisfactory aptitude during a temporary appointment at one of the high courts.[19] At the end of the term, the president of the high court will submit a testimonial on the temporary judge's suitability as a (permanent) judge. These testimonials function as a stamp of approval (or the opposite) and are, as a rule, quite decisive for the chances of later appointment within the judiciary.

While the Judicial Appointments Council safeguards independence and impartiality in the selection process, the Council does not put much weight on a prospective candidate's previous jobs. While old loyalties may give rise to concerns about impartiality and independence, such issues are handled individually when the judge assumes office. If a newly appointed judge, for example, has been involved in a specific case, the judge will recuse him- or herself or be recused by the president of the court.[20] In practice, new judges are subject to a waiting period of a number of years before hearing cases involving their previous clients, colleagues and employers. For example, a former partner at a law firm will have to wait before deciding cases in which that law firm is representing one of

---

[14] This requirement is not expressed in the AJA itself, but is apparent from the *travaux préparatoires*.

[15] Section 34 of the Civil Service Act.

[16] B. Gomard and M. Kistrup, *Civilprocessen*, 8th ed., Karnov Group, Copenhagen 2020, p. 68.

[17] Section 42(2) AJA.

[18] See J.P. Christensen, J.A. Jensen and M.H. Jensen, *Dansk Statsret*, 3rd ed., Jurist- og Økonomforbundets Forlag, Copenhagen 2020, p. 137.

[19] Section 42(4) AJA, which does, however, leave room for exceptions to be made.

[20] See B. Dahl, 'Dommerinhabilitet – strikte jura og fornuftig forsigtighed' in H. Udsen et al. (eds), *Festskrift til Mads Bryde Andersen*, Jurist- og Økonomforbundets forlag, Copenhagen 2018, pp. 169–70, available at https://www.jurabibliotek.dk/view/978877198233 6/9788771982336_0011.xml.

Denmark

the parties.[21] Likewise, a high-ranking member of the Prosecution Authority will not as a judge hear criminal cases initially.

2.2. JUDGES AT INTERNATIONAL COURTS

2.2.1. Appointment Authority

In 2013, a separate Judicial Appointments Council for Candidates for International Judgeships was established.[22] The composition of this Council is different from the composition of the Judicial Appointments Council. It consists of five members appointed following recommendations by the President of the Supreme Court, the presidents of the two high courts, the Danish Bar and Law Society, the Ministry of Foreign Affairs, and the Ministry of Justice.[23] This Council, too, is subject to the rules on impartiality and independence in Chapter 2 of the Public Administration Act.

2.2.2. Judges at the Court of Justice of the European Union

The Treaty on the Functioning of the European Union (TFEU) leaves it to the Member States to enact suitable procedures for selecting and proposing candidates for judgeships at the Court of Justice of the European Union (CJEU).[24] The standard for selection in Denmark is set out in Section 8 of the Rules of Procedure of the Judicial Appointments Council for International Judgeships. However, this provision does nothing more than echo the requirements set out in Articles 253(1) and 254(1) TFEU: candidates for Judge or Advocate General of the Court of Justice must have 'the qualifications required for appointment to the highest judicial offices' or be 'jurisconsults of recognised competence'. Moreover, candidates for the General Court must 'possess the ability required for appointment to high judicial office'. As explained in section 2.1 above, the standards of qualification for domestic judgeships are set out in the Administration of Justice Act. The candidate's adherence to the further formal requirements at the CJEU is considered a non-issue.[25]

---

[21] Ibid., pp. 170–71.
[22] The press release announcing the Council as well as its Rules of Procedure are available at https://um.dk/da/nyheder-fra-udenrigsministeriet/newsdisplaypage/?newsid=da87adf4-2ed2-4ecd-a550-24d65f1c64ec.
[23] Section 2 of the Rules of Procedure of the Judicial Appointments Council for International Judgeships.
[24] Sixth Activity Report of the Panel provided for by Article 255 of the Treaty on the Functioning of the European Union, DOI: 10.2860/662850, p. 11.
[25] Compare, for example, ss. 2 and 4 of the Statute of the Court of Justice of the European Union.

Intersentia

417

It stands to reason that the Judicial Appointments Council for International Judgeships will consider the practice of the so-called Article 255 Panel even though it does not follow explicitly from the Rules of Procedure. As provided for by Article 255 TFEU, the Article 255 Panel assesses the suitability of candidates on behalf of the Union, and the Panel may deny appointments if it is unconvinced that a candidate will be able to perform the duties of Judge or Advocate General.[26] See the Special Non-National Report on Regional Courts, section 3. Consequently, the Council will, for example, ensure that all candidates from Denmark are proficient in EU law, which the Article 255 Panel has invoked as a ground for refusing appointments on previous occasions.[27]

Articles 253(1) and 254(1) TFEU require that candidates be independent 'beyond doubt', but the provisions do not specify that standard. The Council will presumably anticipate whether the Article 255 Panel would express reservations about the candidate's ability to perform his or her duties independently, impartially and with integrity and probity.[28]

2.2.3. Judges at the European Court of Human Rights

For judgeships at the European Court of Human Rights (ECtHR), the Judicial Appointments Council for International Judgeships selects three candidates from the pool of applications. The individual requirements are set out in Section 8(3) of the Rules of Procedure for the Judicial Appointments Council for International Judgeships, which dovetails with Article 21 of the European Convention on Human Rights. Nevertheless, under Section 8(4) of the Rules of Procedure, the Council is to consider relevant recommendations, resolutions, guidelines, etc., by the European Council.

The process and scrutiny thus include the requirements for the selection procedure set out in paragraph 19 of Recommendation 1649 (2004).[29] In 2013, by way of example, a call for the vacant seat was advertised in the trade magazine for lawyers in accordance with paragraph 19.1, although no prospective candidate could have been unaware of the opening.

Of particular importance here is paragraph 19.6 of Recommendation 1649 (2004) on 'Candidates for the European Court of Human Rights', which recommends that candidates whose election might prompt the need to appoint an ad hoc judge not be submitted. This provision addresses a concern about general impartiality

---

[26]   Compare Article 255 TFEU.
[27]   Compare Sixth Activity Report of the Panel provided for by Article 255 of the Treaty on the Functioning of the European Union, pp. 18–19.
[28]   Ibid., p. 19.
[29]   Recommendation 1649 (2004), available at http://assembly.coe.int/nw/xml/xref/xref-xml2html-en.asp?fileid=17193.

and independence, which may for example arise when a former government official would have to recuse him- or herself on grounds that the ECtHR would repeatedly review legislation that the person helped draft.

2.2.4. General Attitude Towards Independence and Impartiality of International Adjudicators

It appears to be the attitude of the ministries that any prospective applicant who meets the bar for being recommended for an international judgeship by Denmark will release him- or herself from any interests of previous employers. As a requirement of simple professionalism and legitimacy of the court, it is expected that all newly appointed judges will assume and act in their new position on its terms and remain immune to outside pressure.

These days, some Danish politicians are concerned that judges may be influenced not by third parties, but by an excessive attachment to their chosen field of law. For example, an overwhelming enthusiasm about EU law and the EU's institutions may introduce a bias in decisions on general issues of EU law. A number of Danish politicians share a view that both the CJEU and the ECtHR interpret their respective sources too dynamically and expansively.

Denmark has appointed judges and advocates general from various backgrounds to the CJEU: high-ranking government officials, esteemed judges, as well as recognised lawyers and academics. Currently, the Danish judge at the CJEU has leave from his office at the Supreme Court, and the former Advocate General from Denmark (2015–2021) was Consumer Ombudsman prior to his appointment at the Court. For the 2015 appointment to the ECtHR, Denmark's list of suggestions comprised the so-called Government Attorney, a high-ranking official from the Ministry of Justice and a high court judge – the latter was chosen for the position. The lists of suggestions for the recent 2022–2023 appointment were made up of three judges.[30]

2.3. INVESTMENT ARBITRATION

Denmark has enacted the ICSID Convention but has, to my knowledge, as of yet only been the respondent in one ICSID case.[31] In that case, the arbitrator appointed by the respondent was chosen by the Ministry of Justice after consultations with its lawyer.[32]

---

[30] The procedure had to be repeated after the first list submitted was rejected due to a lack of diversity among the candidates.

[31] Government decree no. 92 of 12 August 1968.

[32] ICSID Case No. ARB/20/30.

Denmark's contribution to the list of arbitrators at ICSID consists of two Supreme Court justices as well as two attorneys, one of whom is an independent arbitrator.

3. CONSTITUTIONAL PROTECTION, MEASURES AND SANCTIONS CONCERNING THE DOMESTIC JUDICIARY

3.1. CONSTITUTIONAL PROTECTION OF THE JUDICIARY'S INDEPENDENCE

The functional independence of judges is pronounced in Section 64 of the Danish Constitution, which begins with: 'In the performance of their duties, the judges shall be governed solely by the law'. Thus, the judge may not follow, for example, instructions from the government or anyone else. Section 64 of the Danish Constitution protects judges in that they can be dismissed 'by judgment only' or 'if the entire court system is reorganised'.[33] Therefore, a judge does not have to fear negative consequences in relation to, for example, his or her job security when ruling against the government (which is, of course, the judge's ultimate employer). The elimination of possible negative incentives helps maintain independence.

The authority to dismiss judges (by judgment) falls within the exclusive jurisdiction of the Special Court of Indictment and Revision. Founded in 1939, this Court is a separate and independent court competent in, inter alia, cases about complaints against judges and experts in the discharge of their office.[34] The Court is not a court of appeal on substance and will dismiss attempts to have a judgment remanded.[35]

If a judge renders a judgment without being sufficiently impartial and independent, the parties are left with two options. First, the judge's misjudgment in this regard may constitute a ground for retrial, the decision of which rests with the Court of Appeal.[36] Second, the Special Court of Indictment and Revision may sanction the judge personally if his or her conduct in discharging the office has been unjustifiable or unseemly. Not every (honest) misjudgment about one's impartiality and independence amounts to such. The threshold is in the vicinity of gross misconduct.

---

[33] According to s. 64 of the Danish Constitution, a judge who is 65 years of age may be let go but will retain his or her remuneration until the regular retirement age of 70.

[34] Section 49 AJA.

[35] See for example judgment of the Special Court of Indictment and Revision of 10 June 2021 in case no. 21/00229.

[36] Compare M. Ellehauge, *Inhabilitet i dansk retspleje*, Jurist- og Økonomforbundets forlag, Copenhagen 2001, p. 288.

Denmark

Minor infractions not necessarily directly related to the discharge of the office may be sanctioned by the president of the court upon complaint or on the president's own motion. The president may elevate complaints to the Special Court of Indictment and Revision and typically does so in cases that concern (more) serious offences or sanctions or that raise some important point of principle or practice.[37]

3.2. REGULATION AND DISCLOSURE OF EXTERNAL ACTIVITIES

Under Danish law, judges are not prohibited from undertaking salaried activities on the side.[38] To the contrary, the ability to draw on the expertise and knowledge of judges outside the courtroom is considered a strength. Judges are, for example, frequently asked or even encouraged to sit on commissions of inquiry, arbitral tribunals, dispute boards and pre-legislative inquiries. Many judges also contribute to the legal doctrine as authors.

Salaried activities on the side may, of course, create an air of uncertainty about the judge's incentives and priorities.[39] Therefore, the access to pursuing income outside the courtroom is not unfettered. The Administration of Justice Act sets out certain constraints in order to, inter alia, safeguard the independence and impartiality of judges. Under Section 47 a of the Administration of Justice Act, any *permanent* position to be held by a judge must be prescribed by law or require specific and individual permission from the External Activities Review Board.[40]

A crucial element in the preservation of the judge's individual independence and impartiality is found in Section 47 a(3) of the Administration of Justice Act, which concerns external dispute resolution jobs, including as an arbitrator. When holding such positions, the judge must be appointed by the president of the relevant court. For example, parties to arbitral proceedings and party-appointed arbitrators may not appoint a judge as tribunal chair directly but must, instead, ask the president of the court – who keeps track of previous appointments – to do so. To avoid future conflicts, a judge may not serve as a

---

[37] Section 48 AJA. The practical relationship with s. 49 AJA is addressed in P. Sørensen, 'Klager over dommeres adfærd m.v.' in A. Møller-Sørensen and A. Storgaard (eds), *Festskrift til Gorm Toftegaard Nielsen*, Christian Ejlers, Copenhagen 2007, pp. 567–70 and 572–73.

[38] Section 47 AJA. Commission Report no. 1319 of 1993, pp. 343–99.

[39] The rules are also designed to prevent secondary activities from growing to a volume that would interfere with the judge's ability to fulfil his primary work obligation at that court, as well as the possible issue of a lower court judge having to try a decision from a dispute board on which a higher court judge is sitting or presiding. See in this regard B. Dahl, 'Dommerinhabilitet – strikte jura og fornuftig forsigtighed' in H. Udsen et al. (eds), *Festskrift til Mads Bryde Andersen*, Jurist- og Økonomforbundets forlag, Copenhagen 2018, pp. 171–72.

[40] See s. 47 e–f AJA.

Intersentia

421

party-appointed arbitrator but only as a chair appointed jointly by the parties, by the co-arbitrators or by a third party.[41] This appointment procedure is intended to reduce the risk of double-hatting and interference with the impartiality and independence of the courts.

Section 47 b of the Administration of Justice Act limits the allowed remuneration from judges' secondary activities. According to the provision, a judge may not earn more than 50% of his or her salary at the judiciary from such secondary activities. The judge must disclose a detailed report on his or her salaried activities for transparency reasons.[42] If an activity is confidential, which arbitral proceedings may be, the identities of the parties may be kept confidential, but the judge must disclose the names of the lawyers and the method of appointment.

3.3. RECUSAL IN INDIVIDUAL CASES

All judges are subject to standards of impartiality and independence throughout the proceedings. The standards are found in Sections 60 and 61 of the Administration of Justice Act as supplemented by Article 6 of the European Convention on Human Rights.[43] Section 60 of the Administration of Justice Act sets out a 'blacklist' that includes the judge's actual interest in the outcome of the specific case, close family relations to one of the parties or their lawyer, and previous involvement with the case, for example as a witness.[44] Section 61 is a catch-all clause covering *any circumstances* that are likely to give rise to doubt about the complete impartiality of the judge. Every judge is required to ensure compliance with the standards on his or her own motion, and the judge is required to recuse him- or herself when the standards are not met. In addition, either party may challenge the judge. A challenge prompts the court to make a formal decision on impartiality and independence, which, under Section 62 of the Administration of Justice Act, is subject to appeal.

If a judge recuses him- or herself from the proceedings, another judge from the same court will step in. In practice, issues of impartiality and independence are pre-empted by swapping cases between fellow judges before the case is prepared and heard. The sentiment is that there is no reason to jeopardise the sanctity of the procedure. Over the past 30 years, there has been a continuing

---

[41]   Commission Report no. 1465 from 2005, p. 7.

[42]   Section 47 c AJA.

[43]   See in general U.R. Bang-Pedersen, L.H. Christensen and C.S. Petersen, *Den civile retspleje*, Hans Reitzels Forlag, Copenhagen 2020, pp. 44–51 and 85–87.

[44]   See B. Dahl, 'Dommerinhabilitet – strikte jura og fornuftig forsigtighed' in H. Udsen et al. (eds), *Festskrift til Mads Bryde Andersen*, Jurist- og Økonomforbundets forlag, Copenhagen 2018, pp. 174–80.

debate about whether judges recuse themselves too readily.[45] While this appeared to be the case until approximately 10 years ago, the approach has been replaced by a more balanced and objective procedure over the last decade.[46]

In rare instances, the entire court or collegium is disqualified due to an individual judge's – in practice typically the chief judge's – conflict of interest.[47] In such cases, the bench will be filled by judges from a 'sister' court. For example, the entire High Court of Western Denmark recused itself in a case where the defendant in a liability case was married to one of the judges in the court. Similarly, the entire High Court of Eastern Denmark recused itself in a case arising from a commission of inquiry chaired by the president of the court. Moreover, the entire probate court under the Maritime and Commercial Court was recused due to the chief judge's categorical statements about the particular subject matter of the case.[48] Nevertheless, it takes a serious conflict of interest to disqualify an entire court or collegium.

In the Maritime and Commercial Court, industry experts typically serve as judges. The experts provide insight into the technical and commercial side of the disputes. They are appointed by different relevant trade associations and the president of the court.[49] Except for a law degree, the experts must meet the same formal requirements as ordinary judges, and the opinion of the expert judges have the same weight as the opinion of an ordinary judge.[50] From a practical point of view, the technical or commercial insight brought by the expert judges outweighs the possible inclinations towards the specific industries involved.

Tenancy disputes are decided by special so-called 'housing courts' in which lay judges appointed by organisations representing landlords and tenants participate. In these courts, the standards of impartiality and independence are arguably reduced for the lay judges, but their possible preconceptions and sympathies are presumed to balance each other out.

4. INTERNATIONAL ASPECTS

4.1. ENFORCEMENT OF INTERNATIONAL ARBITRAL AWARDS

An increasing number of commercial disputes are international. Those disputes are typically resolved by arbitration. Under the legal framework of the

---

[45] The discussion was started by O. Bisgaard, 'Hvor inhabil kan man være?' in Fuldmægtigen 1992.177.

[46] B. Dahl, 'Dommerinhabilitet – strikte jura og fornuftig forsigtighed' in H. Udsen et al. (eds), Festskrift til Mads Bryde Andersen, Jurist- og Økonomforbundets forlag, Copenhagen 2018, pp. 179–80.

[47] See ibid., pp. 176–78.

[48] See also ibid., pp. 173–74.

[49] Section 93 b(1) and (2) AJA.

[50] Section 93 b(4) AJA.

New York Convention, arbitral awards are generally enforceable around the world. Denmark is a party to the Convention, and the Convention's provisions on enforcement of arbitral awards are set out in Sections 38 and 39 of the Arbitration Act. Section 38 sets out the general rule that arbitral awards be enforced, and Section 39 provides the list of defences.

The absence of legal safeguards, such as an impartial and independent tribunal, may be a ground for refusal of enforcement. Under Section 39(1)(1)(d) of the Arbitration Act, recognition and enforcement may be refused if 'the composition of the arbitral tribunal or the arbitral procedure was not in accordance with the agreement of the parties or with the law of the country where the arbitration took place'. The failure of an arbitrator to meet the required standards of impartiality and independence is within the core of the provision.[51]

As set out in the provision, the required threshold for refusing enforcement depends on the parties' agreement and the lex arbitri. If a conflict of interest is not prohibited by the parties' agreement or the law of the seat of arbitration, the conflict is not a ground for refusing enforcement in Denmark.

If an arbitrator displays actual bias and treats the parties unequally, the issue may be ground for a challenge under Section 39(1)(1)(b) of the Arbitration Act on the parties' right 'to be heard'.[52]

Grave conflicts of interest may prevent enforcement under Section 39(1)(2)(b) of the Arbitration Act on public policy. The provision entitles the court to refuse enforcement on its own initiative or upon the request of a party if the court finds that 'the recognition or enforcement of the award would be manifestly contrary to the public policy of this country'. A conflict of interest would perhaps be grave enough to prevent enforcement under the public policy defence if the arbitrator is a party to the dispute or is influenced by bribery.[53]

4.2. ENFORCEMENT OF FOREIGN JUDGMENTS

Denmark is a party to the Brussels Ia Regulation,[54] which governs the recognition and enforcement of judgments within the EU.[55] Under Article 36 of the Regulation, a judgment from one Member State shall be recognised in other

---

[51]   J. Juul and P. Thommesen, *Voldgiftsret*, 3rd ed., Karnov Group, Copenhagen 2017, p. 274 (referring to p. 291 on challenges under s. 37 of the Danish Arbitration Act on annulment).

[52]   Ibid., p. 288–89.

[53]   J. Tufte-Kristensen, *Voldgiftsdommerens upartiskhed og uafhængighed*, Karnov Group, Copenhagen 2018, p. 205.

[54]   Regulation (EU) No. 1215/2012 of the European Parliament and of the Council of 12 December 2012 on jurisdiction and the recognition and enforcement of judgments in civil and commercial matters.

[55]   Denmark does not participate in the EU's cooperation on Justice and Home Affairs, under which the Brussels I Regulation belongs, but has enacted the Regulation through a so-called

Member States without any special procedure being required. Under Article 39, a judgment from one Member State is also enforceable in other Member States without any declaration of enforceability being required.

Article 45 sets out the defences against recognition and enforcement. The provision does not include a challenge on grounds of a failure to meet the required standards of impartiality and independence. Under Article 45(1)(a) of the Brussels Ia Regulation, recognition and enforcement may be refused if it is 'manifestly contrary to' the ordre public of the Member State addressed, but as mentioned above, only grave conflicts of interest would fall within this category.

Denmark is a party to the 2005 Hague Convention on Choice of Court Agreements.[56] Under Article 8 of the Convention, a judgment from one contracting state designated in an exclusive choice-of-court agreement shall be recognised and enforced in other contracting states. The list of defences in Article 9 is rather similar to the list of defences in Article 45(1)(a) of the Brussels Ia Regulation, but Article 9 of the Hague Convention adds an important element to subsection (e). According to the provision, the recognition and enforcement may be refused if it would be manifestly incompatible with the public policy of the requested state, including 'situations where the specific proceedings leading to the judgment were incompatible with fundamental principles of procedural fairness of that State'. The failure to meet the internal Danish standards of impartiality and independence would probably fall within the provision.

The Nordic countries – Denmark, Finland, Iceland, Norway and Sweden – have made a Convention on the recognition and enforcement of judgments on civil matters.[57] The Convention does not explicitly include a list of challenges, but it requires courts in each contracting state to recognise and enforce judgments from other contracting states 'in accordance with the internal law of that state'.[58] The requirement would arguably entitle a Danish court to refuse the recognition and enforcement of a judgment on grounds of a failure to meet the internal Danish standards of impartiality and independence.

'parallel agreement' with the EU, OJ L 299, 16 November 2005, pp. 61–70, with later opt-in to the recast of the Regulation.

56 Convention of 30 June 2005 on Choice of Court Agreements.

57 Konvention af 11. oktober 1977 mellem Danmark, Finland, Island, Norge og Sverige om anerkendelse og fuldbyrdelse af afgørelser om privatretlige krav.

58 Ibid., Article 1 ('i overensstemmelse med denne stats interne lovgivning').

THE INDEPENDENCE AND IMPARTIALITY OF ADJUDICATORS IN FRANCE

Karim El Chazli*

1. The Selection of Candidates for Positions as International Judges 429
   1.1. The GFCPA: The Main Actor in the Selection Process. 429
        1.1.1. Constitution and Role 429
        1.1.2. The Wide Leeway the GFCPA Enjoys in Selecting French
               Candidates 430
        1.1.3. No Judicial Recourse is Possible against the GFCPA's
               Decisions 431
        1.1.4. Main Criticisms of the Process: Lack of Transparency
               and Professional Protectionism. 431
   1.2. The Outcome of the Selection Process 432
        1.2.1. Prevalence of Judges and State Agents. 432
        1.2.2. Marginal Selection of Academics and its Reasons 433
   1.3. Appointment Process in Specific Courts 434
        1.3.1. International Court of Justice 434
        1.3.2. International Criminal Court 435
        1.3.3. European Court of Human Rights 435
        1.3.4. Court of Justice of the European Union. 436
        1.3.5. International Centre for Settlement of Investment
               Disputes 437
   1.4. National Mechanisms to Ensure Independence and
        Impartiality of International Judges. 437
   1.5. Conclusion on the Selection of Candidates for Positions
        as International Judges. 438
2. Arbitrators' Impartiality in French Law. 439
   2.1. General Remarks: The Law is (Still) under Construction 440
        2.1.1. Reasons Pertaining to the CPC and the Case Law 441
        2.1.2. Peculiar Nature of Impartiality Disputes. 441

---

* The rapporteur would like to thank François Alabrune, Karim Bounab, Eva Litina and Karen Topaz Druckman for their valuable comments on earlier drafts of this report. All errors (and opinions) remain mine. This report is up to date as at July 2022.

Intersentia

	2.1.3.	Recent (Normative and Factual) Developments Affecting Arbitrator's Impartiality................................ 442	
		2.1.3.1. Normative Developments..................... 442	
		2.1.3.1.1. The Emergence of Non-National Sources 442	
		2.1.3.1.2. Leeway for Agreement between the Parties? 443	
		2.1.3.2. Factual Developments........................ 444	
2.2.	Mechanisms to Ensure Impartiality of International Arbitrators ... 444		
	2.2.1.	No Particular Restrictions for Prospective Arbitrators 445	
	2.2.2.	Duty to Disclose...................................... 445	
	2.2.3.	The Main Obstacle to the Implementation of the Impartiality Requirement: The Parties' Duty to Invoke Irregularities in a Timely Manner....................... 447	
2.3.	Circumstances that Could Give Rise to Impartiality Concerns..... 448		
	2.3.1.	Arbitrator's Acts..................................... 448	
		2.3.1.1. Acts Accomplished in the Context of the Adjudicative Function........................ 448	
		2.3.1.2. Acts Unrelated to the Adjudicative Function..... 448	
		2.3.1.3. The Award Itself 449	
	2.3.2.	Arbitrator's Relationships............................ 449	
		2.3.2.1. Relationships under Scrutiny................. 449	
		2.3.2.2. Criteria for the Assessment of the Arbitrator's Relationships............................... 449	
	2.3.3.	Arbitrator's Previous Opinions (Issue Conflict) 450	
2.4.	Impartiality of Party-Appointed Arbitrators 450		
2.5.	The Consequences of Lack of Impartiality: Remedies Strictly Speaking.. 451		
	2.5.1.	Remedies Concerning the Award....................... 451	
		2.5.1.1. Awards Made in France....................... 451	
		2.5.1.2. Awards Made Abroad 452	
	2.5.2.	Remedies Concerning the Arbitrator................... 452	
		2.5.2.1. Challenging the Arbitrator.................... 452	
		2.5.2.2. Civil Liability: A Mere Application of General Rules............................ 453	
		2.5.2.3. Criminal Liability: Potential and Risks.......... 453	
		2.5.2.4. Disciplinary Liability........................ 455	
2.6.	Conclusion on Impartiality of Arbitrators 455		
3.	General Conclusion 455		

This report, written in the context of the International Academy of Comparative Law (IACL) research project on the 'Independence and Impartiality of

International Adjudicators', will address two issues: (i) the French practice of selecting candidates for positions as an international judge, and (ii) French law rules on arbitrators' impartiality.

1. THE SELECTION OF CANDIDATES FOR POSITIONS AS INTERNATIONAL JUDGES

Two main features characterise the French practice regarding the selection of candidates for international adjudicator positions. The first is the central role played by the French Group at the Permanent Court of Arbitration (GFCPA)[1] in the selection process, around which there exists a perceived lack of transparency. The second feature, which concerns the outcome of the selection process, is the clear prevalence of former state agents and judges among the French candidates for positions as an international judge.

1.1. THE GFCPA: THE MAIN ACTOR IN THE SELECTION PROCESS

1.1.1. Constitution and Role

The origin of the GFCPA dates back to the 1907 Convention for the Pacific Settlement of International Disputes. Its Article 44 specifies that '[e]ach Contracting Power selects four persons at the most, of known competency in questions of international law, of the highest moral reputation, and disposed to accept the duties of Arbitrator'.

Article 4 of the International Court of Justice (ICJ) Statute bestowed on the GFCPA a crucial role in selecting ICJ judges. Pursuant to this provision, '[t]he members of the Court shall be elected by the General Assembly and by the Security Council from a list of persons nominated by the national groups in the Permanent Court of Arbitration'. The International Criminal Court (ICC) Statute gives the GFCPA a similar power to nominate candidates for the ICC.[2]

France has extended the role of the GFCPA and involved it in the selection of candidates for the European Court of Human Rights (ECtHR) and Court of Justice of the European Union (CJEU) (even though their texts provide no role for the GFCPA). We stress, however, that, strictly speaking, it is not the GFCPA as such that acts as a selecting authority. In fact, the GFCPA's members

---

[1] This is the abbreviation of 'Groupe français de la Cour permanente d'arbitrage'.

[2] Pursuant to Article 36 of the ICC Statute, '4. (a) Nominations of candidates for election to the Court may be made by any State Party to this Statute, and shall be made either: (i) By the procedure for the nomination of candidates for appointment to the highest judicial offices in the State in question; or (ii) By the procedure provided for the nomination of candidates for the International Court of Justice in the Statute of that Court.'

Intersentia

429

Karim El Chazli

are merely members of an ad hoc committee that usually comprises an external member as well.[3] Moreover, the role of the GFCPA is not the same regarding the selection of candidates for the different courts. While the GFCPA has the exclusive power to nominate the candidates for the ICJ and ICC judgeships, for other courts, the GFCPA, or the ad hoc committee, merely suggests names to the government, which will ultimately decide which name(s) to communicate to the relevant international bodies.[4] The government has always endorsed the GFCPA's recommendations, except in a single case.[5]

The members of the GFCPA are appointed by the government for a six-year mandate. Regarding the constitution of the GFCPA, the most striking feature is probably the significant number of GFCPA members who have held the position of Director of Legal Affairs at the Ministry of Foreign Affairs (French state agents before international courts). The list of the GFCPA's current members provides the best evidence:

- His excellency Mr Gilbert Guillaume, former ICJ judge and former Director of Legal Affairs at the Ministry of Foreign Affairs;
- Ms Edwige Belliard, member of the Conseil d'État and former Director of Legal Affairs at the Ministry of Foreign Affairs;
- Prof. Geneviève Bastid Burdeau; and
- Mr François Alabrune, (current) Director of Legal Affairs at the Ministry of Foreign Affairs.[6]

1.1.2. *The Wide Leeway the GFCPA Enjoys in Selecting French Candidates*

There is no known text spelling out the operation of the GFCPA or the method and criteria it adopts regarding the selection process. France is not unique in indulging in the leeway that the relevant international texts offer[7] and

---

3   For example, for the selection procedure for the position of judge at the ECtHR that took place in 2019, the 'ad hoc Selection Committee' comprised a former ICC judge in addition to the four members of the GFCPA.

4   S. Szurek, 'La composition des juridictions internationales permanentes : de nouvelles exigences de qualité et de représentativité' (2010) 56 *Annuaire français de droit international* 41, 59. With respect to the candidates for the European courts, the practice seems to be that, after conducting interviews, the GFCPA establishes a list of four to six candidates from which the government will choose three. See M. Afroukh and Y. Lécuyer, 'Sur une exception française : la procédure de désignation des candidats au poste de juge à la Cour européenne des droits de l'homme' (2020) *Revue des droits et libertés fondamentales*, http://www.revuedlf.com/cedh/sur-une-exception-francaise-la-procedure-de-designation-des-candidats-au-poste-de-juge-a-la-cour-europeenne-des-droits-de-lhomme/.

5   On this incident, see section 1.3.3.

6   The list of all PCA members is available at https://pca-cpa.org/en/about/structure/members-of-the-court/.

7   For a comparison of the main approaches among European states, see L. Burgorgue-Larsen, 'Des idéaux à la réalité. Réflexions comparées sur les processus de sélection et de nomination des membres des Cours européenne et interaméricaine des droits de l'homme' (2014) 6 *La Revue des droits de l'homme*, §19, http://revdh.revues.org/949. She notably relies on a

France

it does not seem that there is a willingness to relinquish such prerogatives. Furthermore, public information on exactly how the GFCPA performs its duties is scarce. According to Prof. Szurek, the GFCPA seems to have relied, at least until recently, on informal consultations and direct discussions with the best-informed specialists, but in the last decade, application processes have been established and procedures have become more transparent.[8] That said, when it comes to nominating candidates for the ICJ, the GFCPA has always followed the recommendation laid down by Article 6 of the ICJ Statute, which stipulates that '[b]efore making these nominations, each national group is recommended to consult its highest court of justice, its legal faculties and schools of law, and its national academies and national sections of international academies devoted to the study of law.'[9]

1.1.3. No Judicial Recourse is Possible against the GFCPA's Decisions

Can the GFCPA's selection be subject to judicial review? This question was raised by Olivier de Baynast, an unsuccessful candidate for the position of the French nominee for the ICC. The answer of the Conseil d'État (the Supreme Court in administrative law matters) was that judicial review is not possible. The technical reason is that the impugned acts could not be separated (*'les actes contestés ne sont pas détachables'*) from the election procedure of ICC judges by the Assembly of States Parties and thus such acts do not fall within the French administrative courts' jurisdiction.[10]

1.1.4. Main Criticisms of the Process: Lack of Transparency and Professional Protectionism

Although the matter is sensitive, several French academics have expressed their discontent regarding the French practice of selecting candidates for international adjudicator positions. The staunchest criticism has probably come

---

    document titled 'Nomination of candidates and election of judges to the European Court of Human Rights' that was established by the Committee on Legal Affairs and Human Rights of the Parliamentary Assembly of the Council of Europe. This document is available at http://www.assembly.coe.int/CommitteeDocs/2008/20081201_ajdoc52.pdf.

8   S. Szurek, 'La composition des juridictions internationales permanentes : de nouvelles exigences de qualité et de représentativité' (2010) 56 *Annuaire français de droit international* 41, 58–59.

9   As confirmed by a GFCPA member.

10   Conseil d'État, sect., 28 March 2014, *De Baynast*, No. 373064, *Lebon*. Some commentators have explained that the act of choosing the French nominee to the ICC is an 'act of state' (*acte de gouvernement*). See J.-P. Pastor, 'Le choix du candidat français à la Cour pénale internationale est un acte de gouvernement' (2014) *AJDA* 712. See also G. Eveillard, 'Election des juges à la Cour pénale internationale : incompétence de la juridiction adminstrative' (2014) 7 *Droit administratif* comm. 43.

Intersentia   431

Karim El Chazli

from Prof. Burgorgue-Larsen.[11] In her opinion, the constitution of the GFCPA demonstrates obvious and continuous professional protectionism (*corporatisme* · *évident et continu*).[12] She further adds that the presence within the GFCPA of Ministry of Foreign Affairs lawyers and Conseil d'État judges shows the locking (*verrouillage*) of the system in favour of those who have had careers in one of these two institutions. According to her, the fact that academics have never represented a majority in the GFCPA is the reason why they are rarely nominated to occupy positions of international judges.[13]

In 2020, two university professors reiterated the criticism of the French tradition, namely the strong preference for judges (over academics) as candidates for positions at the European courts. From their standpoint, there is a total lack of transparency in the selection of French candidates.[14] But the GFCPA has its defenders as well. According to former ICJ judge G. Guillaume, the success of French judges in international courts demonstrates the quality of the GFCPA's choices. He has further pointed out that the call for applications system sometimes dissuades the most qualified persons from applying because, at the advanced stage of their careers, they might not be willing to go through that sort of exam.[15]

1.2. THE OUTCOME OF THE SELECTION PROCESS

1.2.1. Prevalence of Judges and State Agents

According to Prof. C. Santulli, the recent French practice (with some notable exceptions) tends to select former agents of its foreign legal policy (*anciens*

---

[11]   L. Burgorgue-Larsen, 'Des idéaux à la réalité. Réflexions comparées sur les processus de sélection et de nomination des membres des Cours européenne et interaméricaine des droits de l'homme' (2014) 6 *La Revue des droits de l'homme*, §19, http://revdh.revues.org/949.
       For the sake of transparency, it should be noted that Prof. Burgorgue-Larsen applied to be the French judge at the ECtHR.

[12]   Ibid.

[13]   The Sorbonne professor mentions an exception to this trend: Prof. J.-P. Cot who has been appointed as a judge for the International Tribunal for the Law of the Sea (ITLOS). But then she adds that Prof. Cot was a former minister before being selected by France. Other authors mention older exceptions: R. Cassin (ECtHR 1959–1976) and P.-H. Teigten (ECtHR 1976–1982). That said, it is worth noting that Cassin was also the Vice-President of the Conseil d'État and Teigten was a former minister. Likewise, Prof. Basdevant and Gros – who sat at the ICJ – also worked for the Ministry of Foreign Affairs.

[14]   M. Afroukh and Y. Lécuyer, 'Sur une exception française: la procédure de désignation des candidats au poste de juge à la Cour européenne des droits de l'homme' (2020) *Revue des droits et libertés fondamentales*, http://www.revuedlf.com/cedh/sur-une-exception-francaise-la-procedure-de-designation-des-candidats-au-poste-de-juge-a-la-cour-europeenne-des-droits-de-lhomme/.

[15]   S. Szurek, 'La composition des juridictions internationales permanentes : de nouvelles exigences de qualité et de représentativité' (2010) 56 *Annuaire français de droit international* 41, 58–59. However, this author says, this system allows unsuccessful candidates to better prepare themselves for the following call for applications.

serviteurs de sa politique juridique extérieure), while the German, Italian or US policies overall prefer selecting more independent candidates, often university professors, who might be less loyal but are more influential.[16] Indeed, French candidates are overwhelmingly state agents and judges. Many candidates who are state agents have worked at the Ministry of Foreign Affairs, especially as the Director of Legal Affairs. That said, this experience undoubtedly offers first-hand and unparalleled exposure to the functioning of international courts, thereby justifying their selection as candidates. And a large majority of nominated judges come from the Conseil d'État, which is the Supreme Court for administrative law matters. Some French candidates also come from the Cour de cassation (the Supreme Court for civil and criminal matters), as well as from civil and criminal lower courts.

1.2.2. Marginal Selection of Academics and its Reasons

Some argue that there is a well-established French tradition of avoiding the selection of academics as candidates for international adjudicator positions. Without doubting the qualifications and credentials of the French nominees, many French academics complain that they are de facto excluded even though some of them fulfil the requirements to be selected as international judges.[17] For some observers, the marginal selection of academics is not arbitrary and can be accounted for based on objective factors. According to a former Conseil d'État judge, the overwhelming nomination of judges can be explained by three factors.[18] First, international judicial positions ought to be bestowed on those who have already held a judicial position. Second, given the constitution of French ministerial offices where judges are better represented than academics, judges have more opportunities to intervene in the process of selecting candidates for international adjudicator positions.[19] Third, the selected candidates have demonstrated their competence and deserved to be nominated and to have their mandates renewed.

While agreeing with these factors as an explanation for the lack of academics among French nominees, a former Advocate General at the Cour de cassation

---

[16]   C. Santulli, *Droit du contentieux international*, 2nd ed., LGDJ 2015, p. 479. This author gave those examples in the context of arguing that the more remote the judge is from the appointing authority, the more likely this judge will be able to earn their colleagues' trust and influence the court. The same point was made earlier in more detail by the same author in: J.-M. Sorel and H. Ruiz Fabri (eds), *Indépendance et impartialité des juges internationaux*, Pedone 2010, p. 232.

[17]   See section 1.1.4 and its footnotes.

[18]   B. Genevois in J.-M. Sorel and H. Ruiz Fabri (eds), *Indépendance et impartialité des juges internationaux*, Pedone 2010, p. 143.

[19]   '[D]ans le cas de la France, joue un rôle le fait que les possibilités d'intervention dans les circuits de décisions conduisant aux nominations ne sont pas identiques pour chaque famille de juristes. Il ne faut pas se cacher ce qu'il en est, compte tenu de la composition des cabinets ministériels'.

Intersentia

433

added that this phenomenon is also due to the 'state culture' (*culture d'État*) which militates in favour of selecting those who are more immersed in such culture.[20] A member of the WTO Legal Affairs Division advanced considerations in the same vein. According to him, there is some suspicion towards academics who bring with them unruly reasoning.[21] In contrast, an ambassador sitting on a WTO panel will be more thoughtful of the outcome to be given for the disputed issue, especially if the same issue is likely to arise in relation to his own state. That is why WTO members[22] have a preference for diplomats and state agents. Finally, it is worth mentioning the point of view of a former ICC judge who implied that judges with an academic background might sometimes be less impartial than other judges. This judge believes that it could be difficult for 'academic judges' to sever ties with the academic community that will comment on the decisions they render.[23]

It seems obvious that, in a jurisdiction such as France, finding competent candidates among judges and state agents should not be a difficult task. That said, it is perfectly conceivable that, for a given position, an academic might be more competent than a non-academic.

1.3. APPOINTMENT PROCESS IN SPECIFIC COURTS

1.3.1. *International Court of Justice*

In addition to what has already been mentioned about the process of selecting French candidates, it is worth noting that the five French judges at the ICJ (the academics J. Basdevant and A. Gros, the diplomat G. Ladreit de Lacharrière and

---

[20]   R. De Gouttes in J.-M. Sorel and H. Ruiz Fabri (eds), *Indépendance et impartialité des juges internationaux*, Pedone 2010, p. 145.

[21]   Y. Renouf in J.-M. Sorel and H. Ruiz Fabri (eds), *Indépendance et impartialité des juges internationaux*, Pedone 2010, p. 217–18: 'les académiques vont arriver avec des raisonnements que l'on ne contrôle pas'; 'ils vont venir avec des théories, peut être que ça va nous poser des problèmes'.

[22]   The whole statement here is general in nature. It is not limited to France or to French academics.

[23]   See the interview of B. Cotte (starting from minute 27:30) on https://criminocorpus.org/fr/ bibliotheque/video/2563/. 'Les juges doivent être au-dessus de la mêlée. Ils ne dépendent pas de leurs gouvernements. C'est très clair. Et sur ce plan-là, je peux attester, en tout cas en ce qui me concerne, d'une indépendance totale et absolue. Mais il faut qu'ils se dégagent aussi totalement de la communauté professionnelle d'où ils viennent. Je n'étais pas un magistrat français discutant avec des magistrats français. Je n'étais pas un diplomate restant en lien avec sa communauté de diplomates.

Je pense que pour un juge universitaire, la rupture du cordon ombilical est parfois beaucoup plus difficile à réaliser, car il sait que les décisions rendues par la chambre dont ils font partie seront commentés non pas par des juges, mais par des collègues universitaires.'

the two Conseil d'État judges G. Guillaume and R. Abraham) worked at the Ministry of Foreign Affairs. The last four held the position of Director of Legal Affairs.[24]

1.3.2. International Criminal Court

In 2002, the National Consultative Commission on Human Rights (CNCDH)[25] recommended that the process of selecting candidates be the subject of an official publication specifying the calendar and modes by which applications should be sent to the GFCPA so as to give the latter the time necessary to consult the highest judicial and academic authorities as recommended by Article 6 of the ICJ Statute.[26] The discontent regarding the selection process is also echoed in a written question by a socialist MP pointing out that members of the French coalition for the ICC were worried about the opaqueness surrounding this process. In its response, the Ministry of Foreign Affairs explained that the French candidate fulfilled the various requirements set by the ICC Statute.[27] The selection process has subsequently been reformed and a call for applications was published in 2011.[28]

1.3.3. European Court of Human Rights

According to some observers, the French tradition is to select judges from the Conseil d'État and the Cour de cassation as candidates for European courts.[29] The selection process of candidates for the position of ECtHR judge has become more transparent thanks to the actions of the Council of Europe.

---

[24] A. Marissal, 'Cultures juridiques et internationalisation des élites du droit. Le cas des juges de la Cour internationale de Justice' (2020) 105 *Droit et société* 343, 357.

[25] CNCDH is the abbreviation of 'Commission nationale consultative des droits de l'homme', which is the French National Institution for Human Rights, established in 1947.

[26] Opinion on the implementation of the ICC Statute (Avis sur la mise en oeuvre du Statut de la Cour pénale internationale) adopted by the plenary assembly of the CNCDH on 19 December 2002, available at https://www.cncdh.fr/sites/default/files/02.12.19_avis_mise_en_oeuvre_statut_cpi.pdf.

[27] The question was published on 12 December 2002 in the Official Gazette of the Sénat (the Sénat is the upper house of the French Parliament) and the response on 13 February 2003. Both are available at https://www.senat.fr/questions/base/2002/qSEQ021204661.html.

[28] S. Szurek, 'La composition des juridictions internationales permanentes : de nouvelles exigences de qualité et de représentativité' (2010) 56 *Annuaire français de droit international* 41, 59. The current French judge, appointed in 2015, was a member of the Conseil d'État and he also served in numerous senior positions in the Ministries of Foreign Affairs and Defence as well as in the United Nations Secretariat. He also led the French delegation to the Rome Conference and signed the Rome Statute on behalf of France. Information available at https://www.icc-cpi.int/Publications/JudgesENG.pdf.

[29] M. Afroukh and Y. Lécuyer, 'Sur une exception française : la procédure de désignation des candidats au poste de juge à la Cour européenne des droits de l'homme' (2020) *Revue des droits et libertés fondamentales*, http://www.revuedlf.com/cedh/sur-une-exception-francaise-

In their 2007 answer to a questionnaire established by the Council of Europe's Parliamentary Assembly,[30] French authorities indicated that there is no public call for applications, but it added that the criteria of fairness, transparency and consistency 'are guaranteed by the attachment of the French authorities to the principle of independence of magistrates both on the national and international level'. Moreover, 'French authorities underscore that the selection procedure currently employed has permitted French judges, on two occasions, to be elected presidents of the ECtHR'.

The situation has however evolved towards more transparency. In the 2010 selection process, a call for applications was published, after which the GFCPA communicated five names to the government and recommended two of them. To those two names, the government added the name of a candidate who was not retained by the GFCPA. According to one observer, this purely political nomination pushed the European authorities to reject the French list altogether.[31] Ultimately, a new list following the proposals of the GFCPA was sent to the Council of Europe.

For the selection procedure that took place in 2019, an ad hoc Selection Committee (composed of the four members of the GFCPA and a former ICC judge) was established.[32] A call for candidates with a detailed job description was published on the intranet of the Ministry of Justice, the Ministry of Foreign Affairs, the Ministry of Education and the Ministry of Higher Education, and on the LinkedIn accounts of the last three of these ministries.[33] Out of the 17 applications submitted to the Selection Committee within the deadline, nine candidates were invited for an interview. At the end of the interviews, the Committee shortlisted four candidates whose names were submitted to the government, which chose three of them (they were all judges) to be forwarded to the European authorities.[34]

1.3.4. Court of Justice of the European Union

According to a former CJEU Advocate-General, the French tradition seems to consist of selecting one judge from the Conseil d'État and another one from civil

---

la-procedure-de-designation-des-candidats-au-poste-de-juge-a-la-cour-europeenne-des-droits-de-lhomme/.

[30] Available at http://www.assembly.coe.int/CommitteeDocs/2008/20081201_ajdoc52.pdf.

[31] S. Szurek, 'La composition des juridictions internationales permanentes : de nouvelles exigences de qualité et de représentativité' (2010) 56 *Annuaire français de droit international* 41, 59–60.

[32] Parliamentary Assembly of the Council of Europe, Election of Judges to the European Court of Human Rights – List and curricula vitae of candidates submitted by the Government of France, Doc. 15008 (25 November 2019), available at https://pace.coe.int/pdf/42febc4fb92f893bcdc385afe51e97151abc88d638aeea051ecd39e62604647c/doc.%2015008.pdf.

[33] Ibid.

[34] Ibid.

and criminal courts, and of renewing their mandates.[35] He also disclosed that no academics have been selected, although on each occasion, some academics declared to the government their interest in being selected.[36] He added that some argue that French academics are less powerful as a body than the Conseil d'État or the civil and criminal judges but, according to him, this explanation is doubtful. It is worth noting that for the last procedure for the selection of the French Advocate-General, there was – for the first time – a public call for applications and the selection was made by an ad hoc committee composed of the GFCPA's members as well as a former ICC judge.

1.3.5. *International Centre for Settlement of Investment Disputes*

A public call for applications was published in 2018 in view of the designation of four arbitrators (and four conciliators) to be added to the International Centre for Settlement of Investment Disputes (ICSID) list.[37] Interestingly, this call indicated that successful candidates would be required to refrain from acting as counsel, experts and witnesses in investment arbitral proceedings insofar as such activity could jeopardise their neutrality as to the procedural and legal issues that they might encounter when sitting as arbitrators.

The selection committee comprised two members of the GFCPA, one agent each from the Ministries of Justice and Economy and a former judge. After conducting the interviews, the selection committee communicated the names of six candidates to the Minister of Economy, who in turn chose four names to be communicated to the ICSID Secretary-General. It is worth observing that the outcome of the process was rather diverse: two law professors, one former judge and a practising lawyer (*avocate*).

Although ICSID rules allow states to designate non-nationals, French authorities exclusively selected French nationals. This approach – which is widespread internationally – is perfectly understandable and justifiable given the significant number of highly competent French international lawyers.

1.4. NATIONAL MECHANISMS TO ENSURE INDEPENDENCE AND IMPARTIALITY OF INTERNATIONAL JUDGES

There are no known national codes of conduct that apply to international judges nominated by France. That said, international judges – whether or not

---

[35] P. Léger in J.-M. Sorel and H. Ruiz Fabri (eds), *Indépendance et impartialité des juges internationaux*, Pedone 2010, p. 32.

[36] Ibid., p. 35.

[37] Available at https://www.tresor.economie.gouv.fr/Articles/14ccbbb3-0d29-4bce-8be8-0460692 e6f14/files/ba3e6314-3f33-4482-bb53-709407120b81. For the sake of clarity, we remind the

nominated by France – can be held criminally liable pursuant to Article 435-7 of the Penal Code establishing the offence of passive bribery and trading in influence (*corruption et trafic d'influence passifs*), which specifically mentions international judges (*toute personne exerçant des fonctions juridictionnelles ... au sein ou auprès d'une cour internationale*). This offence is committed when a judge of an international court unlawfully solicits or accepts for himself or another person, at any time, directly or indirectly, any offer, promise, gift, present or advantage of any kind, to carry out or abstain from carrying out an act within his function or facilitated by his function. The punishment provided for by this provision is 10 years' imprisonment and a fine of €1,000,000, which amount can be increased to an amount equal to twice that of the proceeds of the offence.

1.5. CONCLUSION ON THE SELECTION OF CANDIDATES FOR POSITIONS AS INTERNATIONAL JUDGES

It is difficult to say whether independence and impartiality are important parameters for selecting French candidates for positions as international adjudicators. Based on the overwhelming selection of state agents and judges, some authors even suggest that French authorities prefer candidates who are more sympathetic to the French state and its interests.[38] If this analysis is correct, this would mean that, from the French perspective, representativeness would have a significant weight in the selection decision, but this does not appear to be surprising as such. The reason for this is that when selecting their candidates for international courts, states are acting as 'parties'.[39] That is why it is perfectly understandable that choosing the most independent person is not their overarching concern. In fact, it might be overly optimistic, and even naïve, to expect that the incentive to choose independent candidates will naturally emanate from states. Such incentive must come from the international courts themselves or from states acting collectively.

More generally, it should not be forgotten that the statutes of some international courts specifically refer to the importance of representativeness.[40] The drafters of these statutes intended to ensure the choice not only of independent judges but also judges who reflect the legal and cultural diversity of the states parties. In this

---

reader that parties are free to choose arbitrators that are not on the ICSID list, and they usually do so.

[38] See e.g. sections 1.1.4 and 1.2.

[39] One could draw a parallel with arbitration where each party usually appoints an arbitrator.

[40] See e.g. Article 9 of the ICJ Statute: 'At every election, the electors shall bear in mind not only that the persons to be elected should individually possess the qualifications required, but also that in the body as a whole the representation of the main forms of civilization and of the principal legal systems of the world should be assured.'

context, it does not appear to be wholly illegitimate for states to ensure that their nominees share their general perspective and understanding of international law. Put differently, the mere fact that a state and its nominee are on the same page should not be taken as an evidence of a lack of impartiality or independence.

In fact, the most controversial aspect of the French practice appears to be its lack of transparency, especially if compared with a growing number of European states that have adopted transparent procedures set out in legal texts. In other words, in the French context, the process receives more criticism than its outcome. However, there has been undeniable progress in recent years regarding transparency (e.g. a public call for applications, interviews for some candidates, etc.). Moreover, the fact that the GFCPA is involved in the selection procedure (even where its participation is not required by international texts) could be seen as an attenuation of the government's influence in selecting the French candidates.

In any event, although the potential lack of independence or impartiality of the candidate with respect to the nominating state is certainly an issue, this risk can be nuanced. First, given the relatively high number of judges that generally render an international decision (which is particularly true for the ICJ), a potential lack of independence towards the nominating state will presumably have less impact than it would have in (commercial) arbitration where the party-appointed arbitrator constitutes one-third of the tribunal and can weigh even more heavily than that if he or she is particularly active and convincing.[41] Second, international courts are small enough to expect that judges know how their colleagues were nominated. In other words, a potential lack of independence towards the nominating state is likely to be difficult to hide and might be – perhaps wrongly – presumed by other judges. Finally, it has been rightly said on several occasions that partiality is counterproductive because a judge lacking impartiality is likely to lose their credibility and thus be unable to influence their colleagues.

2. ARBITRATORS' IMPARTIALITY IN FRENCH LAW

France is rightly perceived to be one of the friendliest jurisdictions to arbitration. The French arbitration law[42] lies in the Civil Procedure Code (Code de procédure

---

[41] That is what happened in the infamous *Tapie* case: CA Paris, 17.02.2015, no. 13/13278.

[42] For an account of this law in English, See G. Carducci, *Arbitration in France: Law and Practice*, Oxford University Press 2023. On arbitrators' impartiality in French law, some valuable indications could be found in S. Angoura, *The Impartiality and Independence of Arbitrators in International Commercial Arbitration*, Nomos 2022; I. Beimel, *Independence and Impartiality in International Commercial Arbitration*, Eleven 2021.

In French, there are three published PhD dissertations that are entirely devoted to the topic of arbitrators' impartiality (though tackling it from different angles): K. El Chazli, *L'impartialité*

civile, CPC). The last major reform of French law dates back to January 2011 (décret No. 2011-48 of 13 January 2011). French texts are succinct compared to the UNCITRAL Model Law; hence, case law is also important.[43]

Furthermore, France adheres to the dualistic approach to arbitration in the sense that it has different regimes for domestic and international arbitration.[44] That said, numerous provisions (including those on the duty to disclose and the challenging of arbitrators) apply to both domestic and international arbitration.[45] Moreover, there is no indication in the case law that a difference between the regimes of the two types of arbitration exists regarding impartiality.[46]

As a matter of terminology, the word 'impartiality' will be preferred over 'independence' because impartiality (usually understood to be a state of mind) is broad enough to encompass independence (usually understood to be an objective situation), while the reverse is not true. In reality, lack of independence is a problem only because of its threat to the arbitrator's freedom of mind (i.e. because it creates a risk of partiality).[47] Finally, it should be noted that French case law traditionally conflates the two concepts even though several 2021 cases have started to distinguish them.[48]

2.1. GENERAL REMARKS: THE LAW IS (STILL) UNDER CONSTRUCTION

An analysis of French law on arbitrators' impartiality is a difficult task because this law has not yet been clearly settled. The reasons first pertain to the CPC

---

de l'arbitre, LGDJ 2020; C. Castres Saint-Martin, Les conflits d'intérêts en arbitrage commercial international, L'Harmattan 2016; and M. Henry, Le devoir d'indépendance de l'arbitre, LGDJ 2001.

[43] French courts hand down roughly a dozen decisions each year addressing aspects of the impartiality of arbitrators. Cases are regularly reported and commented notably in Revue de l'arbitrage, the Paris Journal of International Arbitration, Recueil Dalloz and Dalloz actualité (website). Given the limited space, this report does not purport to be exhaustive and can only mention some important cases. A trove of case law can be found in T. Clay, Code de l'arbitrage, LexisNexis 2021.

[44] Foreign domestic awards are assimilated to international awards for recognition purposes (Cass. 1re civ., 13.01.2021, EGPC c. NATGAS, no. 19-22.932).

[45] See Article 1506 CPC, which lists the provisions that apply to both domestic and international arbitration unless the parties have agreed otherwise.

[46] In fact, there are no compelling reasons for such a difference to exist.

[47] Another reason to prefer impartiality as a concept is that from a terminological point of view, most relationships (that might impact the arbitrator's judgment, i.e. their impartiality) do not make the arbitrator 'dependent' strictly speaking. In fact, only a small minority of relationships that are characterised by a severe imbalance (such as the employment relationship) might create such dependency.

[48] See e.g. CA Paris, 16.02.2021, Grenwich, no. 18/07442, Rev. arb. 2022, p. 431, note K. El Chazli; CA Paris, 02.03.2021, Rotana, no. 18/16891.

France

and the case law, the peculiar nature of impartiality disputes and the recent (normative and factual) developments affecting arbitrators' impartiality.

2.1.1. Reasons Pertaining to the CPC and the Case Law

Two normative reasons make a description of French law on arbitrators' impartiality difficult: French texts (the CPC) directly concerning impartiality are brief and consistency does not seem to be the main objective of French courts.

The brevity of French texts regarding impartiality can be evidenced by the fact that the words 'independence' and 'impartiality' are only mentioned in the context of the duty to disclose.[49] These words are mentioned neither as duties by which arbitrators must abide nor as a reason for the annulment or denial of recognition of awards.[50] To give the normative regime for arbitrators' impartiality some substance, a judicial trend used to refer to the textual 'grounds for challenge' (*causes de récusation*) that are applicable to judges, but this trend was reversed more than 20 years ago.[51]

Thus, to ascertain the content of French law on arbitrators' impartiality, one needs to revert to the case law. That said, one should note that the French legal system does not adhere to the doctrine of precedent. Thus, judges might not feel obliged to pursue consistency as an English judge would. Although each decision is awaited and dissected by scholars in the hope of clarifying the law, this does not mean that these decisions set new binding principles. Moreover, as will be shown in the following section, impartiality disputes are highly fact-specific and this hinders the 'precedential' value of previous cases. That said, there are some well-established solutions and trends in French case law, but this disclaimer is necessary to be well aware of the limitations of French case law as a source of law on arbitrators' impartiality.

2.1.2. Peculiar Nature of Impartiality Disputes

It is important to keep in mind three characteristics of impartiality disputes that add to the complexity of the regulation of impartiality. First, impartiality disputes arise in very different contexts. Indeed, arbitrators' impartiality can be questioned based on their relationship with a party, their conduct of proceedings,

---

[49] Article 1456 CPC: 'Before accepting a mandate, an arbitrator shall disclose any circumstance that may affect his or her independence or impartiality.'

[50] Impartiality issues are generally argued and decided on the 'improper constitution of the arbitral tribunal' ground or, more rarely, under the 'international public policy' ground.

[51] On this case law, see M. Henry, *Le devoir d'indépendance de l'arbitre*, LGDJ 2001, pp. 296–98. The disconnection between judges' and arbitrators' impartiality is to be commended because they raise different questions and involve different stakes, especially when it comes to party-appointed arbitrators.

Intersentia

a previously held opinion or some passages of their award. Since each category of circumstances raises its own questions and difficulties, it might be sensible for each category to get its own bespoke rules (e.g. specific rules for arbitrators' relationships; other rules for issue conflicts), especially because the impartiality requirement is too broad a principle to offer meaningful assistance in answering such varied questions.

Second, disputes about impartiality are highly fact-specific. Thus, hard-and-fast rules might not be the most appropriate, and solutions of previous cases might not be readily transposed.

Finally, it should be recalled that it is extremely difficult to prove 'evident partiality'.[52] The overwhelming majority of cases are about 'risks' of partiality, which means that, in practice, assessment of impartiality is in essence a matter of probability. Since risks of partiality are not always serious enough to justify in and of themselves radical and costly consequences, such as the annulment of the award, deciding impartiality disputes usually involves in practice some (unspoken) balancing of impartiality with other considerations such as efficiency[53] and the parties' 'right' to appoint arbitrators. In summary, the peculiar nature of impartiality disputes makes it more difficult to craft workable rules that can address the multiplicity of situations and stakes.

2.1.3. Recent (Normative and Factual) Developments Affecting Arbitrator's Impartiality

2.1.3.1. Normative Developments

2.1.3.1.1. The Emergence of Non-National Sources

Until quite recently, the topic of impartiality had not attracted much normative attention from arbitral institutions and national legislators. For decades, the consensus concerning the impartiality requirement seemed to have overshadowed the challenges raised by its implementation. With the increased quest for transparency and awareness of the difficulties (and uncertainties) of implementing impartiality provisions and the duty to disclose, some actors in the arbitration community (such as the IBA and some arbitral institutions) have recently begun to dwell on the impartiality requirement with the aim of filling the gaps in the (hard) law of impartiality.[54]

---

[52] One could also add that biased arbitrators are probably smart enough to hide their bias under the gloss of sophisticated legal arguments.

[53] Annulment of an award obviously has costs that ought to be taken into consideration, especially if the risk of partiality is low.

[54] This trend, while welcome, is not without its disadvantages. In fulfilling the duty to disclose, an arbitrator might potentially need to consider soft law (IBA Guidelines), an

France

From the standpoint of national legal systems, the thorniest question revolves around the weight to be given to such non-national rules. The IBA Guidelines on Conflicts of Interest in International Arbitration have the advantage of having a universal vocation. Many state courts have referred to this text, sometimes praising it[55] and, more rarely, criticising it.[56] It is surprising to note that French courts have apparently referred to the IBA Guidelines in only a single case.[57] That said, one should not deduce from that fact that French courts are hostile to non-national rules. In fact, the reason for refraining from citing these guidelines lies rather in the French courts' traditional reluctance to cite soft law texts in their decisions.

In 2016, the ICC[58] published a Note to Parties and Arbitral Tribunals on the Conduct of the Arbitration, regularly updated, the last version of which dates from January 2021. French decisions have referred to this Note with respect to arbitral proceedings conducted under the ICC Rules.[59] Although it is perfectly justifiable that arbitral institutions' documents be given some value or effect, the multiplication of such documents carries the risk of the fragmentation of the law on arbitrators' impartiality and the lessening of the precedential value of decisions that refer to a given arbitral institution document.

2.1.3.1.2. LEEWAY FOR AGREEMENT BETWEEN THE PARTIES?

Can parties agree that a given kind of circumstance does not jeopardise impartiality? A 2022 decision[60] confirmed that such agreements can have an impact on assessment of impartiality. In a nutshell, several days after the disclosure made by a party-appointed arbitrator, the parties entered into a procedural agreement (*accord procédural*) in which they stipulated that the relationships between the party-appointed arbitrators or their law firms and the

---

arbitral institution's recommendations as well as the law of the seat and the law of the place of enforcement. The plurality of norms to be taken into account can be disconcerting for arbitrators.

55 See e.g. ATF 147 III 65 (Swiss Federal Supreme Court, 22.12.2020, *Sun Yang v. AMA & FINA*, no. 4A_318/2020), cons. 7.4: 'These guidelines ... constitute a useful working instrument that can contribute to the harmonization and unification of the standards applied in the field of international arbitration for the settlement of conflicts of interest, an instrument that cannot fail to have an influence on the practice of arbitration institutions and courts'. A translation of this decision is available at https://www.swissarbitrationdecisions.com/atf-4a-318-2020.

56 [2016] EWHC 422 (Comm), paras 36–37.

57 CA Paris, 23.02.2021, *Lerco*, no. 18/03068.

58 In the rest of this chapter, 'ICC' refers to the International Chamber of Commerce.

59 See e.g. CA Paris, 11.01.2022, *Rio Tinto France*, no. 19/19201. However, the legal value of the ICC Note is not entirely clear. The language of the decision suggests that abidance with this Note is not mandatory ('l'arbitre peut notamment se référer aux recommandations ...').

60 CA Paris, 11.01.2022, *Rio Tinto France*, no. 19/19201.

Intersentia

parties' affiliated entities (concerning matters unrelated to the current dispute) did not constitute, as such, an obstacle for the nomination and confirmation of such arbitrators. When one of the parties challenged the award on the ground that a relationship of the above-mentioned sort was not disclosed, the Paris Court of Appeal relied, among other grounds, on this agreement to dismiss the challenge.[61]

This approach (giving parties some leeway to define what does not constitute a risk of partiality) has the advantage of facilitating the nomination of lawyers affiliated to large law firms, as well as the judge's task in assessing impartiality, since it gives them some substance to decide whether a given circumstance could give rise to reasonable doubts. It is too early, however, to evaluate to what extent French courts will give full legal effect to such agreements. As is usually the case in impartiality matters, it is likely that the value to be given to such agreements will depend upon the circumstances of the case.

2.1.3.2. Factual Developments

Despite being a fundamental principle since time immemorial, the requirement of impartiality must be implemented in light of the new technological challenges as well as the evolution of the arbitration practice. The most important technological challenge obviously comes from the internet, on which relevant information for assessing impartiality can be found. In a significant number of cases since 2013, a preliminary, yet fundamental, issue in deciding an impartiality dispute was to determine whether the complaining party could be presumed to know the information that is available online, in which case it was presumed to have waived its right to invoke this information.[62] The evolution of arbitration practice has also influenced the implementation of the impartiality requirement, notably with the emergence of new actors such as third-party funders that might be interested in the outcome of the dispute.

2.2. MECHANISMS TO ENSURE IMPARTIALITY OF INTERNATIONAL ARBITRATORS

The preceding section stressed the uncertainty surrounding the implementation of the impartiality requirement, since it is a legal area that is still under construction and, consequently, has a significant potential to evolve. This will

---

[61]   '[L]es parties ont entendu par la conclusion d'un accord procédural et leur attitude ultérieurement exclure du champ du doute raisonnable tout lien entre le cabinet d'un arbitre et les entités affiliées aux parties' (§90).

[62]   On this issue, see section 2.2.3.

France

therefore inform our approach to stating impartiality law. Instead of focusing on some recent cases that might become quickly 'outdated', we will rather focus on the more established solutions.

2.2.1. No Particular Restrictions for Prospective Arbitrators

French texts do not place particular restrictions on prospective arbitrators to ensure their impartiality. Nor do French courts. As several cases have held, sharing the nationality of a party does not compromise an arbitrator's impartiality.[63] That said, several cases in 2021[64] suggested, in a debatable *obiter dictum*, that bias might stem from an arbitrator's nationality.[65]

2.2.2. Duty to Disclose

The main mechanism to prevent the nomination of arbitrators who lack impartiality is the duty to disclose, which is enshrined in Article 1456 CPC.[66] That article provides as follows: 'Before accepting a mandate, an arbitrator shall disclose any circumstance that may affect his or her independence or impartiality. He or she also shall disclose promptly any such circumstance that may arise after accepting the mandate.'

As to the scope of the duty, there is no detailed list in French law like those given by the IBA Guidelines or the ICC Note; as a result, there is still some uncertainty as to what, exactly, an arbitrator should disclose. Arbitrators will need to rely on guidance given in the case law (and non-national rules such as the IBA Guidelines and rules laid down by arbitral institutions, if any).[67] It is, however, well accepted that the circumstances to be disclosed go beyond those justifying a finding of lack of impartiality.

An important limitation to the scope of the disclosure duty is to be found in the case law. According to a well-established rule – predating Article 1456 CPC – arbitrators need not disclose circumstances that may affect their impartiality when these circumstances are notorious or of common knowledge (*notoires*). Regarding such circumstances, parties are expected (and, in fact, irrefutably presumed) to know them.

---

[63] See e.g. CA Paris, 25.11.2014, *Electroputere VFU Pascani c. Blue Engineering*, no. 13/11333; CA Paris, 17.02.2005, *Mytilineos Holdings c. The Authority for Privatization and State Equity Administration*, no. 2003/22386.

[64] See e.g. CA Paris, 16.02.2021, *Grenwich*, no. 18/07442, *Rev. arb.* 2022, p. 431, note K. El Chazli; CA Paris, 12.10.2021, *République du Sénégal c. Aboukhalil*, no. 19/21625.

[65] 'L'impartialité de l'arbitre suppose l'absence de préjugés ou de partis pris susceptibles d'affecter le jugement de l'arbitre, lesquels peuvent résulter de multiples facteurs tels que la nationalité de l'arbitre, son environnement social, culturel ou juridique.'

[66] Before being written in the Code, it was recognised by case law.

[67] See section 2.1.3.1.

Intersentia

445

In many cases, 'notoriety' was loosely understood to mean that the mere online availability of a piece of information was enough to make it notorious, thereby (i) considerably (and questionably) alleviating the arbitrator's duty to disclose and (ii) heightening the parties' duty to investigate potential conflicts of interest. In fact, French courts seem to impose upon parties a duty to discover 'online' information that can sometimes be quite stringent.[68] That said, some recent cases have stressed that a given piece of information is notorious only when it can be *easily* accessed, which is not the case when a party must conduct a meticulous examination of online sources in order to find it.[69]

Another important exception to the notoriety rule is that arbitrators should disclose all relevant circumstances that arise *after* the commencement of arbitral proceedings.[70] In other words, parties are not expected to carry out their duty to investigate throughout the arbitral proceedings. It is worth noting as well that there is broad agreement among courts[71] and scholars[72] that so-called scientific or intellectual relationships (*liens d'ordre scientifique ou intellectuel*) need not be disclosed.

Finally, it is admitted that non-disclosure does not, by itself, justify a finding of a lack of impartiality.[73] What counts in the first place is the impact of the undisclosed circumstance on impartiality. That said, some intentional

---

[68] See e.g. CA Paris, 25.05.2021, *Delta Dragon c. Byd Auto*, no. 18/20625; CA Paris, 26.01.2021, *Vidatel*, no. 19/10666.

[69] CA Paris, 25.02.2020, *Sté Dommo Energia c. Sté Barra Energia Do Brazil*, no. 19/15818. See also CA Paris, 11.01.2022, *Rio Tinto France*, no. 19/19201; CA Paris, 17.05.2022, *Sté Billionaire International AG c. SARL Sivendome*, no. 20/18020. On the concepts of notoriety and duty of curiosity, see C. Debourg and E. Teynier, 'Exception de notoriété et obligation de curiosité', *Rev. arb.* 2022, p. 99.

[70] See e.g. CA Paris, 27.03.2018, *Sté Saad Buzwair Automotive (SBA) c. Sté Audi Volkswagen Middle East (AVME)*, no. 16/09386; CA Paris, 11.01.2022, *Rio Tinto France*, no. 19/19201. Cf. Cass. 1re civ., 25.05.2022, *Sté Soletanche Bachy France c. Sté Aqaba Container Terminal*, no. 20-23.148.

[71] See e.g. CA Paris, 17.05.2022, *Sté Billionaire International AG c. SARL Sivendome*, no. 20/18020 (presiding over a conference); CA Paris, 17.05.2022, *Sté Saudi Tumpane Company Ltd c. Sté Pizzarotti Rizzani De Eccher Saudi Ltd*, no. 20/15162 (participation in scientific activities); CA Paris, 14.10.2014, *S.A. Fidelidade Companhia de Seguros c. FC Nantes*, no. 13/14076 (participation in a dinner debate by a think tank); CA Paris, 01.07.2011, *SA Emivir c. SAS ITM Entreprises*, no. 10/10406 (common publication).

[72] See e.g. J.-B. Racine, *Droit de l'arbitrage*, PUF 2016, p. 343. Cf. K. El Chazli, *L'impartialité de l'arbitre*, LGDJ 2020, pp. 162–63.

[73] See e.g. CA Paris, 17.05.2022, *Sté Billionaire International AG c. SARL Sivendome*, no. 20/18020: 'la non-révélation par l'arbitre d'informations qu'il aurait dû déclarer ne suffit pas à caractériser un défaut d'indépendance ou d'impartialité. Encore faut-il que ces éléments soient de nature à provoquer dans l'esprit des parties un doute raisonnable quant à l'impartialité et à l'indépendance de l'arbitre, c'est-à-dire un doute qui peut naître chez une personne placée dans la même situation et ayant accès aux mêmes éléments d'information raisonnablement accessibles.'

non-disclosures can aggravate the doubts about impartiality and be taken as a factor in the assessment of impartiality.[74]

2.2.3. The Main Obstacle to the Implementation of the Impartiality Requirement: The Parties' Duty to Invoke Irregularities in a Timely Manner

Article 1466 CPC (which is not specific to impartiality) provides that:

> A party which, knowingly and without a legitimate reason, fails to object to an irregularity before the arbitral tribunal in a timely manner shall be deemed to have waived its right to avail itself of such irregularity.

Practically speaking, this provision imposes a duty to invoke before the arbitral tribunal the circumstance materialising the risk of partiality in a timely manner, failing which a party loses its right to invoke this circumstance before state courts. This provision is imbued with efficiency purposes and is, in practice, the main obstacle for enforcing the impartiality requirement. It is likely that most impartiality arguments have been held inadmissible by French courts on the ground of Article 1466 CPC.

In fact, the case law holds the complaining party to an even stricter standard than does the wording of this provision. While Article 1466 CPC requires actual knowledge of the relevant circumstance, courts frequently content themselves with presumed or constructive knowledge through the concepts of notoriety and duty of curiosity. In other words, a party may well be deemed to have waived its right to avail itself of a given risk of partiality of which it is not aware.[75]

Courts do sometimes stick to a literal interpretation of Article 1466 CPC, as shown by a recent case[76] in which it was held that objecting before the arbitral institution (ICC Court) was not enough to satisfy the conditions of Article 1466 CPC, since this provision enjoins parties from making such an objection before the arbitral tribunal.[77]

---

[74] See e.g. CA Reims, 02.11.2011, *Tecnimont c. Avax*, no. 10/02888; Cass. 1re civ., 18.12.2014, *Sté VR services c. Sté Dukan de Nitya*, no. 14-11085.

[75] However, a recent decision (CA Paris, 11.01.2022, *Rio Tinto France*, no. 19/19201) may show some hope, stating that the challenging party's knowledge (and waiver) could not be established in relation to a circumstance that the non-disclosing co-arbitrator did not know either.

[76] CA Paris, 15.06.2021, *Pharaon*, no. 20/07999.

[77] The reply to this argument is that Article 1466 CPC (which is not specific to impartiality) enjoins parties to object to irregularities before the arbitral tribunal because for all irregularities the tribunal is in the best position to correct them. For impartiality irregularities, however, it is not the case and the arbitral institution is arguably the place to go to object to this kind of irregularities.

The general impression one gets from the application of this provision in French case law is that courts seek to avoid the situation where parties might use impartiality arguments as ammunition against an unfavourable award. Parties are therefore strongly encouraged to put forward all their objections as early as possible. The drawback of this approach is that it might create an incentive to multiply tactical objections – even for flimsy reasons – just to avoid losing the right to raise these objections after an unfavourable award has been rendered.

2.3. CIRCUMSTANCES THAT COULD GIVE RISE TO IMPARTIALITY CONCERNS

2.3.1. Arbitrator's Acts

2.3.1.1. Acts Accomplished in the Context of the Adjudicative Function

French courts are reluctant to discern signs of partiality from acts accomplished in the context of the adjudicative function, i.e. acts and decisions taken during the proceedings. This approach of deference to arbitrators seems justifiable, since the duty to adjudicate obliges the arbitrator to take several decisions and initiatives related to procedure and evidence. Courts are right to support arbitrators who are willing to perform their duties and reach a correct outcome of the dispute.[78] More generally, it should not be forgotten that even an erroneous decision does not indicate partiality.

However, arbitrators do not have *carte blanche* and if a certain threshold is crossed, a lack of impartiality might be established. For example, arbitrators who lack technical expertise and refrain from seeking an expert valuation could be viewed as willing to circumvent the experts' impartial opinion in order to favour one party at the expense of the other.[79]

2.3.1.2. Acts Unrelated to the Adjudicative Function

Detecting potential partiality from acts that are unrelated to the adjudicative function should be easier, since such acts are not necessary to perform judicial duties and thus are more difficult to justify. This is the case, for example, of an

---

[78] See e.g. CA Paris, 23.06.2015, *CNAN c. CTI*, no. 13/09748, where it was held that there was nothing objectionable about asking a party's counsel and witnesses questions during the hearing since these questions only sought to obtain factual clarifications that were useful for deciding the dispute. The court added that these questions did not demonstrate that the arbitrator held strong views about which he was asking.

[79] CA Paris, 27.05.2014, *Huertas c. Taburno*, no. 12/05975.

arbitrator who sues the defendant in an ongoing arbitration to obtain payment of his fees.[80]

2.3.1.3. The Award Itself

One might have thought that the award is the ideal basis for assessing impartiality since this is where bias, if any, materialises. Nonetheless, French courts are very reluctant to detect partiality based on the award itself. In several recent decisions, the Paris Court of Appeal has relentlessly repeated that it cannot review the reasoning of the award even to assess impartiality.[81] The Court added that the reasonable doubts about an arbitrator's impartiality can only be based on the structure of the award or its terms (*termes*).

2.3.2. Arbitrator's Relationships

2.3.2.1. Relationships under Scrutiny

Risks of partiality can stem from arbitrators' relationships with parties; are there other kinds of relationships that might prove problematic from the impartiality standpoint? In fact, French case law is flexible. In their assessment of impartiality, French courts have been willing to examine the relationships with counsel, other arbitrators and interested third parties.[82]

2.3.2.2. Criteria for the Assessment of the Arbitrator's Relationships

The thorniest issue concerning the assessment of the risk of partiality arising from the arbitrator's relationships is to determine the proper criteria to conduct such an assessment. The case law does not follow a clear approach. Several criteria have been used.[83] That said, the most important (and logical) criterion seems to be 'intensity'.

The case law follows a more settled approach regarding specialist arbitration, such as commodity arbitration, where it is well established that having relationships with parties does not, by itself, impugn an arbitrator's impartiality.[84] This judicial trend is an additional indication that assessment of impartiality does not happen in a vacuum; it necessarily takes into consideration the stakes and peculiarities of (the relevant type of) arbitration.

---

[80] CA Paris, 02.04.2019, *Patrick Desbordes*, no. 16/00136.
[81] See e.g. CA Paris, 28.06.2022, no. 21/06317; CA Paris, 16.02.2021, *Grenwich*, no. 18/07442, *Rev. arb.* 2022, p. 431, note K. El Chazli.
[82] See e.g. K. El Chazli, *L'impartialité de l'arbitre*, LGDJ 2020, pp. 101–12.
[83] See e.g. ibid., pp. 119–51.
[84] See e.g. CA Paris, 17.12.2013, *Oursel c. Sermaplus*, no. 12/13053.

Intersentia

449

2.3.3. Arbitrator's Previous Opinions (Issue Conflict)

It is accepted that risks of partiality can arise from the arbitrator's relationships not only with parties and interested third parties but also with the dispute, the so-called concept of 'issue conflict'.[85] The existence of previously expressed opinions on issues that are part of the current dispute is relevant from an impartiality standpoint because such expressed opinions have the potential to limit an arbitrator's freedom of mind. It is difficult to state French courts' position on this matter since issue conflicts can arise in a variety of very different situations that cannot be resolved the same way.[86] That said, regarding opinions expressed on purely legal issues, it is worth noting that in a relatively old case, the Paris Court of Appeal showed some hostility towards the concept when it ruled that the fact that an arbitrator has decided the same legal issue in a previous case cannot constitute a pre-judgment since the parties were different.[87]

2.4. IMPARTIALITY OF PARTY-APPOINTED ARBITRATORS

There is an agreement among French scholars that in French law, party-appointed arbitrators must be fully impartial, i.e. they have the same impartiality duties as other arbitrators.[88] In fact, it is rare that the case law explicitly addresses this question. While one can find cases insisting that a party-appointed arbitrator must remain independent,[89] other cases seem comfortable with the idea that party-appointed arbitrators have a role specific to them within the arbitral tribunal.[90]

---

[85] Issue conflict is 'an allegation that an arbitrator is biased towards a particular view of certain issues or has already prejudged them. The alleged predisposition or prejudgment involves an arbitrator's purported adherence to his or her pre-existing views on legal and factual questions, developed through experience as an arbitrator, as counsel, writing scholarly articles, and giving interviews or other public expressions of views' (L. Boisson de Chazournes and J. Crook, *Report of the ASIL-ICCA Joint Task Force on Issue Conflicts in Investor-State Arbitration*, 2016, available at http://www.arbitration-icca.org/media/6/81372711507986/asil-icca_report_final_5_april_final_for_ridderprint.pdf).

[86] For the various hypotheses, see K. El Chazli, *L'impartialité de l'arbitre*, LGDJ 2020, pp. 213–50.

[87] CA Paris, 14.10.1993, *Ben Nasser c. BNP et Crédit Lyonnais*, *Rev. arb.* 1994, p. 380, note P. Bellet.

[88] See e.g. C. Seraglini and J. Ortscheidt, *Droit de l'arbitrage interne et international*, LGDJ 2019, p. 727.

[89] See e.g. CA Paris, 28.06.2018, *Me C. c. Le Bâtonnier de l'Ordre des avocats de Paris*, no. 16/16859: 'l'arbitre, même choisi par une partie, doit rester indépendant'.

[90] See e.g. CA Paris, 16.01.2003, *Intelcam c. France Télécom.* no. 2001/03698: the presence of an arbitrator designated by a party within the arbitral tribunal offers a guarantee that its point of view will be heard, even if it is not adopted. See also CA Reims, 02.11.2011, *Tecnimont c. Avax*, no. 10/02888 (suggesting that the chair's duty to disclose is more stringent than that of the party-appointed arbitrators).

The latter group of cases could be interpreted as a common-sense admission that party-appointed arbitrators cannot be always expected to be as impartial as other arbitrators who do not owe their nomination to a single party to the dispute. In fact, as long as the right to appoint arbitrators is viewed as a cornerstone of arbitration, it seems counter-intuitive to deny that this right has any impact on the assessment of impartiality. In any event, it seems that the various (national and non-national) rules on arbitrators' impartiality already condone an attenuated duty of independence and impartiality. To put it differently, if one compares the rules on impartiality of arbitrators and on impartiality of judges, it will become clear that the rules regarding arbitrators are laxer (notably to accommodate the existence of party-appointed arbitrators).

When discussing the degrees of impartiality of the different types of arbitrators, the crucial point appears to be the following: whatever the expectations are concerning party-appointed arbitrators, the impartiality requirements for tribunal chairs and sole arbitrators should be particularly high. Practically speaking, given that there are no specific rules for the chairs of the tribunals and for sole arbitrators, the assessment of their impartiality should be stricter. In other words, it would be sensible to err on the side of caution (i.e. recusal).

2.5. THE CONSEQUENCES OF LACK OF IMPARTIALITY: REMEDIES STRICTLY SPEAKING

A finding of lack of impartiality might have consequences for the arbitrator and/or the award.

2.5.1. Remedies Concerning the Award

2.5.1.1. Awards Made in France

The only (direct) means of recourse against an award made in France in an international arbitration is an action to set aside (Article 1518 CPC)[91] and such action shall be brought before the Court of Appeal of the place where the award was made (Article 1519 CPC). It is interesting to note that although the lack of impartiality is not one of the five limitative grounds that are mentioned in Article 1520 CPC, there is almost a judicial consensus that the ground of lack of

---

[91] An indirect means consists of appealing the order *denying* recognition or enforcement of an international arbitral award made in France (Article 1523 CPC). This provision adds that if the order is appealed, and if one of the parties so requests, the Court of Appeal shall rule on an action to set aside unless the parties have waived the right to bring such action or the time limit to bring such action has expired.

Intersentia

451

impartiality is subsumed within the ground of the improper constitution of the tribunal.[92]

2.5.1.2. Awards Made Abroad

Regarding an award made abroad, impartiality arguments could be raised by appealing the order granting recognition or enforcement of this award (Article 1525 CPC).[93] It should be noted that the Court of Appeal may only deny recognition or enforcement of an award on the grounds listed in Article 1520 CPC (as indicated by Article 1525 CPC). This implies that the difference of treatment between awards made in France and those made abroad relates to procedure, not substance.

2.5.2. Remedies Concerning the Arbitrator

2.5.2.1. Challenging the Arbitrator

Pursuant to Article 1458 CPC, an arbitrator may only be removed with the unanimous consent of the parties. This provision adds that where there is no unanimous consent (which is a common situation in impartiality disputes), the provisions of the final paragraph of Article 1456 CPC shall apply. This paragraph reads as follows:

> If the parties cannot agree on the removal of an arbitrator, the issue shall be resolved by the person responsible for administering the arbitration or, where there is no such person, by the judge acting in support of the arbitration (*juge d'appui*) to whom application must be made within one month following the disclosure or the discovery of the fact at issue.

Decisions made by arbitral institutions and the *juge d'appui* regarding impartiality are not governed by the same legal regime. On the one hand, decisions of arbitral institutions are not *res judicata* and consequently the complaining party can renew its challenge once the award is rendered.[94] On the other hand, decisions of the *juge d'appui* are *res judicata* and cannot be challenged unless new elements arise.[95]

---

[92]   Some recent cases, however, consider that lack of impartiality amounts to a violation of international public policy. See e.g. CA Paris, 15.06.2021, *Pharaon*, no. 20/07999; CA Paris, 12.07.2021, *Fiorilla*, no. 19/11413.

[93]   Such arguments could not be made during enforcement (*exequatur*) proceedings for the simple reason that such proceedings are not adversarial (Article 1516 CPC).

[94]   See e.g. CA Paris, 23.06.2015, *CNAN c. CTI*, no. 13/09748.

[95]   See e.g. Cass. 1re civ., 04.11.2015, *Cool Carriers c. Helvetia*, no. 14-22.643.

France

2.5.2.2. Civil Liability: A Mere Application of General Rules

When an award is annulled for impartiality concerns or for improper disclosure, the arbitrator could be held civilly liable and thus be obliged to compensate the injured party for the harm resulting from such annulment (i.e. expenses incurred as a result of the annulment, not the amount allocated by the award) pursuant to contractual liability rules.[96] That said, since the annulment (or non-recognition) of an award does not presuppose a finding of intentional bias or misconduct, it is perfectly conceivable that the arbitrator would not be held liable despite such an annulment or non-recognition.[97]

2.5.2.3. Criminal Liability: Potential and Risks

Breaching the duty of impartiality can sometimes constitute a criminal offence. Some provisions specifically mention arbitrators, such as Articles 434-9, 435-7 and 435-9 of the Penal Code, which establish the offence of bribery and trading in influence (*corruption et trafic d'influence*), respectively for arbitrators acting under the French arbitration law and those acting under a foreign arbitration law.[98]

More generally, partial arbitrators can also be held criminally liable for other offences committed within the context of their mandate, as well as evidenced by the infamous *Tapie* affair.[99] In what seems to be the last episode of this high-profile case, a party-appointed arbitrator was convicted of fraud (*escroquerie*) for the following reasons:

- working with his appointing party several months before the decision to submit the dispute to arbitration in order to prepare the potential arbitral proceedings;
- agreeing to sit as an arbitrator with the sole goal of furthering the interests of his appointing party;

---

[96] J.-B. Racine, *Droit de l'arbitrage*, PUF 2016, pp. 368–72; P. Stoffel-Munck, 'La responsabilité de l'arbitre' (2017) *Revue de l'arbitrage* 1123. For an application, CA Paris, 12.10.1995, *Raoul-Duval*, *Rev. arb.* 1999, p. 323 (the Chair of the Tribunal was hired by a party the same day the award was rendered, and he did not disclose the underlying negotiations). See also CA Reims, 31.01.2012, *Somoclest*, *Rev. arb.* 2012, p. 209.

[97] See e.g. CA Basse-Terre, 04.07.2022, *Sté AGI*, no. 17/00750: 'La cour d'appel de Paris dans son arrêt de 2014 sur l'exequatur a simplement relevé l'existence d'éléments 'de nature à faire naître dans l'esprit [de la société AGI] un doute raisonnable quant à l'indépendance et l'impartialité de l'arbitre', ce qui constituait une irrégularité dans la composition du tribunal arbitral au sens de l'article 1520 2° du code de procédure civile, sans se prononcer sur l'existence d'une faute objective.'

[98] The offence is basically the same as the one set out in section 1.4.

[99] CA Paris, 24.11.2021, no. 20/00688. On this case, see also C. Sanderson, 'Orange head resigns after guilty verdict in Tapie affair', *Global Arbitration Review* (26 November 2021).

- signing a statement of independence which he knew to be inaccurate;
- concealing longstanding, close and remunerative relationships with his appointing party;
- maintaining secret relationships with his appointing party during the arbitral proceedings; and
- exploiting his authority and experience as a former judge and an arbitration practitioner to exert a preponderant role within the arbitral tribunal and marginalise his colleagues by steering the proceedings and presenting the dispute in a one-sided manner.

The arbitrator was thus given a three-year sentence[100] and fined €300,000, and sums of money corresponding to the value of proceeds were confiscated. The same decision accepted that the act of signing a statement of independence from parties while knowing that this statement is inaccurate (notably because of the existence of undisclosed relationships with those parties) could constitute the offence of forgery (*faux*).[101]

It remains to be seen whether the *Tapie* affair will impact future assessment of arbitrators' impartiality and whether biased arbitrators will be held criminally liable. On the one hand, it could be considered a peculiar case (because of its unusual parties and arbitrators as well as the nature of the dispute and its public interest dimension) that bears no relation to the majority of international commercial arbitration cases. On the other hand, it draws the attention of parties to the availability of criminal law tools to challenge impartiality. Indeed, there are some recent reports of arbitrators being threatened with criminal proceedings.[102]

Whatever the future may bring, one should not expect too much from criminal law as a tool for guaranteeing impartiality. In the vast majority of impartiality cases, criminal law is not an appropriate tool, and it might even be a dangerous one as well. First, criminal law is rarely appropriate because its thresholds are understandably high and require proof of a criminal intent. Thus, criminal law is more likely to sanction evident partiality than a mere risk of partiality. The problem is that usually only a risk of partiality is at stake. Establishing obvious partiality is likely to be difficult, time-consuming and intrusive in any event, as the *Tapie* affair demonstrates. This is why it is highly doubtful that such extensive

---

[100] Due to his age (92 years old), the arbitrator was not imprisoned.

[101] CA Paris, 24.11.2021, no. 20/00688, p. 135. Cf. D. Rebut, 'Les infractions pénales affectant la régularité de l'arbitrage' (2019) *Revue de l'arbitrage* 21, 25–26. In this case, the arbitrator was not convicted of forgery because of the *ne bis in idem* principle (i.e. since the arbitrator had been convicted of fraud because of his signing of the misleading statement of independence, this act could not serve as a basis for convicting him of another offence).

[102] J. Ballantyne, 'Congo accuses Derains of corruption', *Global Arbitration Review* (11 October 2021).

investigations could be a workable solution to quickly decide a challenge or an annulment case.

Another problematic aspect is that criminal law judges might not necessarily be well versed in arbitration practice. With their judicial instincts, they might expect party-appointed arbitrators to be fully independent and impartial, whereas arbitration practice seems to tolerate lower standards for this sort of arbitrator. In other words, there might be a discrepancy or a tension between the idealism (and harshness?) of criminal law and the realism (and laxness?) of arbitration practice.

2.5.2.4. Disciplinary Liability

Disciplinary proceedings against arbitrators do not exist in France. However, a think tank report suggested that it might be appropriate to establish such proceedings before a specialised entity (that is independent from arbitral institutions) in order to sanction arbitrators who, among other things, do not properly comply with their disclosure duty.[103] This approach would have the benefit of targeting the careless arbitrator rather than the award (and indirectly the parties).

2.6. CONCLUSION ON IMPARTIALITY OF ARBITRATORS

Although French law has, for decades, been at the cutting edge of arbitration law and has crafted sophisticated rules for many issues in arbitration law, it seems that French law concerning impartiality of arbitrators is still under construction. Even if the principles seem clear, their implementation is often plagued by uncertainty. In light of this observation, there may be room, and even a need, to develop an international instrument that addresses impartiality issues. This could be an update and enlargement of the scope of the IBA Guidelines or the adoption of 'model rules' developed by bodies such as UNCITRAL. Such an initiative would contribute to more certainty and uniformity.

3. GENERAL CONCLUSION

Is there a single French perspective on the independence and impartiality of international adjudicators? From the foregoing analysis, the answer appears to

---

[103] Club des Juristes, *La responsabilité des arbitres*, 2017, pp. 75, 99–100, available at https://www.leclubdesjuristes.com/wp-content/uploads/2016/03/rapport-club-des-juristes-la-responsabilite-de-larbitre.pdf.

be 'no'. Rather, there are two perspectives depending on the role and position of the state. When the state is acting as a 'party' (i.e. participating in selecting adjudicators that might need to decide disputes in which France is a party), representativeness seems to be a consideration in selecting international adjudicators. However, when the state acts as a neutral third party (e.g. when reviewing commercial arbitral awards), impartiality requirements clearly outweigh representativeness concerns.

THE INDEPENDENCE AND IMPARTIALITY OF ADJUDICATORS IN GREECE

Eva LITINA*

1. The Fundamental Principle of Independence and Impartiality
   of Adjudicators in the Greek Legal System 458
2. The Selection of National Candidates for Positions as International
   Adjudicators. 460
   2.1. European Court of Human Rights. 460
       2.1.1. Call for Applications and Selection Criteria 461
       2.1.2. The Selecting Authority 462
       2.1.3. The Selection Process 463
       2.1.4. Assessment of the Selection Mechanism 464
   2.2. Court of Justice of the European Union 465
       2.2.1. Formal Legal Basis 465
       2.2.2. Call for Applications and Selection Criteria 466
       2.2.3. The Selecting Authority 467
       2.2.4. The Selection Process 468
       2.2.5. Assessment of the Selection Mechanism 469
3. Arbitrators 470
   3.1. Greek Arbitration Law. 470
       3.1.1. Method for Appointing International Arbitrators 471
       3.1.2. Arbitrator Impartiality and Disclosure Duty 471
       3.1.3. Remedies and Enforcement. 473
   3.2. Arbitration Institutions and Associations in Greece and
       Other Special Rules 475
   3.3. International Centre for Settlement of Investment Disputes 476
   3.4. Assessment 477
4. Conclusions 477

---

* The rapporteur would like to thank Karim El Chazli for his valuable comments on an earlier draft of this report and the people of Intersentia, especially Rebecca Bryan, for the insightful editing of this report. All errors remain mine.

Intersentia

1. THE FUNDAMENTAL PRINCIPLE OF INDEPENDENCE AND IMPARTIALITY OF ADJUDICATORS IN THE GREEK LEGAL SYSTEM

The rule of law ensures judicial independence and the right to a fair trial.[1] Article 10 of the Universal Declaration of Human Rights and important international legal texts assert that access to a fair hearing by an impartial tribunal is a fundamental human right.[2] At the national level, it is also found in constitutions and national legislation.

Greece is bound by Article 14(1) of the International Covenant on Civil and Political Rights, Article 6 of the European Convention for the Protection of Human Rights and Fundamental Freedoms (ECHR) and Article 47 of the Charter of Fundamental Rights of the European Union. Article 87 of the Greek Constitution includes provisions on judicial independence with specific reference to decisional and personal independence. Decisional independence means that the judge is free to decide a dispute only bound by the Constitution and the law.[3] Personal independence refers to the service and salary of the judiciary. The supervision of national adjudicators is conducted only by higher-degree judges.[4]

The principle of judicial impartiality derives from Articles 4 (right to equality), 8, 20, para. 1, 29, para. 3, and 87, para. 2 of the Constitution.[5] In accordance with Article 8, no person shall be deprived of the judge assigned by law against his or her will. Judicial committees or extraordinary courts, under any name whatsoever, are forbidden. Article 20, para. 1 provides that every person shall be entitled to receive legal protection from the courts and may plead before them his or her views concerning his or her rights or interests, as specified by law. Article 29, para. 3 refers to the political and ideological impartiality of judges.[6] Greek procedural laws also safeguard judicial impartiality by providing for the exclusion of judges, prosecutors and judicial clerks in the case of

---

[1] The International Bar Association (IBA) has created eight short videos illustrating different elements that make up the rule of law, among which is the independent judiciary and the right to a fair trial, www.ibanet.org/rule-of-law-videos-en.aspx.

[2] International Covenant on Civil and Political Rights, Article 14(1); European Convention for the Protection of Human Rights and Fundamental Freedoms, Article 6; Charter of Fundamental Rights of the European Union, Article 47; American Convention on Human Rights, Article 8.

[3] Constitution, Article 87, para. 2.

[4] Constitution, Article 87, para. 3.

[5] For a more detailed analysis, see D. Raikos, *Judicial Independence and Impartiality*, Sakkoulas, Athens/Thessaloniki 2008, pp. 102–12.

[6] Manifestations of any nature in favour of or against a political party by judges are absolutely prohibited.

special relationships or interest in the proceedings or any other cause of suspicion of bias.[7]

Independence and impartiality of adjudicators are also instrumental in determining the success and legitimacy of international courts and tribunals. This report will explore and assess Greek law and practices on the selection of national candidates for positions as international adjudicators.

In arbitration, the selection of arbitrators is one of the most important expressions of party autonomy and one of the principal reasons to resort to arbitration. Given a valid arbitration agreement in a dispute, the next phase of an international arbitration is the appointment of the arbitral tribunal. According to a commonly used maxim, arbitration is as good as the arbitrator: the selection of arbitrators has significant consequences for the entire arbitral process. The fundamental duty of arbitrators to be independent and impartial is a universally accepted and integral principle that arises from the very nature of arbitration as a method of resolving disputes. Impartiality operates as a safeguard for the integrity of arbitration and limits the otherwise unfettered freedom of the arbitrator.

However, the rules must be considered and structured carefully since challenges to arbitrators may lead to additional costs, delays and ultimately a defeat of the very purpose of arbitration.[8] There is a perception that challenges to arbitrators are being launched to gain a tactical advantage, such as eliminating a specific arbitrator, intimidating the other party, or wasting time and increasing costs to pressure an economically weaker party.[9]

Lack of impartiality not only affects the selection of arbitrators and the arbitration process but also has crucial consequences for the efficiency of arbitration. When arbitrators lack impartiality, the award is susceptible to challenges, which may hinder its enforcement.

To evaluate the method for appointing national candidates to positions as international adjudicators, we will first examine the Greek law and practices as to the selection of national candidates to human rights courts, such as the European Court of Human Rights (ECtHR), and regional courts, such as the

---

[7] Code of Civil Procedure, Article 52, para. 1; Code of Criminal Procedure, Articles 14, 15; Code of Administrative Procedure, Articles 14, 15, 17; Presidential Decree 18/1989 (for the Supreme Administrative Court), Article 40.

[8] H.-L. Yu and L. Shore, 'Independence, Impartiality, and Immunity of Arbitrators – US and English Perspectives' (2003) 52 *ICLQ* 935, 936 suggest that a challenge to an arbitrator's independence or impartiality can be a delaying tactic or an attempt to influence the composition of the arbitral tribunal or an effort to avoid an unfavourable award. K. Calavros, *International Commercial Arbitration*, vol. 1, Sakkoulas, Athens/Thessaloniki 2019, pp. 214–15 refers to the abuse of process caused by such challenges and the repeat challenges aiming to intimidate the arbitrator (so-called guerrilla tactics).

[9] J. Dias, 'Resignation in the Face of Confidentiality?' (2020) 2 *Transnational Dispute Management* 1.

Court of Justice of the European Union (CJEU). Greece has not had a judge at the International Court of Justice (ICJ)[10] and the International Tribunal for the Law of the Sea (ITLOS) for many years.[11] There is also no Greek judge at the International Criminal Court (ICC).[12] Then we will examine the safeguards provided for international arbitrators.

2. THE SELECTION OF NATIONAL CANDIDATES FOR POSITIONS AS INTERNATIONAL ADJUDICATORS

2.1. EUROPEAN COURT OF HUMAN RIGHTS

Article 21(1) of the ECHR stipulates the criteria for selecting adjudicators. Judges shall be of high moral character and must either possess the qualifications required for appointment to high judicial office or be jurisconsults of recognised competence. During their term of office, judges shall not engage in any activity which is incompatible with their independence, impartiality or with the demands of a full-time office.[13] The Parliamentary Assembly of the Council of Europe (PACE) in its Resolution 1646 (2009) provides guidelines on the requirements that states should comply with in their national selection procedures.[14]

In Greece, there is an established procedure for the election of ECtHR judges, but without a formal legal basis. The most recent election of a Greek judge to the ECtHR took place in January 2021.[15] The list of candidates and detailed curricula vitae are available on PACE's website.[16] In the same document, there is also information on the national selection procedure for the position of a judge of the ECtHR.[17]

---

[10]   Greek judges have been appointed as ad hoc judges in four cases: www.icj-cij.org/en/all-judges-ad-hoc; and one Greek judge was a member of the ICJ in 1958–1967: www.icj-cij.org/en/all-members.

[11]   www.itlos.org/en/main/the-tribunal/members-of-the-tribunal-since-1996/.

[12]   www.icc-cpi.int/Publications/JudgesENG.pdf.

[13]   ECHR, Article 21(4).

[14]   Parliamentary Assembly, Resolution 1646 (2009), 'Nomination of Candidates and Election of Judges to the European Court of Human Rights', https://pace.coe.int/pdf/6adfb02a7293ff6403e42946ceceab3785638c90437533634e433df4304607a8/res.%201646.pdf.

[15]   'PACE Elects Ioannis Ktistakis Judge to the European Court of Human Rights in Respect of Greece', https://pace.coe.int/en/news/8181/pace-elects-ioannis-ktistakis-judge-to-the-european-court-of-human-rights-in-respect-of-greece. See 'Elections of Judges to the European Court of Human Rights – Table of Progress by Contracting Party', https://rm.coe.int/forthcoming-elections-for-judges-country-by-country-january-2023-/1680aa06ac.

[16]   Parliamentary Assembly, 'Election of Judges to the European Court of Human Rights, List and Curricula Vitae of Candidates Submitted by the Government of Greece', Doc. 15187 (25.11.2020), https://pace.coe.int/pdf/f0c14e2cc4d19c3c4aa765b85997eacfbc8d71a5bc3a794c7407b0cbf494f563/doc.%2015187.pdf.

[17]   Ibid.

According to this document, the procedure for the nomination of candidates was based on the practice followed during the previous selection of candidates for the position of a Greek judge of the ECtHR, with improvements.[18]

2.1.1. Call for Applications and Selection Criteria

The Ministry of Foreign Affairs published a call for applications due to the end of the term of the former judge and President of the ECtHR Linos-Alexandros Sicilianos.[19] The deadline for the applications was 6 December 2019. The call was published on 1 November 2019 on the website of the Ministry of Foreign Affairs and was accompanied by a model curriculum vitae in English and French and relevant information.

The call was also published in national newspapers with wide circulation, such as *Naftemporiki*,[20] as well as in the specialised legal press, such as *Lawspot*.[21] It was also sent by a letter signed by the Minister of Foreign Affairs and the Minister of Justice to the Presidents of the three Supreme Courts, the President of the Plenary of the country's bar associations, and the rectors of universities with law schools.[22] The Athens Bar Association also published the call.[23] Therefore, the call was made known to all relevant professional and academic institutions.

The call contained a job description, focusing on the requirements set out in the ECHR and PACE's guidelines, i.e. candidates should fulfil the requirements for appointment to high judicial office of the ECtHR, have proven experience in the field of human rights[24] and have excellent knowledge of one of the official languages of the Council of Europe (English or French) and at least passive knowledge of the other.

---

[18]   Ibid.

[19]   Πρόσκληση Εκδήλωσης Ενδιαφέροντος για τη Θέση του Έλληνα Δικαστή στο Ευρωπαϊκό Δικαστήριο Δικαιωμάτων του Ανθρώπου (ΕΔΔΑ) (Call for Expressions of Interest in Greek), www.mfa.gr/epikairotita/eidiseis-anakoinoseis/prosklese-ekdeloses-endiapherontos-gia-te-these-tou-ellena-dikaste-sto-europaiko-dikasterio-dikaiomaton-tou-anthropou-edda.html.

[20]   Πρόσκληση Εκδήλωσης Ενδιαφέροντος για τη Θέση του Έλληνα Δικαστή (ΕΔΔΑ) (Call for Expressions of Interest in Greek), www.naftemporiki.gr/story/1529127/edda-prosklisi-ekdilosis-endiaferontos-gia-ti-thesi-tou-ellina-dikasti.

[21]   Πρόσκληση για τη Θέση του Δικαστή της Ελλάδας στο Ευρωπαϊκό Δικαστήριο Δικαιωμάτων του Ανθρώπου (Call for Expressions of Interest in Greek), www.lawspot.gr/nomika-nea/prosklisi-gia-ti-thesi-toy-dikasti-tis-elladas-sto-eyropaiko-dikastirio-dikaiomaton-toy.

[22]   Parliamentary Assembly, 'Election of Judges to the European Court of Human Rights, List and Curricula Vitae of Candidates Submitted by the Government of Greece', Doc. 15187 (25.11.2020), https://pace.coe.int/pdf/f0c14e2cc4d19c3c4aa765b85997eacfbc8d71a5bc3a794c7407b0cbf494f563/doc.%2015187.pdf.

[23]   Πρόσκληση Εκδήλωσης Ενδιαφέροντος (Call for Expression of Interest in Greek), www.dsa.gr/sites/default/files/news/attached/2019-11-19_2.pdf.

[24]   The ECHR (Article 21) does not itself require experience in the field of human rights. However, see Recommendation 1429 (1999), mentioning that candidates should have practical human rights experience, either as practitioners or as NGO activists.

The call also mentioned that in establishing the list of candidates, the criteria set out in relevant Resolutions and Recommendations of PACE, in particular Resolution 1646 (2009), would be taken into account, while care would be taken to promote the balanced representation of men and women on the Court.

2.1.2. The Selecting Authority

The public call for applications indicated the selection authority for the evaluation of candidatures, which was based on the practice followed in 2010. It referred to a three-member Selection Committee, composed of the Secretary-General of the Ministry of Foreign Affairs, the Secretary-General of the Ministry of Justice and the President of the Legal Council of State.[25] This Committee would consider and evaluate the candidatures and make recommendations to the Minister of Foreign Affairs and the Minister of Justice.

However, it soon became apparent that a Committee composed merely of government officials did not provide the necessary safeguards of independence and impartiality. Therefore, considering the best practices of Council of Europe Member States, the composition of the Selection Committee was amended to include the President of the Council of State (Supreme Administrative Court), as the Chair of the Committee, as well as a former Greek judge of the ECtHR. The Minister of Foreign Affairs and the Minister of Justice issued a Joint Ministerial Decision to this effect.[26]

According to the Decision, the Selection Committee consisted of:[27]

1. Aikaterini Sakellaropoulou, President of the Council of State (Symvoulio tis Epikrateias – the Supreme Administrative Court of Greece), as Chair;
2. Ioannis-Konstantinos Chalkias, President of the Legal Council of State (the Government's Agent before the ECtHR);
3. Themistoklis Demiris, Secretary-General of the Ministry of Foreign Affairs;
4. Panos Alexandris, Secretary-General of the Ministry of Justice; and
5. Christos Rozakis, Emeritus Professor of the National and Kapodistrian University of Athens, former Judge and Vice-President of the ECtHR.

---

[25] In accordance with Article 100A of the Greek Constitution, the competence of the Legal Council of State pertains mainly to the judicial support and representation of the Greek state and to the recognition of claims against it or to the settlement of disputes with the state. It is subject to the Minister of Finance (Article 3, Law 4831/2021). This is a different body and should not be confused with the Supreme Administrative Court of Greece, called the Hellenic Council of State.

[26] Joint Ministerial Decision 378/03.12.2019 of the Ministers of Foreign Affairs and Justice (Government Gazette B 4734/20.12.2019).

[27] Joint Ministerial Decision 378/03.12.2019, para. A.

In January 2020, the Ministerial Decision was amended to replace the Chair of the Committee, who was later elected President of the Hellenic Republic.[28] Ioannis Sarmas, President of the Court of Auditors, was appointed as Chair of the Selection Committee.[29]

2.1.3. The Selection Process

According to the procedure provided for in the Ministerial Decision, the Committee shall select from among all the candidates those to be invited for an interview, then proceeds to the evaluation of candidatures and compiles a list of three leading candidates and a list of up to three candidates to be considered.[30] The lists are submitted to the Ministers of Foreign Affairs and Justice, who decide on the final list of three candidates to be submitted to PACE.

According to the document submitted to PACE, 14 applications were submitted to the competent Directorate of the Ministry of Foreign Affairs by the deadline.[31] Two applicants withdrew their candidatures (one before the first meeting of the Committee and the second before the interviews).[32] The final number of applicants was 12.

In its first meeting, on 27 January 2020, the Committee reviewed the applications and verified their compliance with the selection criteria.[33] 12 candidates participated in the interviews before the Committee, which were held on 18 February 2020 at the building of the Court of Auditors.[34]

The questions addressed to the candidates related to their knowledge of the two official languages of the Council of Europe, the role of the Council of Europe in shaping the international and European legal order, their personal and professional qualifications, their comparative advantage as a judge of the ECtHR, and three questions regarding the ECtHR case law.[35]

Each interview lasted approximately 30 minutes and the candidates were called to answer one question in one language, and to read and summarise a text regarding the case law of the Court in the other.[36] The exact time of the interviews was fixed to protect the privacy of the candidates.[37]

---

[28]   Joint Ministerial Decision 1144/10.01.2020 of the Ministers of Foreign Affairs and Justice, para. A (Government Gazette B 64/21.01.2020).
[29]   Ibid.
[30]   Joint Ministerial Decision 378/03.12.2019, para. B.
[31]   Parliamentary Assembly, 'Election of Judges to the European Court of Human Rights, List and Curricula Vitae of Candidates Submitted by the Government of Greece', Doc. 15187 (25.11.2020), https://pace.coe.int/pdf/6adfb02a7293ff6403e42946ceceab3785638c90437533634e433df430 4607a8/res.%201646.pdf.
[32]   Ibid.
[33]   Ibid.
[34]   Ibid.
[35]   Ibid.
[36]   Ibid.
[37]   Ibid.

In its third session, and after a thorough examination of the candidates' curricula vitae, as well as their performance during the interviews, the Committee shortlisted four candidates, submitted their names to the Minister of Foreign Affairs and the Minister of Justice, who drew up a list of three candidates, from among those shortlisted by the Committee, to be forwarded for opinion to the Advisory Panel of Experts on Candidates for Election as Judge to the ECtHR.[38]

2.1.4. Assessment of the Selection Mechanism

National appointment procedures have an important impact on the independence and impartiality of the international adjudicators. States should follow a fair, transparent and consistent procedure to identify suitable candidates.[39] A close connection between the appointing authority and the state may affect the independence and impartiality of the appointed adjudicator. Ultimately, the result of the selection depends on the appointing authority's independence, the familiarity with the requirements for effectively adjudicating the relevant type of disputes, its understanding of the relevant legal framework and its knowledge of how to identify qualified adjudicators. It is in this way that both the identity of the appointing authority and the procedure affect the independence and impartiality of the adjudicator.

A public call for applications contributes to the fairness and transparency of the selection procedure, giving all potential candidates equal opportunity to apply. The call should also encourage diverse and underrepresented groups such as minorities, LGBTQ individuals and persons with disabilities to apply. In this context, increased transparency may also contribute to promoting diversity initiatives within the ECtHR.

In accordance with international principles on the independence of judges, the selection and appointment of judges must be carried out by an independent body that includes substantial judicial representation.[40] The participation of Supreme Court judges, former judges of the ECtHR, university professors or other professionals with expertise in international human rights law in the Selection Committee ensures understanding of the requirements for effectively adjudicating human rights disputes and the relevant legal framework. Supreme Court judges and university professors are also independent in their posts. Moreover, such an independent Selection Committee should consult with

---

[38] Ibid.

[39] See PACE, 'Procedure for the Election of Judges to the European Court of Human Rights', Information Document SG-AS (2023) 01rev02 (25.01.2023), p. 2, https://assembly.coe.int/LifeRay/CDH/Pdf/ProcedureElectionJudges-EN.pdf.

[40] See the 2017 International Association of Judges Universal Charter of the Judge, www.unodc.org/res/ji/import/international_standards/the_universal_charter_of_the_judge/universal_charter_2017_english.pdf, Article 5; Judges Charter in Europe, Principle 4; European Charter on the Statute for Judges, General Principle 1.3.

interested civil society bodies such as human rights organisations and national bar associations.[41]

On the contrary, the participation of government officials in the Selection Committee politicises the selection, especially when such officials form the majority of members. It is no coincidence that the Selection Committee being composed of government officials raised concerns over its independence in the Greek press.[42] A further issue that Greece needs to address following the PACE Resolution 1646 (2009) is to ensure that the Selection Committee is as gender-balanced as possible. It is evident that the latest Selection Committee lacked gender diversity, since initially only one member was a woman and after her replacement there was none.

The interviews and the assessment of the linguistic skills of the candidates are positive aspects of the selection process. However, despite the reference to lists of leading candidates and candidates to be considered, it is not clear whether the Selection Committee provides reasons for its ranking of candidates.[43]

Against this background, Greece should take further steps to increase the transparency of the selection process for national candidates for the ECtHR. It should involve a more independent Selection Committee consisting primarily of judges and experts on international human rights law and should reconsider the extensive involvement of government officials. Universities and civil society bodies, such as human rights organisations and bar associations, should also play a more active role in the selection process. Last but not least, Greece should strengthen the diversity within the Selection Committee.

2.2. COURT OF JUSTICE OF THE EUROPEAN UNION

2.2.1. Formal Legal Basis

Contrary to the lack of formal legal basis for selection of national candidates for positions as ECtHR judges, there is a formal and detailed legal basis for the selection of judges and advocates general of the Court of Justice of the European Union.

Law 4297/2014 applies to the selection of candidates for judges and advocates general of the CJEU and for judges of the General Court when there is a vacancy due to termination or non-renewal, withdrawal or death.[44] Law 4297/2014

---

[41]   J. Limbach et al., 'Judicial Independence: Law and Practice of Appointments to the European Court of Human Rights', Interights, May 2003, p. 33, www.corteidh.or.cr/tablas/32795.pdf.

[42]   'Τα Μαγειρέματα της Κυβέρνησης για τον Νέο Έλληνα Ευρωδικαστή', www.efsyn.gr/politiki/254290_ta-mageiremata-tis-kybernisis-gia-ton-neo-ellina-eyrodikasti.

[43]   On the importance of the independent body's freedom to rank the candidates, see J. Limbach et al., 'Judicial Independence: Law and Practice of Appointments to the European Court of Human Rights', Interights, May 2003, p. 33, www.corteidh.or.cr/tablas/32795.pdf.

[44]   Law 4297/2014, Article 1.

stipulates a public call for applications published in the Government Gazette and interviews to assess the candidates with the involvement of independent experts.

According to the Recital to Law 4297/2014, the establishment of a method to appoint candidates for the positions of judges at the CJEU and the General Court was necessary to enrich the current practice with useful data derived from similar procedures provided for in Greece and from best practices at the European level.

The first objective of the law is to ensure transparency of the process, which is achieved through the publication of a call for applications and the determination of selection criteria. Furthermore, another essential objective is to ensure a specialised evaluation of the candidates, which is achieved through the participation of an advisory body that is, thanks to its composition, in a position to examine the candidates and submit a reasoned opinion to the decision-making body.

The Recital further refers to the panel provided for in Article 255 of the Treaty on the Functioning of the European Union (TFEU), which gives an opinion on the suitability of candidates nominated by the Member States for judges and advocates general of the CJEU and the General Court. According to the Recital, one of the most important elements taken into account by the panel is the existence of a procedure followed at national level for the selection of the candidate to ensure meritocracy and avoid politicised or partisan appointments.

The integration of the above best practices in the Greek legal order aims to contribute to fairness and transparency, ensure an expeditious process and lead to the selection of the most suitable and qualified candidates.

2.2.2. Call for Applications and Selection Criteria

In accordance with Article 3 of Law 4297/2014, the Ministry of Justice publishes a call for applications in the ASEP Issue of the Government Gazette.[45] The call sets a deadline of 30 days for the submission of the necessary supporting documents by interested candidates starting from its publication.[46] The call is also published on the websites of the Ministry of Foreign Affairs and the Ministry of Justice respectively.[47] The call is further disseminated in the specialised legal press, such as eThemis.[48]

---

[45] See for example, the Ministerial Decision of the Minister of Justice 37367/08.09.2020 (Government Gazette ASEP (Supreme Council for Personnel Selection) Issue 35/15.09.2020).

[46] Law 4297/2014, Article 3.

[47] Ibid. See for example, the Call contained in the Ministerial Decision of the Minister of Justice 37367/08.09.2020 published on the website of the Ministry of Foreign Affairs on 24 September 2020: Πρόσκληση Υποβολής Υποψηφιοτήτων για την Πλήρωση της Θέσεως Έλληνα Δικαστή στο Δικαστήριο της Ευρωπαϊκής Ένωσης, www.mfa.gr/eykairies-stadiodromias/epaggelmatiki-stadiodromia-se-diethneis-organismous/prosklese-upoboles-upopsephioteton-gia-ten-plerose-tes-theseos-ellena-dikaste-sto-dikasterio-tes-europaikes-enoses.html.

[48] Πρόσκληση Υποβολής Υποψηφιοτήτων για την Πλήρωση της Θέσεως Έλληνα Δικαστή στο Δικαστήριο της Ευρωπαϊκής Ένωσης, www.ethemis.gr/jobs/2020/09/24/πρόσκληση-

Greece

The applicants must provide full guarantees of independence and must either possess the qualifications required for appointment to high judicial office in Greece or be jurisconsults of recognised competence.[49] Applicants for a position in the General Court must provide full guarantees of independence and have the necessary capacity to perform high judicial duties.[50]

In evaluating the candidates, the Selection Committee shall consider their ethics and integrity, the nature and standard of their studies, their scientific training, their professional experience and career, their experience in European Union law and their familiarity with the subject matter and the judicial system of the European Union, their knowledge of foreign languages, and their ability to work within collective structures in an international environment.[51]

2.2.3. The Selecting Authority

National candidates for the CJEU and General Court are selected by the Council of Ministers at the recommendation of the Minister of Justice, after obtaining the opinion of a Selection Committee.[52]

The Selection Committee is set up by decision of the Minister of Justice and consists of:[53]

1. the Presidents of the Council of State (Supreme Administrative Court) and the Supreme Court;
2. the former judges and advocates general of the CJEU and former judges of the General Court of the European Union, who had been nominated by Greece, including those who are leaving; and
3. one of the Presidents of the law schools of Greece, who is determined each time by a public draw, held at the headquarters of the National and Kapodistrian University of Athens Law School.

The oldest of the Greek judges of the CJEU, if he or she is at that time President of the Court, President of the Council of State or President of the Supreme Court, is appointed as Chair of the Committee.[54] Participation in the Committee is unpaid.[55] The place and time of the meetings of the Committee and any other

---

υποβολής-υποψηφιοτήτων-για-την-πλήρωση-της-θέσεως-έλληνα-δικαστή-στο-δικαστήριο-της-ευρωπαϊκής-ένωσης.html.

[49] Law 4297/2014, Article 4, para. 1.
[50] Ibid., Article 4, para. 2.
[51] Ibid., Article 7.
[52] Ibid., Article 2.
[53] Ibid., Article 5, para. 1.
[54] Ibid.
[55] Ibid.

Intersentia

467

necessary details regarding its operation are determined by a decision of the Minister of Justice.[56]

The Selection Committee shall select those to be invited for an interview after examining the files of the candidates.[57] Upon completion of the interviews, the Committee provides to the Minister of Justice a reasoned opinion on the qualifications of the candidates and submits a list of the three most suitable candidates.[58] The final selection of the candidates for appointment is made by decision of the Council of Ministers, after a suggestion of the Minister of Justice, from among the three considered by the Selection Committee as the most suitable for each position.[59]

2.2.4. The Selection Process

In accordance with the Ministerial Decision on the operation of the Selection Committee of Law 4297/2014, the Committee, after excluding, with brief reasons, the candidates who do not have the required qualifications, invites the qualified candidates for an interview.[60] The invitation is sent by any appropriate means, at least five days before the scheduled date and states the exact date and time of the interview.[61] The interview does not take place publicly.[62] The duration of the oral interview shall not exceed one hour per candidate.[63]

The objective of the interview is to assess the moral character, integrity and legal qualifications of the candidates.[64] In particular, it examines the candidates' understanding of the law and the judicial system of the European Union, their linguistic skills, primarily in English and French, as well as their ability to work in an environment in which different legal traditions are represented.[65] The Committee also assesses whether the candidates provide the necessary guarantees of independence and impartiality.[66] Unfortunately, the Ministerial Decision does not specify any criteria for this assessment, which is thus necessarily subjective. For the assessment of the qualifications of the candidates, the Committee

---

[56] Ibid., Article 5, para. 2.

[57] Ibid., Article 6.

[58] Ibid.

[59] Ibid., Article 8.

[60] Ministerial Decision of the Minister of Justice 96430/26.11.2014 (Government Gazette B 3262/04.12.2014), Article 3, para. 1.

[61] Ibid.

[62] Ibid., para. 2.

[63] Ibid., para. 3.

[64] Ibid.

[65] Ibid.

[66] Ibid.

considers in particular the nature and duration of their professional experience, as well as their publications.[67]

After conducting the interviews, the Committee shall give a reasoned opinion on the suitability of the candidates and select the three most suitable for each position.[68] This opinion is submitted without delay to the Minister of Justice.[69] The Committee may draw up a detailed report on its work and propose any necessary legislative amendments to the Minister of Justice.[70]

The Directorate of Strategic Planning, Organisation and Operation of Justice of the Ministry of Justice keeps record of the Committee's work.[71] The term of office of the Committee expires upon completion of its work.[72]

2.2.5. Assessment of the Selection Mechanism

The selection mechanism follows a predetermined procedure which has a formal legal basis. The publication of an open call for applications in the Government Gazette, on the ministries' websites and in the specialised press, and the conduct of interviews, contribute to the transparency of the selection mechanism. The assessment of the candidates' experience in European Union law and the judicial system of the European Union and the evaluation of their linguistic skills are positive aspects of the selection process. Therefore, the procedure to identify qualified adjudicators for the CJEU and the General Court is transparent, consistent and fair.

As to the Selection Committee, the participation of Supreme Court judges, university professors and former judges of the CJEU ensures an understanding of the requirements for effectively adjudicating EU law issues and the relevant legal framework. Although the ultimate choice lies with the Council of Ministers at the suggestion of the Minister of Justice, there is no participation of government officials in the Committee. Therefore, we can see a more balanced approach that ensures the independence of the Selection Committee compared to the practice followed for the selection of ECtHR judges. Perhaps this is, to a certain extent, explained by and related to the authority of the ECtHR to rule on applications alleging violations of civil and political rights.

However, this mechanism does not resolve all issues. For example, the Council of Ministers recently selected a candidate for the position of Greek judge at the General Court of the European Union due to the appointment of Dimitrios

---

[67]   Ibid., para. 4.
[68]   Ibid., Article 4, para. 1.
[69]   Ibid.
[70]   Ibid., para. 2.
[71]   Ibid., para. 3.
[72]   Ibid., Article 5.

Gratsias to the position of CJEU judge. At the recommendation of the Minister of Justice, the selected candidate was Evgenia Prevedourou, Professor of the Aristotle University of Thessaloniki Law School.[73] However, her candidacy was, according to the Greek press, rejected by the panel provided for in Article 255 TFEU.[74] The reasons for the rejection remain unclear.

Finally, on 21 December 2021, Ioannis Dimitrakopoulos was appointed to the General Court to fill the position left vacant by Dimitrios Gratsias for the remainder of the term until 31 August 2022.[75] Ioannis Dimitrakopoulos is a judge at the Council of State (Supreme Administrative Court) and is considered to have a long experience in European Union law and human rights law.[76]

3. ARBITRATORS

3.1. GREEK ARBITRATION LAW

In Greece,[77] there is a dual regime for domestic and international arbitration. Articles 867–903 of the Code of Civil Procedure (CCP) govern domestic arbitration. The provisions for international arbitration are found in Law 5016/2023 on International Commercial Arbitration (LICA). Greece has also ratified the New York Convention[78] by Legislative Decree 4220/1961 (in force since 14 October 1962) and applies the reciprocity reservation and the commercial reservation.

Initially, Greece adopted the 1985 UNCITRAL Model Law on International Commercial Arbitration in Law 2735/1999. Reforms to Greek arbitration law were recently adopted. The Ministry of Justice established a special legislative committee in early 2020 to amend the law in accordance with the 2006

---

73 'Ανακοίνωση της Κυβερνητικής Εκπροσώπου Αριστοτελίας Πελώνη για τη Συνεδρίαση του Υπουργικού Συμβουλίου της 30ης Ιουνίου 2021', https://government.gov.gr/anakinosi-tis-kivernitikis-ekprosopou-aristotelias-peloni-gia-ti-sinedriasi-tou-ipourgikou-simvouliou-tis-30is-iouniou-2021/.

74 'Απορρίφθηκε η Ελληνική Υποψηφιότητα για τη Θέση Δικαστή στο Γενικό Δικαστήριο της ΕΕ', https://tvxs.gr/news/ellada/aporrifthike-i-elliniki-ypopsifiotita-gia-ti-thesi-dikasti-sto-geniko-dikastirio-tis-ee.

75 Council of the EU, 'EU Court of Justice: Nine Judges of the General Court appointed', Press Release (21.12.2021), www.consilium.europa.eu/en/press/press-releases/2021/12/21/eu-court-of-justice-nine-judges-of-the-general-court-appointed/.

76 'Ο Ιωάννης Δημητρακόπουλος Είναι ο Νέος Έλληνας Δικαστής στο Γενικό Δικαστήριο της ΕΕ', www.lawspot.gr/nomika-nea/o-ioannis-dimitrakopoylos-einai-o-neos-ellinas-dikastis-sto-geniko-dikastirio-tis-ee.

77 The following abbreviations are used for Greek case law: Supreme Court (SC), Court of Appeals (CA), Multi-member First Instance Court (MFIC), Single-member First Instance Court (SFIC). All the decisions can be retrieved by the Greek commercial legal database NOMOS, unless a different source is specified in the footnote.

78 Convention on the Recognition and Enforcement of Foreign Arbitral Awards, 10 June 1958.

Greece

UNCITRAL amendments.[79] The reform aims to modernise the arbitration legislation but does not intend to change the dual regime for domestic and international arbitration.[80] This report focuses on Greek law on the appointment and safeguards for independence and impartiality of international arbitrators. Domestic arbitration is considered, when appropriate, from a comparative perspective.

3.1.1. Method for Appointing International Arbitrators

In accordance with Article 15, para. 2 of LICA, the parties are free to agree on an appointment procedure.

> Where, under an appointment procedure agreed upon by the parties:
> (a) a party fails to act as required under such procedure, or
> (b) the parties, or two arbitrators, are unable to reach an agreement expected of them under such procedure, or
> (c) a third party fails to perform any function entrusted to it under such procedure,
>
> any party may request the court to take any necessary measure, unless the agreement on the appointment procedure provides other means for securing the appointment.[81]

The court or other authority, in appointing an arbitrator, shall have due regard to any qualifications required of the arbitrator by the agreement of the parties and to any considerations as are likely to secure the appointment of an independent and impartial arbitrator and, in the case of a sole or third arbitrator, shall take into account as well the advisability of appointing an arbitrator of a nationality other than those of the parties and consider the recommendations of the parties.[82]

3.1.2. Arbitrator Impartiality and Disclosure Duty

Article 18, para. 1 of LICA provides for the arbitrator's duty to disclose circumstances giving rise to justifiable doubts as to impartiality or independence. Article 18, para. 2 provides that an arbitrator may be challenged only for justifiable doubts as to impartiality, independence or possession of the qualifications agreed to by the parties. A party may challenge an arbitrator appointed by it, or in whose appointment it has participated, only for reasons of which it becomes aware after the appointment has been made.

The parties are free to agree on a procedure for challenging an arbitrator.[83] Failing such agreement, a party who intends to challenge an arbitrator shall,

---

[79] Ministerial Decision 6943/F.339/27.02.2020 (Government Gazette YODD Issue 199/ 18.03.2020).
[80] Recital to Law 5016/2023, s. A, para. 2.
[81] LICA, Article 15, para. 3.
[82] Ibid., Article 15, para. 5.
[83] Ibid., Article 19, para. 1.

Intersentia

471

within 15 days after becoming aware of the constitution of the arbitral tribunal or after becoming aware of any circumstance referred to in Article 18, para. 2, send a written statement of the reasons for the challenge to the arbitral tribunal.[84] Unless the challenged arbitrator withdraws from his or her office or the other party agrees to the challenge, the arbitral tribunal, after having heard the challenged arbitrator, shall decide on the challenge without the participation of the challenged arbitrator within 30 days after having received the challenge.[85] If the challenge of an arbitrator, under any procedure agreed upon by the parties or under the procedure provided by law, is not successful, or if the arbitral tribunal has not decided on the challenge within 30 days, the challenging party may request the competent Single-member First Instance Court to decide on the challenge.[86] The request must be filed within 30 days after having received notice of the decision rejecting the challenge or after the deadline for the decision on the challenge has passed and the decision of the court shall not be subject to appeal.[87] Pending such a request, the arbitral tribunal, including the challenged arbitrator, may continue the arbitral proceedings and issue an award, unless the parties have agreed otherwise.[88]

The UNCITRAL Model Law standard of 'justifiable doubts' is less stringent than the one used in domestic arbitration. In domestic arbitration, arbitrators may be challenged by the parties if they do not possess full legal capacity (entire or partial incapacity to enter into a contract) or for the same grounds for which judges can be challenged.[89] These grounds include any interest they may have in the arbitration, their family relationship to the parties or any relationship that creates dependence on a party, having acted as counsel or witness in the same case or other forms of prior involvement in the case, and suspicion of partiality.[90] If the party has appointed an arbitrator, it can only challenge the arbitrator for reasons of which it became aware after the appointment of the arbitrator.[91] In contrast to international arbitration, the arbitration proceedings in domestic arbitration are suspended until the decision on the challenge is issued.[92]

---

[84]   Ibid., Article 19, para. 2.
[85]   Ibid.
[86]   Ibid., Article 19, para. 3.
[87]   Ibid.
[88]   Ibid.
[89]   CCP, Article 883, para. 2; SC 1509/1982 NOMOS; CA Athens 6839/1986 NOMOS; SFIC Kerkira 360/2003 NOMOS. For cases addressing abusive challenges in domestic arbitration: SFIC Athens 1202/2008 NOMOS; CA Thessaloniki 2525/2000 NOMOS.
[90]   CCP, Article 52, para. 1.
[91]   Ibid., Article 883, para. 2.
[92]   Ibid.

Greece

3.1.3. Remedies and Enforcement

As in the UNCITRAL Model Law, in LICA the arbitrator's lack of impartiality or independence is stated as a ground for challenge of the arbitrator and does not expressly provide a basis for annulment of the award.[93] The remedies available in cases of breach of the principle of independence and impartiality are challenges to arbitrators during the proceedings or challenges to awards tainted by partiality at the annulment or enforcement stage. Such remedies ensure arbitral independence and impartiality at each stage of the arbitration.

Greek courts have addressed the issue of impartiality of members of the Legal Council of State when they act as arbitrators appointed by the Greek state.[94] In accordance with Article 6, para. 3A of Law 3086/2002 (Regulation of the Legal Council of State), which was added by Article 16, para. 2 of Law 4110/2013, in domestic and international arbitrations concerning contracts concluded with the Greek state or with state legal entities of public or private law that function for the public interest, the arbitrator appointed by the Greek state or state legal entity shall be an active member of the Legal Council of State. In exceptional cases and with an increased majority of two-thirds of the members present at the Plenary Session, an honorary member of the Legal Council of State shall be appointed. A non-member of the Legal Council of State shall be appointed as an arbitrator only if this is required by the nature of the dispute and it is expressly provided in the relevant arbitration clause, which in this case must be signed by the Minister of Finance. This provision was clearly incompatible with the principle of independence and impartiality of arbitrators and the relevant provisions safeguarding independence and impartiality in Greek law.[95] In accordance with the new Regulation of the Legal Council of State (Article 7, para. 5, Law 4831/2021), in domestic and international arbitrations concerning disputes of the state, legal entities of public law and independent authorities whose legal support is carried out by the Legal Council of State, the Legal Council of State gives an opinion and a senior judge or member of the Legal Council of State, with the rank of at least Legal Counsel of State, professor or associate professor of a law school or lawyer at the Supreme Court, is appointed, as long as the latter has proven expertise in the specific subject matter.

---

[93] Allegations of lack of independence or impartiality can be based on the following provisions of LICA: (i) Article 43(2)(a)(ab) because a partial tribunal arguably denies a party an opportunity to present its case; (ii) Article 43(2)(a)(ad) because a partial tribunal is arguably not constituted in accordance with the parties' agreement or with this law; or (iii) Article 43(2)(b)(bb) because a partial tribunal arguably violates international public policy as defined in Article 33 of the Civil Code.

[94] SC 1261/2021; SFIC Athens 4778/2013, *Greek Journal Epitheorisi Politikis Dikonomias (EPolD)* 2013, 677 with notes by Panagiotis Giannopoulos.

[95] It was amended by Article 103, Law 4139/2013 to include also judges, university professors and lawyers at the Supreme Court.

Intersentia

473

In exceptional cases of arbitrations governed by a special regime or conducted before international arbitration centres, the rules of which provide for a special method of appointment of arbitrators, Greek or foreign arbitrators who do not have one of the above capacities may be appointed, provided that they have proven experience and significant expertise in the subject matter of the dispute and in the specific arbitral process and their appointment is compatible with the rules of the international centre before which the dispute is submitted.

In an interesting and relevant case, the court found that what raised suspicions of bias was the objective consideration of the principle of impartiality, as the dispute was between the applicant and the Greek state.[96] The defendant arbitrator was a legal representative of the Greek state, owed a fiduciary duty to it and was in fact subject to liability for acts or omissions against the state.[97] Therefore, following the party-initiated challenge, the court removed the arbitrator. The arbitral tribunal, with the then President of the Supreme Court acting as the presiding arbitrator, had rejected the challenge. Although it seems that the constitutionality of the provision was raised before the arbitral tribunal, the court did not address the issue. However, it is worth noting that the First Instance Court of Athens, comprised of an associate judge, disagreed with a tribunal presided over by the President of the Supreme Court, proving the decisional independence of Greek courts.[98]

Recognition and enforcement of foreign arbitral awards is governed by the provisions of the New York Convention, which, in accordance with Article 28, para. 1 of the Greek Constitution, form an integral part of Greek law and prevail over any contrary provision.

The national rules for the recognition and enforcement of foreign awards are found in Article 45 of LICA, which refers directly to the New York Convention. In accordance with the New York Convention, the arbitrator's lack of impartiality can be a ground for denying recognition and enforcement of an arbitral award under: (i) Article V(1)(b) if a party was unable to present his case; (ii) Article V(1)(d) when the composition of the arbitral authority or the arbitral procedure was not in accordance with the agreement of the parties, or, failing such agreement, was not in accordance with the law of the country where the arbitration took place; or (iii) Article V(2)(b) if the competent authority in the country where recognition and enforcement is sought finds that the recognition or enforcement of the award would be contrary to the public policy of that country.

---

[96]   SFIC Athens 4778/2013.

[97]   The court noted that although Article 100A of the Constitution stipulates that the provisions of Article 88, paras 2 and 5 and Article 90, para. 5 referring to judges apply to the personnel of the Legal Council of State, neither Article 88, para. 1, which refers to security of tenure, nor Article 87. para. 1, which states that judges enjoy decisional and personal independence, apply to the personnel of the Legal Council of State.

[98]   Notes by Panagiotis Giannopoulos, *EPolD* 2013, 680–81.

3.2. ARBITRATION INSTITUTIONS AND ASSOCIATIONS IN GREECE AND OTHER SPECIAL RULES

There are several arbitration institutions and associations in Greece. Greek law (Article 902 of the CCP) stipulates the establishment of permanent arbitration institutions at chambers, stock markets and professional associations by presidential decrees. Article 46 of LICA also provides that arbitration institutions may operate with a declaration submitted by the institution to the Ministry of Justice, following an official inspection of fulfilment of specific requirements. However, despite the presence of specialised arbitration centres in the Greek territory, most disputes involving Greek parties are resolved in the traditional well-established arbitration centres abroad.

Special provisions referring to the appointment and impartiality of arbitrators can be found in every arbitral institution's rules. A permanent arbitration institution is established at the Athens Chamber of Commerce and Industry in accordance with the Presidential Decree 31/1979. Arbitrators are appointed from its roster of arbitrators[99] and the rules for domestic arbitration apply regarding challenges of arbitrators.[100] The EODID Athens Mediation and Arbitration Organisation was founded in March 2016, with the exclusive purpose of providing mediation and arbitration services.[101] Article 7 of the EODID Arbitration Rules provides the procedure for the constitution of the tribunal and Article 8, para. 1 provides that throughout the arbitral proceedings, arbitrators must be independent and impartial in respect of the parties and their representatives.

The Piraeus Association for Maritime Arbitration (PAMA), a private non-profit association founded in 2005, aims to promote the resolution of maritime disputes by arbitration in Piraeus.[102] The PAMA Rules impose a duty of independence and impartiality on arbitrators, as well as the duty to disclose an issue that is likely to arise relating to independence or impartiality.[103] The PAMA Rules also stipulate the appointment of an arbitrator of a different nationality from those of the parties if the nature of the dispute so requires.[104] Another option for maritime arbitration in Greece is arbitration under the auspices of the Hellenic Chamber of Shipping in accordance with the provisions of the Royal Decree 447/1969. Under Article 3 of the Decree, arbitrators are appointed from the Chamber's roster of arbitrators.

---

[99]   Presidential Decree 31/1979, Article 6.
[100] Ibid., Article 9.
[101] EODID Athens Mediation and Arbitration Organisation, www.eodid.org/en/about-us/.
[102] PAMA website, www.mararbpiraeus.eu/index.php/base/en.
[103] PAMA Rules, Article 7, para. 1.
[104] Ibid., Article 7, para. 2.

Recently, bar associations in Greece have also developed arbitration rules to promote the use of arbitration in domestic disputes. The Athens Bar Association Arbitration Rules include detailed provisions on the independence and impartiality of arbitrators.[105] The Bar Association of Thessaloniki has also recently adopted new rules for institutional arbitration under its auspices.[106]

Finally, although there is an ethical code for mediators in Greece, there is no code of ethics for arbitrators. The Lawyers' Code of Ethics applies to counsel and arbitrators who are licensed as attorneys in Greece. The IBA Guidelines on Conflicts of Interest in International Arbitration 2014, though not binding, can serve as guidance.

3.3. INTERNATIONAL CENTRE FOR SETTLEMENT OF INVESTMENT DISPUTES

There is no uniform process concerning how a Member State should identify candidates for the International Centre for Settlement of Investment Disputes (ICSID) panels and each state has discretion as to the approach it adopts. In practice, states have followed various formal and informal approaches, such as consultation with national bar associations or other professional societies, public calls for expressions of interest or searches via a government agency or department with knowledge of international investment or dispute resolution.[107]

In Greece, there is no formal legal basis for the designation of ICSID arbitrators. There is also no formal call for applications as happens in other countries.[108] The most recent designations took place in February 2020.

---

[105] See Presidential Decree 91/2020 approving the Regulation of the Athens Bar Association Arbitration, Article 7.

[106] See Presidential Decree 68/2020 approving the Regulation of the Thessaloniki Bar Association Arbitration.

[107] 'Considerations for States in Designating Arbitrators and Conciliators to the ICSID Panels', https://icsid.worldbank.org/sites/default/files/Considerations_for_States_on_Panel_Designations.pdf.

[108] See for example the UK: 'Appointments to ICSID Panels: Call for Expressions of Interest', www.gov.uk/government/publications/appointments-to-icsid-panels-call-for-expressions-of-interest; and France: 'Appel à Candidatures en vue de la Désignation par la France d'Arbitres et de Conciliateurs auprès du Centre International pour le Règlement des Différends Relatifs aux Investissements (CIRDI)' (03.10.2018), https://www.tresor.economie.gouv.fr/Articles/14ccbbb3-0d29-4bce-8be8-0460692e6f14/files/ba3e6314-3f33-4482-bb53-709407120b81.

The panel of arbitrators designated by Greece, with a term from 4 February 2020 until 4 February 2026, includes two lawyers[109] and two university professors.[110]

3.4. ASSESSMENT

Greece has adopted the UNCITRAL Model Law and is a party to the New York Convention. Therefore, Greece applies the international rules on independence and impartiality of arbitrators and enforcement of arbitral awards. LICA provides for the standard of 'justifiable doubts' for removal of an arbitrator, while the available remedies in cases of arbitrator bias are challenges to the award at the annulment or enforcement stage.

The provisions regarding the appointment of arbitrators by the Greek state in domestic and international arbitrations concerning contracts concluded with the Greek state or with state legal entities were clearly incompatible with the principle of independence and impartiality. This has been confirmed by Greek case law and the relevant legislation has been amended.

As to investment arbitration under the auspices of ICSID, there is no established procedure for the designation of arbitrators. A public call for applications and a more transparent procedure would be a welcome improvement.

4. CONCLUSIONS

This report has examined Greek law and practices on the selection of international adjudicators. It first provided an overview of the principle of independence and impartiality in the Greek legal system. It analysed Greek law and practices relating to the selection of candidates for positions as international adjudicators. It examined the selection mechanism of national candidates to positions as international adjudicators at the courts to which Greece appoints judges, i.e. the ECtHR and the CJEU, and assessed these selection mechanisms and practices. Finally, it discussed the appointment and independence and impartiality of international arbitrators, as well as the remedies available in the event that the principle of independence and impartiality is breached.

---

[109] The lawyers are Nikolas Kanellopoulos and Ioannis Vassardanis. According to their CVs, Nikolas Kanellopoulos is a lawyer and accredited mediator, founder and managing senior partner of a law firm and Ioannis Vassardanis is the managing partner of a law firm, arbitrator and counsel in international arbitrations.

[110] The professors are Glykeria Siouti, Professor of Public Law and Environmental Law at the National and Kapodistrian University of Athens, and founder and managing partner of a law firm, and Dimitris Ziouvas, Associate Professor at Panteion University.

Intersentia

As a general observation, Greece adheres to the best practices on the selection of international adjudicators, although there is room for improvement. As to the CJEU and the General Court, Greece has enacted legislation to integrate European practices on the selection of adjudicators. Greece also follows the best practices and PACE guidelines on the selection of adjudicators to serve at the ECtHR. However, Greece should strengthen both the independence and diversity of the Selection Committee evaluating candidates for the ECtHR. In all cases, universities, relevant non-governmental organisations and bar associations should play a more active role in the selection process. In arbitration, Greece follows the UNCITRAL Model Law standards and is a party to the New York Convention. Greece has recently amended its arbitration law to create a modern and arbitration-friendly regime. The impact of this legislative reform remains to be evaluated. Finally, a more transparent procedure to identify candidates for ICSID panels would be a welcome improvement.

THE INDEPENDENCE AND IMPARTIALITY OF ADJUDICATORS IN HUNGARY

István VARGA

1. Introduction 480
2. The Designation of Domestic Adjudicators 480
   2.1. Legal Sources, Fundamental Principles and Institutional
        Framework 481
   2.2. The Authority Appointing Domestic Adjudicators, the Criteria
        and the Method for Appointment 485
        2.2.1. Appointment (and Transfer) of Judges.................. 485
        2.2.2. Senior Court Officials (Executives) and the Role of the
               Presidents of the NOJ and the Kúria 490
        2.2.3. Appointment of Judges of the Constitutional Court 493
   2.3. Duration of Judges' Tenure and Termination of Office........... 494
   2.4. Designation of Judges in a Specific Case...................... 495
   2.5. Arbitrators... 497
   2.6. Parameters to Ensure that Domestic Adjudicators Act
        Independently and Impartially and Consequences of a
        Breach of this Requirment 498
        2.6.1. Non-Appointment and Recusal of Judges for
               Conflicts of Interest................................ 498
        2.6.2. Judicial Integrity 501
        2.6.3. Evaluation of Judges 502
        2.6.4. Training of Judges and Trainee Judges................. 502
        2.6.5. Increase of Salaries 503
        2.6.6. Service Courts, Disciplinary Matters and Liability
               for Damages and Impeachment 503
               2.6.6.1. Competent Court............................ 503
               2.6.6.2. Disciplinary Matters and Impeachment........ 503
               2.6.6.3. Liability for Damages....................... 506
        2.6.7. Immunity and Criminal Liability 506
        2.6.8. Enforcement of a Final Decision Rendered by a Domestic
               Adjudicator who Breached the Requirement to Act
               Independently and Impartially 506

Intersentia 479

Istv├ín Varga

| | 2.7. | Comments and Relevant Cases | 507 |

2.7. Comments and Relevant Cases 507
    2.7.1. EC Rule of Law Report on Hungary..................... 507
    2.7.2. Recent Cases before the Constitutional Court of Hungary
         Concerning the Judiciary............................. 509
    2.7.3. Academic Discourse on the Hungarian Judiciary 511
3. The Appointment of National Candidates to Positions as International
   Adjudicators... 516
   3.1. Lack of Detailed Rules...................................... 516
   3.2. Selection of Hungarian Candidates for Positions in the Court
      of Justice of the European Union............................ 516
   3.3. Enforcement of a Final Decision Rendered by a Foreign or
      International Adjudicator who Breached the Requirement to
      Act Independently and Impartially 517
4. Conclusion... 518

1. INTRODUCTION

The independence and impartiality of adjudicators are not only among the cornerstones of all dispute resolution processes, but also core constitutional values and unequivocal objectives of any justice system. So that these principles can be secured in practice, a well-designed regulatory framework needs to be introduced that includes proper guarantees and safeguards concerning inter alia the selection and designation of adjudicators, their autonomy when rendering justice and effective remedies, should justified concerns arise with respect to the fulfilment of the relevant criteria. The present report aims to provide an objective overview of the regime applicable to the designation and work of adjudicators in Hungary, focusing primarily on the selection and designation of Hungarian judges working in state courts, relying on the black-letter rules re-codified as of 2012. In addition, where relevant, regard will be had to the designation of members of the Constitutional Court and arbitrators as well. Subsequently, the selection of Hungarian members of international adjudicative organs will be reflected upon.

2. THE DESIGNATION OF DOMESTIC ADJUDICATORS

With respect to the designation of domestic adjudicators in Hungary the focus will be on the current state of the relevant black-letter rules, re-codified with effect as of 1 January 2012. First, the relevant legal sources will be listed, concerning both the judiciary and institutional arbitration in Hungary. This will be followed by the description of the criteria for the selection of domestic adjudicators and the relevant application and procedures. Subsequently, parameters will be identified that can contribute to ensuring the independence and impartiality of domestic adjudicators, followed by the summaries of comments on the system, relevant cases and views expressed in academia.

2.1. LEGAL SOURCES, FUNDAMENTAL PRINCIPLES AND INSTITUTIONAL FRAMEWORK

The present section is aimed at providing an overview of the legal framework in Hungary and the basics of the Hungarian judicial system[1] to provide the background against which the rules of the selection of domestic adjudicators will be summarised.

The regulation of the Hungarian judiciary, including the black-letter rules on the selection and appointment of national adjudicators, is multi-layered: relevant provisions are included in the Hungarian constitution, several acts of Parliament on the judiciary and decrees, as well as other instruments, instructions and codes of conduct.

The new Fundamental Law of Hungary (i.e. the constitution), in force as of 1 January 2012, provides in its Article XXVIII(1) that '[e]veryone shall have the right to have any indictment brought against him or her, or his or her rights and obligations in any court action, adjudicated within a reasonable time in a fair and public trial by an independent and impartial court established by an Act.'[2] Among others, this article sets forth the fundamental right to have matters adjudicated by an independent and impartial court of law. Article 26(1) of the Fundamental Law[3] further specifies that '[j]udges shall be independent and only subordinated to Acts; they shall not be instructed in relation to their judicial activities. Judges may only be removed from office for the reasons and in a procedure specified in a cardinal Act. Judges may not be members of political parties or engage in political activities.'[4]

---

[1] For a more in-depth overview of the Hungarian judicial system cf. István Varga, 'Civil Litigation and Arbitration' in Attila Harmathy (ed.), *Introduction to Hungarian Law*, 2nd ed., Kluwer 2019, Chapter 16, pp. 327–67.

[2] The new Fundamental Law of Hungary is in force as of 1 January 2012 and has been amended nine times. This provision has been unchanged since its promulgation. English translation available at https://njt.hu/jogszabaly/en/2011-4301-02-00.

[3] Note: the Fundamental Law consists of several structural units in which different numbering styles are used (letters, Roman numerals and Arabic numerals).

[4] This provision has been unchanged since its promulgation. English translation available at https://njt.hu/jogszabaly/en/2011-4301-02-00. Note: 'cardinal act' refers to legislation adopted by the National Assembly by a two-thirds majority.

The cornerstones of the appointment of judges and their duties are included in the Fundamental Law itself, which are detailed in further acts.

The above principles are mirrored in Act CLXI of 2011 on the Organization and Administration of Courts (Courts Administration Act), which also provides that judges shall be independent, shall render their decisions in view of the law and pursuant to their conviction, and cannot be influenced or given any instructions in connection with the rendering of their judicial duties.[5] Act CLXII of 2011 on the Legal Status and Remuneration of Judges (Judges Act)[6] also requires judges to be independent when administering justice.[7]

The requirements for the selection of judges, the selection process, tenure, remuneration, etc. are regulated separately in the Judges Act. Also of relevance is the Courts Administration Act, which regulates inter alia the structure of the court system as well as that of courts, the principles of the functioning of courts, the tasks of courts, etc., but also includes rules inter alia on senior court officials (executives).

There are four instances of courts, namely: (i) the 'Kúria', which is the supreme court of Hungary; (ii) five regional courts of appeal; (iii) 20 general courts (having competence for smaller regions); and (iv) 113 district (and urban district) courts.[8]

The long-term tasks of courts are set forth by the National Office for the Judiciary (NOJ), a central administrative organ led by its President and Vice Presidents.[9] Amongst others, the NOJ also issues rules that are binding upon courts, makes recommendations and decisions, and represents courts. The NOJ's President plays an important role in particular in the selection and designation of judges.

There is also an independent supervisory organ over the central administration of the courts called the National Judicial Council (NJC), which is composed of the President of the Kúria (ex officio) and 14 further judges and

---

5   §2(1) Courts Administration Act. For an English summary, see also Annual Report of the President of the National Office for the Judiciary 2018, available at https://birosag.hu/sites/default/files/2020-03/annualreport2018_online.pdf (English version), p. 25.

6   An English translation of the Judges Act (dated 15 February 2012) provided by the Council of Europe is available at https://www.venice.coe.int/webforms/documents/default.aspx?pdffile=CDL-REF(2021)058-e.

7   §1(1) Judges Act.

8   §16(1) Courts Administration Act. See also the English summary in 2021 Rule of Law Report, Country Chapter on the rule of law situation in Hungary, European Commission, Brussels, 20.07.2021, SWD(2021) 417 final (English version), p. 1.

9   Article 25(5)–(6) of the Fundamental Law; §§76 et seq. Courts Administration Act. See also the summary in 2021 Rule of Law Report, Country Chapter on the rule of law situation in Hungary, European Commission, Brussels, 20.07.2021, SWD(2021) 417 final (English version), p. 2.

Hungary

14 substitute members (elected by their peers for a single six-year period).[10] The Constitutional Court of Hungary is not part of the ordinary court system.[11]

Reference needs to be made to Act CXXX of 2016 on the (new) Code of Civil Procedure of Hungary (CCP),[12] Act I of 2017 on the Code of Administrative Court Procedure (CACP)[13] and Act XC of 2017 on the Code of Criminal Procedure (CCrP),[14] which contain rules on the recusal of judges and foresee recourse against court decisions for judges' violations (also independence and impartiality-related) of their duties. Act C of 2012 on the Criminal Code of Hungary[15] contains provisions on the criminal liability of judges for violations of their official duties. Reference will also be made to Act CLI of 2011 on the Constitutional Court (ACC) with respect to members of the Constitutional Court, who can, upon request, be appointed judges too as a result of a recent modification of the law.

On 10 November 2014, a Code of Judicial Conduct was adopted in the Meeting of the NJC,[16] the aim of which is to 'strengthen the public confidence in the judicial system by laying down ethical norms for judges to follow'.[17] The Code defines the expected code of conduct of judges in and out of office, including detailed provisions on independence, impartiality, dignity, diligence, propriety, respect and cooperation, and also includes guidelines for senior court officials (judges in court executive positions). The NJC has since then revised the Code of Conduct and adopted the Draft of the New Code of Judicial Conduct during its session held on 2 December 2020, inviting judges to provide opinions on it.[18]

---

[10] Article 25(5)–(6) of the Fundamental Law; §§88 et seq. Courts Administration Act. The NJC is named in the Fundamental Law as a result of an amendment with effect as of 1 October 2013. See also the summary in 2021 Rule of Law Report, Country Chapter on the rule of law situation in Hungary, European Commission, Brussels, 20.07.2021, SWD(2021) 417 final (English version), pp. 2–3.

[11] See also the summary in 2021 Rule of Law Report, Country Chapter on the rule of law situation in Hungary, European Commission, Brussels, 20.07.2021, SWD(2021) 417 final (English version), p. 2.

[12] In force as of 1 January 2018. An English translation of the CCP is available at https://njt.hu/jogszabaly/en/2016-130-00-00.

[13] In force as of 1 January 2018. An English translation of the CACP is available at https://njt.hu/jogszabaly/en/2017-1-00-00.

[14] In force as of 1 July 2018. An English translation of the CCrP is available at https://njt.hu/jogszabaly/en/2017-90-00-00.

[15] In force as of 1 July 2013. An English translation of the Hungarian Criminal Code is available at https://njt.hu/jogszabaly/en/2012-100-00-00.

[16] The Code of Judicial Conduct came into effect on 1 January 2015. It is available in English at https://birosag.hu/en/code-judicial-conduct. In Hungarian, the Code of Conduct is available at https://birosag.hu/sites/default/files/birak_etikai_kodexe_.pdf.

[17] Code of Judicial Conduct, Preamble. English translation at https://birosag.hu/en/code-judicial-conduct.

[18] See Decision 137/2020 (XII. 2.) OBT at p. 42 of the Protocol available at https://orszagosbiroitanacs.hu/2020-12-02/; see also https://orszagosbiroitanacs.hu/az-etikai-kodex-

Intersentia

483

The debate on the New Code of Judicial Conduct by the NJC was scheduled for the first quarter of 2022.[19]

Whereas the Judges Act and the Courts Administration Act are in force as of 1 January 2012, the arbitration law of Hungary has been updated later, with the entry into force of the new Hungarian arbitration act, i.e. Act LX of 2017 on Arbitration (HAA).[20] In addition to including the 2006 UNCITRAL Model Law on International Commercial Arbitration with some amendments, the latter also regulates the institutional framework of arbitration in Hungary, containing rules inter alia on who can be an arbitrator, as well as the prerequisites for being featured on the list of recommended arbitrators of the sole commercial arbitration institution of Hungary, the Arbitration Court Attached to the Hungarian Chamber of Commerce and Industry (Commercial Arbitration Court).

As noted at the outset, the present report aims to provide an objective description of the Hungarian judiciary and relevant appointment regimes, focusing on the black-letter rules. To provide an efficient overview and reflect views on recent developments from abroad, regard will be had both to the Annual Reports of the President of the NOJ (and other materials available in English on the website of the Hungarian judiciary)[21] as well as the most recently published Rule of Law Report of the European Commission on Hungary,[22] together with the input from Hungary,[23] which also contain general information on the Hungarian judiciary in English.[24]

---

[19] felulvizsgalata/ and https://www.mabie.hu/index.php/1559-felhivas-a-birak-uj-etikai-kodexe-tervezetenek-velemenyezesere.

See the session plan of the NJC available at https://orszagosbiroitanacs.hu/ulesek/.

[20] The HAA is applicable to arbitrations that commence(d) on or after 1 January 2018. The transitory provisions of the HAA came into force already on 16 June 2017. An English translation of the HAA is available at https://njt.hu/jogszabaly/en/2017-60-00-00.

[21] Concise summaries on the Hungarian judiciary are available on the website of the Hungarian judiciary, which also provides content in the English language at https://birosag.hu/en, which is also relied on in the present report. Another useful source of information relied on is the Annual Report of the President of the National Office for the Judiciary (NOJ), which also provides general summaries on the Hungarian judiciary and court system in English. The latest version also available in English (as of 16 March 2022) is the one for the year 2018 (at https://birosag.hu/en/national-office-judiciary/annual-reports). The latest version available in Hungarian is the one for the year 2021, available at https://birosag.hu/en/birosagokrol/birosagi-szervezet/obh/obh-elnokenek-beszamoloi.

[22] Annual Report of the President of the National Office for the Judiciary 2018, available at https://birosag.hu/sites/default/files/2020-03/annualreport2018_online.pdf (English version).

[23] 'European Rule of Law Mechanism: input from Hungary 2021', available at https://commission.europa.eu/system/files/2021-07/hu-input.pdf. An Addendum is available at https://commission.europa.eu/system/files/2021-07/hu-additional_input.pdf.

[24] The English terminology used in the report, including English translations of the relevant legal provisions, are in part taken from the materials on the Hungarian judiciary available in the English language, including the reports mentioned in the previous footnotes, the English translations of the relevant acts and materials available on the English website of the Hungarian judiciary.

2.2. THE AUTHORITY APPOINTING DOMESTIC ADJUDICATORS, THE CRITERIA AND THE METHOD FOR APPOINTMENT

2.2.1. *Appointment (and Transfer) of Judges*

As of 2018, the headcount of the judiciary was about 12,000, about one-quarter of whom were judges.[25]

Appointment as a judge is subject to the fulfilment of cumulative, positive and negative prerequisites laid down in §4 of the Judges Act. Accordingly, in Hungary only such a person of at least 30 years of age can be appointed as a judge who:

1. is a Hungarian citizen;
2. is not under tutelage affecting their legal capacity;
3. has a law degree;
4. has passed the exam to be admitted into the legal profession (unified 'bar' exam for legal professionals);
5. undertakes to make an asset declaration;
6. has, at least for one year, worked as a legal professional (e.g. as a court secretary, (junior) prosecutor, attorney-at-law, notary public, public servant in the government or at a central administrative organ, judge of the Constitutional Court or military judge) or was a judge or exercised duties related to the administration of justice at an organ of the European Union; and
7. was considered suitable for office in view of the results of an aptitude test.

The negative criteria include a criminal conviction, ongoing criminal proceedings, disciplinary sanctions for violation of office (not necessarily as a judge, but also in other positions, e.g. as a public servant, notary public, attorney-at-law, etc.) and having reached the age limit for receiving an old-age pension.

Judges are appointed by the President of the Republic (i.e. the head of state of Hungary).[26] The decision on who can become a judge is, however, not made by the President of the Republic, but is the result of an application procedure initiated by public calls for appointment.[27]

---

[25] Annual Report of the President of the National Office for the Judiciary 2018, available at https://birosag.hu/sites/default/files/2020-03/annualreport2018_online.pdf (English version), p. 61.

[26] §3(2) Judges Act.

[27] Exceptions pursuant to §8 of the Judges Act include a judge's return from a secondment to the NOJ or the Ministry, a change in a court's area of competence that prevents a judge's continued employment at the given court, the reinstatement of a judge following a labour dispute or a successful request by a judge to be transferred to another court. For a description of the

Applications are called for by the President of the NOJ,[28] apart from a few exceptions. Applicants have to file their applications with the president of the court where they are applying for the position of a judge. Subsequently, applicants will be interviewed by the judicial council of the respective court (consisting of judges elected by their peers) that has competence for the ranking of applicants. The judicial council ranks applicants based on scores given in view of – in part objective, in part subjective – criteria set forth in an exhaustive manner in the Judges Act. The criteria include, for example, the evaluation of earlier professional experience, duration of professional experience after the bar exam, result in the required aptitude test, result in the bar exam, academic title, relevant additional legal degree (LLM), studies abroad after graduation from law school, competence in languages, publications, participation in legal trainings, and other relevant additional professional activity. The subjective criteria to be considered include the opinion of the relevant division of the general court, court of appeal or Kúria[29] or the opinion of the president of the relevant district court,[30] as well as the results of the hearing of the applicant by the judicial council of the relevant court.[31] In addition to the Judges Act, further rules applicable to the ranking (including the scores to be given to the aforementioned criteria) are set forth in Decree 7/2011 (III. 4.) by the Minister of Public Administration and Justice on the detailed rules for assessing applications for judges and on the scores awarded during the ranking of applicants ('Scoring Decree', revised as of 1 November 2017).[32] The NOJ made available a number of professional aids (e.g. guides, forms) to promote applicants' preparation.[33]

---

application procedure in English, see also the Annual Report of the President of the National Office for the Judiciary 2018, available at https://birosag.hu/sites/default/files/2020-03/annualreport2018_online.pdf (English version), pp. 63 ff. The evaluation process is described at pp. 68 ff. See also the summary in 2021 Rule of Law Report, Country Chapter on the rule of law situation in Hungary, European Commission, Brussels, 20.07.2021, SWD(2021) 417 final (English version), p. 2.

[28] §9(1) Judges Act.

[29] In the case of applications for positions at the general regional courts, courts of appeal and the Kúria.

[30] In the case of applications for positions at a district court.

[31] §14 Judges Act.

[32] The number of points that can be given in view of each relevant criterion when assessing applications for judge positions are set forth in the table included in Annex no. 1 to the Scoring Decree (English translation of the name of the Decree from the information sheet entitled Information on the practice of the President of the National Office for the Judiciary in the course of the assessment of applications for judicial appointments in 2018, dated 20 February 2019, available at https://birosag.hu/sites/default/files/2019-04/mia_tajekoztato_biroi_palyazatok_2018.pdf). See also Annual Report of the President of the National Office for the Judiciary 2018, available at https://birosag.hu/sites/default/files/2020-03/annualreport2018_online.pdf (English version), pp. 69 ff.

[33] Annual Report of the President of the National Office for the Judiciary 2018, available at https://birosag.hu/sites/default/files/2020-03/annualreport2018_online.pdf (English version), p. 69.

Hungary

The judicial council forwards its final ranking to the president of the relevant court, who will then submit it to the President of the NOJ along with his or her recommendation (the president of the court may agree with the ranking or, giving written reasons, propose that the position be given to the applicant ranked second or third).[34]

If the President of the NOJ (or, in the case of applications for positions at the Kúria, the President of the Kúria)[35] agrees that the applicant ranked first shall fill the post, he or she shall decide on the application by submitting it to the President of the Republic, recommending the appointment of the applicant as judge; if the applicant is already a judge, the President of the NOJ shall decide on the application by deciding on transferring the judge. The NOJ's (or the Kúria's) President can only deviate from the ranking established by the judicial council with the prior consent of the NJC:[36] he or she may deviate from the ranking established by the judicial council by proposing the appointment or transfer of the candidate ranked second or third. In this case, the President of the NOJ (or Kúria) shall send the applications of the first three candidates in the ranking, as well as his or her written reasons for the deviation from the ranking, to the NJC. If the NJC does not agree with the proposal of the President of the NOJ (or Kúria), the President of the NOJ has three options: he or she may (i) recommend the appointment of the candidate ranked first to the President of the Republic or transfer the candidate (if the candidate is already a judge), (ii) make a new proposal to the NJC, or (iii) declare the application procedure unsuccessful.[37] The principles to be followed by the President of the NOJ and of the Kúria are laid down in Decision 3/2013 (I. 21.) of the National Judicial Council on the principles to be taken into account (to be examined and applied) by the President of the NOJ and the President of the Kúria upon a departure from the ranking of applications during the assessment of applications for judicial positions.

The application procedure is unsuccessful if no application is received or all applications have been rejected already by the president of the relevant court[38]

---

34 §16 Judges Act.
35 In the case of positions at the Kúria, the foregoing applies mutatis mutandis to the President of the Kúria, who, if the application procedure is successful, shall approach the President of the NOJ to make the respective recommendation or transfer the judge concerned. §19 Judges Act.
36 See also the summary in 2021 Rule of Law Report, Country Chapter on the rule of law situation in Hungary, European Commission, Brussels, 20.07.2021, SWD(2021) 417 final (English version), p. 2.
37 §§17–18 Judges Act.
38 §20(1)(a) in conjunction with §13 Judges Act (if the application is belated or if the applicant has not remedied the defects of the application within the time limit provided by the president of the court).

Intersentia

487

and if the President of the NOJ or the Kúria does not intend to fill the post with any of the applicants because:

- the appointment would give rise to a conflict of interest;[39]
- the participants involved in the assessment process breached procedural requirements during the assessment procedure;
- the judicial council failed to comply with its obligation to give reasons;
- changes in work organisation, workload or budget occurring after publishing the call for applications make it administratively unreasonable to fill the post; or
- a circumstance arose after publishing the call for applications as a result of which the vacancy is to be filled without a call for applications[40] as laid down by law.[41]

The President of the NOJ notifies the president of the relevant court of the result of the application procedure, who in turn notifies the applicants in writing. Applicants who were not excluded due to their application being belated or incomplete can challenge the result of the application procedure within 15 days of the publication of the decision on the appointment or transfer of the winning applicant. The challenge shall be filed in writing with the president of the court concerned, who will forward it to the President of the NOJ.[42] The President of the NOJ (or the Kúria) shall send the challenge together with its statement to the first-instance service court. If the latter establishes that the winning applicant cannot be appointed as judge or does not comply with the prerequisites foreseen in the call for applications, the court serves its decision on the applicant who filed the challenge and – so that the relevant measures can be taken – with the person who rendered the decision on the application as well as the President of the Republic. Otherwise the first-instance service court dismisses the challenge as unfounded. No further recourse is possible.[43]

Judges also work in administrative positions at the NOJ. Pursuant to the Judges Act, judges working at the NOJ retain their office as judge but cannot carry out adjudicative tasks; when their position at the NOJ comes to an end,

---

[39] See §41 Judges Act (no one can work as a judge at the court or court organ led by his or her relative).

[40] §8 of the Judges Act lists a number of scenarios in which no call for applications needs to be issued.

[41] These scenarios are listed in §20 of the Judges Act. The above list in the English language has been adapted from the information sheet entitled Information on the practice of the President of the National Office for the Judiciary in the course of the assessment of applications for judicial appointments in 2018, dated 20 February 2019, available at https://birosag.hu/sites/default/files/2019-04/mia_tajekoztato_biroi_palyazatok_2018.pdf.

[42] Except in the case of applications for positions at the Kúria.

[43] §21 Judges Act.

Hungary

they need to be delegated to a judge position; such a judge can – in justified cases without an application process – be delegated to be the chair of a panel or transferred to a judge position at least at the level of his or her previous judge position, possibly at the judge's place of residence.[44]

There is also an exceptional way of becoming a judge, available to members of the Constitutional Court of Hungary. Pursuant to a relatively new provision introduced into the Judges Act with effect as of 20 December 2019 and a related provision introduced into the ACC at the same time, members of the Constitutional Court may – through the President of the Constitutional Court – request their appointment as a judge, in which case they shall be appointed by the President of the Republic as a judge for an indefinite period of time without an application procedure.[45] The President of the Constitutional Court shall – simultaneously with forwarding the request to the President of the Republic – notify the NOJ's President of the request. This also means that the NOJ's President has no role in the appointment. In this case the office of the judge (as a judge) is suspended until the termination of his or her office as a member of the Constitutional Court. Subsequently, the President of the Kúria shall transfer said judge to the Kúria.[46]

By default, judges can be assigned to another court to secure the proportionate allocation of cases among courts or to further the professional development of the judge, but only with their consent.[47] However, every three years, and within such a three-year period for a maximum of one year, judges can temporarily be assigned to another court even without their consent.[48]

§103(3)(f) of the Courts Administration Act requires the NJC to publish a report every year on the practice of the Presidents of the NOJ and the Kúria with respect to assessment of applications for judge positions as well as executive positions in the judiciary.[49]

---

[44] §§57–58 of the Judges Act.

[45] §3(4a) of the Judges Act (in force as of 20 December 2019); §69(10) ACC (in force as of 20 December 2019).

[46] §88(3) of the Judges Act (in force as of 20 December 2019).

[47] §31(2) and (4) Judges Act.

[48] §31(3) Judges Act.

[49] Information on the related practice of the President of the NOJ is made available on the website of the Hungarian judiciary available in English at https://birosag.hu/en/appointment-judges. The annual reports of the President of the NOJ are available both in Hungarian (for the year 2021 at https://birosag.hu/en/birosagokrol/birosagi-szervezet/obh/obh-elnokenek-beszamoloi) and in English (the last report available in English is the one for the year 2018, available at https://birosag.hu/sites/default/files/2020-03/annualreport2018_online.pdf). Information sheets are also available. The latest English information sheet entitled 'Information on the practice of the President of the National Office for the Judiciary in the course of the assessment of applications for judicial appointments in 2018', dated 20 February 2019, is available at https://birosag.hu/sites/default/files/2019-04/mia_tajekoztato_biroi_palyazatok_2018.pdf.

Intersentia

489

Istvàn Varga

2.2.2. Senior Court Officials (Executives) and the Role of the Presidents of the NOJ and the Kúria

The Courts Administration Act contains special rules on applications for executive positions,[50] for which appointments are granted for six-year terms[51] to judges appointed for an indefinite term.[52]

The executives of the courts of appeal and the general courts[53] are appointed by the NOJ's President[54] or the president of the relevant court of appeal[55] or general court[56] (depending on the court and the position),[57] whereas the executives of the Kúria[58] are appointed by the President of the Kúria.[59]

The president who has the right of appointment hears the candidates and evaluates their applications in view of the application documents, the applicants' interview and the relevant consultative body's[60] proposal expressed by secret ballot. (The consultative body ranks applicants, prioritising multiple applicants by their votes.)[61] The latter does not bind the appointing president, but he or she must provide written reasoning if he or she makes a different decision.[62] Court presidents who have the right of appointment either appoint the applicant

---

[50]   §§127–134 Courts Administration Act.
[51]   Except for the chairpersons of court chambers, who are appointed for an indefinite term. Presidents and vice presidents of courts can be appointed only two times. However, with the prior agreement of the NJC, they can be appointed for the same position again. §127 Courts Administration Act.
[52]   §127(1) Courts Administration Act.
[53]   President, vice president and heads of divisions.
[54]   §128(2) Courts Administration Act.
[55]   Vice heads of divisions and chairpersons of the chambers of the courts of appeal. §128(4) Courts Administration Act.
[56]   Vice heads of divisions and the chairpersons of the chambers of the general courts and the president, vice president, group head and vice group head of the district courts. §128(5) Courts Administration Act.
[57]   Where the appointment is not made by the president of the given court, the person entitled to make the appointment shall procure the recommendation of the president of the given court. §123 Courts Administration Act. The calls for application shall be issued by the person entitled to make the appointment (except in the case of Vice Presidents of the Kúria, in the case of whom the call shall be issued by the President of the Kúria). §130(2) Courts Administration Act.
[58]   Heads of divisions, vice heads of divisions, chairpersons of chamber as well as the secretary general and vice secretary general.
[59]   §128(3) Courts Administration Act.
[60]   Plenary session, judges' general meeting, division, regional division, all judges or a group. For example, in the case of the Vice President and head of divisions of the Kúria, this is the full plenary session of the Kúria; in the case of the president, vice president and heads of division of the court of appeal and the general court this is the full plenary session of the relevant level, etc. §131(a)–(h) Courts Administration Act.
[61]   §132(1)–(3) Courts Administration Act.
[62]   §132(4) Courts Administration Act. In the case of court presidents appointed by the NOJ's President, the rules of giving an opinion are laid down in NOJ Instruction 6/2015 (30 November).

490

Intersentia

Hungary

or declare the application invalid if they consider the quality of the application inappropriate. Unsuccessful calls for application need to be repeated. If the second call is also unsuccessful, the president may assign a person to hold the relevant position for up to one year.[63]

The Presidents of the NOJ and the Kúria are subject to special additional rules: if they make a decision that deviates from the recommendation of the relevant consultative body, they must provide – simultaneously with the appointment – written reasoning to the NJC and also present their reasons at the next session of the NJC. This does not affect the appointment of the candidate.[64] However, if the President of the NOJ or of the Kúria intends to appoint a candidate who has not won the support of the majority of the consultative body, he or she shall procure the preliminary opinion of the NJC on the candidate, who can be appointed only with the agreement of the NJC.[65]

The Presidents of the Kúria and of the NOJ are nominated by the President of the Republic and elected by the National Assembly by a two-thirds majority, for a nine-year term, from among the judges who have been appointed for an indefinite period of time and who have served at least five years as a judge.[66] Having heard the nominee, the NJC can provide an opinion on him or her,[67] which is, however, not binding. As of 1 January 2020, an additional rule has been introduced into the law with respect to the President of the Kúria. In accordance with this, when calculating the five years of service, experience as a judge or senior legal secretary at an international court, as a member of the Constitutional Court or as senior legal secretary in the Office of the Constitutional Court also has to be taken into account.[68]

The President of the Kúria decides not only on the appointment of the judges of the Kúria[69] (as well as their assignment to chambers),[70] but also on the

---

[63] §133(1)–(2) Courts Administration Act. See also the summary in Annual Report of the President of the National Office for the Judiciary 2018, available at https://birosag.hu/sites/default/files/2020-03/annualreport2018_online.pdf (English version), pp. 59–60.

[64] §132(5) Courts Administration Act.

[65] §132(6) Courts Administration Act.

[66] With respect to the President of the Kúria, see Article 26(3) of the Fundamental Law and §114(1) 1st sentence Courts Administration Act; with respect to the President of the NOJ, see Article 25(6) of the Fundamental Law; §§66–67 Courts Administration Act. See also 2021 Rule of Law Report, Country Chapter on the rule of law situation in Hungary, European Commission, Brussels, 20.07.2021, SWD(2021) 417 final (English version), p. 2, n. 5. The President of the NOJ retains his or her judicial status but may not administer justice (§57(1) Judges Act (generally applicable to all judges posted at the NOJ)).

[67] §103(3)(a) and Courts Administration Act.

[68] §114(1) 2nd sentence Courts Administration Act (in force as of 1 January 2020). Also recalled in 2021 Rule of Law Report, Country Chapter on the rule of law situation in Hungary, European Commission, Brussels, 20.07.2021, SWD(2021) 417 final (English version), p. 5, n. 33.

[69] §§17 and 19 Judges Act.

[70] There can be more than one presiding judge in a chamber. If that is that case, the President of the Kúria designates one of them to perform administrative tasks. 2021 Rule of Law Report,

Intersentia

491

appointment of executives: the presiding judges (i.e. division heads,[71] presiding judges of chambers, and the Secretary General and the Vice Secretary General of the Kúria).[72] Vice Presidents of the Kúria are appointed by the President of the Republic upon the recommendations made by the President of the Kúria.[73]

As of 1 January 2021, the President of the Kúria has received additional powers in organising the functioning of the Kúria, resulting in increased administrative powers.[74] These enable the President of the Kúria to set up five-member judicial panels consisting of a presiding judge and four further judges for certain groups of cases, prior to which the President of the Kúria shall seek the (non-binding) opinion of the relevant division.[75] The introduction of such five-member panels also has to be included in the case allocation scheme of the Kúria,[76] on which the judicial council of the Kúria provides a (non-binding) opinion.[77]

A call for applications for executive positions is unsuccessful if the person entitled to appoint the senior court official does not accept any of the applications. If a call for applications is unsuccessful, a new call for applications shall be issued. If the new call is also unsuccessful, the person entitled to make the appointment may fill the senior court official post by giving a mandate to someone for a maximum of one year.[78]

The records of the interviews of applicants to be appointed by the NOJ's President are public and available on the website of the judiciary together with the application documents.[79]

Country Chapter on the rule of law situation in Hungary, European Commission, Brussels, 20.07.2021, SWD(2021) 417 final (English version), pp. 3–4, n. 17.

[71] Such decisions are made in view of the (non-binding) opinion of the plenary session of the Kúria (in the case of the Vice President or department head of the Kúria) or the relevant department of the respective court (§§131(a) and (c) and 132(4) Courts Administration Act).

[72] §128(3) Courts Administration Act.

[73] §128(1) Courts Administration Act.

[74] 2021 Rule of Law Report, Country Chapter on the rule of law situation in Hungary, European Commission, Brussels, 20.07.2021, SWD(2021) 417 final (English version), pp. 3–6.

[75] The new 1st sentence of §10(2) Courts Administration Act introduced as of 1 January 2021. (The subsequent amendment of the same paragraph with effect as of 1 January 2022 does not affect this provision.)

[76] §10(2) 2nd sentence Courts Administration Act (in effect as of 1 January 2021).

[77] §151(1)(d) Courts Administration Act. 2021 Rule of Law Report, Country Chapter on the rule of law situation in Hungary, European Commission, Brussels, 20.07.2021, SWD(2021) 417 final (English version), p. 3, n. 13.

[78] §133(1)–(2) Courts Administration Act. For all other aspects, §134 of the Courts Administration Act renders the provisions of the Judges Act on applications for judge positions mutatis mutandis applicable to applications for court executive positions too.

[79] See also the summary in Annual Report of the President of the National Office for the Judiciary 2018, available at https://birosag.hu/sites/default/files/2020-03/annualreport2018_online.pdf (English version), pp. 59–60.

Hungary

2.2.3. Appointment of Judges of the Constitutional Court

Reference is made to the appointment of members of the Constitutional Court in view of the aforementioned recent amendment to the law, as a result of which members of the Constitutional Court can request that they be appointed as judges and be transferred to the Kúria after the expiry of their term at the Constitutional Court. Members of the Constitutional Court can become judges (at the Kúria) without an application procedure without having worked as a judge in an ordinary court previously.

The Fundamental Law of Hungary provides that the 15 members of the Constitutional Court be elected by the National Assembly, by a two-thirds majority, for 12-year terms. The President of the Constitutional Court is also elected by the National Assembly, also by a two-thirds majority, from among the members of the Constitutional Court. It is also expressly stated in the Fundamental Law that members of the Constitutional Court cannot be members of any political party and cannot engage in any political activity.[80] Further details are foreseen in the ACC, which provides that members of the Constitutional Court shall be independent and shall be subject only to the Fundamental Law and the acts of Parliament.[81] The ACC also lists the prerequisites for being elected as a member of the Constitutional Court. These include the lack of a criminal record, Hungarian citizenship, a law degree, being aged between 45 and 70, exceptional theoretical knowledge (professor of law or doctor of the Hungarian Academy of Sciences), or at least 20 years of professional experience in law.[82] Members of the Constitutional Court cannot be re-elected.[83] No one can be a member of the Constitutional Court who was a member of the government, a senior official of any party or held a political or senior professional office within four years preceding the day of his or her election.[84] Members of the Constitutional Court are recommended by appointing committees that consist of at least nine and at most 15 delegates of parties represented in the National Assembly.[85] Members of the Constitutional Court cannot undertake any other state position or any position in a self-government, nor any other social, political or economic position or mandate, except positions related to academia and education. They can generate additional income only from the specifically listed activities, which include inter alia scientific, academic, educational, artistic, editorial and

---

[80] Article 24(8) of the Fundamental Law of Hungary.
[81] §5 ACC.
[82] §6(1)–(2) ACC.
[83] §6(3) 2nd sentence ACC.
[84] §6(4) ACC.
[85] Each party shall have at least one delegate in the committee. The persons thus recommended are heard by the committee of the National Assembly in charge of constitutional matters. The recommended persons are elected by the National Assembly in view of the opinion of the committee. §§7 and 8(1) ACC.

Intersentia

493

Ist遠ván Varga

copyright-protected work.[86] The ACC expressly mentions that having been appointed as a judge does not generate a conflict of interest.[87] Members of the Constitutional Court also have immunity.[88]

2.3. DURATION OF JUDGES' TENURE AND TERMINATION OF OFFICE

The first appointment of a judge is, by default, limited to a fixed term of three years; in other cases it is for an unlimited period of time.[89] 120 days prior to the last day of the fixed term of a judge, the president of the court that employs the judge shall procure the judge's statement on whether he or she requests his or her appointment as judge for an unlimited period of time. If yes, the judge's work shall be examined. If the judge is considered to be suitable for appointment, the recommendation for his or her appointment shall be submitted to the President of the Republic.[90] If the judge has not requested his or her appointment for an unlimited period of time, or has been found to be unsuitable in light of the aforementioned assessment, his or her status as a judge ends on the last day of the third year calculated from the day of his or her initial appointment for a fixed term.[91]

A judge's office is terminated if the judge (i) dies; (ii) was initially appointed for a fixed term and does not request that he or she be appointed for an unlimited period of time or is considered to be unsuitable for such appointment in view of his or her assessment; or (iii) is removed from office by the President of the Republic.[92] A judge shall be removed from office if he or she:

1. has resigned from office;[93]
2. has become incapable of serving as a judge for health reasons or has been declared unfit for office in an impeachment procedure;

---

[86]   §10(1) ACC.
[87]   §10(1a) ACC (in force as of 20 December 2019).
[88]   §14 ACC.
[89]   §23(1) Judges Act. However, upon the suggestion of the person evaluating the application, already the first appointment can be made for an unlimited period of time in certain scenarios (when the applicant has worked for three years as a judge or military judge, or a judge of the Constitutional Court, or has been an adjudicator at an international organisation or an organ of the European Union, or has acquired exceptional legal know-how in the field of academia and teaching). §23(2)–(2a) Judges Act.
[90]   Within 30 days before the last day of the three-year term without a call for applications, §24 of the Judges Act. See also §24(3) and Chapter V of the Judges Act entitled 'Evaluation of Judges' Work and Impeachment Procedures'. The outcome of the evaluation may be challenged before the competent court (see §§80 and 101 of the Judges Act).
[91]   §25(1) Judges Act.
[92]   §89 Judges Act.
[93]   With three months' notice. Upon request of the judge, this can be shortened by the NJC and the NJC can also relieve the judge of his or her duties for (part of) said period. §93 Judges Act.

3. a punishment (e.g. jail term etc.) has been imposed upon the judge with *res judicata* effect;
4. has not taken the vow within the prescribed time limit;
5. no longer fulfils the prerequisites for becoming a judge (Hungarian citizenship, unrestricted legal capacity);
6. has been elected or appointed a representative in the National Assembly, the European Parliament or a local self-government, an advocate for a nationality or a senior political executive, or state secretary in charge of administrative matters or deputy state secretary;
7. takes a position (with the consent of the NOJ's President) at an international organisation or at an organ of the European Union as a result of an application procedure to perform adjudicative work or other work related to the administration of justice;
8. reaches the general age for old-age retirement or requests his or her earlier retirement in accordance with the relevant legal provisions;
9. has a motion for his or her removal from office made against him or her as a *res judicata* disciplinary sanction in the course of disciplinary proceedings against the judge;
10. is the subject of challenge proceedings against the result of the application procedure where it is found that the legal prerequisites for his or her appointment are not fulfilled;
11. deliberately fails to make an asset declaration or provides incomplete or incorrect information;
12. does not demonstrate his or her lack of a criminal record (with respect to punishments listed in the law) within the applicable time limit when requested to do so;
13. does not participate in the medical examination imposed by his or her employer;
14. is elected rector of a state institution of higher education or the leader of a research institute that functions as a budgetary organ;
15. terminates his or her status as a judge in an unlawful manner; or
16. a conflict of interest concerning the judge is established in a decision with *res judicata* effect.[94]

2.4. DESIGNATION OF JUDGES IN A SPECIFIC CASE

The Courts Administration Act declares the basic principle that no one can be deprived of his or her judge designated by law,[95] who is the judge of the court

---

[94] §90 Judges Act.
[95] §8(1) Courts Administration Act.

having competence for the case, assigned to the case in accordance with the case allocation scheme of the relevant court. The latter is determined by the president of each court in view of the opinion of the judicial council and the divisions of the court for every year (until 10 December of the previous year).[96]

The concrete panels hearing the cases[97] consist of a presiding judge and two other judges from the same chamber[98] of the respective court. The chambers functioning at a given court are organised into divisions (each regional court and regional court of appeal has a civil and a criminal division; at larger courts, there are also economic divisions; there are also administrative and labour divisions that have jurisdiction over several courts). Cases are distributed among the chambers by the respective head of division in accordance with the case allocation scheme of the given division.[99]

Case allocation schemes shall be determined in view of the significance and workload of cases as well as statistics on incoming cases and proportionate case allocation. The case administration schemes of the courts are publicly available in the courts, on the website of the judiciary and, in the case of courts that also have individual websites, also on the websites of the courts.[100]

In view of the special nature of a given area requiring special skills, the Judges Act provides that for certain cases judges need to be assigned by the President of the NOJ or the Kúria.[101]

---

[96] The case allocation scheme contains which chambers (in which composition) function at the respective court, as well as which judges, chambers and court clerks are in charge of which types of cases, who can they be substituted by, which senior court official is in charge of case allocation and how cases are allocated, which cases are heard by judges in executive positions and how these cases are allocated and which panels proceed in so-called high-profile cases (in view of the amount in dispute pursuant to the CCP and pursuant to the Code on Criminal Procedure). See §§8 et seq. Courts Administration Act.

[97] In Hungarian 'eljáró tanács', i.e. panel proceeding (in a given case). See 2021 Rule of Law Report, Country Chapter on the rule of law situation in Hungary, European Commission, Brussels, 20.07.2021, SWD(2021) 417 final (English version), p. 3, n. 15.

[98] In Hungarian 'ítélkező tanács'. See 2021 Rule of Law Report, Country Chapter on the rule of law situation in Hungary, European Commission, Brussels, 20.07.2021, SWD(2021) 417 final (English version), p. 3, n. 15.

[99] Ibid., n. 17.

[100] §§8–11 Courts Administration Act.

[101] Accordingly, for example judges proceeding in administrative and labour matters are appointed by the NOJ's President (in the case of the judges of the appellate court and the higher regional court upon the suggestion of the president of the respective court; §30(1) and (1a) Judges Act). Judges hearing juvenile criminal cases and judges acting as court mediators are also appointed by the NOJ's President (upon the suggestion of the president of the relevant court). §30(2) Judges Act. In the case of judges of the Kúria, these rights are exercised by the President of the Kúria, which also appoints judges proceeding in matters concerning the review of decrees issued by local self-governments (or when the latter omit to issue decrees; §30(3)–(4) Judges Act). The appointment of a judge is subject to the judge's consent (§30(6) Judges Act).

Hungary

2.5. ARBITRATORS

Whether ad hoc or institutional, arbitrations seated in Hungary are governed by the HAA, which contains provisions both on the arbitral procedure (based on the 2006 UNCITRAL Model Law) and on institutional arbitration in Hungary. Accordingly, the HAA stipulates that the Arbitration Court attached to the Hungarian Chamber of Commerce and Industry (the Commercial Arbitration Court) is the sole standing arbitral institution proceeding in general commercial matters.[102]

The HAA contains some general rules as to who can(not) be an arbitrator in arbitrations seated in Hungary. Accordingly, '[n]o person shall be precluded by reason of his nationality or the lack of it from acting as an arbitrator, unless otherwise agreed by the parties.'[103] The HAA also expressly provides who shall not serve as arbitrators. These are:

1. persons under the age of 24;
2. persons excluded from participating in public affairs by a final and binding court judgment;
3. persons sentenced to imprisonment by a final and binding court judgment, until exonerated from the aggravating consequences of having a criminal record;
4. persons placed under custodianship or supported decision-making affecting their capacity to act;
5. persons disqualified from a profession that is subject to a university degree in law; or
6. persons on probation by a final and binding court judgment, during the probation period.[104]

Further, '[p]ersons formerly participating as a mediator, a representative of one of the parties or an expert in the legal dispute of the parties referred or related to arbitration shall not proceed as an arbitrator in the arbitral proceedings' either.[105]

The HAA also foresees that the Commercial Arbitration Court shall draw up a list of recommended arbitrators, to be published on the website of the Court,

---

[102] There are three further institutions constituted by separate acts of Parliament, namely, the Arbitration Court for Sports, the arbitration court attached to the agricultural chamber and the Concession Arbitration Court. See §59 HAA.

[103] §12(1) HAA. English translation of the HAA available at https://njt.hu/jogszabaly/en/ 2017-60-00-00.

[104] §12(7) HAA. English translation of the HAA available at https://njt.hu/jogszabaly/en/ 2017-60-00-00.

[105] §12(8) HAA. English translation of the HAA available at https://njt.hu/jogszabaly/en/ 2017-60-00-00.

Intersentia

497

Istvàn Varga

which shall have a general part (consisting of a minimum of 60 names) and also include a separate energy section according to the recommendations of the Hungarian Energy and Public Utility Regulatory Authority, as well as a financial and capital market section according to the recommendations of the Budapest Stock Exchange Ltd and the Hungarian Banking Association (containing at least 30 names each). The same person may be included in several parts of the list. The list shall be revised every three years. Modifications to the specific sections are subject to the approval of the two aforementioned authorities.[106] Pursuant to the HAA:

> [t]he list may include the names of lawyers with excellent professional knowledge a) who request it, b) who have at least 10 years of professional experience in a legal profession, c) who passed the professional examination in law or the corresponding professional examination according to his national law, d) who are capable of fulfilling the arbitrator's tasks according to the opinion of the majority of the Presidium, and e) who have not yet reached the age of 70.[107]

The list of recommended arbitrators serves merely informative purposes, and does not mean that arbitrators can be selected only from the list. Parties are therefore free to select arbitrators even in institutional arbitrations administered by the Commercial Arbitration Court. However, pursuant to the default rules in the HAA on the constitution of the arbitral tribunal, if no agreement is reached as to the person of the presiding or sole arbitrator, or a missing arbitrator needs to be appointed, by default, a person on the list of recommended arbitrators shall be appointed by the institution, except when the list does not include any person complying with the qualifications or other prerequisites agreed upon by the parties.[108]

2.6. PARAMETERS TO ENSURE THAT DOMESTIC ADJUDICATORS ACT INDEPENDENTLY AND IMPARTIALLY AND CONSEQUENCES OF A BREACH OF THIS REQUIRMENT

2.6.1. Non-Appointment and Recusal of Judges for Conflicts of Interest

As noted above, the President of the NOJ (or of the Kúria) can decide that an application for a judge position is unsuccessful if the appointment of the applicant as judge would result in a conflict of interest.

---

[106] §63(1)–(4), (7)–(9) HAA. English translation of the HAA available at https://njt.hu/jogszabaly/en/2017-60-00-00.

[107] §63(6) HAA. English translation of the HAA available at https://njt.hu/jogszabaly/en/2017-60-00-00.

[108] §12(3) and (5) HAA.

Detailed rules on the recusal of judges are included in the CCP, the CAP and the CCrP. Accordingly, the following persons shall be recused and cannot participate in the adjudication of cases:

a) a party, a person entitled or subject to the same right or obligation as a party, a person who demands the subject matter of the action or any part thereof for himself, or a person whose rights or obligations may be affected by the outcome of the action,[109]

b) a representative or supporter of a person mentioned in point a), or a former representative or supporter who was involved in the case,[110]

c) a relative of a person specified in points a) or b),[111]

d) a person who was ordered by the court to be interviewed as a witness in the action, who was officially appointed as an expert by the court during the action or who delivered an expert opinion concerning the action,[112]

e) a person who conducted any mediation procedure concerning the action,[113] or

f) a person who may not be expected to assess the matter objectively for any other reason.[114]

---

[109] §12(a) CCP; see §10(1)(a), (b) and (c) CACP (those persons 'who have the right to participate in the court procedure as a party or an interested person', 'who participated in performing the administrative activity subject to the dispute', 'who are officials, members, founders of the party or the interested person; or who are controlling shareholders of a public company limited by shares which is a party or an interested person; or who are engaged in an employment relationship with the party or the interested person, except for budgetary organs, for five years after the termination of that legal relationship'); §14(1)(a) CCrP (a person who 'proceeded in the case as a prosecutor or a member of the investigating authority, or ... is a relative of a person who proceeds or proceeded in the case as a prosecutor or a member of the investigating authority'); §14(1)(a) CCrP (a person who 'participates or participated in the case as a defendant, person reasonably suspected of having committed a criminal offence, defence counsel, aggrieved party, party with a pecuniary interest, party reporting a crime, an aide of any such person, or ... is a relative of any such person'); also §14(1)(d) CCrP (a person who 'adopted a decision permitting secret information gathering concerning the case, regardless of whether or not any piece of information secretly gathered was used in the criminal proceeding').

[110] §12(b) CCP; see §10(1)(d) CACP (those persons 'who are representatives, supporters or former representatives or supporters, having proceeded in the case before, of the persons under points a), b) or c)').

[111] §12(c) CCP; see §10(1)(e) CACP (those persons 'who, according to the Civil Code, are relatives of the persons under points a), b), c) or d)'); §14(1)(a) 2nd alternative, §14(1)(b) 2nd alternative CCrP.

[112] §12(d) CCP; see §10(1)(f) CACP (those persons 'whose hearing as witnesses was ordered by the court, or who were appointed by the court as experts, or provided an expert opinion'); §14(1)(c) CCrP (who 'participates or participated in the case as a witness, expert, or consultant').

[113] §12(e) CCP; see §10(1)(g) CACP (those persons 'who conducted a mediation procedure relating to the action').

[114] §12(f) CCP; see §10(1)(h) CACP (those persons 'who may not be expected to judge the case objectively for other reasons'); §14(1)(e) (who 'cannot be expected to adjudicate the case without bias for any other reason') in conjunction with paras (7) and (8). The above list is adapted from the English translation of the CCP available at https://njt.hu/jogszabaly/en/2016-130-00-00. The English quotes from the CACP are from the English translation of

Further, a judge who participated in the adjudication of the matter at first instance shall also be disqualified from the adjudication of the matter at second instance. A judge shall also be disqualified from the adjudication of a retrial or a review application if he or she participated in the proceedings leading to the adoption of the decision subject to retrial or the decision affected by the review application.[115]

Not only judges but also whole courts can be disqualified if the above scenario (a) applies to the court itself, or if the president or the vice-president of the court is disqualified under (a), (b) or (c).[116]

A judge shall notify the president of the court of a ground for recusal without delay. Grounds for recusal may also be invoked by any party, in any phase of the proceedings until the decision closing the proceedings is rendered. The general ground for recusal pursuant to the above scenario (f) may not be invoked after the commencement of a hearing, unless the party invoking the ground for recusal substantiates that he or she became aware of the fact justifying recusal thereafter and that he or she acted without delay.[117]

The CCP foresees that courts shall seek to ensure ex officio that no recused judge or court is involved in the proceedings. If a ground for recusal is reported by a judge or if a judge acknowledges the ground for recusal invoked by a party, the president of the court arranges for the appointment of another judge or panel.[118] In all other cases, the decision on a ground for recusal concerning a

---

the CACP available at https://njt.hu/jogszabaly/en/2017-1-00-00. The English quotes from the CCrP are from the English translation of the CCrP available at https://njt.hu/jogszabaly/en/2017-90-00-00.

[115] §13 CCP. The list is adopted from the English translation of the CCP available at https://njt.hu/jogszabaly/en/2016-130-00-00. See §10(2) CACP ('The judge who participated in the court procedures preceding the adoption of the decision challenged by the procedural remedy shall also be disqualified from administering the procedural remedy.' English translation available at https://njt.hu/jogszabaly/en/2017-1-00-00). See also §14(3)–(6) CCrP.

[116] §14(1) CCP. These grounds also apply to the district courts in the case of which the general employer's rights over the judges are exercised by the president of the court affected by the action (§14(2) CCP). However, the CCP also lists certain scenarios which shall not in themselves serve as a ground for the disqualification of the proceeding court 'a) other proceedings between the party and the proceeding court are pending, b) a request for the extension of the action could be rejected if the court involved in the matter at the first or second instance were to be involved in the action, or c) the action is brought by virtue of law against a person acting within his administrative, judicial or prosecutorial powers, for an activity subject to the liability obligation of the employer, infringing personality rights, or causing damage, even if the person acting within his judicial powers acted for the proceeding court'; English translation of the CCP available at https://njt.hu/jogszabaly/en/2016-130-00-00). See also §10(3) CACP.

[117] §15 CCP; similarly, §15 CCrP. §10(5) CACP renders the provision of the CCP mutatis mutandis applicable to the submission and administration of the motion for recusal in all other respects.

[118] §16 CCP; §16 CCrP.

Hungary

sole judge shall be made by another sole judge of the same court who proceeds at the same instance; if the ground for recusal concerns the chair or a member of a panel, the decision shall be rendered by another panel of the same court that proceeds at the same instance. If the same court does not have a judge or panel that is not affected by the ground for recusal or the whole court is affected by it, the decision on recusal shall be made by the next highest court. If the ground for recusal was not reported by the judge him- or herself, his or her statement shall be obtained before rendering a decision. A complaint against the dismissal of a motion for recusal can be filed as part of the appeal against the decision closing the proceedings.[119]

A judge who reports a ground for recusal against him- or herself may not proceed in the case until the notice is dealt with. In all other cases the judge concerned by the ground for recusal may proceed but may not participate in the rendering of the decision on the merits until the motion for recusal filed in the above scenarios (a)–(e) is dealt with, unless the same party filed a motion for the recusal of the same judge in the same case after the dismissal of its earlier motion for recusal. Manifestly or repeatedly unfounded motions for the recusal of the same judge shall be sanctioned by imposing a fine upon the party making such motions. Recusal matters shall be decided as a matter of priority.[120]

2.6.2. Judicial Integrity

In view of the State Audit Office's 2018 Integrity Survey, the judiciary displays a high level of integrity.[121]

In the Annual Report of the NOJ's President, a separate chapter is devoted to judicial integrity,[122] which has been reflected in the adoption of numerous integrity-related measures by the NOJ (regulations, instructions, recommendations by the NOJ's President),[123] awareness-raising courses and workshops, and the creation of internal rules of integrity and annual integrity questionnaires for judges, integrity working plans and risk management action plans.

---

[119] §17 CCP; §17 CCrP.

[120] §18 CCP. See §10(4) CACP ('If all the judges or panels of the administrative and labour court meet the grounds for disqualification or the ground for disqualification affects the court as a whole, the matter of disqualification shall be decided upon by the Budapest-Capital Regional Court.' English translation available at https://njt.hu/jogszabaly/en/2017-1-00-00); §18 CCrP.

[121] The average risk (33%) exceeds the average of all respondent institutions by 10%, whereas the control index at 84% is significantly above the average of 54%. Annual Report of the President of the National Office for the Judiciary 2018, available at https://birosag.hu/sites/default/files/2020-03/annualreport2018_online.pdf (English version), p. 105.

[122] Ibid., pp. 105 ff.

[123] These include e.g. NOJ Instruction 7/2018 (11 July) on the rules of procedure for whistle-blowing reports and complaints (designed to increase public trust in courts and improve

Intersentia

501

István Varga

2.6.3. Evaluation of Judges

Detailed rules on the evaluation of judges' work are included in Chapter V of the Judges Act, entitled 'Evaluation of Judges' Work and Impeachment Procedures'. To facilitate the uniformity of evaluation reports in terms of content and structure, the President of the NOJ issued NOJ Instruction 8/2015 (12 December) on the Regulation of the Standard Evaluation of Judges' Activities and Detailed Evaluation Criteria, which is used as standard practice.[124] Evaluations are carried out by examiners[125] whose appointment is subject to the qualifications set forth in the aforesaid Instruction (central training and entry in the Examiners' Register). As a result of the evaluation, judges can be found 'qualified for a higher position with distinction', 'qualified with distinction', 'qualified' and 'unqualified'. Pursuant to the 2018 report of the NOJ's President, whereas the majority fell within the first category, only two out of 258 judges were found 'unqualified'. Judges unsatisfied with the result can turn to the competent court (the Service Court), which may change the evaluation but also order that a new evaluation be made.[126]

2.6.4. Training of Judges and Trainee Judges

The training of trainee judges is regulated in Decree 11/1999 (6 October) of the Minister of Justice on the legal internship and training of trainee judges.[127]

---

court cooperation); NOJ Instruction 10/2018 (19 December) on the performance assessment of court employees or the NOJ President's Recommendation 3/2018 (26 June) on the rules of procedure for managing events violating the organisational integrity of appellate and regional courts; and Recommendation 4/2018 (26 June) on the regulations of integrated risk management at appellate and regional courts. Annual Report of the President of the National Office for the Judiciary 2018, available at https://birosag.hu/sites/default/files/2020-03/annualreport2018_online.pdf (English version), pp. 105 ff., 109–10.

[124] Annual Report of the President of the National Office for the Judiciary 2018, available at https://birosag.hu/sites/default/files/2020-03/annualreport2018_online.pdf (English version), p. 26.

[125] The examination that provides that basis of a judge's assessment is conducted by the head of division or the judge appointed by him (examiner). The judge is notified of who the examiner will be (§71(2) Judges Act). Judges working at the Kúria and the NOJ are evaluated by the Presidents of the Kúria and the NOJ, respectively (§71(3)–(4) Judges Act).

[126] See §§80, 101, 145(2) and 146 of the Judges Act. Presidents and members of the service courts are appointed by the NJC. (Vice presidents are appointed by the presidents.) See §102 Judges Act and §103(3)(g) Courts Administration Act. See also the summaries in the Annual Report of the President of the National Office for the Judiciary 2018, available at https://birosag.hu/sites/default/files/2020-03/annualreport2018_online.pdf (English version), p. 26; as well as 2021 Rule of Law Report, Country Chapter on the rule of law situation in Hungary, European Commission, Brussels, 20 07.2021, SWD(2021) 417 final (English version), p. 7.

[127] Amended by Decree 20/2017 (21 December) of the Minister of Justice. Annual Report of the President of the National Office for the Judiciary 2018, available at https://birosag.hu/sites/default/files/2020-03/annualreport2018_online.pdf (English version), p. 46.

Hungary

The presidents of the courts[128] issue a uniform, common call for applications twice a year. Applicants need to take written and oral exams. The duration of traineeship is three years. As shown above, being a trainee judge is not a mandatory prerequisite for applying for a judge position if the candidate has worked as another legal professional.

2.6.5. Increase of Salaries

A gradual increase of salaries in 2020 and 2021 is also supposed to enhance judicial independence.[129]

2.6.6. Service Courts, Disciplinary Matters and Liability for Damages and Impeachment

2.6.6.1. Competent Court

Disciplinary proceedings against judges, related damages claims, cases concerning the violation of personality rights, disputes arising from the evaluation of the work of judges and court executives, impeachment procedures and procedures concerning conflicts of interest fall within the competence of the Service Courts. The First Instance Service Court functions at the Budapest Regional Court of Appeal and the Second Instance Service Court at the Kúria.[130] The president and the members of the Service Courts are appointed by the NJC.[131]

2.6.6.2. Disciplinary Matters and Impeachment

Pursuant to the Judges Act, '[a] judge commits a disciplinary breach if he culpably a) violates his obligations related to his service relationship or b) curtails or jeopardises the reputation of the judicial profession by virtue of his lifestyle or behaviour.'[132]

---

[128] Those presidents that exercise employers' rights (i.e. all presidents except the presidents of the district courts).

[129] Annual Report of the President of the National Office for the Judiciary 2018, available at https://birosag.hu/sites/default/files/2020-03/annualreport2018_online.pdf (English version), pp. 7–8.

[130] §101 Judges Act. See also the English summary available at https://birosag.hu/en/service-court.

[131] §102(1) Judges Act. The members of the Service Court are recommended by the full plenary session of the Kúria or the court of appeal or general regional court. §102(2) Judges Act. Service Court judges carry out such duties beside their adjudicative or administrative work and receive proportionate remuneration. §102(3)–(4) Judges Act. Further rules inter alia on who cannot be Service Court judges are contained in the Judges Act (§§103–104).

[132] Cf. §108(1): 'If the judge's culpability is minor and the breach did not involve consequences or only involved minor consequences, the institution of disciplinary proceedings may be

Intersentia

503

The Judges Act differentiates between disciplinary breaches committed by senior court officials (holding executive positions) and judges not holding a senior appointment. If the suspicion of a disciplinary breach by the former emerges, 'the person exercising the right of appointment shall initiate disciplinary proceeding before the chair of the service court of first instance.'[133] If criminal proceedings have been instituted against a judge, disciplinary proceedings shall also be instituted.[134] If criminal proceedings are pending, disciplinary proceedings shall be suspended.[135] However, '[n]o disciplinary proceedings may be instituted if the person authorised to institute the proceedings did not initiate proceedings within 3 months of becoming aware of the relevant circumstances or a period of 3 years has elapsed since the termination of the practice constituting the disciplinary breach.'[136]

Preparation for disciplinary proceedings and a preliminary investigation is conducted by an investigating commissioner, who cannot be a judge inferior to the level of the position of the judge concerned.[137] Three-member disciplinary chambers of the First and – following an appeal – the Second Instance Service Courts proceed.[138] Judges are not suspended from office automatically, but there are scenarios foreseen in the Judges Act when they must and others in which they can be suspended.[139]

---

dispensed with.' Paragraph (2) provides that, in that case, the person authorised to institute disciplinary proceedings shall warn the judge, who may, within 15 days of service of the warning, request the institution of disciplinary proceedings. English translation of the Judges Act by the Council of Europe, available at https://www.venice.coe.int/webforms/documents/default.aspx?pdffile=CDL-REF(2012)006-e.

[133] § 106(1) Judges Act. See also paragraphs (2) and (3). English translation of the Judges Act by the Council of Europe, available at https://www.venice.coe.int/webforms/documents/default.aspx?pdffile=CDL-REF(2021)058-e.

[134] § 106(4) Judges Act.

[135] § 107 Judges Act.

[136] § 110(1) Judges Act. English translation of the Judges Act by the Council of Europe, available at https://www.venice.coe.int/webforms/documents/default.aspx?pdffile=CDL-REF(2021)058-e. See also § 110(2) Judges Act (special rules in the case of decisions made in criminal proceedings or administrative infringement proceedings against the judge).

[137] § 113(2) Judges Act. The investigating commissioner shall clarify the circumstances necessary for the establishment of the facts of the case, hear the judge, may hear witnesses and use experts and take evidence otherwise, view the documents of the court, and shall be furnished with all necessary information by judges and court employees, and shall draft a written report on his or her proceedings for the service court chamber within 15 days (§ 120 Judges Act). English translation of the Judges Act by the Council of Europe, available at https://www.venice.coe.int/webforms/documents/default.aspx?pdffile=CDL-REF(2021)058-e.

[138] §§ 112–113 Judges Act. Special rules on the recusal of service court judges are foreseen in § 114 Judges Act. For procedural aspects, see §§ 115–116.

[139] §§ 117–118 Judges Act.

Both the preliminary investigation and the disciplinary proceedings shall not be conducted in public.[140] Further rules on the proceedings and the hearing are included in the Judges Act.[141] The service court chamber may (i) remove the judge from office, (ii) pronounce the judge culpable and impose a disciplinary sanction, or (iii) terminate the proceedings instituted against the judge.[142] The service court chamber is bound by a prior finding of a criminal court in the sense that, if a criminal court has already established the judge's liability due to the act that is the subject matter of the disciplinary proceedings, the service court chamber may not conclude that the judge did not commit the relevant act.[143]

The disciplinary sanctions – to be imposed in view of the gravity and consequences of the breach and the degree of culpability – are: (i) reprimand; (ii) censure;[144] (iii) demotion by one pay grade;[145] (iv) exemption from senior office;[146] and (v) motion seeking removal from the office of judge.[147] Costs shall be covered by the court, except when the judge's liability is established on a final and absolute basis, in which case costs shall be reimbursed by the judge.[148]

The decision of the First Instance Service Court may be appealed by the judge and the person who initiated the disciplinary proceedings.[149] The Second Instance Service Court shall uphold or alter the disciplinary sanction (and the decision on costs), terminate the proceedings or repeal the decision and instruct the First Instance Service Court to conduct the proceedings anew and render a

---

[140] §119 Judges Act. English translation of the Judges Act by the Council of Europe, available at https://www.venice.coe.int/webforms/documents/default.aspx?pdffile=CDL-REF(2021)058-e.

[141] §§121–122 Judges Act.

[142] §123(1) Judges Act. English translation of the Judges Act by the Council of Europe, available at https://www.venice.coe.int/webforms/documents/default.aspx?pdffile=CDL-REF(2021)058-e.

[143] §123(3) Judges Act. English translation of the Judges Act by the Council of Europe, available at https://www.venice.coe.int/webforms/documents/default.aspx?pdffile=CDL-REF(2021)058-e.

[144] This remains in effect for one year. §126(1)(a) Judges Act.

[145] This remains in effect for two years. §126(1)(b) Judges Act.

[146] This remains in effect for two years. §126(1)(b) Judges Act.

[147] This remains in effect for three years. §126(1)(c) Judges Act. The list of sanctions is foreseen in §124 Judges Act. On application, the First Instance Service Court may exempt a judge from the detrimental legal consequences if one half of the aforementioned timeframe has already elapsed, provided that no new disciplinary proceedings are pending. When counting the date of promotion to a higher pay grade, the aforementioned timeframes shall be disregarded (§127 Judges Act). Further consequences are that a judge under the effect of a disciplinary sanction, appointed as a senior court officer (executive position), promoted to a higher pay grade or awarded a title corresponding to a more senior judicial position (§126(3) Judges Act). Pursuant to §128, a disciplinary sanction imposed on a final and absolute basis shall be recorded in the judge's personal file. English translation of the Judges Act by the Council of Europe, available at https://www.venice.coe.int/webforms/documents/default.aspx?pdffile=CDL-REF(2021)058-e.

[148] §124(4) Judges Act.

[149] §125(2) Judges Act. English translation of the Judges Act by the Council of Europe, available at https://www.venice.coe.int/webforms/documents/default.aspx?pdffile=CDL-REF(2021)058-e.

new decision.[150] Disciplinary proceedings against judges posted at the Kúria, the Ministry of Justice and the NOJ may be instituted by the President of the Kúria, the Minister of Justice and the President of the NOJ, respectively; otherwise the aforementioned rules foreseen in the Judge Act shall apply.[151]

2.6.6.3. Liability for Damages

Judges are financially liable for any loss or damage caused to their employer through the wilful or grossly negligent violation of their obligations arising from their service relationship. Further, the employer can also require judges to pay compensation for the violation of personality rights.[152] The liability of the judge, the occurrence of damage and the amount thereof, and the violation of personality rights must be proven by the employer.[153] In the case of damages caused with gross negligence, the judge is liable for up to three months' remuneration. In the case of wilfully caused damages and the violation of personality rights, the judge shall be liable for the whole amount of the damages.[154]

2.6.7. *Immunity and Criminal Liability*

Judges have the same immunity as members of the National Assembly, which can be suspended only by the President of the Republic upon the suggestion of the President of the NOJ.[155]

Certain violations by judges of their duties are also foreseen as criminal offences in the Hungarian Criminal Code. The relevant offence is passive bribery.[156]

2.6.8. *Enforcement of a Final Decision Rendered by a Domestic Adjudicator who Breached the Requirement to Act Independently and Impartially*

If it turns out that a party lost a case in an unlawful manner owing to a criminal offence committed by a judge who participated in the rendering of the judgment (or other decision with the same effect), retrial may be sought against the decision

---

[150] §125(3) Judges Act. English translation of the Judges Act by the Council of Europe, available at https://www.venice.coe.int/webforms/documents/default.aspx?pdffile=CDL-REF(2021)058-e.
[151] §130 Judges Act.
[152] §131(1) Judges Act.
[153] §131(2) Judges Act.
[154] §132 Judges Act.
[155] §2 Judges Act. English translation of the Judges Act by the Council of Europe, available at https://www.venice.coe.int/webforms/documents/default.aspx?pdffile=CDL-REF(2021)058-e.
[156] §296(1)–(2) Criminal Code. English translation from https://njt.hu/jogszabaly/en/2012-100-00-00.

affected by the criminal offence[157] within six months from the date when the decision becomes final and binding or when the party requesting retrial becomes aware of said ground for retrial, but not later than within five years following the date when the contested decision became final and binding.[158]

The rules governing the setting aside of arbitral awards in §47 of the HAA correspond to the relevant provision of the UNCITRAL Model Law. With respect to domestic awards, only the ex officio grounds for the refusal of enforcement are foreseen in the law (non-arbitrability of the subject matter under Hungarian law and the violation of Hungarian public policy).[159]

2.7. COMMENTS AND RELEVANT CASES

2.7.1. EC Rule of Law Report on Hungary

Pursuant to the 2021 Rule of Law Report of the European Commission on Hungary (EC Rule of Law Report), it needs to be mentioned that,[160] 'as regards judicial independence, the justice system has been subject to new developments adding to existing concerns.' Reference was made to the 'new rules allowing for appointment of members of the Constitutional Court to the Supreme Court (Kúria) outside the normal procedure' and 'the election of the new Kúria President, whose position was also endowed with additional powers ... despite a negative opinion of the National Judicial Council'. In this context, the European Commission noted that '[t]he recommendation to strengthen judicial independence ... remains unaddressed', which 'includes the need to formally reinforce the powers of the independent National Judicial Council to enable it to counter-balance the powers of the President of the National Office for the Judiciary',[161] because the NJC 'is facing a series of structural limitations that prevent it from exercising effective oversight regarding the actions of the NOJ President', including lack of legal personality and of the right to propose legislation or to be consulted on relevant legislative proposals.[162]

It is also mentioned in the EC Rule of Law Report that the NOJ's President 'has repeatedly filled vacancies in higher courts, without a call for applications, with judges performing administrative tasks in the NOJ.'[163]

---

[157]   §393(b) CCP.

[158]   §395(1) and (3) CCP; also §122(1) CAP.

[159]   §54 HAA.

[160]   2021 Rule of Law Report, Country Chapter on the rule of law situation in Hungary, European Commission, Brussels, 20.07.2021, SWD(2021) 417 final (English version).

[161]   Ibid., p. 1.

[162]   Ibid., pp. 2–3.

[163]   Ibid., p. 3, with reference to §58(3) of the Judges Act, the Contribution from the European Association of Judges for the 2021 Rule of Law Report, 7 as well as Decisions 83.E/2020 (II. 21.) OBHE and 62.E/2021 (III. 12.) OBHE.

The EC Rule of Law report also notes that, following the above-mentioned recent amendment of the law making this possible, as of 1 July 2020 eight members of the Constitutional Court were appointed as judges of the Kúria by the President of the Republic, six of whom had no experience as a judge in an ordinary court. The Report also mentions that the President of the Republic recommended that the National Assembly elect one of them as President of the Kúria,[164] which indeed happened on 19 October 2020 (for a period of nine years),[165] notwithstanding the fact that, having heard the nominee, the NJC rejected his nomination almost unanimously[166] (except for the vote of the then President of the Kúria, the ex officio member of the NJC, who also assigned said nominee to the Kúria to be a presiding judge in one of the chambers until he took office as President of the Kúria).[167]

The Report notes that, on 21 September 2020, the NJC called on the NOJ's President to propose legislation removing the provision that allows members of the Constitutional Court to request their appointment as judges.[168]

The EC Rule of Law Report also highlights that the President of the NOJ continued the practice of 'annulling the procedures for selecting court presidents and appointing ad interim court presidents without the approval of the National

---

[164] The recommendation of the President of the Republic and the declaration and acceptance of the nomination by the nominee, as well as the draft decision of the National Assembly signed by the Chair of the National Assembly is available (in Hungarian) at https://www.parlament. hu/irom41/13175/13175.pdf.

[165] 2021 Rule of Law Report, Country Chapter on the rule of law situation in Hungary, European Commission, Brussels, 20.07.2021, SWD(2021) 417 final (English version), p. 5, with reference to the Input from Hungary for the 2021 Rule of Law Report, p. 12.

[166] Pursuant to the summary of the decision of the NJC (Decision 120/2020 (X. 9.) OBT) in the Report, the NJC 'recognised the personal qualities and preparedness of the nominee, his academic merits and the experience he gained in the field of justice, in a broader sense, as member of the Constitutional Court and deputy of the Prosecutor General, but explained the rejection by referring to the nominee's lack of courtroom experience and the fact that his candidacy was made possible by legislative amendments which the Council considered were contrary to the constitutional requirement of independence and impartiality of the head of the judicial system'. 2021 Rule of Law Report, Country Chapter on the rule of law situation in Hungary, European Commission, Brussels, 20.07.2021, SWD(2021) 417 final (English version), p. 5, n. 33.

[167] As pointed out in the EC Rule of Law Report, this was criticised by the UN Special Rapporteur on the independence of judges and lawyers and the European Network of Councils for the Judiciary too. 2021 Rule of Law Report, Country Chapter on the rule of law situation in Hungary, European Commission, Brussels, 20.07.2021, SWD(2021) 417 final (English version), pp. 5–6, and n. 37, with reference to the Letter of the UN Special Rapporteur on the independence of judges and lawyers dated 15 April 2021.

[168] I.e. §3(4a) of the Judges Act. The NOJ's President and the representative of the Ministry of Justice were of the view that the NJC had no competence in the matter. See Decision 107/2020 (IX. 21.) OBT, summarised in 2021 Rule of Law Report, Country Chapter on the rule of law situation in Hungary, European Commission, Brussels, 20.07.2021, SWD(2021) 417 final (English version), p. 5, n. 29.

Judicial Council'.[169] The EC Rule of Law Report listed five such cancellations of selection procedures for executive positions in 2020, as a result of which three ad interim court presidents were appointed.[170]

The possibility of the (temporary) transfer of judges without their consent has also been subject to criticism (although not practised since 2012).[171]

With respect to the President of the Kúria, the 2021 EC Rule of Law Report noted that the role of the Kúria's judicial bodies (e.g. the judicial council or the divisions) is 'merely consultative', as a result of which they are 'unable to counter-balance the extensive powers of the Kúria President.'[172]

2.7.2. Recent Cases before the Constitutional Court of Hungary Concerning the Judiciary

A provision of the Code of Judicial Conduct was challenged before the Constitutional Court in 2015. The provision concerned provides that '[a] judge shall refrain from comments that would suggest failure to [his or her] fulfil obligation, decisions made to serve political or other interests on his or her colleagues' side.'[173] According to the motion, said provision restricts judges' freedom of expression[174] as well as the independence of judges[175] to an unjustified extent and thereby violates the Fundamental Law. The Constitutional Court dismissed the constitutional complaint as inadmissible by order without dealing with it on the merits on the grounds that the Code of Judicial Conduct cannot be considered a norm (a provision of law) that could be the subject of a procedure before the Constitutional Court.[176]

---

[169] 2021 Rule of Law Report, Country Chapter on the rule of law situation in Hungary, European Commission, Brussels, 20.07.2021, SWD(2021) 417 final (English version), p. 6.

[170] Ibid., p. 6, n. 41, with reference to Decisions 373.E/2020 (X. 1.) OBHE, 388.E/2020 (X. 19.) OBHE, 415.E/2020 (XI. 12.) OBHE, 443.E/2020 (XI. 30.) OBHE, 444.E/2020 (XI. 30.) OBHE.

[171] 2021 Rule of Law Report, Country Chapter on the rule of law situation in Hungary, European Commission, Brussels, 20.07.2021, SWD(2021) 417 final (English version), p. 7, n. 52, with reference to GRECO Fourth Evaluation Round – Second Interim Compliance Report, recommendation xi, para. 27; Committee of Ministers of the Council of Europe Recommendation CM/Rec(2010)12, para. 52.

[172] Footnotes omitted. 2021 Rule of Law Report, Country Chapter on the rule of law situation in Hungary, European Commission, Brussels, 20.07.2021, SWD(2021) 417 final (English version), pp. 4–5.

[173] English translation at https://birosag.hu/en/code-judicial-conduct.

[174] Foreseen in Article XI of the Fundamental Law.

[175] Foreseen in Article 26(1) of the Fundamental Law.

[176] The Order of the Constitutional Court (3003/2016 (I. 15.) AB végzés) and the constitutional complaint (and its amendment) are available in Hungarian at http://public.mkab.hu/dev/dontesek.nsf/0/B7F10C5FFDE065D9C1257E65005876F5?OpenDocument.

Intersentia

By contrast, the Constitutional Court quashed parts of Order 6/2016 (V. 31.) OBH of the NOJ's President on the Integrity Code[177] for its being unconstitutional.[178] In the constitutional complaint, it was requested that the whole Integrity Code be quashed for its being unconstitutional or, alternatively, certain provisions of it (listed in the complaint). In the applicant's view, the independence of judges inherently means that rights and obligations can be foreseen for judges by law (i.e. in acts of Parliament) only. The applicant argued that the challenged Order fell short of this and pointed out that the procedure resulting in a judge's removal from office could only be foreseen in an act of Parliament adopted by a two-thirds majority. Further, the Order entrusted the NOJ's President with future, unknown powers by providing that integrity means inter alia 'compliance with the goals, values and principles determined in the instructions and recommendations of the NOJ's president and conduct and operation in compliance therewith', which not only covered the existing Order but also involved the danger of 'quasi governance by decree instead of laws', which could jeopardise the functioning of the judiciary as an independent branch of power. Further, the Order did not provide the possibility to challenge the consequences of a certain breach of integrity.

In this case, the Constitutional Court found that the Order was a norm that could be challenged before the Constitutional Court and admitted the complaint (considering all the prerequisites thereof fulfilled). The Constitutional Court pointed out that, according to the Order, the NOJ's President could issue 'not only mandatory orders but also non binding recommendations applicable to courts, judges and judicial staff members, containing a required conduct the violation of which may result in launching a proceeding against the judge.'[179] The Constitutional Court found that 'rules of conduct affecting judicial independence may not be determined in such a document without binding force as it is not subject to constitutional supervision' and 'annulled the part of the Order regulating recommendations.'[180] The Constitutional Court also noted that the Order provided for rules of conduct but did not contain any provision guaranteeing the right to a legal remedy, which would be essential concerning the violation of such rules. As

---

[177] Available in Hungarian at https://birosag.hu/obh/szabalyzat/62016-v31-obh-utasitas-az-integritasi-szabalyzatrol-0, in its unified version as amended and effective as of 1 July 2018.

[178] The Decision of the Constitutional Court (33/2017 (XII. 6.) AB határozat), the constitutional complaint and the statement of the NOJ submitted in the proceedings before the Constitutional Court are available in Hungarian at https://alkotmanybirosag.hu/ugyadat lap/?id=B8B4A549C5C37B1FC1257FF0005876C0. An English summary of the decision is available on the website of the Constitutional Court at https://hunconcourt.hu/kozlemeny/ the-order-issued-by-the-president-of-the-national-office-for-the-judiciary-is-in-conflict-with-the-fundamental-law-in-many-respect.

[179] English summary on the website of the Constitutional Court available at https://hunconcourt. hu/datasheet/?id=B8B4A549C5C37B1FC1257FF0005876C0.

[180] Ibid.

a result, the Constitutional Court held that 'the examined provisions, for example the establishment of the violation of integrity, initiating the calling to account for a breach of obligation as well as the application of legal consequences violate both the right to legal remedy and the independence of judges'. The Constitutional Court found that the relevant provisions of the Order were contrary to the Fundamental Law and quashed them.[181]

2.7.3. Academic Discourse on the Hungarian Judiciary

In the present subsection, certain developments will be mentioned that have also caught media attention.

In 2018, an article by Viktor Vadász,[182] a former judge and member of the NJC, entitled 'Crisis in the Hungarian judicial administration?' was published in MTA[183] Law Working Papers (i.e. in the series of the Hungarian Academy of Sciences).[184] The article is also available in English on the website of the Hungarian judiciary.[185] An answer to Vadász's article rebutting his arguments was also published in the same series, authored by another judge, Csaba Virág, with the title 'Reflections on Viktor Vadász's paper entitled "Is There a Crisis in The Administration of The Courts?"'.[186]

Vadász noted that in 2011 the central administration of courts was put into the hands of a single person, the President of the NOJ, with broad powers inter alia regarding the distribution of judicial positions and the appointment of judges and court executives.[187] Vadász also pointed out that while the President

---

[181] Ibid.

[182] Former judge of the Metropolitan Court of Budapest (a general court), head of the criminal law division (on mandate) and a member of the NJC and former Director of the Hungarian Academy of Justice. The author later resigned from his positions in the Hungarian judiciary and was elected the new Director of Programmes of the Academy of European Law (ERA) in January 2022. The announcement on the website of ERA is available at https://www.era.int/cgi-bin/cms?_SID=1cb9bbd1dcb19d97a17b358e06cfd01d6cc00b2500828869334711&_sprache=en&_bereich=artikel&_aktion=detail&idartikel=131148.

[183] MTA is the abbreviation for Magyar Tudományos Akadémia, i.e. the Hungarian Academy of Sciences.

[184] The Hungarian version of the article dated 19 June 2018, entitled 'Krízis a bírósági igazgatásban?', MTA Law Working Papers 2018/13, is available at http://real.mtak.hu/121520/1/2018_13_Vadasz.pdf.

[185] The English version of the article entitled 'Crisis in the Hungarian judicial administration?', with minor changes finalised on 12 July 2018, is available at https://birosag.hu/sites/default/files/users/2018.%20j%C3%BAlius_Crisis%20in%20the%20Hungarian%20Judicial%20Administration%2012.07.2018%20vadaszv.pdf.

[186] Csaba Virág, 'Reflections on Viktor Vadász's paper entitled "Is There a Crisis in The Administration of The Courts?"', MTA Law Working Papers 2018/17, available at https://birosag.hu/sites/default/files/2019-01/reflections.pdf. The Hungarian version of the article entitled 'Észrevételek Vadász Viktor "Krízis a bírósági igazgatásban?" című írásához', MTA Law Working Papers 2018/17, is available at http://real.mtak.hu/121518/1/2018_17_Virag.pdf.

[187] Ibid., p. 1.

of the NOJ acquired a personalised apparatus, the NJC has no infrastructure and, since it lacks legal personality, it cannot execute procurements necessary for its operation, maintain an office or hire employees.[188] Despite the allocation of some budget to the NJC, the NJC has to conclude an annual agreement about it with the President of the NOJ.[189]

Vadász also noted that the President of the NOJ is elected by the National Assembly, which embodies the legislative branch (the appointment thus depending on government majority and party will), and not the NJC, which would embody judicial self-governance.[190] As Vadász summarised, in the sense of public law, 'OBT [Hungarian abbreviation for NJC] and judicial self-governance guarantee the rule of law and embody the independence of the judicial branch of power, since judicial self-governance must of necessity exercise supervision over the political appointee President of OBH [Hungarian abbreviation of NOJ] concerning the most important status issues.'[191]

Vadász noted, though, that 'judges are selected via application, in a transparent way', and that the majority of points that can be given when scoring applicants for judge positions are based on objective criteria.[192] He also noted that judicial councils and divisions of courts embody judicial self-governance at local level because they represent the collective will of judges.[193] Vadász also considers it to be a positive aspect that the President of the NOJ may – ex officio or on the motion the president of the court concerned – derogate from the ranking, for example when a judge with a longer service period applies for a job in another part of the country but another applicant with a shorter service period has higher objective scores. In the case of derogations, the necessary agreement of the NJC ensures the legitimacy of the decision.[194] At the same time, Vadász also noted that the President of the NOJ can 'bypass judicial self-governance' by declaring the application proceedings unsuccessful.[195]

Vadász had concerns about the right of the President of the NOJ not to appoint anyone and declare an executive application unsuccessful. He argued that 'the high number of persons not supported by the judges who are nevertheless fulfilling important executive positions projects an alarming democracy deficit', the relevant 'method' being that, 'after declaring the second round of applications for an executive position unsuccessful, the President of OBH [Hungarian abbreviation for NOJ] assigns someone for one year ... to fill the position, and when new application proceedings are initiated one year later, that person is usually the

---

[188]   Ibid., p. 2.
[189]   Ibid., p. 2 and n. 4; §104 Courts Administration Act.
[190]   Ibid., pp. 2–3.
[191]   Ibid., p. 3.
[192]   Ibid., pp. 5–6.
[193]   Ibid., p. 6.
[194]   Ibid., p. 6.
[195]   Ibid., p. 6.

only candidate', in which case persons who have not submitted an application and were not evaluated by their peers (the judicial council) can be appointed as judges. Vadász noted that 'assigning an executive function to a person who had not even submitted an application against a candidate supported by the judges is completely contrary to the aim of the legislator and to the international minimum standards'.[196] Vadász noted that, upon requests by the general conferences of the Metropolitan Court and the Regional Court of Appeal of Győr, the NJC ordered an inquiry concerning the lawfulness of the practice of the President of the NOJ to declare application proceedings of judges and executives unsuccessful. The President of the NOJ did not comment on the report.[197] Vadász noted that, as a result of the resignation of a judge from the NJC, the session of the NJC of 2 May 2018, where actions would have been required of the NOJ's President, was unable to act according to the previous written notification of the President of the NJC, who did not attend the session.[198] The session was still held and the report of the NJC was also summarised there, with the most serious identified error being the lack of reasoning either for or against declaring application proceedings unsuccessful.[199] Vadász also noted that, pursuant to the Judges Act, the NJC was operable and severely criticised the erroneous legal interpretation of the President of the NOJ.[200] In view of the erroneous legal interpretation on the operability of the NJC, the NJC addressed an open letter to the judiciary.[201]

---

[196]   Ibid., pp. 7–8.

[197]   Ibid., p. 8. See the protocol and summary of the NJC's session of 22 February 2018 and the decisions made there at https://orszagosbiroitanacs.hu/2018-02-22/. At this session, the NJC rendered a decision inter alia on the setting up of a specialised committee to examine the practice of the President of the NOJ annulling applications for judge and executive positions (Decision 20/2018 (II. 22.) OBT).

[198]   Ibid., p. 8; see also the Summary on the Session of the NJC held on 2 May 2018 available (in Hungarian) at https://orszagosbiroitanacs.hu/2018-05-02/.

[199]   Viktor Vadász, 'Crisis in the Hungarian judicial administration?', MTA Law Working Papers 2018/13, pp. 8–9 (English version). The English version of the article entitled 'Crisis in the Hungarian judicial administration?', with minor changes finalised on 12 July 2018, is available at https://birosag.hu/sites/default/files/users/2018.%20j%C3%BAlius_Crisis%20in%20 the%20Hungarian%20Judicial%20Administration%2012.07.2018%20vadaszv.pdf. See also the Summary on the Session of the NJC held on 2 May 2018 available (in Hungarian) at https:// orszagosbiroitanacs.hu/2018-05-02/.

[200]   Viktor Vadász, 'Crisis in the Hungarian judicial administration?', MTA Law Working Papers 2018/13, pp. 9–10 (English version). The English version of the article entitled 'Crisis in the Hungarian judicial administration?', with minor changes finalised on 12 July 2018, is available at https://birosag.hu/sites/default/files/users/2018.%20j%C3%BAlius_Crisis%20 in%20the%20Hungarian%20Judicial%20Administration%2012.07.2018%20vadaszv.pdf.

[201]   Available on the website of the Hungarian Association of Judges at https://mabie.hu/index. php/981-kozlemennyel-fordult-magyarorszag-biraihoz-az-orszagos-biroi-tanacs. Viktor Vadász, 'Crisis in the Hungarian judicial administration?', MTA Law Working Papers 2018/13, p. 10 (English version). The English version of the article entitled 'Crisis in the Hungarian judicial administration?', with minor changes finalised on 12 July 2018, is available at https://birosag. hu/sites/default/files/users/2018.%20j%C3%BAlius_Crisis%20in%20the%20Hungarian%20 Judicial%20Administration%2012.07.2018%20vadaszv.pdf.

Istvan Varga

As 'the main deficiency of the current system', Vadász identified the issue
'that the body of judicial self-governance that is meant to exercise supervision
over a political appointee endowed with strong powers does not have a legal
status and adequate powers that would give it equal weight' and suggested
that '[c]onsolidating the legal status of OBT would promote the more efficient
fulfilment of the constitutional role of "checks and balances" and thus secure the
independent, accountable and quality administration of justice all at once' and
formulated proposals *de lege ferenda*.[202]

Virág argues that Vadász has not supported his claim of a violation of judicial
independence when criticising the current model of court administration.[203]
Virág noted that the President of the NOJ may exercise his or her powers in
accordance with the Courts Administration Act, 'a piece of legislation with
constitutional force',[204] i.e. an act of Parliament adopted by a two-thirds majority.
Virág argues that 'it is not the legitimising decisions of a judicial council referred
to by the author that can justify the powers of the President of the NOJ', and that
'the appointment of judges by a judicial body would amount to the prohibited
self-legitimisation of judicial power'.[205] He also noted that, pursuant to the
Courts Administration Act, the Presidents of the NOJ and the Kúria assume no
political or legal liability towards the National Assembly.[206]

With respect to the exercise of the appointing powers of the President of
the NOJ, Virág submitted that well-founded conclusions can be drawn from
individual cases only via a correlation analysis based on a larger sample.[207] With
respect to the appointment of senior court officials (executives), Virág pointed
out that the President of the NOJ is responsible only for the appointment
of 15.8% of altogether 753 executives.[208]

With respect to the applications for vacant positions, Virág recalled the 2017
statistics (for judge positions, 274 invitations, 1,919 applications and 15 cases in
which the President of the NOJ declared the application procedure unsuccessful,
in four of which no applications were submitted), and also noted that in 2018 the

---

[202] Viktor Vadász, 'Crisis in the Hungarian judicial administration?', MTA Law Working
Papers 2018/13, p. 12 (English version). The English version of the article entitled 'Crisis
in the Hungarian judicial administration?', with minor changes finalised on 12 July 2018,
is available at https://birosag.hu/sites/default/files/users/2018.%20j%C3%BAlius_Crisis%20
in%20the%20Hungarian%20Judicial%20Administration%2012.07.2018%20vadaszv.pdf.

[203] Csaba Virág, 'Reflections on Viktor Vadász's paper entitled "Is There a Crisis in The
Administration of The Courts?"', MTA Law Working Papers 2018/17, https://birosag.hu/
sites/default/files/2019-01/reflections.pdf, p. 3.

[204] Ibid., pp. 3–4.

[205] Ibid., pp. 4–5.

[206] Ibid., pp. 5–6.

[207] Ibid., p. 6.

[208] Ibid., p. 6. As Virág summarised, 38 managers are appointed by the President of the Kúria,
48 by the presidents of the five regional courts of appeal, 548 by the presidents of the 20 high
courts, and 119 managers by the President of the NOJ (2017 data).

514

Intersentia

President of the NOJ did not deviate from the rankings suggested by the NJC (223 out of 251 calls for applications were successful).[209] Virág also summarised the statistics concerning executive positions (in 2017, 16 calls, eight appointments, five calls declared unsuccessful for lack of applications, two for lack of the opinion-giving body's support, and one because the President of the NOJ exercised a power of discretion provided for by law not to appoint the applicant; between 1 January and 31 October 2018, 35 invitations, five unsuccessful for lack of applications, two due to the revocation of the sole application, in nine no support of the majority of the opinion-giving body, and in five[210] the President of the NOJ decided not to appoint the applicant having received the majority support of the opinion-giving body on grounds of reasoned professional objections).[211] In view of these data, Virág claimed that the President of the NOJ accepted the position of the relevant opinion-giving body and the appointments were made in accordance with the rankings in 97% of cases, and deviated only in a small number of cases, submitting reasoned proposals to the NJC.[212] In the case of vacant manager positions, the ratio was 84.6% over the same period. Virág noted that the deviations concerned positions in the central region of Hungary, the judicial system's particularly important geographical area.[213]

In the context of judicial self-governance, Virág mentioned the 'protected legal status' of members of the NJC (the prohibition of administrative measures against them, independent disciplinary tribunal).[214]

In response to Vadász's arguments on the necessity of a self-legitimising and self-administrative model, Virág noted that '[i]n 2011, the legislator decided to set up a system in which the principle of personal responsibility prevails, a single person is entrusted with strong operative powers with regard to the central administration of the courts' to which the NJC merely contributes, 'instead of the previous model in which there had been a collegiate body responsible for the courts' central administration.'[215] In Virág's view, such a model would result in 'the judges' excessive power without any appropriate control institutions in a public law sense', and would lead to 'adverse selection' by peers.[216]

---

[209] Ibid., pp. 6–7.

[210] Two of these cases concerned the same position, the post of President of the High Court of Budapest.

[211] Csaba Virág, 'Reflections on Viktor Vadász's paper entitled "Is There a Crisis in The Administration of The Courts?"', MTA Law Working Papers 2018/17, available at https://birosag.hu/sites/default/files/2019-01/reflections.pdf, pp. 6–7.

[212] Ibid., p. 8.

[213] Ibid., p. 9.

[214] Ibid., p. 27.

[215] Ibid., p. 10.

[216] Ibid., pp. 10–11.

Istvan Varga

3. THE APPOINTMENT OF NATIONAL CANDIDATES TO POSITIONS AS INTERNATIONAL ADJUDICATORS

3.1. LACK OF DETAILED RULES

In Hungary, there are no detailed legal provisions or rules with respect to the designation of national candidates to positions as international adjudicators comparable to the above rules on the selection of domestic adjudicators.

3.2. SELECTION OF HUNGARIAN CANDIDATES FOR POSITIONS IN THE COURT OF JUSTICE OF THE EUROPEAN UNION

Relevant provisions are included in §70 of the Act XXXVI of 2012 on the National Assembly, which provides that Hungarian candidates for positions in institutions including the Court of Justice of the European Union and the General Court[217] are proposed to the institution having competence to decide on the appointment of candidates by the Hungarian government.[218] Prior to that, the government shall notify the National Assembly, which may hear the candidate before the government makes its proposal to the relevant institution.

Relevant information is also included in Resolution 10/2014 (II. 24.) OGY on certain provisions of the Rules of Procedure of the National Assembly (Parl. Res. 10/2014),[219] which specifies that the candidate may be heard by the committee of the National Assembly dealing with European Union matters,[220] i.e. the Committee on European Affairs[221] of the National Assembly. The latest candidate

---

[217] The Court of Justice has one judge from each EU country, whereas the General Court has two judges from each EU country. See https://european-union.europa.eu/institutions-law-budget/institutions-and-bodies/search-all-eu-institutions-and-bodies/court-justice-european-union-cjeu_en.

[218] Note: the same provision also lists the European Commission, the European Audit Office and the European Investment Bank.

[219] Available in English at https://www.parlament.hu/documents/125505/138409/Resolution+on+certain+provisions+of+the+Rules+of+Procedure/968f2e08-f740-4241-a87b-28e6dc390407.

[220] §141 of Parl. Res. 10/2014 ('If the Government makes a proposal for filling a position in the European Union as defined in the Act on the National Assembly, the committee dealing with European Union affairs and the standing committee competent with regard to the activity connected to the position in the European Union may hear the candidate').

[221] Information on the Committee on European Affairs is available on the website of the National Assembly at https://www.parlament.hu/web/house-of-the-national-assembly/greetings-of-the-chairman.

was heard in February 2021.[222] In light of the minutes, the Minister of Justice notified the Chair of the parliamentary Committee on European Affairs that the government was proposing the candidate as the Hungarian member of the Court of Justice of the European Union. The CV of the candidate was circulated among the members of the Committee before the hearing. In the course of the hearing, the candidate gave a presentation, followed by questions from the members of the Committee. As also noted during the session, the Committee itself makes no decision on the fitness of the candidate given that there is no legal relationship between the candidate and the Parliament.[223]

One member of the parliamentary Committee asked the candidate, among other things, about the question of the independence of judges, on which the candidate – who had been a judge in the General Court for five years – commented that judges must be independent from the Member State that has delegated him or her in the strictest sense.[224]

3.3. ENFORCEMENT OF A FINAL DECISION RENDERED BY A FOREIGN OR INTERNATIONAL ADJUDICATOR WHO BREACHED THE REQUIREMENT TO ACT INDEPENDENTLY AND IMPARTIALLY

Hungary being a Member State of the European Union, the recognition and enforcement of foreign judgments rendered in civil and commercial matters in other Member States of the European Union in Hungary is governed by Regulation (EU) No. 1215/2012 of the European Parliament and of the Council of 12 December 2012 on jurisdiction and the recognition and enforcement of judgments in civil and commercial matters (Brussels Ia Regulation).[225] Article 45(1)(a) of the Brussels Ia Regulation provides that '[o]n the application of any interested party, the recognition of a judgment shall be refused: (a) if such recognition is manifestly contrary to public policy (ordre public) in the Member State addressed'. Pursuant to Article 46, this is also a ground for the refusal of enforcement. Where the breach of the requirement of independence and impartiality by a foreign judge amounts to a breach of public policy, the recognition and enforcement of the judgment affected by such a breach in Hungary can be refused in view of these provisions.

---

[222] The minutes of the relevant session of said parliamentary committee are available on the website of the Hungarian National Assembly. Session no. EUB-1/2021. Minutes available in Hungarian at https://www.parlament.hu/documents/static/biz41/bizjkv41/EUB/2102151.pdf.

[223] Ibid., p 6.

[224] Ibid., pp 10–11.

[225] OJ L 351, 20.12.2012, p. 1–32.

Arbitral awards can only be challenged at the seat of arbitration. The recognition and enforcement of foreign arbitral awards in Hungary is governed by the 1958 New York Convention on the Recognition and Enforcement of Foreign Arbitral Awards. Relevant grounds for the refusal of recognition and enforcement are included in Article V(1)(d) (improper composition of the tribunal, including grounds for challenge) and Article V(2)(b) (violation of public policy).

4. CONCLUSION

In view of the foregoing, the selection and designation of judges is subject to a detailed legal framework, newly codified with effect as of 2011 in conjunction with the re-codification of the law of procedure in all areas. Over the past decade, the system has been subject to a number of amendments. The black-letter rules are quite detailed as regards the designation of domestic adjudicators, with certain solutions and practices having been subject to criticism and discourse, and some having been annulled by the Constitutional Court. At the same time, the appointment of national candidates for positions as international adjudicators is largely unregulated, with the exception of the Court of Justice of the European Union.

After the editorial finalisation of the present report, Parliament enacted Act X of 2023 on the Amendment of Certain Laws on Justice related to the Hungarian Recovery and Resilience Plan. This new law was mainly triggered by the above-described criticism relating to nomination practice and to the imbalance of power between the NOJ and NJC. The cornerstones of the new Act, which entered into force on 1 June 2023, embrace the following. The NJC is now vested with substantially greater powers in terms of controlling a series of NOJ decisions in the form of a right to consent, including nomination proceedings. In addition, the NJC has been accorded a right to consent with respect to a series of law-making initiatives of the Minister of Justice. Further, the Act repeals the possibility of nominating Constitutional Court judges as Kúria judges and also strengthens the professional preconditions for the election of the President of the Kúria. Lastly of relevance for this report are a series of new rules aiming at the thorough automation of the process of individual task allocation within the Kúria. All new provisions have however been introduced without a specific intertemporary regime, which means that the situation and personal setting, including nominations already effectuated as described in this report, remain valid and unaltered, and the new provisions will apply only to future nominations and other judicial organisational processes.

THE INDEPENDENCE AND IMPARTIALITY OF ADJUDICATORS IN ITALY

Marco Torsello

1. Introduction 520
2. Criteria for the Selection of Adjudicators 524
   2.1. Selection of Domestic Adjudicators............................ 525
        2.1.1. Judges 525
        2.1.2. Arbitrators 528
   2.2. Selection of National Candidates to Positions as International
        Adjudicators 531
3. The Authority Appointing Adjudicators 533
   3.1. The Appointment of Domestic Adjudicators 533
        3.1.1. Judges 533
        3.1.2. Arbitrators 534
   3.2. The Appointment of National Candidates to Positions
        as International Adjudicators 535
4. The Method for Appointing Adjudicators............................. 536
   4.1. The Appointment of Domestic Adjudicators 536
        4.1.1. Judges 536
        4.1.2. Arbitrators 536
   4.2. The Appointment of National Candidates to Positions
        as International Adjudicators 537
5. Methods to Balance the Appointing Authority's Influence
   on the Appointment of Adjudicators 538
   5.1. The Appointment of Domestic Adjudicators 538
        5.1.1. Judges 538
        5.1.2. Arbitrators 538
   5.2. The Appointment of National Candidates to Positions
        as International Adjudicators 540
6. Parameters to Ensure that Adjudicators Act Independently
   and Impartially 540
   6.1. Parameters for Domestic Adjudicators......................... 540
        6.1.1. Judges 540
        6.1.2. Arbitrators 543

Intersentia 519

Marco Torsello

6.2.	Parameters for Nationals Appointed to Positions as International Adjudicators	544
7.	Consequences for an Adjudicator of a Breach of the Requirement to Act Independently and Impartially	545
7.1.	Consequences for Domestic Adjudicators	545
7.1.1.	Judges	545
7.1.2.	Arbitrators	546
7.2.	Consequences for Nationals Appointed to Positions as International Adjudicators	548
8.	Enforcement by a Domestic Court of Decisions Rendered by an Adjudicator who Breached the Requirement to Act Independently and Impartially	549
8.1.	Enforcement of Decisions Rendered by Domestic Adjudicators	549
8.1.1.	Decisions Rendered by Judges	549
8.1.2.	Decisions Rendered by Arbitrators	550
8.2.	Enforcement of Decisions Rendered by International Adjudicators	552
9.	Final Remarks	552

1. INTRODUCTION

In most legal systems, commentators have extensively explored the independence and impartiality of domestic adjudicators. Italy is no exception.[1] However, legal literature is more sparse concerning the independence and impartiality of 'international' adjudicators.

---

[1] See, ex multis, S. Rodotà, 'Obiettivo 1 – Tutela dei diritti e imparzialità della magistratura – Giudici, diritti fondamentali, democrazia' (2003) *Questione Giustizia* 324; L. Ferrajoli, 'Obiettivo 1 – Tutela dei diritti e imparzialità della magistratura – Democrazia plebiscitaria e giurisdizione' (2003) *Questione Giustizia* 332; A. Pizzorusso, 'Obiettivo 1 – Tutela dei diritti e imparzialità della magistratura – Principio democratico e principio di legalità' (2003) *Questione Giustizia* 340; R. Romboli, 'In materia di diritto ad un giudice indipendente ed imparziale' (2004) IV *Foro italiano* 565; E. Bruti Liberati and D. Salas, 'Imparzialità e apparenza di imparzialità dei magistrati in Europa' (2006) *Questione Giustizia* 377; G. Oberto, 'Judicial independence and judicial impartiality: international basic principles and the case-law of the European Court of Human Rights' (2006) *Rivista di diritto privato* 485; G.U. Rescigno, 'Note sulla indipendenza della magistratura alla luce della Costituzione e delle controversie attuali' (2007) *Costituzionalismo.it*, https://www.costituzionalismo.it/wp-content/uploads/Costituzionalismo_242.pdf; V. Accattatis, 'Indipendenza, imparzialità, autonomia, neutralità' (2007) *Il Ponte* 40; R. Bin, 'Sull'imparzialità dei giudici costituzionali' (2009) *Giurisprudenza costituzionale* 4015; M. Patrono, 'L'indipendenza della magistratura in Europa: un quadro comparato' (2010) *Diritto pubblico comparato ed europeo* 1613; see also the various contributions collected in G. Ferri and A. Tedoldi, *La responsabilità civile dei magistrati*, ESI, Naples 2019; M. Chiavario, 'Indipendenza e responsabilità del magistrato: il contributo del Giuliani "interdisciplinare"' (2012) *Rivista di diritto processuale* 668;

Italy

The subject matter addressed in this report requires some preliminary clarifications and definitions to detail the precise scope of the study. The first notion that requires an explanation is that of an 'adjudicator'.[2] Unlike the definition of judge, judiciary or arbitrator, there seems to be no generally accepted definition of an adjudicator. This report will use the term adjudicator to refer to an institution, whether operating on a stable or temporary (ad hoc) basis, composed of one or more individuals and called upon to decide a dispute based on predetermined legal rules, according to predetermined procedures and through a decision that is binding on the parties to the dispute.

As it applies to purely domestic matters, the notion of an adjudicator shall include reference to domestic courts and the individual magistrates sitting in domestic courts; it shall also refer to arbitrators and arbitral tribunals. Conversely, the analysis will not include public prosecutors, although their recruitment in Italy occurs through the same national competition as other magistrates. The reason for excluding public prosecutors is that they are not called upon to 'adjudicate' (that is, decide) cases. Instead, in criminal and other selected proceedings, they are required to represent the public interest in an adversarial position against the accused.[3]

Moreover, the domestic notion of adjudicator used in this work will not include administrative agencies or governmental bodies, which may be called upon to make decisions and resolve disputes. The reason for this exclusion is that administrative agencies or governmental bodies do not operate in the same independent manner as courts and other adjudicators since they are usually entrusted with pursuing the ultimate goals of the governmental branch within which they operate.[4] Conversely, the domestic notion of adjudicator includes administrative courts and the judges sitting in those courts.[5] Administrative courts are often called upon to review the decisions of administrative agencies or

---

P. Ferrua, 'Indipendenza e imparzialità' (2020) *Legislazione penale* 8; A. Angeli, 'Il principio di indipendenza e imparzialità degli organi del potere giudiziario nelle recenti evoluzioni della giurisprudenza europea e polacca' (2021) *Federalismi* 1.

[2] For a paper addressing the issue of the forms and limits of adjudication, see L. Fuller, 'The Forms and Limits of Adjudication' (1978) 92 *Harvard Law Review* 353.

[3] For a study on the independence and impartiality of public prosecutors, see F. Donati, 'Indipendenza e responsabilità dei pubblici ministeri: principi europei e modello italiano' (2021) *Questione Giustizia* 54, 54–58; A. Rosanò, 'La chimera e il pubblico ministero: considerazioni relative alla giurisprudenza della Corte di giustizia dell'Unione europea e della Corte europea dei diritti dell'uomo in materia di indipendenza del pm' (2021) *Questione Giustizia* 74, 74–84.

[4] For further references, see M. Avvisati, 'Neutralità, imparzialità e azione amministrativa. Riflessioni su pubblica amministrazione e controllo di costituzionalità' (2020) *Federalismi* 15.

[5] On the independence and impartiality of administrative judges and courts, see P. Tanda, 'Profili istituzionali, processuali e comparatistici dell'indipendenza e dell'imparzialità del giudice amministrativo' (2020) *Giurisprudenza italiana* 697; A.L. Di Stefano, 'Il Consiglio di Stato e le perplessità sulla sua indipendenza' (2018) *Giustizia Amministrativa.it* 31; M. Vanini, 'L'indipendenza e l'imparzialità dei consiglieri di Stato' (2013) *Giustizia Amministrativa.it* 4.

governmental bodies. It is unquestioned that such revision does not constitute an appeal, thus confirming that the findings of administrative agencies or governmental bodies lack the characteristics of decisions rendered by an adjudicator, according to the notion of adjudication adopted here.

Compared to the domestic one, the notion of 'international' adjudication is less univocal. It is used to designate disparate methods for the settlement of international disputes. Relevant disputes include those between private parties, a private party and a state, and between states. Therefore, the notion of an international adjudicator refers to various and exceedingly diverse adjudicating bodies, including ad hoc arbitral tribunals, institutional arbitral tribunals, arbitral tribunals established by treaty, claim tribunals, international administrative tribunals, WTO panels, regional courts and permanent international courts.

From a public international law perspective, an adjudicating body of the kind considered here may be viewed as an 'international' one if it is constituted through an agreement between states or law-making procedures based on such an agreement (as in the case of decisions adopted within international intergovernmental organisations).

As far as commercial arbitration is concerned, the situation is more complex. In cross-border commercial disputes, the notion of internationality does not apply, stricto sensu, to the arbitral tribunal but instead to the dispute submitted to arbitration. The underlying transaction in dispute, not the tribunal, must be connected to more than one jurisdiction for the arbitration to be international.[6] When the parties in conflict have different nationalities or domiciles, it is common practice for the members of the arbitral tribunal (or at least the presiding arbitrator) to be of a nationality other than those of the parties. However, this rule is not mandatory, and the parties may derogate from it.[7] Moreover, irrespective of the nationality of its members, the arbitral tribunal and the arbitration proceedings are 'seated' in one specific state under whose legal system (and according to whose legal rules) the arbitral adjudication takes place. Therefore, rather than international, the arbitral tribunal and the arbitration proceedings may be either domestic or foreign, thus leading to what has been referred to as a 'national international commercial arbitration'.[8] This report will take both types (domestic and foreign arbitral tribunals) into account, provided that the interest in the activity of domestic arbitral tribunals is greater (although not exclusive) when they are in charge of deciding an international dispute.

Furthermore, this report investigates the 'independence' and 'impartiality' of international adjudicators. Independence and impartiality are often used as

---

[6] Cf. G. Cordero-Moss, *International Commercial Contracts*, Cambridge University Press, Cambridge 2014, pp. 3–5.

[7] Accordingly, M. Benedettelli, *International Arbitration in Italy*, Kluwer Law International, Alphen aan den Rijn 2020, p. 182.

[8] For a similar statement, see F. Ferrari, 'National International Commercial Arbitration' (2022) 32 *American Review of International Arbitration* 439.

hendiadys, and this survey will mainly use them as such. A distinction, however, is possible and not infrequent.[9] 'Independence' refers to the absence of objective personal or financial connections between the adjudicating subject and those affected by the decision. 'Impartiality' refers to the subjective mindset of the adjudicator, which may be affected by a situation of lack of independence, but may also be biased for other personal reasons. Therefore, adjudicators may lack impartiality even if they are objectively independent, as in the event of an adjudicator who, despite not having any objective connection, is biased against a party merely due to the party's race, gender, origin, age, etc. On the other hand, adjudicators may be impartial (and thus capable of rendering an unbiased decision), notwithstanding the lack of independence. The latter situation could lead one to reduce the relevance of the independence requirement. However, it is a universally accepted principle that adjudicators must not only *be* unbiased, they must also *appear* neutral and unbiased, as often stated by the European Court of Human Rights (ECtHR).[10] Therefore, both the impartiality and the independence of adjudicators must be regarded as essential.

The most relevant legislative reference to the independence and impartiality of adjudicators in the Italian legal system is laid out in Article 111(2) of the Italian Constitution, which states, in the relevant part, that 'any proceedings … take place before a judge, third and impartial'.[11] This provision, affirming the fundamental status of the right to a fair trial, is often read in conjunction with Article 6 of the European Convention on Human Rights (ECHR).

As a prerequisite of impartiality, the adjudicator's (appearance of) independence is a right of every person who may be subject to the binding decision of the adjudicator. At the same time, the adjudicator's independence is a prerogative of the judge as an individual and the judiciary as a whole.[12]

As emphasised by the Consultative Council of European Judges (CCJE), a consultative body of the Council of Europe:

> Judicial independence is a pre-requisite to the rule of law and a fundamental guarantee of a fair trial. Judges are 'charged with the ultimate decision over life, freedoms, rights, duties and property of citizens' (recital to UN basic principles,

---

[9]   See e.g. W.W. Park, 'Arbitrator Integrity: The Transient and the Permanent' (2009) 46 *San Diego Law Review* 635.

[10]   Cf. L. Seminara, 'L'indépendance des magistrats dans la Convention Européenne des droits de l'homme: conjugaison d'apparences et d'éléments substantiels' (2016) *Rivista della cooperazione giuridica internazionale* 99.

[11]   Article 111(2) of the Italian Constitution: 'ogni processo si svolge nel contraddittorio tra le parti, in condizioni di parità, davanti a giudice terzo e imparziale. La legge ne assicura la ragionevole durata'.

[12]   M.G. Civinini, 'Indipendenza e imparzialità dei magistrati' (2019, Special Issue) *Questione Giustizia*, https://www.questionegiustizia.it/speciale/articolo/indipendenza-e-imparzialita-dei-magistrati_67.php#:~:text=1%20(2001)%20sull'indipendenza,e%20libera%20da%20 influenze%20esterne.

Intersentia

echoed in Beijing declaration; and Articles 5 and 6 of the European Convention on Human Rights). Their independence is not a prerogative or privilege in their own interests, but in the interests of the rule of law and of those seeking and expecting justice. … Judicial independence presupposes total impartiality on the part of judges. When adjudicating between any parties, judges must be impartial, that is free from any connection, inclination or bias, which affects – or may be seen as affecting – their ability to adjudicate independently. In this regard, judicial independence is an elaboration of the fundamental principle that 'no man may be judge in his own cause'. This principle also has significance well beyond that affecting the particular parties to any dispute. Not merely the parties to any particular dispute, but society as a whole must be able to trust the judiciary. A judge must thus not merely be free in fact from any inappropriate connection, bias or influence, he or she must also appear to a reasonable observer to be free therefrom. Otherwise, confidence in the independence of the judiciary may be undermined.[13]

Based on the questionnaire prepared by Professor Giuditta Cordero-Moss, the general rapporteur on 'Independence and Impartiality of International Adjudicators' for the 21st Congress of the International Academy of Comparative Law,[14] this report provides an overview of the topic from the perspective of Italian law.

In the forthcoming sections, the report will consider various prerequisites, operative rules, monitoring and implementing tools, and enforcement mechanisms concerning the principle of independence and impartiality of adjudicators. Each different aspect will be analysed by presenting the Italian law concerning international adjudicators or mechanisms for selection, appointment and removal of domestic candidates for positions as international adjudicators. However, with a view to complementing the presentation with the parallel rules concerning domestic adjudicators, each topic will first be addressed by presenting the current state of the law concerning domestic adjudicators, making a distinction between domestic courts (and judges) and arbitral tribunals (and arbitrators) seated in Italy.

2. CRITERIA FOR THE SELECTION OF ADJUDICATORS

Determining the criteria for selecting adjudicators is critical to assessing a legal system's approach to implementing the principle of adjudicators' independence and impartiality.

---

[13] CCJE, 'Opinion No. 1 (2001)' of 23 November 2001 for the attention of the Committee of Ministers of the Council of Europe on 'Standards concerning the independence of the judiciary and the irremovability of judges (Recommendation No R(94) 12 on the independence, efficiency and role of judges and the relevance of its standards and any other international standards to current problems in these fields)', https://rm.coe.int/1680747830.

[14] Held in Asunción, Paraguay, on 23–28 October 2022.

2.1. SELECTION OF DOMESTIC ADJUDICATORS

First, the question will be addressed by considering domestic adjudicators, including judges and arbitrators.

2.1.1. Judges

Under Article 104 of the Italian Constitution, the judiciary constitutes an autonomous order independent of any other power. The independence and autonomy under consideration have mainly been interpreted as concerning the relations between the judiciary and the government. However, they must also be understood as the absence of any external conditioning. Moreover, independence must be understood both as internal and as external and intended to protect the function performed, as well as the structure of the judicial power.

The judiciary's independence is primarily ensured by the existence of the High Council of the Judiciary (Consiglio Superiore della Magistratura, CSM),[15] a body of self-government of the judiciary in charge of all matters concerning the careers of its members (promotions, disciplinary proceedings, etc.).[16] Moreover, the CSM is called upon to safeguard the judiciary's independence from other powers. The head of state, who is also the head of the CSM, is called upon to regulate these relations. Article 1(1) of Law No. 195/1958 governs the composition of the CSM. It provides that it is presided over by the head of state and composed of the Justice in Chief of the Court of Cassation, the Attorney-General of the Court of Cassation, 16 judges elected from different judicial offices, and eight members elected by the Parliament with a qualified majority from among Italian universities' law professors and lawyers with at least 15 years of experience. Therefore, the majority of the members of the CSM are judges.

In discussing the issue of the criteria for the 'selection' of domestic adjudicators, it is worth distinguishing between the selection requirements applied at the stage of recruitment of new members to the judiciary and those utilised to allocate cases to the different judges or panels within a single court.[17]

The criteria adopted at the two stages share the same underlying goal: they aim to ensure the maximum possible degree of independence and impartiality

---

[15] For a recent overview of the discussion about the reform of the CSM, see T.F. Giupponi, 'Il Consiglio superiore della magistratura e le prospettive di riforma' (2021) *Quaderni Costituzionali* 45.

[16] See G. Grasso, 'Trasparenza e semplificazione nelle delibere del Consiglio superiore della magistratura' (2015) *Foro italiano* 47; for a comparative perspective, see S. Franzoni, 'I Consigli di giustizia in Europa e "il CSM che si vorrebbe": da modello a involuzione?' (2014) *Lo Stato* 225.

[17] See M. Fresa, 'Il sistema di progressione in carriera e la valutazione della professionalità dei magistrati tra il vecchio ed il nuovo ordinamento giudiziario' (2006) *Diritto e formazione* 122, 122 ff. and 274 ff.

of the selected judges. However, the same underlying goal is pursued through different rules due to the different contexts in which the rules operate.

Under Article 106(1) of the Italian Constitution and Articles 1 et seq. of Legislative Decree (D.Lgs.) No. 160/2006, the selection of new judges and their admission to the judiciary takes place through a public competition open to Italian citizens holding a law degree, based on written and oral examinations. Candidates must meet other alternative requirements that ensure their competence. Such requirements consist of having completed an 18-month traineeship in a judicial office, attended a post-graduate specialisation school, obtained a PhD in law, or been admitted to practice law in Italy.

The recruitment of administrative judges also occurs through a similar selective competition. However, candidates must meet specific requirements, partly different from those of ordinary judges, and based on previous professional experience as public servants or experienced lawyers (Article 14 of Law 6 December 1971, No. 1034 and Article 16 of Law 27 April 1982, No. 186 (Administrative Judiciary Act)).

There are some exceptions to the recruitment of judges by competition. The first exception concerns the jurors sitting in court as members of the jury. Another exception concerns honorary magistrates, who exercise judicial functions part-time. Honorary judges are assigned to cases of lower value or limited complexity. Moreover, they are selected based on their previous professional experience, a mechanism that may lead to the lack of (appearance of) independence and impartiality. For this reason, Article 5 of D.Lgs. 13 July 2017, No. 116 provides a detailed list of situations of conflict of interest preventing the taking of office as an honorary judge.[18] The third exception is provided for by Article 106(3) of the Italian Constitution, as implemented by Law 5 August 1998, No. 303. Accordingly, the CSM may appoint justices to the Court of Cassation for 'distinguished merits', law professors employed in Italian universities, and lawyers with long and qualified experience.

Upon taking over their position, all judges must take an oath, which includes the commitment to act independently and impartially. The language of the oath for ordinary judges is still a matter of somewhat surprising debate. Article 9 of the Royal Decree (R.D.) of 30 January 1941, No. 12 on the judicial system required a commitment referring to the judge's acting 'faithfully to the Emperor King'.[19] Following the advent of the Republic, the formula was replaced by Article 4 of Law No. 478/1946, under which judges were required to swear

---

[18] On the independence and impartiality of justices of the peace, see A. La Mendola and N. Morrone, 'Giudice di pace: imparzialità e indipendenza nell'esercizio delle funzioni giurisdizionali' (2012) *Il Giudice di Pace* 262.

[19] 'I magistrati prestano giuramento col rito prescritto dal regolamento e con la formula seguente: "Giuro di essere fedele al Re Imperatore, di osservare lealmente lo Statuto e le altre leggi dello Stato e di adempiere coscienziosamente i miei doveri di magistrato"'.

their faithfulness to the Italian Republic and its head of state.[20] However, it is apparent that even the judge's commitment to the head of state is at odds with the requirement of complete independence and impartiality of the judiciary. It is also in contrast with Article 101 of the Italian Constitution, under which: 'Justice is administered in the name of the people. Judges are subject only to the law'. Moreover, a rather improper legislative intervention aimed at reducing and rationalising the Italian legislative system abolished (rather than amending) the entire Article 4 of Law No. 478/1946, thus formally making the old oath referring to the King applicable again, a result that, in substance, is clearly incompatible with the Italian Constitution. However, the improper intervention has created a vacuum regarding the current formula of the judges' oath.

As for the courts' jurors, their oath upon taking office appears to be more in line with the general principles of independence and impartiality of adjudicators and the approach adopted in most jurisdictions. Under Article 30 of Law 10 April 1951, No. 287 (last replaced by Article 37 of Presidential Decree 22 September 1988, No. 449), upon taking office, jurors must take an oath according to the following formula, which includes separate references to the objective independence and the subjective impartiality of the jurors:

> With the firm will to fulfil as a person of honour all my duties, conscious of the supreme moral and civil importance of the office that the law entrusts to me, I swear to listen diligently and to examine with serenity evidence and reasons of the prosecution and defence, to form my inner conviction judging with rectitude and impartiality, and to keep away from my soul any feeling of aversion and favour, so that the judgment will succeed as society should expect it: affirmation of truth and justice. I also swear to maintain secrecy.[21]

In light of the foregoing, it seems correct to posit that to ensure the independence and impartiality of domestic judges and jurors the Italian legal system relies primarily, if not exclusively, on the existence of the general duty to abide by the principle of independence and impartiality, and on the taking of the corresponding oath. Conversely, at no stage are judges and jurors subject to a duty to disclose circumstances that may affect their independence and impartiality. Of course, this observation is not meant to suggest that judges and

---

[20]   'Giuro di essere fedele alla Repubblica italiana e al suo Capo, di osservare lealmente le leggi dello Stato e di adempiere con coscienza i doveri inerenti al mio ufficio'.

[21]   'Con la ferma volontà di compiere da persona d'onore tutto il mio dovere, cosciente della suprema importanza morale e civile dell'ufficio che la legge mi affida, giuro di ascoltare con diligenza e di esaminare con serenità prove e ragioni dell'accusa e della difesa, di formare il mio intimo convincimento giudicando con rettitudine ed imparzialità, e di tenere lontano dall'animo mio ogni sentimento di avversione e di favore, affinché la sentenza riesca quale la società deve attenderla: affermazione di verità e di giustizia. Giuro altresì di conservare il segreto'.

Intersentia

Marco Torsello

jurors are not required to abstain in case of a conflict of interest. Indeed, they certainly are. However, the duty to abstain is not coupled with a duty to disclose circumstances that might be suspicious in the eyes of the parties.

The allocation of cases to judges within a court is intended to ensure compliance with the right to a 'natural judge', which is enshrined in Article 25 of the Italian Constitution.[22] The principle requires that specific criteria are predetermined based on which cases filed with a court are assigned among the judges in that court. For the ordinary judiciary, this principle has been implemented through the tabular system, which establishes objective, predetermined and non-discretionary criteria for forming panels and allocating cases to chambers and individual judges (Articles 7-*bis* and 7-*ter*, R.D. No. 12/1941 (Judiciary Act)).[23]

2.1.2. Arbitrators

The criteria for selection are remarkably different when the adjudication is assigned to arbitrators. When arbitration proceedings are seated in Italy, the criteria for selecting the arbitrators result from a combination of the parties' consent and the need to ensure the level of neutrality that characterises the judiciary. As a means of resolution of disputes essentially based on the parties' will, arbitration cannot operate in the absence of a manifestation of consent by the parties. However, starting from a landmark decision rendered by the Italian Constitutional Court on 28 November 2001,[24] it is now unquestioned that:

> arbitration constitutes a procedure provided for and regulated by the Code of Civil Procedure for the objective application of the law in the concrete case, for the purpose of resolving a dispute, with the guarantees of due process and impartiality typical of ordinary civil jurisdiction.[25]

---

[22]   Cf. A. Pizzorusso, 'Giudice naturale' in *Enciclopedia giuridica Treccani*, vol. XV, Istituto della Enciclopedia italiana, Rome 1989, pp. 3 ff.; M. Bove, 'Responsabilità civile dei magistrati: individuazione del giudice naturale e struttura del diritto risarcitorio da illecito giudiziario' (2018) *Giurisprudenza italiana* 2129.

[23]   Cf. A. Nicolì, 'Precostituzione del giudice e nuova circolare sulle tabelle degli uffici giudicanti' (2018) *Giustiziacivile.com* 16.

[24]   See C. Cost., 28.11.2001, No. 376, concerning the entitlement of an arbitral tribunal to raise a constitutional issue before the Constitutional Court. For a comment on the decision, see G. Ruffini, 'Arbitri, diritto e costituzione (riflessioni a margine della sentenza della Corte Costituzionale, 28 novembre 2001, n. 376)' (2002) *Rivista trimestrale di diritto e procedura civile* 263, 263–79.

[25]   '[L]'arbitrato costituisce un procedimento previsto e disciplinato dal codice di procedura civile per l'applicazione obiettiva del diritto nel caso concreto, ai fini della risoluzione di una controversia, con le garanzie di contraddittorio e di imparzialità tipiche della giurisdizione civile ordinaria. ... il giudizio arbitrale non si differenzia da quello che si svolge davanti agli organi statali della giurisdizione'.

Italy

The position held by the Constitutional Court in 2001[26] was a dramatic change compared to previous decisions.[27] Before that, the Constitutional Court had embraced the assumption that Article 102 of the Constitution, in combination with Articles 24 and 25, granted a monopoly to the judiciary in the exercise of the judicial power.[28] The new approach, which allocates a considerable share of the judicial power to private arbitrators, is remarkable. Scholars have suggested that it should be considered in conjunction with the contemporary legislative change brought about by Article 4 of Constitutional Law 18 October 2001, No. 3, which amended Article 118 of the Italian Constitution, thus assigning administrative functions based on the principle of (horizontal) subsidiarity, i.e. as a rule to the municipality as the body closest to the citizens and, therefore, better able to pursue their interests. It has been held[29] that the constitutional opening to a broader role for private actors vis-à-vis public interventionism has also impacted the allocation of jurisdictional powers, paving the way for a 'jurisdiction without state'.[30] From this perspective, the authoritative jurisdictional intervention becomes an extrema ratio available to litigants when alternative solutions do not seem to achieve the goal. Therefore, the subsidiarity of jurisdiction implies favouring the parties' access to a series of alternative solutions to the ordinary judicial resolution of disputes: from mediation and conciliation[31] to arbitration.

The new constitutional paradigm has impacted the most recent reforms of the Italian rules on arbitration, including the rules on the selection of arbitrators. Reference is made here not only to the reform introduced by D.Lgs. 2 February 2006, No. 40, but also to the recent reform of Italian civil procedure that came into

---

[26]   The change of approach was soon embraced also by the Italian Court of Cassation: see Cass., 25.10.2013, No. 24153, stating that 'anche gli arbitri esercitano una funzione giurisdizionale', thus overruling the contractual approach upheld in its decision of Cass., 03.08.2000, No. 527.

[27]   See, in particular, the following decisions that the Italian Constitutional Court rendered prior to 2001: C. Cost., 12.02.1963, No. 2, holding that: 'manca all'arbitro il potere di produrre atti sostanzialmente identici a quelli promananti dalla potestà del giudice'; C. Cost., 26.05.1966, No. 50, holding that: 'i poteri demandati al collegio di conciliazione ed arbitrato non hanno affatto natura decisoria, e vien meno perciò la premessa che darebbe luogo al problema di una eventuale violazione dell'art. 102 della Costituzione'; C. Cost., 04.07.1977, No. 127, holding that a mandatory arbitration was void 'nella parte in cui non riconosce la facoltà dell'inventore e del datore di lavoro di adire l'a.g.o.'

[28]   This position, opposing arbitration, dates back to the enactment of the Italian Code of Civil Procedure of 1940 and to the position expressed by the then Minister of Justice, Grandi, who regarded arbitration as causing harm to the unitary jurisdiction of the state ('una menomazione e corrosione dell'unità di giurisdizione dello Stato'): Minutes of the Legislative Assembly, 18 January 1940, no. 57.

[29]   For this position, see T.E. Frosini, 'Un nuovo paradigma di giustizia: le *Alternative Dispute Resolution*' (2011) *Analisi giuridica dell'economia* 1.

[30]   The expression 'giurisdizione senza Stato' is used by C. Punzi, 'Le nuove frontiere dell'arbitrato' (2015) *Rivista di diritto processuale* 14.

[31]   In recent years several legislative interventions in Italy have incentivised resort to mediation. See D.Lgs. 4 March 2010, No. 28.

force on 28 February 2023, which is based on the guiding principles outlined in Law 26 November 2021, No. 206, as implemented by D.Lgs. 10 October 2022, No. 149.

The Italian reform of arbitration adopted in 2006[32] introduced some innovations and clarifications regarding the selection of arbitrators. As a general rule, parties enjoy broad freedom concerning the number, qualities and names of arbitrators, their rights and duties, relevant remedies, and the procedures for their appointment, replacement, and removal.[33] The only limits to party autonomy stem from specific requirements that arbitrators must fulfil in consideration of the judicial function they are called upon to perform.[34] In particular, there must be an odd number of arbitrators.[35] The constitution of the arbitral tribunal must conform to the principle of parties' equality. All subjects who are bound by the disputed legal relationship must be granted the opportunity to participate in the arbitral proceedings.[36]

Article 810 of the Italian Code of Civil Procedure (CCP) governs the appointment of the arbitrators. It provides for suppletive (i.e. non-mandatory) rules on the process for the selection by the parties.[37] It also provides for the judicial appointment of arbitrators in the event of inertia of one party or failure to reach an agreement on the appointment of the third arbitrator. Moreover, under Article 832 CCP, one or more members of the arbitral tribunal can be appointed by an arbitral institution when the arbitration agreement submits the dispute to the institution's arbitration rules or when it grants the institution the role as appointing authority in an ad hoc arbitration. Combined with the rules on the recusal of arbitrators (Article 815 CCP),[38] these rules provide a balanced solution between the need to ensure the consensual basis of arbitration and to enforce the constitutional requirements applicable to the jurisdictional function assigned to arbitrators.

The attention to balancing the autonomy of the parties and the need to ensure the independence of the arbitrators is particularly apparent in the legislative reform of Italian company law adopted in 2003.[39] The 2003 reform introduced

---

[32] D.Lgs. 2 February 2006, No. 40.

[33] See F. Benatti, 'La "figura" dell'arbitro' in D. Mantucci (ed.), *Trattato di diritto dell'arbitrato*, vol. III, *Il tribunale arbitrale*, ESI, Naples 2021, p. 1.

[34] E. Zucconi Galli Fonseca, 'Il numero degli arbitri. Il principio di equidistanza del Tribunale arbitrale. La nomina in caso di pluralità di parti' in D. Mantucci (ed.), *Trattato di diritto dell'arbitrato*, vol. III, *Il tribunale arbitrale*, ESI, Naples 2021, p. 99.

[35] See Article 809(1) CCP.

[36] M. Benedettelli, *International Arbitration in Italy*, Kluwer Law International, Alphen aan den Rijn 2020, p. 182.

[37] S. Maroni, 'La nomina giudiziale dell'arbitro: tra "libertà" e vincoli' (2017) *Corriere giuridico* 1245; for an overview of the rules applicable in public procurement contracts, see e.g. F. Tizi, 'La costituzione del tribunale arbitrale nel recente Codice dei contratti pubblici' (2016) *Rivista dell'arbitrato* 375.

[38] On arbitrators' recusal and liability, see, ex multis, F. Carpi, 'L'indipendenza e la imparzialità dell'arbitro. La sua responsabilità' (2018) *Rivista trimestrale di diritto e procedura civile* 239.

[39] D.Lgs. No. 5/2003.

special arbitration proceedings in the field of company law.[40] This choice has been confirmed by the most recent reform of Italian arbitration law, introduced by D.Lgs 10 October 2022, No. 149, which incorporated into the Italian Code of Civil Procedure the 2003 rules on company law arbitration. Under the new Article 838-*bis* (which reproduces the text of Article 34 of D.Lgs. No. 5/2003), companies may refer disputes to arbitration, provided that listed companies, making use of the risk capital market, cannot. However, the arbitration clause must provide for the number and manner of appointment of the arbitrators, which, in all cases, confers the power of appointment on a third party unrelated to the company.[41] In the event of failure to identify an appointing authority, the law entrusts the president of the court of first instance for the place where the company has its registered office with the relevant power.

2.2. SELECTION OF NATIONAL CANDIDATES TO POSITIONS AS INTERNATIONAL ADJUDICATORS

Identifying the criteria for the selection of national candidates for positions as international adjudicators is more challenging. The notion of international adjudicators used here is rather broad.[42] It is not confined to international courts in a strict sense, namely international adjudicating bodies in charge of the resolution of international disputes between states, or between states and international organisations (the most notable examples of such international adjudicators in a strict sense being the International Court of Justice, the International Tribunal for the Law of the Sea, and the WTO Appellate Body). The notion adopted here encompasses a broader range of courts, including those entitled to hear cases filed by or against individuals and private entities (such as the ECtHR, international criminal courts and tribunals), as well as regional-integration courts, such as the Court of Justice of the European Union (CJEU).[43]

---

[40]   Cf. S. Cerrato, 'Il ruolo dell'autonomia privata nell'arbitrato societario' (2016) *Rivista trimestrale di diritto e procedura civile* 223; D. Corapi, 'Appunti in tema di arbitrato societario' (2015) *Rivista di diritto commerciale e diritto generale delle obbligazioni* 1; E. Dalmotto, 'Profili processuali dell'arbitrato societario in Italia' (2014) *Giurisprudenza italiana* 1528 1528–34; P. Montalenti, 'L'arbitrato societario: appunti' (2013) *Rivista trimestrale di diritto e procedura civile* 1275; A. Fusaro, 'La clausola compromissoria negli statuti societari. L'elaborazione giurisprudenziale' (2013) *Rivista di diritto privato* 81; N. Soldati, 'L'arbitrato societario alla luce della riforma' (2007) *Contratti* 825; E. Zucconi Galli Fonseca, 'L'arbitrato societario nell'applicazione della giurisprudenza' (2007) *Giurisprudenza commerciale* 935.

[41]   '[P]revedere il numero e le modalità di nomina degli arbitri conferendo, in ogni caso, a pena di nullità il potere di nomina ad un soggetto estraneo alla società'.

[42]   See supra, section 1.

[43]   For a similar definition, see T.R. Treves, 'Corti e tribunali internazionali' in *Enciclopedia Treccani*, Istituto della Enciclopedia italiana, Rome 2013.

Notwithstanding the variety of different international courts and tribunals considered, it is challenging to identify transparent, predetermined criteria for selecting national candidates to positions as members of the said courts or tribunals. It is widely acknowledged that in the international legal order, the judicial function is carried out in a fragmented manner, using an assortment of forms and methods that are neither correlated nor coordinated.[44] The absence of a central apparatus comparable to that of the state means that there is no organised and hierarchically structured system of courts of justice of the kind known in domestic legal systems. Instead, the adjudication of disputes is entrusted from time to time to ad hoc arbitrators or international judges operating in entirely separate and autonomous spheres.

Moreover, the judicial function is exercised sporadically since only agreements between states can confer jurisdiction, and the enforcement of decisions must rely on spontaneous compliance or cooperation.

In light of the foregoing, it cannot come as a surprise that the appointment of judges to positions as members of international adjudicators is often highly politicised. States that support a candidate engage in actual campaigning in which bargaining and deals are not infrequent. Competence and independence are not necessarily at the core of the process of selection.

Re-election is often permitted (this is the case, for instance, at the International Court of Justice and the International Tribunal for the Law of the Sea, but it has been banned at the International Criminal Court),[45] and relatively frequent in practice. This per se creates a potential conflict of interest, considering that the re-election depends on the state(s) from which the candidate for re-election seeks a vote.

The overall model seems to be primarily influenced by the need to ensure the representation of states. A significant indication of this approach is the principle followed by the International Court of Justice and the International Tribunal for the Law of the Sea, according to which, where no judge is sitting in the court having the nationality of one of the parties to the dispute, that party may designate an ad hoc judge. Similarly, in human rights courts,[46] the presence in the panel of a judge of the nationality of the state against which the claim is filed is always ensured. Conversely, this principle is not accepted by the WTO Appellate Body.

The selection of national candidates to positions as international adjudicators is made by the government (usually the Minister of Foreign Affairs) using an opaque process. A recent survey of a reputable NGO focused on the nomination

---

[44]   M. Pedrazzi, 'Corti internazionali' in *Enciclopedia Treccani, scienza sociali*, Supplemento I, Istituto della Enciclopedia italiana, Rome 2001.

[45]   Cf. P. Bargiacchi, 'La Corte penale internazionale: singolarità giuridiche e ostilità politiche' (2020) *Rivista della cooperazione giuridica internazionale* 48; I. Piccolo, 'Giustizia penale internazionale' (2016) *Diritti dell'uomo* 11.

[46]   Cf. F. Pocar, 'Diritti umani: la difficile ricerca di equilibrio tra le giurisdizioni delle Corti internazionali' (2011) *Guida al diritto* 9.

Italy

of candidates to the International Criminal Court[47] reported that individuals familiar with the Italian nomination process described it as 'lacking transparency'. There is no legal framework that guides the process nor an established, transparent procedure. In the large majority of cases, there is no public call for applications, candidates are not interviewed and their competencies are not assessed. The government approaches a small circle of people, and the general public is not informed of the nomination process or the candidates. Most judges do not even know about the possibility of an appointment to international adjudicators, much less that Italy seeks to appoint judges.

3. THE AUTHORITY APPOINTING ADJUDICATORS

Not only the selection criteria but also the identity of the appointing authority are critical for assessing the effective implementation of the principle of independence and impartiality.

3.1. THE APPOINTMENT OF DOMESTIC ADJUDICATORS

3.1.1. Judges

As far as domestic judges are concerned, the public competition to enter the ordinary judiciary is organised by the Ministry of Justice. However, the procedure is run under the supervision of the CSM.

The examining committee, appointed by a decree of the Ministry ratifying a prior decision by the CSM, is presided over by a senior judge and composed of 20 magistrates, five university professors and three lawyers admitted to practice before the high courts.[48] Under the relevant legislation,[49] magistrates, university professors and lawyers who, in the previous 10 years, have been teaching in schools preparing for the national recruitment competition cannot be members of the committee.

Once the exams are completed, the committee forms the ranking list, and the winners are appointed to the judiciary by a decree of the Ministry.[50]

A similar procedure applies to the competition to become an administrative judge. Under the Administrative Judiciary Act,[51] the Prime Minister appoints commissioners from among administrative judges and university professors.

---

[47] Open Society Justice Initiative (ed.), 'Raising the Bar. Improving the nomination and election of judges to the International Criminal Court' (2019), https://www.justiceinitiative.org/uploads/a43771ed-8c93-424f-ac83-b0317feb23b7/raising-the-bar-20191112.pdf.

[48] D. Ferranti, 'La formazione professionale dei magistrati: il Consiglio Superiore della Magistratura' (2002) *Diritto e formazione* 1301.

[49] Article 5 D.Lgs. No. 160/2006.

[50] Article 8 D.Lgs. No. 160/2006.

[51] Article 16 Law No. 186/1982.

Intersentia

533

Marco Torsello

Within judicial offices, the allocation of cases to chambers is done by the court's president, while under the Judiciary Act,[52] the allocation of cases to panels or to single judges is up to the president of each chamber. The CSM appoints the presidents of the court.

3.1.2. Arbitrators

As far as the appointment of arbitrators is concerned, parties generally appoint them following the rules established in the arbitration agreement.[53]

The parties are free to grant the power to appoint arbitrators to third parties of their choice. When the arbitration agreement makes the arbitration subject to institutional rules[54] or when, in the context of an ad hoc arbitration, the parties grant the power to appoint arbitrators to an appointing authority, one or more members of the arbitral tribunal are designated by such an appointing authority.

According to Article 832(4) CCP, professional or business associations cannot act as appointing authorities in disputes where their associates (or other subjects belonging to the relevant business sector) are in opposition to third parties.[55]

Under Article 810 CCP, when parties (or persons designated by the parties) fail to appoint an arbitrator, any interested party may obtain the appointment from the president of the court of first instance for the seat of arbitration or, when the seat is abroad, from the president of the court of first instance of Rome.[56] The president's order can be appealed according to Articles 739 and 742-*bis* CCP before the competent court of appeal.

The recent reform of Italian civil procedure implemented by D.Lgs. No. 149/2022 introduced a remarkable innovation to the text of Article 810 CCP. When in charge of appointing an arbitrator, the president of the court of first instance must comply with criteria 'that ensure transparency, rotation, and efficiency'. Moreover, to that end, a notice of the appointment is published on the judicial office's website.

---

[52] Article 7-*ter* R.D. No. 12/1941.

[53] E. Zucconi Galli Fonseca, *Diritto dell'arbitrato*, Bononia Univeristy Press, Bologna 2021, pp. 66 ff.

[54] For Italian scholarly writing devoted to institutional arbitration see, ex multis, V. Vigoriti, 'L'arbitrato amministrato' (2013) *Contratto e impresa* 364; S. Azzali, 'Arbitrato amministrato e arbitrato *ad hoc*' in G. Iudica (ed.), *Appunti di Diritto dell'Arbitrato*, Giappichelli, Turin 2012, pp. 101 ff.; C. Punzi, 'Brevi note in tema di arbitrato amministrato' (2009) *Rivista trimestrale di diritto e procedura civile* 1325; E. Zucconi Galli Fonseca, 'La nuova disciplina dell'arbitrato amministrato' (2008) *Rivista trimestrale di diritto e procedura civile* 993; R. Sali, 'Arbitrato amministrato', *Digesto delle discipline privatistiche. Sezione civile*, Aggiornamento ***, UTET, Turin 2007, pp. 67–77; E.F. Ricci, 'Note sull'arbitrato amministrato' (2001) *Rivista di diritto processuale* 1.

[55] See e.g. G. Canale, 'Estraneità e neutralità nell'arbitrato' (2020) *Rivista dell'arbitrato* 31.

[56] For a comment on this provision, see e.g. A. Briguglio, 'Art. 810' in A. Briguglio, E. Fazzalari and R. Marengo (eds), *La nuova disciplina dell'arbitrato*, Giuffrè, Milan 1994, p. 35.

An exception to the parties' power to appoint arbitrators is set forth by Article 838-*bis* CCP (which reproduces the text of Article 34 of D.Lgs. No. 5/2003), regulating corporate disputes submitted to arbitration.[57] An arbitration clause contained in the deed of incorporation of a company incorporated under Italian law, providing for the submission of corporate disputes to arbitration, must grant the power to appoint all the members of the arbitral tribunal to a subject who is independent of the relevant company on penalty of nullity.

3.2. THE APPOINTMENT OF NATIONAL CANDIDATES TO POSITIONS AS INTERNATIONAL ADJUDICATORS

The appointment of candidates to positions as international adjudicators is usually a two-step process, including a domestic phase where the national government selects and proposes the candidates and a subsequent phase at the international level where the candidates are examined and possibly appointed.

At the international level, the second phase occurs through the rules and agreements provided for each court. Domestic law does not play any role in the second phase. Instead, domestic law governs the first phase, where domestic candidates are selected. National candidates for positions as international adjudicators are typically appointed by the government, specifically by the Ministry of Foreign Affairs.

The mechanisms of appointment of national candidates to positions as international adjudicators conform to a model of party appointment. Given that most international adjudicators are courts in charge of resolving international disputes among states, not unlike many other governments, the Italian one is primarily concerned with having a national judge sitting in the court. This approach, however, does not duly ensure either the independence and impartiality or the competence of the selected candidates. It has been noted that, when governments have the power to nominate candidates for a post as international adjudicators,

> there should be guarantees to ensure that the procedures to appoint judges are transparent and independent in practice and that the decisions will not be influenced by any reasons other than those related to the objective criteria mentioned above.[58]

However, this goal is rarely achieved in practice.

---

[57] P. Biavati, 'Il procedimento nell'arbitrato societario' (2003) *Rivista dell'arbitrato* 27; F. Corsini, 'L'arbitrato nella riforma di diritto societario' (2003) *Giurisprudenza italiana* 1285; E. Zucconi Galli Fonseca, 'La convenzione arbitrale nelle società dopo la riforma' (2003) *Rivista trimestrale di diritto e procedura civile* 929.

[58] European Commission for Democracy Through Law, 'Report on the Independence of the Judicial System – Part I: The Independence of Judges', 16 March 2010, CDL-AD, 2010, 004.

4. THE METHOD FOR APPOINTING ADJUDICATORS

4.1. THE APPOINTMENT OF DOMESTIC ADJUDICATORS

4.1.1. *Judges*

The appointment of national judges is based on a national competition. The examining committee assesses the candidates' written and oral examination according to merit criteria, and the winners are formally appointed by the Ministry of Justice (or the Prime Minister for administrative judges). The competition for administrative judges is based on the examination and the candidates' curricula vitae (i.e. previous professional experiences).

In the ordinary judiciary, the criteria for the formation of chambers within each court and for the definition of the internal competence of each chamber, which is generally based on the subject matter of the proceedings, are established every three years by decree of the Minister of Justice in accordance with the decisions of the CSM taken on the proposals of the Presidents of the Courts of Appeal, after hearing the local Judicial Councils.[59] As for the allocation of cases to specific judges or panels within each chamber, it is done randomly based on objective and predetermined criteria set forth in instructions issued by the CSM.[60] However, deviations from the tabular criteria for allocation of cases to single judges within a court do not cause the voidness of the acts and orders issued by the judge so appointed. Such deviations are only subject to a possible disciplinary sanction.

4.1.2. *Arbitrators*

In arbitration, the parties are free to choose whether to submit their disputes to a sole arbitrator or to a panel of arbitrators, to determine the number of members of the arbitral tribunal, to agree on their names or on specific qualities which the arbitrators must possess, and to set up procedures for the arbitrators' appointment, replacement and removal.[61]

However, in consideration of the adjudicatory function of arbitrators, parties are bound by fundamental principles of procedural public policy.[62] According

---

[59] Article 7-*bis* Judiciary Act.

[60] Article 7-*ter* Judiciary Act.

[61] Article 809(2) CCP. For further details, see C. Giovannucci Orlandi, 'Art. 810' in F. Carpi (ed.), *Arbitrato. Titolo VIII libro IV del codice di procedura civile. Artt. 806–840*, Zanichelli, Bologna 2007, p. 256.

[62] For a work devoted to this matter, see S. Turatto, *L'impugnazione del lodo arbitrale per contrarietà all'ordine pubblico*, Giappichelli, Turin 2020, pp. 215 ff.

to Article 809(1) CCP, arbitral tribunals must be composed of an odd number of members; all parties, even in the case of multi-party arbitrations,[63] must have equal rights to decide on the constitution of the arbitral tribunal, and when the legal relationship cannot be adjudicated without the participation of all interested subjects, all the subjects must be given a chance to take part in the arbitral proceedings, and to equally participate in the appointment of the arbitral tribunal.

4.2. THE APPOINTMENT OF NATIONAL CANDIDATES TO POSITIONS AS INTERNATIONAL ADJUDICATORS

As already mentioned, in most cases, national candidates for positions as international adjudicators are appointed by the government based on an opaque private consultation. Therefore, the methodology cannot fully ensure the effective implementation of the principle of independence and impartiality.

In recent years, a notable exception to this approach has emerged. It concerns the appointment of national candidates to the CJEU. Law No. 234/2012, although leaving the initiative with the government, provides that the Prime Minister or the Minister of Foreign Affairs shall report to the Parliament, indicating the procedure to follow and presenting the candidates' curricula vitae. In addition, in 2018, the government made an open call for applications concerning two positions as Italian judges at the CJEU.[64] Based on an open call for applications, the same approach was adopted for the position as candidate to become a judge at the ECtHR.[65]

In both reported cases, the actual appointment also required a positive assessment of a consultative panel, and it was ultimately made in accordance with the public international law rules governing the relevant institution. The change concerning the appointment method of national candidates to positions as international adjudicators is remarkable. It ensures transparency and objectivity in the process and favours the competence and independence of the proposed candidates.

---

[63] C. Perazzo, 'Pluralità di parti e arbitrato amministrato' (2014) *Foro padano* 57, 57.

[64] Cf. F. Battaglia, 'Il sistema di selezione dei membri della Corte di giustizia dell'Unione europea fra valutazioni di merito e problemi di trasparenza' (2019) *Eurojus* 22.

[65] See the online call at: https://www.governo.it/it/articolo/procedura-di-selezione-dei-candidati-l-elezione-giudice-componente-della-corte-europea-dei. See also D. Cardamone, 'La procedura di elezione dei giudici della Corte Edu' (2019) *Questione giustizia*, Special Issue, April 2019, https://www.questionegiustizia.it/speciale/articolo/la-procedura-di-elezione-dei-giudici-della-corte-edu_34.php. For a broader, international perspective, see the contributions collected in J. Limbach (ed.), *Judicial independence: law and practice of appointments to the European Court of Human Rights*, Interights, London 2003.

5. METHODS TO BALANCE THE APPOINTING AUTHORITY'S INFLUENCE ON THE APPOINTMENT OF ADJUDICATORS

5.1. THE APPOINTMENT OF DOMESTIC ADJUDICATORS

5.1.1. *Judges*

The Italian Constitution and implementing statutes protect the judicial independence of ordinary judges from the executive and legislative powers.[66] Judges hold a permanent position, and they serve until retirement. They cannot, directly or indirectly, be disciplined or deprived of their post, salary or functions, except for cause after adjudication by the CSM. As already noted, two-thirds of the members of the CSM are elected by judges from their own ranks, and a joint session of Parliament elects one-third from among professors of law and lawyers who have had 15 years of practice.

Under the Italian Constitution, '[j]udges are subject only to the law'[67] and '[m]agistrates are distinguished from one another only by the diversity of their functions'.[68]

Therefore, in the relations between magistrates, there can be no hierarchical relationship, as this would compromise the independence of the judges serving in an inferior hierarchical position. Similar guarantees are established by statute for administrative judges, whose independence is protected in a very similar fashion.[69]

Moreover, to ensure the full autonomy and freedom of each justice, under Article 276 CCP (and, implicitly, Articles 525 et seq. of the Code of Criminal Procedure, and Article 76 of the Code of Administrative Proceedings) deliberations are secret, and drafting dissenting opinions is not permitted.

5.1.2. *Arbitrators*

Moving to arbitration, it is worth noting that Italian arbitration law does not provide general rules to balance the influence of the appointing authority over

---

[66] See R. Martino, 'Separazione dei poteri, ruolo del giudice e responsabilità civile del magistrato' (2016) *Giusto processo civile* 305; for a comparative perspective, see N. Mykhailiuk, G. Mykhailiuk and L.A. Di Matteo, 'Advancing the Rule of Law: Creating an Independent and Competent Judiciary' (2021) *Italian Law Journal* 61.

[67] Article 101(2) Constitution.

[68] Article 107(3) Constitution.

[69] See Articles 24 et seq. Administrative Judiciary Act.

arbitrators. One exception is the already mentioned rules applicable to professional or business associations charged with the administration of arbitral proceedings. These professional or business associations cannot appoint arbitrators when the dispute at stake puts their associates, or other subjects belonging to the relevant business sector, in opposition to third parties.[70] Another exception concerns corporate disputes submitted to arbitration.[71] An arbitration clause contained in the deed of incorporation of a company must grant the power to appoint all the arbitral tribunal members to a subject independent of the relevant company on penalty of nullity.

The recent reform of Italian civil procedure is worth mentioning here.[72] With Article 1(15)(a) of Law No. 206/2021, the Parliament instructed the government to strengthen the guarantees of impartiality and independence of arbitrators by introducing a duty of disclosure. D.Lgs. No. 149/2022 implemented the legislative guidelines by amending Articles 83 and 815 CCP. Before the reform's entry into force, arbitrators were not subject to a duty to disclose. Conversely, under the new regime, upon accepting the appointment, arbitrators will be required to disclose any circumstances that, although not impacting their independence and impartiality, are capable of raising reasonable doubts in the eyes of the parties. Therefore, following the reform's entry into force on 28 February 2023, the arbitrators' duty to disclose is generally applicable in all cases.

The reform had not significantly changed the situation as regards administered arbitration. In particular, notwithstanding the absence of a legislatively imposed duty to disclose, Article 20 of the Arbitration Rules for the Milan Chamber of National and International Arbitration,[73] the most authoritative Italian arbitral institutions, already provided that, in their declaration of independence, arbitrators must disclose, specifying the period and duration: any relationship with the parties, their counsel and any other person involved in the arbitration,

---

[70]   Article 832(4) CCP.

[71]   Pursuant to Article 838-*bis* CCP.

[72]   Law 26 November 2021, No. 206 on the reform of civil procedure, providing the government with the legislature's guidelines for the reform of civil proceedings, as implemented by D.Lgs. 10 October 2022, No. 149. For a comment on the possible impact of the reform on Italian arbitration law, see M. Benedettelli, A. Briguglio, A. Carlevaris, A. Carosi, E. Marinucci, A. Panzarola, L. Salvaneschi and B. Sassani, 'Commento ai principi in materia di arbitrato della legge di delega n. 206 del 21 novembre 2021, art. 1, c. 15' (2022) *Judicium*, https://www.judicium.it/commento-ai-principi-in-materia-di-arbitrato-della-legge-di-delega-n-206-del-21-novembre-2021-art-1-c-15/.

[73]   For a commentary on the rules, see L. Castelli, G.P. Coppola, S. Sanzo and F. Rosti, *Commentario pratico al Regolamento della Camera Arbitrale di Milano*, Cedam, Padua 2021.

whether personal, professional or financial, that is relevant to the arbitrator's impartiality and independence; any personal or economic interest, direct or indirect, relating to the dispute; and any prejudice or reservation with respect to the matter in dispute.[74]

5.2. THE APPOINTMENT OF NATIONAL CANDIDATES TO POSITIONS AS INTERNATIONAL ADJUDICATORS

The implementation of the principle of independence and impartiality appears much less effective with respect to the methods to balance the appointing authority's influence on the appointment of national candidates to positions as international adjudicators.

At present, the appointing authority (the government) has a great influence on such appointments. Methods to balance the appointing authority's influence are deployed mainly at the international level. They include precluding the possibility of reappointment, which has been introduced at the International Criminal Court. Conversely, balancing methods or initiatives at the national level are still extremely rare and ineffective.

6. PARAMETERS TO ENSURE THAT ADJUDICATORS ACT INDEPENDENTLY AND IMPARTIALLY

6.1. PARAMETERS FOR DOMESTIC ADJUDICATORS

6.1.1. Judges

As a general rule, judges may not hold public or private office or employment to avoid any conflict of interest.[75] Moreover, they cannot engage in any industry or commerce or have a separate profession. Judges are also precluded from acting as arbitrators unless duly authorised by the CSM, and only in cases where the state is a party to the arbitral proceedings.[76] Furthermore, judges serving in

---

[74] The Milan Rules refer to the well-known IBA Guidelines on Conflicts of Interest in International Arbitration, adopted by resolution of the IBA Council on 23 October 2014: https://www.camera-arbitrale.it/Documenti/IBA-guidelines-on-conflict-of-interest-nov2014.pdf.

[75] For a recent comparative overview of the treatment of the issue of judges' political involvement, see A. Morelli, 'La libertà di associazione partitica dei magistrati: analisi comparata del rischio di politicizzazione del potere giudiziario nei sistemi di "civil law" e "common law"' (2022) *Rivista dell'associazione italiana dei costituzionalisti* 42.

[76] Article 16 Judiciary Act.

Italy

courts of first instance and courts of appeal may not belong to judicial offices in which their relatives up to the second degree, first-degree relatives-in-law, spouse or partner habitually practice law.[77]

With regard to individual civil proceedings, Article 51(1) CCP imposes on judges the obligation to abstain:

1. if they have an interest in the case or in another case involving the same point of law;
2. if they or their spouse or partner are a relative up to the fourth degree, or a cohabitant or habitual companion, of one of the parties or of any of the defendants;
3. if they or their spouse or partner have pending lawsuits or serious enmity or credit or debt relationships with one of the parties or any of their counsel;
4. if they have given advice or acted as counsel in the case, or have given evidence in it as a witness, or have served as a judge at another stage of the proceedings or as an arbitrator, or have participated as an expert witness;
5. if they are a guardian, administrator, procurator, agent or employer of one of the parties; or
6. if, in addition, he or she is a director or manager of a body, firm, association, committee, corporation or establishment which has an interest in the case.[78]

Furthermore, a judge may voluntarily ask his or her head of office for authorisation to abstain if there are 'relevant reasons of convenience' (Article 51(2) CCP).

Article 17 of the Code of Administrative Proceedings extends to administrative proceedings the grounds and procedure for abstention provided for in the CCP.

Under Articles 34 et seq. of the Code of Criminal Procedure (CCrP), a series of rules are provided which add further grounds of incompatibility, abstention and recusal.[79] In particular, according to Article 34, a judge who delivered a judgment or performed his or her functions as a judge in one phase of the proceedings shall not perform those functions in subsequent instances or phases, nor may he or she serve as a judge if he or she previously served as public prosecutor; carried out police actions; rendered service as a lawyer, proxy, administrator of a party, witness, expert or technical consultant; submitted a report, complaint, petition or request; or issued the authorisation to proceed in the same proceedings.

Article 35 CCrP establishes the incompatibility to serve as judges in the same proceedings for individuals who are spouses, relatives or relatives-in-law up to

---

[77]   Article 18 Judiciary Act.

[78]   For further details and a thorough analysis of this matter, see A. Tedoldi, 'Art. 51–56. Astensione, ricusazione e responsabilità dei giudici' in S. Chiarloni (ed.), *Commentario del Codice di Procedura Civile*, Zanichelli, Bologna 2015, pp. 1 ff.; see also L. Dittrich, 'Incompatibilità, astensione e ricusazione del giudice civile', Cedam, Padua 1991, *passim*.

[79]   E. Zappalà, *La ricusazione del giudice penale*, Giuffrè, Milan 1989, pp. 151 ff.

the second degree of kinship. Article 36 lists eight grounds for abstention, not only referring to the cases of incompatibility set forth in Articles 34 and 35, but also providing for a duty to abstain:

1. if the judge has interests in the proceedings or if one of the private parties or counsel is a debtor or creditor of the judge, the judge's spouse or the judge's children;
2. if the counsel, representative or administrator of one of the parties is a relative of the judge or the judge's spouse;
3. if the judge advised or expressed an opinion on the subject of the proceedings outside the performance of his or her judicial function;
4. if any of the judge's relatives or the judge spouse's relatives is the victim or injured person of the offence; or
5. if the judge's relatives or the judge spouse's relatives currently serve or have served as public prosecutor.

Incompatibility may also arise based on any other serious reasons of convenience.

The abstention is always conditional on the authorisation of the president of the court. Article 37 CCrP establishes that the judge may be recused by the parties in cases falling under Article 36 (with the exception of abstention for serious reasons of convenience). Moreover, the judge may be recused if, while performing his or her function and prior to the delivery of the judgment, he or she improperly expresses a personal view of the case.[80]

At times, the rules on territorial competence are also derogated from to ensure the full independence and impartiality of criminal judges. First, according to Article 11 of the CCrP, proceedings which involve a magistrate (public prosecutor or judge) as a suspect, accused, victim or injured person, and which would fall within the competence of a judicial office located in the same district of the court of appeal where the magistrate serves or served when the criminal act was committed, shall be conducted by the court with subject-matter competence of the neighbouring court of appeal district. Another derogation from rules on territorial competence is provided under Articles 45 et seq. CCrP, which provide for the transfer of a trial if contextual circumstances, which cannot be eliminated, may prejudice the progress of the trial, so as to affect the freedom of determination of the persons involved in the proceedings, endanger public security or safety or raise reasonable reasons of suspicion. Under these circumstances, the Court of Cassation decides on the request for transfer of the trial. The transfer, however, remains an exceptional deviation from the rule, and orders upholding such a request are extremely rare.

---

[80] By its decision of 14 July 2000 (C. Cost., No. 283/2000), the Constitutional Court extended the scope of the ground for recusal to cases where the judge expresses an opinion in distinct proceedings, yet on the same facts, and against the same accused.

6.1.2. Arbitrators

As to the parameters to ensure that arbitrators act independently and impartially,[81] Article 815 of the CCP deals with the recusal of arbitrators.[82] It sets out the requirements considered essential to guarantee independence and impartiality, many of which reproduce the regime governing the recusal of judges under Article 51 CCP. In addition, Article 832(5) CCP explicitly establishes that institutional rules can provide additional recusal grounds.

According to Article 815 CCP, arbitrators may be challenged:

1. if they do not have the qualification expressly agreed upon by the parties;
2. if they, or a body, association or corporation which they direct, have an interest in the case;
3. if they or their spouses are relatives up to the fourth degree or the cohabitant or habitual companion of one of the parties, or legal representatives of one of the parties, or of any of the defendants;
4. if they or their spouses have a pending lawsuit or a serious enmity with one of the parties, their legal representatives, or any of the defendants;
5. if they are linked to one of the parties, to a company controlled by one of the parties, to the entity that controls it, or to companies subject to joint control, by an employment relationship or a continuous consultancy or paid work relationship, or by other relationships of a financial or associative nature that compromise their independence; furthermore, if they are guardians or curators of one of the parties; or
6. if they offered advice, assistance or representation to one of the parties at an earlier stage of the proceedings or acted as witness.

The recent reform of Italian civil procedure implemented by D.Lgs. No. 149/2022 has introduced a new ground for the recusal of arbitrators. Under Article 815(6-*bis*) CCP, arbitrators are also subject to challenge 'if serious reasons of convenience exist, such as to impact on the arbitrator's independence and impartiality'.

The new provision is consistent with the guidelines concerning the reform of Italian civil procedure issued by the Parliament to strengthen the guarantees of arbitrators' independence and impartiality and to reintroduce a ground for recusal based on serious reasons of convenience.[83] However, although consistent

---

[81] In addition to the bibliography contained in previous notes, see V. Di Gravio, 'L'indipendenza dell'arbitro' (2018) *Rivista dell'arbitrato* 195; L. Dittrich, 'L'imparzialità dell'arbitro interno ed internazionale' (1995) *Rivista di diritto processuale* 52.

[82] For a commentary on this provision, see G. Ruffini and J. Polinari, 'Art. 815' in M. Benedettelli, C. Consolo and L. Radicati di Brozolo (eds), *Commentario breve al diritto dell'arbitrato nazionale ed internazionale*, Cedam, Padua 2017, pp. 205 ff.

[83] See Article 1(15)(a) of Law No. 206/2021, referring to 'gravi ragioni di convenienza'.

with the rule applicable to Italian judges, the inclusion of the new ground for recusal appears questionable due to its lack of specificity. Such lack of specificity, combined with the arbitrators' generalised duty to disclose any circumstances that may appear relevant in the eyes of the parties (a duty to which judges are not subject), may result in too high a degree of uncertainty as to what arbitrators must disclose in practice.

According to Article 815(2) CCP, a party cannot challenge an arbitrator who it has appointed or to whose appointment it has contributed unless the grounds for recusal have become known to it after the appointment.

6.2. PARAMETERS FOR NATIONALS APPOINTED TO POSITIONS AS INTERNATIONAL ADJUDICATORS

The legal framework is less settled when it comes to determining the national parameters to ensure that nationals appointed to positions as international adjudicators act independently and impartially.

As mentioned above, the only parameters implemented at the national level to ensure that nationals proposed for positions as international adjudicators act independently and impartially consist in publishing a call for applications for the position that specifies the requirements for the position. This measure has been recently introduced for the appointment of Italian nationals to positions at the CJEU and the ECtHR. However, it is not a generalised measure, and there is no certainty that it will be adopted for other international courts or tribunals, or even for future appointments of Italian candidates to the CJEU and the ECtHR. The only measure that has been introduced by specific legislation[84] relates to the appointment of Italian candidates to the CJEU. It provides that the Prime Minister or the Minister of Foreign Affairs reports to the Parliament, indicating the procedure followed and presenting the candidates' curricula vitae.

Both measures indicated above may only indirectly ensure that Italian nationals appointed to positions as international adjudicators act independently and impartially. The main goal of the measure is the transparency of the process and an open competition favouring the selection of the most knowledgeable candidates. There is no doubt that transparency of the process and competence of the appointees are prerequisites for independent and impartial action. The innovation to the process is thus to be welcomed. However, more can certainly be done at the national level to pursue more effectively the goal of ensuring the independence and impartiality of international adjudicators.

---

[84] Law No. 234/2012.

7. CONSEQUENCES FOR AN ADJUDICATOR OF A BREACH OF THE REQUIREMENT TO ACT INDEPENDENTLY AND IMPARTIALLY

7.1. CONSEQUENCES FOR DOMESTIC ADJUDICATORS

7.1.1. *Judges*

If judges fail to abstain from hearing a case in a situation where their independence and impartiality are impaired, the parties may challenge their participation in the case. This is done through special recusal proceedings (*ricusazione*) to be initiated within peremptory time limits.[85]

According to Articles 52 et seq. CCP, pending the recusal, the civil proceedings may be stayed, unless the challenge is manifestly groundless. The recusal is decided by a panel of three judges sitting in the same court (generally, but not necessarily, in a different chamber). After hearing the challenged judge and taking evidence where necessary, the decision is given in the form of a final order, which is not subject to appeal.[86]

Articles 17 and 18 of the Code of Administrative Proceedings extend to administrative proceedings the grounds for abstention and the procedure for recusal set forth in the CCP. However, one important difference exists in that the decision on the recusal of an administrative judge is rendered by the same panel of judges where the recused was in office after the replacement of the recused judge.

In criminal proceedings, according to Articles 37 et seq. CCrP, the recusal of a judge of a court of first instance is decided by the court of appeal. The Court of Cassation decides the recusal of a judge of the court of appeal. A different chamber of the court decides the recusal of a judge of the Court of Cassation. Pending the recusal, the recused judge does not have to stay the proceedings but cannot issue a judgment (Article 37(2) CCrP).

As for the judges' liability, all judges are subject to disciplinary measures issued by the CSM.[87] Based on the severity of the judge's breach, these measures range from a mere warning to removal from office and possible criminal prosecution. Moreover, the Italian legislator introduced in the system a special regime of civil

---

[85]   See A. Tedoldi, 'Art. 51–56. Astensione, ricusazione e responsabilità dei giudici' in S. Chiarloni (ed.), *Commentario del Codice di Procedura Civile*, Zanichelli, Bologna 2015, pp. 55 ff.

[86]   Not even to appeal to the Court of Cassation under Article 111 Constitution. Accordingly, ex multis, Cass., 07.09.2020, No. 18611.

[87]   Cf. G. Ferri, 'Il diritto a un giudice indipendente e imparziale previsto dalla CEDU e la Sezione disciplinare del CSM (a proposito del caso "Di Giovanni c. Italia")' (2014) *Giurisprudenza costituzionale* 553.

liability of judges.[88] The liability may be affirmed only provided that the judge (i) is liable for a 'manifest disregard of the law' (including EU law); (ii) grossly misappreciated the facts or the evidence; (iii) affirmed a fact whose existence was unequivocally denied by the records; (iv) denied a fact whose existence was unequivocally affirmed by the records; or (v) issued an interim measure outside the cases contemplated by the law or without reasons.

As for the proceedings, the law provides that the injured party may claim compensation for damage only against the state, not against the judge who is liable. Thereafter, it is for the state, if held accountable, to file for recourse against the judge within two years of the judgment ascertaining the judge's liability. Except for cases of wilful misconduct, judges' liability is capped at half the amount of their annual salary.

7.1.2. Arbitrators

As for arbitrators, according to Article 815(3) CCP, a recusal against them is filed through an application to the president of the court of first instance for the place of the seat of arbitration. The application must be filed within a peremptory time limit of 10 days of the notification of the appointment or knowledge of the cause for recusal.[89] The president of the court of first instance issues a final order after hearing the challenged arbitrator and the parties and, where necessary, after obtaining summary information. The decision on the recusal is not subject to appeal.[90]

Under Italian law, parties may agree on different rules governing the challenge of arbitrators, including rules delegating the challenge to an arbitral institution. In the event of an agreed procedure for the challenge, it is unclear whether, under what grounds and to what extent judicial review of the institution's decision on the challenge is possible. Arguably, in the absence of any provision similar to Article 13(3) of the UNCITRAL Model Law,[91] it is

---

[88] Law 13 April 1988, No. 117.

[89] See L. Salvaneschi, 'Arbitrato. Libro quarto: Procedimenti speciali art. 806–840' in S. Chiarloni (ed.) *Commentario del Codice di Procedura Civile*, Zanichelli, Bologna 2014, pp. 111 ff.

[90] Cass., 31.08.2017, No. 20615.

[91] See Article 13(3) of the UNCITRAL Model Law: 'If a challenge under any procedure agreed upon by the parties or under the procedure of paragraph (2) of this article is not successful, the challenging party may request, within thirty days after having received notice of the decision rejecting the challenge, the court or other authority specified in article 6 to decide on the challenge, which decision shall be subject to no appeal; while such a request is pending, the arbitral tribunal, including the challenged arbitrator, may continue the arbitral proceedings and make an award'.

not possible for the challenging party to request the court of the seat to decide on the challenge. Moreover, an in-depth analysis of the innovations brought about by the 2006 reform to the recusal proceedings under Article 815 CCP supports the conclusion that the proceedings for recusal of the arbitrator and those for the challenge of the award under Article 829 CCP are separate and incompatible.[92]

The situation described above has partly changed as a result of the reform of Italian civil procedure. Law No. 206/2021, outlining the Parliament's guidelines to the government for the reform, provided that the implementing legislative decree should determine the invalidity of the arbitrator's acceptance of appointment in case of breach of the duty to disclose relevant circumstances impacting the arbitrator's independence and impartiality. Moreover, a breach of the disclosure obligation would constitute grounds for removal from office and recusal of the arbitrator. The implementing legislation (D.Lgs. No. 149/2022) followed the Parliament's guidelines. Under the new text of Article 823(1) CCP, it is mandatory for each arbitrator, on penalty of nullity, to disclose any circumstances that might be susceptible to problematic assessments of independence and impartiality. The lack of disclosure prevents the finalisation of the acceptance and, thus, the appointment as arbitrator. It is expected that the declaration will be made anew in case of circumstances that arise during the proceedings. Any failure to make the declaration, and also any omission of relevant circumstances, entitles the parties concerned to apply to the president of the court of first instance for the disqualification of the arbitrator. The application must be filed within 10 days from the acceptance made without the declaration or from the discovery of the relevant circumstance not declared.

As for liability of arbitrators, Article 813-*ter* CCP grants arbitrators a broad immunity by providing that they can be sued for damages by the parties only in a limited number of cases.[93] In particular, arbitrators are liable for damages caused to the parties if: (i) they wilfully or grossly negligently omit or delay to perform any act that is due, provided that they have been disqualified on those grounds; (ii) resign without a justified reason; (iii) wilfully or grossly negligently omit or prevent the issue of an award within the fixed time limits; or (iv) commit

---

[92] For more details, see infra, section 8.
[93] On arbitrators' liability, see R. Rordorf, 'La responsabilità degli arbitri' in D. Mantucci (ed.), *Trattato di diritto dell'arbitrato*, vol. III, *Il tribunale arbitrale*, ESI, Naples 2021, pp. 365 ff.; as for other remedies available to the parties in case of arbitrators' lack of independence and impartiality, see M. Benedettelli, *International Arbitration in Italy*, Kluwer Law International, Alphen aan den Rijn 2020, pp. 225–28.

wilful misconduct or gross negligence within the limits provided for judges' liability.[94]

Moreover, if the award is rendered, a liability claim against the arbitrators may only be filed following the successful setting aside of the award by means of a final judgment, and for the reasons for which the award was set aside. Conversely, during the arbitration proceedings, a liability claim can be filed only in cases of disqualification for omissions or delays in the performance of any act.

Except in cases of wilful misconduct, the amount of the compensation may not exceed three times the agreed remuneration or, in the absence of an agreement, three times the remuneration laid down in the applicable tariff.

It is debated whether arbitrators may be criminally liable for corruption.[95] The prevailing solution in the case law is negative.[96] This solution rests on the principle *nulla poena sine lege*, as Article 813(2) of the CCP expressly establishes that arbitrators are not public officers, nor are they in charge of a public service, a circumstance that constitutes a prerequisite for the crime of corruption under the Italian Criminal Code. A different interpretation, overcoming the literal interpretation of the rule, would seem at odds with the prohibition of extensive interpretation *contra reum* in criminal law.

7.2. CONSEQUENCES FOR NATIONALS APPOINTED TO POSITIONS AS INTERNATIONAL ADJUDICATORS

At the national level, the consequences of a breach of the requirement to act independently and impartially for nationals appointed as international adjudicators are primarily, if not exclusively, of a political nature.

Other than the possible 'political' stigma and denial of reappointment, at the national level there are no consequences for nationals appointed to positions as international adjudicators of a breach by the adjudicator of the requirement to act independently and impartially. In addition, in case law there seem to be no reported cases of criminal charges against Italian international adjudicators based on alleged circumstances or conduct that might have impaired their independence and impartiality.

The observed situation is consistent with the more limited availability of instruments implementing the principle of independence and impartiality of international adjudicators. However, it is also a clear indication that mechanisms to implement the principle are necessary.

---

[94] The limits are set by Law No. 117/1988.
[95] Under one of the delicts punished by Articles 318, 319 and 319-*ter* CCrP.
[96] See Cass., 08.03.2013, No. 5901.

Italy

8. ENFORCEMENT BY A DOMESTIC COURT OF DECISIONS RENDERED BY AN ADJUDICATOR WHO BREACHED THE REQUIREMENT TO ACT INDEPENDENTLY AND IMPARTIALLY

8.1. ENFORCEMENT OF DECISIONS RENDERED BY DOMESTIC ADJUDICATORS

The final question to be addressed in this report concerns the enforceability by a domestic court of decisions rendered by an adjudicator who breached the requirement to act independently and impartially.

8.1.1. Decisions Rendered by Judges

The analysis starts from the hypothesis of a national judge breaching the requirement to act independently and impartially. As a general rule, the violation of the judge's duty to abstain can be denounced by a party only by means of a request for recusal within the applicable time limits. If the recusal is not proposed in a timely manner, the judgment issued at the end of the proceedings cannot be challenged on those grounds.

If the recusal proposed in civil proceedings is rejected, the challenging party can appeal the judgment rendered by (or with the participation of) the unsuccessfully recused judge on the same grounds, denouncing the wrongfulness of the order dismissing the recusal.

If the recusal is filed in criminal proceedings and it is rejected, the decision on the recusal can be challenged before the Court of Cassation.[97]

Once a civil judgment becomes final, Article 395 CCP provides for the remedy of revocation, an exceptional means for challenging final judgments. Revocation can be invoked after the elapse of the term for appeal when the decision is affected by material injustice because, inter alia, it is the product of judicial fraud (*dolo*). However, the existence of fraud cannot be proved in the revocation proceedings. Instead, it must have been ascertained in a judgment that has acquired *res judicata* effects. The relevant notion of fraud includes any wilful violation of the duty to pronounce a judgment impartially and pursuant to law.

Moreover, final criminal judgments of conviction are subject to revision if it is proven that the judgment was delivered as a consequence of false documents or statements provided during the trial or any other criminal act deemed an offence by law, including the corruption or fraud of a judge.[98]

---

[97]   Article 41 CCrP.
[98]   Article 630 CCrP.

Intersentia

549

8.1.2. Decisions Rendered by Arbitrators

The legal scenario is rather different in the case of a decision rendered by an arbitral tribunal that breached the requirement to act independently and impartially. Arbitral awards are final. However, they are subject to challenge under Articles 827–831 CCP.[99] The annulment of arbitral awards has a much narrower scope than appeals against court judgments. Unlike the latter, which enables a full review of the first instance decision, the subject matter of the proceedings for annulment of an arbitral award is limited to the ascertainment of the existence of one of the specific, numerus clausus, grounds for annulment listed in Article 829 CCP.[100]

Under Article 829(1) no. 2 CCP, an award may be annulled if the arbitrators have not been appointed with the formalities and modalities agreed by the parties or prescribed by the law, subject, however, to the relevant issue having already been raised in the arbitral proceedings.

As Article 829 is silent on this point, it is debated whether the lack of independence and impartiality can be raised as a ground for annulment under Article 829(1) no. 2 CCP. It is also unsettled if the award may be challenged when the recusal was not proposed pursuant to Article 815 CCP, in particular in situations where the challenge of the arbitrator was raised under some institutional rules.

As already stated, an in-depth analysis of the innovations brought about by the 2006 reform to the recusal proceedings under Article 815 CCP supports the conclusion that the proceedings for recusal of the arbitrator are separate and somewhat incompatible from those for the challenge of the award under Article 829 CCP. The most recent reform implemented by D.Lgs. No. 149/2022 does not affect this position.

Indeed, Article 815 CCP states that the recusal ordered by the president of the local court of first instance determines the ineffectiveness (not the invalidity) of any act carried out with the participation of the recused arbitrator. This ineffectiveness also affects the arbitral award. Therefore, the challenging party can raise the ineffectiveness on any occasion on which the award rendered by (or with the participation of) the recused arbitrator is invoked against it.

---

[99] Cf., ex multis, L. Salvaneschi, 'I motivi di impugnazione del lodo: una razionalizzazione?' (2015) *Rivista dell'arbitrato* 233; M. Bove, 'L'impugnazione per nullità del lodo rituale' (2009) *Rivista dell'arbitrato* 19; for a comparative overview, see E. Marinucci, 'Esito ed effetti dell'impugnazione giudiziaria del lodo arbitrale: note di diritto comparato' (2000) *Rivista trimestrale di diritto e procedura civile* 1327; F. Ferrari and F. Rosenfeld (consultant ed.: J. Fellas), *International Commercial Arbitration: A Comparative Introduction*, Edward Elgar, Cheltenham/Northampton 2021, pp. 170 ff.

[100] Accordingly, M. Benedettelli, *International Arbitration in Italy*, Kluwer Law International, Alphen aan den Rijn 2020, pp. 399–400.

Article 829(1) CCP, on the other hand, deals with defects concerning the process of appointment of the arbitral tribunal. The consequence of the defect is the annulment (not the ineffectiveness) of the arbitral award. The annulment must be asserted using the appropriate appeal on penalty of the award becoming final.

It is not only the effects of recusal and annulment that differ. The procedures also diverge significantly, and such a divergence supports the conclusion that the grounds for recusal cannot be converted into grounds for setting aside the award. To be admissible, the recusal must be proposed within the 'peremptory term of ten days from the notification of the nomination or from the subsequent knowledge of the cause for objection' (Article 815(3) CCP).

Within this peremptory term, the petition for recusal must be brought to the attention of the judicial authority (the president of the court of first instance), not of the arbitrators. The arbitrators will most likely acquire knowledge of the recusal, but there is no peremptory term to notify them to ensure the admissibility of the objection. Therefore, if within the 10-day period indicated by Article 815 CCP the party merely raises the grounds for recusal before the arbitral tribunal, the recusal subsequently proposed before the competent president of the court of first instance would be inadmissible. On the other hand, the ground for annulment under Article 829 CCP requires that the party objects to the violation of the rules on the arbitral tribunal's constitution 'in the first instance or defence following the violation' (Article 829(2) CCP). Therefore, not only does nothing ensure that this term coincides with the peremptory term of Article 815 CCP, but certainly the activity imposed by Article 815 CCP (filing before the president of the court of first instance) would not be sufficient to prevent the forfeiture of the ground of annulment under Article 829(2) CCP, which requires that the defence is raised before the arbitrators.

In conclusion, the current system of recusal of arbitrators under Article 815 CCP, introduced by the arbitration reform of 2006, provides for an autonomous mechanism for challenging arbitrators, with its own rules and procedure, leading to a decision on the recusal, which is not subject to review in the form of a challenge of the arbitral award. This conclusion, however, is not without exceptions. In particular, the separation between the recusal proceedings and the challenge of the award cannot go as far as to conflict with the public policy principle under which 'no one can be a judge in his or her own case'. Accordingly, the challenge of the award for reasons of public policy should still be admissible in the event of an award that is directly affected by the conflict of interest of the arbitrator.[101]

---

[101] This conclusion is supported by the decision rendered by the ECtHR in the *BEG* case: *BEG SpA v. Italy*, ECtHR decision of 20 May 2021, application no. 5312/11. For a comment on the decision, see D. Pauciulo, 'Imparzialità degli arbitri secondo la Corte Europea dei diritti dell'uomo nel caso "BEG S.p.A. c. Italia"' (2021) *Diritto del commercio internazionale* 1083.

On a different note, Article 831 CCP extends to arbitral awards the remedy of revocation of court judgments. Accordingly, the remedy at hand allows for an appeal against the award, even after the acquisition of *res judicata* effects, in the event, inter alia, of fraud by the arbitrators.

8.2. ENFORCEMENT OF DECISIONS RENDERED BY INTERNATIONAL ADJUDICATORS

As mentioned above, international courts and tribunals rely primarily on spontaneous compliance and cooperation for the enforcement of their decisions. In particular, at the domestic level, arguments opposing the enforcement of an international judgment are typically based on the notions of sovereignty and immunity, rather than on the inherent flaws of the decisions. That said, it is apparent that the (political) arguments aimed at the rejection of the decision's enforcement at the domestic level would only be reinforced in the event of a breach of the requirement to act independently and impartially in deciding the case. After all, compliance with the requirements of the adjudicator's independence and impartiality is unquestionably a public policy principle. This applies in most jurisdictions, and Italy is no exception.

9. FINAL REMARKS

The purpose of this report was to provide an overview of the independence and impartiality of international adjudicators from the perspective of Italian law. After providing a definition of what meaning would be attached to the notion of an adjudicator, various prerequisites, operative rules, monitoring and implementing tools, and enforcement mechanisms concerning the principle of independence and impartiality of adjudicators have been analysed. Each different aspect has been analysed by accompanying the presentation of Italian law concerning international adjudicators with the domestic rules concerning national adjudicators, thus including rules concerning both judges and arbitrators seated in Italy.

With this focus, the report has reviewed the criteria for selection of adjudicators, the authority appointing domestic adjudicators and national candidates to positions as international adjudicators, the methods for appointing those domestic adjudicators and candidates, the balancing of the appointing authority's influence, the parameters to ensure that adjudicators act independently and impartially, and the enforceability by a domestic court of decisions rendered in breach of the requirement to act independently and impartially.

The review has highlighted a sharp difference in the methodology and degree to which the principle of independence and impartiality is implemented with respect to domestic, as opposed to international, adjudicators. The principle is fully implemented with respect to Italian judges and arbitrators seated in Italy. Some possible changes and amelioration are clearly possible. However, overall no serious flaws or critical situations have been detected. Conversely, the approaches adopted as regards the selection and appointment of national candidates for positions as international adjudicators are primarily political. Therefore, the guiding principles and legal mechanisms in place are primarily focused on pursuing the goal of selecting international adjudicators chiefly guided by the protection of national interests. In this context, it cannot come as a surprise that the principle of independence and impartiality is mostly overlooked, and the process of selection is often opaque. Without hampering the policy needs to protect national interests in international institutions, this report suggests that Italy could effectively take action, especially in the process of selecting national candidates for positions as international adjudicators, to better implement the transparency of the process and the principle of independence and impartiality of international adjudicators appointed by Italy.

THE INDEPENDENCE AND IMPARTIALITY OF ADJUDICATORS IN MEXICO

Rafael QUINTERO GODÍNEZ

1. Introduction 555
2. Historical Context of the 2021 Judicial Reform 557
3. Criteria for the Selection of Adjudicators 560
    3.1. Federal Adjudicators 561
        3.1.1. The Supreme Court of Justice of the Nation 561
        3.1.2. The Electoral Tribunal 563
        3.1.3. Circuit Magistrates and District Judges 565
    3.2. The Method for Appointing National Candidates to Positions
          as International Adjudicators 568
4. The Methods to Balance the Appointing Authority's Influence 569
5. Parameters to Ensure that Adjudicators Act Independently and
    Impartially 570
6. Consequences for Domestic Adjudicators of a Breach of the
    Requirement to Act Independently and Impartially 572
    6.1. Political Impeachment 572
    6.2. Administrative Responsibility Procedure 573
    6.3. Criminal Charges 574
7. Enforcement of Final Judgments Rendered by Adjudicators in
    Breach of the Requirement to Act Independently and Impartially 575
8. Conclusion 576

1. INTRODUCTION

Judicial independence is a goal democracies strive to achieve.[1] If the judiciary is free of constraints that undermine its impartial judgement, it will be in a better position

---

[1]   As pointed out by Gibler and Randazzo: '[n]ewly independent judiciaries are sometimes created in unstable states and are unable to stop antidemocratic reversals': 'Testing the Effects of Independent Judiciaries on the Likelihood of Democratic Backsliding', *American Journal of Political Science* 55, no. 3 (2011): 707.

Intersentia

Rafael Quintero Godínez

to develop judicial review that defends the rule of law, protects the separation of powers, and promotes due process of law.[2] To accomplish this, the judiciary should be independent from the parties to a conflict, autonomous from the political institutions of a government, and independent from contested political ideologies.[3] In other words, the judiciary cannot be an extension of the legislative and executive arms of the government.[4] However, the formation of an independent judiciary may be hampered by institutional legacies, insufficient training and support for judges, and the power of strong political players.[5] Without the ability of courts to render independent judgments, democratic development stalls and the likelihood of the state reverting to an authoritarian regime increases.[6]

Strengthening judicial independence so that courts hold political actors accountable (judicial review) is symptomatic of an improving democracy.[7] 'Why should any authoritarian regime', Shapiro asks, 'allow a small group of persons, not themselves, to make public policy decisions contrary to, or at least independent of, their preferences'.[8] But without judicial independence, courts cannot effectively and democratically intervene in the political process.[9] Institutional guarantees to safeguard judicial independence are therefore extremely important.[10]

Since 1994, Mexico has initiated a wave of judicial reforms aimed to strengthen judicial independence and impartiality. Although there have been shortcomings along the way, improvements have been made. The latest judicial reform (2021) has precisely aimed to improve the criteria for selecting adjudicators and the methods to balance the appointing authority's influence. To understand the process of this reform, we provide a historical context.

---

[2] Charles G. Geyh, 'The Endless Judicial Selection Debate and Why It Matters for Judicial Independence', *The Georgetown Journal of Legal Ethics* 21 (2008): 1260.

[3] Paul W. Kahn, 'Independence and Responsibility in the Judicial Role', in *Transition to Democracy in Latin America: The Role of the Judiciary*, ed. Irwin P. Stotzky (Routledge, 2018), 73.

[4] Erik S. Herron and Kirk A. Randazzo, 'The Relationship Between Independence and Judicial Review in Post-Communist Courts', *The Journal of Politics* 65, no. 2 (2003): 423.

[5] Shapiro argues that 'the political parties–court connection is not always and necessarily a negative one': 'The Success 1 of Judicial Review and Democracy', in *On Law, Politics, and Judicialization* (Oxford University Press, 2002), 160.

[6] Gibler and Randazzo, supra n. 1, 707. According to Moohyung the real challenge to promoting judicial independence lies in maintaining it, rather than in establishing it. This because autocratic regimes may grant judicial independence, provided that it does not strongly constrain their opportunism. 'Rethinking Judicial Independence in Democracy and Autocracy' (Doctor of Philosophy, Duke University, 2020), 19.

[7] Cf. Annabelle Lever, 'Is Judicial Review Undemocratic?', *Public Law* (2007): 280.

[8] Martin Shapiro, 'Judicial Power and Democracy', in *Judicial Power: How Constitutional Courts Affect Political Transformations*, ed. Christine Landfried (Cambridge University Press, 2019), 22.

[9] Carlo Guarnieri and Patrizia Pederzoli, *The Power of Judges: A Comparative Study of Courts and Democracy*, trans. Cheryl Thomas, Oxford Socio-Legal Studies (Oxford Scholarship Online, 2012), 18.

[10] Theunis Roux, *The Politico-Legal Dynamics of Judicial Review: A Comparative Analysis*, Comparative Constitutional Law and Policy (Cambridge University Press, 2018), 12.

Our report proceeds as follows. Section 2 explains the historical context of the latest judicial reform, which situates the evolution of the Mexican judiciary in the structural trend of judicialisation – the process whereby adjudicatory bodies increasingly dominate the making of public policies.[11] Section 3 explains the criteria for the selection of adjudicators as well as the authorities that design them – in particular, we focus on the judicial bodies at the federal level. Section 4 explains the methods to balance the appointing authority's influence, which, for the most part, is limited to appealing the results of the competitive examinations and ratifying magistrates and district justices. Section 5 discusses the parameters to ensure that federal adjudicators act independently and impartially. Section 6 explains the three punishments for federal adjudicators who do not act independently and impartially: political impeachment, administrative responsibility procedure, and criminal charges. Finally, section 7 explains the consequences of violating *res judicata* if adjudicators act in violation of the principles of impartiality and independence.

2. HISTORICAL CONTEXT OF THE 2021 JUDICIAL REFORM

The post-war period brought about an era of dictatorial and authoritarian regimes in Latin America.[12] Judiciaries were servile institutions to political and military systems;[13] judicial independence and impartiality were not attainable aspirations, but uncharted territories.[14] For example, in Peru, the government of General Juan Velasco replaced the entire Supreme Court with judges ideologically sympathetic to his regime.[15] In El Salvador, the judiciary lacked independence and failed to examine cases of serious human rights violations.[16]

Similarly, in Mexico, the Justices of the Supreme Court of Justice of the Nation (SCJN) acquired the role of 'regime supporters'.[17] Between 1944 and

---

[11] C. Neal Tate, 'Why the Expansion of Judicial Power?', in *The Global Expansion of Judicial Power*, ed. C. Neal Tate and Torbjörn Vallinder (New York University Press, 1995), 28.

[12] Alexandra Barahona de Brito, *Human Rights and Democratization in Latin America: Uruguay and Chile*, Oxford Studies in Democratization (Oxford University Press, 1997), 2–5.

[13] Elin Skaar, *Judicial Independence and Human Rights in Latin America Violations, Politics, and Prosecution* (Palgrave Macmillan, 2011), 2–4.

[14] Margaret Popkin, 'Fortalecer La Independencia Judicial', in *En busca de una justicia distinta. Experiencias de reforma en América Latina*, ed. Luis Pásara (UNAM 2004), 410.

[15] By 1975, the Peruvian regime had replaced 504 out of 643 lower-level judges. Linn A. Hammergren, *The Politics of Justice and Justice Reform in Latin America: The Peruvian Case in Comparative Perspective* (Westview Press, 1998), 144.

[16] Margaret Popkin, *Peace without Justice: Obstacles to Building the Rule of Law in El Salvador* (Pennsylvania State University Press, 2000), 3.

[17] Andrea Castagnola and Saul Lopez Noriega, *Judicial Politics in Mexico: The Supreme Court and the Transition to Democracy* (Routledge, 2016), 24.

1994, the majority of presidents appointed more than half of the justices during their tenure, and over 40% of them served for fewer than five years, arriving and departing according to the presidential term.[18] This resulted in a judiciary that primarily employed a legalist standard of judicial interpretation that condoned state abuse.[19]

Against this backdrop, which included 65 years of the rule of a severely delegitimised political party, i.e. the Institutional Revolutionary Party (IRP), and several local electoral defeats, the newly elected Mexican president, Ernesto Zedillo, launched a new judicial reform in 1994.[20] At its core, there was a change of personnel along with an expansion of the jurisdiction of the SCJN so as to secure its independence.[21]

On the one hand, the number of justices was lowered from 25 to 11; life appointments were replaced with 15-year appointments; and the president now nominates justices, who must be confirmed by a Senate majority of two-thirds.[22] On the other hand, two new mechanisms of constitutional control were introduced.[23] First, the Court could resolve disagreements between various governmental branches over the constitutional legality of their respective actions (constitutional controversies). Second, qualified minorities of legislative bodies at the federal, state and municipal levels, as well as the Attorney General, could challenge the constitutionality of federal and state laws and international treaties, directly before the Court, by filing a constitutional action. Finally, the reform created the Federal Judicial Council (FJC), charged with administering the federal judiciary – namely, selecting judges and determining their promotions.[24]

Some scholars have argued that the 1994 reform was an insurance policy designed to protect the weakening IRP, which was operating in an unstable political environment.[25] However, ex post explanations which try to capture

---

[18] Beatriz Magaloni, 'Authoritarianism, Democracy and the Supreme Court: Horizontal Exchange and the Rule of Law in Mexico', in *Democratic Accountability in Latin America*, ed. Scott Mainwaring and Christoper Welna (Oxford University Press 2003), 288–89.

[19] Arianna Sánchez, Beatriz Magaloni and Eric Magar, 'Legalist versus Interpretativist: The Supreme Court and the Democratic Transition in Mexico', in *Courts in Latin America*, ed. Gretchen Helmke and Julio Rios-Figueroa (Cambridge University Press, 2011), 190.

[20] Jorge A. Vargas, 'The Rebirth of the Supreme Court of Mexico: An Appraisal of President Zedillo's Judicial Reform of 1995', *American University International Law Review* 11, no. 2 (1996): 299.

[21] Miguel Schor, 'An Essay on the Emergence of Constitutional Courts: The Cases of Mexico and Colombia', *Indiana Journal of Global Legal Studies* 16, no. 1 (2009): 181.

[22] Juan Gonzalez Bertomeu, 'Judicial Politics in Latin America', in *Handbook of Law and Society in Latin America*, ed. Tatiana Alfonso, Karina Ansolabehere and Rachel Sieder (Routledge, 2018), 172.

[23] Josafat Cortez Salinas and Grisel Salazar Rebolledo, 'La Construcción de La Independencia y Del Poder de La Suprema Corte de Justicia En México. Explicando La Reforma Judicial de 1994', *Estudios Políticos (México)*, no. 46 (2019): 219.

[24] Magaloni, supra n. 18, 294.

[25] Jodi Finkel, 'Judicial Reform as Insurance Policy: Mexico in the 1990s', *Latin American Politics and Society* 47, no. 1 (2005): 88.

hidden motivations are hard to study.[26] Instead, here it is argued that this and the following reforms have taken place in the wider context of making the judiciary independent to advance democratic governance in Latin America:[27] a process which tries to politically insulate the judiciary from institutions under popular control,[28] while increasing its intervention in political processes through various forms of judicial review.[29]

The latest breakthroughs in the transformation of the Mexican judiciary support this thesis. First, between 2009 and 2011, a series of judicial decisions and reforms brought about a paradigm shift in the jurisprudence of the SCJN, which marked the start of the 10th epoch of the court's jurisprudence.[30] It set forth the diffuse control of constitutionality and conventionality. This meant that any Mexican judge or court could examine whether a law – or, more specifically, any other legal element – is contrary to the Constitution and, if so, refuse to apply it in resolving a specific case.[31] Necessarily, this new form of constitutional judicial review renders Mexican courts unable to effectively make or block public policies.[32]

However, a series of controversial designations of the SCJN Justices and nepotistic practices within the FJC prompted a downshift in safeguarding the independence of the Mexican judiciary.[33] Caballero notes two controversial appointments: first, the obscure designation process of Justice Eduardo Medina Mora (2015), who had been criticised because of his previous performance at the Center for Investigation and National Security and as Attorney General of the Republic;[34] and second, the controversial designation of Yazmín Esquivel Mossa, given that she is the wife of businessman José Mara Riobóo, a contractor and consultant for the current Mexican administration.[35] Additionally, a recent study shows the existence of clientelist networks in Mexico's judicial system, in which a high percentages of judicial officials have relatives in the circuit they represent – in some instances, up to 66%.[36]

---

26   Gonzalez Bertomeu, supra n. 22, 171.
27   Michael Dodson, 'Assessing Judicial Reform in Latin America', *Latin American Research Review* 37, no. 2 (2002): 201.
28   Owen M. Fiss, 'The Right Degree of Independence', in *Transition to Democracy in Latin America: The Role of the Judiciary*, ed. Irwin P. Stotzky (Routledge, 2018), 62.
29   Guarnieri and Pederzoli, supra n. 9, 18.
30   Eduardo Ferrer Mac-Gregor and Rubén Sánchez Gil, *Control Difuso de Constitucionalidad y Convencionalidad* (Suprema Corte de Justicia de la Nación, Oficina en México del Alto Comisionado de las Naciones Unidas para los Derechos Humanos y Comisión de Derechos Humanos del Distrito Federal, 2013), 14–15.
31   Ibid., 15.
32   Shapiro, supra n. 8, 21.
33   José Antonio Caballero, 'La Reforma Judicial de 2021. ¿Hacia Dónde va La Justicia?', *Nexos* (blog), 5 October 2021; Sociedad, 'Organizaciones Exigen Cambiar El Proceso Para Designar a Los Ministros', *Expansión Política*, 13 March 2019.
34   Also, in 2019, Medina Mora resigned with no official explanation.
35   Caballero, supra n. 33; Sociedad, supra n. 33.
36   Felipe Borrego Estrada, 'Estudio Sobre Redes Familiares y Clientelares En El Consejo de La Judicatura Federal', *Reforma Judicial. Revista Mexicana de Justicia*, no. 29–30 (2017): 159–63.

These controversies alone triggered the 2021 judicial reform.[37] The reform project indicates the need to combat nepotism within the judiciary.[38] It underscores that federal judges do not always conduct themselves with independence and impartiality; neither has the judicial career system been successful in ensuring that those who become judges are the most honest and best prepared; nor has it been possible to banish corruption. If anything, inbreeding and cronyism have produced deep-rooted clientelist networks, in which positions are trafficked, favours are exchanged, or worse, a price is put on justice.[39]

The reform considers two major aspects – namely, jurisdiction and governance. Given the scope of this report, we concentrate on the latter.[40] The main governance focus is to address the way people enter a judicial career, to reduce clientelism within the judiciary.[41] To that end, the reform limits the ability of judges and magistrates to appoint their staff; it underscores the immovability of judges; it establishes the Federal Judicial Training School – charged with implementing the processes of formation, training and updating of the jurisdictional and administrative personnel of the judiciary,[42] as well as of conducting competitive examinations; and, finally, it introduces gender parity criteria.[43]

3. CRITERIA FOR THE SELECTION OF ADJUDICATORS

The manner in which judges are recruited has an impact not only on the professional makeup of the judiciary, but also on the connections it develops with other political actors.[44] The European Court of Human Rights (ECtHR) has determined that to decide whether a body can be deemed independent,

---

[37] Carlos Martín Gómez Marinero, 'La Reforma Judicial de 2021', *Hechos y Derechos*, no. 65 (2021).

[38] José Antonio Caballero, *La Reforma Judicial de 2021 ¿Hacia Dónde va La Justicia?*, Serie Estudios Jurídicos, No. 360 (Universidad Nacional Autónoma de México and Instituto de Investigaciones Jurídicas, 2021), 13 and 17.

[39] Poder Judicial de la Federación, *Reforma Judicial Con y Para El Poder Judicial* (México, 2020), 3.

[40] For a comprehensive overview of the reform's whole scope, see: Caballero, supra n. 38, 29–81.

[41] Ibid., 88.

[42] Formation refers to the process of developing a new judicial profile with the highest technical standards and human quality (Escuela Federal de Formación Judicial' (2023), available at https://escuelajudicial.cjf.gob.mx/), while training is the process of learning specific tasks and techniques to respond to the specific needs of judicial officers (Consejo de la Judicatura Federal and Escuela Federal de Formación Judicial, 'Informe de Actividades 2022' (2022), 27).

[43] Political Constitution of the United Mexican States (1917) Article 100, paras 7–8; Judicial Career Law of the Judicial Branch of the Federation (2021).

[44] Guarnieri and Pederzoli, supra n. 9, 18–19.

the way in which its members are appointed and their tenure in office must be examined.[45] In the same vein, a report concerning the judicial independence of the ECtHR finds that the practice of appointments is important in relation to two factors. First, given that the legitimacy and credibility of any judicial institution are contingent upon public faith in its independence, it is essential that judicial nomination processes adhere to recognised principles of judicial independence.[46] Second, the likelihood of judges lacking the necessary skills and capacities to carry out their profession increases if there are neither objective nor transparent standards of appointment, based on appropriate professional qualifications.[47]

3.1. FEDERAL ADJUDICATORS

In this section, we analyse the designation process, along with the criteria for selecting adjudicators of the Mexican judiciary at the federal level.[48] This includes the Justices of the SCJN, the Magistrates of the Electoral Tribunal, and circuit magistrates and district judges. We do not consider the designation process of the Councillors of the FJC, given that its organisational nature is more administrative than adjudicatory.

3.1.1. The Supreme Court of Justice of the Nation

The SCJN is the country's highest constitutional court and the head of the federation's judiciary.[49] It is composed of 11 Justices[50] with a 15-year tenure.[51] Among its responsibilities are to defend the legal order established by the Federal Constitution, to maintain the balance of power between the various branches

---

45   See, for instance, the recent decision of the ECtHR against Poland, in which it found that the procedure for appointing judges had been unduly influenced by the legislative and executive powers, which 'amounts to a fundamental irregularity adversely affecting the whole process and compromising the legitimacy of a court composed of judges so appointed'. *Reczkowicz v. Poland*, ECtHR decision of 22 July 2021, application no. 43447/19, para. 276.

46   Jutta Limbach et al., 'Judicial Independence: Law and Practise of Appointments to the European Court of Human Rights' (Interights, 2003), 5–6; United Nations, 'Basic Principles on the Independence of the Judiciary', Pub. L. No. Resolutions 40/32 of 29 November 1985 and 40/146 of 13 December 1985.

47   Limbach et al., supra n. 46, 5–6.

48   Political Constitution of the United Mexican States, Article 94, paras 1–6; Organic Law of the Federal Judiciary 2021, Article 1.

49   Political Constitution of the United Mexican States, Article 94, para. 3; Organic Law of the Federal Judiciary, Article 2.

50   Political Constitution of the United Mexican States, Article 94, para. 3; Organic Law of the Federal Judiciary, Article 2.

51   Political Constitution of the United Mexican States, Article 94, para. 14; Organic Law of the Federal Judiciary, Article 8.

and spheres of government, and to definitively resolve matters of great social importance.[52]

The process of appointing the SCJN Justices begins with the President of Mexico submitting a list of three candidates for consideration to the Senate. Following a hearing, the Senate appoints a Justice by a vote of two-thirds of the senators present. If the Senate does not make a decision within 30 days, the person designated by the President will occupy the position of Justice. However, if the Senate rejects the entire list of three candidates, the President must submit a new one. If this second slate is also rejected by the Senate, then the President will name the new Justice.[53]

The Constitution suggests that appointments of the SCJN Justices shall preferably be made from among those persons who have served with efficiency, capacity and probity in the administration of justice, or who have distinguished themselves for their honourability, competence and professional background in the exercise of legal praxis.[54] Additionally, to be elected a Justice of the SCJN, it is required that the officeholder should:

1. be a Mexican citizen by birth, in full exercise of political and civil rights;
2. be at least 35 years of age on the day of the appointment;
3. possess, on the day of the appointment, at least 10 years of seniority and a professional law degree issued by an authority or institution legally empowered to do so;
4. have a good reputation, and not have been convicted of a crime punishable by more than one year's imprisonment;
5. have resided in the country during the two years prior to the day of the appointment; and
6. not have been Secretary of State, Attorney General of the Republic, a senator, a federal deputy, or head of the executive power of any federal entity during the year prior to the day of appointment.

This process of electing SCJN Justices has been criticised. Allier has noted four procedural flaws.[55] First, the President is not obliged to motivate the candidacies he or she proposes to the Senate. Second, there is no law establishing objective criteria for the selection of aspiring ministers, which would provide certainty to the appointment system. Third, there is a lack of participation by both the

---

[52] SCJN, '¿Qué Es La Suprema Corte de Justicia de La Nación?', n.d., https://www.scjn.gob.mx/conoce-la-corte/que-es-la-scjn. The complete list of attributions is set forth in Organic Law of the Federal Judiciary, Article 10.

[53] Political Constitution of the United Mexican States, Article 96, para. 2.

[54] Ibid., Article 95, para. 2.

[55] Jaime Allier Campuzano, 'Nuevo Procedimiento para la Designación de Ministros de la Suprema Corte de Justicia de la Nación', *Revista del Instituto de la Judicatura Federal*, no. 47 (2019): 4.

federal judiciary and civil society in the selection and appointment process. Fourth, this process endorses the prevalence of presidentialism and particracy. To correct these flaws, Allier suggests that the candidate be knowledgeable about constitutional law, human rights and the branches of law that correspond to the chambers of the SCJN.[56]

Another proposal to reform the designation process comes from José and Miguel Carbonell:[57] they consider that the system of shortlists should be replaced and, to that end, that the Senate should have exclusive authority to nominate and appoint individuals. Likewise, they recommended holding extensive hearings to fully assess the qualifications and expertise of applicants for the top post in the federal judicial branch, as well as to create a more expedited approach in the case of an unexpected SCJN vacancy.

We consider that both the Allier and Carbonell approaches may serve as gateways to addressing the problems of nepotism and controversial designations that triggered the judicial reform. Certainly, reducing the President's discretion to nominate SCJN Justices while incorporating the views of the federal judiciary and civil society would help to democratise the selection process.

3.1.2. The Electoral Tribunal

The Electoral Tribunal is a specialised judicial body of the Federal Judiciary, and the highest judicial authority in electoral matters.[58] It settles, in the last instance, any challenge or controversy that may arise in federal and local electoral processes.[59] The Electoral Tribunal operates on a permanent basis with a Superior Chamber, seven Regional Chambers and a Specialised Regional Chamber.[60] Magistrates at the Superior and Regional Chambers have a tenure of nine years, which cannot be extended.[61]

In addition to meeting the criteria to be a Justice of the SCJN,[62] the Organic Law of the Judiciary of the Federation (OLJF) considers that an electoral magistrate of the Superior Chamber must:[63]

---

[56] Ibid.

[57] José Carbonell and Miguel Carbonell, 'El Nombramiento de Los Ministros de La Suprema Corte: Una Propuesta de Reforma', in *Estado Constitucional, Derechos Humanos, Justicia y Vida Universitaria. Estudios En Homenaje a Jorge Carpizo*, vol. III (Universidad Nacional Autónoma de México, 2015), 71–72. José Carbonell and Miguel Carbonell, 'El Nombramiento de Los Ministros de La Suprema Corte: Una Propuesta de Reforma', *Quid Iuris* 23, no. 8 (2014): 77.

[58] Political Constitution of the United Mexican States, Article 99; Organic Law of the Federal Judiciary, Article 164.

[59] Organic Law of the Federal Judiciary, Article 165.

[60] Political Constitution of the United Mexican States, Article 99, para. 2; Organic Law of the Federal Judiciary, Article 165.

[61] Political Constitution of the United Mexican States, Article 99, paras 12 and 13.

[62] Ibid., Article 99, para. 12.

[63] Organic Law of the Federal Judiciary, Article 193.

1. have a voting card with a photograph;
2. be able to prove his or her knowledge of electoral law;
3. not hold or have held the position of President of the National Executive Committee or equivalent of a political party;
4. not have been registered as a candidate for any office of popular election in the last six years immediately preceding the appointment; and
5. not hold or have held a national, state, district or municipal leadership position in any political party in the six years immediately preceding the appointment.

The OLJF sets forth three additional conditions to the selection of magistrates of the Regional Chambers; namely, they must be at least 35 years old at the time of designation; have a clean record and not have been convicted of an intentional offence punishable by more than one year's imprisonment; and possess a legally recognised law degree and a minimum of five years of professional experience.[64] Although it is not expressly stated in the OLJF, these three additional criteria are also applicable to the selection of Superior Chamber Magistrates, given that the Constitution expresses that they should meet also the criteria to be a Justice of the SCJN.

The process of designating a Magistrate of the Electoral Tribunal (either at the Superior Chamber or at the Regional Chambers) is more rigorous than that for the SCJN Justices.[65] It combines a nomination process carried out by the SCJN and a designation by the Senate. First, the Plenary of the SCJN issues a general call for applications; namely, any person who meets the legal requirements listed above can apply. Additionally, applicants should submit their résumé and write a 10-page essay on an electoral topic chosen at the discretion of the SCJN.[66] After examining and evaluating the candidates, the SCJN shortlists a number of candidates to undergo an oral and public examination. Each of the shortlisted candidates is examined by one of the SCJN Justices concerning the functioning of the Superior or Regional Chamber, as appropriate. Afterwards, each of the candidates presents, before the Plenary of the SCJN, the key points of their essay; they are then examined on those points by one Justice.[67] Finally, the Justices vote upon whom they consider to be the most appropriate candidates to comprise the trio from which the Senate elects one magistrate.[68]

---

[64] Ibid., Article 194, sections II, III and IV.
[65] Political Constitution of the United Mexican States, Article 99, para. 11.
[66] SCJN Pleno, 'Acuerdo Número 6/2016' (2016).
[67] SCJN Pleno, 'Acuerdo Número 14/2016' (2016).
[68] SCJN Pleno, 'LISTA Aprobada Por El Pleno de La Suprema Corte de Justicia de La Nación En Su Sesión Pública Celebrada El Dieciséis de Agosto de Dos Mil Dieciséis, de Los Cuarenta y Dos Candidatos a Integrar Las Ternas Que Serán Propuestas a La Cámara de Senadores Del Congreso de La Unión Para La Designación de Magistrados de La Sala Superior Del Tribunal Electoral Del Poder Judicial de La Federación' (2016).

Second, the Justice Commission of the Senate carries out a hearing process in which, after evaluating the candidates' compliance with the formal legal requirements, it proposes to the Plenary of the Senate of the Republic one person from each slate proposed by the SCJN to occupy the positions in question.[69]

The appearances are in trios; each of the three members presents for five minutes. The nominees discuss the significance and fitness of their candidacy, the substance of their essays, and the role they aim to establish as a Magistrate of the Electoral Tribunal, if selected.[70] Following the presentation of the three candidates, the senators who are members of the Justice Commission have up to two minutes to ask questions. The selection procedure concludes after four days, following the final appearance. Once this procedure is completed, the names of candidates for appointment as Magistrates of the Electoral Tribunal are presented to the Plenary of the Senate of the Republic, who will decide by a vote of two-thirds of the members present.[71]

In a General Agreement, the Justice Commission has set forth that the decision of the senators to elect the Magistrates of the Electoral Tribunal should be motivated following the parameters of the candidates' excellence in preparation and their professional experience; their theoretical and practical training; their knowledge of and familiarity with electoral matters; the jurisdictional impartiality they can ensure; and the relevance and suitability of their candidacy.[72]

3.1.3. Circuit Magistrates and District Judges

The circuit magistrates are the adjudicators of the different collegiate tribunals in Mexico, which have the powers of constitutional courts of cassation.[73] There are three types of circuit tribunals – collegiate tribunals of appeal,[74] circuit collegiate tribunals,[75] and regional plenary[76] – each of which are distributed across 32 judicial circuits in the national territory.[77] Each tribunal is made up of three circuit magistrates, who may specialise in one area or several (civil, criminal, administrative and labour).[78]

---

69 Rules of Procedure of the Senate of the Republic (2010), Article 257, section II.
70 Senado Comisión de Justicia, 'Acuerdo de la Comisión de Justicia por el que se establece el procedimiento para la comparecencia y dictaminación de los candidatos presentados por la Suprema Corte de Justicia de la Nación para Magistrados de las Salas Regionales del Tribunal Electoral del Poder Judicial de la Federación' (2013), section 2.
71 Political Constitution of the United Mexican States, Article 99, para. 12.
72 Comisión de Justicia, supra n. 70.
73 Fabiola Martínez Ramírez and Edgar Caballero González, 'El Recurso de La Casación', *Revista Iberoamericana de Derecho Procesal Constitucional*, no. 12 (2009): 149.
74 The Organic Law of the Federal Judiciary, Article 35 lays down the full list of their competence.
75 Ibid., Article 38 lays down the full list of their competence.
76 Ibid., Article 42 lays down the full list of their competence.
77 Ibid., Article 1, sections III, IV and V.
78 Federal Law of Responsibilities of Public Servants (1982), Article 2.

On the other hand, district judges are the judicial bodies of first instance of the federal judicial branch. They hear disputes arising from the enforcement or application of federal laws in civil, criminal and administrative matters, and resolve indirect *amparo* lawsuits in those same subjects.[79]

Both magistrates and judges are appointed for a probation period of six years, at the end of which, if ratified, they can only be removed due to political impeachment or serious administrative misconduct, as outlined below in sections 6.1 and 6.2.[80]

As we have mentioned, a series of controversies triggered a judicial reform,[81] which established the Judicial Career Law of the Judicial Branch of the Federation (JCLJBF). The JCLJBF establishes the guiding procedures to appoint judicial personnel. In line with the text of the Constitution, the JCLJBF states the FJC is the authority in charge of appointing circuit magistrates, as well as district judges, based on objective criteria and in accordance with internal or external competitive examinations.[82]

Circuit magistrates and district judges must meet the same formal legal requirements, except for the age criterion. These include:[83]

1. being a Mexican citizen by birth, without having acquired another nationality;
2. being in full enjoyment and exercise of their civil and political rights;
3. being over 35 years of age for magistrates and 30 for judges;
4. having a good reputation;
5. not having been convicted of a felony punishable by deprivation of liberty; and
6. having a law degree legally issued and at least five years of professional experience.

Although the formal requirements for circuit magistrates and district judges are identical, the entry process differs, in that only district judges and Secretaries of Study and Account of the SCJN can participate in the competitive examinations to fill the positions of circuit magistrate.[84]

First, there are two procedures for the competitive examination for the appointment of district judges: school-based and non-school-based.[85] The former

---

[79] Organic Law of the Federal Judiciary, Articles 49–62.

[80] Political Constitution of the United Mexican States, Article 110, para. 3. The comprehensive list of reasons for impeachment is found in Federal Law of Responsibilities of Public Servants, Article 7.

[81] There have been allegations of exam leaks in the organisation of the competitive examinations. See José Antonio Belmont, 'Destituyen e Inhabilitan a Magistrado Por Filtración de Exámenes Para Jueces', *Milenio*, 5 August 2020.

[82] Political Constitution of the United Mexican States, Article 100, paras 7, 10 and 11.

[83] Judicial Career Law of the Judicial Branch of the Federation, Articles 11 and 12, respectively.

[84] Ibid., Article 22, para. 5.

[85] Ibid., Article 24.

is carried out through a training course given by the Judicial School,[86] while the latter refers to open or internal competitive examinations, which include the completion of a questionnaire whose content deals with subjects related to the function of the position for which the candidate is applying.[87] Access to both the training courses and the competitive examinations is both internal (for those already part of the judiciary) and external (available to anyone), provided they meet the above criteria.[88]

The competitive examinations for both circuit magistrates and district judges consist of two stages. The first stage consists of a multiple-choice test – 50 questions for magistrates[89] and 100 for judges[90] – a practical test, consisting of writing a draft judgment, and a 15-minute oral exam before a jury. Finally, district judges who successfully pass the examination undergo an induction and specialisation course to strengthen and improve the performance of the judicial function.[91] The appointments are made by the Plenary of the FJC[92] and published in Mexico's Official Gazette.[93]

As we have mentioned, after successfully completing a probation period of six years, the FJC determines whether to ratify the magistrate or the judge. To do so, it evaluates:[94]

1. whether they have not been sanctioned for serious misconduct as a result of an administrative complaint during their tenure as a district judge or circuit magistrate;
2. whether they have a satisfactory evaluation as a federal judge, in accordance with the following:
   a. judicial functioning, based on the following:
      i. results of inspection visits, and
      ii. performance, evaluated based on productivity derived from statistical information;

---

[86] Ibid., Article 25.
[87] Ibid., Article 26, paras 3 and 4.
[88] Ibid., Article 20, section II.
[89] FJC Pleno, 'Acuerdo General Del Pleno Del Consejo de La Judicatura Federal, Que Establece El Procedimiento y Lineamientos Generales Para Acceder al Cargo de Magistrado de Circuito, Mediante Concursos de Oposición Libres' (2021), Décima Quinta, 1.
[90] FJC Pleno, 'Acuerdo General Del Pleno Del Consejo de La Judicatura Federal, Que Reforma El Diverso Que Establece El Procedimiento y Lineamientos Generales Para Acceder al Cargo de Juez y Jueza de Distrito Especializado En Materia de Trabajo Mediante Concursos Abiertos de Oposición' (2020), Décima Quinta, 1.
[91] Ibid., Vigésima Segunda.
[92] Political Constitution of the United Mexican States, Article 97.
[93] Judicial Career Law of the Judicial Branch of the Federation, Articles 25, para. 5; 26, para. 7; and 27, para. 7.
[94] Ibid., Article 67.

Intersentia

567

b. suitability, where the following is accredited:

iii. that they have conducted themselves without intent to deceive the various administrative instances of the Council in its surveillance processes, visits, statistics, discipline, work conflicts or in compliance with the judicial policies implemented, especially those to combat nepotism;

iv. that they hold the appropriate law degrees, as well as refresher and specialisation courses;

v. that they have not been sanctioned for crimes or misdemeanours that, regardless of their individual qualification, as a whole are considered serious because they reflect patterns of conduct that are far from the constitutional standards of excellence, objectivity, impartiality, professionalism and independence; and

vi. that they have not incurred a systematic breach of labour standards, for which disciplinary proceedings, labour disputes and ordinary visit rulings may be reviewed; and

3. any other issues deemed pertinent by the FJC, provided that they are included in general agreements published six months prior to the date of ratification.

The weight assigned to points 1, 2 and 3 must be determined in the respective general agreement and shall be stated in the resolutions of the FJC in which the ratification is agreed upon.[95]

3.2. THE METHOD FOR APPOINTING NATIONAL CANDIDATES TO POSITIONS AS INTERNATIONAL ADJUDICATORS

Although Mexican citizens have occupied several positions as international adjudicators,[96] there are no formal methods to nominate them to the relevant international adjudicatory bodies. This is particularly concerning if we consider that in 2019 Mexico obtained, worldwide, the highest number of elected candidacies to bodies of the multilateral system, with a total of 32, at a 100% success rate in its nominations.[97] The internal regulations of the Secretariat

---

[95] Ibid., Article 67, para. 2.

[96] To name a few examples, Bernardo Sepúlveda Amor was a justice at the International Court of Justice; Ricardo Ramírez Hernández was a member and president of the Appellate Body of the World Trade Organization; and Sergio García Ramírez and Eduardo Ferrer Mac-Gregor Poisot have been judges and presidents of the Inter-American Court of Human Rights.

[97] Secretaría de Relaciones Exteriores, 'Durante 2019 México Obtuvo El Número Más Alto de Candidaturas Electas a Organismos Multilaterales', 2 January 2020, https://www.gob.mx/sre/prensa/durante-2019-mexico-obtuvo-el-numero-mas-alto-de-candidaturas-electas-a-organismos-multilaterales.

of their Economy and Internal Affairs consider provisions on nominating personnel to international organisations, but no formal criteria or standards are put forward.[98]

In light of the above, the nomination and designation of María del Socorro Flores Liera as justice of the International Criminal Court in 2019 sparked controversy as to the method whereby Mexico nominated her.[99] As Martínez and Guzmán note, her selection procedure did not meet the criteria set forth in Article 36(4)(a)(i) of the Rome Statute, because neither did the Mexican President provide a shortlist of candidates, nor was the Senate consulted during the selection process.[100]

This is symptomatic of a bigger problem. Mexico lacks a policy or legal framework governing judicial nominations to international organisations. Additionally, there is no impartial and independent selection body to make such nominations, which would ensure fairness and the suitability of those nominated. In this sense, Martínez and Guzmán suggest the Senate and the Secretariat of Foreign Affairs establish a clear selection method that ensures equal opportunity for all applicants: one in which the nomination process provides a set of transparent, merit-based criteria that certify impartiality and appropriately assess the candidate's profile, abilities, knowledge and experience.[101]

4. THE METHODS TO BALANCE THE APPOINTING AUTHORITY'S INFLUENCE

As we have discussed, the process of electing SCJN Justices and Electoral Magistrates is carried out between two governmental branches. Concerning the former, the president nominates and the Senate chooses, while for the latter, the SCJN nominates and the Senate appoints. However, neither the decisions to nominate nor to appoint can be recursed.

Similarly, the decisions of the FJC to appoint magistrates and judges cannot be appealed. Only the results of the competitive examinations may be challenged before the Plenary of the FJC.[102] The appeal for administrative review must be filed within five working days following the date on which the notification of the

---

[98] Internal Regulations of the Secretariat of Economy (2019), Article 5, section XVIII; Internal Regulations of the Secretariat of Internal Affairs (2019), Article 5, section XVIII.

[99] Rodolfo González Espinosa, 'La Nueva Jueza Mexicana En La Corte Penal Internacional: Una Oportunidad Perdida', *Nexos*, 7 January 2021.

[100] Graciela Martínez Manzo and Olga Guzmán Vergara, 'ICC 2020 Judicial Elections: Mexico Aims for a Seat on the Bench', *International Justice Monitor*, 2 January 2020, https://www.ijmonitor.org/2020/09/icc-2020-judicial-elections-mexico-aims-for-a-seat-on-the-bench.

[101] Ibid.

[102] Political Constitution of the United Mexican States, Article 100, para. 11; Judicial Career Law of the Judicial Branch of the Federation, Article 74.

results of the competitive examination has taken effect or has become known.[103] Decisions declaring the administrative review appeal well founded may correct the score or annul the competitive examination, order that the appellant be re-examined, or order any other measure to correct the violation suffered by the appellant.[104]

The decisions of the FJC referring to the ratification of magistrates and district judges may be appealed before the Plenary of the SCJN, which should only verify whether they have been adopted in accordance with the rules established by the Constitution, the JCLJBF, internal regulations and general agreements issued by the FJC.[105] The appeal for administrative review must be filed within five working days following the date on which the notification of the resolution to be challenged becomes effective.[106] Finally, the resolutions declaring the appeal for review to be well founded shall be limited to declaring the nullity of the challenged act, so that the Plenary of the FJC may issue a new resolution within a term not to exceed 30 calendar days.[107]

Although the positive impact of the new process of admission into the federal judiciary may be tangible in the short term, it will be hard to tackle nepotistic difficulties without modifying the structure of the judicial office and its system of responsibilities. This is because, as Caballero notes, within the judicial office structure responsibility is often centred on the head of the jurisdictional unit – either the circuit magistrate or the district judge. As a result, adjudicators prefer to place a premium on trust in their employees rather than competence, a trait that creates an inbuilt incentive for clientelist partnerships.[108]

5. PARAMETERS TO ENSURE THAT ADJUDICATORS ACT INDEPENDENTLY AND IMPARTIALLY

The World Justice Project places Mexico in the bottom four countries in Latin America, and among the 30 countries with the most corrupt public servants.[109] This is why institutional mechanisms ensuring adjudicators behave impartially and independently are important in combating corrupt practices. Although

---

[103] Judicial Career Law of the Judicial Branch of the Federation, Article 76.
[104] Ibid., Article 78.
[105] Political Constitution of the United Mexican States, Article 100, para. 10; Judicial Career Law of the Judicial Branch of the Federation, Article 68.
[106] Judicial Career Law of the Judicial Branch of the Federation, Article 70.
[107] Ibid., Article 73.
[108] Caballero, supra n. 38, 93–96.
[109] World Justice Project, 'Rule of Law Index', 2020, 17–18.

real efforts have been made, these problems have been persistent within the judiciary.[110]

As we have mentioned, controversial designations of SCJN Justices and nepotistic practices within the FJC have prompted internal responses within the judiciary. In light of this, the FJC set forth the Comprehensive Plan to Combat Nepotism. The Plan includes[111] strengthening of the methods of selection of judicial personnel; a digital register of family relationships;[112] the fact that hiring persons related to other incumbents by blood or affinity within the fifth degree will require the non-binding opinion of an Integrity Committee; and an electronic mailbox for reporting cases of nepotism.

Another important instrument to ensure the impartiality of Mexican adjudicators is the Code of Ethics of the Judicial Branch of the Federation (CEJBF). The CEJBF sets forth the judicial principles, rules and virtues applicable to guide the conduct of federal judges and their assistants, as well as to facilitate ethical reflection on the various aspects of judiciary praxis.

The Code is divided into five chapters. The first four chapters define the four fundamental guiding principles of judicial ethics (independence, impartiality, objectivity and professionalism). The fifth chapter does not include a guiding concept of judicial ethics, but rather presents a variety of judicial characteristics that collectively comprise the ideal profile of a good judge under the term 'excellence': a competent judge's ideal profile.[113]

Although ethical codes are not a panacea to solve a lack of impartiality, they are definitely important. If applied seriously, their usage can create an ethical environment or culture, as part of a learning process that includes the promotion, inculcation, reinforcement and assessment of ethical behaviour.[114] In addition, they are helpful in certain situations, such as preventing technical infringements and increasing scrutiny both inside and outside public organisations.[115]

Additionally, the JCLJBF considers that members of the judiciary have the duty to act in conformity with the judicial function's independence, ensuring the prompt, complete, expeditious and impartial administration of justice.[116]

---

[110] In the latest Corruption Perception Index of Transparency International, Mexico ranks 124 out of 180. See https://www.transparency.org/en/cpi/2020/index/mex.

[111] FJC Pleno, 'Acuerdo Del Pleno Del Consejo De La Judicatura Federal Por El Que Se Establece El Plan Integral De Combate Al Nepotismo', Pub. L. No. CJF-002 (2019).

[112] In order for all public servants to declare, under oath, their family relationships in the judiciary, by affinity and consanguinity up to the fifth degree.

[113] Suprema Corte de Justicia de la Nación, Consejo de la Judicatura Federal and Tribunal Electoral, *Código de Ética Del Poder Judicial de La Federación* (Suprema Corte de Justicia de la Nación, 2004), 5–6.

[114] Alan Doig and John Wilson, 'The Effectiveness of Codes of Conduct', *Business Ethics: A European Review* 7, no. 3 (1 July 1998): 146–47.

[115] Maíra Martini, 'The Effectiveness of Codes of Conduct for Parliamentarians' (Transparency International, 2012).

[116] Judicial Career Law of the Judicial Branch of the Federation, Article 44, section VII.

6. CONSEQUENCES FOR DOMESTIC ADJUDICATORS OF A BREACH OF THE REQUIREMENT TO ACT INDEPENDENTLY AND IMPARTIALLY

The Mexican legal system considers three consequences for the federal adjudicators that we have discussed if they do not act with independence and impartiality: political impeachment, administrative liability trial, and criminal charges.

6.1. POLITICAL IMPEACHMENT

Political impeachment is a judicial proceeding entrusted to the legislative branch,[117] whose purpose is to investigate the conduct of high-ranking public officials, including the federal adjudicators listed in sections 3.1.1–3.1.3,[118] in order to ascertain political responsibility and to impose an appropriate sanction.[119] The procedure starts with a complaint, which could be made by any Mexican citizen, and is overseen by the legislative branch in two phases. The first stage is before the Chamber of Deputies, which serves as the investigating and accusing body; and the second stage is before the Chamber of Senators, which serves as the jury of judgment and conducts the trial of responsibility[120] in accordance with the provisions of Articles 22 et seq. of the Federal Law on Public Servants' Responsibilities (FLPSR).[121]

Article 7 of the FLPSR establishes a numerus clausus list of conduct in relation to which political impeachment can be initiated, among which the violation of human rights stands out:[122] the Charter of the Rights of Persons before the Judiciary, in the Ibero-American Judicial Area, 'recognises a fundamental right of the population to have access to independent, impartial, transparent, accountable, efficient, effective and equitable justice'.[123] In this sense, it is possible to assume that if an adjudicator violates the right to independent and impartial justice, political impeachment will follow.

---

[117] Political Constitution of the United Mexican States, Article 109.
[118] The full list is set forth in ibid., Article 110, paras 1–2.
[119] Abelardo Esparza Frausto, *El Juicio Político* (Cuadernos de la Judicatura, 2001), 43.
[120] Political Constitution of the United Mexican States, Article 110, paras 5 and 6.
[121] Marisol Luna Leal, 'Algunos Aspectos de Procedimiento Del Juicio Político En México', *Letras Jurídicas*, no. 21 (2010): 173.
[122] It is worth noticing that the Chamber of Deputies has approved a new law on political impeachment, the Ley de Juicio Político y Declaraciones de Procedencia, which is currently being discussed in the Senate. See Redacción, 'Ley de Juicio Político: 11 Puntos Clave Para Entenderla', *El Financiero*, 2 September 2021, https://www.elfinanciero.com.mx/nacional/2021/09/02/ley-de-juicio-politico-11-puntos-clave-para-entenderla/.
[123] Charter of the Rights of Persons before the Judiciary in the Ibero-American Judicial (n.d.) Preamble and Article 17.

Mexico

The sanctions this procedure considers are the dismissal or permanent disqualification from performing activities, employment, posts or commissions of any kind in the public service.[124] But when the conduct of the adjudicator is of a criminal nature, the Chamber of Deputies would issue a declaration of proceeding, which effectively *activates* the possibility of initiating criminal proceedings against, in this case, the relevant adjudicator.[125]

6.2. ADMINISTRATIVE RESPONSIBILITY PROCEDURE

The SCJN determines that administrative liability arises for public servants who fail to comply with legality, honesty, loyalty, impartiality and efficiency in public office.[126] When that happens within the federal judiciary, the comptrollers of the SCJN, the Federal Judiciary Council and the Electoral Tribunal[127] initiate the administrative responsibility procedure, whose purpose is to 'sanction conduct that harms the proper functioning of the public administration'.[128]

The General Law of Administrative Responsibilities (GLAR) considers two types of administrative misconduct, i.e. non-serious and serious. Among non-serious misconduct[129] is non-compliance with the relevant codes of ethics, such as the CEJBF,[130] while serious misconduct includes taking over, processing or resolving matters in which an adjudicator has a conflict of interest.[131] Additionally, the OLJF considers that any behaviour that threatens the independence of the judicial function, such as accepting or exercising instructions, pressures or commissions, or any action that generates or implies undue subordination with respect to any person would trigger administrative liability.[132]

The penalties applicable to these administrative misconducts consist of: private or public warning; private or public reprimand; economic sanction;

---

[124]   'Diccionario de Derecho Parlamentario' (Fundación Mexicana, 1993), 212.
[125]   Political Constitution of the United Mexican States, Article 111; Federal Law of Responsibilities of Public Servants, Article 7.
[126]   SCJN Pleno, Responsabilidades de Servidores Públicos. Sus Modalidades de Acuerdo con el Titulo Cuarto Constitucional, No. P. LX/96 (1996).
[127]   These are the organisations responsible for the control and inspection of compliance with the administrative operating rules governing the federal judiciary's bodies and public servants, Organic Law of the Federal Judiciary, Article 105.
[128]   Marco Antonio Castro Rojas, 'Ponencia VI. Los Sujetos de Responsabilidad', *Revista Mexicana de Justicia* V, no. 3 (1987): 111.
[129]   There are additional 10 types of non-serious misconduct. See General Law of Administrative Responsibilities (2016), Articles 49 and 50.
[130]   Ibid., Article 49, section I.
[131]   General Law of Administrative Responsibilities, Article 58. The full list of serious administrative misconduct is set forth in Articles 51–64.
[132]   Organic Law of the Federal Judiciary, Article 110, section I.

Intersentia

573

suspension; removal from office; and temporary disqualification from holding jobs, positions or commissions in the public service.[133]

Finally, it is important to mention that administrative responsibility procedures remain confidential. Although this is in line with the United Nations Basic Principles on the Independence of the Judiciary,[134] as Caballero notes, this makes it difficult to follow up on cases, to effectively combat corruption or to at least be informed about it.[135]

6.3. CRIMINAL CHARGES

According to Article 111 of the Federal Constitution, the Justices of the SCJN and the Magistrates of the Superior Chamber of the Electoral Tribunal may not be prosecuted for criminal actions unless the Chamber of Deputies approves, by an absolute majority of its members, a 'declaration of procedural immunity'. The SCJN has explained that the recognition of this constitutional immunity is a characteristic element of a democratic state, consisting of protecting the constitutional functions performed by certain public servants – a protection that has as its ultimate objective the avoidance of possible obstructions for political purposes or retaliation from light, malicious or irresponsible accusations that seek to interrupt such constitutional functions of an essential nature for the constitutional order.[136]

It is important to notice that the 'declaration of procedural immunity' is only addressed to the heads of the highest bodies of the judiciary. According to SCJN Justice Fernando Franco, this legal figure must be interpreted as aimed at safeguarding autonomy and independence from external interference or pressures imposed by external agents through complaints lodged against those in the highest positions in the respective government branches.[137] In this sense, only Magistrates of the Regional Chambers of the Electoral Tribunal, circuit magistrates and district judges can be prosecuted for federal crimes without a prior 'declaration of procedural immunity'.

The Federal Criminal Code includes a comprehensive list of crimes against the administration of justice. In particular, we note that the following may be against the principles of judicial impartiality: first, hearing matters which the adjudicator is legally impeded from hearing;[138] and second, issuing a decision on

---

[133]   Ibid., Article 135. Additionally, this law establishes that misconduct shall be assessed and, if applicable, punished in accordance with the criteria set forth in Articles 75–80 of the GLAR.
[134]   United Nations, Basic Principles on the Independence of the Judiciary, sec. 17.
[135]   Caballero, supra n. 38, 21–22.
[136]   SCJN Pleno, Controversia Constitucional 99/2016 (24 September 2019), para. 81.
[137]   José Fernando Franco González, Constitutional Controversy 207/2017, Concurring Vote (SCJN 2020).
[138]   Federal Criminal Code (1931), Article 225, section I.

574

the merits or a final judgment that is unlawful because it violates a precept of the law or is contrary to the proceedings of the trial, or omitting to issue a procedural decision on the merits or a lawful final judgment within the parameters established by law.[139] The first situation is not allowed because, in line with the Federal Code of Civil Procedures (FCCP), judges, magistrates or justices shall not hear legal disputes that may affect their impartiality, including having a direct interest in the subject matter of the dispute or being an acquaintance or relative of any of the parties to the dispute.[140] In the second situation, the sanction for the former is imprisonment of three to eight years and a monetary fine, while the latter carries a penalty of four to 10 years' imprisonment and a pecuniary fine.

7. ENFORCEMENT OF FINAL JUDGMENTS RENDERED BY ADJUDICATORS IN BREACH OF THE REQUIREMENT TO ACT INDEPENDENTLY AND IMPARTIALLY

In 2004, the Code of Civil Procedures of Mexico City was reformed to include a new chapter, 'The Action for Nullity of a Concluded Judgment', which contained seven sections that contemplated various situations in which the action for annulment of a concluded judgment could be exercised. According to Ovalle Favela, 'these seven sections allowed the nullity action to be exercised in very broad and flexible cases, which undoubtedly seriously affected the authority of res judicata.'[141] Moreover, several members of the Legislative Assembly of Mexico City, along with the Attorney General, filed an action of unconstitutionality (No. 11/2004). After resolving these unconstitutionality lawsuits, the SCJN found five of the seven portions of Article 737-A of the Code of Civil Procedures of Mexico City unconstitutional, which, ultimately, were reduced to two and changed.[142]

One of the sections of Article 737-A provided that the judgment could be annulled if the sentences were 'the product of the fraud of the judge', such as if an adjudicator hears legal disputes in which there is a *cause of origin* affecting his or her impartiality – as listed in Article 39 of the FCCP. However, the SCJN found that despite the existence of fraudulent conduct by the judge, this cannot be considered as a defect in the process that transcends the result of the

---

[139] See the complete list of the cases of impediment to attain jurisdiction in: Federal Code of Civil Procedures (1943), Article 39.

[140] Federal Criminal Code, Article 225, section VI.

[141] José Ovalle Favela, 'La Nulidad de La Cosa Juzgada', *Reforma Judicial. Revista Mexicana de Justicia*, no. 18 (2011): 97.

[142] Ibid.

judgment or as a defect in the judgment itself, and therefore considered that such assumptions are contrary to the guarantee of legal certainty.[143]

The SCJN has affirmed this line of thought in subsequent decisions. It has been determined that when there is a definitive pronouncement derived from a jurisdictional conflict in which an adjudicatory body has established its competence to hear a matter, such a resolution acquires the category of *res judicata*, which is irrebuttable, indisputable and unmodifiable. Therefore, in the appeal for review in which the judgment of indirect *amparo* is challenged, the appellate court can no longer question that decision.[144]

Having that said, there are instances in which, during the course of a trial, unforeseeable or previously unknown events arise; they may modify the situation that prevailed at the time the jurisdictional decision to hear the dispute was made, one which directly influences the competence of the adjudicator, which is known as 'supervening incompetence'.[145] When the above occurs, such as the emergence of any of the situations listed in Article 39 of the FCCP, the adjudicatory body must declare itself legally incompetent.[146] In this sense, the actions of the court declared incompetent are null and void, and the nullity only operates from the moment at which the incompetence occurred.[147] However, supervening incompetence can only be claimed before a final decision has been rendered by either a circuit collegiate tribunal or the SCJN, when they function as constitutional courts of last resort.

8. CONCLUSION

Since 1994, the Mexican judiciary has undergone a serious transformation towards achieving more independence and impartiality. However, controversial appointments of SCJN Justices along with nepotistic practices within the judiciary triggered a legitimacy crisis which, ultimately, resulted in the 2021 judicial reform. Although the reform underscores important elements of safeguarding the impartiality and independence of the judiciary, including limiting circuit

---

[143] SCJN Pleno, Nulidad de Juicio Concluido. El Artículo 737 A, Fracciones I y VI, del Código de Procedimientos Civiles para el Distrito Federal Viola la Garantía de Seguridad Jurídica, No. P./J. 87/2008 (2008).

[144] SCJN Segunda Sala, Recurso de Revisión. Debe Prevalecer la Autoridad de la Cosa Juzgada Respecto de las Determinaciones Sobre Cuestiones Competenciales, No. 2a./J. 126/2012 (10a.) (2012).

[145] Federal Code of Civil Procedures, Article 17.

[146] Tribunales Colegiados de Circuito, Competencia en el Juicio de Amparo Indirecto. El Juez de Distrito Debe Declararse Legalmente Incompetente, Después de Celebrada la Audiencia Constitucional, Si en el Trámite del Asunto se Modificó el Supuesto que la Originaba, Aun Cuando Esta Determinación Sea Consecuencia de lo Resuelto en un Conflicto Competencial, No. II.2o.P.12 K (10a.) (2014).

[147] Federal Code of Civil Procedures, Article 17, paras 1 and 2.

magistrates' and district judges' capacity to appoint their staff, emphasising judicial immovability, and establishing the Federal Judicial Training School, it fails to address the structure of the judicial office and its system of responsibilities.

Overall, the method of appointing Magistrates of the Electoral Tribunal, circuit magistrates and district judges aims at securing meritocracy and independence. Unfortunately, the same cannot be said concerning the designation of the SCJN, which remains heavily influenced by the roots of Mexican presidentialism and particracy. More problematic, however, is the lack of a legal framework governing judicial nominations to international organisations.

Decisions to nominate and appoint SCJN Justices and Magistrates of the Electoral Tribunal cannot be recursed, only the results of the competitive examinations for circuit magistrates and district judges. Likewise, the decisions referring to their ratification may be appealed before the SCJN.

To ensure that members of the federal judiciary act impartially and independently, the FJC has established the 'Comprehensive Plan to Combat Nepotism'. Likewise, the SCJN has established a Code of Ethics, which, although not magic, if implemented efficiently may create an ethical environment. In this sense, we recall that violations of the principles of independence and impartiality may trigger three types of liabilities: political, administrative and criminal.

Finally, in the event that a final judgment is rendered by partial and non-independent adjudicators, the Mexican legal system does not provide for any legal recourse. This is because the SCJN considers that legal certainty is a principle that overrides the existence of fraudulent conduct by the judges or parties to the dispute.

THE INDEPENDENCE AND IMPARTIALITY OF ADJUDICATORS IN PARAGUAY

Raúl PEREIRA FLEURY

1. Selection Criteria and Appointment Method..........................579
    1.1.   Domestic Adjudicators 579
    1.2.   Domestic Arbitration..582
    1.3.   International Adjudicators 582
2. Appointing Authorities 583
    2.1.   Domestic Adjudicators 583
    2.2.   International Adjudicators 583
3. Counterbalancing the Selecting Authority's Influence 584
4. Code of Conduct for Adjudicators..................................585
5. Consequences of Breaching the Duties of Independence and
    Impartiality 586
    5.1.   Domestic Adjudicators 586
    5.2.   Arbitrators..588
6. Conclusion..589

1. SELECTION CRITERIA AND APPOINTMENT METHOD

1.1. DOMESTIC ADJUDICATORS

The Paraguayan Constitution establishes that domestic adjudicators are selected by a body named the Consejo de la Magistratura[1] and confirmed by the Supreme Court of Justice,[2] except for the Justices of the Supreme Court, who are selected by the Senate and confirmed by the President.

---

[1]   Paraguayan Constitution, Article 264.
[2]   Ibid., Article 251.

Intersentia

In order to apply for a judgeship, candidates must first comply with objective criteria:

Table 1. Judgeship objective criteria

Position	Requirements
Justice of the Supreme Court	– Paraguayan nationality; – 35 years of age; – SJD or PhD in Law; – Notorious reputation; and – For at least 10 years, jointly, separately or alternatively: • has practised the legal profession; • has served as a judge; or • has taught law at university level.
Court of Appeal and Administrative Court Judges	– Paraguayan nationality; – 35 years of age; – Law degree; – Good reputation; and – For at least 10 years, jointly, separately or alternatively: • has practised the legal profession; • has served as a judge; • has taught law at university level; or • has served in the judicial branch, the Public Prosecutor's Office or the Ministry of Public Defence.
First Instance Judges	– Paraguayan nationality; – 30 years of age; – Law degree; – Good reputation; and – For at least 5 years, jointly, separately or alternatively: • has practised the legal profession; • has served as a judge; • has taught law at university level; or • has served in the judicial branch, the Public Prosecutor's Office or the Ministry of Public Defence.
Small Claims Judgeship	– Paraguayan nationality; – 25 years of age; – Law degree; and – Good reputation.

Moving forward to the subjective criteria, under the rules of the Consejo de la Magistratura[3] (Selection Rules), candidates for a judgeship must go through a three-stage evaluation process.

---

[3] Reglamento que Establece los Criterios de Selección, Evaluación de Meritos y Aptitudes para la Elección de Postulantes y para la Conformación de Ternas por el Consejo de la Magistratura.

First, the candidates must take a General and Specific Knowledge Test.[4] This test has two stages: a test on general constitutional law and one on the specific legal field that the candidate is applying for, i.e. civil and commercial law. There is a minimum score to advance to the second stage of the process and the list of candidates who pass is publicised.

The candidates that score above the minimum established for the General and Specific Knowledge Test can move forward to the second part of the evaluation process, consisting of a Psychotechnical and Vocational Test.[5] At this stage, the candidates are evaluated on the following criteria: (i) adequate knowledge of the Spanish and Guaraní languages,[6] broad knowledge and experience in the field, broad knowledge of the national social reality, superior general intelligence, capacity for abstract and critical judgement, capacity for analysis and synthesis, objectivity, capacity for oral and written expression, ability to use legal vocabulary;[7] and (ii) high self-esteem, self-confidence, independence of judgement, autonomy, prudence, responsibility, self-reliance, sense of justice and fairness, equanimity, and reasonableness and balance in his or her decisions.[8]

The third and last stage before the Consejo de la Magistratura consists of an interview with two members of said body.[9] According to the Selection Rules, the interview is designed to evaluate personal attributes that are otherwise difficult to assess through other procedures, such as ethics, independence of criteria, initiative, interpersonal relations, conflict management, responsibility, motivation, office management, and general knowledge of the Spanish and Guaraní languages.

After the three-stage process is completed, the Consejo de la Magistratura draws up a shortlist of candidates with the highest scores to be sent to the Supreme Court of Justice, which will decide which candidate to select from the shortlist.[10]

In addition to the scores a candidate may obtain in the three stages before the Consejo de la Magistratura, other relevant factors that can increase a candidate's score are his or her academic background (postgraduate studies such as a PhD, master's degree, specialisations and others), university teaching experience, professional experience and publications.[11]

---

[4]   Selection Rules, Article 8.
[5]   Ibid., Article 16.
[6]   According to its Constitution (article 140), Paraguay has two official languages: Spanish and Guaraní, the latter being the language of the natives that inhabited (and still do) Paraguay in pre-colonisation era. According to a survey conducted in 2022 by the National Institute of Statistics, 33.4% of the Paraguayan population has Guaraní as its main language.
[7]   These criteria are referred to as '*Cognitive and Communicational Abilities*'.
[8]   These criteria are referred to as '*Personality Traits*'.
[9]   Selection Rules, Article 21.
[10]   Paraguayan Constitution, Article 251; Law No. 609/1995, Article 3(c).
[11]   Selection Rules, Article 31.

The Justices of the Supreme Court go through an identical process before the Consejo de la Magistratura. However, the shortlist of candidates is referred to the Senate, who must select its candidate and that candidate must then be confirmed by Paraguay's President.[12]

1.2. DOMESTIC ARBITRATION

Arbitration proceedings seated in Paraguay, both domestic and international, are governed by Law No. 1879/2002 (Arbitration Act). Article 3(d) of the Arbitration Act defines an arbitral tribunal as the body of one or more arbitrators designated by the parties to decide their conflict. Furthermore, Article 12 establishes that the parties are free to choose the arbitrators.

Therefore, no selection criteria are provided for in the Arbitration Act and, therefore, whether an arbitrator is qualified will depend on what each party is looking for in an arbitrator or on the agreement of the parties.[13] In this context, Article 13(f) of the Arbitration Act provides that, when a judge is called to appoint an arbitrator, either because of a reluctant party or because the parties cannot reach an agreement in nominating a single arbitrator, said judge shall have due regard to any qualifications required of the arbitrator by the agreement of the parties.

It is worth noting that the Paraguayan Mediation and Arbitration Center (CAMP), has a closed list of arbitrators, from which the parties must select if the arbitration is a domestic one.[14] Likewise, the CAMP has a list of qualifications for persons that wish to join its list of arbitrators. These qualifications include: (i) a law degree; (ii) a minimum of five years of professional practice; and (iii) a clean judicial and criminal record.[15]

1.3. INTERNATIONAL ADJUDICATORS

Paraguayan legislation does not contemplate special laws or rules determining the criteria for the selection of national candidates to positions as international adjudicators. As such, the Paraguayan President (in charge of making such a selection) will normally look to the requirements that each international

---

[12] Paraguayan Constitution, Article 264(1).

[13] For further discussion on arbitrators' qualifications, see Emmanuel Gillard and John Savage (eds.), *Fouchard, Gaillard, Goldman on International Commercial Arbitration* (Kluwer Law International, 1999), pp. 458–59; Paul D. Friedland, *Arbitration Clauses for International Contracts* (JurisNet, 2007), p. 71.

[14] CAMP Arbitration Rules, Article 7(3).

[15] CAMP Rules for Arbitrators, available at https://www.camparaguay.com/es/descargas-3/reglamentos-vigentes.

organisation has for a person to join its list of international adjudicators and make a decision accordingly.

For international arbitration proceedings, the Arbitration Act does not provide for specific criteria. It will depend on the parties and their agreement.

2. APPOINTING AUTHORITIES

2.1. DOMESTIC ADJUDICATORS

As indicated above, the appointment of domestic adjudicators depends on the level of judgeship. First-instance and court of appeals judges are selected by the Supreme Court from a shortlist prepared by the Consejo de la Magistratura. On the other hand, Justices of the Supreme Court are selected by the Senate from a shortlist prepared by the Consejo de la Magistratura, and then confirmed by Paraguay's President.

Arbitrators in domestic arbitrations are selected, primarily, by the parties.[16] If, for any reason, one or more arbitrators cannot be selected, the parties may resort to a national judge seated at the place of the arbitration to appoint the arbitrator(s). If that is the case, the judge called upon to select the arbitrator(s) shall have due regard for the particular circumstances of the case in order to secure the appointment of an independent and impartial arbitrator(s).[17]

2.2. INTERNATIONAL ADJUDICATORS

The selection of national candidates to positions as international adjudicators in bodies such as the International Court of Justice or ICSID is made by the Paraguayan President, pursuant to Article 238(7) of the Paraguayan Constitution.[18] In selecting these candidates, the President will normally look at each institution/convention's requirements for their adjudicators; however, the President may also apply his or her own criteria and Paraguayan foreign policy concerns.

As for international arbitration proceedings, the same rules as for domestic arbitration apply.

---

16 Arbitration Act, Article 13(c).
17 Ibid., Article 13(f).
18 Paraguayan Constitution, Article 238(7): 'The president of the Republic shall have the following duties and powers: ... 7) manage the Republic's foreign relations'.

Intersentia

583

3. COUNTERBALANCING THE SELECTING AUTHORITY'S INFLUENCE

As indicated above, the selection of domestic adjudicators is left entirely to the Consejo de la Magistratura, while the supervision of the judges' performance is left to a similar body, the Jurado de Enjuiciamiento de Magistrados (JEM).[19] As such, the JEM has the authority to remove judges from office for bad performance of their duties, which includes lack of independence and impartiality[20] or the commission of a crime.

This division aims to safeguard the integrity of the selection made by the Consejo de la Magistratura, because the body that will evaluate judges' performance is an entirely different one. However, neither body is exempt from possible influence peddling by its members. In a recent judgment, a criminal court in Asunción sentenced a former senator to two years' imprisonment for influence peddling during his term as a member of the JEM.[21]

Judges are also prohibited from practising while holding their judgeship, thus preventing the risk of double-hatting.[22] This prohibition does not exist for attorneys who also act as arbitrators.

The Arbitration Act does not bar double-hatting in this field, i.e. arbitrators may also act as counsel. However, lack of independence and impartiality of an arbitrator may result in the arbitration award (either foreign or domestic) being annulled or not recognised.[23]

Finally, it is worth mentioning the incompatibilities applicable to judges. As such, the Constitution indicates that during their judgeship, judges and magistrates are banned from holding other public or private positions (paid or not) and from exercising commerce and any professional or political activity. However, judges may engage in teaching or scientific research.[24] In this context, the Supreme Court has indicated that '[t]he service of justices, guaranteed by our Constitution, would be disturbed and damaged by the simultaneous performance of two positions or activities by the magistrates. If this were the case, it would be literally impossible to fulfil the value of justice with impartiality and objectivity'.[25]

---

[19] Paraguayan Constitution, Article 253.
[20] Law No. 3759/2009, Articles 14(c) and 14(g).
[21] *Oscar A. Gonzalez Daher et al s/ Trafico de influencias, asociación criminal y otros*, Criminal Court 35, Decision No. 2 dated 28.12.2020.
[22] Code of Judicial Organisation, Article 97.
[23] Arbitration Act, Articles 40 and 46.
[24] Paraguayan Constitution, Article 254.
[25] *Acción de Inconstitucionalidad E. T., O. v. Art. 1 de la Ley N° 5534/15*, Supreme Court of Justice, Decision No. 889 dated 02.10.2018.

Paraguay

4. CODE OF CONDUCT FOR ADJUDICATORS

Domestic adjudicators' conduct is governed by a Code of Judicial Ethics[26] issued by the Supreme Court of Justice. The Code is applicable to every Paraguayan judge, including the Justices of the Supreme Court.[27]

The Ethics Code lists 13 essential duties that judges must observe: (i) justice; (ii) honesty; (iii) correctness; (iv) independence; (v) impartiality; (vi) caution; (vii) responsibility; (viii) dignity; (ix) authority; (x) moral strength; (xi) good faith; (xii) respect; and (xiii) judicial decorum and image.[28] Each of these duties are explained in the Code.

With regard to the duty of independence, the Ethics Code indicates that a judge must exercise his or her judicial function with absolute independence from factors, criteria or motivations that are not strictly juridical or legal. As such, judges must strive for the judicial branch's institutional, political and economic independence; maintain their independence from political parties; and abstain from participating in political-partisan rallies, occupying positions within a party and voting in party elections. Judges must also refrain from seeking partisan support, of any kind, and must exercise their judgeship with the purpose of administering justice through the applicable law.[29]

Regarding impartiality, the Ethics Code provides for the judges' obligation to avoid incompatibilities applicable to their judgeship; treat the parties equally during the procedure, avoiding attitudes that may imply the judge is privileging one of the parties; refrain from joining associations that practice or promote, directly or indirectly, discrimination based on race, colour, sex, religion, political or other opinion, national or social origin, economic position, birth or condition; refrain from exercising their judgeship based on guidelines issued by institutions or associations they are a part of; avoid the influence of family and friends in making their decisions; refrain from accepting gifts and presents from the parties, their counsel or other people interested in the litigation; and avoid being associated with law firms.[30]

The duty of independence and impartiality has been recognised in Paraguayan case law as well. As indicated by the Supreme Court, decisions must be 'reasoned and supported by objective legal criteria ... so as not to violate the principles of *impartiality*, reasonableness and equality inherent to the jurisdictional function.'[31]

---

26 Supreme Court of Justice Resolution No. 390, dated 18 October 2005 (Ethics Code).
27 Ethics Code, Article 1.
28 Ibid., Articles 7–19.
29 Ibid., Article 10.
30 Ibid., Article 11.
31 *RHP G. M., N. B. v. Itaipú Binacional y otro s/ Indemnización de daños y perjuicios por responsabilidad extracontractual y otros*, Supreme Court of Justice, Decision No. 889 dated 04.12.2020.

Intersentia

When it comes to arbitrators, the Arbitration Act only requires independence and impartiality, nothing else. Notwithstanding this, the CAMP has a Code of Ethics for arbitrators acting under their rules.[32] This Code mandates that arbitrators must be, at all times, transparent, honest, impartial and diligent towards the parties. Regarding impartiality, the Code defines the term as the 'absence of favouritism or bias, of any kind, towards a party or the matters involved, and the commitment to serve the parties and not one of them.'[33]

CAMP's Code of Ethics also mandates that arbitrators must reveal any circumstances that may give rise to suspicions as to their bias towards a party, in which case the arbitrator must decline the appointment. The Code also establishes the arbitrators' obligation to reveal any and all conflict of interest, real or potential, of any nature, such as kinship, friendship, enmity, business, knowledge of one of the parties or of the dispute by having acted for any of the parties as counsel, advisor, arbitrator, judge, prosecutor, witness or any other role, as well as any other circumstance indicating a conflict of interest.

5. CONSEQUENCES OF BREACHING THE DUTIES OF INDEPENDENCE AND IMPARTIALITY

5.1. DOMESTIC ADJUDICATORS

Under Paraguayan civil procedure law, a judge must recuse him- or herself from hearing a case if he or she finds him- or herself within one or more of the reasons established in Article 20 of the Code of Civil Procedure (CPC):[34]

1. kinship;
2. interest in the conflict;
3. having a current conflict with one of the parties;
4. being a creditor, debtor or guarantor of one of the parties;
5. being, or having been, a complainant or accuser of one of the parties, or being or having been denounced or accused by one of the parties;
6. having acted as counsel or issued a legal opinion regarding the conflict, either before or after the commencement of the legal procedures.
7. having received presents or favours from one of the parties or his or her next of kin;
8. being the former guardian or conservator of one of the parties or formerly being under the guardianship or conservatorship of one of the parties;

---

[32] CAMP Code of Ethics for arbitrators and mediators, dated 10 August 2002, available at https://www.camparaguay.com/es/descargas-3/reglamentos-vigentes.

[33] CAMP Code of Ethics for arbitrators and mediators, Article 3.

[34] The list is not exhaustive, that is, a judge must also avoid hearing a case if other reasons exist that give rise to serious issues of decorum or decency (CPC, Article 21).

9. friendship with one of the parties; or
10. enmity with one of the parties.

While 'lack of independence and/or impartiality' is not expressly stated among the list of reasons, each reason describes a circumstance that could give rise to doubts as to a judge's independence and impartiality.

Regarding the challenge of a judge by one of the parties, each party has one opportunity to challenge a judge without cause.[35] Once this opportunity is exhausted, a party challenging a judge must prove one of the reasons of Article 20 indicated above.

Case law has established that, firstly, judges have a duty to recuse themselves from hearing a case if one of the grounds of Article 20 CPC arises.[36] At the same time, since the recusal of a judge is an extraordinary event, the grounds for such a decision must be interpreted restrictively.[37]

Depending on the challenged judge's category, different bodies will decide on such a challenge. Challenges to Supreme Court Justices and judges from the courts of appeals are heard by the Supreme Court of Justice,[38] while challenges to judges from lower courts are heard by the court of appeals.[39]

In both cases, once the judge is challenged, he or she is separated from the case, until a decision is rendered. If the challenge is accepted, the judge in question is permanently removed from the case, which will be further decided by another judge of the same category.[40] It is worth mentioning that the successful challenge of a judge does not strip him or her of his or her judgeship. It only means that the judge is not suitable to hear and decide that particular case, but remains in his or her role as a judge.

However, the challenge may relate to bad performance of his or her role as a judge, and this would be a reason to remove the person from that role. Article 14(c) and (g) of Law No. 3759/2009 empowers the JEM to remove a judge from office for lack of independence and impartiality. In this context, it has been said that this regime clearly demonstrates the interest of the Paraguayan legal system in guaranteeing a judge's impartiality as this is essential to a person's right to defence.[41]

---

[35]   CPC, Article 24.
[36]   *Arévalo M., María del Carmen v. Sra. Sung Choi Prop. Supermercado 'Mbocayá' s/ cobro de guaraníes*, Labor Court of Appeals of Asunción, Chamber 1, Decision No. 257 dated 16.06.2005.
[37]   *Sanatorio Cristina S.R.L. v. Rojas González, Beatriz y otro*, Civil and Commercial Court of Appeals of Asunción, Chamber 5, Decision No. 1009 dated 26.12.2002.
[38]   CPC, Article 31.
[39]   Ibid., Article 34.
[40]   Ibid., Article 36.
[41]   Marcela Gómez Navarro, *Enemistad, odio o resentimiento v. Imparcialidad*, comments to *Felicidad Chamorro de Ataia s/ sucesión*, Supreme Court of Justice, Civil Chamber, Decision No. 1910, available at https://www.pj.gov.py/ebook/monografias/nacional/procesal/Marcela-Gomez-Navarro-Enemistad-odio-resentimiento.pdf.

5.2. ARBITRATORS

As indicated, the Paraguayan Arbitration Act only requires that arbitrators be independent and impartial in their duties. In particular, Article 14 establishes that an arbitrator may be challenged if *justified doubts* exist regarding his or her independence or impartiality.[42] As of the date of this report, there is no case law (either in ordinary courts or arbitral proceedings) available regarding the interpretation of the 'justifiable doubts' standard adopted by the Arbitration Act. However, we may resort to the Arbitration Act's source in order to interpret this standard.

In this context, the Paraguayan Arbitration Act replicated almost in its entirety the UNCITRAL Model Law on International Commercial Arbitration of 1985 as amended in 2006. Therefore, commentaries and case law interpreting the Model Law as well as arbitration laws based on the Model Law are valid sources in order to understand the 'justifiable doubts' standard adopted by the Arbitration Act.

Leading authorities agree that the standard of independence and impartiality required by the Model Law is an objective one, and that it does not require a certainty or likelihood of partiality or dependence, but only objectively justified doubts.[43] Therefore, it is not necessary to demonstrate that the arbitrator actually lacks independence or impartiality. It is, instead, sufficient to show that there is enough 'doubt' or 'suspicion' as to an arbitrator's impartiality to justify removing the arbitrator.[44]

It is also important to mention that the standard of proof of independence and impartiality under the Model Law must be analysed from the point of view of a 'disinterested, reasonable person',[45] rather than from the point of view of one of the parties or the arbitrators. As one tribunal put it, '"justifiable doubts" are those of an informed and fair-minded observer'.[46]

Moving forward, if an arbitrator is successfully challenged, he or she will only be removed from the tribunal in that particular case. That is, the Arbitration Act does not foresee a personal sanction for the arbitrator. However, under the CAMP's Code of Ethics for arbitrators and mediators, an arbitrator's failure to observe his or her duties of independence and impartiality may result, depending on the gravity, in either the suspension or exclusion of the arbitrator from the CAMP's list.[47]

---

[42] Arbitration Act, Article 14.

[43] Gary B. Born, *International Commercial Arbitration* (3rd ed., Kluwer Law International, 2021), pp. 1894–95; Fernández Rozas, 'Clearer Ethics Guidelines and Comparative Standards for Arbitrators' in M. Fernández-Ballesteros and D. Arias (eds.), *Liber Amicorum Bernardo Cremades* (La Ley, 2010), pp. 420–25.

[44] Gary B. Born, *International Commercial Arbitration* (3rd ed., Kluwer Law International, 2021), p. 1911.

[45] Ibid., p. 1913.

[46] Decision in LCIA No. UN3490 of 21 October 2005, Challenge Digest (2011) 27 *Arb. Int'l* 377, para. 4.11.

[47] CAMP Code of Ethics for arbitrators and mediators, Articles 6(3) and 7(6).

Another important and grave consequence of an arbitrator's lack of independence and impartiality is that the award rendered by such an arbitrator (whether acting as a sole arbitrator or a co-arbitrator) may be set aside or denied recognition.

In this context, it is important to note that the Arbitration Act – as indicated above – has its source in the Model Law, incorporating the same grounds for setting aside and denial of recognition of arbitral awards. Moreover, these are also identical to the grounds provided for in Article V of the New York Convention on the Recognition and Enforcement of Foreign Arbitral Awards.

Therefore, although not expressly provided for in the Model Law, scholars and case law recognise that an annulment or denial of recognition of an arbitral award for an arbitrator's lack of independence or impartiality can be based on a number of the grounds established in the Model Law:

> Claims of lack of independence or impartiality can potentially be based on Article 34(2)(a)(ii) of the UNCITRAL Model Law, because a partial tribunal arguably denies a party an opportunity to present its case; or on Article 34(2)(a)(iv), because a partial tribunal is arguably not constituted in accordance with the parties' agreement or with applicable law; or on Article 34(2)(b)(2), because a partial tribunal arguably violates conceptions of procedural (or other) public policy.[48]

Regarding the application of the New York Convention, courts have found an arbitrator's lack of independence and impartiality to be a breach of due process and procedural public policy.[49]

To the best of my knowledge, at the time of writing, no arbitral award has been set aside or refused recognition in Paraguay on these grounds.

6. CONCLUSION

Under Paraguayan law, independence and impartiality of both domestic and international adjudicators play a fundamental role in the process of delivering justice. They are vital parts of the judicial machinery, and, for that matter, the inobservance of these duties may have negative consequences not only for the adjudicator, but also for the decisions they render. That is, the consequences go beyond the adjudicator's sphere, and affect the people that seek justice either within the judicial branch or through alternative means, such as arbitration.

---

[48] Gary B. Born, *International Commercial Arbitration* (3rd ed., Kluwer Law International, 2021), p. 3564.

[49] UNCITRAL Secretariat Guide on the Convention on the Recognition and Enforcement of Foreign Arbitral Awards (New York, 1958), 2016 ed., p. 253.

THE INDEPENDENCE AND IMPARTIALITY OF ADJUDICATORS IN ROMANIA

Lucian Bojin and Sorina Doroga

1. Preliminary Remarks 592
2. Criteria for Selection of Adjudicators 592
   2.1. Domestic Adjudicators 592
   2.2. National Candidates for Positions as International Adjudicators 593
       2.2.1. National Candidates for the Position of Judge at the
              ECtHR. 594
       2.2.2. National Candidates for the Position of Judge at the CJEU
              and the General Court 595
3. Authority Appointing the Adjudicators and Methods for Appointing
   the Adjudicators 596
   3.1. Domestic Adjudicators 596
   3.2. National Candidates for Positions as International
        Adjudicators 597
       3.2.1. National Candidates for the Position of Judge
              at the ECtHR 597
       3.2.2. National Candidates for the Position of Judge at the
              CJEU or the General Court 599
4. Methods to Balance the Appointing Authority's Influence on the
   Appointment of Adjudicators 601
   4.1. Domestic Adjudicators 601
   4.2. National Candidates for Positions as International Adjudicators 603
5. Parameters to Ensure that Adjudicators Act Independently
   and Impartially 604
   5.1. Domestic Adjudicators 604
   5.2. Nationals Appointed to Positions as International Adjudicators 605
6. Consequences for Adjudicators in Case of a Breach of the
   Requirement to Act Independently and Impartially 607
   6.1. Domestic Adjudicators 607
   6.2. Nationals Appointed to Positions as International
        Adjudicators 608

Intersentia

591

7. Enforcement of a Final Decision Rendered by an Adjudicator in
   Breach of the Requirement to Act Independently and Impartially 608
   7.1. Domestic Adjudicators 608
   7.2. Foreign or International Adjudicators. 609
8. Conclusion. 610

1. PRELIMINARY REMARKS

The present report describes the national rules and practices applicable in the Romanian legal system concerning the independence and impartiality of domestic adjudicators, as well as of national candidates to positions as international adjudicators.

Following the guidelines provided by the general rapporteur, the Romanian report explains the state of the law and of the legal debates concerning issues such as the criteria for selection of adjudicators, appointment procedures and appointing authorities, mechanisms to balance the influence of appointing authorities, as well as other parameters and rules intended to ensure the observance by adjudicators of the requirements of independence and impartiality in their activity.

From a structural perspective, the report dedicates separate subsections, under each of the issues examined, to domestic adjudicators and to national candidates to positions as international adjudicators, respectively. The categories of domestic adjudicators discussed include national judges and arbitrators in domestic arbitration procedures.

Under the category of national candidates to positions as international adjudicators, the report focuses on two international adjudicative bodies in which Romania participates: the European Court of Human Rights (ECtHR) and the Court of Justice of the European Union (CJEU). The limitation to these two categories is due to the scarcity of legal rules and information available concerning Romania's practices in respect of selection and appointment of other types of international adjudicators, such as international arbitrators. Nonetheless, the existing legal framework offers sufficient information to allow for an overview of the general approach on procedures concerning national candidates to positions as international adjudicators.

2. CRITERIA FOR SELECTION OF ADJUDICATORS

2.1. DOMESTIC ADJUDICATORS

As indicated above, there are two professional categories that we include under the label of 'domestic adjudicators': domestic judges and arbitrators in domestic arbitration procedures. Our report will deal with both categories. It should be borne in mind that while being a domestic judge is, in principle, a lifelong career, domestic arbitrators act rather occasionally in this capacity, in specific arbitration proceedings. This essential difference is reflected in almost all topics under consideration in the present report.

According to Law No. 303/2004 concerning the status of judges and public prosecutors, domestic judges are selected from among law graduates. They must be Romanian citizens, reside on Romanian territory, have no criminal or tax record, know the Romanian language, and be medically and psychologically apt to exercise the profession. The candidates must pass an admission exam organised by the National Institute of Magistracy,[1] with the approval of the Superior Council of Magistracy.[2]

There are two alternative ways to be selected as a judge, both involving the admission exam. One concerns law graduates without requirements of professional experience. If they pass the admission exam, they are enrolled at the National Institute of Magistracy for two years, at the end of which they must pass a completion exam. After that, they become trainee judges for two years, at the end of which they must pass the capacity exam. Once the capacity exam is passed, they are appointed as judges.

The second selection route concerns law graduates with previous experience in a legal profession of a minimum of five years. They must pass the admission exam as well, after which they are enrolled at the National Institute of Magistracy for a training period of six months.

Domestic arbitrators are selected, in ad hoc arbitration procedures, by the parties, without any specific requirements. In arbitral procedures organised by arbitration institutions, the latter publish lists of arbitrators (composed mainly of well-recognised professionals in the legal field or law professors), but selecting the arbitrators from these lists is not mandatory for the parties.[3]

2.2. NATIONAL CANDIDATES FOR POSITIONS AS INTERNATIONAL ADJUDICATORS

As indicated in the introduction, the information comprised in this report refers to existing Romanian legislation and practices concerning the appointment of international adjudicators, in the context of Romania's participation in two regional and human rights jurisdictional mechanisms: the CJEU and the ECtHR.

While Romania does participate in international arbitral proceedings, the rapporteurs could not identify publicly available national rules or practices

---

[1]   See section 3 below.
[2]   See section 3 below.
[3]   Art. 618(1) of the Romanian Civil Procedure Code.

concerning the appointment of adjudicators in the context of international arbitral proceedings involving Romania.

2.2.1. National Candidates for the Position of Judge at the ECtHR

As far as the selection of national candidates for the position of judge at the ECtHR is concerned, the Romanian legislation includes the general criteria for selection, while the specific eligibility criteria are those indicated under Articles 20–22 of the European Convention on Human Rights (ECHR) and under various relevant resolutions of the Parliamentary Assembly and of the Committee of Ministers of the Council of Europe.[4]

According to the provisions of the Government Ordinance (GO) No. 94/1999, national candidates for the position of judge at the ECtHR shall be designated:

> from among individuals with a high moral and civic standing, who fulfil the requirements for the performance of high judicial functions or who are jurists of recognised professional reputation and who satisfy the criteria for the selection of judges, as provided for in the relevant legal instruments adopted by the Council of Europe.[5]

The most recent call for applications for the selection of the Romanian candidates was published in view of the vacancy of the position of ECtHR judge appointed on behalf of Romania on 17 December 2022.[6] The call contains references to the provisions of Articles 20–22 of the ECHR, as well as the eligibility requirements resulting from the relevant resolutions of the Parliamentary Assembly and of the Committee of Ministers of the Council of Europe. Furthermore, it indicates that:

> [f]or the duration of their mandate, appointed judges may not exercise any activities incompatible with the requirements of independence, impartiality and availability, as required by the permanent character of the activity to be performed at the Court.[7]

---

[4] See, for instance, Resolution 1366 (2004) of the Parliamentary Assembly of the Council of Europe, as amended; Resolution 1646 (2009) of the Parliamentary Assembly of the Council of Europe; Resolution CM/Res (2009) 5 of the Committee of Ministers of the Council of Europe; Resolution CM/Res (2010) 26 of the Committee of Ministers of the Council of Europe.

[5] Art. 5(13) GO No. 94/1999 on the participation of Romania in the proceedings before the European Court of Human Rights and the Committee of Ministers of the Council of Europe and on the exercise by the state of the right to redress following judgments and friendly settlements.

[6] Call for applications published by the Romanian Ministry of Foreign Affairs on 12.10.2021, available at https://www.mae.ro/node/48704.

[7] Ibid.

As far as specific criteria for selection are concerned, the call for applications indicates that the evaluation of the candidates is to be made according to the following criteria:

a)   fulfilment of the eligibility requirements;
b)   legal qualification of the candidate and his/her knowledge of human rights law and of the case-law of the Court;
c)   professional experience, including scientific notoriety, if applicable;
d)   the capacity to exercise high judicial functions or being a jurist of recognised professional or scientific reputation;
e)   language skills;
f)   the ability to handle the challenges raised by the workload and the role of the Court;
g)   the ability to work in a multicultural environment which reflects different legal systems;
h)   the lack of any apparent doubt concerning the independence, impartiality, probity and integrity of the candidate.[8]

2.2.2.   National Candidates for the Position of Judge at the CJEU and the General Court

The general rules for selection and appointment of judges at the EU judicial bodies are contained in the Treaty on the Functioning of the European Union (TFEU) and in the Statute of the European Court of Justice. In the Romanian system, the selection procedures for candidates are described by government memoranda issued for each individual vacancy. This report describes the most recent selection procedures carried out by Romania for the position of judge at the CJEU and for the position of judge at the General Court of the EU (both vacancies filled on 7 October 2021). While adopted through distinct government memoranda, the two procedures include almost identical provisions, steps and criteria for the selection of candidates.

According to the Procedures for the selection of the Romanian candidates for the position of judge at the Court of Justice of the European Union[9] and at the General Court of the EU respectively,[10] as approved by memoranda

---

8   Ibid.
9   Call for applications and Procedure for selection published by the Romanian Ministry of Foreign Affairs, available at https://www.mae.ro/sites/default/files/file/anunȚ_referitor_la_selecția_candidatului_româniei_pentru_funcția_de_judecător_la_curtea_de_justiție_a_uniunii_europene_.pdf.
10   Call for applications and Procedure for selection published by the Romanian Ministry of Foreign Affairs on 19.04.2021, available at https://www.mae.ro/sites/default/files/file/anul_2021/2021_pdf/anunt_referitor_la_selecția_candidatului_româniei_pentru_funcția_de_judecător_la_tribunalul_uniunii_europene.pdf.

by the Romanian government (hereinafter Procedures for selection for the CJEU/General Court), candidates must be selected from among:

> personalities who offer full guarantees of independence and who meet the requirements for exercising in Romania the highest jurisdictional functions, in accordance with Article 253 of the Treaty on the Functioning of the European Union.[11]

The common provisions of Article 5 of the Procedures for selection for the CJEU/General Court include the following criteria for evaluation of the candidates:

a) legal qualification of the candidate and his/her knowledge of EU law and institutions;
b) professional experience;
c) the capacity to exercise judicial functions;
d) language skills;
e) the ability to work in a multicultural environment, reflecting different legal systems;
f) the lack of any apparent doubt concerning the independence, impartiality, probity and integrity of the candidate.[12]

While the criteria for selection of national candidates to positions as judges at the ECtHR and the CJEU are not identical, they are largely similar. Both selection procedures place great emphasis on professional or academic experience, substantive knowledge of the relevant legal field, language skills, and the high standing of the candidates from the perspective of their reputation, integrity, independence and impartiality.

3. AUTHORITY APPOINTING THE ADJUDICATORS AND METHODS FOR APPOINTING THE ADJUDICATORS

3.1. DOMESTIC ADJUDICATORS

Domestic judges are appointed by the President of Romania upon the proposal of the Superior Council of Magistracy. Proposals are made on the basis of having passed the admission exam and, in the case of law graduates without prior professional experience, on having passed the capacity exam. The President has no discretion to reject the proposals of the Council. Therefore, after passing the relevant exams, appointment as a judge is automatic.

---

[11] Art. 4 of the Procedures for selection for the CJEU/General Court.
[12] Ibid., Art. 5(4).

Domestic arbitrators are appointed by the parties to the dispute. If the parties cannot reach an agreement (in the case of a single arbitrator) or if one party does not appoint an arbitrator (in the case of a tribunal composed by more members), such appointment is made by the president of the arbitral institution.[13] In other cases, if the arbitrators appointed by the parties do not reach an agreement on who to appoint as president of the arbitral tribunal, such appointment is made by the executive board of the arbitral institution.[14] In ad hoc arbitrations, if the parties do not agree on the sole arbitrator to be appointed, or when the tribunal is composed of three arbitrators, if one party does not appoint its arbitrator or if the party-appointed arbitrators cannot reach an agreement on the president of the tribunal, the courts may intervene, upon request of one party, in order to appoint the arbitrator or the president of the arbitral tribunal.[15] The competent court is the departmental tribunal of the place of arbitration.

3.2. NATIONAL CANDIDATES FOR POSITIONS AS INTERNATIONAL ADJUDICATORS

3.2.1. National Candidates for the Position of Judge at the ECtHR

National candidates to the position of judge at the ECtHR are appointed by the government, with the prior approval of the joint legal and human right commissions of the Senate and the Chamber of Deputies, upon the proposal of a selection commission.[16] The members of the selection commission must exercise their mandate individually, independently and in accordance with their own personal views. They are:

1. the Minister of Justice;
2. the Minister of Foreign Affairs;
3. the governmental agent for the ECtHR;
4. the Director of the European Affairs and Human Rights Directorate of the Ministry of Justice;
5. a member of the Superior Council of Magistracy;
6. a judge from the High Court of Cassation and Justice;
7. the People's Advocate (the Ombudsman); and

---

13 Art. 19(2) and (3) of the Rules of procedure of the International Commercial Arbitration Court attached to the Romanian Chamber of Commerce and Industry in Bucharest (these rules also constitute a model for regional commercial arbitration courts).
14 Ibid., Art. 19(4).
15 Art. 561 of the Romanian Civil Procedure Code.
16 Art. 5(1) of GO No. 94/1999.

8. two law professors from advanced research and education universities in Romania (the professors are selected by the other members of the selection commission, from the lists proposed by the law faculties).[17]

The work of the selection commission is presided over by the Minister of Justice. It may adopt its decisions with a majority of the members present (a quorum of at least five members is required).[18]

The selection commission publishes a call for applications, indicating the requirements for occupying the position, the necessary documents to be submitted, as well as the time and place of selection and the deadline for submission of applications.[19]

After the expiry of the application deadline, the commission organises a hearing for the eligible persons and selects three candidates to include on the list of proposals to be submitted to the government. If possible, the commission will also submit a reserve list comprising three other candidates. The lists are published on the website of the Ministry of Justice and the minutes of the selection procedures include reasons for the content of the two lists.[20]

If the government agrees with the commission's proposals, it will submit the list of candidates to the legal and human rights commissions of the Senate and the Chamber of Deputies for consultative approval. The joint parliamentary commissions will conduct a hearing for the proposed candidates.[21]

If the government disagrees with one or several of the proposed candidates submitted by the selection commission, it will provide reasons for its decision and request the submission of alternative proposals. The alternative proposals may include one or several of the candidates on the reserve list. However, if the government disagrees with all of the proposed candidates (including the ones on the reserve list), the entire selection procedure is restarted, under the rules indicated above.[22]

After having received the consultative approval of the parliamentary commissions, the government adopts and sends to the Council of Europe the list of the three candidates proposed on behalf of Romania for the position of judge at the ECtHR.[23]

In cases where the Convention provides for the appointment of an ad hoc judge, such appointment is made by the Minister of Foreign Affairs, upon the proposal of the governmental agent of Romania.[24]

---

[17] Ibid.
[18] Ibid., Art. 5(1^1).
[19] Ibid., Art. 5(1^2).
[20] Ibid., Art. 5(1^4)–(1^5).
[21] Ibid., Art. 5(1^6).
[22] Ibid., Art. 5(1^7)–(1^8).
[23] Ibid., Art. 5(1^9).
[24] Ibid., Art. 5(2).

3.2.2. National Candidates for the Position of Judge at the CJEU or the General Court

National candidates to the position of judge at the CJEU or the General Court are appointed by the government, based on the proposal of a selection commission.[25] The selection commission is composed of the following members, who must exercise their mandate individually, independently and in accordance with their own personal views:

1. the Minister of Justice;
2. the Minister of Foreign Affairs;
3. the governmental agent for the CJEU;
4. the Director of the European Affairs and Human Rights Directorate of the Ministry of Justice;
5. a member of the Superior Council of Magistracy, designated by its plenary body, upon invitation of the Minister of Justice;
6. two judges from the High Court of Cassation and Justice, designated by its management body, upon invitation of the Minister of Justice;
7. two law professors from advanced research and education universities in Romania, upon invitation of the Minister of Justice; and
8. two deans of the Bar Associations which members of the National Union of the Romanian Bars, upon invitation of the Minister of Justice – these additional members of the commission are included only in the procedure for the selection of national candidates to the position of judge at the General Court of the EU.

The selection commissions must meet in full for the procedures for hearing, deliberation and selection of candidates. For all other activities, the selection commissions require a quorum of at least five[26] or seven members, respectively.[27] If one of the members of the selection commissions is unable to take part in the activities, for objective reasons, he or she must ensure his or her replacement, exclusively for the duration of the objective impossibility of participating in the work of the commission.[28]

The decisions of the commissions are adopted in a written procedure, by a simple majority vote, with the exception of the decision concerning the selection of the Romanian candidate and two reserve proposals for the position of judge at the CJEU, which must be adopted by a two-thirds majority.

---

[25] Art. 1 of the Procedures for selection for the CJEU/General Court.
[26] In the case of the procedure for selection of national candidates to the position of judge at the CJEU.
[27] In the case of the procedure for selection of national candidates to the position of judge at the General Court of the EU.
[28] Art. 1(3) of the Procedures for selection for the CJEU/General Court.

The work of the selection commissions is presided over by the Minister of Justice and meetings may take place either in person or by videoconference, as needed.[29]

Each selection commission publishes a call for applications indicating the requirements for occupying the position, the necessary documents to be submitted, as well as the time and place of selection and the deadline for submission of applications.[30]

After the expiry of the application deadline, the commission organises a hearing for the eligible persons and conducts recorded interviews with the candidates. The time allocated to each candidate is at least 15 minutes, up to a maximum of one hour.[31]

The commission selects one candidate as the Romanian proposal for the position of judge and two other candidates on the reserve list.[32] The results are published on the websites of the Ministry of Justice, the Ministry of Foreign Affairs, the Superior Council of Magistracy, the High Court of Cassation and Justice and the National Union of the Romanian Bars.

The final proposed candidate and the reserve list are communicated to the government for approval.[33] If the government does not agree with the proposed candidate submitted by the commission, it may select one of the candidates included on the reserve list, by means of a reasoned decision.[34] If the government rejects all three proposals of the selection commission, it shall provide reasons for its decision and the selection procedures are restarted, following the steps indicated previously.[35]

The government submits its proposed candidate for the position of judge at the CJEU or at the General Court to the EU Council and informs the Parliament which proposed candidate it has adopted.[36]

While the steps and requirements of the procedures for selecting national candidates to the position of judge at the ECtHR or the CJEU are largely similar, we note the highly detailed and more predictable character of the former (regulated by means of a Government Ordinance), as compared to the latter (for which no permanent national rules exist and the procedures are managed on a case-by-case basis when a vacancy arises).

In both cases, while the appointments are subject to clear procedural steps and are not discretionary, the process is primarily controlled by the executive

---

[29]   Ibid., Art. 2.
[30]   Ibid., Art. 3.
[31]   Ibid., Art. 5.
[32]   Ibid., Art. 6(1).
[33]   Ibid., Art. 6(3).
[34]   Ibid., Art. 7(1).
[35]   Ibid., Art. 7(2).
[36]   Ibid., Arts 8–9.

branch, with limited participation of the judiciary and parliamentary bodies. The involvement of other legal professional categories in the selection process, apart from magistrates, is very limited. For instance, representatives of attorneys are involved only in the selection of candidates to the position of judge at the General Court, but are not included in any of the other selection processes.

4. METHODS TO BALANCE THE APPOINTING AUTHORITY'S INFLUENCE ON THE APPOINTMENT OF ADJUDICATORS

4.1. DOMESTIC ADJUDICATORS

In the case of domestic judges, although two authorities are involved in the process of appointment (the President and the Superior Council of Magistracy), the role of the President is merely formal, as he or she has no discretion to reject a proposal for appointment of a judge.[37] Therefore, we can speak of a single appointing authority, namely the Superior Council of Magistracy. The elements of influence balancing are provided by the composition and rules of functioning of the Council.

The Superior Council of Magistracy is an independent agency, a body which is mentioned by the Constitution itself as the 'guarantor of the independence of the judiciary'.[38] The Council is composed of 19 members, as follows: nine judges elected by professional assemblies of judges and confirmed by the Senate; five public prosecutors elected by the professional assemblies of prosecutors and confirmed by the Senate; two legal professionals with a high moral and professional reputation, elected by the Senate as 'representatives of the civil society'; the Minister of Justice; the President of the High Court of Cassation and Justice; and the General Prosecutor. Among the nine judges who are members of the Council, two are judges of the High Court of Cassation and Justice, three are judges of courts of appeal, two are judges of departmental tribunals and two are judges of first-instance courts (the lower courts). This shows that while higher courts (and thus the more experienced judges) do exercise a greater influence in the Council, the latter has represented within it all categories of judges, including ones from the lower courts. The nine judges who are members of the Council, together with the President of the High Court of Cassation and Justice and the Minister of Justice, form the Section for Judges of the Council, which is

---

[37] Arts 31(3) and 33(11) of Law No. 303/2004 concerning the status of judges and public prosecutors.

[38] Art. 133(1) of the Romanian Constitution.

responsible for most decisions concerning the career of judges, including their appointment.[39]

The purpose of establishing the Council was to insulate, to a certain extent, decisions relevant to the appointment and career of magistrates from the political sphere. Therefore, seeing the central role of the Council in selecting, appointing and removing judges, one understands that the mechanism put in place was meant to give the judicial profession itself greater weight in the decision-making process. Of course, no mechanism is perfect and criticism of 'corporatism' has been sometimes put forward.[40] However, it is undeniable that the institutional architecture of the Council and its central place in the governance of the judiciary were meant to balance the influence of the political factor in decisions regarding the judiciary.

An independent factor tempering the influence of the appointing authority is the irremovability of the judge provided by Romanian Constitution in Article 125(1). Once a person enters the profession, this is in principle a lifelong career choice which is guaranteed by the Constitution and by the applicable laws. The course of the person's career may be influenced by two types of events: (i) promotion and (ii) removal from office for proven inaptitude or as a disciplinary measure. The Superior Council of Magistracy manages both procedures. Promotion depends on several factors, including a periodic assessment by the president of the court and two colleagues, which gives some influence over the personal career of judges to the presidents of the courts. However, the most important criterion for promotion is an exam organised by the Council, through its 'training branch', the National Institute of Magistracy. Removal from office is quite rare in practice, so as not to constitute in practice a sword of Damocles for judges. It can be concluded, therefore, that the reasonable promise of a lifelong career within the judiciary is a relatively effective guarantee against influence of the appointing authority over the judge.

Concerning domestic arbitrators, the role of the president of the arbitration institution (or the executive body of it) is not meant to balance the influence of the parties in appointing the arbitrators, but just to replace one party's input in the procedure or the possible lack of agreement of the two members of the tribunal. By doing so, however, the institution itself does balance, in a way, the parties' influence on the appointment of arbitrators.

---

[39] Art. 41(1)(c) of Law No. 317/2004 on the Superior Council of the Magistracy.
[40] See e.g. B. Iancu and E.S. Tănăsescu, 'Introduction' in B. Iancu and E.S. Tănăsescu (eds), *Governance and Constitutionalism. Law, Politics and Institutional Neutrality*, Routledge, 2019, p. 30.

Romania

4.2. NATIONAL CANDIDATES FOR POSITIONS AS INTERNATIONAL ADJUDICATORS

As described above, the appointment of national candidates to positions as international adjudicators is a government-led and controlled process. In the selection of national candidates to positions as judges at the ECtHR and the CJEU, the government retains the final power to appoint or reject any (or even all) of the proposed candidates submitted by the selection commissions.

The mixed composition of the selection commissions is intended as one of the mechanisms to balance the influence of the appointing authority – they include, in all cases, in addition to ministers and other members of the executive, representatives of the legal profession (predominantly magistrates) and law professors. Nonetheless, the impact of the mixed composition should not be overstated, given that in certain cases (for instance, in the appointment of CJEU candidates) the magistrates and academics forming part of the selection commission are nominated by invitation of the Minister of Justice, who thus retains an indirect control over the selection process.

Another factor balancing the government's authority concerns the detailed and precise character of the steps of the procedures, as well as the inclusion of clear criteria for the selection of candidates. However, we note in this respect that while the selection of ECtHR candidates is based on permanent, predictable rules adopted by Government Ordinance, the selection of CJEU candidates is based on practices (rather than on permanent national rules), with the selection process described in government memoranda adopted when individual vacancies arise.

The appointing authority's influence may be considered to be further tempered by certain procedural rules applicable during the selection process, such as:

- the requirement to provide reasons for the refusal to nominate the candidate proposed by the selection commission (or another candidate on the reserve list);
- the requirement to submit the list of accepted candidates to the parliamentary commissions for consultative approval (applicable for the selection of ECtHR candidates); and
- transparency requirements, such as the obligation to publish the call for applications, the list of proposed candidates and the reserve list, as well as to record the candidate interviews (in the case of CJEU candidates).

We conclude on this point that the selection procedures for both ECtHR and CJEU candidates are not discretionary and include several rules and guarantees that contribute to modulating the influence of the appointing authority.

Intersentia

603

However, the appointment process remains heavily controlled by the executive branch and involves the participation of only a limited number of the relevant legal actors at the national level.

5. PARAMETERS TO ENSURE THAT ADJUDICATORS ACT INDEPENDENTLY AND IMPARTIALLY

5.1. DOMESTIC ADJUDICATORS

The independence of domestic judges is provided for expressly in the Romanian Constitution in Article 124(3). Moreover, Article 2(3) of Law No. 303/2004 provides for the requirement of impartiality in rendering their judgments. To ensure such independence and impartiality, several constitutional and legal requirements, and procedures to assess their fulfilment, have been put in place.

First, there are incompatibilities and prohibitions, inobservance of which triggers the ineligibility for, or removal from, office. According to Article 125(3) of the Constitution, a judge cannot hold any public office or a private job, except for teaching in a university. Law No. 303/2004 makes this rule more specific: judges are not allowed to exercise commercial activities directly or indirectly, to be partners or managers of companies or to be arbitrators.[41] In order to preserve the independence of the judiciary, they are not allowed to be members of political parties.[42] Instead, they may be members of NGOs or of scientific or academic associations and they can publish articles, studies and books (including literature), except those with a political character.

There is also a general duty to refrain from judicial activity whenever there is a conflict between their private interests and the public interest of due process.[43] Finally, Articles 6 and 7 of Law No. 303/2004 provide for a prohibition on being a judge in respect of persons who were collaborators of the former communist secret service (*Securitate*) or are agents of an existing intelligence service.

A breach of incompatibilities and prohibitions triggers a disciplinary procedure, dealt with by the Superior Council of Magistracy, and will trigger removal from office or, in less severe situations, the loss of a professional degree.[44]

Moreover, a judge is under a duty to abstain from adjudicating cases on which he or she has previously expressed an opinion, where he or she has a conflict of interests (various scenarios are expressly listed by the law), or when there is legitimate doubt concerning his or her impartiality.[45] Among the cases

---

[41] Art. 8(1) of Law No. 303/2004 concerning the status of judges and public prosecutors.
[42] Ibid., Art. 9(1).
[43] Ibid., Art. 5(2).
[44] Arts 99 and 100.
[45] Art. 42 of the Romanian Civil Procedure Code.

of conflicts of interests provided by the law are the following: when the judge was a lawyer, witness, prosecutor, arbitrator or mediator in the same case, when he or she (or his or her spouse or relative) has an interest in the case, when he or she is married to one of the parties or one of the lawyers of the parties (this specific provision indicating that there are families in the same profession, where one spouse is a judge and the other is a lawyer), when he or she (or his or her spouse or relative) has participated in the judgment which is under review (for appeal judges), or when he or she (or his or her spouse or relative) is has relations of enmity with one of the parties.

For domestic arbitrators, the cases of judges' incompatibility to adjudicate a specific case also apply.[46] Moreover, the law provides for specific cases of incompatibility or conflicts of interests for arbitrators. These are as follows: when a company in which the arbitrator is a partner or a member of the management board has an interest in the case, when the arbitrator is an employee of one of the parties (or of a person belonging to the same group of companies as one of the parties), when the arbitrator has other contractual relations with one of the parties (or of a person belonging to the same group of companies as one of the parties), or when the arbitrator has given advice to one of the parties, has represented a party or has been a witness in the previous stages of the dispute.[47]

Both domestic judges and domestic arbitrators, when in a situation of incompatibility to adjudicate or to arbitrate, incur a duty to abstain. If they do not abstain, any of the parties may recuse them. The request for recusal of judges is decided by another formation of judges of the same court. In institutional arbitration, the request for recusal of arbitrators is decided upon by a commission appointed by the president of the arbitral institution.[48] In ad hoc arbitration, the request for recusal is decided upon by the departmental tribunal of the place of arbitration.[49] The decision to deny the request can only be appealed together with the decision on the merits of the case. If the case is being heard in the final instance, the decision to deny the request can be appealed within five days from the communication of the decision.

5.2. NATIONALS APPOINTED TO POSITIONS AS INTERNATIONAL ADJUDICATORS

Apart from the relevant criteria applicable at the stage of selection, the Romanian system does not contain specific rules intended to ensure that nationals appointed

---

[46] Ibid., Art. 562(1).
[47] Ibid. See also Art. 21 of the Rules of procedure of the International Commercial Arbitration Court attached to the Romanian Chamber of Commerce and Industry in Bucharest.
[48] Art. 23(6) and (7) of the Rules of procedure of the International Commercial Arbitration Court attached to the Romanian Chamber of Commerce and Industry in Bucharest.
[49] Art. 563 of the Romanian Civil Procedure Code.

as international adjudicators act independently and impartially throughout the duration of their mandate. The rules governing the exercise of their functions as international adjudicators are those specific to the judicial body where they perform their duties.

Nonetheless, it is worth reiterating that, as a condition of participating in the selection process, candidates for ECtHR or CJEU positions must prove that they meet the necessary requirements to occupy a (high) judicial function and that there are no circumstances affecting their independence, impartiality, reputation or probity. Such conditions are meant to ensure, at least in principle, that the selected candidates will act independently and impartially once they are appointed as international adjudicators.

More specifically, according to the calls for applications published for both ECtHR[50] and CJEU selection procedures,[51] candidates must include, among the documents necessary for their application, the following:

- a written affidavit declaring that the candidate has no criminal record and is not subject to any other circumstances that would prevent them from effectively performing their judicial functions at the ECtHR (or the CJEU/ General Court), and additionally that he or she meets the requirements of Article 6 and 7 of Law No. 303/2004, in the sense that he or she was not an agent or collaborator of the former communist secret service (*Securitate*), and that he or she is not currently an agent of an intelligence service;
- a written affidavit 'to accept the nomination as a candidate on behalf of Romania (implying, among others, the willingness to cease all other activities incompatible with the status of a judge at the ECtHR, if nominated), as well as to confirm that there are no declarations or acts of the candidate which, if made public, could prejudice the reputation of the Court'.[52]

The latter disclosure requirement, although applicable in the selection process for ECtHR candidates, may be regarded as a true commitment to maintaining independence and impartiality for the duration of the mandate as an international adjudicator.

---

[50] Call for applications published by the Romanian Ministry of Foreign Affairs on 12.10.2021, p. 2, available at https://www.mae.ro/node/48704.

[51] Call for applications and Procedure for selection published by the Romanian Ministry of Foreign Affairs, p. 2, available at https://www.mae.ro/sites/default/files/file/anunŢ_referitor_la_selecţia_candidatului_româniei_pentru_funcţia_de_judecător_la_curtea_de_justiţie_a_uniunii_europene_.pdf; Call for applications and Procedure for selection published by the Romanian Ministry of Foreign Affairs on 19.04.2021, p. 2, available at https://www.mae.ro/sites/default/files/file/anul_2021/2021_pdf/anunt_referitor_la_selecţia_candidatului_româniei_pentru_funcţia_de_judecător_la_tribunalul_uniunii_europene.pdf.

[52] Call for applications published by the Romanian Ministry of Foreign Affairs on 12.10.2021, p. 3, available at https://www.mae.ro/node/48704.

6. CONSEQUENCES FOR ADJUDICATORS IN CASE OF A BREACH OF THE REQUIREMENT TO ACT INDEPENDENTLY AND IMPARTIALLY

6.1. DOMESTIC ADJUDICATORS

Domestic judges are subject to three types of legal responsibility: civil liability, disciplinary responsibility and criminal responsibility.[53] Civil liability applies, according to the general rules, when four conditions are met: wrongfulness, fault, damage and a causal link between wrongfulness and the damage.[54] There are no specific rules on civil liability for breaching the requirements of independence and impartiality; therefore the general rules will apply.

There are, instead, specific rules concerning the disciplinary responsibility of domestic judges which apply in cases of breach of the requirement to act independently and impartially. A breach of the rules concerning the incompatibilities and prohibitions presented above is specifically qualified as misconduct under Article 99(b) of Law No. 303/2004 concerning the status of judges and public prosecutors. A breach of the rules concerning the duty to abstain from adjudicating certain cases is qualified as misconduct under Article 99(d) of the same law. For the first type of breach, only the two most severe types of penalties may be applied: the loss of a professional degree or removal from office.[55] For the second type of breach (that of the duty to abstain), any of the available penalties may be applied. These include, besides the two already mentioned, the following: a warning, a 25% reduction of the gross wage, relocation to a different court for a period of between one and three years, or suspension from office for a maximum of six months.

Disciplinary proceedings are organised in a trial-like manner, with the Section for Judges of the Superior Council of Magistracy acting as a court.[56] The disciplinary action is conducted by the Judicial Inspection, a separate structure within the Council, acting similarly to the role of a public prosecutor within this procedure. The decisions of the Council concerning disciplinary proceedings are subject to appeal before the High Court of Cassation and Justice.[57]

Domestic judges can be subject to criminal responsibility for acts that would also qualify as breaches of the duty to act independently and impartially (such as bribery, corruption, etc.). The judgment is rendered by criminal courts, but the criminal investigation is conducted by the Section for Investigating Crimes

---

[53]   Art. 95 of Law No. 303/2004 concerning the status of judges and public prosecutors.
[54]   Art. 1357 of the Romanian Civil Code.
[55]   Art. 100(2) of Law No. 303/2004 concerning the status of judges and public prosecutors.
[56]   Art. 44(1) of Law No. 317/2004 on the Superior Council of the Magistracy.
[57]   Ibid., Art. 51(3).

related to the Judiciary (SIIJ), a department within the Public Prosecution Office attached to the High Court of Cassation and Justice.[58] The Section is currently at the centre of a heated political and legal debate due to accusations of pressuring judges and affecting the independence of the judiciary. The CJEU recently decided that some specific issues concerning the SIIJ (in particular the interim appointments) fail to observe the principle of the rule of law.[59]

There are no specific provisions for domestic arbitrators who breach their duty to act independently and impartially by not abstaining from intervening in cases where they should have done so. However, as this is a breach of law, civil or criminal liability can be triggered, provided that the legal requirements are fulfilled. Rules of the arbitral institutions usually contain clauses limiting liability to gross negligence or bad faith.[60]

6.2. NATIONALS APPOINTED TO POSITIONS AS INTERNATIONAL ADJUDICATORS

Romanian legislation does not contain specific rules concerning the breach by an international adjudicator of the requirement to act independently and impartially. There are no national provisions concerning the potential removal of an international adjudicator, as such rules are generally comprised in the statute of the international adjudication body.

7. ENFORCEMENT OF A FINAL DECISION RENDERED BY AN ADJUDICATOR IN BREACH OF THE REQUIREMENT TO ACT INDEPENDENTLY AND IMPARTIALLY

7.1. DOMESTIC ADJUDICATORS

Decisions rendered by domestic judges that breached the requirement to act independently and impartially are subject to revision and, if the request for revision is granted, the decision is annulled and no longer enforceable (or, if it has been already enforced, the *status quo ante* must be re-established). The scenario

---

[58] Art. 88[1]–88[11] of Law No. 304/2004 concerning the organisation of the judiciary.

[59] European Court of Justice, Judgment of Grand Chamber of 18 May 2021 in joined cases C-83/19, C-127/19, C-195/19, C-291/19, C-355/19 and C-397/19, available at https://curia. europa.eu/juris/document/document.jsf?text=&docid=241381&pageIndex=0&doclang=en &mode=req&dir=&occ=first&part=1&cid=40892101.

[60] Art. 53 of the Rules of procedure of the International Commercial Arbitration Court attached to the Romanian Chamber of Commerce and Industry in Bucharest.

of breach of the duty to act independently and impartially may qualify under two separate cases for revision. The first is the scenario provided by Article 509(1), point 3 of the Civil Procedure Code: where the judge who rendered or took part in the judgment has been convicted by a final decision for a crime related to that case. This would be the case for corruption or other similar crimes related to that particular case. The second scenario is provided by Article 509(1), point 4 of the Civil Procedure Code: where the judge has been subject to a final disciplinary penalty for exercising his or her office in bad faith or gross negligence and such acts influenced the decision rendered in that case. The refusal to abstain would amount to bad faith, according to Article 99^1 of Law No. 303/2004 concerning the status of judges and public prosecutors.[61] A failure to abstain would qualify as gross negligence according to the same article.[62] The request for revision must be presented within 30 days from the date the person concerned knew about the occurrence of these scenarios, but no later than one year after the final decision to convict or to impose a disciplinary penalty has been rendered.

Arbitral awards issued by domestic arbitrators who breached the requirement to act independently and impartially are susceptible to being annulled under the action for annulment provided by the Romanian Civil Procedure Code as being against the public order.[63] However, the action for annulment may be lodged only within one month after the communication of the arbitral award. Therefore, if the breach is discovered after that point, only a criminal conviction of the arbitrator might trigger the annulment of the award.

7.2. FOREIGN OR INTERNATIONAL ADJUDICATORS

The Romanian legislation does contain express rules concerning the specific situation in which a decision of a foreign or international tribunal was rendered by an adjudicator in breach of their obligation to act independently and impartially.

However, in the field of recognition and enforcement of foreign judicial decisions and arbitral awards, the Romanian Civil Procedure Code contains rules allowing domestic courts to refuse recognition and/or enforcement in situations where the foreign judgment is manifestly contrary to the public order,[64] a scenario that could include situations of failure to observe the requirements of impartiality and independence.

---

61 Art. 99^1(1) of Law No. 303/2004 concerning the status of judges and public prosecutors: 'There is bad faith when the judge or the public prosecutor knowingly breaches the substantive or procedural rules, with the purpose of harming a person or accepting that harm will occur'.
62 Ibid., Art. 99^1(2): 'There is gross negligence when the judge or public prosecutor does not observe, with severe, undoubtable and inexcusable fault, the substantive or procedural rules'.
63 Art. 608(1)(h) of the Romanian Civil Procedure Code.
64 See ibid., Arts 1097(1)(a) and 1104(2).

Intersentia

8. CONCLUSION

Our analysis in the present report has sought to highlight the most important rules and practices concerning the requirements of independence and impartiality of adjudicators, in both a domestic and an international context.

On a very basic, quantitative level, our research has shown, as was to be expected, that the rules contained in the national legal system focus predominantly on ensuring the functioning of the domestic judiciary in accordance with the principles of independence and impartiality, with fewer rules dedicated to domestic arbitrators or candidates to positions as international adjudicators. Both the institutional design of the judiciary and the rules applicable to the performance of the duties of judges contribute towards ensuring the observance of the requirements of independence and impartiality.

From the perspective of the degree of discretion afforded in the process of selection of adjudicators to appointing authorities, we note that as far as domestic adjudicators (and especially judges) are concerned, such discretion is very limited – almost inexistent. As the process of selection of domestic judges relies, in all cases, on a competence-based admission exam, the procedures are insulated from the influence of other authorities or of the political sphere. As far as domestic arbitrators are concerned, affording the parties more latitude in the selection and appointment process is part of the very essence of arbitral proceedings, but there are sufficient procedural guarantees in place to ensure the observance of the principles of independence and impartiality.

On the other hand, the selection process for national candidates to positions as international adjudicators is (as is perhaps to be expected) highly political and the level of discretion afforded to the appointing authorities is relatively high. Such discretion is tempered, as illustrated in various parts of this report, by clear selection criteria and procedural mechanisms aiming to ensure that the nominated candidates comply with the requirements of independence, impartiality and probity. This is exemplified, for instance, by the emphasis placed on the profile of the candidates or by the requirement to disclose potential conflicts of interest and to declare that the candidate has not collaborated with the former communist secret service and that he or she is not currently involved in any other intelligence activities.

THE INDEPENDENCE AND IMPARTIALITY OF ADJUDICATORS IN SLOVENIA

Vasilka SANCIN and Domen TURŠIČ

1. Introduction 611
2. Appointment of Adjudicators 612
   2.1. Appointment of Domestic Adjudicators....................... 612
   2.2. Appointment of International Adjudicators................... 614
3. Independence and Impartiality of Adjudicators..................... 617
   3.1. Independence and Impartiality of Domestic Adjudicators 617
   3.2. Independence and Impartiality of International Adjudicators 619
4. Conclusion... 619

1. INTRODUCTION

The appointment of adjudicators in the Republic of Slovenia is governed by the Constitution of the Republic of Slovenia[1] and further legislation (e.g. the Constitutional Court Act (CCA)).[2] Moreover, Slovenia has specific legislation regarding the appointment of international adjudicators, i.e. the Act on Nomination of Candidates from the Republic of Slovenia for Judges at International Courts (ANCJIC).[3] Nevertheless, Slovene practice of appointing candidates for international adjudicators, particularly when it comes to 'potential adjudicators',[4] varies and does not always strictly adhere to the requirements of the ANCJIC.

The requirement of independence and impartiality of domestic adjudicators is expressly regulated in the Constitution and legislation. There exist however no

---

[1] Official Gazette of the Republic of Slovenia, No. 33/91-I, 42/97 – UZS68, 66/00 – UZ80, 24/03 – UZ3a, 47, 68, 69/04 – UZ14, 69/04 – UZ43, 69/04 – UZ50, 68/06 – UZ121, 140, 143, 47/13 – UZ148, 47/13 – UZ90, 97, 99, 75/16 – UZ70a and 92/21 – UZ62a.

[2] Official Gazette RS, No. 64/07 – official consolidated text, 109/12, 23/20 and 92/21.

[3] Official Gazette RS, No. 64/01 and 59/02.

[4] Members of lists from which parties to a dispute can, but are not obligated to, select adjudicators (e.g. PCA arbitrators or ICSID conciliators and arbitrators).

Intersentia

specific provisions that would demand the competent authorities to be guided by the need to ensure independence and impartiality of international adjudicators when selecting appropriate candidates.

The report will present the appointment of domestic (section 2.1) and international adjudicators (section 2.2), describing the role of the appointing authority, the criteria for appointment and the method of appointment. The report will then describe the existing mechanisms for ensuring the independence and impartiality of domestic (section 3.1) and international adjudicators (section 3.2).

2. APPOINTMENT OF ADJUDICATORS

2.1. APPOINTMENT OF DOMESTIC ADJUDICATORS

Slovenia's Constitution provides the initial legal framework for the appointment of judges. Article 130 of the Constitution provides that judges are elected by the National Assembly, which is a house of Slovenia's parliament that consists of 90 elected representatives. The National Assembly elects judges based on a proposal of the Judicial Council. Article 131 of the Constitution provides that the Judicial Council consists of 11 members, five of which are elected by the National Assembly on the proposal of the President of Slovenia from among university professors of law, attorneys and other lawyers, while six members are elected by judges amongst themselves.

The Constitution therefore provides that the appointing authority for domestic judges is the legislative branch of the government. This may be criticised from the perspective of the independence of the judiciary from the other branches of government. When drafting the Constitution, a proposal was put forward that aimed at limiting the influence of the legislative branch over the judiciary by making the President of Slovenia the appointing authority for judges (still based on a proposal by the Judicial Council). However, this proposal was not adopted.[5]

Article 129 of the Constitution provides that the office of a judge is permanent and that the age requirement and other conditions for election are determined by law. These conditions and requirements for the election of judges are further stipulated in the Judicial Service Act (JSA).[6] Article 8 of the JSA provides eight cumulative conditions for a person to be eligible to be elected to the office of a judge:

---

[5]   J. Sovdat, 'Ustavnopravni vidik neodvisnosti sodstva' (2017) 321 *Revija Pravnik* 332.
[6]   Official Gazette RS, No. 94/07, 91/09, 33/11, 46/13, 63/13, 69/13, 95/14 – ZUPPJS15, 17/15, 23/17 – ZSSve and 36/19 – ZDT-1.

1. the person must be a Slovene national;
2. the person must master the Slovene language;
3. the person must have legal competence and sufficient health to be able to perform the judicial function;
4. the person must be 30 years of age;
5. the person must have a Bachelor of Law (pre-Bologna) or Master of Law degree (second Bologna cycle) obtained in Slovenia or a comparable degree, recognised in Slovenia, from a foreign institution;
6. the person must have passed the state legal exam (bar exam);
7. the person must not have been convicted of an intentionally committed criminal offence; and
8. there must not be a final indictment against the person or a scheduled main hearing based on an indictment proposal for an intentionally committed criminal offence that is prosecuted ex officio.

In order to be promoted or directly appointed to the position of a Higher Court judge (second instance), a person must have successfully exercised the functions of a judge for at least six years or have at least nine years of post-qualification experience as a lawyer. Alternatively, a university teacher of law may be elected as a judge of the Higher Court if they fulfil the conditions from Article 8 of the JSA and have been elected to the position of at least Assistant Professor (*docent*).

Similarly, a person may be elected as a Supreme Court judge if they have successfully exercised the judicial function for at least 15 years or have at least 20 years of post-qualification experience as a lawyer. Alternatively, a university teacher of law may be elected to the position of a Supreme Court judge if they have been elected to the position of at least Associate Professor.

Once a person has been elected as a judge by the National Assembly, the decision regarding their promotion to the position of a judge of a Higher Court is made by the Judicial Council. Their promotion to the second instance is therefore not in the hands of the legislator. However, it is again the National Assembly that elects judges of the Supreme Court based on the proposal of the Judicial Council.

The appointment of judges of the Constitutional Court of Slovenia has a separate legal basis compared to the rest of the judiciary. Article 163 of the Constitution provides that the Constitutional Court is composed of nine judges, elected on the proposal of the President of Slovenia by the National Assembly in a manner provided by law. It also stipulates that the judges are elected from among 'legal experts'. The CCA then further specifies the manner in which the National Assembly elects judges to the Constitutional Court as it provides that the National Assembly shall hold a secret ballot when voting on the candidates proposed by the President of Slovenia. The CCA also further specifies the eligibility criteria for Constitutional Court judges. Article 9 of the CCA stipulates that a person can be elected as a judge of the Constitutional Court if they are a Slovene national, if they are a legal expert and if they are at least 40 years of age. The minimum age limit is also a particularly relevant eligibility criterion for the appointment of candidates for international adjudicators, as further explained in the next section.

2.2. APPOINTMENT OF INTERNATIONAL ADJUDICATORS

The appointment of international adjudicators is not regulated by the Constitution of Slovenia. However, in 2001, the National Assembly adopted the ANCJIC, which is applicable to both the nomination and election of candidates for adjudicators in international courts or tribunals as well as the nomination and election of international adjudicators that are appointed directly by Slovenia. The ANCJIC also stipulates that it applies to the nomination or election of representatives of Slovenia to other international judicial organs and for 'members of an international arbitration tribunal from Slovenia' (i.e. arbitrators appointed by Slovenia).

Article 2 of the ANCJIC stipulates that candidates for international adjudicators must meet the requirements set by the ANCJIC. The ANCJIC sets out these requirements in Article 3, stipulating that a candidate must be proficient in at least one of the official languages of the relevant international court or tribunal and must meet either of the two disjunctive set of criteria:

1. the criteria for the election to the Supreme Court, as set out in Article 12 of the JSA; or
2. the criteria for the election to the Constitutional Court, as set out in Article 9 of the CCA.

In most cases, the most favourable set of requirements for candidates will be the one from Article 9 of the CCA, as it only requires a candidate to be a Slovene national, a legal expert (a term that is not clearly defined) and of sufficient age (minimum 40 years old). Thus, only when a university teacher of law who is younger than 40 fulfils all the cumulative conditions under the first paragraph of Article 8 of the JSA and has the title of (at least) Associate Professor would the set of requirements under the JSA be more favourable, as the candidate can also be between 30 and 40 years of age.[7] Nevertheless, even in the case of candidates who have at least the title of Associate Professor and work, for example, in the field of international law, they would not qualify if they have not also successfully passed the state legal exam (bar exam) – which can only be taken after a minimum period of judicial or other traineeship. These requirements effectively prevent the occurrence of such

---

[7] For candidates under 40 years of age who are not associate professors of law, the JSA would not be more favourable. Even though the JSA does not include an age requirement per se,

hypothetical cases, since it would be extremely difficult, although theoretically not impossible, to cumulatively satisfy all these criteria.

The Constitutional Court of Slovenia was faced with the issue of the constitutionality of the age requirement included (by reference) in the ANCJIC. An applicant for the position of a judge of the Joint Supervisory Body of Eurojust was not yet 40 years of age when applying to become a candidate for the position. When his application was dismissed for not meeting the basic requirements of Article 3 of the ANCJIC, the applicant argued that the age requirement was arbitrary and discriminatory and therefore violated the Constitution. The Constitutional Court, however, noted that differentiating between applicants based on age was in direct connection with the object of regulation, as it is not unreasonable to demand that a candidate for an international judge has some 'life experience'. According to the Court, this sentiment is echoed in the Constitution as well, as the Constitution envisages in Article 129 that the legislator may impose age requirements for eligibility to become a judge.[8]

The second paragraph of Article 2 of the ANCJIC, however, adds that if the rules of an international court or a treaty which is binding on the Republic of Slovenia provide special conditions for election of international court judges, a person who could be considered for nomination and election as a candidate for the position of international court judge also needs to comply with any such conditions. This means that the second paragraph potentially provides for additional requirements for prospective candidates, rather than alternative ones to those stipulated in paragraph 1 and further listed in Article 3. Thus, regardless of the fact that treaties feature above laws in Slovenia's legal hierarchy, and the latter must be in conformity with generally accepted principles of international law and with valid treaties ratified by the National Assembly,[9] candidates who fulfil all the requirements under the specific treaty establishing an international court or tribunal cannot apply for a position as an international adjudicator if they do not also fulfil the requirements under the ANCJIC. Nevertheless, it is interesting to note that the provision not only mentions requirements that would arise out of a treaty that is binding on Slovenia, since treaties are usually rather general when it comes to conditions for judges/arbitrators, but also specifically refers to the rules of an international court, which in fact may also contain more specific requirements, including those demanding independence and impartiality of adjudicators. Consequently, Slovenia must take any such requirements into account when selecting appropriate candidates.

---

it does require at least 15 years of experience as a judge (i.e. being at least 45 years of age, as one must be at least 30 years of age to become a judge) or 20 years of post-qualification experience (it is virtually impossible to become a qualified lawyer in Slovenia before the age of 20 – much more likely 25 and over – making it highly improbable that such a candidate would be younger than 40 years of age).

8   Constitutional Court, U-I-120/04, decision of 1 July 2004.
9   Article 153(2) of the Constitution.

Pursuant to Article 4 of the ANCJIC, the Ministry of Justice must publish a call for applications for a vacancy in the Official Gazette. Pursuant to Article 6 of the ANCJIC, the government and the Judicial Council must provide an opinion to the President of Slovenia on the applications received. The President of Slovenia then decides which candidates are to proceed to the election procedure in the National Assembly. The National Assembly holds a secret ballot in which a candidate must receive at least 46 votes (of the 90 total votes) in order to be nominated or elected to the position of an international adjudicator.

The ANCJIC also provides that if the rules of an international court or the relevant treaty provide that an alternate judge must be appointed for a specific case, such alternate is to be appointed by the government based on a proposal by the Minister of Justice, who must obtain the opinion of the Judicial Council beforehand. Therefore, in the case of alternate judges for specific cases, the legislator has no role in appointing an international adjudicator.

It must be noted that, in practice, the requirements and the procedure of the ANCJIC are not always abided by. For example, the Ministry of Finance (and not the Ministry of Justice) published a call for applications on its website (and not in the Official Gazette) for arbitrators and conciliators to be appointed to the list of arbitrators and/or conciliators at the International Centre for Settlement of Investment Disputes (ICSID). The call for applications included requirements that departed from the ones in the ANCJIC. Additionally, the call for applications stated that the decision regarding who to nominate would be made by a committee of two representatives of the Ministry of Finance and one representative of the Ministry of Economic Development and Technology.[10] Thus, the call for applications completely departs from the ANCJIC not only with respect to the role of the National Assembly in appointing international adjudicators, but also with respect to the roles of the Minister of Justice, the Judicial Council and the President of Slovenia. In comparison, the appointment to the list of Members of the Court at the Permanent Court of Arbitration (PCA) is traditionally done through the process envisioned by the ANCJIC.[11]

The inconsistency of the application of the ANCJIC is also evidenced by the fact that the ANCJIC was the legal basis for the appointment of an arbitrator in the matter of an arbitration under the Arbitration Agreement between the Government of the Republic of Croatia and the Government of the Republic of Slovenia, signed on 4 November 2009,[12] who was a Slovene national, but not for his replacement, after he stepped down, when Slovenia selected the then President of the ICJ, Judge Ronny Abraham. Moreover, the ANCJIC was also

---

[10] Available at https://www.gov.si/assets/ministrstva/MF/Generalni-sekretariat/DOKUMENTI/Delovna-mesta/VLASTA/Javni_poziv_ICSID_2021_P.pdf.

[11] See for example the Decision on the election of a Member of the PCA, Official Gazette of the Republic of Slovenia 34-1506/2019, 24 May 2019, 4006.

[12] For details about the case see https://pca-cpa.org/en/cases/3/; Decision on the election of an arbitrator, Official Gazette of the Republic of Slovenia 76/2011, 9879.

Slovenia

not observed for the appointment of arbitrators in the three publicly known international investment cases where Slovenia appeared as the respondent.[13]

Therefore, the ANCJIC should be revised to accommodate the different requirements and reasons for appointment of international adjudicators. Such revision, encompassing a broader range of appointments, would increase the consistency of its application in practice.

3. INDEPENDENCE AND IMPARTIALITY OF ADJUDICATORS

3.1. INDEPENDENCE AND IMPARTIALITY OF DOMESTIC ADJUDICATORS

The Constitution of Slovenia provides for the independence and impartiality of judges. Article 23 of the Constitution provides that everyone has the right to have any decision regarding his or her rights, duties and any charges brought against him or her made without undue delay by an independent, impartial court constituted by law. Additionally, Article 125 provides that judges shall be independent in the performance of the judicial function.

The Constitutional Court has noted that:

> [T]he constitutional principle of the independence of judges, the bearers of which are judges, cannot be regarded as their privilege, but foremost as an essential element for ensuring the protection of the rights of persons who are parties to judicial proceedings. Ensuring the right to judicial protection and within this framework also the right to an independent judge can entail an essential element of the possibility to exercise all other rights. The implementation of the principle of the independence of the judiciary is thus not intended (only) for judges as such, but especially for those who need judicial protection of their rights. In addition, the independence of judges is a prerequisite for their impartiality in concrete judicial proceedings and thereby for the credibility of the judiciary as well as the trust of the public in its work.

According to Article 23 of the Constitution, only a judge duly appointed pursuant to rules previously established by law and by judicial regulations may judge an individual. If there are any reasons that put in doubt a judge's independence or impartiality, a judge must recuse him- or herself.[14] Moreover, procedural legislation provides for reasons when a judge cannot be deemed to be independent or impartial (*iudex inhabilis*) or when there are reasons for doubting the independence or impartiality of a judge (*iudex suspectus*).

---

[13] A list of these cases is available at https://investmentpolicy.unctad.org/investment-dispute-settlement/country/192/slovenia.

[14] Wedam-Lukič.

Intersentia

The Contentious Civil Procedure Act, for example, provides in Article 70 that:

A judge or a lay judge shall be prohibited to exercise the judicial function:

1. if he himself is a party to the litigation or their statutory representative or attorney; or their co-obligee, co-obligor or recourse debtor; or if in the litigation concerned he was heard as a witness or an expert witness;
2. if he is permanently or temporarily employed by a party, or if he is a partner in a general partnership, limited partnership or a limited liability company, or the silent partner in a silent partnership which is a party to the litigation;
3. if a party or their statutory representative or attorney is his relative in direct line, irrespective of removals, or in lateral line up to four removals, or his spouse or an in-law up to two removals, regardless of whether the marriage has terminated or not;
4. if he is a guardian, adoptor or adoptee of a party, or their statutory representative or attorney;
5. if in the litigation concerned he has taken part in the proceedings before a lower court, arbitration tribunal or another body;
6. if other circumstances render his impartiality doubtful.[15]

The first five reasons are grounds for exclusion, whereas the sixth reason is a ground for refusal. The main differences between them are that the grounds for exclusion are an exhaustive list of reasons that the courts must consider as sufficient for disqualifying a judge ex officio, whereas the ground for refusal is a general clause that must be invoked by a party to the proceedings and where it must be established whether the circumstances are such as to cast doubts on the impartiality of a judge.[16] It is not necessary to establish that a judge was indeed partial. The appearance of partiality is sufficient. The appearance of partiality must not only be viewed through the eyes of the party to the procedure, but also objectively, so that a reasonable third person would have serious doubts regarding the impartiality of the judge.[17] If a judgment is rendered by a judge who ought to have been disqualified, such a judgment can be set aside by the appellate court.[18]

The requirement of independence and impartiality of domestic adjudicators more broadly can also be seen from the Arbitration Act,[19] Article 14 of which

---

[15] Official Gazette RS, No. 73/07, 45/08 – ZArbit, 45/08, 111/08 – decision CC, 57/09 – decision CC, 12/10 – decision CC, 50/10 – decision CC, 107/10 – decision CC, 75/12 – decision CC, 40/13 – decision CC, 92/13 – decision CC, 10/14 – decision CC, 48/15 – decision CC, 6/17 – decision CC, 10/17, 16/19 – ZNP-1 in 70/19 – decision CC.

[16] L. Ude, 'Izločitev' in L. Ude et al., *Pravdni postopek: zakon s komentarjem*, Uradni List: GV Založba, Ljubljana 2005, pp. 301–12; Similar provisions can be found in other procedural legislation, e.g. Article 39 of the Criminal Procedure Code, Official Gazette RS, No. 176/21.

[17] A. Galič, 'Pravica do sodnega varstva v civilnih zadevah' in L. Šturm (ed.), *Komentar Ustave Republike Slovenije, dopolnitev – A*, Fakulteta za državne in evropske študije, Kranj 2011, pp. 337–85.

[18] E.g. Article 339 of the Contentious Civil Procedure Act; Article 371 of the Criminal Procedure Code.

[19] Official Gazette RS, No. 45/08.

provides that in case of a failure of a party to an arbitration agreement or an appointing authority to appoint an arbitrator, the court appoints an independent and impartial arbitrator.

3.2. INDEPENDENCE AND IMPARTIALITY OF INTERNATIONAL ADJUDICATORS

The ANCJIC does not explicitly provide for the requirement of international adjudicators to be independent or impartial. Nevertheless, such a requirement can be inferred from the fact that independence and impartiality of (domestic) adjudicators is a constitutionally regulated matter, which must be respected in appointing adjudicators under both the JSA and the CCA, which are in turn referenced in the ANCJIC. Moreover, the Judicial Council should flag any potential issues regarding independence and impartiality of an applicant in its opinion to the President of Slovenia, before the latter proposes candidates to be elected or nominated by the National Assembly. Furthermore, as discussed above (section 2.2), the requirement of independence and impartiality may be explicitly included in the rules of international courts and tribunals, which Slovenia, under Article 2(2) of the ANCJIC, needs to observe when selecting appropriate candidates for international adjudicators. The practice so far, however, does not demonstrate that any special attention had been accorded or particular procedures undertaken in Slovenia for this purpose in the selection and appointment of international adjudicators.

In any case, it would be advisable to include an explicit requirement for candidates for international adjudicators to be independent and impartial directly in the ANCJIC as well as mechanisms for dealing with instances where a lack of independence or impartiality is discovered after the appointment of an adjudicator. Of course, in such cases, the rules of the specific international court or tribunal may be more pertinent to tackle the issue of dependence or partiality discovered ex post.

Moreover, the mechanisms in the ANCJIC that could increase the scrutiny of an international adjudicator's independence and impartiality may have little practical effect if the appointment of certain international adjudicators is done without reference to the ANCJIC, as has occasionally been the case.

4. CONCLUSION

The election of judges in Slovenia by the National Assembly raises issues regarding the division of powers. However, this apparent dependence of the judiciary on the legislative branch of the government is offset by the permanent mandate of judges. Moreover, the independence and impartiality of domestic adjudicators is regulated by the Constitution, as well as relevant procedural legislation.

The ANCJIC provides for the procedure of the election or nomination of international adjudicators from Slovenia and the criteria applicants must meet in order to be considered. However, the application of the ANCJIC is not extended to all international adjudicators appointed or nominated by Slovenia. The ANCJIC does not explicitly provide for the requirement of independence and impartiality of international adjudicators. However, this can be inferred from the Constitution, from referenced legislation and from importation of requirements of any applicable rules of an international court or a treaty which is binding on the Republic of Slovenia, which may provide special conditions for election of international court judges, including a requirement of independence and impartiality.

While theoretically speaking the regulation embedded in the ANCJIC may be seen as an example of good practice, this may be the case only for those positions of international adjudicators where Slovenia has a right to appoint a judge or an arbitrator, meaning that the place is reserved for 'its judge or arbitrator'. It is particularly in such instances that the requirements of independence and impartiality may sound counterintuitive, but are in fact still relevant and an important guarantor of fair and just decision-making of an international body.

However, and as discussed above, the ANCJIC is not always followed in practice and the choices of when it will be applied or not seem rather coincidental and consequently arbitrary.

Perhaps more problematic still is the fact that when the ANCJIC is applied, it requires lengthy proceedings, which de facto hamper any real chances of success for candidates for international adjudicators, who after having been selected as candidates by Slovenia (or its National Group in the case of election of ICJ judges) still need to compete for actual election at the international level. This is because after procedures in Slovenia are finally completed, there usually remains little time for any effective international campaign.[20] In any event, the independence and impartiality of candidates nominated by Slovenia in such circumstances unfortunately seem to stand a rather slim chance of being considered properly (and in a timely manner) in the decision-making by the relevant electoral body.

---

[20] A similar concern was expressed also by (a former Constitutional Court) Judge Mirjam Škrk in her separate dissenting opinion, where she stated that the ANCJIC is problematic from the perspective of any efficient or successful candidacy of professionally established and internationally recognised experts, who would stand as candidates from Slovenia for international adjudicators. See U-I-120/04 of 1 June 2004, para. 3, available at http://odlocitve.us-rs.si/sl/odlocitev/US23592.

THE INDEPENDENCE AND IMPARTIALITY OF ADJUDICATORS IN TURKEY

Didem KAYALI

1. Introduction 622
2. Judges 622
   2.1. Selection and Appointment 622
       2.1.1. General Judicial Courts of First Instance, Administrative
               Courts and Tax Courts 622
       2.1.2. Specialised Judicial Courts of First Instance 626
       2.1.3. Regional Courts of Appeal and Regional Administrative
               Courts 627
       2.1.4. The Court of Cassation and the Council of State 627
       2.1.5. The Constitutional Court 628
       2.1.6. The Court of Jurisdictional Disputes 629
       2.1.7. The Court of Accounts 629
   2.2. Independence and Impartiality 630
       2.2.1. Related Legislation 630
       2.2.2. The Court of Cassation's Code of Judicial Conduct 632
       2.2.3. Related Court Judgments 632
3. Arbitrators 633
   3.1. Selection and Appointment 633
   3.2. Independence and Impartiality 634
       3.2.1. Related Legislation 634
       3.2.2. Istanbul Arbitration Association Arbitrator's Code
               of Ethics 635
       3.2.3. Related Court Judgments 635
4. Selection of National Candidates to Positions as International
   Adjudicators 637
5. Conclusion 639

Intersentia

621

Didem Kayalı

1. INTRODUCTION

The independence and impartiality of an adjudicator is a crucial factor for protecting the legitimacy of any system of dispute settlement, because a dispute settlement method, whether in courts or through arbitration, needs to be fair. The right to a fair trial is a fundamental right which is protected by Article 6 of the European Convention for the Protection of Human Rights and Fundamental Freedoms, and an independent and impartial tribunal is one of the components of a fair trial. Although Article 6(1) of the Convention is directly binding on the courts of the contracting states, it is disputable whether it extends to arbitration procedure and binds arbitrators as well.[1] Apart from the ongoing discussions about the relationship of Article 6(1) with arbitration, it could be argued that since arbitrators resolve disputes in a final and binding way, and thus use a judicial power, they have to be independent and impartial to ensure a fair trial. Considering its importance, Turkish law has introduced mechanisms to safeguard the independence and impartiality of both judges and arbitrators.

2. JUDGES

2.1. SELECTION AND APPOINTMENT

Since the selection and appointment of judges differ with respect to the type of court, it would be useful to have an overview of the judicial system in Turkey.

2.1.1. General Judicial Courts of First Instance, Administrative Courts and Tax Courts

The selection and appointment of judges for general judicial courts of first instance (general criminal courts and general civil courts), administrative courts and tax courts are regulated in the Code of Judges and Prosecutors (Code No. 2802). According to Article 9 of this Code, considering the needs of the judicial system and receiving the opinion of the Justice Academy of Turkey, each year the Ministry of Justice determines the number of intern judges to be recruited.

---

[1]   See in general J.D.M. Lew, L.A. Mistelis and S.M. Kröll, *Comparative International Commercial Arbitration*, Kluwer Law International, The Hague 2003, pp. 91–94; S. Besson, 'Arbitration and Human Rights' (2006) 24 *ASA Bulletin* 395, 399–401; M.S. Kurkela and S. Trunen, *Due Process in International Commercial Arbitration*, 2nd ed., Oxford University Press, New York 2010, p. 2; A. Jaksic, *Arbitration and Human Rights*, Peter Lang International Academic Publishers, Berlin 2002, pp. 185–86, 218; G. Petrochilos, *Procedural Law in International Arbitration*, Oxford University Press, New York 2004, pp. 152–53.

Turkey

Table 1. Court System in Turkey

A – JUDICIAL COURTS				
COURT OF CASSATION	REGIONAL COURTS OF APPEAL	JUDICIAL COURTS OF FIRST INSTANCE	CRIMINAL COURTS	General Courts	Justiceship of Peace
					Criminal Courts of First Instance
					Heavy Criminal Courts
				Specialised Courts	Juvenile Criminal Courts of First Instance
					Juvenile Heavy Criminal Courts
					Courts of Enforcement
					Criminal Courts of Intellectual and Industrial Property Rights
					Justiceship of Execution
			CIVIL COURTS	General Courts	Civil Courts of Peace
					Civil Courts of First Instance
				Specialised Courts	Commercial Courts of First Instance
					Family Courts
					Labour Courts
					Cadastral Courts
					Consumer Courts
					Civil Courts of Intellectual and Industrial Property Rights
					Courts of Enforcement

B – ADMINISTRATIVE COURTS		
COUNCIL OF STATE	REGIONAL ADMINISTRATIVE COURTS	Administrative Courts
		Tax Courts

C – CONSTITUTIONAL COURT

D – COURT OF JURISDICTIONAL DISPUTES

E – COURT OF ACCOUNTS

Intersentia

In order to be an intern judge, the following requirements must be met by the candidate (Code No. 2802, Article 8):

1. be a Turkish citizen;
2. be under the age of 35 as of 1 January of the year in which the entrance exam is held;
3. for candidates for judicial courts, hold a law degree (LLB); for candidates for administrative and tax courts, hold a law degree (LLB) or a bachelor's degree in political science, administrative science, economics or finance which offers a certain amount of law courses in its curriculum;
4. not be prohibited from public service due to a criminal conviction;
5. be successful in the Entrance Exam for Legal Professions or the Administrative Jurisdiction Pre-Exam;
6. have completed or be exempt from compulsory military service;
7. be mentally and physically healthy to continually serve as a judge all over the country;
8. not have been convicted of or prosecuted for certain categories of crimes;
9. be successful both in the written exam and the interview; and
10. not have engaged in inappropriate behaviour for the profession.

The exams mentioned in the fifth requirement were introduced by an amendment which entered into force on 24 October 2019. These exams are mandatory for students enrolled in the degree programmes mentioned in the third requirement after the date of the amendment. Therefore, starting with the graduates of 2024, candidates will have to be successful in the Entrance Exam for Legal Professions or the Administrative Jurisdiction Pre-Exam in order to be eligible to sit the written exam mentioned in the ninth requirement, which will be followed by an interview process. On the other hand, students who were already enrolled in the degree programmes mentioned in the third requirement before 24 October 2019 only have to pass the written exam and the interview.

The details of the written exam, application process, qualifications of the candidates and number of vacant positions are publicly announced by the Ministry of Justice at least 15 days before the deadline for applications.

According to Article 9(A) of Code No. 2802, the written exam is held by the Student Selection and Placement Centre of Turkey. The exam consists of multiple-choice questions regarding different areas of law, which are worth 80 points in total, as well as questions regarding general knowledge of the Turkish language, maths, citizenship, etc., which are worth 20 points in total. The candidates have to score at least 70 points from the written exam. For the interviews, the candidates are ranked according to their written exam scores and the number of candidates to be interviewed is twice the number of vacancies announced. For example, when 100 vacancies are announced, 200 candidates, beginning with the person who achieves the highest score, are shortlisted for the interviews.

Interviews are held by a committee of seven members presided over by the Deputy Minister of Justice. Other members are the Head of the Inspection Board, the General Director for Legal Affairs, the General Director for Criminal Affairs, the General Director for Personnel Affairs from the Ministry of Justice, the General Secretary of the Council of Judges and Prosecutors, and a person selected by the Advisory Board of the Justice Academy of Turkey.

During the interviews the candidates are evaluated on the following abilities and characteristics:

- discernment;
- ability to comprehend, summarise and express an issue;
- suitability of the candidates' physical appearance, behaviour and reactions to the profession;
- general skills and cultural background; and
- openness to contemporary scientific and technological developments.

In order to succeed in the interviews, the candidates must score at least 70 points. After the interviews have finished, the final list of successful candidates is prepared, with the written exam making up 70% of the candidates' final score and the interview 30%, and these listed candidates are appointed as intern judges. According to Article 10 of Code No. 2802, the probationary period for intern judges is two years, which consists of education and practice phases.

At the end of the probationary period, intern judges have to take both written and oral exams. Interns who achieve at least 70 points in the written exam are eligible to take the oral exam. The questions of the written exam are prepared by the lecturers who teach at the Justice Academy of Turkey. The oral exam is held by a committee composed of the President of the Justice Academy of Turkey, the Head of Inspection Board, the General Director of Personnel Affairs of the Ministry of Justice, and two lecturers. In order to be deemed successful at the end of the probationary period, intern judges have to score at least 70 points, calculated on the basis of the written exam making up 60% of the final score and the oral exam making up 40%. Unsuccessful interns are appointed to positions classified as administrative services at the Ministry of Justice upon their request. The successful interns are appointed as judges by the Council of Judges and Prosecutors (the Council) to different cities, which are determined by casting lots.

The Council is established by the Code of the Council of Judges and Prosecutors (Code No. 6087). It is composed of 13 members, including the Minister of Justice (the head of the Council) and the Deputy Minister of Justice. Four other members are appointed by the President of Turkey from among the first-grade judges or prosecutors, and seven members by the Grand National Assembly of Turkey from among the judges of the Court of Cassation and the Council of State, lecturers at law faculties, and lawyers who have at least 15 years of experience. According to Code No. 6087, the Council is independent in fulfilling its duties and exercising its powers; no organisation, authority or person may give orders or instructions to the Council. In addition, the Council performs its duties according to the principles of fairness, impartiality, accuracy, honesty, consistency, equality, competence and qualification.

2.1.2. Specialised Judicial Courts of First Instance

The Juvenile Criminal Courts of First Instance and Juvenile Heavy Criminal Courts are established by the Code of Child Protection (Code No. 5395). According to Article 28, the judges of judicial courts, who preferably have expertise in child law or have received an education in the field of child psychology and social services, are appointed to these courts by the Council.

The Justiceship of Execution is established by the Code of Justiceship of Execution (Code No. 4675), and according to Article 3, judges and prosecutors of judicial courts can be appointed as a judge of execution by the Council.

The Family Courts are established by the Code of Establishment, Duty and Proceedings of Family Courts (Code No. 4787). According to Article 3 of the Code, the judges of judicial courts, who are preferably married with children, at least 30 years old and have a master's degree in family law, can be appointed to the family courts by the Council.

Both the Criminal and Civil Courts of Intellectual and Industrial Property Rights are established by the Code of Industrial Property (Code No. 6769). The Courts of Enforcement are authorised by the Code of Enforcement and Bankruptcy (Code No. 2004) to render decisions in both civil and criminal cases related to attachment and execution proceedings. The Commercial Courts of First Instance are authorised by the Turkish Commercial Code (Code No. 6102) to hear all commercial disputes which are defined in the same Code. The Labour Courts are established by the Code of Labour Courts (Code No. 7036). The Cadastral Courts are established by the Cadastral Code (Code No. 3402). The Consumer Courts are authorised by the Code of Consumer Protection (Code No. 6502) to deal with disputes arising from consumer transactions. Although these are specialised courts, there are no specific provisions regarding the appointment of judges to these courts in the relevant codes. On the other hand, according to the Code of Council of Judges and Prosecutors, appointment of all judges is under the authority of the Council. Therefore, appointment to these courts is made by the Council from among existing judicial judges.

Turkey

2.1.3. Regional Courts of Appeal and Regional Administrative Courts

Regional Courts of Appeal are established by the Code of Establishment, Duty and Authority of the Judicial Courts of First Instance and Regional Courts of Appeal (Code No. 5235). There are four grades of judges in the Turkish judiciary and judges serving successfully for 10 years can be second-grade. After serving successfully for three years, second-grade judges can be first-grade. According to Article 43 of the Code, presidents of the courts and presidents of the divisions within the courts are appointed from among first-grade judges, members of the courts are appointed from among at least second-grade judges, and prosecutors of judicial courts are appointed by the Council. The head of the chambers and the members of the Court of Cassation, upon their request, may also be appointed as presidents of the courts or divisions by the Council.

Regional Administrative Courts are established by the Code of Establishment and Duty of the Regional Administrative Courts, Administrative Courts and Tax Courts (Code No. 2576). According to Article 3/E of the Code, presidents of the Regional Administrative Courts and presidents of the divisions within the courts are appointed from among first-grade judges, members of the courts are appointed from among at least second-grade judges, and prosecutors of administrative courts are appointed by the Council. The head of the chambers and the members of the Council of the State, upon their request, may also be appointed as presidents of the courts or divisions by the Council.

2.1.4. The Court of Cassation and the Council of State

The Court of Cassation is established by the Court of Cassation Code (Code No. 2797). According to Article 29 of the Code, members of the Court of Cassation are selected by the Council from among first-grade judges and prosecutors of judicial courts.

The Council of State is established by the Council of State Code (Code No. 2575). According to Article 8 of the Code, the members of the Council of State are selected from among the people holding the following positions:

1. administrative judge and prosecutor;
2. minister, Vice-President, vice-minister, undersecretary, deputy undersecretary, ambassador or governor;
3. general or admiral;
4. General Secretary of the Presidency, Head of the Administrative Affairs of the Presidency or General Secretary of the Grand National Assembly of Turkey;
5. General Secretary of the Council of Judges and Prosecutors;

Intersentia

627

Didem Kayalı

6. general manager or head of the inspection board of a public institution, or head of an independent regulatory agency;
7. professor in law, economics, finance or public administration at a university; or
8. chief legal counsel, first legal counsel, head of legal services or head of legal affairs of a public institution.

To be eligible, administrative judges and prosecutors should be first-grade. Those who hold administrative positions must have worked for at least 15 years in the public services, must be first-grade civil servants and must have the morals and character required for the office of judge. Three-quarters of the members of the Council of State are elected from among administrative judges and prosecutors by the Council of Judges and Prosecutors, and one-quarter from among other professions selected by the President of Turkey.

2.1.5.   *The Constitutional Court*

The Constitutional Court is established by the Code of Establishment and Proceedings of the Constitutional Court (Code No. 6216). According to Article 6 of the Code, the Court consists of 15 members. In order to be elected to the Court, one of the following qualifications should be held:

1. being a member or a head of chamber of the Court of Cassation, Council of State or Court of Accounts;
2. being a rapporteur of the Constitutional Court for at least five years;
3. being at least 45 years old, holding a bachelor's degree and having no condition that prevents being accepted to the office of judge; and
    a.   being a law, economics or political science professor or associate professor at a university; or
    b.   being a lawyer with at least 20 years' experience; or
    c.   being the president or a member of the Council of Higher Education, the rector or dean of a university, or a deputy minister, undersecretary, deputy undersecretary, ambassador or governor with at least 20 years of public service experience; or
    d.   being a first-grade judge or prosecutor with at least 20 years' experience, including the probationary period.

The Grand National Assembly of Turkey selects two members of the Constitutional Court from among three candidates from the members of the Court of Accounts nominated for each vacant position by the General Assembly of the Court of Accounts, and one member from among three candidates from self-employed lawyers nominated by the presidents of the bar associations.

The President of Turkey selects:

- three members of the Constitutional Court from among three candidates from the members of the Court of Cassation nominated for each vacant position by the General Assembly of the Court of Cassation;
- two members from among three candidates from the members of the Council of State nominated for each vacant position by the General Assembly of the Council of State;
- three members, at least two of whom must be law professors, from among three candidates from the professors of law, economics and political sciences nominated for each vacant position by the Council of Higher Education; and
- four members from among high-level bureaucrats, self-employed lawyers, first-grade judges and prosecutors and rapporteurs of the Constitutional Court with at least five years' experience.

Elections are held to designate the candidates who will be nominated by the general assemblies of the Court of Cassation, the Council of State and the Court of Accounts, and by the Council of Higher Education and the presidents of the bar associations. The three people who receive the most votes are deemed to be nominated.

2.1.6. The Court of Jurisdictional Disputes

The Court of Jurisdictional Disputes is established by the Code of Establishment and Mechanism of the Court of Jurisdictional Disputes (Code No. 2247). The Court is the final authority for settling disputes concerning verdicts and competencies of the judicial and administrative courts. According to Article 2 of the Code, the Court consists of a President, six principal and six alternate members. The President of the Court is selected by the Constitutional Court from among its members. Three principal and three alternate members are selected by the Assembly of the Civil Chamber of the Court of Cassation from among its own members, and the other principal and alternate members are selected by the General Assembly of the Council of State from among its own members.

2.1.7. The Court of Accounts

The Court of Accounts is regulated by the Code of the Court of Accounts (Code No. 6085). The Court is responsible for auditing the revenues, expenditures and property of public administrations on behalf of the Grand National Assembly of Turkey and carries out functions required by the Code related to inquiry, auditing and judgment. According to Article 12 of the Code, the President and

Didem Kayalı

the members of the Court must hold a bachelor's degree in the field of law or economics and administrative sciences, and must have at least 16 years of public service experience.

In addition, the President must have worked as a member of the Court of Accounts, as a minister, undersecretary, governor, rector, general director or head of the inspection board at the ministries or as the head of an independent regulatory agency for at least one year. To be elected as a member of the Court, candidates must also have similar work experience or must have worked as a deputy undersecretary, first-grade auditor, chief prosecutor, prosecutor, professor, second-grade judge or prosecutor at the judicial or administrative courts, or auditor at the ministries for at least one year. The President and the members of the Court are selected by the Grand National Assembly of Turkey.

2.2. INDEPENDENCE AND IMPARTIALITY

2.2.1. *Related Legislation*

Due to its importance, the principle of independence and impartiality is secured by the Turkish Constitution. Article 9 of the Constitution states that judicial power shall be exercised by independent and impartial courts on behalf of the Turkish nation. In addition, Article 138 reads as follows:

> Judges shall be independent in the discharge of their duties; they shall give judgment in accordance with the Constitution, laws, and their personal conviction conforming to the law.

> No organ, authority, office or individual may give orders or instructions to courts or judges relating to the exercise of judicial power, send them circulars, or make recommendations or suggestions.

> No questions shall be asked, debates held, or statements made in the Legislative Assembly relating to the exercise of judicial power concerning a case under trial.

> Legislative and executive organs and the administration shall comply with court decisions; these organs and the administration shall neither alter them in any respect, nor delay their execution.

Finally, Article 139 states that judges and public prosecutors shall not be dismissed, or unless they request shall not be retired before the age prescribed by the Constitution; nor shall they be deprived of their salaries, allowances or other rights relating to their status, even as a result of the abolition of a court or a post. There are exceptions indicated in law relating to those convicted for an offence requiring dismissal from the profession, those who are definitely established as unable to perform their duties because of ill health, or those determined as unsuitable to remain in the profession.

630

Intersentia

The Code of Judges and Prosecutors includes provisions regarding independence which replicate the aforementioned provisions of the Constitution.[2] There are also some provisions in the Code of Civil Procedure (Code No. 6100) which serve to protect the independence and impartiality of judges.

First of all, Article 34 of Code No. 6100 provides that judges cannot handle certain specific cases and even if there is no objection they must withdraw from the case. These cases are as follows:

1. his or her own cases or those directly or indirectly related to the judge;
2. cases of his or her spouse even if they are divorced;
3. cases of his or her descendants or ascendants or his or her spouse's descendants or ascendants;
4. cases of anyone who has an adoption relationship with the judge;
5. cases of his or her relatives by blood up to and including the third degree and relatives by marriage up to and including the third degree even if the marriage is over;
6. cases of his or her fiancé(e); and
7. cases in which he or she acts as the lawyer, guardian, custodian or legal counsel of one of the parties.

According to Article 36, one of the parties may challenge the judge or the judge may withdraw for an important reason which causes doubts as to his or her impartiality. In particular, the following situations are deemed to be a reason for challenge:

1. the judge has given legal advice to one of the parties;
2. the judge has declared his or her opinion about the case to one of the parties or a third party even if it is not required by the law;
3. the judge was a witness or expert witness or acted as a judge, arbitrator, mediator or conciliator in the case;
4. one of the parties is the collateral relative (up to and including the fourth degree) of the judge; or
5. there is an ongoing litigation or hostility between the judge and one of the parties.

'An important reason which causes doubts as to the judge's impartiality' is the general ground for challenging a judge, and the above-mentioned situations are examples of important reasons which may lead to a challenge.[3]

---

[2] See Articles 4 and 44 of the Code of Judges and Prosecutors.
[3] R. Akcan and C. Kaya, 'Medeni ve İdari Yargıda Hakimin Davaya Bakmaktan Yasaklılığı ve Reddi' (2010) 68 *İÜHFM* 171, 179.

Intersentia

631

Didem Kayalı

2.2.2. The Court of Cassation's Code of Judicial Conduct

The Court of Cassation's Code of Judicial Conduct[4] was prepared within the scope of the Ethics, Transparency and Trust Project of the Court of Cassation, which was financed by the Court of Cassation and implemented by the Court of Cassation and the United Nations Development Programme. The Code of Judicial Conduct was adopted unanimously on 8 December 2017 by the Grand Plenary Assembly of the Court of Cassation. The aim of the Code is to provide guidance to the bench members and rapporteur judges of the Court of Cassation by establishing the standards of ethical conduct, to enable the members of the legislature and executive, lawyers and the public to better understand the judiciary, and to provide support to the judiciary, to complement binding rules of professional conduct for judges.[5]

There are six values and accordingly six principles in the Code of Conduct. The first value is independence and the related principle says: 'Judicial independence is a pre-requisite to the rule of law and a fundamental guarantee of a fair trial. A judge shall therefore uphold and exemplify judicial independence in both its individual and institutional aspects.' Following the principle, eight rules have been drawn up regarding the conduct of judges to safeguard the principle of independence.

The second value is impartiality and the related principle states: 'Impartiality is indispensable for the proper discharge of the judicial office. It applies not only to the decision in the appeal process but also to the process by which the decision is made.' Following the principle, seven rules have been drawn up regarding the conduct of judges to safeguard the principle of impartiality.

The Judicial Ethics Advisory Committee was also established under the Code of Conduct on 9 July 2018 to advise judges on the propriety of their conduct and provide models for their possible conduct in relation to ethical values.

2.2.3. Related Court Judgments

The Court of Cassation, in its various decisions, has not accepted the situations listed below as grounds for challenging a judge:

- the judge had awarded damages against the defendant in another case;[6]
- the judge's son was a student at the school of the defendant;[7]
- the grandmother of the defendant and the grandfather of the judge were siblings;[8]

---

[4]   https://www.yargitay.gov.tr/documents/CourtOfCassationCodesOfConduct.pdf.
[5]   See Preamble of the Code of Judicial Conduct.
[6]   Y. 20. HD E.2003/4042, K.2003/5618, T.09.07.2003.
[7]   Y. 20. HD E.2005/1299, K.2005/1864, T.01.03.2005.
[8]   Y. 20. HD E.2010/15448, K.2010/16428, T.21.12.2010.

Turkey

- one of the parties filed a complaint against the judge during the course of proceedings;[9] and
- the lawyer of the respondent and the spouse of the judge were friends from college.[10]

On the other hand, the Court did accept a challenge against a judge who said to the claimant during the course of proceedings that, 'It is a car accident, you cannot claim for nonpecuniary damages', which means he stated his opinion before rendering the judgment.[11] In another case, the judge had a professional and social relationship with the claimant and the respondent, who were also judges. The Court argued that knowing both of the parties, since they were all colleagues working at the same courthouse, did not cause doubts as to the judge's impartiality, but having a social relationship with both of the parties and their spouses did.[12]

3. ARBITRATORS

In Turkey there are two different codes for domestic and international arbitration. However, since both of them are based on the UNCITRAL Model Law on International Commercial Arbitration, they consist of similar provisions, except the nuances arising from the national or international character of the arbitration. Domestic arbitration is regulated under the Code of Civil Procedure (Code No. 6100) and related provisions of the Code are applicable to disputes that do not include foreign elements and when the place of arbitration is in Turkey. On the other hand, the Code of International Arbitration (Code No. 4686) is applicable to disputes that include foreign elements and when the place of arbitration is in Turkey or the Code is chosen by the parties as the applicable law.

3.1. SELECTION AND APPOINTMENT

According to Article 416 of Code No. 6100, the parties are free to agree on a procedure for appointing the arbitrator(s). Unless otherwise agreed by the parties, the following procedure is applied:

1. Only real persons can be selected as arbitrators.
2. If a sole arbitrator is to be selected and the parties are unable to agree on the arbitrator, he or she shall be appointed, upon request of one of the parties, by the court.

---

9   Y. 20. HD E.2012/13574, K.2012/14189, T.10.12.2012.
10   Y. 20. HD E.2014/8621, K.2014/10584, T.16.12.2014.
11   Y. 20. HD E.2015/13366, K.2015/12087, T.03.12.2015.
12   Y. 20. HD E.2016/3456, K.2016/4496, T.14.04.2016.

Intersentia

Didem Kayalı

3. If three arbitrators are to be selected, each party shall appoint one arbitrator, and the two arbitrators thus appointed shall appoint the third arbitrator. If a party fails to appoint an arbitrator within one month of receipt of a request to do so from the other party, or if the two arbitrators fail to agree on the third arbitrator within one month of their appointment, the appointment shall be made, upon request of one of the parties, by the court. The third arbitrator will be the chair.
4. If more than three arbitrators are to be selected, the arbitrators who shall appoint the last arbitrator are determined equally by the parties.
5. If there are three or more arbitrators, at least one of them shall be a jurist with at least five years' experience in his or her field.

Even if the parties have agreed on the procedure to be followed, (i) if one of the parties does not abide by this agreement, (ii) if the parties or the arbitrators cannot reach a mutual agreement on the arbitrator selection when they are supposed to do so, or (iii) if the authorised third party or institution does not select the arbitrator(s), then the arbitrator(s) shall be appointed, upon request of one of the parties, by the court. The court considers the agreement of the parties and the principle of independence and impartiality.

Code No. 4686 contains a similar provision in Articles 7/A and 7/B with regard to the selection and appointment of arbitrators. However, the above-mentioned condition in point (5) is not a requirement in international arbitration. In addition, if the court is appointing an arbitrator, it shall also consider the nationality of the parties and the arbitrator.

3.2. INDEPENDENCE AND IMPARTIALITY

3.2.1. *Related Legislation*

Both Codes contain exactly the same provision regarding the duty of disclosure and challenging arbitrators, which reads as follows:

> When a person is approached in connection with his or her possible appointment as an arbitrator, he or she shall disclose any circumstances that give rise to justifiable doubts as to his or her impartiality or independence. The arbitrator shall without delay disclose any such subsequent circumstances to the parties unless they have already been informed of them by him or her.

> An arbitrator may be challenged if he or she does not possess the qualifications that were agreed to by the parties, if there exists a reason for challenge in accordance with the arbitration procedure agreed by the parties, or if the existing circumstances give rise to justifiable doubts as to his or her impartiality or independence.

Turkey

3.2.2. Istanbul Arbitration Association Arbitrator's Code of Ethics

The Istanbul Arbitration Association (ISTA) was founded as a non-governmental organisation in 2015 with the aim of transforming Istanbul into one of the world's leading arbitration centres. ISTA considered the issue of ethics in arbitration to be one of the problematic areas of arbitration in Turkey and introduced its Arbitrator's Code of Ethics on 15 March 2018.[13] The Code includes modern rules with regard to the duty of independence and impartiality:

- The prospective arbitrator may accept an appointment provided that he or she is confident that he or she is able to carry out his or her duties in an impartial and independent manner. If the prospective arbitrator has any doubts, he or she must decline appointment (Rule 2.1).
- From the moment the arbitrator accepts the appointment, he or she must be impartial and independent and must remain impartial and independent throughout the arbitration proceedings (Rule 3.1).
- If the arbitrator is or subsequently becomes aware that he or she cannot act impartially and independently as expected, he or she shall promptly take all steps as may be required under the circumstances including recusing him or herself or withdrawing. If all parties ask the arbitrator to withdraw then the arbitrator must withdraw (Rule 3.3).
- Prior to accepting the appointment, the prospective arbitrator must notify the parties as to whether:
  - he or she has any direct or indirect economic or personal interest in the outcome of the arbitration;
  - he or she, or his or her family, employees or business partners, have any known current or past economic, professional or personal relationships that could affect the arbitrator's independence or impartiality in the mind of any party;
  - he or she possesses any previous knowledge regarding the dispute as well as the scope and extent of such knowledge; or
  - there are any other matters, relationships and interests as may be required to be disclosed under the agreement between the parties, applicable institutional rules or the law governing the arbitration (Rule 4.1).

3.2.3. Related Court Judgments

Apart from other reasons, arbitral awards contrary to public policy may be challenged under Article 439/2 of the Code of Civil Procedure or Article 15/A of

---

[13] See https://ista.org.tr/hakkimizda/hakemlerce-uyulmasi-gereken-etik-kurallar-belgesi/.

the Code of International Arbitration, depending on the national or international character of the arbitration. Public policy is also a ground to refuse recognition and enforcement of foreign arbitral awards under the Code of International Private and Procedural Law (Code No. 5718),[14] in addition to the New York Convention on Recognition and Enforcement of Foreign Arbitral Awards.[15]

Considering the *nemo iudex in causa sua* principle, the Court of Cassation has ruled, in various decisions regarding the challenge of arbitral awards, that the arbitrator should be a third person who has no interest in the case, and this aspect of arbitration relates to public policy.[16]

Independence and impartiality of arbitrators is regarded by Turkish scholars[17] and Turkish courts[18] as being within the scope of public policy when also dealing with enforcement of foreign arbitral awards. Some scholars argue that violation of public policy occurs only if the doubts regarding the independence and impartiality of the arbitrator become concrete in the arbitral award.[19] However, it is not realistic to expect an arbitrator, whose reputation is as important as his or her experience and knowledge, to be partial and record it in the arbitral award. Accordingly, there is no requirement of proof of partiality of arbitrators concerning the duty of disclosure and challenging arbitrators in any of the national and international regulations. Therefore, the 'justifiable doubts' standard should also be applicable when considering the refusal of enforcement because of a violation of public policy.

The main discussion regarding the lack of independence and impartiality of arbitrators as a ground to refuse enforcement within the violation of public policy stems from a decision of the Court of Cassation. In a decision from 1976, the Court refused enforcement of an ICC award, arguing that the scrutiny of the award by the ICC Court was in conflict with the principle of the independence of arbitrators, and thus with public policy.[20] While some scholars

---

[14]   Article 54/1/c.
[15]   Turkey ratified the Convention by Code No. 3731 of 08.05.1991.
[16]   See Y. 4. HD E.1964/8868, K.1964/5220, T.09.11.1964; Y. 13. HD E.1974/2385, K.1974/2161, T.26.09.1974; Y. 20. HD E.2002/1955, K.2002/2791, T.28.03.2002; Y. 15. HD E.2005/5778, K.2006/93, T.18.01.2006.
[17]   T. Kalpsüz, *Türkiye'de Milletlerarası Tahkim*, 2nd ed., Yetkin, Ankara 2010, p. 230; S. Tanrıver, 'Yabancı Hakem Kararlarının Türkiye'de Tenfizi Bağlamında Kamu Düzeninin Etkisi' (1997–98) 27 *MHB* 467, 481–84; E. Nomer, 'Yabancı Hakem Kararlarının Tenfizinde Hakem Mahkemesinin Bağımsızlığı' (1984) 9 *MHB* 29, 29; C. Şanlı, *Uluslararası Ticari Akitleri Hazırlanması ve Uyuşmazlıkların Çözüm Yolları*, 5th ed., Beta, Istanbul 2013, p. 398.
[18]   İstanbul BAM 14. HD E.2019/2100, K.2020/74, T.30.01.2020.
[19]   E. Nomer, 'Yabancı Hakem Kararlarının Tenfizinde Hakem Mahkemesinin Bağımsızlığı' (1984) 9 *MHB* 29, 31; Z. Akıncı, *Milletlerarası Ticari Hakem Kararları ve Tenfizi*, Dokuz Eylül Üniversitesi Hukuk Fakültesi, Ankara 1994, p. 166; B. Şit, *Kurumsal Tahkim ve Hakem Kararlarının Tanınması ve Tenfizi*, İmaj, Ankara 2005, p. 223.
[20]   Y. 15. HD E.1975/1617, K.1976/1052, T.10.03.1976.

Turkey

supported this decision,[21] others argued that the purpose of the scrutiny was to assist the arbitrators in producing an enforceable award, and since the Court did not have the authority to require the arbitrators to consider its comments regarding substance, the scrutiny procedure was not contrary to public policy.[22] In later decisions, the Court of Cassation changed its interpretation and reached a conclusion that the authority of the ICC Court regarding scrutiny does not require the intervention of public policy.[23]

4. SELECTION OF NATIONAL CANDIDATES TO POSITIONS AS INTERNATIONAL ADJUDICATORS

The national selection procedure for candidates for the post of judge at the European Court of Human Rights is conducted by the Ministry of Foreign Affairs in cooperation with the Ministry of Justice. The selection procedure and the qualifications required are publicly announced by these ministries. The application requirements are determined in line with the decisions and guidelines of the Council of Europe and the Parliamentary Assembly, and the qualified candidates apply to the Ministry of Justice with the relevant documents.

According to the latest announcement regarding the selection procedure,[24] applicants were required to have the following qualifications:

- be a Turkish citizen;
- have high moral character;
- be between the ages of 35 and 60;

---

[21] S. Tanrıver, 'Yabancı Hakem Kararlarının Türkiye'de Tenfizi Bağlamında Kamu Düzeninin Etkisi' (1997–98) 27 *MHB* 467, 483; B. Kuru and E. Yılmaz, 'Türkiye'de Yabancı Hakem Kararlarının Tanınması' in *Yabancı Hakem Kararlarının Türkiye'de Tanınması ve Tenfizi, II. Tahkim Haftası, Bildiriler-Tartışmalar*, Banka ve Ticaret Hukuku Araştırma Enstitüsü, Ankara 1984, p. 200.

[22] N. Ekşi, 'Yargıtay Kararları Işığında ICC Hakem Kararlarının Türkiye'de Tanınması ve Tenfizi' (2009) 67 *Ankara Barosu Dergisi* 54, 61–62; E. Nomer, 'Yabancı Hakem Kararlarının Tenfizinde Hakem Mahkemesinin Bağımsızlığı' (1984) 9 *MHB* 29, 30; T. Kalpsüz, 'Hakem Kararlarının Milliyeti' (1978) 9 *BATİDER* 601, 625; Z. Akıncı, *Milletlerarası Ticari Hakem Kararları ve Tenfizi*, Dokuz Eylül Üniversitesi Hukuk Fakültesi, Ankara 1994, p. 166; R. Koral, 'Hakemliğin Milliyeti ve Yargıtay XV. Hukuk Dairesinin 1976 Tarihli Kararının Eleştirisi' in *Prof. Dr. Hıfzı Timur'a Armağandan Ayrı Bası*, Fakülteler Matbaası, Istanbul 1979, p. 468; M. Birsel, 'Milletlerarası Ticaret Odasının Uzlaştırma ve Tahkim Hükümlerine Göre Verilen Hakem Kararlarının 2675 Sayılı Kanun Hükümleri Dairesinde Türkiye'de Tenfizi' in *Yabancı Hakem Kararlarının Türkiye'de Tanınması ve Tenfizi, II. Tahkim Haftası, Bildiriler-Tartışmalar*, Banka ve Ticaret Hukuku Araştırma Enstitüsü, Ankara 1984, pp. 148–49.

[23] Y. 15. HD E.1991/2383, K.1991/3667, T.10.07.1991; Y. 15. HD E.1996/2781, K.1996/3533, T.20.06.1996; Y. 19. HD E.2003/2061, K.2003/7606, T.10.07.2003.

[24] For the latest announcement dated 20.04.2018 see https://www.mfa.gov.tr/avrupa-insan-haklari-mahkemesine-hakim-adayi-belirlenmesine-iliskin-duyuru_-19-nisan-2018.tr.mfa.

Intersentia

637

Didem Kayalı

- be fluent in English or French, and have intermediate knowledge of the other;
- have a law degree or be a graduate of a political sciences or economics and administrative sciences programme with an appropriate amount of law lectures;
- have knowledge of the Turkish law system and public international law;
- not have been convicted of any crime;
- undertake not to deal with another business which does not accord with his or her independence and impartiality or which prevents him or her from fulfilling his or her obligations as a full-time judge in the event of appointment;
- be in good health; and
- have experience in the field of human rights.

Besides these qualifications, the applicants were also asked to fulfil one of the following requirements:

- for academics, to be at least an associate professor;
- for judges or prosecutors, to have been first-grade for at least three years;
- to be a member of the high court;
- for lawyers, to have at least 15 years' experience;
- for other candidates who are public officers, to have at least 15 years' experience in the public service, and for those who are not public officers, to have at least 15 years' work experience.

The applicants were subject to a preliminary assessment by a committee consisting of officials from the Ministry of Foreign Affairs and the Ministry of Justice. The committee determined whether the applicants possessed the required qualifications and were thus eligible for the interview.

The interview committee comprised the Undersecretary or Deputy Undersecretary of the Prime Minister's Office, the Undersecretary or Deputy Undersecretary of the Ministry of Justice, the Undersecretary or Deputy Undersecretary of the Ministry of Foreign Affairs, the General Secretary of the Constitutional Court, a member assigned by the President of the Court of Cassation, a member assigned by the President of the Council of State, and a member assigned by the President of the Council of Higher Education.

The interview committee listed the eligible candidates in conformity with the qualifications required, and the decisions and the guidelines of the Council of Europe and the Parliamentary Assembly. The candidates shortlisted by the interview committee were submitted to the Council of Ministers by the Prime Minister's Office. The final list of candidates was determined by the Council of Ministers and submitted to the Council of Europe by the Ministry of Foreign Affairs.

Other than the European Court of Human Rights, there are Turkish panellists in the WTO Indicative List of Governmental and Non-Governmental Panellists,[25] and Turkish nationals among the members of the Permanent Court of Arbitration[26] and the ICSID Panels of Conciliators and of Arbitrators.[27] Unfortunately, the rapporteur could not find any sources about the national designation or selection procedures for these international adjudicative bodies.

5. CONCLUSION

Under Turkish law, the independence and impartiality of judges is protected first of all by the objective selection and appointment procedures. Judges are also protected from any external intervention, especially by legislative and executive bodies, which is extremely important when performing their duties. In addition, in some specific situations judges are prevented from hearing cases even if there are no objections. Challenging a judge is also possible when there are doubts as to his or her impartiality. On the other hand, it is not always easy to concretise and decide on the concepts of independence and impartiality. Therefore, the Court of Cassation's Code of Judicial Conduct is an important step in terms of providing guidance.

With regard to arbitration, Turkish law has two instruments, both based on the UNCITRAL Model Law. Therefore, it could be argued that the selection, appointment and challenge of arbitrators and challenge of arbitral awards are in line with modern global regulation. In addition, since Turkey is one of the 172 contracting states of the New York Convention, recognition and enforcement of foreign arbitral awards are mostly conducted in accordance with the provisions of the Convention, and independence and impartiality of arbitrators are considered by Turkish scholars and Turkish courts within the scope of public policy.

---

[25]   See WTO Indicative List of Governmental and Non-Governmental Panelists, https://docs. wto.org/dol2fe/Pages/SS/directdoc.aspx?filename=q:/WT/DSB/44R52.pdf&Open= True.

[26]   See List of the Members of the Permanent Court of Arbitration, https://docs.pca-cpa. org/2021/11/2021/11/9a588797-pca-184006-v96k-current_list_annex_1_members_of_the_ court.pdf.

[27]   See Members of the ICSID Panels of Conciliators and of Arbitrators, https://icsid.worldbank. org/sites/default/files/documents/2021_Oct_ICSID.rev.pdf.

THE INDEPENDENCE AND IMPARTIALITY OF ADJUDICATORS IN THE UNITED STATES OF AMERICA

Jarrod WONG

1. Introduction 641
2. US Judges 642
    2.1. Federal Judges 642
    2.2. State Judges 645
3. Arbitrators in the US 647
4. International Adjudicators in the US 653
    4.1. Appointments to International Arbitral Tribunals 653
    4.2. Appointments to International Courts 655

1. INTRODUCTION

This national report examines the law and practice concerning the independence and impartiality of adjudicators, including both judges and arbitrators, in the US legal system. Its content, along with that of all other national reports, will be synthesised into a comparative general report on the issue of the independence and impartiality of international adjudicators. For this project, the national rapporteurs have been asked to review the mechanisms for safeguarding the independence and impartiality of both domestic adjudicators, and national candidates in the position of international adjudicators. To the extent possible, the national rapporteurs are to identify who selects the adjudicator and through what method, consider the criteria for selecting the adjudicator and what interests they serve to protect, and also assess the relevant parameters for the adjudicator's conduct and the remedies available in the event independence and impartiality have been compromised (including the consequences for the offending adjudicator and the fate of any decision rendered by that adjudicator).

Jarrod Wong

2. US JUDGES

The US Constitution, the supreme law of the land in the United States, creates a federalist system of government in which power is shared between the federal and state governments. In line with this division, the federal government and each of the state governments have their own respective court systems.

2.1. FEDERAL JUDGES

Under the US Constitution, federal judges are nominated by the President and confirmed by the Senate.[1] The names of potential nominees are often recommended by senators or sometimes by members of the House who are of the President's political party.[2] In the case of Court of Appeals and district court judges, the White House may consult with the senators who represent the state in which the appointment will occur. In turn, these 'home state senators' may recommend candidates to the White House by conducting exhaustive searches through the state bar for candidates or creating selection committees made up of leading attorneys in the state. The White House will then conduct a thorough vetting of the candidate's background involving investigations by the FBI and the Department of Justice, as well as a non-partisan but non-binding peer review by the American Bar Association's Standing Committee on the Federal Judiciary. The Standing Committee rates the candidate as 'well qualified', 'qualified' or 'not qualified' based on criteria that includes the candidate's reputation for integrity and impartiality.[3] Upon the President's nomination, the Senate Judiciary Committee typically conducts confirmation hearings for the nominee. If the nominee is voted favourably out of committee, the nomination is forwarded to the Senate for a full vote. If the Senate confirms the nominee, the judicial appointment begins.

The President has substantial control over the selection of Supreme Court nominees, and their political partisan or policy preferences may well be conveniently aligned. The often active involvement of a home state senator in the selection of a lower court nominee, however, renders any such connection more tenuous, and the lower court nominee may more closely reflect the policy preferences of the particular senator.[4]

---

[1]   *See* US Const. art. II, §2, cl. 2.

[2]   *See* United States Courts, *FAQs: Federal Judges*, available at https://www.uscourts.gov/faqs-federal-judges.

[3]   *See* Center for American Progress, *Federal Judicial Nominations: 9 Steps from Vacancy to Confirmation* (Jan. 29, 2013), available at https://www.americanprogress.org/issues/general/news/2013/01/29/50996/federal-judicial-nominations-9-steps-from-vacancy-to-confirmation/.

[4]   *See* Michael W Giles et al., *Picking Federal Judges: A Note on Policy and Partisan Selection Agendas*, 54 POLITICAL RESEARCH QUARTERLY 623, 627 (Sept. 2001).

The nine judges on the US Court of International Trade (USCIT) are similarly appointed by the President with the consent of the Senate.[5] The USCIT is a specialised federal court that has subject matter jurisdiction over civil suits that arise out of import transactions and federal transactions affecting international trade.[6] Unusually and uniquely, the governing statute provides that '[n]ot more than five of such judges shall be from the same political party.'[7] This political party restriction has been criticised for apparently violating the Appointments Clause and for being an unjustifiable anachronism that should be eliminated.[8] Notwithstanding earlier congressional attempts to remove it, however, the restriction remains.[9]

Once appointed, Article III of the Constitution states that the judges to which it applies, which includes Supreme Court justices, federal circuit and district judges, and the USCIT judges (Article III judges), 'hold their office during good behavior'. This means that Article III judges have lifetime appointment, except under very limited circumstances. The Constitution also provides that these judges' salaries cannot be reduced while they are in office. These constitutional safeguards, which were designed to secure the independence of federal judges, are vital in light of the ongoing debate as to whether the selection process leaves too much room for political partisanship and the consideration of judges' ideology.[10]

Article III judges can be removed from office only for 'treason, bribery, or other high crimes and misdemeanors', and through impeachment by the House of Representatives and conviction by the Senate.[11] There is disagreement as to what crimes meet this constitutional standard, but it is at least reasonably clear that Congress cannot remove judges based simply on its disagreement with their legal decisions.[12] Impeachment of Article III judges is rare, and removal is rarer still. Since 1803, the House of Representatives has impeached only 15 judges and only eight of those impeachments were followed by convictions in the Senate.[13] Successful impeachments include charges of abuse of contempt power and other

---

[5] *See* 28 USC 251(a).
[6] See Gregory W. Carman, *The Jurisdiction of the United States Court of International Trade: A Dilemma for Potential Litigants*, 22 Stetson L. Rev. 157, 160–62 (1992).
[7] 28 USC 251(a).
[8] *See generally* Adam J. Rappaport, *The Court of International Trade's Political Party Diversity Requirement: Unconstitutional Under Any Separation of Powers Theory*, 68 U. Chi. L. Rev. 1429 (2001).
[9] *See id.* at Part I(B).
[10] *See generally* Vicki C. Jackson, *Packages of Judicial Independence: The Selection and Tenure of Article III Judges*, 95 Geo. L.J. 965 (2007).
[11] US Const. art. II, §4.
[12] *See* Michael J. Gerhardt, The Federal Impeachment Process 50 (1996).
[13] *See* Federal Judicial Center, *Impeachment of Federal* Judges, available at https://www.fjc.gov/history/judges/impeachments-federal-judges.

misuses of office, improper relationship with litigants, and favouritism in the appointment of bankruptcy receivers.[14]

In addition to Article III judges, the federal judiciary includes magistrate and bankruptcy judges.[15] Magistrate judges are judicial officers appointed for a renewable term of eight years by majority vote of the US district judges of the relevant court. They handle a variety of judicial proceedings, including pre-trial motions and hearings in civil and criminal cases. By federal law, magistrate judges must meet specified eligibility criteria, including at least five years as a member in good standing of a state or territory's highest court bar, and be vetted by a merit selection panel that consists of lawyers and non-lawyers from the community. Bankruptcy judges are also judicial officers of the district court, but who preside exclusively over bankruptcy proceedings and cases. Bankruptcy judges are appointed to renewable 14-year terms by a majority of the judges of the US Court of Appeals for their circuit with assistance from the circuit council. Bankruptcy judges must meet eligibility criteria, including being a member of the bar in good standing. Circuit councils may appoint a merit selection panel, consisting of judges and other legal professionals, to review and recommend candidates for appointment.[16]

All federal judges except US Supreme Court justices are subject to the Code of Conduct for United States Judges, a set of ethical guidelines initially adopted by the Judicial Conference on 5 April 1973 and revised substantially over the years.[17] The Code's various canons broadly provide that a judge should inter alia 'uphold the integrity and independence of the judiciary', 'avoid impropriety and the appearance of impropriety in all activities', 'perform the duties of the office fairly, impartially and diligently', and 'refrain from political activity'.[18] The Code requires a judge to disqualify him- or herself in proceedings in which the judge's impartiality might reasonably be questioned, including, for example, where the judge was a lawyer or material witness in the matter in controversy, or has a financial interest in it.[19] Not every violation of the Code leads to disciplinary action. Whether disciplinary action is appropriate, and the degree of discipline, should be determined through a reasonable application of the text and should depend on such factors as the seriousness of the improper activity, the intent of

---

[14]   *See id.*

[15]   *See* United States Courts, *About Federal Judges*, available at https://www.uscourts.gov/judges-judgeships/about-federal-judges.

[16]   *See id.*

[17]   *See* United States Courts, *Code of Conduct for United States Judges*, available at https://www.uscourts.gov/judges-judgeships/code-conduct-united-states-judges.

[18]   Judicial Conference of the United States, *Code of Conduct for United States Judges (Mar. 12, 2019)* Canons 1–5 (2019), available at https://www.uscourts.gov/sites/default/files/code_of_conduct_for_united_states_judges_effective_march_12_2019.pdf.

[19]   *See id.* Canon 3(C).

United States of America

the judge, whether there is a pattern of improper activity, and the effect of the improper activity on others or on the judicial system.[20]

Additionally, the Judicial Conduct and Disability Act of 1980 establishes a process by which any person can file a complaint alleging inter alia that a federal judge has engaged in 'conduct prejudicial to the effective and expeditious administration of the business of the courts'.[21] More specifically, the Rules for Judicial-Conduct and Judicial-Disability Proceedings, as amended on 12 March 2019, provide mandatory and nationally uniform provisions governing the substantive and procedural aspects of judicial conduct and disability proceedings under the Act.[22] As defined in the Rules, cognisable misconduct includes: 'using the judge's office to obtain special treatment for friends or relatives'; 'accepting bribes, gifts, or other personal favors related to the judicial office'; 'engaging in improper ex parte communications with parties or counsel for one side in a case'; 'engaging in partisan political activity or making inappropriately partisan statements'; and 'intentional discrimination on the basis of race, color, sex, gender, gender identity, pregnancy, sexual orientation, religion, national origin, age, or disability'.[23] As might be expected, the judicial conduct and disability review process cannot be used to challenge the correctness of a judge's decision in a case.

2.2. STATE JUDGES

Each of the 50 states in the US has its own court system. Over the course of American history, state judges have been appointed by one of four basic methods: appointment by elected officials, partisan election, non-partisan election, and selection by a technocratic commission.[24] In several states, there are different methods for selecting judges for different levels of courts. Often, trial court judges are elected, while appellate court judges are appointed in some way. In a few states, the method for selecting trial court judges can even vary from county to county.[25]

In terms of appointment by elected officials, it is the state governor who appoints judges in many states, often, although not always, from a list of

---

[20]   *See id.* Canon 1 cmt.

[21]   28 USC §351(a).

[22]   Judicial Conference of the United States, *Rules for Judicial-Conduct and Judicial-Disability Proceedings (Mar. 12, 2019)*, available at https://www.uscourts.gov/sites/default/files/judicial_conduct_and_disability_rules_effective_march_12_2019.pdf.

[23]   *See id.* Rule 4(a).

[24]   Brian T. Fitzpatrick, *The Ideological Consequences of Selection: A Nationwide Study of the Methods of Selecting Judges*, 70 VAND. L. REV. 1729, 1729–30 (2017).

[25]   Institute for the Advancement of the American Legal System, *Judges in the United States, Quality Judges Initiative: FAQS*, 3–4 (2014), available at https://iaals.du.edu/sites/default/files/documents/publications/judge_faq.pdf.

Intersentia

645

candidates submitted by a judicial nominating commission. Judges, attorneys and laypersons can serve on judicial nominating commissions, which screen judicial applicants and recommend shortlists of the best-qualified candidates.[26] Before making the appointment, however, the governor's office will often investigate each nominee's professional and personal background and interview each nominee. Most states place a time limit on the governor's appointment decision, ranging from 15 to 60 days. If the governor fails to make the appointment in the time allowed, the chief justice usually makes the appointment. In various states, the governor's appointment must be confirmed by the state legislature or the governor's council.[27]

Partisan elections of judges operate similarly to partisan elections for other offices. Candidates compete first in a primary election to win their party's nomination and then in the general election against the other party's candidate. Judges of the court of last resort are chosen in partisan elections in nine states, and intermediate appellate court judges are selected this way in seven states. Judges of major trial courts may be chosen in partisan elections in 14 states.[28]

In states with non-partisan judicial elections, candidates compete in a non-partisan primary. In most of these states, if one candidate does not get at least 50% of the vote, the top two candidates compete in the general election. Candidates are not identified on the ballot as a member of a political party. Judges of the court of last resort are chosen in non-partisan elections in 13 states, and intermediate appellate court judges are selected this way in 11 states. Judges of major trial courts may be chosen in non-partisan elections in 20 states.[29]

In states where judges are elected, judicial vacancies may arise between elections or when the legislature is not in session that need to be filled. Midterm, or interim, vacancies in these states may be filled via commission-based appointment by the governor (with or without confirmation), appointment by the governor (with or without confirmation), special election, or supreme court appointment.[30]

The debate is longstanding on whether appointment or election represents the 'best' selection method in yielding an independent, highly qualified but yet accountable judiciary, and what empirical evidence we have does not resolve the question.[31] While appointive systems are generally thought to maximise independence, opponents could argue that appointment by a political executive begets more political beholdenness than election.[32] Not surprisingly, proposals

---

[26]   See id. at 4–5.
[27]   See id.
[28]   See id. at 5.
[29]   See id.
[30]   See id. at 6.
[31]   See generally Rebecca D. Gill, Beyond High Hopes and Unmet Expectations: Judicial Selection Reforms in the States, 96 JUDICATURE 278 (2013).
[32]   Id. at 283.

have been introduced by legislators, governors, courts and citizens' groups in nearly every state to limit the role of politics in the selection of state judges. Regardless, because most state judges stand for periodic election, they are, to that extent, less independent of the public they serve than their federal counterparts. Decisional independence of state judges is nonetheless promoted by a variety of other means, such as longer terms between election cycles than other elected officials, selection regimes that reduce the likelihood of electoral defeat, such as retention elections in which judges run unopposed, and state codes of judicial conduct.[33]

Codes of judicial conduct are the primary means by which judicial conduct is regulated in state courts.[34] The revised Model Code of Judicial Conduct was adopted by the American Bar Association (ABA) in 1990, and amended most recently in 2010. Every state and the District of Columbia has a code based on some version of the ABA model.[35] This widespread adoption of state codes based on an ABA model provides some uniformity and is the foundation for a national body of law concerning judicial conduct. In broad terms, the Model Code requires judges to uphold the integrity and independence of the judiciary, avoid impropriety and the appearance of impropriety in all of their activities, and perform the duties of their office impartially and diligently.[36]

Historically, judicial misconduct in the United States was dealt with primarily through the traditional procedures of impeachment, address, or recall.[37] These procedures were often inappropriate, not least because they provided for just the one draconian remedy of removal. In response, states began to establish permanent state commissions charged with regulating judicial conduct. Today, there are judicial conduct organisations in all 50 states and the District of Columbia is vested with authority to investigate, prosecute and adjudicate cases of judicial misbehaviour, as well as to impose or recommend to a higher authority sanctions ranging from censure to removal, where it has been determined that misconduct has occurred.[38]

3. ARBITRATORS IN THE US

Consistent with the US Supreme Court's recognition of arbitration as a strict matter of contract,[39] selection of the arbitrator or arbitrators in the US typically occurs through the parties' agreement. Parties can name the specific arbitrator

---

[33] JAMES J. ALFINI & JAMES SAMPLE, JUDICIAL CONDUCT AND ETHICS §1.02. (6th ed. 2020).
[34] *See id.* at §1.03.
[35] *See id.*
[36] *See id.*
[37] *See id.* at §1.05.
[38] *See id.*
[39] *See* Jarrod Wong, *Arbitrating in the Ether of Intent*, 40 FLA. ST. U. L. REV. 165, 170 (2012).

Jarrod Wong

in their agreement or, more commonly, will specify a procedure for selecting the arbitrator in a pre-dispute agreement, for instance by committing to arbitrate according to the rules of an arbitral institution, such as the American Arbitration Association (AAA). Continuing with that example, under the AAA Commercial Arbitration Rules, if the parties have not appointed an arbitrator and have not provided any other method of appointment, the AAA sends the parties a list of 10 potential arbitrators.[40] Each party gets to strike the potential arbitrators to which it objects, and ranks the remaining candidates in order of that party's preference. The AAA invites the candidate with the highest combined ranking to serve as the arbitrator. If the process fails to yield an arbitrator, the AAA picks one.[41]

Agreeing to tripartite arbitration is another method of selecting arbitrators that can serve as an alternative to relying on an institution's arbitration rules.[42] In tripartite arbitration, each party picks one arbitrator and the two arbitrators agree on the third.[43]

US courts place limits on the selection of arbitrators in at least two ways.[44] First, courts have declined to enforce executory arbitration agreements when dissatisfied with the agreement's method of selecting the arbitrator. For instance, courts have refused to enforce arbitration agreements reserving to the drafting party complete discretion over the selection of the arbitrator,[45] or those naming a close affiliate of the drafting party as the arbitrator.[46] Second, courts have refused to enforce arbitration awards on the ground that the parties selected an arbitrator who had an undisclosed substantial relationship with one of the parties. This second limit has an added layer of complexity in the case of tripartite arbitration as it raises legal and ethical issues about the extent to which the party-appointed (as opposed to the presiding) arbitrator may be partial rather than neutral. Under section 10(a)(2) of the Federal Arbitration Act (FAA), which broadly applies to any written arbitration agreement in any transaction involving interstate or international commerce,[47] a court may vacate an arbitration award where 'there was evident partiality or corruption in the arbitrators'.[48] However, conduct that may be regarded as partial in a single arbitrator – for example, ex parte communications with just one party – may be acceptable in tripartite arbitration in the US.[49] In some circumstances, party-appointed arbitrators in tripartite

---

[40]   See AAA, *Commercial Arbitration Rules*, R-12(a) (2013).

[41]   See id. R-12(b).

[42]   See, e.g., id. R-16.

[43]   See, e.g., Delta Mine Holding Co. v. AFC Coal Properties, Inc., 280 F.3d 815, 817 (8th Cir. 2002).

[44]   See Stephen J. Ware & Ariana R. Levinson, Principles of Arbitration law 113 (2017).

[45]   See, e.g., Hooters of America, Inc. v. Phillips, 173 F.3d 933, 938–39 (4th Cir. 1999).

[46]   See, e.g., Graham v. Scissor Tail, Inc., 171 Cal. Rptr. 604 (Cal.1981).

[47]   See 9 USC §§1–2.

[48]   Id. §10(a)(2).

[49]   See, e.g., U.S. Life Ins. Co. v. Superior Nat. Ins. Co., 581 F.3d 1167, 1171 n. 1 (9th Cir. 2010).

United States of America

arbitration are allowed and even expected to be partisan in representing the interests of the party appointing them. Indeed, Judge Easterbrook of the Seventh Circuit noted that, 'in the main[,] party-appointed arbitrators are *supposed* to be advocates. In labor arbitration a union may name as its arbitrator the business manager of the local union, and the employer its vice-president for labor relations. Yet no one believes that the predictable loyalty of these designees spoils the award.'[50] On the other hand, both the AAA Commercial Arbitration Rules and the Code of Ethics for Arbitrators in Commercial Disputes approved by the AAA and the ABA establish a presumption of neutrality for all arbitrators, including party-appointed arbitrators, unless the parties have specifically agreed otherwise.[51]

Arbitral awards may be vacated under section 10(a)(2) of the FAA not just when the arbitrators exhibit 'evident partiality' in their conduct of the arbitration, but also, and perhaps more importantly, when the arbitrators fail to make relevant disclosures. The leading US judicial decision on the failure to disclose – and on the independence of arbitrators generally – is *Commonwealth Coatings Corp. v. Continental Casualty Co.*, a 1968 US Supreme Court decision.[52] There, the Supreme Court vacated an arbitral award because the presiding arbitrator had failed to disclose his four-to-five-year consulting work for one party to the arbitration that had earned him $12,000, including compensation, on the very same projects at issue in the arbitration.[53] Although there was no claim of actual bias or prejudice on the part of the presiding arbitrator, the divided Court ultimately vacated the award, with a plurality stating that the non-disclosure of any dealings creating 'an impression of possible bias' or 'even an appearance of bias' warranted vacating:

> It is true that arbitrators cannot sever all their ties with the business world, since they are not expected to get all their income from their work deciding cases, but we should, if anything, be even more scrupulous to safeguard the impartiality of arbitrators than judges, since the former have completely free rein to decide the law as well as the facts and are not subject to appellate review. We can perceive no way in which the effectiveness of the arbitration process will be hampered by the simple requirement that arbitrators disclose to the parties any dealings that might create an impression of possible bias. ... [A]ny tribunal permitted by law to try cases and controversies not only must be unbiased but also must avoid even the appearance of

---

[50] Sphere Drake Ins., Ltd. v. All Am. Life Ins. Co., 307 F.3d 617, 620 (7th Cir. 2002) (emphasis in original).

[51] *See* AAA, *Commercial Arbitration Rules*, R-13(b) (2013); *Code of Ethics for Arbitrators in Commercial Disputes* (Mar. 1, 2004).

[52] 393 U.S. 145 (1968).

[53] *See id.* at 146.

Intersentia

649

bias. We cannot believe that it was the purpose of Congress to authorize litigants to submit their cases and controversies to arbitration boards that might reasonably be thought biased against one litigant and favorable to another.[54]

Muddying this otherwise straightforward directive, Justice White wrote a separate opinion concurring in the result but articulating a very different standard of impartiality requiring the disclosure of only non-trivial relationships:

> The Court does not decide today that arbitrators are to be held to the standards of judicial decorum of Article III judges, or indeed of any judges. It is often because they are men of affairs, not apart from but of the marketplace, that they are effective in their adjudicatory functions. This does not mean the judiciary must overlook outright chicanery in giving effect to their awards; that would be an abdication of our responsibility. But it does mean that arbitrators are not automatically disqualified by a business relationship with the parties before them if both parties are informed of the relationship in advance, or if they are unaware of the facts but the relationship is trivial.[55]

As Gary Born has noted in criticising this tension:

> [n]ot surprisingly, U.S. lower courts have had difficulty developing a single standard of impartiality and independence from the Commonwealth Coating opinions (which the Supreme Court has not subsequently revisited). Thus, one court remarked that Commonwealth Coatings 'provides little guidance because of the inability of a majority of Justices to agree on anything but the result,' while another correctly observed that '[t]he various federal and state courts that have addressed "evident partiality" have struggled with the concept.'[56]

As a result, some US courts have vacated awards based on an appearance or 'a reasonable impression' of bias, relying on the plurality's view that arbitrators should be held to a higher level of impartiality than judges. For instance, the Eleventh Circuit Court of Appeals determined that because an arbitrator neglected to disclose his relationship to some of the parties, vacating the arbitration award was proper because of the reasonable appearance of bias.[57]

Meanwhile, other courts have vacated awards only where the arbitrator had failed to disclose a non-trivial relationship, and a reasonable person would have to conclude that an arbitrator was partial to one party to the arbitration, following Justice White's analysis that arbitrators are not necessarily to be held to the same standards as judges on account of their inevitable business connections. For instance, the Fifth Circuit Court of Appeals in an *en banc* decision reversed

---

[54] *Id.*at 149.
[55] *Id.* at 150.
[56] GARY BORN, INTERNATIONAL COMMERCIAL ARBITRATION 1768 (2nd ed. 2014).
[57] *See* Middlesex Mut. Ins. Co. v. Levine, 675 F.2d 1197, 1204 (11th Cir. 1982).

a lower court decision that had vacated an award because an arbitrator had failed to disclose he had been co-counsel with counsel of one of the parties in a complex case.[58] Even though the arbitrator and his then co-counsel had signed many of the same papers, they had never met nor spoken to each other. Relying on Justice White's concurrence, a majority of the court held that vacatur was only appropriate where the disclosure created 'a concrete, not speculative impression of bias'.[59] Indeed, some courts adopting a similar analysis have articulated even more stringent standards, holding that '[t]he conclusion of bias must be ineluctable, the favorable treatment unilateral' before an award may be vacated.[60]

Compounding this already serious confusion, other authorities have suggested yet additional standards for establishing the 'evident partiality' of arbitrators for purposes of vacating awards. For example, the American Law Institute's draft Restatement (Third) U.S. Law of International Commercial Arbitration provides that evident partiality exists 'when there is proof that would cause an objective, disinterested observer who is fully informed of the relevant facts relating to the arbitrators' conduct or alleged conflicts to have a serious doubt regarding the fundamental fairness of the arbitral proceedings'.[61]

Given these different authorities, the particular standards of impartiality and independence of arbitrators (both domestic and international) will remain unsettled under US law without further guidance from the US Supreme Court.[62] Of course, even if there were agreement and clarity on a particular 'evident partiality' standard, the determination of whether particular dealings or relationships crossed the line or required disclosure would still have to be examined on a case-by-case basis in a fact-intensive inquiry.[63] In this regard, the Fourth Circuit has identified four facts to be considered:

> (1) the extent and character of the personal interest, pecuniary or otherwise, of the arbitrator in the proceeding (2) the directness of the relationship between the arbitrator and the party he is alleged to favor; (3) the connection of that relationship to the arbitration; and (4) the proximity in time between the relationship and the arbitration proceeding.[64]

---

[58] Positive Software Solutions, Inc. v. New Century Fin. Corp., 476 F.3d 278 (5th Cir. 2007) (*en banc*).

[59] *Id.* at 286.

[60] *See id.* at 1769 (citations omitted).

[61] RESTATEMENT (THIRD) OF THE U.S. LAW OF INT'L COMMERCIAL & INV'R-STATE ARBITRATION §4.18 (AM. LAW INST., Proposed Final Draft 2019). Among the factors to be considered by the reviewing court is whether the arbitrator satisfied the 'duty to conduct a reasonable investigation into potential conflicts.' *Id.* §4.18, Reporters' note b.

[62] *See* BORN, *supra* note 56, at 1770.

[63] *See* WARE & LEVINSON, *supra* note 44, at 150.

[64] ANR Coal Co., Inc. v. Cogentrix of North Carolina, Inc., 173 F.3d 493, 500 (4th Cir. 1999).

Examples of situations where the court had vacated the award include where the arbitrator had failed to disclose that he was co-counsel in extensive litigation with the lawyer representing the winning party,[65] that the arbitrator had represented investors with similar claims against the predecessor-in-interest to the respondent,[66] and that the arbitrator's law firm had represented the corporate parent of a party in multiple cases over 35 years ending less than two years before the arbitration.[67]

It bears observing that recourse to the courts is not always required to resolve impartiality issues. Many arbitration agreements adopt the rules of arbitral institutions such as the AAA (but which may provide for a standard of impartiality that varies from 'evident partiality'). 'In most cases such contractual mechanisms, which permit issues of partiality and personal interest to be addressed as they arise, play a significant role in policing such conflicts and make recourse to the courts less likely.'[68] For instance, Rule 17(a) of the AAA Commercial Arbitration Rules provides that the arbitrator:

> shall disclose to the AAA any circumstance likely to give rise to justifiable doubt as to the arbitrator's impartiality and independence, including any bias or any financial or personal interest in the result of the arbitration or any past or present relationship with the parties or their representatives. Such obligation shall remain in effect throughout the arbitration.[69]

Further, Rule 18(a)(i) provides that the arbitrator 'shall be impartial and independent and shall perform his or her duties with diligence and in good faith, and shall be subject to disqualification for partiality or lack of independence.'[70] Should a party object to an arbitrator, or even on its own initiative, the institution (AAA) gets to determine whether the arbitrator should be disqualified, and whose decision is final and conclusive.[71] The ability to have an arbitrator disqualified and removed under institutional rules is significant as the primary remedy afforded under section 10(a)(2) is the vacatur of the award for evident partiality. The FAA makes no provision for interlocutory judicial challenges to or removal of an arbitrator and does not directly address the standards of impartiality and independence required for arbitrators.[72] While certain commentators offer that during the

---

[65]   Positive Software Solutions, Inc. v. New Century Mortgage Corp., 436 F.3d 495 (5th Cir. 2006).

[66]   Wages v. Smith Barney Harris Upham Co., 937 P.2d 715 (Ariz.Ct.App. 1997).

[67]   Schmitz v. Zilveti, 20 F.3d 1043 (9th Cir. 1994).

[68]   Ian R. McNeil, Richard E. Speidel & Thomas J. Stipanowich, Federal Arbitration Law §28.2.6.1, at 28:57 (Supp. 1999).

[69]   AAA, *Commercial Arbitration Rules*, R-17 (2013).

[70]   *Id.* R-18(i).

[71]   *Id.* R-18(c).

[72]   *See* Born, *supra* note 56, at 1765.

United States of America

arbitrator-selection process, one may conceivably challenge the appointment of an arbitrator on the ground that the arbitrator is partial to the other party and thereby seek the arbitrator's disqualification, 'there is little FAA case law dealing with challenges to arbitrator partiality before an award.'[73] That is, almost all US judicial decisions considering arbitrators' independence and impartiality under the FAA have been rendered in the context of actions to vacate or to recognise awards, rather than interlocutory challenges to an arbitrator. This serious remedial limitation has been criticised.[74] One consequence is that these decisions should be applied with care when evaluating the standards applied to arbitrator independence and impartiality during the course of arbitral proceedings (and, particularly, in the context of actions to remove an arbitrator under institutional rules).[75]

4. INTERNATIONAL ADJUDICATORS IN THE US

This section examines the rules of and practices in the US legal system in the appointment of US candidates to positions of international adjudicators insofar as they implicate mechanisms for ensuring their independence and impartiality. Because special rapporteurs have been appointed to consider the rules and practices of particular international fora, such as the International Court of Justice (ICJ) and the World Trade Organization (WTO), this section will only consider substantially the relevant issues arising specifically from US law or practice.

4.1. APPOINTMENTS TO INTERNATIONAL ARBITRAL TRIBUNALS

With regard to appointments to ad hoc tribunals in international commercial arbitration, the selection of arbitrators is typically governed by the institutional rules of the arbitral forum chosen by the parties. Accordingly, sole arbitrators are chosen jointly by the parties or failing agreement, by whatever method is prescribed in the applicable rules in those circumstances. In tripartite arbitrations, each party usually appoints an arbitrator, and both party-appointed arbitrators select the presiding arbitrator. Those same rules will often generically require the arbitrator to be independent and impartial, and may impose disclosure obligations on the arbitrator and allow for a party to challenge an

---

73   MCNEIL, SPEIDEL & STIAPNOWICH, *supra* note 68, §28.1.1.
74   *See* Ronán Feehily, *Neutrality, Independence and Impartiality in International Commercial Arbitration, A Fine Balance in the Quest For Arbitral Justice,* 7 PENN ST.J.L& INT'L.AFF. 88, 99 (2019).
75   *See* BORN, *supra* note 56, at 1765.

Intersentia

653

arbitrator for lack of independence or impartiality.[76] In connection with the United Nations Convention on the Recognition and Enforcement of Foreign Arbitral Awards (the New York Convention),[77] where US law relating to independence and impartiality may intrude, however, is at the end of the process after the arbitration is concluded. Specifically, this may occur in the context of any attempt by a party to set aside an award issued in an arbitration seated in the United States. The United States ratified the New York Convention in 1970 and implemented it in Chapter 2 of the FAA.[78] The New York Convention provides that '[e]ach Contracting State shall recognize arbitral awards as binding and enforce them.' Exceptionally, under Article V(1)(e) of the New York Convention, a national court may refuse such recognition and enforcement where the award 'has been set aside or suspended by a competent authority of the country in which, or under the law of which, that award was made.'[79] Critically, the New York Convention leaves the standards of vacatur to the national law of the seat of the particular arbitration.[80] As such, for awards issued in international arbitrations seated in the United States, the standards for their vacatur are controlled by the FAA, including section 10(a)(2) of the Act, which as discussed above, allows an award to be vacated for 'evident partiality'.[81] This means the same confusion that afflicts US domestic case law on the interpretation of 'evident partiality' likewise impacts the vacatur of awards issued in international arbitrations seated in the US that is sought on the basis of the arbitrator's lack of impartiality and independence. Accordingly, the reader is referred back to the earlier discussion in this report on the vacatur of US arbitral awards.[82]

With respect to appointments to international investor-state arbitrations involving the United States as the respondent, the Office of the Legal Adviser of the State Department typically takes the lead in selecting the arbitrator to be appointed by the United States, although it often consults with US government offices, including the Department of Commerce, the Treasury and the Office of the US Trade Representative.[83] Perhaps unsurprisingly, there is, however, little information on the selection criteria employed by the State Department in that process.

---

[76] As explained above, such rules of particular international fora will be addressed by special rapporteurs and are outside the scope of this report.

[77] Convention on the Recognition and Enforcement of Foreign Arbitral Awards, June 10, 1958, 21 U.S.T. 2517, 330 U.N.T.S. 3.

[78] *See* USC §§201–208.

[79] New York Convention, *supra* note 77, art. V(1)(e).

[80] *See* Karaha Bodas, Co., L.L.C. v. Perusahaan Pertambangan Minyak Dan Gas Bumi, 364 F.3d 274, 287–88 (5th Cir. 2004) (stating that 'the courts of the country of the arbitral situs ... may apply their own domestic law in evaluating a request to annul or set aside an arbitral award').

[81] *See supra* section 3.

[82] *See id.*

[83] Chiara Giorgetti, *Who Decides Who Decides in International Investment Arbitration?*, 35 U. Pa. J. Int'l L. 431, 446 (2013). *See generally* Jeremy Sharpe, *Representing a Respondent*

United States of America

Whether in international commercial or investor-state arbitration, challenges initiated against arbitrators based on an alleged lack of independence or impartiality, as well as the applicable impartiality and independence requirements, will ordinarily be governed by the rules of the particular arbitral forum, and as such are outside the scope of this national report.

4.2. APPOINTMENTS TO INTERNATIONAL COURTS

There are various international courts whose composition includes or has included US nationals as adjudicators. There is however often little transparency and public information concerning the process, never mind the precise selection criteria, relied upon in the nomination or appointment of those adjudicators. To complicate matters, while the most typical form of judicial selection procedure in international courts involves the nomination of candidates by a state (and then the election of judges from among those candidates by an intergovernmental body),[84] this is not always the case. For example, and most prominently, with regard to the ICJ, it is the relevant Permanent Court of Arbitration (PCA) national group rather than the state that formally nominates ICJ candidates, even if the state may continue to have influence over the process.[85]

The ICJ comprises 15 judges from different states.[86] Since the ICJ's founding, the tradition has been for each of the five permanent Member States of the United Nations Security Council, including the United States, to have a seat on the Court. This is the case even though the text of the Statute says nothing in this regard, and is an expression of power politics at play.[87] As indicated above, PCA national groups play a central role in the ICJ nomination process.[88] Each national group can nominate up to four ICJ candidates, although 'not more than two of whom shall be of their own nationality.'[89] With regard to the US national group, there is a convention that the current legal adviser to the Department of

---

State in Investment Arbitration, in LITIGATING INTERNATIONAL INVESTMENT DISPUTES: A PRACTITIONER'S GUIDE (C. Giorgetti ed., 2014).

[84] See Ruth Mackenzie, The Selection of International Judges, in INTERNATIONAL ADJUDICATION 737, 743–47 (Cesare PR Romano, Karen J. Alter & Yuval Shany eds., 2014).

[85] See id. at 749.

[86] See ICJ Statute, art. 3.

[87] See Davis R. Robinson, The Role of Politics in the Election and the Work of Judges of the International Court of Justice, 97 AM. SOC'Y INT'L L. PROC. 277, 278 (2003); Mackenzie, supra note 84, at 745.

[88] A national group is a group of up to four persons appointed by a Member State of the PCA. Each national group has the exclusive right to nominate candidates for the election of judges to the ICJ. See ICJ Statute, art. 4. See generally Remy Jorritsma, National Groups (Permanent Court of Arbitration), MPILux Research Paper Series 2017 (2017), available at www.mpi.lu.

[89] ICJ Statute, art. 5(2).

Intersentia

655

State and the legal adviser of the former administration are members, ensuring bipartisan participation.[90] The other members of the US national group have typically included other former legal advisers and representatives of the academic community.[91] The US national group functions quite independently from the government.[92] Indeed, it has twice nominated candidates (Philip Jessup in 1960 and Richard Baxter in 1978) who were not favoured by the government. In both instances, the US national group resisted pressure to nominate the US government's preferred candidate and the government eventually agreed to carry the candidature through to election.[93] Nonetheless, the US national group will more likely see to it that the nominees proposed are acceptable to the government.[94] Since 1960, the national group of the United States has consulted widely with a range of bodies at the domestic level to seek suggestions as to potential candidates.[95] For example, when Judge Schwebel's resignation was announced in November 1999, the US national group invited recommendations from the American Society of International Law, the ABA (Section of International Law and Practice, and Standing Committee on Law and National Security), the American Branch of the International Law Association, the Association of American Law Schools, the Association of the Bar of the City of New York, the Federalist Society and the Chief Justice of the United States.[96] Notwithstanding such consultation, some commentators have criticised the nomination process as suffering from a 'serious democratic deficit' and being 'far removed from popular oversight' with no input from ordinary citizens.[97] In any event, once the national groups have drawn up their lists, the General Assembly and Security Council elect the Court's members, voting separately and by simple majority. Domestic governments do not have a say at this stage of the process,[98] which is thus outside the scope of this national report.

Another adjudicatory institution that effectively locks up a seat for a US national notwithstanding silence on the issue in the governing instrument is the

---

[90] Ruth MacKenzie et al., Selecting International Judges: Principle, Process, and Politics 71 (2010).

[91] See Lori Fisler Damrosch, The Election of Thomas Buergenthal to the International Court of Justice, 94 Am. J. Int'l. L. 579 (2000).

[92] See Davis R. Robinson, Politics and Law in International Adjudication, 97 Am. Soc'y Int'l. L. Proc. 277, 279 (2003) (noting as reflective of the US national group's independence the instance 'when the Carter Administration supported former Supreme Court Justice Arthur Goldberg for election but the national group selected Harvard Law School Professor Richard Baxter instead').

[93] MacKenzie et al., supra note 90, at 92–93.

[94] Jeffrey Golden, National Groups and the Nomination of Judges of the International Court of Justice: A Preliminary Report, 9 The International Lawyer 333, 341 (1975).

[95] MacKenzie et al., supra note 90, at 91–92.

[96] Damrosch, supra note 91, at 581.

[97] Mark L. Movsesian, Judging International Judgments, 48 Va. J. Int'l L. 65, 97 (2007).

[98] See id.

Appellate Body of the WTO.[99] Even more concerning, however, is the extent to which the United States can and did influence the selection of Appellate Body members.

Formally, Appellate Body members are selected by a consensus decision of the Dispute Settlement Body (DSB), which is convened by the General Council of the WTO and consists of representatives from all WTO Member States.[100] In practice, however, the process of selecting Appellate Body members is carried out by a Selection Committee composed of the director-general and the chairs of the General Council, the DSB, the Council for Trade in Goods, the Council for Trade in Services and the TRIPS Council.[101] In reviewing prospective candidates, the Selection Committee has consulted with other members. It is at this stage of the process that the United States has enjoyed 'special privileges' enabling it to object to some candidates, amounting as such to a veto power.[102] This unilateral veto is apparently used regularly by the United States to ensure that the candidates selected to serve on the Appellate Body are not exceedingly activist, biased or expansive lawmakers. Typically, the general counsel of the Office of the United States Trade Representative (USTR) and the assistant USTR for monitoring and enforcement, in coordination with the assistant USTR for WTO affairs, carefully vet each candidate by reading his or her past work and judicial decisions (if any), and interviewing each in Washington or Geneva, before deciding whether to endorse the candidacy. These interviews have tended to focus on the candidate's qualifications and approach to judicial decision-making, and would appear to address US fears of judicial activism.[103]

More recently, the United States has controversially employed its more direct veto power to decimate the Appellate Body. Recall that the appointment of Appellate Body members requires the consensus of all WTO members so that any member can veto a candidate's selection.[104] For a number of years now, partly in response to China's rise as a more strategic litigator and the US losing cases at the WTO regarding antidumping, countervailing duty and safeguard

---

99 *See* Erik Voeten, *The Politics of International Judicial Appointments*, 9 CHI. J. INT'L L. 387, 402 (2009) (noting that '[t]he US and the EU are de facto assured of a seat on the [WTO appellate] body and are widely thought to set the acceptable boundaries for candidates from other countries as well'); Petros C. Mavroidis, in REFLECTIONS ON THE CONSTITUTIONALISATION OF INTERNATIONAL ECONOMIC LAW: LIBER AMICORUM FOR ERNST-ULRICH PETERSMANN 243, 247 (Marise Cremona et al. eds., 2014) (noting that 'the EU, Japan and the US have always had a seat in the AB').

100 *See* Understanding on Rules and Procedures Governing the Settlement of Disputes, art. 2, Apr. 15, 1994, Marrakesh Agreement Establishing the World Trade Organization, Annex 2, 1869 U.N.T.S. 401 (DSU).

101 Richard H. Steinberg, *Judicial Lawmaking at the WTO: Discursive, Constitutional, and Political Constraints*, 98 AM. J. INT'L L. 247, 264 (2004).

102 *See id.*

103 *See id.*

104 *See* DSU, art. 2.4.

measures, the USTR increasingly challenged Appellate Body decisions against it and expressed its discontent by taking more aggressive positions in the Appellate Body selection process.[105] For example, under the Bush and Obama administrations, the USTR twice refused to re-nominate the current US member to the Appellate Body for a second term to signal US dissatisfaction, and replaced each with a new US member. The Trump administration, however, took it to a whole new level. Over the last few years, the Trump administration repeatedly blocked the selection of new tribunal members when their predecessors' terms expired. The end result is that on 10 December 2020, the Appellate Body ceased to exist when its last member left.[106] While various observers had expected the Biden administration to reverse course, it has so far adopted the same position, and has declined to consent to new appointments to the Appellate Body.[107] These dramatic developments present a sober cautionary tale. Although the decision by consensus requirement – and therefore unilateral veto power by each WTO member – is ostensibly democratic, and empowers any state to protest perceived partiality on the part of the Appellate Body as the United States has done, such an institutional design also permits the same state unilaterally to hijack and hold the tribunal hostage at the expense of all other end users of the adjudicatory system.

Finally, as with international arbitration, challenges initiated against adjudicators in international courts based on an alleged lack of independence or impartiality, as well as the applicable impartiality and independence requirements, will ordinarily be governed by the rules of the particular judicial forum, and as such are outside the scope of this national report.

---

[105] Gregory Shaffer, *A Tragedy in the Making? The Decline of Law and the Return of Power in International Trade Relations*, 44 YALE J. INTL. L. ONLINE 37, 40–41 (2018).

[106] Gregory Shaffer and Henry Gao, *It's essential to bring back binding WTO dispute settlement*, The Hill (Oct. 27, 2021, 3:00 PM), available at https://thehill.com/opinion/international/578148-its-essential-to-bring-back-binding-wto-dispute-settlement.

[107] *See id.*

THE INDEPENDENCE AND IMPARTIALITY OF ADJUDICATORS IN VIETNAM

Nguyen Thi Hoa and Tran Hoang Tu Linh

1. Introduction 660
2. The Principle of Independence and Impartiality of Adjudicators
   in the Vietnamese Legal System 660
3. Mechanism to Ensure the Principle of Independence and
   Impartiality of Adjudicators 662
   3.1. Independence of Adjudicators 662
      3.1.1. The Institutional Independence of the Judiciary and
             Adjudicators from the Other Branches of Government 662
         3.1.1.1. Independence of the Courts and Judges and
                  their Relationship with Other Authorities 663
         3.1.1.2. Independence of Judges and the Internal
                  Organisation of Courts in Vietnam. 666
            3.1.1.2.1. Appointing Judges 667
            3.1.1.2.2. Assigning Court Cases to Judges. 669
            3.1.1.2.3. Independence of Each Member
                       of a Trial Jury 670
      3.1.2. Independence of Adjudicators from the Parties
             to Dispute. 671
   3.2. Impartiality of Adjudicators 672
4. Enforcement of an Arbitral Award or a Judgment Breaching the
   Principle of Independence and Impartiality of Adjudicators 673
   4.1. Enforcement of an Arbitral Award that Breaches the
        Principle of Independence and Impartiality of Adjudicators. 673
   4.2. Enforcement of a Judgment that Breaches the Principle of
        Independence and Impartiality of Adjudicators 675
      4.2.1. Conditions to Appeal for Cassation Review and Retrial. . . . 675
      4.2.2. Disputing a Party's Right to Appeal for Cassation
             Review and Retrial 677
5. Conclusion. 677

Intersentia

659

1. INTRODUCTION

Independence and impartiality are without doubt considered crucial elements of any system of justice, including arbitration. This important role is also found in Article 10 of the Universal Declaration of Human Rights, which states that the independence and impartiality of a tribunal in a hearing is one of the elements assuring human rights. So, the question arises: to what extent are the independence and impartiality of adjudicators guaranteed in the Vietnamese legal system? The answer to this question will be found in this report through the analysis below relating to: (i) recognising the principle of independence and impartiality of adjudicator in the legal system of Vietnam; (ii) the mechanism to ensure that this principle will apply in practice and in the event of a breach of this principle; and (iii) whether this influences the enforcement of an arbitral award or a judgment.

2. THE PRINCIPLE OF INDEPENDENCE AND IMPARTIALITY OF ADJUDICATORS IN THE VIETNAMESE LEGAL SYSTEM

Regarding adjudicating, in Vietnam the two entities with this power are national judges and arbitrators. In the judicial branch in Vietnam there are separate provisions for criminal, administrative and civil procedure. Due to the scope of this report for the purposes of the General Congress, it is devoted to exploring laws on civil procedure.

Relating to independence and impartiality, it has been recognised that these two elements are pivotal for the legitimacy of each decision issued by an adjudicating body.[1] Due to the significance of independence and impartiality in adjudicating, in Vietnam it is recognised in the Constitution[2] that 'the judges and assessors are independent and shall only obey laws; interference with the trials of the judges and assessors by bodies, organizations, and individuals is strictly prohibited.'[3] Impartiality of the judges is thus not mentioned by this provision. As a result, it may be asked whether the impartiality of the national courts is not necessary. The response to this question must be negative. Although the notion of 'impartiality' is not directly mentioned in the Constitution, it is explained that:

---

[1] Flavia Marisi, 'Independence and impartiality: The role of soft law in international arbitration' (2019) 85(4) *Arbitration: The International Journal of Arbitration, Mediation and Dispute Management* 326.

[2] The Constitution of the Socialist Republic of Vietnam adopted on 28 November 2013 by the Thirteenth National Assembly, and took effect on 1 January 2014.

[3] Constitution, Article 103, para. 2.

Independent trial does not mean arbitrary trial, but the trial must comply with the provisions of laws within the framework of laws. Independence and only obeying laws are two unifying sides of a fundamental principle in proceedings. Independence is to obey laws and obey laws to be independent. If only obeying laws without independence, it is only formal and ineffective compliance. It shows that the judgments and decisions of the trial panel must be consistent with the objective facts of the case.[4]

Therefore, under the Constitution, the judges must be impartial to be independent and only obey laws. Thus, Vietnam's Civil Procedure Code of 2015 (CPC)[5] provides that the judge cannot conduct the proceedings if there is reasonable evidence to consider that he or she will not be impartial.[6] In addition, Vietnam's Law on Organisation of the People's Court (LOPC)[7] requires that 'judges need to be independent, impartial, objective, and uphold justice in the trial; abide by the code of conduct, professional ethics of judges, and protect the prestige of the court'.[8] Furthermore, the independence and impartiality of adjudicators also exists in commercial arbitration. Namely, under the second paragraph of Article 4 of Vietnam's Law on Commercial Arbitration of 2010 (LCA),[9] arbitrators must be independent, impartial and obey laws. However, it is regrettable that the notion of independence is not mentioned in the Labour Code with regard to the principles of dispute resolution through arbitration. Therefore, a question can be raised as to whether the arbitral tribunal in a labour dispute is only impartial and does not need to be independent. To answer this question, it is necessary to understand whether there is a difference between independence and impartiality.

Regarding independence and impartiality in hearings, there is a point of view that:

> The notion of independence is generally used to refer to the institutional independence of the judiciary and adjudicators from the other branches of government. In addition, independence is also used to designate the absence of legally relevant relationships between the adjudicator and the parties to a dispute. The notion of impartiality, in turn, refers to the lack of prejudgment of the decision-maker in relation to the case or to the parties before her. It encompasses both the actual absence of pre-disposition and conflicts of interest and the perception thereof.[10]

---

4   Trần Thị Thu Hằng, 'Nguyên tắc Thẩm phán, Hội thẩm xét xử độc lập và chỉ tuân theo pháp luật – Thực tiễn thực hiện và kiến nghị' [Principles that judges and jurors are independent and only obey the law – Practical implementation and recommendations], *Online Revue of People's Court under leadership of the Supreme People's Court*, available at https://www.tapchitoaan.vn/bai-viet/phap-luat/nguyen-tac-tham-phan-hoi-tham-xet-xu-doc-lap-va-chi-tuan-theo-phap-luat-thuc-tien-thuc-hien-va-kien-nghi.

5   Vietnam's Civil Procedure Code of 2015 (Law No. 92/2015/QH13).

6   Ibid., Article 16, para. 1.

7   Vietnam's Law on Organisation of the People's Court (Law No. 62 /2014/QH13).

8   Ibid., Article 76.

9   Vietnam's Law on Commercial Arbitration of 2010 (Law No. 54/2010/QH12).

10   Chiara Giorgetti et al., 'Independence and impartiality of adjudicators in investment dispute settlement: Assessing challenges and reform option' (2020) 21 *Journal of World Investment & Trade* 441.

However, there is also the point of view that 'these terms are also to a certain extent intertwined – some have even suggested that the terms are "legally synonymous"'[11] or that 'independence is a necessary condition of impartiality'.[12] If this is the case, the fact that the Labour Code of Vietnam does not clearly provide that arbitral tribunals must be independent does not amount to the fact that the tribunal in labour dispute settlement can be dependent. Moreover, arbitration laws in the labour field are recent and protect employees/weaker contractual parties; therefore, there are special provisions. Thus, the arbitration laws for labour disputes will not be discussed in this report.

3. MECHANISM TO ENSURE THE PRINCIPLE OF INDEPENDENCE AND IMPARTIALITY OF ADJUDICATORS

As mentioned above, there is a point of view that there are differences in the requirements of independence and impartiality. Therefore, the analysis below will clarify elements of the independence (section 3.1) and impartiality (section 3.2) of adjudicators.

3.1. INDEPENDENCE OF ADJUDICATORS

As explained above, the notion of independence of adjudicator is used to refer to two situations: first, the institutional independence of the judiciary and adjudicators from the other branches of government (section 3.1.1); and second, the absence of legally relevant relationships between the adjudicator and the parties to a dispute (section 3.1.2).

3.1.1. *The Institutional Independence of the Judiciary and Adjudicators from the Other Branches of Government*

It has been recognised that there are many principles for a fair trial, but the first and most important one is that the judges should be absolutely independent of the government.[13] Thus, according to the Basic Principles on

---

[11]   Laurens J.E. Timmer, 'The Quality, Independence and Impartiality of the Arbitrator in International Commercial Arbitration' (2012) 78(4) *Arbitration: The International Journal of Arbitration, Mediation and Dispute Management* 348.

[12]   Diego M. Papayannis, 'Independence, impartiality and neutrality in legal adjudication' (2016) 28 *Revus* 33, available at https://journals.openedition.org/revus/3546#quotation.

[13]   A.T. Denning, 'The independence and impartiality of the Judges' (1954) 71(4) *South African Law Journal* 345.

662   Intersentia

Independence of the Judiciary formulated by the United Nations in 1985,[14] the independence of the judiciary is to ensure that 'the judiciary shall decide matters before them impartially, based on facts and in accordance with the law, without any restrictions, improper influences, inducements, pressures, threats or interferences direct or indirect from any quarter or for any reason' and 'the principle of the independence of the judiciary entitles and requires that judicial proceedings are conducted fairly and that the rights of the parties are respected'.

Pursuant to the Constitution, the state's power is unified and divided into the executive, legislative and judicial branches with reciprocal control.[15] Therefore, a concern may be raised as to whether the independence of the courts is guaranteed if other authorities have a degree of control over the court.

3.1.1.1. Independence of the Courts and Judges and their Relationship with Other Authorities

Indeed, the other authorities do exercise some external control over the judiciary. Firstly, control over the courts is exercised by the legislative branch – the National Assembly. Constitutionally, the National Assembly can supervise the courts' observance of the Constitution and the laws. However, in Vietnam, there is not a Constitutional Council to inspect whether the courts are observing the Constitution. Constitutionally, however, the National Assembly's influence over the courts can be exerted through the power to elect or dismiss the Chief Justice of the Supreme People's Court.[16] Nevertheless, when the Chief Justice is nominated, he or she will act autonomously and only obey laws, and under Article 82 of the LOPC he or she can be dismissed if he or she does not observe the law. Moreover, the National Assembly controls the judiciary through the enactment of laws and the Constitution.

The second control over the courts exists in the proceedings of the People's Procuracy system.[17] The People's Procuracy must:

> appeal to competent authorities against acts, judgments or decisions of competent authorities or individuals in judicial activities which seriously violate laws, infringe on human rights, citizen's rights and interests of the State, lawful rights and interests of organisations and individuals. These authorities must settle this appeal of the People's Procuracy in accordance with laws.[18]

---

[14] United Nations Basic Principles on the Independence of the Judiciary Adopted by the Seventh United Nations Congress on the Prevention of Crime and the Treatment of Offenders held at Milan from 26 August to 6 September 1985 and endorsed by General Assembly Resolutions 40/32 of 29 November 1985 and 40/146 of 13 December 1985, available at https://www.ohchr.org/en/professionalinterest/pages/independencejudiciary.aspx.

[15] Constitution, Article 2, para. 3.

[16] Ibid., Article 70.

[17] Ibid.

[18] LOPC, Article 5, para. 1.

In a hearing, this role of the People's Procuracy shows through the power to appeal a judgment of a first-instance court that has not yet taken effect to the Appellate Court, or to appeal an effective judgment to the superior court for cassation review or retrial.[19] At first glance, it is understandable that this control may make judges dependent on the People's Procuracy. However, if we look into this mechanism in more detail, the independence of the judges is reflected. Namely, a prosecutor can take part in hearings to present his or her point of view about the case. However, the judge has discretionary power to settle a dispute. As a result, in Vietnam, it is not uncommon for the court to decide against the opinion of the People's Procuracy. Moreover, as previously analysed, the role of the People's Procuracy is to monitor the independence and impartiality of judges in terms of their observance of laws when adjudicating.

Furthermore, the People's Procuracy is only competent to appeal a judgment to a higher court but not to review it. As a result, the fundamental principle of the independence of the judiciary, i.e. that 'the judiciary shall have jurisdiction over all issues of a judicial nature and shall have exclusive authority to decide whether an issue submitted for its decision is within its competence as defined by law',[20] is respected. Therefore, it is understandable that even though the other authorities are supervised, this supervision is to reinforce the independence and impartiality of judges. Thus, it has been commented that 'this control is to actively prevent and handle law violations, infringing on judicial activities which reduce the effectiveness and efficiency of state power in general and on legitimate rights and interests of legal entities in society in particular'.[21] According to Montesquieu, 'constant experience shows us that every man invested with power is apt to abuse it'.[22] As a consequence, the independence and impartiality of the judiciary would not be guaranteed if there were no supervision by the other authorities. Thus, the supervision of the Procuracy is an element to ensure the independence of the courts and does not form a barrier to the independence of judges.

Apart from the control exercised by the National Assembly and People's Procuracy, as just described, the influence of Communist Party Agencies is

---

[19]   CPC, Articles 278 and 315.

[20]   United Nations Basic Principles on the Independence of the Judiciary Adopted by the Seventh United Nations Congress on the Prevention of Crime and the Treatment of Offenders held at Milan from 26 August to 6 September 1985 and endorsed by General Assembly Resolutions 40/32 of 29 November 1985 and 40/146 of 13 December 1985, available at https://www.ohchr.org/en/professionalinterest/pages/independencejudiciary.aspx.

[21]   Phạm Hồng Phong, 'Kiểm soát quyền tư pháp của Toà án Việt Nam' [Controlling judicial power of Vietnamese Courts] (2018) 24(376) *Legislative Studies Review*, available at http://lapphap.vn/Pages/tintuc/tinchitiet.aspx?tintucid=208350.

[22]   C. de Montesquieu, *The Spirit of Laws* (first published 1748), Prometheus Books, Amherst 2002. See R. Shackleton, *Montesquieu: A Critical Biography*, Oxford University Press, Oxford 1961, p. 150.

considerable. This can be seen in Article 41 of the Communist Party Charter, according to which:

1. The Party leads the State and socio-political organisations by means of the political Party platform, strategies, policies; by ideological work, organisation, staff and inspection and supervision of the implementation.
2. The Party introduces qualified cadres to stand for election or be appointed to State agencies and socio-political organisations.

Therefore, the state apparatus is under the leadership of the Communist Party. For this to work, in Vietnam the Communist Party's organisational system is established in correspondence with the state's organisational system. The Communist Party's agencies at each level are groups of communists of each state body at that level, including the People's Courts. Usually, the President or Vice-President of the People's Committee of each level is the leader of the Party agency of that level, who might consequently influence judges. To further understand this influence of the Communist Party's agencies, it is necessary to explore the relationship between the judiciary and the executive and the Communist Party apparatus as follows.

Figure 1. The relationship between the judiciary, the executive and the Communist Party apparatus

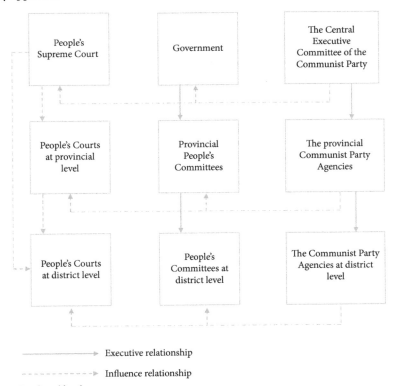

Source: Produced by the rapporteurs.

This leading role of the Communist Party is mentioned in the Communist Party Charter but not in any piece of legislation. Therefore, there is a point of view that:

> the Party's leadership over adjudication activities is currently not clearly and specifically legislated, which leads to the fact that many Party organizations or Party Committees have been leading 'directly and comprehensively' the activities of the Court and interfered in settlement of some cases that may affect the independence of the trial, such as the land corruption in Do Son case, the Farm in the Hau River case.[23]

As a result, Dr Nguyen Son, former Deputy Chief Justice of the Supreme People's Court, has pointed out that the Supreme People's Court had proposed two solutions: (i) to have a separate Party Committee for the Supreme People's Court that is directly under the leadership of the Politburo; and (ii) to establish regional first-instance People's Courts that do not depend on administrative units, instead of People's Courts at the district level.[24]

So, in principle, judges must be independent and impartial and only obey laws. However, the independence is not absolute because external authorities' ability to potentially interfere in judicial activities remains worrisome, which is one of the disadvantages of the courts compared to arbitration. This is because, like in other countries in the world, arbitral institutions in Vietnam are also independent and the LCA permits each party to appoint an arbitrator constituting the tribunal. Therefore, the arbitral tribunal does not represent the state in the hearing. Thus, it can be said that, organisationally, arbitral institutions and arbitrators are not influenced by state power, as the judiciary is. Apart from external control over the courts, can there be any internal control over judges in Vietnam?

3.1.1.2. Independence of Judges and the Internal Organisation of Courts in Vietnam

There can be no independence of judges in hearings if the other stages of proceedings are not declared independent, namely, if the livelihoods of judges

---

[23] La Thị Quế, 'Giải pháp nâng cao tính độc lập xét xử của Toà án trong Nhà nước pháp quyền ở Việt Nam hiện nay' [Solutions to improve the judicial independence of the courts in the current rule of law in Vietnam], *Industry and Trade Magazine of the Ministry of Industry and Trade*, available at https://tapchicongthuong.vn/bai-viet/giai-phap-nang-cao-tinh-doc-lap-xet-xu-cua-toa-an-trong-nha-nuoc-phap-quyen-o-viet-nam-hien-nay-57327.html.

[24] Minh Đức, 'Những trăn chở về độc lập xét xử' [Concerns about judicial independence], *Laws magazine under the leadership of the Department of Justice of Ho Chi Minh City*, available at https://plo.vn/phap-luat/nhung-tran-tro-ve-doc-lap-xet-xu-949679.html; see more details in the Resolution No. 49-NQ/TW of 2 June 2005 of the Politburo on the judicial reform strategy until 2020, in which the Party directed that it is necessary to prepare the conditions for the establishment of regional courts at the first-instance level and step by step renovate the organisation of the People's Court system at all levels.

Vietnam

are still dependent on the legislature, the executive and other powerful bodies of the state, such as governmental agencies and Party leadership agencies at a local and central level.[25] Therefore, it is crucial to study the independence of judges by looking at the mechanism for appointing judges in Vietnam.

3.1.1.2.1. APPOINTING JUDGES

In Vietnam, to become a judge, an individual must: (i) be a Vietnamese citizen, loyal to the Fatherland and the Constitution of the Socialist Republic of Vietnam; (ii) have good moral qualities, a strong political will, a courageous spirit and be resolute regarding justice protection, and in his or her integrity and honesty; (iii) possess a bachelor's degree in law or higher; (iv) have been trained in adjudication; (v) have at least five years of practical legal experience; and (vi) be in good health to complete his or her assigned tasks.[26] In addition, each individual must pass the exam organised by the National Judge Selection and Supervision Council. In addition, he or she might have to satisfy a requirement of the Communist Party that is not legislated as analysed above. Individuals satisfying these requirements will be chosen, following the recruitment needs of the Court system, by the Chief Justice of the Supreme People's Court, who shall submit to the National Assembly a list of proposed judges for approval.[27] The first mandate of a judge is five years; if reappointed, the next mandate is 10 years.[28]

According to the above procedure for appointing judges, it can be seen that the judges of the lower courts are organisationally dependent on the Chief Justice of the Supreme People's Court. For instance, if the judges of the lower courts do not follow the instruction of the Chief Justice, their judgments could be subsequently vacated; as a result, they would not be reappointed at the end of their mandate. Namely, relating to reappointment, Decision No. 120/QD-TANDTC[29] provides that judges cannot be reappointed at the end of their appointment if the total number of judgments and decisions set aside due to subjective fault accounts for more than 3% of the total number of cases settled or tried by the judge.[30] If this is the case, not being reappointed significantly affects the reputation and psychology of the judge. As a result, independence and impartiality are not guaranteed. Research or practice on the implementation

---

[25] Nguyễn Đăng Dung, 'Cải cách tư pháp trong cơ cấu quyền lực Nhà nước' [Judicial reform in the State power structure] (2009) 03(52) *Vietnamese Journal of Legal Sciences* 40, available at https://tapchikhplvn.hcmulaw.edu.vn/module/xemchitietbaibao?oid=c86813f7-b4ce-4d16-94d0-46c38ab70b61.

[26] LOPC, Article 67.

[27] Ibid., Article 72, para. 1.

[28] Ibid., Article 74.

[29] Decision No. 120/QD-TANDTC of 19 June 2017 of the Supreme People's Court of Vietnam promulgating regulations on handling responsibilities of judicial cadres in people's courts.

[30] Ibid., Article 13, para. 1.

Intersentia

667

of the principle show that judges adjudicate independently and obey only laws as follows:

> The current Constitution does not stipulate the administrative relationship between courts at all levels. There are no superior courts and lower courts, only first-instance and appellate courts, courts performing the functions of cassation and reopening. These courts exercise their judicial powers independently of each other ... However, there is still a situation where the superior courts manage the lower courts in terms of organization, finance, and professional direction. In some cases, the intervention of court leaders in adjudication activities has deeply interfered with the judge's adjudication activities. There are even cases for personal interests the Chief Justice instructs and orients the Trial Panel. In fact, the status that judges consult court leaders is still high. The fact that provincial and district judges consult with the President of Court at each level about the case's solution still accounts for a large proportion.[31]

Due to this situation, there have been recommendations that:

> Judges must have a long mandate, possibly even a lifetime mandate, a commensurate salary, and not be influenced by the political activities of the legislature and the executive. If judges are only appointed for a short term in any way or by any branch/authority, they will not have an independent and determined spirit. Moreover, a judge is a particular profession that is constantly under pressure from public opinion and threatened by dangerous forces in society. So without a long mandate and solid salary regime, it would be difficult to recruit talented, virtuous, fair, and impartial people in judicial activities. The independence of judges is an important factor in meeting the rule of law requirements in terms of limiting State power and ensuring the implementation of democratic and human rights.[32]

It can be said that, due to the importance of the independence of judges, proposals to extend the mandate of judges have also been supported by many experts in Vietnam.[33] However, this proposal has not yet been accepted by Vietnamese legislators.

---

[31] Trần Thị Thu Hằng, 'Nguyên tắc Thẩm phán, Hội thẩm xét xử độc lập và chỉ tuân theo pháp luật – Thực tiễn thực hiện và kiến nghị' [Principles that judges and jurors are independent and only obey the law – Practical implementation and recommendations], *Online Revue of People's Court under leadership of the Supreme People's Court*, available at https://www.tapchitoaan.vn/bai-viet/phap-luat/nguyen-tac-tham-phan-hoi-tham-xet-xu-doc-lap-va-chi-tuan-theo-phap-luat-thuc-tien-thuc-hien-va-kien-nghi.

[32] Nguyễn Đăng Dung, 'Cải cách tư pháp trong cơ cấu quyền lực Nhà nước' [Judicial reform in the State power structure] (2009) 03(52) *Vietnamese Journal of Legal Sciences* 40, available at https://tapchikhplvn.hcmulaw.edu.vn/module/xemchitietbaibao?oid=c86813f7-b4ce-4d16-94d0-46c38ab70b61.

[33] Nguyễn Sơn Hà, 'Những điều kiện đảm bảo cho thẩm phán xét xử độc lập và chỉ tuân theo pháp luật' [Conditions for ensuring judges to adjudicate independently and obey only the law] (2013) 11(243) *Journal of Legislative Studies*, available at https://thuvienphapluat.vn/van-ban/Bo-may-hanh-chinh/Hien-phap-nam-2013-215627.aspx.

Thus, the pressure on judges to take responsibility if a lot of their judgments are set aside is different from that on arbitrators in Vietnam. Namely, the LCA does not include any provision on adverse consequences for the arbitrator if his or her award is set aside by the national court. On that point, commenting on the Law, Associate Professor Van Dai Do, who is also an arbitrator, has pointed out that:

> The responsibility of the arbitrator should not be laid down too easily. This does not amount to the fact that the arbitrator is entirely irresponsible for his work ... It is necessary to have specific rules for the arbitrator's responsibilities. The clearer the arbitrator's obligations is provided, the more trust and prestige the arbitrator gains ... Therefore, the Law must regulate the arbitrator's responsibility if he intentionally violates laws or has serious negligence in the arbitral proceedings.[34]

According to these analyses of Associate Professor Dai, the fact that an arbitrator or judge has to assume responsibility if a judgment or an arbitral award is set aside due to his or her fault does not affect the independence or impartiality of the adjudicator. But 'assign[ing] responsibility too easily to the arbitrator will make the arbitrator feel insecure when adjudicating'.[35] However, regarding what is meant by an 'intentional violation' of arbitrator or the 'subject fault' of a judge, as provided in Decision 12/QD-TANDTC above, Huynh Nghia, a Congressman, has explained that any fault committed by arbitrators during the arbitral proceedings must be considered intentional or subjective.[36] According to this explanation, if a judgment or an arbitral award is set aside, this naturally amounts to there having been a deliberate fault of the judge or arbitrator. Consequently, the risk that this judge is unable to be reappointed is considerable. This can affect the independence of judges. Therefore, in his research, Tran Anh Tuan has suggested that 'the Supreme People's Court must explain clearly and specifically what is meant by "subjective fault" of the judge'.[37]

3.1.1.2.2. ASSIGNING COURT CASES TO JUDGES

Apart from these issues, regarding the internal relationship between judges at each court level, attention must also be paid to the assignment of cases to judges by the president of the court. The CPC provides that 'assigning procedure-conducting persons must ensure that they will be impartial and objective when

---

34 Đỗ Văn Đại and Trần Hoàng Hải (eds), *Pháp luật về trọng tài thương mại* [Laws on commercial arbitration], Chính Trị Quốc Gia, 2011, p. 200.

35 Ibid., p. 199.

36 Ibid., p. 198.

37 Trần Anh Tuấn, 'Quyền được xét xử bởi một toà án độc lập, khách quan theo một thời hạn hợp lý trong tố tụng dân sự' [Right to a trial by an independent, impartial court within a reasonable period of time in civil proceedings] (2018) 12 *Ha Noi Law Review* 49.

performing their tasks and powers'.[38] Under Article 47 of the CPC, the president of the court is competent to assign cases to judges of his or her court. So, in this situation, judges might be dependent on the president of the court; otherwise, they might not have cases to adjudicate because the laws do not contain specific provisions on the process of assigning cases to judges. Moreover, random assignment may lead to complex and thorny cases being given to unqualified people. This is worrisome because, in practice, 'there are the judges who want to avoid these thorny cases, especially disputes relating to finance, banking, redundancy, property design, land use boundaries … which might influence on objectivity in hearing the case'.[39] There is even the case of a judge of a district court in a rural area who, in order to get reappointed, created 57 false lawsuit records.[40] Therefore, it has been suggested that it is necessary to develop an electronic online system that publicly publishes the list of judges of each court and the cases assigned to them.[41]

3.1.1.2.3. INDEPENDENCE OF EACH MEMBER OF A TRIAL JURY

Finally, another question is whether the adjudicator's independence includes the independence of each adjudicator from the rest of the adjudicating panel. This question was raised because, in practice, there was a case where an arbitral award was subject to a request to set aside on the grounds that the tribunal was not independent and impartial because the arbitrator appointed by the claimant and the one appointed by the defendant worked in the same university and had a superior–subordinate relationship. However, the People's Court of Ho Chi Minh City[42] rejected this request, judging that only a superior–subordinate relationship in the same organisation is not grounds for asserting that the arbitrators are not 'independent, objective, impartial'; thus, the request was unfounded.

In the case at hand, there was only speculation as to the colleague relationship between the arbitrators and no evidence to prove the non-independence

---

[38]   CPC, Article 16, para. 2.

[39]   Vũ Thanh Tuấn, 'Một số bất cập của bộ luật tố tụng dân sự năm 2015 và phương hướng hoàn thiện' [Some inadequacies of the Civil Procedure Code 2015 and directions for finishing] (2021) 9 *Legal Profession Review*, available at https://iluatsu.com/dan-su/mot-so-bat-cap-cua-bo-luat-to-tung-dan-su-nam-2015-va-phuong-huong-hoan-thien/.

[40]   Anh Tuấn, 'Vụ tòa huyện lập 57 hồ sơ khống: Hành vi vi phạm pháp luật nghiêm trọng' [The district court made 57 false records: Serious violation of laws], *Online Magazine of the Communist Party*, 19 June 2021, available at https://dangcongsan.vn/ban-doc/luat-su-cua-ban/vu-toa-huyen-lap-57-ho-so-khong-hanh-vi-vi-pham-phap-luat-nghiem-trong-583361.html.

[41]   Vũ Thanh Tuấn, 'Một số bất cập của bộ luật tố tụng dân sự năm 2015 và phương hướng hoàn thiện' [Some inadequacies of the Civil Procedure Code 2015 and directions for finishing], (2021) 9 *Legal Profession Review*, available at https://iluatsu.com/dan-su/mot-so-bat-cap-cua-bo-luat-to-tung-dan-su-nam-2015-va-phuong-huong-hoan-thien/.

[42]   Decision No. 147/2017/QĐ-PQTT of 17 February 2017 of the People's Court of Ho Chi Minh City.

Vietnam

and objectivity of the arbitrator. It follows that if one party can prove that non-independence exists between arbitrators, the court can set aside the award. This amounts to the independence of an adjudicator being required not only in relationships with external subjects but also in the relationships between members of the tribunal themselves. The CPC stipulates that judges must refuse to hear a case if they are on the same panel as a relative;[43] in this case, only one person can proceed with the case.

3.1.2. *Independence of Adjudicators from the Parties to Dispute*

The principle that adjudicators must be independent in adjudication also requires the absence of legally relevant relationships between adjudicators and the parties to a dispute. An arbitrator must refuse to settle the dispute, and the parties have the right to request the replacement of an arbitrator to settle the dispute, in the following situations:

a) The arbitrator is a relative or representative of a party;
b) The arbitrator has a related interest in the dispute; …
d) the arbitrator had been a mediator, representative or lawyer of any party before the dispute was brought to arbitration unless otherwise agreed in writing by the parties.[44]

Under this provision, there are different situations in which arbitrators are considered relevant to the parties to the dispute. In any of these situations, either the arbitrator must actively refuse to settle the dispute, or a party can request the replacement of the arbitrator. This is the same in judicial proceedings. Namely, the procedure-conducting persons must refuse to conduct proceedings or must be replaced if:

1. They are concurrently the involved parties, representatives, and relatives of the involved parties;
2. They had participated in the proceedings as defenders of the legitimate rights and interests of the involved parties, witnesses, experts, and interpreters in the same case.[45]

From all the foregoing, the independence of adjudicators in a hearing requires that they must be independent from all other subjects, such as external authorities, the superior court, the president of the court and other members of the trial panel.

---

[43] CPC, Article 53, para. 2.
[44] LCA, Article 42.
[45] CPC, Article 53.

Intersentia

671

3.2. IMPARTIALITY OF ADJUDICATORS

As regards the impartiality of adjudicators, it has been considered that:

> Impartiality consists of two notions: the subjective impartiality and the objective impartiality. The subjective impartiality refers to the personal convictions and behavior of the members of the court or tribunal. It requires that a judge does not act with a personal bias towards one of the parties and that he or she hears a matter without a pre-conceived view on the merit. The personal impartiality of a judge or a court will be presumed unless there is proof of actual bias ... Considerations relevant to the objective impartiality of a court or tribunal will often be similar to those relating to its independence from the executive and the parties.[46]

According to this theory, objective impartiality relates to the independence of a court or tribunal from the executive and the parties, which has been analysed above and will therefore not be mentioned again. Thus, the present section will only be devoted to the subjective impartiality of adjudicators, which refers to the personal convictions and behaviours of the members of the court or tribunal in each specific situation. Because this concerns the personal convictions and behaviours of adjudicators, it will be difficult to define a scope. As a result, on this matter, Vietnamese laws provide in a general manner that adjudicators must refuse to settle the dispute or be replaced if 'there is clear ground to believe that they might not be impartial while performing their task'.[47]

In practice, for example, in arbitration, one party applied to set aside an award on the ground that the arbitrators were not impartial because they had incorrectly applied provisions of the LCA relevant to determining when the claimant knew or ought to have known about the product defect. However, this appeal was not admitted by the People's Court of Ho Chi Minh City, judging that 'apart from the above argument, the plaintiff had not produced any other evidence to prove that the arbitrator is not independent, objective, impartial or does not comply with the provisions of the Law, affecting the objectivity and fairness of the arbitral award'.[48]

Thus, according to this reasoning, it is necessary to have evidence to prove that an arbitrator is not impartial and the burden of proof falls on the claimant's shoulders. Another illustration can be found in a case in which the claimant argued that the arbitral tribunal was not impartial and independent because it did not respect the agreement of the parties. However, the Appellate Court of

---

[46] Ben Olbourne, 'Independence and Impartiality: International Standards for National Judges and Courts' (2003) 2 *Law & Practice of International Courts & Tribunals* 97.

[47] LCA, Article 42; CPC, Article 53.

[48] Decision No. 509/2015/QĐ-PQTT of 27 May 2015 of the People's Court of Ho Chi Minh City.

the Supreme People's Court did not accept this argument because the claimant did not produce any evidence.[49] This burden of proof on the claimant is the same in judicial proceedings. Namely, in a case relating to a dispute on the division of property in a divorce, the wife asked to change the judge because the latter was not impartial when accepting the husband's request. However, the Court rejected this request because the wife had failed to prove that the judge was not impartial.[50] The question can therefore be raised as to what element can affect the independence or impartiality of the adjudicator? On that point, the Council of Judges of the Supreme People's Court has explained that if a disputing party provides evidence that the arbitral award was made through coercion, deception, intimidation or bribery, it can be considered as breaching the principle of independence and impartiality of arbitrators.[51]

The right to have an independent and impartial trial is enshrined in the Constitution and specific laws, as can be seen from the foregoing. In the event of the absence of independence and impartiality of adjudicators, they can be replaced. So, the question is: what are the consequences for the enforcement of an arbitral award or a judgment made in breach of this principle?

4. ENFORCEMENT OF AN ARBITRAL AWARD OR A JUDGMENT BREACHING THE PRINCIPLE OF INDEPENDENCE AND IMPARTIALITY OF ADJUDICATORS

On this point, the analysis below will explore successively the issue in relation to arbitral awards and judgments.

4.1. ENFORCEMENT OF AN ARBITRAL AWARD THAT BREACHES THE PRINCIPLE OF INDEPENDENCE AND IMPARTIALITY OF ADJUDICATORS

Relating to an award, there are two different legal regimes for enforcement of domestic and foreign arbitral awards.

A foreign award can be recognised and enforced under the New York Convention of 1958 or the CPC if the award originates from a country not

---

[49] Decision No. 05/2010/KDTM-PQTT of 15 January 2010 of the Appellate Court of the Supreme People's Court in Ho Chi Minh City.

[50] Decision No. 13/2019/HNGD-ST of 28 March 2019 of People's Court of District of Thai Thuy of Thai Binh Province.

[51] Article 14, para. (d) of Resolution No. 01/2014/NQ-HĐTP instructing implementation of some provisions of the Law on Commercial Arbitration.

party to the New York Convention of 1958. It has been recognised that the New York Convention of 1958 does not have any provision directly mentioning the principle of independence or impartiality of an arbitrator. And the grounds permitting refusal of an application for recognition and enforcement of a foreign award are similar to those provided in Article 459 of the CPC. However, according to the New York Convention Guide, there are many countries that have implemented the Convention in such a manner that an award that breaches the principle of independence and impartiality of arbitrators is contrary to the procedural public policy of these countries and can be refused for exequatur.[52] On that point, according to information published by the Ministry of Justice of Vietnam, between 2012 and now, it has been the case that foreign awards were not recognised due to being contrary to the public policy of Vietnam but neither of them relating to breaching the principle of independence and impartiality of arbitrators.[53] In addition, there have been no awards refused directly on the grounds of breach of the principle of independence and impartiality of arbitrators.

For a national award, a defective award can be set aside under Article 68 of the LCA. As far as independence and impartiality of arbitrators is concerned, this Law provides that the court can annul an award made by 'arbitrators who receive money, property or other material benefits of a disputing party and [whose] conduct affects the objectivity and fairness of the arbitral award'.[54] According to this provision, there must be three elements to set aside an award on grounds of a breach of the principle of independence and impartiality of arbitrators: (i) the arbitrator must have received material benefits, but not moral benefits; (ii) these benefits must come from a disputing party; and (iii) the defective conduct of the arbitrator must be such that it 'affects the objectivity and fairness of the arbitral award'. On that point, some believe that 'if, in a three-member tribunal, only one member has a defective conduct and his/her views are minor, this conduct is also not considered as affecting the fairness of the award; and as a result, the award is unable to be set aside'.[55] This shows that Vietnam is indeed conscious of limiting interference with arbitration

---

[52]   The New York Convention Guide, available at https://newyorkconvention1958.org/index. php?lvl=cmspage&pageid=10&menu=626&opac_view=-1.

[53]   Website on international laws of the Ministry of Justice, available at https://moj.gov.vn/tttp/ Pages/dlcn-va-th-tai-Viet-Nam.aspx?fbclid=IwAR2z5ftEuTBmx94OyKzkCh08ZFUZyta1f tj_q4pYtz8X7DI_ohChvqcwhdI#.

[54]   LCA, Article 68, para. d.

[55]   Phan Thông Anh, 'Căn cứ huỷ phán quyết trọng tài liên quan đến chứng cứ và sự khách quan của trọng tài viên trong tố tụng trọng tài-Bất cập và hướng hoàn thiện' [Grounds for annulment of arbitral awards related to evidence and arbitrator's impartiality in arbitral proceedings – Inadequacies and directions for improvement] (2015) 06(91) *Vietnamese Journal of Legal Science* 57, available at https://tapchikhplvn.hcmulaw.edu.vn/module/ xemchitietbaibao?oid=5279a326-763f-4cee-b6a8-d20c552b0c4a.

activities, except in extreme cases listed in Article 68 of the LCA. When there is a request to set aside an award, its enforcement will be suspended until there is a court decision rejecting the request.[56] The national court's decision to admit or refuse this request becomes final and binding without being subject to any appeal. However, this mechanism led to the fact that different solutions for the same issue referred to different courts relating to setting aside an award in practice, which can make citizens suspicious of the justice system. Thus, it has been suggested that appeal for cassation against a court's decision on a request to set aside an award must be admitted.[57]

Apart from these issues reflecting Vietnam's support for arbitral activities, another point worth noting is that the statute of limitations for a request to set aside an award is short, specifically 30 days from receipt of the arbitral award under Article 69 of the LCA.

4.2. ENFORCEMENT OF A JUDGMENT THAT BREACHES THE PRINCIPLE OF INDEPENDENCE AND IMPARTIALITY OF ADJUDICATORS

As analysed above, in Vietnam, a judgment of the first instance can be reviewed at the Appellate Court and a judgment of the latter can be appealed to the superior court for cassation review or retrial.

4.2.1. Conditions to Appeal for Cassation Review and Retrial

As regards appealing against a judgment at first instance, this right is enshrined in the CPC without any condition for doing so. Thus, it is understandable that a disputing party can freely refer the judgment at first instance to the Appellate Court provided that this appeal is within the statute of limitations of 15 days from the pronouncement of the judgment or from the receipt of the judgment by the party who was absent from the hearing for a reasonable causes.[58] However, the fact that there are no conditions for appeal to the Appellate Court does not mean that this appeal can be admitted at first instance without any condition. For example, as regards the principle of independence and impartiality of judges, as mentioned in the previous section, a judgment can only be vacated if

---

[56] LCA, Article 66.
[57] Nguyễn Thị Hoa, 'Hoàn thiện pháp luật trọng tài ở Việt Nam hiện nay' [Completing the arbitration law in Vietnam today] (2021) 12(436) *Journal of Legislative Studies*, available at http://lapphap.vn/Pages/TinTuc/210862/Hoan-thien-phap-luat-trong-tai-o-Viet-Nam-hien-nay.html.
[58] CPC, Article 273.

the appellants can produce evidence to prove that the court of first instance was not independent or impartial in its hearing.

As for appealing for cassation review, the first paragraph of Article 326 of the CPC provides conditions as follows:

a) The conclusion in the judgment or decision is not consistent with the objective details of the case and causes damages to the lawful rights and interests of the involved parties;

b) There is a serious procedural violation that makes the involved parties unable to perform their procedural rights and obligations and results in their legitimate rights and interests not being protected under law;

c) There is a mistake in the application of the law leading to the issuance of incorrect judgments or decisions, causing damage to the lawful rights and interests of the involved parties, infringing upon public interests and the interests of the State, the legal rights and interests of a third party.

This provision thus does not directly mention that a breach of the principle of independence and impartiality of judges is a condition to appeal for cassation review. As a consequence, question arises whether such a breach would be considered a serious procedural violation as provided for in point (b) of the first paragraph of Article 326 of the CPC above and would be subject to an appeal for cassation review. Because the CPC is not clear, there is an opinion that the Supreme Court needs to give specific instructions about this provision.[59] Therefore, recently, the Council of Judges of the Supreme People's Court has drawn up a Resolution Draft, and its Article 14 instructs that the fact that the persons conducting the procedure are not replaced when there is clear evidence that they will be not independent or impartial in the hearing can be considered a serious procedural violation under the Article 326 of the CPC.[60]

Apart from being subject to an appeal for cassation review, a judgment made by a judge who is not independent or impartial is also subject to an appeal for retrial. This is because Vietnam permits an appeal against a judgment if the judge intentionally falsifies the case files or intentionally reaches illegal conclusions.[61] It follows that if a judge is not impartial and reaches an illegal conclusion, his or her judgment can be vacated under the retrial procedure.

---

[59] Thạch Phước Bình, 'Kháng nghị giám đốc thẩm trong tố tụng dân sự' [Appeal for cassation review in civil proceedings] (2020) 13(413) *Journal of Legislative Studies*, available at http://lapphap.vn/Pages/tintuc/tinchitiet.aspx?tintucid=210590.

[60] Text No. 132/TANDTC-PC of 20 August 2020 relating to seeking comments on the Resolution Draft guiding a number of provisions on cassation review and retrial, available at https://www.toaan.gov.vn/webcenter/ShowProperty?nodeId=/UCMServer/TAND137744.

[61] CPC, Article 352, para. 3.

Vietnam

4.2.2. Disputing a Party's Right to Appeal for Cassation Review and Retrial

The analyses above indicate that a defective judgment made by a judge who is not independent or impartial can be subject to an appeal for cassation review or retrial. However, it should be noted that under the CPC disputing parties do not have the right to directly appeal to the Supreme Court. They can only file a request with the People's Procuracy[62] and the head of the latter will decide whether it is necessary to appeal for cassation review or retrial in each case.[63]

5. CONCLUSION

From all the foregoing, it can be said that the principle of independence and impartiality of adjudicators is enshrined in Vietnamese law. However, it is sometimes the case that this principle is breached in practice. Nevertheless, according to the information published by the Supreme Court,[64] the latter is developing, under the leadership of the Communist Party, a strategy for judicial reform at the People's Court to 2030, with a vision to 2045. Thus, elements that have a negative influence on the independence and impartiality of adjudicators, as analysed above, will be subject to reform, such as issues relating to salary, judges' qualifications, and particularly re-organisation of the judiciary by the establishment of regional courts at the first-instance level, which is considered a key element to improve the independence of the courts. Therefore, one may look forward to seeing a higher quality of justice in Vietnam in the coming years.

---

[62]   Ibid., Article 70, para. 23.
[63]   Ibid., Article 57, para. 1.
[64]   Website of the Supreme People's Court: https://www.toaan.gov.vn/webcenter/portal/tatc/chi-tiet-tin?dDocName=TAND189785.

Intersentia

APPENDIX

QUESTIONNAIRE

Special Non-National Reports

The *special non-national rapporteurs* are kindly asked to explain, for the relevant type of international adjudication, the state of the law, of the legal debate and of practice on the issues listed in sections 3–10 of the Comments, summarised below:

1. Criteria for the selection of the adjudicators
    Examples of issues that can be analysed: Criteria for selecting the adjudicators; underlying interests: representation, independence, combination
2. Which authority appoints the adjudicators?
    Examples of issues that can be analysed: Appointing authority (based on closeness to the dispute or on independence), party appointment (bias and double-hatting versus qualification), combination
3. The method for appointing the adjudicators
    Examples of issues that can be analysed: Election, appointment, consent, combination; random allocation, by rotation, discretionary assignment
4. Methods to balance the appointing authority's influence on the appointment of the adjudicators
    Examples of issues that can be analysed: Reappointment, service period; double-hatting, issue conflict; confidentiality of deliberations, ban of dissenting opinions; financing of the adjudication activity
5. Parameters to ensure that the adjudicators act independently and impartially
    Examples of issues that can be analysed: Guidelines, codes of conduct, binding rules; conflict of interest; repeat appointments, double-hatting, issue conflict; disclosure; quarantine
6. Consequences for the adjudicator of a breach by the adjudicator of the requirement to act independently and impartially
    Examples of issues that can be analysed: Removal as sanction, as undue influence; removing authority; party-initiated challenge
7. Enforceability of a final decision that was rendered by an adjudicator who breached the requirement to act independently and impartially
    Examples of issues that can be analysed: Finality of the decision; control of validity, enforcement; national or international standards; public policy

Intersentia

679

Appendix: Questionnaire

QUESTIONNAIRE

Rapports Spéciaux Non Nationaux

Les *rapporteurs spéciaux non nationaux* sont priés de bien vouloir expliquer, pour le type de résolution internationale des différends traité, l'état du droit, du débat juridique et de la pratique sur les questions énumérées dans les sections 3 à 10 des observations, résumées ci-dessous :

1. Critères pour la sélection des décideurs
   Exemples de problèmes pouvant être analysés : critères de sélection des décideurs ; intérêts sous-jacents : représentation, indépendance, combinaison
2. Quelle autorité nomme les décideurs ?
   Exemples de problèmes pouvant être analysés : autorité de désignation (basée sur la proximité au litige ou sur l'indépendance), désignation par les parties (parti pris et double casquette versus qualification), combinaison
3. Mode de désignation des décideurs
   Exemples de problèmes pouvant être analysés : élection, désignation, consentement, combinaison ; désignation aléatoire, par rotation, désignation discrétionnaire
4. Méthodes permettant d'équilibrer l'influence de l'autorité de désignation sur la désignation des décideurs
   Exemples de problèmes pouvant être analysés : désignation répétée, période de service ; double casquette, problème de conflit ; confidentialité des délibérations, interdiction des opinions dissidentes ; financement de l'activité de résolution des différends
5. Paramètres garantissant que les décideurs agissent de manière indépendante et impartiale
   Exemples de problèmes pouvant être analysés : lignes directrices, codes de conduite, règles contraignantes ; conflit d'intérêt ; désignations répétées, double casquette, problème de conflit ; divulgation ; quarantaine
6. Conséquences pour le décideur d'un manquement du décideur à l'obligation d'agir de manière indépendante et impartiale
   Exemples de problèmes pouvant être analysés : le retrait comme sanction, comme influence indue ; autorité de retrait ; récusation initiée par une partie
7. Possibilité d'exécution d'une décision finale rendue par un décideur n'ayant pas respecté l'exigence d'agir de manière indépendante et impartiale
   Exemples de problèmes pouvant être analysés : finalité de la décision ; contrôle de validité, exécution ; normes nationales ou internationales ; ordre public

680

Intersentia

Appendix: Questionnaire

QUESTIONNAIRE

Special National Reports

The *special national rapporteurs* are kindly asked to explain the state of the law, of the legal debate and of practice on the issues listed in sections 3–10 of the Comments, summarised below:

1. Criteria for the selection of domestic adjudicators
2. Criteria for the selection of national candidates to positions as international adjudicators
   Examples of issues that can be analysed: Criteria for selecting the adjudicators; underlying interests: representation, independence, combination
3. Which authority appoints domestic adjudicators?
4. Which authority appoints national candidates to positions as international adjudicators?
   Examples of issues that can be analysed: Appointing authority (based on closeness to the dispute or on independence), party appointment (bias and double-hatting versus qualification), combination
5. The method for appointing domestic adjudicators
6. The method for appointing national candidates to positions as international adjudicators
   Examples of issues that can be analysed: Election, appointment, consent, combination; random allocation, by rotation, discretionary assignment
7. Methods to balance the appointing authority's influence on the appointment of domestic adjudicators
8. Methods to balance the appointing authority's influence on the appointment of national candidates to positions as international adjudicators
   Examples of issues that can be analysed: Reappointment, service period; double-hatting, issue conflict; confidentiality of deliberations, ban of dissenting opinions; financing of the adjudication activity
9. Parameters to ensure that domestic adjudicators act independently and impartially
10. National parameters (if any) to ensure that nationals appointed to positions as international adjudicators act independently and impartially
    Examples of issues that can be analysed: Guidelines, codes of conduct, binding rules; conflict of interest; repeat appointments, double-hatting, issue conflict; disclosure; quarantine

Intersentia

Appendix: Questionnaire

11. Consequences for the domestic adjudicator of a breach by the adjudicator of the requirement to act independently and impartially
12. Consequences (if any) for nationals appointed to positions as international adjudicators of a breach by the adjudicator of the requirement to act independently and impartially
Examples of issues that can be analysed: Removal as sanction, as undue influence; removing authority; party-initiated challenge
13. Enforcement of a final decision by a domestic court, if the decision was rendered by a domestic adjudicator who breached the requirement to act independently and impartially
14. Enforcement of a final decision by a foreign or international tribunal, if the decision was rendered by a foreign or international adjudicator who breached the requirement to act independently and impartially
Examples of issues that can be analysed: Finality of the decision; Control of validity, enforcement; national or international standards; public policy

QUESTIONNAIRE

Rapports Spéciaux Nationaux

Les *rapporteurs spéciaux nationaux* sont priés de bien vouloir expliquer, l'état du droit, du débat juridique et de la pratique sur les questions énumérées dans les sections 3 à 10 des observations, résumées ci-dessous :

1. Critères de sélection des décideurs nationaux
2. Critères de sélection des candidats nationaux aux postes de décideur international

   Exemples de problèmes pouvant être analysés : critères de sélection des décideurs ; intérêts sous-jacents : représentation, indépendance, combinaison
3. Quelle autorité nomme/désigne les décideurs nationaux ?
4. Quelle autorité nomme/désigne les candidats nationaux aux postes de décideur international ?

   Exemples de problèmes pouvant être analysés : autorité de désignation/ nomination (basée sur la proximité au litige ou sur l'indépendance), désignation par les parties (parti pris et double casquette versus qualification), combinaison
5. La méthode de désignation/nomination des décideurs nationaux
6. La méthode de désignation/nomination des candidats nationaux aux postes de décideur international

   Exemples de problèmes pouvant être analysés : élection, désignation/ nomination, consentement, combinaison ; désignation/nomination aléatoire, par rotation, désignation discrétionnaire
7. Méthodes permettant d'équilibrer l'influence de l'autorité de désignation/ nomination sur la désignation/nomination des décideurs nationaux
8. Méthodes permettant d'équilibrer l'influence de l'autorité de désignation/ nomination sur la désignation/nomination des décideurs nationaux aux postes de décideur international

   Exemples de problèmes pouvant être analysés : désignation répétée, période de service ; double casquette, problème de conflit ; confidentialité des délibérations, interdiction des opinions dissidentes ; financement de l'activité de résolution des différends
9. Paramètres garantissant que les décideurs nationaux agissent de manière indépendante et impartiale
10. Paramètres (s'ils existent) garantissant que les nationaux nommés à un poste de décideur international agissent de manière indépendante et impartiale

Appendix: Questionnaire

Exemples de problèmes pouvant être analysés : lignes directrices, codes de conduite, règles contraignantes ; conflit d'intérêt ; désignations répétées, double casquette, problème de conflit ; divulgation ; quarantaine

11. Conséquences pour le décideur national d'un manquement du décideur à l'obligation d'agir de manière indépendante et impartiale

12. Conséquences (si elles existent) pour les nationaux nommés à un poste de décideur international en cas de manquement du décideur à l'obligation d'agir de manière indépendante et impartiale

    Exemples de problèmes pouvant être analysés : le retrait comme sanction, comme influence indue ; autorité de retrait ; récusation initiée par une partie

13. Possibilité d'exécution d'une décision finale rendue par une cour nationale, lorsque cette décision a été rendue par un décideur national n'ayant pas respecté l'exigence d'agir de manière indépendante et impartiale

14. Possibilité d'exécution d'une décision finale rendue par une cour internationale ou étrangère, lorsque cette décision a été rendue par un décideur international ou étranger n'ayant pas respecté l'exigence d'agir de manière indépendante et impartiale

    Exemples de problèmes pouvant être analysés : finalité de la décision ; contrôle de validité, exécution ; normes nationales ou internationales ; ordre public

COMMENTS TO THE QUESTIONNAIRES

1. THE INCREASED ATTENTION TO INDEPENDENCE AND IMPARTIALITY OF INTERNATIONAL ADJUDICATORS

International adjudication is a notion used to designate disparate methods for the settlement of international dispute resolution. It refers to a variety of disputes – ranging from private or commercial disputes, to disputes between a private party and a state, or disputes between states. The notion also refers to a variety of adjudicating bodies – ranging from ad hoc arbitral tribunals, to institutional arbitral tribunals, arbitral tribunals established by treaty, claim tribunals, international administrative tribunals, WTO panels, regional courts or permanent international courts.

The need to solve international disputes has grown in parallel with the increasing internationalisation that we witnessed in the second half of the 20th century, and it does not seem that it is decreasing at the current moment, which is instead characterised by decreasing globalisation and signs of emerging re-localisation. Possibly as a side effect of the emerging reversal of globalisation, international adjudication is the object of increasing criticism.

This applies, to varying degree, to all forms of international adjudication.

The International Court of Justice, for example, is criticised for, inter alia, its restricted jurisdiction, its ineffectiveness and also possible bias.[1]

The WTO Dispute Resolution System is criticised for possible bias and for exceeding its power.[2] Its ability to be operative is threatened since the US in 2018 declined to contribute to the appointment of new members, as a reaction to the Appellate Body's judicial overreach.[3]

The type of adjudication that has probably attracted the loudest criticism in recent years is investment arbitration.

---

[1] Gleider Ignacio Hernandez, 'Impartiality and Bias at the International Court of Justice' (2012) 1(3) *Cambridge Journal of International and Comparative Law* 183; Eric A. Posner and Miguel de Figueiredo, 'Is the International Court of Justice Biased?' (2005) 34(2) *The Journal of Legal Studies* 599.

[2] https://www.wto.org/english/thewto_e/10anniv_e/future_wto_chap6_e.pdf.

[3] https://www.wto.org/english/news_e/news18_e/ab_22jun18_e.htm.

Criticism of investment arbitration led to, among other things, a mandate by the UNCITRAL to its Working Group III to work on the possible reform of investor-state dispute settlement. Among other points, the criticism regards the impact of party appointment on the impartiality and independence of arbitrators.[4]

The European Union's active position against investment arbitration resulted, inter alia, in the agreement for the termination of bilateral investment treaties between the Member States of the European Union, signed in May 2020.

Commercial arbitration is also increasingly criticised for having become unnecessarily costly and time-consuming, as well as overregulated.[5] In part, this development is due to arbitral tribunals' increasing concern of avoiding suspicion of being partial. Arbitral tribunals more and more indulge the parties in sometimes unreasonable requests that new claims or new evidence be admitted, that terms be extended, etc. – falling for what is often called 'due process paranoia' and unnecessarily inflating the duration and cost of the proceedings.

While the requirement of independence and impartiality is not the only basis for the growing criticism against international adjudication, it constitutes an important element.

2. THE PURPOSE OF COMPARATIVE RESEARCH

The requirement that adjudicators shall be impartial and independent is a fundamental principle that can be found both in national law, usually at the level of the constitution, in international law[6] and in transnational soft law.[7] In addition, it is affirmed in rules of arbitrations, codes of ethics of international courts and codes of conduct of free trade agreements.

---

[4]   Working Group III (Investor-State Dispute Settlement Reform), Thirty-fourth session, Vienna, 27 November–1 December 2017, Possible reform of investor-State dispute settlement (ISDS) – Note by the Secretariat, A/CN.9/WG.III/WP.142, para. 20.

[5]   Queen Mary and White&Case 2015 Survey, 'Improvements and Innovations in International Arbitration', available at http://www.arbitration.qmul.ac.uk/media/arbitration/docs/2015_International_Arbitration_Survey.pdf.

[6]   See the European Convention on Human Rights, Article 6; the Universal Declaration of Human Rights, Article 10; the International Covenant on Civil and Political Rights, Article 14. Charles T. Kotuby Jr and Luke A. Sobota, *General Principles of Law and International Due Process*, Oxford University Press 2017, 157–202, identify independence and impartiality of the adjudicator as one of the elements of the principle of due process.

[7]   See, for example, Article 1 of the ALI/UNIDROIT Principles of Transnational Civil Procedure. The text of the Principles and the accompanying commentary, adopted by the American Law Institute (ALI) in May 2004 and by the International Institute for the Unification of Private Law (UNIDROIT) in April 2004, is available at https://www.unidroit.org/english/principles/civilprocedure/ali-unidroitprinciples-e.pdf.

Each type of dispute and each type of adjudicating body has its own legal framework. Some of these rely on national law or on uniform law (i.e. national law that has been harmonised by international conventions); some rely on public international law; some on a combination. Some are constituted ad hoc for a certain dispute; others are permanent. It is not necessarily evident that features from one adjudication system can be automatically transferred to all other systems.

Comparative research can highlight the specific content of the principle of independence and impartiality by assessing the criteria and mechanisms that each system puts in place to ensure that the principle is respected.

The aim is not necessarily to harmonise the various criteria and mechanisms. To the extent it exists, a convergence among the systems will be highlighted. More importantly, however, the interests that justify a divergence will be exposed and analysed. The intention is to provide an assessment of the different meanings that the principle of independence and impartiality may have and of how the different mechanisms may serve this diversity.

To this end, it is useful to assess the relevant criteria, mechanisms and remedies applicable in each system for the purpose of ensuring independence and impartiality of adjudicators.

Each special rapporteur is kindly asked to prepare a report explaining how the given national legal system (for special national rapporteurs) or the given type of international adjudication (for special non-national rapporteurs) deals with the different aspects of the principle of independence and impartiality, as described in sections 3–10 below.

3. BREAKING DOWN THE PRINCIPLE OF INDEPENDENCE AND IMPARTIALITY

To fully understand the implications of the principle of independence and impartiality in international adjudication, it is necessary to examine the issue from different angles.

Firstly, it is necessary to assess the criteria for selecting the adjudicators and to analyse what interests they intend to protect.

Secondly, it is necessary to assess who carries out the selection and, thirdly, on the basis of what mechanism. This may permit to assess whether the selection process actually permits to achieve the protection of the interests that the selection criteria intend to protect.

Fourthly, it is necessary to assess the parameters for the conduct of the adjudicators.

Finally, it is necessary to assess the remedies available in case the principle of independence and impartiality has been breached. This can, in turn, be divided into two parts: fifthly, the effects that the breach has on the adjudicator (e.g. removal from office); and sixthly, the effects that the breach has on the decision that was rendered by an adjudicator who was not independent or impartial (e.g. invalidity or unenforceability).

4. THE SELECTION CRITERIA

The criteria for selecting the adjudicators have a significant impact on the adjudicators' independence and impartiality. There are two main competing interests in the selection of adjudicators: representation and independence.

Representation assumes that the adjudicator is selected from the environment that is involved in the dispute: for example, a judge with the same nationality as the respondent state, or an arbitrator active in the specific business area in which the dispute arose. Representation ensures that decisions are taken by an adjudicator who is familiar with the legal system, the underlying issues, the branch uses, or other parameters that may be relevant. This ensures that the adjudicator has the necessary background to understand the issues in dispute. It also favours accountability of the adjudicator. On the other hand, familiarity with the underlying values may expose the adjudicator to bias, and accountability may create the risk of the adjudicator rendering a decision that is in favour of the party to which he or she is accountable.

Independence assumes that the adjudicator does not have any connection with the interests in dispute. While this may decrease the risk of bias, it may create the risk of misunderstandings due to the lack of familiarity with the involved legal system, the underlying issues, etc.

Different adjudication systems seem to address the need to balance representation and independence in different ways: the African Court on Human and Peoples' Rights, for example, always includes in the panel a judge from the respondent state, and so does the European Court of Human Rights. In arbitration, to the contrary, usually arbitrators, and certainly the presiding arbitrator, do not have the nationality of one of the parties. Common nationality is a criterion for qualification in the former and for disqualification in the latter.

Issues: Criteria for selecting the adjudicators; underlying interests: representation, independence, combination

5. THE SELECTING AUTHORITY

The identity of the selecting body is crucial to the selection of the adjudicator and may thus have a significant impact on the adjudicator's independence and impartiality. There are two main approaches: selection can be carried out by an appointing authority, or the adjudicators may be appointed by the parties involved. A combination may also be found: in arbitration, for example, a panel of three often consists of one arbitrator appointed by each of the parties, and a presiding arbitrator appointed by the party-appointed arbitrators.

The appointing authority may be a selection committee, a court or other body. Too close a connection between the appointing authority and one of the parties to the dispute may affect the independence of the appointed adjudicator. On the other hand, the result of the selection will depend on the appointing authority's familiarity with the requirements for effectively adjudicating the relevant type of disputes, its understanding of the relevant legal framework and its knowledge of how to identify qualified adjudicators. The identity of the appointing authority, therefore, may have a considerable impact not only on the independence and impartiality of the adjudicator, but also on the efficiency of the process.

Party appointment is often deemed to prejudice the legitimacy and accountability of the adjudicators. This has been recently argued in respect of investment arbitration. Arbitrators appointed by the parties are suspected of being biased and of being inclined to decide in favour of the party who appointed them, for the purpose of being appointed again by the same party in new disputes. The system of party appointment is also criticised for preventing diversity by confirming pre-existing connections, and for creating conflict of interests when professionals belonging to the same environment appoint each other or alternatively appear as counsel and as arbitrator (so-called double-hatting).

On the other hand, party appointment is the fundamental basis of a dispute settlement mechanism such as arbitration. It permits to select arbitrators for their expertise and their understanding of the specific area of the dispute. There may be few qualified experts in sophisticated areas, and it may be more important to ensure that the tribunal understands the law and the underlying issues than to avoid appointing anyone who has involvement in similar disputes. When called upon to scrutinise the appointment mechanism of the Court of Arbitration for Sport (CAS), the European Court of Human Rights found that it did not violate the principle of independence and impartiality laid down in Article 6 of the European Convention of Human Rights.[8]

The Hague Rules on Business and Human Rights Arbitration[9] emphasise that arbitration can assist in implementing the UN Guiding Principles on

---

[8]   *Mutu and Pechstein v. Switzerland*, ECtHR decision of 2 October 2018, application nos 40575/10 and 67474/10, paras 150 ff.

[9]   Hague Rules on Business and Human Rights Arbitration, launched 12 December 2019, by the Centre for International Legal Cooperation and the Business and Human Rights Arbitration Working Group, chaired by former ICJ Judge Bruno Simma, available at https://www.cilc. nl/cms/wp-content/uploads/2019/12/The-Hague-Rules-on-Business-and-Human-Rights-Arbitration_CILC-digital-version.pdf.

Business and Human Rights.[10] The Hague Rules are based on the UNCITRAL Arbitration Rules and, therefore, prefer party appointment,[11] additionally spelling out the requirements that arbitrators shall be of high moral character and exercise independent and impartial judgment,[12] and that the presiding arbitrator shall have demonstrated expertise in international dispute resolution and in areas relevant to the dispute.[13]

> *Issues: Appointing authority (based on closeness to the dispute or on independence), party appointment (bias and double-hatting versus qualification), combination*

6. THE SELECTION MECHANISM

The method for selecting the adjudicators may have a significant impact on the selecting authority's influence on the outcome of the selection, and thus, indirectly, on the adjudicator's independence and impartiality. The more the selecting authority may influence the outcome of the selection, the more the adjudicator is exposed to the risk of being not independent or biased.

There are various methods: the adjudicator may be elected, may be appointed by each of the parties or by the authority, or may be appointed by consent of the parties to the disputes or by consent of the represented parties.

Often a combination of these methods may be found: the election may regard a shortlist of candidates appointed by the different parties, or a roster of candidates agreed between the parties. Variations may also be found: the selection may be based not on the election of one adjudicator, but on the exclusion of all but one candidates on a list agreed between the parties.

Another aspect of the selection mechanism regards the allocation of cases to the different panels that may be formed within an adjudicating body. The composition of the panels and the allocation of the cases to the panels may be based on a random system enhancing objectivity, on predetermined criteria for rotation, or on discretionary assignment. An objective or random allocation reduces the possibility to steer the allocation of specific cases to certain adjudicators, thus reducing the possible impact on the adjudicators' independence and impartiality. However, this also reduces the possibility to allocate disputes according to the specialisation of the adjudicators, and thus may give inefficient results.

---

[10] Hague Rules on Business and Human Rights Arbitration, Preamble, Comment No 2. The UN Guiding Principles are available at https://www.ohchr.org/Documents/Publications/GuidingPrinciplesBusinessHR_EN.pdf.

[11] Ibid., Article 11(1)(c).

[12] Ibid., Article 11(1)(b).

[13] Ibid., Article 11(1)(c).

Issues: Election, appointment, consent, combination; random allocation, by rotation, discretionary assignment

7. COUNTERBALANCING THE SELECTING AUTHORITY'S INFLUENCE

The more the selecting authority may influence the outcome of the selection, the more the adjudication system is exposed to raising the suspicion of not being independent. The adjudicator may be suspected of rendering decisions that the adjudicator assumes may be pleasing for the selecting authority. There are some mechanisms to reduce any incentives that the selection system may give. However, these mechanisms may lead to disqualifying many professionals with the relevant qualifications and experience, thus giving inefficient results.

An adjudicator may be interested in the prospect of being reappointed. This may expose the adjudicator to the suspicion of rendering decisions that are likely to encourage new appointments. A possible way to reduce the influence of this incentive is to ban reappointments. Another possible way is to provide for full-time terms that are so long that seeking other appointments under the term is excluded, and reappointments are unlikely.

An adjudicator may be interested in being appointed to, or may hold, other functions within the dispute resolution system, such as expert witness or counsel in other disputes. This may expose the adjudicator to bias and may raise suspicion of the adjudicator rendering decisions that may serve the interests that the adjudicator represents in other disputes (double-hatting). A possible way to reduce the influence of this incentive is to restrict the possibility to exercise double-hatting.

An adjudicator may have held in the past functions within the dispute resolution system which may have led to developing certain opinions on issues of law or of fact. This may expose the adjudicator to the suspicion of bias if those issues arise in the dispute (issue conflict). A possible way to reduce the influence of this bias is to restrict the possibility to exercise double-hatting.

An adjudicator may be interested in showing to the selecting authority the extent to which the selecting authority's interests have been given consideration in the deliberations. A possible way to reduce the accountability of the adjudicator towards the selecting authority is to draft the decision in a way that does not show the different positions within the adjudicating body, and to ban dissenting opinions.

There are other ways of detaching the adjudication system from the states or the parties involved. Some of these ways are more organisational than merely legal, and regard, for example, the financing of the adjudication activity.

Intersentia

Comments to the Questionnaires

Issues: Reappointment, service period; double-hatting, issue conflict; confidentiality of deliberations, ban of dissenting opinions; financing of the adjudication activity

8. THE PARAMETERS FOR THE ADJUDICATOR'S CONDUCT

An adjudicator is bound to comply with the requirements of independence and impartiality.

To render these requirements more specific, sources of soft law have been developed such as the International Bar Association (IBA) Guidelines on Conflicts of Interest in International Arbitration,[14] a soft law instrument that enjoys widespread success.[15]

Among the more detailed codes of conduct that are being developed,[16] mention can be made of the Draft Code of Conduct for Adjudicators in Investor-State Dispute Settlement, released in May 2020 by ICSID and the UNCITRAL Working Group III.[17] This Code of Conduct is intended to be a binding set of rules, rather than a set of guidelines.

Among the specifications of what could constitute a conflict of interest, and thus affect the adjudicator's independence and impartiality, is the conduct described in section 7 above: repeat appointment, double-hatting, issue conflict.

Among the duties imposed on adjudicators to support the principle of independence and impartiality is the duty to disclose any interests that may give rise to suspicion about the adjudicator's independence and impartiality.

Some instruments impose on adjudicators the duty to refrain from acting, after the proceedings, in a way that can create suspicion that they were not independent or impartial under the proceedings. Some instruments impose a quarantine in respect of the parties involved in the proceedings.

Issues: Guidelines, codes of conduct, binding rules; conflict of interest; repeat appointments, double-hatting, issue conflict; disclosure; quarantine

---

[14] https://www.ibanet.org/Document/Default.aspx?DocumentUid=e2fe5e72-eb14-4bba-b10d-d33dafee8918.

[15] Although not all of its provisions are always deemed to reflect sound principles, see the English High Court case [2016] EWHC 422 (Comm) and the Austrian Supreme Court case 15 May 2019 Docket 18 ONc 1/19w.

[16] For an overview and summary of the main codes of conduct, see https://uncitral.un.org/sites/uncitral.un.org/files/media-documents/uncitral/en/annex_b_summary_of_fta_coc.docx (Annex B – Summary of Code of Conducts in Free Trade Agreements (update as of 8 May 2020, including new treaties and updated references)).

[17] Available, with annotations and commentary, at https://uncitral.un.org/en/codeofconduct.

Comments to the Questionnaires

9. BREACH: REMOVAL FROM OFFICE

The effectiveness of the principle of independence and impartiality may be measured by reference to the consequences that follow if the principle is breached. This section refers to the consequences for the adjudicator who is in breach.

Removal from office may be a sanction against conduct in breach of the principle of independence and impartiality. However, the power to remove the adjudicator may be abused in order to exercise undue influence on the adjudicator.

There are different approaches to who can remove an adjudicator from office as a consequence of breach of the principle of independence and impartiality: the decision may be taken by the court to which the adjudicator belongs, by the appointing authority, or by a third party.

There are also different approaches to who can take the initiative for the removal: the adjudicator's colleagues, a party represented in the court (typically, a state), a party to the specific dispute, or the party who appointed the adjudicator.

Issues: Removal as sanction, as undue influence; removing authority; party-initiated challenge

10. BREACH: EFFECTIVENESS OF THE DECISION

The effectiveness of the principle of independence and impartiality may be measured by reference to the consequences that follow if the principle is breached. This section refers to the consequences for the decision rendered by an adjudicator who breached the principle.

In arbitration, national courts may exercise a certain control over awards rendered both in commercial disputes and in investment disputes that were subject to commercial arbitration rules. National courts may verify the validity of an award rendered on their territory, and the criteria for validity are laid down in national law. If the arbitral tribunal was not independent or impartial, in most legal systems the court may set aside the award.

To avoid exposing arbitral awards to possible abusive influence by local courts, the enforceability of awards in countries different from the country where the arbitral tribunal had its seat is regulated by uniform law. According to the prevailing view, an award that was set aside by a national court in the award's country of origin may not be enforced in other countries under the New York Convention on Recognition and Enforcement of Foreign Arbitral Awards (the most important instrument of uniform law on this matter). However, sometimes the New York Convention is interpreted so as to permit

Intersentia

693

enforcement of an award notwithstanding that it was set aside in its country of origin.

Enforcement of awards is uniformly regulated by the New York Convention, which permits the enforcement court to set aside or refuse enforcement of awards rendered by a tribunal that was not impartial or independent. Although most of the criteria for refusing enforcement are uniformly regulated, the national enforcement court has a certain leeway.

On the one hand, it interprets the uniform principle of independence and impartiality. Interpretation of international instruments is expected to be autonomous, i.e. it shall reflect the international nature of the instrument and not the peculiarities of the court's legal tradition. However, national courts do not always apply international standards to the interpretation or application of uniform law.

On the other hand, the New York Convention in some instances refers to national law – for example, the procedural law of the seat of arbitration and the public policy of the enforcement court. The prevailing view is that this refers the court to the national law as it is interpreted and applied in its domestic context. However, sometimes courts apply an international standard to interpret the national law.

To avoid exposing investment arbitration to the influence of national courts, under the ICSID Convention the validity of an award is decided by a special committee, and the enforcement is subject to the same enforcement regime that applies to final judgments rendered by a court in the enforcement country. This does not necessarily mean that a breach of the principle of independence and impartiality would not have effect on the enforceability of the award. In some legal systems, under exceptional circumstances, a decision may be refused enforcement even though it is final, for example if its enforcement would violate public policy.

Issues: Finality of the decision; control of validity, enforcement; national or international standards; public policy

11. THE REPORTS

The *special non-national rapporteurs* are kindly asked to explain the state of the law, the legal debate and practice concerning the given type of adjudication on the issues described in sections 3–10 above.

The *special national rapporteurs* are kindly asked to explain the state of the law, of the legal debate and of practice on the issues described in sections 3–10 above as far as concerns: (i) domestic adjudicators in the given state, and (ii) international adjudicators.

The former may permit to verify to what extent there is, among the domestic legal systems, a convergence of criteria, mechanisms and remedies regarding domestic adjudication. In turn, this can be basis for developing international principles.

The latter may permit to assess, in the various legal systems, the approaches to international adjudication. This, in turn has relevance to two aspects: (i) as far as concerns the selection of international adjudicators, there may be domestic rules, guidelines or practices for the implementation of the relevant international tribunal's rules on the selection of the adjudicators; (ii) as far as concerns the effects of breaching the principle of independence and impartiality, of particular interest are the domestic criteria, mechanisms and remedies regarding the validity and enforceability in the given state of a decision rendered by an international adjudicator.

Both special national and non-national rapporteurs are invited to integrate the list of issues described in sections 3–10 with any matters that they deem relevant.

Both special national and non-national rapporteurs are encouraged to write any comments they may have on the effectiveness of the system that they present.

INDEX

A

accountability 45
allocation of cases 37, 268, 386, 528, 670
annulment of the decision 57, 130–131, 169, 229, 281, 550, 575, 608, 649
anonymous separate opinions 45
appearance *see* standard, objective
appointing authority 27–30, 38–39, 62, 70, 72, 91–94, 97–99, 120, 137, 140, 163, 208–210, 240, 250, 266, 288–293, 533

C

CETA Code of Conduct 271, 279–280
challenge 55, 76–77, 79, 81, 106–113, 127–130, 145–146, 152, 154, 169, 185, 187, 224, 226–229, 261, 280, 299, 346, 370, 373, 388, 391, 409, 452, 471, 541, 543, 545–546, 645
codes of conduct 52, 166
collegial body 25–26, 38, 43, 61, 94, 139, 183, 195, 215, 266, 439, 464, 469, 601
competence 21–24, 27, 30, 34, 43, 59, 88, 159, 206, 224, 240, 265, 279, 285, 307–308, 314, 316, 339, 358, 379, 433, 469, 537, 570, 596
confidentiality 48
conflict of interests 15–19, 167, 403

D

disciplinary action 644; *see also* immunity
disclosure 11, 40, 46–50, 48, 50, 60, 76–78, 100–104, 108, 122–124, 144, 152, 225–226, 240, 251, 278, 281, 344, 368, 405, 422, 445–447, 539, 547, 649
   adjudicator's diligence 48
   breach of duty 50, 78, 108, 225, 278, 281, 446, 547, 649
   parties' diligence 48, 226, 446–447
disqualification 280; *see also* challenge
dissenting opinions 45, 275–276, 294, 328, 538
diversity 25, 39, 136, 207, 309, 379, 465
double hatting 23, 30, 40–42, 60, 159, 165, 186, 189, 207, 226–227, 240, 271–273
due process 8, 13, 218, 240, 407, 528, 636

E

equality of the parties 14, 27, 30, 38, 61, 63, 141, 151, 201, 214–221, 241, 250, 407, 473, 530, 648
evocation 230
extraneity 19–20, 28

F

familiarity 19–21, 24, 28, 59, 159, 224, 438
financial safeguards 643; *see also* immunity
full-time position 60, 62–63

I

IBA Guidelines on Conflict of Interests 17–18, 160, 225, 251, 270, 443
ICSID/UNCITRAL draft Code of Conduct 10, 14, 41, 46, 269, 272, 278
immovability 643; *see also* immunity
immunity 12, 51–54, 62, 105–106, 125–126, 184, 294, 328, 384, 453–455, 545, 547, 572–575, 607, 643, 669
impeachment 643; *see also* immunity
incompatibility 16, 185, 190, 294, 327, 387, 421, 540
issue conflict 23, 42–46, 60, 188, 270, 273–274, 404, 450

L

lack of independence 10
long-term position 39, 60, 183, 294, 320, 323, 356, 362, 538, 668

M

moral standard 24–25, 31, 59, 79, 172, 184, 240, 265, 285, 307, 387
multiple appointments 23, 39–40, 60, 158, 160–162, 165, 224, 240

N

nationality 20–22, 69–72, 75, 116–117, 135–137, 160, 184, 189, 207, 236, 240, 264–265, 285, 306, 310–312, 316, 324, 344, 355, 357, 379, 445, 532
nomination 33–34

O

organic links 217

P

party appointment 30–32, 61–62, 69, 72, 96–97, 120, 163, 210, 241, 265
political considerations 27, 34, 182, 432, 465, 532, 535, 553, 642, 646, 666
post-term duties 50–51, 271
public policy 8, 151, 636; *see also* due process

Intersentia

697

Index

R

reasonable doubts   11; *see also* standard, objective
recognition and enforcement of decisions 392
refusal of recognition or enforcement   57–58, 130–131, 149, 169
removal   209, 280; *see also* challenge
repeat appointments   269–270
revocation   57, 168, 549, 552
roster   194, 204–205, 215, 266, 339, 355, 379

S

secrecy of deliberations   45, 75, 166, 274–275, 294, 327, 369, 538
selecting body   26–32
selection mechanism   32–37, 139, 141–144, 250, 267–268, 288–293, 313–316, 507–509
selection method   342–343
self-recusal   185; *see also* withdrawal
separation of powers   12, 28, 384, 399, 414, 512, 525, 538, 559, 663
standard   9–11, 44, 46–47, 60, 74–75, 101, 114, 145, 188, 218, 222–223, 251, 368, 370, 401, 406, 445, 450–451, 472, 543, 648–650

arbitration   9–10, 222, 406, 543, 649
arbitrators   451
chair of the arbitral tribunal   10, 44, 74, 251, 451
co-arbitrators   10, 74, 251, 450, 648
court   9–10, 222
disclosure   11, 46, 368, 445
disqualification   11, 47, 370
objective   10–11, 46, 60, 75, 101, 114, 145, 188, 218, 222–223, 401, 472, 650
subjective   10, 218, 401
structural independence   214; *see also* equality of the parties

T

transparency   34–36, 186, 196, 215–216, 308, 314, 317, 431–432, 436, 439, 465, 469, 532, 537, 544, 560, 569, 603

V

voluntary arbitration   221, 224

W

waiver   13–14, 17, 48, 115, 152–153, 155, 222, 236, 410, 443, 447
withdrawal   54, 76, 109, 148, 182, 185–186, 228, 261, 325, 371, 541

ABOUT THE SERIES

As globalisation proceeds, the significance of the comparative approach in legal scholarship increases. The IACL / AIDC with almost 800 members is the major universal organisation promoting comparative research in law and organising congresses with hundreds of participants in all parts of the world. The results of those congresses should be disseminated and be available for legal scholars in a single book series which would make both the Academy and its contribution to comparative law more visible. The series aims to publish the scholarship emerging from the congresses of IACL / AIDC, including: 1. of the General Congresses of Comparative Law, which take place every 4 years (Brisbane 2002, Utrecht 2006, Washington 2010, Vienna 2014, Fukuoka 2018 etc.) and which generate (a) one volume of General Reports edited by the local organisers of the Congress; (b) up to 30 volumes of selected thematic reports dealing with the topics of the single sections of the congress and containing the General Report as well as the Special Reports (national and non-national) of that section; these volumes would be edited by the General Rapporteurs of the respective sections; 2. the volumes containing selected contributions to the smaller (2–3 days) thematic congresses which take place between the International Congresses (Mexico 2008, Taipei 2012, Montevideo 2016 etc.); these congresses have a general theme such as "Codification" or "The Enforcement of Law" and will be edited by the local organisers of the respective Congress. All publications may contain contributions in English and French, the official languages of the Academy.

More information about this series at: www.larcier-intersentia.com/en/series/ius-comparatum.html

Académie Internationale de Droit Comparé
International Academy of Comparative Law

Printed in the USA
CPSIA information can be obtained
at www.ICGtesting.com
LVHW080800100724
784400LV00003B/52